Improbable Voices

Improbable Voices:

A History of the World Since 1450
Seen From Twenty-Six Unusual Perspectives

Derek Dwight Anderson

ISBN-13: 9798640294163

Cover design by Marci Velando

Cataloging Data

Improbable voices: a history of the world since 1450 seen from 26 unusual perspectives / Derek Dwight Anderson

Sausalito, California

Includes bibliographic references and index.

1. World history, 1500-   2. Biography—Collections

909.08—dc23

For additional resources and information visit: improbablevoices.com

In honor of my students and my great teachers—
especially Marty, Terry, and Valerie

TABLE OF CONTENTS

ACKNOWLEDGEMENTS

Libraries and museums stand at the foundation of historical research, and this project would have been impossible without the help of a good many of them. First and foremost, I want to acknowledge the good folks at the University of San Francisco's Gleason Library, without whom this project never would have gotten off the ground. Thank you for the access and the friendship. I am also mindful of and very grateful for the role my local public libraries—Sausalito Public Library and San Rafael Public Library—played in helping me obtain interlibrary loans efficiently and without charge. Dominican College of California's Alemany Library often provided me with an agreeable place to work, while its stacks showcase what strategic collection development can do in a small college library. Further afield, I benefited from the expertise and enjoyed a warm welcome from all those affiliated with:

- Alexander Turnbull Library, Wellington, New Zealand
- Amsterdam Museum, Amsterdam, Netherlands
- Duke University's Perkins-Bostock, Lilly, Divinity School Libraries, Durham, NC
- Herbert Hoover Presidential Library, West Branch, IA
- Het Scheepvaartmuseum, Amsterdam, Netherlands
- Hoover Institution Archives and Hoover Institution Library, Stanford, CA
- Indiana State University's Cunningham Library, Terre Haute, IN
- Indiana University's Lilly Library, Bloomington, IN
- Mitchell Library/State Library of New South Wales, Sydney, Australia
- National Library of Australia, Canberra, Australia
- The Ringling Art Library, John and Mable Ringling Museum of Art, Sarasota, FL
- San Francisco Airport Commission Aviation Library, San Francisco, CA
- Spakenburg Museum, Bunschoten-Spakenburg, Netherlands
- Stanford University's Green Library, Stanford, CA
- University of Hawai'i's Hamilton Library/Special Collections, Honolulu, HI
- University of Iowa's Main Library, Iowa City, IA
- University of Otago's Hocken Collections, Uare Taoka o Hākena, Dunedin, NZ
- Wellington City Library's Central Branch, Wellington, New Zealand
- William Penn University's Wilcox Library, Oskaloosa, IA

In addition to these institutions and the individuals who share images on Wikimedia Commons, I want to recognize those museums and libraries which make so much of their non-copyrighted art work digitally available to the public for free. These organizations provided me with many of the illustrations for the book, and I am cognizant of how much better it is with these visual accompaniments.

- Art Institute Chicago, Chicago, IL
- Brooklyn Museum, Brooklyn, NY
- Boston Public Library, Boston, and the Norman B. Leventhal Map Center
- Library of Congress, Washington, DC
- Los Angeles County Museum of Art, Los Angeles, CA
- Metropolitan Museum of Art, New York, NY
- National Army Museum, London, U.K.
- National Archives, Washington, DC

- National Archives of the Netherlands, The Hague, Netherlands
- National Gallery of Art, Washington, DC
- National Museum of Korea, Seoul, Korea
- National Museum, Stockholm, Sweden
- Newberry Library, Chicago, IL
- New York Public Library, New York, NY
- Rijksmuseum, Amsterdam, Netherlands
- Wellcome Library, London, U.K.
- Yale University Art Gallery, New Haven, CT

I am especially grateful to all those who believed in me and the possibility of this project. Topping the list are the professional historians who critically read individual chapters and offered me essential feedback: Don Baker, Michael Burger, M.A. Claussen, John Cole, Katrina Olds, Gary Gibbs, Heather Hoag, Joan Hoff, Uldis Kruse, Scott McElwain, Kathy Nasstrom, Elliot Neaman, Stephen Roddy, Michael Stanfield, Michael V. Woodward, and Taymiya Zaman. Omid Ahmadian, Trevor Calvert, Jen Coté, Constance Freeman, J O'Malley, and Chiquita Rollins were also important chapter readers. Conversations with Rachel Crawford, Joe Garity, Candice Hamilton, Lois Lorentzen, and Tami Spector always illumined. All of these women and men saved me from countless errors, pointed me in fruitful directions, offered inspiration, and gave me the confidence to press onwards.

I am also quick to remember those who provided crucial translation assistance, including Hideko and Takako Akashi, Karen Bouwer, Ginger da Silva, Uldis Kruse, Shuyu Liu, Jessie Liu, Marjolein Oele, John Petrovsky, Joshua Tanzer, Karsten Windt, and Yinshun Wang. These people enriched the text, as well as my appreciation of linguistic nuance, and the result is a measurably better book. Arie ter Beek, Karen Brown, Elisa Hansen, and Judith and Jacques Keene provided personalized tours for me that decidedly advanced my understanding and appreciation of art, architecture, and its cultural context.

My colleagues and students at Marin Academy, both past and present, have provided important emotional and practical support for this book during the eight years of its creation. I would like extend my gratitude to Jon Bretan, Liz Gotliebb, Anita and Robert Mattison, Kevin Rees, and Mark Stefanski for their assistance in helping me understand complex mathematical and scientific issues; to Bill and Mae Henley, Mallory Powers, and Erin and Connor Van Gessel for visiting (or trying to visit!) relevant historical sites on my behalf; to David Gutierrez for rescuing months of work; and to Travis Brownley for granting me a semester leave of absence in 2015. Nicole Stanton understood the ways in which my research connected with my teaching and awarded me the school's E. E. Ford grant that same year so that I could afford to travel to Australia and New Zealand for research. All of my Marin Academy history department colleagues took a deep interest in my project from the outset, and I am grateful for the way in which they value what I have learned along the way. It has been a great department to call home. Special thanks to Jennifer DeForest, Pam Maffei, Bill Meyer, Betsy Muir, James Shipman, and Tom Woodward. I want to acknowledge MA colleagues Rebecca Abbey, Susan Adams, Chris Alexander, Randi Bakken, Katherine Boyd, Ellie Beyers, Alexandria Brown, Mary Collie, Annie Elias, Evelyn Flory, Karen Jacobsen, Evie Koh, Kim Martin, Lisa Shambaugh, and KaTrina Wentzel for their encouragement and support for this project. I have also benefited from working with dozens of other MA colleagues for one, two, or three decades, and I don't take that time or their influence for granted. I have to trust they know who they are and what I mean. Those in MA's technology department, especially Sachi DeCou, Russ Thibeault, and Kyle Vitale, have been endlessly patient with me.

Once I had completed the first draft of the manuscript and began looking for a publisher, Bodie Brizendine championed my work, quite true to form. I'll never forget her generosity. Jason Rezaian also served as a vocal advocate. I appreciate the advice and help of Robert Elias, Naomi Gibbs, Connor Guy, Christopher O'Sullivan, Rhea and Rajan Dev, Catherine Price, and Marie Szuts as I attempted to understand the quickly-changing world of modern publishing. Once I determined the best route to take, Valerie Anderson, Pam Jacklin, Joani Lacey, and Marci Velando proved indispensable with their help and expertise. Linda Steck's editorial work on the manuscript affirmed the depth of her insight, critical engagement with words, and personal kindness. I have always treasured collaborating with her and now owe her a debt that cannot be repaid. Continued words of encouragement from David and Jan Anderson, Dorothy Anderson, Chris Blumenthal, Scott Buxton, Tim Conn, Chad Dawson, Jon Denton-Schneider, Helen Harper, Rob and Sandy Jacklin, Robert Pierce, Brian Rowett, Brendan Schmonsees, Johanna Stefanski, Nanci Tangeman, and Michael Wilson were especially important for me during this phase of the project.

Because this book is dedicated to my students and my great teachers, I want to acknowledge the myriad of ways I have learned from my students over the past 35 years, just as I want to remember those who influenced me the most during my educational development: Lincoln Middle School teachers Suzanne Brown and Gary Swenson; Pullman High School teacher Dutch Day; Grant High School teachers Ruth Alcorn, Jim Conover, Gene Jenkins, Ron Sobottka, Jan Shaffer, Sunny Stautz, and Leonard Whitlow; and Bates College professors Peter Bergmann, Loring Danforth, John Cole, Steve Hochstadt, and Tom Tracy. Mentors Bill Hiss, Cleve Latham, and Bruce Shaw were also critically important in my development and career.

Finally, there are friends and family who have supported me long before I began working on *Improbable Voices*. What I call "my army of mothers and a few good men" includes Joan Bouchard, John S. Bouchard, Louise Carpenter, Ellen Evans, Leonard Girard, Donna Granville, Jan Harris, Joan Hoff, Pam Jacklin, Shirl Lipkin, Earl Muir, Gus Nasmith, Chiquita Rollins, Marcia Rae Wells, Marlene Woodward, and Thomas Woodward. All these people have influenced me in transformative ways, probably more than they realize. This book is also a testament to how they have helped me flourish.

INTRODUCTION

On a sleepless night in March 2012, I lay in bed thinking about my world history class and the text I was using that year, Neil MacGregor's *The History of the World in 100 Objects*. As my mind wandered, I thought about other ways a world history could be told. People were an obvious choice, but how many people and which people? What would the criteria be for inclusion and exclusion? I then remembered a book I'd been given in 1978 as a high school freshman to support my budding interest in the past: Michael H. Hart's *The 100: A Ranking of the Most Influential Persons in History*. I enjoyed that book very much at the time, but as a teacher with thirty-five years of classroom experience, I knew that looking at history through the accomplishments of famous people would not offer the world anything new. What might? *Improbable Voices* is the outcome of my attempt to answer that question. I hope it offers engaged students and general adult readers something original.

The purpose of this book is to try to explain the history of the world since 1450 without either focusing upon history's most well-known personalities or ignoring the importance of individuals in shaping human events. My general rule of thumb in developing my list was that if a person had more than passing reference in a standard world history textbook, then they couldn't be one of my chosen figures. Darwin and DaVinci, Hobbes and Hokusai, and Suleiman and Steinem aren't discussed here because their stories and contributions have been told so well elsewhere. This also means that I explicitly question Thomas Carlyle's famous conclusion that "The History of the world is but the Biography of great men."[1] Instead, this book hopes to remind us that lesser known individuals also make lasting impressions on the fabric of history. They too had rich experiences that helped to shape the world's past and present. Operating from this premise, I thought about how much I struggled as a teacher and librarian to find accessible materials that offered both the vivid depth and expansive breadth I wanted in a text. I quickly realized that a book about fifty or a hundred unfamiliar figures might provide breadth, but could not offer a sufficient depth to do my selections justice. I also believed I needed a clear organizational principle to structure and justify my choices for inclusion. Eventually, I arrived at the A-Z format presented here.

The selection of the twenty-six figures constituted a fascinating puzzle. Because standard world history texts tend to emphasize certain periods more than others, I knew I wanted to have a balanced chronological distribution. This led me to distribute the twenty-six chapters so that the fifteenth/sixteenth, seventeenth, eighteenth, nineteenth, and twentieth centuries each have five chapters. This left me with one chapter for the twenty-first century and that seemed appropriate since so much of its history has yet to be told. I also knew that I wanted to offer a wide geographical distribution so that I might address the planet's enormous cultural diversity. Issues of class, customs, family, gender, language, race, religion, and sexuality had, therefore, to be addressed in

---

[1] Thomas Carlyle, *On Heroes, Hero-Worship, and the Heroic in History* (Berkeley: University of California Press, 1993), 26, EBSCOebooks. In May 1840, Scottish historian and social critic Thomas Carlyle delivered six public lectures in London on the essential importance heroes played in the development of human history, from Muhammad to Shakespeare, from Luther to Napoleon. These lectures were published in 1841 and received high acclaim in Victorian Britain, but have also been a source of historical debate ever since. Today, many find Carlyle's interpretation quite limiting, for it minimizes the importance of women, the power of nature, the role of culture, and the element of luck in the development of historical events.

meaningful and substantial ways. To help facilitate this, many of the figures I selected have a transcontinental component to their lives. Finally, I wanted to offer more than just a political or socio-economic history. Consequently, my selection includes generals and musicians, aristocrats and artists, businessmen and suffragists, missionaries and doctors, monarchs and scientists.

There are several other important points to note. First, *Improbable Voices* is more than a mere biographical collection of people who are not household names. Rather, it also addresses the broader historical forces these twenty-six individuals faced. It is, then, both an attempt to understand people in the context of their time and to understand a given era through the lives of specific individuals. For me, people shape history and history shapes people. Second, beliefs—be they political, economic or spiritual—both unite people and divide people. Much of the history of humanity, therefore, is about what one group believes, what it does not, and how it interacts with other groups in the world with different belief systems. This is why I have devoted significant attention to defining major political, economic, and religious concepts and institutions through the narrative, while using accessible language and minimizing the secondary and tertiary details as much as possible. I chose to do this because I couldn't imagine encountering a figure in southern India without discussing the basic tenets of Hinduism or meeting an early modern European businessman without discussing mercantilism. By understanding the fundamental beliefs of various cultures and subcultures, and how they differ, I believe that we can gain a better understanding of the world's collective history. Third, I have sought to present the twenty-six worldviews as best I can, even when I found that worldview to be disagreeable. This is the job of historians, for as Audrey Truschke wrote in the introduction to her book *Aurangzeb: The Life and Legacy of India's Most Controversial King*, "historians seek to comprehend people on their own terms, as products of particular times and places, and explain their actions and impacts. We need not absolve our subjects of study of guilt, and we certainly do not need to like them."[2] I have tried to see the world through these twenty-six people's lives, but I do not always support the values they represent. Finally, while each chapter can stand alone, the later chapters do assume the knowledge of earlier ones; the discussion of Confucianism in Chapter N, for example, assumes the information presented in Chapter K. The index will guide readers of selected chapters to further information.

Even with a history of this length, I am aware of its incompleteness. I also know that it would be a better book if I read Arabic and Chinese, German and Latin. There are also unrepresented nationalities, neglected sources, and missed opportunities. I ask for readers' forgiveness for these oversights, choices, and limitations. I have done the best I could with the resources and skills available to me. No history of the world may be considered complete, but I hope that readers will find this one satisfying nonetheless.

---

[2] Audrey Truschke, *Aurangzeb: The Life and Legacy of India's Most Controversial King* (Stanford, California: Stanford University Press, 2017), 9, EBSCOebooks.

ILLUSTRATIONS

All of these illustrations respect copyright law.
For additional supporting illustrations visit: improbablevoices.com

Page 485   1) "Mr. Buzacott's Church at Avarua, 1853," illustration in Aaron Buzacott, *Mission Life in the Islands of the Pacific* (London: John Snow and Co., 1866), 209; 2) "Makea," illustration in William Gill, *Gems from the Coral Islands* (London, Ward and Co., 1856), 140.

Page 488   "A Comparative View of the Polynesian Dialects," in George Turner, *Nineteen Years in Polynesia* by (London: John Snow, 1861), n.p.

Page 492   Map for Chapter U: Europe, by the author.

Page 493   "German Bridge Train," photograph by Bain News Service, 1914 or 1915, courtesy of the Library of Congress, Washington, DC, 2014697825.

Page 495   "Soviet Poster Dedicated to the 5th Anniversary of the October Revolution and IV Congress of the Communist International," poster by Ivan Vasilyevich Simakov, 1922, courtesy of Wikimedia Commons.

Page 499   Print by the British Caricaturist KEM," cartoon by Kimon Evan Marengo, 1939, courtesy of the National Archives of the Netherlands, The Hague, 2.24.05.02. In the cartoon, Hitler and Stalin walk with handcuffed legs along the Eastern Frontier, seemingly friendly, but ready to shoot the other too.

Page 505   "Zentralbild-Vitanova Berlin," photograph by anonymous, 1946, courtesy of Wikimedia Commons and Allgemeiner Deutscher Nachrichtendienst – Zentralbild, 183-H26222.

Page 507   "Potsdam Conference [with] Churchill, Truman and Stalin Together in Front of Churchill's Residence," photograph by War Office, July 23, 1945, courtesy of the National Archives of the Netherlands, The Hague, 2.24.05.02

Page 508   Map for Chapter U: East Germany, by the author.

Page 514   "Pieck's Successor, Walter Ulbricht," photograph by anonymous, September 1960, courtesy of the National Archives of the Netherlands, The Hague, 2.24.01.09.

Page 516   "East Germans Fortify Border," photograph by anonymous, November 1961, courtesy of the Central Intelligence Agency, Langley, VA, https://www.flickr.com/photos/ciagov/albums. In the photo, East Berlin is on the left, West Berlin on the right. The Brandenburg Gate stands in the background as GDR forces expand the concrete wall and added a barbed-wire fence.

Page 527   Map for Chapter V: Brazil, by the author.

Page 528   "Amazonas Theater in Manaus, Amazonas, Brazil," photograph by Ivo Brasil, 2017, courtesy of Wikimedia Commons.

Page 529   "Arthur Rubinstein," photograph by anonymous, n.d., courtesy of Wikimedia Commons and Arquivo Nacional/ Brazilian National Archives, BR_RJANRIO_PH_0_FOT_40677_006.

Page 534   "Copacabana, Rio de Janeiro, Brazil," photograph by American Red Cross, October 1921, courtesy of the Library of Congress, Washington, DC, 2017679513.

Page 540   "President Getúlio Vargas inaugurates Santos Dumont Airport," photograph by anonymous, November 1936, courtesy of Wikimedia Commons and Arquivo Nacional/ Brazilian National Archives, BR_RJANRIO_EH_0_FOT_EVE_00655_0015.

Page 541   Model of Brazil's pavilion for the 1939 World's Fair in New York, photograph by the author at a Lúcio Costa exhibition, National Museum, Brasilia, July, 2006.

Page 545   "Pan American Airways System," baggage sticker, c. 1935, author's personal collection.

Page 546   "Bidú Sayão and Villa Lobos," photograph by anonymous, 1945, courtesy of Wikimedia Commons and Arquivo Nacional/Brazilian National Archives, BR_RJANRIO_PH_0_FOT_41392_026. Bidú Sayão was a leading soprano for the Metropolitan Opera in New York between 1937 and 1952.

Page 549   "*The Emperor Jones* by Eugene O'Neill with Ralph Chesse's Marionettes," poster by the Work Projects Administration for the Federal Theatre Project, 1937, courtesy of the Library of Congress, 97514066.

Page 552   Congressional Buildings, Brasília, Brazil, photograph by the author, 2010.

Page 555   "George Fox,' print by Lehman & Duval, 1835, courtesy of Library of Congress, Washington, DC, 2003670321,

Page 558   Map for Chapter W: Kenya, by the author.

Page 559   Map for Chapter W: Nyanza District, by the author.

Page 563   Miriam Khamadi [Were] in 1964 yearbook, courtesy of Wilcox Library, William Penn University, Oskaloosa, IA.

Page 564   Miriam Khamadi [Were] in 1964 yearbook, courtesy of Wilcox Library, William Penn University, Oskaloosa, IA.

Page 568   Map for Chapter W: central Africa, by the author.

A

Afonso de Albuquerque

1453-1515

In 1925, the Portuguese poet Fernando Pessoa wrote a guidebook for tourists that unapologetically celebrated his nation's people and history. In his passage describing a park dedicated to Afonso de Albuquerque in Lisbon's Belém neighborhood, Pessoa lauds the "ample space, with gardens, in the middle of which stands the monument to that great historic figure, the greatest of viceroys of India and the founder of modern imperialism."[1] It is an apt description, if an unintentionally ironic one, for the memorial reveals so much about how perceptions of the past change. What was once happily celebrated with patriotism is often viewed today with skepticism, hostility or embarrassment.

Erected through an endowment provided by a prominent Portuguese historian, the Albuquerque monument was constructed in 1901.[2] Near the base, still sufficiently close to eye-level, four friezes heroically depict defining moments in Albuquerque's career. The first, on the southeast side of the monument, shows Albuquerque refusing Muslim gifts, his head held high in indignation, as the gift-givers' hands gesture their disbelief. The second, facing northeast, shows

---

[1] Fernando Pessoa, *Lisbon: What the Tourist Should See* (Exeter, U.K.: Shearsman Books, 2008), 62. It should be noted that Albuquerque was never actually appointed viceroy as his predecessor had been and his successors were; rather, he simply held the title of governor. For a critique of Pessoa's guidebook, which was originally published in English, see Danielle Alves Lopes, Rita Baleiro, and Sílvia Quinteiro, "Os Guias De Viagens De Fernando Pessoa e De Manuel Bandeira: Uma Leitura Comparada." *Acta Scientiarum. Language and Culture* 39, no. 1 (2017): 93-102, ProQuest Central.

[2] The historian was Simão José da Luz Soriano (1802-1891). The sculptor was Costa Mota and the architect was Silva Pinto. Many websites list the inauguration date as 1902, but the inscription on the statue says 1901.

two men on bended knees presenting Albuquerque with the keys to the Indian city of Goa. In the third, on the northwest side, Albuquerque rallies his men in the conquest of the Malaysian port of Malacca, his sword pointing toward the direction of victory. In the final frieze, on the southwest side, Albuquerque descends the steps of a dais in Hormuz to initiate a murderous deception.[3] Above the friezes four angelic figures, three female and one male, rest upon the heads of elephants. The female figures all wear long-sleeved, nineteenth-century dresses with high collars. One carries a flag and a banner with Albuquerque's name emblazoned upon it; the second carries the Ten Commandments and a sword; and the third holds a book and a rudder. The male figure, mostly naked, carries a sword and a shield. Between the angels are four identical carvings of carracks, the revolutionary ships that aided Portuguese exploration. Above the carracks and the angels a tall column rises, which is capped with Portugal's coat of arms and armillary spheres. At the top of the column stands a large bronze statue of the tall, bearded governor, looking with conviction towards the horizon. His left hand rests on the hilt of a long sword, while his right points to the weapons gathered at his feet. All told, it is a monument that celebrates Portuguese imperial righteousness and Albuquerque's importance in the development of the modern world. Like any memorial, however, it only tells part of the story.

Afonso de Albuquerque was born in 1453, the same year that Ottoman Sultan Mehmed II took Constantinople and destroyed the Byzantine empire.[4] This seems apt, since so much of

---

[3] Pessoa describes the four friezes in his guidebook. After I visited the memorial in April 2018, I agree with him about the content of three of the four panels, but believe he misidentified the southwestern frieze. Pessoa states that the fourth panel shows "the Reception of the Ambassador of the Kings of Narcinga," which was what the Portuguese once called the Indian empire of Vijayanagara. See Pessoa, *Lisbon: What the Tourist Should See*, 62. It is worth noting that there was a 25-year lapse between when the statue was constructed and when Pessoa wrote, and that Pessoa makes other minor errors in the guidebook, including a misattribution of a plaque at the Torre de Belém. With regards to the damaged southeastern frieze involving Albuquerque's refusing of gifts or bribes, it is not clear to me exactly where this took place. It may be a tribute to repeated episodes during Albuquerque's interactions in the Indian Ocean. One specific event that the frieze could depict occurred at Calayate (today's Qalhat, Oman) and is described later in this chapter. For a description of the actual reception of the Vijayanagara ambassador, see [Braz] Afonso de Albuquerque, *The Commentaries of the Great Afonso Dalboquerque*, Volume 4, Walter de Gray Birch (trans.) (London: The Hakluyt Society, 1888), 122. Braz de Albuquerque was Afonso de Albuquerque's illegitimate son, who was born in 1500. Albuquerque had him legitimized six years later and entrusted his education and upbringing to Manuel I's court. Upon Albuquerque's death in 1515, Manuel changed Braz's name to Afonso. To help distinguish other primary source citations by Afonso and Braz's *Commentaries*, I have added Braz's name to the relevant citations.

[4] The exact date of Albuquerque's birth is not known, but most agree that it occurred sometime in 1453.

Albuquerque's life ended up being defined by his vengeful struggle against Islam.[5] It also fits with

his family's long history of service to the Catholic kings of Portugal and Castile and the resurgence of anti-Muslim sentiment in Europe in the wake of the fall of Constantinople.[6]   Because of his family's connections, Albuquerque was raised in the royal palace where he obtained a solid education.   He also developed a close friendship with the heir to the throne, the future João II. The two boys grew up in a country both poor and minor—a place with few natural resources, a small population, and a continuing problem with famine.[7] These difficult economic circumstances encouraged fifteenth century Portuguese kings to look beyond their borders, especially towards Morocco, Madeira, and the Azores.[8] They hoped to conquer territories and settle new lands that would enrich Portugal's grain supply and improve its gold reserves.[9]   In 1458, João's father seized the Moroccan port

of Alcácer-Seguer as part of this effort, and in 1471 Albuquerque and João II fought together in the

[5] The intent of this book is to present history from the perspective of the individuals selected. Albuquerque's documented hatred of Islam does not, however, imply that there has been an automatic or inevitable "clash of civilizations" between Muslims and Christians. While wars can begin for ideological reasons, they also are often rooted in economic competition, individual egos, particular circumstances, and even chance. For a discussion of the "clash of civilizations" paradigm, see, for example, Richard W. Bulliet, *The Case for Islamo-Christian Civilization* (New York: Columbia University Press, 2006); and Chiara Bottici and Benoît Challand, *The Myth of the Clash of Civilization* (New York: Routledge, 2012).

[6] For information on the family background and upbringing, see [Braz] Afonso de Albuquerque, *The Commentaries*, *Volume 4*, 213-217; or John Villiers, "Introduction: Faithful Servant and Ungrateful Master," in *Albuquerque: Caesar of the East: Selected Texts by Afonso de Albuquerque and His Son*, T. F. Earle and John Villiers (eds.) (Warminster, U.K.: Aris & Phillips, 1990), 2. For the effects of the fall on Constantinople on the European mindset, see Roger Crowley, *1453: The Holy War for Constantinople and the Clash of Islam and the West* (New York: Hyperion, 2005), 238-239.

[7] Felipe Fernández-Armesto, "Portuguese Expansion in a Global Context," *Portuguese Oceanic Expansion, 1400-1800*, Francisco Bethencourt and Diogo Ramada Curto (eds.) (New York: Cambridge University Press, 2007), 484-485 and Roger Crowley, *Conquerors: How Portugal Forged the First Global Empire* (New York: Random House, 2015), xxi. Portugal's population in 1415 was about one million; a hundred years later, it had grown to about 1.5 million, but this was still a quarter of Castile's population and about half of England's for the early sixteenth century.

[8] For a detailed discussion of the settlement of Madeira and the Azores, see Peter Russell, *Prince Henry "the Navigator:" A Life* (New Haven, Connecticut: Yale University Press, 2000), 85-100 and 99-106.

[9] Ines G. Županov and Ângela Barreto Xavier, "Quest for Permanence in the Tropics: Portuguese Bioprospecting in Asia (16th-18th Centuries), *Journal of The Economic & Social History of The Orient*, 57, no. 4 (November 2014): 511-548. EBSCOhost and Vincent J., Cornell, "Socioeconomic Dimensions of Reconquista and Jihad in Morocco: Portuguese Dukkala and the Sadid Sus, 1450-1557." *International Journal of Middle East Studies*, no. 4 (1990): 379-418, EBSCOhost.

Portuguese capture of Arzila—a battle which resulted in the killing of 2,000 inhabitants and taking of 5,000 captives. The terror inflicted upon Arzila was so traumatic that the residents of nearby Tangier abandoned their city without a fight, lest they too be victimized by Portuguese brutality.[10]

Like many noblemen, Albuquerque remained in Morocco after the capture of Arzila, for a culture of medieval chivalry persisted within the Portuguese elite that required stories of glory, looked to profit from the spoils of war, and sought continued revenge against the Infidel.[11] For these *fidalgos*, knighthood was, in the words of one king, "a combination of virtue and honourable power," and weapons were "a means to gain honour." Furthermore, knights were "obligated to sacrifice their lives for their religion, for their country, and for the protection of the [Christian] helpless."[12] Albuquerque believed these words fervently and so spent the better part of his twenties in Morocco, probably based in Arzila. During this period he developed a deep hatred for Muslims while honing his brutal approach to war.[13] Chivalrous war did not preclude violence against civilians; in fact, it helped define it in the proper circumstances.[14]

João II was particularly interested in economic issues, which is why he directed many of the Moroccan campaigns in the 1470s toward ports that could facilitate the trade of Moroccan grain and horses for Portugal and Moroccan textiles for sub-Saharan Africa. Through a combination of force and negotiation, Portugal's success was such that most the people along Morocco's Atlantic coast came to accept Portuguese domination; a burgeoning demand for trade proved more enticing than war.[15] Such accommodation did not diminish Albuquerque's convictions regarding Muslims, however, for new threats and indignities emerged. In late July 1480, Ottoman Sultan Mehmed II landed an army to take the city of Otranto as a first step in an Ottoman conquest of the Italian states. After a successful fifteen-day siege, the Ottomans killed thousands of Otranto's residents and sold thousands more into slavery. The 800 men who were defending the Catholic cathedral refused to renounce their Christian faith when Mehmed II forced open its doors. All were subsequently executed on a hill outside of town.[16] The archbishop, who refused to leave the cathedral, was sawn in two upon the altar.[17] Outraged, Albuquerque joined the Portuguese response to these atrocities, for he was on one of the twenty-five ships Portugal sent to help repulse the Turks as part of the pope's coalition to defend the King of Naples.[18] The effort came to naught, however,

[10] Bailey W. Diffie and George D. Winius, *Foundations of the Portuguese Empire, 1415-1580* (Minneapolis, Minnesota: University of Minnesota Press, 1977), 145. João II's father was Afonso V (1438-1481). Alcácer-Seguer (today's Ksar es-Seghir) is about 20 miles northeast of Tangier. Arzila (today's Asilah) is about 25 miles southwest of Tangier.
[11] Malyn Newitt, "Introduction," *The Portuguese in West Africa, 1415-1670: A Documentary History*, Malyn Newitt, ed., (New York: Cambridge University Press, 2010), 4, 25; Crowley, *Conquerors*, 123.
[12] Afonso V quoted in C. R. Boxer, *The Portuguese Seaborne Empire, 1415-1825* (New York: Alfred A. Knopf, 1969), 316. These words were delivered at João's knighting ceremony on August 24, 1471.
[13] Villiers, "Introduction," *Albuquerque: Caesar of the East*, 3. Some scholars, including Villiers, indicate that Albuquerque was stationed at Anafé or Anfa (modern Casablanca), instead of at Arzila during this decade.
[14] Richard W. Kaeuper, *Medieval Chivalry* (New York: Cambridge University Press, 2016), 5, 9, 14-15, 163-167.
[15] A. R. Disney, *A History of Portugal and the Portuguese Empire*, Volume 2 (New York: Cambridge University Press, 2009), 7-8.
[16] Valentina Giuffra, and Gino Fornaciari, "Research Paper: Pulverized Human Skull in Pharmacological Preparations: Possible Evidence from the "Martyrs of Otranto" (Southern Italy, 1480)." *Journal of Ethnopharmacology* 160 (February 3, 2015): 133-139. *ScienceDirect*, EBSCOhost.
[17] Hugh Thomas, *Rivers of Gold: The Rise of the Spanish Empire, from Columbus to Magellan* (New York: Random House, 2003), 73.
[18] Nicolao Pagliarini, "To the Reader," *The Commentaries of the Great Afonso Dalboquerque*, Volume 1, Walter de Gray Birch (trans.) (London: The Hakluyt Society, 1875), xxxviii. The pope was Sixtus IV (r. 1471-1484).

because the Portuguese arrived too late to be of any service: upon Mehmed II's death in May 1481, the Ottomans withdrew their troops from Otranto to help defend Mehmed's oldest son in a struggle over the succession.[19]

When João II became king upon his father's death in 1481, he appointed Albuquerque his chief equerry or master of horse.[20] Because both men were known for their intelligence, sense of duty, and deep religiosity,[21] João wanted Albuquerque as part of his inner circle of advisors. This access gave Albuquerque access to the secret intelligence coming back from the continuing exploratory voyages along the western coast of Africa. These voyages began in 1434, when Gil Eanes sailed south into waters which medieval Europeans thought to be so filled with monsters and trickery that they were judged impossible to navigate.[22] The voyages continued in 1445 with Alvise Cadamosto's voyage to Cape Verde in Senegal and up the Gambia River and with Fernão Gomes' caravels*[23] reaching Ghana's Gold Coast. The Portuguese also crossed the Equator off Gabon by 1474. In the 1480s, João sent Diogo Cão on three voyages, during which he left stone markers to demarcate Portugal's claim, sailed a hundred miles up the Congo River, traveled overland into modern Angola to make contact with the king of Kongo, and sailed as far south as Cape Cross in central Namibia.[24] Bartolomeu Dias completed Portugal's exploration of Africa's Atlantic coast when he rounded the Cape of Good Hope and sailed into the Indian Ocean in 1488. This fifty-four-year, inch-by-inch exploration of the 7,500-mile coastline may seem rather timid to the modern eye, but given the vast array of technological, logistical, climatic, navigational, and financial challenges these fifteenth

---

[19] The Portuguese may have dallied in Rome and in Naples, compounding the problems of their late arrival. Mehmed's eldest son was Bayezid II (1447-1512), but a much younger son, Cem (1459- 1495) presented military challenges for Bayezid for a year. See Lord Kinross, *The Ottoman Centuries: the Rise and Fall of the Turkish Empire* (New York: Morrow Quill Paperbacks, 1977), 161-163; and Ludwig Pastor, *The History of the Popes from the Close of the Middle Ages*, Volume 4, Frederick Ignatius Antrobus (ed.), (2nd ed.) (London: Kegan Paul, Trench, Trübner & Co.,1900), 344-345.

[20] The title in Portuguese was *estribeiro-mor*.

[21] It is always difficult to prove that the faith witnessed later in life had been present in those when younger, and this is particularly true for Albuquerque since so little is written about his life prior to 1503. For a discussion of the religious atmosphere of the Avis court, see Maria De Lurdes Rosa, "Espiritualidade(s) na corte (Portugal, c. 1450-c. 1520): que leituras, que sentidos?" [Spirituality(ies) in the Court (Portugal, c. 1450-c.1520): Interpretations and Meanings], *Anuario De Historia De La Iglesia* no. 26 (2017): 217, EBSCOhost. For a reference specifically to João's faith see A. R. Disney, *A History of Portugal and the Portuguese Empire*, Volume 1 (New York: Cambridge University Press, 2009), 133.

[22] Richard Humble, *The Explorers* (Alexandria, Virginia: Time-Life Books, 1978), 19. This cape was known as Cape Bojador in the fifteenth century, but Peter Russell shows quite clearly that the place was actually today's Cape Juby in southern Morocco. The modern Cape Bojador is in the Western Sahara but this is not the point Eanes reached in 1434. Russell also notes that 1) the Portuguese may not have been the first Europeans to sail to this part of the world since the French may have been there earlier in the century; and 2) it was in the Moroccans' interest to feed European impressions of the dangers of "Cape Bojador" as a way of protecting their overland trade. See Russell, *Prince Henry "the Navigator,"* 111-116, 129-130.

[23] Terms with an asterisk in the text are defined in the glossary.

[24] A. R. Disney, *A History of Portugal and the Portuguese Empire*, Volume 2 (New York: Cambridge University Press, 2009), 33-37. Cão probably died on the return voyage of the final trip in 1486, but many of the details of his voyages have been lost because the surviving records are fragmentary. At some point between the mid-1440s and the early 1470s, the Portuguese learned that if they tacked northwest from the African coast until they reached the latitude of the Azores, they could pick up the westerly winds that would take them to the Portuguese coast. This shortened the return trip considerably. See Philip Curtin, Steven Feierman, Leonard Thompson, and Jan Vansina, *African History* (New York: Longman, 1984), 185.

century explorers faced as they ventured into the complete unknown, it is little wonder that each returning voyage was celebrated heartily by the court in Lisbon.

Conversely, however, there was great concern in the Portuguese court when Christopher Columbus arrived in Lisbon in March 1493, gloating before a king who had once rejected his overtures for sponsorship, with the shocking news that he had reached India by sailing west.[25] João II immediately wrote to Spain's monarchs, Ferdinand and Isabella, complaining that Columbus had violated the 1479 Treaty of Alcáçovas. According to this treaty, which ended the War of the Castilian Succession, Portugal had renounced its claim to the Castilian throne and had recognized Castilian control of the Canary Islands in exchange for Castile's recognition of Portugal's claims to Madeira, the Azores, and lands in Africa "discovered and to be discovered."[26] Because this recognition included a monopoly on all trade from these lands,[27] João believed that Columbus had violated this agreement. Ferdinand and Isabella appealed to the pope, who set the line of control between Spain and Portugal at 350 miles west of the Cape Verde Islands. João thought this too limiting and in 1494 secured through subsequent negotiations in the Spanish town of Tordesillas a new treaty that placed the dividing line 950 miles further west.[28] This redrawing meant that Brazil would become Portuguese instead of Spanish. It was João's greatest legacy; he died legally childless just sixteen months later.[29]

João's premature death at forty had serious repercussions for Albuquerque. Because João mistrusted his cousin, Manuel I, and refused to endorse his succession,[30] Albuquerque's close association with João was deeply suspect. His advice unwanted, Albuquerque left the court and returned to Morocco where he spent the next eight years.[31] With the coastal regions secured by Portuguese forts, much of Albuquerque's energy was devoted to raiding the Moroccan interior for grain, sheep, and men who could be sold or ransomed. Portuguese success was facilitated by the political and economic disarray northwest Africa experienced in the late fifteenth century.[32] The Muslims, bickering among themselves and unable to combat the economic changes Portugal's maritime exploits produced, were at their nadir. Protecting Lusitanian interests in Africa was essential work since through the course of the 1480s Portugal's African trade in gold, slaves, grain, and textiles generated enough income for the treasury that João II was able to stabilize Portugal's

[25] Crowley, *Conquerors,* 26. João rejected Columbus' bid because Columbus wanted exclusive control over his discoveries. See Newitt, "Introduction," *The Portuguese in West Africa, 1415-1670,* 10.

[26] A. J. R. Russell-Wood, "Patterns of Settlement in the Portuguese Empire, 1400-1800," *Portuguese Oceanic Expansion, 1400-1800,* 164-165. The death of Castile's Enrique IV in 1474 left two female claimants to the throne: Isabella I and Juana, who was the niece of Portuguese king Afonso V. Afonso married his niece and declared war on Castile in May 1474.

[27] Newitt, "Introduction," *The Portuguese in West Africa, 1415-1670,* 9.

[28] Humble, *The Explorers,* 91.

[29] João II had one legitimate son, Prince Afonso, but the prince died in a riding accident on July 12, 1491. João also had one illegitimate son, Jorge de Lencastre (1481—1550), but João was never able to secure his legal recognition. Therefore, when Joao died on October 25, 1495, the throne passed to João's cousin, Manuel I.

[30] Disney, *A History of Portugal and the Portuguese Empire,* Volume 1, 136-137.

[31] Villiers, "Introduction," *Albuquerque: Caesar of the East,* 4.

[32] R. Montran, "North Africa in the Sixteenth and Seventeenth Centuries," *The Cambridge History of Islam,* Volume 2, P. M. Hold, Ann K. S. Lambton, and Bernard Lewis (eds.) (Cambridge, U.K.: Cambridge University Press, 1970), 238-239.

currency before his death.[33] In fact, 45% of the Crown's total revenues in the late fifteenth century came from Portugal's growing empire.[34]

When Vasco da Gama's returned from his first trip to India in 1499, Manuel I quickly organized larger and better-prepared fleets to make the seven-month voyage to the subcontinent. There were departures in February or March 1500, 1501, and 1502. Needing experienced commanders for the growing overseas enterprise, Manuel put aside his suspicions about Albuquerque, and in early 1503 gave him command of three ships to travel to the Malabar coast and establish a fort at Cochin.[35] Albuquerque's cousin, Francisco de Albuquerque, commanded three additional ships, but neither man was given overall command of the venture because of Manuel's deep suspicion of concentrated power.[36] Afonso departed from Belém first, in early April, but arrived in Cochin two weeks after Francisco did, having encountered such foul weather that he lost one of his three ships. Upon his arrival, Afonso learned that Francisco had not only gained the glory of a battle but had already purchased all the pepper available in the city.[37] That annoyed the ever-competitive Afonso considerably since pepper was the essential commodity that drove the spice trade. Although there were far more exotic spices grown in Asia, pepper was the most well-known and commonly used Asian spice: its mass appeal made it particularly profitable. What had once been hoarded by Roman emperors and used as currency[38] had become an almost obligatory part of aristocratic tables by the eleventh century.[39] By the early fifteenth century, what had once belonged to dukes and counts had become an expectation for much of the peasantry. In fact, in 1400 it was possible for a skilled craftsman in England to buy a half a pound of pepper with a day's wages.[40] Most of this pepper came from the Malabar Coast, which is why Manuel I recruited Afonso and ordered him and Francisco to build a fortress in Cochin to protect Portugal's commercial interests. By late January 1504, Afonso and Francisco had done so with the consent of the local ruler, and Afonso had obtained the pepper he needed from a nearby port.[41] He set sail for home on January 25 and arrived in Lisbon's port of Belém in late July, having stopped in the Cape Verde Islands to repair his leaky ships. Francisco left the Malabar coast February 5, but he and his men were never heard from again: they became a part of the 35% of sailors who left Lisbon and failed to return.[42]

Once in Lisbon, Albuquerque and Manuel I developed a geopolitical strategy to further Portuguese interests in the Indian Ocean. In this, Portugal adopted an approach which differed

[33] M. Malowist, "The Struggle for International Trade and Its Implications for Africa," *General History of Africa, Volume V: Africa from the Sixteenth to the Eighteenth Century* (Berkeley, California: University of California Press/UNESCO, 1984), 3.

[34] Jorge M. Pedreira, "Costs and Financial Trends in the Portuguese Empire, 1415-1822," *Portuguese Oceanic Expansion, 1400-1800*, 54.

[35] Cochin is known today as Kochi.

[36] Crowley, *Conquerors,* 162-163.

[37] Crowley, *Conquerors,* 125.

[38] Andrew Dalby, *Dangerous Spices* (London: British Museum Press, 2000), 91.

[39] Jack Turner, *Spice: The History of Temptation* (Alfred A. Knopf, New York, 2004), 101.

[40] Turner, *Spice,* 138.

[41] This port was Coulão, today's Kollam, which is 80 miles south of Cochin. See [Braz] Afonso de Albuquerque, *The Commentaries of the Great Afonso Dalboquerque,* Volume 1, Walter de Gray Birch (trans.) (London: The Hakluyt Society, 1875), 8-10.

[42] [Braz] Afonso de Albuquerque, *The Commentaries,* Volume 1, 17-19; and Crowley, *Conquerors,* 130. At times the fatality rates were much higher. In 1571 of the 4,000 men who left Lisbon, only 2,000 arrived in Goa. See C. R. Boxer, *Four Centuries of Portuguese Expansion, 1415-1825: A Succinct Survey* (Berkeley, California: University of California Press, 1969), 20.

considerably from the way Spain initially approached its newly claimed lands. For voyages to the Spanish New World, private individuals like Columbus had to finance their voyages on their own; the crown only provided the necessary permission to travel. For the Portuguese, however, the state held the monopoly; it provided all of the necessary financing, took all of the risk, and retained most of the profits. The crown was the entrepreneur.[43] In an effort to promote this state monopoly, Manuel wanted to eliminate as much competition as possible. As he told the court in February 1505, Portugal's goal was to impose its power thoroughly in the Indian Ocean so that "all India should be stripped of the illusion of being able to trade with anyone but ourselves."[44] To accomplish this, Portugal would establish a series of trading stations and fortresses along Africa's eastern coast, in the Middle East, and on India's western coast, and would use its superior navy to patrol all maritime traffic. It was a remarkably bold initiative for a small country whose geographers just twenty years before had believed, like Ptolemy, that the Indian Ocean was a landlocked sea.

To execute this strategy, Manuel outfitted a fleet in February 1506 for Albuquerque and his cousin, Tristão da Cunha. True to form, Manuel appointed Cunha as the overall commander of the operation, but gave Albuquerque secret instructions that appointed him governor of India three years hence.[45] Manuel also gave Albuquerque authority to govern over Portuguese interests in the western half of the Indian Ocean in the meantime. These incentives certainly helped to soothe Albuquerque's sizable ego. There were, however, significant delays in the fleet's departure from Belém and in its progression through the Atlantic.[46] In fact, by the time the fleet arrived in the Indian Ocean, they had missed the favorable seasonal winds that could take them to India.[47] There

---

[43] Diffie and Winius, *Foundations of the Portuguese Empire, 1415-1580*, 311-312; and Thomas, *Rivers of Gold*, 160, 167, 226.

[44] Manuel I, quoted in Crowley, *Conquerors*, 138.

[45] [Braz] Afonso de Albuquerque, *The Commentaries*, Volume 1, 20. This meant that the appointment as governor was for 1509.

[46] These delays included an outbreak of plague, difficulties procuring pilots, and tussles between Albuquerque and Cunha. See Crowley, *Conquerors:* 163-165.

[47] In the spring and summer months, warm air over the Indian subcontinent rises, drawing moisture to the land and generally creating humid, monsoonal winds which blow from the southwest to the northeast. In the fall

was still time, however, to make contact with the Christian community on Socotra Island at the mouth of the Gulf of Aden. When Cunha and Albuquerque arrived off Socotra in July 1507, "with flags flying from all the ships in holiday trim" and an honorary artillery salute, they were surprised to find the island's fort was occupied by Muslims.[48] The anticipated joyful reunion of long-separated Christians turned into a seven-hour, ultimately successful, battle for a fortress. The next day Cunha, Albuquerque, and all their men followed a Franciscan priest in a procession to the island's main mosque to reconsecrate it as a Christian church. The priest began his exorcism as his ecclesiastical predecessor had in 1415 in Ceuta, when the Portuguese first conquered an overseas possession from the Muslims. A cauldron of salt and water was prepared and a prayer recited:

> Almighty God, we piously ask that with your infinite mercy you will bless and sanctify this salt, which by your holy grace you have given for the health and the benefit of the human race. Almighty God, we piously ask that with your infinite mercy you will bless and sanctify this water, which by your holy grace you have given for the health and the benefit of the human race.[49]

The salted water was then spread around the newly-christened Our Lady of the Victory, an altar raised, and mass held.[50] This important business taken care of and Socotra secured, Cunha left Albuquerque with six dilapidated and decaying ships and four hundred men to secure the seas between Mozambique and Iran; Albuquerque's only advantages were superior firepower, the capture of an excellent Arab pilot on Socotra, and his own righteous certainty.[51]

These assets, as well as Albuquerque's willingness to employ brutal methods to enforce his will, were put to considerable use over the next seven weeks as he made his way along the Arabian coast towards the *entrepôt* of Hormuz to put an end to Muslim trading through the Persian Gulf.[52] At the town of Curiate, for example, the Portuguese suppressed the inhabitants and then looted the city, collecting "as much spoil as they could carry," before setting fire to

---

and winter, the situation is reversed with rising ocean air drawing cooler air from the land and generally creating dry winds which blow from the northeast to the southwest. Traders traveled between the Arabian peninsula and India in accordance with the prevailing winds. The 1506 fleet arrived off the Mozambique coast too late to take advantage of this cycle. During the Atlantic portion of the voyage, part of the fleet discovered a group of remote islands in the South Atlantic that they named after Tristão da Cunha; Albuquerque was the one who suggested that the largest island in the group be named after Cunha. [Braz] Afonso de Albuquerque, *The Commentaries*, Volume 1, 24.

[48] [Braz] Afonso de Albuquerque, *The Commentaries of the Great Afonso Dalboquerque*, Volume 1, Walter de Gray Birch (trans.) (London: The Hakluyt Society, 1875), 45.

[49] Gomes Eanes de Zurara, quoted in "The Portuguese Celebrate Mass in the Mosque in Ceuta, 1415," *The Portuguese in West Africa, 1415-1670*, 27.

[50] [Braz] Afonso de Albuquerque, *The Commentaries*, Volume 1, 52. Albuquerque says that the priest was a member of the Order of St. Francis, Father Antonio do Loureiro. More commonly, however, the priests accompanying Portuguese ships were Dominicans. See Pamila Gupta, *The Relic State: St. Francis Xavier and the Politics of Ritual in Portuguese India* (Manchester, U.K.: Manchester University Press, 2014), 30.

[51] Crowley, *Conquerors*, 163-170, and [Braz] Afonso de Albuquerque, *The Commentaries*, Volume 1, 52. Unfortunately for the Portuguese, Socotra proved to be too far from the Arabian coast to be of much use in monitoring non-Portuguese trade. See Diffie and Winius, *Foundations of the Portuguese Empire, 1415-1580*, 235.

[52] Albuquerque's original orders were to take Aden and block maritime traffic out of the Red Sea, but Albuquerque made the decision on his own to go to Hormuz instead.

some houses in which the bulk of the supplies were, to prevent the Moors [*sic*] from making use of them; and the fire was so fierce that there was not a house, not a building, nor the mosque, which was one of the most beautiful ever seen, left standing. [Albuquerque] ordered also that they should cut off the ears and noses of the Moors who were captured there, and then send them away to Hormuz to bear witness to their disgrace.[53]

Similarly, in Muscat, when Albuquerque perceived the Arabs to have reneged on their promise to become Manuel's vassals by not providing everything that Albuquerque asked of them, he attacked the city, giving no quarter. Not only did the Portuguese pursue women retreating to the hills to kill them, but women and children found hiding in their homes were put to the sword. The city's large mosque, built of finely carved timber, had its supports cut out from underneath before being set on fire, and thirty-four ships in Muscat's harbor were set ablaze. Albuquerque's final order before disembarking was once again that the remaining prisoners have their ears and noses cut off.[54] He wanted some left alive to be able to tell of the terror the Portuguese instilled.

There were times, however, when Albuquerque's contact with Muslims did not turn violent. In the port of Calayate for example, Albuquerque refused to accept the gift of "oranges, lemons, pomegranates, and fowls, and some sheep," from the local governor, despite desperately needing the supplies, because he "would not accept anything from those against whom he would have to declare war if they refused to be vassals of the King of Portugal."[55] The governor responded by

strategically suggesting that Albuquerque proceed to Hormuz and leave Calayate unharmed; if the Portuguese were unable to reach an agreement with the King of Hormuz, who ruled Calayate, then Calayate would become Manuel's vassals instead. Albuquerque agreed to this proposal but insisted upon paying for the supplies Calayate's residents had provided.[56] Albuquerque was certainly brutal, but he was also relentlessly scrupulous in his transactions. This is why the southeastern frieze on Albuquerque's commemorative statue in Belém shows him refusing Muslim gifts with resolute conviction, much to the astonishment of the gift-givers. As Albuquerque wrote in 1513 about a similar encounter, "The messenger…then came back with a present of lemons, oranges, chickens, and lambs. I was doubtful about accepting them and said that it was not my habit to receive presents from rulers of cities with whom we had not concluded treaties of peace."[57]

---

[53] [Braz] Afonso de Albuquerque, *The Commentaries*, Volume 1, 71. Curiate is known today as Qurayat, Oman.

[54] [Braz] Afonso de Albuquerque, *The Commentaries*, Volume 1, 73-74, 79, 82.

[55] [Braz] Afonso de Albuquerque, *The Commentaries*, Volume 1, 63. Calayate is known today as Qalhat, Oman.

[56] [Braz] Afonso de Albuquerque, *The Commentaries*, Volume 1, 65.

[57] Afonso de Albuquerque to Manuel I, December 4, 1513 in *Albuquerque: Caesar of the East*, 211, 213.

When Albuquerque's six ships crossed the Straits of Hormuz to the island of Hormuz near the Iranian shore in late September 1507, they found Hormuz's harbor full of vessels, including 200 oared galleons and fifty armed vessels. The largest ship was the *Meri*, which belonged to the King of Cambay and carried a thousand men. Albuquerque quickly found his squadron surrounded, and, when he became convinced that the Muslims were about to attack with their clear numerical advantage, he ordered a bombardment with large cannons. The opening salvo sunk two key ships and Albuquerque engaged the *Meri* in a fierce battle. As the Muslim response collapsed, with men throwing themselves overboard, the Portuguese boarded small boats. In his report to Manuel, Albuquerque noted that men in the skiffs "killed countless of [the Muslims] in the water." In fact, "there was one man that day who killed eighty men in the sea." Then, "having vanquished the fleet, we went in pursuit of the galleons…and we captured thirty of them, killing many of their men, and then setting them on fire, casting them loose and watching them drifting out to sea ablaze."[58] The representatives of the infant king of Hormuz quickly sued for peace, and Albuquerque "accepted their surrender of the kingdom and took possession of it." He then "ordained that the king should rule in the name of the king of Portugal" and imposed a steep annual tribute on the kingdom to be paid in gold, silver, and pearls.[59]

Albuquerque's men profited handsomely from the capture of Hormuz and the looting of other ports in the region. In fact, it took them eight days to retrieve all the valuables from the 900 men that were floating in the bay in the aftermath of the battle.[60] These men did not, however, share their commander's conviction that it was necessary for the Portuguese to construct a fortress in Hormuz to protect the crown's long-term interests. Albuquerque was insistent that the fortress be built, however, and ordered the captains of the other ships to participate in the manual labor. This infuriated the captains, who took the order as an insult to their honor. After four crewmen deserted and converted to Islam in order to escape the work, Albuquerque flew into a rage, opened fire on the city's walls, poisoned its cistern by filling it with human corpses and dead horses, and attacked one of his captains for disobeying an order.[61] In January 1508, three of the six Portuguese captains mutinied, believing that Albuquerque had become unstable and was unfit for command; they sailed from Hormuz for Cochin, where they planned to petition the viceroy for amnesty in the wake of Albuquerque's unwarranted behavior. Left with only three ships and facing a fast-approaching Muslim fleet from other parts of the Persian Gulf, Albuquerque had no choice but to abandon Hormuz. He returned to Socotra Island to resupply the men stationed there and then sailed to India to defend the charges against him and to claim his governorship.[62] Many surprises awaited.

[58] Afonso de Albuquerque to Manuel I, November 1507 in *Albuquerque: Caesar of the East:* 55.

[59] Afonso de Albuquerque to Manuel I, November 1507 in *Albuquerque: Caesar of the East,* 57. At the time of Albuquerque's arrival, the government was in the hands of royal eunuchs because internal rivalries had reduced the royal family to a collection of infants, women, and blind men. See Valeria Fiorani Piacentini, "Salghur Shāh, Malik of Hormuz, and His Embargo of Iranian Harbours (1475-1505), *Revisiting Hormuz: Portuguese Interactions in the Persian Gulf in the Early Modern Period*, Dejanirah Couto and Rui Manuel Laureiro (eds.) (Wiesbaden, Germany: Harrassowitz Verlag, 2008), 12.

[60] Afonso de Albuquerque to Manuel I, November 1507 in *Albuquerque: Caesar of the East,* 57.

[61] [Braz] Afonso de Albuquerque, *The Commentaries,* Volume 1, 141-143, 160, 165, 173, 177, 188.

[62] [Braz] Afonso de Albuquerque, *The Commentaries,* Volume 1, 195. On the voyage to India from Socotra, Albuquerque also returned briefly to Hormuz and imposed a temporary blockade.

~

Hinduism is not an indigenous term to India; it is the designation those from outside the subcontinent use to describe the eclectic combination of faith, social standing, and custom which dominates much of India today and which derives its heritage from traditions going back thousands of years. Though notoriously difficult to define,[63] Hinduism may be seen as a system and as a way of life, rather than just a theological belief. Hinduism is about faith, and it is about social order; Hinduism is about religion, and it is about society.

The reason for this dual nature rests in the concept of reincarnation. All living things are judged by their actions, or karma, and upon death are evaluated accordingly. Those who have lived an honorable life—a life lived in accordance with the universal law or dharma—will be reincarnated more prosperously, while those who have not will be reborn with less wealth, or less intelligence, or less opportunity. The better people behave, the better their next life will be; the less pure their actions, the worse their next life will be. Hindu society in India codifies the concepts of karma and dharma in the caste system. The caste system is a social hierarchy in which those born to parents of a certain status become a part of that same group and cannot change their societal position through the course of their lives, regardless of ability or circumstance or even luck. Therefore, the son of a priest becomes a priest; the daughter of a slave remains a slave her whole life.

Like most Hindus today, those in the sixteenth century had a faith in a Creator or universal Supreme Being, often known as Brahma, but they emphatically embraced the multitude of forms God can take. For Hindus, the greatest expression of the divine is found in the almost infinite expression of multiplicity. It is in God's diversity that faith is revealed. In fact, it may be better to think about "hinduisms" instead of Hinduism as a unified system since so many different traditions can be found within the vast subcontinent.[64] It is also true, however, that most sixteen century Hindus focused on one of these forms above all others. The founders of the Vijayanagara Empire, for example, were followers of Shiva.[65] Shiva is frequently known as the Destroyer, but he is also seen as the deity of sexuality and self-control, of life-giving rains and terrible storms, of poisonous herbs and healing. He is frequently represented either as a bull or as a figure dancing in a ring of fire, but he is also symbolized by the *linga*—a phallus-shaped object placed at the center of his temples. Taken together, these traits and symbols embrace the notion of balance and emphasize the idea that it is only through destruction that a truly new beginning can occur. Like a pine cone needing a forest fire to release new seeds, destruction is the basis of creation. Another important form of God in the Hindu pantheon is Vishnu. Vishnu is generally more loved than feared for he is frequently known as the Preserver.[66] Vishnu helps maintain the balance in the world between

---

[63] Wendy Doniger, *The Hindus: An Alternative History*, (New York: Penguin Group, 2010), 24-28. In 2014, this book was found by an Indian court to be in violation of the nation's blasphemy law and Penguin withdrew the work from publication in India and pulped the remaining copies. See Wendy Doniger, "Banned in Bangalore," *New York Times*, March 6, 2014, A24, ProQuest Historical Newspapers; and Ellen Barry, "A Book Vanishes, Rattling India's Intellectuals," *New York Times*, February 16, 2014, 1, ProQuest Historical Newspapers.

[64] Kim Knott, *Hinduism: A Very Short Introduction* (New York: Oxford University Press, 1998), 2.

[65] The Vijayanagara Empire was founded in 1336; the Sangamas Dynasty (1336-1485)'s family deity was Virupaksha, a form of Shiva. See Catherine B. Asher and Cynthia Talbot, *India Before Europe* (New York: Cambridge University Press, 2006), 64.

[66] Westerners often learn that Shiva is counterbalanced by Vishnu. Wendy Doniger notes, however, that the popular notion of a Hindu trinity (Brahma as the Creator, Shiva as the Destroyer, and Vishnu as the Preserver)

good and evil, between right and wrong, and as a result of this responsibility, he has had to intervene in earthly affairs nine times, taking a different form each time. The rulers of Vijayanagara recognized the equilibrium Vishnu provides when they constructed a large temple to one of Vishnu's avatars, Lord Rama. In addition to these two cults, the followers of Shiva and Vishnu may also subscribe to a multitude of other expressions of God, including female forms and local deities. This is why the towers of Hindu temples and gates feature a plethora of statues to represent this diversity.

The second largest religious community on the Malabar Coast, the Muslims, held very different beliefs. In fact, it is difficult to imagine two more divergent assumptions about the nature of God than those that exist between Hindus and Muslims. In Islam, the fundamental tenets and the religious rituals are clear and succinct in comparison with Hinduism, as evidence by the Five Pillars of the Muslim faith:

> *Shahada*: publicly proclaiming, "There is no god but God and Muhammad is the
>   only true messenger of God;"
> *Salah*: praying five times a day in direction of Mecca in a prescribed manner;
> *Zakat*: providing alms to the poor;
> *Sawm*: fasting during daylight hours during the month of Ramadan;
> *Hajj*: making the pilgrimage to Mecca, if financially able to do so.

These pillars emphasize the unity of both faith and experience: all who know God must know God in the same way and be able to demonstrate this knowledge in the same manner. For a Muslim, the greatness of God rests in His unifying singularity and in the purity of Muhammad's message that he was God's last and final prophet.

There were other religious groups on the Malabar Coast, including small communities of Jews and Jains,* but it was the presence of a group of Christians that drew Portuguese attention. The St. Thomas Christians trace their church's history to its apostolic origins, when the Apostle Thomas brought Christianity to India and began converting people of all castes. Tradition holds that he also established seven churches on the Malabar Coast, and the church successfully maintained contact with Christian communities in the Middle East from at least the sixth century.[67] By the time of Vasco da Gama's arrival in India, these churches and others in South India had 70,000 to

---

probably developed as response to Christianity: "The idea that Brahma is responsible for creation, Vishnu for preservation or maintenance, and Shiva for destruction does not correspond in any way to the mythology, in which both Vishnu and Shiva are responsible for both creation and destruction and Brahma was not worshiped as the other two were." See Doniger, *The Hindus,* 384.

[67] While apostolic succession cannot be proven, the evidence for its validity is similar to that for St. Peter and St. Paul. The seven churches are at Cranganore, Quilon, Paravur, Kokkamangalam, Niranam, Palayur and Cayal. The St. Thomas Christians are also known as Syriac Christians. See Samuel Hugh Moffett, *A History of Christianity in Asia, Volume I: Beginnings to 1500* (Maryknoll, New York: Orbis Books, 1998), 31, 34, 501; Ian Gillman and Hans-Joachim Klimkeit, *Christianity in Asia before 1500* (Ann Arbor, Michigan: University of Michigan Press, 1999), 159. Interestingly, Western Europe may have first learned of these Christians when a man claiming to be "Patriarch John" arrived in Rome and spoke to Pope Calixtus II in 1122 about a wealthy Christian land in India where St. Thomas awoke each year to bless the faithful. See Keagan Brewer, "Introduction," *Prester John: The Legend and its Sources* (Farham, U.K.: Ashgate Publishing Limited, 2015), 4-6.

100,000 members,[68] but the Portuguese struggled to see them as fellow Christians because so many of their liturgical practices differed from those of early modern Catholicism.[69] One of the most disturbing local conventions centered on the lack of images or statues in St. Thomas churches. To Catholic eyes, the absence of figures revealed an insufficient respect for the Virgin Mary and the saints.[70] These churches were also suspect because of their decorative similarity to mosques and the absence of human iconography. This dissonance the Portuguese experienced upon entering the churches of St. Thomas led them to draw erroneous conclusions about Hindu temples. They repeatedly mistook the statuary in Hindu temples to be representations of a schismatic Christian sect. They saw Brahma, Shiva, and Vishnu as a form of the Holy Trinity and drew other parallels based on their own faith and experience.[71] As one member of Vasco da Gama's crew wrote,

> They took us to a large church….In the center of the body of the church rose a chapel, all built of hewn stone, with a bronze door sufficiently wide for a man to pass, and stone steps leading up to it. Within this sanctuary stood a small image which they said represented Our Lady….Many other saints were painted on the walls of the church, wearing crowns. They were painted variously, with teeth protruding an inch from the mouth, and four or five arms.[72]

It was in this unique religious mix on the western coast of India that Albuquerque sought to establish the Portuguese trading monopoly. Doing so required him to reconsider his usual geopolitical equation, for India was more than just another battlefield between Catholics and Muslims.

~

Albuquerque's first port of call upon his arrival in India in early December 1508 was Cannanore, where Viceroy Francisco de Almeida was busily making preparations to avenge his son's death at

---

[68] Alexander Henn, *Hindu-Catholic Encounters in Goa: Religion, Colonialism, and Modernity* (Bloomington, Indiana: Indiana University Press, 2014), 22 and Samuel Hugh Moffett, *A History of Christianity in Asia, Volume II: 1500-1900* (Maryknoll, New York: Orbis Books, 2005), 5.
[69] The division of Christianity between Catholicism and Orthodox Christianity connects directly to the dissonance the Portuguese experienced. This division and its consequences are explored at length in Chapters B and C.
[70] Moffett, *A History of Christianity in Asia, Volume II: 1500-1900*, n.p. (chapter 1), Google Books. Some St. Thomas Christian churches did have images of certain animals, like peacocks.
[71] The Portuguese chronicler Duarte Barbosa (1480-1521), for example, wrote that the Hindu priests "hold the number three in great reverence; they hold that there is God in three persons, who is not more than one….They honor the Trinity and would, as it were, desire to depict it. The name which they give it is Bermabesma Maceru, who are three persons and only one God, whom they confess to have been since the beginning of the world. They have no knowledge nor information concerning the life of our Lord Jesus Christ." Duarte Barbosa, *The Book of Duarte Barbosa*, Volume II, Mansel Longworth Dames (ed. and trans.) (London: Hakluyt Society, 1921), 37. Bermabesma Maceru is Brahma, Vishnu, and Shiva. Part of the reason for this misidentification rests in the "very human, and humane, desire to find familiar things" when encountering new ones. See M.N. Pearson, *The Portuguese in India* (Cambridge: Cambridge University Press, 1987), 116.
[72] Álvaro Velho quoted in Henn, *Hindu-Catholic Encounters in Goa*, 19. According to Henn, the quote is "most likely" from Velho.

the Battle at Chaul in March 1508.[73] Albuquerque asked Almeida to surrender his office by order of the king, but Almeida repeatedly refused, saying that his term did not end until January. Unable to effect the change he wanted, Albuquerque decided there was little to do but head south to the Portuguese base at Cochin as Almeida headed north to Diu to seek his revenge.[74] Eight weeks later, when Almeida arrived in Cochin having obliterated the Egyptian fleet, Albuquerque joined the clergy, officers, and other notables on the beach to welcome and congratulate the viceroy on his tremendous victory at Diu. Almeida snubbed Albuquerque on the shoreline, failing to acknowledge his successor's presence, and proceeded to the church. After mass, Albuquerque confronted Almeida at the entrance to the Cochin fortress:

> Sir, seeing that God has given you so complete a victory, and you have avenged the death of your son with so much honour....I beg you of your grace let there be no differences between us, but deliver to me the government of India by these provisions which I here hold from the king.[75]

Almeida steadfastly refused to relinquish his power. Instead, in the following weeks, Almeida indicted Albuquerque on ninety-six charges of gross mismanagement, arrested him, destroyed his house in Cochin, confiscated his household goods, and had him imprisoned in the fort at Cannanore so that he would not be able to interfere with Almeida's work in Cochin. Three months later, in late October 1509, a high-ranking nobleman, Fernando Coutinho, arrived in Cannanore with fifteen ships from Portugal. He freed Albuquerque, sailed to Cochin, and demanded that Almeida surrender his post. Almeida finally gave way.[76] He boarded his ship on November 5 and waited for five days as the cargo and all of his possessions were loaded; it took so long because Almeida took all of the furnishings from the Portuguese headquarters, thereby establishing the tradition that each viceroy or governor needed to provide for all of his own household goods.[77]

Coutinho brought two very specific orders with him from Manuel. The first was that the Portuguese had to punish the city of Calicut—the premier port on the Malabar Coast. Calicut had achieved this position despite the disadvantages of its poor harbor because of the atmosphere its ruler, the zamorin or lord of the ocean, had created. The zamorins were Hindus, but the city's

---

[73] The Battle of Chaul in March 1508 pitted an Egyptian fleet of forty-five vessels of differing capabilities against Lourenço de Almeida's 500 men on nine ships with superior guns. In the three-day battle, the Portuguese missed the opportunity to destroy the Egyptian fleet at the outset and subsequently suffered the loss of its flagship, the *São Miguel*; Lourenço was killed by cannon shot; his body was sunk to prevent it from becoming a trophy. The Egyptian victory cost its commander, Musrif Hussain, about 80% of his men and failed to stop Portuguese interference in the spice trade. See Crowley, *Conquerors,* 177-192.

[74] [Braz] Afonso de Albuquerque, *The Commentaries of the Great Afonso Dalboquerque,* Volume 2, Walter de Gray Birch (trans.) (London: The Hakluyt Society, 1877), 1-4. At the Battle of Diu in February 1509, Almeida's fleet obliterated its foe, sinking, capturing, or burning every Egyptian ship. The Malmuk Sultanate's credibility as the defenders of Islam suffered a fatal blow. In the aftermath, Almeida also tortured surviving Egyptians to death and then displayed their dismembered bodies down the coast. See Crowley, *Conquerors,* 201-210.

[75] Afonso de Albuquerque quoted in [Braz] Afonso de Albuquerque, *The Commentaries,* Volume 2, 17.

[76] [Braz] Afonso de Albuquerque, *The Commentaries,* Volume 2, 36, 44, 46-48.

[77] Pedro Dias, "The Palace of the Viceroys in Goa," *Goa and the Great Mughal,* Jorge Flores and Nuno Vassallo e Silva (eds.) (London: Scala Publishers, 2004), 68; and [Braz] Afonso de Albuquerque, *The Commentaries,* Volume 2, 48. Dias' article is about the traditions developed at the Fortaleza Palace in Goa, not Almeida's residence in Cochin, but given how long the loading process took and how reluctant Almeida was to surrender his post, it seems likely that Almeida was the one who established the tradition of removing all valuables and selling off the everyday items, like kitchen utensils, at the end of their tenure in India.

commercial establishment was predominately Muslim.[78] Working effectively together, the zamorins and the traders promoted the pepper trade by providing a safe port for all and by not taking advantage of endangered or damaged ships.[79] This allowed Calicut to become so wealthy and strong in the years before the Portuguese arrived that other cities on the coast, such as Cochin and Cannanore, could not sell their pepper on the open market: they had to ship it to Calicut first.[80] The reason Manuel wanted this city punished, however, was as much a matter of pride as it was a matter of economics. Vasco da Gama had been belittled there as a new trader with substandard goods in 1498. Two years later Pedro Álvares Cabral, the first European in Brazil and the man who had negotiated the rights for Portugal's first European trading post in India, had witnessed Muslim traders destroy the outpost and murder its staff. Cabral and Manuel blamed the zamorin for the deaths and the damage. On his second trip to India in 1502, da Gama inflicted heavy damage when he bombarded Calicut with Portugal's heavy, state-of-the-art cannons, but this did not make the zamorin become a Portuguese vassal.[81] Manuel wanted complete submission, which is why Fernando Coutinho and Albuquerque set sail for Calicut with twenty ships in January 1510. Even though the zamorin and most of his troops were not in the city, the Portuguese attack did not go well; it quickly devolved into a looting mission. Rather than securing a base of operations, Coutinho focused on reaching the zamorin's palace. This required marching through narrow lanes for three miles from the shore. Albuquerque advised against moving so far away from the fleet's protective cannons, but Coutinho proceeded anyway. He reached the palace with only minor interference. As the looting began, however, the zamorin's reinforcements arrived. The Portuguese were then forced to retreat through the narrow streets as the Indians hailed projectiles down upon them. Coutinho was soon dead and Albuquerque received an arrow in his left arm, a dart in his neck, and a gunshot wound in the chest. His men carried him on a shield back to the beach, where the ships' cannons made an evacuation possible.[82] Calicut had been vandalized but not defeated. Manuel had envisioned something more and Calicut remained a thorn in Portugal's side.

The king's second order was for Portugal to capture Goa.[83] While Cochin was an excellent base for the pepper trade, it was too far south to police Muslim trade along the whole Indian Ocean coast. Portugal needed a permanent presence near its midpoint, and the island of Goa filled that role nicely. A Hindu pirate named Timoji may have also influenced the decision for he provided Albuquerque with a valuable orientation to the Goa region in hopes that he might win a land grant once the Portuguese were in power.[84] What Timoji knew was that Goa sat in the borderland region between the Bijapur Sultanate, which was Muslim, and the Vijayanagara Empire, which was Hindu.

---

[78] N. Venkataramanayya, "The Kingdom of Vijayanagara," *The Delhi Sultanate*, R. C. Majumdar (ed.) (Bombay: Bharatiya Vidya Bhavan, 1967), 418.

[79] Catherine B. Asher and Cynthia Talbot, *India Before Europe* (New York: Cambridge University Press, 2006), 78.

[80] Venkataramanayya, "The Kingdom of Vijayanagara," *The Delhi Sultanate*, 418.

[81] Disney, *A History of Portugal and the Portuguese Empire*, Volume 2, 126-127.

[82] Crowley, *Conquerors*, 215-225, and [Braz] Afonso de Albuquerque, *The Commentaries* Volume 2, 63-71.

[83] Diffie and Winius, *Foundations of the Portuguese Empire, 1415-1580*, 248-249. Other historians believe that Albuquerque acted on his own; see, for example, Disney, *A History of Portugal and the Portuguese Empire*, Volume 2, 130.

[84] Teotónio R. De Souza, "Portuguese Impact Upon Goa: Lusotopic, Lusophonic or Lusophilic?" *Creole Societies in the Portuguese Colonial Empire*, Philip J. Havik and Malyn Newitt (eds.) (Newcastle-Upon-Tyne, U.K.: Cambridge Scholars Publishing, 2015), 201, 204, EBSCOebooks. The land grant holder was known as *jaggirdar*.

The two states had fought incessantly with one another for generations.[85] When Bijapur captured Goa in 1470, it denied Vijayanagara access to its principal port on the west coast, thereby limiting its access to the Persian and Arabian horses that were so essential for Vijayanagara's military campaigns.[86] Having the chance to correct this problem and form an alliance with Vijayanagara could work to Albuquerque's advantage. He might also further good will by adjusting several Bijapur policies, for the sultanate had imposed crippling policies upon Goa's Hindu population, most of whom were followers of a Shiva cult that rejected the caste system.[87] Under Bijapur's rule of Goa land taxes doubled and payment had to be made in cash instead of in kind. Taxes were also assessed on the village level instead of on the family level. These policies produced profound and unwelcome changes to Goa's predominantly agrarian society.[88] In addition, a new sultan had recently inherited the Bijapur throne and was busy fighting in the interior. Timoji knew Goa was not well defended, and its population was restive. In other words, as a result of a wide variety of cultural, economic, and military factors, the time was right for a Portuguese move.

Albuquerque began cautiously. Rather than simply sail up the five-mile estuary of the Mandovi River and start shelling the town, he ordered the bar sounded at low and high tide to make sure there was sufficient depth to let his fleet pass and sent out teams to reconnoiter the city and its

defenses.[89] There were brief skirmishes with the Muslims stationed in the outer defensive towers and earthworks, but when representatives from the city arrived to sue for peace it was clear that Goa would be no Calicut. This is why the formal surrender of the city on March 1, 1510 was chosen for the northeastern frieze of Albuquerque's commemorative statue in Belém. In it, Albuquerque stands proudly above a turbaned man, who on bended knee offers the governor a silk pillow upon which the keys to the city rest. A crucifix-carrying Dominican friar and a captain bearing the royal

---

[85] In the fifteenth century, Vijayanagara fought the larger Bahmani Sultanate under which Bijapur was simply one of its provinces. By 1500, however, weaknesses in the Bahmani Sultanate allowed Bijapur to become essentially an independent sultanate of its own. The fighting between the Muslim and Hindu states continued. See Asher and Talbot, *India Before Europe*, 57.

[86] Venkataramanayya, "The Kingdom of Vijayanagara," *The Delhi Sultanate*, 297-298.

[87] P.P. Shirodkar, "Socio-cultural Life in Goa During the 16th Century," *Goa and Portugal: Their Cultural Links*, Charles J. Borges and Helmut Feldmann (eds.) (New Delhi: Concept Publishing Company, 1997), 29. Goans were members of the Nath cult. Also known as the Yoga, Siddha or Avadhut cults, it holds that "the Shakti creates the universe, Siva nurtures it, and time destroys it, and Natha brings *mukti* (freedom)."

[88] Pearson, *The Portuguese in India*, 88-89.

[89] In nautical terms, a bar is a long ridge of sand or gravel near the surface of the water that obstructs navigation near the mouth of the river into a harbor. "Sounding the bar" means to measure it.

standard stand at Albuquerque's shoulders, surrounded by other officers and soldiers with sharpened pikes as the crenelated walls and stout towers of the fortress rise above.[90]

Those walls were not in the prime condition the frieze suggests and upon inspection Albuquerque found them quite wanting. He immediately set both local residents and his soldiers to work to improve the foundations and, as in Hormuz, Albuquerque insisted that the captains participate in the labor.[91] In the end, there was not enough time or sufficient supplies to complete the necessary repair work. When the sultan of Bijapur, Ismael Adil Shah, returned to Goa in April, he did so with an army of 50,000 men, and the Portuguese were eventually forced to abandon the city. Interestingly, the sultan offered Albuquerque peace and the opportunity to construct a fortress elsewhere on the island, but the governor quickly rejected the offer.[92] For him, the city of Goa was an all-or-nothing proposition. This is why in November 1510 Albuquerque returned to Goa with his fleet repaired and supplemented with new ships. He then abandoned caution: with 1,600 men, who were supported by thousands of local inhabitants opposed to Bijapur rule, Albuquerque ordered an assault on the front gate at dawn. His men forced it open and the attack was successful; four days of looting and bloodshed followed. No quarter was given to any Muslim for Albuquerque's "determination was to leave no seed of this race throughout the whole of the island."[93] Those who weren't killed by sword or pike and then fed to the crocodiles were rounded into a mosque before it was set ablaze.[94]

~

With the capture of Goa, Portugal was well positioned to exert additional pressure on the spice trade, even if Manuel's kingdom was already enjoying considerable success, as statistics from Venice reveal. In 1495, before the Portuguese arrived in India, Venetian merchants purchased 3.5 million pounds of spices in Alexandria, Egypt; ten years later, they could only procure one million pounds. Meanwhile, Portuguese spice imports jumped from less that 250,000 pounds in 1501 to 2.3 million pounds in 1505.[95] Portugal replaced Venice as the main supplier of pepper and other spices for the European market. Albuquerque, however, was not one to settle: that there were *any* spices still passing through the traditional Middle Eastern trading channels was unacceptable to the governor. He had been ordered to establish a monopoly and that is exactly what he intended to do by taking three decisive steps.

First, he sought to control the local coastal trade more effectively. Therefore, all ships had to purchase a *cartaz* or pass which permitted travel between specific points and required ships to stop and pay customs duties at key ports. Along the west coast of India, these taxes ranged from 3.5% in Diu to 8% in Chaul in 1569.[96] Ship captains also had to leave a cash deposit at their point of

[90] The depiction of this frieze closely follows the description offered by Albuquerque's son. In it, the flag is "made of white satin with a cross of Christus worked in the centre." See [Braz] Afonso de Albuquerque, *The Commentaries,* Volume 2, 97-98.

[91] [Braz] Afonso de Albuquerque, *The Commentaries,* Volume 2, 101.

[92] Crowley, *Conquerors,* 235; and Diffie and Winius, *Foundations of the Portuguese Empire, 1415-1580,* 252.

[93] [Braz] Afonso de Albuquerque, *The Commentaries of the Great Afonso Dalboquerque,* Volume 3, Walter de Gray Birch (trans.) (London: The Hakluyt Society, 1880), 16.

[94] Crowley, *Conquerors,* 252.

[95] Stanley A. Wolpert, *A New History of India,* 2nd ed. (New York: Oxford University Press, 1982), 138.

[96] Diffie and Winius, *Foundations of the Portuguese Empire, 1415-1580,* 321.

departure to ensure their return voyage.[97] These regulations, and the capital outlay they required, forced the local merchants into Portuguese hands since they could not make a sufficient profit if they stopped at each required port to pay the necessary fees. Enforced by Portuguese military might, this system discouraged illegal trade, fought piracy, and boosted prices in India and profits in Lisbon. The pass system also applied to Muslims traveling to Mecca on the *hajj*, which was particularly offensive since the passes came emblazoned with a picture of the Virgin Mary and Jesus. The fact that even being on a ship holding such a pass could be interpreted as an act of grave idolatry only made the Portuguese presence in the Indian Ocean more resented.[98]

Second, and most ambitiously, Albuquerque sought to establish a real colony in Goa instead of a mere trading fort. This was a very complex process, involving virtually every aspect of society. It began immediately upon Albuquerque's conquest of Goa, when he strongly encouraged his soldiers to marry the widows of the Muslim soldiers, especially those with lighter skin tones.[99] It continued with the governor's decision to cut tax assessments and to preserve traditional legal mechanisms for settling disputes.[100] Albuquerque also sought to encourage the establishment of a lasting colony by making Goa a center for diplomatic and religious life. Albuquerque formally received delegations from Vijayanagara and Gujarat, Iran, and Ethiopia. The setting for the ceremonies would have been modest in the early days of the Portuguese colony, but the diplomatic network these encounters produced rivaled those of many contemporary European monarchs. Eventually it grew so fruitful that one of Albuquerque's successors boasted that he had "spies in all the courts of the kings of India."[101] Significantly, Portuguese became the language of diplomacy throughout Asian ports until the mid-eighteenth century,[102] which meant Portuguese influence extended long after the might of their cannons, thanks to Albuquerque's farsighted efforts. Naturally, Catholicism also played a key role in Albuquerque's vision, but he allowed Hindus to continue practicing their faith with the exception of *sati*, the practice of Hindu women immolating themselves upon their dead husbands' pyres.[103] These policies collectively allowed Albuquerque to write "the peoples of India now realize that we have come to settle permanently in this land, for they see us planting trees, building houses of stone and lime, and breeding sons and daughters."[104]

---

[97] Pearson, *The Portuguese in India*, 38.

[98] Ellison B. Findly, "The Capture of Maryam-un-Zamāni's Ship: Mughal Women and European Traders," *Journal of the American Oriental Society*, Vol. 108, No. 2 (April- June, 1988), 227-238, EBSCOhost.

[99] Pearson, *The Portuguese in India*, 101, 105.

[100] Pearson, *The Portuguese in India*, 94; Diffie and Winius, *Foundations of the Portuguese Empire, 1415-1580*, 332; and Disney, *A History of Portugal and the Portuguese Empire*, Volume 2, 130.

[101] Miguel de Noronha quoted in Anthony Disney, "Portuguese Expansion, 1400-1800, Encounters, Negotiations and Interactions," *Portuguese Oceanic Expansion, 1400-1800*, 297.

[102] Disney, "Portuguese Expansion, 1400-1800," *Portuguese Oceanic Expansion, 1400-1800*, 290.

[103] [Braz] Afonso de Albuquerque *The Commentaries, Volume 2*, 94; and Disney, *A History of Portugal and the Portuguese Empire*, Volume 2, 130. This practice is also called *suttee*. Wendy Doniger notes that: 1) *suttee* may have been symbolic in the Vedic period, but was then later used as scriptural evidence for the actual practice; 2) in the Mughal period Akbar opposed *suttee* but did not ban it; 3) women's motivations for participation in *suttee* varied substantially; and 4) the practice was deeply embedded in cultural understandings of gender. See Doniger, *The Hindus*, 124, 570, 613-614.

[104] Afonso de Albuquerque quoted in C. R. Boxer, *The Dutch Seaborne Empire 1600-1800* (New York: Penguin Books, 1973), 212. Significantly, as the fundamental security of the colony was no longer in question, and as elements of Western civilization became more obvious, racial prejudice increased rather than decreased in Goa. By the late seventeenth century one Jesuit priest wrote, "the Portuguese character...naturally despises all these Asiatic races." See Francisco de Sousa, S.J. quoted in Boxer, *Four Centuries of Portuguese Expansion*, 42. Portuguese men became less willing to marry local women and establish families with them. Similarly, religious

Another way in which Albuquerque worked to establish a lasting colony in Goa involved the creation of durable governmental systems. This was essential for the long-term success of the colony because the Portuguese kings, fearing the power their viceroys possessed, usually limited their appointments to three-year terms. Therefore, the only way any meaningful knowledge about local conditions could be passed down was through some type of institution run by those who were going to live in a colony long-term. The best way to do this, Albuquerque reasoned, was to try to replicate as far as possible the municipal institutions of Portuguese towns. This would allow colonists to draw upon established traditions and help to recreate the familiar in an unfamiliar land. In Portugal, the *oficiais da câmara,* or municipal council, usually consisted of three to four aldermen, two justices of the peace, a town attorney, and representatives of the trade guilds,* all of whom had voting rights. In addition, market inspectors, the treasurer, the accountant, the ensign bearer, and the sergeant-at-arms attended meetings as non-voting members. All of these officeholders were selected by lot after a rather complex nomination process.[105] In Goa, Albuquerque had to make adjustments for different conditions and fewer eligible office holders. In the end, this municipal council, the first one established in the Portuguese empire, included the three aldermen drawn from the nobility; two ordinary judges; the city prosecutor; and four trade guild representatives. In the largest departure from tradition, a military captain of the city, who was appointed by the crown, also attended and had two votes. Initially all of these men were Iberian born, but by the mid-sixteenth century those of mixed Portuguese-Indian heritage also served the city in this way.[106]

Interestingly, the Goa council sought to preserve the political, economic and social rights and privileges European towns had slowly won through the course of the Middle Ages. As viceroy, Albuquerque could not interfere in the day-to-day dealings of the *câmara*, and he at least had to listen to the advice the *câmara* gave him regarding war strategy, civil defense, monetary policy, and handling those officials who abused their offices. Moreover, Albuquerque had to uphold the free trading rights of council members in all goods except spices, he had to treat them with a dignity usually reserved for members of the royal household, and he had to ensure that the rights and privileges of the Portuguese citizens of Goa were protected.[107] In turn, the Goa council had to promise to provide for the upkeep of basic infrastructure such as walls, roads, and bridges.[108] This

accommodation evaporated as European power grew. Religious life became more formalized and doctrinaire: Goa received its first bishop in 1538, its first Jesuits in 1542, and its first representatives of the Inquisition in 1560. These men set higher standards for literacy and liturgy, but they also sought to obliterate any resistance to Catholicism, punishing supposed converts who lived as Hindus at home. In fact, the Inquisition forbade everything from cooking rice without salt to wearing traditional undergarments, from refusing to eat pork to sending gifts at traditional times. These regulations produced 3,800 Inquisition cases in Goa between 1561 and 1623 and 16,172 cases between 1561-1774. See Pearson, *The Portuguese in India*, 120. Those who did not convert also suffered. In 1567, for example, a captain led his force into the Goan countryside raiding and pillaging, spending "nights and nights" destroying 280 temples as part of the iconoclasm movement that swept Goa in the mid-sixteenth century. See Rajiv Malik, "Surviving a Troubled Past, Thriving in a Progressive Present," *Hinduism Today*, 33, 4 (Oct.-Dec., 2011), 19-29, ProQuest Central; and Henn, *Hindu-Catholic Encounters in Goa*, 41-43.

[105] C.R. Boxer, *Portuguese Society in the Tropics: The Municipal Councils of Goa, Macao, Bahia and Luanda, 1510-1800* (Madison: University of Wisconsin Press, 1965), 5-6.

[106] Boxer, *Portuguese Society in the Tropics,* 34-35.

[107] Boxer, *Portuguese Society in the Tropics,* 13-14. Significantly, the Goa *câmara* wrote to the crown at least 10 times between 1520 and 1680 to obtain on-going affirmations of these prerogatives.

[108] Boxer, *Portuguese Society in the Tropics,* 19.

may seem excessively bureaucratic and formal for a tiny colony halfway around the world from Lisbon, but it was precisely because of the enormous distances involved that Portuguese monarchs wanted power to be shared between the viceroy and the municipal council. These kings wanted a system of checks and balances which would keep their viceroys accountable, their soldiers loyal, and their civic officials dependent on royal support.   From Lisbon's perspective, and from Albuquerque's as well, this was the best way to keep the profits from the spice trade flowing fast.

Once Albuquerque had secured local maritime traffic and given Goa a colonial foundation, he set his sights upon the third decisive step to secure the Portuguese spice monopoly: capturing two cities that stood as the sentries guarding the opposite doorways for Muslim access to the Indian Ocean. The first was Malacca, which overlooked the strait separating Sumatra from the Malay Peninsula. Ruled by a sultan, it connected Indian Ocean trade with that from the South China Sea because it stood at the edge of two different monsoonal weather systems, In addition, its early leaders promoted peaceful trade, respected cultural differences, discouraged piracy, and built a reputation as a reliable place to transact business.[109] Porcelain, nutmeg, silk, tin, breadfruit, gold, opium, pepper, pomegranates, rice, cotton fabrics, cloves, and rugs intermingled in a Babel of tongues and currencies. It was an *entrepôt* the Portuguese both wanted and needed if Albuquerque and Manuel's dreams were to be secured.

Departing Goa with 18 ships, 900 Portuguese soldiers and 200 Indian mercenaries, Albuquerque set sail in April 1511 to attack an enemy 2,500 miles away through seas he'd never sailed. Seizing a Gujarati merchant ship off the coast of Sri Lanka allowed him to capture knowledgeable navigators to help mitigate the uncertainties,[110] but the inherent difficulty of an amphibious assault on a town with 20,000 defenders remained.   That wasn't about to stop the governor: he audaciously announced his arrival in Malacca in early July with trumpets blaring, guns blasting, and flags waving.[111] Negotiations with the sultan quickly froze as Albuquerque refused to discuss terms until twenty Portuguese hostages, captured during Portugal's first visit to Malacca in 1509, had been released, but the sultan refused to release the detainees until Albuquerque promised that he was willing to trade in peace and on equal terms with other parties.[112] The standoff between the two obstinate men lasted until July 24 when Albuquerque made his first attempt to take the city—one designed to capture the bisected city's only bridge. The sultan responded to the assault on the city by leading twenty war elephants with swords swinging from their trunks against the invaders. Two *fidalgos* managed to stab the lead elephant in the eye and belly to stop the charge, but as arrows and poisoned darts flew, Albuquerque's men were not able to secure the bridge and had to return to their ships.[113] Albuquerque's second attempt came on August 10, when his men loaded onto a tall, commandeered junk that drifted with the incoming tide towards the bridge. The height advantage from the junk allowed archers to keep the sultan's troops occupied as the Portuguese disembarked. Soon the defenders were dislodged from their posts, and Albuquerque's men gained control of the

---

[109] Donald B. Freeman, *The Straits of Malacca: Gateway or Gauntlet?* (Montreal, Canada: McGill-Queen's University Press, 2003), 85-88, EBSCOebooks.

[110] [Braz] Afonso de Albuquerque, *The Commentaries, Volume 3*, 58.

[111] [Braz] Afonso de Albuquerque, *The Commentaries, Volume 3*, 66.

[112] [Braz] Afonso de Albuquerque, *The Commentaries, Volume 3*, 66-67; and Crowley, *Conquerors*, 258-259. Diogo Lopes de Sequeira arrived in Malacca in 1509, but his effort to impose Portuguese dominance was rebuffed and some of his men were captured.

[113] [Braz] Afonso de Albuquerque *The Commentaries of the Great Afonso DAlboquerque, Volume 3*, Walter De Gray Birch (trans.) (London: Hakluyt Society, 1877), 103-104, 106-108; and Roger Crowley, *Conquerors: How Portugal Forged the First Global Empire* (New York: Random House, 2015), 260-261.

bridge. Then the Portuguese dig in, fortified their position, and held it for twenty days until the sultan decided to abandon the city.[114] Once this happened, Albuquerque moved his men out. He had trained them to fight in such situations as a phalanx, a tight, maneuverable rectangular formation of men wielding pikes that did not break formation for individual combat. The phalanx proved to be extraordinarily and brutally effective in taking control of the rest of Malacca and ridding the city of its Muslim population, for as Albuquerque ordered in Curiate, Muscat, and Goa, no quarter was given to any Muslim, regardless of age, profession, or gender.[115]   The ruthless purge of Malacca is the scene depicted on the northwestern frieze of Albuquerque's commemorative monument in Belém, although the phalanx formation is not present. Instead, Albuquerque rallies his men to move forward as the noblemen shout their battle cry, "Santiago!" The two *fidalgos* who are already engaged in combat against men with bows or swords have shoved their pikes into the torsos of two of the city's hapless defenders who scream out in pain, disbelief, and horror. One Muslim man has already decided the fight is hopeless and has turned his back on the scene to flee. There are no women or children depicted in the frieze although they too suffered from the Portuguese wrath. Once the city was secured, Albuquerque authorized the looting of the city "as recompense for past labours." His men had "free power to keep or dispose of everything they took," but they could not touch the property of Malacca's Hindu or Chinese residents.[116]

The plunder from Malacca rivaled that of Hernán Cortés in Mexico and Francisco Pizarro in Peru. Had it not been lost to the sea in a typhoon as Albuquerque sailed for Goa in December 1511, the treasures abroad the flagship *Frol de la Mar* would have made Manuel I the envy of Europe's monarchs.[117] As it was, Albuquerque's prize for Manuel was Portugal's firm command of the eastern doorway to Indian Ocean trade, thanks to the construction of a major fortress at water's edge that was capable of withstanding naval assaults.[118] It was a present of continuous reward—one that would serve Portugal for generations. Little wonder that despite the loss of the *Frol de la Mar*, Albuquerque was able to write to Manuel with pride and confidence:

---

[114] Crowley, *Conquerors*, 263-264.

[115] [Braz] Afonso de Albuquerque, *The Commentaries, Volume 3*, 127; and Crowley, *Conquerors*, 263.

[116] [Braz] Afonso de Albuquerque, *The Commentaries, Volume 3*, 126-127.

[117] Diffie and Winius, *Foundations of the Portuguese Empire, 1415-1580*, 258, 260. Built in 1502, the *Frol de la Mar* was an intimidating 400-ton carrack with forty guns distributed over three decks but after a decade of service, it was in such poor shape that many Portuguese sailors refused to sail it. See Crowley, *Conquerors*, 268.

[118] Freeman, *The Straits of Malacca*, 129-130, EBSCOebooks.

> There is no need for any *naus* [large ship] to be kept permanently in Malacca, other than those you decide should be used for trading in those parts….Your men have left behind them such a good reputation that these pirates will not dare to return as far as the port of Malacca, as they used to in the time of [Muslim] rule.[119]

The construction of the Albuquerque's fortress, known as A Famosa (the Famous), defended Portugal's interests in Malacca for 130 years until the city finally fell to the Dutch in 1641.[120]

With the eastern doorway secure, Albuquerque set his sights on the western doorway to the Indian Ocean, the citadel of Aden, near the entrance of the Red Sea. Capturing this port had been a part of Manuel I's instructions to Albuquerque in 1506, but at that point Albuquerque simply didn't have sufficient manpower to conquer the city.[121] The sixteenth-century city was uniquely situated: sitting on the floor of an extinct volcano, Aden was protected on three sides by the crater's tall rim while an intimidating, man-made wall faced the sea on the fourth. The only land access to the city came via an isthmus that flooded at high tide and through a single narrow pass on the northwest side of the crater's rim. Capturing the city required scaling the wall, taking several fortifications and towers, securing the pass, and overcoming Aden's main geographical curse: a lack of water.[122] On Good Friday 1513, Albuquerque and his captains agreed to scale the wall facing the sea in two places and then proceed as quickly as possible to the city gate facing the mountain pass. Controlling this gate was essential because through it the Muslims "could bring so many troops into the city that we would be overwhelmed," Albuquerque noted.[123] The governor was clear that "we needed to fight well" in order to have the plan succeed; if the first assault failed, the Portuguese would have to retreat because they did not have enough fresh water to stay off shore for very long.[124] As dawn broke the next day Albuquerque and his men boarded skiffs and rowed towards the beach. At the last minute the governor changed the battle plan because

> it seemed to me that our numbers were too small for scaling the wall and that we had too few ladders….I considered that, if we scaled the walls from two directions, we would not be able to put a body of men on top of them… and accordingly I decided that we should

[119] Afonso de Albuquerque to Manuel I, April 1, 1512 in *Albuquerque: Caesar of the East*, 127.

[120] For an account of the Dutch seizure of Malacca in 1641, see Dianne Lewis, *Jan Compagnie in the Straits of Malacca* (Athens, Ohio: Ohio Center for International Studies, Ohio University, 1995), 12-28. Lewis also notes that the Portuguese capture of Malacca in 1511 did not end trade all by Malays. Rather, the capture simply fragmented the trade as other ports compensated and developed. It is also important to note that the Malays did not passively accept the Portuguese presence. As Lewis notes on page 9, there were Malay attacks on Malacca in 1517, 1520, 1521, 1558, 170, and 1575.

[121] Diffie and Winius, *Foundations of the Portuguese Empire, 1415-1580,* 237. This is why Albuquerque proceeded to Hormuz instead in 1507.

[122] For more on the Aden's geography, fortifications, and water issues, see Roxani Eleni Margariti, *Aden and the Indian Ocean Trade: 150 Years in the Life of a Medieval Arabian Port* (Chapel Hill, North Carolina: University of North Carolina Press, 2007), 34-52 and 87-94. Portuguese intelligence on Aden in 1513 was so weak that Albuquerque didn't know if Aden was an island or on a peninsula. It was only after the battle, when Albuquerque sailed into the bay to the west of the city, that he learned Aden was on a peninsula. See Afonso de Albuquerque to Manuel I, December 4, 1513 in *Albuquerque: Caesar of the East*, 221.

[123] Afonso de Albuquerque to Manuel I, December 4, 1513 in *Albuquerque: Caesar of the East*, 213.

[124] Afonso de Albuquerque to Manuel I, December 4, 1513 in *Albuquerque: Caesar of the East*, 213.

make a joint attack at one spot, so that twice as many men could get to the wall and we could assist one another.[125]

Unfortunately for the Portuguese, this change in strategy did not work. In fact, nothing seemed to go right for them that morning: the landing required the men to get into the water; the gunpowder got wet as they splashed ashore; the *fidalgos* failed to coordinate the placement of the ladders as they competed for the honor of being the first to scale the walls; the ladders were not long enough to quite reach the top of the wall; and the ladders broke and had to be repaired in the middle of the battle. Despite all of these setbacks, about fifty men successfully scaled the wall and some descended to the opposite side and began fighting in the streets.[126] Portuguese cannons even opened a hole in the wall, but the *fidalgos* failed to take advantage of the situation, perhaps because Albuquerque's nephew let his pride get in the way: António Garcia de Noronha is reported to not have entered the breech because the men already inside the city's walls had already won the glory; without *fidalgo* leadership, none of the other soldiers acted.[127] In contrast, the Muslims defended their city forcefully. By noon, the Portuguese were in full retreat, evacuating to their ships.

In the aftermath of the Aden debacle, Albuquerque admitted that his faulty strategy also played a role in the defeat. As he told Manuel I, "I think that, if I had reconnoitered Aden beforehand, I would not have attacked where we did."[128] Albuquerque remained convinced, however, that not only was Aden conquerable, but that it was essential for Portugal to do so in order to secure the spice monopoly and undermine Arab markets. He noted with satisfaction that merely sailing into the Red Sea had generated panic in Jeddah and Cairo, for in doing so, the Portuguese had "touched them on the raw in the place where they felt most secure.[129] Albuquerque concluded that if Manuel captured Aden and established a fortress on Massawa Island to control the Red Sea trade, "you will have the riches of the whole world in your hands."[130] Such steps would require an investment in ships and manpower, but Manuel's priorities were not exclusively focused upon Asian trade. Instead, the king chose to continue to expand Portugal's presence in Morocco. In 1513, he sent 18,000 troops to capture Azamor; in 1514, he sent 120 ships to facilitate the construction of the nearby Mazagão fortress; and in 1515, he sent 200 ships to the mouth of the Sibu River to build a fortress there.[131] This was the type of support and commitment Albuquerque believed was necessary for the success of the *Estado da Índia*. And that level of commitment only seemed fair since in the 1510s 65% to 68% of the crown's revenue came from the overseas trade, and the taxes generated from the spice trade alone exceeded those from all domestic sources.[132] As he bitterly complained to Manuel,

---

[125] Afonso de Albuquerque to Manuel I, December 4, 1513 in *Albuquerque: Caesar of the East*, 215.
[126] Afonso de Albuquerque to Manuel I, December 4, 1513 in *Albuquerque: Caesar of the East*, 217.
[127] Crowley, *Conquerors*, 291.
[128] Afonso de Albuquerque to Manuel I, December 4, 1513 in *Albuquerque: Caesar of the East*, 255.
[129] Afonso de Albuquerque to Manuel I, December 4, 1513 in *Albuquerque: Caesar of the East*, 257, 259.
[130] Afonso de Albuquerque to Manuel I, December 4, 1513 in *Albuquerque: Caesar of the East*, 257, 259.
[131] Susannah Humble Ferreira, *The Crown, the Court, and the Casa da Índia: Political Centralization in Portugal 1479-1521* (Leiden, Netherlands: Brill, 2015), 145-146, EBSCOebooks. The effort at the Sibu River ended in failure when a changing tide left the Portuguese ships stranded on sandbars; in the subsequent Muslim attack with 3,000 cavalry 30,000 infantry, many members of the Portuguese nobility were captured and then ransomed at high cost. This brought an end to the period of Portuguese expansion in Morocco.
[132] The 65% figure is from 1506 and the 68% figure is from 1518-19. See Disney, *A History of Portugal and the Portuguese Empire*, Volume 1, 147-148.

I also notice, Sire, that you do not send me arms or men or any military equipment....If Your Highness had sent the equipment, the men and the arms with which to carry out your orders, I would neither have had to put my men twice under fire in Malacca and twice in Goa, nor would the [Muslims] have taken control of your fortress which I had begun to build in Ormuz.[133]

Without sufficient support from Lisbon, Albuquerque had little hope of securing the spice trade's western door.

~

The fourth and final frieze on Albuquerque's memorial in Belém depicts the governor about to instigate a murderous plot in Hormuz in April 1515. In this scene, Albuquerque is walking with considerable gravitas down the steps of a three-tiered dais, having just risen from an ornate and amply upholstered chair that could be mistaken for a throne. A large tapestry hangs on the wall behind it, again drawing attention to the chair as the focal point of the room. Standing immediately

---

[133] Afonso de Albuquerque to Manuel I, April 1, 1512 in *Albuquerque: Caesar of the East,* 103, 105.

at Albuquerque's left is a poised boy holding a partially-obscured sword in his left hand. The man Albuquerque approaches wears a long, double strand of pearls, a bejeweled headdress, and a luxurious sash around his waist. He bows deeply with his arms crossed in front of his chest before the governor. Eight Portuguese *fidalgos* observe this formal, diplomatic interaction with different expressions on their faces: two of them are coldly inscrutable, three have a vague look of anticipation, one has puckered his lips to take a deep breath, and one has just cracked the first hint of a smile. The final observer, with a Cheshire cat grin and knowing glance, reveals that the bowing visitor is about to die.

The memorial's sculptor naturally took some artistic liberties to create this vivid scene, but he did faithfully capture the essence of Albuquerque's overall scheme for April 18, 1515. When the governor arrived in Hormuz on the first of the month, he found the rich city-state in political turmoil: both the young king, Turan Shah, and his chief vizier were at the mercy of a man named Rais Ahmed, who had entered the king's bedroom one night, held a knife to this throat, and forced the young ruler to beg for his life. The king did so and surrendered all meaningful political control to Ahmed.[134] Albuquerque's arrival changed the equation and allowed Turan Shah to demonstrate a degree of independence: he gave formal permission for the Portuguese to disembark and to construct a stockade between the beach and the palace.[135] Several days later Albuquerque asked to meet with Rais Ahmed and the king. After some diplomatic haggling over the arrangements they agreed to meet unarmed on neutral ground. Albuquerque ordered that a large reception room of finished earthen walls be built near the beach for this meeting. It was decorated with cloth and "a brocaded dais, furnished with two chairs of crimson velvet, fringed with gold," as well as benches "covered in cushions for the captains."[136] When Ahmed arrived at the hall, carrying a sword, dagger, and shield, Albuquerque asked why he had come with weapons. Insulted by the implied lack of trust and the break with Arab custom, Ahmed turned back towards the doorway just as Turah Shah entered. Albuquerque's men immediately locked the doors behind the king; as Ahmed turned to object, Albuquerque bellowed, "Kill him!" The *fidalgos* daggers impaled Ahmed from all directions, and he was dead before his head hit the floor. Stunned by the quick turn of events, Turah Shah became full of dread that he would be next to fall, but Albuquerque took his hand, reassured the boy, and led him to the dais to sit in the chair as king.[137] The Portuguese had won Turah Shah's complete loyalty.[138]

Albuquerque then demanded that a Portuguese fortress be built in Hormuz, thereby rectifying the problem his captains created when they mutinied in 1509. The work proceeded through the summer with the men mostly working by torchlight to avoid the blistering heat of the day, but dysentery set in and workers began to die. Albuquerque too fell victim in August, but refused to leave Hormuz until he could be certain that the fort was a viable defensive structure.[139] On November 8 he finally set sail for Goa, slipping away without bidding Turah Shah a formal farewell

---

[134] Rais Ahmed always stood next to "the king's chair, holding a short sword, with one hand placed on his dagger" so that "the king would never answer any more than what this man told him." [Braz] Afonso de Albuquerque, *The Commentaries, Volume 4*, 140, 148-149.

[135] Crowley, *Conquerors*, 307-308.

[136] [Braz] Afonso de Albuquerque, *The Commentaries, Volume 4*, 157.

[137] [Braz] Afonso de Albuquerque, *The Commentaries, Volume 4*, 158-159.

[138] Roger Crowley aptly describes these events as "a perfect coup." Crowley, *Conquerors,* 311.

[139] Crowley, *Conquerors*, 312-314. For a discussion of the evolution of the fortress, see João Lizardo, "The Evolution of the Fortress of Hormuz up to its Renovation by Inofre de Carvalho," *Revisiting Hormuz: Portuguese Interactions in the Persian Gulf in the Early Modern Period*, 135-148.

as a result of his rapidly deteriorating health. He left his nephew, Pero de Albuquerque, in command of the fortress.[140] Off the coast from Calayate, the fleet encountered a ship carrying the news that Manuel I had appointed a new viceroy of India—a man who was from an anti-Albuquerque faction within the court.[141] Heartbroken by the news from Lisbon, the dying governor exclaimed, "It were well that I were gone."[142] Without the faith of his king, Albuquerque felt his life was over. He had worked so hard to further Portuguese interests in the Indian Ocean and to obtain revenge for Christendom against Islam, but it had not been enough. He had failed to take Aden and without securing the Red Sea, the dream of a Portuguese monopoly in the spice trade could not be realized.

Albuquerque clung to life until his ship approached Goa. He met with his secretary, dictated his last will and testament, and asked to be clothed in the surcoat of Santiago so that he might die in the uniform of a Crusader. He then sipped some Portuguese red wine, called for his confessor, accepted the Last Rights, and was absolved of his sins in the Catholic tradition. As dawn broke on December 15, 1515, Albuquerque asked to be carried to his cabin's window so that he might have one last look at the Goan skyline. He died holding a crucifix, thinking of his city and what awaited, both for it and for him, as a tropical breeze blew across the land.[143]

~

António de Oliveira Salazar began his thirty-six-year rule as Portugal's authoritarian prime minister in 1932.[144] As an integral part of his campaign to instill the values of tradition, morality, and pride in the nation, the Salazar government sought to celebrate 1940 as the Double Centenary of National Independence—the eight hundredth anniversary of Portugal's founding and the three hundredth anniversary of Portugal's regaining its independence after a sixty-year period of Spanish rule.[145] As a part of the observance, the government sponsored the Exposition of the Portuguese

[140] [Braz] Afonso de Albuquerque, *The Commentaries, Volume 4*, 191-192.

[141] Albuquerque's replacement was Lopo Soares de Albergaria (c. 1460 – c. 1520), who had the opportunity in 1517 to take Aden for the Portuguese and destroy a Muslim fleet at Jeddah but timidly failed to take advantage of either situation. Historian Matteo Salvadore describes the Portuguese court as having an imperial faction and a mercantile* faction. Albuquerque and Manuel were imperialists, but with Manuel's death in 1521 the mercantile faction under João III came to dominate. See Matteo Salvadore, *The African Prester John and the Birth of Ethiopian-European Relations, 1402-1555* (New York: Routledge, 2016), 154.

[142] Afonso de Albuquerque quoted in [Braz] Afonso de Albuquerque, *The Commentaries, Volume 4*, 195.

[143] [Braz] Afonso de Albuquerque *The Commentaries of the Great Afonso DAlboquerque, Volume 4*, Walter De Gray Birch (trans.) (London: Hakluyt Society, 1877), 196.

[144] The degree to which Salazar's government was fascist is a subject of intense historical debate. Labels such as "fascistic," "para-fascist," and "proto-fascist" have been used to note the similarities and the differences. For more detail about the degree that the Portuguese experience fits the fascist model see among other sources David D. Roberts, *Fascist Interactions: Proposals for a New Approach to Fascism and Its Era, 1919-1945* (New York: Berghahn, 2016), 29-30, 131, 138, 194; Robert O. Paxton, *The Anatomy of Fascism* (New York: Alfred A. Knopf, 2004), 150, 217-218; and Ellen W. Sapega, *Consensus and Debate in Salazar's Portugal: Visual and Literary Negotiations of National Text, 1933-1948* (University Park, Pennsylvania: Pennsylvania State University, 2008), 2, EBSCOebooks.

[145] When Portuguese king Sebastião I was killed without an heir in Morocco at the Battle of Alcácer Quibir (1578), he was succeeded by his great uncle Henry who was a cardinal and had served as regent during Sebastião's minority. When Henry died in 1580 without appointing a successor, there was a succession crisis. Spain's Philip II did not have the best claim to the throne, but upon sending an army to Lisbon, he secured it. Spanish kings ruled Portugal until 1640 when João IV established the House of Braganza.

World. Like a World's Fair but only involving Portugal, Brazil, and the Portuguese colonies in Africa and Asia, the Exposition was held in Lisbon's Belém neighborhood in the shadows of the sixteenth-century Jerónimos Monastery and near the port from which Eanes, Cão, Dias, Gama, and Albuquerque all sailed. It was a purposefully and unapologetically didactic festival,[146] one designed to help Salazar's people remember Portugal's Golden Age and to witness the nation's recovery from the Republican era (1910-1926). In this way, the 1940 Exposition served the same function as Paris' *Exposition Universelle* of 1900, which sought show France's recovery from the Franco-Prussian War,* or as San Francisco's Panama–Pacific International Exposition of 1915, which attempted to show the city's recovery from the 1906 earthquake.[147] The fair also celebrated the contrast between Portugal's peaceful stability and Spain's recent Civil War and the rest of the continent's descent into World War II.[148] What truly made Salazar's fair exceptional, however, was that its focus was the past instead of the future, for as Salazar said,

> Through the centuries and generations, we have always kept alive the same spirit and, in coexistence with the most perfect territorial identity and national identity in Europe, one of the greatest vocations of Christian universalism."[149]

The Age of Exploration, in particular, was glorified with messianic messages, and the value of Portuguese imperialism to the world was reinforced with the government slogan "Portugal: Not a Small Country."[150] To emphasize the connection between the past and the present, the Exposition's paternalistic official guide for visitors explained the optimal way in which the pavilions and exhibits should be viewed. It specifically held, "Your visit should begin at the main entrance, located at Afonso de Albuquerque Square."[151] This meant that the visitors who followed the prescribed plan would begin their exploration of Portugal's past through the lens of Albuquerque's life, looking up at the resolute man staring towards the sea.

---

[146] Sapega, *Consensus and Debate in Salazar's Portugal*, 25. Sapega also has another article about the Belém site: Ellen W. Sapega, "Remembering Empire/Forgetting the Colonies," *History & Memory*, 20, 2 (Fall/Winter 2008), 18-38, ProQuest Central.

[147] David Corkill and José Carlos Pina Almeida, "Commemoration and Propaganda in Salazar's Portugal: The Mundo Português Exposition of 1940." *Journal of Contemporary History*, 44, no. 3 (July 2009): 381-399, EBSCOhost.

[148] Joana Ramalho, "The *Mise-en-scène* of the Empire: the 1940 Portuguese World Exhibition," *Media and the Portuguese Empire*, José Luís Garcia, Chandrika Kaul, Filipa Subtil and Alexandra Santos (eds.) (Cham, Switzerland: Palgrave Macmillan, 2017), 209.

[149] António de Oliveira Salazar quoted in Ramalho, "The *Mise-en-scène* of the Empire," *Media and the Portuguese Empire*, 203.

[150] Corkill and Pina Almeida, "Commemoration and Propaganda in Salazar's Portugal," *Journal of Contemporary History*, 381-399, EBSCOhost; and Felipe Fernández-Armesto, "Portuguese Expansion in a Global Context," *Portuguese Oceanic Expansion, 1400-1800*, 483. The "Portugal Não é um País Pequeno" slogan was shown on maps that superimposed Portugal's colonial possessions on a map of Europe. On this scale, Mozambique, Angola, Portuguese Guinea, São Tomé and Príncipe, Timor, Goa, Diu, Macau and other holdings stretched from Gibraltar to Russia.

[151] *Guia Oficial Exposição do Mundo Português* quoted in Ellen W. Sapega, *Consensus and Debate in Salazar's Portugal*, 30.

B

Ivan Bersen-Beklemishev

?-1525

"Of men here I do say that there is no truth among them."[1]

So said a Russian nobleman, Ivan Bersen-Beklemishev,[2] at his trial in 1525 for sedition and treason against the increasingly powerful state of Muscovy[3] and its grand prince Vasilii III. Beklemishev's statement wasn't spontaneous or impulsive, and his supposed subversion and disloyalty wasn't even particularly unique. In fact, Beklemishev's opinion was in many ways the natural conclusion to a decision made 1200 years before.

In 284 CE, the Roman Emperor Diocletian made the monumental decision to divide his empire into two parts, an east and a west.[4] His motivations for doing so involved a complex variety of political, administrative, and economic issues, but from that moment on the two halves of the empire slowly but steadily began to develop in different ways. For Beklemishev, it was the divergence in religious traditions that mattered the most. In the west, that tradition became

---

[1] Ivan Bersen-Beklemishev quoted in V.O. Kluchevsky, *A History of Russia* Volume 2, C. J. Hogarth (trans.) (New York: Russell & Russell, 1960), 62.

[2] There are multiple variations to the spelling of Ivan's name, perhaps because literacy in fifteenth-century Muscovy, even among nobles, was so low. See Robert M. Croskey, *Muscovite Diplomatic Practice in the Reign of Ivan III* (New York: Garland Publishing, Inc., 1987), 109; and Nancy Shields Kollmann, *By Honor Bound: State and Society in Early Modern Russia* (Ithaca, New York: Cornell University Press, 1999), 21.

[3] By 1300 Muscovy was one of several principalities on the Russian plain that was subject to Mongol domination. By 1400 Muscovy had successfully begun to expand its territorial holdings, and between 1450 and 1480 gradually lessened the Golden Horde's influence on Moscow. Technically, Ivan IV (Ivan the Terrible, 1530-1584) was the first to use the title of tsar formally and Muscovy was the Grand Principality of Moscow, but for convenience I have, like other writers, occasionally used the terms "Russia" and "tsar" for Beklemishev's lifetime as well. See Nancy Shields Kollmann, The Russian Empire, 1450-1801 (New York: Oxford University Press, 2017), 9.

[4] For an analysis of this decision and its consequences for the Roman Empire, see Judith Herrin, *The Formation of Christendom* (Princeton, New Jersey: Princeton University Press, 1987), 22-24, 137-138.

Catholicism; in the east, the tradition became Orthodox Christianity. While both are Christian communities with a common debt to Judaism and a common faith in Jesus as humanity's savior, the two churches hold some very different opinions about how they should be governed, how they view the relationship between the Father and the Son, and how the faithful should express their beliefs. Today, a billion Catholics and 200 million Orthodox Christians hold different beliefs as a result of Diocletian's decision to divide his empire. Though not a clergyman, Beklemishev symbolizes the consequences of these differences in a provocative way.

~

Upon his Resurrection, Jesus told the Apostles to go forth in his place, spread Christianity, and administer the sacraments to converts who believed in Christ as their Savior. According to the Orthodox interpretation of the scriptures, this directive was given equally to all twelve of the Apostles, for as Jesus says to his disciples in John 20-19, "As the Father has sent me, so I send you." Logically, therefore, all the leaders of the church should have an equal say over the governance of church policies and practices. Catholics, on the other hand, believe that Jesus gave the Apostle Peter a special role to go forth and direct the building of the faith: "And I tell you, you are Peter, and on this rock I will build my church" [Matthew 16:18]. Therefore, it follows that there should be a single leader, the bishop of Rome, to oversee the administration of the church.[5] This Orthodox and Catholic disagreement over who held ultimate authority was a major factor in causing Christianity's largest split before the Protestant Reformation.

Another important issue involved the differences in how the Orthodox and Catholics saw the relationship between God and Jesus. At the Council of Nicaea in 325, the bishops wrote a profession of faith detailing exactly what it meant to be a Christian. What became known as the Nicene Creed held that the Holy Spirit proceeded from the Father alone. In 589, however, a council of bishops meeting in Spain stated that the Holy Spirit proceeded from both the Father and the Son. This was a deeply troubling proposition for the Orthodox because it seemed to diminish the Holy Spirit and to make the Father and Jesus completely equal.[6] A third key theological difference centered on the proper type of bread to use for communion. As one Russian Metropolitan* noted, if leavened bread "symbolizes the consubstantiality of Christ's body with ours," the "use of unleavened bread" by Catholics was "an attack on the very heart of eastern Christian theology."[7] Orthodox Christians and Catholics also came to different understandings about the correct language for the mass, the right of priests to marry, the purpose of a sermon, the proper way to make the Sign of the Cross, the doctrine of purgatory,* the number of sacraments, the proper ritual for baptism, the value of mysticism, the practice of venerating saints, the most desirable style of

[5] David N. Bell, *Orthodoxy: Evolving Tradition* (Collegeville, Minnesota, Liturgical Press, 2008), 37-41; and Theodore Stylianopoulos, "Concerning the Biblical Foundation of Primacy," *The Petrine Ministry: Catholics and Orthodox in Dialogue*, Cardinal Walter Kasper (ed.) (New York: The Newman Press, 2006), 57-58.
[6] Bell, *Orthodoxy: Evolving Tradition*, 55-56.
[7] Metropolitan Hilarion Alfeyev, *Orthodox Christianity, Volume I: The History and Canonical Structure of the Orthodox Church* (Yonkers, New York: St. Vladimir's Seminary Press, 2011), 112. Hilarion Alfeyev (1966-) is currently the Metropolitan of Volokolamsk, Russia.

church architecture, the use of silk vestments, and more.[8] By 1054, the religious gulf between Christians in Western Europe and those in Eastern Europe was so pronounced and the animosity so great that the pope's legate traveled to Constantinople and excommunicated the patriarch of the Greek Orthodox Church and all of his followers for heresy. The Orthodox patriarch subsequently returned the favor and excommunicated the pope and all of his Catholic followers.[9] Both sides were satisfied to go their own way in the eleventh century, confident that they were being faithful to the intentions of Jesus Christ and the practices of the original church.

The home of Orthodox Christianity was Hagia Sophia, a massive, thoroughly innovative church in Constantinople, which many have called it the greatest building ever constructed.[10] Designed by a mathematician and a physicist in 532, Hagia Sophia's uniqueness rests in its utilization of a series of cascading arches to support a vast dome so beautiful that, according to the Byzantine historian

Procopius, "it seems not to rest upon solid masonry, but to cover the space with its golden dome [as if] suspended from Heaven."[11] Hagia Sophia's exterior was quite plain, but its interior was adorned with huge gold mosaics, colorfully-veined marble walls and floors, an iconostasis* with twelve delicate silver columns, and a gold altar studded with precious stones and covered by a silver canopy.[12] It was considered such a holy place that Muhammad prophesied that the first Muslim to pray under the great dome would go to Heaven.[13] Hagia Sophia's lavishness and fame, however, also made it a target. In 1204, Catholics on a Crusade to Jerusalem ransacked Constantinople and looted the church, carrying back to Venice many of its treasures, including relics, statues, books, and gold. Orthodox Christians experienced an even greater misfortune in 1453 when Byzantium finally fell to the Ottomans, and Hagia Sophia was transformed into a mosque.[14]

---

[8] Some Orthodox saw these differences in ritual as rather trivial as compared to the key issues of the primacy of the pope and of *filioque*—the addition of "and the Son" to the Creed. See Anthony Edward Siecienski, *The Papacy and the Orthodox: Sources and History of a Debate* (New York: Oxford University Press, 2017), 253.

[9] Alfeyev, *Orthodox Christianity,* 113. It is worth noting that the temperament of the papal legate, Humbert of Silva Candida (d. 1061), was ill-suited for a diplomatic mission and succeeded in exacerbating the tensions. See Anthony Edward Siecienski, *The Papacy and the Orthodox: Sources and History of a Debate* (New York: Oxford University Press, 2017), 249-252.

[10] John Freely and Ahmet S. Cakmak, *Byzantine Monuments of Istanbul* (New York: Cambridge University Press, 2010), 90.

[11] Procopius quoted in Freely and Cakmak, *Byzantine Monuments of Istanbul,* 95.

[12] Freely and Cakmak, *Byzantine Monuments of Istanbul,* 115-116.

[13] W. Eugene Kleinbauer, Antony White, and Henry Mathews, *Hagia Sophia* (London: Scala Publishers, 2004), 81.

[14] Hagia Sophia remained a mosque until 1935, when the founder of the Republic of Turkey, Mustafa Kemal Atatürk, transformed the building into a museum as part of his secularization program. Hagia Sophia remained

The loss of Orthodoxy's home to Islam had profound consequences for the faith. Since re-conquest was improbable, the most practical choices were to either accept the primacy of Rome and merge with Roman Catholicism or else to forge a new path and create a new foundational center for Orthodox Christianity. Both choices were quite antithetical to the principles for which Orthodoxy had stood for well over a thousand years, but something had to change if the religion was to survive. As it turned out, the Russian Orthodox Church was quite eager to take over this leadership role. In fact, there were many in Moscow who believed that the fall of Constantinople was a just punishment for the way the Byzantines had agreed to a reunification with Catholicism in 1439. In particular, the head of the Russian national church, Metropolitan Iona, held that it was Russia's destiny in 1453 to seize the leadership position since Constantinople had lost God's grace.[15] Henceforth, Moscow's grand princes would be the guardians of the faith, providing for the salvation of true Christian souls in conjunction with the church leadership. In the best of Byzantine tradition, the church and the state would act as two sides of the same coin, harmonious and inseparable.[16] This doctrine became known as the Third Rome because from the Orthodox perspective Rome was no longer faithful and neither was Constantinople. Moscow was to be the third and final home of true Christianity.[17] In time, this conviction grew so much that Russians began portraying Muscovy as the New Israel—a land surrounded by Catholic, Lutheran, Muslim and pagan infidels.[18]

The men within the Russian church that was the most comfortable assuming this mantle were largely followers of Iosif Volotskii, an abbot who founded a monastery dedicated to a tightly regulated and communal monastic life. Frequently known as the Possessors, Iosif's followers believed that monasteries had a duty to support the state vigorously when the ruler acted in accordance with God's laws,[19] that monasteries should be allowed to accumulate wealth for their own benefit and purpose, and that monks should work aggressively to root out heresy of any sort.[20] As one Possessor argued,

> God's holy churches and monasteries must not suffer injury or violence, and their lands and belongings must not be taken away….For all church and monastery [property], as well

a museum until July 2020, when Turkish president Recep Tayyip Erdoğan signed a decree to restore the building as a mosque.

[15] David B. Miller, "The Orthodox Church," *The Cambridge History of Russia, Volume 1: from Early Rus' to 1689*, Maureen Perrie (ed.) (Cambridge, UK: Cambridge University Press, 2006), 338.

[16] Robert O. Crummey, *The Formation of Muscovy, 1304-1613* (New York: Longman, Inc., 1987), 139.

[17] The doctrine was summarized in a letter by Abbot Filofei of the Eleazorov Monastery in Pskov, who wrote in 1510, "Two Romes fell down, the third is standing, and there will be no fourth." See George Vernadsky, *A History of Russia, Volume IV: Russia at the Dawn of the Modern Age* (New Haven, Connecticut: Yale University Press, 1959), 169. Some, however, argue that the letter dates from as late as 1523. See Janet Martin, *Medieval Russia, 980-1584* (New York: Cambridge University Press, 1995), 261. Isaiah Gruber describes the quote as "infamous" and notes that there is "significant controversy…over the correct interpretation" of Filofei's words, with some seeing them as apocalyptic, while others see them as an attempt to limit the power of the state. See Isaiah Gruber, *Orthodox Russia in Crisis: Church and Nation in the Time of the Troubles* (DeKalb, Illinois: Northern Illinois Press, 2012), 33-34.

[18] Gruber, *Orthodox Russia in Crisis*, 24.

[19] Donald Ostroski, "The Growth of Muscovy, 1462-1533," *The Cambridge History of Russia, Volume 1: from Early Rus' to 1689*, Maureen Perrie (ed.) (Cambridge, UK: Cambridge University Press, 2006), 228.

[20] Miller, "The Orthodox Church," *The Cambridge History of Russia, Volume 1,* 351-352.

as the fruits of the monks' labor, are dedicated to God and are spent only on the poor…and the most essential needs of the churches, the monasteries, and the monks.[21]

Conversely, those within the church who were less comfortable with Russia adopting a new leadership role were known as the Non-Possessors. They were largely followers of Nil Sorskii and were *skete* monks: men who lived primarily on their own, eating and working and praying in isolation, but who gathered once a week for divine service. *Skete* monasteries were the predominant type of monastic community in Russia through the fourteenth and fifteenth centuries. These men shunned politics, wanting nothing to do with the state or the nobility, and they were adamantly opposed to monks owning property.[22] Nil worried that it was too easy for monks living communally to be tempted by luxuries, vices, and the labor of others.[23] As Nil himself had said, it was in silence and simplicity that a monk might best find God, since "it is not becoming to monks to own villages."[24] He also maintained that "no one was ever judged for not decorating a church," that monks should drive from themselves "any desire for gold, silver, and property," and that they should only use things that were "cheap, unadorned and easily obtainable."[25] But by the time of Nil's death in 1508, it was clear that tide had turned against the individualistic monastic life in Russia. *Skete* monasteries were in decline.[26] Instead, the wealthier, communal monasteries, whose orientation aligned more closely with those of the church's episcopal authorities and the increasingly powerful monarchy, ensured that Russia would assume the responsibility of becoming Orthodoxy's Third Rome.[27]

~

Like many nobles, Ivan Beklemishev was someone who struggled with change for he both benefited from and trusted in the power of tradition. The problem for Beklemishev was that in the late fifteenth and early sixteenth centuries, Russia was full of political, economic, and social change, and there seemed to be nothing he could do to stop it.

[21] "Joseph of Volokolamsk on Church Property, ca. 1503," in *A Sourcebook for Russian History from Early Times to 1917*, Volume 1, George Vernadsky, Ralph T. Fisher Jr., Alan D. Ferguson, Andrew Lossky, and Sergei Pushkarev (eds.) (New Haven, Connecticut: Yale University Press, 1972), 154.

[22] Bell, *Orthodoxy: Evolving Tradition*, 147.

[23] Kollmann, *The Russian Empire, 1450-1801*, 251.

[24] Nil Sorskii quoted in Miller, "The Orthodox Church," *The Cambridge History of Russia, Volume 1*, 351.

[25] Nil Sorskii quoted in Alexsandra Sulikowska, *The Icon Debate: Religious Images in Russia in the 15th and 16th Centuries* (Frankfurt am Main, Peter Lang, 2016), 113, 176.

[26] Paul Bushkovitch, *Religion and Society in Russia: The Sixteenth and Seventeenth Centuries* (New York: Oxford University Press, 1992), 10.

[27] It is critical to note that despite these differences in emphasis between Nil and Iosif on the best nature of a monastic community, they were not as adversarial as one might suppose, according to recent scholarship. In fact, they agreed on many issues, such as the ways in which they upheld *starchestvo*, the ideal master-disciple relationship. See David Goldfrank, "Nil's and Iosif's Rhetoric of 'Starchestvo'," *Russian History*, 39, 1/2 (2012), 42-76, EBSCOhost. Where the two men had differences, they were more in emphasis than dogma. Iosif still "fostered poverty and asceticism for individual monks," while desiring wealth for the Church as a whole, and Nil clearly "benefitted from his hermitage's connection to the immensely rich Kirillo Belozersk Monastery." See Gruber, *Orthodox Russia in Crisis*, 52-53.

As best Beklemishev could tell, all of his and all of Russia's problems began on November 12, 1472. On that day the niece of the last Byzantine Emperor arrived in Moscow to marry Muscovy's grand prince Ivan III,[28] accompanied by a hundred-horse caravan carrying her luggage.[29] Ivan's choice of a bride was completely inappropriate as far as Beklemishev was concerned: her family had advocated for a reunification with Catholicism in 1439 at the Council of Florence,[30] she had lived in Rome as a ward of the pope since 1460, and had become a practicing Catholic. She had even given up her Greek birth name, Zoe, to become Sophia. If Sophia had been quiet or dim-witted perhaps everything would have turned out all right, but that too was a problem: Sophia was bright and charming. According to the Austrian ambassador Sigismund von Herberstein, Sophia was "very artful," able to assess complex situations quickly and then exert considerable influence over her husband's actions.[31] Beklemishev thought she was responsible for changing the whole character of the court, robbing it of its traditional informality and imposing upon the Kremlin a host of cumbersome, elaborate Byzantine customs and procedures for conducting business.[32] Access to the Ivan III became far more restricted after Sophia's arrival, making it seem as if she were intent upon making the crown prince the heir to all of Byzantium with all its pomp and circumstance. She certainly brought an understanding of bureaucracy and how to utilize it.[33] Once Sophia started to receive ambassadors and dignitaries on her own, she was nicknamed "Despina."[34] Beklemishev thought it quite apt. He once said,

> Since the time that the Greeks came hither, our land hath been thrown into confusion, even though it did once live in peace and quietness. Straightaway when the Suzerain Princess Sophia did come hither with those Greeks...there hath arisen among us great strife....She hath come hither to our undoing.[35]

---

[28] V.O. Kluchevsky, *A History of Russia,* Volume 2, 64.

[29] Catherine Merridale, *Red Fortress: The Secret Heart of Russia's History* (London: Allen Lane/ Penguin Books, 2013), 51.

[30] In November 1437, Byzantine Emperor John VIII Palaeologus (1425-1448), Patriarch Joseph II (1416-1439), and other key representatives of the Eastern Church travelled to Italy in hopes of obtaining military assistance from Pope Eugene IV and Western Christendom to stop Ottoman advances and save Byzantium. A council began meeting in Ferrara on April 9, 1438 and moved to Florence in February 1439. At the Council of Florence, after almost a year and a half of discussions to resolve the key theological differences between the Orthodox and the Catholics, the Latins issued an ultimatum demanding that the Greeks accept the Catholic view that the Holy Spirit proceeded from both the Father and the Son in order to receive military help against the Ottomans. Eugene IV also demanded that the Greeks accept Catholic teachings on purgatory, transubstantiation, and the supremacy of the pope. Thirty-three members of the Greek delegation ended up signing the act of union. Upon the agreement's distribution, the Russian Orthodox Church became the first to reject it. The official Russian chronicle describes the Council of Florence agreement as a "pernicious deceit." See "The Voskresensk Chronicle Concerning the Council of Florence and its Aftermath, 1437-1441" in *A Sourcebook for Russian History from Early Times to 1917*, Volume 1, 126. For a detailed account of the Council of Florence from the Orthodox perspective, see Alfeyev, *Orthodox Christianity, Volume I,* 112-114.

[31] Sigismund von Herberstein, *Notes Upon Russia,* Volume 1, R. H. Major (trans.) (London, The Hakluyt Society, 1851), 21.

[32] Kluchevsky, *A History of Russia,* Volume 2, 17-18.

[33] Donald Ostroski, "The Growth of Muscovy, 1462-1533," *The Cambridge History of Russia, Volume 1: from Early Rus' to 1689*, Maureen Perrie (ed.) (Cambridge, UK: Cambridge University Press, 2006), 233.

[34] A despina is a female despot or autocrat. See Arthur Voyce, *The Art and Architecture of Medieval Russia* (Norman, Oklahoma: University of Oklahoma Press, 1967), 148-149.

[35] Ivan Bersen-Beklemishev quoted in Kluchevsky, *A History of Russia,* Volume 2, 64.

Merely two years after her arrival in Moscow, Sophia convinced Ivan III that Moscow was too provincial as a capital city and that experts from Italy should be brought in immediately to help Russia build structures worthy of its status as a strong, new country. This was but one example of how the courts of Europe imported Italian expertise in the late Renaissance period, for it was Italy that defined cultural prestige and social refinement.[36] Italian artists in this era happily accepted these foreign commissions for they were eager to leave behind Italy's overly-controlling clients and regain artistic freedom.[37] A cultural transfer took place,[38] and the Kremlin was soon awash in Italian artists and architects, who began a complete reconstruction of the fortress and its buildings. Leading the team was Ridolfo Fioravanti, a man who resembled Leonardo da Vinci in the diversity of his talents and interests. As an engineer, Fioravanti had successfully relocated a campanile in Bologna to a site 18 miles distant, straightened subsiding towers in Venice and Mantua, constructed and repaired numerous canals, and built military fortifications for the Sforzas in Milan and for the king of Hungary to defend against the Ottomans' invasion. He also designed buildings.[39] Upon Fioravanti's arrival in Moscow in 1475, he designed new exterior walls for the Kremlin, established a brick manufacturing plant to produce the necessary materials for the reconstruction, and made sure the that the whole site was safe from the adjacent Moscow River.[40] He also built a new cannon works in 1479 so that both the latest European military technology and fine church bells could be made in Moscow.[41] As an architect, Fioravanti designed and built a new cathedral in accordance with Orthodox tradition, but he did so while incorporating Italian touches. This gave the Cathedral of the Dormition an interior spaciousness that was unlike any previous building in Russia.[42] As a traditionalist, Beklemishev easily could have found it scandalous that the construction of the seat

[36] Robert Casillo and John Paul Russo, *The Italian in Modernity* (Toronto, Ontario: University of Toronto Press, 2011), xvi-xvii, EBSCOebooks. In addition to the arrival of the Italians, numerous Greeks also followed Sophia to Moscow, including artisans, engineers, architects, physicians, merchants, and noblemen. See William K. Medlin and Christos G. Patrinelis, *Renaissance Influences and Religious Reforms in Russia: Western and Post-Byzantine Impacts on Culture and Education* (Geneva: Librairie Droz, 1971), 42-43.

[37] Fernand Braudel, *Out of Italy 1450-1650*, Siân Reynolds (trans.) (Paris, Flammarion, 1991), 62.

[38] Braudel, *Out of Italy 1450-1650*, 79.

[39] David Hemsoll, "Fioravanti, Aristotele," *Dictionary of Art*, Jane Turner (ed.), vol. 11 (New York: Oxford University Press, 1996), 115-116.

[40] Voyce, *The Art and Architecture of Medieval Russia*, 152-153.

[41] Edward Williams, *The Bells of Russia: History and Technology* (Princeton, New Jersey: Princeton University Press, 1985), 42, EBSCOebooks.

[42] George Heard Hamilton, *The Art and Architecture of Russia* (Baltimore, Maryland, Penguin Books, 1954), 124. Specifically, Fioravanti utilized deep foundations and "specially hardened lightweight bricks and iron tie-rods for the vaults." He also omitted the usual galleries to enhance the visual height of the church and made the aisle and nave bays equal in size to create a sense of greater openness. See Hemsoll, "Fioravanti, Aristotele," *Dictionary of Art*, Volume 11, 116.

of the Orthodox faith was entrusted to a foreigner and a schismatic, but like many others he easily could have admitted that the outcome of Fioravanti's work was magnificent.[43] Later, other Italian architects added two more churches to the area to create Cathedral Square and then began replacing the Kremlin's collection of wooden residences with stone buildings. These additions included a limestone palace and a separate throne room, known as the Palace of Facets, where Ivan III and Sophia received audiences under its groin-vaulted arches and colorful, religious frescos.[44]

Sophia was also instrumental in creating a designated area within the city of Moscow for foreigners. Because she resented the vestiges of Muslim Tartars'* domination of Muscovy, she found the presence of an embassy building for the Tartars within the Kremlin walls to be deeply offensive. This motivated Sophia to secure its removal. First, she sent generous gifts to a Tartar queen, followed by excessively deferential letters, begging for permission to remove the embassy so that a church might be built on the site. Then Sophia also offered to find another good building in Moscow for the Tartar embassy, should the queen approve. In the interests of diplomatic relations, the approval came. Once it did, Sophia had the embassy burnt and a church built, but the Tartars never received another building in compensation.[45] Sophia's message was clear: the Kremlin was for Russians. Henceforth, foreigners increasingly found themselves more comfortable if they remained in a neighborhood outside its walls, which eventually became known as the German Quarter. This proved satisfactory to most since early sixteenth-century Moscow was "tolerably large" with "gardens and spacious court-yards in every house" and "confined by no settled boundary" like a city wall, according to Ambassador Herberstein.[46] He went on to add that the city was constructed almost entirely of wood, was "very dirty," and had a lot of stagnant water as a result of surrounding marshes. Only the Kremlin impressed him, since it was "so large that...it might itself be taken for a city" thanks to the large stone palace and the domes of so many churches.[47]

The changing appearance of the Kremlin mirrored a transformation in Russia's social fabric. Beklemishev may have very well found this change even more disorienting. He could see change in nearly every aspect of his life and he noted the sea of complaints these changes produced. On his own lands, for example, peasants had lost their freedom of movement, which greatly diminished the traditionally clear distinctions between peasants, who were free men, and slaves, who were chattel. According to a new legal code passed in 1497, peasants could only move during a two-week window each November,[48] and in order to do so they had to pay the nobleman one ruble prior to departure.[49] This was an almost impossible sum for most peasants: a ruble could buy 300 bushels of oats, 200 bushels of barley, 150 bushels of rye, *and* 120 bushels of wheat, and most peasant

[43] Voyce, *The Art and Architecture of Medieval Russia*, 155.

[44] For an overview of the work of the Italians in Moscow during this period, see Alexander Mozhaev, "The Italians (Who Built The Third Rome)," *Russian Life*, January/February 2015, 28-36, EBSCOhost.

[45] Sigismund von Herberstein, *Notes Upon Russia*, Volume 1, R. H. Major (trans.) (London, The Hakluyt Society, 1851), 25.

[46] Herberstein, *Notes Upon Russia*, Volume 2, 4.

[47] Herberstein, *Notes Upon Russia*, Volume 2, 5.

[48] Richard Hellie, "The Peasantry," *The Cambridge History of Russia, volume 1: from Early Rus' to 1689*, Maureen Perrie (ed.) (Cambridge, UK: Cambridge University Press, 2006), 295-296. This law did not create the system of serfdom that dominated Russian life in later centuries, but it was the first step in tying all peasants to a specific piece of land in order to stabilize the labor force and raise tax revenues.

[49] "Extracts from the Law Code of 1497," in R. E. F. Smith, *The Enserfment of the Russian Peasantry* (Cambridge, U.K., Cambridge University Press, 1968), 82.

families harvested just ten percent of those figures.[50] They were trapped. One possible escape was for peasants to sell themselves into slavery to cover debts, but this decision then condemned generations to a life of bondage.[51] Another important change came in the way in which the land was farmed. As late as the mid-fifteenth century, each family in a commune managed its own land as it saw fit, and different families had fields of different sizes as a result of exchanges and inheritances. In some areas, peasants were so independent that they bought and sold land among themselves, virtually independent of the lord.[52] By 1500,

however, each household tilled an equal proportion of the commune's land, and the village assembly determined who received which plots of land to farm, when crops were planted, and how to punish non-taxpayers. This system bound the peasants more closely together socially and economically.[53] It also helped bring about the adoption of the three-field system* in Russia, hundreds of years after its adoption in Western Europe. Unfortunately, this improvement was coupled by a surge in taxes, which increasingly had to be paid with coin instead of in kind. This made the burden on peasants who lived on lands like Beklemishev's particularly onerous.[54]

The peasants weren't the only ones complaining about changes: Beklemishev's peers also had their grievances. In Beklemishev's father's time, the old Muscovy nobility, the boyars, were a collection of eight to ten families, which regularly consulted with the grand prince on matters of governance. Indeed, the grand prince was more referee than autocrat in those days.[55] Muscovy's successful expansion, however, had changed the nature and character of this relationship, and this particularly mattered in a culture that prized precedence and honor.[56] In fact, the social construction of honor was so embedded in Muscovy that people of all social ranks were believed to possess honor, including slaves and peasant women. All had the right to sue in court if they believed their honor had been tarnished in the least; all were expected to uphold their honor lest their clan's social status slip even slightly in relation to others within their class.[57] For Beklemishev and others

---

[50] Jerome Blum, *Lord and Peasant in Russia from the Ninth to the Nineteenth Century* (Princeton, New Jersey: Princeton University Press, 1971), 111-112.

[51] "Note of a deed of full [bondage] of Nastasiya Onanya and her Daughter," in R. E. F. Smith, *The Enserfment of the Russian Peasantry* (Cambridge, U.K., Cambridge University Press, 1968), 78-79.

[52] Blum, *Lord and Peasant in Russia,* 93, 510-511.

[53] Jules Koslow, *The Despised and the Damned: The Russian Peasant Through the Ages* (New York: Macmillan Company, 1972), 11-13.

[54] Blum, *Lord and Peasant in Russia,* 228-229.

[55] Paul Bushkovitch, *Religion and Society in Russia: The Sixteenth and Seventeenth Centuries* (New York: Oxford University Press, 1992), 33.

[56] Nikolaos Chrissidis, "*Whoever does not drink to the end, he wishes evil*: Ritual Drinking and Politics in Early Modern Russia," *The New Muscovite Cultural History: A Collection in Honor of Daniel B. Rowland* (Bloomington, Indiana: Slavica Publishers and Indiana University Press, 2009), 115.

[57] Kollmann, *By Honor Bound,* 1, 25, 47, 133, 248.

like him, who were not as wealthy and established as the most elite boyar families,[58] this was particularly important. With the addition of new princes and aristocrats from places like Perm, which was incorporated into Muscovy in 1472, competition for societal position had never been greater. Like others, Beklemishev would have attempted to substantiate his status by developing a detailed genealogical table which showed birth order and length of service to the crown.[59] The problem was that thanks to treaties and strategic marriages, the struggle for precedence only grew with the addition of Novgorod in 1478, Tver in 1485, and Pskov in 1510. By that time, Ivan III and Sophia were dead and Vasilii III had ascended to the throne.[60]

As a monarch, Vasilii was determined to solidify his father's and grandfather's territorial acquisitions by adopting innovative policies regardless of the costs. He was happy to discard long-standing relationships with noble families and break with established traditions in order to fortify his position and advance his vision for a strong, unified Russia.[61] Specifically, Vasilii sought to expand his own direct power vis-à-vis the Duma.* He also established diplomatic relations with the Ottoman Empire, formed a new political coalition with the khans of the steppe, reopened trade with the Hanseatic League,* encouraged domestic industries, modernized the army, pursued war against Lithuania, rescinded the tax exemptions traditionally given to monasteries, and tripled the tax burden on the peasantry.[62] His actions were so sweeping that von Herberstein noted that "in the sway which he holds over his people" Vasilii "surpasses all the monarchs of the whole world."[63] In achieving this stature, Vasilii fulfilled his father's express wish that royal authority become concentrated in the hands of his oldest son.[64] When Vasilii's armies finally took Smolensk in 1514 from the Lithuanians, the circle of the aristocracy expanded once again.[65] This further eroded the status of longstanding, lower-ranking nobles from Muscovy.   It was at this point that Beklemishev openly complained that his voice was being squeezed out by that of the newcomers, who in order to have influence only had to "swear upon the cross that they would serve the sovereign grand prince of all Russia"[66] and post a security bond financially guaranteeing their commitment.[67] This changed the honorific order in which

[58] Vernadsky, *A History of Russia, Volume IV*, 137.

[59] Kollmann, *By Honor Bound*, 1, 10, 134-138.

[60] Sophia died in 1503 and Ivan III died in 1505.

[61] Crummey, *The Formation of Muscovy, 1304-1613*, 86.

[62] Martin, *Medieval Russia, 980-1584*, 271, 275, 300, 323, 324, 362.

[63] Sigismund von Herberstein, *Notes Upon Russia*, Volume 1, (R. H. Major, trans.) (London, The Hakluyt Society, 1851), 30.

[64] "The Last Testament of Ivan III, 1504," in *A Sourcebook for Russian History from Early Times to 1917*, Volume 1, 120.

[65] In 1500, Ivan III began his war with Lithuania and besieged Smolensk in 1502 but was unsuccessful in securing the important trade center. Vasilii renewed the effort against the Lithuanians in 1507, but it wasn't until July 31, 1514 that Smolensk finally fell to the Russians. See "The Voskresensk Chronicle on the Annexation of Smolensk, 1514," in *A Sourcebook for Russian History from Early Times to 1917*, Volume 1, 131-132; and Jeremy Black, *European Warfare, 1494-1660* (London: Routledge, 2002), 90, EBSCOebooks.

[66] "The Voskresensk Chronicle of an Appanage Prince's Transfer to Muscovy, 1500 in *A Sourcebook for Russian History from Early Times to 1917*, Volume 1, 96.

[67] Blum, *Lord and Peasant in Russia*, 140.

the boyars sat when in the presence of the crown prince[68]—unfairly Beklemishev thought. His public objection drew Vasilii's ire. The grand prince expelled Beklemishev from the meeting chamber, bellowing, "Begone, smerd! I have no further need of thee!"[69] This public condemnation of Beklemishev as a peasant was an acute insult to the boyar's honor.

Despite his temporary banishment from court, there was truth in Beklemishev's criticism, which Vasilii recognized when he perpetuated the use of the *mestnichestvo*. This system of ranks positioned families, as well as individuals within those families, in carefully delineated positions of hierarchy. But it did not compensate sufficiently for the social changes Beklemishev found so troubling. The new system only seemed to make everyone more dependent on the crown prince for appointments to military or governmental positions.[70] Men like Beklemishev missed the old days when a long-established, but not particularly wealthy, nobleman could gain the crown prince's ear in the informal setting of the boyars' meetings. Indeed, Beklemishev epitomized the resentment generated by the fact that a man no longer had to be born as a boyar but could be promoted to be one.[71]

Dissenters need confidants, and fortunately Beklemishev had one—a man known as Maksim the Greek, who was the most sophisticated theologian in sixteenth-century Russia. He was born in Arta, Greece, but in 1493 travelled to Italy to complete his education. Maksim lived in Ferrara, Milan, Padua, and Venice before eventually settling in Florence, where he became a Dominican friar. His spiritual training gave him a strong understanding of Catholic theology and how it differed from the faith of his youth. By 1506, however, Maksim found Orthodox practice more compelling. He returned to Greece to become an Orthodox monk on the Athos peninsula. Ten years later, when Russian emissaries came in search of a translator, Maksim agreed to go to Moscow.[72] His tasks were to translate religious texts, help prosecute heresy, and advise Vasilii III and the Metropolitan on how to construct an ideal state and society.[73] He was received in the Kremlin with great honors in March 1518, and his initial interactions went well. Unfortunately, Maksim didn't know Russian and few Russians knew Greek; therefore, all of Maksim's work had to be translated twice (usually Greek to Latin, then Latin to Russian); this opened up his work to criticism from both Vasilii and the Metropolitan. That criticism, as well as Maksim's overall celebrity, was more than enough to attract Beklemishev, who soon became a regular visitor to Maksim's cell in the St. Simeon Monastery. Other disaffected boyars joined them. It wasn't long before the group's frequent and extensive discussions became subversive,[74] for in sixteenth-century Russia religious issues were political issues because the church and the state worked so closely together.[75] Beklemishev once said, for example, that he admired Maksim because he was "a wise man, able to assist us and enlighten us when we inquire how a sovereign should order the land, how

---

[68] Kollmann, *By Honor Bound*, 143.

[69] Kluchevsky, *A History of Russia*, Volume 2, 62.

[70] Greta Bucher, *Daily Life in Imperial Russia* (Westport, Connecticut: Greenwood Press, 2008), 13-14, and Kollmann, *By Honor Bound*, 166. According to the *mestnichestvo* system, no one had to serve in the military or the government in a position that would place him below a person with a higher precedence. Seniority trumped merit, which created obvious problems on the battlefield or in government.

[71] Kluchevsky, *A History of Russia*, Volume 2, 45.

[72] Medlin and Patrinelis, *Renaissance Influences and Religious Reforms in Russia*, 20-23.

[73] Vernadsky, *A History of Russia, Volume IV*, 160.

[74] Vernadsky, *A History of Russia, Volume IV*, 160.

[75] Gruber, *Orthodox Russia in Crisis*, 25.

people should be treated, and how a Metropolitan should live."[76] Those were dangerous words. What saved Maksim, Beklemishev, and the other boyars from Vasilii's wrath was that Metropolitan Varlaam largely agreed with Maksim's writings on monasticism. These were extremely critical of the greed and wealth of Russian communal monasteries and the way this greed affected Russian society as a whole.[77] As long as a Non-Possessor was the Metropolitan, Maksim, Beklemishev and their compatriots were safe.

That situation changed in 1522, when Varlaam died and a new Metropolitan was elected by the council of bishops. Daniil had succeeded Iosif Volotskii as abbot of the Volokolamsk Monastery and, as such, was an ardent Possessor—someone who believed that monasteries could rightfully become wealthy institutions for their own benefit. Ironically, he was also a harsh critic of the monasteries, for Daniil believed that most monks were morally lax and most of their institutions were too insular.[78] Since the monasteries were no longer providing sufficient role models for the laity, Daniil concluded that priests and the bishops would have to fill the spiritual void. He wanted peasants to turn to their local church for pastoral care rather than to a monastery since monasteries had become suspect and were generally not subject to his authority anyway. Like his mentor, Daniil also believed in the church's duty to support the state, but Daniil had fewer qualms about offering any limitations. By advocating for greater centralization and control within the church and by giving his full support for the growth of royal authority, Daniil formed a powerful alliance with Vasilii.[79] This alliance proved to be quite important since Vasilii wanted a new wife.

Vasilii was married to Solomonia Saburova in 1505, but after eighteen years of marriage the couple remained childless. In 1523, Vasilii announced at a regular meeting of the Duma that he wanted to divorce Solomonia and remarry. Since the Orthodox tradition only provided for divorce in cases of adultery, the chamber erupted in astonishment. Several members of the Duma, and almost certainly Beklemishev, thought the proposal to be a scandalous sacrilege.[80] To them it was an insult to everything Muscovy once stood for, as well as an insult to the mantle of Russia as the Third Rome. Perhaps most distressingly, Vasilii's announcement came on the heels of the Shemiakin Affair, in which a minor prince who had been granted safe conduct to Moscow by the Metropolitan was subsequently arrested by Vasilii's guard.[81] Beklemishev took great exception to the breach of protocol and pointedly and directly accused Daniil of perjury and dishonor.[82] Given the Metropolitan's closeness to the Grand Prince, this accusation represented a direct challenge to

---

[76] Ivan Bersen-Beklemishev quoted in Miller, "The Orthodox Church," *The Cambridge History of Russia, Volume 1,* 353.

[77] Paul Bushkovitch, *Religion and Society in Russia: the Sixteenth and Seventeenth Centuries* (New York: Oxford University Press, 1992), 17.

[78] Bushkovitch, *Religion and Society in Russia,* 30. Ambassador Herbertsein noted this too, describing monastic rules as "gradually falling into disuse and becoming obsolete." See Herberstein, *Notes Upon Russia,* Volume 1, 58.

[79] Vernadsky, *A History of Russia, Volume IV,* 136.

[80] Martin, *Medieval Russia, 980-1584,* 291. I cannot be certain that Beklemishev objected to the divorce but given the depth of his known conservatism and his penchant for tradition, it is difficult to imagine him not belonging to this faction.

[81] The prince, Vasili Shemiakin, was accused of involvement in the suspicious death of another apanage prince and of conducting secret diplomatic relations with King Sigismund of Lithuania. Daniil promised Shemiakin safe passage to Moscow for questioning in 1523, but the prince was arrested and imprisoned. Shemiakin died in prison in 1529. See Vernadsky, *A History of Russia, Volume IV,* 136, 157-158.

[82] Vernadsky, *A History of Russia, Volume IV,* 136.

Vasilii, who saw Beklemishev as guilty of gross insubordination. Vasilii vowed to get his revenge and a new wife. Within three years he had both.

Beklemishev's last public event may have been the great ceremony of Epiphany,* which was held on January 6, 1525.[83] The Blessing of the Waters ceremony in Moscow was always the most magnificent event of the liturgical year. The ceremony commenced with the 9:00 a.m. bell, which was about an hour before sunrise that time of year. Daniil, Vasilii, dozens of bishops, over a hundred priests, and the Moscow boyars gathered in the Cathedral of the Dormition to begin their unhurried procession to the frozen Moscow River. As the Daniil approached the river, dressed in

white vestments with silver embossing and a white rounded mitre with gold embroidery, he paused.[84] The Metropolitan then said a prayer and made the sign of the cross "first touch[ing] the forehead, then the breast, then the right and lastly the left" with his thumb, index and middle finger joined.[85] He then walked across the ice to join the bishops and priests already assembled in a circle around a large square hole. After readings and prayers celebrating Christ's baptism in the Jordan River, the Metropolitan approached the hole and plunged a large cross into it,[86] breaking the thin layer of ice that had formed since the ceremony began, saying, "Great is the cross that shined in the pool: slaves of sin are going down and coming up children of incorruption, receiving a second light and having been clothed in Christ, the pearl."[87] Once the water had been made holy, the Metropolitan scooped a little of it in his hands and cast it on the crown prince and upon certain boyars.[88] Daniil then took a gold pitcher and filled it with the frigid water; later in the day, he would sprinkle this blessed water on rooms in the palace, icons, and regimental army banners.[89] Other members of the clergy then filled vessels so that they might use the blessed Epiphany waters for

---

[83] The Orthodox Church originally set its own feast calendar at the Second Council of Trullo in 692, but by the late fifteenth century there were at least 35 additional indigenous feast days in Russia, including those for Stefan of Perm, Leontii of Rostov, and the Dedication of the Church of St. George in Kiev. By elevating the role of these feasts and by associating these feasts with Muscovy, the Church helped the grand princes to integrate new territories into Muscovy. See Richard D. Bosley, "The Changing Profile of the Liturgical Calendar in Muscovy's Formative Years," *Culture and Identity in Muscovy 1359-1584*, A. M. Kleimola and G. D. Lenhoff (eds.) (Moscow: ITZ-Garant, 1997), 26, 35, 37-38.

[84] In order to complete this description of the sixteenth century Epiphany ceremony, I have utilized a few sources from other periods. This portion comes from Walter Duranty, "River at Moscow Blessed Once More," *New York Times*, January 2, 1922, 21, ProQuest Historical Newspapers.

[85] Herberstein, *Notes Upon Russia*, Volume 1, 80. This is unique to the Orthodox tradition; Catholics make the sign of the cross with two fingers raised instead of three and move from left to right.

[86] Bushkovitch, *Religion and Society in Russia*, 42.

[87] *Alleluia, Troparion, Sinai 99, and Sinai 974* quoted in Nicholas E. Denysenko, *The Blessing of Waters and Epiphany: The Eastern Liturgical Tradition* (Farnham, Surrey, England: Ashgate Publishing Limited, 2012), 72.

[88] Robert Best (attributed), *The Voyage, wherein Osep Napea, The Muscovite Ambassadour Returned Home* (1558) in *Russia Under Western Eyes, 1517-1825*, Anthony Cross (ed.) (London: Elek Books, 1971), 65.

[89] Bushkovitch, *Religion and Society in Russia*, 42.

communion instead of the Eucharist.[90] After closing prayers and benedictions, the clergy and nobility processed back to the Kremlin. Then the residents of Moscow descended upon the hole in the river in great numbers, filling their earthenware containers with the holy water,

> for that Moscovite which hath no part of that water, thinks himselfe unhappy. And [then] very many went naked into the water, both men and women and children: after the [press] was a little gone, the Emperours [sic]…horses were brought to drinke of the same water, and likewise many other men brought their horses thither to drinke, and by that means they make their horses as holy as themselves."[91]

Afterward, these residents of Moscow went home to eat as nice meal as they could afford, making sure to drink to the tsar's health for the new year ahead.[92]

Those who returned to the Kremlin enjoyed the feast day as well. Their celebration featured "indulging…drunkenness and elegant attire" at a formal banquet, according to an English witness.[93]

The banquet began with each nobleman and ambassador giving a gift to Vasilii. The Crown Prince then returned the honor in the traditional fashion by presenting loaves of bread to his guests. These loaves were "used by the prince to express his favour towards anybody, but when he [also] sends salt, it is intended to express affection" since "it is not possible for him to show greater honour to any one at an entertainment given by himself than by sending his salt from his own table."[94] With the introductory formalities concluded, brandy was then brought as an apéritif, followed by a main dish of roasted swans served with vinegar, sour milk, cucumbers, and prunes. After the consumption of much food and Greek and Hungarian wine by all, the meal concluded with a prescribed series of hymns and prayers for Vasilii's longevity, God's protection, and the intercession of the saints.[95] Finally, there was the formal drinking of the tsar's cup, during which Vasilii offered each nobleman or dignitary, and Daniil offered each clergyman, a full glass of wine in accordance with their rank. All were expected to enthusiastically consume the entire cup, and, to show that all of it had been relished, each man turned the glass upside down on his head. This part of the ceremony affirmed Muscovy's carefully delineated hierarchy with the grand prince standing above all but God.[96] While this ritualized consumption of alcohol may have been intended to control and even moderate intake,[97] visitors interpreted the series of toasts as attempts "to make

[90] Denysenko, *The Blessing of Waters and Epiphany,* 150-151.
[91] Robert Best (attributed), *The Voyage,* 65.
[92] Nikolaos Chrissidis, "*Whoever does not drink to the end,*" 108-109.
[93] Robert Best (attributed), *The Voyage,*79.
[94] Herberstein, *Notes Upon Russia*, Volume 2, 128.
[95] Chrissidis, "*Whoever does not drink to the end,*" 111-112. These hymns included a troparion, a kontakion, and a theotokion.
[96] Chrissidis, "*Whoever does not drink to the end,*" 113-115; and Herberstein, *Notes Upon Russia*, Volume 2, 132.
[97] Chrissidis, "*Whoever does not drink to the end,*" 121.

each other drunk."[98] The relative state of inebriation did not, however, detract from the importance of the feast day for the people of Moscow.

It is unclear if Beklemishev attended these events, but because he had managed to remain out of Vasilii's vengeful path for several years prior to the Epiphany celebration, it is likely that he did. Everything changed quite suddenly in February 1525, however, when the crown prince put Beklemishev on trial for treason. That Beklemishev's trial was public is noteworthy for it illustrates both the importance of civic involvement in the Russian legal system and the limits of autocracy.[99] Indeed, Beklemishev's fellow boyars expected to witness and participate in trials, and a grand prince rarely acted as summarily as many suppose. It was socially important for Beklemishev to have the opportunity to defend his honor. As a defendant in a capital crime, Beklemishev may have been tortured in hopes of obtaining a confession,[100] but what is clear is that he refused to admit any wrongdoing. Beklemishev exercised his right to speak for himself against Vasilii's charges, as the rare surviving extract of the trial's minutes show. After kissing the Cross to indicate his promise to give truthful testimony,[101] Beklemishev noted that he and his family had served the princes of Muscovy for generations. His father, Nikita, had been ambassador to both the Volga Tartars and khan of Crimea. Ivan III had also entrusted him with the custodianship of a suspected Italian spy.[102] What could be more loyal than protecting the monarch from international intrigue? Beklemishev also noted his own service as a diplomat, for Ivan III had appointed him as ambassador to Poland, ambassador to Crimea, and ambassador to Moldavia.[103] Didn't these appointments speak of loyalty? The defendant then explained how Ivan III gave at least the appearance of listening to the expertise of the boyars and to accepting occasional criticism from them. This contrasted starkly with Vasilii, who possessed "highmindedness," "asking not of counsel" and ignoring time-honored administrative methods. Beklemishev said,

> Behold, ye have Tsars...who do oppress you, and who have brought you upon evil times....[Vasilii] pitieth not men, nor yet yieldeth. Likewise, he loveth not contrary speech, but doth conceive anger against them who do speak it.[104]

---

[98] Sigismund von Herberstein, *Notes Upon Russia*, Volume 2, 130-132.

[99] Kollmann, *By Honor Bound*, 17, 112, 252.

[100] Nancy Shields Kollmann, "Torture in Early Modern Russia," *The New Muscovite Cultural History*, 161.

[101] Ann M. Kleimola, *Justice in Medieval Russia: Muscovite Judgement Charters (Pravy Gramoty) of the Fifteenth and Sixteenth Centuries* (Philadelphia, Pennsylvania: American Philosophical Society, 1975), 59. The practice of kissing the Cross began in the early 16th century, so I have assumed that it was in use in the Grand Prince's Court, which was the highest court in the land, by 1525. Kleimola notes that boyars served as judges on an *ad hoc* basis (page 13) and that all Russians could appear in courts as plaintiffs, including women, children (13-14), and slaves (21). It seems likely, therefore, that as a boyar, Beklemishev would have had some trial experience prior to his defense in February 1525.

[102] Vernadsky, *A History of Russia, Volume IV*, 21-22; and Croskey, *Muscovite Diplomatic Practice*, 112. The Venetian spy's name was Trevizano, who was arrested for fraud. The Khan of Crimea was Mengli Giray, who entered into an alliance with Muscovy in 1480 against Poland-Lithuania and the Great Horde. For a detailed account of this diplomacy and the complex geo-politics across the vast region during Ivan III's reign, see Dariusz Kołodziejczyk, *The Crimean Khanate and Poland-Lithuania: International Diplomacy on the European Periphery (15th-18th Century)* (Leiden, Netherlands: Koninklijke Brill NV, 2001), 23-30.

[103] Croskey, *Muscovite Diplomatic Practice in the Reign of Ivan III* (New York: Garland Publishing, Inc., 1987), 109. Various circumstances, such as the death of Poland's Casimir IV in June 1492, meant that Beklemishev didn't actually leave Moscow to complete these ambassadorships, but the multiple appointments show that he had Ivan III's confidence.

[104] Ivan Bersen-Beklemishev quoted in Kluchevsky, *A History of Russia*, Volume 2, 63.

Beklemishev was particularly disgusted with the fact that Vasilii kept conducting state business with two or three favored advisors in his private apartments instead of in open council. If someone's actions had been treasonous, it was the Crown Prince's, not Beklemishev's. The accused boyar had nothing to hide; did Vasilii? Beklemishev then concluded his statement by arguing,

> The land which doth forsake its ancient customs standeth not for long. Behold, here is our Suzerain Prince beginning to change our ancient usage. What honour, therefore, should he look for from us?[105]

It was a grand gesture and a reasoned commentary from a marginalized nobleman about the threatening social changes that came to Russia in the late fifteenth and early sixteenth centuries, but it was not nearly enough of a self-defense. Beklemishev was beheaded in a Kremlin dungeon on the day he gave his impassioned testimony defending the customs and traditions he had once benefited from so much. His dismembered body likely joined those of other state criminals along the banks of the moat on the east side of the Kremlin.[106] Such was the fate of those who challenged Vasilii so directly[107] and who refused to change.

Beklemishev wasn't the only one to suffer ill fortune. In 1526, Daniil annulled Vasilii's marriage to Solomonia and had her forcibly removed to a convent. There, the Metropolitan himself gleefully cut off her hair as she sobbed in disbelief and frustration. When she refused the veil, throwing it to the ground and then stamping upon it, Daniil ordered Solomonia beaten with a scourge. In the end, she too surrendered to her fate, but "in the presence of all" proudly made it clear that "she took the hood unwillingly and under compulsion, and invoked the vengeance of God on her behalf for so great an injury."[108] Others who stood in Vasilii's way fared no better. Maksim the Greek was put on trial for his collusion with Beklemishev, his refusal to recognize the independence of the Russian church from the patriarch in Constantinople, his mistranslations, and his questioning of Vasilii's decision-making in times of crisis.[109] He was found guilty and imprisoned in the Volokolamsk Monastery, where he was tortured.[110] Six years later, in 1531, Maksim was charged with "Hellenic and heretical sorcery," for people believed the Greek possessed the ability to change the grand prince's disposition when he rubbed his palms together.[111] The court proved unwilling to execute

---

[105] Ivan Bersen-Beklemishev quoted in Kluchevsky, *A History of Russia,* Volume 2, 64.
[106] Arthur Voyce, *The Moscow Kremlin: its History, Architecture and Art Treasures* (Berkeley, California: University of California Press, 1954), 133.
[107] Some have argued that the challenge Vasilii objected to was a personal one against Beklemishev, rather than "the very idea of political, administrative, and legal conservatism." See Tamara I. Lipich, et al. "Legal Status of Moskovia During 16-17th Centuries," *Journal of History, Culture & Art Research*, *Tarih Kültür Ve Sanat Arastirmalari Dergisi* 6, no. 4 (September 2017): 1305-1313, EBSCOhost.
[108] Herberstein, *Notes Upon Russia*, Volume 1, 50-51.
[109] Maksim believed that the Russian Metropolitans had to be confirmed by the Greek Patriarch to be consecrated. The crisis involved Vasilii's handling of the Crimean Tartar siege of Moscow in 1521. See Donald Ostrowski, "The Moscow Councils of 1447 to 1589 and the Conciliar Period in Russian Orthodox Church History," *Tapestry of Russian Christianity: Studies in History and Culture*, Nickolas Lupinin, Donald Ostrowski, and Jennifer B. Spock (eds.) (Columbus, Ohio: Department of Slavic and East European Languages and Cultures and the Resource Center for Medieval Slavic Studies, The Ohio State University, 2016), 136.
[110] Medlin and Patrinelis, *Renaissance Influences and Religious Reforms in Russia,* 23.
[111] Valerie A. Kivelson, "Political Sorcery in Sixteenth Century Muscovy," *Culture and Identity in Muscovy 1359-1584*, A. M. Kleimola and G. D. Lenhoff (eds.) (Moscow: ITZ-Garant, 1997), 267. The full charge was that

the scholar on the basis of the evidence, but did exile Maksim to the more remote Otroch Monastery in Tver, where he remained imprisoned for another sixteen years until Daniil's death in 1547. Maksim died in Russia in 1556, having never returned to Greece. Other Non-Possessors and opponents of political and ecclesiastical centralization were also prosecuted and silenced, including a former bishop named Vassian, who was starved to death in the Volokolamsk Monastery in 1532 on Vasilii's orders.[112] Only Vasilii died happily, having remarried a young Lithuanian woman named Elena. She gave birth to two sons, including the future Ivan the Terrible. Ivan would conclude the process of securing autocracy in Russia, symbolized by his coronation as "Tsar of all the Russians" in 1547.

~

On the southeast corner of the Kremlin fortress, the Beklemishev Tower proudly stands overlooking the Moscow River, Red Square, and the land which once belonged to Ivan Bersen-Beklemishev. Designed by an Italian architect in 1487 to endure the ravages of weather and time, the tower's rounded, smooth, red-brick base is stout and virile. It rises confidently to an overhanging rim, called a machicolation, which allowed Kremlin defenders to drop boiling oil on would-be attackers. Narrow-slatted windows called arrow loops dot the tower's base and enhance both its defensive merit and its intended purpose. Designed to maximize sight lines and be an independent fortress in times of crisis, it is not a structure to be taken lightly. Even the addition of a lofty, decorative spire at the end of the seventeenth century does not detract from the unyielding obstinacy of the base of Kremlin's second oldest tower.[113] It also serves as a metaphor for Beklemishev's personality and life, a reminder of how he defended his interests, confronted repressive forces, refused to compromise, and then died for his beliefs in during a period of significant social and religious change in Russia. From the Caribbean to the Deccan, from the Andes to the Low Countries, millions more would make the same choices and meet with the same fate before the bloody sixteenth century reached its merciful terminus.

Maksim, "writes words on his palms with salves and rubs them together, hand over hand, and then comes to the grand prince and from that moment the grand prince's anger towards him is alleviated and [he] begins to laugh."

[112] Vernadsky, *A History of Russia, Volume IV*, 161. As a Non-Possessors, Vassian once argued that "what we hand out to the poor, the devil himself cannot steal." See Vassian Patrikeyev quoted in Sulikowska, *The Icon Debate*, 113.

[113] Voyce, *The Moscow Kremlin*, 20, 25, 30, 133; and Merridale, *Red Fortress*, 59. The Italian architect was Pietro Antonio Solari, 1445-1493, who worked for the Sforza family and was one of the architects for the Milan Cathedral.

C

Wolfgang Fabricius Capito

1478-1541

Both heroes and villains—be they historical, mythical or literary—are best sculpted in high relief, with distinctive features and clear trajectories. They are definitive in both character and action. And they drive stories with clear morals and clear resolutions, whether for good or bad. The Protestant Reformation seems full of such decisive characters, but the era's most illuminating figures are actually those who wavered in the face of a new theology. Those who were full of trepidation, those who feared both the temporal and the eternal consequences of adopting a new form of Christianity, illustrate the political, economic, and spiritual trauma of the Reformation in Europe far better than those who embraced the Reformation's changes wholeheartedly from the outset. Wolfgang Capito was one of those initial fence-sitters.

Prior to 1512, Capito's life shared a remarkable commonality and parallelism with that of Martin Luther. Both were born in small German towns to ambitious fathers named Hans, who became members of the bourgeoisie* and who served on city councils. Both Capito and Luther complained bitterly about their early educational experiences and neither man was a particularly distinguished student in his youth, but both did sufficiently well in Latin in grammar school to gain a university placement. Both men then earned their bachelor's degree within a year of one another (1504 for Luther and 1505 for Capito) and their Master of Arts degree soon after. Both men took clerical vows against their fathers' explicit instructions, with Capito doing so over his father's deathbed wish. By 1509, both were teaching university students while pursuing their degree in theology, with Capito lecturing at the University of Freiburg and Luther lecturing at the University of Erfurt.[1]

These two universities adhered to a particular theological tradition known as the *via moderna* or modern way. Its fundamental premise held that God purposely chose to reveal himself to

---

[1] For more detailed information on Capito's and Luther's early life, see two books by James M. Kittelson: *Wolfgang Capito: from Humanist to Reformer* (Leiden, Netherlands: E.J. Brill, 1975), 9-15 and *Luther the Reformer: The Story of the Man and his Career* (Minneapolis, Minnesota: Augsburg Publishing House, 1986), 31-67. The letter in which Capito discusses his father's plea not to enter the priesthood and his father's idea that "a chaste marriage was much preferable to a sinful celibacy," can be found in Wolfgang Capito, *The Correspondence of Wolfgang Capito Volume 1, 1507-1523*, ed. and trans. Erika Rummel with the assistance of Milton Kooistra (Toronto, Canada: University of Toronto Press, 2005), 157.

humanity in certain, specific, and very limited ways, and that as a result of this decision it was impossible for humans to make sense of everything they encountered in the world. Those things that humans did not understand—whether about death or the heavens or their station in life—were a direct result of the fact that God did not want them to be able to do so. Human reasoning was useless in such situations.[2] Indeed, God was the all-powerful force in the universe; humans were flawed creatures who had to place their trust in God if they hoped to find peace and happiness. Humans had to accept the idea that God knew best, and that He would care for those who actively demonstrated their faithfulness. As a leading fifteenth century German theologian succinctly put it, "do what is in you" and let God take care of the rest.[3]

While this may have meant one thing to Europe's leading theologians, for most parish priests and their humble faithful, demonstrating faithfulness meant participating in the rituals and practices of the Catholic Church. These centered upon the seven sacraments (baptism, confirmation, confession, communion, marriage, holy orders, and last rights) and continued with other "good works," such as going on a pilgrimage, lighting a candle at a local shrine, praying at the Stations of the Cross in a church, abstaining from meat on Fridays, praying at the relics of a saint, and giving alms to the poor. All of these actions were manageable things the penitent could do in

this life to minimize their punishment in purgatory* after death.[4] They showed an individual's desire to earn Christian salvation and they formed the fundamental basis for how all Christians in Western Europe practiced their religion prior to the Reformation.

In 1512, having earned his degree in theology, Capito resigned his professorship and became a canon and preacher associated with the Benedictine monastery at Bruchsal. Canons were those priests who were tied to a particular church or monastery, but who did not take the same vows as monks (who removed themselves from the

---

[2] The opposing school of thought, the *Via Antiqua* or Traditional Way, was based on the writings of Thomas Aquinas (1225-1274) and held that human reason was one of God's gifts which could be utilized to discover truth. Both the *Via Moderna*, championed by William of Ockham (1288-1347), and the *Via Antiqua* were critically examined in medieval universities through specific rules of inquiry and discussion in an attempt to reconcile the teachings of Aristotle with Holy Scripture. This technique of precise didactic investigation was known as scholasticism.

[3] Gabriel Biel (1420-1495) quoted in James D. Tracy, *Europe's Reformations, 1450-1650* (Lanham, Maryland: Rowman & Littlefield Publishers, 2002), 37.

[4] Steven Ozment, *The Age of Reform, 1250-1550: An Intellectual and Religious History of Late Medieval and Reformation Europe* (New Haven, Connecticut: Yale University Press, 1980), 216-217.

outside world and dedicated their lives to prayer and contemplation, usually in austere and ascetic circumstances). Canons typically earned income by saying masses for the dead, which was another good work, and by preaching to the public. The Bruchsal canons were not known, however, for their zeal and devotion to religious practices. Most of them were the younger sons of noblemen who had been pensioned off, unable to inherit land by the rules of primogeniture.[*5] This atmosphere did not suit Capito particularly well, for he had always been someone who took his religious studies and responsibilities quite seriously. In Bruchsal he was, therefore, rather isolated and doubtful that he'd made the right career choice.[6] Fortunately, Capito quite unexpectedly received the invitation to become the cathedral preacher in Basel in 1515. He immediately accepted the post and soon found himself in a cosmopolitan metropolis filled with humanists, who embraced different traditions than the ones Capito had learned during his time in Freiburg.

Early modern humanism is notoriously difficult to define as a result of its diversity,[7] but it centered upon a different sensibility as to how to best understand the human experience, the intentions of God, and methods of reforming the Catholic Church. Whereas the scholastics[*] of both the *via moderna* and the *via antiqua* schools hoped to achieve understanding by examining and reconciling the views of authorities from the past, humanists emphasized returning to the original Latin, Greek, and Hebrew texts in order to find truth. In other words, humanists tended to investigate texts on their own instead of in the context of an established tradition of interpretation.[8] In this way, humanists believed it was possible for religion to be freed from the limitations of a systematic theology, and they hoped that this freedom would make it possible for European society to participate in a moral renewal.[9] Such a reorientation helped promote an independent spirit that valued of the experiences of the individual; fifteenth and sixteenth century humanists hoped this shift would create a rich civic life with cities full of individuals doing good deeds. For many humanists, this secular goal was more important than making sure everyone in a community adhered to a particular set of rigidly defined beliefs.[10] It also meant that the true purpose of education rested not in pre-professional training but in personal enhancement and edification.

The most important humanist of the era, Desiderius Erasmus of Rotterdam, was staying in Basel, working on his edition of the Greek New Testament, when Capito arrived in the city to accept his position as cathedral preacher and professor of theology at the University of Basel. Erasmus had secured his standing as "the prince of the humanists" in 1511 with his publication of *Praise of Folly*. This book was written in a week for the amusement of Sir Thomas More in 1509, was full of allusions to ancient mythology and sacred texts, and was in part a reaction to the three years Erasmus had just spent in Italy. While Erasmus found the wealth of libraries, manuscripts, and scholars appealing, he was deeply disturbed by the pagan atmosphere in Rome and Julius II's corrupt and temporally-oriented papacy.[11] *Praise of Folly* mercilessly satirized the clergy, whom he described as being "universally loathed," "gloriously self-satisfied," "boorish," and "shameless." He specifically criticized them for believing that "it's the highest form of piety to be so uneducated that they can't even read," baying "like donkeys in church, repeating by rote the psalms they haven't

[5] Kittelson, *Wolfgang Capito*, 19.
[6] Kittelson, *Wolfgang Capito*, 15, 19, 22.
[7] Euan Cameron, *The European Reformation* (Oxford, U.K.: The Clarendon Press, 1991), 64.
[8] Ozment, *The Age of Reform, 1250-1550,* 307.
[9] Kittelson, *Wolfgang Capito*, 23-24.
[10] Ozment, *The Age of Reform, 1250-1550,* 307.
[11] A. H. T. Levi, "Introduction," Erasmus of Rotterdam, *Praise of Folly and Letter to Martin Dorp, 1515* (New York: Penguin Books, 1971), 41. Julius II was pope from 1503-1513.

understood," and making "a good living out of their squalor and beggary" at the expense of "all the other beggars." Erasmus also scolded the clergy for its

> practice of doing everything to rule, as if they were following mathematical calculations which it would be a sin to ignore. They work out the number of knots for a shoe-string, the material and width to a hair's breadth of a girdle, the shape and capacity (in sacksful) of a cowl, the length (in fingers) of a hair-cut, the number of hours prescribed for sleep.

Erasmus objected to these traditions because "this equality applied to such a diversity of persons and temperaments will only result in inequality, as anyone can see."[12] In *Praise of Folly*, Erasmus also criticized the Church's leading theologians for their unimaginativeness, arguing that these men were merely "fortified with an army of schoolmen's definitions, conclusions and corollaries, and propositions" and were only able to "interpret hidden mysteries to suit themselves," while dwelling in a "sort of third heaven." When their quibbling was met with the least criticism, these theologians reacted by denouncing humanists like Erasmus "as a heretic on the spot, for this is the bolt they always loose on anyone to whom they take a dislike."[13] Such criticism was quite daring, and it made *Praise of Folly* quite a sensation in Western Europe's learned community in the early fifteenth century. In other writings, Erasmus also made it clear that relics, vows, pilgrimages, and other hallmarks of medieval piety were centered upon worthless, corrupt practices.[14]

As a newcomer to Basel, Capito was naturally attracted to Erasmus' fame. The two men met, Erasmus asked Capito for assistance with some Hebrew translations, and the two men struck up a friendship that was to influence Capito's career greatly. In fact, Erasmus' public acknowledgement of Capito's assistance substantially increased Capito's reputation, and soon the young preacher's pulpit was Basel's most popular and consequential.[15] By the end of 1516, Erasmus had seemingly blessed Capito as his heir apparent, regularly praising his unusual facility with three ancient languages[16] and proclaiming in a letter that was later published that Capito is "in life so very upright, in morals so holy that I have never seen anyone more unspoiled."[17]

Such accolades, as well as the publication in 1518 of Capito's book of Hebrew grammar, won the attention of the ambitious archbishop in Mainz, Albrecht von Hohenzollern. Albrecht wanted to draw humanists to his court in hope of establishing a center of learning which would rival those in Italy, thereby enhancing his influence and power.[18] Albrecht's use of money and his personal ambition epitomized many of the problems in the pre-Reformation Catholic Church; he was an extreme example of a European nobleman exploiting the Church for the benefit of his own family's

---

[12] Erasmus of Rotterdam, *Praise of Folly*, Betty Radice (trans.) (New York: Penguin Books, 1971), 164-165.

[13] Erasmus of Rotterdam, *Praise of Folly*, 153-154.

[14] Carlos M. N. Eire, *Reformations: The Early Modern World, 1450-1650* (New Haven, Connecticut: Yale University Press, 2018), 110-112.

[15] Kittelson, *Wolfgang Capito*, 25.

[16] Those who could read Hebrew, Greek, and Latin were in the elite of scholarly circles. See Hughes Oliphant Old, *The Reading and Preaching of the Scriptures in the Worship of the Christian Church, Volume 4: The Age of Reformation* (Grand Rapids, Michigan: W.B. Eerdmans, 2002), 69. Capito's knowledge of Hebrew was not, however, as nuanced as he professed. See Debra Kaplan, *Beyond Expulsion: Jews, Christians, and Reformation Strasbourg* (Stanford, California: Stanford University Press, 2011), 126-130.

[17] Erasmus of Rotterdam quoted in Kittelson, *Wolfgang Capito,* 27.

[18] Miriam Usher Chrisman, *Strasbourg and the Reform: A Study in the Process of Change* (New Haven, Connecticut: Yale University Press, 1967), 89.

fortune.[19] Albrecht became Archbishop of Magdeburg in 1513 at the age of twenty-three (seven years before he was supposed to be eligible for the job) because his family purchased the office for him. At the time, Albrecht also held title over another diocese, which wasn't normally allowed, but the payment to the Vatican of another handsome fee allowed the young man to keep both appointments. Then, in 1514, the archbishopric in Mainz became vacant and Albrecht wanted it too, but he did not want to resign from the other two offices since doing so would mean surrendering the income these offices produced. The Mainz archbishopric was worth going to extraordinary lengths to secure because its holder also served as one of the seven electors of the Holy Roman Empire.* Holding this office would enhance Hohenzollern influence in central Europe since Albrecht's older brother already controlled another one of the seven offices. Control of two of the seven seats would give the Hohenzollerns an influence which would rival that of the Habsburgs.[20] The problem was if it was unusual for an archbishop to hold two offices, it was scandalous for a single man to hold three holy offices simultaneously. Obviously, a special deal would have to be struck.

Pope Leo X was eager to make a deal because he desperately needed money to move the renovations of St. Peter's Basilica in Rome forward. By the mid-fifteenth century, the original St. Peter's, which was built in the fourth century, was falling apart with huge cracks compromising the walls and fracturing the floors. Repair efforts began in the mid-fifteenth century during the papacy of Nicolas V, but it wasn't until 1505, during the papacy of Julius II, that major renovations began in earnest and much of the old basilica was dismantled. This left Leo with little more than a construction site for the home of Catholicism. Something dramatic and unprecedented had to be done.[21] Leo allowed Albrecht to purchase the Mainz archbishopric for 10,000 ducats and arranged for Albrecht to be able to borrow the large sum from the Fugger banking family. Leo also decided to allow Albrecht to retain the other two archbishoprics and to issue exclusive indulgences throughout his dioceses for a period of eight years. These indulgences were another example of a good work. They were purchased by the faithful in order to shorten the time that the purchaser (or members of the purchaser's family, whether alive or deceased) spent in purgatory. They had a long and established tradition in the Catholic Church. In this case, roughly half the proceeds would go towards repaying the Fugger loans (which together with Albrecht's other office purchases totaled 26,000 ducats) and the other half would help finance the rebuilding of St. Peter's.[22] To make sure that these plenary indulgences, which absolved the recipient of all sins committed since baptism, received wide popular support, Leo X sent a great Dominican preacher and salesman, Johannes Tetzel, to Germany to promote their distribution. Tetzel arrived in Germany in 1517 with great fanfare and quickly began selling indulgences by the score.[23] He even had a catchy slogan to

---

[19] Diarmaid MacCulloch, *The Reformation* (New York: Viking, 2004), 117.

[20] The Habsburgs were the leading royal family of Europe in the 16th century with powerful branches in both Austria and Spain. Thanks to a combination of key marriages, lucky inheritances, and the military successes of Frederick the Great (1712-1786), the Hohenzollerns were eventually able to become as important to northern Germany as the Habsburgs were to the rest of central Europe.

[21] Keith Miller, *St. Peter's* (Cambridge, Massachusetts: Harvard University Press, 2007), 54, 68-75.

[22] Ozment, *The Age of Reform, 1250-1550*, 251.

[23] Tetzel, who was employed by both the papacy and the Fugger family, also took a cut of the profits of the sales of indulgences, and he certainly wasn't above using raw intimidation to increase sales. See Martin Marty, *Martin Luther* (New York: Penguin Group, 2004), 29.

advertise his mission: "Once the coin into the coffer clings, a soul from purgatory heavenward springs!"[24]

On October 31, 1517, Martin Luther famously responded to Tetzel's mission by posting his 95 Theses on a door of the Wittenberg church. Luther didn't object to all indulgences on principle; rather, he objected to Leo and Albrecht's indulgences for St. Peter's because they did not seem to require real repentance. Tetzel's indulgences only seemed to require money.

During the next two and a half years, Catholic officials responded to Luther's assertions by engaging him in a series of interviews, each of which was designed to get Luther to recant the positions he outlined in the 95 Theses. Luther proved himself to be a strong debater, however, because as a man of extremes, he refused to acknowledge that an opponent might have a good point or that there might be room for compromise.[25] Luther also repeatedly benefited from political issues within the Holy Roman Empire, which ensured that he did not face imprisonment or excommunication during these early years of protest. The process of debating proved to be particularly important because it gave Luther the chance to solidify his views, which became more radical with each passing month. By the time Luther and a papal representative met in Leipzig in June and July 1519, Luther had come to believe that the problem wasn't just with one pope and one set of indulgences but involved the very nature of the papacy and the practice of good works in general. He asserted that Scripture had to be the final authority rather than the pope, since the papacy was a human creation rather than a creation of the word of God. Luther was also well on his way to articulating his doctrine of Justification by Faith Alone, meaning that salvation comes to those who truly believe rather than to those who merely participate in the rituals of the Church.[26] Salvation is about believing, not about doing, as the medieval practices of the Church seemed to imply.

It was into this swirling theological sea that Capito arrived in Mainz in May 1520 to become Albrecht's advisor and personal chaplain. His primary responsibility was to oversee all of the archbishop's written correspondence with Rome. It was a prestigious appointment, but given Albrecht's Machiavellian* political appetite, Capito's friends worried for his soul. In the words of Erasmus, "Capito is wholly of the [Mainz] court and is taking on its characteristics."[27] Indeed, Capito's decision to accept the position in Mainz surprised many of his friends because he initially had written so positively about Luther's actions in Wittenberg. In July 1518, for example, Capito wrote an introduction to a pamphlet, saying that Luther

> deserves an aureole, as they say, for being the first clearly to tear to pieces the abuses involving indulgences, at which so many thousand theologians have winked over so many years....Everywhere the world is coming to its senses.[28]

Capito also attempted to build support for Luther by saying to Erasmus, "I implore you not to disparage Martin [Luther]'s work in public."[29] Capito even offered Luther tactical advice in September 1518 to help ensure his success: "You should studiously avoid offending the Pope" and

---

[24] Kittelson, *Luther the Reformer*, 103-104.
[25] Marty, *Martin Luther*, 50-51.
[26] Kittelson, *Luther the Reformer*, 135, 138.
[27] Erasmus of Rotterdam quoted in Kittelson, *Wolfgang Capito*, 52.
[28] Capito, *The Correspondence of Wolfgang Capito Volume 1, 1507-1523*, 29-30. An aureole is similar to a halo, but surrounds the whole body in a religious painting.
[29] Wolfgang Capito quoted in Kittelson, *Wolfgang Capito*, 39.

"You will succeed by small, repeated strokes, where you would not have been able to accomplish anything by violence."[30]

By the summer of 1520, however, it was clear to Capito that as a member of the Mainz court he could not remain such an advocate for Luther. This was especially clear after Luther published his *Address to the Christian Nobility of the German Nation* in August, which advanced his belief in the Priesthood of All Believers. This doctrine held that all Christians possessed the power of faith within them and therefore could be considered priests. Luther also called upon secular leaders to implement change since the Catholic hierarchy had proven so resistant to it. This work was followed by the October publication of *On the Babylonian Captivity of the Church*, which reduced the number of valid sacraments to two (baptism and communion), held that common parishioners were entitled to partake of the wine during mass, and maintained that priests did not have any special power or authority. This was the treatise that struck a dagger into the heart of late medieval piety.[31] The Church no longer seemed essential to Christianity since so many of its practices no longer mattered. Wholly troubled by the increasing polarization these publications caused in Germany, Capito responded forcefully, writing to Luther in December 1520: "There are those who fear that every semblance of piety may be obliterated by that uproar of yours"[32] and "do not preach the Word of Christ contentiously, but with charity."[33]

In truth, Capito's motivations for resisting Luther's assault against traditional Catholicism were not purely theological. There was a clear economic component at work for him as well. By 1520, Capito had achieved economic security as a result of his appointment in Mainz, and he was deeply

---

[30] Wolfgang Capito quoted in Kittelson *Wolfgang Capito*, 40.

[31] Kittelson, *Luther the Reformer*, 154.

[32] Wolfgang Capito quoted in Kittelson, *Wolfgang Capito*, 62

[33] Capito, *The Correspondence of Wolfgang Capito Volume 1, 1507-1523*, 110.

afraid of sliding back into the tenuous economic status of his young adulthood. In fact, Capito had his eye on an easy source of substantial and continuous income, which was contingent upon maintaining much of the status quo: a prebend at the chapter of St. Thomas in Strasbourg. A prebend was an ecclesiastical appointment with an endowment attached to it.[34] The income generated from the endowment came from sources such as tolls and tithes.* In Strasbourg in the mid-1520s and early 1530s, the Church owned 39% of the land surrounding the city, and the tax revenues from these lands supported both the local bishop and the Papacy, and specific officeholders like the one Capito coveted.[35] As long as there was unity within the Christian community in Western Europe, there was a reasonable chance that Capito could win the pope's blessing for the St. Thomas prebend. If Luther led Europe into irreconcilable religious turmoil, however, Capito would have to choose a side; choosing a side meant risking his future economic well-being. Since Capito was certainly not the only one in such an uncertain financial situation, papal officials understood the situation well from afar. In February 1521, a papal legate recommended that Albrecht's aide be awarded the prebend to keep Capito in the Catholic camp. Capito is "just as capable of being a service as doing harm" as a result of his eloquence and connections, the legate wrote.[36]

Leo X excommunicated Martin Luther in January 1521 for the multitude of objectionable writings and unwillingness to recant them. At this point Capito could have easily abandoned his friend, who was now in a precarious state since Church courts had proclaimed that it was no longer a sin to kill him. Capito, however, believed that Luther deserved a chance to air his evolving understanding of the Gospel in a fair and complete way, and he was instrumental in securing this opportunity for Luther.[37] The meeting, known as the Diet of Worms, was held through the spring of 1521 and brought the most powerful men in Europe together on a grand stage. The newly elected Holy Roman Emperor, Charles V, had promised as a condition of his election that no German would be condemned of heresy without a fair trial; therefore, he guaranteed Luther safe passage to and from the assembly. Luther agreed to acknowledge the summons, albeit with considerable trepidation, and arrived in Worms in a covered wagon, surrounded by cheering, drunken crowds who saluted him as a conquering hero.[38] On April 17, he entered the great hall dressed in the simple black habit of an Augustinian monk and stood before a vast assortment of distinctive hats and gold crowns, ermine collars and sumptuous robes. Charles V sat on a raised dais in the center of the room, which was covered by a canopy emblazoned with the double-headed eagle of the Holy Roman Empire. Carrying the imperial scepter in his right hand, Charles, even at twenty-one, looked intimidating as he glared at Luther and the collection of books stacked high on the table between them. A papal representative stepped forward and asked Luther if he had written all of these books. Luther approached the table, examined them, and affirmed that he was indeed the author. The papal representative then asked if Luther would now renounce them before this august body. Expecting a real debate instead of a tribunal, Luther was taken aback and asked for time to consider his answer. This request confused and startled many in the room, but Charles granted the former monk a one-day recess.[39] The next evening, with the hall bathed in candlelight, the Diet

[34] There were also situations in which prebends did not have an administrative office or duties attached to them.

[35] Thomas A. Brady, Jr., *Ruling Class, Regime and Reformation at Strasbourg, 1520-1555*, 145.

[36] Girolamo Aleandro quoted in Capito, *The Correspondence of Wolfgang Capito Volume 1, 1507-1523*, xxi.

[37] Kittelson, *Wolfgang Capito*, 67.

[38] Marty, *Martin Luther*, 67.

[39] Marty, *Martin Luther*, 67.

reassembled to hear Luther's answer. He said, "Should I recant at this point, I would open the door to more tyranny and impiety, and it will be all the worse should it appear that I had done so at the insistence of the Holy Roman Empire." The papal legate, Johann Eck retorted in Latin,

> How can you assume that you are the only one to understand the sense of Scripture? Would you put your judgment above that of so many famous men and claim that you know more than all of them? You have no right to call into question the most holy orthodox faith, instituted by Christ the perfect Lawgiver....I ask you Martin—answer candidly and without distinctions—do you or do you not repudiate your books and the errors which they contain?[40]

In German, Luther responded without hesitation:

> Since then your serene majesty and your lordships seek a simple answer, I will give it in this manner, neither horned nor toothed. Unless I am convinced by the testimony of the Scriptures or by clear reason (for I do not trust either in the pope or in councils alone, since it is well known that they have often erred and contradicted themselves), I am bound by the Scriptures I have quoted and my conscience is captive to the Word of God. I cannot and will not retract anything, since it is neither safe nor right to go against conscience.[41]

Luther then paused and concluded, "I cannot do otherwise, here I stand. May God help me, Amen."[42]

Charles V refused to hear any more blasphemy and quit the room with an entourage of color following in his wake. He did adhere to his promise for temporary safe passage, and Luther was able to leave Worms unmolested. The lines, however, were clearly drawn. There would be no compromise or reconciliation between the two camps, as Capito had hoped.

When Capito returned with Albrecht to Mainz, the discussion centered upon whether Albrecht should accept the pope's appointment to become an inquisitor general, which would give him the responsibility of enforcing Charles V's Edict of Worms throughout Germany. This edict described Luther as a "devil in the habit of a monk" whose actions threatened the collapse of Christendom as he "sullied marriage, disparaged confession," and "encouraged the laity to wash their hands in the blood of the clergy," in order to create "rebellion, division, [and] war." The edict ordered that "no one is to harbor" Luther, his "followers are to be condemned," and "his books are to be eradicated from the memory of man."[43] Albrecht was initially tempted to accept the appointment as a way of winning increased favor in Rome, but Capito was eventually able to convince the archbishop that it would be foolhardy for him to do so. In August 1521, Capito wrote Albrecht a long letter which outlined thirteen major reasons why the appointment had to be refused. Capito noted, for example, that Lutheranism was already so entrenched that "one cannot hope to disparage it even with the greatest possible effort," and that even trying to do so would be a very expensive proposition. Therefore, Albrecht would take on "all of the labor and great risk, effort and work, but not get anything here or in Rome except mockery, disgrace and loss." He would be "deprecated, despised

---

[40] Johann Eck quoted in Will Durant, *The Reformation: A History of European Civilization from Wyclif to Calvin, 1300-1564* (New York : Simon and Schuster, 1957), 361.

[41] Martin Luther quoted in Durant, *The Reformation,* 361.

[42] Martin Luther quoted in Marty, *Martin Luther,* 69.

[43] Charles V, "Edict of Worms," quoted in Durant, *The Reformation,* 362-363.

and driven into the ground" for taking forceful actions and seen as "disloyal to the Roman see" if he responded in a "measured way." Never had there been "a more dangerous commission" in Germany, which is why it would be far wiser for Albrecht to wait until "this tempest is over" before accepting the job, Capito wrote.[44] Albrecht's decision to take Capito's advice and refuse the appointment was an important moment in the history of the Reformation for it meant that there would be no equivalent of the Spanish Inquisition in Germany.[45] That Albrecht never signed the Edict of Worms, as tradition demanded, meant that Martin Luther lived for another quarter century. Capito literally helped save Luther's life. As time passed, however, the politics of the Mainz court, Capito's growing frustration over Luther's intransigence, and the increasing fear of peasant unrest all began to take a personal toll on the forty-three-year old man who abhorred disorder and cherished predictability. As early as January 1522, Capito wrote that he wished to retire from Albrecht's court, move to Strasbourg, and return to his scholarly studies.[46] A little over a year later, his wish came true.

As a boat took him up the Rhine to his new home in June 1523, Capito was still very much a man caught between two opposing camps, both practically and theologically. Because he hoped to please so many different people he respected and because he repeatedly wrote contradictory statements in an effort to appeal to different audiences, it is difficult to assess what Capito truly believed during this transitional period. Capito would not commit to one side or the other because to his mind both sides had serious flaws. There were also financial risks. Therefore, what he wrote in 1521 was still his view as he approached Strasbourg: "I keep to myself and will not join anyone's party....People everywhere are carried away by insane passion rather than wise and pious moderation."[47] This would not, however, be a position Capito would be able to keep for long.

~

In the sixteenth century, the city of Strasbourg sat on an island in the middle of the Ill River just before it emptied into the Rhine. The 466-foot, flamboyant Gothic spire of the cathedral's north tower dominated the flat, bountiful countryside for miles around. Its markets were a regional center of commerce, not only for its own cloth, printing, and wine industries, but also for goods passing from Italy and southern France to northern Europe. As an Imperial Free City within the Holy Roman Empire, Strasbourg enjoyed a high degree of political independence. It levied its own taxes, provided for its own defense, and formulated its own foreign and immigration policies. As one early sixteenth-century visitor wrote, "All things are found in over-abundance in this city, especially wine and grain, for she lies in a noble land....There is nothing like it to be found in all Germany."[48]

The people who would have agreed the most with that assessment were those who stood nearest the top of the Strasbourg social pyramid. This hierarchy wasn't quite typical of the Middle Ages for while the nobility and the wealthiest guild* members had different historical origins, by 1500 they

---

[44] Capito, *The Correspondence of Wolfgang Capito Volume 1, 1507-1523*, 160-166.
[45] Kittelson, *Wolfgang Capito*, 69.
[46] Capito, *The Correspondence of Wolfgang Capito Volume 1, 1507-1523*, 188.
[47] Capito, *The Correspondence of Wolfgang Capito Volume 1, 1507-1523*, 182.
[48] Miriam Usher Chrisman, *Strasbourg and the Reform: A Study in the Process of Change* (New Haven, Connecticut: Yale University Press, 1967) 3-4.

were indistinguishable in terms of their political influence.[49] In Strasbourg, wealth had become more important than class by the early modern period, which meant that a wealthy merchant could stand as a noblemen's equal in the city.[50] In fact, 70% of the city's wealth was controlled by 10% of the population, and many of the men that held this wealth also served as city magistrates. These men dominated both the guilds and the key civic offices, perpetuating Strasbourg's oligarchical rule by a few families.[51] Below this elite group stood lesser merchants, other guild officers, and civil servants, followed by common artisans, day laborers, and the poor. This social stratification was further delineated within the middle class as a result of a strict hierarchy within the city's twenty recognized guilds, with shippers, butchers, and innkeepers standing at the top of the social ladder and carpenters, gardeners and masons grasping its bottom.[52] Everyone in the community had a very precise social standing. The town honored this social structure once a year at an oath-taking ceremony.[53] At 9:00 a.m. on the first or second Tuesday of the new year, the city hall's bell rang. The five highest-ranking magistrates descended a covered staircase from the Gothic brick building onto a cobblestone street near Place Gutenberg, carrying the city's mace and plaques with the town's coat of arms. They regally led a procession of several thousand men through the streets to Cathedral Square, where they mounted a tall, temporary wood platform, decorated in the city's colors of red and white. The members of each of the twenty guilds, led by an honored standard-bearer, followed next into the square and were saluted by piercing trumpets and booming kettledrums played by colorfully-dressed musicians. Banners fluttered in every direction in the January wind. The guild officers joined the officials on the platform while the rest of each guild's membership stood in assigned areas on the square, looking up at their leaders. Then the noblemen entered the square and took a prominent place on the platform. Once everyone had assembled, the city secretary read a summary of the city's constitution and the people raised two fingers and swore to defend the city and abide by the city's laws. The city secretary responded by saying, "May God grant you and all of us luck, health, prosperity and long life!," at which point the crowd quickly departed to get out of the cold.[54] This oath-taking soothed the potential animosity Strasbourg's social hierarchy might create. It made all of the citizens believe that they were part of the ruling class and that power was broadly shared, even if this wasn't true.[55]

Strasbourg's religious community had a parallel hierarchy of prestige and station. At its apex stood the cathedral and the collegiate church of St. Thomas, both of which housed a chapter of canons.[56] The cathedral chapter's members were drawn from the highest ranks of the German

---

[49] John D. Derksen, *From Radicals to Survivors: Strasbourg's Religious Nonconformists over Two Generations, 1525-1570* (Utrecht, Netherlands: Hes & DeGraaf Publishers, 2002), 23.

[50] Miriam Usher Chrisman, *Lay Culture, Learned Culture: Books and Social Change in Strasbourg, 1480-1599* (New Haven, Connecticut: Yale University Press, 1982), xxix.

[51] Lorna Jane Abray, *The People's Reformation: Magistrates, Clergy and Commons in Strasbourg, 1500-1598* (Ithaca, New York: Cornell University Press, 1985), 53-54. Abray notes on page 11 that there were about 550 magistrates on different city councils in the 16th century.

[52] Derksen, *From Radicals to Survivors*, 22.

[53] Abray, *The People's Reformation*, 50-51.

[54] Abray, *The People's Reformation*, 51. Some of this description is also based upon Robert Darnton, *The Great Cat Massacre and Other Episodes in French Cultural History* (New York: Vintage Books, 1985), 116-117.

[55] It is important to realize that the residents of Strasbourg and the citizens of Strasbourg were not one and the same. Citizenship was a privilege, acquired either by birth or purchase. This meant that native Strasbourgers could be of any class, but those who purchased citizenship were people of means.

[56] Monks are often priests who live together in a community secluded to some degree from the rest of the world, while parish priests are those members of the clergy who care for the pastoral needs of a particular

nobility, while those of St. Thomas enjoyed the benefits of vast land holdings, like Capito's prebend.[57]   These priests controlled the spiritual life of the city because they determined the appointments to Strasbourg's parish churches, said masses for the dead, and issued indulgences. Below these two institutions, there were two other collegiate churches, nine parish churches, nineteen religious houses (including those for Franciscans, Dominicans, Augustinians, Carthusians, Knights Hospitaller, and the Teutonic Knights) and 200 chapels.[58] The nine parishes were frequently dominated by particular guilds, which contributed to their relative wealth, prestige, and character. For example, St. Aurelie at the west end of the city served independently-minded gardeners and domestic servants, while St. Stephen at the eastern gate served more traditional rivermen and fishermen.[59] The Strasbourg laity complained regularly about clerical greed and laziness, as well as clerical ignorance and incompetence, but for all of this pre-Reformation anticlericalism and resentment over clerical tax exemptions, Strasbourg was a city with a rich and full religious life.[60]

It was in this complex setting that a priest named Matthew Zell began preaching Luther's evangelical message. Zell began reading Luther in 1518 and by 1521 was arguing that the Wittenberg reformer was not a heretic. By late 1521, Zell was attracting such large crowds that he outgrew one of the side chapels and needed to preach in the cathedral's nave. When the bishop refused to grant Zell access to the nave's stone pulpit, the carpenters' guild constructed a wooden one, which was rolled in for the revolutionary preacher.[61] By the spring of 1523, the city was restless with pro-Zell and anti-Zell fliers posted around town, and the bishop, the canons, and the city magistrates all anxiously awaited what might happen next.

~

Capito arrived in Strasbourg in June 1523. He had hoped that his move would protect him from the politics of the Reformation, but this was not to be. Soon after his arrival in the city, Capito complained to Erasmus that "the Lutherans attack me with pictures and slanderous books. The papists on the other hand consider me...a complete Lutheran because of false testimonies."[62] As a man who held a prominent position within the community, he would be expected to choose a side, even if he hoped to reconcile his desire to remain in the Church with his agreement with Luther about the centrality of the Gospel. In the end, it was Matthew Zell who pushed Capito into the Lutheran camp. When the two men first met, Capito accused Zell of promoting "nothing but bitterness, rebellion and perfidy among the people,"[63] while Zell, unintimidated by the more learned and sophisticated man, accused Capito of trying "to create a reputation and to gain favor and

---

congregation. Canons are in a separate category. They are priests who live together in chapters but are not secluded and have no responsibilities to a parish. With less responsibility than a parish priest and less asceticism than a monk, the life of a canon attracted many nobles who could not inherit land because of the rules of primogeniture.

[57] Chrisman, *Lay Culture, Learned Culture*, xxiii.
[58] Derksen, *From Radicals to Survivors*, 26.
[59] Chrisman, *Strasbourg and the Reform*, 139.
[60] Abray, *The People's Reformation*, 24-26.
[61] Chrisman, *Strasbourg and the Reform*, 100.
[62] Wolfgang Capito quoted in Kittelson, *Wolfgang Capito*, 89.
[63] Wolfgang Capito quoted in Kittelson, *Wolfgang Capito*, 91.

approval of the world...so with your brilliance you make the Word of God weak and powerless."[64] Zell told Capito to let go of his vanity and to commit himself to his real duty: to convey the Gospel to the common people so that they might be saved. Capito came to find these words convincing and decided to support both the Strasbourg and Wittenberg reformers. His was a calculating, political decision, rather than a spiritual one. As Capito wrote several years later:

> In an uprising of this sort by the common people, I felt that it was my responsibility to God to help according to the best of my ability. I felt I must help the cause of peace and unity, create understanding and propagate the Word of God....Thus it was that I went into the pulpit of some of the chapter churches and gave three or four [evangelical] sermons for the priest.[65]

In July 1523, Capito purchased Strasbourg citizenship and took an oath that his first loyalty was the city. This gave him the protection of the city magistrates should he ever need it, but the notable shift in loyalties from religious authorities to secular ones was certainly something the local bishop noticed.

The Reformation was not yet complete, and through the course of the next two and a half years, between July 1523 and December 1525, Capito found himself, like so many others in central Europe, in a period of on-going transition. Some of the Reform developments he readily embraced, but from others he instinctively recoiled. For example, he supported the right of parishes to appoint their own preachers, and he accepted an invitation from the parishioners of the church of New St. Peter to become their preacher in February 1524. He also turned away from the Catholic tradition of clerical celibacy, endorsed the marriage of priests, and married Agnes Roettel, a daughter of a magistrate in August 1524. Finally, Capito supported the movement to abolish the mass in April 1525 in order to keep the emphasis on the Scriptures. On the other hand, Capito objected to guild members refusing to pay the tithe to the Church (1523) and to the stripping of altars and the removal of the statues of saints from churches (winter 1524-1525). He condemned the Peasants' War and the social revolution it represented (April 1525). Taken together, these conflicting reactions to the progress of the Reformation show how individualistic responses to this period of significant religious change could be.

~

Capito and his wife lived in a typical Strasbourg house of the era.[66] It was a three-story, half-timbered home, which sat above a street-level shop. Its beams were dark and thick, which contrasted nicely with the white-washed plaster that hid the straw insulation underneath. The beaver-tail-shaped tiles flowing off its steeply-pitched roof were uniformly dark, except for one which was glazed and decorated with a bouquet of flowers, an Alsatian sign of prosperity. Each of its windows consisted of six circles of greenish glass set in lead frames, surrounded by painted shutters. Because it was the house of a prominent member of the community, the exterior of

---

[64] Matthew Zell quoted in Chrisman, *Strasbourg and the Reform*, 109.
[65] Wolfgang Capito quoted in Chrisman, *Strasbourg and the Reform*, 111.
[66] This description of a typical house is based on an April 2013 visit to the Alsatian Museum in Strasbourg. For more information about the museum, see https://en.musees.strasbourg.eu/alsatian-museum

Capito's home also featured decorative elements others lacked. The carved wood gargoyles and cherubs were reminiscent of those covering the facade of the late Gothic cathedral and its tower, and the thin, looping wood molding over parts of the white plaster finished everything off with an ornamental flourish. Inside, the rooms were cozy, edging towards claustrophobic, with their low ceilings, heavy beams, small sleeping alcoves and bulky armoires. It wasn't quite as impressive or as well-decorated a house as those of Strasbourg's wealthiest merchants, but it made a definitive statement on the street near New St. Peter, where Capito was preacher.

It was in this home that Capito entertained a controversial group of guests on December 20, 1526.[67] Despite significant differences in their views, the men were lumped together as Anabaptists and as such were members of the one sect most every other Christian in Europe held in contempt. It was bad enough that some Anabaptists were separatists and pacifists (who refused to take civic oaths) or that some were millenarians (who proclaimed the imminence of Christ's Second Coming) or that some were proto-socialists (who sought political revolution and a redistribution of wealth). What goaded other Christians the most was that the Anabaptists did not believe in the value of infant baptism. Rather, all Anabaptists held that only fully cognizant adults could commit themselves to Christ. This was an utter heresy to all other Christians because without baptism all children were unredeemable and doomed to Hell. Both secular authorities and many members of the clergy saw Anabaptist doctrines as significant threats to the social order since they challenged the bonds which held so much of Europe's early modern society together.[68] Many towns expelled Anabaptists or persecuted them ruthlessly. One leader, Michael Sattler, had his tongue cut out and his body gripped by red-hot tongs five times before being burned at the stake.[69]

Capito, however, advocated a different approach, believing that the use of force was both counterproductive and immoral. He admired the Anabaptists because, as he noted in July 1526, they lived good Christian lives and avoided "gambling, drinking, gluttony, adultery, fighting, murder, slander, and living according to the desires of the flesh."[70] He argued that persecution of the Anabaptists only made them more stubborn, but that patient conversation and leniency would help them understand their theological errors and would produce civic peace.[71] "They confess their

[67] The guests were Hans Denck (1495-1527), Martin Cellarius (1499-1564), and Ludwig Hetzer (1500-1529). See R. L. Williams, "Martin Cellarius and the Reformation in Strasbourg," *The Journal of Ecclesiastical History*, 32. 4 (October, 1981), 477-497, EBSCOhost.

[68] Thomas A. Brady, Jr., *The Politics of the Reformation in Germany: Jacob Strum (1489-1553) of Strasbourg* (Atlantic Highlands, New Jersey: Humanities Press International, 1997), 144.

[69] Wolfgang Capito, *The Correspondence of Wolfgang Capito Volume 2, 1524-1531*, ed. and trans. Erika Rummel with the assistance of Milton Kooistra (Toronto, Canada: University of Toronto Press, 2009), 280.

[70] Capito, *The Correspondence of Wolfgang Capito Volume 2, 1524-1531*, 282.

[71] Capito, *The Correspondence of Wolfgang Capito Volume 2, 1524-1531*, 330.

error out of fear, yet cling to their former belief in their heart."[72] Consequently, between 1525 and 1532 Capito regularly met with Anabaptists and provided long-term room and board for several of them. As he wrote in 1527, "There are good men among them, whom the fear of God, which is a virtue, has driven to error. They...superstitiously involve themselves in minutiae, and go beyond limits, but they are wretched rather than evil." "They sin without malice, if they sin at all."[73] Three years later, he put it even more succinctly: the Anabaptists were "enslaved more by the letter than by the Spirit."[74] Such an understanding was virtually unique among sixteenth century Reformation leaders.[75] Such uniqueness would eventually bring Capito a notoriety he did not wish.

The man who ultimately challenged Capito's independent approach was Strasbourg's other leading reformer, Martin Bucer, who was a more charismatic and less subtle man than Capito. He was also significantly younger and, as Capito's ill health began to take an increasing toll, Bucer became an increasingly prominent figure within the city. A former Dominican, Bucer was far less willing to accommodate the Anabaptists than Capito was. In fact, he regularly disparaged all who disagreed with him, publicly attacking theological rivals from the pulpit.[76] Bucer's aim was to take the Reformation in Strasbourg to a purer level—one which would mandate behavior and provide a systematic unity between civic and religious authorities, just as John Calvin would later do in Geneva. In June 1533, Bucer and his political ally, Jacob Sturm, held a synod which completely reconstructed Strasbourg's political-theological landscape, shattering the relative toleration Capito had cultivated in order to preserve peace.[77] Capito's work "to quell the uprisings on both sides" in order to find "a basis on which an  understanding could be reached by both sides" was quite undone.[78] The new ecclesiastical constitution established Christian doctrine for the city and imposed more disciplinary measures within it. Soon, the Anabaptists had to swear that they would fulfill their civic duties and not criticize their city's approved theology in public, but they were permitted a freedom of conscience in private.[79] During the synod, Capito acquiesced quite completely before the assembly, admitting that he had been too permissive of dissent in the preceding years. He was not a man whose convictions would allow him to gamble his well-being in the face of almost certain defeat. He was not willing to sacrifice his personal security for what he believed. Capito also realized that he had been beaten by a more dogmatic, more confident man. As he ruefully wrote a friend in September 1534, "Bucer is our bishop."[80]

---

[72] Capito, *The Correspondence of Wolfgang Capito Volume 1, 1507-1523*, xxxi.

[73] Capito, *The Correspondence of Wolfgang Capito Volume 1, 1507-1523*, xxxi.

[74] Wolfgang Capito quoted in Kittelson, *Wolfgang Capito,* 174.

[75] Kittelson, *Wolfgang Capito,* 175.

[76] Chrisman, *Strasbourg and the Reform,* 125.

[77] Thomas A. Brady, Jr., "'The Earth is the Lord's, and our Homeland as Well': Martin Bucer and the Politics of Strasbourg," *Martin Bucer and Sixteenth Century Europe,* Christian Krieger and Marc Lienhard (ed.), Volume 1 (Leiden, Netherlands: E.J. Brill, 1993), 132.

[78] Wolfgang Capito quoted in Chrisman, *Strasbourg and the Reform,* 129.

[79] Derksen, *From Radicals to Survivors,* 84.

[80] Wolfgang Capito quoted in Brady, Jr., "'The Earth is the Lord's, and our Homeland as Well,'"*Martin Bucer and Sixteenth Century Europe,* 133.

Once Capito had capitulated, he followed Bucer's lead on all other issues of the day. The most important of these was the on-going Sacramentarian Controversy, which involved the purpose, meaning, and integrity of the mass. In the Catholic tradition, the priest transforms the bread into the body of Christ through a process known as transubstantiation; the priest does this so that another's soul may be physically nourished with Christ's body. Similarly, a Catholic priest transforms the wine literally into Christ's blood. By the early 1520s, however, many Protestant reformers, including Huldrych Zwingli of Switzerland, were arguing that what happened in the mass was symbolic, not real: the bread and the wine were merely symbols of Jesus' body and blood, not the actual things themselves. This was a position Luther absolutely refused to accept. He believed that the Catholics were correct in their interpretation of the mass and that when the priest said, "the body of Christ" during the Eucharist, the body of Christ was exactly what the parishioner received during communion.

For his part, Capito hedged his bets in the early years of the Sacramentarian Controversy, not taking a definitive stand in hope that a compromise position might be found. In 1524, for example, he wrote that the Eucharist is "a recollection of Christ's death on the cross. We refresh our memory and clearly affirm it by accepting the Lord's bread and wine," but then also quickly added, "We know, however, that we become blessed through the body and blood alone."[81] The first sentence was written for the Zwinglians, while the second was clearly written to appeal to the Lutherans. Over time, however, Capito came to find the symbolic interpretation more and more satisfying, even though it was most important to him to find a meaningful way for the various Protestant groups to reconcile. Only this could prevent social disorder, public confusion, and a resurgence of Catholicism. From Capito's point of view, there had to be a Eucharistic language upon which all parties could agree since they were all Christians. As Capito once wrote, "Our salvation does not consist of words, but of the power of God."[82]

There were attempts to find common ground. In fall 1529, for example, the Landgrave Philip I of Hesse invited leading theologians to come to his castle at Marburg to discuss their differences.[83] He hoped that they could reach a collective understanding on the nature of the Eucharist, which in turn could pave the way for a German-Swiss confederation of Protestants to stand against the military power of Charles V.[84] Luther and Zwingli accepted Philip's invitation, as did Luther's key ally, Philipp Melanchthon. Capito's best friend, Johannes Oecolampadius, and other leading reformers also participated. Strasbourg sent Bucer to Marburg instead of Capito, who was in poor health at the time and who was still being punished for his close association with the Anabaptists.[85] At the Marburg Colloquy in early October, the pivotal moment came when Luther wrote, "*Hoc est corpus meum*" ("This is my body") on a table with a piece of chalk, covered the table with a velvet cloth, and challenged Zwingli and Oecolampadius to "prove that Christ's body is not there where the Scripture says, this is my body." "I request…valid scriptural proof to the contrary." Zwingli and Oecolampadius responded by saying that the words had to be read figuratively. Oecolampadius quoted the Gospel according to John (6, 63): "It is the spirit that gives life; the flesh is of no avail." Therefore, Oecolampadius said, Jesus "repudiated once and for all the physical eating of his flesh." Luther responded, "If you interpret the Lord's Supper figuratively, why not do the

[81] Capito, *The Correspondence of Wolfgang Capito Volume 1, 1507-1523*, xxvii.
[82] Wolfgang Capito quoted in Kittelson, *Wolfgang Capito*, 170.
[83] Landgrave is a noble title, equivalent to that of a count.
[84] Roland H. Bainton, *Here I Stand: A Life of Martin Luther* (New York: Abingdon Press, 1950), 318.
[85] Erika Rummel, "Introduction," *The Correspondence of Wolfgang Capito Volume 2, 1524-1531*, xi.

same with these words—"He was taken up into Heaven." The debate continued until Luther removed the velvet cloth and said,

> "This is my body"! Right here is our Scripture. You haven't torn it away from us yet like you promised to do….My esteemed lords, as long as the text of my Lord Jesus Christ is there…then truly I cannot pass over it, but must confess and believe that Christ's body is there."[86]

The contrast between Luther's literalness and Zwingli and Oecolampadius' figurativeness meant that the theologians could not find agreement on the Eucharist in Marburg. Each side left disappointed that they had not been able to convince the other, even if there was still personal affection between many of the participants.[87]

In June 1530, Charles V made his own attempt to unify Western Christianity by calling for a meeting known as the Diet of Augsburg. It was a conference of electors, sovereigns, free city

representatives, and theologians—each of which met as a separate college.[88] Charles' impetus for convening the Diet came from the threat posed by the Ottoman Empire. Suleiman the Magnificent had laid siege to Vienna in late September 1529 and, while that attack was thwarted, Charles V knew that the sultan and his troops would return. The Holy Roman Empire was both vulnerable and less formidable as a result of its religious divisions, and Charles hoped to be able to find religious unity.[89] He also hoped to manage the religious issue quietly behind closed doors.[90] Unfortunately for this approach, Catholic prelate Johann Eck arrived in Augsburg armed with a list of 404 statements from reformers' writings that he considered to be heretical. He wanted a confrontation. As for the Protestants, many still hoped to reach a reconciliation with the Catholics.[91] To attain such unity, several key participants prepared statements outlining their theological positions in generous terms. Philipp Melanchthon prepared the most important one, which became known as the *Confession of Augsburg*. It drew a sharp distinction between Lutheran beliefs and those of Zwingli and the Anabaptists, and it did not reject papal authority outright. Melanchthon's *Confession* did, however, maintain the correctness of offering the bread and the wine to the faithful, of permitting the marriage of priests, of prohibiting mandatory fasting, of eliminating private masses, and of abolishing monastic vows.[92] Capito and Bauer wrote a separate confession for the city of Strasbourg

---

[86] "The Debate at the Colloquy of Marburg, 1529," in Michael W. Bruening, A *Reformation Sourcebook: Documents from an Age of Debate* (Toronto: University of Toronto Press, 2017), 96-99, EBSCOhost.

[87] "The Debate at the Colloquy of Marburg, 1529," in Bruening, A *Reformation Sourcebook*, 96-99.

[88] For more information how the Diet operated, see Krodel G. Gottfried, "Law, Order, and the Almighty Taler: The Empire in Action at the 1530 Diet of Augsburg," *The Sixteenth Century Journal* 13, no. 2 (1982), 75-106, EBSCOhost.

[89] William Maltby, *The Reign of Charles V* (New York: Palgrave, 2002), 51-52. In addition to the religious issues and the Ottoman threat, the Diet was convened to consider improving government and public well-being. James M. Kittleson disagrees with this assessment and asserts that Charles never had any intention of compromising on the theological issues. See Kittleson, *Wolfgang Capito,* 154.

[90] Gottfried, "Law, Order, and the Almighty Taler."

[91] Lewis W. Spitz, *The Protestant Reformation, 1517-1559* (New York: Harper & Row, 1985), 116.

[92] Scott H. Hendrix, *Martin Luther: Visionary Reformer* (New Haven: Yale University Press, 2015), 214, 219, 221.

known as the *Tetrapolitana Confession*.[93]   In genuine Capitoian character, the *Tetrapolitana* attempted to find the middle ground between the literalist Lutherans and the figurative Swiss. This didn't always make for the most elegant prose. At times, it was purposely ambiguous.[94] Capito declared, for example, "In the sacrament, Christ gives his true body truly to eat and his blood truly to drink, for the nourishment of their souls and eternal life, that you may remain in him and he in you."[95]   Not only did this compromise language fail to sway the Swiss, but it also isolated Strasbourg's representatives to the Diet. In fact, Capito subsequently suffered a series of personal humiliations as a result of his perceived fence sitting. His former employer, Albrecht von Hohenzollern, Luther, and Melanchthon all refused to meet with Capito.[96] He left the Diet before its conclusion as a result of these snubs, admitting that he was sometimes a poor judge of character.[97]

After the failure of the Diet of Augsburg, a group of Protestant German states formed a defensive alliance in early 1531 known as the Schmalkaldic League. The League's aim was to prevent Charles V and the Holy Roman Empire from re-imposing Catholicism by force in Germany. Membership in the League was conditional upon agreeing to uphold various Lutheran principles. Strasbourg's magistrates worried that the city would be too vulnerable to Charles' armies unless it joined the League, and so sent Capito and Bucer to negotiate with Luther and win Strasbourg's membership in the League. For its part, the League wanted Strasbourg's support because of its commercial wealth and strategic location. Therefore, in May 1536, Capito and Bucer travelled to Wittenberg to meet with Luther and other Reformation leaders, including Melanchthon and representatives from key cities such as Augsburg, Constance, Eisenach, Frankfurt, and Ulm.[98] Capito had not seen Luther in ten years,[99] but they had resumed their correspondence in August 1535.[100] The animosity present at the Diet of Augsburg had dissipated by the time Capito arrived in Wittenberg. On May 25, 1536, the attendees signaled the commonality by sharing in the Lord's Supper during the festival of Christ's Ascension, and by May 29 Melanchthon had drafted a statement of agreement.[101] Known as the Wittenberg Concord, the document proclaimed a universal understanding of the meaning of the Eucharist, but its wording ("through sacramental unity the bread is the body of

---

[93] It took this name because it was eventually adopted by four imperial cities as their statement of belief. These cities were Strasbourg, Konstanz, Memmingen, and Lindau.
[94] Abray, *The People's Reformation,* 41.
[95] Capito, *The Correspondence of Wolfgang Capito Volume 1, 1507-1523,* xxviii.
[96] Rummel, "Introduction," *The Correspondence of Wolfgang Capito Volume 2, 1524-1531,* xii. Luther did not actually attend the Diet of Augsburg because there was still a warrant out for his arrest within the Holy Roman Empire, but Luther did travel as far as Coburg, Saxony to monitor the proceedings.
[97] Capito, *The Correspondence of Wolfgang Capito Volume 2, 1524-1531,* 426.
[98] The participants were: Johannes Bugenhagen, Caspar Cruciger, and Justus Jonas (who were Luther's close associates), Matthäus Alber (Reutlingen), Johannes Bernhardi (Frankfurt), Martin Frecht (Ulm), Martin Germanus (Fürfeld in Kraichgau), Justus Menius (Eisenach), Wolfgang Musculus (Augsburg), Friedrich Myconius (Gotha), Jacob Otter (Esslingen), Johannes Schradin (Reutlingen), Gervasius Schuler (Memmingen), Boniface Wolfhart (Augsburg), and Johannes Zwick (Constance). See Wolfgang Capito, *The Correspondence of Wolfgang Capito Volume 3, 1532-1536*, ed. and trans. Erika Rummel with the assistance of Milton Kooistra (Toronto, Canada: University of Toronto Press, 2015), 402, EBSCOhost.
[99] Scott H. Hendrix, *Martin Luther: Visionary Reformer* (New Haven: Yale University Press, 2015), 249.
[100] Capito did not write to Luther in 1532, 1533, or 1534. Capito's first letter is on behalf of the Strasbourg clergy and is dated August 19, 1535. See Capito, *The Correspondence of Wolfgang Capito Volume 3, 1532-1536,* 349.
[101] Hendrix, *Martin Luther,* 250.

Christ") still allowed for multiple interpretations.[102] It was exactly what Capito had sought for the previous dozen years: the theology was flexible and Strasbourg's safety was secure. Little wonder he left Wittenberg so satisfied.

Capito, Bucer, Luther, and the other signatories then began a campaign to promote the Wittenberg Concord across Germany. They visited towns, met with influential figures, wrote commentaries, and gathered intelligence. As Capito wrote in June,

> I fear greatly that inexperienced people will make slanderous remarks about matters of small importance….Furthermore, there are even among us rather contrary, not to say, treacherous people, who have promised us concord up front, by in fact nurse discord. If anything is written about this to the Doctor [Luther]…please inform me of it at once – this I ask through Christ and for the salvation of the churches.[103]

By late July 1536, these efforts began to bear fruit with Augsburg, Frankfurt, Worms, and Strasbourg all signing the Concord. At the end of the year even places that had been resistant, like Ulm, had affirmed the convent. Only the Swiss and the city of Constance refused to join.[104] This resolution sufficiently solidified the strength of Lutheranism in Germany that even military losses could not dislodge the reformed faith in central Europe.[105]

In the last five years of his life, Capito continued his attempts to resolve conflicts, build Christian consensus, and write new works. His most important text in this late period was *Hexameron Dei opus explicatum* (1539), a commentary on Genesis. In Capito's explication, he tried to embrace *Hebraica Veritas*—the concept that Christian truth and authenticity could be found in Hebrew sources—but he did so while simultaneously distancing himself from the rabbinical readings of those texts. The result is a work with decidedly anti-Semitic passages[106] that were not dissimilar to those of Luther's later years.[107] One of the men who took note of *Hexameron* was John Calvin.[108] Once Calvin arrived in Strasbourg after his expulsion from Geneva in May 1538, he and Capito became personally acquainted. Capito helped the Genevan to expand his circle of Reformation

---

[102] Christopher W. Close, "Augsburg, Zurich and the Transfer of Preachers During the Schmalkaldic War," *Central European History*, 42, 4. (December, 2009), 595-619.

[103] Capito, *The Correspondence of Wolfgang Capito Volume 3, 1532-1536*, 443.

[104] Rummel, *The Correspondence of Wolfgang Capito Volume 3, 1532-1536*, 437-438.

[105] In the Schmalkaldic War, Charles V's army routed the Protestants at the Battle of Mühlberg on April 24, 1547, but this victory did not result in the enforcement of the Edict of Worms. Protestantism was too entrenched by the mid-century to allow this to happen.

[106] Debra Kaplan, *Beyond Expulsion: Jews, Christians, and Reformation Strasbourg* (Stanford, California: Stanford University Press, 2011), 119, 133-134. Kaplan also notes how the relationship between Jews and Christians in Strasbourg changed over the course of the sixteenth century: before the Reformation, Jews lived side by side with Christians, and prior to 1550 there was considerable contact as a result. By the later sixteenth century, city magistrates sought to limit these interactions and by 1570 even economic contact had nearly stopped altogether. See Kaplan, 1-10.

[107] The scholarship on Luther's attitudes towards Jews and the publication of two key works, *Against the Sabbatarians* (1538) and *Jews and Their Lies* (1543), is vast. One particularly helpful discussion can be found in Hendrix, *Martin Luther*, 264-266 and 274-275. One concise discussion that challenges the conventional view that Luther changed his attitudes towards the Jews as he grew older is Craig L. Nessan, *Tikkun* (Duke University Press), Summer 2017, Vol. 32 Issue 3, 34-38, EBSCOhost.

[108] Erik A. De Boer, "'Portrait of a New Prophet': John Calvin Moonlighting as a Pamphleteer in Strasbourg (1539)," *Reformation & Renaissance Review: Journal of the Society for Reformation Studies* 12, no. 2/3 (August 2010): 329–48. EBSCOhost.

acquaintances and contacts.[109] Capito also urged Calvin to lecture publicly as a way of increasing the thirty-year old's exposure.[110] This mentorship was simultaneously paired with Capito's ongoing campaign urging Calvin to moderate the language of his written works, for the older man typically found Calvin's tone to be too confrontational and divisive. In fall 1536, for example, Capito cautioned Calvin not to publish a series of letters that excoriated the Catholic Church, especially those that criticized Catholics who held evangelical beliefs.[111] When Calvin described Catholics as "monsters" and the Church as a place where "detestable sacrileges, pollutions, and filthiness swarm,"[112] Capito thought the Genevan had gone too far. Such language didn't fit with Capito's unifying, diplomatic sensibilities. Similarly, Capito opposed the publication of Calvin's seminal work *Psychopannychia* because of the controversy it might generate.[113] These tensions meant that Capito would not play a key role in the development of Calvin's doctrine.[114] Rather, it was the younger and more prominent Bucer who imparted the greater theological influence on the Genevan during his three years in Strasbourg.[115]

~

In 1681, one hundred and forty years after Capito died of the plague at age sixty-three,[116] France's staunchly Catholic king Louis XIV captured the city of Strasbourg and extended France's borders

---

[109] Heiko A Oberman, "Calvin and Farel the Dynamics of Legitimation in Early Calvinism." *Reformation & Renaissance Review: Journal of the Society for Reformation Studies*, no. 1 (June 1999): 7, EBSCOhost.

[110] John Calvin, *Letters of John Calvin: Compiled from the Original Manuscripts and Edited with Historical Notes, Volume 1*, (Jules Bonnet, ed. and trans.) (Philadelphia, Pennsylvania: Jesper Harding & Son, 1858), 106.

[111] Bruce Gordon, *Calvin* (New Haven, Connecticut: Yale University Press, 2009), 77.

[112] John Calvin quoted in Gordon, *Calvin*, 77.

[113] Bruce Gordon, *Calvin* (New Haven, Connecticut: Yale University Press, 2009), 43, EBSCOhost. *Psychopannychia* explores what happens to the soul upon death; Calvin argues that the soul remains alive and does not sleep until Resurrection.

[114] John Calvin lived in Strasbourg between September 1538 and September 1541. Upon Calvin's return to Geneva, an ecclesiastical ordinance based on the Strasbourg model was adopted by the city's magistrates. The Strasbourg model for its educational program was also adopted in the Swiss canton. Theologically, Calvin emphasized the concept of predestination far more than either Bucer or Luther, arguing that at the moment of Creation God chose a few individuals ("The Elect") for Heaven and condemned all others to eternal damnation. The selection was not made on the basis of individual merit, but for the purpose of God's own divine pleasure. There was nothing humans could do on earth to change their fate. See Ozment, *The Age of Reform, 1250-1550,* 363-366, 379-380; and Eire, *Reformations,* 290-296.

[115] Heiko A Oberman, "Calvin and Farel the Dynamics of Legitimation in Early Calvinism." *Reformation & Renaissance Review: Journal of the Society for Reformation Studies*, no. 1 (June 1999): 7, EBSCOhost. In December 1541, however, Calvin wrote to Guillaume Farel from Geneva, expressing his sadness over Capito's death the previous month. Calvin admitted, "I was so overpowered by the sad intelligence of the death of Capito that since that time I have neither been well in body nor in mind." See John Calvin, *Letters of John Calvin, Volume 1*, 310. This, combined with the numerous times Calvin evokes Capito's name between April 1537 and December 1541, shows that although the two reformers disagreed with one another there was affection and appreciation between them.

[116] Just before he died, Capito had asked Bucer to care for his second wife, Wibrandis Rosenblatt. Wibrandis had been the widow of Capito's best friend Johannes Oecolampadius before marrying Capito. When Bucer's own wife, Elizabeth, realized that she too would succumb to the plague just a few weeks after Capito's death, Elizabeth urged Bucer to marry Wibrandis. Hence, Wibrandis was married to three of the Reformation's key

to the Rhine. The Sun King then forced the city to accommodate its Catholic subjects in a more equitable manner, which included the restoration of the Strasbourg Cathedral and several other parish churches to the Catholic fold. Others, like St. Thomas, were allowed to remain Protestant. Interestingly, there was no mention of Capito's church, New St. Peter, in the surrender treaty. In true Capito fashion, however, the canons and the parishioners struck a deal: they constructed a massive wall which completely divided the nave from the choir, creating in essence two separate churches. The Catholics used the choir, which they embellished with green and gold paneling and which featured a new Baroque altar; the Protestants used the pulpit-dominated nave, which they kept whitewashed and simplified. The choir became an architectural expression of the Catholic view of God as being infinitely complex and magnificent, while the nave became an architectural expression of the Protestant view of the purity and importance of Scripture. This compromise lasted until 1898, when the Catholics agreed to move to a new church within Strasbourg's growing city limits. The Protestants had the dividing wall demolished and restored the medieval frescoes that had been covered with whitewash.[117] Today, Capito's portrait hangs on a pier in the nave, overlooking the congregation. His expression is pensive and a bit anxious, full of caution and some uncertainty. He seems quite at home.

---

reformers. See Willem van't Spijker, "Bucer's Doctrinal Legacy as Formulated in his Last Three Wills and Testaments," *Reformation & Renaissance Review: Journal of the Society for Reformation Studies,* Jun2001/Dec2001 (Vol. 3, Issue 1/2), EBSCOhost.

[117] F. Westphal, *Saint-Pierre-Le-Jeune: Protestant Church Strasbourg,* J.+ J. Osborne (trans.) (Strasbourg: Ligne Á Suivre, 2005), 7-9.

$\mathcal{D}$

John Dee

1527-1609

Looking up into the night sky on November 6, 1572, a Benedictine abbot in Sicily named Maurolycus and a group of Korean astronomers working in the court of King Seonjo all realized a new light shone from the heavens. Five nights later, clear skies allowed the Danish nobleman Tycho Brahe to resume his astronomical studies, and he too saw a new star shining in the constellation Cassiopeia. The Koreans reported that it was as bright as Venus; a few days later, Chinese chroniclers recorded that the new star was so bright that it could be seen even in daylight.[1] Plainly, this was a major astronomical event, but what did it mean? What did it portend? And whom could a monarch trust to reveal and interpret such vital intelligence? For England's Elizabeth I, the choice was an easy one: she turned to her favorite astrologer, John Dee.

The arrival of a new star challenged the very foundations of sixteenth century cosmology and bolstered fears that the Apocalypse was imminent. Even those who accepted Copernicus' new heliocentric model of the universe continued to believe that the stars were fixed entities in an immutable, incorruptible celestial realm, as Aristotle and Ptolemy maintained. Suddenly there was manifest evidence that this was not so. Even more frighteningly for Elizabeth, if the perceived cosmological order wasn't true, then by implication the political and religious order could be questioned as well.[2] Moreover, in the late sixteenth century it was also commonly believed that the day of reckoning was at hand. The enormous changes caused by the Reformation fed popular anxiety; since the only acknowledged occasion when a new star had appeared in the heavens was with the birth of Christ and the arrival of the Star of Bethlehem, it made sense that the arrival of the new star in 1572 foretold an event of Biblical proportions. It would take the expertise of an especially learned professional to navigate this problem, and everyone agreed that John Dee had

---

[1] David A. Green and F. Richard Stephenson, "The Historical Supernovae," *Supernovae and Gamma-Ray Bursters*, K.W. Weiler (ed.) (New York: Springer-Verlag, 2003), 10-11.
[2] Benjamin Woolley, *The Queen's Conjuror: The Life and Magic of Dr. Dee* (London: Flamingo, 2002), 153.

the necessary credentials and experience. He was quickly summoned to Windsor Castle. The specific details of Dee's meeting with Elizabeth have not survived, but Dee believed that Haniel, the archangel associated with Venus, governed female rulers in the sixteenth century. Because he had calculated that the 1572 supernova appeared within Venus' sphere, Dee believed that this astrological influence would intensify. Dee also believed the arrival of a new light in the sky signaled the end of a decayed world and the emergence of a politically and religiously unified continent. He even held that new star would allow him to discover the long sought-after substance which could turn inferior metals into gold.[3]

Five years later, a great comet appeared. As with the supernova, this was interpreted as a sign that significant change loomed, and many in the court worried that the comet foretold of devastating plague and famine. Again, Elizabeth called for her Renaissance magus, who told the queen not to fear it. Rather, Dee urged Elizabeth to embrace the comet as another sign of her impending greatness. In the presence of her courtiers who refused to look into the sky, Elizabeth looked out a window, gazed directly at it, and said, "*Iacta est alea*," the die is cast.[4] Elizabeth then promised to protect Dee as he furthered his study and practice of magic and alchemy.[5] Clearly, Dee was a man Elizabeth respected, someone who she could trust to explain the inexplicable.

~

Most people today would agree that astronomy and astrology are completely different disciplines, with the former having significantly more legitimacy than the latter. The same is true for chemistry and alchemy. During the Renaissance, however, this was not the case. Alchemy was a legitimate field of experimental science, and astrology was simply thought of as applied astronomy, just as mechanical engineering is seen today as being a form of applied physics. For many Elizabethans, astrology had a deep authority and authenticity since it professed to answer questions in a systematic way, using a precise mathematical method. Every action had an astrological explanation, based on the positions of the planets, the sun, the moon, and the constellations of the zodiac at a given moment in time. Astrology explained the natural order of things, offered an answer when no other authority could, and seemingly had as good a rate of success as anything else.[6] In fact, Copernicus, Brahe, Kepler, and Galileo all cast horoscopes for clients, indicating that astronomers did not see astrology as an unrelated, incompatible, or illegitimate field.[7] For these men and for society as a whole, there was a causal relationship between astral influences and everyday life. But people distinguished between ordinary horoscopes that made generalized predictions about a person's life and "judicial horoscopes," which sought to answer very specific questions.[8] To make one of these elevated horoscopes, a conscientious astrologer needed to be able to differentiate

---

[3] Glyn Parry, *The Arch-Conjuror of England: John Dee* (New Haven, Connecticut: Yale University Press, 2011) , 47, 98, 107.
[4] Woolley, *The Queen's Conjuror*, 161-162.
[5] Parry, *The Arch-Conjuror of England*, 97.
[6] Keith Thomas, *Religion and the Decline of Magic* (New York: Charles Scribner's Sons, 1971), 324, 327, 338.
[7] Dan Burton and David Grandy, *Magic, Mystery and Science: The Occult in Western Civilization* (Bloomington, Indiana: Indiana University Press, 2004), 97.
[8] Francis Young, *Magic as a Political Crime in Medieval and Early Modern England: A History of Sorcery and Treason* (London/New York: I.B. Tauris, 2018), 82.

among 25,000 individual planetary conjunctions.[9] Such precision and authority is what led one London astrologer, Simon Forman, to see over a thousand clients a year between 1597 and 1601. These customers came from all walks of life and asked Forman's predictions about marriages, pregnancies, debts, journeys, legal actions, bets, political events, battles, missing persons, and hidden treasure.[10] Clearly, many in early modern England saw astrology as a rational approach to answering questions about the future.

Magic had a similar standing before the Reformation because the boundary between magic and religion was an imprecise one. Priests used a type of magic to change the essence of the host and the wine during communion. Similarly, practices like casting out evil spirits from dwellings with holy water or visiting a shrine to cure disease or protect from misfortune made it hard for many people to distinguish between the priest's rituals and a magician's spells. The main difference in the common mind between prayers and spells was that prayers didn't always work, but spells always did.[11] By the mid-sixteenth century, magic had become far more suspect as a result of the Reformation, but in times of personal crisis people might well to turn to a magician for assistance. This was particularly true when people believed that black magic had been used against them. In this case, it was legitimate to seek a practitioner of white magic to counteract black magic's power.[12] Elizabeth, for example, hoped early in her reign that Dee's knowledge of the occult could counteract that of Nostradamus, who at the time was working for Catherine de Medici in France. Similarly in 1578, when a wax image of Elizabeth was found full of pig bristles, the queen's Privy Council demanded that Dee counteract the magic and speedily "prevent the mischief" of this Catholic plot.[13] Even the passage of witchcraft laws in 1563 and 1604 and the English clergy's repeated denunciations of magic proved unable, however, to reduce the popularity of its practice.[14]

Alchemy was a third occult practice that held significant respect in sixteenth century Europe. Its goal was to transform commonplace metals into gold by placing them in contact with the philosopher's stone: an as-yet-undiscovered substance so sublime that it could turn dead matter into living. Its most base practitioners were only interested in creating enormous wealth quickly, but for someone like Dee there was a deeply spiritual element involved in the process as well. Philosophical alchemy maintained that the process that turned lead into gold would also transform the alchemist's soul, thereby making the alchemist almost divine.[15] Astrology played a role in this process as well since the sun, the moon, and the planets were each associated with were a particular

[9] J.L. Heilbron, "Introductory Essay," in Wayne Shumaker (trans. and ed.), *John Dee on Astronomy: Propaedeumata Aphoristica (1558 and 1568) Latin and English*, (Berkeley, California: University of California Press, 1978), 12. To assist with these calculations, astrologers used established tables and astrolabes to determine the positions of the planets at a particular moment. They then correlated this information to the zodiac's astrological houses, which governed a person's familial relationships, personal health, careers, and more. See William Eamon, "Astrology and Society," *A Companion to Astrology in the Renaissance*, Brendan Dooley (ed.) (Leiden: Brill, 2014), 156-157.
[10] Thomas, *Religion and the Decline of Magic*, 307-312, 316-317, 319.
[11] Thomas, *Religion and the Decline of Magic*, 29, 33, 41.
[12] Thomas, *Religion and the Decline of Magic*, 246.
[13] Parry, *The Arch-Conjuror of England*, 49, 132.
[14] Thomas, *Religion and the Decline of Magic*, 250-251. These laws were aimed at preventing the use of astrology for political purposes, especially in cases of sedition. See Eamon, "Astrology and Society," 229.
[15] Deborah E. Harkness, *John Dee's Conversations with Angels: Cabala, Alchemy and the End of Nature* (Cambridge, England: Cambridge University Press, 1999), 200.

metal.[16] The alchemist's method was often threefold. It began with the "black stage," which destroyed the properties of the original substance to create a powder. This powder was then combined with a metal like mercury so that it could be reconfigured in the transitional "white stage." After repeatedly applying processes of heat, fermentation, and condensation, the "red stage" would produce the philosopher's stone if each of the calculations and steps had been completed accurately.[17] Of course, no one actually succeeded in producing gold from lead in antiquity, the Middle Ages, or the early modern period. But the fact that so many tried with the blessings and support of their political and religious leaders shows how blurred the distinctions between science, religion, and the occult were for many Europeans before the Scientific Revolution.*

~

Dee began learning about the occult disciplines as a student at St. John's College, Cambridge, where he began his studies in November 1542. They were not a part of the official curriculum, but rather became Dee's focus in private tutorials. He would have also encountered logic, Aristotelian philosophy, medieval scholasticism,* humanism, classical languages, geometry, astronomy, cosmology, and music.[18] From a very early point in his intellectual career, Dee was attracted to the philosophy of Neoplatonism: that all existence emanates from a single source, and that it is it possible for individuals to connect to that source through spiritual or mystical means. As time went on, Dee became increasingly convinced that this single source was mathematical in nature. He began a life-long religious quest to understand divinity and the cosmos, and for many decades he did so through mathematical means.[19]

Upon earning his bachelor's degree, Dee secured an auxiliary faculty position at newly-established Trinity College, Cambridge in December 1546, thanks to his father's connections to the court of Henry VIII.[20] The most important event of Dee's Trinity experience involved his production of Aristophanes' comedy *Pax*. The play calls for a scarab or dung beetle to carry the protagonist, Trygaeus, to Mount Olympus to try to meet Zeus. Dee wanted to make a lasting impression with the production; he wanted to do something no one else had done and produce an effect no one would ever forget. Inspired by fifteenth-century occultist Heinrich Cornelius Agrippa von Nettesheim, who held that the magician must be well versed in applied mathematics, Dee constructed a flying machine, which may well have been the first seen in England.[21] At a time when audiences went to *hear* a play more than *see* one, the effect of Dee's scarab flying high above the

[16] The sun was gold; the moon, silver; Mercury, mercury; Venus, copper; Mars, iron; Jupiter, tin; and Saturn, lead. See Burton and Grandy, *Magic, Mystery and Science*, 78.
[17] Burton and Grandy, *Magic, Mystery and Science*, 82-83.
[18] Nicholas H. Clulee, *John Dee's Natural Philosophy: Between Science and Religion* (New York: Routledge, 1988), 23-25.
[19] Clulee, *John Dee's Natural Philosophy*, 15.
[20] Dee's father was a prominent cloth merchant who provided fabrics to the king and his palaces. He later was responsible for monitoring for the crown all merchandise shipped through London. See Woolley, *The Queen's Conjuror*, 6, 29.
[21] Frances A. Yates, *Theater of the World* (London: Routledge & Kegan Paul, Ltd., 1969), 30-32.

audience was quite terrifying.[22] Even his educated audience assumed Dee's stagecraft involved an act of unnatural levitation. Dee was accused of conjuring demons in order to achieve his theatrical effect. It was an accusation that would dog him for the rest of his life.

As a result of the suspicious atmosphere the play created for him at Cambridge, Dee sought to expand his circle of acquaintances. The continent beckoned. He made an investigatory trip to the Low Countries, returned to Cambridge to complete his Master of Arts degree in May 1548, and then enrolled in a law course at the Catholic University of Louvain outside Brussels. This was a typical course of action for English gentlemen preparing for government service, but with the rise of a more radical Protestantism during the reign of Edward VI, this choice might have drawn suspicion since Louvain was very much a Catholic university. Dee didn't seem to notice. He was more interested in the people he met at Louvain than the university's legal curriculum or its religious orientation.[23] In fact, Dee devoted most of his attention over the next two years to the remarkable group of mathematicians assembled around Gemma Frisius, a professor of medicine and mathematics who used trigonometry to pioneer triangulated land surveys. Under his influence, Louvain became a center of scientific measurement. Its scholars constructed precise instruments, and its cartographers, including Gerard Mercator, produced the most accurate maps and globes yet known.[24] Dee and Mercator developed a close friendship, largely because of their shared interest in a mathematical approach to astrology. Both men theorized that the angle of a star's relationship to earth determined that star's power and influence. Astrology, therefore, became a measurable, scientific endeavor for them. After Mercator built a disc which could measure the angles of stars, Dee began to make and record thousands of detailed observational measurements. Because Dee believed the precise moment of birth determined the tenor of one's astrological chart, he also recorded the patterns of his wife's menstrual cycles and the times of their sexual couplings in order to predict the planetary influences upon any conceived children.[25]

In July 1550, Dee traveled to Paris, where he gave a public lecture on Euclidean geometry.* His presentation sought to explain Euclid's theorems as they related to the physical world of everyday life, the celestial world of the planets and stars, and even to the supernatural, ethereal world of God. Inspired by Agrippa's *De occulta philosophia* and what he had learned at Louvain, Dee sought

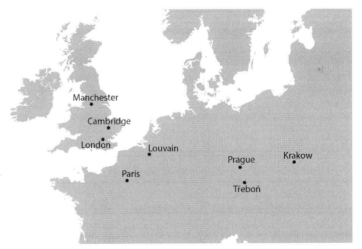

[22] Deborah E. Harkness, "Shows in the Showstone: A Theater of Alchemy and Apocalypse in the Angel Conversations of John Dee (1537-1608/9), *Renaissance Quarterly*, 49.4 (Winter, 1996), 707-737, ProQuest Central.

[23] Clulee, *John Dee's Natural Philosophy*, 27.

[24] Woolley, *The Queen's Conjuror*, 19-20. These maps and globes sought to project the curved surface of the earth onto a flat, rectangular map using mathematical principles. Today the Mercator Projection is the basis of the maps which hang in many classrooms and which show Greenland to be larger than Africa. This is because this projection is most accurate at the equator and least accurate at the poles.

[25] Peter J. French, *John Dee: The World of an Elizabethan Magus* (London: Routledge & Kegan Paul, 1972), 17-19.

to present his first unified explanation for everything in the universe. Since Agrippa's teachings were controversial in France, Dee's presentation created a significant stir.[26] Suddenly everyone wanted to meet the twenty-three-year old. Many Renaissance monarchs sought to attract famous scholars to their courts, and Dee was soon offered a royal position in France. He turned it down, in hopes of securing a similar offer in England. But given how frequently the political sands shifted in England in the 1550s, as the royal succession passed from Edward VI to Mary I to Elizabeth I, Dee might have enjoyed more affectionate and less strenuous patronage had he remained in France.

~

Elizabeth's reign was dominated by three intertwining issues: the nation's religious landscape, the monarchy's succession issues, and the direction of England's foreign policy. All three were a direct product of Henry VIII's famous decision in 1533 to dissolve his twenty-four-year marriage with Catherine of Aragon and make himself the head of the official church in England. Twenty-five years of turmoil followed between traditional Catholics, the new Anglicans, and the Calvinist Puritans, who wanted England to adopt a radical form of Protestantism. By the 1560s, Elizabeth and Parliament had passed legislation that created a practical religious equilibrium in England. This legislation sought to accommodate Catholics by retaining much of the Catholic liturgy and style, as well as the familiar episcopal structure of governance by bishops. It sought to accommodate the different types of Protestants by making English the language of worship, allowing the clergy to marry, and offering communion with both bread and wine. The doctrinal language was kept purposefully broad, but weekly church attendance was obligatory, the use of the Book of Common Prayer was required, and all political and religious officials, and all candidates for university degrees had to take an oath of allegiance to Elizabeth, recognizing her as supreme governor of the Church of England. Taken together, these compromising policies and Elizabeth's orientation as a *politique** saved England, unlike France, from a religious civil war. As a result, this religious compromise represents one of Elizabeth's greatest achievements.[27] It wasn't until quite late in her reign that Elizabeth authorized the persecution of Catholics or Puritans who aggressively criticized her religious settlement.[28]

    Both the succession and foreign policy issues were tied to the fact that none of Henry VIII's three direct heirs had children. Edward VI died before he was able to marry, Mary I never became pregnant, and Elizabeth repeatedly refused to marry despite considerable pressure and opportunity to do so. This meant that the person with the best claim to the English throne was Mary Stuart, Queen of Scots. From the beginning of Elizabeth's reign, Mary Queen of Scots represented a serious threat to the Virgin Queen. Mary herself took the title as Queen of England in 1558 and repeatedly

---

[26] French, *John Dee,* 30-31.

[27] For a recent scholarly exploration of the Elizabethan Settlement and the defense of the Church of England, see the essays collected in *Defending the Faith: John Jewel and the Elizabethan Church*, Angela Ranson, André A. Gazal, and Sarah L. Bastow (eds.) (University Park, Pennsylvania: Pennsylvania State University Press, 2018), EBSCOebooks.

[28] For interesting examinations of these persecutions, see Jessie Childs, *God's Traitors: Terror and Faith in Elizabethan England* (Oxford, U.K.: Oxford University Press, 2014); and the opening chapters of Michael P. Winship, *Hot Protestants: A History of Puritanism in England and America* (New Haven, Connecticut: Yale University Press, 2018).

refused to renounce it because she considered Elizabeth to be an illegitimate heir. Mary also challenged Elizabeth's religious settlement: she was an ardent Catholic who stirred the imaginations of recusant Catholics hoping that England might return to the old religion. And Mary represented a military threat since she had the potential to raise an army and invade England from its northern border, perhaps even with French assistance. Fortunately for Elizabeth, Mary proved to be a rather inept ruler in Protestant Scotland. In 1567, Mary's lords rebelled against her, forcing her to flee to England, where Elizabeth quickly had her imprisoned. Mary spent many of her nineteen years as a prisoner actively participating in Catholic conspiracies against Elizabeth, including several plots to murder the Virgin Queen. In 1587, Elizabeth finally ordered Mary's execution, even though this decision transformed the incompetent queen into a Catholic martyr.

Sixteenth-century English foreign policy was also deeply intertwined with the political situation in the Low Countries since this was the chief market for England's most important export, woolen cloth. When the Dutch began to revolt against Spanish rule in the late 1560s, a vocal group of Elizabeth's advisors urged her to intervene on behalf of the rebellion. A decade later, the Dutch Republic's key legislative body begged Elizabeth to send an army. There was even talk of the Virgin Queen becoming the sovereign of the United Provinces as a way of further thwarting Spanish power.[29] Elizabeth, however, was cautious and preferred subversive actions against Spain's king Philip II to direct ones: she sent the Dutch funds from her depleted treasury instead of declaring war, she labeled English ships that seized Spanish galleons as "privateers" instead of admitting her sponsorship, and she portrayed raids against Spanish ports like Cadiz as retaliations instead of acts of aggression. Even her decision to behead Mary Queen of Scots was calculated to minimize its impact.[30] By this point, however, Philip II had lost his patience and began the preparations for the Spanish Armada* to sail to England and depose Elizabeth.

The three issues of religious tranquility, succession, and foreign policy were complicated by Elizabeth's drive to portray herself as a monarch as competent and forceful as any male ruler. She needed to overcome the liabilities of her gender in sixteenth century Europe. Elizabeth rejected matrimony, for example, because she realized that to maintain her authority, she needed to create an image of herself that nobles, ambassadors, and the general public would recognize as virtuous and strong. Elizabeth did this by embracing the concept of the Virgin Queen. Only in this way could no male possess her.[31] As she said in 1559, "And in the end this shall be for me sufficient that a marble stone shall declare that a Queen, having reigned such a time, lived and died a virgin."[32] Elizabeth reinforced this image through portraiture. In the "Armada Portrait," for example, Elizabeth's dress is covered in pearls and bows, which are both symbols of virginity. Even more symbolically, the painting features a more delicate white bow and especially large pearl just below her waist, where a codpiece would appear in a man's portrait of the era. In other words, Elizabeth was seeking to show that her potency and effectiveness as a ruler rested upon her virginity.[33] Her concerted effort to control the gender dialogue about her can also be seen in the way in which

[29] Parry, *The Arch-Conjuror of England*, 107, 126-127.
[30] Elizabeth ordered that Mary's execution was not to be held in public, anything that could be turned into a relic of the Catholic queen was secretly buried or destroyed, and all English ports were closed for three weeks in an effort to delay the spread of the news to the continent. See Antonia Fraser, *Mary Queen of Scots* (New York: Delacorte Press, 1969), 528, 540-541, 543.
[31] Susan Frye, *Elizabeth I: The Competition for Representation* (New York: Oxford University Press, 1996), 15.
[32] Elizabeth I quoted in *The English Renaissance: An Anthology of Sources and Documents,* Kate Aughterson (ed.), (New York: Routledge, 2002), 102.
[33] Susan Doran, *Queen Elizabeth I* (New York: New York University Press, 2003), 122.

Elizabeth upheld various court traditions. She continued the practice, for example, of washing the feet of the poor on Maundy Thursday* as had many English kings since the Norman Conquest, and she expanded the drama of the ceremony by drawing a cross on each foot as she finished. Similarly, she promoted the tradition of healing by royal touch, but instead of limiting this ceremony to one particular season Elizabeth utilized it year-round. By taking these ceremonies seriously and by increasing their frequency and elaborateness, they became a potent political force that allowed Elizabeth to claim the rights and prerogatives of earlier English kings.[34]

~

Dee first met Elizabeth in April 1555, when she invited the astrologer to Woodstock Palace in order to cast her horoscope.[35] Elizabeth wanted to know if she would survive her half-sister's reign, if she would be recognized as the legitimate queen, and, if so, would enjoy a long life. She also wanted Dee to cast horoscopes for Mary I and Philip II.[36] Although the actual horoscopes do not survive, Dee must have been encouraging: he certainly ended up being right. Three years later, when he confirmed the desirability of the date the Privy Council proposed for Elizabeth's coronation, Dee

---

[34] Carole Levin, *The Heart and Stomach of a King: Elizabeth I and the Politics of Sex and Power* (Philadelphia: University of Pennsylvania Press, 1994), 31-33.

[35] Parry, *The Arch-Conjuror of England*, 31.

[36] Young, *Magic as a Political Crime in Medieval and Early Modern England*, 82. The casting of these horoscopes led to accusations of treason against Dee, who was subjected to arrest, questioning, and possibly torture during the summer of 1555. In late August the Star Chamber dismissed the charges against Dee, perhaps because it had become clear that Mary would not give birth to an heir. See Young, 83-84.

also expressed his affirmation for the young queen's future.[37] These early positive contacts and correct predictions helped Elizabeth trust Dee's word even when others didn't. In his relationship with Elizabeth, Dee seems to upheld the advice outlined in *The Book of the Courtier*: "since the princes of today are so corrupted by evil customs" and "since men seek to gain their favor by means of lies and flatteries," the courtier must "captivate the mind of his prince that he may have free and sure access to speak to him of anything whatever without giving annoyance."[38] Throughout her reign, Elizabeth repeatedly demonstrated her faith in Dee. This is perhaps best seen in October 1578, when Elizabeth gave Dee a bottle containing her urine and dispatched him to consult with a German physician about an intense pain in her face and the possibility that she might have been poisoned.[39] Such a mission required diplomacy, delicacy, and discretion, and Elizabeth clearly believed that Dee possessed these qualities, as well as the scientific knowledge to cure her.

In the 1570s and early 1580s Dee had three experiences which promoted his public stature in England. The first came in the field of mathematics. Even though he was not included in a contemporary compendium of the century's chief mathematicians, Dee attracted significant recognition. The reason for this discrepancy is that Dee's contributions were largely pedagogical rather than theoretical.[40] The purpose of his "Mathematicall Praeface" to a new publication of Euclid's *Geometry* was to promote ancient mathematical knowledge for the common man. Published in 1570 in English instead of Latin, Dee hoped to expand knowledge broadly. He wanted to help artisans, mechanics, and navigators appreciate the beauty of mathematics, and he provided improved Euclidean diagrams to make these geometrical concepts more accessible to them.[41] In doing so, Dee wrote for the benefit of the commonwealth as a whole, instead of for a community of scholars.[42] This is why there are sections within the text showing how geometrical concepts can be applied to a vast array of subjects, including astronomy, anthropology, architecture, artistic perspective, astrology, clock-making, hydrology, music, military formations, and mining.[43] As Dee said, an expanded knowledge of geometry would help England "forsake and abandon the grosse and corruptible Objects of our [out]ward senses" and ascend to things "Intellectual, Spirituall, aeternall, and such as concerne our Blisse euerlasting."[44] It was an ambitious goal—one Dee failed to reach it because so much of his text was not as accessible as he intended it to be—but the publication of the "Mathematicall Praeface" shows the depth of the Renaissance values Dee held. Interestingly, Dee's preface also references magical elements and applications, but these passages are obscure, perhaps deliberately so.[45] Overall, this text brought Dee the attention of needed patrons

---

[37] Dee's positive horoscope contrasted with that of Dee's life-ling nemesis, John Prestall. A loyal Catholic, Prestall prophesied a catastrophic reign for Elizabeth. He lived until 1579 in part because he was able to convince William Cecil that he could transmute silver into gold whereas Dee could not. See Young, *Magic as a Political Crime in Medieval and Early Modern England,* 132-133.

[38] Baldesar Castiglione, *The Book of the Courtier*, Charles S. Singleton (trans.) (New York: Anchor Books, (1959), 293.

[39] Parry, *The Arch-Conjuror of England,* 135-136. It turned out that that pain was actually from Elizabeth's rotting teeth and gums.

[40] Heilbron, "Introductory Essay," 17.

[41] Heilbron, "Introductory Essay," 22.

[42] Clulee, *John Dee's Natural Philosophy,* 176.

[43] Adam Max Cohen, "Tudor Technology in Transition," *A Companion to Tudor Literature*, Kent Cartwright, (ed.) (Malden, Massachusetts: Wiley-Blackwell, 2010), 96-97.

[44] John Dee, *The Mathematicall Praeface to Elements of Geometrie of Euclid of Megara*, Project Gutenberg, July 13, 2007, ebook #22062, http://www.gutenberg.org/files/22062/22062-h/main.html

[45] Clulee, *John Dee's Natural Philosophy,* 169.

and illustrates how much faith in the 1560s and 1570s the polymath had in mathematics and its applications to provide him with a key to universal understanding.

The second of Dee's significant experiences during the first decades of Elizabeth's reign involved a renewed English attempt to find the fabled Northwest Passage to China and Dee's argument for establishing England as a colonial power. The effort began in the mid-1570s, when a wealthy merchant founded a new investment company, attracted stakeholders, and hired Martin Frobisher to command a fleet of three tiny vessels.[46] The stockholders asked Dee to "examine and instruct" Frobisher on the "rules of Geometry and Cosmography" and the use of the latest navigational equipment. Partly because Frobisher lacked the mathematical background to make effective use of Dee's advice, and partly because both men used an erroneous map of the North Atlantic, Frobisher was never where he thought he was in the summer of 1576. What he mistook for the mythical island of Frieseland was actually Greenland, and what he mistook for Greenland was actually Baffin Island. Still, Frobisher returned to England convinced that he had found the approach to the Northwest Passage. He also brought back a captured Inuit, who remained quite a curiosity in London as long as he lived, and a black rock which "glistened with a bright marquesset of gold."[47] This challenged the prevailing belief that gold existed almost exclusively in the tropics as a result of the sun's heat, and triggered something of a gold rush in influential English circles.[48] The next summer, Frobisher set off on his second exploratory voyage, but this time the focus was on gold rather than cartography, and this time both Elizabeth and Dee, along with many other prominent Elizabethans, helped underwrite the enterprise.[49] Such heightened interest in the North Atlantic encouraged Dee write a series of manuscripts between 1576 and 1580; taken together, they represent a remarkably bold and imaginative vision for England's future.

Dee's work, *General and Rare Memorials Pertayning to the Perfecte Arte of Navigation,* had four parts. In the first section, he called for the creation of a competitive royal navy to defend England's coastline, its expanding commercial interests, and a new overseas empire. It was to consist of at

---

[46] Each of the ships weighed between 20-25 tons, whereas Albuquerque's flagship, *Flor de la Mar,* which sank after the capture of Malacca, weighed 400 tons.

[47] Woolley, *The Queen's Conjuror,* 115-123. Frobisher named the snowcapped peaks of what was actually Greenland "Dee's Pinnacles" after his geographical instructor, but the place name has not withstood the test of time.

[48] Mary C. Fuller, "Making Something Of It: Questions of Value in the Early English Travel Collection," *Bringing the World to Early Modern Europe: Travel Accounts and Their Audiences* (Peter Mancall, ed.) (Leiden, the Netherlands: Koninklijke Brill NV, 2006), 27.

[49] Forbisher's second trip yielded only trace samples of gold. A third expedition left with fifteen ships in late May 1578. It too returned essentially empty-handed with only rock containing mica and iron pyrites. In the end, the thousands of pounds of rock brought back from Canada were used to repair roads in Kent. See Brenden Lehane, *The Northwest Passage* (Alexandria, Virginia: Time-Life Books, 1981), 32.

least sixty ships weighing over 160 tons and at least twenty barques of at least twenty tons.[50] Dee also argued that every sovereign had the right to access all the world's seas and that the Portuguese and Spanish were wrong to restrict passage in any way. He based his arguments not upon England's tradition of common law,* but instead upon the legal code of the Roman emperor Justinian: "by natural law, the following things are free to all men, namely: air, running water, the sea, and for this reason, the shores of the sea. No one, therefore, is prohibited from approaching the seashore."[51] By basing his arguments on Roman law, Dee utilized the legal tradition of all of Europe and made his justification more universal. The second part of *General and Rare Memorials* consisted of detailed navigational tables of longitude and latitude for the north polar region, which were to be used in conjunction with something Dee called his "Paradoxical Compass." This may have been a projection map drawn with the north pole as its focus or it may have a device Dee used to calculate the data in his tables.[52] The reason for the uncertainty is that this portion of Dee's four-part opus has not survived. The third part no longer exists either. Dee may have burned it because he worried that it was too secret or too politically dangerous for distribution.[53] The fourth, called *Of Famous and Rich Discoveries* was written to promote Frobisher's second voyage and Francis Drake's circumnavigation of the world. It was a call to action, urging England to become a colonial power alongside Portugal and Spain. Such a declaration was too provocative since Drake's mission was confidential and since Dee's work contained so many geographical secrets. Elizabeth, therefore, forbade Dee from distributing his work except to a few members of her Privy Council. Consequently, some sixty copies of *General and Rare Memorials* remained on the shelves of Dee's personal library in 1583.[54]

This didn't mean that Elizabeth wasn't interested in what Dee had to say. Shortly after ordering the suppression of *General and Rare Memorials*, Elizabeth summoned Dee to court and asked him to prepare a new document so that she might learn more about Dee's vision for England's future. His influential response, *Brytanici Imperii Limites* or *The Limits of the British Empire*, developed the rationale for England's new course. Dee again utilized Justinian's Code, showing that any claim to a new territory required actual possession and habitation: "there can be no acquisition of possession by intent alone," according to Justinian. Therefore, England was perfectly within its rights to establish colonies in North America in those territories "which the Spaniard occupieth not." [55] This argument became the basis of royal patents for colonization, as well as for rebutting the Spanish ambassador's September 1580 complaints about Francis Drake's voyage and his claims to New Albion. In a separate document, Dee also reiterated his argument that Elizabeth had the right to reclaim the lands once ruled by King Arthur, which for Dee included Scotland, Ireland, Scandinavia, France, the Low Countries, Iceland, Greenland, and other parts of North America.[56]

---

[50] Much of England's existing fleet was not sufficiently sea-worthy. By comparison, the Spanish had over 200 naval ships at this time, including many larger ones. Woolley, *The Queen's Conjuror,* 132.

[51] Ken MacMillan, "Discourse on History, Geography and Law: John Dee and the Limits of the British Empire, 1576-80, *Canadian Journal of History*, 36.1 (April, 2001), 1-25, ProQuest Central.

[52] Lesley B. Cormack, *Charting an Empire: Geography at the English Universities 1580-1620* (Chicago, Illinois: University of Chicago Press, 1997), 99.

[53] Woolley, *The Queen's Conjuror,* 133; and French, *John Dee,* 183.

[54] MacMillan, "Discourse on History, Geography and Law."

[55] MacMillan, "Discourse on History, Geography and Law."

[56] In *General and Rare Memorials* Dee maintained that King Arthur, Welsh King Malgo, and Irish cleric St. Brendan had either conquered or settled Iceland, Greenland, and Atlantis in the sixth century. Therefore, Elizabeth's claims in the Americas were much older than those of the Iberian powers. These claims were

In fact, because Dee believed Elizabeth was the rightful queen of Scotland, he was one of the first to use the term "British Empire."

Dee's third moment in the limelight came in December 1582, when the Privy Council consulted with him about the possibility of replacing the traditional calendar of Julius Caesar with a new calendar adopted in Catholic territories by order of Pope Gregory XIII. By eliminating ten days, the new Gregorian calendar brought predictable celestial events like the rising of a new moon back into alignment with holy days like Easter. As an astrologer, Dee believed that it was vitally important to have the calendar correspond with movement of planets, but he asked for time to confirm the validity of Rome's calculations. Two months later, he presented a sixty-two page treatise to Elizabeth's key minister, William Cecil, arguing that the correction actually needed to be eleven days and fifty-three minutes. For Dee, it made more sense to begin the calculations with the birth of Christ than with the Council of Nicaea as the Gregorian calendar did. Dee showed how his detailed proposal accounted for the lost days without disrupting any laws or church festivals, and he argued that his perpetual calendar would guide Christendom and glorify Elizabeth for centuries.[57] Although Dee had been more logical and more precise than his counterparts in Rome, his Elizabethan calendar was not to be. Cecil wanted to be in harmony with at least one of the systems used on the continent. He eventually convinced Dee to amend his proposal to a modification of ten days. Later, the Archbishop of Canterbury rejected the idea entirely, arguing that the very idea of a calendar reform was akin to a Papist conspiracy to increase Rome's authority in Protestant countries.[58] As a result of this objection and the importance of the independence of the Church of England it illustrated, the English would not adopt the Gregorian calendar until 1752.

The essential problem for Dee was that none of these three episodes brought Dee the satisfaction he wanted. The reason was that he wanted to be listened to and admired all of the time, not just some of it. He aspired not just for the private, quiet approval of a monarch or the occasional recognition of her council but for the adulation of the entire English court. In fact, he wanted to be for Elizabeth what Aristotle was for Alexander the Great: a great philosopher whose wisdom and secret knowledge was so profound that he could enhance the ruler's political power and the nation's glory.[59] This was a remarkably unrealistic goal given the competing egos of Elizabeth's advisors, the court's constantly competing factions, Dee's merchant class background, and Elizabeth's instinct not to trust any person more than necessary. Dee's inability to attain the social and financial stature he thought he deserved, as well as his inability to acquire the key to all knowledge and the profound wisdom of the philosopher's stone after decades of work, left him open to the enticing words of those who appeared to have new paths of discovery. Dee was about to enter the most controversial period of his life.

~

In the dead of the night of September 21-22, 1583, Dee and his companions boarded a large rowed boat and headed with the current to the mouth of the Thames to meet a ship to take them to Europe.

---

reinforced, according to Dee, by Edward III's settlement of four great northern islands in 1380 and Welsh Prince Madoc's discovery of Florida in 1170. See MacMillan, "Discourse on History, Geography and Law."
[57] Parry, *The Arch-Conjuror of England,* 150.
[58] Woolley, *The Queen's Conjuror,* 194-195.
[59] Clulee, *John Dee's Natural Philosophy,* 190.

The choice of the departure time stemmed from the fact that Dee's creditors were demanding payment, and he was in financial trouble. Joining Dee were his wife Jane, their first three children, a debt-ridden Polish nobleman named Albert Laski, and a scryer named Edward Kelley, who had had his ears cropped, probably for counterfeiting. It was hardly an august assemblage. Their luggage included six hundred books and one hundred manuscripts, largely dealing with alchemy and medicine, as well as a polished obsidian mirror, two crystal balls, and a Holy Table. This table featured a large circle divided into forty equal parts, and was inscribed with numbers, letters, fantastic creatures, and symbols of the occult, including a secret symbol or sigil at its center. The table had been constructed in accordance with the instructions given to Dee through Kelley by the Archangel Michael eighteen months earlier.[60]

Dee may have begun his attempts to communicate with angels for help with his philosophical studies as early as 1568, two years before he finished the "Mathematicall Praeface."[61] He hoped to find through them the true wisdom of God which "no vulgar Schole doctrine or human Invention"

could provide.[62] He also wanted to place himself in the tradition of angelic magic.[63] Dee's difficulty was that, not possessing the gift of second sight himself, he had to rely on a third party to call the angels forth and to translate their messages for him. Dee dismissed many of those attempting to provide these services as obvious frauds, but he eventually came to believe that Kelley possessed a special gift.[64] The two men first met in March 1582, when Kelley came to Dee's house using a false name. Dee initially dismissed Kelley as another charlatan, but when Kelley returned and offered to show Dee his skill, Dee acquiesced: Kelley's visions were so dependably frequent and so rich in detail that Dee developed a deep trust in Kelley. In fact, in most of their séances, or "Actions" as Dee called them, Dee never doubted that the spirits Kelley heard were real and present, even if the angel's messages were occasionally obscure.[65] By the time Dee and Kelley were en route to the continent, the two men had developed a symbiotic and seemingly amicable relationship. The events of the next three and a half years would test that relationship to the breaking point.

Since Elizabeth's succession in 1558, Dee had been dependent upon noble or royal patronage. Albert Laski had looked to be a promising benefactor before the departure for Europe, but by the time Dee reached Poland in February 1584 it was clear that learned Englishman would have to find another patron. More talk than substance, Laski was going to be of little help. The natural choice was the most powerful man in central Europe, the Holy Roman Emperor Rudolf II. After spending several months in Krakow, Dee, his family, and Kelley made their way to Prague in hope of attracting the support of the emperor, who was known for sponsoring a host of artists, musicians,

[60] *The Diaries of John Dee*, Edward Fenton (ed) (Charlbury, U.K.: Day Books, 1998), 36, 60.

[61] Woolley, *The Queen's Conjuror*, 167. Dee also took a manuscript of St. Augustine (Oxford University's Corpus Christi 125) that included information about magic. Dee annotated this manuscript and kept track of those St. Augustine manuscripts he did not own. See Sophie Page, *Magic in the Cloister: Pious Motives, Illicit Interests, and Occult Approaches to the Medieval Universe* (University Park, Pennsylvania: Pennsylvania State University Press, 2013), 133, 135.

[62] "Schole doctrine" is scholasticism. See Harkness, "Shows in the Showstone."

[63] Page, *Magic in the Cloister*, 140.

[64] *The Diaries of John Dee*, 25; and Woolley, *The Queen's Conjuror*, 180.

[65] Clulee, *John Dee's Natural Philosophy*, 197, 205.

and scientists; for being a reasonable Catholic in a predominantly Protestant land; and for his interests in alchemy and the occult.[66]

By the time Dee and Kelley arrived in Prague in August 1584, their relationship had taken a decided change. At times, it had become downright combative. Even in Krakow, their Actions took on a different character than those they had shared in England. Some of the cooperative spirit had faded and Kelley's behavior had become erratic, for he exhibited happiness some days and fierce anger on others. At one point, Kelley refused to participate in the Actions altogether.[67] Once in Prague, Kelley was clearly more interested in finding hidden treasure and asking questions about alchemy than in the pursuit of philosophical and spiritual truth.[68] Even worse, the evening before Dee's audience with Rudolf, a drunken Kelley picked a fight with Dee's bodyguard, Alexander. When Dee tried to patch things up the next morning, Kelley flew into rage and ran out of the house, throwing rocks at Alexander "as after a dog....The rage and fury was so great in words and gestures" that Dee feared for his own safety. That Kelley's actions drew the attention of a watchman made the situation worse. Dee fretted for his reputation and wrote that it would be "to my great grief, discomfort and most great discredit" should the truth "have come to the Emperor's understanding."[69]

Rudolf never heard about the brawls between the members of Dee's entourage, but the audience with the Emperor still did not go well. Rather than seeking to ingratiate himself and find common ground with an interest in the occult, Dee presented himself as the equivalent of an Old Testament prophet and reprimanded the emperor fiercely:

> The Angel of the Lord hath appeared to me, and rebuketh you for your sins. If you will hear me, and believe me, you shall triumph. If you will not hear me, the Lord, the God that made Heaven and earth (under whom you breathe and have your spirit) putteth his foot against your breast, and will throw you headlong down from your seat.[70]

Dee concluded his remarks by saying that if Rudolf did as Dee ordered the emperor would quickly subdue the ever-threatening Ottoman Empire, which for sixteenth-century Habsburgs was the Devil incarnate. This may have led Rudolf to respond as graciously as he did to Dee's impertinence, saying that he "would hear and understand more" at another time.[71] As repeatedly had happened in England, Dee did not read the room correctly. He didn't understand that he was being dismissed, that his report of his angelic conversations was not valued. So obtuse was Dee to the situation that even Rudolf's letter nine days later came as a surprise to Dee:

> Since he is not perfectly skilled in the Latin tongue in every detail: and furthermore being occupied with many divers[e] affairs of State, will not always have the leisure to grant an

---

[66] Peter Demetz, *Prague in Black and Gold: Scenes in the Life of a European City* (New York: Hill and Wang, 1997), 180-181, 196.

[67] Woolley, *The Queen's Conjuror*, 236.

[68] Wayne Shumaker, *Renaissance Curiosa* (Binghamton, New York: Center for Medieval and Renaissance Studies, 1982), 32.

[69] John Dee, *The Diaries of John Dee* (Edward Fenton, ed.) (Charlbury, U.K.: Day Books, 1998), 141.

[70] Dee, *The Diaries of John Dee*, 143.

[71] Dee, *The Diaries of John Dee*, 143.

audience: it seems to his Majesty that the said Master Dee should be willing to entrust his business to the magnificent Master Dr. Curtz.[72]

In other words, Dee was being handed off to an imperial official. By the end of the month these court officials had made it clear that they "earnestly reviled" Kelley and had no faith that the Actions would produce anything fruitful.[73] Even worse, the two Englishmen were becoming a target of the Counter Reformation, the Catholic Church's effort to reform governance, reduce corruption, and reassert itself in Protestant areas while retaining its fundamental doctrinal beliefs.[74] Central Europe was one of the key areas of the Counter Reformation's focus, and as early as 1584 Dee and Kelley had been identified as a threat to the goal of bringing Prague back into the Catholic fold. There were also concerns in the Habsburg court that Dee was an English spy.[75] In March 1586, the pope's ambassador interviewed Dee and tried to trap him into admitting to illegal activities. Dee escaped this initial investigation unscathed, but then just two months later a new ambassador wrote to Rudolf, accusing Dee of necromancy and conjuring evil spirits. After intense lobbying from papal officials, Rudolf expelled Dee and Kelley from Habsburg lands on May 29, 1586.

This might have brought an end to Dee's continental sojourn, but one of Bohemia's most powerful nobles, Vilém Rožmberk, unexpectedly came to Dee's rescue. Rožmberk had been married three times but had yet to produce a legitimate heir. He hoped that Dee's knowledge of the occult and his now well-known conversations with angels might help him gain a son. He asked Rudolf to rescind his expulsion order. The emperor agreed as a favor to Rožmberk, as long as Dee and Kelley kept out of the limelight. They certainly shouldn't be seen in Prague. This was perfect for Rožmberk, who was also interested in alchemy and who wanted to learn the truth of the rumors about Kelley's abilities as an alchemist. Rožmberk arranged for the men and their families to settle in a small town called Třeboň near the modern border with Austria.[76]

Over the next two years Kelley and Dee worked and lived together, but Dee was no longer the architect of the relationship. Kelley directed their labors and he did so increasingly towards alchemy. In December 1586, he made almost an ounce of "gold" in the presence of two visitors from England, and when this news spread Kelley found himself to be a man in high demand. He began making regular visits to Prague without Dee. The ultimate expression of their reversed relationship, came in April 1587 when, during one of the increasingly infrequent Actions, the childless Kelley reported that an angel carried a written message which said, "Nothing is unlawful which is lawful to God." The angel also said, "Behold, you are [to] become free. Do that which most pleaseth you." It soon became clear that Kelley's vision involved him having sex with Dee's wife while Dee had sex with Kelley's wife. Dee was horrified that the angels would propound "so impure a doctrine" and troubled that he had offered up his "soul as a pawn" in his belief that the angels were benevolent.[77] When Dee broke the news of the visions to his wife Jane, she wept with anger and a sense of betrayal. Dee found himself doubting Kelley, the angels, and God's mysterious decision which countered millennia of Judeo-Christian tradition. In early May, however, the two couples signed an agreement, swearing all, upon pain of death, to utmost secrecy about the "most

[72] Dee, *The Diaries of John* Dee, 146.
[73] Dee, *The Diaries of John* Dee, 149-150.
[74] For an updated look at the Counter Reformation, see Anthony D. Wright, *The Counter-Reformation: Catholic Europe and the Non-Christian World* (London: Routledge, 2017).
[75] Woolley, *The Queen's Conjuror,* 263, 270.
[76] Woolley, *The Queen's Conjuror,* 276.
[77] Dee, *The Diaries of John* Dee, 215-217.

new and strange doctrine" they were about to uphold. Dee clearly saw this as a test, similar to God's testing of Abraham with Isaac's life. Dee felt he had to submit or else admit that all of his conversations were fake, and he was a victim of Kelly's elaborate hoax.[78] Three weeks later, on May 21, 1587, Dee recorded just two mournful words in his diary in Latin: "Pactum factum."[79] The agreement had been fulfilled. Almost exactly nine months later, Jane gave birth to a boy, but Dee never made reference to the boy's parentage.[80]

In December 1587, two men arrived in Třeboň with a message from Elizabeth. She ordered Kelley to return to England immediately so that she might utilize the alchemist's skills as England prepared for war with Spain. Specifically, she and William Cecil wanted Kelley back on English soil so that he might make enough gold to finance resistance to the impending Spanish Armada. The order did not mention Dee, but he realized that he had to act as if it did, especially when the agents returned a year later to collect Kelley. Even after the Armada failed to accomplish its mission, it was clear to Dee by late 1588 that his future in the Elizabethan court depended upon Kelley's actions.[81] Dee, therefore, wrote to Elizabeth on November 10, 1588, lauding her victory over the Spanish Armada, offering both his and Kelley's loyal service to their "Most gracious Sovereign Lady," and promising to "untangle" themselves from Třeboň as soon as possible.[82] That Dee wrote in the first person plural is significant: he was desperate to present the impression that he was still of vital importance to Kelley's work. The reality, however, was that Kelley had left Dee behind. The

Docta etiam sanos Plantis haurire liquores,   Pour guarir maladie et tant mal qu'endommage,   3t distileren hier wynden, en spereryen,
Quèis ægro medicam sedula præstet opem.   Ils distilent ici diverse herbe en breuuage.   Sté van oerr sijn ghebuecsie in serer vuer Barban

[78] Shumaker, *Renaissance Curiosa*, 42.
[79] Dee, *The Diaries of John* Dee, 220, 223.
[80] Woolley, *The Queen's Conjuror*, 295.
[81] Parry, *The Arch-Conjuror of England*, 201-202.
[82] John Dee, "Letter to Queen Elizabeth [1588]," *John Dee*, Gerald Suster (ed.) (Berkeley, California: North Atlantic Books, 2003), 97-98.

two men last saw each other in February 1589 when Kelley left for Prague to join Rudolf's court as the Baron of Bohemia.[83]

Dee returned to England where he lived for another twenty years. His initial focus was to recover the 500 books missing from his library and to reestablish his position at court. While a mob never ransacked his home on the Thames as was once thought, Dee did suffer a significant financial loss during his European travels. He estimated the loss of the books and the damage to other valuables to be almost £400, which was a small fortune.[84] In an effort to promote his standing at court and to remind Elizabeth of all of the service he had provided England, Dee wrote a promotional autobiography in 1592 entitled "Compendious Rehearsal" and asked the queen to appoint him to a position which would allow him to live in the style he believed he had earned. This autobiography and his effort did not secure nearly what Dee hoped, but he was not out of favor entirely: two of Dee's daughters had godparents who were members of the nobility, and Dee had so many visitors to his home that he nicknamed it the "Mortlake Hospice for Wondering Philosophers.[85] Eventually Dee won an administrative appointment from Elizabeth that provided him with some dependable income: in 1595, he became the Warden of Manchester Collegiate Church. It was an unhappy appointment, however, with Dee becoming enveloped in a labyrinth of financial difficulties and becoming caught between the radical Protestant church leaders and the area's conservative gentry.[86] He spent much of his time in London.

The opening years of the seventeenth century brought Dee little but woe. England's new king, James I, refused Dee's request to be put on trial for witchcraft so that he might clear his name for conjuring evil spirits. He also suffered the deaths of wife Jane and most of his children. In his final years, Dee continued to try transmute metals and to find a universal key to understanding. He renewed his conversations with angels with another scryer and consulted sources in his library, but it was a quixotic quest. He died in the home of the executor of his will, probably in 1609.[87]

~

001.9
133.0931
133.43092
133.93
192
508

---

[83] Without Dee, no one recorded the details of Kelley's life precisely, so it has been lost in legends. He was arrested in April 1590 for unclear reasons, released in the fall of 1593, re-imprisoned in November 1596, and then either committed suicide, died of injuries trying to escape prison, or was slain. Other stories say he survived and moved to Russia. See Woolley, *The Queen's Conjuror*, 299-301.

[84] *The Diaries of John Dee*, 246.

[85] Madinia was baptized in 1590, Margarite in 1595. See William H. Sherman, *John Dee: The Politics of Reading and Writing in the English Renaissance* (Amherst, Massachusetts: University of Massachusetts Press, 1995), 16, 40.

[86] Parry, *The Arch-Conjuror of England*, 246, 254.

[87] Woolley, *The Queen's Conjuror*, 322.

516.2

526.0942

792.0942

820.9003

942.055

These numbers are part of a code. The smallest possible number in the code is 000.001, while the largest number is 999.999. This range represents the vast array of everything known and unknown, everything that has happened and will happen, anywhere in the universe. As such, it would have appealed to the man who owned the largest private library in sixteenth-century England and who devoted his life to solving a mystery hidden in secret processes.

The numerical code is the Dewey Decimal Classification system, one method librarians use to categorize all human knowledge. The system was copyrighted by Melvil Dewey in 1876. The above eleven numbers represent specific books with different foci which have been written about John Dee. 001.9 stands for controversial knowledge and 133.43092 denotes biographies involving magic and witchcraft; 192 is the number for British philosophy, while 516.2 represents Euclidean geometry; 526.0942 signifies English cartography and 792.0942 designates English theater; 820.9003 is the code for history and criticism in English literature between 1558-1625, while 942.055 corresponds to the history of England during the reign of Elizabeth I. Taken together, these numbers and the array of books they represent show how much Dee personified the tenor of the English Renaissance. It was an age of curiosity and risk-taking, of ambition and competition. Dee possessed an inquisitiveness which refused to be confined, but which blinded him to practical realities. He was similar to Leonardo da Vinci, who is routinely thought of as the embodiment of Renaissance ideals.[88] Like Leonardo, Dee struggled to secure the patronage he wanted, refused to spend sufficient time attending to the vicissitudes at court, alienated potential allies, and allowed his curiosity to cause him trouble. Like Leonardo, Dee also fascinates because he refuses simple classification. Little wonder then that Dee has been the inspiration for many characters in literature, theater, film, and opera, including Prospero in *The Tempest*, and Albus Dumbledore of *Harry Potter* fame.[89]

---

[88] Some of the more important recent scholarship on Leonardo da Vinci includes: Carmen Bambach, *Leonardo da Vinci Rediscovered*, Volumes 1, 2, 3, 4 (New Haven, Connecticut: Yale University Press, 2019); and Walter Isaacson, *Leonardo da Vinci* (New York: Simon & Schuster, 2017).

[89] For a detailed discussion of many of these roles, see Robert W. Barone, *A Reputation History of John Dee, 1527-1609: The Life of an Elizabethan Intellectual* (Lewiston, New York: The Edwin Mellen Press, 2009), 169-171 and György E. Szönyi and Rowland Wymer, "John Dee as a Cultural Hero," *European Journal of English Studies*, Vol. 15, No. 3, December, 2011, 189-209, accessed July 10, 2020, https://tinyurl.com/y4hvdw6y

ℰ

Eleni

1430-1522

Atop a promontory in the Ethiopian Highlands some 200 miles north northwest of Addis Ababa, a compound of rather mysterious fifteenth and sixteenth century ruins overlooks the community of Mertula Maryam. Because no extensive archeological excavations have been conducted on these ruins, scholars remain uncertain as to the purpose of the site. With some of the walls rising more than thirty feet tall and with some surviving ornamentation exhibiting expert craftsmanship, it is clear that these ruins were once a part of an exceptional complex. Specific construction features point to foreign influences in the design and assembly: the cut and fitting of the stones, the style of the two surviving arches, the pattern of the lintels, the deep relief of floral carvings, the presence of anthropomorphic stone figures, and the arrangement of drainage outlets. This adds further intrigue. Local lore holds that this Home of Mary compound, finished about 1510, once comprised the most splendid buildings in Ethiopia, thanks to the presence of two altars of solid gold and a gold-sheeted roof.[1] Local tradition also maintains that the palace-monastery complex of Mertula Maryam was built for a remarkable Ethiopian queen and regent named Eleni.[2] This understanding

---

[1] The description of Mertula Maryam is based upon four sources: 1) Paul Henze, "Consolidation of Christianity around the Source of the Blue Nile," *The Nile: Histories, Cultures, Myths*, Haggi Erlich and Israel Gershoni (eds.) (Boulder, Colorado, Lynne Rienner Publishers, 2000), 41-54; 2) Paul B. Henze, *Layers of Time* (New York: Palgrave, 2000), 74-76; 3) Paul B. Henze, "The Monastery of Märṭula Maryam: Questions and Speculations about its Architecture and Ornamentation," *The Indigenous and the Foreign in Christian Ethiopian Art: On Portuguese-Ethiopian Contacts in the 16th and 17th Centuries*, Manuel João Ramos and Isabel Boavida (eds.) (Aldershot, U.K.: Ashgate Publishing Limited, 2004), 49-57; and 4) J. J. Hespeler-Boultbee, *A Story in Stones: Portugal's influence on Culture and Architecture in the Highlands of Ethiopia, 1493-1634* ([Terrance], British Columbia, Canada: CBB Publishing, 1999), 82-91.

[2] English does not have standardized spellings of Ethiopian personal names or place names. Mertula Maryam, for example, can also be spelled Mertola Maryam, Mertule Maryam, Martula Mariam, and Märṭula Maryam. Eleni can be spelled Eléni, Elenī, Elēni, Elena, Illena, and Illénī. Consequently, I have avoided most diacritical marks in this chapter and used the most common spellings. It should also be noted that Ethiopians have no family names in a Western sense, which is why the queen is simply known as Eleni. See Manuel João Ramos and Isabel Boavida, "Introduction," *The Indigenous and the Foreign in Christian Ethiopian Art*, xxii; and Mohammed Hassen, *The Oromo and the Christian Kingdom of Ethiopia, 1300-1700* (Woodbridge, Suffolk, U.K.: James Currey, 2015), xvi.

befits honoring a woman who personified her era as much as regents Catherine de Medici in sixteenth century France and Cixi in nineteenth century China.

Eleni wasn't destined for greatness. She was born in 1430 to the Muslim ruler of Hadiya, which

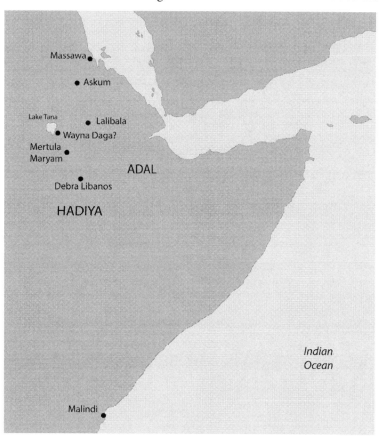 for Christian Ethiopians was a rather contentious, if agriculturally-rich,[3] tributary state.* Because Hadiya's people were not particularly loyal subjects, members of the Ethiopian court regularly sought to establish political alliances with key Hadiya families through arranged marriages.[4] By strategically marrying into these families, the court hoped to provide effective indirect rule over the restive region and to secure the handsome tax revenues Hadiya produced as a result of its agricultural wealth.[5] Eleni was one of the brides obtained through the negotiations between the Ethiopian court and Hadiya's sultan. When she left Hadiya in 1445 to join the Ethiopian court, she dutifully converted to Christianity as the marriage agreement specified. No one expected her to do much more than give birth to healthy heirs.

The mobile Ethiopian court was a vast tent city of 20,000 souls and arrival there was an intimidating experience for any visitor, let alone for a fifteen-year-old girl sent to marry a forty-six-year-old king.[6] As Eleni's entourage approached the encampment from the west, as tradition

---

[3] Hassen, *The Oromo and the Christian Kingdom of Ethiopia, 1300-1700*, 139.

[4] Taddesse Tamrat, *The Church and State in Ethiopia, 1270-1527* (London: Oxford University Press, 1972), 297.

[5] Hassen, *The Oromo and the Christian Kingdom of Ethiopia, 1300-1700*, 139. Hassen also notes that Hadiya was known for its trade, cavalry, infantry and "production of eunuchs."

[6] While there is no record of Eleni's arrival at court, there are surviving accounts of the arrival of other visitors, including the one by the Portuguese missionary and explorer Francisco Álvares. His account, *Verdadera Informaçam das terras do Preste Joam das Indias*, was first published in Lisbon in 1540. Álvares supplemented the portions written in Ethiopia with additional material upon his return to Portugal in 1527. The translation I have used extensively for this chapter is Francisco Alvares, *The Prester John of the Indies: A True Relation of the Lands of the Prester John Being the Narrative of the Portuguese Embassy to Ethiopia in 1520*, C.F. Beckingham and G.W.B. Huntingford, (eds.) (Cambridge, U.K.: Cambridge University Press, 1961.) The description of Eleni's arrival in the Ethiopian court is based upon Alvares, *The Prester John of the Indies*, 267-270; and Tamrat, *The Church and State in Ethiopia*, 269-275. The size of the court and its impact on the land meant that it could not

demanded, a large party on fine Arabian steeds greeted her. She was escorted past four captive lions, held back with heavy chains staked deeply into the earth, and through twenty archways wrapped alternately in red and white cloth. Hearing drums pounding in the distance as she passed through the arcade's last arch, Eleni came to a large gate where she was told to dismount. Curtains, again alternating red and white, stretched from the gate to form a circle a mile in diameter and sentries guarded the exterior of the curtain wall. As she passed through the gate, Eleni saw the members of the court standing in straight rows on both sides of the path, motionless and silent. Ecclesiastics wearing richly embroidered robes and pointed caps of crimson silk stood in front, holding the symbols of Eleni's new church, as men and women, some stripped to the waist, stood behind dressed in white cloth. Eleni's escort slowed his pace, allowing every set of eyes to evaluate the young bride. After the quarter mile walk of inspection, Eleni came to a second, tighter ring of curtains, which formed a smaller concentric circle inside the first. Passing through another gateway, Eleni saw the great white tent of the emperor with its flaps open. An old man slowly approached her and asked her who she was and what business she had with the emperor. Eleni replied that she had come from Hadiya as the daughter of Mehmad to be the emperor's wife. "But the emperor already has a wife," the Guardian of Court Traditions and second person of the kingdom retorted. Realizing that she was being tested, Eleni again asserted her purpose. The guardian then turned, slowly walked towards the great tent, entered it, and conferred in soft voices with someone inside. When he returned, the guardian asked Eleni again, "What is your purpose here, young woman?" Again, Eleni stated her intention and again the guardian conferred with someone inside the tent. The consultative ritual was then repeated a third time until finally Eleni was allowed to enter the tent to meet Zara Yaqob. The emperor must have liked what he saw for the wedding proceeded as planned.[7]

The next day, Eleni and Zara Yaqob sat upon a wood divan in the open air near the king's tent, surrounded by the inner circle of red and white curtains. The head of the Ethiopian Church, the Abun, and his assistants began the wedding ceremony with chanting and then walked around the couple three times, carrying a gold cross and swinging a silver thurible. The musty aroma emanating from the thurible's incense would have still been quite unfamiliar to Eleni and must have added to the mysteriousness of the moment. The Abun laid his hands on the couple's heads and told them "to observe that which God had commanded in the Gospel; and that they were no longer two separate persons, but two in one flesh; and that so in like manner should their hearts and wills be."[8] Then the Abun read a contract about the penalty each would pay for dissolving the marriage, and led the couple into a nuptial mass. Finally, one of the Abun's assistants handed the patriarch a knife, which he used to cut a lock of hair from the emperor and a lock of hair from Eleni. These black locks were washed with honey wine and then exchanged so that Eleni's lock became a part of Zara Yaqob's hair and the emperor's lock part of hers. The Abun then sprinkled holy water on each of their heads, and pronounced them husband and wife in the eyes of God.

---

remain in one place for more than four months and could not return to the same place for ten years. See Richard Pankhurst, *The Ethiopians* (Malden, Massachusetts: Blackwell Publishers, 2001), 67.

[7] Zara Yaqob's visual approval of the bride is based upon an account of his great-grandson rejecting another bride from Hadiya because the woman's front teeth were too large. See *The Portuguese Expedition to Abyssinia in 1541-1543 as Narrated by Castanhoso,* R.S. Whiteway (ed.) (London: Hakluyt Society, MDCCCCII, [1902]), xxviii. Admittedly, this inspection may have been done by a court official rather than the emperor.

[8] Alvares, *The Prester John of the Indies,* 107. Other parts of the wedding description are from Alvares, 106-108.

~

Given certain patriarchal traditions and Zara Yaqob's competence, Eleni's rise to prominence surprises. Initially she wasn't even the emperor's favorite wife.[9] The explanation for her ascent rests partially on the fact that there was no clear, absolute line of male succession in the Ethiopian monarchy: primogeniture,* personal friendships, individual wealth, and the ability to attract followers all entered into the succession equation.[10] This meant that each member of the royal family might become a rallying point for divergent political factions within the court.[11] It also explains why potential male claimants to the throne were separated from the court at an early age. Over time, Eleni proved able to exploit this charged environment by skillfully building alliances to become an important force within the court. Tradition also played an important role in Eleni's rise. In Africa, strong female leadership was valued in a way that wasn't true in Europe or other parts of the world.[12] In Ghana and the Cote d' Ivoire, for example, the Akan people of the fourteenth and fifteenth centuries were ruled by queens, and in later centuries political authority was shared by kings and queens in this highly centralized state.[13] Similarly, in Chad queen mothers held a preeminent role in the court of the Kanem Empire.[14] In medieval Mali, one empress possessed sufficient strength to lead a rebellion against her husband, and in the Songhay Empire, where female leadership was less common, one woman is nonetheless known to have led troops into battle.[15] In Ethiopia, the Abyssinian royal house proclaimed the Queen of Sheba as the mother of the dynasty's founder.[16] This linked a woman to the country's political and religious foundations in a unique and compelling way, and provided Ethiopians with a powerful, honored female role model. People in the mountainous kingdom thus thought of female leadership differently than in other Christian states. Over time, this orientation resulted in a particular deference to royal mothers and gave other women political roles.[17] Finally, Eleni's force of personality also played a key role in her rise to prominence. She developed both a strong sense of ambition and acute powers of observation. From early on she must have wanted to be something more than just an additional, inconsequential wife. Therefore, Eleni set forth to gain a thorough appreciation of her husband's interests, methods,

---

[9] Tamrat, *The Church and State in Ethiopia, 1270-1527*, 243.

[10] Pankhurst, *The Ethiopians*, 64.

[11] Tamrat, *The Church and State in Ethiopia, 1270-1527,* 275-276.

[12] John Reader, *Africa: A Biography of a Continent* (New York: Alfred A. Knopf, 1998), 377.

[13] P. Kipre, "From the Ivory Coast Lagoons to the Volta," *UNESCO General History of Africa, IV: Africa from the Twelfth to the Sixteenth Century*, D.T. Niane (ed.), (Berkeley, University of California Press and UNESCO, 1984), 338.

[14] D. Lange, "The Kingdoms and Peoples of Chad," *UNESCO General History of Africa, IV,* 248.

[15] Michael A. Gomez, *African Domination: A New History of Empire in Early and Medieval West Africa* (Princeton, New Jersey: Princeton University Press, 2018), 1, 149-150, 298-300. The Mali woman was named Qāsā or Kassi and the Songhay woman was named Yānū.

[16] According to the story outlined in the *Kebre Negast*, or *The Glory of the Kings*, the Queen of Sheba, Makeda, went to Jerusalem in the 10th century B.C., was impregnated by King Solomon of the Jews, and returned to Ethiopia to raise her son, Menilek. Menilek went to Jerusalem as a young man and stole the Ark of the Covenant with God's blessing, making Ethiopians the chosen people. See Harold G. Marcus, *A History of Ethiopia* (Berkeley, California: University of California Press, 2002), 17-19; and Pankhurst, *The Ethiopians*, 53-57.

[17] Larry Williams and Charles S. Finch, "The Great Queens of Ethiopia," *Black Women in Antiquity*, (Ivan Van Sertima, ed.) *Journal of African Civilizations*, Vol.6, No. 1 (April, 1984), Revised ed., September 1987, 16., New Material, 1988, Fourteenth printing, 2010, Google Books, n.p..

and personal preferences. She emerged as Zara Yaqob's favorite within a few years, becoming, according to the emperor's official chronicle:

> accomplished in everything: in front of God, by practicing righteousness and having a strong faith; by praying and receiving Holy Communion; as regards worldly matters she was accomplished in the preparation of food, in her familiarity with books, in her knowledge of the law, and in her understanding of the affairs of state.[18]

What began, then, as an arranged marriage for political reasons became a successful partnership and romantic union between two people originally thought to have little potential.[19]

Through the course of her twenty-three-year marriage to Zara Yaqob, Eleni developed a deep appreciation for managing the complexities of imperial rule in three major ways. The first centered on promoting a unity in faith. The emperor's primary goal was to settle a key religious controversy that had divided the Orthodox nation since the mid-fourteenth century, when an abbot named Ewostatewos rose to prominence. Ewostatewos maintained that the Sabbath should be observed on both Saturdays and Sundays so as to honor the traditions of both the Old Testament and the New. Despite persecution, this Ewostathian practice became increasingly popular as the decades passed until it was finally legitimized by Zara Yaqob's father in 1403. The court remained quite divided between Sabbatarians and traditionalists. Even more problematically, the Church's ecclesiastical and episcopal authority came into question since the Ewostathians refused to accept ordination by Egypt's Coptic bishops, as had been the Ethiopian Church's tradition since the early fourth century.[20] These divisions pointed towards the potential for an outright schism. Zara

---

[18] Official chronicle of Zara Yaqob quoted in Henze, *Layers of Time*, 75.

[19] Zara Yaqob was the youngest son of Dawit I, who ruled from 1382 to 1413. This birth order made Zara Yaqob an unlikely candidate to become emperor. In fact, there were six other Ethiopian emperors in between the reigns of Dawit I and Zara Yaqob. This is why as a boy Zara Yaqob was seen as having little potential. For information on Zara Yaqob's childhood and upbringing, see Tamrat, *The Church and State in Ethiopia, 1270-1527*, 278-282.

[20] Marcus, *A History of Ethiopia*, 7, 23-24. While the Ethiopian Orthodox Church officially maintains that Christianity came to the nation in the first decades after Christ's crucifixion, the first historical mention of the Ethiopian Church is in 305, when the kingdom received its first bishop from the Patriarch in Alexandria, Egypt. As a member of the Oriental Orthodox Churches, the Ethiopians separated from much of the rest of Christianity in 451, when they refused to accept the ruling of the Council of Chalcedon that Jesus has two natures, one divine and one human. Instead, the Ethiopian Orthodox Church is monophysitistic, holding that Jesus is one person with a single, united, and indivisible nature. See David N. Bell, *Orthodoxy: Evolving Tradition* (Collegeville, Minnesota: Liturgical Press, 2008), 27-29.

Yaqob believed he could exploit the situation for political gain by resolving the conflicts and finding a way of promoting faith within his kingdom. Therefore, in 1450 Zara Yaqob decided to convene a Church council.   Attendees included two Coptic bishops from Egypt, the followers of Ewostatewos, and the abbots of key monasteries. Zara Yaqob played the decisive role in helping the two sides reach a compromise: the practice of the dual Sabbath remained intact and all Ethiopian priests pledged to receive their Holy Orders from Egyptian prelates.[21] Armed with this victory, Zara Yaqob set forth to solve other key problems in the Church, including an inadequately educated clergy, an insufficient number of recruits for the priesthood, and persistent paganism among recent converts. He began by asking the patriarch in Alexandria to appoint a second bishop in Ethiopia. This sparked considerable enthusiasm in the monasteries.[22] He then instituted inspection tours of monasteries, improved the training of monks, and established a scriptorium to expand religious book production. At the parish level, Zara Yaqob promoted weekly mass attendance, required strict observance of fasting days, encouraged the creation of a library at every church, and utilized village chiefs "to pillage the houses and seize the goods of priests who would not follow [his] prescriptions," according to the official Ethiopian chronicle.[23] In regard to paganism, the emperor ordered the construction of new churches, frequently situated on pagan sites, and ordered put to death those who consulted with shamans or used magic. Zara Yaqob's religious zeal is well documented, for the official chronicle relates the story of how Zara Yaqob also made good on his father's promise to build a church in Amhara atop "a high and beautiful mountain" by requiring "everyone, rich and poor alike...even the chiefs" to "carry stones" up the mountain "with the result that this edifice was speedily erected."[24] He also fostered new cults to the Virgin Mary by introducing a new icon in her honor and by adding thirty-two new feast days dedicated to her.[25] The emperor even ordered crosses affixed to all belongings of Christians and proclaimed that all good Christians should have the names of the Father, Son and Holy Ghost branded onto their foreheads.[26]

The second area in which Eleni obtained valuable observational experience during her marriage to Zara Yaqob involved the strategic distribution of favors. To ensure that his decrees were followed, Zara Yaqob used an intricate system of rewards to counterbalance the punishments so many Ethiopians came to fear. Ethiopian emperors distributed their patronage primarily through the *gult*. This was a land tenure system that provided the *gult* holder with both a tax exemption to the state and the income produced from the land grant. It was a system that could make those in the emperor's favor quite prosperous. Annual dues from tenants were usually assigned in proportion to crop yields, with a fifth of the crop constituting the typical payment. But the *gult*

[21] Tamrat, *The Church and State in Ethiopia, 1270-1527*, 230. One reason that the Ethiopian Church remained acephalous and dependent on appointments from the Patriarch of Alexandria was that the appointment of a neutral Egyptian helped soothe ethnic and regional conflicts within Ethiopia. It also helped maintain good relations with Egypt. See Matteo Salvadore, *The African Prester John and the Birth of Ethiopian-European Relations, 1402-1555* (New York: Rutledge, 2017), 7. This made the Ethiopian Church quite different from the Russian Orthodox Church as discussed in Chapter B.
[22] Tamrat, *The Church and State in Ethiopia, 1270-1527*, 236.
[23] *The Ethiopian Chronicles,* Richard K.P. Pankhurst (ed.) (Addis Ababa, Oxford University Press, 1967), 40.
[24] *The Ethiopian Chronicles,* 35.
[25] Marilyn E. Heldman, "Fre Seyon: A Fifteenth-Century Ethiopian Painter," *African Arts*, 31.4 (Autumn, 1998), 48-55+, ProQuest Central.
[26] Tamrat, *The Church and State in Ethiopia, 1270-1527*, 239.

holder could assess a quarter or even a third of the harvest as the tax amount due.[27] Payments came in the form of harvested grain, cattle, or additional *corvée* labor. Ethiopian historians have resisted comparing this system to fiefs in medieval Europe or feudal estates in pre-Tokugawa Japan because the military connection was not as extensive and because Ethiopian nobles never directed a manorial economy: the tenant farmers were always in control of when, where, and what to plant.[28] The system did, however, create a clear class structure in Ethiopia. It also allowed the emperor to reassign *gult* grants as he deemed necessary, even on a whim.[29] Another way in which Zara Yaqob distributed patronage and punished misbehavior was to transfer court offices and governorships to those who remained in his good graces. One fascinating example of this came later in Zara Yaqob's reign, when he became so disappointed in a group of office holders that according to the official chronicles, he transferred six important governorships to his daughters and one important to his niece.[30] While he eventually transferred these offices back to himself in an effort to centralize his government and begin a process of direct rule, Zara Yaqob continued to honor his daughters by giving two of them the title of *Bitwoded* ("Beloved One"). This was the highest-ranking secular office in the court. This varied system of patronage and punishment helped keep local chiefs, governors, and the fractious court in check during the emperor's thirty-four-year reign.

The third area in which Eleni gained valuable observational governing experience concerned the necessity of versatility in foreign affairs, for Ethiopia was often in a precarious geopolitical situation. Eleni learned from Zara Yaqob that if the Christian kingdom were to survive, Ethiopia could not allow itself to become isolated by the Islamic lands that surrounded it. The Prophet Muhammad had told his followers to leave the Ethiopians alone, which meant that for hundreds of years Muslims and Christians had collaborated and coexisted in the Red Sea trade basin.[31] With the rise of Ethiopia's Solomonic dynasty in the late thirteenth century, however, the equilibrium shifted dramatically. Zara Yaqob's predecessors came to see Islam as a threat and Christian Europe as an ally that could provide the military technology to counterbalance the danger. Europe was also recognized as a valuable source for skilled artisans. The first Ethiopian attempt to make direct contact with Western Europe came in 1306, when an embassy sent by Emperor Wedem Arad visited Pope Clement V in Avignon. Although nothing tangible came of this mission, the Ethiopian initiative to find a Christian ally, reaching out into the unknown, set an important precedent that would not be forgotten by either the Ethiopians or Europeans.[32] In fact, it helped cultivate the legend of Prester John: the idea that a vastly rich and virtuous line of emperors, who ruled over an idyllic land as both kings and priests, would aid Western Christendom to defeat the enemies of Christ.[33] In the early fifteenth century, Zara Yaqob's father attempted to make contact again, when

---

[27] Donald Crummey, *Land and Society in the Christian Kingdom of Ethiopia* (Urbana, Illinois: University of Illinois Press, 2000), 42.

[28] Crummey, *Land and Society in the Christian Kingdom of Ethiopia*, 2.

[29] Stuart Munro-Hay, *Ethiopia, the Unknown Land: A Cultural and Historical Guide* (New York: I.B. Tauris Publishers, 2002), 25.

[30] *The Ethiopian Chronicles*, 32.

[31] Matteo Salvadore, "The Ethiopian Age of Exploration: Prester John's Discovery of Europe, 1306-1458," *Journal of World History*, 21, 4 (December 2010) 593-627, ProQuest Central.

[32] Salvadore, *The African Prester John and the Birth of Ethiopian-European Relations, 1402-1555*, 2-4.

[33] Keagan Brewer, "Introduction," *Prester John: The Legend and Its Sources* (Farnham, U.K.: Ashgate Publishing Limited, 2015), 10. Brewer particularly documents how this legend grew from its identification with a single individual to a line of monarchs. The first surviving written reference to Prester John is from about 1145 (page 6), but by the end of that century references to the emperor were commonly appearing in diplomatic communications, geographical treatises, songs, propaganda, works of fiction and more (17-18).

he gave a visiting Florentine merchant a twelve-carat pearl and charged him to bring a piece of the True Cross back to Ethiopia. Antonio Bartoli did so in 1403. Bartoli also provided the emperor a silver chalice with a Latin inscription.[34] Zara Yaqob pursued his father's overture in 1449, when he sent a diplomatic mission to meet with Alfonso V, King of Aragon, Naples, and Sicily.[35] Alfonso responded by promising technical assistance and arranging for joint marriages between his grandchildren and those of Zara Yaqob. Alfonso also proposed a military alliance against the Muslims and asked Zara Yaqob to "promptly stop the waters that run to Cairo," believing that as Prester John the Ethiopian monarch had the power to stop the Nile.[36] This shows that while the logistical difficulties were great, both Ethiopians and Europeans valued the importance of on-going contact, finding unity in the perception of a common foe.[37]

Zara Yaqob soon found, however, that he couldn't wait for European assistance to arrive. He had to act with the resources he had available to him. He fought tooth and nail to establish and then preserve Christian access to the Red Sea, where he eventually developed his own port.[38] He also sought to check Muslim incursions into the central Ethiopian highlands from the east and south. An important victory came against the rebellious tributary sultanate of Adal in 1445. According to the official chronicle's account of the key battle, Zara Yaqob initially found himself significantly outmanned, but invoking the David and Goliath story to his troops and then creating an imposing spectacle by ordering his men to raise the royal umbrellas, blow the trumpets, and beat the drums, the emperor's troops advanced quickly. Zara Yaqob killed the sultan in battle, plunging his lance into the rebel's neck. The Muslims turned to flee, but the Christian troops caught and killed them all.[39] Further afield, relationships with Egypt were also quite complicated because of the on-going tensions between the ruling Burji Mamluk sultans and the Patriarch of Alexandria. In his correspondence with the Mamluks, Zara Yaqob described himself as a strong yet magnanimous leader. He noted the kindness he extended to his Muslim subjects by allowing them to dress as they wished and by exempting them from particular taxes. But Zara Yaqob also made it clear that he was not a man to be provoked. Evoking the mighty reputation of Prester John, the emperor wrote that he could divert the Nile River if he wished to bring great misery upon the Egyptian people.[40]

---

[34] Salvadore, *The African Prester John and the Birth of Ethiopian-European Relations, 1402-1555*, 24-26, 34.
[35] Between 1403 and 1449, there were a surprising number of contacts between Ethiopians and Europeans, as Matteo Salvadore has thoroughly documented. There was a mission to Rome in 1404; Ethiopian observers attended the Council of Florence in 1441; and at least five Ethiopian monks walked the Camino de Santiago in 1430. In 1427, Zara Yaqob's half-brother, Yeshaq I (r. 1414-1429) proposed a double marriage between his family and Alfonso V's. According to the proposal, Yeshaq would send an Ethiopian princess to marry Alfonso's brother Pedro (1406-1438) and Joana d'Urgell (1415-1445) would be sent to marry Yeshaq. Significantly too, Europeans also came to Ethiopia, including a man named Rombulo who lived in Ethiopia for 37 years in the early fifteenth century, and a painter of Marian icons in Zara Yaqob's court named Fre Seyon. Alfonso V sent missions in January 1452 and July 1453, but neither group arrived in Ethiopia. See Salvadore, *The African Prester John and the Birth of Ethiopian-European Relations, 1402-1555*, 37, 39-40, 42, 48, 54, 58.
[36] Alfonso V to Zara Yaqob, September 18, 1450 in Salvadore, *The African Prester John and the Birth of Ethiopian-European Relations, 1402-1555*, 48.
[37] I use the term "perception" here quite purposefully, for as I said in footnote 5 for Chapter A, I do not mean to imply that there has been an automatic or inevitable "clash of civilizations" between Muslims and Christians.
[38] Marcus, *A History of Ethiopia*, 26-27. Today, this is the port of Gherar, near Massawa, Eritrea.
[39] *The Ethiopian Chronicles*, 36-38.
[40] Tamrat, *The Church and State in Ethiopia, 1270-1527*, 262.

Zara Yaqob died in 1468. His thirty-four-year reign left the country far more secure internationally and far more stable domestically. Eleni should have disappeared from the center of court life at this point since the next emperor was not her son but the son from Zara Yaqob's first marriage. This son, twenty-year old Baeda Maryam, had endured "much ill treatment" at his father's hands, including the death of his mother who had been beaten to death on Zara Yaqob's orders six years before.[41] Perhaps because of the absence of his own mother, Baeda Maryam invited Eleni to come to his coronation in Askum, the ancient city Ethiopians associated with the Queen of Sheba and the Arc of the Covenant.[42] Eleni took her place with "all the chiefs and soldiers...dressed in rich robes according to their rank," and saw how "following the ancient custom, a buffalo and a lion were brought to [Baeda Maryam] in order that he should slay them with his own hand" as part of the ceremony. Eleni then noted how Baeda Maryam refused the honor, asking "others to kill the buffalo and to let the lion live" as a sign of his magnanimity.[43]

Baeda Maryam was so reliant upon Eleni's knowledge and advice that his stepmother essentially ruled as co-monarch during the decade of his reign.[44] Indeed, by this time Eleni was so well versed in the affairs of state she had developed her own sense for what constituted good policy and what did not. She was particularly concerned with issues regarding Ethiopia's frontiers,[45] and she knew that Zara Yaqob's model of direct rule upset important local traditions. Therefore, Eleni had Baeda Maryam appoint local figures as provincial governors and "thus made his kingship respected everywhere."[46] Eleni also noted how Zara Yaqob's personal decisions in theological matters upset the Ethiopian clergy, as happened when he enforced saying the correct prayers at the correct canonical hours.[47] Therefore, she urged Baeda Maryam to issue decrees affirming the primacy of the Church in making theological decisions for the country. In order to protect the reputation and power of the youthful emperor, Eleni tolerated little criticism of Baeda Maryam. She charged the army with bringing critics to court for punishment and made sure that the punishments were harsh. As the official chronicle of Baeda Maryam noted, "These punishments inspired such a fear in his subjects that they said among themselves, 'This King is even more severe than his father.'"[48] Through her stepson, Eleni declared, "moderate from now on your words, O men of Ethiopia, and stay within the law."[49] Baeda Maryam was so grateful to Eleni for her wisdom and strength that he symbolically made her his wife so that she might have as great a position in the court as possible. As the official chronicle notes, Baeda Maryam loved Eleni "exceedingly" and "considered her like his own mother."[50]

In 1478, Baeda Maryam died unexpectedly at the age of thirty. His oldest son, Iskinder, was only a boy of six so the Ethiopian court faced a severe, factional crisis over the succession and

---

[41] Baeda Maryam's mother was Tseyan Mogasa, who Zara Yaqob accused of treason for having "made contact with all the holy persons in monasteries and churches" and for attempting to put Baeda Maryam on the throne prematurely. Zara Yaqob had her flogged to death in 1462. See *The Ethiopian Chronicles*, 41.

[42] For information on this legend, see E. Littmann, *Bibliotheca Abessinica, Studies Concerning the Languages, Literature, and History of Abyssinia: the Legend of the Queen of Sheba in the Tradition of Axum* (Leyden, Netherlands: E. J. Brill, 1904), accessed January 2, 2020, https://archive.org/details/legendqueensheb00shebgoog/page/n6

[43] *The Ethiopian Chronicles*, 45.

[44] Henze, *Layers of Time*, 75.

[45] Marcus, *A History of Ethiopia*, 29.

[46] *The Ethiopian Chronicles*, 44.

[47] *The Ethiopian Chronicles*, 35.

[48] *The Ethiopian Chronicles*, 46.

[49] *The Ethiopian Chronicles*, 46.

[50] Tamrat, *The Church and State in Ethiopia, 1270-1527*, 288.

regency. On one side stood Eleni and those who favored a continuity of leadership, and on the other stood allies of Iskinder's mother, Romna, and the forces in favor of change.[51] This latter group, supported by a strong coalition of nobles, emerged victorious in the subsequent power struggle. Eleni was banished from court. There is no known written record about what Eleni exactly did for the next eight years, but thanks to her effective use of political patronage during Baeda Maryam's reign, Eleni was eventually able to win sufficient support to stage a *coup d'état* for control of the regency. By 1486, Eleni's name was first on the list of Iskinder's regents.[52] This was a remarkable political feat for a woman in her position: she overcame both gender and genealogy to lead the court for a second time. Dominating a government is not the same thing as governing a country, however, and for some years after the *coup d'état*, Eleni and her officials were not in complete control of the situation.[53] The army rioted and looted repeatedly, and the nation's clerics objected to every slight. One example involved the presence and influence of a Franciscan priest, Ioane de Calabria, at the court. Father Ioane arrived in Ethiopia in 1482 and sought an audience with Iskinder. He was rebuffed by the members of Romna's regency but remained in the country anyway, hoping to win an audience eventually. Eleni, ever mindful of the importance of European allies, reoriented policy in Iskinder's court, seeing to it that Father Ioane was received with honors. The Ethiopian clergy complained that the young emperor had "joined the religion of the Franks" as he prescribed changes to the Ethiopian Sabbath and prohibitions on food,[54] but Eleni had once again ensured that European Catholics were welcome in the House of Solomon's court.

Patrilineal monarchies can struggle to perpetuate a clear male line with capable heirs. In 1494, Iskinder, like his father, unexpectedly died, sending the kingdom into disarray once more. The power struggle that followed the twenty-two-year-old's death was so intense that it has been described as a civil war with regional and religious overtones between court factions.[55] After six months of conflict, Iskinder's brother Na'od became emperor. He ruled for fourteen years with Eleni serving as his advisor. Drawing upon her Muslim upbringing, Eleni worked to maintain peaceful and commercially beneficial relationships with Ethiopia's Muslim neighbors, including Adal, but some of the region's emirs periodically attacked anyway.[56] In 1508, during an attempt to suppress Muslim raids, Na'od was killed in battle. This time, however, there was no dynastic crisis or civil war. Court officials, including Eleni, chose a boy named Lebna Dengel to become king.[57] Eleni, now with the full support of the court,[58] became the regent of Ethiopia for the third time in forty years. This is the regency for which she is best remembered.

[51] The crisis was so acute that one of these two factions, although it is not clear which, requested assistance from the Oromo, a preliterate, pastoral, monotheistic (but not Christian or Muslim) ethnic group that began migrating north in the sixteenth century, pressuring Ethiopian Christian communities. See Hassen, *The Oromo and the Christian Kingdom of Ethiopia, 1300-1700*, 17, 86-88, 154.
[52] Tamrat, *The Church and State in Ethiopia, 1270-1527*, 287.
[53] Tamrat, *The Church and State in Ethiopia, 1270-1527*, 290.
[54] Ethiopian priest quoted in Tamrat, *The Church and State in Ethiopia, 1270-1527*, 291. "Franks" is a term that was often used to describe Western Europeans. Tamrat says "no definite conclusions can as yet be drawn" about the Franciscan's experience with the court, but because this narrative seems so logical, given what else is known about Eleni, I chose to remove the conditionalities.
[55] Tamrat, *The Church and State in Ethiopia, 1270-1527*, 292-293.
[56] Henze, *Layers of Time*, 84.
[57] Cates Baldridge, *Prisoners of Prester John: the Portuguese Mission to Ethiopia in Search of the Mythical King, 1520-1526* (Jefferson, North Carolina: McFarland & Company, 2012), 146.
[58] Francisco Alvares, *Narrative of the Portuguese Embassy to Abyssinia During the Years 1520-1527*, Lord Stanley of Alderley (trans.) (London, The Hakluyt Society, MDCCCLXXXI [1881]), 143.

Shortly after Eleni became Lebna Dengel's regent, two unexpected but very welcomed visitors appeared in the Ethiopian court. They had travelled initially by ship from the East African trading station of Malindi, which the Portuguese established with the blessing of the local sultan in 1499.[59] Eleni saw to it that merchants Fernão Gomes and João Sanchez were well received, for she understood that their arrival represented a new possibility for her kingdom. Eleni realized that the Portuguese presence in the Indian Ocean gave her a new ally against the growing Muslim threat to Ethiopia. It was a gift from God. Eleni quickly decided to send an emissary to the King of Portugal to request his aid. She declared,

> We can supply you with mountains of provisions, and men like unto the sands of the sea!...to wipe the Moors from the face of the earth! We by land, and you, brother, on the sea!...[N]ow is the moment come for the fulfillment of the promise made by Christ and Holy Mary, His Mother, that in the last time there would arise a king among the Franks who would make an end to the all the Moors![60]

In addition to the military alliance, Eleni proposed that the two crowns unite in marriage, just as the Ethiopians had proposed once before. She told Portugal's Manuel I, "give us your daughters for our sons, or take our sons for your daughters—which will be more fitting."[61] To demonstrate her sincerity, Eleni included with her letter the piece of the True Cross, which Antonio Bartoli had brought to Ethiopia from Europe in 1403.[62]

Eleni's choice to lead the mission to Portugal was an Armenian man named Mateus, who had been in service to the Ethiopian court for many years. The problem with the embassy was that it was not appropriate by the etiquette of the day for a diplomatic mission to travel with merchants like Gomes and Sanchez. Mateus would have to make his way to Goa in order to obtain the necessary diplomatic *entrée*. Afonso de Albuquerque received Mateus as a distinguished royal envoy in December 1512 and issued orders for his safe passage to Lisbon. Manuel I received Mateus and the piece of the True Cross Eleni had sent with tears of joy.[63] There were, however, suspicions about Mateus' credibility in Lisbon because his lighter complexion didn't fit with the expectations people had for a representative of the Ethiopian court.[64] Many did not trust him or his story. Consequently, it wasn't until 1515 that Manuel allowed Mateus to begin his return journey. Mateus

---

[59] Pankhurst, *The Ethiopians*, 83. The Portuguese were able to establish the trading post at Malindi (which is in modern Kenya) easily because the sultan believed the Portuguese could help him with his rivalry with Mombasa. See A. R. Disney, *A History of Portugal and the Portuguese Empire*, Volume 2 (New York: Cambridge University Press, 2009), 123.

[60] Eleni quoted in Baldridge, *Prisoners of Prester John*, 45.

[61] Eleni to Manuel I, 1509 in Salvadore, *The African Prester John and the Birth of Ethiopian-European Relations, 1402-1555*, 109.

[62] Salvadore, *The African Prester John and the Birth of Ethiopian-European Relations, 1402-1555*, 113.

[63] Bailey W. Diffie and George D. Winius, *Foundations of the Portuguese Empire, 1415-1580* (Minneapolis: University of Minnesota Press, 1977), 352. While Mateus' arrival in Lisbon was certainly noteworthy, many in Lisbon were more captivated by the arrival of a white elephant and white rhino, which Albuquerque probably sent at the same time. Manuel sent both animals on to Italy with much fanfare, but both soon died. The rhino was the one Albrecht Dürer famously drew without having actually seen it. See Roger Crowley, *Conquerors: How Portugal Forged the First Global Empire* (New York: Random House, 2015), 282-283.

[64] Mateo may have been an Armenian, but his exact ethnicity remains unclear. There may have also been relief in Lisbon that Mateo did not have black skin, for "almost all of the literature and iconography concerning Prester John" showed the king of Ethiopia to be a white. See Baldridge, *Prisoners of Prester John*, 45.

was accompanied by a Portuguese ambassador, who bore magnificent gifts for the Ethiopian emperor. Unfortunately, the party did not reach Ethiopia for another five years for there were continuing rumors that Mateus was a spy. When Mateus finally arrived in the Ethiopian port of Massawa in 1520, however, he was immediately recognized and warmly welcomed, putting all Portuguese anxieties aside.[65] The embassy had taken twelve long years, and Ethiopia's situation was more delicate than ever.

~

Upon reaching his majority in 1516, Ethiopia's emperor, Lebna Dengel, sought to end the perennial Muslim raids into the Ethiopian highlands for cattle and slaves. These raids frequently came at Lent, when the Muslims knew the Ethiopians would be weak from fasting. They resulted in great numbers of cattle and slaves being carried off each year. After a quarter century of being caught unprepared, Lebna Dengel was determined to catch the culprits. In 1517, the young emperor's troops ambushed the Muslim forces in a highland gorge. Lebna Dengel then challenged their emir,

Mahfuz, to a duel, but an Ethiopian monk stepped forward and stood in the emperor's place. The monk killed the emir and the Muslim troops quickly fled, fearing for their lives.[66] Lebna Dengel then ordered his troops to pursue them into Adal. After laying waste and destroying a castle at Zankar, the young emperor returned to the Ethiopian court a hero at twenty-one.[67] Therefore, when the Portuguese embassy arrived three years later, it had to deal with a king who was quite certain his prowess required no allies. In fact, Lebna Dengel was apprehensive that Ethiopia's request for assistance might cause the Portuguese to turn his lands into a colony.[68] Only Eleni, who remained an important member of the court at age eighty-six, seemed to realize that Ethiopian and Portuguese interests coincided.

An embassy of thirteen men arrived in Ethiopia to negotiate a permanent alliance on the basis of Eleni's invitation from twelve years earlier. Rodrigo de Lima led the party, accompanied by a priest, Francisco Álvares, who documented what he saw and experienced in expansive detail. The embassy took five months to reach the tented, mobile court after its arrival in Massawa, partly because Mateus died shortly after his return to Ethiopia, leaving the embassy without a guide. On October 19, 1520, the embassy finally reached its destination. Its members changed into their finest clothes and approached the tent city, which was arranged in the way Eleni had seen it seventy-five years earlier. Proceeding past the lions and arches and curtain walls and court officials standing in straight lines, the party came to the Guardian of Court Traditions, the second person of the kingdom, who asked them what they wanted and where they came from. Lima said that he was bringing an embassy to Prester John from the King of Portugal. The man Álvares called the Cabeata turned towards the large tent and conferred with its occupants, Lebna Dengel and Eleni. The

[65] Pankhurst, *The Ethiopians*, 83.
[66] Pankhurst, *The Ethiopians*, 81-82.
[67] J. Spencer Trimingham, *Islam in Ethiopia* (London: Frank Cass & Company, 1965), 84.
[68] Baldridge, *Prisoners of Prester John*, 121-122.

Cabeata returned to Lima, asked him the same questions, and again returned to the royal tent to report on the visitors. The Cabeata slowly came back to Lima a third time and again asked what they wanted and where they were from. At this point, Lima said, "I do not know what to say." The Cabeata responded, "Say what you want, and I will tell it to the King." Lima replied that he would not "deliver his embassy except to His Highness" and that they were there only to "kiss his hands" and give "great thanks to God for having fulfilled their desires [of] bringing Christians together with Christians."[69] The Cabeata consulted with Lebna Dengel and Eleni once more, and this time returned with the announcement that the emperor would like to see presents sent to him by the King of Portugal. Lima and his men presented the gifts one by one to a court official, who announced each of them so all the assembled could hear. There was "a rich sword, a rich dagger, four pieces of tapestry," body armor, a helmet, two cannons, four guns, two barrels of gunpowder, a map of the world, and some musical instruments.[70] The Portuguese also included four bales of pepper with their European goods because in the five years between when Manuel dismissed Mateus in Lisbon and the embassy's arrival in Massawa, a significant portion of the treasure intended for the Ethiopian court had been stolen. Lebna Dengel and Eleni were not impressed with the gifts they'd seen and this slight represented a notable lapse diplomatic protocol.[71] Lebna Dengel believed that the Portuguese were holding back, while Eleni thought that a gold or silver cross should be bestowed upon the court in exchange for the piece of the True Cross she had sent King Manuel in 1508. After seventeen days of keeping the Portuguese waiting and wondering what was going to happen, Lebna Dengel sent a message asking if anyone in the Portuguese embassy had a gold or silver cross. Álvares responded that no one did, but sent his wooden crucifix to the emperor in hopes that it might soothe Lebna Dengel and Eleni's frustrations. The emperor returned Álvares' cross to the priest via a courier, "saying that he rejoiced much that we were Christians." When Lima offered chests of clothes and an additional amount of pepper, Lebna Dengel sent a message back that he had no need for European clothes and that the four bales of Portuguese pepper had already been distributed to the poor.[72] That's how large the gulf was between the Ethiopian expectations and the Portuguese ability to meet them. The makeshift presents were not fit for a king: they were best suited for the poor! Had it not been for Eleni's international orientation and influence, it is likely that Lebna Dengel would have banished the Portuguese from his lands immediately.

With the passage of a few more weeks, Lebna Dengel's curiosity got the better of him. He sent messages to the Portuguese, asking a multitude of military questions, ordering the Portuguese to demonstrate their fencing skills, and instructing the visitors to sing and dance for his entertainment.[73] There were also important moments of exchange, such as when Lebna Dengel and Eleni showed Álvares the silver chalice with the Latin inscription that Florentine merchant Antonio Bartoli had brought back to Ethiopia in 1403.[74] Because of his devoutness, Lebna Dengel was particularly interested in how his Orthodox Christianity differed from that of the Álvares' Catholicism. In early November 1520, Lebna Dengel asked Álvares to bring him the Catholic Host, to dress himself in his vestments, "to say mass," and "to tell him what each of the pieces signified."[75]

---

[69] Alvares, *The Prester John of the Indies,* 271.

[70] Alvares, *The Prester John of the Indies,* 63.

[71] C.F. Beckingham and G.W.B. Huntingford, "Introduction," *The Prester John of the Indies,* 3.

[72] Alvares, *The Prester John of the Indies,* 280.

[73] Alvares, *The Prester John of the Indies,* 286-287.

[74] Alvares, *The Prester John of the Indies,* 298.

[75] Alvares, *The Prester John of the Indies,* 290.

In mid-November, the emperor ordered his entire court to attend a Catholic mass, and by December he was asking to witness the sacrament of confession so that he could see how it was done. Lebna Dengel even put aside the court's own traditions on Christmas and had his wife, his mother, the Cabeata, Eleni, and other courtiers observe Álvares conduct the Christmas mass. Afterwards, Lebna Dengel asked, "What reason had we for allowing laymen to come into the church the same as the clergy?"[76] since in the Orthodox tradition the two groups are physically separated from one another, often by an iconostasis.* Eleni asked Álvares why he didn't carry the incense himself since in the Orthodox tradition "incense ought to go in the hand of a priest."[77] And so the questions continued until near dawn.

The fascination over different religious traditions continued into January when the Portuguese had the opportunity to observe Ethiopian Epiphany.* The ceremony began at midnight with priests gathered around a large hole, "cut very straight in the earth," "lined with planks" and "thick waxed cotton" and filled with water from a pipe connected to a creek.[78] The liturgy featured seven Old Testament readings, significant antiphonal participation, and the blessing and signing of the water three times with a cross of lighted tapers. It also included the recitation of the "Great are You" prayer, which captured the essence of why the baptismal water in the plank-lined hole was so important and how it reflected Christ's entrance into the River Jordan.[79] It read in part:

> Make it [the water] a source of incorruption, a gift of sanctification, a remission of sins, a protection against disease, a destruction to demons…that all who draw from it and partake of it may have it for the cleansing of their soul and body, for the healing of their passions, for the sanctification of their dwellings, and for every purpose that is expedient.[80]

While this prayer was the focal point of many Orthodox Epiphany ceremonies, in Ethiopia the key moment came with the full re-baptism of each participant. The king's re-baptism came first, followed by those of the head of the Ethiopian Church, Lebna Dengel's wife, and Eleni. Then the other members of the court followed, each entering the tank as naked "as their mothers bore them," and with their backs to the Emperor, who sat on an enclosed wooden platform behind a curtain of blue taffeta. Descending the steps, members of the court approached the Emperor's chaplain, who stood naked in water up to his shoulders, shivering in the mountain cold. The priest put his hands on each person's head "and put them under water three times," saying, "I baptize thee in the name of the Father, of the Son and of the Holy Spirit."[81] Each person blessed for another year, then climbed the stairs out of the tank, this time facing Lebna Dengel. The ceremony concluded with the priest offering the benediction from Psalm 28, 9: "O Lord, save Thy people and bless Thine

---

[76] Alvares, *The Prester John of the Indies*, 329.
[77] Alvares, *The Prester John of the Indies,* 329.
[78] Alvares, *The Prester John of the Indies,* 345.
[79] The evidence for the origins and early development of the Blessing of the Water ceremony is limited. Because the various Eastern Orthodox Churches are acephalous, they did not (and still do not) have a single, universal liturgical order for their ceremonies. The passage of time and the isolation of the Ethiopian Church further complicates the situation. This description does extrapolate from what the Portuguese account says. See Nicholas E. Denysenko, *The Blessing of Waters and Epiphany: The Eastern Liturgical Tradition* (Farnham, U.K.: Ashgate Publishing Limited, 2012), 24, 69-70, 193.
[80] Denysenko, *The Blessing of Waters and Epiphany,* 1.
[81] Alvares, *The Prester John of the Indies,* 345-346.

inheritance. Feed them and lift them up forever." As the assembled departed, the priest touched his hand to each person's forehead, blessing them individually.[82]

While Álvares and the rest of the Portuguese embassy were clearly scandalized by the nakedness of the ceremony's participants, and refused to take part in the ritual because of their belief that a person should only be baptized once, Álvares' account leaves little doubt that they were grateful for the opportunity to witness the ceremony, just as the Ethiopians had been for the opportunity to witness Catholic Christmas. These exchanges illustrate how much Ethiopians and Europeans had to learn about one another in the sixteenth century: so connected in some ways, yet so disparate in many others.[83]

~

In 1487, Portugal's João II sent two diplomats on an overland, undercover expedition to find Prester John. Disguised as Muslim honey merchants, the two men seemed to have disappeared without a trace until Rodigo de Lima and Francisco Álvares arrived at the Ethiopian court in 1520 and found one, Pêro da Covilhã, very much alive.[84] Covilhã had, in fact, been living in Ethiopia for twenty-eight years, and during that long interval had developed a close association with Eleni. Records show that Eleni favored Covilhã with a *gult* the size of Portugal and ordered him to go to Mertula Maryam to oversee the construction of the famed gold altars.[85] It may be that Covilhã designed and built Mertula Maryam with Portuguese touches as a way of honoring his own heritage and Eleni's worldly outlook.[86] What is clearer is that in 1521 Eleni withdrew from the court and travelled to 9,000-foot Mertula Maryam. Now in her final months, it seems that Eleni wanted to die surrounded by the prayers of monks rather than the commotion of everyday life in a mobile camp. She wanted to breathe her last on consecrated ground. That end came in April 1522. Eleni was ninety-five.

When the news of her death arrived at the court, it deeply affected everyone. One measure of this grief is that even three years after her passing, Eleni's tent in the royal compound remained standing as a cenotaph where mourners continued to gather.[87] As Álvares wrote, "they said that since she had died all of them had died great and small and that while she lived, all lived and were

[82] *The Liturgy of the Ethiopian Church*, Marcos Daoud and H.E. Blatta Marsie Hazen (trans.) (Kingston, Jamaica: Ethiopian Orthodox Church, 1959), 9,accessed January 2, 2020,
http://www.ethiopianorthodox.org/biography/englishethiopianeira.pdf
[83] One historian has argued, rather convincingly, that Álvares concealed the extent of the theological differences in his account, for while the priest may not have been a thoroughly trained theologian, it must have been clear to him from the art work alone that the Ethiopians were monophysites—Christians who believed that God and Jesus were of same substance, instead of being both fully divine and fully human, as Catholic theology holds. For sixteenth century Catholics, monophysites were guilty of an unforgivable heresy, which is why Álvares obfuscated the differences. See Baldridge, *Prisoners of Prester John,* 2, 93-94, 152-153.
[84] Pêro da Covilhã travelled with Afonso de Paiva. The two men separated from each other en route, perhaps in Aden, and it remains unclear what became of Afonso de Paiva. Before his arrival in Ethiopia, Covilhã travelled to Goa, Hormuz, Mecca, and Medina. See Hespeler-Boultbee, *A Story in Stones,*37-39; and Alvares, *Narrative of the Portuguese Embassy to Abyssinia During the Years 1520-1527*, 267-270.
[85] Hespeler-Boultbee, *A Story in Stones,* 40.
[86] Hespeler-Boultbee, *A Story in Stones,* 87. According to Hespeler-Boultbee, the necessary craftsmen may have come from Goa.
[87] Baldridge, *Prisoners of Prester John,* 240.

defended and protected; that she was the father and the mother of all."[88] What a perfect epitaph for a woman who alone embodied Ethiopian royal authority and continuity for seven decades of dynastic crises and global change.

Eleni was fortunate not to have lived much longer. In 1526, Portuguese embassy departed in frustration, unable to conclude a formal alliance with Lebna Dengel.[89] A year later, a Muslim imam* and general named Ahmad ibn Ibrahim al-Ghazi prevented Adal from paying its tribute to the Ethiopian court and then rallied the troops from neighboring sultanates to attack the Christian kingdom.[90] In this war, al-Ghazi inflicted heavy losses upon Lebna Dengel's forces in both 1529 and 1531. These victories allowed al-Ghazi to capture most of Ethiopia and reduced Lebna Dengel to a fugitive, fighting a guerrilla war in his own land. He remembered Eleni's advice about the strategic use of *gults* and issued more of them than any of his predecessors. He also did so over a broader geographic range in a desperate attempt to retain allies, but it was to no avail.[91] By 1535, his situation was so grim that he had to take refuge in a monastery accessible only by baskets pulled up by ropes.[92] At this point Lebna Dengel decided to heed Eleni's most important and enduring advice and seek an alliance with the Portuguese. With an urgent call for help, he dispatched to Lisbon a physician, João Bermudes, who remained behind from Álvares' and Lima's embassy. A follow-up letter to Bermudes shows the emperor's thinking in this period: "All my chiefs have rebelled against me to help the Moors, and have wasted and violently taken possession of my countries; in fear of this, I asked the King, my brother, for men....I beg you to bring many pioneers."[93] The Portuguese responded to the request for help with a military expedition led by the son of Vasco da Gama, but it wasn't until February 1541 that the 400 well-armed men arrived at Massawa.[94] Then, under a white flag embroidered with a red cross, the Portuguese marched into the Ethiopian Highlands and engaged al-Ghazi's forces three times. In the definitive battle of Wayna Daga near Lake Tana on February 21, 1543, the Portuguese killed al-Ghazi with a musket shot, captured the imam's son, and brought a swift end to the war.[95]

---

[88] Alvares, *The Prester John of the Indies,* 434. Álvares wrote this passage when there was a rumor of Eleni's death in 1521, but the sentiments would have held true a year later.

[89] Lebna Dengel rarely let foreigners leave his country so the Portuguese departure came only with his permission. At one point the Portuguese were held as prisoners as the Ethiopians sought to referee between two Portuguese factions. See Baldridge, *Prisoners of Prester John,* 169, 171-177.

[90] Al Granzi began his career as a common soldier, but his military prowess allowed him to become sufficiently powerful that he overthrew a sultan and took the title of imam. An important part of his trajectory centered upon his marriage to an imam's daughter named Bati Del Wanbara. She developed a reputation for advocating magnanimity in victory, but as will become clear, she was frequently unsuccessful in these appeals. See John Labrand, *Bringers of War: Portuguese in Africa During the Age of Gunpowder and Sail from the Fifteenth to the Eighteenth Century* (London: Frontline Books, 2013), 90-91.

[91] Crummey, *Land and Society in the Christian Kingdom of Ethiopia*, 32, 33, 43, 48. According to Curmmey, Lebna Dengel gave a grant every three quarters of a year, compared to an average of one every two and a half years. Most of Lebna Dengel's grants were to individuals, which also differed from the norm of awarding land grants to institutions.

[92] The place was Debre Damo in Tigray. See Labrand, *Bringers of War,* 93.

[93] Lebna Dengel to João Bermudes, c. 1540, in *The Portuguese Expedition to Abyssinia in 1541-1543 as Narrated by Castanhoso,* 107-108.

[94] Interestingly, the Portuguese were met by another dowager queen of Ethiopia, Sabla Wengal, who was a wife of Lebna Dengel and mother of King Galawdewos. See Labrand, *Bringers of War,* 71.

[95] There is a legend that al-Ghazi was not killed in the battle by the Portuguese but instead when an Ethiopian princess betrayed him. According to the story, the al-Ghazi fell in love with and married the princess; later, she convinced him into take a bath in a hot spring and then arranged for her friends to murder him. See Girma

While historians concur on many of the basic facts of this conflict, there is little agreement on their meaning. The differences in interpretation center upon the definition of who is considered an Ethiopian. If Ethiopia is defined solely as an Orthodox Christian nation, then al-Ghazi's war pits his foreign Muslim invaders against an increasingly vulnerable Christian monarch, who finally reached out to the Portuguese for assistance. Prior to the Portuguese arrival, however, the Muslims inflicted massive destruction on the kingdom and created a cultural wasteland. As a part of the subjugation, fifty major churches were stripped of their wealth and burned. The destruction included Eleni's Mertula Maryam, the seat of Ethiopian scholarship and learning at Debra Libanos, and the place where Ethiopian emperors were crowned, Aksum. At Makana-Selassie, or the Church of the Holy Trinity in Wollo, al-Ghazi destroyed something so grand he rhetorically asked, "Is there anywhere in the Byzantine Empire, in India, or in any other land, a building such as this, containing such figures and works of art?"[96] Also according to this interpretation, the demographic and spiritual effects of the foreign Muslim invasion were as significant as the physical ones because al-Ghazi's troops forced mass conversions upon Ethiopian Christians.[97] The official Christian chronicle noted that large numbers of "young men and women and children of both sexes" were "led into captivity" and "sold...as slaves." Of those who remained, it was "doubtful if one in ten retained his faith."[98] Little wonder the chronicle sadly concluded, "The Imam is master of the kingdom of Abyssinia."[99]

Alternatively, if Ethiopia is defined as a multicultural nation that includes Muslims, Jews, pagans, and Christians, then al-Ghazi's campaign was really a civil war that the Muslims won.[100] Al-Ghazi ruled most of Ethiopia for fourteen years, and united Muslims from the lowland areas like Adal with those Muslims who were already scattered across the Highlands. This school of thought allows for greater recognition and inclusion of the Oromo people, who increasingly migrated back into the Christian-controlled Highlands in the fifteenth and sixteenth centuries. Their presence contributed significantly to the difficulties Lebna Dengel and his son Galawdewos faced because by the 1550s it meant there was a tripartite struggle between Oromos, Christians, and Muslims for control of Ethiopia's lands.[101] As for the destruction to churches, royal palaces, and the countryside during Al Grazi's domination, some have argued that the devastation could not

---

Fisseha, "Ahmad Grañ and the Portuguese in Ethiopian Folk Painting," *The Indigenous and the Foreign in Christian Ethiopian Art,* 115.

[96] Jean Doresse, *Ethiopia,* Elsa Coult (trans.) (New York: G. P. Putnam's Sons, 1959), 128, 145. Apparently there were still a few things as grand since the rock churches of Lalibela, which al-Ghazi admired, were spared from destruction as a result of their uniqueness.

[97] Pankhurst, *The Ethiopians,* 88-89. Those who resisted conversion were often put to death, but there were exceptions—especially if this religious resistance had not been accompanied by military opposition. In these cases, Christians had to pay a tax known as the *jizyah.* For more information this tax, see Chapter J.

[98] *The Ethiopian Chronicles,* 50.

[99] *The Ethiopian Chronicles,* 65.

[100] Mukerrem Miftah champions this view and states that there were Muslims scattered throughout Ethiopia and Eritrea in the early modern period. See Mukerrem Miftah, "Key Dimensions in Abyssinia-Ottoman Relations in the Sixteenth and Seventeenth Centuries: A Critical Review of Literatures," *Journal of Pan African Studies,* vol. 10, no. 1 (2017): 265-279, EBSCOhost. Taddesse Tamrat notes that the Ethiopian Jews and pagans joined Muslims in looting and destroying Christian villages during al-Ghazi's campaign. See Tamrat, *The Church and State in Ethiopia, 1270-1527,* 299.

[101] Mohammed Hassen argues that the Oromo were not foreign invaders, but rather migrating Ethiopians. See Hassen, *The Oromo and the Christian Kingdom of Ethiopia, 1300-1700,* ix-x, 5, 63-64, 86, 88, 127, 168, 339.

have been as extensive as was reported in the official Christian chronicle since such a scale of destruction would have made recovery nearly impossible.[102]

Regardless of which of these interpretations finds greater acceptance in the decades ahead, it remains clear that at the battle of Wayna Daga the Portuguese not only saved Christianity in the kingdom of Prester John. They also proved Eleni right.

---

[102] Henze, *Layers of Time*, 87.

F

Diego Fernández de Córdoba

1578-1630

In their treatment of Latin America, most world history texts move with astonishing speed from Cortés, Pizarro, and the Conquest in the sixteenth century to Bolívar, San Martín, and Independence in the nineteenth. The period in between, particularly the seventeenth century, stands as something of a lost, untold epoch of Spanish rule in the Americas. But during the 1600s the work of rather cautious government officials like Diego Fernández de Córdoba y López de las Roelas allowed Spain to solidify its lasting cultural impact on Latin America. In doing so, Fernández helped realize Philip II's dream of creating a vast Catholic empire.

Fernández de Córdoba came from a noble family with a long history of serving the Spanish crown. His forefathers led decisive military campaigns against the Moors in Granada, Algeria, and Navarre. Subsequently, they then served important administrative roles in these areas and in Toledo, Córdoba, Italy, and the Low Countries.[1] Diego's uncle, Luis Fernández de Córdoba y Portocarrero, for example, became a key ecclesiastical figure, serving as bishop to Salamanca and Málaga and as archbishop to Santiago de Compostela and Seville.[2]

Fernández's family background and his being a cousin[3] to King Philip III gave him the *entrée* to the Spanish court as a young man. His first major assignment for the crown came in 1598, when he traveled to Graz, Austria as the personal representative of the Spanish king.[4] Fernández's mission was to escort fifteen-year-old Margaret of Austria safely to Spain for her betrothal to twenty-one-

---

[1] For detailed information on the family, see Yuen-Gen Liang, *Family and Empire: The Fernández de Córdoba and the Spanish Realm* (Philadelphia, Pennsylvania: University of Pennsylvania Press, 2011), especially pages 1-7.

[2] Sarai Pérez Herrera, "Linaje, Poder y Cultura De La Nobleza De Guadalcázar. Aproximación Al Eclesiástico Luis Fernández De Córdoba y Portocarrero/Lineage, Power and Culture of the Guadalcázar Nobility. Approximation to the Ecclesiastic Luis Fernández of Córdoba y Portocarrero." *Anales De Historia Del Arte* 23, (2013): 419-427, ProQuest Central. Luis Fernández de Córdoba y Portocarrero (1555-1625) was bishop of Salamanca from 1602 to 1615; bishop of Málaga from 1615 to 1622; archbishop of Santiago de Compostela from 1622 to 1624; and archbishop of Seville in 1625, when he died.

[3] Marilyn Norcini, "The Political Process of Factionalism and Self-Governance at Santa Clara Pueblo, New Mexico," *Proceedings of the American Philosophical Society* 149.4 (2005), 544-590, ProQuest Central.

[4] Sarai Pérez Herrera, "Diego Fernández de Córdoba y el palacio del marquesado de Guadalcázar," *Tiempos Modernos*, 21 (February, 2010), accessed January 2, 2020, https://tinyurl.com/y6nor62g

year-old Philip III, thereby reinforcing the relationship between the two main branches of the Habsburg family. The journey was successful and the young couple married in Valencia on April 18, 1599.

Margaret's arrival at the Spanish royal palace in Madrid proved essential to Fernández's fortunes. Margaret became a significant political figure within the court. Having brought her own retinue to Spain, including her own confessor and ladies-in-waiting, she became an unofficial representative of the Austrian Habsburgs in Madrid and an important counterweight to Philip III's primary advisor, the Duke of Lerma.[5] Margaret also influenced Fernández's life in three significant ways. First, she introduced Fernández to her best friend, Maria Sidonia Riderer, who in turn helped pave the way for Fernández's marriage to Mariana Riderer Paar. This made Fernández the brother-in-law of Margaret's closest friend.[6] Second, Margaret probably facilitated Fernández's promotion to marquis in 1609, three years after the death of Fernández's father, the Lord of Guadalcázar.[7] This noble rank allowed the new Marqués de Guadalcázar to win an honorary position in the royal household as gentlemen of the bedchamber, serving essentially as a chamberlain to the king.[8] This post gave Fernández coveted access to Philip III, a monarch who cherished his privacy.[9] In turn, this increased familiarity between the king and the Marqués de Guadalcázar facilitated Margaret's third and most important intervention on Fernández's behalf. Just before her death in childbirth, Margaret convinced Philip III to appoint Fernández the viceroy of New Spain[10] over other candidates whose bribes and backroom negotiations made the appointment difficult to obtain.[11] Fernández, then, owed both his family and his career to Margaret.

Fernández and Mariana arrived in Veracruz, Mexico in October 1612 after a voyage of about seventy-five-days[12] across the Atlantic and through the Caribbean. They were then two of the most important people in the New World. This status stemmed from both viceroy's vast physical jurisdiction and the immense duties entrusted to him. Fernández formally governed what is today Mexico, Central America, most of the Caribbean, Venezuela, New Mexico, Florida, and the

[5] Magdalena S. Sánchez, *The Empress, the Queen and the Nun: Women and Power at the Court of Philip III of Spain* (Baltimore, Maryland: 1998), 2-4, 21-22.

[6] Sánchez, *The Empress, the Queen and the Nun,* 29; and Pérez Herrera, "Diego Fernández de Córdoba y el palacio del marquesado de Guadalcázar."

[7] There was an "inflation of honors" during Philip III's reign. Fernández's elevation was one of thirty to the level of marquis; there were also three new dukes and thirty-three new counts in the Spanish nobility by 1630. See J. H. Elliott, *Imperial Spain 1469-1716* (New York: Penguin Books, 1990), 314.

[8] The official title in Spanish is *Gentilhombres de cámara con ejercicio.* See Pérez Herrera, "Diego Fernández de Córdoba y el palacio del marquesado de Guadalcázar."

[9] Sánchez, *The Empress, the Queen and the Nun,* 11.

[10] Sánchez, *The Empress, the Queen and the Nun,* 29.

[11] Hector Jaime Trevino Villarreal, "Diego Fernandez." *El Norte,* Mar 13, 1999, 8, ProQuest Central.

[12] Murdo J. Macleod, "Spain and America: The Atlantic Trade 1492-1700," *The Cambridge History of Latin America, Volume 1, Colonial Latin America,* Leslie Bethell (ed.) (New York, Cambridge University Press, 1984), 353.

Chihuahua
Sierra
Madre
Occidental
Durango
Zacatecas
Mexico City
Veracruz
Acapulco
Atlantic Ocean
Pacific Ocean
Trujillo
Lima
Huancavelica
Arequipa
Potosi

Philippines. He supervised the tax collection for the Crown, managed the treasury and the distribution of coinage, and enforced Spain's restrictive commercial policies. He appointed and removed officials from various offices, commanded troops, built military fortifications, modified royal orders, distributed land, guaranteed titles, founded new towns, oversaw hospitals and schools, maintained food stores for emergencies, and directed public projects like roads and aqueducts.[13] In addition, the viceroy had a responsibility for promoting Catholicism in his role as the primary propagator of the faith in the Spanish colonies. Fernández both not only authorized the construction and maintenance of all churches, convents and monasteries, but he also oversaw religious orders, held the archbishop and the diocesan clergy accountable, and had the final word on the appointment of all church offices within New Spain.[14] In short, the Marqués de Guadalcázar was the personification of the king in North America, which is why his arrival was met with

---

[13] Lillian Estelle Fisher, *Viceregal Administration in the Spanish-American Colonies* (Berkeley, California: University of California Press, 1926), 2, 19, 58, 91-94, 129-130, 182, 251, 303.

[14] All of this was a function of Spain's unique relationship with the Papacy. In the papal bull *Eximiae devotionis* of November 16, 1501, Pope Alexander VI granted Spanish kings the right to collect tithes, build churches, and provide support for the clergy on the Papacy's behalf. In 1583, these powers were entrusted to the viceroy for New Spain. See Fisher, *Viceregal Administration in the Spanish-American Colonies*, 182-183, 186, 191,197, 215.

elaborate welcoming ceremonies, including an inauguration day that drew upon the Roman tradition of an emperor's triumphal entrance into a city.[15] This too was great political theater.

On October 28, 1612,[16] the colony's officialdom, dressed in their most fanciful and splendid attire, lined up and processed into Mexico City in a highly prescribed order: university professors and bureaucrats near the front, members of the city council (*cabildo*) and the city's chief magistrate (*corregidor*) in the middle, and the judges (*oidores*) of district-level judicial tribunals (*audiencias*) near the end.[17] At the rear of the procession, in the place of most importance, came the viceroy, shaded by a sixty-foot tawny canopy and riding a white horse with a black saddle, gold stirrups and gold bridal. He was dressed in gold-threaded garments so impressive that it seemed the sun itself rode the stallion.[18] The impact on the crowd would have been one of collective delight, jubilation, and awe.[19]

The procession's first destination was the Plaza of Santo Domingo, where a free-standing, ninety-foot triumphal arch had been constructed by the *cabildo* for the oath-taking ceremony. Decorated with paintings and statuary to evoke works from antiquity and emblazoned with poems and text, the arch's iconography honored the viceroy's position and challenged him to perform his duties faithfully.[20] Fernández then took his oath, received a symbolic key to the city, and walked through the arch as the city's ruler and defender. From the Plaza of Santo Domingo, the procession passed through the heart of the city to the main square and the cathedral, where the archbishop received Fernández and the canons sang *Te Deum laudamus*, an ancient hymn reserved for the most solemn occasions.[21] After high mass, Fernández and Mariana crossed the Zócalo, or main square, and as night fell, they entered the Baroque viceregal palace for the first time.[22] The financial costs of the day's events were high, but, in a society that equated displays of magnificence and expenditure with effective government, the day's ceremonies required grandeur.[23] Only in this way could the town leaders ensure that the community would pay homage as the *cabildo* gained the opportunity to buy influence.

Despite all this fanfare for the viceroy, there were significant limitations on his power. Many of these derived from the overlapping jurisdictions of the complex bureaucracy in the Spanish empire. On the political side, these counterbalances included district-level judicial tribunals called

---

[15] Anna More, *Baroque Sovereignty: Carlos de Sigüenza y Góngora and the Creole Archive of Colonial Mexico* (Philadelphia, Pennsylvania, 2013), 111.

[16] Domingo Francisco de San Antón Muñón Chimalpahin Cuauhtlehuanitzin, *Annals of His Time: Don Domingo de San Antón Muñón Chimalpahin Quauhtlehuanitzin*, James Lockhart, Susan Schroeder, and Doris Namala (ed. and trans.) (Stanford, California: Stanford University Press, 2006), 231.

[17] Alejandro Cañeque, *The King's Living Image: The Culture and Politics of Viceregal Power in Colonial Mexico* (New York: Routledge, 2004), 123-124.

[18] This description is based on the procession in 1640 but is representative of the inaugural processions of other viceroys. See Linda A. Curcio-Nagy, *The Great Festivals of Colonial Mexico City: Performing Power and Identity* (Albuquerque, New Mexico: University of New Mexico Press, 2004), 16.

[19] Jacqueline Holler, "Of Sadness and Joy in Colonial Mexico," *Emotions and Daily Life in Colonial Mexico*, Javier Villa-Flores and Sonya Lipsett-Rivera (ed.) (Albuquerque, New Mexico: University of New Mexico Press, 2014), 36.

[20] Anna More, *Carlos de Sigüenza y Góngora and the Creole Archive of Colonial Mexico* (Philadelphia, Pennsylvania, 2013), 112.

[21] Cañeque, *The King's Living Image*, 124-125.

[22] Chimalpahin, *Annals of His Time*, 231.

[23] Curcio-Nagy, *The Great Festivals of Colonial Mexico City*, 18. In September 1603, Viceroy Monterrey's eight-day reception for his successor, the Marqués de Montesclaros, cost Monterey a year's salary. See *The Works of Hubert Howe Bancroft, Volume XI, History of Mexico, Volume III, 1600-1803*, 5.

audiencias, which included judges (*oidores*) and crown attorneys (*fiscals*). What gave the *audiencia* real power in relation to the viceroys was its ability to communicate directly with royal officials in Madrid. In turn, members of the *audiencia* were held in check by local town councils (*cabildos*), who could appeal directly to the viceroy. Viceroys also typically had to face a visitor-general, an inspector sent directly by the king to audit both the viceroy and the *audiencia*. Thus every level of the bureaucracy had some built-in redundancy so that when disputes arose every institution had somewhere to appeal. It possessed a certain democratic sophistication, but it was not an efficient system. This was especially true because of the pervasive attitude at all levels of government that it was permissible to acknowledge rules without necessarily obeying them.[24] Reaching a final decision on any issue was almost impossible,[25] and Fernández swam in an ocean of paper as a result, corresponding with the various constituencies above and below him.

The political system's overlapping jurisdictions were further complicated by the state's unique relationship with the Church. The Spanish Church's autonomy from Rome meant no papal nuncio* was ever allowed to visit the New World to inspect Spanish churches, review church appointments, or evaluate its missionary efforts. The Church's dependence on the viceroy also meant frequent conflicts between bishops and viceroys over policy, status, and authority as the Church grew to thirty-four bishoprics and archbishoprics in the Spanish colonies by 1620.[26] The growth of religious orders in New Spain and the competitiveness between groups like the Franciscans, Dominicans, Augustinians, Carmelites, and Jesuits further complicated the situation. These groups fought with one another and the regular clergy over doctrinal issues central to the salvation of souls, mission territory, and the loyalty of the people. The orders opposed the establishment of one another's houses in certain cities, they tangled over their relative processional order in public ceremonies, and they quarreled about the use of devotional symbols. Each order also experienced internal turmoil over how strictly to adhere to their particular rules.[27] Two episodes during Fernández's term as viceroy provide excellent illustrations of the religious issues in New Spain in the seventeenth century.

The first involved a prominent and outspoken Jesuit preacher named Father Gómez. On August 13, 1618, Gómez criticized Fernández's sale of prestigious offices to Spaniards born in the Americas, or Creoles. The practice of selling offices was not in and of itself controversial or new. In fact, in an effort to increase revenues, Philip II began selling offices in 1591. Fifteen years later, Philip III amplified the practice, as well as the problem, by allowing current office holders to sell their own positions if the Crown received in taxes one third to one half of the purchase price.[28] Gómez, however, argued that the sale of offices to Creoles threatened the established privileges of the *Peninsulares*, who he argued were by definition more competent administrators than those born in

[24] J. H. Elliott, "Spain and America in the Sixteenth and Seventeenth Centuries," *The Cambridge History of Latin America, Volume 1, Colonial Latin America*, Leslie Bethell (ed.) (New York, Cambridge University Press, 1984), 303.

[25] Jeffery A. Cole, *The Potosí Mita, 1573-1700: Compulsive Labor in the Andes* (Stanford, California: Stanford University Press, 1985), 69.

[26] Elliott, "Spain and America in the Sixteenth and Seventeenth Centuries," 300-301.

[27] Karen Melvin, *Building Colonial Cities of God: Mendicant Orders and Urban Culture* (Stanford, California: Stanford University Press, 2012), 10, 144, 187, 194.

[28] Louisa Schell Hoberman, *Mexico's Merchant Elite, 1590-1660: Silver, State and Society* (Durham, North Carolina, Duke University Press, 1991), 11. Hoberman also notes that this practice generally diminished the quality of office holders over time.

the Americas.[29] In his utter denigration of the Creoles, Gómez asserted that they were incapable of running anything, even a hen pen, let alone a city or a district.[30] In reality, though, the Creoles were often wealthier than the appointees from Spain.

These statements inflamed Gómez's largely Creole audience at the chapel of the San Hipólito hospital that August morning. By the end of the second decade of the seventeenth century, Creoles were deeply involved in creating their own sense of identity: they were on the verge of using the term "criollo" with a sense of pride and ownership.[31] Gómez's audience responded to his denigration by drawing their swords, ending the mass in turmoil and acrimony, and calling for Gómez's censure. Archbishop Pérez de la Serna responded to the situation by revoking Gómez's license to preach, but this produced Jesuit indignation since archbishops have no authority over the members of the Jesuit order. The controversy simmered for a month with the archbishop ordering each church in the city to give a sermon praising Creoles on September 20, while the Jesuits stood by Gómez and brought in a special counsel to defend him. The archbishop upped the ante by arresting this counsel, while the Jesuits, in turn, appealed to Fernández for assistance. The viceroy, who had no personal affection for the archbishop, sided with the Jesuits, and with the cooperation of the *audiencia*, successfully freed the special counsel from the archbishop's jail. Thus the viceroyalty's most prominent authorities were at loggerheads, each working to undermine every other, but all knew that this much open conflict threatened the established order. A face-saving compromise had to be found in order to preserve the legitimacy of the archbishop, the Jesuits, Gómez, the special counsel, and Fernández. In the end, the viceroy brokered an agreement. It allowed Gómez to deliver the official Jesuit New Year's sermon for 1619, but then required him to leave the city for many months.[32] This compromise restored the appearance of harmony between colonial leaders.

Another example from Fernández's term that illustrates the overlapping jurisdictions and rivalries in early seventeenth century New Spain involved the doctrine of Immaculate Conception. Early Christian and medieval theologians had long wrestled with the quandary of the Virgin Mary and original sin: How was it possible for Mary to be both conceived by human parents and free of original sin? By the seventeenth century, the twelve-hundred-year-old debate had coalesced into two camps: one led by the Dominicans, who followed the scholastic* tradition and Thomas Aquinas; and one led by Franciscans, who followed Duns Scotus and the humanist tradition. The Dominicans argued that only Christ was free of original sin because only Christ was conceived without sexual intercourse. Having human parents, Mary could not have been conceived without original sin, and she

---

[29] Interestingly, these tensions between *Peninsulares* and Creoles also occurred within the mendicant orders themselves, where by 1610 Creoles dominated the membership of both the Dominicans and the Augustinians. The Franciscans also had a large number of Creoles and experienced significant bitterness between those who were Spanish-born and those who were not. See J.I. Israel, *Race, Class and Politics in Colonial Mexico, 1610-1670* (London: Oxford University Press, 1975), 103.

[30] Israel, *Race, Class and Politics in Colonial Mexico, 1610-1670*, 85.

[31] More, *Baroque Sovereignty*, 8-12.

[32] Israel, *Race, Class and Politics in Colonial Mexico, 1610-1670*, 84-86.

too needed Christ's power of salvation.[33] To claim otherwise was to deny Christ's power as the universal redeemer, and that was an untenable proposition for any Christian. Conversely, the Franciscans emphasized the corruption of the soul instead of the body through sexual intercourse, thereby breaking the connection between the body, procreation, and original sin posited by St. Augustine. For the Franciscans, God made Mary free of sin at the moment of her conception, providing the greatest example of Christ's power to save souls.[34]

Philip III endorsed the Franciscan position in 1616 and the first large-scale, public celebration of the Immaculate Conception occurred in New Spain two years later. As part of the preparations for the event, the silversmith's guild* in Mexico City constructed a four-foot statue of the Virgin Mary in pure silver. They also made blue cloaks emblazoned with the words, "Mary conceived without original sin" in silver. On the feast day, Fernández, the *audiencia*, Archbishop Juan Pérez de la Serna, his clergy, and the members of the male mendicant orders processed through the streets and triumphal arches to collect the statue and bring it to the cathedral. Along the way, the procession stopped at the Franciscans' primary church, where congratulatory fireworks were set off, and at a Franciscan nunnery, where the nuns greeted the parade with music. Once in the cathedral, the silver statue and the concept of Immaculate Conception were then celebrated continuously for the next week as large crowds venerated the new statue.[35]

The Dominicans did not accept Philip III's endorsement of the doctrine and responded to the public celebration by writing sonnets poking fun at the members of the other orders. The sonnets ridiculed Franciscans for their spurious theology, the Augustinians for their problematic humanism, the Carmelites for their excessive wealth, and the Jesuits for preaching little of value. Not to be outdone as poets, representatives of these now-abused orders then wrote sonnets of their own and distributed them to artisans and merchants throughout Mexico City.[36] This spurred considerable conversation and debate between laypeople and clergy alike, but the Dominicans' efforts to discredit their fellow clerics and to decide the theological question did not work. In 1662, the news reached Mexico that the pope had prohibited anyone from saying that Mary had been conceived with sin and had ordered the Inquisition to investigate anyone who said she had been.[37]

Philip II established the Holy Office of the Inquisition in the Americas in 1569 to protect the Catholic faith "in all the purity and completeness necessary" so that the New World might be "free from errors and false and suspicious doctrines." The pious king also ordered that all officials in the viceroyalties of New Spain and Peru cooperate with the inquisitors "with due and decent reverence and respect," aiding the Holy Office "whenever it is requested...in order to arrest whatever heretics or suspects in faith they may find."[38] The Inquisition's purpose was to identify and root out heresy, blasphemy, adultery, bigamy, witchcraft, idolatry, and homosexuality among the people and

---

[33] Sarah Jane Boss, "The Development of the Doctrine of Mary's Immaculate Conception," *Mary: The Complete Resource*, Sarah Jane Boss (ed.) (New York: Continuum, 2007), 212.

[34] Boss, "The Development of the Doctrine of Mary's Immaculate Conception," 208-209, 212-214.

[35] Melvin, *Building Colonial Cities of God*, 207, 210.

[36] Melvin, *Building Colonial Cities of God*, 208-209.

[37] Melvin, *Building Colonial Cities of God*, 212. Since the Spanish Inquisition was independent of the Inquisition elsewhere, this edict would not have technically applied to New Spain, but the effect was pronounced nonetheless. In 1854, Pope Pius IV issued a papal bull finalizing the Church's position in favor of Franciscan viewpoint. See Pius IX, "*Ineffabilis Deus*: The Immaculate Conception," *Papal Encyclicals Online*, accessed January 2, 2020 https://www.papalencyclicals.net/pius09/p9ineff.htm

[38] "Royal Order Issued by King Philip II Establishing the Foundation of the Holy Office of the Inquisition in the Indies," *The Inquisition in New Spain, 1536-1820: A Documentary History*, John F. Chuchiak IV (ed. and trans.) (Baltimore, Maryland: The Johns Hopkins University Press, 2012), 81-82.

immorality within the clergy. All of these behaviors represented perceived threats to the social order. By censoring books and other printed works and by investigating suspicious individuals and bringing them to trial, the Inquisition acted as the colonies' moral disciplinarian.[39] During Fernández's term as viceroy, for example, the Holy Office issued an edict in 1616 that ordered the population to denounce practitioners of astrology and other forms of divination and to surrender all books relating to such practices. It also prohibited the use of peyote in 1620, describing its hallucinogenic effects as "vile illusions" triggered by the devil in order to "trick the simple minds" of Indians who possess "a natural inclination towards idolatry."[40] And it reprimanded a parish priest in 1614 for stepping far beyond his authority in illegally conducting trials and punishments of the indigenous population.[41]

Despite its reputation for vitriolic and sadistic judges who quickly handed down pre-determined verdicts, the Inquisition was a complex bureaucracy with a well-defined legal process.[42] This process involved a preliminary investigation and required collaborating eyewitness testimony, proof without *any* doubt (as opposed to proof beyond a reasonable doubt), and a review by a council that examined the transcripts and verdicts before sentencing. Throughout the process, the Inquisition protected witnesses by granting them complete anonymity. It could use torture to obtain information and confessions, but defendants had to reaffirm their statements while not being tortured in order for these statements to have validity.[43] At the conclusion of a trial, the Holy Office regularly showcased its authority and its teachings during a public ceremony, an *auto-de-fé*, in which the convicted publicly performed a penance. For the most egregious offenses, usually involving individuals who refused to recant or were repeat offenders, the Inquisition ordered the guilty to be burned alive.

Unfortunately for Philip II and those who fervently desired to establish a kingdom of God in the Americas, by the early seventeenth century the Inquisition was less ferocious and omnipresent in New Spain than its reputation today would suggest. Between 1571-1700, the Holy Office held 1,913 trials in New Spain: 29.7% involving minor religious crimes, 27.5% dealing with formal heresy, 24.1% entailing sexual crimes, and 7.2% comprising witchcraft. Significantly, these 1,913 cases represented just 5% of those tried in peninsular Spain.[44] Even more tellingly, the punishments meted out were more lenient than in Spain itself. In New Spain, the death penalty was only used in 1% of the cases. The second highest level of punishment (a loss of property, public flogging, imprisonment followed by forced labor) occurred in 18.3% of the cases, as opposed to 70% of the cases in peninsular Spain. Taken together, these statistics show how much less intense the Inquisition was in the Americas than in Spain itself. In short, the Inquisition was not a daily concern

---

[39] C.H. Haring, *The Spanish Empire in America* (New York: Harbinger Books, 1963), 189.

[40] "Edict of Faith that Requires All to Denounce the Practitioners of Astrology, Necromancy, Geomancy..." and "Edict of Faith Concerning the Illicit Use of Peyote," in *The Inquisition in New Spain, 1536-1820*, 110-114.

[41] J. Richard Andrews and Ross Hassig, "Editor's Introduction," *Treatise on the Heathen Superstitions that Live Among the Indians Native to this New Spain* (Norman, Oklahoma: University of Oklahoma Press, 1987), 7.

[42] Irene Silverblatt, *Modern Inquisitions: Peru and the Colonial Origins of the Civilized World* (Durham, North Carolina: Duke University Press, 2004), 5-7.

[43] John F. Chuchiak IV, "The Holy Office of the Inquisition in New Spain (Mexico): An Introductory Study," *The Inquisition in New Spain, 1536-1820*, 33-45.

[44] Chuchiak, "The Holy Office of the Inquisition in New Spain (Mexico)," 7. The remaining 11.5% involved solicitation, civil crimes, and idolatry. Formal heresy involved things like practicing Judaism, Islam, or Protestantism or professing schismatic propositions or false mysticism.

for most of those under Fernández's jurisdiction, even if those in Mexico City felt the Inquisition's presence more than those in other parts of New Spain.[45]

One of the reasons for this decreased emphasis centered upon the attitude of government officials. The Holy Office was as an arm of the state rather than the Church, so the Holy Office's mission required active cooperation between the viceroy and the inquisitors. Government officials, however, frequently boycotted required Holy Office events. Even numerous viceroys failed to attend occasions that the Holy Office saw as essential.[46] Fernández seems to have been one of the officials with a rather lackadaisical attitude about the Inquisition's mission. Between 1610-1619, only 83 cases came before New Spain's inquisitors. The majority of these involved bigamy (22), blasphemy (9) and witchcraft (5), and there were only two cases about heresy.[47] Even more tellingly, no *auto-de-fé* was held during Fernández's term as viceroy.[48]

Another reason for the limited success of the Inquisition in seventeenth century Mexico was that the Holy Office frequently came into conflict with members of the diocesan clergy and officials in the Church hierarchy, who once had the responsibilities now given to the Inquisition.[49] Rivalry and jealousy over moral authority also hampered the Inquisition. With key institutional and societal leaders only marginally supporting the Holy Office, its unpopularity spread to the general population. People refused to surrender their banned books, and individuals even openly ridiculed Inquisition judges. In 1615, for example, one woman in Mexico City publicly described the inquisitors as "nothing but a bunch of drunks and fools who do not know what they are doing."[50]

Nonetheless, the Inquisition pursued certain cases with particular assiduousness. Frequently these cases involved Jews.

~

Judaism is arguably the oldest of the world's monotheistic religions, but the method by which Jews honored God's singularity changed irrevocably in 70 CE, when the Romans destroyed the Temple in Jerusalem and expelled the Jews from the city. No longer able to perform ritual animal sacrifices in their only House of God, Jews had to create a new liturgical tradition. They became the People of the Book. They studied the Torah (the first five books of the Hebrew Bible) and the Talmud (the rabbinical commentary which forms the basis of Jewish law) and came to believe that studying was the proper way to understand God, rather than performing animal sacrifices. Not everything about Judaism changed, however. Jews continued to profess that God is not a physical being but an essence that is all-powerful and all-knowing. Many also maintained their belief that upon death

---

[45] Chuchiak, "The Holy Office of the Inquisition in New Spain (Mexico), xv, 48.

[46] Martin Austin Nesvig, *Ideology and Inquisition: The World of the Censors in Early Mexico* (New Haven, Connecticut: Yale University Press, 2009), 191.

[47] Nesvig, *Ideology and Inquisition,* 171.

[48] Elkan Nathan Adler, *Auto de Fé and Jew* (London: Oxford University Press, 1908), 154. Adler does list one *auto-de-fé* occurring in 1621, but does not give the specific date. It is very unlikely that this occurred before Fernández left Mexico for Peru in March 1621, especially given the nature of Fernández's departure detailed below.

[49] Elliott, "Spain and America in the Sixteenth and Seventeenth Centuries," 302.

[50] Ana de Aranda quoted in Martin Austin Nesvig, *Ideology and Inquisition: The World of the Censors in Early Mexico* (New Haven, Connecticut: Yale University Press, 2009), 191. Ana de Aranda was not punished for these words even if the Holy Office found them to be "scandalous and offensive to pious ears."

humans are judged by Him, and many continued to trust that God will vindicate his Chosen People by one day creating a perfect society on Earth.

Jews migrated to the Iberian peninsula as early as the third century. They flourished in the early years of Islamic Spain in the eighth century, as Muslims frequently left Jews in charge of managing the towns they had conquered.[51] Through the course of the Middle Ages, however, tensions came to mark the interactions between Jews, Muslims, and Christians, even as all three communities also interacted regularly as a result commercial, scientific, or other professional reasons.[52] There were particularly vicious persecutions of Jews in Spain in 1391 and 1449. Then in 1492, Christian forces captured Granada, and the victorious Spanish monarchs, King Ferdinand and Queen Isabella, ordered the expulsion of all Jews from Spain in an effort to create a purely Christian kingdom. Some Jews, called *conversos*, converted to Christianity rather than leave Spain.[53] Others departed for Islamic North Africa, and as many as 100,000 migrated to Portugal, where they were able to purchase admission to the country. Just five years later, however, the Portuguese king, Manuel I, began forcing Christian baptism upon Jews, perhaps to improve his chances of marrying Ferdinand and Isabella's daughter.[54] This created more *conversos,* many of whom continued to practice Judaism in secret. Others hid their identities and migrated to the Americas, despite repeated Spanish royal decrees in the sixteenth century that prohibited Jews from entering the New World.[55] During the first decade of the seventeenth century, however, the situation changed when Philip III began allowing open migration to his colonies. The number of descendants of *conversos* moving to the Americas grew considerably between 1601 and 1609 as a result. So many Jews, crypto-Jews, and former Jews came from Portugal to New Spain that Inquisition records use the words for "Jews" and "Portuguese" as virtual synonyms.

Once in the viceroyalty of New Spain, most Jews became shopkeepers, peddlers, and craftsmen, but the wealthiest members of the Jewish community were members of the commercial elite, specializing in the trade of slaves, cacao, and textiles.[56] Jews in places like Mexico City usually had to appear to be proper Christians in public. They had to be creative in the ways they hid their Judaism, from being less literal about kosher dietary laws, feigning illness to avoid working during the Sabbath, creating synagogues in private homes, and using a modified, longitudinal circumcision in the teenage years instead of at birth.[57] They had little knowledge of Hebrew, but knew the basic tenets of Jewish law.[58] Over time, New Spain's Jews also incorporated elements of Catholicism into

---

[51] Chris Lowney, *A Vanished World: Muslims, Christians, and Jews in Medieval Spain* (New York: Oxford University Press, 2006), 96.

[52] Joseph Pérez, *History of a Tragedy: The Expulsion of the Jews from Spain*, Lysa Hochroth (trans.) (Urbana, Illinois: University of Illinois Press, 2007), 8-18.

[53] *Conversos* were also known as "New Christians," but many were thought to be crypto-Jews, who had not truly accepted the Catholic faith and who continued to practice Judaism in private. This led long-standing Christian Spaniards to pass blood purity laws ("Limpieza de sangre"), forcing people to prove their multi-generational Christian ancestry as a test of the sincerity of faith.

[54] François Soyer, The Persecution of the Jews and Muslims in Portugal: King Manuel I and the End of Religious Tolerance (Leiden, The Netherlands: Brill NV, 2007), 177.

[55] When Spain's Philip II became King of Portugal in 1580 as a result of a dynastic struggle in Portugal, many *conversos* temporarily returned to Spain and then migrated to the Spanish colonies in the Americas. The crowns remained united until 1640.

[56] Israel, *Race, Class and Politics in Colonial Mexico, 1610-1670*, 128.

[57] Seymour B. Liebman, *The Jews in New Spain: Faith, Flame and the Inquisition* (Coral Gables, Florida: University of Miami Press, 1970), 57, 64, 71-72, 76-77.

[58] Israel, *Race, Class and Politics in Colonial Mexico, 1610-1670*, 129.

their rituals, such as praying with outstretched arms, believing in purgatory,* and employing the intervention of saints.[59] But Judaism survived: according to mid-sixteenth century records, Jews comprised 22% of Mexico City's White[60] population during the first half of the seventeenth century, and *conversos* controlled at least 20% of New Spain's Atlantic trade. Jews, however private about their religious practices, played an important role in Mexico City, Puebla, and other major communities in New Spain.[61]

The Inquisition in New Spain pursued cases against Jews erratically, but the periods of persecution tended to be intense. The worst came between 1590 and 1600 and between 1640 and 1650. At an *auto-de-fé* on April 11, 1649 in Mexico City, for example, 65 Jews were burnt in effigy, 9 were banished, 19 reconciled, 12 whipped to death and then burnt, and one was burnt alive.[62] Not all cases ended up in convictions, however. In 1615, for example, a learned man in the town of Zacatecas was accused by multiple witnesses of being a Jew; he questioned Jesus' standing as the Messiah as a result of Jesus being the son of a carpenter and being crucified. The man denied in court the interpretation these witnesses ascribed to his words and was apparently set free since the Holy Office never arrested him or sequestered his property.[63] Overall, cases against Jews between 1571 and 1700 formed 6.8% of the total cases tried by the Holy Office.[64]

~

Diego Fernández de Córdoba, the Marqués de Guadalcázar, faced a number of other challenges during his eight-and-a-half years as viceroy of New Spain. Some of these were perennial, faced by every viceroy; others were particular to Fernández's term. In the eyes of the Mexico City wealthiest, the most important issue for any viceroy was to manage involved commercial activity. Consequently, one of the first groups to seek an audience with the Marqués de Guadalcázar was the merchant community's elite.

By the second decade of the seventeenth century, Mexico City was an emporium of the world's merchandise because Spain was near the zenith of its economic influence, connecting Asian, American, and European goods as its galleons plied the Atlantic and the Pacific Oceans.[65] Mexico City's markets filled with European clocks, Chinese silks, Persian rugs, Japanese screens, Indonesian

---

[59] Liebman, *The Jews in New Spain,* 72.

[60] In the wake of the protests following George Floyd's death in Minneapolis, Minnesota on May 25, 2020, the National Association of Black Journalists (NABJ) released the following statement: "it is important to capitalize 'Black' when referring to (and out of respect for) the Black diaspora. NABJ also recommends that whenever a color is used to appropriately describe race then it should be capitalized, including White and Brown." I have adopted this style recommendation as a result, except when quoting from a primary source. See National Association of Black Journalists, "NABJ Statement on Capitalizing Black and Other Racial Identifiers," June 2020, accessed August 27, 2020, https://www.nabj.org/page/styleguide

[61] Liebman, *The Jews in New Spain,* 21, 42.

[62] Elkan Nathan Adler, *Auto de Fé and Jew* (London: Oxford University Press, 1908), 155.

[63] Liebman, *The Jews in New Spain,* 74, 208.

[64] "Trials and Testimonies Against Jewish and Crypto-Jewish Practices," *The Inquisition in New Spain, 1536-1820: A Documentary History,* John F. Chuchiak IV (ed. and trans.) (Baltimore, Maryland: The Johns Hopkins University Press, 2012), 235-236.

[65] Israel, *Race, Class and Politics in Colonial Mexico, 1610-1670,* 21.

spices, Cambodian ivory, Angolan slaves, Guatemalan cacao, and Peruvian wine.[66] While 50% of all shipping between Spain and the New World passed through Mexico during this period, the Pacific trade was of even greater concern for the city's elite merchants since only they possessed the resources to handle the high costs incumbent in trading between Acapulco and Manila.[67] In fact, between 1610 and 1619, just seventeen men controlled 94% of the Pacific trade, and the vast majority of them were Spanish-born.[68] These men petitioned Fernández repeatedly to expand trade in the Pacific and to reduce the number of regulations governing it. These merchants pointed out that when the Mexico-Philippine trade began in 1567 no regulations existed. The free market determined both the goods exchanged and their prices. This made it more attractive for New Spain's merchants to obtain goods from Asia than from Spain. In fact, by 1597 the amount of Mexican silver leaving Acapulco for the Philippines exceeded the value of all Mexican trade to Spain.[69] Royal officials in Madrid, however, were mercantilists,* who believed that colonies existed for the benefit of the mother country, and that the economy had to be controlled to be effective and prosperous. These officials also believed that the Pacific trade should further Spanish political and religious goals in Asia, which ranged from limiting Dutch expansion to supporting a base from which Christianity might be brought to China. Consequently, Philip II began imposing regulations on the Pacific trade in 1582. In an effort to prevent the drainage of South American silver to Asia, he also imposed regulations on the trade between New Spain and Peru. By 1604, royal regulations held that only three galleons of no more than 400 tons could sail between Acapulco and Lima, and these ships were expressly forbidden to carry Asian goods.[70] The merchants meeting with Fernández found these rules far too constraining and pointed out that demand for Asian goods far outstripped what three ships per year could carry. They repeatedly urged the viceroy to change the regulations so that honorable merchants could remain in accordance within the law and help the Crown fight piracy. Fernández, however, could not convince Spanish court officials to allow more

---

[66] Rainer F. Buschmann, Edward R. Slack, Jr., and James B. Tueller, *Navigating the Spanish Lake: The Pacific in the Iberian World, 1521-1898* (Honolulu, Hawai'i: University of Hawai'i Press, 2013) 26.

[67] Hoberman, *Mexico's Merchant Elite, 1590-1660,* 32.

[68] Hoberman, *Mexico's Merchant Elite, 1590-1660,* 39, 41.

[69] Elliott, "Spain and America in the Sixteenth and Seventeenth Centuries," 325.

[70] Hoberman, *Mexico's Merchant Elite, 1590-1660,* 214-216. Madrid's mercantilist fervor only grew over time as it tried to squeeze revenues out of the colonies in the Americas. In 1631, the Crown banned all direct trade between Peru and Mexico to direct as much silver as possible to Spain.

trade, so the problem of illegal trading worsened. By 1618, the estimated value of illegal trade between Acapulco and the Philippines was at least 100% of the value of the legal trade.[71]

One reason Fernández made such little headway regarding royal economic policies was that Spanish manufacturers were angry about the competition from colonial manufactured goods. They complained that their exports had fallen since the peak in 1608.[72] One reason for the decline was that by the seventeenth century New Spain didn't need Spanish goods as much as it had in the sixteenth. Because Spanish wine and oil could not arrive in Peru or Chile before it turned to vinegar or became rancid, these areas developed their own production. Similarly, in the textile industry it became easier and cheaper to produce cloth and clothing locally than to import these items from Spain. By 1604, therefore, Mexico City had 25 textile mills and ten hat factories.[73] In Peru, Europeans used local cloth to supplement their fashions.[74] As the colonies became increasingly independent economically, the balance of power between Spain and New Spain shifted.[75] Significantly, Fernández understood these changes, bragged about an increase in production of textiles from Puebla in 1612, and concluded that this revealed the colony's strength.[76] Since this ran quite contrary to their goals, officials in Spain were not impressed with this news. Their frustration only grew as the century progressed, for as the colonies developed their own illicit trade within the Americas, Spain experienced a sharp decrease in both the number of arriving ships and the tonnage of the cargo.[77]

One of the best illustrations of the complexities of Spanish commerce can be seen in the various attempts to establish trade with Japan. Upon the urging of Franciscan missionaries in Japan, the Japanese sent their first envoys to Mexico in 1610 during the viceroyalty of Fernández's predecessor.[78] In response to this contact, the viceroy authorized explorer Sebastian Vizcaino to sail to Japan in March 1611 with six barefoot Franciscans, establish commercial relations with the Japanese, and spend time learning about the Japanese archipelago and its customs. This effort was partially thwarted by the Dutch, who convinced many Japanese officials that the Spanish were more interested in missionary activity than trade.[79] But Japanese lord Date Masamune was very keen to generate more diplomatic and commercial relations with the West and so made arrangements for one of his vassals, Hasekura Tsunenaga, to travel to Madrid and to Rome. The *San Juan Bautista* sailed from Japan in October 1613 with 180 men on board, including its captain Vizcaino and a

[71] Hoberman, *Mexico's Merchant Elite, 1590-1660*, 220.
[72] Macleod, "Spain and America," 370. This was the peak in both volume and variety.
[73] Israel, *Race, Class and Politics in Colonial Mexico, 1610-1670*, 20.
[74] Karen B. Graubart, *With Our Labor and Sweat: Indigenous Women and the Formation of Colonial Society in Peru, 1550-1700* (Stanford, California: Stanford University Press, 2007), 155.
[75] John Lynch, *Spain Under the Habsburgs, Volume II: Spain and America, 1598-1700* (New York: Oxford University Press, 1969), 13.
[76] Hoberman, *Mexico's Merchant Elite, 1590-1660*, 271.
[77] Geoffrey Parker, Global Crisis: *War, Climate Change, and Catastrophe in the Seventeenth Century* (New Haven, Connecticut: Yale University Press, 2013), 466-468. In fact, by 1650, the quantity of goods transported from the Americas to Spain had fallen to less than half the volume of 1600. Parker notes that the diversification of the economy and the retention of wealth in the Americas allowed the region to avoid the worst effects of climatic challenges caused by the seventeenth century's Little Ice Age and "General Crisis."
[78] The viceroy of New Spain from July 2, 1607 to June 19, 1611 was Luís de Velasco, Marquess of Salinas (1534-1617). The Japanese delegation did not have to go all the way to Madrid since, as the king's representative, the viceroy could negotiate on his behalf.
[79] *The Works of Hubert Howe Bancroft, Volume XI, History of Mexico, Volume III, 1600-1803*, 3-4.

sixty-member Japanese embassy led by Hasekura.[80] The voyage to Mexico took the Spanish three months as a result of several debilitating storms, but they reached Acapulco in January 1614, and were greeted by a warm welcome with horns and drums booming. Upon the ship's arrival, the crew had their weapons confiscated, lest they might misbehave in a new land, but the Japanese seemed pleased with their reception.[81]

This auspicious beginning suffered a significant blow, however, when a Japanese officer beat and stabbed Captain Vizcaino for trying to take possession of the gifts the Japanese intended for Fernández, King Philip III, and Pope Paul V. Apparently the captain believed he deserved a reward for delivering the Japanese safely and with none forthcoming, he took matters into his own hands. The Japanese saw Vizcaino's attempted theft as a dishonorable act and acted accordingly, thereby illustrating the differences in cultural expectations that make trade and diplomacy so delicate. The Japanese worried about the impression the arrival of a bloodied Spanish captain would make and so sent an advance party to Mexico City. This contingent marched into the capital at twelve noon on March 4 with the soldiers dressed in "something like a tunic," their hair tied "at the back of their

necks," and carrying "long, narrow, black poles, maybe their lances" in the lead, according to one eyewitness. The officers proudly followed on horseback.[82] By the time Hasekura and most of the rest of the delegation arrived on March 24, having taken a leisurely journey across the mountains from the coast, Vizcaino had had a chance to tell his side of the story but to little avail. Fernández saw to it that Hasekura and his officers were properly accommodated at a house near the San Francisco Monastery and the dispute with Vizcaino was forgotten.[83] Of greater concern to Fernández were those members of the New Spain business community who feared that trade with Japan would adversely affect the established trade with the Philippines. Fernández had to weigh these fears, while making sure that his Japanese guests were not offended by hostility they received from some quarters.[84] Such was the life of a viceroy: forever balancing

---

[80] Thomas Christensen, *1616: The World in Motion* (Berkeley, California: Counterpoint, 2012), 330

[81] Takashi Gonoi, *Hasekura Tsunenaga* (Tokyo, Japan: Yoshikawa Kobunkan, 2003), 77. I am indebted to Takako and Hideko Akashi for their assistance in translating passages from this work into English for me.

[82] Chimalpahin, *Annals of His Time*, 273, 275. During the visit in 1610, Chimalpahin's journal entries describe the Japanese as a "bold, not gentle and meek people, going about like eagles." (171), and yet he is also surprised by their having beardless "faces like women…whitish and light" (173). Chimalpahin also comments at length on the hair of the men: "Their hair begins at their temples, all going around towards the nape of their necks. They are long-haired…[and] look like girls because of the way they wear their hair…[which] they tie in twisted, intertwined fashion, reaching to the middle of the head with close shaving. It really looks like a tonsure that they display on their heads." (171). Significantly, however, Chimalpahin's entries in 1614 do not dwell on these physical details; the Japanese have become far more known and far less foreign to him by then.

[83] According to Chimalpahin, during the Japanese visit in 1610 the viceroy sent his personal carriage to pick up the delegation's leader. Chimalpahin also briefly mentions a formal reception and meal at the viceroy's palace. By 1614, such accommodations did not deserve mention in his mind; it was a given. See Chimalpahin, 173, 275-276.

[84] Gonoi, *Hasekura Tsunenaga*, 87, 93. A more recent source notes that Fernández issued a specific order to maintain the peace in spite of the Japanese presence. He charged Dr. Antonio de Morga with the job of ensuring that the Japanese right to sell their merchandise was not infringed upon by other businessmen or the

various constituencies with contrasting needs and agendas, while maintaining proper diplomatic decorum and viceregal dignity. Since forty-two members of the Japanese delegation were baptized as Catholics in Mexico City in April 1614,[85] and since the majority of the delegation peacefully remained in Mexico City while Hasekura proceeded to Europe with twenty men, it is clear that Fernández proved able to establish an equilibrium.[86] He did, however, write to the Council of the Indies on October 30, 1614, questioning the wisdom of developing trade relations with the Japanese, given how poorly defended Spain's holdings on the Pacific coast were.[87]

A second major issue Fernández dealt with in his tenure as viceroy of New Spain was the flooding caused by the unusual topography surrounding the viceregal capital. Because it sat in a basin with no outlet for runoff water, excess precipitation drained into a shallow lake which covered about 19% of the valley floor.[88] The Aztecs subdivided this lake with causeways, constructed floodgates, built floating gardens, and rerouted rivers in a successful effort to control flooding during the rainy season; their work also segregated brackish water, and increased food production in the area.[89] During the early colonial period, the Spanish failed to appreciate the complexity of the region's hydrology. Combined with increased soil erosion and little maintenance of Aztec water containment systems, this ignorance set the stage for significant problems.[90] In 1551, 1580, and 1604 the capital experienced substantial flooding and each attempt to correct the problem failed.[91] When another flood hit the city in 1607, the viceroy, Luís de Valesco, argued that the existing systems were "not strong or effective enough to assure this city's safety and perpetuity."[92] He convinced local elites to agree to a solution originally proposed five centuries earlier: drain the lakes out of the Valley of Mexico by constructing a drainage tunnel that led to rivers flowing to the Pacific Ocean. Funded by a tax on every slaughtered animal in the city, a tax on wine, and a one-time property assessment of 1.5%, and built with compulsory indigenous labor, the drainage project

---

public. See Cornelius Conover, *Pious Imperialism: Spanish Rule and the Cult of the Saints in Mexico City* (Albuquerque, New Mexico: University of New Mexico Press, 2019), 50, 204.

[85] Chimalpahin, *Annals of His Time,* 277, 279.

[86] Hasekura did meet with King Philip III and Pope Paul V in 1614, but his embassy did not produce meaningful results. He returned to Mexico, traveled to the Philippines, and returned to Japan in 1620. Just after Hasekura departed Japan in 1613, Shogun Tokugawa Ieyasu expelled most Christians from Japan, making his mission impossible to fulfill. I have not been able to find any account of Fernández's impressions of the Japanese arrival or departure, either in 1614 or 1616. For more information about the event and its significance see Inaga Shigemi, "Japanese Encounters with Latin America and Iberian Catholicism (1549-1973): Some Thoughts on Language, Imperialism, Identity Formation, and Comparative Research." *The Comparatist* 32, (May, 2008): 27-35, ProQuest Central.

[87] Cornelius Conover, *Pious Imperialism: Spanish Rule and the Cult of the Saints in Mexico City* (Albuquerque, New Mexico: University of New Mexico Press, 2019), 204.

[88] Vera S. Candiani, *Dreaming of Dry Land: Environmental Transformation in Colonial Mexico City* (Stanford, California: Stanford University Press, 2014), 16.

[89] Ivonne Del Valle, "On Shaky Ground: Hydraulics, State Formation and Colonialism in Sixteenth Century Mexico," *Hispanic Review,* 77.2 (Spring 2009), 197-220, ProQuest Central.

[90] Candiani, *Dreaming of Dry Land,* 28-29.

[91] By the seventeenth century, the one lake separated by causeways was no more. Instead, a series of separate lakes existed in the valley. The main, central lake, Texcoco, was closest to the capital city, had the lowest elevation, and was brackish. To the south stood the freshwater lakes of Chalco and Xochimilco, which were about five feet higher in elevation than Texcoco. To the north stood the freshwater lakes of Cristóbal and Zumpango, which were about ten feet and twenty-seven feet higher than Texcoco respectively. In the rainy season, Zumpango's overflow ran into Cristóbal, Cristóbal's overflow ran into Texcoco, and the city flooded. See *The Works of Hubert Howe Bancroft, Volume XI, History of Mexico, Volume III, 1600-1803,* 8.

[92] Luís de Valesco quoted in Candiani, *Dreaming of Dry Land,* 49.

represented a massive undertaking. It required the construction of a fifteen-mile-long diversion dam, a four-mile-long trench, and a four-mile-long tunnel, which was eight feet wide and nine feet tall at the point of its greatest volume.[93] All this work and more took just ten months, due to efforts of 60,000 Indian laborers. On September 17, 1608 water flowed out of the Valley of Mexico for the first time.[94]

By the time of Fernández's inauguration in December 1612, serious problems had crept into the project. The tunnel was too small to handle the required volume of water and the tunnel's slope was too steep; this eroded the tunnel's walls because they had no revetments. With the tunnel crumbling and water not draining properly, the city's property owners complained that their tax money had been wasted and Indian labor had been commandeered from important agricultural work.[95] These complaints reached Philip III, who in May 1613 asked his ambassador to France to find an engineer who could solved the hydrology issues in Mexico City. Five months later, Adrian Boot, who was paid an alluring hundred ducats a day, arrived in the capital and met with Fernández.[96] The viceroy commissioned a party to escort the Flemish engineer on his inspection of the basin's water management system. After twenty-four days in the field, including a detailed inspection of the tunnel, Boot reported to Fernández that the drainage tunnel project was indeed "a grand work," but that it was "useless for the purpose of freeing the City of Mexico from the risks it faces and the dangers to come." Boot concluded that it would be impossible to drain the lakes of the basin because the cost would be too "extraordinary to be sustainable."[97] As an alternative, Boot proposed that the city invest in a system of twenty new sluice gates and a new eleven-kilometer canal to take water away from the city. He estimated that the canal would cost 340,000 pesos and take three years to complete.[98] Fernández respected Boot's candor and thoroughness, but in January 1615 he rejected the engineer's proposal as impractical because of the political fallout it would generate. The city's elite were vehemently opposed to Boot's plan because of its high costs and the amount of Indian labor it would require.[99] Fernández didn't believe it was prudent to spend the necessary political capital on a project which might or might not work. Such cautiousness generally characterized Fernández's administrative approach as viceroy.[100]

A third issue Fernández dealt with during this time in Mexico, and one that affected him personally, was disease. First came the death in 1613 of the viceroy's oldest daughter, after just a year of life, and then came the death of his wife Mariana, who made her will on February 25, 1619.[101]

---

[93] Candiani, *Dreaming of Dry Land,* 50-51, 56-57.

[94] W. Michael Mathes, "To Save a City: The Desague of Mexico-Huehuetoca, 1607," *The Americas*, 26, 4 (April, 1970), 419-438, EBSCOhost. Mathes notes that during construction only ten men died from accidents in the tunnel and 63 died of diseases.

[95] Candiani, *Dreaming of Dry Land,* 62, 64-65.

[96] Rivera Cambas, *Diego Fernández de Córdoba,* 6.

[97] Adrian Boot quoted in Candiani, *Dreaming of Dry Land,* 75-76.

[98] Candiani, *Dreaming of Dry Land,* 76.

[99] Trevino Villarreal, "Diego Fernandez."

[100] Such antipathy for taxes combined with administrative caution had consequences: in 1629 a massive flood kept much of Mexico City underwater for five years. Another example of Fernández's administrative cautiousness involves English incursions into Florida; he waited for a decision from Philip III about how to proceed in Florida, rather than acting on his own as soon as the news reached him. See Rivera Cambas, *Diego Fernández de Córdoba,* 7.

[101] Pérez Herrera, "Diego Fernández de Córdoba y el palacio del marquesado de Guadalcázar." Before she died, Mariana gave birth to three children in Mexico, two girls and a boy. Mariana Manuela was born January 2, 1613 and lived just under a year; Brianda was born January 13, 1614. I have not been able to find an exact birth

The viceroy mourned the loss of his wife deeply. He knew Spanish law prohibited viceroys and other key officials from marrying women within their jurisdictions so as to prevent a concentration of wealth and influence which might undermine royal authority.[102] Fernández was going to be alone for the foreseeable future. He responded to this grief by designing an elaborate funeral to honor Mariana. The arrangements included a protocol-breaking funeral procession and the construction of a platform for her coffin which was larger than the one made for Margaret of Austria in 1611. He also ordered the *oidores* to wear mourning clothes while hearing cases, something which was only normally done upon the death of a king or queen. When this news reached Madrid, the Crown responded negatively, fining Fernández 4,000 ducats for his ceremonial abuses. The viceroy replied to the rebuke, arguing that the colony's remoteness required extra pomp and that he had only been trying to honor the dignity of the viceregal office, not his wife. But in the eyes of most, whether in Mexico City or Madrid, Fernández had gone too far and overstepped his station.[103] He may have been the embodiment of the Crown in New Spain, but he was not the king and Mariana was not the queen.

   The rest of the city was certainly not immune from the misfortune that had befallen the viceregal family. The infant mortality rate in the seventeenth century for *Peninsulares* and Creoles was 20%. It was higher for those of mixed race and higher still for Indians.[104] As a result of the Columbian Exchange,* diseases devastated adult populations too. Historians estimate that about 20 million people lived in central Mexico in 1520, but by 1548 there were only six million as the multitudes fell victim to diseases for which they had no immunity.[105] Although no one has found evidence that the Spanish purposefully sought to infect Indians as happened in New England and in the American West, the indigenous population continued to fall through the opening decades of the seventeenth century, as wave after wave of contagions swept across the continent.[106] As soon as one disease began to fade away, another followed, with new diseases like yellow fever and malaria entering into the mix. At the same time, the strains of familiar diseases like smallpox and measles became increasingly virulent as time passed, probably as a result of the growth of the Atlantic slave trade.[107] In 1615, for example, smallpox and measles epidemics hit the Valley of Mexico, reaching the highest levels of infection in the first three months of 1616.[108] As with previous episodic arrivals of these diseases, the results were painful to witness. With smallpox, the pustules usually began covering the victim's feet, hands, face, arms and neck, occasionally blending together into a single, massive sore,

---

date for Francisco, but it was between 1614-1619. For confirmation of the girls' birth dates, see Chimalpahin, *Annals of His Time*, 233, 271.

[102] This requirement explains why so many Spanish officials came to the Americas with wives; only merchants were exempt from this rule. It also explains why Fernández never remarried. See María Emma Mannarelli, *Private Passions and Public Sins: Men and Women in Seventeenth Century Lima*, Sidney Evans and Meredith D. Dodge (trans.) (Albuquerque, New Mexico: University of New Mexico Press, 2007), 23, 25.

[103] Cañeque, *The King's Living Image*, 144.

[104] Nicolá Sánchez-Albornoz, "The Population of Colonial Spanish America," *The Cambridge History of Latin America, Volume 2, Colonial Latin America*, Leslie Bethell (ed.) (New York, Cambridge University Press, 1984), 23.

[105] Israel, *Race, Class and Politics in Colonial Mexico, 1610-1670*, 13.

[106] David Cook, *Born to Die: Disease and New World Conquest, 1492-1650* (New York: Cambridge University Press, 1998), 214-215. In 1763, for example, Sir Jeffery Amherst advocated for the purposeful infection of Native Americans with smallpox. See Elizabeth A. Fenn, *Pox Americana: The Great Smallpox Epidemic of 1775-82* (New York: Hill and Wang, 2001), 88-89.

[107] Cook, *Born to Die*, 173.

[108] Cook, *Born to Die*, 167. Cook indicates (173) that the repeated outbreaks of smallpox and measles between 1614-1620 is enough to suggest pandemics rather than epidemics.

but in some patients, the legions formed internally, leading to subcutaneous hemorrhaging from the eyes, nose, mouth and anus. In other cases, smallpox victims mysteriously died even before any skin lesions appeared.[109] There was, however, little Fernández or anyone else could do about these horrific epidemics except pray.

The fourth major issue which faced Fernández as viceroy of New Spain was rebellion, and one of the major rebellions during his administration was directly connected to disease. In 1616, the Tepehuan Indians in Sierra Madre Occidental mountains between Durango and Chihuahua rose up in a rebellion which was thought at the time to be "one of the greatest outbreaks of disorder, upheaval and destruction...seen in New Spain since the Conquest."[110] The Tepehuanes had experienced significant societal stress before the start of seventeenth century, as they, like so many other tribes, had abandoned traditions and beliefs, moved to mission villages, and endured coerced labor. The waves of earlier epidemics had convinced many Tepehuanes that their gods were not powerful enough to stop the widespread deaths, and they had converted to Christianity. With the passage of time, however, the Christian God had proven no more able to terminate the plagues, which hit the Tepehuanes in 1594, 1601-1602, 1606-1607.[111] In fact, they came to see churches and baptisms by Jesuit missionaries as the direct cause of death.[112] Then, in 1615, a charismatic shaman named Quautlatas called upon the Tepehuanes to rise up against Spanish for enslaving them. He proclaimed that all Christians had to be killed in order to honor the old Tepehuan gods and that anyone dying in the revolt would be brought back to life. These messages were well received, and by November 1616 the Tepehuanes were ready to strike, having six commanders and key alliances with surrounding tribes.

The coordinated attack on numerous strategic targets resulted in the death of over 200 Spaniards, including eight Jesuits, one Franciscan, and one Dominican, all of whose bodies were mutilated. The Tepehuanes destroyed church altars, flogged statues of the Virgin Mary, urinated on Hosts, drank communion wine, killed livestock, and burned buildings.[113] Spanish commanders in Durango dispatched small contingents of troops as quickly as they learned the news in December 1616. By March 1617 these troops had captured all six of the Tepehuan leaders and put them to death. This brought much of the revolt to a close as Tepehuan allies quickly sued for peace. The entire episode cost the Crown over a million pesos in expenses and loss of revenue from the silver mines; over 300 Spaniards and 1,000 Indians lost their lives.[114] The peace remained tenuous and there were additional Indian revolts later in the century.

The Tepehuan Revolt illustrates both the problems the viceregal government faced in attempting to rule such vast territories and the success it had in doing so. On the one hand, the three companies of soldiers Fernández sent from the capital didn't arrive in Durango until ten

---

[109] Fenn, *Pox Americana,* 16-18.

[110] Andrés Pérez De Ribas quoted in Charlotte M. Gradie, *The Tepehuan Revolt of 1616: Militarism, Evangelism, and Colonialism in Seventeenth Century Nueva Vizcay*a (Salt Lake City: University of Utah Press, 2000), 165.

[111] Gradie, *The Tepehuan Revolt of 1616,* 168, 170. Another author cites different dates for the outbreaks: 1590 for smallpox and 1596-1597 for smallpox and measles, but concurs with Gradie for the events in 1601-1602 (measles, smallpox, and perhaps typhus) and 1606-1607 (measles and smallpox). See Susan M. Deeds, *Defiance and Deference in Mexico's Colonial North: Indians Under Spanish Rule in Nueva Vizcaya* (Austin, Texas: University of Texas Press, 2003), 16.

[112] Susan M. Deeds, "First Generation Rebellions in Seventeenth Century Nueva Vizcaya," *Native Resistance in the Pax Colonial in New Spain*, Susan Schroeder (ed.) (Lincoln, Nebraska: University of Nebraska Press, 1998), 11. Deed's 2003 book cited above puts this rebellion into a broader historical context.

[113] Deeds, "First Generation Rebellions in Seventeenth Century Nueva Vizcaya," 9-10.

[114] Deeds, "First Generation Rebellions in Seventeenth Century Nueva Vizcaya," 11.

months after the rebellion began, while on the other hand Fernández wrote to Philip III to inform him of the situation and to get advice as quickly as he probably could.[115] It took months for Fernández to receive word back from Spain, but when it came Philip made the Spanish position clear: "the uprising must be put down, and if this doesn't happen through the measures taken by the present [provincial] Governor, send someone with more experience for the period of time the war lasts."[116] Fernández, therefore, had to assess the situation, determine the best course of action, restore as much harmony as he could, and balance his dual responsibilities of protecting the Indians and promoting the spread of the Catholic faith. Fernández's decree of January 10, 1618 shows his solution. He ordered that peaceful Indians be treated kindly, and he gave the remaining rebellious Indians a sixty days in which to surrender without facing retribution. Those who failed to accept his offer of amnesty would suffer the consequences.[117] This balanced approach fit with Fernández's political instincts, but also replicated the procedures of the Inquisition when it entered a town to begin its investigations. In the minds of many Spanish administrators, the power to inflict punishment should be moderated by a desire to dispense clemency.[118]

Another rebellion which occurred during Fernández tenure in New Spain involved the viceroyalty's Black population. The status of Blacks was particularly complicated in the Spanish colonies because many were free, many were runaway slaves (known as maroons), and many, whether slave or free, had freedom of movement in places like Mexico City.[119] Spaniards saw owning an African slave as a sign of prestige, but then employed them as overseers for Indian workers and allowed them to purchase their freedom by earning wages.[120] Such circumstances did not limit racial tensions between Blacks and Whites. In fact, these tensions were at an all-time high just prior to Fernández's arrival in the colony. In 1611, a Black female slave was flogged to death in Mexico City by her master. The injustice caused more than 1,500 Blacks to join in an organized march in which they carried the woman's body through the streets to the palaces of the archbishop, the Inquisition, the viceroy, and finally to the house of the slave's owner. When the *audiencia* deported the organizer of the march, Blacks began plotting a *coup d'état* for Holy Thursday 1612. Their intent was to replace the viceroy with a Black king and queen.[121] Word of the plot reached colonial authorities, however, and the *audiencia* suspended the Holy Week processions and re-imposed old laws: the dawn-to-dusk curfew for all Blacks, whether slave or free; the ban on carrying weapons; a prohibition on meetings of three or more Blacks at any time; and a rule against wearing luxurious clothing. Then, on May 2, 1612, twenty-nine men and seven women were hanged on nine gallows for their involvement in the plot and their heads were severed and paraded through

---

[115] The date of Fernández's letter to Philip was February 15, 1617, and the troops arrived in Durango on September 22, 1617. See Gradie, *The Tepehuan Revolt of 1616,* 159, 164.

[116] Philip III quoted in Gradie, *The Tepehuan Revolt of 1616*, 165.

[117] Gradie, *The Tepehuan Revolt of 1616,* 165.

[118] Alejandro Cañeque, "The Emotions of Power: Love, Anger, and Fear, or How to Rule the Spanish Empire," *Emotions and Daily Life in Colonial Mexico*, Javier Villa-Flores and Sonya Lipsett-Rivera (ed.) (Albuquerque, New Mexico: University of New Mexico Press, 2014), 103.

[119] Jane G. Landers, "*Cimarrón* and Citizen: African Ethnicity, Corporate Identity, and the Evolution of Free Black Towns in the Spanish Circum-Caribbean," *Slaves, Subjects and Subversives: Blacks in Colonial Latin America*, Jane Landers, and Barry Robinson (eds.) (Albuquerque, New Mexico: University of New Mexico Press, 2006), 119.

[120] Israel, *Race, Class and Politics in Colonial Mexico, 1610-1670*, 72-73.

[121] Landers, "*Cimarrón* and Citizen," 119-120.

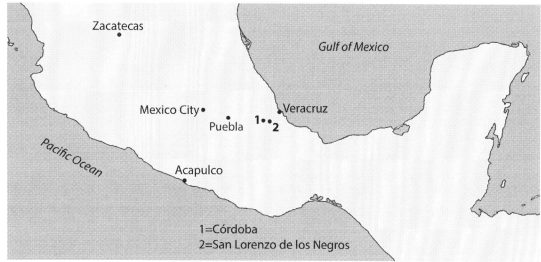

the streets on pikes to warn other Blacks from rebellion.[122] By the time Fernández arrived in Mexico City that fall, Spanish ardor had cooled, but as his term progressed new tensions arose.

The greatest of these were the return of maroon raids on the vital Veracruz-Mexico City road and an uprising by maroons in 1617-1618. Like several of his predecessors, Fernández dispatched troops to restore order, but as in the past his military commanders found it impossible to combat the guerrilla-style warfare of the maroons in the mountains. In the end, the Spanish simply renewed an existing agreement with the maroon leader Yanga: in exchange for their freedom and independence from Spanish harassment, the maroons would stop raiding the Veracruz-Mexico City road and return any new runaway slaves who attempted to join their community. This time, however, the Spanish also formally recognized the right of the Blacks to have a permanent town with their own *cabildo*. The town took the name San Lorenzo de los Negros.[123] Fernández then granted the Black community sufficient lands surrounding San Lorenzo to support the town. As an additional precaution, in 1618 Fernández founded the Spanish town of Córdoba in the heart of maroon territory so Spanish troops could protect supply routes and watch for runaway slaves.[124] By the end of his term as viceroy of New Spain, relations between Whites and Blacks were far less tense than when Fernández took office.

Despite his even-handed approach to viceregal administration and a reasonable record of accomplishment (including the establishment of colleges and the construction of a 900-arch aqueduct), Fernández's term ended ignominiously: his *audiencia* staged a *coup d'état* against him. Its members may have had authorization from Spain, but it is more likely that they acted on their own, realizing that with Philip III's impending death Fernández would lose the basis of his support in Madrid. Fernández had certainly made enemies. He had, for example, angered Archbishop Pérez

---

[122] Israel, *Race, Class and Politics in Colonial Mexico, 1610-1670*, 70-71.

[123] Today the town is called Yanga in honor of the maroon leader.

[124] Jane G. Landers, "*Cimarrón* and Citizen: African Ethnicity, Corporate Identity, and the Evolution of Free Black Towns in the Spanish Circum-Caribbean," *Slaves, Subjects and Subversives: Blacks in Colonial Latin America*, Jane Landers, and Barry Robinson (ed.) (Albuquerque, New Mexico: University of New Mexico Press, 2006), 125-128. Yanga, who claimed to be an African chief, began his community in the 1570s in the mountains west of Veracruz. Yanga and followers lived in settled, agricultural communities for almost forty years before the founding of San Lorenzo de los Negros.

de la Serna and violated direct orders from the court by refusing to allow the archbishop to evaluate the competence of the assistants to parish priests who were members of religious orders. In January 1620, the members of the *audiencia* began virulently attacking what they described as Fernández's "tyrannical" rule.[125] The viceroy's last day in office was March 14, 1621.[126]

What happened next is unclear because Fernández didn't arrive in Lima to begin his term as the viceroy of Peru for sixteen months after being removed from office in Mexico City. He probably lived in Mexico City as a private citizen, awaiting news of a new appointment from Philip IV.[127] At some point, he made his way to Acapulco, accompanied by his two surviving children, a boy and a girl. Once in Acapulco, Fernández saw the impressive, five-bastion* fortress of San Diego for the first time. How ironic the structure must have seemed to the viceroy, who in an effort to secure the Manila trade in the face of new Dutch encroachments into the Pacific, had authorized the fort's construction in 1615 without waiting for approval or financial support from Spain.[128] Designed by Adrian Boot and erected in just seven months, the fort dominated the entire crescent moon harbor. It undoubtedly stood in Fernández's mind as a symbol of effective leadership. Yet he was leaving Mexico under a cloud without the pomp that had greeted him upon his arrival. He could take some comfort in the fact that he had an even more prestigious appointment awaiting him.

~

Ynes Quispi's simple canopy in the market in the Plaza Mayor faced both Lima's newly-completed cathedral with its two rather squat bell towers and three great portals, and the archbishop's residence, which a Jesuit described in 1629 as having "splendid windows." To her left stood "the largest and most luxurious structure" in the kingdom, the viceregal palace, which was "resplendent" despite having only one story. Behind Quispi, on the west side of the square, rose the "imposing and magnificent" town hall for the *cabildos*; to her right stood a row of commercial buildings "featuring stone columns, a brick arcade and many large balconies with windows." The market offered "anything a well-supplied republic could desire for its sustenance and comfort," while

---

[125] Israel, *Race, Class and Politics in Colonial Mexico, 1610-1670*, 137, 141.

[126] The next viceroy, Marques de Gelves, arrived in New Spain in 1621 on a mission to end corruption. As a result of his authoritarian style, Gelves quickly alienated the archbishop, the members of the *audiencia*, and the merchant community. He was ousted from office in 1624.

[127] Israel, *Race, Class and Politics in Colonial Mexico, 1610-1670*, 137. This appointment came as the result of Fernández's having sufficiently pleased royal officials in Spain during his tenure as viceroy of New Spain. See Rivera Cambas, *Diego Fernández de Córdoba*, 17.

[128] The Dutch captain Joris Van Spilbergen's fleet of five ships, 150 guns and 800 men entered the Pacific and defeated the Spanish off the coast of Peru on July 17-18, 1615. Spilbergen proceeded north, arriving in Acapulco on October 11, 1615, where he agreed to exchange fresh provisions and prisoners instead of destroying the town. Later, Spilbergen sailed for the Moluccas having never encountered the Manila galleons, but his appearance prompted Fernández's actions and the fort's construction. See Engel Sluiter, "The Fortification of Acapulco, 1615-1616," *The Hispanic American Historical Review*, 29, 1 (February, 1949), 69-80, EBSCOhost.

surrounding stores specialized in the fashionable goods Lima's elite sought.[129]   Quispi's simple produce and clothing stand might not look like much, but its simplicity belied both her personal ambition and her overall economic importance to the community.

Quispi was an Andean woman from the highlands about a hundred miles southeast of Lima. Although illiterate, she owned land in the countryside and a house in the city, managed a business, employed at least one person in Lima to help her sell her goods, and understood Spanish property law quite thoroughly.[130]   Quispi raised fruits and vegetables on land outside of Lima she and her husband worked together, but her will of 1623 makes it clear that she saw herself as an independent economic entity, noting the amount of money she put into the business over the years and the amount of her original dowry.   She also owned a large amount of high-quality clothing. Documenting her financial status was important to Quispi because she also served as an unofficial financier for many of the other vendors on the Plaza Mayor.

One can imagine Quispi surveying the market scene one crisp morning as *limeños* began their day. It was a busy place, for in the words of one early seventeenth century commentator, "everyone [in Lima] is a merchant, even if it is through a third party or on the sly."[131]   Quispi easily could have chatted with an Andean woman under the awning on her left or with a free Black woman under the canopy on her right, for all of these women were members of a shared economic community with social ties.[132] In fact, they probably lived as neighbors in Lima's largest parish, where in 1619 women composed 38% of the parish's Andean population, and 46% of its Black population.[133] As for social and economic interactions, any of these women might have hired a Black slave as a day laborer since it was common for slaves to work for wages, give a percentage of their wages to their masters, and keep the rest so that in time they could buy their freedom.[134] Alternatively, these women might have had an apprentice.[135] The Iberian men who owned the stores may have dominated the highest levels of Lima's commerce, but the things of everyday life were sold by women like Quispi, utilizing multiethnic networks.[136]

Other people would have caught Quispi's eye that morning: the elite Spanish women carried in sedan chairs through the streets[137] or the multitude of shoppers, noble or not, who would spend "incredible sums" on "all kinds of silks, fabrics, brocades, delicate linens and fine textiles" since

---

[129] Bernabé Cobo, "Viceregal Lima in the Seventeenth Century," *I Saw a City Invincible: Urban Portraits of Latin America*, Sharon Kellum (trans.) (Wilmington, Delaware, 1996), 62-63. Cobo wrote his account of the history of Lima between 1611-1639; this description of the Plaza Mayor is from 1629.

[130] Graubart, *With Our Labor and Sweat,* 70-72. All of the subsequent information on Quispi also comes from these pages.

[131] Anonymous, "Pedro de León Portocarrero's Description of Lima Peru," *Colonial Latin America: A Documentary History*, Kenneth Mills, William B. Taylor and Sandra Lauderdale Graham (ed.) (Wilmington, Delaware: Scholarly Resources, Inc., 2002), 193. As the editors note, the text was not signed, but many historians believe that the description of Lima was authored by Pedro de León Portocarrero, a *converso* who hid his identity to emigrate to the Americas.

[132] Graubart, *With Our Labor and Sweat,* 90.

[133] María Emma Mannarelli, *Private Passions and Public Sins: Men and Women in Seventeenth Century Lima*, Sidney Evans and Meredith D. Dodge (trans.) (Albuquerque, New Mexico: University of New Mexico Press, 2007), 20.

[134] Henry Louis Gates, Jr., *Blacks in Latin America* (New York: New York University Press, 2011), 96.

[135] Graubart, *With Our Labor and Sweat,* 92.

[136] Graubart, *With Our Labor and Sweat,* 70.

[137] Graubart, *With Our Labor and Sweat,* 87.

there was "no moderation at all in this part of the world."[138] There were carpenters and silversmiths, orphans and vagabonds, government officials and priests.   There were also seductively posed, flirtatious women looking out from wood-latticed balconies or riding in carriages or simply walking down the street, their heads wrapped up so a passerby could only see one eye.

These women were not prostitutes. They were *tapadas*: women dressed in the most expensive fashions, purposely showing the lace of their undergarments; they used a shawl to conceal their identity and maintain their anonymity so that they might break social conventions and do as they pleased.[139] Some saw their mystery as defining sexual desirability. Others saw their unrecognizability as a threat to social order in a racially diverse, economically stratified city. If husbands couldn't identify their own wives, if fathers couldn't recognize their own daughters, if men could dress as women without anyone knowing, then the value of Christian modesty signified little.[140] This is why, soon after his arrival in Lima as the new viceroy, Fernández de Córdoba found himself beseeched by male petitioners to do something about what they described as the social menace of the *tapada*. These petitioners had not had viceregal support in the past.   One of Fernández's predecessors argued that "since I have seen that each  husband cannot control his own wife, I have no confidence whatsoever that I will be able to control all of them together."[141] Fernández felt an obligation to try to address a situation that had the potential to create unruliness. He issued an ordinance that as of December 10, 1624, all women, regardless of class or whereabouts, had to leave their faces "uncovered so that they may be seen and recognized at all times."[142] Read in every Peruvian town, the ordinance specified punishments, which were substantially harsher than any previously issued for the offense. All women found in violation would be fined sixty pesos, but the prison terms differed by race and class; noble women faced a prison term of ten days, while Black and mixed race women faced prison terms of thirty days.[143] Those who were found guilty of a second violation were to be banished from their communities for a year.[144] These punishments did not, however, provide a sufficient deterrent for Peruvian women. The *tapadas* tradition continued well into the nineteenth century.

The status of every Peruvian viceroy ultimately rested upon something far more material and tangible than divergent social mores: the amount of silver transported from the colony to Spain. Most of this metal came from Potosí, a single 15,800-foot mountain in modern Bolivia which contained one of the world's largest concentrations of silver ore. Between 1574 and 1735 miners

138 Bernabé Cobo, "Viceregal Lima in the Seventeenth Century," 67-68.
139 Luis Martín, *Daughters of the Conquistadors: Women of the Viceroyalty of Peru* (Dallas, Texas: Southern Methodist University, 1983), 281, 299.
140 Laura R. Bass, Amanda Wunder and Enrique Garcia Santo-Tomás, "The Veiled Ladies of the Early Modern Spanish World: Seduction and Scandal in Seville, Madrid and Lima," *Hispanic Review*, 27.1 (2009), 97-146, ProQuest Central.
141 Juan de Mendoza y Luna, Marquess of Montesclaros, quoted in Martín, *Daughters of the Conquistador,* 303.
142 Diego Fernández de Córdoba quoted in Martín, *Daughters of the Conquistadors,* 304.
143 Bass, Wunder and Garcia Santo-Tomás, "The Veiled Ladies of the Early Modern Spanish World."
144 Martín, *Daughters of the Conquistadors,* 304.

extracted almost 20,000 tons of silver from Potosí.[145] The Crown took one fifth of the production, which it used to help finance its military needs and defend Catholicism around the globe. The supply of silver from Potosí was essential because its liquidity allowed Spain to pay its troops and obtain necessary loans.[146] This is why Fernández received such acclaim for successfully defending Lima's port of Callao in the face of a Dutch attack in 1624. It is also why it was fortuitous that he had ordered the Spanish treasure fleet carrying nine million pesos of silver to depart Callao for Panama just five days before the Dutch arrived.[147] Potosí's silver was Spain's lifeblood.

The production of ore necessary for these coins came at a significant human cost. Because all of the easily accessible ore had been removed from Potosí by 1572, Viceroy Francisco de Toledo had created a compulsory Andean labor system to extract silver. This system was called the *mita*. Pressed into service as vassals to the crown, all Andean men between eighteen and fifty who lived in one of sixteen high-altitude provinces had to report to Potosí once every seven years for a twelve-month contract. This system created a workforce of 13,500 laborers, who worked in one-week shifts followed by two weeks of rest. Originally, workers received wages, had the costs of transportation costs to Potosí funded, and worked from dawn to dusk Tuesday through Saturday, spending their nights above ground.[148] This system was prone to significant abuse. Men were forced, for example, to stay in the mines overnight or were beaten to meet illegal production quotas.[149] Whereas Toledo had specified that miners could only make two trips hauling rock out of the mines a day, by the 1590s the Andean miners regularly carried nineteen. The conditions were horrific, as noted by a priest in the 1590s:

> They labor in these mines in perpetual darkness, not knowing day from night. And since the sun never penetrates to these places…the air is very thick and alien to the nature of men….The ore is generally hard as flint, and they break it up with iron bars. They carry the ore on their backs up ladders made of three cords of twisted rawhide joined by pieces of wood that serve as rungs….Each man usually carries on his back a load of [fifty-five

---

[145] Nicolas A. Robin and Nicole A. Hagan, "Mercury Production and Use in Colonial Andean Silver Production: Emissions and Health Implications," *Environmental Health Perspectives*, 120.5 (May 2012), 627-31, ProQuest Central. This includes the 25% presumably lost to contraband. Significantly, this huge influx of specie into the European economy created inflation; when silver supplies began to shrink, the Spanish economy contracted.

[146] Elliott, "Spain and America in the Sixteenth and Seventeenth Centuries," 322.

[147] Lynch, *Spain Under the Habsburgs, Volume II: Spain and America, 1598-1700*, 181. The Dutch never caught the Spanish treasure fleet, partially because they attacked Guayaquil. Interestingly, when this fleet reached Acapulco in October 1624, Fernández's and Adrian Boot's fort there withstood the attack. Perhaps as a result of his experiences with rebellion in Mexico, as part of the preparations to defend Lima Fernández established a regiment of black mercenaries to put down any Andean or black rebellion in the moment of crisis. See Benjamin Schmidt, "Exotic Allies: the Dutch-Chilean Encounter and the (Failed) Conquest of America," *Renaissance Quarterly*, 52.2 (1999), 440-473, ProQuest Central.

[148] Peter Bakewell, "Mining in Colonial Spain America," *The Cambridge History of Latin America, Volume 2, Colonial Latin America,* Leslie Bethell (ed.) (New York, Cambridge University Press, 1984), 124-125. One historian notes that in Toledo's tenure, the *mita* was a widely-praised solution to the labor issues and became so embedded that it lasted until 1825, when Simón Bolívar finally ended it. See Kris Lane, *Potosí: The Silver City that Changed the World* (Oakland, California: University of California Press, 2019), 71-72.

[149] Kenneth J. Andrien, *Andean Worlds: Indigenous History, Culture and Consciousness Under Spanish Rule, 1532-1825* (Albuquerque, New Mexico, University of New Mexico Press, 2001), 61.

pounds] of silver ore tied in a cloth, knapsack fashion....They climb a great distance, often more than [980 feet]—a fearful thing, the mere thought of which inspires dread.[150]

Once the rock was on the surface, it went to one of the 124 refineries located in the town at the base of the mountain, where it was crushed into the consistency of flour. Once sufficiently ground, Andeans then mixed a combination of copper pyrite, salt, and mercury into the rock and ore with their bare legs for six to eight weeks so that the mercury would amalgam with the silver. Once the silver and the mercury were sufficiently integrated, the composition was shoveled into vats and washed to carry off the waste rock. The remaining silver and mercury were then heated to allow the mercury to evaporate, leaving pure silver and creating toxic clouds of vapor.[151]

The conditions were so bad that Andeans went to great lengths to avoid the Potosí *mita* altogether. They ran away from the towns they had been assigned to live in by colonial officials or hired replacements to fulfill their service. Andeans who survived their first tour of duty frequently stayed in Potosí and found less-risky work as wage employees to avoid the jobs assigned to those under the *mita* contract.[152] Some even went further: a mid-seventeenth century report noted that "many mothers maim their infant sons in the arms or legs so that when they are older they will be exempt" from *mita* service, especially if they thought that service would be in the deadly mercury mines of Huancavelica.[153]

Fernández became convinced early in this term that the Potosí *mita* was an unsustainable enterprise. Analyzing the data available to him, he concluded that the towns of the high Andean plain could not support the required draft numbers for very much longer. Consequently, Fernández wrote to Philip IV, urging the Crown to reduce the number of required draftees, regardless of the effects on silver production. Surprisingly, but echoing both his father's and his grandfather's concern for the indigenous peoples of the Americas, Philip IV agreed to Fernández's

---

[150] Jeffery A. Cole, *The Potosí Mita, 1573-1700: Compulsive Labor in the Andes* (Stanford, California: Stanford University Press, 1985), 24.

[151] Bakewell, "Mining in Colonial Spain America," 115-116.

[152] By 2010, so much rock and ore had been removed from the mountain that a sinkhole began opening near the summit, risking the collapse of tunnels far below. In June 2014, UNESCO warned that the summit was in danger of collapse, threatening the still-operating mine shafts below. The following month, the Bolivian government moved to close mines above 14,435 feet, but miners continue to work there under brutal conditions. See William Neuman, "For Miners, Increasing Risk on a Mountain at the Heart of Bolivia's Identity," *The New York Times*, September 16, 2014, A9, ProQuest Historical Newspapers. Attempts to regulate conditions have not been effective. See Kenneth Dickerman and Simone Francescangeli, "What Life is Like for the Teenage Miners of Potosi, Bolivia," *The Washington Post*, 2018, ProQuest Central.

[153] Ann M. Wightman, *Indigenous Migration and Social Change: The Forasteros of Cuzco, 1570-1720* (Durham, North Carolina: Duke University Press, 1990), 50.

proposal. This royal agreement should have produced a dramatic change in the *mita* system, but when he got the news from Madrid, Fernández wavered: he decided to wait for individual communities to request a reassessment of their *mita* quotas instead of making a sweeping directive.[154]

Fernández's hesitancy rested in his fear of disorder, and this fear had some justification. In 1618, a civil war broke out in Potosí after years of bitter animosity between the Spanish and the Basques, who owned most of the mines and dominated the *cabildo*, mint, and royal treasury.[155] According to one contemporary account, the Basques lorded their position and wealth over everyone else in Potosí, treating all others "disdainfully and vituperously."[156] The Spaniards, both *Peninsulares* and Creoles, resented the Basques' status and resorted to violence. Between 1622 and 1624, five thousand people died in their conflict. This level of bloodshed between Whites in the Spanish colonies was unprecedented. It is possible that the conflict went beyond ethnic and financial jealousy: the violence may have actually been a consequence of widespread mercury poisoning.[157] Whatever the cause, the violence became so disruptive that Fernández travelled to Potosí in 1624 to negotiate a settlement, rather than send a subordinate as would have been customary.[158] Fernández believed that the peace settlement he negotiated favored both sides equally.[159] It provided for the marriage of a Castilian girl to the son of a Basque leader, thereby helping to restore honor and soothe ethnic tensions,[160] but the consequences of visible unrest between Whites threatened the social fabric of Peru; this was something Fernández could not risk any more than he could gamble on the flow of silver from Potosí. In the end, Spain's goal of protecting the indigenous population of the Americas was incompatible with its goal of combating the twin evils of Islam and Protestantism in the late sixteenth and early seventh century; it needed the wealth of the mines to pay for the armies to fight the English, the Dutch, and Ottomans, and the only way to operate them efficiently was with indigenous labor. Old World realities trumped New World aspirations.

Ironically, the opposite was true in the Andeans' practice of Catholicism: New World realities trumped Old World aspirations. By the time Fernández arrived in Peru in 1621, a rigorous campaign against idolatry, superstition, and witchcraft had been underway for a dozen years. It began with great enthusiasm in Lima in 1609, where an *auto-de-fé* resulted in the beating of an Andean shaman and the burning of idols and ancestral mummies just before Christmas. In subsequent years, the clergy became deeply divided as to the campaign's merits and necessity, partly because it utilized the procedures of the Inquisition. The most ardent proponents of the campaign believed that the Andeans were "so persistent in their idolatry that almost all of them have relapsed into paganism."[161] These clerics argued that it was appropriate to instill "fear and terror" in the

[154] Cole, *The Potosí Mita, 1573-1700*, 77-78.

[155] Kris Lane, *Potosí: The Silver City that Changed the World* (Oakland, California: University of California Press, 2019), 113. Lane notes that the animosity between then Spanish and the Basques also stemmed from long-standing rivalries in peninsular Spain.

[156] William A. Douglass and Jon Bilbao, *Amerikanuak: Basques in the New World* (Reno, Nevada, University of Nevada Press, 2005), 82.

[157] Robin and Hagan, "Mercury Production and Use in Colonial Andean Silver Production."

[158] Fisher, *Viceregal Administration in the Spanish-American Colonies*, 257.

[159] Diego Fernández de Córdoba, Marqués de Guadalcázar in *Colección de las Memorias o Relaciones que Escribieron los Virreyes del Perú Acerca del Estado en que Dejaban Las Cosas Generales del Reino*, Tomo 11 (Madrid, Spain: Imprenta Mujeres Españolas, MCMXXX (1930)), 226.

[160] Douglass and Bilbao, *Amerikanuak: Basques in the New World*, 82-83.

[161] Anonymous letter quoted in Joseph de Arriaga, *The Extirpation of Idolatry in Peru*, L. Clark Keating (ed. and trans.) (Lexington, Kentucky, University of Kentucky Press, 1968), 140.

Andeans in order to end this "plague."[162] At the other end of the spectrum, the provincial of the Augustinians stated that "not even a trace" of idolatry could be found in his jurisdiction,[163] and the bishops of Arequipa and Trujillo argued that even if idolatry could be found, the appropriate response was preaching and education, not torture.[164] In reality, there was an incompleteness to the Andeans' Christianization, but there was also a significant incorporation of Catholic ritual and belief. This was possible because priests sought to utilize native religiosity, carefully substituted local deities for Christian figures, and encouraged the blending of Andean and European clothing in religious festivals.[165] Indeed, many Andeans in the seventeenth century enthusiastically participated in Catholic festivals and ceremonies and readily used Catholic prayers and devotional objects, but they also honored their cultural past by continuing to worship local deities and to venerate their ancestors in customary ways.[166] While there were those who refused to accept Spanish rule and culture well into the seventeenth century, in most regions a blending of religious traditions occurred.[167] One example is the way the Andean Earth Mother goddess, Pachamama, became transformed into the Virgin Mary.[168] For his part, Fernández saw himself as the "healer and protector" of the Andeans and stated that their conversion and education was one of his most important obligations as viceroy. This belief led him to establish new schools and to urge the Crown to continue financing idolatry inspections.[169] A strong indication of Fernández's sense of moderation rests in the fact that the periods of the idolatry campaign's greatest intensity came before and after his term as viceroy.[170] Indeed, Fernández's held the same general attitude toward the idolatry campaign in Peru that he had held towards the Inquisition in Mexico.

Some of the best evidence of the syncretism which emerged in the Spanish colonies can be found in a large painting hanging prominently in the cathedral in Cuzco, Peru. Painted by Marcos Zapata in the mid-eighteenth century, *The Last Supper* merges conventional Christian iconography with Andean customs. Jesus and the Apostles sit around a rectangular table with only Judas looking away from Christ. Judas bears a clear resemblance to conquistador Francisco Pizarro and holds a bag of money under the table. Instead of the bread and the wine being the focus of their meal, a cooked guinea pig rests on its back on a large platter in the middle of the table. The guinea pig, or *cuy*, was an important source of protein in the Andean diet, as well as an important element in

---

[162] Gonzalo de Campo quoted in Nicolas Griffiths, *The Cross and the Serpent: Religious Repression and Resurgence in Colonial Peru* (Norman, Oklahoma: University of Oklahoma Press, 1996), 36.

[163] Francisco de la Serna quoted in Griffiths, *The Cross and the Serpent*, 56.

[164] Griffiths, *The Cross and the Serpent*, 56-59.

[165] Carolyn Dean, *Inka Bodies and the Body of Christ: Corpus Christi in Colonial Cuzco, Peru* (Durham, North Carolina: Duke University Press, 1999), 16, 122, 159.

[166] Kenneth J. Andrien, *Andean Worlds: Indigenous History, Culture and Consciousness Under Spanish Rule, 1532-1825* (Albuquerque, New Mexico, University of New Mexico Press, 2001), 154-160, 190-191.

[167] The Araucanian Indians of Chile, for example, persisted in a guerrilla war against the Spanish deep into the colonial period. Fernández's nephew, Luis Fernández de Córdoba y Arce, became the governor of Chile in 1625 and despite his ruthless attempts to subjugate the indigenous people, Luis had no more success in reaching his goals than either his predecessors or his successors. See Brian Loveman, *Chile: The Legacy of Hispanic Capitalism* (New York: Oxford University Press, 1979), 65-66.

[168] Carol Damian, *The Virgin of the Andes: Art and Ritual in Colonial Cuzco* (Miami Beach, Florida: Grassfield Press, 1995), 26.

[169] Fernández de Córdoba, *Colección de las Memorias o Relaciones que Escribieron los Virreyes del Perú Acerca del Estado en que Dejaban Las Cosas Generales del Reino*, 238, 268-269.

[170] The periods of greatest intensity were 1609-1622 and 1649-1670. During Fernández's term, there was one year of intense extirpation (1625-1626), created by the appointment of a new archbishop, who died soon into his term. See Griffiths, *The Cross and the Serpent*, 10, and Andrien, *Andean Worlds*, 154-160, 173-177.

Incan religious rituals; it was frequently used as a sacrificial offering.[171] The *cuy*'s inclusion in the painting, hung in a Baroque church situated on the site of an important Incan temple, shows how Andean beliefs and practices were not completely supplanted by Catholicism, despite the campaigns against idolatry. In the long run, the Church learned that the best way for Christianity to become meaningful in the Andes was to accommodate local sensibilities while remaining true to its fundamental tenets.[172] Only in this way could Philip II's vision of a great Catholic empire in the New World become a reality.

~

After sixteen years of service to the Crown in the Americas, Diego Fernández de Córdoba wrote to Philip IV, asking for permission to return to Spain. He wanted to retire. He wanted to enjoy the luxurious palace constructed for him in the Andalusian town of Guadalcázar while he was in the New World.[173] In his summary account of his time in Peru, Fernández indicated that he had done his best to improve upon what he had found during his tenure.[174] The king granted Fernández's request, and in January 1629, the viceroy sailed for home with his teenage children, Brianda and Francisco. Fernández died just twenty-two months later, in October 1630, at the age of fifty-two, not having enjoyed his newly-constructed palace for very long.

It is easy to find zealots in the pages of history, but Fernández does not stand as one of them. A dutiful bureaucrat for the Spanish Crown, he liked constancy and order so much that he told his successor in Lima, "As you now enter government, it would be better not to make any innovations in these regulations until, having more experience, you can consult with the King" about them.[175] This may not make Fernández a particularly exciting or morally righteous figure, but he also didn't persecute or abuse those he governed. Unlike those more famous in the sixteenth and seventeenth centuries, he was a cautious and prudent man, who seemed to understand human frailties and to have the capacity to work with them. Never dogmatic or totalitarian, Fernández wouldn't have been particularly troubled by the appearance of the guinea pig in *The Last Supper*, even if he would have strongly objected to any association between the deeds of Judas and those of Pizarro.

---

[171] Allison Lee Palmer, "The Last Supper by Marcos Zapata (c. 1753): A Meal of Bread, Wine, and Guinea Pig," *Aurora, The Journal of the History of Art*, 9 (Annual, 2008), 54+, EBSCOhost.

[172] Gabriela Ramos, *Death and Conversion in the Andes: Lima and Cuzco, 1532-1670* (Notre Dame, Indiana: University of Notre Dame Press, 2010), 222. Similarly, in Mexico, beatification of Fray Felipe de Jesús de las Casas, the first saint from the Americas, offered colonial leaders the chance to celebrate Mexico's contributions to the Empire and the Catholic Church, while accommodating local sensibilities. See Conover, *Pious Imperialism,* 61, 64, 83.

[173] Pérez Herrera, "Diego Fernández de Córdoba y el palacio del marquesado de Guadalcázar." Financing for the palace largely came from the wealth Fernández accumulated as viceroy, which is why many historians accuse him of considerable corruption. J. H. Elliot says, for example, that during Fernández's administration of New Spain, "government was lax, corruption rampant, and collusion between royal officials and a handful of leading families led to the further enrichment of a privileged few." See Elliott, "Spain and America in the Sixteenth and Seventeenth Centuries," 317.

[174] Fernández de Córdoba, *Colección de las Memorias o Relaciones que Escribieron los Virreyes del Perú Acerca del Estado en que Dejaban Las Cosas Generales del Reino*, 216.

[175] Diego Fernández de Córdoba quoted in Wightman, *Indigenous Migration and Social Change*, 37.

G

Go-Mizunoo

1596-1680

Kyoto's residents witnessed two remarkable turning points in the life of Go-Mizunoo, Japan's 108th emperor. The first came on a humid afternoon in June 1620, when Go-Mizunoo's bride-to-be, Tōfukumon'in, passed through the city streets on her way to the imperial palace, accompanied by a long procession of notables and attendants.[1] Bystanders beheld an unparalleled spectacle, for Tōfukumon'in was the daughter of Hidetada, the second shogun* of the Tokugawa family, and this wedding was to be the first between a shogun family and the imperial family in more than four hundred years. As the official in charge of the wedding arrangements wrote, "There are no limits to the plans...[and] we must prepare everything as carefully as possible. It may entail great expense, but we should plan as if expenses are of no concern."[2] The procession featured porters carrying the hundreds of chests which composed Tōfukumon'in's trousseau, samurai* warriors flashing their long swords in the sun, musicians with their instruments, and nobles riding horseback, shielded from the heat with red parasols carried by their servants. The procession included also six carriages for ladies-in-waiting and many palanquins for important dignitaries. Tōfukumon'in's black lacquered carriage, pulled by two black oxen and emblazoned with the Tokugawa family crest in gold leaf, drew the most attention.[3] The stark beauty of the carriage's design, its expert craftsmanship, and the expense it represented "amazed the tens of thousands of spectators,"

---

[1] Upon their death, Japanese emperors and certain other members of the royal family received a posthumous name; both Go-Mizunoo and Tōfukumon'in are examples of this. Following the convention adopted in the nineteenth century, I have used Go-Mizunoo throughout the chapter to identify the emperor, but during his life he was known by other names, including Kazuhito and Kotohito. His posthumous name is also spelled in a variety of ways, such as Go-Mizuno-o, Gomizunoo or Gomizuno-o. Tōfukumon'in was also known as Tokugawa Masako and Kazuko. For a discussion of the development of naming protocol, see Herschel Webb, *The Japanese Imperial Institution in the Tokugawa Period* (New York: Columbia University Press, 1968), 71-72. Some sources say that the Go-Mizunoo and Tōfukumon'in's marriage occurred in July 1620, but June 18, 1620 seems to be the actual date. See Cecilia Segawa Seigle, "Tokugawa Tsunayoshi and the Formation of Edo Castle Rituals of Giving," *Mediated by Gifts: Politics and Society in Japan 1350-1850*, Martha Chaiklin (ed.) (Leiden, Netherlands: Brill, 2016), 123.

[2] Doi Toshikatsu quoted in Elizabeth Lillehoj, *Art and Palace Politics in Early Modern Japan 1580s-1680s* (Leiden, Netherlands: Koninklijke Brill, 2011), 127.

[3] Lillehoj, *Art and Palace Politics in Early Modern Japan 1580s-1680s,* 128-130.

according to one eyewitness account.[4]   This was the
intention of the Tokugawa family, who saw this
procession as its opportunity to make a memorable
statement about their power and success as the rulers of
Japan.

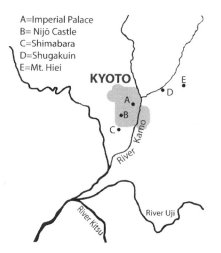

A=Imperial Palace
B= Nijō Castle
C=Shimabara
D=Shugakuin
E=Mt. Hiei

Six years later, on a crisp autumn day in 1626, the
people of Kyoto witnessed another impressive spectacle
and turning point in Go-Mizunoo's life. This came when
the emperor, Tōfukumon'in, and other members of the
imperial family visited Kyoto's Nijō Castle at the behest of
the nation's third shogun, Tokugawa Iemitsu, and his
retired father Hidetada.[5]   This time the procession
featured two long, parallel rows of palanquins, nobles on
horseback, musicians, and an entourage of thousands of
servants. Men dressed all in white surrounded Go-Mizunoo's phoenix-decorated palanquin as the
procession made its way through the orthogonal streets of Kyoto.[6] It too was an event the crowd
would remember, even if most observers had little understanding of how politically charged these
two processions were. The marriage event had been decades in the making, and the visit to Nijō
Castle required two years of preparation. Both were well worth the effort since they realized the
Tokugawa family's long-standing dream: the recognition of their legitimate rule of a unified nation
firmly under their control.

Such an outcome was not guaranteed during much of the fifteenth and sixteenth centuries, when
equally-matched, perpetually-battling regional warlords dominated Japan. During this Warring
States or Sengoku Period, neither the emperor nor the shogun wielded meaningful centralized
authority in Japan. In fact, the political order dissipated so completely that there was more strength
and stability in peripheral regions and islands than in the nation's traditional heartland.[7] Only the
introduction of firearms by Portuguese traders altered the military equation enough to change the
pattern of near-ceaseless war. A warlord named Oda Nobunaga proved particularly adept at
adapting traditional military strategy to utilize the new technology: by 1575 he had won a string
important battles, brutally subdued opponents in conquered lands, captured Kyoto, built Nijō
Castle in its center, and imposed regulations limiting the actions and prerogatives of the emperor
and other leaders. For all intents and purposes, Nobunaga was the king of Japan, which is how a
Jesuit missionary in the 1560s referred to him.[8] After Nobunaga's assassination in 1582 by a
resentful vassal, two of his generals, first Toyotomi Hideyoshi and then Tokugawa Ieyasu, finished
the process of pacification and unification of Japan. By 1603, Ieyasu was the nation's new shogun
and its most commanding individual.

---

[4] Horin Shōshō quoted in Elizabeth Lillehoj, "Tōfukumon'in: Empress, Patron and Artist," *Woman's Art Journal*,
Vol. 17, No.1 (Spring-Summer, 1996), 28-34, EBSCOhost.
[5] Shoguns frequently retired before their deaths in order to give greater legitimacy and continuity to their sons
as heirs, but they retained most of the actual power. The first Tokugawa shogun, Ieyasu, held the formal title
only two years (1603-1605) but lived until 1616. His son, Hidetada, held the office from 1605-1623 but died in
1632. The third Tokugawa shogun, Iemitsu, was the first shogun to hold the office until his death (1651).
[6] Lillehoj, *Art and Palace Politics in Early Modern Japan 1580s-1680s*, 161-162.
[7] Marius B. Jensen, *The Making of Modern Japan* (Cambridge, Massachusetts: The Belknap Press of Harvard
University Press, 2000), 4-5.
[8] Jensen, *The Making of Modern Japan*, 15.

The first Tokugawa shogun was not satisfied with this accomplishment. Ieyasu wanted to be more than another one of history's conquerors. He craved legitimacy. He wanted to create a proud legacy built upon a durable stability. This desire led Ieyasu to devote the last thirteen years of his life to obtaining this for himself, the Tokugawa family, and Japan. Upon being named shogun, Ieyasu began issuing regulations and taking actions to bring order to the realm. These included issuing a coinage with a fixed weight, encouraging agricultural output, improving highways and canals, and authorizing more trade missions to China in order to expand foreign trade. He also relocated regional lords to new lands, built and expanded castles in strategic areas, wrote a new military code to promote less bellicose behavior, and ordered Buddhist temples to focus on scholarly pursuits.[9] Additionally, Ieyasu established a new capital city, Edo, in order to lessen the importance of the imperial capital, Kyoto. Perhaps most significantly, Ieyasu drafted sweeping new regulations for the imperial family. These fundamentally changed the nature of the relationship between the emperor and the shogun for the next two hundred and fifty years. These rules redefined the system of court ranks, gave the shogun the right to veto the emperor's court appointments, regulated court dress, established punishments for the misbehavior of courtiers, and instructed the emperor to devote himself to scholarship and the arts instead of national politics.[10]

All of these regulations were enforced by Ieyasu's administration with the assistance of regional lords. Most members of the administration, the *bakufu*, were former samurai, who became bureaucrats as a result of the peace produced by unification. They held jobs as chamberlains, city commissioners, inspectors, tax collectors, and magistrates.[11] Significantly, these officials preserved their high social rank despite this change in vocation. Under Ieyasu's rule, the imperial aristocracy, or *daimyo*, also retained their status. They also maintained considerable autonomy over their lands as long as they submitted to Tokugawa will, managed to keep the tax revenue flowing, and after 1635 lived in the new capital of Edo in alternate years.[12] These relationships, institutions, and policies ensured that Japan made a successful transition from a country torn apart by centuries of war to a nation of peace and growing prosperity. It was a remarkable achievement, especially because it challenged a fundamental Japanese tenet.

In the Shinto* tradition, two primeval deities created Japan, and the emperor is a direct descendent of these gods. By his very nature the emperor possesses sacrosanctity. He is inviolable and cannot be removed or replaced, even if he is an utterly unreasonable or incompetent ruler.[13] To do so would be to challenge the gods, demonstrate infidelity, jeopardize the uniqueness of Japan, and risk losing the nation's intermediary to the gods. For the Japanese people, maintaining imperial continuity was absolutely paramount.[14] This was a very different attitude from that in China, where its Mandate of Heaven allowed for the removal of China's emperor in times of natural disaster,

[9] Conrad Totman, *Early Modern Japan* (Berkeley, California: University of California Press, 1993), 51, 52, 70, 72, 76.

[10] Webb, *The Japanese Imperial Institution in the Tokugawa Period*, 60-63.

[11] Louis G. Perez, *Daily Life in Early Modern Japan* (Westport, Connecticut: Greenwood Press, 2002), 23.

[12] The tradition of paying homage to the shogun in Edo began decades before 1635, but the requirement to live in Edo only became institutionalized in 1635-1636. See Jensen, *The Making of Modern Japan*, 56.

[13] David Magarey Earl, *Emperor and Nation in Japan: Political Thinkers of the Tokugawa Period* (Seattle, Washington: University of Washington Press, 1964), 12-13.

[14] Webb, *The Japanese Imperial Institution in the Tokugawa Period*, 161-165.

military defeat, or other calamities. In Japan, the shogun might rule supreme, but he needed the emperor in order to give that rule legitimacy.[15]

A notable illustration of this dynamic came in 1617, when Go-Mizunoo named Ieyasu as Tōshō Daigongen, the "Great Incarnation Illuminating in the East." This compared Ieyasu to the Sun Goddess and made him a *de facto* member of the imperial family as well as a Shinto deity. It was the highest possible honor Go-Mizunoo could bestow, and he did so with great care by personally writing the Chinese characters on dark blue silk and having them retouched in gold leaf.[16] While this may seem like Go-Mizunoo simply yielded to Tokugawa pressure, in fact, it shows how well the young emperor understood the symbiotic relationship between Edo and Kyoto: the shoguns needed imperial blessing for legitimacy, while the emperors needed Tokugawa recognition and financial support to provide the continuity which was so important to the well-being of the nation.

This is not to say that there weren't significant tensions between the two parties. The negotiations for Go-Mizunoo and Tōfukumon'in's wedding, for example, were fraught with issues of honor, prestige, tradition, and politics. In 1608, Ieyasu began contemplating the possibility of this marriage when his granddaughter was an infant and Go-Mizunoo was twelve. Formal negotiations began may have begun by 1612, but when a lady of the imperial court gave birth to Go-Mizunoo's first son six years later, a new urgency filled the air. The birth of a daughter in 1619 added more pressure. The shogun responded by ordering the imperial court's three marriage negotiators into exile. Go-Mizunoo tried to abdicate in protest over such Tokugawa interference in court appointments, but the shogun refused to allow it and essentially forced the emperor to marry Tōfukumon'in as soon as the necessary arrangements could be made.[17]

Upon her arrival at the imperial court on that humid June day, the thirteen-year-old Tōfukumon'in and the twenty-four-year-old Go-Mizunoo exchanged gifts and each drank from a cup of sake three times to seal their vows. Tōfukumon'in then retired to her newly constructed palace which was grander and more imposing than anything built in the imperial compound in generations. Like the wedding procession and the huge allowance provided to facilitate her entry into the court, Tōfukumon'in's new palace was a piece of Tokugawa propaganda.[18] The palace resembled those of Go-Mizunoo, which in itself was a departure from tradition; it included separate buildings for rituals, waiting guests, formal receptions, servants' quarters, and her private residence. Tōfukumon'in's private rooms featured exquisite sliding door panels of white and pink peonies in a garden and screens of red plums painted on gold paper by artists of the highest caliber. Other rooms featured gold wall paintings of men, women and children playing a form of badminton,

---

[15] Tokugawa scholars expended considerable effort trying to reconcile these two different traditions, especially in the context of the *bakufu*'s adoption of Confucianism as an official doctrine. (See Chapter K for an overview of the fundamental principles of Confucianism.) Hayashi Razan (1583-1657), for example, argued that the Mandate of Heaven applied to the shogun instead of the emperor. Kumazawa Banzan (1619-1691) argued that the emperor, being a deity, had a fundamentally different nature than other men, which meant that it was improper for him to be involved in Japanese political life. Yamaga Soko (1622-1685) held that Japan, not China, was the center of the civilized world, and, therefore, China's concept of the Mandate of Heaven was flawed. See Earl, *Emperor and Nation in Japan: Political Thinkers of the Tokugawa Period*, 21, 26, 44.

[16] Lillehoj, *Art and Palace Politics in Early Modern Japan 1580s-1680s*, 100. Ieyasu died on June 1, 1616, so the award was made posthumously.

[17] Lillehoj, *Art and Palace Politics in Early Modern Japan 1580s-1680s*, 127.

[18] Tōfukumon'in's allowance was equivalent to the amount given to all courtiers over a 70-year period. This gave her enormous purchasing power, which she used quite effectively. See Lillehoj, *Art and Palace Politics in Early Modern Japan 1580s-1680s*, 127, 131. For other examples of the ways in which royal women used their income to project their political and cultural influence, see Chapters I and J.

surrounded by tall pines near an important shrine.[19] These works created the impression of an idyllic realm, but Tōfukumon'in initially faced considerable opposition from members of the court, who resented her usurping the imperial marriage traditions and thought her to be a Tokugawa spy. Fortunately, she and Go-Mizunoo developed affection for one another as time passed. The birth of their first child in 1624 improved Tōfukumon'in's standing with the court, and Go-Mizunoo named her empress as a result. They royal couple eventually had seven more children together.[20]

The 1620s were transformational for Go-Mizunoo. Subject to continual Tokugawa oversight and essentially imprisoned within the imperial palace, the proud young man needed to find a purpose. He had to find a way to exploit the restrictions and limitations he faced. Since the shoguns decreed that the emperor should devote himself to scholarship and the arts, why not do this more thoroughly and wholeheartedly than anyone imagined? Why not make the court the guardian of *all* Japanese traditions? Let the shoguns manage the world of politics. The emperor would instead focus on those things which mattered most: the arts, scholarship, and faith.

~

Siddhartha Gautama, the man who became the Buddha, was born into a royal family in the fifth or sixth century BCE in what is today southern Nepal.[21] According to the traditional narrative, Siddhartha Gautama's life as a prince was highly protected. Encouraged to enjoy the pleasures of a privileged court life, he grew up having never seen suffering or pain or hunger or old age or death. The only world he knew was artificial, one full of delights and indulgences, decadence and debauchery. As he grew older, Gautama became restless, finding that he could not take pleasure in trivial things as did the other residents of the court. Even marriage and the birth of his son produced no bliss. One day, riding through the royal estate with his chariot driver Channa, Gautama saw an old man for the first time. He was shocked but curious to learn more. On subsequent trips, he saw a sick man and a dead man. As a result of these encounters, Gautama learned that life is full of suffering and that human existence, from birth to death, is defined by pain. This was a reality he could not ignore. He decided to leave his family and the material comforts of the palace to experience the realities of the outside world. In Buddhism, this is known as "Going Forth." Gautama spent six years exploring the plethora of sixth century India's spiritual communities, most of which believed in reincarnation. Eventually Gautama joined a small group of ascetics, who encouraged him to deny himself as much human pleasure and comfort as he possibly could, including food, clothing, shelter, sex, and sleep. He even consumed his own urine and feces and tried not to breathe.[22] As he approached death, however, Gautama realized his passing would not bring him any fulfillment, for he would simply be reincarnated in a different

[19] Lillehoj, *Art and Palace Politics in Early Modern Japan 1580s-1680s*, 131-143.
[20] The imperial household was polygamous. While Go-Mizunoo only had one principal wife, Tōfukumon'in, he had intimate relationships with many other palace women, fathering thirty-seven children. Most of those who reached adulthood became Buddhist monks or nuns. See Webb, *The Japanese Imperial Institution in the Tokugawa Period*, 83-85.
[21] Traditionally, Siddhartha Gautama's birth date is 563 BCE, but some historians put his birth closer to 479 BCE. As with Christianity and Islam, the details of the prophet's life were not written down until years after his death. See Karen Armstrong, *Buddha* (New York: Viking Penguin, 2001), xiii-xiv, 189.
[22] Armstrong, *Buddha*, 63.

form. His suffering would not end. Upon this realization, he broke with the ascetics, began to replenish his body, and devoted himself to discovering how to break the endless cycle of birth, suffering, death, and rebirth.

One day, sitting under a bodhi tree, the former prince reached enlightenment and became the Buddha. He then spent the next forty-five years teaching what he now knew to be true: the Middle Way, the Four Noble Truths and the Eight-Fold Path. The Middle Way holds that neither the path of sensual indulgence or the path of harsh asceticism will bring humanity true satisfaction. Both extremes are traps, but a life of moderation is not. The Four Noble Truths are: 1) all life entails suffering; 2) all suffering is caused by desire; 3) the cooling of desire (Nirvana) brings about enlightenment; and 4) the way to cool desire is to follow the Eight Fold Path. In other words, our desire for wealth, for power, for belonging, for longevity, or for sex is what makes us miserable. The best way to alleviate our misery is to follow eight prescribed practices, which allow us to be right in the world. These practices include Right Understanding (embracing the Four Noble Truths), Right Thought (practicing non-violence and love), Right Speech (not lying, gossiping, or offending), Right Action (not stealing or killing, or defrauding), Right Livelihood (not causing harm to others by one's profession), Right Effort (cultivating a positive state of mind), Right Mindfulness (being aware of one's feelings and body), and Right Concentration (practicing deep meditation).

After living a life following these precepts and sharing them with his followers, the Buddha knowingly ate tainted or poisoned food, lay down on his right side, and departed this earthly life. His final words were, "All contingent things pass away; strive on toward Nirvana with diligence."[23] As time passed, the Buddha's followers came to understand these words in different ways. In Japan, China, and Tibet, most Buddhists are members of the Mahayana tradition. This practice holds that the Buddha exists in each and every person and that enlightened figures called *bodhisattvas* intervene in earthly affairs to assist each of us in the process of realizing our individual potential for enlightenment. For followers of this tradition, humans are not alone in their journey; they receive the Buddha's help when they practice the Eight Fold Path faithfully. The Mahayana tradition also encourages its adherents to study the records of the oral teachings (*sutras*) of the Buddha closely. Over time such study led Buddhist scholars to take different philosophical positions either on the sutras or on early scholarly commentaries. Hence, in the Mahayana tradition, there are multiple interpretations and elaborations of Buddha's teachings.

Japan developed an array of different Buddhist sects as a result of these Mahayana roots, but these sects generally coexisted with one another benignly. Because each sect focused its attention on different sutras and commentaries, they came to different conclusions. The sects may have disagreed over the preeminent path for attaining enlightenment, but they did not go to war over differences in doctrine as Christian denominations did in Europe. The founder of the Tendai school, Kūkai, and the founder of the Shingon school, Saichō, were close friends who admired one another's spirituality, but they could not agree on Buddha's teachings and how they were transmitted.[24] This meant that Kūkai and the Tendai school concentrated upon the importance of Buddha's last sermon, the *Lotus Sutra*. This advocated for universal salvation, holding that all humans have the capacity for Buddhahood, not just those in the religious elite. Saichō and his

---

[23] The Buddha quoted in Kevin Trainor, "The Career of Siddhartha," *Buddhism: The Illustrated Guide*, Kevin Trainor (ed.) (New York: Oxford University Press, 2004), 41.

[24] Thierry Robouam, "The Role of Esoteric Buddhism in Contemporary Japan: Whether Esotericism Appears to Remain Concealed in the World Depends on the Trend of the Times," *Esoteric Buddhism and the Tantras in East Asia*, Charles D. Orzech, Henrik H. Sørensen and Richard K. Payne (eds.) (Leiden, Netherlands: Koninklijke Brill, 2011), 1033.

Shingon school followers instead centered their practice upon the use of devotional gestures (*mudras*), the interpretation of visual diagrams (*mandalas*), the recitation of sutras, and the practice of yoga to reach enlightenment. By synthesizing these practices, Shingon adherents believe that they can evoke the power of *bodhisattvas* and the Buddha.[25] Other schools of Japanese Buddhism, such as the Pure Land School, contended that it was necessary to put one's faith solely in a single divine entity, the Buddha of the boundless light or Amida, and to call to him for salvation and transportation to the western realm of the universe upon death.[26] Conversely, the different sects within the Zen Buddhist tradition all emphasized the central importance of self-discovery and realization. They all held that enlightenment could only be attained through strict discipline and with the guidance of a master. Such commonalities did not prevent the Zen sects from differing on essential doctrines and practices, however, for they too belonged to the Mahayana tradition. The Sōtō Zen sect stressed the gradual attainment of enlightenment by sitting in mediation without a particular focus, while the Rinzai Zen sect employed discussions about conundrums (*koans*), which could help disciples reach enlightenment in a sudden moment of inspiration.[27] Most importantly, the Japanese integrated all of these Buddhist traditions with the indigenous spirit religion of Shinto. This was because many didn't see a conflict between them. As the general and regent Toyotomi Hideyoshi once wrote, the kami (spirits) "are thus the root and source of all phenomena. They are in India under the name of Buddhism; they are in China under the name of Confucianism; they are in Japan where they are called Shinto. To know Shinto is to know Buddhism and Confucianism."[28] Such attitudes meant that differences in Japan's religious landscape did not cripple the nation with sectarian war.

Go-Mizunoo drew his spiritual beliefs from many of these schools and beliefs, for he saw himself as the preserver of all Japanese religious tradition. In 1623, he demonstrated this by reviving an eight-hundred-year old tradition. Developed by the founder of the Shingon school, Kūkai, the Imperial Rite of the Second Seven Days of the New Year, or Mishuhō, complemented another Buddhist new year's rite, and empowered the monarch by associating his authority with his promises to follow Buddhist teachings.[29] Go-Mizunoo put considerable effort into the preparations for the potent and secretive ceremony, consulting a twelfth-century scroll to provide him with the necessary details, including the placement of the appropriate accoutrements. During the ceremony, monks chanted mantras from the Golden Light Sutra, whose words had the power to transform the emperor into a legendary Buddhist ruler wise and virtuous enough to rule the world.[30] Then an abbot sprinkled scented water on Go-Mizunoo's robes and proclaimed him the chief protector of

---

[25] Charles D. Orzech and Henrik H. Sørensen, "Mudrā, Mantra, and Mandala," *Esoteric Buddhism and the Tantras in East Asia*, Charles D. Orzech, Henrik H. Sørensen and Richard K. Payne (eds.) (Leiden, Netherlands: Koninklijke Brill, 2011), 83.

[26] H. Paul Varley, *Japanese Culture: A Short History* (New York: Praeger Publishers, 1973), 51, 69-70. The Pure Land School divided into two groups over the doctrinal issue of how many times a person had to call for Amida. Those who believed that a single instance was sufficient formed the True Sect of the Pure Land School.

[27] Varley, *Japanese Culture,* 73.

[28] Toyotomi Hideyoshi quoted in Herman Ooms, *Tokugawa Ideology: Early Constructs, 1570-1680* (Princeton, New Jersey: Princeton University Press, 1985), 46.

[29] ELillehoj, *Art and Palace Politics in Early Modern Japan 1580s-1680s*, 108-110.

[30] Ryūichi Abé, "Scholasticism, Exegesis, and Ritual Practice: On Renovation in the History of Buddhist Writing in the Early Heian Period," *Heian Japan: Centers and Peripheries,* Mikael Adolphson, Edward Kamens, and Stacie Matsumoto (ed.) (Honolulu, Hawai'i: University of Hawai'i Press, 2007), 206.

Buddhism in the Land of the Rising Sun.[31] This revival of an esoteric Buddhist tradition annoyed the Confucian-oriented Edo government considerably.

That reaction contributed to the shogun's decision to present Go-Mizunoo and Tōfukumon'in with the irrefusable invitation to come to Nijō Castle for a five-day visit in the fall of 1626. The first day began with shogun Iemitsu coming to the imperial palace to escort the royal couple through the streets of Kyoto to the newly expanded castle with its new suites, audience rooms, private areas, and gardens for Go-Mizunoo, Tōfukumon'in, and Tōfukumon'in's mother to enjoy. The Tokugawa also dismantled and moved a multistoried *donjon*, or castle keep, from Fushimi Castle and placed it in the Nijō Castle grounds to provide the guests with a viewing platform from which to see the entire city now firmly under Tokugawa control. The paintings in Go-Mizunoo's suite reaffirmed this message: they featured images of warrior-class dominance, including historical scenes with Mongols and Tartars.*[32] After five days of artistic performances, exulted tributes and lavish gifts, Iemitsu escorted the emperor and his entourage back to the imperial palace. The message was no less subtle when Iemitsu marched 300,000 troops through the streets of Kyoto in 1634.[33] The shogun reigned supreme.

Iemitsu's supremacy resulted in the *Pax Tokugawa* and helped make Japan a prosperous exception in the second half of the seventeenth century. Whereas so much of the world endured an economic contraction and a reduction in a standard of living as a result of the Little Ice Age* and warfare, Japan's authoritarian peace allowed it to experience striking population growth, a dramatic increase in crop yields, an impressive expansion of urbanization, and greater productivity.[34] Peace became prized in a culture that had long been torn by warfare. As the eighth Tokugawan shogun wrote,

> it is worthy of celebration that bows and arrows are kept in bags and swords in wooden cases. That the shogun's men keep their armor in merchants' storehouses means that Japan is now enjoying unprecedented peace….You should not be sorrowful that swords and bows rot in pawnshops.[35]

The only serious exception to the *Pax Tokugawa* came as the result of external influences rather than domestic ones. Seventy-seven years earlier, in August 1549, Jesuit missionary Francis Xavier brought Christianity to Japan. Through the second half of the sixteenth century, the faith spread quickly from its base in Nagasaki, despite the unease it caused in the minds of Japan's pre-Tokugawa military-political leadership. Warlord Oda Nobunaga and leading general Toyotomi Hideyoshi both took steps to limit Catholicism's visibility and influence, but the religion remained quietly ensconced in southern Japan. Then in October 1596, a shipwrecked but brazen Spanish captain changed the equilibrium when he bragged that the Spanish could easily colonize Japan.

[31] Lillehoj, *Art and Palace Politics in Early Modern Japan 1580s-1680s*, 111.
[32] Lillehoj, *Art and Palace Politics in Early Modern Japan 1580s-1680s*, 156-161.
[33] Morgan Pitelka, "Warriors in the Capital: Kobori Enshū and Kyoto Cultural Hybridity," *Kyoto Visual Culture in the Early Edo and Meiji Periods: The Arts of Reinvention*, Morgan Pitelka and Alice Y. Tseng (eds.) (New York: Routledge, 2016), 19.
[34] Geoffrey Parker, *Global Crisis: War, Climate Change and Catastrophe in the Seventeenth Century* (New Haven, Connecticut: Yale University Press, 2013), 484-485, 487, 504-505, 668,
[35] Tokugawa Yoshimune (1684-1751) quoted in Constantine Nomikos Vaporis, "Introduction," *Voices of Early Modern Japan: Contemporary Accounts of Daily Life During the Age of the Shoguns* (Santa Barbara, California: Greenwood/ABC-CLIO, 2012), xvii.

When Hideyoshi learned about this insult and threat, he ordered the retributive execution of six Franciscan missionaries, three Jesuits, and seventeen Japanese laymen.[36] On February 5, 1597, the Twenty-Six Martyrs were crucified in front of 4,000 witnesses, who collected the martyrs' dripping blood in cloths.   Rather than deter Catholicism, the haunting scene reinforced adherents' convictions and the clothes became relics.[37]   By 1614, the Tokugawa Shogunate began to systematically persecute Catholics, but the increasingly underground faith endured.[38] Two decades passed, but in December 1637 a rebellion arose near Nagasaki. Prompted by discontent over high taxes, the Shimabara Uprising quickly became an expression of Catholic discontent over religious persecution. Led by the sixteen-year old son of a samurai, 37,000 peasants rose up in rebellion.[39] They based themselves in Hara Castle, an abandoned fortress in some need of repair, which sat on a peninsula surrounded by the sea on three sides. As Shogun Iemitsu's army moved to quell the revolt, a ship from the Dutch East India Company also moved into range. Hoping to present themselves as loyal vassals of the shogun, secure a monopoly with Japan, and undercut the Catholic presence in East Asia, the Dutch fired hundreds of shells at Hara Castle over a two-week period and helped suppress the revolt.[40] In the end, the Catholic Church gained another 37,000 martyrs, the Dutch became the only Europeans allowed to trade with Japan, and the shoguns rid themselves of a considerable foreign influence.

~

In written Japanese, most nouns are expressed as *kanji*—adapted Chinese characters that are ideograms. Most kanji have more than one meaning, and the way in which kanji are combined changes the meaning of the word.[41] The concept of suffering caused by desire in Buddhism, for example, combined the kanji for "sorrow," "grief," and "world." In the seventeenth century, people began mischievously substituting the verb "to float" for "sorrow." This created the new concept of

---

[36] Jurgis Elisonas, "Christianity and the Daimyo," *The Cambridge History of Japan*, Volume 4, John Whitney Hall, ed., (New York: Cambridge University Press, 1991), 331, 360-364.

[37] Yoshiko Okuyama, "Christian Martyrdom in Japanese Contexts: The Amakusa-Shimabara Revolt and Christian Martyrs," *International Journal of Religion & Spirituality in Society,* vol. 5, no. 3 (September 2015), 33-40, EBSCOhost. These executions sent shock waves throughout the Spanish empire. Eulogies for the Nagasaki martyrs could be heard in Manila, Buenos Aires, and Brussels. See Cornelius Conover, *Pious Imperialism: Spanish Rule and the Cult of the Saints in Mexico City* (Albuquerque, New Mexico: University of New Mexico Press, 2019), 37-38.

[38] Kevin Michael Doak, *Xavier's Legacies: Catholicism in Modern Japanese Culture* (Vancouver, British Columbia: University of British Columbia Press, 2011), 2, EBSCOebook.

[39] Yoshiko Okuyama, "Christian Martyrdom in Japanese Contexts: The Amakusa-Shimabara Revolt and Christian Martyrs," *International Journal of Religion & Spirituality in Society,* vol. 5, no. 3 (September 2015), 33-40, EBSCOhost.

[40] Adam Clulow, *The Company and the Shogun: The Dutch Encounter with Tokugawa Japan* (New York: Columbia University Press, 2014), 17, 95-96, 121-123, 125, 127, EBSCOebook. The Dutch East India Company is discussed at length in Chapter H.

[41] Lucien Ellington, *Japan* (Santa Barbara, California: ABC-CLIO, 2009), 223. To account for the different sounds in spoken Japanese and Chinese, as well as other linguistic issues, the Japanese supplemented the kanji with two syllabaries, the Hiragana and the Katakana. This makes Japanese one of the most difficult languages to learn to write. See Ellington, 228.

ukiyo or the "floating world," a space where desires were to be celebrated instead of rejected.[42] Kyoto had long had a lively entertainment district alongside the Kamo River—a place where the combination of teahouses, taverns, and open-air stages, each with its own musicians, actors, drummers, jugglers, jesters, puppeteers, or exotic animal trainers, created a carnival-like atmosphere day and night.[43] But in 1640, a new pleasure quarter opened on the southwest outskirts of the city that catered to those with greater means.[44] Enclosed by an earthen wall and surrounded by a moat, Shimabara was widely considered to be the most glamorous part of town.[45] It featured a refined and elegant atmosphere with everything a man who had money to spend could want, including the city's best entertainment, intelligent conversation, and government-sanctioned prostitution. Best of all, it wasn't limited to the daimyo the way the old prostitution district had been.[46] Instead, it was a place where men of many backgrounds might escape from Japan's stringent social norms.[47] This made it an ideal place for merchants to go to impress their clients.[48] Significantly too, a visit to Shimabara brought no sense of shame since many in seventeenth-century Japan believed that sex within marriage was for producing heirs, while sex outside of marriage was for enjoyment.[49]

The Floating World created in Shimabara, and in its counterpart of Yoshiwara in the capital city of Edo, was made possible largely through a well-established system of sex trafficking and sexual slavery. Usually sold by impoverished peasant families when they were six or seven, girls were initially contracted for ten years of service. During this period, they became the property of the brothel owner. In the opening years of the contract, the girls worked as maids. Later, they were taught how to be a proper attendant to a courtesan. Throughout this training period, these girls incurred debts for everything they wore or ate. This meant that by the time the girls started working as courtesans themselves at thirteen or fourteen, they faced enormous bills that kept many women working until their late twenties.[50] At this point, a woman might leave Shimabara or Yoshiwara by marrying or becoming a concubine of a client. Alternatively, she might remain in the pleasure quarter, helping to train and supervise newly recruited girls. Others simply committed suicide.[51]

Clients were enticed to come and then subsequently return to Shimabara by more than the excellent food, the beautiful music, and the pleasures of a sexual encounter. There was also the allure of prestige and status. A ranking system of the courtesans ensured that there were always

---

[42] Laura W. Allen, "Introduction," *Seduction: Japan's Floating World* (San Francisco, California: Asian Art Museum, 2015), xiii.

[43] Lesley Downer, *Women of the Pleasure Quarters: The Secret History of the Geisha* (New York: Broadway Books, 2001), 32.

[44] Donald H. Shively, "Popular Culture," *The Cambridge History of Japan*, Volume 4, John Whitney Hall (ed.) (New York: Cambridge University Press, 1991), 742.

[45] There may be some connection between the name of the Kyoto entertainment district and the Shimabara Uprising near Nagasaki, but the evidence is not clear.

[46] Tatsurō Akai, "The Common People and Painting," *Tokugawa Japan: The Social and Economic Antecedents of Modern Japan*, Chie Nakane and Shinzaburō Ōishi, (eds.), Conrad Totman (trans.) ([Tokyo]: University of Tokyo Press, 1991), 180. The prostitute district in Kyoto from 1602-1640 was Rokujō Misuji-machi. See Shively, "Popular Culture," 742.

[47] Allen, "Introduction," xiii.

[48] Downer, *Women of the Pleasure Quarters,* 41.

[49] Liza Dalby, *Geisha* (London: Vintage, 2000), 58.

[50] Downer, *Women of the Pleasure Quarters,* 42-44.

[51] Cecilia Segawa Seigle, *Yoshiwara: The Glittering World of the Japanese Courtesan* (Honolulu, Hawai'i: University of Hawai'i Press, 1993), 182-183.

women of higher standing to spark the imagination. These were the women who wore the latest fashion, had the best training, and had the right to refuse to have sex with a customer.[52]

For many men, the combination of heightened etiquette, titillation, and risk of rejection made these most elite women difficult to resist[53] and these repeat clients helped to make Shimabara a decidedly profitable enterprise.[54] In fact, the Floating World became an outright industry, employing countless seamstresses and gardeners, painters and hairdressers, chefs and musicians, laundresses and garbage collectors.[55] As its popularity and economic importance grew, detailed guide-books to the pleasure quarters began appearing to help new visitors navigate their options and manage their expectations. Published as early as early as 1642, these guidebooks provided practical information, advertisements, and rankings of prostitutes with their rates.[56] Such advice helped clients understand and follow the rules for proper behavior in Shimabara, so that they were not dismissed as crude boors— the laughingstocks of the pleasure quarter.[57]

Depending on the evening and the venue, a client's sexual partners could have easily been male instead of female since Tokugawa Japan never developed a strong hostility to male homosexuality and many men

---

[52] Shively, "Popular Culture," 745.

[53] Totman, *Early Modern Japan*, 211.

[54] The pleasure quarter of Yoshiwara generated the income equivalent to an amazing $877,200 per day. See Melinda Takeuchi, "Seduction: Japan's Floating World," *Seduction: Japan's Floating World* (San Francisco, California: Asian Art Museum, 2015), 11.

[55] Takeuchi, "Seduction: Japan's Floating World," 11.

[56] Takeuchi, "Seduction: Japan's Floating World," 9; and Shively, "Popular Culture," 745-746. In 1700, Kyoto had 308 registered courtesans, who were divided into four ranks. Only 13 women held the top rank of Tayū.

[57] Richard Lane, *Images from the Floating World* (New York: Konecky & Konecky, 1978), 22.

were habitually bisexual.[58] The society also accepted a diversity of gender expression as evidenced in the development of Kabuki theater, where many of the early skits featured women playing men and men playing women. As with the Shakespearean stage, this created opportunities for humorous confusion. But unlike in England, the chief function of an early seventeenth century kabuki performance was to sell something more than theatrical entertainment: the true objective was to facilitate prostitution.[59] The administrators of the Tokugawan *bakufu* banned women from the stage in 1629 as a result of male violence triggered by the provocative performances and post-production sexual liaisons. As a consequence, boys assumed the female theatrical roles, but a change in personnel did not change the importance of prostitution. Violence between men fighting over boys instead of fighting over women led to another *bakufu* intervention: the banning of boys from the stage in 1652.[60] Tokugawa officials always feared disruption in the social order and wanted to limit potential triggers for violence and mayhem whenever possible. Severing the association between theater and prostitution was one way to do this.[61] This regulation did not mean the end to pederastic relationships within Japanese society. Intergenerational sexual relations occurred everywhere from the imperial palace to Buddhist monasteries, from samurai castles to battlefields.[62] In all of these settings, there was usually a significant age discrepancy between the participants, as older men embraced *wakashudō*, or the way of youths.[63] Boys between the ages of twelve and fifteen were generally considered to be too immature, while young men between eighteen and twenty were thought to be almost past their prime. Ages fifteen to seventeen represented the ideal.[64] According to the established sexual construct, only anal sex held cachet, with the older man taking the position of the penetrator.[65] In Kyoto's Shimabara and in Edo's Yoshiwara, male prostitutes also had rankings and could command large fees.[66]

While such pedophilic relationships are at odds with contemporary Western values, world history is full of examples of all-male sexual unions. In ancient Athens, men and boys of aristocratic birth entered into intimate relationships, but there were laws to protect boys against unwanted advances. There was a cultural concern for the reputation of the boy should he agree to be anally

---

[58] Gary P. Leupp, *Male Colors: The Construction of Homosexuality in Tokugawa Japan* (Berkeley, California: University of California Press, 1995), 94-95.
[59] Masakatsu Gunji, "Kabuki and its Social Background," *Tokugawa Japan: The Social and Economic Antecedents of Modern Japan*, Chie Nakane and Shinzaburō Ōishi (eds.), Conrad Totman (trans.) ([Tokyo]: University of Tokyo Press, 1991), 201.
[60] Only in the late seventeenth century, when adult men played all of the stage roles did kabuki attain its status as a legitimate form of theater. Many of these actors lived as transvestites off-stage and were accepted into the women's side of public bathhouses. See Shively, "Popular Culture," 752-754.
[61] Gregory M. Pflugfelder, *Cartographies of Desire: Male-Male Sexuality in Japanese Discourse, 1600-1950* (Berkeley, California: University of California Press, 1999), 113.
[62] In medieval Japan, the samurai took youths with them on military campaigns to serve as their primary sexual partners, and samurai were known to fight duels over these boys. When Francis Xavier arrived in Japan in 1549, he was shocked by the openness of homosexuality, so it is clear that the behaviors in medieval Japan did not change in the early modern period, even if the role of samurai did. See David F. Greenberg, *The Construction of Homosexuality* (Chicago, Illinois: University of Chicago Press, 1988), 260-261.
[63] Both Shoguns Hidetada and Iemitsu practiced *wakashudō*. As an adult, Hidetada had several page-boy lovers, while as a boy Iemitsu had an affair with an older male. See Louis Crompton, *Homosexuality & Civilization* (Cambridge, Massachusetts: The Belknap Press of Harvard University Press, 2003), 439.
[64] Pflugfelder, *Cartographies of Desire*, 31.
[65] Leupp, *Male Colors*, 109.
[66] Takeuchi, "Seduction: Japan's Floating World," 6.

penetrated too often or by too many partners.[67] In China, there was a forthright acceptance of homosexuality for twenty-four centuries.[68] Both the Han Dynasty and the Ming Dynasty had numerous emperors who openly and happily preferred male sexual companions. In the southern province of Fujian, it was common for non-aristocratic men to live together like a married couple for decades and then choose mutual suicide over being forced into a heterosexual marriage.[69] In the Middle East, Arab culture may have condemned sexual contact between men, but it also exalted homoerotic love in its literature and poetry.[70] In nineteenth century Iran, homosexuality was illegal for the non-elite, but it was perfectly acceptable for a privileged man to hire a boy to provide both sexual and non-sexual services.[71] In Central Asia, it was fashionable for Mughal aristocrats to practice pederasty and other forms of homosexuality.[72] Similarly, in the Ottoman Empire, sultans, diplomats, judges, soldiers, and poets regularly had relationships with boys.[73] In the Americas, there is evidence that several pre-Columbian cultures, including the Aztecs, Mayans, Toltecs, and Incans practiced some form of ritualized homosexuality.[74] In some cultures, alternative sexual practices protected the very fabric of the civilization. In the New Guinean highlands, for example, the young men of the Sambia tribe, typically ages fifteen to twenty, orally inseminated boys between the ages of seven and fourteen in order to provide the boys with the essence they needed to become warriors and fathers.[75]

Documentation of lesbian relationships is far less abundant in the historical record due to differences in literacy rates, the absence of laws criminalizing the behavior, and the prevalence of misogyny, both in the past and by historians.[76] It is clear, however, that intimate relationships occurred between women in many cultures. There are depictions of lesbian relationships in pottery from the Moche and Chimú civilizations in northern Peru, numerous texts from ancient India, and love poems by female poets like Sappho of ancient Lesbos and Wallada bint al-Mustakfi of medieval Islamic Spain. Popular novels from Ming dynasty China provided explicit details of relations between women and documented marriage ceremonies between women in Guangdong, known as

[67] Kirk Ormand, *Controlling Desires: Sexuality in Ancient Greece and Rome* (Westport, Connecticut: Praeger Publishers, 2009), 51.

[68] Crompton, *Homosexuality & Civilization*, 215. Many cultures, including China, did not use the term homosexuality to describe male-male sex; even in the West, it wasn't until 1892 that the word homosexuality became part of the English language. See David M. Halperin, *One Hundred Years of Homosexuality and Other Essays on Greek Love* (New York: Routledge, 1990), 15.

[69] Crompton, *Homosexuality & Civilization*, 218, 225-227.

[70] Crompton, *Homosexuality & Civilization*, 172.

[71] Janet Afary, *Sexual Politics in Modern Iran* (New York: Cambridge University Press, 2009), 104.

[72] Abraham Eraly, *The Mughal World: India's Tainted Paradise* (London: Weidenfeld & Nicolson, 2007), 105, 119

[73] Khaled El-Rouayheb, *Before Homosexuality in the Arab-Islamic World, 1500-1800* (Chicago: University of Chicago Press, 2005), 21, 33-34, 64, 84, 93, 155-156, EBSCOhost.

[74] Greenberg, *The Construction of Homosexuality*, 163-168. Greenberg notes that most of the sources for this activity come from Spanish colonialists, who may have exaggerated the extent of the practice as a way of justifying their policies; alternatively, however, informers may not have been honest about homosexuality practices since they quickly understood Spanish opposition.

[75] Gilbert Herdt, *The Sambia: Ritual, Sexuality and Change in Papua New Guinea* (Belmont, California: Thomson Wadsworth, 2006), 56-57, 60. Once a man becomes a father, he is expected to stop participating in this ritual (page 119). This practice continued until into the 1980s, but by 1998 had ceased in the wake of increased Westernization. See Bruce Knauft, "What Every Happened to Ritualized Homosexuality? Modern Sexual Subjects in Melanesia and Elsewhere," *Annual Review of Sex Research*, 14 (2003), 137-159, ProQuest Central.

[76] Katherine Crawford, *European Sexualities, 1400-1800* (New York: Cambridge University Press, 2007), 161-162, 206-207. Crawford notes how frequently historians present female relationships in desexualized terms.

Golden Orchid Associations. In many different tribes in across central Africa, lesbian relationships were common between the co-wives of chiefs and kings, and it was not unusual for girls to engage in sexual activities with one another while in school in the late twentieth century. In Europe, the Byzantine Empire did not punish lesbian relations harshly, Renaissance texts tended to present female eroticism in a positive light, and records from eighteenth century Amsterdam document numerous intimate relationships between women of different classes.[77]

Human history is replete with other forms of sexual expression. In Pharaonic Egypt, members of the royal family were often incestuous in order to protect the familial lineage, even if this behavior was not common with Egyptian society at large.[78] In India, the famous textbook of erotic love, *Kamasutra*, devotes its entire fifth book to the art of seducing the wives of other men.[79] In Northern Peru, the Moche civilization documented heterosexual anal sex in their pottery, perhaps reflecting their belief that anal sex was what provided nursing babies with milk.[80] On the island of Grande Terre in the South Pacific, it was an honor for a father to sleep with his son's wife.[81] The context of the liaison mattered substantially in some cultures. In the Arab world, for example, Islam sanctioned sex between Muslim conquerors and the women of their foes (whether these women were married nor not), unlike the expectations men had of one another in regard to their own wives. Other boundaries also varied. Libertine French aristocrat Marquis de Sade practiced sadomasochism for sexual gratification and held that "cruelty is the energy in man civilization has not yet altogether corrupted: therefore, it is a virtue, not a vice."[82] Men in Queensland, Australia in the late-nineteenth and early twentieth century went to considerable length to practice bestiality.[83] This was also a common sexual practice for young men in rural Brazil.[84] In both Native American and Nordic Sami cultures, there are numerous examples of women assuming cross-gender roles.[85] From all these examples, it is clear that the history of human sexuality is as diverse as the world itself. It is important, therefore, not to see either *wakashudō* or the Floating World of Tokugawa Japan as a particular aberration in the human experience.

---

[77] Leila J. Rupp, *Sapphistries: A Global History of Love Between Women* (New York: New York Press, 2009), 4, 26-27, 32-33, 47, 51-52, 55-56, 109, 115, 205; James Neill, *The Origins and Role of Same-Sex Relations in Human Societies* (Jefferson, North Carolina: McFarland and Company, 2009), 53, 261-262; and Crawford, *European Sexualities, 1400-1800*, 206. Tribes with co-wives in lesbian relationships included the Azande of Sudan, Nupe of Nigeria, Nyakyusa of Tanzania, and Mongo of the Congo. The Zande people feared lesbian relationships.

[78] Joyce Tyldesley, "Marriage and Motherhood in Ancient Egypt." *History Today* 44, no. 4 (04, 1994): 20, ProQuest Central.

[79] Vatsyayana Mallanaga, *Kamasutra*, Wendy Doniger and Sudhir Kakar (trans.) (New York: Oxford University Press, 2002), 104-130.

[80] Mary Weismantel, "Moche Sex Pots: Reproduction and Temporality in Ancient South America." *American Anthropologist* 106.3 (2004): 495-505, ProQuest Central.

[81] Ta'unga quoted in R. G. and Marjorie Crocombe, *The Works of Ta'unga: Records of a Polynesian Traveller in the South Seas, 1833-1896* (Canberra, Australia: Australian National University Press, 1968), 103. For more detail on customs in the South Pacific, see Chapter T.

[82] Marquis de Sade, "Philosophy in the Bedroom," *The Marquis de Sade: Three Complete Novels: Justine, Philosophy of the Bedroom,* Eugénie de Franval and other Writings, Richard Seaver and Austryn Wainhouse (trans.) (New York: Grove Press, 1966 [1981, twelfth printing]), 254.

[83] Anne-Maree Collins, "Women or Beast? Bestiality in Queensland, 1870-1949," *Hecate* 17.1 (1991): 36, ProQuest Central.

[84] Giberto Freyre, *The Masters and the Slaves: A Study in the Development of Brazilian Civilization*, Samuel Putnam (trans.) (New York: Alfred A. Knopf, 1946), 154-155.

[85] Rupp, *Sapphistries*, 82-85.

~

Just as the Tokugawan shoguns sought to control Japan's politics and social life, they also sought to influence Japan's Buddhist monasteries. In 1627, Iemitsu began enforcing the decrees originally issued by his grandfather a dozen years earlier. These regulations differed by sect, but they generally clarified the organizational structure of and relationship between Buddhist temples, established clear standards for clerical qualifications, and redefined the appointment process for awarding promotions within the clergy.[86] They also developed new regulations for the daily life of monks.[87] Furthermore, the general populace had to register with its local Buddhist temple, and these temples had to certify that no Christians lived within their jurisdictions.[88] These regulations did not trouble Go-Mizunoo, but the new regulations surrounding the appointments of Buddhist monks to the highest rank—those with the right to wear the purple robe—most certainly did. As far as he was concerned, these appointments were the emperor's to make and for a dozen years he simply ignored the *bakufu*'s regulations and continued to make purple robe promotions without Tokugawa approval. Iemitsu and his administration were determined to end this autonomy; in 1627, the shogun stripped 150 clerics from different sects of their robes and titles since the *bakufu* had not confirmed their appointments. This revocation not only affected the ability of these men to attract followers since they had lost the prestige of wearing the purple robe, but also prevented them from earning higher fees for funeral rites. In addition, the new fees monks would pay as part of the promotion process would be sent to Edo instead of to the imperial palace.[89] This was all part of the Tokugawa goal of redirecting power away from Kyoto.

Go-Mizunoo was indignant about this Tokugawa attack on a long-standing imperial privilege. He urged his purple robe appointees to write officials in Edo to object to the shogun's actions and to affirm the emperor's right to make the appointments as a Buddhist tradition.[90] One Rinzai Zen monk, Takuan Sōhō, led the criticism, arguing that the *bakufu*'s regulations were arbitrary and superficial: the notion that a monk's training wasn't complete until he had answered 1,700 koans— such as "what sound does one hand clapping make?"—made no sense to Takuan since he believed effectively solving even a single conundrum might merit promotion.[91] The *bakufu* viewed such objections as inappropriate sophistry. In 1629, they responded to the complaints by exiling the leading critics to remote northern provinces for three years.[92] In addition, monks from many sects were stripped of their purple robe titles. Furious and deeply insulted, Go-Mizunoo abruptly abdicated the throne, writing:

---

[86] Duncan Williams, "The Purple Robe Incident and the Formation of the Early Modern Soto Zen Institution," *Japanese Journal of Religious Studies*, 36, no. 1 (Winter, 2009), 27-43, ProQuest Central.

[87] Ooms, *Tokugawa Ideology*, 172.

[88] Jurgis Elisonas , "Christianity and the Daimyo," *The Cambridge History of Japan*, Volume 4, John Whitney Hall (ed.) (New York: Cambridge University Press, 1991), 371.

[89] Williams, "The Purple Robe Incident and the Formation of the Early Modern Soto Zen Institution."

[90] Lillehoj, *Art and Palace Politics in Early Modern Japan 1580s-1680s*, 197.

[91] Bitō Masahide, "Thought and Religion: 1550-1700," *The Cambridge History of Japan*, Volume 4, John Whitney Hall (ed.), Kate Wildman Nakai (trans.) (New York: Cambridge University Press, 1991), 413-414.

[92] With a child on the throne, the *bakufu* were able to assert control over the awarding of purple roles, but they were less successful in dominating Buddhist institutions. Instead, some regulations were ignored and a dialog developed between the monasteries and the government. See Williams, "The Purple Robe Incident and the Formation of the Early Modern Sōtō Institution."

O Land of Reed Plains,
If you must grow rank and wild
Then grow wild at will,
For this world is grown a wilderness,
In which the True Path can no longer be seen.[93]

Go-Mizunoo named his oldest surviving child, seven-year old Meishō, as his successor. This action caught both the shogun and the imperial court by surprise since Meishō, the daughter of Tōfukumon'in, would be the first empress to reign in 865 years.[94] Go-Mizunoo then sought to use his daughter's installation as an affirmation of imperial tradition by reviving a version of the accession ceremony that hadn't been used since the fourteenth century. He believed it was a more somber and dignified rite, and he planned the whole installation carefully, just as in 1623, when he revived the Rite of the Second Seven Days of the New Year. This was Go-Mizunoo's way of recreating imperial prestige as it once was.[95]   Despite this detailed expression of tradition, his frustration with the shogun and the *bakufu* remained pronounced, as Go-Mizunoo clearly expressed in his New Year's poem for 1630. While tradition urged optimism for the occasion, Go-Mizunoo's tone is anything but:

Unexpectedly, this spring,
even I have faced reproach—
as the ancient saying goes,
"the longer a man lives,
the greater the shame he faces."[96]

~

When Go-Mizunoo abdicated the throne in 1629, he was thirty-three years old. His wife Tōfukumon'in was twenty-two. Each had a lifetime ahead of them, and each found fulfillment through the middle decades of the seventeenth century by pursuing a devotion to the arts, scholarship, and faith. Go-Mizunoo's goal was to fight what he described as "this degenerate age," when "our words have no effect," unlike antiquity when "imperial edicts commanded obedience in

[93] Go-Mizunoo quoted in George Sansom, *A History of Japan, 1615-1867* (Stanford, California: Stanford University Press, 1963), 27.
[94] Despite the surprise, there was also some delight because Go-Mizunoo's resignation also meant that Ieyasu's great-granddaughter would sit on the imperial throne. In Japanese history, it was rare for the descendants of a military family to hold this position. Elizabeth Lillehoj, "From Kyoto to Edo and Back: Karasumaru Mitsuhiro as a Seventeen-Century Diplomatic and Cultural Emissary," *Kyoto Visual Culture in the Early Edo and Meiji Periods*, 46.
[95] Lillehoj, *Art and Palace Politics in Early Modern Japan 1580s-1680s*, 202.
[96] Go-Mizunoo quoted in Lillehoj, *Art and Palace Politics in Early Modern Japan 1580s-1680s*, 198.

all matters."[97] By promoting culture over politics, Go-Mizunoo sought to seize the leadership role in an area of vital importance to the Japanese people and to revitalize the nation.

This orientation can be seen in many different forms, first and foremost with calligraphy. Calligraphy's importance in Japanese culture is exceptional because the script possesses a spiritual, artistic sensibility.[98] Go-Mizunoo's began his calligraphic studies at an early age, under the guidance of a Tendai abbot known for his calligraphic mastery. He later learned a different method from a Shingon monk. Eventually, Go-Mizunoo developed his own distinctive calligraphic style with crisp, slender characters and a decidedly sober mood.[99] This style caught the attention of senior Tendai Buddhist officials, who in 1643 allowed Go-Mizunoo to examine the *Jubokushō*, a highly influential fourteenth-century treatise on calligraphy that promoted individual spiritual cultivation and Buddhist enlightenment by its practitioners.[100] Even Iemitsu admired Go-Mizunoo's work. The shogun twice asked the former emperor to write part of the text scroll trumpeting Ieyasu's accomplishments as the unifier of Japan and founder of Tokugawa Japan. Iemitsu believed that Go-Mizunoo's hand would increase the prestige of the documents, which shows the extent to which the imperial legacy and authenticity mattered to the shogun and his administration even after Go-Mizunoo's abdication.[101] The first request came in 1633, which was the twenty-first anniversary of Ieyasu's death. Go-Mizunoo completed most of his work in time for the anniversary and the arrival of a Korean delegation sent to reestablish diplomatic relations. In 1639, Iemitsu made a second request, which Go-Mizunoo resisted, complaining of muscle pains. The shogun's representative in Kyoto insisted that the work be completed by the twenty-fifth anniversary of Ieyasu's death in 1640, and the former emperor complied, completing the calligraphy for the final two chapters of the scrolls. The first presented a rather optimistic version of the Tokugawa lineage, while the second commemorated Iemitsu's sighting of a pair of auspicious, white-necked cranes near the shrine for Ieyasu in Edo Castle.[102] It can't have been a very enjoyable endeavor. Fortunately, there were other forms of expression. Go-Mizunoo also promoted poetry, becoming a champion of preserving aristocratic verse and an expert in turning prose texts into verse forms. One of his surviving poems illustrates why he thought this work was so important and the value of tradition to him:

> May it endure forever,
> passed down faithfully
> from the age of the gods
> to the world of men—
> the way of Japanese poetry.[103]

[97] Go-Mizunoo quoted in Bob Tadashi Wakabayashi, "In Name Only: Imperial Sovereignty in Early Modern Japan." *Journal of Japanese Studies*, vol.17, no. 1 (Winter, 1991), 25-57, EBSCOhost.

[98] Louise Boudonnat and Harumi Kushizaki, *Traces of the Brush: The Art of Japanese Calligraphy* (San Francisco, California: Chronicle Books, 2003), 44.

[99] Lillehoj, *Art and Palace Politics in Early Modern Japan 1580s-1680s*, 116-117.

[100] Gary DeCoker, "Secret Teachings in Medieval Calligraphy: Jubokushō and Saiyōshō." *Monumenta Nipponica*, vol. 43, no. 2 (Summer, 1988), 197-228, EBSCOhost.

[101] Lillehoj, *Art and Palace Politics in Early Modern Japan 1580s-1680s*, 205.

[102] Lee Bruschke-Johnson, "Insincere Blessings? Court-Bakufu Relations and the Creation of *Engi* Scrolls in Honour of Tokugawa Ieyasu," in *Uncharted Waters: Intellectual Life in the Edo Period: Essays in Honour of W.J. Boot*, Anna Beerens, Mark Teeuwen, and W. J. Boot (eds.) (Leiden, Netherlands: Brill, 2012), 162-170, EBSCOebooks.

[103] Go-Mizunoo quoted in Lillehoj, *Art and Palace Politics in Early Modern Japan 1580s-1680s*, 114-115.

Go-Mizunoo nourished other cultural arts as well. He encouraged flower arranging and the tea ceremony. He promoted the publication of ancient texts, held poetry competitions, sponsored salons for the comparatively free exchange of ideas, and commissioned many works of art. Most significantly, he did this while allowing for direct and unprecedented social connections between the court and a wide array of Kyoto's artisans and merchants.[104] Although he still possessed moral power, many of the social barriers that separated the emperor no longer applied. Go-Mizunoo understood that by ignoring the traditional rules of the established social hierarchy, he created the opportunity to build a broader, more lasting cultural legacy. This would give a renewed importance to the imperial court. His associations and interactions challenged the traditional view that the merchant class lacked any virtue.[105] Reconstituting Kyoto's relationships for artistic purposes was especially important because officials in Edo wanted art to reflect its own definition of good government, conduct, and virtue.[106]

Go-Mizunoo similarly influenced Japanese architecture and landscape design. In 1647, the imperial couple went on an outing to Shugakuin in the Mt. Hiei foothills northeast of the imperial palace. Ostensibly their purpose was to look for mushrooms, but they actually went to find a site for a retirement residence. Their final choice was idyllic, with its clear water, and sweeping views of valleys, mountains, and the city of Kyoto. Designed by Go-Mizunoo, the retreat's construction began in 1650 with funds from Tōfukumon'in's family, and nine years later the couple held a party to show off their new retreat and to thank those who had been involved in the project.[107] Go-Mizunoo's plan included the construction of villas on two levels and the damming of a creek to create an ornamental lake large enough for boating at the higher elevation. The lake's three islands, which were hilltops before the flooding, inspired the name "Pond of the Bathing Dragon."[108] The water reflected the moods in different hours of the day and seasons of the year,[109] while the carefully landscaped terrain fused landscaped trees and bushes in the foreground with the surrounding wild hills to give the illusion of a never-ending garden. The ambulatory paths, constructed with maze-like hedges, further emphasized this effect.[110] It was a monument to rustic simplicity and to Go-Mizunoo's appreciation of nature.[111] It must have been a welcomed change in scenery and space from the confines of the imperial palace with its surrounding fifteen-foot high walls, warren of individual enclosures and small living quarters of no more than 120 square feet.[112] Indeed, retirement and abdication must have been liberating for Go-Mizunoo, who, while continuing to

[104] Lillehoj, *Art and Palace Politics in Early Modern Japan 1580s-1680s*, 167-168.
[105] Ryan Lagrill, "The Evolution of Merchant Moral Thought in Tokugawa Japan," *The Journal of Philosophical Economics*, 5.2 (Spring, 2012), 109-122, ProQuest Central.
[106] Totman, *Early Modern Japan*, 189.
[107] Lillehoj, *Art and Palace Politics in Early Modern Japan 1580s-1680s*, 214, 217.
[108] Bruce A. Coats, "Shugakuin Detached Palace," Kyoto §IV, 11, (vol. 18), *Dictionary of Art*, Jane Turner (ed.) (New York: Oxford University Press, 1996), 566-567. In 1682, after Go-Mizunoo's death, a middle level was added as part of the addition of a Buddhist monastery to the site.
[109] Elizabeth Bibb, *In the Japanese Garden* (Washington, DC: Starwood Publishing, 1991), 65.
[110] Bruce A. Coats, "Kyoto §IV: Buildings and Gardens, Part 11: Shugakuin Detached Palace," *Dictionary of Art*, Vol. 18, Jane Turner (ed.) (New York: Oxford University Press, 1996), 566-567. This also gave the impression that Go-Mizunoo's power was greater than it actually was. See Louise Wickham, *Gardens in History: A Political Perspective* (Havertown, Pennsylvania: Windgather Press, 2012), 225, EBSCOebooks.
[111] Cecilia Segawa Seigle, "Shinanomiya Tsuneko: Portrait of a Court Lady," *The Human Tradition in Modern Japan*, Anne Walthall (ed.) (Wilmington, Delaware: SR Books, 2004), 9, 20.
[112] Webb, *The Japanese Imperial Institution in the Tokugawa Period*, 66-67.

influence court politics from afar, was no longer burdened with the stultifying atmosphere of daily court life or the responsibility of leading over 180 ceremonies a year.[113]   He also had far more personal freedom, which allowed him to enjoy the company of people in informal settings, to visit family members far more frequently, and to shower his guests with gifts.[114] Go-Mizunoo had the freedom to pursue what mattered to him most, including faith.

When the shogun Iemitsu died in April 1651, Go-Mizunoo seized the opportunity to complete a long-standing wish: he became a Buddhist monk.[115] Taking his tonsure and announcing his ordination just two weeks after Iemitsu's death was a decidedly improper move since the period of mourning had just begun, but Go-Mizunoo probably used this timing as a calculated protest of Tokugawa policies.[116] By taking the religious name Enjō Dōkaku Hōō and by assuming the title of Dharma Emperor, Go-Mizunoo became Japan's chief Buddhist representative in affairs of state and enhanced his already-important religious stature.[117] He chose to join the Rinzai sect with its focus on solving koans in order to attain enlightenment, but he did not retreat to a monastery. Instead he continued to live in his retirement palace. Following Zen tradition, Go-Mizunoo worked with a series of masters, the most important of whom was Ryōkei Shōsen. The two men first met in 1636, and Ryōkei instructed Go-Mizunoo several times through the course of the 1640s. In 1651, the former emperor granted Ryōkei a purple robe and appointed him as abbot of an important Rinzai temple, Myōshin-ji. This increased their association[118] and in the 1660s, Ryōkei formally became Go-Mizunoo's Zen master. By the end of the decade, he certified that the former emperor had resolved a Rinzai mystery, achieved enlightenment and become a *bodhisattva*. According to the Obaku tradition, Ryōkei even transferred his Dharma lineage or sacred genealogy to Go-Mizunoo so that Ryōkei's teachings might continue.[119]

Go-Mizunoo died in 1680, having lived for eight and half decades. While he cared about his own reputation and the emperor's institutional status vis-à-vis that of the shoguns, most of his life was devoted to a deepening appreciation for aesthetics rather than politics. In embracing the world of calligraphy, painting, architecture, and literature, and in committing himself to the pursuit of spiritual enlightenment, Go-Mizunoo came to embody those things which make Japanese culture so distinctive. His life was about restrained and refined beauty, or *shibui* in Japanese; it was about finding harmonious tranquility or *wabi*, in the face of raw domination. And it was about aging gracefully or *sabi*. In other words, Go-Mizunoo's last fifty years embraced the essential triad of

---

[113] Webb, *The Japanese Imperial Institution in the Tokugawa Period*, 83, 116. Go-Mizunoo's involvement with the court included appointing not just Meishō as his successor in 1629, but also his sons Go-Kōmyō, Go-Sai, and Reigen as emperors in 1643, 1654, and 1663, respectively.

[114] Cecilia Segawa Seigle, "Shinanomiya Tsuneko: Portrait of a Court Lady," *The Human Tradition in Modern Japan*, Anne Walthall (ed.) (Wilmington, Delaware: SR Books, 2004), 8.

[115] One measure of this faith can be seen in the way a renowned Ōbaku Zen monk named Kōsen Shōton (1633-1695) noted how Go-Mizunoo "announced an edict, which commanded ten monks to transcribe the Lotus Sutra in the proper manner, to aid the [spirit of the] previous emperor in his journey towards the Buddhist paradise in the afterlife." Kōsen Shōton quoted in Patricia Jane Graham, *Faith and Power in Japanese Buddhist Art, 1600–2005* (Honolulu, Hawai'i: University of Hawai'i Press, 2007), 52, EBSCOebooks.

[116] Helen J. Baroni, *Obaku Zen: The Emergence of the Third Sect of Zen in Tokugawa Japan* (Honolulu, Hawai'i: University of Hawai'i Press, 2000), 173.

[117] Lillehoj, *Art and Palace Politics in Early Modern Japan 1580s-1680s*, 218.

[118] Baroni, *Obaku Zen*, 173. Presumably, these honors were given with the *bakufu*'s approval, but the text does not specifically indicate this.

[119] Baroni, *Obaku Zen*, 176-178. On his deathbed, Go-Mizunoo transferred this Dharma lineage to another monk to preserve Ryōkei's teachings, but his choice created considerable controversy and split the sect.

Japanese aesthetics.[120]   Little wonder his surviving children revered him, and, following the Buddhist tradition, created relics to venerate in his memory.[121]

---

[120] Boyé Lafayette De Mente, *The Japanese Have a Word for It: The Complete Guide to Japanese Thought and Culture* (Lincolnwood, Illinois: Passport Books, 1997), 308-309.

[121] These relics included a shrine made by Go-Mizunoo's eldest daughter featuring inscriptions honoring the Buddha made from Go-Mizunoo's fingernails. Several tooth relics and a clay statue with Go-Mizunoo's hair attached also survives. Go-Mizuno seems to have facilitated this by collecting some of these materials himself. See Patricia Fister, "Creating Devotional Art with Body Fragments: the Buddhist Nun Bunchi and Her Father Emperor Gomizuno-o," *Japanese Journal of Religious Studies*, 27, 3/4 (Fall, 2000), 213-238, EBSCOhost.

H

Gijsbert Heeck

1619-1669

As a man approaching his thirtieth birthday, Gijsbert Heeck intended to savor the comfortable life of an experienced seventeenth-century surgeon living in Europe's most prosperous country, the Dutch Republic. He had survived not one but two voyages to the Spice Islands of Southeast Asia; his new medical practice was growing; he was married to an Amsterdam woman named Susanna, whom he held most dear; and he adored his two children, a boy named Joost and a girl named

Jannetien. Everything indicated that Heeck would enjoy a contented, safe life in the place of his birth, the village of Bunschoten in the district of Utrecht.

But it was not to be. Heeck's daughter died as a six-month-old in 1648 and Susanna followed two years later. Heeck remarried, but his second wife died in 1654, a year after giving birth to another son, Pieter.[1] As a widower with two young children, Heeck, who had once "fully resolved to leave the high seas (and its inherent dangers) behind me for good," changed his mind and reenlisted for a third three-year stint as a surgeon with the Dutch East India Company or VOC.[2] As part of his preparations for the expedition, Heeck rented out his house, left his younger son Pieter with

[1] Oth Dekkers, *Onder dokters handen: Drie eeuwen artsen in Bunschoten Spakenburg eemdijk* (Bunschoten: Historische Vereniging 'Bunscote,' 1986), 9-11. Heeck's name is also spelled Heecq in some sources.
[2] Gijsbert Heeck, *A Traveler in Siam in the Year 1655: Extracts for the Journal of Gijsbert Heeck*, Barend Jan Terwiel (trans.) (Bangkok, Thailand: Silkworm Books, 2008), 25. The departure information also comes from this source. VOC is the Dutch acronym for the *Vereenigde Oost-Indische Compagnie*.

his second wife's family, and obtained permission for Joost (now nine years old) to accompany him on the voyage. Father and son then visited seven cities and towns, saying goodbye to friends, family, and associates. Their final stop before traveling by barge to the province of Zeeland for embarkation in November 1654 was Amsterdam.

Mid-seventeenth-century Amsterdam was a city of canals and markets, ambition and sin, immigrants and profit, affluence and tolerance. Built on land reclaimed from the sea, Amsterdam was the hub of a complex network of Dutch trade, part of which was exotic and intercontinental and much of which was European and rather routine. The great merchant ships from Java, Sri Lanka, the Caribbean, and North America anchored off shore, their cargo loaded and unloaded by crews rowing skiffs and barges, while smaller ships sailed into the center of town on the Damrak canal to be packed and unpacked dockside. There were over 700 sea-going vessels flying the Dutch colors and over 400 distinct goods—from prized Chinese porcelain and everyday salted herring—available in the city of 150,000.[3] Complained René Descartes, "Everyone is so preoccupied by his own profit that I could live here for all my life without ever being noticed by anyone."[4]

Much of this atmosphere was captured in Johannes Lingelbach's 1656 painting, "Dam Square with the New Town Hall Under Construction."[5] Under the imposing façades of the Nieuwe Kerk, the Weigh House, and the rising Town Hall, the energy of the city's commercial activity is palpable. Everyone seems to be negotiating with someone for something. The square is full of people coming and going, hustling and bustling, carrying trunks, pushing barrels, leading horses, and directing porters, who are identified by their red, white and blue caps. Burghers from the Stock Exchange, dressed in black with white lace collars, bargain after hours in the late afternoon light, while Ottoman Turks in long robes seek directions from a Dutch passer-by. Monkeys draw a crowd's attention under a blue parasol. Women from the countryside, sporting clean, white aprons, hawk

---

[3] Geert Mak, *Amsterdam* (Cambridge, Massachusetts: Harvard University Press, 2000), 99, 102, 120.
[4] René Descartes quoted in Mak, *Amsterdam*, 100.
[5] Detailed information about this recently restored painting was obtained through personal correspondence with Dr. Judith van Gent of the Amsterdam Museum, August 19, 2013.

their garden vegetables, fresh fish, and cakes. A man sells a peacock to an owner of a country estate, men deeply bow in greeting, and couples stroll through the square parading the latest fashions. One man with a purposeful stride wears an embroidered red cape as dogs eagerly search for food or play with children in various parts of the square. The depiction of a mustached Spaniard in the square illustrates how Amsterdam's reputation for open-mindedness allowed bitter former enemies to thrive in the cosmopolitan metropolis.[6] The scene celebrates Amsterdam's importance and its affluence, but which also hints at the city's problems: three men read a notice of the latest tally of the plague ("896 dead"); a woman cries out as if robbed; a boy, dressed in his orphanage's red and black uniform, walks alone through the crowded square; a poor fisherman carries his long poles and empty bag over his shoulder; and a woman in black pleads with two men, her arms outstretched in helplessness. This is the atmosphere Heeck and his son would have experienced as they made their way to Zeeland for their departure aboard the *Vereenigde Provintien* in November 1654. A wondrous, frightening world awaited.

That ship was the property of Dutch East India Company, which was founded in 1602 as a joint stock trading company with a twenty-one-year monopoly on all Dutch trade to and from Asia. The VOC also had the power to negotiate treaties with Asian rulers, build fortifications, and employ troops. As such, it was a private corporation designed to generate profits for its investors, and it was also an extension of the Dutch state. It was both an economic entity and a political one. The company was governed by a board of directors, the *Heeren XVII*, which was composed of eight representatives from the chief port of Amsterdam, four from Zeeland, and one each from the ports of Delft, Enkhuizen, Hoorn, and Rotterdam; there was also one rotating member. As with the national government, this federalist structure allowed each port autonomy and balanced Amsterdam's natural dominance, while distributing the economic risk and promoting common interests. It proved to be a very successful formula: seventeenth-century VOC profits were high with individual stockholders regularly securing profits of 10% to 20% a year. Some individual ships brought 1000% return on the company's investment for the voyage.[7] One reason for this success was that the company held frugality in high esteem as a way to maximize its profits at every turn. It worked feverishly to establish monopolies on the clove, nutmeg, mace, and cinnamon trade; it brutally suppressed Indonesians who refused to trade on terms the Dutch found agreeable; it provided stingy salaries and carefully regulated rations to its sailors and soldiers; it rewarded captains who completed their journeys in the shortest time; and it strove to maintain peaceful relations with local governments in order to boost trade. As the *Heeren XVII*'s 1650 instructions said, "Special attention must be paid to driving a peaceful trade throughout all Asia, which keeps the cooking going in the kitchens of the fatherland."[8]

The VOC's policies were an expression of the economic practice of mercantilism.* According to this economic theory, there is a finite amount of wealth in the world and the acquisition of wealth is a zero-sum equation. Governments should, therefore, try to control markets through a system of careful regulations. Doing so will not just maximize profits for the regulating nation, but also

---

[6] Protestants in the Low Countries fought an eighty-year war of independence against Catholic Spain between 1568 and 1648. The first phase (1566-1609) is known as the Dutch Revolt.* After a twelve-year truce, war resumed as part of the Thirty Years' War.* In 1648, the Peace of Münster (which was part of the Treaty of Westphalia) Spain recognized the Dutch Republic as a sovereign nation; most of what is today Belgium remained Catholic and in Spanish control.

[7] Mike Dash, *Batavia's Graveyard* (New York: Three Rivers Press, 2002), 63-64.

[8] "*Punten en artikelen in form van Generale Instructie,*" April 26, 1650, quoted in C. R. Boxer, *The Dutch Seaborne Empire* (New York: Penguin Books, 1973), 107.

take away profits from other countries. In the sixteenth century, Afonso de Albuquerque had tried to establish such a system by force in order to control the spice trade, but in the last quarter of that century, Portugal's established reliance on the merchants, financiers, and ships from the Low Countries to distribute Asian goods to the rest of Europe broke down. When Spain's Philip II became the king of Portugal in 1581 and subsequently banned the Dutch from trading in Lisbon as a result of the Dutch Revolt,* the Dutch began sailing to Asia on their own. The creation of the VOC was seen as the most lucrative and effective method to replace the Portuguese as Europe's largest Asian traders.[9]

The three-masted *Vereenigde Provintien* was a huge ship for the seventeenth century, one of the largest in the VOC fleet. At 1,100 metric tons, it was almost three times the size of the ship Afonso de Albuquerque lost off the coast of Malacca a hundred and fifty years earlier. Armed with more than thirty guns, decorated with an elaborately-carved stern, and trimmed with square-rigged sails, the East Indiaman was designed to both impress and frighten. It looked and maneuvered like a warship. In fact, only thing that distinguished ships like the *Vereenigde Provintien* from ones in the Dutch navy was the number and size of its cannons.[10]

As the *Vereenigde Provintien*'s appointed surgeon, it was Heeck's responsibility to care for the health of the crew and to protect the VOC's investment. This was an exceptional challenge: the ship was crowded with 380 men (and an unrecorded number of women and children), nine months of provisions, chests of bullion, armaments, and bricks for construction of buildings in Batavia, the capital of Dutch Asia. The crew's quarters below deck had little ventilation or light; were perpetually infested with fleas, lice, bedbugs, rats, and cockroaches; and were routinely contaminated with urine, excrement, and vomit since men frequently became seasick and ignored the regulations to use the latrine.[11] Typhus, malaria, scurvy, beriberi, and dysentery were all common as a result of the unsanitary conditions, the unvaried diet, and the incessant infestations. Even divergent conditions like hypothermia and heat stroke were possibilities, given the drastic changes in climate over the course of a single voyage, from the frigid North Sea to the stifling Tropics. This was a lot to manage, which is why from the company's beginning the VOC staffed its ships with doctors. The only things these VOC doctors would not treat were sexually transmitted diseases and injuries caused by fighting between employees.[12] In fact, the VOC was so committed to the health of its crews that even employees who returned home ill had their medical care paid for by the company. Employees who lost an eye or a limb as a result of their employment were entitled to compensation.[13]

What Heeck and other ship's surgeons had to combat this array of conditions was a medicine chest full of herbs, oils, ointments, powders, vinegars, and acids; a collection of saws, lances, cups,

---

[9] For more information on the transition in the late sixteenth and early seventeenth centuries, see Martha Howell, "Into the East: European Merchants in Asian Markets During the Early Modern Period," *Across the Ocean: Nine Essays on Indo-Mediterranean Trade*, Marco Maiuro and Federico De Romanis (eds.) (Leiden: Brill, 2015), 155-157, EBSCOhost. Although the Dutch came to dominate the Asian markets, the Portuguese won the struggle against the Dutch in Brazil and held their own in Africa. See Stuart B. Schwartz, "The Economy of the Portuguese Empire," *Portuguese Oceanic Expansion, 1400-1800*, Francisco Bethencourt and Diogo Ramada Curto (eds.) (New York: Cambridge University Press, 2007), 33.

[10] J.R. Bruijn, F.S. Gaastra and I. Schöffer, *Dutch-Atlantic Shipping in the 17th and 18th Centuries*, Volume 1 (The Hague, Netherlands: Martinus Nijhoff, 1987), 38.

[11] Boxer, *The Dutch Seaborne Empire*, 85-86.

[12] Iris Bruijn, *Ship's Surgeons of the Dutch East India Company: Commerce and the Progress of Medicine in the Eighteenth Century* (Leiden, Netherlands: Leiden University Press, 2009), 59.

[13] Bruijn, *Ships Surgeons of the Dutch East India Company*, 90

and funnels; and a set of medicinal theories which hadn't significantly changed since antiquity.[14] The seventeenth century had no knowledge of bacteria or viruses and an incomplete understanding of organs. In cities and large towns, there was a distinction between surgeons (who set broken bones, treated wounds, and shaved beards) and physicians (who practiced internal medicine and were held in significantly higher esteem), but in village communities and at sea, barber-surgeons were responsible for curing all of the medical issues their neighbors or crew encountered.[15] Men like Heeck sought to restore the proper balance of fluids within the body by bloodletting, cupping, purging, and clystering. They believed that removing polluted fluids from the body would cure their patients. Ship surgeons created plasters from ingredients in their medicine chests, performed amputations, set fractures, trepanned skulls, and ordered changes in diet. They also used opium as a painkiller and as a cure for dysentery.[16] Given the inherent dangers of the long voyage and the state of medical knowledge, it is striking that between 1650 and 1660, only 4.2% of the crews died on the voyage between the Dutch Republic and the Cape of Good Hope, and only 7.6% died between Europe and Asia.[17] Casualty rates for the return voyages to Europe were significantly lower than this as a result of a smaller number of returning passengers, shorter trip durations, and adapted immune systems.[18]

The *Vereenigde Provintien* arrived at the new Dutch settlement at Table Bay, near the Cape of Good Hope, in early April 1655, after eighteen weeks at sea. The ship had stopped for a week at the Cape Verde Islands to obtain fresh water, but the long subsequent journey left the crew in dire circumstances and great misery, according to Heeck's journal.[19] Once this was reported to Jan Van Riebeeck, the founder of the Dutch colony in South Africa, he had "cabbage and other earth and garden fruits" sent aboard the *Vereenigde Provintien* and the other five ships in the harbor. He also decided to "supply them with some more every day for the proper refreshment of the crews as long as they are lying here."[20] This certainly helped the conditions on board the six ships. It also illustrated why the settlement at the Cape had been established in 1652: it was to be a supply depot for the VOC. As Van Riebeeck wrote, the colony's gardens "will always have to be cultivated zealously so as to enable us properly to accommodate the ships with adequate refreshments, now that they are compelled to call here."[21] Heeck, however, was not completely mollified. In his entry of April 3, he criticized the *Heeren XVII* for placing such a premium on speed that ships could not

[14] The Roman physician Galen applied the Hippocratic idea that the body possessed four fluids (blood, yellow bile, black bile, and phlegm) to the concept that people also possessed four temperaments (sanguine/optimistic, melancholic/ depressed, choleric/easily angered and phlegmatic/calm.) Galenic medicine sought to maintain the proper balance in the fluids and temperaments, and it still formed the foundation of medicine in the mid-seventeenth century.

[15] Bruijn, *Ships Surgeons of the Dutch East India Company*, 17, 29, 35.

[16] Hans Derks, *History of the Opium Problem: The Assault on the East, ca. 1600-1950* (Leiden, The Netherlands: Koninklijke Brill NV, 2012), 196.

[17] Bruijn, Gaastra and Schöffer, *Dutch-Atlantic Shipping in the 17th and 18th Centuries*, Volume 1, 163.

[18] Bruijn, *Ships Surgeons of the Dutch East India Company*, 75.

[19] During the voyage, Heeck kept a daily log, but the text of the journal was written upon his return to the Dutch Republic. I am grateful to Dr. Karen Bouwer of the University of San Francisco whose knowledge of Afrikaans allowed her to provide me with approximate translations for key passages of the seventeenth-century Dutch.

[20] Jan Van Riebeeck, *Journal of Jan Van Riebeeck, Volume 1, 1651-1655*, H.B. Thom (ed.) (Cape Town, South Africa: A. A. Balkema, 1952), 304-305.

[21] Riebeeck, *Journal of Jan Van Riebeeck, Volume 1, 1651-1655*, 304.

stop at the island of St. Helena for fresh water before proceeding to the Cape.[22] He understood, as a result of his two previous voyages to the East Indies, how important it was for the crew to have fresh water, fruits, and vegetables throughout the voyage. Like other surgeons, Heeck didn't know that a deficiency in vitamin C caused scurvy, but he did understand from practical experience that men who ate fruits and vegetables stayed healthier. Indeed, Heeck's practical experience contributed to the fact that only four of the 380 men aboard the *Vereenigde Provintien* died on the trip between Europe and southern Africa—75% less than the norm.[23]

The *Vereenigde Provintien* spent twelve days restocking supplies while anchored at Table Bay, and Heeck took full advantage of the opportunity to explore the area since the Dutch settlement had not existed during his previous trips to the East Indies. He was a man of intense curiosity, and like Charles Darwin aboard the *Beagle* 180 years later, this fascination with a new land compelled him to record his impressions, both good and bad. Commenting at length on the flora and fauna, the geology and weather, the indigenous people, and the Dutch settlers, Heeck's entries show him to be much more than a typical village barber. He is a careful, if biased, observer. In his entry of April 4, 1655, for example, Heeck describes the Khoikhoi as the poorest people he has ever seen; he deplores their living in tiny straw huts with rounded tops like Dutch ovens, eating the uncooked innards of animals, and having no knowledge of sowing and reaping crops or even fishing. He pities the Khoikhoi for living like wild beasts and is embarrassed by their "immodest," "ugly" women. But Heeck also notes with some admiration that the men are well built and fast runners; that they refuse to sell any of their cattle for any price; and that they raise good-looking sheep with fat tails, which was a seventeenth-century Dutch delicacy. He is also able to see cultural differences between indigenous peoples, for he comments upon the Khoikhoi practice of celebrating the apogee of the full moon and of using scarification as beauty marks. He notes how the Khoikhoi have a different color skin tone than other Africans he had seen.[24] Another example of Heeck's observational powers and natural curiosity involves his decision on April 11 to climb Table Mountain with a small group of men. After a five-hour ascent through rough and varied vegetation, Heeck looked down upon Fort Hope and the surrounding gardens, noting how small and fragile it seemed against the vastness of the sea and the emptiness of the land. It was a "horrifying" sight downwards for a man from the flat Lowlands. Heeck and his compatriots didn't make it back to the fort until well after nightfall, at which point they gave God thanks for His protection.[25]

Well-stocked with cabbages, radishes, carrots, fish, firewood, and water from the Cape, the *Vereenigde Provintien* set sail on April 15 for Batavia on the island of Java. Her route was directly across the Indian Ocean, rather than following the coastline as the Portuguese had done. This was because captain Henrik Brouwer found in 1616 that by heading directly east and then turning north toward the Indonesian archipelago, VOC ships could save thousands of miles and halve the travel time. Since less time at sea meant lower casualty rates and increased profits for the VOC, the choice

---

[22] Gijsbert Heecq, *De derde voyagie van Gijsbert Heecq naar Oost Indijen*, L'Honoré Naber, S. P. (ed.) (Den Haag : Vereniging van Marine-officieren ; Den Helder : N.V. Drukkeru Voorheen C. De Boer, 1911), 30.

[23] In addition to these four, three men also died aboard the *Vereenigde Provintien* while it was still in port in Zeeland. This is why VOC records list the number of casualties for the trip to the Cape seven deaths. Van Riebeeck began his career with VOC as an assistant surgeon, so he also understood the connection at sea between diet and health.

[24] Heecq, *De derde voyagie van Gijsbert Heecq naar Oost Indijen*, 32-34.

[25] Gijsbert Heeck quoted in *Cape Good Hope 1652-1702: The First Fifty Year of Dutch Colonisation as Seen by Callers* (R. Raven-Hart, trans.), Vol. 1 (Cape Town, South Africa: A. A. Balkema, 1971), 41-42, *Digitale bibliotheek voor de Nederlandse letteren*, accessed August 31, 2019, https://tinyurl.com/y2v8x72m

was logical but risky: with no way to determine longitude accurately in the seventeenth century, ships could underestimate their speed in the strong winds of the Roaring Forties and end up running aground off the unforgiving and unsettled coast of Western Australia.[26]

After two months at sea, the *Vereenigde Provintien* arrived in Batavia (modern Jakarta) on June 19, 1655. Heeck was amazed by what he saw. The town had grown significantly since his last visit in 1643, let alone since his first visit in 1636, when the Dutch community lived behind the walls of a bamboo fort and the population of the whole town and its environs was only 8,000 people.[27] Heeck noticed how the markedly improved stone fortress with four bastions* and defensive moats dominated the harbor, while a new stone-walled channel provided access to the town by small boat. The town was

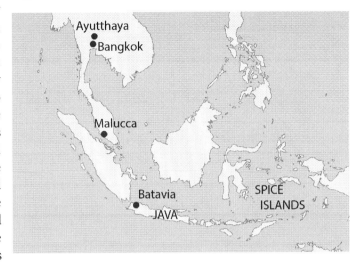

laid out on a grid of interconnected canals. A new stone drawbridge connected the east and west sides of the community, Heeck noted with pleasure, since it made travel within Batavia far more convenient. There were several grand new houses, the city hall had been updated with more doorways to the surrounding gardens, and bamboo dwellings had been outlawed within the town because of the fire danger.[28] For Heeck, Batavia felt like an established community rather than an outpost. For many of its Dutch residents, the town seemed like a bit of Holland transported to the tropics.

By the mid-seventeenth century, Batavia was the focal point of all Dutch trade in Asia. Structured like a modern airline hub route system, all goods the VOC procured came to Batavia before being shipped to Europe. Persian silk traveled east to Batavia before being shipped west to the Dutch Republic, just as Japanese lacquerware was transferred in Batavia before heading to the Amsterdam market. Such a concentration of trade helped create Batavia's distinctive atmosphere, which was both diverse and divided. On the one hand, its residents included Balinese Hindus and Javanese Muslims, Chinese traders and Indian slaves, and German Lutherans and Portuguese Catholics.[29] On the other hand, most VOC officials had very little interest in developing a colony the way Albuquerque did in Goa. Their focus involved simply securing and protecting company profits, instead promoting intermarriage and local self-government as Albuquerque had. Over

---

[26] Watchmaker John Harrison was not awarded the prize for inventing an accurate timepiece to determine longitude accurately until 1773. For details on this invention and the problem of longitude, see Dava Sobel, *Longitude: The True Story of a Lone Genius Who Solved the Greatest Scientific Problem of His Time* (New York: Penguin Books, 1995), 4-10, 106-110.

[27] Ulbe Bosma and Remco Raben, *Being "Dutch" in the Indies: A History of Creolisation and Empire, 1500-1920*, Wendie Shaffer (trans.) (Athens, Ohio: Ohio University Press, 2008), 15.

[28] Heecq, *De derde voyagie van Gijsbert Heecq naar Oost Indijen*, 53-55.

[29] Those with non-Christian beliefs were allowed to practice their religions in temples outside the walls of the city, but Christians who were not members of the Dutch Reformed Church had no such venue. The first Lutheran church was not built in Batavia until 1743, and the first Catholic church was not allowed until 1829.

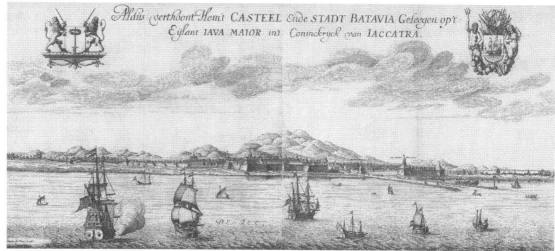

time, the main consequence of this orientation was that the Dutch Batavians created a segregated, rigidly hierarchical society devoted to the accumulation of wealth. At the top of the social pyramid stood the highest-ranking VOC employees and their European-born wives. Below them were VOC employees of lesser rank. Together, these individuals were the most preoccupied with enforcing minute social gradations, from determining who could wear what clothing to who could ride in which vehicle.[30] When in town, those with higher rank were followed by a retinue of slaves to publicize their wealth and status with as much pomp as possible. Below the VOC employees stood the non-VOC employees of European origin, who were known as "free citizens." Most of these individuals were either former-VOC employees who had elected to stay in the Indies once their contracts came due or were descendants of Portuguese immigrants to Asia. They had a rather liminal status, having more standing than Asians but being severely limited as to their employment options and confined to a small part of the town. Many became money-lenders,[31] who financed the illicit trade upon which virtually all VOC employees depended since their official company salaries were often insufficient to cover basic living expenses.[32]

The status of those who were not of European origin was confused since social biases didn't match well with human needs in the multicultural environment. Although an official declared in 1650 that children of mixed marriages invariably inherited the disagreeable characteristics of the mother, leading to "a filthy and debauched life," 41% of the marriages performed in Batavia that same year were between European men and Asian women who had been baptized.[33] By the time Heeck arrived in Batavia for the third time, the earliest children of such marriages were adults and some clarification of their status was necessary. The VOC ruled that mixed-race children possessed the same rights as Dutch citizens, but continued to prohibit Asians from immigrating to the Dutch Republic.[34] The sizable Chinese community in Batavia had its own neighborhood and was governed by its own official, who reported to the Dutch Governor General. Since few Chinese women emigrated to Java in the seventeenth century, many of the Chinese men married Javanese

[30] Boxer, *The Dutch Seaborne Empire*, 236.
[31] Bernard H.M. Vlekke, *Nusantara: A History of the East Indian Archipelago* (Cambridge, Massachusetts: Harvard University Press, 1943), 169, 173.
[32] Boxer, *The Dutch Seaborne Empire*, 225.
[33] Bosma and Raben, *Being "Dutch" in the Indies*, 23, 29, 37.
[34] Vlekke, *Nusantara*, 132.

and other Asian women. At the bottom of the social ladder were the slaves, most of whom in the mid-seventeenth century were Hindus from Bali or India. These slaves could earn money and eventually purchase their freedom, unlike in many slave-owning societies.

On his first day in Batavia, Heeck reported to the hospital in the fortress, submitted his account of the medical issues encountered abroad the *Vereenigde Provintien,* and was given new orders. He could have been stationed in one of four wards of the VOC hospital, assigned to provide medical care on a ship returning to the Dutch Republic, or ordered to join a ship heading for another Asian port. The fortress' head surgeon instructed Heeck to join the crew of *De Walvisch* (The Whale) to replace its recently deceased surgeon.[35] Therefore, on July 3, 1655, Heeck began his illuminating voyage to Siam.[36]

On the morning of September 7, Heeck arrived in Bangkok, which in the seventeenth century was a city "shoddily built on high stilts," full of houses made from bamboo beams, straw mat walls, and palm tree leaf roofs. The surrounding area's bountiful "coconut palms, orange trees, lemons, bananas," and betel nut palms meant that it supported one of the Chao Phraya River's best markets, which was conducted "mainly on large and small boats" and annually produced "a large income for the king from trade duties."[37] Heeck also took note of the city's "idolatrous temples," which he described as being "very elegant in their heathen way and constructed at no little cost." He praised them for being built "purely of stone masonry," possessing "gables on both ends," which are "artfully carved and usually gilded," and roofs decorated with colorful tiles.[38] That afternoon, Heeck went inside one of the Thai temples, which he described in fascinating detail:

> Inside, more than twenty-five statues, all very well executed, were placed on a stone dais or elevation. All were gilded, except for one that was still lacquered pitch black. We guessed it to be new, because it is on such smooth black surfaces that the gilding is laid. The [figures] sat cross-legged as tailors do, which is here generally the common manner of sitting among both the Moors and the heathens. The largest of these figures sat at the rear, flanked by two somewhat smaller ones, although these two were still some six times taller than an ordinary man. In front of them stood a series of gradually smaller [figures], the last one very small. Some of the latter were metal and copper. Facing this group were two man-sized figures [standing] upright with folded hands, looking up toward heaven in the devout manner of priests. Among the many images were some of the feminine shape. Some were [portrayed] sitting with their eyes closed as if sleeping, others half open and others again with completely open eyes. Some looked sad, almost crying, while others were quite merry and happy. Usually the left hand lay on the thigh, the palm turned upwards and the right [hand] straight down on the right thigh near the knee. Some of these had been honored and covered with torn pieces of cloth, dirty and quite dusty. In front of the entrance to this temple stood three low pyramids, and directly behind them eight rather high ones, all carefully made and preciously gilded. They had stairways for climbing up

---

[35] Built in 1632, *De Walvisch* was a one-thousand-ton ship with a proud history, having served as the expedition ship of Jan Van Riebeeck when he established Fort Hope in South Africa in 1652. Being assigned to this ship would not have represented a demotion for Heeck or a disparagement of his ability as a ship's surgeon. For detailed information on VOC ship history, see Jaap van Overbeek, *The VOC Site,* http://www.vocsite.nl/schepen/index.html.

[36] Field Marshal Plaek Phibunsongkhram changed the name of the country from Siam to Thailand in 1939.

[37] Heeck, *A Traveler in Siam in the Year 1655,* 41.

[38] Heeck, *A Traveler in Siam in the Year 1655,* 41.

part of them, but the highest steeples could not be reached. Directly before the entrance stood some wooden lattices where red flowers without scent were hung as a sign of offering. Also, in front of the images [had been placed] some elegant artificial flowers; both the flower and the flowerpots were completed gilded and painted in many colors, with a stone censer adjacent to them for offering incense.[39]

What Heeck saw, of course, was a Buddhist temple with its stupas, symbolic ornamentation, and Buddha figures sitting in the pose of calling the earth to witness. He had no understanding of this religion, but neither did any other Westerner of his era since most Europeans had little desire to appreciate Asian cultures on their own terms until well into the eighteenth century.[40] It is important to note that this Buddhist temple came from a very different tradition than that of Go-Mizunoo's Japan. Instead of being a part of the Mahayana school, the temple Heeck saw belonged to the Theravada school, whose followers believe that Buddha gave us the tools to complete our own journeys to reach Nirvana and enlightenment, but that we must each do so individually. The Buddha is not involved in this process in any way. He does not intervene in our daily lives, and there are no *bodhisattvas*. Theravadins emphasize the purity of Buddhist teachings and believe that those who begin striving towards enlightenment need to become a part of a monastic community to complete their journey. There is, therefore, a distinct separation between monks and members of the laity in Theravadin societies. Today this is the dominant school of Buddhism in Sri Lanka, Burma, Laos, Cambodia, and Thailand.

By September 8, 1655, Heeck had arrived at the Thai capital, Ayutthaya, a walled city of soaring spires, broad canals and lively markets on an island in the middle of the Chao Phraya River, ninety miles upriver from the Gulf of Siam. Just downstream of the island stood the Dutch factory or trading station compound, which was home to some forty employees. It was rather typical of a minor VOC outpost. The main lodge was a two-story, whitewashed brick structure with a double outside staircase leading to a teak dining room and officers' quarters. Below, an airy and spacious warehouse with barred windows comprised the whole first floor. This building was surrounded by small outbuildings which were the living quarters for the surgeon, the cook, carpenters, the blacksmith, and other employees. Other elements of the compound included a horse stable, a garden, animal pens, a kitchen, a prison, and a cemetery. These structures were enclosed by a bamboo fence and a deep moat. The factory's closest neighbors included a similar Portuguese encampment, a tavern run by a French national, and a small village where the concubines of VOC employees lived.[41]

At many of the small factories, VOC men, regardless of their rank or position, sought relationships with Asian women, most of whom were ethnic minorities in Siam such as Mon and Lao peoples.[42] The men were expected to provide a house and financial support for their mistresses. When the employees left Ayutthaya, these vulnerable women demanded that the company provide them with a large severance payment in order to live well and care for any children. Heeck found this arrangement objectionable, primarily because to his mind the VOC men in Ayutthaya did not treat the women with enough respect: "How wrong [they are] is sufficiently clear from their own deeds and words, since they seldom refer to them other than as whore, trollop, slut and the like."[43]

[39] Heeck, *A Traveler in Siam in the Year 1655,* 45-46.
[40] Edward W. Said, *Orientalism* (New York: Vintage Books, 1994), 117, 120.
[41] Heeck, *A Traveler in Siam in the Year 1655,* 54.
[42] Bosma and Raben, *Being "Dutch" in the Indies,* 9-10.
[43] Heeck, *A Traveler in Siam in the Year 1655,* 57.

While Heeck worried about the fate of the children of these relationships, many of the offspring became VOC employees in their own right, frequently serving as important liaisons between the company and various Asian courts and societies as a result of their multilingual skills.[44] Formal marriages and long-term relationships also occurred. In one notable case, a French-born surgeon for the VOC, Daniel Brochebourde, joined King Narai's court in 1672 and married a Thai woman. Two of their sons and one grandson also served the Ayutthaya court as surgeons, meaning that the associations lasted for generations.[45] In another case, a Mon woman named Cao Soet, who was partly raised by the Dutch, had three daughters with a VOC directors, one son with a free Dutch merchant, and a long and public relationship with another director. Thanks to key friendships with a queen and other high-ranking women, Soet had unparalleled access to members of the Ayutthaya court. From this advantage, she applied considerable influence to official Dutch-Thai trade negotiations. She also became the only local merchant with whom the VOC traded in the late 1640s, allowing Soet to manipulate rice, coconut oil, and sappanwood prices to her own advantage.[46]

The most important Thai-Dutch trade centered upon deer and water buffalo hides because these were in high demand in Japan. The Japanese had strong cultural and religious taboos against producing hides themselves but needed them for armor, quivers, shields, helmets, and horse tack.[47] This demand allowed the Dutch to transport 150,000 hides a year to Japan and make an average profit of 132% at the height of the trade.[48] But Japanese demand was only part of the economic equation. By providing the Japanese with hides purchased with silver, the Dutch acquired the money they needed to buy Asian products that were in high demand in Europe. This fit well with the VOC goal of increasing its intra-Asian trade because these voyages had higher profit margins than trips between Asia and Europe.[49] The intra-Asian routes were also popular with VOC employees because they allowed ample opportunity for smuggling by crew members. Far from the watchful eyes of the *Heeren XVII*, ledgers could be faked and merchandise could be "lost" or "stolen." Bribes were seen as a legitimate way to supplement VOC salaries and almost all crew members participated in some type of illegal trading. So omnipresent was the smuggling that ships sometimes found it hard to load the official cargo with so many illicit goods already on board.[50] But even with all the graft, the VOC's stockholders still made solid profits. There was simply that much money to be made.

The Dutch became commercially dominant in the seventeenth century for several reasons, including their establishment of monopolies in key spice markets, their capture of vital Portuguese

---

[44] Bosma and Raben, *Being "Dutch" in the Indies*, 9.

[45] Dhiravat na Pombejra, "Ayutthaya as a Cosmopolitan Society: A Case Study of Daniel Brochebourde and His Descendants," *Court, Company, and Campong: Essays on the VOC Presence in Ayutthaya* (Ayutthaya, Thailand: Ayutthaya Historical Study Center, 1992), 27-28, 34.

[46] Pombejra, "Okya Sombatthiban and the VOC, c. 1648-1656," *Court, Company, and Campong,* 11-12. Cao Soet's name is also sometimes spelled Chao Sut. She was also known as Ososet Pegu.

[47] Louis G. Perez, *Daily Life in Early Modern Japan* (Westport, Connecticut: Greenwood Press, 2002), 213-214.

[48] George Vinal Smith, *The Dutch in Seventeenth Century Thailand: Center for Southeast Asian Studies Special Report, Number 16* ([DeKalb, Illinois]: Northern Illinois University Press, 1977), 79. The Dutch had a monopoly on exporting Thai hides in 1634 and from 1646 to 1653, which helps explain these numbers. See Smith, page 61. For a detailed account of the development of Japanese and Dutch diplomatic and trade relations, see Adam Clulow, *The Company and the Shogun: The Dutch Encounter with Tokugawa Japan* (New York: Columbia University Press, 2014).

[49] Bhawan Ruangsilp, *Dutch East India Company Merchants in the Court of Ayutthaya: Dutch Perceptions of the Thai Kingdom, c. 1604-1765* (Leiden, The Netherlands: Koninklijke Brill NV, 2007), 6.

[50] Boxer, *The Dutch Seaborne Empire*, 228.

territories in Sri Lanka and Malacca,[51] their superiority in naval technology, and, in the case of Japan, their lack of a missionary zeal. Indeed, because the Dutch really only cared about trade, they quickly learned how to adapt to local conditions in essential markets. In Ayutthaya, the Dutch understood that in a monarchy with no established rules for succession and in a court rife with intrigue, it was better to meet each king on his own terms, to adhere to local protocol whenever possible, and to avoid imposing Dutch values outside of the economic sphere.[52] Naturally, there were times of disagreement and diplomatic tension, but the Dutch generally tried to be accommodating in Siam in the 1650s. One illustration of this is the way the VOC contributed to the construction of Thai temples when asked to do so.[53] Similarly, Heeck commented that while he found the Thai practice of women shaving their heads a sign of mourning to be strange, he believed that the Dutch should adhere to the old saying, "When in Rome do as the Romans do."[54]

Heeck was amazed by the "large rambling city" of Ayutthaya, which became the capital of the Thai state in 1350. He approved of its "suitable battlements," "many gates on all sides," and the convenience of its "fine, wide canals," which "traverse the city, receiving their water from the surrounding river." He also appreciated the way each nationality lived "in its own area" and had "the free exercise of religion" with "its own clergy and priests." That it felt like Amsterdam and had the same design as Utrecht helped Heeck to like it even more. As in Bangkok, Heeck took special note of the city's temples and visited several of them, marveling not just at their wealth ("glittering with gold and gemstones like a gilded mountain"), but also with a growing appreciation for their symbolic elements. At one temple Heeck noted, "on every side an awe-inspiring, large man of stone guards the entrance, each with a tiger standing before him, a tiger which it is said, he fought and vanquished." At another, he was intimidated by a Buddha figure, whose "knees seemed like small mountains" and whose "back was so broad it looked like the wall of a lofty church," but whose "mouth, nose, eyes and ears were all matching and so well proportioned that we could see little or no reason to judge it too thick or too thin, too long or too short, too broad or too narrow." For Heeck, this Buddha was "beyond a person's imagination unless he has seen it himself. It truly seems incredible." Such passages affirm the singular importance of Heeck's journal—especially since so many of Thai records of the period did not survive the Burmese invasion and destruction of Ayutthaya in 1767—but it is important to note that Heeck was also a product of his times. He repeatedly criticized the Thais for their "heathenish superstitions," such as trying to protect the royal elephants from a disease by wrapping a rope around the entire city. He admitted that he could not keep himself from "laughing at [the] silliness" of watching the Thais pray with their hands "clasped together and their heads bowed" in the *wai,* the traditional Thai greeting. Similarly, as a devout follower of the Calvinist Dutch Reformed Church, he sometimes unflatteringly compared the ornateness of Thai architecture to that of Roman Catholic "papistry."[55]

After almost a week in Ayutthaya and its environs, Heeck and his medical assistant travelled downstream to rejoin *De Walvisch* near the mouth of the Chao Phraya River. They found it loaded with supplies for Batavia, including rice to supplement the city's food supplies, large timber beams for ship repairs, and coconut oil for lamps. The ship also carried valuables like sappanwood, resins,

[51] For an account of the Dutch seizure of Malacca in 1641, see Dianne Lewis, *Jan Compagnie in the Straits of Malacca* (Athens, Ohio: Ohio Center for International Studies, Ohio University, 1995), 12-28.
[52] Ruangsilp, *Dutch East India Company Merchants in the Court of Ayutthaya,* 10, 221, 224.
[53] Smith, *The Dutch in Seventeenth Century Thailand,* 107.
[54] Heeck, *A Traveler in Siam in the Year 1655,* 43.
[55] Heeck, *A Traveler in Siam in the Year 1655,* 59-65.

and ambergris for re-export to various markets. With the arrival of a strong wind on October 18, Heeck and *De Walvisch* left Thai waters bound for Java.[56]

Heeck's adventures continued in Batavia and on subsequent assignments aboard ships bound for Sri Lanka and India, but because the second volume of his journal has never been found the details of many of his experiences have vanished. He likely began his return to the Dutch Republic with the 1657 Christmas fleet and arrived home in June 1658. As he passed through Amsterdam on his way back to the village of Bunschoten, Heeck would have looked with pride upon the newly-opened town hall, which some said could only be compared in scale and grandeur to St. Peter's Basilica, Spain's El Escorial, and Venice's Palazzo Ducale.[57] He would have learned of the deaths of friends in the plague of 1655, which killed 16,727 people in Amsterdam and 20% of Leiden's population in six months.[58] He also would have heard of the absence of a *stadholder* and of the continuing prosperity of Dutch export industries.[59] And he would have encountered concern over the growing influx of Jews from central and eastern Europe.

~

A leading figure in the early seventeenth century wrote that to be a Jew and live in Amsterdam was to "enter under the wings of the Divine Presence."[60] This was because, unlike in so many other European cities, Amsterdam did not require Jews to wear identifiable clothing, obey a curfew, or live in a walled-off ghetto. They did not face targeted attacks in times of natural disasters. Rather, by the mid-seventeenth century, Amsterdam's wealthy Jews were well-integrated into the city's economic community. They could participate freely in the stock exchange, they possessed the same rights in commercial ventures as other citizens of the Republic, and they could join guilds.*[61] The

richest Jews lived in palatial homes, hired servants, and had access to a wide array of luxury goods, just as other affluent residents of the city did.[62] More typical members of the merchant class specialized in importing sugar, tobacco, and spices from lands bordering the Atlantic, rather than joining the Baltic Sea trade of herring and salt, timber, and grains. Though small in number,

[56] Heeck, *A Traveler in Siam in the Year 1655*, 66, 73.

[57] Simon Schama, *The Embarrassment of Riches: An Interpretation of Dutch Culture in the Golden Age* (New York: Vintage Books, 1997), 225.

[58] Jonathan Israel, *The Dutch Republic: Its Rise, Greatness and Fall, 1477-1806* (New York: Oxford University Press, 1995), 625.

[59] Israel, *The Dutch Republic*, 611.

[60] Miriam Bodian, *Hebrews of the Portuguese Nation: Conversos and Community in Early Modern Amsterdam* (Bloomington, Indiana: Indiana University Press, 1997), 63. The figure may have been Joseph Pardo.

[61] Schama, *The Embarrassment of Riches*, 587, 590, 593.

[62] Allan Levine, *Scattered Among the Peoples: The Jewish Diaspora in Twelve Portraits* (Woodstock, New York: The Overlook Press, 2003), 124.

these groups of prosperous Jews were so well integrated economically that they could have appeared in Johannes Lingelbach's painting of the town hall without being readily identifiable. Indeed, because Amsterdam's artists were not confined to stereotypical characterizations, numerous works by Rembrandt and other Dutch artists seem to celebrate Jewish life and Jewish themes.[63]

Amsterdam's Jewish community did have its difficulties and challenges. There were, for example, rules by which Jews alone had to abide. They could not proselytize, criticize Christianity, or publish anything in the Dutch language. They were excluded from pubs and welfare societies. Until 1660, Jews legally were treated as foreigners instead of as Dutch citizens. The Jewish community's leaders also placed restrictions on Jewish residents, believing that Jews should be discrete in public places. In 1639, they declared that "bridegrooms and mourners must not travel in procession" and that Jews should "avoid being noticed" by Amsterdam's Christian communities in order to preserve social order and interdenominational relations.[64] In addition, Jews were not well integrated into Amsterdam's social life. As a result of their different dietary rules, Sabbath, and holiday calendar, the Jewish community could not participate in the social milieu of the city. Consequently, Jews did not have significant relationships with Christians outside of the economic arena, and so they were largely excluded from even Amsterdam's informal political life. This isolated and marginalized them in many ways.

Two identity issues within the Jewish community compounded these challenges. First, Amsterdam's earliest Jews, who were Sephardic Jews from Spain and Portugal, struggled to determine what it meant to be Jewish and to practice Judaism. Until 1603, no rabbis lived in the city, there were no ritual baths, and there was no Kosher slaughterer. The first Torah didn't arrive in Amsterdam until 1606.[65] Everything had to be constituted and constructed from scratch. More problematically, the Sephardic Jews themselves came from families with diverse experiences and practices, just as was true in Mexico. Some came from families that had continuously practiced Judaism. Others were *conversos*, or crypto-Jews. Hence, many Jews who arrived in Amsterdam either practiced a folkloric Judaism or knew little of what being Jewish meant.[66] In fact, many of the Sephardic men in Amsterdam even refused circumcision.[67] Mid-seventeenth century rabbis, then, faced significant challenges to get their congregants to adhere to Jewish law, and it often took charismatic figures to be able to do it.[68]

The second identity issue involved the arrival of the Jews from Germany, Poland, and Lithuania, especially in the aftermath of the Thirty Years' War* in 1648. The Ashkenazi were, as a whole, far poorer than their Sephardic brethren. Coming from central and eastern Europe, they had a different cultural heritage and spoke a different language. This led to social tensions within the Jewish community and sparked conversation in the general public. In 1656, for example, when 300 Ashkenazi arrived in Amsterdam, the Sephardic residents provided the new refugees with food, clothing and shelter, according to Jewish custom, but encouraged them to move elsewhere by providing financial assistance for them to be able to do so.[69] Conditions elsewhere in Europe kept

---

[63] The motivations for Rembrandt's painting Jewish-themed works is a subject of historical debate. See Steven Nadler, *Rembrandt's Jews* (Chicago, Illinois: University of Chicago Press, 2003), 44-48.

[64] Bodian, *Hebrews of the Portuguese Nation*, 62.

[65] Bodian, *Hebrews of the Portuguese Nation*, 29, 45.

[66] Miriam Bodian, *Hebrews of the Portuguese Nation: Conversos and Community in Early Modern Amsterdam* (Bloomington, Indiana: Indiana University Press, 1997), 10.

[67] Levine, *Scattered Among the Peoples*, 127.

[68] Nadler, *Rembrandt's Jews*, 118.

[69] Bodian, *Hebrews of the Portuguese Nation*, 127, 142.

the immigrants coming to Amsterdam, however, and by 1690 two thirds of Amsterdam's 7,500 Jews were Ashkenazi.[70] This imbalance, combined with the Ashkenazim's belief in their own spiritual pre-eminence,[71] threatened the Sephardim, who wanted to retain their Portuguese heritage as much as their Jewish identity. The two communities divided and built separate synagogues. Jewish disunity seemed to be the price for living in a tolerant city.

~

The seventeenth century is often described as the Golden Age of the Dutch Republic. It was a time of mounting affluence and prosperity with a growing population, greater urbanization, rising wages, improving nutrition, later marriage ages, and declining family sizes. With the rest of Europe facing far more adverse conditions, the Dutch Republic was the great exception.[72]

Despite the pleas of Calvinist ministers for moderation and circumspection, many Dutch indulged in the benefits of the age. They believed that momentous events, like a birth of a child or a friend's return from overseas, deserved a celebratory feast so large most other Europeans would have found it nauseating. In 1703, for example, just seven men consumed fourteen pounds of beef, eight pounds of veal, six fowl, and a wide assortment of stuffed cabbages, fruit, nuts, and bread— all washed down with twenty bottles of red wine and twelve bottles of white wine.[73] Heeck's arrival in Bunschoten would have allowed his friends and neighbors prepare a banquet of similar proportions, which was most likely held at a local tavern.[74] The platters of food would have been presented with considerable flourish and there would have been elaborate toasts all around, just as happened at guild meetings and militia gatherings.[75] The wood floor would have become became strewn with broken glassware as the participants, after gulping down their wine, threw their glasses over their heads and against the wall as signs of their affluence and their desire to celebrate the honored guest.[76] Heeck would have been elected the "glutton of the assembly" and would have presided over the festivities with a cooking pot for a crown and a serving spoon as a scepter.[77] And the room would have been heavy with smoke as both men and women sucked their clay pipes well into the night. Indeed, the seventeenth century Dutch saw smoking and drinking as an essential

---

[70] Schama, *The Embarrassment of Riches,* 594.

[71] Nadler, *Rembrandt's Jews,* 31.

[72] Schama, *The Embarrassment of Riches,* 224. Noted historian Geoffrey Parker confirms this conclusion but notes that at key times the Dutch "suffered the same appalling weather as other parts of the world" and helped trigger their own decline in 1651, when the Great Assembly of the States General refused to appoint a new Stadholder. This absence of central authority undercut the Republic's ability to coordinate its military and naval operations and led to a series of British victories as the century progressed. See Geoffrey Parker, *Global Crisis: War, Climate Change, and Catastrophe in the Seventeenth Century* (New Haven, Connecticut: Yale University Press, 2013), 236, 239.

[73] Schama, *The Embarrassment of Riches,* 151-152.

[74] Paul Zumthor, *Daily Life in Rembrandt's Holland,* Simon Watson Taylor (trans.) (London: Weidenfeld and Nicolson, 1962), 172.

[75] Schama, *The Embarrassment of Riches,* 179-182, 185.

[76] Julie Berger Hochstrasser, *Still Life and Trade in the Dutch Golden Age* (New Haven, Connecticut: Yale University Press, 2007), 84.

[77] Zumthor, *Daily Life in Rembrandt's Holland,* Simon Watson Taylor (trans.) (London: Weidenfeld and Nicolson, 1962), 172.

part of the national identity, and as such, they were a people quite addicted to both alcohol and tobacco.[78]

Dutch still life paintings document this extravagance handsomely, as well as the underlying trade that fathered it. In Jan Davidszoon de Heem's *Still Life with Parrots* (c. 1645), for example, a thick wood table, covered in a delicately embroidered rust and gold fabric supports an outlandish cornucopia of enticements for the palette: luscious oysters on the half shell, a burst pomegranate

---

[78] Schama, *The Embarrassment of Riches*, 189, 200.

with scattered seeds, and a basket overflowing with ripe peaches and succulent grapes accompany a translucent lemon with its corkscrewed skin still attached, a cluster of oranges, and a cantaloupe full of seeds. An ornate silver pitcher, a bulbous gold goblet, a stout salt cellar, an overturned pepper shaker, and a towering flute of red wine crowd what little empty space is left on the table. A Brazilian scarlet macaw and a gray African parrot look down on this scene, bickering over a piece of fruit and symbolizing the vastness of the Dutch trading network and the exoticism of the goods it produced. The foreground features giant seashells from the East and West Indies, while in the background an open black curtain reveals the claws and head of an enormous lobster sitting on a blue box next to a half-full glass of white wine. In the distance a single Doric column stands overlooking a cloud-covered landscape. De Heem's *pronkstilleven,* or luxurious still life, captures both the unprecedented lavishness of the era, but also the fear that it will all rot or fade away, much like a shelled oyster or ancient Athens.[79]

De Heem's paintings usually sold for very high prices,[80] but the influx of wealth into the Dutch Republic allowed middle class and even peasant households to purchase art. Paintings hung in such profusion in so many homes that the Dutch created the first mass market for art in European history.[81] Many of these works celebrated everyday life and the Republic's growing national identity, in contrast with the religiously-oriented works of the Renaissance.[82] From still lifes of bread and cheese to people ice skating on a local canal, from flattering portraits to maritime landscapes, the Dutch public of all classes covered the walls of their homes so that no bare space remained. This profusion of art work documents in a tangible way the success and the impact of the Dutch trading networks.

The seventeenth-century Dutch Republic was as rare and noteworthy as a surviving Vermeer. Its government was decentralized and democratic in a time dominated by monarchies and notions of Absolutism.* Its women were educated, retained significant financial and property rights, and enjoyed unprecedented social freedoms at a time when women stood as second class citizens in so much of the world. Its children were showered with affection and were encouraged to explore the world at a time when most parents emphasized discipline and provinciality. Its streets, stoops, and houses were brilliantly clean, whereas so many urban settings in the seventeenth century stunk with refuse and excrement.[83] And its ports exchanged the world's goods with a profitable efficiency everyone envied. It was truly a Golden Age, and Heeck was very much a part of it, having had the income and status to enjoy a comfortable life in his final years.[84]

On September 29, 1660, the now forty-one-year-old married a woman named Christiana Greve and settled into domestic life as Bunschoten's premiere surgeon. He had four children with Christiana between 1662 and 1668 and worked with his son Joost, who survived the trip to Asia,

---

[79] Hochstrasser, *Still Life and Trade in the Dutch Golden Age,* 86-88 and Virginia Brilliant, *The John and Mable Ringling Museum of Art: Curator's* Choice (London: Scala Publishers Ltd., 2010), 79. Normal dietary fare was still voluminous by most European standards. For most Dutch, cured meats, sausages, fresh vegetables, fruits, butter, eggs, cheese, and salted and fresh fish were all affordable. *Hutsepot,* a hearty meat and vegetable stew, had become the national dish by 1650, but tea was still expensive and coffee had yet to generate a large demand. See Schama, *The Embarrassment of Riches,* 169-172, 176.

[80] Sybille Ebert-Schifferer, *Still Life, a History* (New York: Harry N. Abrams, 1999), 154.

[81] Schama, *The Embarrassment of Riches,* 318.

[82] Zumthor, *Daily Life in Rembrandt's Holland,* 197-198.

[83] Schama, *The Embarrassment of Riches,* 375-379, 402-407, 485, 491.

[84] Schama, *The Embarrassment of Riches,* 315.

returned to Bunschoten, married, and also became a surgeon.[85] Heeck spent several years preparing the manuscript that described his experiences in Asia. It was clearly a labor of love, for Heeck's penmanship is uniform and careful.[86] He wanted posterity to know what he had done and what he had seen.

In 1903, Heeck's wish was finally fulfilled when the Utrecht town archivist received a bequest from a local aristocrat containing a stack of seventeenth and eighteenth-century papers. The first volume of Heeck's journal was in that donation, but the location of Heeck's manuscript between the author's death and the beginning of the twentieth century is unknown. At some point the first and second volumes became separated and only the first has reemerged.

Little known except to academic specialists, Heeck's account of his third voyage to Asia stands as one of the great travel narratives of the seventeenth century. Although he shared in the prejudices of many of his European contemporaries, Heeck also exhibited a high degree of curiosity and open-mindedness. In some ways, this isn't surprising since he was a product of Dutch Republic who pursued a profession dedicated to the well-being of others. His journal reflects the relative toleration of his homeland, as well as his own selflessness. Heeck's work also possesses a surprisingly universal quality about it, for he proved himself to be a botanist, a climatologist, an anthropologist, and an explorer all rolled into one. A million people may have traveled aboard VOC ships to Asia in the seventeenth and eighteenth centuries, but there was only one surgeon who examined new shores with such distinguished liberality.

---

[85] Dekkers, *Onder dokters handen,* 11-12. Christiana was from Harderwijk, a port town about 16 miles east of Bunschoten. Their four children were: Harmen, born 11/19/1662; Cornelia, born 5/26/1664; Lijsbetjen, born 1/31/1666; and Jannetjen, born 7/5/1668. Joost was married on November 1, 1668 at age 22 to Jacomijntze Zas, who was from Eemnes. They had ten children, the oldest of whom was named Gijsbert in honor of his grandfather. Joost died in 1688.

[86] Barend Jan Terwiel, "Introduction," *A Traveler in Siam in the Year 1655: Extracts for the Journal of Gijsbert Heeck,* (Bangkok, Thailand: Silkworm Books, 2008), 3.

I

Ibrahim I

1615-1648

> I that of Ott'man blood remain alone,
> Call'd from a prison, to ascend a throne.
> My silly mind I bend to soft delights.
> Hating th' unpleasant thoughts of naval fights.
> Till mad with wanton loves, I fall at first
> Slave to my own, then to my people's lust.[1]

Every time a key entered the worn but durable metal lock, Ibrahim instinctively flinched in fear. His reaction was the natural outcome of his twenty-three-year imprisonment in the Cage: perhaps today was the day his jailors would kill him.

Ibrahim was the second oldest son of the Ottoman sultan Ahmed I. In 1617, at the tender age of two, Ibrahim was removed from Topkapı Palace's harem and consigned to a small compound, where the brothers and sons of reigning sultans were held in secluded captivity. Known as the Cage, Ibrahim's new home consisted of a two-story pavilion, a courtyard enclosed by a high wall, and a series of small rooms assigned for the Cage's servants and concubines.[2] The top floor of the pavilion featured tile-covered walls evoking Eden, inspiring domed ceilings, a bronze fireplace, and windows

---

[1] Sir Paul Rycaut, *History of the Turkish Empire from the Year 1640 to the Year 1677* (London: Printed by J.M. for J. Starkey, 1679-80), n.p. (opposite page 1). In the interest of clarity, I have modernized the spelling and punctuation of this poem.

[2] There has never been a thorough archeological survey of the harem, and the specific rooms that constituted the Cage changed over time. See Ilber Ortayli, "House of Sultan," *House of the Sultan: Topkapı Palace, the Imperial Harem* (Istanbul: Topkapı Palace Museum, 2012), 9. The former director of the Topkapı Palace notes that "we have no idea how the occupants [of the harem] were housed during the reign of Sultan Ibrahim," or "exactly where the suite occupied by Kösem Sultan was situated." See Hayrullah Örs quoted in H. Canan Cimilli, "Topkapı Palace Harem," *House of the Sultan: Topkapı Palace, the Imperial Harem*, Alev Taşkin (ed.) (Istanbul, Turkey: Topkapı Palace Museum, 2012), 23. My description is based on a wide variety of sources, a personal visit to the Topkapı Palace in June 2012, and a bit of imagination.

overlooking the courtyard.[3] Below, on ground floor, the rooms were windowless, dark, and dank.[4] While the two floors of the pavilion differed in ambience, both were a prison. In order to eliminate all unauthorized communication with the outside world, many of Ibrahim's caretakers and servants in the compound were congenital deaf mutes, which the Ottoman court began using in the 1470s. By the sixteenth century, these servants had developed a highly sophisticated sign language that was handed down from generation to generation. They were also used as the sultan's trusted agents outside the court.[5] Ibrahim's only other companions in the Cage were other potential male heirs and sterile women, thereby eliminating any possibility of unauthorized procreation. This meant that Ibrahim grew up in such relative isolation that he had more in common with convicts in solitary confinement than with the heirs of the world's other powerful kingdoms and empires.[6]

Isolation and exclusion had long been a part of Ibrahim's life, but circumstances changed in 1632, when Ibrahim's older brother Murad IV assumed full authority as sultan. During his first year on the throne, Murad had two of his and Ibrahim's brothers assassinated. Five years later, another brother met the same fate,[7] which meant that Ibrahim's fear only grew. So when Ibrahim heard the key in the lock on February 9, 1640, he barricaded the door with furniture and refused to let the men with the keys enter the room. When the men enthusiastically proclaimed that he was now the ruling sultan, Ibrahim did not believe them: it had to be a trick, and these men had come to assassinate him, he believed. The men continued their pleas through the heavy wood doors, but Ibrahim did not budge. Instead, he demanded to see physical evidence. The men withdrew, a bit astonished, but returned soon enough and invited Ibrahim to see for himself. Cautiously, Ibrahim approached the window, opened it and the wood shutters beyond. A cold February wind blew onto his face as he looked out to the waters of the Golden Horn. In the courtyard below, Ibrahim saw the body of his dead brother, Murad IV, lying on the cold marble.[8] It was true: Ibrahim had become the eighteenth sultan of the Ottoman Empire. He was twenty-four years old.

Ibrahim's investiture followed the traditions established by Ahmed I in 1603.[9] It began with his being escorted to the sultan's private apartments in a part of the palace he had never seen. Here, the chief minister and the Grand Mufti, a key religious official, became the first to pledge their

[3] The Cage that tourists see today was influenced by eighteenth-century French Rococo; it was presumably less intricate during Ibrahim's imprisonment. See N. M. Penzer, *The Harem: An Account of the Institution as It Existed in the Palace of the Turkish Sultans with a History of the Grand Seraglio from its Foundation to Modern Times* (London: Spring Books, 1965), 199.
[4] A. D. Alderson, *The Structure of the Ottoman Dynasty* (Oxford, U.K.: The Clarendon Press, 1956), 34.
[5] Sara Scalenghe, *Disability in the Ottoman World, 1500-1800* (New York: Cambridge University Press, 2014), 21, 46-47.
[6] Many did not do well with the isolation of the Cage: 115 sons of sultans died early without having fathered children between 1566-1839 because of their confinement. See Alderson, *The Structure of the Ottoman Dynasty*, 33. Many also suffered emotionally in the Cage. This is not surprising, for as modern studies show that solitary confinement exacerbates mental illness. See Seena Fazel and Jacques Baillargeon, "The Health of Prisoners," *The Lancet*, 377. 9769 (March 12-March 18, 2011): 956-965, ProQuest Central. Perhaps the earlier Ottoman practice of quick strangulation was the more humane policy for managing male heirs.
[7] Gabor Agoston and Bruce Masters, *Encyclopedia of the Ottoman Empire* (New York: Facts on File, 2009), 263. The assassinated brothers were Bayezid and Suleiman (1632), and Kasim (1637).
[8] Noel Barber, *The Sultans* (New York: Simon and Schuster, 1973), 87.
[9] Colin Imber, *The Ottoman Empire, 1300-1650: The Structure of Power*, Third ed. (London: Red Globe Press, 2019), 88.

HIBRAIM IMPERATOR TVRCARVM.
VLTIMVS DOMVS OTTOMANNICÆ.
P. de Iode excudit

loyalty and allegiance.[10] Then Ibrahim proceeded to the Gate of Felicity, which separated the administrative portion of the palace from the inner court. Here, government and court officials, military officers, and foreign diplomats paid homage to the new sultan.[11] In a matter of minutes Ibrahim had gone from prisoner to sovereign of an empire that stretched from Algiers to Azov, from Budapest to Aden. Several days later, Ibrahim saw the hectic streets of Istanbul and bustling Golden Horn for the first time as he proceeded to the tomb of Abu Ayyub al-Ansari. Once a close companion of Muhammad's, Al-Ansari also served as standard-bearer in the First Arab Siege of Constantinople in 674. By proceeding to the tomb on the city's outskirts, Ibrahim was symbolically reenacting the Muslim conquest of Constantinople. In another key symbolic moment, Ibrahim was presented with a sword of historical significance, such as the one belonging to Muhammad.[12] He also prayed in Hagia Sophia.

Ibrahim is usually known as "Ibrahim the Mad." Even in the nineteenth century, this portrayal was so common that Nathaniel Hawthorne's most popular story during his lifetime evoked the sultan's image as part of the New Englander's commentary on excessive zeal.[13] Since then, historians have characterized Ibrahim as analogous to the Roman emperor Caligula as they look for new ways to describe him. Ibrahim was "simple-minded"[14] and "incompetent,"[15] "rapacious" and "bloodthirsty,"[16] and "detestable" and "debauched."[17] One historian even concluded that Ibrahim "plumbed the depths of human inadequacy lower than ever before."[18] Even one of the best plays written about Ottoman history is called *Ibrahim the Mad* and features a sultan ruined by "sexual,

[10] Aysel Çötelioğlu, "Ceremonies, Processions, and Celebrations in the Imperial Harem," *House of the Sultan: Topkapı Palace, the Imperial Harem*, Alev Taşkin (ed.) (Istanbul, Turkey: Topkapı Palace Museum, 2012), 63. The Chief Mufti of Istanbul was also known as the *Şeyhülislam*, which was a title given to an honored Islamic scholar. Additionally, the Chief Mufti was a jurisconsult or legal expert and the major spokesman for the *'ulama* —the community of Islamic religious scholars. See Joshua M. White, "Fetva Diplomacy: The Ottoman Şeyhülislam as Trans-Imperial Intermediary." *Journal of Early Modern History* 19 (2/3) (2015): 199–221, EBSCOhost; and Michael M. Pixley, "The Development and Role of the Şeyhülislam in Early Ottoman History," *Journal of the American Oriental Society*, 96, no. 1 (1976): 89-96, EBSCOhost.

[11] Mehradad Kia, *Daily life in the Ottoman Empire* (Santa Barbara, California: Greenwood Press, 2011), 38.

[12] Imber, *The Ottoman Empire, 1300-1650*, 90-91; and Jane Hathaway, *The Chief Eunuch of the Ottoman Harem: From African Slave to Power-Broker* (New York: Cambridge University Press, 2018), 97.

[13] Luther S. Luedtke, *Nathanial Hawthorne and the Romance of the Orient* (Bloomington, Indiana: Indiana University Press, 1989), 93-102; and G. Harrison Orians, "The Sources and Themes of Hawthorne's 'The Gentle Boy'," *The New England Quarterly*, 14, 4 (December 1941), 664-678, EBSCOhost.

[14] Caroline Finkel, *Osman's Dream: The History of the Ottoman Empire* (New York: Basic Books, 2006), 208.

[15] Leslie Peirce, *The Imperial Harem: Women and Sovereignty in the Ottoman Empire* (New York: Oxford University Press, 1993), 107.

[16] Sir Edward S. Creasy, *History of the Ottoman Turks* (Beirut, Lebanon: Khayats, 1961), 259.

[17] Barber, *The Sultans*, 87.

[18] Lord Kinross, *The Ottoman Centuries: The Rise and Fall of the Turkish Empire* (New York: Morrow Quill Paperbacks, 1977), 313.

political, and spiritual power."[19] Many of these descriptions, however, seem focused more upon characterizing Ibrahim's sexual gratification than the pressures he felt as the sole remaining heir to the Ottoman dynasty. Stories get told and retold as to how he had the city's *hammams** "scoured" to find additional beautiful women for his harem,[20] or how he associated "sensuous delight" with physical size, sending agents out to find the largest women in the empire for his obsessive pleasure,[21] or how he was so virile that he could enjoy the intimate company of 24 women in 24 hours.[22] Yet these accounts contrast with stories of Ibrahim's "protracted bouts of impotence" "caused by a curious sexual streak in nature—an insatiable passion for women beyond his reach."[23] The reason for these disparities ultimately rests in Western misunderstandings as to the character and purpose of the harem, as well as a rather lurid Western obsessiveness over what literary critic and social commentator Edward Said called the "ineradicable distinction between Western superiority and Oriental inferiority."[24] Indeed, the stories reveal more about the values of the historians writing about Ibrahim than they do Ibrahim himself.

To call Ibrahim "mad" means that he regularly exhibited behavior that was objectively, subjectively, *and* culturally objectionable.[25] The problem is that while aspects of Ibrahim's behavior upset members of the court, and while there were psychological consequences for living in the Cage, the objective criteria for madness cannot be fully met. There is not a sufficient body of evidence to show that the eighteenth sultan suffered from schizophrenia, paranoia, or dissociative or bipolar disorders, as defined by modern psychiatry.[26] He didn't even suffer from communication disorders or agoraphobia as a result of his long imprisonment in the Cage. Nor can Ibrahim be seen as delusional. Significantly, Ibrahim also doesn't fit well into any of the main categories of madness that were utilized in other parts of the Muslim world in the seventeenth century.[27] Instead, the

---

[19] Talat S. Halman, "Deli Ibrahim," *The Turkish Muse: Views and Reviews*, Jayne L. Warner (ed.) (Syracuse, NY: Syracuse University Press, 2006), 249. For more information on depictions of the Ottoman sultans in drama, see Esin Akalin, *Staging the Ottoman Turk: British Drama, 1656–1792* (Stuttgart, Germany: Ibidem Press, 2016), 222-231, EBSCOebooks.

[20] Kinross, *The Ottoman Centuries,* 313.

[21] Andrew Wheatcroft, *The Ottomans* (New York: Viking, 1993), 37.

[22] Wheatcroft, *The Ottomans*, 37.

[23] Barber, *The Sultans*, 88-89.

[24] Edward W. Said, *Orientalism* (New York: Vintage Books, 1994), 42. Ibrahim is also accused of ordering many members of the harem executed by drowning for sexual infidelity, but because the numbers vary dramatically, the story may be a fabrication based on the biases Said expresses.

[25] Mick Power, *Madness Cracked* (New York: Oxford University Press, 2014), 191-193, EBSCOebooks. Power develops a Venn diagram with the circles "Objective Madness," "Subjective Madness" and "Socially Constructed Madness." He argues that the areas where any two of the three circles meet constitutes a definition of madness. Given the cultural differences between seventeenth-century Ottomans and twenty-first century Americans, it seems reasonable to be more restrictive and limit the definition to the intersection of all three circles.

[26] For these definitions, see *Diagnostic and Statistical Manual of Mental Disorders*, 5th ed. (Washington, DC: American Psychiatric Association, 2013), 99-105, 123-132, 197-202, 292-298.

[27] In the early modern Islamic world, at least among Arabs, these types of madness included idiocy (a mental disability such as a neurodevelopmental disorder), Holy Folly (someone chosen by God to exhibit odd behavior), bestial madness (in which someone behaved like a predatory animal), possession by spirits, hypochondriacal melancholia (which involved delirium, unpredictable anger, a love of solitude, or taciturnity), and other forms of melancholia often triggered by environmental factors. The best case for Ibrahim being mad is that he suffered from the latter form of melancholia, but there was usually sympathy for those affected by circumstance, and this was not the situation with Ibrahim and the Cage. See Scalenghe, *Disability in the Ottoman World, 1500-1800*, 89, 92-95, 100-110.

source of Ibrahim's "madness" may rest more with cultural practices and politics in the Topkapı court. The Ottomans regularly relied on chiromancy and physiognomy: reading palms and using physical appearance to evaluate inner character was common practice. Undesirable or unwanted individuals could be ostracized, regardless of their true mental state or capability.[28] In this way, mental illness in the Ottoman court can be seen a cultural construct, as Michel Foucault held, rather than as an absolute condition.[29] In this light, defining Ibrahim as mad shows him to be the victim of court intrigue and political maneuvering, rather than from mental illness.

In fact, Ibrahim was rightly worried about the possibility of assassination, and once installed as sultan, he was also deeply concerned about preserving the dynastic line. Prior to 1600, the House of Osman practiced extended fratricide: the execution of any male family member who posed a possible threat to the reigning sultan.[30] Uncles, cousins, nephews, sons, and grandsons could be killed in order to avoid struggles for the throne and to enhance the potential for success of the favored son. The reasoning behind this was that there could only be one definitive ruler and that rivals had to be eliminated to prevent civil war. By the mid-1400s this Ottoman custom had legal sanction, for as Mehmed II said, "For the welfare of the state, the one of my sons to whom God grants the sultanate may lawfully put his brothers to death. A majority of the ʻulama consider this permissible."[31] Therefore, when Ibrahim's grandfather had nineteen of his brothers executed on a single night, he did so with complete legal justification. Moreover, Ibrahim's brother, Murad IV, had issued orders on his deathbed for Ibrahim's assassination even though this would mean the end of the dynastic line. Since Murad wanted to ensure his place in history as the last Ottoman sultan, Ibrahim was being quite rational about the precariousness of his status and situation.

When Ibrahim became sultan in 1640, he was thrown into the highly politicized world of the Topkapı Palace where five different factions competed for power. If Ibrahim was to have a successful reign, he would have to manage these different factions effectively. The first faction was the Janissaries—the elite, musket-carrying infantry units that were the first permanent infantry regiments in Europe.[32] They also formed the sultan's household troops and personal bodyguard. Originally the Janissaries were recruited by enslaving about one in every forty Christian peasant boys who showed particular physical and intellectual promise. These forced recruits, who could have contact with their families but who could not marry, were sent to Turkish homes, circumcised, converted to Islam, and given special military training.[33] By the time a boy was in his early twenties,

---

[28] Miri Shefer Mossensohn, *Ottoman Medicine: Healing and Medical Institutions, 1500-1700* (Albany, New York: State University of New York Press, 2009), 95, EBSCOebooks. Most of the descriptions of Ibrahim are unflattering, but one Ottoman bureaucrat and chronicler, Mustafa Naima, found him to have an imposing presence. See Lucienne Thys-Şenocak, *Ottoman Women Builders: The Architectural Patronage of Hadice Turhan Sultan* (Aldershot, U.K.: Ashgate, 2006), 24.

[29] Roy Porter, *Madness: A Brief History* (New York: Oxford University Press, 2002), 3; and Michel Foucault, *Madness: The Invention of an Idea*, Alan Sheridan (trans.) (New York: HarperPerennial, 2011), 99-106. For a recent work on constructionist mental illness, see Michelle O'Reilly and Jessica Nina Lester, *Examining Mental Health through Social Constructionism: The Language of Mental Health* (Cham, Switzerland: Palgrave MacMillan / Springer, 2017).

[30] Alderson, *The Structure of the Ottoman Dynasty*, 25.

[31] Mehmed II quoted in Munis D. Faruqi, *The Princes of the Mughal Empire, 1504-1719* (New York: Cambridge University Press, 2012), 14.

[32] Burak Kadercan, "Strong Armies, Slow Adaptation," *International Security* 38, no. 3 (Winter 2013/2014), 117-152, EBSCOhost.

[33] Douglas E. Streusand, *Islamic Gunpowder Empires: Ottomans, Safavids, Mughals* (Boulder, Colorado: Westview Press, 2011), 83.

he was ready to join a military corps of men, which was segregated from the rest of society and known for exceptional discipline. The Janissaries turned the tide in many Ottoman battles and were feared by the empire's enemies because of their early practice of equipping infantry forces with firearms.[34] By the middle of the seventeenth century, the Janissaries had become such an important institution that they exercised political as well as military power, making them as worrisome to the sultan and the court as to enemy soldiers on the Ottoman frontiers. Seeing themselves as the institutional guardians of the state, the Janissaries started playing the role of kingmaker, demanding the right to approve the order of succession for the sultanate.[35] Their power was not absolute, however, for there were other military forces within the empire. The most important of these were the Sipahis—light cavalry units from the provinces whose commanders had been given lands in conquered territories for their meritorious service. The Sipahis formed the bulk of the Ottoman troops, but because they were seasonal soldiers drawn together from different parts of the empire, they often suffered a lack of cohesion.[36] In times of dynastic crisis, however, they could offer some military counterweight to the Janissaries.

The second faction vying for power in Topkapı Palace was the harem. This institution was not the place of lascivious debauchery and heterosexual male fantasy depicted in nineteenth century paintings like Jean-Leon Gerome's *The Harem on the Terrace*, Jean-Auguste-Dominique Ingres' *The Turkish Bath*, or Vincenzo Marinelli's *The Dance of the Bee in the Harem.* It was not the place one mid-twentieth century historian described as being "a hotbed of unnatural vices."[37] Nor was the harem an imaginary world of sexual slavery and masculine despotism[38] or so sequestered that no one ever travelled outside the palace.[39] Rather, it was a practical, bona fide social organization with political identity, rules, and traditions. These conventions began with the harem's hierarchy. At the bottom of the pyramid were the household domestics—slaves who performed chores such as food preparation, laundry, laying fires, and drawing baths. Above them were members of the household staff—slaves with managerial responsibilities and titles such as laundry supervisor or tasting mistress. Next came the concubines, who were subdivided into different classes, further emphasizing the hierarchical nature of the harem. The lowest-ranking concubines were the novices, foreign slave girls about ten years old, who were purchased for their beauty and potential. They received extensive training in music and dance during their youth. After several years, these concubines could proceed through the ranks:

> Privileged one—had personal contact with the sultan
> Favored one—had sexual relations with the sultan
> Fortunate one—had an on-going relationship with the sultan
> Lady Favorite—a mother of the sultan's daughters
> Princess Favorite—a mother of the sultan's sons

---

[34] Streusand, *Islamic Gunpowder Empires,* 83. Streusand says that the Janissaries were "perhaps the first standing infantry force equipped with firearms in the world."

[35] Kia, *Daily life in the Ottoman Empire,* 65; and Finkel, *Osman's Dream,* 234.

[36] Kadercan, "Strong Armies, Slow Adaptation."

[37] Barber, *The Sultans,* 90.

[38] Kia, *Daily life in the Ottoman Empire,* 40.

[39] One example of Ottoman harem women leaving Topkapı Palace occurred in September 1659, when Turhan Sultan journeyed with her son, Mehmed IV, and court officials to Bursa, Edirne, and two newly-constructed fortresses at the entrance to the Dardanelles. See Thys-Şenocak, *Ottoman Women Builders,* 107.

Haseki—or favorite concubine[40]

Ranking above all these women in the harem was the valide sultan, the mother of the reigning sultan. These women exerted enormous influence upon the court as a result of their exalted status,[41] and in several cases ruled the empire directly as regents for young sons. Even when the valide sultan was not a regent, she held sufficient power that she could approve promotions or release prisoners on her own authority.[42] During the first half of the seventeenth century, as Topkapı harems grew dramatically, from 276 members in 1603 to 436 members in 1652, the power of the valide sultan grew correspondingly.[43] Harems could not grow forever, however, because court tradition dictated that upon the death of a sultan, all the members of his harem would be banished from Topkapı and sent to an old palace in central Istanbul so that a new harem might be created. Alternatively, enslaved members of the harem could purchase their freedom and then marry if they chose to do so. Such women were important contacts with the outside world for those women still in the harem or in retirement.[44]

The harem's hierarchy, power structure, and reproductive politics were reflected in palace budgets.[45] All members of the court were given a daily allowance, which signified their relative importance:

Position	Stipend per day in Aspers[46]
Valide sultan	2,000-3,000
Haseki	1000
Sultan's sisters	400
Princesses prior to marriage	100
Household staff	40
Household domestics	6

The importance of high-ranking women and their ability to influence policy through payments for favors becomes especially clear in the context of salaries of prestigious males in the mid-seventeenth century:

Position	Stipend per day in Aspers
Vizier (government minister)	1,000
Mufti (interpreter of Islamic law)	750
Chief Justice of Anatolia	563
Head of the Janissaries	500
Princes	100

[40] Alderson, *The Structure of the Ottoman Dynasty*, 79-80.
[41] Wheatcroft, *The Ottomans*, 36.
[42] Ebru Boyar, "The Public Presence and Political Visibility of Ottoman Women," *Ottoman Women in Public Space,* Boyar, Ebru, and Kate Fleet (eds.) (Leiden: Brill, 2016), 233.
[43] Peirce, *The Imperial Harem*, 122. The Topkapı's budget increased during this period from almost 65,000 aspers in 1603 to just over 200,000 aspers in 1652.
[44] Leslie Peirce, "Beyond Harem Walls: Ottoman Royal Women and the Exercise of Power," *Servants of the Dynasty: Palace Women in World History*, Anne Walthall (ed.) (Berkeley, CA: University of California Press, 2008), 90.
[45] Peirce, *The Imperial Harem*, 126-132. All of the following statistics also come from these pages.
[46] In the mid-seventeenth century, one gold piece was worth between 120-180 aspers. See *The Intimate Life of an Ottoman Statesman: Melek Ahmed Pasha (1588-1662) as Portrayed in Evliya Çelebi's Book of Travels*, Robert Dankoff (trans.) (Albany, New York: State University Press of New York Press, 1991), 78.

With valide sultans commanding two or three times the income of the viziers, they were able to influence the court in powerful ways, just as Tōfukumon'in did with her extensive income in Tokugawa Japan. This affluence, combined with the harem's fertility and traditions, ensured its importance to the Ottoman state.

The harem was guarded and served by a third faction vying for power within Topkapı Palace, the eunuchs. These castrated males came from different racial groups and served different functions. The White Eunuchs (who hailed primarily from the Caucasus and Balkans) were traditionally the guardians of the harem, while the Black Eunuchs (who hailed primarily from Sudan, Ethiopia, and Kenya) were traditionally the administrators. Initially, White Eunuchs held more influence in the Ottoman court, but by 1600 the Black Eunuchs were in ascendance because the bureaucracy and management of the empire had become so important. Ibrahim's older brother Murad IV established the office of Chief Black Eunuch and gave him the responsibility for overseeing the imperial endowments that funded mosques, *hammams*, hospitals, libraries, soup kitchens, bridges, fountains, and other public works.[47] Control over this enormous amount of money, daily contact with the sultan and the harem, and the supervision of the daily education of the crown prince made the Black Eunuchs a significant force in the Ottoman court.[48] As was true in many other world empires,[49] Ottoman sultans were willing to delegate this power because they liked having castrated males with fewer personal attachments serve as their bureaucrats.[50] Eunuchs also helped project an image of the monarch's purity, sanctity, and dynastic legitimacy.[51]

A fourth faction Ibrahim would have to manage effectively was the grand vizier and his ministers. These men assembled in all-day council meetings several times a week to manage the day-to-day affairs of the Ottoman government. Agenda items might include listening to citizen

---

[47] Finkel, *Osman's Dream,* 167. Finkel also notes that as the power of the black eunuchs and the harem increased after 1600, the role of the grand vizier (chief minister) declined.

[48] Kia, *Daily life in the Ottoman Empire,* 43.

[49] Examples of empires that utilized eunuchs include the Neo-Assyrian (911-612 BCE), Achaemenid (550-331 BCE), Byzantine (330-1453 CE), and all of the Chinese dynasties after the Zhou (1045-771 BCE). See Hathaway, *The Chief Eunuch of the Ottoman Harem,* 4.

[50] Said Amir Arjomand, "Coffeehouses, Guilds and Oriental Despotism in Government and Civil Society in Late 17th to Early 18th Century Istanbul and Isfahan and as Seen from Paris and London," Archives Européennes de Sociologie, 45.1 (April 2004): 23-42, ProQuest Central.

[51] Hathaway, *The Chief Eunuch of the Ottoman Harem,* 5-6.

complaints, receiving foreign ambassadors, adjudicating legal cases, appointing officials, and acting upon petitions. The grand viziers would present a summary of the day's actions to the sultan.[52] Technically, as the sultan's first minister and absolute deputy, the grand vizier was supposed to put the sultan's interests first. In practice, however, grand viziers had minds of their own and could act in ways which were not always in accordance with a sultan's best interests. As a check on ministerial power, therefore, sultans frequently appointed new men to the position of grand vizier. In the fifty years between July 1601 and August 1651, for example, 33 men held the office.

Although the valide sultan would usually be considered as a part of the harem's faction, Ibrahim's mother, Kösem Mahpeyker, proved the exception. A woman of remarkable talent and ambition, she represented a fifth and separate faction in her own right. A woman of Greek birth, who entered the harem at a young age and who rose through the ranks to become Ahmed I's *haseki*, Kösem became a pivotal Topkapı figure in the middle of the seventeenth century. She has been characterized as selfish and manipulative, cold-hearted and power-hungry.[53] This negative reputation rests in part on the fact that as regent she almost certainly gave the order to separate Ibrahim from the court when he was two and to imprison him in the Cage. What is so interesting about Kösem's action and her resulting reputation, however, is that if a king put his country's interests above those of his offspring, he might very well be lauded as a noble, sacrificing statesman. But contemporaries and historians have often failed to give women such credit, which is why Kösem has received so much sexist criticism. The reality is that Kösem strategically guided her empire through a time of dynastic transition, as Eleni did in Ethiopia 150 years before. Kösem arranged for the marriages of her daughters and granddaughters to secure the support of influential pashas.[54] This built important political alliances. She argued that peasant farmers seeking better economic opportunities in Istanbul should not be forced to return to unproductive farms in order to increase tax revenues.[55] This minimized civil unrest at a critical moment. Anticipating increased foreign aggression, Kösem ordered the construction of better defenses in the Dardanelles.[56] This proved to be farsighted. She also took the necessary steps to eliminate those who threatened the balance of power within the palace. This preserved palace tradition.[57] In addition, Kösem sought a peace treaty with Spain and helped postpone a war with Venice, thereby trying to solve or at least postpone the budgetary problems facing the empire.[58] Indeed, Kösem dominated Ottoman politics for the better part of three decades, serving formally as sole regent for twelve years.

During the first four years of his reign, Ibrahim managed these five factions well, acting rationally and practically. He recognized the limitations that his long stay in the Cage produced and accepted his unreadiness to be sultan. He utilized Kösem's expertise and retained the talented Kemankes Kara Mustafa as grand vizier. He also monitored Topkapı politics carefully, asked for written reports regularly, and responded to them in his own handwriting, showing that, despite his reputation, Ibrahim was well-educated and accepted the responsibilities of ruling the empire.[59]

---

[52] Kia, *Daily life in the Ottoman Empire*, 57-60.

[53] Peirce, *The Imperial Harem*, 106.

[54] Peirce, "Beyond Harem Walls," 53-54.

[55] Finkel, *Osman's Dream*, 211.

[56] Finkel, *Osman's Dream*, 263.

[57] Wheatcroft, *The Ottomans*, 37.

[58] Peirce, *The Imperial Harem*, 224-226.

[59] Agoston and Masters, *Encyclopedia of the Ottoman Empire*, 263. Both Ibrahim's learning curve and literacy are confirmed by Geoffrey Parker, *Global Crisis: War, Climate Change and Catastrophe in the Seventeen Century* (New Haven, Connecticut: Yale University Press, 2013), 196.

During this period, Ibrahim's government sponsored a tax reform for the peasantry, reduced of the size of the Janissaries and the Sipahis, stabilized the currency by limiting loans, and eliminated redundant offices and unnecessary salaries.[60] Ibrahim also managed the pressure to produce an heir for the empire and took advantage of the privileges his newly-acquired freedom afforded. Like newly-released prisoners today who are more likely to engage in high-risk sexual activities during their transition to public life,[61] Ibrahim was sexually promiscuous, especially in the first years of his reign. One of his motivations must have been the need to father sons. As the last surviving heir to the House of Osman, he took necessary steps to ensure the continuity of the 340-year-old dynasty within the customs his culture allowed. Before his death, Ibrahim fathered eighteen children, of whom four sons and three daughters survived infancy. Since three of these sons eventually became sultans, Ibrahim clearly saved the dynasty.

Unfortunately for the Ottoman Empire, this efficiency and tranquility did not last. The factionalism of the court reappeared: by 1644 Ibrahim had become influenced by harem rivals of Kösem and ministerial rivals of Kemankes. Just as his health was failing and his headaches were becoming more pronounced, Ibrahim agreed to have his mother forcibly sent to the Old Palace, to have Kemankes assassinated,[62] and to have the Chief Black Eunuch deposed.[63] Ibrahim's endorsement of this *putsch* was a significant mistake, for he was soon surrounded by less talented individuals. The inexperienced sultan also wasted considerable political capital by repeatedly pardoning a particularly corrupt religious figure, magician, and exorcist named Cinci Hoca, with whom the sultan was beguiled.[64] A greater mistake came when Ibrahim fell in love and decided to marry his *haseki*, a woman named Humasah, who was once a slave. This broke with established court etiquette since it muddled the ranks within the harem hierarchy and brought no political or diplomatic benefit for the empire.[65] In addition, marriages were not really necessary: according to Islamic law, all children acknowledged by the father were legitimate, regardless of the mother's status.[66] Hence, there were only three formal marriages to sultans after 1520, and all three of them were controversial and politically disruptive; Ibrahim's was one of these. When he showered his wife with sable furs, wore diamonds in his beard, and craved amber scents, Ibrahim generated more criticism and scandal. If all this hadn't been enough, Ibrahim overreacted to an international incident that shattered seventy years of peace with Venice.

~

Venice's maritime empire, known as *Stato da mar* or the Territory of the Sea, was born in the wake of the sack of Constantinople during the Fourth Crusade. According to the treaty that partitioned the Byzantine Empire in October 1204, Venice gained control of a string of important ports and

---

[60] Finkel, *Osman's Dream*, 224.

[61] Fazel and Baillargeon, "The Health of Prisoners." Even historians who are quite critical of Ibrahim acknowledge that excessive indulgence was a natural consequence of growing up in the Cage. See Penzer, *The Harem*, 198.

[62] Agoston and Masters, *Encyclopedia of the Ottoman Empire*, 263.

[63] Hathaway, *The Chief Eunuch of the Ottoman Harem*, 98. The Chief Black Eunuch was Sünbüllü Agha.

[64] Mehrdad Kia, *The Ottoman Empire: A Historical Encyclopedia*, Volume 2 (Santa Barbara, California: ABC-CLIO, 2017), 91. Cinci Hoca was executed in 1648.

[65] Alderson, *The Structure of the Ottoman Dynasty*, 95.

[66] Alderson, *The Structure of the Ottoman Dynasty*, 102.

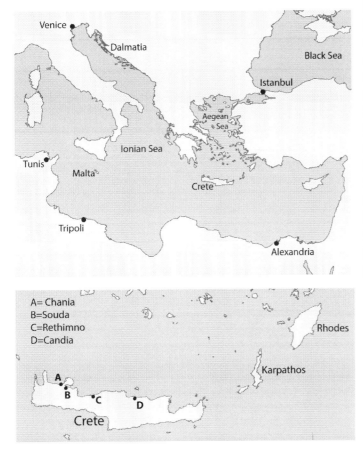

islands in the Ionian and Aegean Seas, as well as critical parts of Constantinople, including its docks and arsenal. From the outset, the *Stato da mar*'s focus was on securing and expanding profits.[67] In 1205, Venice purchased the island of Crete for 5,000 gold ducats from the leader of the Fourth Crusade, Boniface of Montferrat, and began using it as the *entrepôt* of its Eastern Mediterranean trade. Ships arrived in Venice's new Cretan ports from the Black Sea, Syria, and Egypt, and brought slaves and spices, silks and perfumes, sandalwood and carpets for sale in Western Europe.[68] Once transported to and sold in Venice, this trade helped to make the Most Serene Republic the center of the world economy by 1500.[69] This three-hundred-year domination came to an end with Portugal's exploitation of the all-water route to India and with the Ottoman Empire's threat to Venice's territorial network. The sultan and *doge*'s first naval battle came in 1416 at Gallipoli. While the Venetians routed the Ottomans in that battle of oar and arrow, these two empires fought four subsequent wars between 1463 and 1573. Venice suffered important territorial losses in each.

Other Christians also experienced noteworthy defeats as a result of Ottoman expansion in the Mediterranean. Rhodes had been ruled by the Knights of the Order of St. John (Knights Hospitaller) since 1309. By the early modern period, these Knights had become aggressive anti-Muslim corsairs—pirates who have the blessing of a government to seize and plunder.[70] The Knights believed that the seizure of Ottoman or European ships that carried Muslim or Jewish passengers, or any goods that originated from Ottoman ports, was a righteous act since it inflicted economic pain on those they considered infidels.[71] In 1522, Suleiman the Magnificent laid siege to Rhodes. He saw the Knights simply as unethical pirates, and he forced them to vacate Rhodes after a six-month siege. Then, in 1530, Holy Roman Emperor Charles V awarded the Knights the islands

---

[67] Roger Crowley, *City of Fortune: How Venice Ruled the Seas* (New York: Random House, 2011), 117- 119; and Peter Ackroyd, *Venice: Pure City* (New York: Nan A. Talese/Doubleday, 2009), 102.

[68] Crowley, *City of Fortune*, 120, 125.

[69] Ackroyd, *Venice*, 107.

[70] Ayşe Devrim Atauz, *Eight Thousand Years of Maltese Maritime History: Trade, Piracy, and Naval Warfare in the Central Mediterranean* (Gainesville, Florida: University Press of Florida, 2008), 62.

[71] Atauz, *Eight Thousand Years of Maltese Maritime History,* 148.

of Malta as a new, powerful base for their corsair operations. This proved to be a significant security threat to the Ottomans since the Knights continually disrupted trade and since the Ottomans could not dislodge them from their Maltese stronghold.[72]

On September 28, 1644, corsairs operating with the consent of the Knights Hospitaller seized an Ottoman galleon off the coast of Karpathos, halfway between Rhodes and Crete. The ship was carrying 380 *hajj* pilgrims and other passengers from Istanbul to Alexandria, including the former Chief Black Eunuch, who was accompanied by his fortune, and a newly appointed judge for Mecca. The pirates held sixty hostages, killed the other passengers, and took the ship to Venetian-owned Crete, where they distributed their plunder on a deserted beach in accordance with the established rules for Maltese corsairs.[73] When the news of the attack reached the Topkapı Palace, demands for a strong response quickly emerged, led by the influential exorcist Cinci Hoca.[74] Ibrahim subsequently accused the Venetians of providing the pirates with a safe harbor and declared war. In reality, Venice actively sought to limit the actions of the Knights, and in the seventeenth century generally sought peace with the Ottoman Empire since war was so detrimental to trade.[75] This is why the Venetian ambassador in Istanbul denied providing shelter and reported that his government was going to sequester the Knights' commanders.[76] Ibrahim, however, was not satisfied. Ottoman honor had been violated, and he believed that the insult had to be redressed. Like many in the court, Ibrahim believed that Crete would fall quickly and that it was the right time to strike. The pro-war camp reasoned that Europe was consumed with the Thirty Years' War* and Istanbul has already secured a favorable peace with Iran's Safavid Dynasty after almost 150 years of conflict.[77]

Preparations for war with Venice began at once. This included sending letters to the Empire's unruly North African provinces, calling for additional ships to support a coordinated campaign in the spring. Despite their desire for autonomy, the pashas in Algiers, Tunis, and Tripoli complied

---

[72] Joshua M. White, *Piracy and Law in the Ottoman Mediterranean* (Stanford, California: Stanford University Press, 2018), 5, EBSCOebooks. As a way of measuring the level of disruption to Ottoman trade, White notes that the Knights issued 280 privateering licenses between 1600 and 1624 (page 150). For more on the development of the Knights of the Order of St. John and the unsuccessful Ottoman siege of Malta in 1565, see Roger Crowley, *Empires of the Sea: The Siege of Malta, the Battle of Lepanto and the Contest for the Center of the World* (New York, Random House, 2008).

[73] The 380 passengers included both men and women. The former Chief Black Eunuch was Sünbül Ağa; he was killed in the corsairs' attack. The judge was Esiri Mehmed Efendi of Bursa (d. 1681), who was a prisoner on Malta for five years. According to the regulations, corsairs were required to give the Grandmaster of the Knights of the Order of St. John 10% of the loot, while the ship's captain and pilot received 1% each; the rest was divided between the ship's owner and the crew. See Molly Greene, *A Shared World: Christians and Muslims in the Early Modern Mediterranean* (Princeton, New Jersey: Princeton University Press, 2000), 14; White, *Piracy and Law in the Ottoman Mediterranean*, 72; and Atauz, *Eight Thousand Years of Maltese Maritime History*, 149, 248.

[74] Greene, *A Shared World*, 16-17.

[75] Mustafa Soykut, *Italian Perceptions of the Ottomans: Conflict and Politics through Pontifical and Venetian Sources* (Frankfurt am Main, Germany: Peter Lang, 2011), 194.

[76] Soykut, *Italian Perceptions of the Ottomans,* 152.

[77] The Treaty of Zuhab in 1639 helped define the borders between the Ottoman and Safavid empires, promoted long-term stability, and gave the Ottomans control of Baghdad and much of Mesopotamia. See Ernest Tucker, "Ottoman-Iranian Diplomacy through the Safavid Era," *Iran and the Word in the Safavid Age*, Willem Floor and Edmund Herzig (eds.) (London/New York: I.B. Tauris & Company Limited, 2012), 81, 85-86.

with the request from the Topkapı Palace.[78] This allowed Ibrahim to bring some 400 ships and 100,000 men together for his war of revenge.[79]

After feigning an attack on Malta, the combined armada arrived off the northwestern coast of Venetian-owned Crete on June 23, 1645 and began an attack on the fortified port of Chania.[80] After two intense assaults, the town capitulated August 17 with the condition that Venetian troops be allowed to retreat in good order with their arms and standards, and that the townspeople who chose to remain in the city would have a guarantee for their lives and possessions.[81] The Ottomans accepted these conditions and took possession of Chania on August 23. In spring 1646, after a winter respite when key naval commanders were executed for their leniency and failure to return to Istanbul with a sufficiently impressive booty from Chania, the campaign resumed.[82] This resulted in the successful conquest of another port along Crete's northern coast, Rethimno, late in the year.[83] In spring 1647, the Ottomans added Souda to their list of captured Venetian ports.[84] This left only the capital city of Candia (Heraklion) to secure. Candia was guarded by a fortress designed to withstand considerable firepower, and the Ottomans proved unable to enforce a blockade as a result of reinforcement problems, naval defeats, and pirates, among other issues.[85] Consequently, the Cretan War, which expanded into other areas like Dalmatia, dragged on for almost a quarter century.[86] By the time a peace agreement was signed in September 1669, the war was consuming three-quarters of the imperial budget and more than 130,000 Ottoman troops had died in the conflict,[87] but the Ottomans finally gained control of the eastern Mediterranean.

Ottoman control of Crete resulted in Muslims, Catholics, and Orthodox Christians living together on the island for the first time. This made for a religiously fluid and confusing situation, especially since the four hundred and fifty years of Venetian rule in Crete left bitter resentments among the Orthodox population. Cretans had been pressed into military service, forced to rip out grape vines to grow wheat, and made to pay higher taxes.[88] In addition, Venetian regulations forbade Orthodox bishops to visit Crete, Orthodox property was confiscated, and local priests were required to recognize Rome's supremacy.[89] When the Ottomans arrived, the Orthodox Cretans retained significant resentments, but were divided about which side to support in the war. Rural

[78] White, *Piracy and Law in the Ottoman Mediterranean*, 166.
[79] Martin Sicker, *The Islamic World in Decline: From the Treaty of Karlowitz to the Disintegration of the Ottoman Empire* (Westport, Connecticut: Praeger, 2001), 22. Other historians cite different numbers but may be excluding the forces of the North African pashas. See, for example, Parker, *Global Crisis,* 197.
[80] Greene, *A Shared World,* 14.
[81] Alethea Wiel, *The Navy of Venice* (London: John Murray, 1910), 283.
[82] Sicker, *The Islamic World in Decline,* 22.
[83] Greene, *A Shared World,* 18.
[84] Wiel, *The Navy of Venice,* 289.
[85] Greene, *A Shared World,* 18; and White, *Piracy and Law in the Ottoman Mediterranean,* 167.
[86] The primary areas of conflict were in modern Croatia as Venetian and Ottoman forces fought for control of Klis, Knin, Split, and Kotor. For information on the Dalmatian campaigns, see "Domagoj Madunić, "Frontier Elites of the Ottoman Empire During the War for Crete (1645-1669): The Case of Ali-Pasha Čengić," *Europe and the 'Ottoman World': Exchanges and Conflicts, Sixteenth to Seventeenth Centuries,* Gábor Kárman and Radu G. Păun (eds.) (Istanbul, Turkey: The Isis Press, 2013), 50-81.
[87] Parker, *Global Crisis,* 197.
[88] Molly Greene, "Ruling an Island Without a Navy: A Comparative View of Venetian and Ottoman Crete," *Oriente Moderno* 20 (81) no.1 (2001), 193-207, EBSCOhost.
[89] Rossitsa Gradeva, "Orthodox Christians and Ottoman Authority in Late Seventeenth Century Crete," Rossitsa Gradeva (ed.) *Frontiers of Ottoman Space, Frontiers in Ottoman Society* (Istanbul, The Isis Press, 2014), 75.

communities generally favored Ottoman rule more than urban areas,[90] despite the Catholic clergy's willingness to incorporate local Orthodox saints into Catholic liturgy.[91] When the Ottomans captured Chania, they converted only one Orthodox church into a mosque.[92] Instead, they chose to utilize Catholic churches for their mosques as was often true on rest of the island.[93] In the port of Rethimno, officials named one of these converted churches after Kösem, thereby making her the first Ottoman royal woman to have a religious building named after her in a conquered city.[94] Interestingly too, landowners and peasants, both Catholic and Orthodox, converted to Islam in significant numbers in order to maintain or improve their socio-economic influence and standing.[95]

In May 1648, the Venetians successfully blockaded the Dardanelles, thereby bringing the war to Istanbul's doorstep. The people of Istanbul panicked,[96] fearing food shortages and economic disruptions, if not invasion. This social unrest, which coincided with a growing dissatisfaction within Topkapı Palace, helped to create a volatile mix of opposition to Ibrahim's rule. Then, as worshippers prayed in mosques on a Friday in June, a major earthquake hit Istanbul. Not only did the damage cause the collapse of Hagia Sophia's four minarets and the rupture of city's primary aqueduct, but the tremors killed several thousand worshippers in a mosque built by Ibrahim's father.[97] Any one of the factors—the war with Venice; the resentment of Ibrahim's marriage to a former slave; Ibrahim's forcing his sisters to serve his wife; the perception of Ibrahim's irresponsible expenditures; reductions in the Janissaries' ranks; a devastating natural disaster—would not have been sufficient to bring about change, but the combination meant that Ibrahim's days were numbered. But none of the court's factions, from the eunuchs and the harem to the vizier and Janissaries, dared move against the sultan until a ruling had been issued against him in accordance with Islamic law. That ruling had to indicate that Ibrahim was insane because Islamic law held that a mentally compromised man cannot govern the community of Muslim believers.[98] The judge with the proper jurisdiction to issue the *fatwa** in this case, a man named Hanefizade, refused to do so until he consulted with Kösem.   Hanefizade felt the need to bow to the traditional power of the valide sultan, and to her five decades of court experience. For the *coup d'état* to have a legal justification, Kösem had to agree that her son should be deposed. Hidden behind a black veil, Kösem listened carefully as Hanefizade called her "the mother of all true believers" and argued that "the law of a madman ought not to reign whatever be his age; but rather, let a child that is gifted with reason be upon the throne."[99] Kösem could not appear too eager to condone her son's downfall, but she also knew that she was being presented with the opportunity to return to the

[90] Charles A. Frazee, *Catholics and Sultans: The Church and the Ottoman Empire, 1453-1923* (New York: Cambridge University Press, 1983), 123.

[91] Ackroyd, *Venice,* 169. The Catholic church in Crete also modified Latin ecclesiastical rites to conform with Greek practices, but neither of these accommodations won over the majority of the rural population on Crete.

[92] Gradeva, "Orthodox Christians and Ottoman Authority in Late Seventeenth Century Crete," 69.

[93] Frazee, *Catholics and Sultans,* 122-123. In 1630, Crete had 32 Latin churches and 77 Greek ones.

[94] Muzaffer Özgüleş, *The Women Who Built the Ottoman World: Female Patronage and the Architectural Legacy of Günuş Sultan* (London: I. B. Tauris & Company Ltd., 2017), 52.

[95] Gradeva, "Orthodox Christians and Ottoman Authority in Late Seventeenth Century Crete," 65; and Frazee, *Catholics and Sultans,* 123.

[96] Sicker, *The Islamic World in Decline,* 22.

[97] Parker, *Global Crisis,* 198.

[98] Peirce, *The Imperial Harem,* 264.

[99] Hanefizade quoted in Creasy, *History of the Ottoman Turks,* 266.

Topkapı Palace to rule as regent, this time for her grandson.[100] Kösem finally said, "So be it. I shall fetch my grandson, Mehmed, and place the turban on his head."[101] As she crowned the empire's nineteenth and youngest-ever sultan and established herself as regent (over the vigorous objections of the Mehmed IV's mother, Turhan), Kösem once again proved herself to be a masterful politician. In August 1648, she manipulated the harem, the eunuchs, the vizier, the Janissaries, and Ottoman tradition to her advantage and to her sense of the best interests of the dynasty and the empire. Kösem also ordered her son confined to the Cage for the second time.[102]

Ten days later, on August 18, 1648, Ibrahim heard the familiar key enter the durable lock. He did not try to stop the men from entering the Cage as he had eight years earlier; he just kept reading the Quran.[103] The grand vizier and the chief mufti entered. With them was a deaf mute, carrying a bowstring because Ottoman custom forbade the spilling of royal blood.[104] The Grand Mufti declared,

> You have ruined the world by neglecting the affairs of *shari'a*, and the religion of the people. You spent your time with entertainment and slothfulness while bribery became widespread and wrongdoers fell upon the world. You wasted and squandered the state treasury.[105]

Ibrahim protested, "Is there no one of all those who have eaten my bread, that will pity and protect me?"[106] The executioner's quick answer was to throw the bowstring around the thirty-two-year-old's neck. Ibrahim was strangled to death as the Cage's blue-green tiles depicting the gardens of Paradise stood in silent witness. With three of his sons past infancy, Ibrahim had completed his job of procreating. He understood this. His final words were, "I am the father of a dynasty!"[107] In the end, Ibrahim was assassinated not because he was insane, but because he was no longer necessary.

~

Fourteen months after Ibrahim's assassination, in October 1650,[108] the new sultan, Mehmed IV, was circumcised in a Topkapı Palace pavilion that Ibrahim built in 1640 in hope that he would have sons to perpetuate the House of Osman. Kösem and Turhan stood opposite one another in the small, predominantly blue-tiled room, jealously watching each other from behind their veils. As water poured into a marble basin to hide unbecoming noises emanating from the pavilion, the

---

[100] Peirce, *The Imperial Harem,* 264.

[101] Kösem Sultan quoted in Kinross, *The Ottoman Centuries,* 317.

[102] Ibrahim's second imprisonment prompted an uprising by the Sipahis, the provincial light cavalry units, which remained loyal to Ibrahim. This uprising convinced many in the Court that Ibrahim would have to be assassinated. See John Anthony Butler, "Introduction," Sir Paul Rycaut, *The Present State of the Ottoman Empire,* 6th ed. (1686) (Tempe, Arizona: Arizona Center for Medieval and Renaissance Studies, 2017), 58.

[103] Butler, "Introduction," 59.

[104] M. Miles, "Signing in the Seraglio: Mutes, Dwarfs and Jesters at the Ottoman Court, 1500-1700," *Disability & Society,* 15.1 (January 2000), 115, ProQuest Central.

[105] Grand Mufti of Istanbul quoted in Parker, *Global Crisis,* 199.

[106] Ibrahim quoted in Creasy, *History of the Ottoman Turks,* 268.

[107] Ibrahim quoted in Peirce, *The Imperial Harem,* 260.

[108] Tülay Artan, "Arts and Architecture," *The Cambridge History of Turkey,* Vol. 3, Suraiya N Faroqhi (ed.) (New York: Cambridge University Press, 2006), 432.

sultan's chief surgeon cut and the eight-year-old tried to stop crying. In accordance with royal custom, Turhan received the foreskin as the prince's mother, and Kösem received the surgeon's knife as the valide sultan.[109] In normal circumstances, Istanbul's men and women[110] would have witnessed a grand festival in the days leading up to Mehmed IV's circumcision. The celebration to honor the boy's symbolic passage into manhood would have included parades and mock battles, fireworks and athletic competitions, performances and animal sacrifices. All of the public buildings would be decorated, giraffes and elephants would be seen in the streets, and unusual foods would be prepared for the banquets offered foreign dignitaries.[111] The trade guilds* would showcase their finest goods before the sultan, and in turn, the sultan would give the tradesmen money for their works and effort. The sultan would travel outside the city and present the earth his *nahils*, a wooden pole decorated with flowers, ribbons and gold in the shape of a pyramid. Speeches would be given around this phallic symbol of virility, vitality, and fertility, praying that the boy would father a great family. Everyone would comment upon the sumptuous garden made of expensive spun sugar, which surrounded the site of the ceremony.[112] If it was like the circumcision festival of 1582, the people of Istanbul would talk about it for years.[113] In conjunction with this celebration, boys from poor families in Istanbul would have been circumcised *en masse* in the Hippodrome and other venues.[114] Similarly, there would have been corresponding commemorations in towns and villages throughout the empire, featuring the circumcision of thousands of pre-pubescent boys.[115]

But these were not normal times: there was a female regent, factionalism plagued the court, the war with Venice dragged on, the environmental consequences of the Little Ice Age* caused widespread rural poverty in Anatolia and the Balkans,[116] and the government faced a serious monetary crisis from a reduction in tax revenues and a debasement of the currency.[117] Consequently, there was no major public celebration of Mehmed IV's circumcision.[118] Instead the

---

[109] Alderson, *The Structure of the Ottoman Dynasty*, 104. Of course, this was problematic since Mehmed was already sultan and Kösem should not have been the valide sultan. If custom had been followed, Turhan would have received both the foreskin and the knife in this situation. For a detailed primary account of a royal circumcision, see that of poet Mustafa Âlî of Gelibolu (1541-1582) in Aysel Çötelioğlu, "Ceremonies, Processions, and Celebrations in the Imperial Harem," *House of the Sultan: Topkapı Palace, the Imperial Harem*, Alev Taşkin (ed.) (Istanbul, Turkey: Topkapı Palace Museum, 2012), 62.
[110] Non-harem women were regularly seen in public as they attended events, visited *hammams*, and shopped in markets. They certainly attended major public events like circumcision festivals. See Edith Gülçin Ambros, Ebru Boyar, Palmira Brummett, Kate Fleet and Svetla Ianeva, "Ottoman Women in Public Space: An Introduction," *Ottoman Women in Public Space*, Ebru Boyar, and Kate Fleet (eds.) (Leiden: Brill, 2016), 8.
[111] Kia, *Daily life in the Ottoman Empire*, 51.
[112] Faroqhi, *Subjects of the Sultan*, 165.
[113] For a detailed account of the 50-day circumcision festival that Sultan Murad III (r. 1574-1595) held for his son Prince Mehmed in 1582, see Derin Terziolğlu, "The Imperial Circumcision Festival of 1582: An Interpretation," *Muqarnas*, 12 (1995), 84-100, EBSCOhost.
[114] Çötelioğlu, "Ceremonies, Processions, and Celebrations in the Imperial Harem," 61.
[115] There is no set age for the circumcision ceremony to occur, which is why Muslim families often combined the event for several brothers and why poor boys of many ages could be circumcised *en masse* in Istanbul and other cities. For more information on Muslim circumcision, see David Gollaher, *Circumcision: A History of the World's Most Controversial Surgery* (New York: Basic Books, 2000), 44-52.
[116] Parker, *Global Crisis,* 185, 188, 197.
[117] Finkel, *Osman's Dream*, 240.
[118] There may have been some type of public festival, but I have not been able to find a reference to it, and I am convinced that there was not a major one. Instead, it is likely that Kösem and Turhan simply distributed gifts to members of the court. According to a miniature painting, this is how Ibrahim commemorated the

animosity between Kösem and Turhan dominated life in Topkapı Palace. For the next three years, neither Ibrahim's mother or Ibrahim's *haseki* proved able to dislodge her rival. The confederations ebbed and flowed, with the Janissaries generally aligning with Kösem and the Black Eunuchs aligning with Turhan. This tension could not, however, last indefinitely. Something had to give— especially since members of the provincial Sipahis, who supported Ibrahim and were angered by his assassination, had begun to ride in protest towards the capital.[119] In the end, it was Kösem who, in true character, made the decisive move. In August 1651, she decided to replace Mehmed IV as sultan with one of his younger brothers. This move would force Turhan into retirement and allow Kösem to rule as regent without opposition. As she set her plan in motion, an unexpected twist came when one of Kösem's longtime servants betrayed her mistress and informed Turhan of the plot.[120] Turhan didn't hesitate. She ordered her eunuchs to apply the silk rope to Kösem's experienced neck. Kösem, however, did not give in easily. When she heard unexpected footsteps approach, she extinguished the candles in her room and hid in a wardrobe under quilts and carpets. Once found, Kösem offered her executioners money to spare her life, but the men simply took what they wanted instead, pulling diamond earrings off her ears and stripping rings and bracelets off her limbs. They dragged Kösem out of the harem to a courtyard and brought the silk cord towards her neck. Even then she did not surrender to her fate, applying her toothless gums to the thumb of the hand holding the rope, biting so hard that she won a temporary reprieve and gained the satisfaction of resistance.[121] Ibrahim's mother met her death moments later, on September 2, 1651, having finally been outmaneuvered.

~

Elite Ottoman women, be they from the harem or the wife of a grand vizier, used architectural patronage to assert their authority, legitimize their leadership, and publicize the profundity of their faith.[122] Turhan, and to a lesser degree Kösem, participated in such projects, and both left important buildings that stand today.[123] In Istanbul, these works include Turhan's New Mosque and the nearby Spice Bazaar in the Eminönü district overlooking the Golden Horn, and Kösem's Büyük Valide Han—a large, double-tiered caravanserai* just north of the Grand Bazaar. It is, however,

---

circumcision of one of his sons. See John Freely, *A History of Ottoman Architecture* (Ashurst, Southampton, U.K.: WIT Press, 2011), 169.

[119] Finkel, *Osman's Dream*, 235-236, 242, 244.

[120] Peirce, "Beyond Harem Walls," 91.

[121] Rycaut, *The History of the Present State of the Ottoman Empire*, Book I, 35-38.

[122] Thys-Şenocak, *Ottoman Women Builders*, 67, 73, 76, 83, 85, 89.

[123] Kösem spent "enormous sums of money" on philanthropy, but prior to 1640 she generally preferred other types of gift than architectural endowments, including providing for the practical needs of *hajj* pilgrims and helping the poor. This may have been due to her delicate political situation. See Leslie Peirce, "Gender and Sexual Property in Ottoman Royal Women's Patronage," *Women, Patronage, and Self-Representation in Islamic Societies*, D. Fairchild Ruggles (ed.) (Albany, New York: State University of New York Press, 2000), 63-64. She also "paid the debts of imprisoned people, [and] supplied the trousseaus of daughters of poor families." See Aylin Görgün-Baran, "A Woman Leader in Ottoman History: Kösem Sultan (1589-1651)," *Women Leaders in Chaotic Environments: Examinations of Leadership Using Complexity Theory*, Şefika Şule Erçetin (ed.) (Cham, Switzerland: Springer International, 2016), 83.

along the banks of the Bosporus and the Dardanelles that the architectural rivalry between Ibrahim's mother and Ibrahim's *haseki* played out in the most interesting ways.

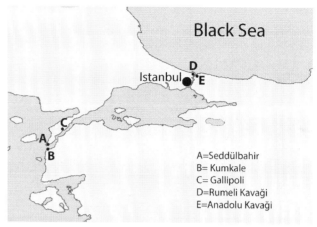

A=Seddülbahir
B= Kumkale
C= Gallipoli
D=Rumeli Kavaği
E=Anadolu Kavaği

Just prior to her assassination, Kösem appointed an architect to determine how to modernize the military fortifications defending the southern entrance to the Dardanelles.[124] She reasoned that this was the only way to prevent Venetian blockades from wreaking havoc on her capital, as had happened repeatedly between 1648 and 1657, when the Ottoman and Venetian navies fought for control of the vital sea lanes.[125] It was, however, Turhan who actually realized Kösem's vision: the new valide sultan's first architectural commission was the construction of the Seddülbahir and Kumkale fortresses on each side of the strait in 1659.[126] Seddülbahir, on the European side, featured two large, crenelated round towers and a strong, crenelated sea wall with rows of gun ports for both heavy and small artillery.[127] The Ottoman traveler Evliya Çelebi visited Seddülbahir on the European side while it was under construction,[128] and with some exaggeration described it as having "huge" bastions* and

> such a wide and deep moat…on the land side of the castle that one dares not look down. The walls on this side are double-layered and 40 paces thick. The circumference of the castle is 1,300 paces. The big harbor on its north side is well-suited for anchoring, and the 80 galleys of the imperial fleet [can be] comfortably moored here.[129]

Evliya was also impressed with the cannons, whose shots spit "like a seven-headed dragon" and could cause heavy damage by ricocheting along the surface of the water.[130] He concluded that Turhan's new fortress could only be described as "impregnable."[131] Though somewhat smaller,

---

[124] Finkel, *Osman's Dream,* 263.

[125] Selcuk Aksin Somel, *Historical Dictionary of the Ottoman Empire* (Lanham, Maryland: The Scarecrow Press, Inc., 2003), xxxix- xi.

[126] Thys-Şenocak, *Ottoman Women Builders,* 109-110.

[127] David Nicolle, *Ottoman Fortifications 1300-1710* (Oxford, U.K.: Osprey Publishing, 2010), 51.

[128] Hakan T. Karateke, "Preface," *Evliya Çelebi's Journey from Bursa to the Dardanelles and Edirne: From the Fifth Book of the Seyahatname* Hakan T. Karateke (ed. and trans.) (Leiden: Brill, 2013), 3, EBSCOebooks.

[129] Evliya Çelebi quoted in *Evliya Çelebi's Journey from Bursa to the Dardanelles and Edirne,* 117.

[130] Çelebi said that the cannon shots could almost reach the island of Bozcaada, 15 miles to the south of Seddülbahir. In reality, seventeenth century Ottoman cannons could not even reach the opposite bank of the Dardanelles, a distance of about two and a half miles. The combined cannons of Seddülbahir and Kumkale did, however, considerably shrink the area through which an invading fleet could safely pass. It wasn't until the twentieth century that shots could be fired all the way across the strait. See Nicolle, *Ottoman Fortifications 1300-1710,* 28, 51.

[131] Evliya Çelebi quoted in *Evliya Çelebi's Journey from Bursa to the Dardanelles and Edirne,* 117.

Kumkale on the Asian side was also a formidable defensive structure.[132] Together, the forts stood as symbolic sentinels of Turhan's effectiveness and ability to protect the empire. Their inauguration helped to present Turhan as a strong, legitimate leader, who was preparing her son for rule, serving the public interest effectively,[133] and following in the footsteps of great Ottoman military leaders, such as Mehmed the Conqueror and Suleiman the Magnificent.[134] As laudatory as such historical comparisons were, Turhan may have been more desirous of a favorable comparison to Kösem.

To gain this reputation, Turhan may have looked north: her architectural triumph at the southern end of the Dardanelles can be balanced against Kösem's projects at the northern end of the Bosporus. In 1623, Kösem financed the construction of mosque for the village of Anadolu Kavaği,[135] near where the cool waters of the Black Sea join the Bosporus on their way to the warmer Mediterranean.[136] This was a significant departure from Kösem's normal philanthropy during the early years of her first regency, and members of the palace would have taken note of it. But in 1624, about the time the mosque's construction was completed, Ukrainian Cossacks raided villages along the Bosporus, proving that they were as adept at sea as they were on land.[137] To compensate for these deeply troubling incursions, the Ottomans quickly built a new fortress with 30-foot walls adjacent to Kösem's mosque in Anadolu Kavaği.[138] Kavak Kalesi, or the Fortress of the Poplars, is typically associated with Murad IV as the reigning sultan, but since he was only twelve in 1624 and didn't begin to assert his independence for another four years,[139] Kösem's connection to the new fortification is solid, even if she didn't personally finance it as she did the village's mosque. By 1625, therefore, Kösem's mosque and fortress in Anadolu Kavaği stood as early symbols of her fortitude and commitment. Given Kösem and Turhan's clear antipathy for one another, it is not hard to imagine Turhan wanting to surpass this symbol, even decades later. Circumstantial evidence indicates that in 1683, the year before she died, Turhan ordered the construction of a mosque on the opposite bank from Anadolu Kavaği, in the town of Rumeli Kavaği.[140] If these two mosques, facing one another across the treacherous channel, were the product of the patronage of rival regents, they serve as a metaphor for life in the Topkapı Palace after Ibrahim's death. The two resolute women, separated by a river of political ambition, knew there could be no meaningful

[132] At 1,100 paces, Kumkale was 200 paces smaller in circumference. See Hakan T. Karateke, "Synopsis," *Evliya Çelebi's Journey from Bursa to the Dardanelles and Edirne: From the Fifth Book of the Seyahatname* Hakan T. Karateke (ed. and trans.) (Leiden: Brill, 2013), 166, EBSCOhost.
[133] Part of this public service came through the financing of public works, such as mosques, schools, and fountains. These helped ameliorate public discontent. See Özgüleş, *The Women Who Built the Ottoman World*, 57.
[134] Thys-Şenocak, *Ottoman Women Builders*, 115, 180.
[135] Thys-Şenocak, *Ottoman Women Builders*, 279.
[136] For information on comparative sea temperatures, see https://seatemperature.info/ For this description, I compared temperatures at Yalta, the Bosporus and Mykonos.
[137] Finkel, *Osman's Dream*, 219. The raids included one on the village of Yeniköy, about eleven miles north of the Topkapı Palace.
[138] Thys-Şenocak, *Ottoman Women Builders*, 279. This fortress was dismantled in the nineteenth century.
[139] Finkel, *Osman's Dream*, 208.
[140] According to one primary source, the Valide Mosque of Rumeli Kavaği was dedicated to Turhan's brother, Yusuf Ağa, but it is uncertain that Turhan actually had a brother. There is also a letter to Turhan "asking for permission to patrol the fortresses of the upper Bosporus" and letters from Turhan asking that property and endowments be transferred to a man named Yusuf Ağa. The mosque in Rumeli Kavaği no longer stands, which makes it difficult to be certain that it was constructed on Turhan's orders. See Thys-Şenocak, *Ottoman Women Builders*, 278-279.

common ground. There would be one winner and one loser in their power struggle to succeed Ibrahim.

The waters of the Bosporus were treacherous indeed.

J

Jahanara Begum

1614-1681

Unprecedented Persian eulogies, written in Arabic script, frame the great arched central entrance of the Jami Masjid in Agra, India, which was finished in 1637. The words offer tribute to the person who paid for the mosque's construction, lauding the patron for being of great dignity and wisdom and for holding the place of greatest honor amongst the Mughal emperor's children. The inscription even makes a comparison between the benefactor and the brightness of the sun. Then comes the surprise: it hails the patron as "the most revered of the ladies of the age, the pride of her gender, the princess of the realm…Jahan Ara Begum."[1] This inscription, and the woman it celebrates, challenges Western stereotypes of Muslim women, just as Jahanara's life helps illustrate the similarities and differences between the Mughal empire and its Ottoman counterpart twenty-eight hundred miles west.

Through the course of her sixty-seven years, four individuals played central roles in the renowned princess' life. The first was her father, Shah Jahan, the fifth emperor of the Mughal Empire and builder of the Taj Mahal. They seemed to share a special affinity since the princess was the emperor's oldest surviving child, but the events of June 17, 1631 transformed the father-daughter relationship. As Jahanara and Shah Jahan were playing a game of chess, waiting for the news of Jahanara's mother's most recent labor, a servant brought word that Mumtaz Mahal needed to see her daughter immediately. Jahanara went to her mother's bedside and saw the pools of blood; Mumtaz Mahal's fourteenth child would not emerge from the womb after thirty hours of labor, and the physicians and midwives despaired for her life. Jahanara rushed to share the news with Shah

---

[1] Afshan Bokhari, "The 'Light' of the Timuria: Jahan Ara Begum's Patronage, Piety, and Poetry in 17th Century Mughal India," *Marg*, vol. 60, no. 1 (September 2008), 52-61. Ruby Lal notes that Jahanara was only the third imperial woman to commission a mosque. The first was Emperor Jahangir's mother, Harkha, who built the Begum Shahi in Lahore in 1611; the second was Jahangir's wife and Jahanara's grandaunt, Nur Jahan. Lal argues that Jahanara was inspired by Nur and emulated her in many ways. See Ruby Lal, *Empress: The Astonishing Reign of Nur Jahan* (New York: W. W. Norton & Company, 2018), 224-225.

Jahan, who ran to his wife's bedside, "shedding tears like rain-water," according to one account.[2] Neither the tears nor the prayers helped and Mumtaz Mahal died just after giving birth to a daughter.[3] One of the midwives turned the empress' face towards Mecca. Following Muslim tradition, a female body washer bathed the queen in cold camphor water and wrapped her in white. She was buried the next day at dawn, her body taken out through a special hole in the fortress' walls, head first to prevent the spirit from finding its way back inside the palace.[4]

Shah Jahan went into deep mourning. He refused to listen to music and never again wore perfume. He also began to age quickly, with his hair and beard turning white within a week to match white mourning clothes he wore for two years. He even thought about abdicating.[5] Fortunately, Jahanara proved able to ease some of the burden. She became the *de-facto* queen of the Mughal empire in her mother's stead and the dominate female at court.[6] She began to monitor affairs of state by listening from behind a lattice screen to the information presented to her father[7] and by simultaneously receiving news from secret intelligence reports, which emperors usually opened in the harem.[8] It also meant Jahanara became the protector of the imperial seal, which showed the name of the ruling emperor in the center of a circle and the names of his predecessors in a surrounding orbit of smaller circles; she was responsible for affixing the seal to all imperial edicts, thereby confirming their legitimacy.[9] In addition, as the most important woman in the royal family, Jahanara took responsibility for arranging the weddings of three of her four brothers and for supervising the upbringing of her

---

[2] Fergus Nicoll, *Shah Jahan: The Rise and Fall of the Mughal Emperor* (London, U.K.: Haus Publishing, 2009), 176-177.

[3] Mumtaz Mahal gave birth to fourteen children between 1613 and 1631; seven survived past childhood.

[4] Waldemar Hansen, *The Peacock Throne: The Drama of Mughal India* (New York: Holt, Rinehart and Winston, 1972), 111.

[5] See Hansen, *The Peacock Throne,* 112 and Nicoll, *Shah Jahan,* 180.

[6] Hansen, *The Peacock Throne,* 117.

[7] Ruby Lal, *Domesticity and Power in the Early Mughal World* (Cambridge, U.K.: Cambridge University Press, 2005), 44.

[8] Abraham Eraly, *The Mughal World: India's Tainted Paradise* (London, U.K.: Weidenfeld & Nicolson, 2007), 131; and Rukhsana Iftikhar, "The Imperial Households of the Great Mughals," *Journal of the Research Society of Pakistan,* vol. 47, no. 1, June, 2010), ProQuest Central.

[9] Annabel Teh Gallop, "The Genealogical Seal of the Mughal Emperors of India," *Journal of the Royal Asiatic Society,* Vol.9, No. 1 (April 1999), 77-140, EBSCOhost.

youngest brother, Murad, who was seven when Mumtaz Mahal died.[10] These duties, as well as her close relationship with her father, allowed Jahanara to influence imperial policy[11] for, as even official dynastic chroniclers acknowledged, women could govern and participate in factional conflicts quite readily.[12]

There were two reasons why Jahanara could do all of this effectively. The first was that she was bright and had received a strong education in her youth. Tutored by carefully selected and experienced teachers, she studied Persian, Arabic, theology and history.[13] In time, she knew the Quran by heart, developed a deep sense of spirituality, and became a noted poet.[14] She was, in fact, a part of the Mughal court tradition of women authors writing works of literary merit that are still enjoyed today.[15] The second reason was that she was independently wealthy and not dependent on income from the state treasury, as were women like Tōfukumon'in in Kyoto or Kōsem in Istanbul. Much of this income came from Jahanara's monopoly on the royal fees collected from the customs house at Surat—the empire's most important port on the Arabian Sea.[16] In addition, Jahanara owned ships of her own, which she contracted out to Dutch and English traders to generate additional income through Indian Ocean trade.[17] All of this income came on top of her annual imperial salary of one million rupees, the gifts bestowed upon her by Shah Jahan (such as 200,000 gold coins and 400,000 rupees given her upon his ascension to the throne in 1628), and her inheritance of half of her mother's estate of twenty million rupees.[18] Altogether, the princess' annual income was about ten million rupees a year. This allowed her to maintain her own household and her own battalion of soldiers.[19] What Jahanara's relationship with her father couldn't influence, her wealth could.

---

[10] Munis D. Faruqui, *The Princes of the Mughal Empire, 1504-1719* (New York: Cambridge University Press, 2012), 72, and Steven P. Blake, "Contributors to the Urban Landscape: Women Builders in Safavid Isfahan and Mughal Shahjahanabad," in *Women in the Medieval Islamic World: Power, Patronage and Piety*, Gavin R. G. Hambly (ed.) (New York: St. Martin's Press, 1998), 416. One illustration of Jahanara's wealth and importance is the amount she spent on her brother Dara Shukoh's wedding: Rs 16,000,000 for pearls, jewels, clothing, carpets, elephants, Arabian horses, and cash gifts, which were ready for presentation on January 25, 1633. This budget was supplemented with Rs 10,000,000 from his mother-in-law, and Rs 6,000,000 form the royal treasury. See Qamar Jahān Begam, *Princess Jahānāra Begam Her Life and Works* (Karachi, Pakistan: S.M. Hamid 'Ali/P.E.C.H. Society, [1992]), 22.

[11] Edward S. Holden, *The Mogul Emperors of Hindustan* (New York: Charles Scribner's Sons, 1895), 313.

[12] Gregory C. Kozlowski, "Private Lives and Public Piety: Women and the Practice of Islam in Mughal India," in *Women in the Medieval Islamic World: Power, Patronage and Piety*, Gavin R. G. Hambly (ed.) (New York: St. Martin's Press, 1998), 470.

[13] Rukhsana Iftikhar, "Cultural Contribution of Mughal Ladies," *South Asian Studies* 25, no 2 (July, 2010): 323-339, ProQuest Central.

[14] Diana and Michael Preston, *Taj Mahal: Passion and Genius at the Heart of the Moghul Empire* (New York: Walker & Company, 2007), 206.

[15] Begum Shaista Suhrawardy Ikramullah, "The Role of Women in the Life and Literature of Pakistan," *Journal of the Royal Society of Arts*, Vol. 106, No. 5025 (August, 1958), 713-726, EBSCOhost.

[16] William Foster, *The English Factories in India, 1655-1600* (Oxford, U.K.: Clarendon Press, 1921), 15. Surat's wealth was such that the Portuguese in Goa had long coveted it. See Jorge Flores and Nuno Vassallo e Silva, "Introduction," *Goa and the Great Mughal*, Jorge Flores and Nuno Vassallo e Silva (eds.) (London: Scala Publishers, 2004), 12.

[17] Satish Chandra, "Commercial Activities of the Mughal Emperors During the Seventeenth Century," in Satish Chandra, *Essays on Medieval Indian History* (New Delhi, India: Oxford University Press, 2005), 232.

[18] Kozlowski, "Private Lives and Public Piety." 476.

[19] Faruqui, *The Princes of the Mughal Empire, 1504-1719*, 164.

Jahanara spent a significant amount of this income helping her father bring the empire's new capital city, Shahjahanabad, to life. Construction began in 1639 upon Shah Jahan's orders. The emperor, keenly interested in architecture, found his father's and grandfather's capital of Agra to be too confining for the imperial pageantry he desired. His new choice allowed him to take advantage of the Delhi area's tradition as a capital city.[20] Initial construction took nine years, and Shah Jahan moved the court to his new city in April 1648. At the inauguration ceremonies, the court presented the emperor with appropriately luxurious gifts, while Shah Jahan in turn conferred titles, honors, money, and presents on princes, nobles, architects, and craftsmen. Poets marked the occasion by writing chronograms—works whose letters, when transcribed into numbers, add up to a particular date—and the festive celebration continued for nine days.[21]

Shahjahanabad was laid out in accordance with both ancient Hindu designs and rules for architecture and Islamic sensibilities. In the Hindu tradition, the city's walls reflected the curvature of a bow, its north-south streets represented the bowstring, and one major east-west street, Chandi Chowk, signified the archer's arm. In the Muslim tradition, the plan of the city emulated human anatomy with the royal palace as the head, a central bazaar as the backbone, the major mosque as the heart, and the *hammams*,* schools, and travelers' lodgings as other vital organs.[22] Its 1,500 acres, surrounded by a twenty-seven-foot-high wall running 3.8 miles, housed 250,000 to 300,000 people in 1650, and as many as another hundred thousand lived in the city's immediate environs.[23]

Of the eighteen important buildings and gardens built by nine Mughal women between 1648 and the 1730s, five were Jahanara's.[24] Three of the five were public works, all of which ran along the archer's arm of Chandi Chowk. The first of these was a shopping esplanade with a canal down its center. The street was broad and long, accommodating over fifteen hundred shops under arcades, each with a small warehouse behind it for extra merchandise on the lower floor and living quarters above. Here Syrian and Chinese merchants competed with their Zanzibari and Dutch counterparts as everything from rubies, hookahs, and camels to weapons, perfumes, and "cures" for venereal disease might be had after considerable haggling.[25] Most of all, the bazaar was a very social place, and as such an area full of gossip about the imperial family and prominent members of the court. Shah Jahan, for example, was regularly criticized by the general public for being haughty as a result of his preference for rigid formality. He was also seen as lascivious,[26] which fed persistent rumors among European travelers about an incestuous relationship with his daughter.

---

[20] The Delhi area saw the rise of seven distinct cities with fortified palaces between the tenth and seventeenth centuries; Shahjahanabad was the seventh. See R. Nath, "Delhi: History and Urban Development," *Dictionary of Art* (Jane Turner, ed.), Volume 8: Cossiers to Diotti (New York: Grove/Oxford University Press, 1996), 670-676.

[21] Susan Stronge, "The Land of 'Mogor,'" *Goa and the Great Mughal*, Jorge Flores and Nuno Vassallo e Silva (eds.) (London: Scala Publishers, 2004), 145. Shahjahanabad was the only capital city in the world to be entirely constructed in the mid-seventeenth century. See Geoffrey Parker, *Global Crisis: War, Climate Change, and Catastrophe in the Seventeenth Century* (New Haven, Connecticut: Yale University Press, 2013), 399.

[22] Blake, *Shahjahanabad,* 32-35.

[23] Blake, *Shahjahanabad,* 31, 67.

[24] Blake, "Contributors to the Urban Landscape," 411, 416.

[25] Blake, "Contributors to the Urban Landscape," 421.

[26] Catherine B. Asher and Cynthia Talbot, *India Before Europe* (New York: Cambridge University Press, 2006), 207.

In reality, many of the travelers who relished the gossip simply struggled to believe that Jahanara's influence on the court could have legitimate merit.[27]

The second of Jahanara's public works was a two-story, ninety-room caravanserai* situated near the midpoint of the nearly mile-long Chandi Chowk. Jahanara wrote that she wanted the lodging for wealthy merchants and travelers to be "large and fine" without any parallel in India. With towers on each of its four squared corners and a garden full of flowers, trees, and fountains in its courtyard, the structure was imposing yet welcoming. There was also a mosque inside for prayer. Jahanara must have been proud of the outcome for she wrote, "The wander[er] who enters its courts will be restored in body and soul and my name will never be forgotten."[28] Across the street from the inn, Jahanara built the third of her major public works, one of the city's largest *hammams*. Nearby, there was an enclosed fifty-acre park for which Jahanara served as the landscape architect.[29] She designed it as a private space for the women and children of the imperial household to meet with the noble families outside of the palace. It featured silver fountains, fruit-bearing trees, and shading pavilions.[30] Like the gardens surrounding the Taj Mahal, Jahanara's garden evoked the Quran's vision for the afterlife: unending leisure spent in a gloriously lush and productive walled garden.[31]

In addition to these four works, Jahanara designed and financed her own mansion within the palace grounds. Symbolically situated in between the harem and the Hall of Special Audience, where the court's most important work was conducted, Jahanara's mansion overlooked the Yamuna River. Because her mansion was destroyed in the eighteenth and nineteenth centuries, along with the harem, it is unclear what the mansion looked like. It certainly would have displayed many of the features of mid-seventeenth century Mughal design, including proportion, symmetry, uniformity, hierarchy, symbolism, and luxurious attention to detail.[32] The building's handcrafted decorative patterns would have featured significant balance and repetition, and they would have built towards an apex symbolizing the glory of God and the strength of the Mughal empire. Each decorative element, such as a row of flowers or an intertwining vine, would have highlighted each architectural element, such as a column or a lintel.[33] The few surviving descriptions of the mansion, all fragmentary, indicate that the walls and ceilings were colorfully painted and encrusted with small pieces of glass to dazzle the eye. There was also a gracefully carved marble screen facing the river.[34] This screen was important because Mughal women were generally subject to the *purdah* system: they wore white veils to cover their faces when in public and lived in segregated quarters protected

[27] Lisa Balabanlilar, "The Begims of the Mystic Feast: Turco-Mongol Tradition in the Mughal Harem," *The Journal of Asian Studies*, 69, no. 1 (February, 2010), 123-147, ProQuest Central.

[28] Jahanara quoted in Blake, "Contributors to the Urban Landscape," 421. Unfortunately, the caravanserai no longer stands, having been replaced by a municipal building.

[29] Jyoti P. Sharma, "The British Treatment of Historic Gardens in the Indian Subcontinent: The Transformation of Delhi's Nawab Safdarjung's Tomb Complex from a Funerary Garden into a Public Park," *Garden History*, Vol. 35, No. 2 (Winter, 2007), 210-228, EBSCOhost. The name of the park was Begam-ka Bagh.

[30] Sadia Dehlvi, *The Sufi Courtyard: Dargahs of Delhi* (Noida, India: HarperCollins Publishers India, 2012), n.p., Google Books.

[31] Giles Tillotson, *Taj Mahal* (Cambridge, Massachusetts: Harvard University Press, 2008), 62, 66.

[32] Ebba Koch, *The Complete Taj Mahal and the Riverfront Gardens of Agra* (New York: Thames & Hudson, Inc., 2006), 104.

[33] Ebba Koch, "The Lost Colonnade of Shah Jahan's Bath in the Red Fort of Agra," *The Burlington Magazine*, Vol. 124, No. 951 (June, 1982), 331-339, EBSCOhost.

[34] Blake, *Shahjahanabad*, 39-40.

by palace guards. But unlike in the Ottoman seraglio, men did occasionally win the honor of entering the Mughal harem and were able to see royal women uncovered.[35] The Ottoman harem also differed from the Mughal one because the role of concubines was different. In India, a hierarchical ranking system of concubines never developed. This meant that only wives and daughters retained political influence.[36] Furthermore, these royal women, unlike their Ottoman counterparts, did not have to have children in order to secure this authority.[37] Taken together, these differences meant that women like Jahanara had a thorough understanding of what happened in the most important room of the palace: the Hall of Special Audience.

This white marble pavilion with four gold domes, the most ostentatious structure of the palace complex, had interior walls inlaid with pearls and agates and paintings of colorful flowers and trees laden with fruit. The ceiling featured gold rings and small pieces of embedded glass which reflected sunlight around the room, as in Jahanara's mansion. At the center of the room stood the Peacock Throne: a canopied gold chair with twelve columns, studded with diamonds, rubies, emeralds, sapphires, and pearls. Atop the canopy stood a peacock statue with its bejeweled tail fully-fanned. With one of the rubies being three fingers wide and two fingers long, according to a contemporary account, the throne effectively embodied the vast wealth of Mughal India during the reign of Shah Jahan.[38] It was, in fact, a wealth far greater than that of the Ottoman Empire, for Mughal India benefited—in ways that Istanbul simply did not—from brisk economic growth as a result of increases in European trade and the influx of silver from Potosí.[39]

In 1644, Shah Jahan stopped conducting government business in the Hall of Special Audience as a result of a serious accident. On March 26, as Jahanara passed down a corridor between the emperor's quarters and her own, a candle's flame caught a piece of her flowing dress. Two of her female attendants immediately fell upon the princess in an effort to douse the ensuing flames, but their own dresses quickly caught fire too. Before the fire was quashed, Jahanara suffered significant burns on her back, side and arms; she spent the next four months in critical condition. Shah Jahan attended to his daughter for weeks, personally applying medicines and staying by her bedside as much as possible. He prayed, annulled debts, released prisoners, and gave alms in an effort to win God's mercy and alleviate his own sin.[40] After four months, Jahanara developed diarrhea and began to expel blood. This triggered a change in physicians.[41] Finally, in late November, Jahanara recovered completely, and the court rejoiced, Shah Jahan most of all.

Jahanara then went on a pilgrimage to the tomb of the Sufi Muslim saint Moinuddin Chishti in the city of Ajmer.[42] Even before the accident, Jahanara was a deeply spiritual person, but she was not someone who found comfort in a precise or literal theology. Rather, the mystical, esoteric sects of Sunni Islam drew her. Like other Sufis, the princess found fulfillment in trying to create a state of mind that allowed for revelation, rather than adhering to a strict set of rules.[43] She particularly

---

[35] Soma Mukherjee, *Royal Mughal Ladies and their Contributions* (New Delhi, India: Gyan Publishing House, 2001), 46-47.
[36] Lal, *Domesticity and Power in the Early Mughal World*, 223.
[37] Balabanlilar, "The Begims of the Mystic Feast."
[38] Holden, *The Mogul Emperors of Hindustan*, 290-291. This throne no longer exists. In 1739, the Persians sacked Shahjahanabad and took the throne back to Persia as war tribute. It was subsequently dismantled.
[39] Faruqui, *The Princes of the Mughal Empire, 1504-1719*, 17-18.
[40] The two attendants died in the accident. See Hansen, *The Peacock Throne*, 126-127; and Qamar Jahān Begam, *Princess Jahānāra Begam Her Life and Works*, 26-28.
[41] Qamar Jahān Begam, *Princess Jahānāra Begam Her Life and Works*, 28.
[42] Mukherjee, *Royal Mughal Ladies and their Contributions*, 42.
[43] Karen Armstrong, *Islam: A Short History* (New York: The Modern Library, 2000), 74.

admired the approach of Moinuddin—a thirteenth-century saint who wrote a treatise connecting Islamic and Hindu mysticism through yoga,[44] and who believed that listening to specific music was crucial for spiritual enlightenment. These songs began with tributes to the Prophet, proceeded to songs of love designed to produce strong emotions, and concluded with music hoping to lead to mystical annihilation and the divine presence.[45] This interpretation was inherently controversial. Many Muslims considered it quite dangerous, while very conservative Muslims considered it idolatrous. Even Sufi texts indicate that this form of Islamic expression should be reserved for those with sufficient sophistication to understand its power.[46] Jahanara supposed herself to have sufficient aptitude, for she believed herself to be part of the sacred group bound for Paradise. Others affirmed this expertise, for she earned the rank of *piri-muridi* or master-disciple, the highest rank a Sufi woman could earn.[47] She also saw her position within the imperial family as unique, writing, "In our family no one took the step on the path to seek God or the truth that would light the Trimuid lamp eternally. I was grateful for having received this great fortune and wealth. There was no end to my happiness."[48] As a result of these beliefs, Jahanara timed her visit to Ajmer to coincide with special events surrounding Chishti's death anniversary. During her visit, she prayed in the mosque Shah Jahan had recently built, perhaps as she had the year before during a similar pilgrimage to Ajmer:

> With an hour of daylight remaining, I went to the holy sanctuary and rubbed my pale face on the dust of that threshold. From the doorway to the blessed tomb I went barefoot, kissing the ground. Having entered the dome, I went around the light-filled room of my master seven times, sweeping it with my eyelashes, and making the sweet-smelling dust of that place the mascara of my eyes.

> At that moment, a marvelous spiritual state and mystical experience befell this annihilated one, which cannot rightly be written. From extreme longing I became astonished, and I do not know what I said or did.

> Finally with my own hand I put the highest quality of *attar* [rose petal oil] on the perfumed tomb of that revered one, and having taken off the rose scarf that I had on my head, I place it on top of the blessed tomb.[49]

---

[44] William Dalrymple, "Under the Spell of Yoga," *The New York Review of Books*, Vol. LXI, No. 4 (March 6, 2014), 30.

[45] Carl W. Ernst, *The Shambhala Guide to Sufism* (Boston, Massachusetts: Shambhala Publications, 1997), 186-187. It is not dissimilar to the technique and goals of the Mevlevi Order or Whirling Dervishes.

[46] Ernst, *The Shambhala Guide to Sufism*, 58, 188-189.

[47] Bokhari, "Between Patron and Piety," 122.

[48] Jahanara quoted in Bokhari, "Between Patron and Piety," 126.

[49] Jahanara, "*The Confident of Spirits*," in Carl W. Ernst and Bruce B. Lawrence, *Sufi Martyrs of Love: the Chishti Order in South Asia and Beyond* (New York: Palgrave Macmillan, 2002), 89. Ernst and Lawrence date this quote from November 1643.

~

Jahanara shared her deep spirituality and her interest in Sufism with the second important person in her life: her brother Dara Shukoh. Born one year after Jahanara, Dara Shukoh has traditionally been seen as much more of a scholar and poet than a warrior and imperial administrator.[50] He enjoyed spending time in Kashmir, where he converted a ruined Buddhist monastery into a garden, the Pari Mahal, and where he devoted his energies to consulting with Sufi masters.[51] Jahanara spent a significant amount of time with Dara Shukoh in Kashmir, making repeated trips so that she might learn from his teachers there.[52] This training was so inspiring that she began writing two of her most significant works, "Confident of Spirits" and "Message of the Madame." Together they detail her motivations for seeking spiritual enlightenment, and they link Sufism to Islam's earliest history in order to document Sufism's legitimacy.[53] While Jahanara may have utilized familiar Mughal tropes such as describing herself as "a weak, lowly person," who had "wasted [my] own life in

worldly matters,"[54] she made a point of documenting her ideas with what she believed to be the most "reliable and respected sources" available, including primary sources from the thirteenth century.[55] Through her writings, Jahanara sought to establish herself as a legitimate scholar and to point others in a true spiritual direction.

Jahanara did not, however, remove herself from the imperial court. Instead, she moved repeatedly between the sacred life she found in Kashmir with Dara Shukoh and the practical life she found with the entourage of Shah Jahan. She also tried to connect these two worlds in tangible ways. After her Kashmiri trip in 1638, she asked her father for the right to finance the construction of the Jami Mosque in Agra.[56] This allowed her a way to demonstrate both her financial power within the court and the strength of her spirituality. As for Dara Shukoh, the prince stayed in Kashmir. As part of his studies he wrote a hagiography, which documented the miracles of a seventeenth-century

---

[50] A new biography of Dara Shukoh challenges this traditional historiography and presents him as a far more complex figure. See Supriya Gandhi, *The Emperor Who Never Was: Dara Shukoh in Mughal India* (Cambridge, Massachusetts: Belknap Press of Harvard University Press, 2020).

[51] Pushpesh Pant, "A Taste of Paradise," *India International Centre Quarterly*, Vol. 37, No. 3/4, (A Tangled Web: Jammu & Kashmir) (Winter 2010-Spring 2011), 324-333, EBSCOhost.

[52] Jahanara made four trips to Kashmir during her life: 1634-1635, 1638-1640, 1645-1646, 1651-1653. See Qamar Jahān Begam, *Princess Jahānāra Begam Her Life and Works* (Karachi, Pakistan: S.M. Hamid 'Ali/P.E.C.H. Society, [1992]), 40. During her second trip, Jahanara wrote poetry, sent letters, and prepared a meal of flatbread and leafy vegetables to honor Sufi spiritual leader Hazrat Mullā Shāh Badakhshi. He ignored Jahanara for a month but eventually agreed to meet. Jahanara then "accepted him as my spiritual guide." See Qamar Jahān Begam, 44-45.

[53] Bokhari, "Between Patron and Piety," 120, 126, 141.

[54] Jahanara quoted in Bokhari, "Between Patron and Piety," 129-130.

[55] Jahanara quoted in Bokhari, "Between Patron and Piety," 129.

[56] Catherine B. Asher, *Architecture of Mughal India* (New York: Cambridge University Press, 1992), 189-190. The mosque was not completed until 1648.

female saint, and published handbooks to the Qadiriyya Sufi order to which he belonged.[57] His religious interests also extended beyond Sufism. He engaged in lengthy discussions with Jesuit missionaries, and he translated foundational Hindu texts such as the *Upanishads* and the *Bhagavad-Gita* into Persian. In time, he came to believe that these works from antiquity contained the basis of hidden meanings within the Quran. He argued that the fundamental nature of Hinduism was identical to that of Islam, that the Hindu soul and the Muslim soul were one and the same. In doing so, he echoed the religious curiosity of his great-grandfather, Akbar,[58] but he also angered more conservative Muslims who saw him as an apostate.[59]

Such a position naturally had political consequences, and Dara Shukoh soon found himself on the defensive, especially because Mughal princes were expected to compete against one another for the right to succeed the imperial throne. Unlike their Ottoman counterparts after 1600, Mughal princes continued the practice of leaving royal palaces to gain experience as warriors.[60] In this process and through their appointments as governors and military commanders, Mughal princes were expected to articulate their own vision and assemble their own achievements, thereby attracting an ever-widening circle of loyal supporters.[61] Initially, Dara Shukoh held the best position as the oldest brother who had the overt support of Shah Jahan as his heir apparent. His controversial religious views and his lack of military success, however, opened the door for his younger brothers to challenge his position. But Jahanara proved to be Dara Shukoh's strongest ally in the imperial family. She once wrote, "I love my brother Dara extremely both in form and in spirit. We are, in fact, like one soul in two bodies and one spirit in two physical forms."[62] In fact, she believed that Dara Shukoh would be the heir to both the exoteric (what can be understood by the general public) and the esoteric (what can be understood by the enlightened few).[63] For Jahanara, her brother epitomized everything a just monarch should be.

Dara Shukoh's ultimate test came in September 1657, when Shah Jahan fell seriously ill. Unable to urinate for three days, he was on the verge of death.[64] While few knew the details, the emperor's inability to attend to his public duties, such as receiving petitions from the general public, sent

[57] Hansen, *The Peacock Throne*, 148. The saint was Bibi Jamal Khatum, who died in 1647. Her miracles included making a fish glow, feeding a crowd with a single rooster, and generating milk from a small bottle of oil. See Ernst, *The Shambhala Guide to Sufism*, 67-68.

[58] Akbar was the Mughal Empire's third emperor, reigning for almost 50 years from January 1556 to October 1605. He is popularly remembered for originating a policy of religious toleration in the subcontinent and for setting an important precedent for the Mughal Empire. Some historians have argued that this reputation needs revaluation, for "the religious controversy surrounding Akbar must be reinterpreted in light of the institutions and knowledge of sacred kingship that had developed in early modern Iran and India." This includes Timur, for Akbar also "drew upon conjunction astrology, messianic and millennial myths, and claims of royal and saintly authority." See A. Azfar Moin, *The Millennial Sovereign: Sacred Kingship and Sainthood in Islam* (New York: Columbia University Press, 2012), 131-132, 166. As one reviewer of Moin's book noted, "Akbar clearly exploited commonalities of themes in divergent faiths and their histories and legends," and he was "exceptionally curious about other belief systems, customs, and peoples," but official Mughal records "do not exalt Akbar's interfaith effort or even name it." See Jamsheed K. Choksy, "The Millennial Sovereign: Sacred Kingship and Sainthood in Islam," *The Journal of the American Oriental Society*, no. 3 (2015), 619-621, EBSCOhost.

[59] John F. Richards, *The Mughal Empire* (New York: Cambridge University Press, 1993), 152.

[60] Kozlowski, "Private Lives and Public Piety," 473.

[61] Faruqui, *The Princes of the Mughal Empire, 1504-1719*, 7-12.

[62] Jahanara quoted in Hansen, *The Peacock Throne*, 151.

[63] Faruqui, *The Princes of the Mughal Empire, 1504-1719*, 178.

[64] Bamber Gascoigne, *The Great Moghuls* (New York: Dorset Press, 1971), 206.

rumors flying through the empire.[65] Dara Shukoh, who at the time was the only son at court in Shahjahanabad and who had Jahanara's full confidence and support, assumed command. He arrested his brothers' allies and censored all communications.[66] Meanwhile, Shah Jahan's other three surviving sons, Aurangzeb, Murad, and Shuja, began preparing their troops for war. Murad and Shuja were so brazen that each crowned themselves as emperor. Jahanara's sisters also picked sides with one choosing Aurangzeb, one choosing Murad.[67] The royal family was torn apart. The ensuing war did not go well for Dara Shukoh, despite Jahanara's help financing the campaign and her strong contacts in Punjab, Gujarat, and Rajasthan.[68] At the battle of Samugarh on May 29, 1658, Dara Shukoh's forces were routed as a result of Aurangzeb's superior artillery, and Dara Shukoh dismounted his elephant and fled the battlefield. Aurangzeb occupied the capital and imprisoned Shah Jahan.

With her father imprisoned, her favorite brother on the run, and the rest of her family factionalized, Jahanara decided to step forward and present a diplomatic solution to the dynastic war. She requested a meeting with Aurangzeb, who received his sister on June 10, 1658. His decision to do so was a sign of his respect for her intelligence and her stature as the oldest sibling.[69] It also stemmed from the legacy of women helping to establish royal traditions and governmental practices in the early years of the Mughal dynasty,[70] and from the general Mughal acknowledgement that women could legitimately govern.[71] In the meeting, Jahanara proposed a five-way partition of the empire: Dara Shukoh would rule the Punjab, Aurangzeb would rule much of north and central India, Shuja would rule Bengal, Murad would rule Gujarat, and Aurangzeb's oldest son would rule the Deccan.[72] Aurangzeb rejected the proposal, knowing that such a compromise was impossible. Like all of his brothers, Aurangzeb believed he had the right to rule all of India, not just part of it. He thought there could be no alternatives to the concentration of power in a single monarch. In this way Mughal dynastic struggles had a Darwinian character to them: from the time sons reached maturity and fathers showed age, everyone knew that only the fittest would survive.

For a year after Jahanara and Aurangzeb's meeting, as the subcontinent suffered massive famine as a result of another failed monsoon season,[73] Dara Shukoh remained on the run. Finally, an Afghan chief betrayed him. The prisoner-prince arrived in Delhi in August 1659 to find Aurangzeb

---

[65] According to the Hindu custom of *darshan*, anyone could petition the ruler; Shah Jahan received these petitions every morning at a special balcony overlooking the banks of the Yamuna River. See Blake, *Shahjahanabad*, 91. This tradition of formerly presenting the emperor to receive petitions also distinguished Mughal governance from that of Ottoman sultans, who had no responsibility to present themselves directly to the people. See Catherine B. Asher, "Sub-Imperial Palaces: Power and Authority in Mughal India," *Ars Orientalis*, Vol. 23, Pre-Modern Islamic Palaces, 1993, 281-302.

[66] Richards, *The Mughal Empire*, 158.

[67] In the succession struggle, the middle sister, Roshanara picked Aurangzeb, while the youngest sister, Gauharana, opted for Murad. See Audrey Truschke, *Aurangzeb: The Life and Legacy of India's Most Controversial King* (Stanford, California: Stanford University Press, 2017), 25.

[68] Faruqui, *The Princes of the Mughal Empire, 1504-1719*, 164.

[69] Hansen, *The Peacock Throne*, 266.

[70] Lal, *Domesticity and Power in the Early Mughal World*, 1.

[71] Kozlowski, "Private Lives and Public Piety," 470.

[72] Faruqui, *The Princes of the Mughal Empire, 1504-1719*, 40. Jahanara was not above playing politics. She contacted Aurangzeb's son to see if he might be willing to work against his father and side with Jahanara and Dara Shukoh in the dynastic war.

[73] Parker, *Global Crisis*, 403, 409. Parker notes that the annual monsoon, upon which the subcontinent depends for 90% of its rainfall, failed four times in the seventeenth century: 1613-1615, 1630-1632, 1658-1660, and 1685-1687. Each of these climate crises killed millions despite imperial attempts to provide relief.

firmly in command, having skillfully dispatched his other brotherly rivals. Aurangzeb had Dara Shukoh paraded through the streets to humiliate him and then ordered Dara Shukoh's execution in accordance with Mughal law.[74] Having supported her favorite brother in the succession fight, Jahanara could have found herself in a precarious situation, but that was not the Mughal tradition. The princely winners were generally magnanimous once their male rivals to the throne had been eliminated.[75] In fact, Jahanara could have joined the court in Shahjahanabad, but she instead chose to live with her imprisoned father in the Red Fort in Agra. For the next eight years, from 1658 to 1666, Jahanara consoled her grieving father. Legend has it that he passed the time forlornly looking out windows and from balconies at the Taj Mahal, longing for death and his reunion with his beloved wife Mumtaz Mahal.[76]

Jahanara envisioned a grand funeral for her father. She wanted "officers of the state carrying the coffin on their soldiers" and all of the "rich men and nobles of Agra" and "all of the scholars, theologians, and popular leaders…walking beside the bier with bare heads and feet" with "common people in their tens of thousands forming the rear of the procession" and with "gold and silver being scattered on both sides every now and then as they moved" towards the Taj Mahal for burial.[77] Aurangzeb, however, had not made any arrangements for his father's funeral and was not in Agra the night he died. Without authorization for an illustrious funeral, Jahanara's hands were tied. Instead, she informed the Red Fort's commander of the death of the emperor and summoned the legal and religious authorities.[78] At dawn, Shah Jahan's body was taken head first out of the Red Fort, carried to the river for transport, and by noon his body lay next to his wife's in the crypt underneath the main floor of the Taj Mahal.

The third critical relationship in Jahanara's life, and the one most important during its last third, was with her brother Aurangzeb. Upon receiving the news of their father's death, Aurangzeb wrote to Jahanara, asking,

> What shall I write, and how can writing suffice, to express what passes in my sorrow-stricken mind at this inevitable occurrence? Has the pen the power to write one word about this heart-breaking pain? Where has the tongue the strength enough to express this patience-robbing grief?[79]

These words seem genuine, for by all appearances, Aurangzeb's own grief was real.[80] His grief was that of the rejected son, who could never win his father's approval. As he told Jahanara in a letter thirteen years before, he would rather die than continue to suffer his father's rejection: if "I alone should spend my life in dishonor and die in obscurity… it is better that by order of His Majesty, I should be relieved from the disgust of such a life."[81] After Shah Jahan's death, however, Aurangzeb

---

[74] Richards, *The Mughal Empire*, 160-161. Shuja and Murad were both executed in 1661, ending any succession controversy.

[75] Faruqui, *The Princes of the Mughal Empire, 1504-1719*, 255.

[76] Tillotson, *Taj Mahal*, 37-39.

[77] Jahanara quoted in Hansen, *The Peacock Throne*, 431.

[78] Tillotson, *Taj Mahal*, 39.

[79] Aurangzeb quoted in Jadunath Sarkar, *Studies in Aurangzeb's Reign* (Hyderabad, India: Orient Longman, 1989), 105.

[80] Diana and Michael Preston, *Taj Mahal: Passion and Genius at the Heart of the Moghul Empire* (New York: Walker & Company, 2007), 249.

[81] Aurangzeb quoted in Faruqui, *The Princes of the Mughal Empire, 1504-1719*, 98.

told Jahanara he was coming to see her to try to comfort her and to pay his respects to his father. He said that he was praying for his father's soul and reminded her, "the thing that will be useful to the late Emperor at this time is the conveying [to his soul] the religious merit of reciting the Quran and giving alms to beggars. Exert yourself to the utmost in this matter, and offer the merit of these acts as a present to the resplendent soul of His late Majesty."[82] Jahanara responded by recounting her being "sunk in an ocean of grief" until "the rays of the Sun of this loving brother's grace shone forth" with the news of Aurangzeb's impending arrival. Interestingly, however, Jahanara balanced this flamboyant prose with an insightful understanding of the political situation: "It is evident and clear that henceforth the full care of all those left behind by him will depend upon your favour and attention. In these circumstances what can I write that is not obvious to you?"[83]

Fortunately, their reunion in the harem of the Red Fort went well. Jahanara presented Aurangzeb with a large gold basin full of gems, which included some of hers and some of Shah Jahan's, as well as a pardon she had managed to get Shah Jahan to sign, absolving Aurangzeb of all sins committed against him. Aurangzeb was deeply moved by these gestures and forgave Jahanara for remaining loyal to their father instead of to him. Before leaving Agra, Aurangzeb presented Jahanara with 100,000 gold pieces, awarded her an annual salary of 1.7 million rupees, and proclaimed her *Padishah Begum*.[84] Jahanara's rehabilitation was complete. She moved back to Shahjahanabad in October 1666 as Aurangzeb's confidante.[85]

Aurangzeb's reign, the second longest in Mughal history after Akbar's, is difficult to characterize succinctly, especially because of the ways in which the historical memory of his 48-year-long rule inflames religious animosities in both India and Pakistan today.[86] He is, and perhaps always has been, a polarizing figure. According to an interpretation that gained traction during the period of British colonialism,[87] Aurangzeb broke with Akbar's tradition of religious toleration because he: 1) believed his predecessors had sinned by not enforcing *Shari'a*, Islamic religious law; 2) needed to reward his supporters in the succession war, many of whom were conservative Muslims and religious scholars with high expectations for societal change; and 3) wanted to punish those who

[82] Aurangzeb quoted in Sarkar, *Studies in Aurangzib's Reign*, 106-107.

[83] Jahanara quoted in Sarkar, *Studies in Aurangzib's Reign*, 106-107.

[84] This is a double honorific that includes designations for both genders. *Padishah* means sovereign at the same level as a king or sultan. *Begum* means lady or queen. One might think of Jahanara, therefore, as being the king of queens.

[85] Hansen, *The Peacock Throne*, 448.

[86] Taymiya R. Zaman, "Nostalgia, Lahore, and the Ghost of Aurangzeb," *Fragments: Interdisciplinary Approaches to the Study of Ancient and Medieval Pasts,* Volume 4, (2015), accessed April 23, 2019, https://tinyurl.com/y6jc8z8y. A film about Aurangzeb, entitled *Takht*, is expected to be released in 2021. Its leading actor says he is "a little bit terrified" to play the role because he has to "get to a place where his [Aurangzeb's] cruel choices make sense to me. The film will undoubtedly continue to inflame the rhetoric surrounding the Mughal king. See Rajeev Masand, "Making Sense of Aurangzeb," *Open*, April 19, 2019, EBSCOhost. For more on the misrepresentation of Aurangzeb, see Mohamed, Dheen. "Towards an Islamic Theology of Hindu-Muslim Relations." *Muslim World* 107, no. 2 (April 2017): 156, EBSCOhost. For information on the relationship between the presentation of history and Hindu nationalism, Hindutva, see Abu Lilia Sulani, "Hindutva and History: The Assault on the Academy." *Muslim World Book Review* 38, no. 1 (October 2017): 6, EBSCOhost. For additional information on Hindutva, see Jyotirmaya Sharma, *Hindutva: Exploring the Idea of Hindu Nationalism*, New Delhi: Penguin Books, 2011; and *Hindu Nationalism: A Reader*, Christophe Jaffrelot (ed.), Princeton, New Jersey: Princeton University Press, 2007.

[87] Taymiya R. Zaman, "Nostalgia, Lahore, and the Ghost of Aurangzeb."

had been disloyal and refused to make amends.[88] One way in which Aurangzeb implemented his changes was to adopt a tax policy that discriminated against Hindus. This included collecting a tax on Hindu pilgrims, imposing a tax on the honoring of Hindu dead in the Ganges,[89] and making Hindu merchants pay a 5% customs duty instead of the 2.5% imposed on Muslims.[90] He also re-imposed the *jizyah*, a poll tax on non-Muslims, after a hundred-year hiatus. Although meant for charity, it also enriched the religious scholars responsible for distributing these alms.[91] Some claim that Aurangzeb's pro-Muslim orientation resulted in the destruction of thousands of Hindu temples, forced conversions, terrorism, and even genocide.[92] The reality, however, was more nuanced, as respected historians have recently articulated. Aurganzeb did not order large-scale conversions, destroy thousands of temples, or commit genocide. Instead, he sought to act as just king who, in accordance with Islamic law, protected his subjects and usually offered them the freedom to worship in their own ways.[93]

This is not to say that Aurganzeb's rule was opposition-free. In fact, many of his policies sparked significant hostility. The port of Surat, the wealthy city from which Jahanara collected customs revenue, provides an example of these tensions. In 1669, the Islamic judge for the city sought to take advantage of the new regulations and began extorting money from Hindus to prevent the destruction of their temples and to prevent forced conversions. The community's leading Hindus, most of whom were merchants, responded to these threats with an ingenious protest: 8,000 men vacated the city, leaving their wives and children in Surat and bringing trade to a halt for months. Only Aurangzeb's promise of upholding Hindus' freedom of religion and the appointment of a new

[88] Ashirbadi Lal Srivastava, *The Mughal Empire (1526-1803 A.D.)* (Agra, India: Shiva Lal Agarwala & Company, 1966), 339; and Satish Chandra, "*Jizyah* and the State in India in the Seventeenth Century," in Satish Chandra, *Essays on Medieval Indian History* (New Delhi, India: Oxford University Press, 2005), 317.

[89] Ashirbadi Lal Srivastava, *The Mughal Empire (1526-1803 A.D.)* (Agra, India: Shiva Lal Agarwala & Company, 1966), 335.

[90] Farhat Hasan, *State and Locality in Mughal India: Power Relations in Western Asia, c. 1572-1730* (Cambridge, U.K.: Cambridge University Press, 2004), 117.

[91] Chandra, "*Jizyah* and the State in India in the Seventeenth Century," 311, 320-321.

[92] Vashi Sharma, *The Naked Mughals: Forbidden Tales of Harem and Butchery* ([New Delhi]: Agniveer, 2017), n.p. (chapter 7), Google Books. More reasoned but still critical accounts note that Aurangzeb dismantled important Hindu temples and replaced them with mosques to punish recalcitrant people who had violated long-established alliances and relationships. See Asher, *Architecture of Mughal India*, 253-254. In the town of Mathura, for example, Aurangzeb ordered a temple to Lord Krishna destroyed and decreed that many of its gold statues should be buried under the steps of a Jahnara's Jami Masjid mosque in Agra. This was done in retaliation for a sustained rebellion of Hindu farmers and herders in the Mathura region. See Richards, *The Mughal Empire*, 175.

[93] Truschke, *Aurangzeb*, 9, 12, 79. Truschke estimates the number of Hindu temples that were demolished or converted into mosques to be about a dozen, rather than the thousands cited elsewhere.

Islamic judge resolved the crisis.[94] There was also opposition closer to home: Hindus in Delhi once blocked the emperor's path, begging for a remission of the tax, but an insulted Aurangzeb ordered his elephants forward, trampling the assembled poor.[95] Resistance also came from within the imperial court, with Jahanara leading the way. Not only did she oppose the re-imposition of the *jizyah*,[96] but she also took strong objection to Aurangzeb's prohibition of alcohol in the court.[97] To protest the liquor ban, Jahanara invited the wives of the theologians and conservative nobles to her mansion and got them drunk. When Aurangzeb appeared at the party and became angry, Jahanara simply asked why he and the husbands were so ineffective at controlling their households if they objected so much to the behavior.[98] Similarly, once Aurangzeb refused to listen to musical performances because they transgressed his sense of propriety and sobriety, Jahanara continued to hire them so that music in Delhi would continue to thrive.[99] These actions show how well Jahanara retained both her ecumenical orientation and her independent spirit after the wars of succession. Her actions and comportment did not change simply because her father was no longer the emperor. Rather, her actions help illustrate how Aurangzeb's reign was not as absolutist and draconian as once thought. A dialog continued within the court and within Mughal society at large, and this dialog allowed Jahanara to emerge as an elder stateswoman, honored for her insight and experience.

~

India is the cradle of many religions and as such a meaningful understanding of any portion of the subcontinent's history involves more than a discussion of Hindus and Muslims. In the late fifteenth century, a man named Nanak struggled to find spiritual fulfillment. After a period of intense reflection, which culminated in his realization of a sense of divine calling, Nanak began to travel extensively, perhaps visiting places as disparate as Mecca and Sri Lanka. He developed a thorough understanding of Buddhism, Hinduism, Jainism,* and Zoroastrianism,* and he visited key Hindu and Muslim religious sites, discussing theology with leading figures.[100] Guru Nanak's followers came to see these debates, and his disagreements with these other religions, as his way of pointing the true path towards salvation, which became known as Sikhism. A decided monotheist, Guru Nanak held that God was the "eternally unchanging Formless one," who is beyond our ability to

---

[94] Richards, *The Mughal Empire*, 176.

[95] Sarkar, *Studies in Aurangzeb's Reign*, 8.

[96] Satish Chandra, "*Jizyah* and the State in India in the Seventeenth Century," *Essays on Medieval Indian History* (New Delhi, India: Oxford University Press, 2005), 321.

[97] Aurangzeb was not the first Mughal emperor to try to ban alcohol at court or in the empire. His grandfather and Akbar's son, Jahangir (r. 1605-1627) attempted to ban the production and sale of wine and narcotics, despite being addicted to both alcohol and opium. See Dirk Collier, *The Great Mughals and their India* (New Delhi: Hay House Publishers, 2016), no page (chapter 3), Kindle edition. In the end, Aurangzeb's attempt to ban alcohol was a "spectacular policy failure," as was his ban on opium. See Truschke, *Aurangzeb*, 72-73.

[98] Hansen, *The Peacock Throne,* 449-450.

[99] Katherine Butler Brown, "Did Aurangzeb Ban Music? Questions for the Historiography of his Reign," *Modern Asian Studies*, 41, 1 (2007), 77-120, EBSCOhost. Brown shows that Aurangzeb refused to allow music to be performed in his presence, but that he did not seek to ban music throughout the Mughal Empire as many historians have asserted.

[100] Doris R. Jakobsh, *Sikhism* (Honolulu, Hawai'i: University of Hawai'i Press, 2012), 16.

comprehend.[101] Because God surpasses description, Nanak believed it was inappropriate to create images of God for worship as did Hindus, Buddhists, and many Christians. He also differed with Hindus in that he repudiated the construction of a society based on difference, including gender and caste, saying "be there the lowest among the low, or even lower, and Nanak is with them."[102] Although the singularity of God and the disavowal of representational art for God had parallels with Islam, Guru Nanak's rejection of Muhammad as the Prophet and his endorsement of the Hindu tenets of karma and the cycle of rebirth distinguished his thinking from that of the Muslims. In fact, while it may be tempting to see Sikhism as a blending of Hinduism and Islam, borrowing ideas from each, such a view diminishes the unique synthesis Guru Nanak's followers believed he articulated.[103] Guru Nanak saw the human soul as possessing a fundamentally positive nature, but felt that human attachment to the things of the world made the soul easily corruptible. He argued that remaining attached to God's earthly creation or attributing acts to one's own skills promotes self-centeredness and obscures the Truth.[104] In order to realize spiritual liberation, humans must practice meditation through five stages, from merely possessing a sense of obligatory religious duty to developing an awareness and understanding to finally reaching a realm which cannot be described, only experienced.[105] At this fifth and amorphous level, union with God occurs. But Guru Nanak did not mean for his religion to be for those seeking escape from the problems of the world. Rather, he held that the true test of the faithful was to remain fully involved in the practical world and to appreciate God's presence in everyday society, from the marketplace to the home. Access to God was not just for the elite or for those at a temple. It was for everyone, and it could be shown by singing hymns to God.[106] These ideas appealed to shopkeepers and traveling salesmen, herders and farmers, all of whom held a low social rank in the Hindu caste system. Therefore, Sikhism steadily grew. It proved to be a growth Mughal emperors often found troubling as the sixteenth century turned into seventeenth.

In 1664, the eighth Sikh guru died of smallpox.[107] This triggered a succession crisis in which twenty-two men proclaimed themselves to be the ninth guru.[108] Eventually, Guru Tegh Bahadur, the youngest son of the sixth guru, emerged as the consensus leader and assumed the mantle of authority to become Sikhism's ninth spiritual guide. This development did not, however, end the

[101] Guru Nanak quoted in J. S. Grewal, *The Sikhs of the Punjab* (New York: Cambridge University Press, 1990) 7, 34.

[102] Guru Nanak quoted Grewal, *The Sikhs of the Punjab*, 29. Although Sikh women have the same access to spiritual liberation as men, Sikh society is patriarchal and women are barred from some important Sikh rituals. See Jakobsh, *Sikhism*, 72-73. Guru Nanak did, however, denounce *sati* (the Hindu practice of wives burning themselves to death on the funeral pyres of their husbands) and regulations of *purdah*.

[103] *World Religions: From Ancient History to the Present* (Geoffrey Parrinder, ed.) (New York: Facts on File, 1971), 251.

[104] Grewal, *The Sikhs of the Punjab*, 36-37.

[105] Jakobsh, *Sikhism*, 49-50.

[106] Jakobsh, *Sikhism*, 18-19.

[107] Grewal, *The Sikhs of the Punjab*, 69. His name was Guru Har Krishan. He was eight years old.

[108] Eraly, *The Mughal World*, 333.

community's crisis. By 1669, it was clear to Guru Tegh Bahadur that the Sikh community faced grave dangers. Emperor Aurangzeb had grown exasperated by the spread of Sikh temples through the key towns of the empire and had ordered their demolition. Guru Tegh Bahadur responded to this decree by initiating a missionary campaign to win additional converts, annoying Aurangzeb even more. The guru's military organizing, his family connections to supporters of Dara Shukoh,[109] and Aurangzeb's undying hatred for his better-loved brother[110] contributed to Aurangzeb's decisive actions. In 1675, Aurangzeb had Guru Tegh Bahadur arrested and brought to Delhi, where he was asked to perform a miracle as proof of his authenticity. The guru refused to participate in the demeaning exercise. He also refused to convert to Islam at Aurangzeb's behest. Even witnessing the execution of three of his followers did not sway Guru Tegh Bahadur's mind. He was beheaded on November 11, 1675 in a square along Jahanara's Chandi Chowk shopping esplanade.[111] It was the second time a Mughal emperor had ordered the execution of a Sikh Guru.[112]

Sikhism's tenth guru, Gobind Singh, was only nine when he assumed leadership of the Sikh community, but in time, he became the most important guru since Guru Nanak, for he changed the practice of religion significantly. In 1699, Guru Gobind Singh called upon all Sikhs to meet in Anandpur. Before a large crowd he asked for someone in the community to come forward and submit to execution as a sign of devotion to him. Out of the stunned assemblage, one man eventually stepped forward. Four more then followed, each from a different caste. Guru Gobind Singh named them the "five beloved ones" and inducted them into the *Khalsa* through a baptism ceremony in which he used a knife dunked into sugar-sweetened water. The *Khalsa* was a brotherhood of warrior-saints who were loyal to him over any other claimants for the leadership of the Sikhs. The members of this brotherhood were to identify themselves by their manner of dress. They were to wear an undergarment which would not encumber a warrior, keep their hair unshorn as a sign of God's will, wear a steel ring to protect their sword-carrying wrist, and carry a comb and a dagger.[113] According to Guru Govind Singh, Sikhs were also no longer permitted to have sexual relations with Muslims or to consume meat butchered in accordance with Islamic law. While not all Sikhs adopted this new orientation, Guru Gobind Singh successfully transformed his followers into a paramilitary fraternity. He declared that he would "convert jackals into tigers and sparrows into hawks," proclaiming that "the sword is God and God is the sword."[114] To the Mughals, this militarization was a threatening expression of disloyalty, but the guru's 1706 letter to Aurangzeb, accusing the Mughals of dishonor, led Aurangzeb to agree to discuss Sikh complaints.[115] Unfortunately, the emperor died before he and the guru could meet and relations between Muslims, Sikhs, and Hindus has remained strained into the early twenty-first century.

---

[109] Barbara D. Metcalf and Thomas R. Metcalf, *A Concise History of Modern India* (New York: Cambridge University Press, 2006), 21.

[110] Taymiya R. Zaman, email message to author, January 5, 2019.

[111] Grewal, *The Sikhs of the Punjab*, 71-72.

[112] The fifth Sikh guru, Guru Arjan, was executed by Shah Jahan's father, Jahangir, in 1606. Mughal accounts of the guru's death say that he was beheaded; Sikh accounts say that Guru Arjan was burned alive. See Jakobsh, *Sikhism*, 28.

[113] Jakobsh, *Sikhism*, 35-36. These five symbols of the *Khalsa* are known as the Five K's: *kirpan* (dagger), *kara* (steel bangle), *kachh* (breeches), *kesh* (uncut hair), and *kangha* (comb).

[114] Guru Gobind Singh quoted in Eraly, *The Mughal World*, 333-334.

[115] Grewal, *The Sikhs of the Punjab*, 79.

~

The fourth critical relationship in Jahanara's life was with her niece Jahanzeb Banu Begum, the daughter of Dara Shukoh. When Jahanzeb's mother committed suicide in Lahore after Dara Shukoh's defeat and death in 1659, the teenage girl came to live with Jahanara.[116] Jahanara then supervised her niece's education and helped arrange for the girl's marriage to her cousin Azam, Aurangzeb's third son. Jahanara and Jahanzeb seemed to be close, for the girl understood how devoted Jahanara and Dara Shukoh were to one another. At Jahanzeb and Azam's colorful wedding in 1669, the grounds were covered with gold and silver. Aurangzeb presented elaborate gifts to his relatives, including a jeweled sword and turban worth 80,000 rupees to Azam, two elephants to Jahanzeb and a detachment of elephant troops to Jahanara.[117] Like her aunt, Jahanzeb possessed both significant aptitude and charisma. She was particularly adept on the battlefield, where she led Mughal troops on three occasions. The first came in 1679, when Azam received a summons from Aurangzeb to appear at court, despite being in the middle of a military campaign. Jahanzeb took control of the royal army for three weeks while Azam made his way to and from Aurangzeb's encampment. Three years later, Jahanzeb went further and took matters into her own hands, even though her husband was also on the battlefield. This time, she mounted her elephant to lead the charge, vowing to commit suicide if the Mughal army failed to win the battle. Jahanzeb also went into battle in 1685-1686 in an effort to raise troop morale during an invasion of Bijapur. At other times, Jahanzeb proved adept at mollifying court egos, whether between her husband and key members of the retinue or between her husband and their sons.[118] This ability to both soothe and motivate, cajole and inspire, shows how well Jahanara passed along her skills and spirit to her niece, just has Jahanara herself had learned these traits from her grand aunt Nur Jahan.[119] Little wonder that in her will Jahanara bequeathed her finest jewels to Jahanzeb.[120] She was quite proud of her protégé.

~

Jahanara never married and never had children because she never really needed to do so. Quite unlike the tradition in the Ottoman harem, where women only held rank when their sons were sultans, Jahanara held her status on her own merits. This stemmed in part from the ways the Mughal court kept alive many Mongol traditions, including those which allowed women to intervene in dynastic politics, obtain a sophisticated education, own property, and make independent decisions.[121] Through her writings and fervent Sufism, Jahanara supplemented this tradition with a deep and recognized spiritual authority, for she did not see her gender as an impediment to holiness. She concluded that she had a religious proficiency comparable to that of

---

[116] Lal, *Domesticity and Power in the Early Mughal World*, 44.
[117] Iftikhar, "The Imperial Households of the Great Mughals."
[118] Faruqui, *The Princes of the Mughal Empire, 1504-1719*, 110.
[119] Lal, *Empress*, 224-225.
[120] Hansen, *The Peacock Throne*, 452. This also fits with Ruby Lal's idea that Mughal women served as role models for one another and how Nur Jahan served as Jahanara's inspiration. See Lal, *Empress*, 224-225.
[121] Balabanlilar, "The Begims of the Mystic Feast."

Muhammad and his companions. After a profound dream in which she met "the Holy Prophet Muhammad… the Four Friends, noble Companions and great saints" she wrote that she needed "to include myself among and on the mantle with this blessed group."[122] Hence, Jahanara stood as both a political force and a religious force in seventeenth century Mughal India. She was righteous, diplomatic, and remarkably successful. While women of power and influence can be found in almost every generation of Mughal rule,[123] Jahanara made the most of the opportunities her life presented.

---

[122] Jahanara quoted in Afshan Bokhari, "Between Patron and Piety: Jahān Ārā Begam's Sufi Affiliations and Articulations in Seventeenth Century Mughal India," in *Sufism and Society: Arrangements of the Mystical in the Muslim World, 1200-1800*, John J. Curry and Erik S. Ohlander (ed.) (New York: Routledge, 2012), 130.
[123] Balabanlilar, "The Begims of the Mystic Feast."

$\mathcal{K}$

Kim Hong-do

1745-1806

In his painting "Village School," Korean artist Kim Hong-do[1] depicted eight students and a teacher sitting on the floor in a circle, watching a ninth student roll up his trousers to present his bare calves

for a beating as he simultaneously wipes away tears of embarrassment and anticipatory fear from his face with his left hand. The boy's book, perhaps tossed in frustration, lies open on the floor with its curled pages offering a pointed reminder of what he doesn't know. The black-hatted, bearded teacher sits behind a bare, low tabletop, staring at the back of the delinquent student with an expression of frustrated annoyance and a touch of sympathy. A cane or switch is within his easy reach. The boy's classmates, who vary in ages as was the custom in village schools, seem quite amused by the situation, for each is either smiling or laughing out loud. Two temper this amusement, however, with an offer of help: one classmate seems to be trying to whisper the correct answer to the

---

[1] There have been two main systems of transliteration between Korean and English, the McCune-Reischauer system and the Revised Romanization of Korean, which the South Korean government adopted in 2000. For this chapter I have generally used the newer system, but I made exceptions for those nouns, such as Kim, that are still better known today by the McCune-Reischauer form. His name in the Revised Romanization of Korean is Gim Hongdo.

boy, while the other is turning a page in the book to show the boy where to look for the correct answer.[2] It is a poignant, illuminating scene, one to which many eighteenth century Koreans could relate since virtually every village in the country had at least one such primary school.[3] Kim's deceivingly simple work also encapsulates the Confucian values that dominated Joseon Dynasty (1392-1910) culture.[4]

The tossed book in the "Village School" was likely *A Primer for Youth*, which had been the basic elementary school text since the sixteenth century. King Yeongjo ordered the book re-issued and widely distributed in the early 1740s because he wanted to ensure that students understood a fundamental purpose of education: appreciating the proper relationships in society. These relationships were defined in Confucian terms:

> Between parent and child there is to be affection; between ruler and minister, righteousness; between husband and wife, differentiation; between elder and younger, precedence; between friends, trust. Human beings who do not understand these Five Moral Relations are hardly different from birds and beasts. It is only when parents are compassionate and children filial, the ruler right (moral) and the minister loyal (true), the husband harmonious and the wife compliant, the elder brother fraternal and younger brother deferential, and friends helpful in the mutual achievement of humaneness that one can speak of them as human beings.[5]

If this admonition was too abstract for certain students, the text provided more specifics about the proper behavior for a faithful son, who "does not presume to consider his body his own" and who holds his parents in such regard that "when they treat him badly, he holds them in fear but does not hold it against them." The primer continued, "if in anger they beat him, though bleeding from it, he does not hold it against them. While his parents are living he has utmost reverence for them, in serving them he has utmost joy, in nursing them utmost concern, in their death utmost grief, and in ancestral rites utmost solemnity."[6]

Such values stemmed from the fifth-century BCE Chinese philosopher Confucius. Confucius lived in a politically unstable period and reasoned that if people lived according to a hierarchy of harmonious relationships, a governmental system could restore order to the land. For Confucius, these hierarchical relationships began with the patriarchal family and proceeded upwards to the monarch, who ruled over his lands as a father did over his wife and children. By honoring the duty to family over the needs of the individual, and by honoring the needs of the community over the needs of the family, an ideal society could emerge. Confucius also believed in the power of merit: all who possessed talent and skill should be rewarded, regardless of their socio-economic status.

---

[2] Jin Jun-hyun, "Kim Hong-do: Captures the Essence of Joseon Society," *Koreana* 23, no. 3 (Autumn, 2009): 52-55. *Art Full Text (H.W. Wilson)*, EBSCOhost.

[3] These village schools were privately operated. See Key P. Yang and Gregory Henderson, "An Outline of Korean Confucianism: Part II: The Schools of Yi Confucianism," *The Journal of Asian Studies*, Vol. 18, No. 2, (February, 1959), 259-276, EBSCOhost.

[4] The Joseon Dynasty is called the Chosŏn Dynasty in the McCune-Reischauer system. Similarly, this system calls the Korean rulers Yŏngjo (1724-1776) and Chŏngjo (1776-1800).

[5] "A Primer for Youth," Jinhong Kim and Wm. Theodore de Bary (trans.) *Sources of Korean Tradition: Volume II: from the Sixteenth to the Twentieth Centuries*, Yŏng-ho Ch'oe, Peter H. Lee and Wm. Theodore de Bary (eds.) (New York: Columbia University Press, 2000), 39.

[6] "A Primer for Youth," *Sources of Korean Tradition: Volume II,* 42.

Consequently, he founded a school and enrolled students from diverse social backgrounds who demonstrated the proper spirit and ability. One of Confucius' most important followers, Mencius, took his idea further, arguing that only through the pursuit of education could each man achieve his potential. By the second century BCE, the emperor of China had established Confucianism as the state doctrine, and by the seventh century CE this doctrine had become manifest in a system of national examinations that were used to determine government appointments. These exams tested mastery of Confucian classical texts, knowledge of history, and literary skill.

Eighteenth-century Korea used a similar examination system to select male candidates for government jobs.[7] There were three types of exams: one for lawyers, translators, accountants, physicians, and astronomers; one for military officials; and one for public office holders. The latter had two subdivisions of its own: a classics exam and literary exam. These two exams were only given once every three years. In order to pass, a candidate had to earn one of the top one hundred scores on either the classics exam or the literary exam. These two hundred candidates could then sit for a three-part palace exam. The thirty-three highest scoring individuals on the palace exam were considered to have passed the final test and won appointments to civil offices.[8] It was a highly competitive system designed to create a talented bureaucracy. Korea was not, however, able to maintain a commitment to the pure, merit-based qualification system envisioned by Confucius.

Rather, the *yangban* came to dominate Joseon society. The *yangban* (meaning "two orders") were the civilian and military officials who occupied government posts. Although there was no legal prohibition against commoners taking the exams and winning royal appointments, in reality a process of careful intermarriage and cultural discrimination against an aspiring merchant class created a self-perpetuating social structure and an entrenched civil bureaucracy.[9] Combined with the ability of members of the *yangban* to bypass the preliminary rounds of tests,[10] this arrangement stacked the deck against those of other socio-economic backgrounds. The *yangban* dominated the examination system and, therefore, the entire bureaucracy of Korea.

This educational system rested, as it does around the world today, on the elementary school classroom like the one Kim depicted in "Village School." Interestingly, this painting may have been drawn from Kim's personal experience as an adult, rather than from a childhood memory. In 1791, Kim was appointed as a county magistrate by King Yeongjo's grandson, King Jeongjo, who reigned

---

[7] While Korean women were excluded from the exam system, they did receive a basic education. It was seen as important for women to be literate in order to fulfill their responsibilities within the family. See JaHyun Kim Haboush, "Women's Education," *Sources of Korean Tradition: Volume II*, 46.

[8] JaHyun Kim Haboush, *A Heritage of Kings: One Man's Monarchy in the Confucian World* (New York: Columbia University Press, 1998), 89-90.

[9] Gregory N. Evon, "Korea's Aristocratic Moods: Re-examining Choson Social and Political History," *Asian Studies Review*, 35, 2. (June, 2011), 253-262, EBSCOhost.

[10] Haboush, *A Heritage of Kings,* 90.

from 1776 to 1800.[11] According to the official policy, one of Kim's key responsibilities as magistrate was to promote education by identifying boys who did more than simply memorize material: "higher grades [scores] shall be given to those who genuinely comprehend the meaning" of Confucian tenets and who "put their understanding into actual practice" over those who "merely recite the texts." The policy held that all boys who were "capable of learning" should receive a basic education, but once every three months officials like Kim needed to consult with school officials and select boys over the age of fifteen from "scholar families" with "superior intelligence," and "good conduct," for an appointment to the county secondary school. The student who earned the highest grade had his work forwarded to the provincial governor for further recognition received "paper, writing brush, and ink" as a reward.[12] If the best students in a local elementary school were well-connected, they could qualify for a provincial college instead of the secondary school. Those with the greatest talents and the best connections were recommended to the Confucian Academy in Seoul, where only 126 applicants were admitted each year in the mid-eighteenth century.[13] Because each stage of this hierarchical examination system was more selective, the exams procured well-qualified officials for government service. In 1774, for example, only eighteen men passed the Deungjunsi Military Examination. In honor of this accomplishment, these men had their portraits painted and included in a special album, which became a part of the court archives.[14] Even with this high degree of selectivity, however, by Kim's period there were far more men with elite diplomas than there were jobs available.[15] Hence, while many members of the *yangban* earned degrees, most did not work in government positions.[16]

~

Kim's career as a painter both did and did not fit well with the Confucian value system. On the one hand, he demonstrated quite early in life that he possessed unusual artistic gifts and much of the success he enjoyed as a painter can be attributed to his raw talent. Nothing in his family background suggested that he would become a royal painter. Kim's father's family came from non-officer military stock, and his mother's family were mainly interpreters and accountants.[17] Kim's forebears were decidedly *jungin* (meaning "middle people"), and since most royal painting positions were hereditary, Kim's arrival at the Joseon court was largely a result of his talent. On the other hand,

---

[11] Kim was the magistrate of Yeonpung in Chungcheong Province between 1791-1795. See Burglind Jungmann, *Pathways to Korean Culture: Paintings of the Joseon Dynasty, 1392-1910* (London: Reaktion Books, 2014), 244.

[12] "Cho Hyŏnmyŏng: County Magistrate's Guide for Promoting Education," *Sources of Korean Tradition: Volume II*, 44-45.

[13] This educational hierarchy should not be confused with the *Seowon*, the Confucian academies which were centers for elite scholars and which over time attracted the best teachers and best students from the *yangban*. The *Seowon* was a separate institution which promoted Confucianism in Korea. See Yang and Henderson, "An Outline of Korean Confucianism: Part II."

[14] In addition, each of the eighteen men received a copy of the portrait album. See *Treasures from Korea: Arts and Culture of the Joseon Dynasty, 1392-1910*, Wyunsoo Woo (ed.) (Philadelphia, Pennsylvania: Philadelphia Museum of Art, 2014), 194-195.

[15] Haboush, *A Heritage of Kings*, 91.

[16] Evon, "Korea's Aristocratic Moods."

[17] Oh Ju-seok, *The Art of Kim Hong-do*, Lim Seon-young and Yang Ji-hyun (trans.) and revised by Mark S. Turnoy (New York: Art Media Resources, 2005), 31-32.

not all of Kim's good fortune fit with Confucian ideals. He also benefited from the practicality of knowing influential people. When Kim was in his late teens, his work caught the attention of a high-ranking court painter. The recommendation of this official secured Kim's appointment and allowed him to by-pass much of the examination system.[18] Cherry-picked to join a world for which he had little social context, Kim soon found himself in Changdeokgung, the royal palace in the center of modern Seoul.

As with the palaces of Go-Mizunoo, Ibrahim, and Jahanara, Changdeokgung contained various areas of exclusivity. There were public audience halls, restricted administrative buildings, and private quarters for the royal family, but these were not laid out in a strict linear progression. Rather, the architectural goal of Changdeokgung was to epitomize the Korean value for blending in with the natural environment. In Changdeokgung, there is no progression from a main gate to a first courtyard to a second gate to a second courtyard. Rather, Changdeokgung was designed to impress as a refined work of art, rather than overwhelm with grandeur.[19] Kim must have made the adjustment to this world quickly, for his first major assignment came in 1765. It was to assist in the painting of a screen, "Banquet of Offering Wine at Gyeondhyeondang," which documented the formal recognition of King Yeongjo as an elder statesman after reigning for forty years.[20]

Kim entered a royal court full of acrimony, remorse, and confusion. Three years before his arrival, the tense relationship between King Yeongjo and his only surviving son, Prince Sado, came to a climax. Beginning in the 1740s Sado began to fear his father, causing the prince to become tongue-tied and tentative whenever he was around the king. This infuriated Yeongjo, who wanted to leave his throne to a strong, confident heir. Sado tried to win forgiveness for his shortcomings, once lying prostrate in the snow for hours, but such acts had little effect. By the late 1750s Sado's mental state unraveled under the continual disapproval. He became erratic and eventually violent, killing people at random. In 1757, for example, he attacked a eunuch, severed the man's head, and then paraded it, still dripping blood, in front of the court's ladies-in-waiting.[21] These women were horrified by Sado's act and began to live in fear of the crown prince since all of them were subject to his sexual desires.[22] This fear proved justified since a few months later Sado, enraged by a palace woman's resistance, beat her until she bled and then raped her.[23]

By May 1762, Sado's mental state was so troubled that the prince dug a crypt-like underground chamber. Two months later he asked for permission to commit suicide, pounding his head on the ground, begging for emancipation and relief. Despite the chaos Sado perpetrated upon the court, Yeongjo was unwilling to order the execution of his son since court tradition prohibited any bleeding or disfigurement of a royal body. Sado had to die of natural causes. Self-strangulation was a possibility, and Sado attempted hanging himself several times without success. Yeongjo's

---

[18] The painter was Kim Huiseong, who died at some point after 1763. See Jungmann, *Pathways to Korean Culture*, 243.

[19] Stephen Henkin, "Korea's Best-Kept Secret," *The World & I*, 14.8 (August 1999), 134-139, ProQuest Central.

[20] Jungmann, *Pathways to Korean Culture*, 243.

[21] Lady Hyegyŏng, *The Memoirs of Lady Hyegyŏng: The Autobiographical Writings of a Crown Princess of Eighteenth-Century Korea*, JaHyun Kim Haboush (trans.), (Berkeley, California: University of California Press, 1996), 282.

[22] Like their Topkapı Palace counterparts in Istanbul, ladies-in-waiting were largely recruited as young girls, were classified by a complex system of ranks, were assigned to a specific palace department, and were managed carefully. At Changdeokgung, the management was by the Bureau of Inner Court Ladies. See JaHyun Kim Haboush, "The Vanished Women of Korea: The Anonymity of Texts and the Historicity of Subjects," *Servants of the Dynasty: Palace Women in World History*, Anne Walthall (ed.) (Berkeley, California: University of California Press, 2008), 282, 284, 293, 297.

[23] Lady Hyegyŏng, *The Memoirs of Lady Hyegyŏng*, 283.

eventual solution was to order his son to crawl inside a wood rice chest that offered very little ventilation. Sado died of suffocation on July 12, 1762 after eight days of suffering in the oppressive summer heat.[24]

The Sado affair divided the court between those who supported the king's order and those who did not.[25] This was unfortunate for Yeongjo, who had devoted considerable attention in the early decades of his reign to ending the factionalism that had previously dominated the court. In fact, upon his accession in 1724, Yeongjo had adopted a policy of impartiality, refusing to favor one of the existing court factions over another. But Prince Sado's death revived the factional tensions within the court, forcing newcomers like Kim to choose sides. He must have chosen well: at the end of Yeongjo's reign in 1776, Kim won the honor of helping to paint a decorative cloth for the king's coffin. It is difficult to be more precise about other aspects of Kim's early years at Changdeokgung and what he painted because his oldest surviving work, "A Taciturn Man," only dates from 1773. In fact, of the estimated 12,000 works Kim created in his lifetime, fewer than 300 still exist.[26]

One reason for Kim's rise to prominence stemmed from the interplay of his talent and his unique relationship with the new king, Jeongjo. Their first major interaction came in 1773, when Kim served as the assistant painter who was responsible for painting the bodies and robes in a joint portrait of Jeongjo and Yeongjo. Being selected to paint the monarch was the highest honor a royal painter could receive, and Kim earned this opportunity at twenty-eight. Like Go-Mizunoo, Jeongjo possessed considerable talent in his own right as an artist and calligrapher, and thus noticed the finest details in a work. Because Jeongjo took pride in being able to judge works of art with authority and because he held his artists to the highest standards, the king promoted those he respected the most. Kim quickly became Jeongjo's favorite. In fact, as a contemporary noted, every painting Kim submitted immediately won the king's approval.[27] Kim also distinguished himself as a musician and as a poet.[28] This range of skills helped Kim stand above the other thirty painters in the court, and facilitated his winning more desirable assignments. While his colleagues drafted the illustrations that documented court events—works that were seen more as didactic records than works of art[29]—and submitted them to the palace archives, Kim worked only on paintings commissioned by the king.[30] One of Jeongjo's first assignments was for Kim to paint the king's pride and joy: Gyujanggak, a two-story library and administrative center Jeongjo had built upon his accession to house his personal writings and the government documents produced during his reign. Until this time, Korean monarchs, unlike their Chinese counterparts, did not have a formal library system, but Jeongjo believed that the entire bureaucracy needed to undergo a major retrofitting to prepare Korea for the nineteenth century; Gyujanggak was to be a symbol of Korean modernity, as well as an educational center. Jeongjo invited those government officials he believed

---

[24] Haboush, *A Heritage of Kings*, 175, 201, 203, 221, 230-231.

[25] Homer Bezaleel Hulbert, *Hulbert's History of Korea*, Volume II, Clarence Norwood Weems (ed.), (New York: Hillary House Publishers Ltd., 1962), 180.

[26] Oh, *The Art of Kim Hong-do*, 13, 85, 87.

[27] Oh Joosok, "The Life and Art of Kim Hong-do," *The International Journal of Korean Art and Archaeology*, Volume 1 (2007), 34-45.

[28] Oh, *The Art of Kim Hong-do*, 51.

[29] Jungmann, *Pathways to Korean Culture*, 208, 211, 268.

[30] Oh, "The Life and Art of Kim Hong-do."

to have the greatest promise to study classics in his library so that they might better understand their roles and learn about Jeongjo's vision for Korea.[31] He also moved the Royal Bureau of Painting from outside the palace into the library so that he might commission works directly, rather than through intermediaries. That the king asked Kim to paint this building illustrates how much Jeongjo valued Kim's talent.[32]

Another example of the symbolically important and highly personalized assignments Jeongjo gave Kim pertained to the tomb of the king's father, Sado. Confucianism holds that when a man dies his spirit remains in the world of the living and that the duty of his heir is to perform the ancestral rites until the spirit fades into another world. Those with sufficient funds honored these spirits by building shrines to house wooden tablets inscribed with the names of their kin. Commoners used pictures of shrines as surrogates, but all used the tablets, shrines, pictures, and portraits to focus their worship, just as Orthodox Christians used icons.[33] The problem with Sado's tomb was that it had been inauspiciously sited. Jeongjo came to believe that this positioning undercut his effectiveness in honoring his father and fulfilling his filial duties as respectfully as possible. According to Sado's wife, Lady Hyegyeong, after several decades of careful and exhaustive planning, Jeongjo decided to move Sado's tomb. The purpose of the 1789 move was to resituate Sado's grave to an exceptional site with pleasing feng shui.[34] In doing this, Jeongjo sought to demonstrate the depth of his Confucian piety, but the king faced awkward circumstances because of his father's questionable credentials for merit within the Confucian system. Jeongjo's politically savvy solution was to construct a Buddhist temple and a palace next to the new site chosen for the tomb. Although Buddhism had been officially suppressed in Korea by the eighteenth century, it was still practiced in rural monasteries and private homes, and it provided a way for Jeongjo to have continual prayers said on his father's behalf without challenging the state's official Confucian precepts.[35] The preparations for the transfer of the tomb and the construction of the palace and temple were so meticulous that Jeongjo sent Kim to China in 1789 to study both

---

[31] Yi Tae-Jin, "King Chŏngjo: Confucianism, Enlightenment, and Absolute Rule," *Korea Journal*, Vol. 40, No. 4 (Winter, 2000), 168-201.

[32] Jungmann, *Pathways to Korean Culture*, 211.

[33] Insoo Cho, "Confucianism and the Art of the Joseon Dynasty," *Treasures from Korea: Arts and Culture of the Joseon Dynasty, 1392-1910*, 9.

[34] Lady Hyegyŏng, *The Memoirs of Lady Hyegyŏng*, 113, 203.

[35] Evon, "Korea's Aristocratic Moods." For information on the status of Buddhism see Robert E. Buswell, Jr., "Buddhism Under Confucian Domination: The Synthetic Vision of *Sŏsan Hynjŏng*," *Culture and the State in Late Chosŏn Korea*, JaHyun Kim Haboush and Martina Deuchler (ed.) (Cambridge, Massachusetts: Harvard University Asia Center, 1999), 134-158.

Buddhist paintings and the Western paintings in a Jesuit church in Beijing. Upon Kim's return, Jeongjo named him as the supervising painter for the Yongjusa Temple's most important work, "Three Tathagatas," or "Three Generations of Buddhas."[36] In the Mahayana school tradition, this work depicts Buddha in the past, present and future, all dressed in red robes with green trim. At the center sits prince Gautama Siddhartha. To his right is the Buddha of healing and medicine, and to his left is the savior Buddha who brings a life in paradise to those who call his name.[37] Surrounding these three-seated Buddhas stand eight *bodhisattvas*, a multitude of other Buddhist figures, and four Heavenly Kings or guardians, one in each corner. All of the figures in the crowded mural are in realistic proportions, and guardians' faces have a heightened ferocity due to Western painting techniques such as chiaroscuro.*[38] This was Kim's special touch. Jeongjo sought to honor his father with a uniquely positioned and artistically sophisticated temple, and he relied on Kim to fulfill his aspirations.

Five years later, in 1795, Jeongjo asked Kim to lead the team of royal painters to document the visit of the court and its 6,000-person retinue to Sado's tomb and the Yongjusa Temple for the king's mother's sixtieth birthday. Though visits to the temple were annual events, this particular visit merited commemoration for several reasons: it was five days longer than the normal shrine visit, an altered procession route had required renovation of roads and villages, and Jeongjo had ordered the construction of a pontoon bridge so that the procession could cross the Han River for the first time.[39] Kim and his team responded by producing twenty-one sets of eight silk screens, which represented an experimental departure from the traditional scroll or album leaves format.[40] The "Royal Visit to the City of Hwaseong," the oldest surviving documentary painting of its type in Korea, shows the king's visit to a Confucian shrine, the holding of a special round of civil and military examinations, a banquet honoring Lady Hyegyeong, reception of national elders, military exercises, ceremonial archery with fireworks, the return procession, and the crossing of the Han River on the pontoon bridge. Each of these panels is presented from a bird's-eye viewpoint, but the overall artistic goal is not to emphasize realism. Rather, the primary goal is to demonstrate the importance of Confucian relationships, such as honoring one's elders. Given the politics surrounding Sado's death, the desire to support the state ideology trumped the necessity for visual realism. Kim certainly had the ability to utilize the techniques of Western perspective if that had been the objective, but confirming the sociopolitical philosophy of the state meant more in this instance.[41] Significantly, Jeongjo's personal visit to his father's tomb is not one of the eight screens, despite Jeongjo's participation in the artistic development of the project. According to court records, Jeongjo was so overwhelmed by grief during his visit to the tomb that he refused to allow

[36] Yi Sŏng-mi, *Searching for Modernity: Western Influence and True-View Landscape in Korean Painting of the Late Chosŏn Period* (Seattle, Washington: University of Washington Press, 2015), 43.

[37] The painting depicts Shakyamuni, Bhaishajyaguru, and Amitabha. Shakyamuni is the prince Gautama Siddhartha, the founder of Buddhism. Bhaishajyaguru and Amitabha are other forms of Buddha within the Mahayana tradition. Baishiajaguru is the Buddha doctor who alleviates suffering and cures the diseases of those who follow him. Amitabha is a monk who promised that upon attaining enlightenment, he would provide life in paradise for those who followed him.

[38] Yi, *Searching for Modernity,* 43-44.

[39] Hyongeong Kim Han, *In Grand Style: Celebrations in Korean Art During the Joseon Dynasty* (San Francisco, California: Asian Art Museum, 2013), 64-65.

[40] Han, *In Grand Style,* 72. Four complete sets of the eight-paneled screens have survived to the present day, as well as seven separate panels from other sets.

[41] Jungmann, *Pathways to Korean Culture,* 215-226.

documentation of his emotional display.[42] In the eight screens, the king chose to celebrate the life of his mother instead of emphasizing the death of his father.[43]

King Jeongjo balanced his desire to reinforce the ideals of the Confucian hierarchy with humaneness. Just as a father had the responsibility to care for his family, the king had a responsibility to care for his people. Authority had to be balanced with kindness, or what in the classical tradition was known as the virtue of humanity.[44] Therefore, Jeongjo sought to understand the condition of everyday Koreans. He expanded the use of a petition system, which permitted commoners to communicate directly with the king: when Jeongjo processed through the streets, he allowed commoners to approach him with their petitions of grievances.[45] This followed the precedent established by Jeongjo's grandfather, who walked through the market district to listen to the candid concerns of merchants and tradesmen.[46] A ruler committed to reform, Jeongjo decreed that people from the northern provinces had an equal right to hold government office as their southern counterparts,[47] issued regulations to prohibit the use of implements of torture during the interrogation of suspected criminals,[48] and sought to combat the effects of inflation on the poor by providing grain at below-market value to destitute families.[49] In an effort to alleviate the tax burden, he reduced the quantity of abalone Jeju Island residents had to send to him in tribute, lessened the amount of ginseng expected of residents of the western provinces,[50] and helped distribute wealth by requiring the state to purchase high-quality silk in cities around the country instead of just from merchants in Seoul.[51] The king was particularly attuned to the needs of the Korean people during periods of famine and epidemics. In 1783, for example, the king issued regulations to provide for the care of orphans in times of famine.[52] He also wrote an edict that year expressing concern for the people. He noted that "the ninth month is usually a time when good things accumulate in farmhouses: the fields are filled with yellow clouds of ripe crops that invite harvest machines; song and music soar, wine is poured from village to village, and the season overflows with merriment." This year, however, drought, insects, and winds had destroyed the harvest, making it impossible for the people to pay their taxes or feed themselves. Consequently, Jeongjo said that "regardless of whether a village is designated a disaster area or not, all past loans will be cancelled" and the year's taxes might be paid with "substitute crops." The king noted this "measure embodies what is meant

[42] Just before Yeongjo ordered Sado to crawl inside the rice chest, Jeongjo, then ten years old, had been brought before his grandfather to beg for his father's life. Yeongjo responded by kicking the boy so hard that it sent Jeongjo reeling. The day must have scared Jeongjo, which helps explain the intensity of the king's emotional response at his father's new burial site. See Hulbert, *Hulbert's History of Korea*, Volume II, 178.
[43] Jaebin Yoo, "The Politics of Art under King Jeongjo Exemplified by 'Events from King Jeongjo's Visit to Hwaseong in 1795,'" in Kim, *In Grand Style: Celebrations in Korean Art During the Joseon Dynasty*, 109.
[44] Judith A. Berling, "Confucianism," *Focus on Asian Studies* Vol. II, no. 1, *Asian Religions* (fall 1982), 5-7, accessed February 22, 2020, https://tinyurl.com/yxg4lkfs
[45] Han Sang-Kwon, "Social Problems and the Active Use of Petitions During the Reign of King Chŏngjo," *Korea Journal*, Vol. 40, No. 4 (Winter 2000), 227-246.
[46] Yi, "King Chŏngjo."
[47] Hulbert, *Hulbert's History of Korea*, Volume II, 184.
[48] Han, "Social Problems and the Active Use of Petitions."
[49] Ko Donghwan, "Development of Commerce and Commercial Policy during the Reign of King Chŏngo," *Korea Journal*, Vol. 40, no. 4 (Winter, 2000), 202-225.
[50] Yi, "King Chŏngjo."
[51] Soo-chang Oh, "Economic Growth in P'Yongan Province and the Development of Pyongyang in the Late Choson Period." *Korean Studies* 30, (2006): 3-22, 132, ProQuest Central.
[52] Anders Karlsson, "Famine Relief, Social Order, and the State Performance in Late Chŏson Korea," *The Journal of Korean Studies*, Vol. 12, No. 1 (Fall, 2007), 113-141, EBSCOhost.

by sharing felicity and effecting compassionate government. The people of the six provinces who suffered damage should not fear and [should] have faith in me. By announcing this, I wish to bring some measure of security and relief" to the people of Korea.[53] Similarly, after a series of poor harvests in the 1790s, Jeongjo asked the general population to submit accounts of their agricultural practices and the problems they faced. These reports confirmed what the king suspected: in an effort to increase yields, more Korean farmers were growing rice using a water-intensive wet-field system instead of using the less bountiful, but more reliable, dry field method. Combined with poor maintenance of dams and reservoirs, the replacement of food-producing rice paddies with fields for tobacco and tea, and a scarcity of rain, there simply wasn't enough rice produced to feed the nation. Jeongjo responded as he had a decade earlier by having the Office of Relief Works requisition food from the national network of government granaries. He also limited his own consumption of food so that he might suffer along with his people.[54]

When epidemics struck, Jeongjo's response was similarly personalized and bold. In 1786, Korea experienced an outbreak of *hongyeok*, the red epidemic or what medical historians believe to have been the measles. In an effort to combat the disease, Jeongjo ordered the Medical Bureau to dispatch royal doctors to provide for the medical needs of the residents of Seoul and the Public Dispensary to supply 27,000 preventative pills to the public. Free services and medicines were provided to those too poor to pay. By establishing this emergency medical relief system, by requesting that doctors in the provinces present their drug formulas to the court, and by personally composing a ritual invocation against the demons of pestilence, Jeongjo fought the disease in an unprecedented fashion.[55] Even if these efforts did nothing to cure the measles outbreak, the king's actions demonstrate the depth of his concern for the welfare of his nation.

The direct management of famine relief and disease prevention usually fell to county magistrates.[56] It was, therefore, important for Jeongjo to have men he trusted in these positions. In 1791, the king appointed Kim as the county magistrate of Yeonpung in Chungcheong-do Province. During the drought of 1792, when three thousand of the area's five thousand residents faced starvation, Kim sought to demonstrate the depth of royal concern for the people by making offerings at important local temples, paying for the restoration of Buddhist paintings, and re-gilding Buddhist statues from his own salary.[57] However well-intentioned Kim's approach might have been, his personal sacrifice did not sit well with the local townspeople, who were angered by the his decision to try to manage the drought without tapping government's grain provision. Kim's use of his own salary provided insufficient relief in the eyes of the residents of Yeonpung.[58]

In 1795, with the drought in its third year, Jeongjo dispatched royal investigators to inspect the effectiveness of the relief efforts and to measure the severity of the conditions. The investigator

[53] Chŏngjo, "King Chŏngjo's Yunŭm to the People of the Six Provinces," *Epistolary Korea: Letters in the Communicative Space of the Chŏson, 1392-1910*, (JaHyun Kim Haboush (ed.) (New York: Columbia University Press, 2009), 25-26.

[54] Karlsson, "Famine Relief, Social Order, and the State Performance in Late Chŏson Korea." In addition to the advantage of higher yields, the wet cultivation system requires less weeding than dry cultivation does. The fact that wet cultivation required less work and produced larger crops led farmers to use the technique in areas which did not always have sufficient water to do so.

[55] Shin Dongwon, "Measures Against Epidemics During Late 18th Century Korea: Reformation or Restoration?," *Extrême-Orient, Extrême-Occident*, 2014, Vol. 37, 91-110, EBSCOhost.

[56] Karlsson, "Famine Relief, Social Order, and the State Performance in Late Chŏson Korea."

[57] Oh, *The Art of Kim Hong-do*, 182-183, 189.

[58] Oh, *The Art of Kim Hong-do*, 189-190.

who visited the village of Yeonpung wrote an alarming report about Kim and his administration, accusing Kim of an abuse of power, corruption, and fraud. Upon reading the report, a court official added a commentary of his own, which called for Kim's immediate punishment:

> Kim Hong-do plundered his subordinates of livestock, inflicted unheard-of harsh punishments, requisitioned soldiers for his hunting trips, and levied a rice tax on those who did not obey. The villagers were in contempt of Kim. Such a man of humble origin never thought of repaying the king's kindness but committed hideous crimes. It is not enough to dismiss him from office. An order must be issued to the relevant department to keep him in custody, interrogate him, and bring his crimes to light.[59]

This report's damaging commentary led Jeongjo to dismiss Kim from office, but the king also pardoned his favorite artist within ten days of that decision, and ordered Kim to return to court. While it is certainly possible that Kim was a corrupt official who took advantage of his post, it is also possible that Jeongjo realized Kim had been targeted by those who objected to his status. Kim was not a member of the *yangban*, he had not earned his position through competitive state examinations, and he was from a different part of the country. Kim was an outsider in Yeonpung, and the king may have recognized the enormous prejudice that could have coalesced against him. By the eighteenth century, Korean nobles were, in fact, looking for ways to reassert their authority and social importance in the wake of the increasing prominence and power of the commercial sector. Boosting familial ties within officialdom was an effective method of doing this,[60] and Kim was in the way. Moreover, Jeongjo thought about the fundamental tensions between the Confucian duty to family and the Confucian obligation to defer to the state regularly; he wrote at length about how the desire to help one's family corrupted the mores of many government bureaucrats.[61] It possible that the king saw Kim as an honest official and so pardoned the artist as someone who had been victimized by circumstances beyond his control.

~

King Jeongjo's personal sensibilities directly affected the development of Korean art in the late eighteenth century. The king supported the incorporation of Western-style realism and perspective in painting,[62] and this had a noticeable effect on Kim's work and that of other court painters. In fact, Jeongjo's progressive values and Kim's paintings embodied an aesthetic distinct from the influential artistic traditions of China.

The forces which prompted this maturation were complex. First, Korea had been a tributary state* to China, and the Korean king recognized the emperor of China as his overlord. In fact, in the Confucian hierarchy of relationships, only China could be the heart of civilization: every other nation was peripheral to the Middle Kingdom and should expect to be treated as such. Because

---

[59] Oh, *The Art of Kim Hong-do*, 192, 194.
[60] Han Sang-kwon, "Social Problems and the Active Use of Petitions During the Reign of King Chŏngjo," *Korea Journal*, Vol. 40, no. 4 (Winter, 2000), 227-246. (print.)
[61] Sungmoon Kim, "Trouble with Korean Confucianism: Scholar-Official Between Ideal and Reality," *Dao: A Journal of Comparative Philosophy*, 8.1 (March, 2009), 29-48, ProQuest Central.
[62] Oh, *The Art of Kim Hong-do*, 146, 166.

they looked to China for guidance and inspiration, this hierarchical relationship remained generally acceptable to the Koreans until 1644, when the Ming Dynasty fell to the Manchurians. With the establishment of the Qing (Manchu) Dynasty, Joseon Korea came to see itself as the protector of Confucian values and ideals.[63]   To court officials, the Koreans, rather than the Manchurian "barbarians" were the rightful heirs of the Confucian tradition.[64] The Koreans saw the Manchus as lacking culture, sophistication, and a scholarly tradition.[65] This is why the Koreans insisted upon wearing Ming-styled fashions when they met with Qing officials, who had imposed their own clothing and hairstyles on the Chinese court.[66] Second, Chinese tradition distinguished between painters of different social backgrounds, consigning each to specific work. Professional painters working for the court produced art in accordance with court tradition, while amateur literati officials of noble lineage who painted did so from inspiration. In Korea, by contrast, distinctions were grounded in the tradition an artist followed rather than the social class from which he came.[67] By the mid-eighteenth century, in fact, the relationship between a painter's style and a painter's social status was quite fluid, making it possible for artists of different backgrounds to create a wide variety of works.[68] Kim exemplifies this trend since he was not from the *yangban* elite. Third, Korea had become deeply influenced by the School of Practical Learning or *Sirhak* movement, which advocated for political, economic, and intellectual reforms. It attracted those who were dissatisfied with the political inertia of Joseon state and the apathy of its ruling elite.[69] One of its leading figures, Yi Ik, believed that painting should reflect reality instead of imaginary worlds. As Yi wrote, "When I look at landscape paintings of the past and present, I am stunned by their strangeness and falsehood. I am sure there is no such scenery on earth. They were painted only to please the viewers."[70] Yi's views and the *Sirhak* movement influenced the work of many artists who embraced what became known as the True-View approach to landscape painting. These artists found that traditional Chinese brush strokes could not capture realistic scenes fully and faithfully, so they created their own brushstrokes in order to paint what they saw.[71] Over time this helped distinguish Korean painting from its Chinese counterpart.

Kim was a part of the second phase of True-View landscape painting, along with one of his mentors, Gang Se-hwang, who was the most influential literati painter of the eighteenth century.[72] The lives of Gang and Kim intersected several times. When Kim was young, the master taught him what Gang once described as "the secrets of painting."[73] Later, the two men worked together briefly

---

[63] Haboush, *A Heritage of Kings,* 21-26.

[64] Yi, *Korean Landscape Painting,* 93.

[65] Yi Sŏng-mi, "Artistic Tradition and the Depiction of Reality: True-view Landscape Painting of the Chosŏn Dynasty," *The Arts of Korea,* Judith G. Smith (ed.) (New York: The Metropolitan Museum of Art, 1998), 340.

[66] Marion Eggert, "Friendship with Foreigners," *Epistolary Korea,* 204.

[67] Ahn Hwi-joon, "A Scholars Art: The Chinese Southern School," *Korean Cultural Heritage, Volume 1, Fine Arts: Painting, Handicrafts, Architecture* (Seoul: The Korea Foundation, 1994), 62.

[68] Yi, *Searching for Modernity,* 129.

[69] Mark Setton, *Chŏng Yagyong: Korea's Challenge to Orthodox Confucianism* (Albany, New York: State University of New York Press, 1997), 10.

[70] Yi Ik (1681-1763), in Yi Sŏng-mi, "Artistic Tradition and the Depiction of Reality: True-view Landscape Painting of the Chosŏn Dynasty," *The Arts of Korea,* Judith G. Smith (ed.) (New York: The Metropolitan Museum of Art, 1998), 342. Yi Ik lived 1681-1763.

[71] Yi, *Searching for Modernity,* 2.

[72] Jungmann, *Pathways to Korean Culture,* 162. Gang Se-hwang lived from 1713 to 1791.

[73] Gang Se-hwang in Yi Song-mi, *Korean Landscape Painting: Continuity and Innovation Through the Ages* (Elizabeth, New Jersey: Hollym International Corporation, 2006), 122.

in the court bureau responsible for palace gardens and vegetable fields and they developed a friendship.[74] Their most celebrated interaction came in 1788, when they unexpectedly met in northeastern Korea, near Mount Geumgang. Kim traveled there at King Jeongjo behest to paint the region's famed scenery, while Gang was there to visit his eldest son, who had been recently appointed to a local office in the region.[75] Gang's account of the events says that Kim painted more than one hundred sketches of Mount Geumgang and its environs during his visit. Kim used these sketches to create a fifty-meter scroll, which won Jeongjo's significant praise. Unfortunately, this scroll did not survive a palace fire in the early nineteenth century,[76] but Gang's account and Jeongjo's reaction make clear that Kim's contemporaries regarded him as a masterful landscape painter, who both followed in the *Sirhak* and True-View traditions and exercised considerable artistic freedom in his compositions.[77] He was, therefore, an important figure in the development of Korean painting.[78]

Kim is perhaps best known for his genre paintings: works with secular themes relating to everyday life.[79] Their existence stems from the fact that Jeongjo broadened what was considered to be appropriate and desirable subjects for paintings. The king wanted art to depict common people doing commonplace things. Kim responded to these preferences.[80] Kim's "Village School" is a fine example of genre painting; Kim's other genre paintings survive in a variety of formats, most commonly as painted silk screens and as ink paintings on album leaves. The painted screens are the more formal works, while the album leaves have a more colloquial quality to them. Even upon a cursory glance, the two types of works possess very different energy and personality.[81] There are several possible reasons for these stylistic differences. Court painters could sell to the public,[82] and such works did not necessarily have the same style and formality of works painted for the court. This could explain the different impressions left by the two formats. It is also possible that Kim drew the drawings now in the album leaves as preliminary sketches, rather than as finished works.[83] A difference in purpose between the album drawings and the formal court screens would explain the different stylistic outcome.

Kim's stylistic diversity may be seen in two works depicting the processing of rice after its harvest. In the screen version, which is the sixth panel in an eight-panel folding screen entitled "Pictorial Records of Travel" (1778), a couple on a journey comes upon four barefoot men beating bundles of rice on the ground to release the panicle's mature grains. A fifth man sweeps up the rewards of their effort. These men are dressed in loose fitting pants, which come to just below their knees, and they wear double-breasted jackets, which are held in place with a cloth belt. Behind the workers, a supervising aristocrat dressed in a luxurious robe overcoat the flat-brimmed, horsehair

---

[74] Yi, *Searching for Modernity,* 132.

[75] Oh, *The Art of Kim Hong-do,* 154.

[76] Oh, *The Art of Kim Hong-do,* 156.

[77] Yi, *Searching for Modernity,* 136.

[78] Some scholars have questioned the authenticity of works ascribed to Kim Hong-do, including the surviving album leaves. See Yi, "Artistic Tradition and the Depiction of Reality," *The Arts of Korea,* 359-362.

[79] Huh Young-hwan, "Chosŏn Landscape and Genre Painting," *Korean Cultural Heritage, Volume 1,* 60.

[80] Jungmann, *Pathways to Korean Culture,* 246.

[81] These stylistic differences have led some art historians to question the authenticity of some of Kim's genre works as well as his landscapes, believing them instead to be the work of nineteenth century artists. See Jungmann, *Pathways to Korean Culture,* 245-246, 342.

[82] Huh Young-hwan, "Chosŏn Landscape and Genre Painting," *Korean Cultural Heritage, Volume 1,* 60.

[83] Kumja Paik Kim, "Kim Hongdo: The Theme of Celebrating a Man's Life," in *In Grand Style: Celebrations in Korean Art During the Joseon Dynasty* (San Francisco, California: Asian Art Museum, 2013), 195.

hat of the *yangban*, sits formally with his legs crossed and his back straight. He is full of composure. A jug, a cup, and other belongings lie carefully positioned by his side. Behind him a stone wall blends into a landscape dominated by a lush pine tree, the trunk of a leafless hardwood, and tall, rolling hills. The screen sends the message of confident order in the land.

This impression contrasts with that of "Rice Threshing" from the *Album of Genre Paintings*. In this version of the threshing scene, Kim did not paint any background, increasing the impression of it being a sketch. Four men with bare chests or opened jackets beat the long, bound stocks over a log to release the rice as another laborer in the foreground sweeps the bounty towards himself. As these men toil with smiles on their faces, a sixth laborer carries bundles of harvested grain on

his back to the worksite. The reason for the smiles lies in the demeanor of the supervising aristocrat. Rather than exhibiting attentiveness and good posture, the blanket-sitting aristocrat has propped himself up against a bundle of grain, with his bent left arm holding up his head, and his left leg crossing over his right knee. The *yangban*'s flat-brimmed, horsehair hat is askew, his shoes have been tossed to the foot of a blanket, and his belongings sit just out of reach. A long pipe juts from his mouth. He seems to be drunk.[84] With its greater sense of energy and movement, this version pokes fun at a lazy *yangban*—something anyone of any other class would have found entertaining. The painting sends a message of playful social uncertainty.

Not all of Kim's genre paintings have a droll quality to them. One interesting example is "Plowing the Field" from another collection of his works on paper, the *Danwaon-jeolsebo Album*. In this painting, a cooperative ox pulls a plow through a field as a farmer guides the plow with his

[84] Jungmann, *Pathways to Korean Culture*, 251.

right foot. He directs the ox along a straight row with the reins in his hands. A curious dog stands between the man and a jumbled rock pile in the foreground, watching with ears perked. These figures are framed by a large, gnarled tree whose trunk first juts left and then right, eventually rising to a crown of branches and a bird's nest. A magpie, representing good news or good luck, perches above the nest, watching over the farmer, ox, and dog, as two *yangban* converse underneath the tree's branches.[85] While the same class division between laborer and non-laborer exists in this work, the image evokes a somberness that is far more akin to the sixth panel of "Pictorial Records of Travel" than to the playfulness of "Rice Threshing." Its commentary on Korea's hierarchical society remains subtle.

One reason for this subtlety is that Kim chose not to reveal the exact social status of the farmer. Given the presence of the *yangban*, the man plowing the field is probably a tenant farmer, working the large holdings of the chatty aristocrats. This would fit with the dominant socioeconomic pattern of late eighteenth-century Korea, where as much as 70% of the population rented all or part of their land and where as much as 62.3% of the land was owned by just 5.4% of the population. In such cases, tenants gave half of their crop to the landowner, out of which the owner paid the 10% tax due to the state.[86] The problem with this interpretation of the painting is that by the end of the eighteenth century, changes in agricultural practices created substantial increases in yields. Increased yields led to the emergence of entrepreneurial farmers who used the income from increased production to buy land or to hire farm laborers of their own. Over time, these wealthier farmers became important private landowners, squeezing out poorer farmers, who lost their land and became hired hands of their peasant neighbors.[87] Therefore, the farmer in Kim's painting might have no employment connection to the *yangban*. Rather, he could easily have been working the land of another member of the peasant class. There is also a third possibility: the farmer could be a slave. By 1780, less than ten percent of Korea's population fell into this category, down from as much as a third in the early Joseon dynasty period, but these slaves still provided important labor for the society.[88] As chattel, Korean slaves could be sold at any time, were transferred through inheritances, and had few legal protections. They rarely had surnames since their kinship had no social value.[89] Although slaves could purchase their freedom after 1718, the adoption of matrilineal law for slaves in 1731 made the status of female slaves worse. The children of female slaves held the status of their mothers, rather than of their fathers, as would be customary in a Confucian society. Slave women then became less desirable marriage partners for either slave or free men. As a result

[85] *Masterpieces of the Ho-Am Art Museum, II: Antique Art 2*, Samsung Foundation of Culture, ed., (Seoul: Samsung Foundation of Culture, 1996), 61, 220.
[86] Gi-Wook Shin, *Peasant Protest and Social Change in Colonial Korea* (Seattle, Washington: University of Washington Press, 1996), 22-23. These figures are from particular districts or provinces, not from the nation as a whole. Historians have had to extrapolate because no reliable national figures exist.
[87] Ki-baik Lee, *A New History of Korea* (Edward W. Wagner with Edward J. Shultz, trans.) (Cambridge, Massachusetts: Harvard University Press, 1984), 227. One example of the change in agricultural practices involved transplanting rice seedlings to paddy fields, which meant that a single plot of land could be used to grow another crop, such as winter barley. This double-crop system increased production considerably. It also required less labor needed since there was less weeding and crop-tending during the early growth of rice seedlings.
[88] James B. Palais, "Slavery," *Sources of Korean Tradition: Volume II,* 157-158.
[89] James B. Palais, *Confucian Statecraft and Korean Institutions: Yu Hyŏngwŏn and the Late Chosŏn Dynasty* (Seattle, Washington: University of Washington Press, 1996), 210-211.

of this diminished social standing, many slave women ran away to cities or remote islands in hope of changing their social status.[90]

Several other of Kim's genre paintings provide additional insight into the demographics of eighteenth-century Korea. In "Peddlers by the Castle Wall," for example, two traveling salesmen pause on a pathway alongside the tall, stone wall of the palace, one facing the viewer, the other turned away. Both peddlers are hunched over as they struggle to continue carrying the weight on their backs. They are certainly tired, possibly even beaten: unable to continue, but unwilling to turn around. Above the two figures, a leafy branch of a tree pokes its way between the wall's crenellations offering hope to the peddlers should they have the energy or thought to raise their eyes aloft. The overall mood of the painting is again somber. It evokes sympathy for these hardworking peddlers and the challenges they face.

Peddlers like these stood at the bottom of the Joseon distribution system. Prior to the late eighteenth century, government-licensed merchants controlled Korean commerce, holding monopolies on essential goods. These merchants either sold directly to consumers or to mid-level wholesalers who in turn sold to peddlers for door-to-door sales. But with Jeongjo's Commercial Equalization Enactment of 1791, private merchants were legally allowed to compete in the marketplace. These men quickly came to control the Korean economy at both the wholesale and retail levels, making significant profits in the process.[91] In fact, these merchants became so powerful that they could manipulate the price of rice in Seoul at will.[92] This commercial power can also be seen in the salt market. Private merchants began transporting salt in 1740, and by 1753, they threatened the viability of the government-licensed shops.[93] Such success made one salt merchant, Kim Hantae, the wealthiest private citizen in the capital and enabled him to wear luxurious clothes, throw lavish parties, and build a huge residence, much to the chagrin of the *yangban*. This wealth also allowed Kim Hantae to become a frequent patron of Kim Hong-do's.[94] Life for itinerant peddlers, however, did not change. They continued to carry goods on their backs, traveling from market to market, futilely trying to undercut prices, or from door-to-door, hoping to entice a spontaneous purchase. Subjected to taxes once a month and exploited by merchants able to deal in greater volume, these peddlers formed a guild* in the nineteenth century to represent their interests.[95] They were, however, victimized by the changing economic climate which characterized late eighteenth century Korea—a fact that Kim must have appreciated when he painted his peddlers in front of the palace walls.

[90] Milan Hejtmanek, "Devalued Bodies, Revalued Status: Confucianism and the Plight of Female Slaves in the Late Chŏson Korea," *Women and Confucianism in Chŏson Korea: New Perspectives*, Youngmin Kim and Michael J. Pettid, (ed.), (Albany, New York: State University Press of New York, 2011), 142-145.
[91] Ko, "Development of Commerce and Commercial Policy during the Reign of King Chŏngo." The king did, however, insist on maintaining the monopoly for government-licensed shops for six products: cotton cloth, ramie cloth, silk, thread, paper and fish.
[92] Kang Man-gil, "The Role of Hangang River Merchants and the Commercial Development in Late Joseon Dynasty," *Korean History: Discovery of its Characteristics and Developments*, (Elizabeth, New Jersey: Hollym International Corporation, 2004), 315.
[93] Kang, "The Role of Hangang River Merchants and the Commercial Development in Late Joseon Dynasty," *Korean History*, 313.
[94] Jungmann, *Pathways to Korean Culture*, 271.
[95] Chung Seung-mo, *Markets: Traditional Korean Society* (Cho Yoon-jung and Min Eun-young, trans.) (Seoul: Ewha Womans University Press, 2006), 56-57, 65.

~

Life in the Changdeokgung palace changed dramatically in 1800, when King Jeongjo unexpectedly died at forty-eight.   Factionalism returned to the court in a pronounced way with Jeongjo's grandmother assuming the regency for Jeongjo's ten-year-old son.[96] In an effort to reorient court loyalties, the Queen Dowager sought to eliminate many of the officials Jeongjo had appointed and nurtured during his twenty-four-year reign.   Therefore, she launched a purge of the court. She initially justified this action as a crackdown on Catholicism, but her real goal was to destroy Jeongjo's political support.[97]

Unlike in Japan, Catholicism came to Korea without the aid of foreign missionaries. Koreans instead learned of the faith through books obtained in China, and they brought the faith to the peninsula themselves. The first Korean was baptized in China in 1784, and when he returned to Korea, Yi Seung-hun began converting his friends. By 1790, there were approximately one thousand Korean converts. A decade later, there were 10,000 Korean Catholics from a wide variety of social classes; there was also a trained clergy to lead them.[98] The Korean establishment saw the arrival and growth of Catholicism as a direct threat to the state, believing it to be a hitherto unknown sect of Buddhism since Catholicism also had a celibate clergy and focused its attention upon one's soul in the afterlife.[99] Because so much of Confucian belief centers upon the responsibilities an individual has to others, instead of the spiritual and personal needs of the individual, Confucianists believed Catholics threatened the bonds which held their society together. Confucianists accused Catholics of tempting people away from their obligations in this life in exchange for an illusory promise in the next.[100] As one contemporary critic said, the difference between "Confucianism and Catholicism is the difference between selflessness…and selfishness."[101] From the establishment's perspective, Catholicism seemed to involve magic and sorcery, which made it similar to the discredited practices of shamanism.[102]

The threat posed by Catholicism was amplified because the Joseon court believed the nation had to epitomize Confucian values par excellence. King Jeongjo sought to meet this goal by limiting the influence of Catholicism as much as possible. In 1787, he issued detailed instructions to an embassy departing for the Qing court forbidding the importation of any materials that deviated from Confucian teachings.[103] A year later, he ordered all Catholic books in Korea to be destroyed. Then, in 1791, he ordered the execution of two Catholics who refused to follow Confucian death

---

[96] Queen Dowager Jeongsun (1745 –1805) was the archenemy of the Hong family, from which Jeongjo's wife, Lady Hyegyeong (1735–1816), came. See JaHyun Kim Haboush, "Introduction," *The Memoirs of Lady Hyegyŏng: the Autobiographical Writings of a Crown Princess of Eighteenth Century Korea*, JaHyun Kim Haboush (trans.) (Berkeley, California: University of California Press, 1996,) 3.

[97] Yi, "King Chŏngjo."

[98] JaHyun Kim Haboush, "Letters of Catholic Martyrs," *Epistolary Korea*, 359. Yi Seung-hun lived from 1756 to 1801.

[99] Evon, "Korea's Aristocratic Moods."

[100] Don Baker, "A Different Thread: Orthodoxy, Heterodoxy, and Catholicism in a Confucian World," *Culture and the State in Late Chosŏn Korea*, 206-207.

[101] An Chŏngbok quoted in Don Baker, "A Different Thread," *Culture and the State in Late Chosŏn Korea*, 209.

[102] Gregory N. Evon, "Tobacco, God and Books: The Perils of Barbarism in Eighteenth-Century Korea," *The Journal of Asian Studies*, Vol. 73, Issue 03 (August 2014) 641-659, accessed February 21, 2020, https://tinyurl.com/y3wg2lka

[103] Evon, "Tobacco, God and Books."

rituals.[104] The king hoped that these executions would be exceptional, rather than typical. He wrote,

> If we want to save our way of life from corruption, there is no better course of action than to clarify the truth. We need a policy that gets the general population working with us to encourage proper behavior and discourage evil. Only then can we expect to get some results. If we fall back on relying primarily on harsh punishments to correct the way people behave, are we really teaching the people anything?[105]

Unfortunately for Korea's Catholics, Jeongjo's sudden death put an end to any possibility of restraint. In 1801, the government began arresting Catholics and executing those who refused to recant their beliefs. One Catholic aristocrat wrote to a bishop in China saying that "the Catholic community here is in imminent danger of extinction" and called for a Chinese-sponsored invasion of Korea.[106]

Kim Hong-do's life also changed dramatically with the death of King Jeongjo. By 1804, he was merely another of the thirty painters-in-waiting. For the first time in his career, Kim had to compete in the examination process, often facing artists a generation younger. Between the summer of 1804 and the summer of 1805, Kim competed in fifteen examinations, some only days apart. These exams asked him to paint a painting entitled, "Lotus Flower Blossoming in the Clean Water," or "Lee Gwang Shoots an Arrow into the Tiger-Shaped Rock." Once he had the choice between "Every Shop Advertises Curious Products," "Storing Rice in the Shed," or "Rich Family Receives a Son-in-Law." In almost half of these competitions, he earned the highest score possible, but he also suffered through days of humiliation in which he finished last among the competitors.[107] These results must have damaged the pride of a man who had painted kings and been described by a contemporary as "a man of exceptional skills" whose "pictures were in harmony with nature" and whose brush strokes "never missed even by a hair's width."[108]

Broken of spirit and in failing health, Kim left Changdeokgung in the fall of 1805. Three days after the winter solstice, he painted his last dated work, "Ode to the Sound of Autumn." It illustrates a poem by the eleventh-century Chinese poet Ouyang Xiu, telling of a fall evening when an old man, reading a book, hears a strange noise outside and orders his young servant to investigate. Finding nothing, the servant points to the sky and says, "Only the stars and the moon are shining brightly and there are no human traces at all. The sound comes from between the trees."[109] In Kim's homage to this poem, the old man sits on the floor in front of a desk, his head turned towards

---

[104] In 1790, the news reached Korea that the pope had forbidden Catholics from participating in Confucian death rituals. A year later, when Paul Yun Chich'ung's mother died, he decided not to make an ancestral tablet as tradition demanded. He also had all of his family's other tablets burned. Officials objected more to the departure from ritual than in Yun's actual belief. Jeongio confirmed the order to execute Yun and his cousin in December 1791, making the two men Korea's first Catholic martyrs. See Baker, "A Different Thread," *Culture and the State in Late Chosŏn Korea*, 217-220.

[105] Jeongjo, "King Chŏngjo: How to Combat the Spread of Catholicism," Donald Baker (trans.), *Sources of Korean Tradition: Volume II,* 135.

[106] Hwang Sayŏng, "Hwang Sayŏng: An Appeal for Aid," Donald Baker (trans.) *Sources of Korean Tradition: Volume II,* 135.

[107] Oh, *The Art of Kim Hong-do,* 219-229.

[108] Lee Yong-hyu quoted in Oh, *The Art of Kim Hong-do,* 41. Oh identifies Lee (1708-1782) as the "best writer of the time."

[109] Ouyang Xiu quoted in Oh, "The Life and Art of Kim Hong-do."

the viewer so that he might look out of a round, curtained window of his one-story, thatched cottage. The home sits in a dell, surrounded by foreboding outcroppings and many leafless trees, most of which are straight and tall and one of which is painfully twisted. The servant stands in the courtyard, pointing towards the still-rising full moon on the left side of the painting, while a large, proud mountain balances the composition on the right. The old man and the servant seem inconsequential in the face of the cold, moody landscape. The accompanying inscription reads in part:

> Alas! Although trees and grass do not have emotions, they shed leaves against the wind when the time comes. Unlike other animals, man has a soul. All kinds of worries grieve my head, and everything pains my body....Why would I compete with trees and grass for prosperity? Who kills and hurts them? Why do I lament the sound of autumn?"[110]

"Ode to the Sound of Autumn" is significant as Kim's culminating work. It powerfully encapsulates and integrates Kim's oeuvre in genre and landscape painting, as well as his ability to evoke emotion. It succeeds by combining the touching sympathy and perceptive narrative so characteristic of his genre works[111] with an integration of traditional brush strokes, close observation of nature, and compositional freedom so characteristic of his landscapes.[112] It also respects Korea's cultural connection to China, while celebrating Joseon independence. "Ode" does this by honoring the eleventh-century poet and by upholding the Daoist* tradition of painting humans as unobtrusive figures in landscapes to show the value of harmony with nature. The painting also, however, illustrates the pride of True-View landscapes that characterized eighteenth-century Korea.[113] It is a fitting tour-de-force from the final weeks of Kim's life.

~

Kim's contemporaries described him as a tall, gregarious man with a sturdy frame, who enjoyed laughter and hearty companionship.[114] Many admired him for his extroverted personality, even if they were amazed by how little his regular and voluminous alcohol consumption affected his work. As one low-ranking official noted in a poem about Kim:

> When he was about to paint
> He would take off his coat

---

[110] Ouyang Xiu quoted in Oh, *The Art of Kim Hong-do*, 231.

[111] Ahn Hwi-joon, "Development of Painting in the Choson Period," *Masterpieces of the Ho-Am Art Museum, II: Antique Art 2*, Samsung Foundation of Culture, ed., (Seoul: Samsung Foundation of Culture, 1996), 195.

[112] Yi, *Searching for Modernity*, 132, 136.

[113] Yi Song-mi, *Korean Landscape Painting: Continuity and Innovation Through the Ages* (Elizabeth, New Jersey: Hollym International Corporation, 2006), 10, 15.

[114] Since the mean height for Korean military recruits between the ages of twenty and forty years old was 165.69 cm in this period (or a little over 5'4"), Kim must have been at least 5'6" to be considered a tall man. See James B. Lewis, Seong Ho Jun and Daniel Schwekendiek, "Toward an Anthropometric History of Chosŏn Dynasty Korea, Sixteenth to Eighteen Century," *The Journal of the Historical Society*, Vol. 13, Issue 3, (September 2013), 239-270, EBSCOhost.

His breath reeked of alcohol
Jokes would escape from his mouth
Nothing seemed to be on his mind
But his brushstroke told the truth.[115]

Kim seems to have reveled in this exceptionality, adopting pen names such as "a drunken painter" or an "old man who gets drunk easily."[116]   He certainly wasn't one who modified his behavior frequently, for as the king's favorite painter he had a latitude other members of the court did not. The boisterously-spirited Kim even possessed the strength of personality to speak his mind in the presence of the king.   In 1791, for example, Kim presented Jeongjo with three different royal portraits. The king then gathered his ministers together for comment, urging them to pick the best one. The ministers all followed Jeongjo's lead, choosing between the two the king clearly preferred and dismissing the one Kim liked best—a vibrant work that he had quickly completed that morning. While none of the three drafts survive, eyewitness accounts show that Kim wasn't afraid to contradict his superiors or modify his opinion for political expediency.[117] He possessed a robust ego.

The acclaim for Kim's work today rests not only on the enormous diversity of his work, but also because his oeuvre provides Koreans a window to understand both their past and their present. Although other eighteenth-century painters also served as the mediators between different social classes,[118] Kim was the one who purposefully documented the breadth of Korean society in his paintings. His work allows Koreans to understand both the life of the court and the life of the commoner during a period celebrated in Korean history for its sound royal leadership and extended peace. Moreover, Kim's close observations of both landscape and laborer allow Koreans to see themselves today. This is because Kim's artistry captured *haan*—a quality many Koreans identify as being central to their national character. *Haan* is a powerful sorrow, mixed with a sense of unfairness, and accompanied by the suppression of anger.[119] It is a characteristic that has been ingrained into generations of Korean children and the way they are taught to see Korean art.[120] In Kim's work, *haan* is the weariness of the peddlers along the castle wall, the amusement of the workers threshing rice, and the frustration of the boy about to be whipped by his teacher. Significantly, however, Kim often balanced this underlining, tacit sadness with a way of resolving *haan* called *haan-puri*. *Haan-puri* is realized anticipation, and it too is part of the Korean identity.[121]   In Kim's "Plowing the Field," for example, *haan-puri* is the magpie in the tree, foreseeing good news and encompassing, like so much of his work, both hopefulness and sadness. This was Kim's magic: he possessed the ability to show Korean pathos while anticipating a promise of something better.

---

[115] Park Yun-muk quoted in Oh, *The Art of Kim Hong-do*, 62.

[116] Oh, *The Art of Kim Hong-do*, 38-39.

[117] Oh, *The Art of Kim Hong-do*, 59-61.

[118] Jungmann, *Pathways to Korean Culture*, 211.

[119] Sung Kil Min, "The Politics of *Haan*: Affect and the Domestication of Anger in South Korea," *The Political Economy of Affect and Emotion in East Asia*, Jie Yang (ed.) (New York: Routledge, 2014), 200-201. The word is also spelled "han" in many sources.

[120] Sunghee Choi, "Re-Thinking Korean Cultural Identities at the National Museum of Korea," *National Museums: New Studies from around the World*, Simon J. Knell et al (ed.) (New York: Routledge, 2011), 292. Choi argues that the development of the *haan* identity in Korea is a product of Japanese colonialism and oppression between 1910 and 1945.

[121] Sung, "The Politics of *Haan*," *The Political Economy of Affect and Emotion in East Asia*, 203.

$\mathcal{L}$

Jeanne Julie Éléonore de Lespinasse

1732-1776

Newly returned from his sixteen-month journey to Moscow and the court of Catherine the Great, Enlightenment* leader Denis Diderot knew he would soon have to pay a visit to the residence of Julie de Lespinasse. The reason was simple: there was no better indoor space in Paris in October 1774 where one could meet to discuss ideas freely, converse with foreign visitors, indulge in gossip, and learn the latest from Versailles. Mademoiselle de Lespinasse's salon at the intersection of rue Bellechasse and rue Saint-Dominique in the Faubourg Saint-Germain was a Parisian institution, a place where those with great minds met, and Diderot hoped that after so much time abroad its hostess would receive him with enthusiasm.[1]

Diderot climbed the stairs to the second floor of the building, where a footman invited him into an anteroom and took his cloak. Upon entering the main salon, Diderot found an ample room decorated in the very latest style. The exuberant, sensuous curvature of Rococo favored by the apartment's former occupants had been replaced with the transitional Louis XVI style, featuring greater symmetry, cleaner lines, and a purposeful homage to antiquity and rationalism. The walls were lined in white wainscoting and accented with mirrors, Greco-Roman medallions, flower garlands, and rectangular, gilded moldings. The half-moon-shaped lunettes above each doorway included engravings replicating popular works by the painter Jean-Baptiste Greuze, such as *The Village Bride* and *The Little Girl Weeping for her Dead Bird*. The ceiling was painted light blue to look like the sky, and an Aubusson carpet with a flower motif and a geometric border lay on top of a well-polished parquet floor. The marble mantle above the fireplace supported an expensive clock, with busts of noted Enlightenment figures Jean le Rond d'Alembert and François-Marie Arouet de Voltaire on each end. Sixteen armchairs and couches, chiefly upholstered in a rich crimson fabric that matched the color and luxuriousness of the window drapes, and tables inlaid with tropical woods, each designed for a specific purpose, furnished the room. A screen separated this guest area

---

[1] By the early twentieth century, the building which housed Mlle. de Lespinasse's apartment no longer stood. See Camilla Jebb, *A Star of the Salons: Julie de Lespinasse* (London, Methuen & Co., 1908), 193. Diderot called upon Lespinasse on October 26, 1774. See Arthur M. Wilson, *Diderot* (New York: Oxford University Press, 1972), 657.

from the hostess' work space, which accommodated bookcases and a rosewood *secrétaire-armoire*. Since Mlle. de Lespinasse's salon began at 6:00 p.m., a large chandelier and several three-candle sconces along each wall provided illumination as Diderot arrived that late October evening.[2]

Lespinasse's influential position in her final years belied the circumstances of her birth. Born out-of-wedlock in a midwife's home in an unfashionable, artisan neighborhood in Lyon on November 9, 1732, she was the child of a noble woman, Julie d'Albon, and an unknown man. When Julie d'Albon brought the newborn to the local parish church for baptism the next day, she took precautions to create the illusion of legitimacy for the child. The girl's baptismal record indicated that she was the "legitimate daughter of Claude Lespinasse, burgher of L[y]on and of the dame Julie Navarre his wife." Both of these names were fictitious. The record also listed a licensed surgeon and his wife as godparents, and in the absence of the father's signature, two witnesses attested with their signatures as to the legitimacy of the birth. Years later, however, someone using a different ink inserted an "il" before the word "legitimate" and crossed out the words "his wife" in the church's record.[3] Lespinasse's secret past eventually became known.

Lespinasse didn't know about these circumstances until she neared her nineteen birthday. One reason for this long concealment was that although Julie d'Albon misrepresented the birth for the baptismal record, she did not renounce her daughter. Rather, once the child was weaned, d'Albon brought her to Chateau d'Avauges to live with her two legitimate children: a daughter, Diane, and a son, Camille. Convention allowed Julie de Lespinasse to be treated as an adoptive daughter but not as an heiress.[4] She seems to have had a happy childhood as a result, at least until 1748, when d'Albon died, leaving the unmarried fifteen-and-a-half year old in a precarious state. Fortunately, Lespinasse's half-sister Diane invited her to come to Champrond, the family estate of Diane's husband Gaspard de Vichy, which was located 60 miles northwest of Lyon. Lespinasse's first two years at Champrond were ones of relative contentment and freedom. She passed her days reading, riding, hunting, and teaching Diane and Gaspard's two sons how to read and write.[5] It was a

---

[2] This description comes from several sources: 1) Jebb, *A Star of the Salons,* 194-195; 2) Janet Aldis, *Madam Geoffrin: Her Salon and her Times, 1750-1777* (New York: G. P. Putnam's Sons, 1905), 176; 3) Olivier Bernier, *Pleasure and Privilege: Life in France, Naples, and America 1770-1790* (New York: Doubleday & Company, 1981), 46, 49; 4) three articles from *The Dictionary of Art,* Jane Turner (ed.) (New York: Grove-Oxford University Press, 1996): a) Monique Riccardi-Cubitt, "Louis XVI Style," Volume 19, 724; b) John Wilton-Ely, "Neo-Classicism," Volume 22, 734-742; c) A. Pradère, "France Furniture, 1719-93," Volume 11, 590-597; and 5) material from the Metropolitan Museum of Art website, including an unsigned article from the *Metropolitan Museum of Art Bulletin* (Vol. 18, No.12, Part 1, November, 1923), entitled "Three Louis XVI Rooms." The article describes the opening of three rooms in the museum from the Hôtel Gaulin in Dijon. These rooms were constructed between 1770 and 1780. The article notes how they are representative of early neo-classicism for those without the unlimited budgets of Versailles and Fontainebleau; hence they are probably more representative of Lespinasse's salon than more famous rooms. Additional material from the website came from the Museum's descriptions of its galleries featuring European Sculpture and Decorative Arts, accessed February 22, 2020, https://tinyurl.com/y24ydqo2

[3] Marquis de Ségur, *Julie de Lespinasse*, P. H. Lee Warner (trans.) (New York: Henry Holt and Company, 1907), 2.

[4] Jebb, *A Star of the Salons,* 5. Julie d'Albon and her husband, Claude d'Albon, did not have a happy marriage. Upon Camille's birth in 1724, Claude returned to his family's estate in Roanne, never to return. Perhaps as a result of this situation, Julie d'Albon also had an illegitimate son, Hilaire, born twenty months before Julie de Lespinasse. Hilaire was also registered as the son of two fictitious people, was raised in a monastery, and became a Franciscan in 1750. See de Ségur, *Julie de Lespinasse,* 5-7.

[5] Jebb, *A Star of the Salons,* 17, 26. Julie de Lespinasse became especially close to the older son, Abel, who was then ten, with the two of them remaining close for the rest of their lives.

pleasant life. Everything changed, however, in 1751, when Diane and Gaspard returned from a winter in Paris, and Lespinasse learned the full truth about her parentage.[6] It was "a compound of circumstances, so calamitous, so horrible," Lespinasse wrote years later, "that it proves the truth is often incredible."[7] Besides being her half-sister's husband, Gaspard de Vichy was also Julie de Lespinasse's father.

As intolerable as she found the betrayal and the new atmosphere at Champrond with Diane and Gaspard treating her like a hired governess and servant instead of a member of the d'Albon family, Lespinasse faced a situation with few alternatives. She had no prospects for marriage.[8] After Camille wrote saying that it was "impossible…for me to give you any financial help [since]…the advancement of my children must be secured," it became clear to Lespinasse that her only viable option was to join a religious order.[9] The nineteen-year old entered a convent in Lyon in October 1752 as a method of escape, despite having little enthusiasm for the religious life.

A few weeks before Julie de Lespinasse entered the convent, she met Gaspard's sister, Marie de Vichy-Champrond, now Madame du Deffand. It was a meeting that would change Julie's fate, for the two women immediately took a liking to one another. They also needed one another. Now in her mid-fifties, Deffand was almost blind and in need of assistance and companionship from a woman of her own class, and Lespinasse wanted an alternative to a nun's life. Madame du Deffand proposed that Lespinasse come to Paris to live with her. There were a number of obstacles to this proposal, not the least of which was Lespinasse's own fear that as a provincial girl she would be ignored or abandoned in the hubbub of the sophisticated city. She wrote Deffand, "I fear that I might become so depressed that I should only be a burden to you, and you would repent of having taken me." Madame du Deffand responded reassuringly:

> When strangers are present I shall treat you not only with politeness but with ceremony, to make people from the first understand that they must do the same….The essential thing is to begin by establishing your position on the strength of your own merits….You have plenty of brains, you can be lively, and you are not wanting in feeling. With all these good gifts you will be charming, if you only allow yourself to be natural.[10]

That concern overcome, Deffand had to turn her attention to the objection of her brother Gaspard, who was adamantly opposed to the proposal, lest his daughter reassert a claim to the d'Albon inheritance once she was in Paris. Madame du Deffand negotiated and beseeched for several months, but eventually put her foot down. She told her brother that Lespinasse had entered the convent of her own free will and that Gaspard had no rights over her whatsoever. His consent was desirable, but not required. By April 1754, Deffand had made arrangements through Lyon's archbishop to have Lespinasse escorted on a *carrosse de diligence*, or stagecoach, to the largest city in Europe.[11] She had also issued a caution to her niece:

---

[6] de Ségur, *Julie de Lespinasse*, 28-29.

[7] Julie de Lespinasse quoted in Helen Clergue, *The Salon: A Study of French Society and Personalities in the Eighteenth Century* (New York: G.P. Putnam's Sons/The Knickerbocker Press, 1907), 202.

[8] de Ségur, *Julie de Lespinasse,*, 29-30; and Jebb, *A Star of the Salons,* 63.

[9] Camille d'Albon quoted in de Ségur, *Julie de Lespinasse*, 59.

[10] Julie de Lespinasse and Madame du Deffand quoted in Jebb, *A Star of the Salons:* 67-69.

[11] Jebb, *A Star of the Salons,* 65-66, 72.

> I am naturally distrustful, and all those in whom I detect slyness become suspicious to me to the point of no longer feeling the slightest confidence in them. I have two intimate friends, Formont and d'Alembert; I love them passionately, but less for their agreeable charms and their friendship for me than for their absolutely truthfulness. Therefore, you must, my queen, resolve to live with me with the utmost truth and sincerity, and…without subterfuge.[12]

That was a warning Lespinasse would eventually fail to heed.

~

When Deffand told Lespinasse to be "natural," she didn't mean that the young woman could simply be herself or do what she pleased. Rather, the blind woman meant that her niece would need to learn how to become naturally comfortable in the salon setting. This was not an easy task, for there was a tremendous amount to learn. Not only would Lespinasse would have to learn how to prepare for conversation with a diverse group of men and women, but also how not to let that preparation show. She would need to learn how to speak the laudatory, hyperbolic language of Versailles and apply it to the particular social setting of the salon without being seen as superficial.[13] She would have to perfect her body language since the gestures and facial expressions had to match her words and tone for her to have salon credibility. She would also have to demonstrate sincere interest, allow for poignant silences, and employ playful teasing with panache.[14] Perhaps Jean-Jacques Rousseau best described the ideal atmosphere of the salon:

> The tone of conversation is flowing and natural, it is neither weighty nor frivolous; it is knowledgeable but not pedantic, cheerful but not loud, polite but unaffected, gallant but not moony, ironic but not equivocal. You hear neither dissertations nor cast-away wit; there is discussion without argument.[15]

This is what it meant to possess *sociabilité*, the defining characteristic of the salon, and to be a participant in a salon meant that someone was a part of *le monde*, the world of polite society. *Le monde* brought diplomats, notable foreign visitors, and carefully selected members of the aristocracy together with the authors, artists, *philosophes,* and scientists who comprised the Republic of Letters, to create a unique, intimate social atmosphere. Given the social diversity in a salon, maintaining the balance Rousseau described was not always easy. This is why the hostess of the salon, the *salonnière*, held such an essential role. She had to be equitable to all, ensuring that all were heard and pleased with the outcome of the conversation. She had to establish social rules and

---

[12] Madame du Deffand to Mlle. de Lespinasse, February 13, 1754 in *Letters of Mlle. de Lespinasse with Notes on her Life and Character by D'Alembert, Marmontel, De Guibert, etc.*, Katharine Prescott Wormeley (trans.) (Boston, Massachusetts: Hardy, Pratt & Company, 1903), 25-26.

[13] Antoine Lilti, *The World of the Salons: Sociability and Worldliness in Eighteenth Century Paris* (New York: Oxford University Press, 2015), 145-146.

[14] Benedetta Craveri, *The Age of Conversation*, Teresa Waugh (trans.) (New York: New York Review of Books, 2005), 346-350.

[15] Jean-Jacques Rousseau quoted in Bernier, *Pleasure and Privilege*, 161.

cultivate a culture of politeness.[16] By doing this and by guiding the discussion, the *salonnières* also became the arbiters of culture, helping to define collective responses to a new piece of literature or a theatrical performance. In this way, the *salonnières* presided over the fate of authors and artists, making the careers of some, ruining the careers of others.[17] This significant responsibility is one reason Lespinasse spent a decade, from April 1754 to April 1764, developing her skills under the tutelage of her blind aunt.

Hosting a salon was a major financial undertaking for those catering to *le monde*. Madame du Deffand's expenses were almost 39,000 *livres* a year, at a time when the rent for most one-room apartments in Paris cost between 40 and 200 *livres* a year.[18] She spent 18,000 for food; 6,000 for wages for her domestic servants and their uniforms; 4,000 for her carriage and three horses; 4,000 for wood and candles; 2,000 for renting her apartment in the convent; and 4,000 for what she described as "my own upkeep." In 1770, her regular income was 35,190 *livres*, which meant that without the annual grant of 6,000 *livres* from the crown, Deffand would have lived beyond her means, as did many *ancien régime** nobles.[19] That food constituted Deffand's largest expenses is not surprising, given the fact that a summer afternoon dinner party for fifteen people usually lasted three to four hours and had five services. A typical menu consisted of:

First Service:	Two soups (cucumber and green pea) and four appetizers (fried mutton feet, veal roast in pastry, small Pâtés, melons).
Second Service:	Boiled leg of mutton, roast veal marinated in cream, duckling with peas, squab with herbs, two chickens with little white onions, rabbit steaks with cucumbers.
Third Service:	1 small turkey, one capon, four partridges, six squabs roasted like quails, two green salads.
Fourth Service:	Apricot tartlets, scrambled eggs, vine-leaf fritters, cookies, small white beans in cream, artichokes with butter sauce.

[16] Dena Goodman argues that male education between antiquity and the late eighteenth century nurtured competitiveness over cooperation. The only way to overcome this tradition, as well as the practice of settling disputes through duels, was to create an atmosphere where politeness was prized and flaunted. She argues that women were uniquely able to do this. See Dena Goodman, *The Republic of Letters: A Cultural History of the French Enlightenment* (Ithaca, New York: Cornell University Press, 1994), 92-97, 102, 104.

[17] Vera Lee, *The Reign of Women in Eighteenth Century France* (Cambridge, Massachusetts: Schenkman Publishing Company, 1975), 116.

[18] In 1799-89, 58% of the one-room rents were between 40-200 livres. See Daniel Roche, *France in the Enlightenment*, Arthur Goldhammer (trans.) (Cambridge, Massachusetts: Harvard University Press, 1998), 655. In terms of wages, English traveler Arthur Young reported that on the eve of the French Revolution, when prices were at their highest, a Provencal gardener made 300 *livres* a year and a Provencal housemaid earned no more than 70 *livres*. This stood in contrast to a Parisian abbot, who had an income of 300,000 *livres* a year. See Arthur Young, *Travels in France During the Years 1787, 1788, and 1789*, Jeffry Kaplow (ed.), (Garden City, New York: Anchor Books, 1969), 70, 197. Between these two extremes, a beginning journalist for the *Gazette de France*, Jean-Baptiste-Antoine Suard (1732-1817), made 2500 *livres* a year. See Robert Darnton, *The Literary Underground of the Old Regime* (Cambridge, Massachusetts: Harvard University Press, 1982), 4.

[19] Lilti, *The World of the Salons*, 32. Lilti points out that the number of families with an annual income of 50,000 *livres* or more was small: 100 of them were noble families residing at Versailles, 60 were noble families not living at Versailles, and 50 were wealthy bourgeois financiers.

Fifth Service:	Four compotes (peaches, prunes, pears, green grapes), four plates of ice cream, one plate of cream cheese, one plate of pastries.[20]

And, of course, there would be wine to accompany all of this, including champagne, which had been invented in 1714 by Dom Pérignon and had become quite popular by 1770.[21]

What did people actually talk about in the salons? Unfortunately, there are few descriptions of this and certainly no recorded minutes to help historians identify exactly who was where, when, and what they said.[22] It is certain, however, that many salon members wanted to enjoy a lively repartee, full of insightful quips that could be easily memorized and repeated. They liked delightful anecdotes, curious facts, puns, and other verbal amusements. This included playing charades or word games, such as picking two synonyms and competing to see who could offer the most clarifying definition.[23] Many salons featured public readings from novels or recently published treatises, frequently by their authors. Publication of controversial works undoubtedly generated discussions. One example was Rousseau's *Émile*, which challenged the established practices of binding infants and wet nursing, and held that children should not be exposed to ideas they cannot yet understand, such as morality.[24] Gossip certainly played a significant role in salon conversations with everything from hairstyles to sexual dalliances considered fair game. Any rumor about the royal family was definitely worth repeating, which is why Deffand was so pleased to be the first to report that the young *dauphin** had knocked over his chamber pot.[25] Any news from the other courts of Europe was equally noted, which is why ambassadors and government officials were frequently in attendance. Other foreign visitors received considerable attention as well. As Scottish philosopher, historian, and diplomatic attaché David Hume noted in a letter to Scottish historian William Robertson, recounting his first months in Paris: "I eat nothing but Ambrosia, drink nothing but Nectar, breathe nothing but Incense, and tread on nothing but Flowers."[26] Similarly, in a letter to social philosopher and political economist Adam Smith, Hume wrote:

> I have been three days at Paris and two at Fontainebleau, and have everywhere met with the most extraordinary honours which the most exorbitant vanity could wish or desire....There is not a courtier in France who would not have been transported with joy to have had half of these obliging things said to him.[27]

---

[20] Bernier, *Pleasure and Privilege,* 97-98. There was no fish course because of the lack of refrigeration during summer (page 99).
[21] Bernier, *Pleasure and Privilege,* 95.
[22] Steven Kale, *French Salons: High Society and Political Sociability from the Old Regime to the Revolution of 1848* (Baltimore, Maryland: The Johns Hopkins University Press, 2004), 2.
[23] Lilti, *The World of the Salons,* 139, 141, 160-161.
[24] George R. Havens, *Jean-Jacques Rousseau* (Boston, Massachusetts: Twayne Publishers, 1978), 95-96. By the last 1770s, *Émile* was owned by anyone who could afford it See Robert L. Dawson, *Confiscations at Customs: Banned Books and the French Booktrade during the Last Years of the Ancien Régime,* SVEC 2006:07 (Oxford, U.K.: The Voltaire Foundation, 2006), 45.
[25] Lilti, *The World of the Salons,* 194.
[26] David Hume to William Robertson, December 1, 1763 in *New Letters of David Hume,* Raymond Klibansky and Ernest C. Mossner (ed.) (New York: Oxford University Press, 2011), 74.
[27] David Hume quoted in Aldis, *Madam Geoffrin,* 209-210.

Other topics also generated conversation. Scandals drew rapt attention, such as the one in March 1766 in which the English were accused of poisoning a horse before a key race.[28] Legal proceedings, such as the separation suit the Marquise de Mézières filed against her husband in September 1770 for financial mismanagement and physical abuse, stirred conversation.[29] Salon participants also offered their opinions on specific events, like the unveiling of a commissioned painting[30] or the concert series Wolfgang and Maria Anna Mozart gave as childhood prodigies in 1764 and 1766.[31] Complaints about the weather, future travel plans, health concerns, and family matters rounded out the topics of conversation. As a whole, eighteenth-century Parisian salons were rather catty and indulgent establishments, full of what Hume described as "frivolous vanity."[32]

It is important to note that regardless of the topic of conversation or the professed desire to allow those of different social backgrounds to fraternize, most salons could not remove themselves from the socio-political realities of the outside world. They did not promote a fully egalitarian atmosphere.[33] Noted mathematician Jean le Rond d'Alembert, for example, found that he was greeted differently by nobles than by those from his own class. D'Alembert wasn't actually surprised by this behavior, for he noted that in every social situation, "all attentions will be for rank."[34] Even honored guests like Hume were occasionally mocked by the elite, as happened the evening he was chosen to play the part of a sultan in a charade as a result of his imperfect French.[35] The punishment for overstepping one's station within *ancien régime* society was ridicule. Since scornful disdain and mockery was something at which Deffand was quite adept, she had little difficulty keeping her guests in line and upholding what she considered to be proper behavior. For Deffand, this meant upholding social rank, ignoring the large philosophical questions of the day, and using even the casual reference to morality, religion, or politics as another opportunity for teasing and *bon mots*.[36]

By the time Lespinasse was in her mid-thirties, she began to find the chatter of Deffand's salon wanting. She hungered for something more meaningful. She also found herself chafing against the incessant and exacting demands of her aunt. Lespinasse complained, "God does not require so much as she. With her, a single venial sin cancels in one moment the services of many years."[37] Since Deffand preferred to sleep through the day and stay up all night, it wasn't hard to create an opportunity for a bit of independence. Lespinasse and her good friend d'Alembert began to meet with a small group of other like-minded individuals an hour before Deffand's salon began. What

---

[28] *The Yale Edition of Horace Walpole's Correspondence*, W. S. Lewis (ed.), Volume 30, (New Haven, Connecticut: Yale University Press, 1937), 218.

[29] Mary Trouille, *Wife-abuse in Eighteenth Century France*, SVEC 2009: 01 (Oxford, U.K.: The Voltaire Foundation, 2006), 107.

[30] In October 1754, for example, Anne-Thérèse Rodet, Madame Geoffrin (1699-1777), unveiled a work she had commissioned from Carle Van Loo. See Emma Barker, "Mme. Geoffrin, Painting and *Galanterie*: Carle Van Loo's Conversation Espagnole and Lecture Espagnole," *Eighteenth Century Studies*, 40.4 (Summer 2007): 587-590, 592-596, 598-614, ProQuest Central.

[31] Eva Rieger, "Wolfgang Amadeus Mozart, Travels, 1763-73," *The New Grove Dictionary of Music and Musicians*, Stanley Sadie (ed.), Vol.17, (New York: Oxford University Press, 2001), 277.

[32] David Hume quoted in Annette C. Baier, *The Pursuits of Philosophy: An Introduction to the Life and Thought of David Hume* (Cambridge, Massachusetts: Harvard University Press, 2011), 110.

[33] Kale, *French Salons,* 25-26.

[34] Jean-Baptiste le Rond d'Alembert quoted in Lilti, *The World of the Salons,* 78.

[35] Baier, *The Pursuits of Philosophy,* 112.

[36] de Ségur, *Julie de Lespinasse,* 151.

[37] Julie de Lespinasse quoted in Jebb, *A Star of the Salons,* 178.

they called the "*petite salon de contrabande*," met in Lespinasse's bedroom, upstairs from Deffand's rooms. This arrangement served the conspirators well until one day in mid-April 1764, when something disturbed the blind woman, and she rose earlier than usual. Climbing the stairs, Deffand found Lespinasse's bedroom full of conversation and laughter. As the men made a hasty retreat, Madame du Deffand cried, "So mademoiselle, you would rob me of my friends! It is by such treason that you show your gratitude! You shall remain no longer under my roof. I have had enough of nursing a viper in my bosom!" Lespinasse responded by saying, "I would not stay here longer if you asked me. I have friends of my own, real friends, who will treat me very differently from you!"[38]

A variety of people came to the now-homeless Lespinasse's rescue. The most important of these was Madame Geoffrin, who had trained for many years in the salon of Claudine Alexandrine Guérin de Tencin and who had overcome her husband's opposition to establish one of Paris' most prestigious salons.[39] A key rival of Deffand's, Geoffrin granted Lespinasse an annual pension and made arrangements for her to obtain an additional annual stipend from the royal coffers to set up her own salon. The Maréchale de Luxembourg provided all of the necessary fashionable furnishings.[40] To expand her circle of acquaintances, Geoffrin also provided Lespinasse with a standing invitation to her famous Monday and Wednesday afternoon dinners. She was the only woman to enjoy this honor.

With the establishment of her own salon, Lespinasse sought to create a different atmosphere from either Deffand's or Geoffrin's, which was known for its hostess' firm hand in order to direct conversation and to avoid controversial issues and scandal.[41] Lespinasse loathed the superficiality that characterized many salon discussions, just as she resented the favoritism and bigotry she saw as being characteristic of the *ancien régime*.[42] To help correct for these faults, she created a nursery for ideas, a laboratory where both established and nascent intellectuals were free to express themselves candidly.[43] Thus she attracted the major intellectuals of the era, stealing many from Deffand's circle. The rivalry between niece and aunt became so intense that these women made *le monde* declare for one side or the other, including foreign guests like Hume. Lespinasse wrote to the Scottish philosopher, "I was one of the first to recognize your work. I am proud of it, and I sincerely desired to be your friend....Whether or not custom licenses or tolerates the alliance of a friend with an enemy, I cannot tell. I do know the demands of friendship."[44] Hume had hoped to avoid dispute entirely, but, like so many others, he sided with Lespinasse and wrote to Deffand on August 5, 1766 to announce his decision. It was impossible for him to patronize Lespinasse's salon while maintaining a close friendship with Deffand.[45] Others also cast their lots with Lespinasse, including leading members of the French Republic of Letters: social critic Friedrich Melchior Grimm, writer and historian Jean-François Marmontel, economist André Morellet, and journalist Jean-Baptiste-Antoine Suard. For twelve years, these and other men frequently met in Lespinasse's salon, which she held between 6:00 p.m. and 9:00 p.m. every day that she didn't go to the opera or theater. Since she did not have the financial resources to be able to provide her guests with meals

---

[38] Jebb, *A Star of the Salons,* 181.
[39] Craveri, *The Age of Conversation*, 298. Her full name was Marie Thérèse Rodet Geoffrin (1699-1777).
[40] Aldis, *Madam Geoffrin,* 176.
[41] Craveri, *The Age of Conversation,*301-302.
[42] Craveri, *The Age of Conversation*, 309.
[43] Frank Hamel, *Famous French Salons* (New York: Brentano's, 1908), 235.
[44] Julie de Lespinasse quoted in de Ségur, *Julie de Lespinasse*, 190.
[45] *The Letters of David Hume, Volume II*, J. Y. T. Greig (ed.), (Oxford, U.K.: The Clarendon Press-Oxford University Press, 1932), 72.

and entertainment as others did, Lespinasse relied upon her conversational abilities and her reputation for allowing freedom of speech to attract those she wanted to come to her door. This approach created a salon unlike any other in Paris. Marmontel hailed her exceptional talent for "casting out a thought and giving it for discussion," as well as for her "own talent in discussing it with precision" and for "bringing forth new ideas." He also said, "Nowhere was the conversation more lively, more brilliant or better regulated than at her house."[46] Grimm echoed this assessment, asserting that Lespinasse had "great knowledge of the world" and that she

> possessed [to] an eminent degree that art so difficult and so precious—of making the best of the minds of others, of interesting them, and of bringing them into play without any appearance of constraint or effort. She knew how to unite the different styles of mind, sometimes even the most opposed, without appearing to take the slightest pain to do so; by a word adroitly flung in, she sustained the conversation, animating and varying it as she pleased.[47]

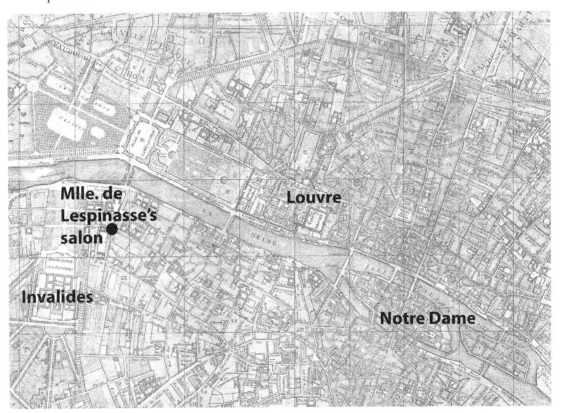

In other words, Lespinasse was like a great classroom teacher: establishing a conducive atmosphere for learning and exchange, bringing out the best qualities in her guests, and relinquishing the need to be the center of attention. Furthermore, as with other important *salonnières*, she prepared for her salon each day in the way teachers prepare for class: she focused

---

[46] Jean-François Marmontel quoted in "Notes," *The Letters of Mlle. de Lespinasse,* 35.
[47] Friedrich Melchior Grimm quoted in "Notes," *The Letters of Mlle. de Lespinasse,* 35.

her thinking through a daily process of reading and writing.[48] These efforts allowed her and her guests to be able to talk about ideas without the risk of untoward confrontation.[49] Consequently, when Adam Smith visited to Paris in 1766 and attended Lespinasse's salon, there could well have been forceful but amicable discussion about the moral philosophy Smith outlined in his newly-translated *The Theory of Moral Sentiments* (1759)[50] or his reaction to the free trade ideas of Physiocrat* François Quesnay. There were certainly conversations about commercial theory, banking, and public credit.[51] Similarly, when political philosopher and statesman Edmund Burke argued with those gathered in Lespinasse's salon in February 1773,[52] the debate easily could have centered upon his *Enquiry into the Origin of Our Ideas of the Sublime and Beautiful:* that Enlightenment rationalism cannot explain our interest in art or why artistic expression is so essential to the human experience.[53] For Burke, there was still a place for wondrous incomprehensibility that all the writings of the rational *philosophes* could not illumine.[54] Certainly not everyone in the room would have agreed. Perhaps the best examples come from Hume because he spent three years in Paris in the mid-1760s and was a regular participant in Lespinasse's salon. Hume enjoyed her salon because he believed that only by discussing his beliefs with observant companions could he be certain of his own interpretations.[55] One of the issues the group would have repeatedly discussed involved God and the proper role of religion. As his works *A Treatise of Human Nature* and *Enquiry Concerning Human Understanding* make clear, Hume was a skeptic, but not an atheist. He could not be certain if God exists, but he opposed the dogma of many Christian denominations.[56] Not everyone in Lespinasse's circle agreed with Hume's position. Some

---

[48] James Van Horn, *The Rise of the Public in Enlightenment Europe* (Cambridge, U.K.: Cambridge University Press, 2001), 207.

[49] Voltaire believed that this salon atmosphere gave France a distinctiveness: "The continued commerce between the sexes, so lively and polite, has introduced a politeness quite unknown elsewhere. Society depends on women." Similarly, *salonnière* Suzanne Necker noted, "Everyone in these assemblies is [now] convinced that women fill the intervals of conversation and of life, like padding that one inserts in cases of china; they are valued at nothing, and [yet] everything breaks without them." See Van Horn, *The Rise of the Public in Enlightenment Europe*, 205, 208.

[50] *The Theory of Moral Sentiments* was first translated into French in 1764. See Gilbert Faccarello and Philippe Steiner, "The Diffusion of the Work of Adam Smith in the French Language: An Outline History," originally published in: *A Critical Biography of Adam Smith*, Keith Tribe (ed.) (London, U.K.: Pickering and Chatto, 2002) and accessed January 10, 2020, http://ggjff.free.fr/textes/Smith_in_French_2002.pdf

[51] Ian Simpson Ross, *The Life of Adam Smith* (New York: Oxford University Press, 1995), 210.

[52] *The Yale Edition of Horace Walpole's Correspondence*, 103.

[53] David Bromwich, *The Intellectual Life of Edmund Burke: From the Sublime and Beautiful to American Independence* (Cambridge, Massachusetts: Belknap Press of Harvard University, 2014), 62-63, 77. *Enquiry into the Origin of Our Ideas of the Sublime and Beautiful* was first published in England in 1757 and was first translated into French in 1765. See Louise Pelletier, *Architecture in Words: Theatre, Language and the Sensuous Space of Architecture* (New York: Routledge, 2006), 138.

[54] Russell Kirk, *Edmund Burke: A Genius Reconsidered* (New Rochelle, New York: Arlington House, 1967), 33.

[55] Baier, *The Pursuits of Philosophy,* 110.

[56] Baier, *The Pursuits of Philosophy*, 126-127. Baier argues that *Enquiry Concerning Human Understanding* is a really a mature refinement of *A Treatise of Human Nature*, which Hume wrote when he was only twenty-five (Baier, 60, 67-70). Parisians would have had access to *Enquiry* since it was translated into French in 1758, but not to *Treatise* since it was not translated until 1878. See Jean A. Perkins, *The Concept of the Self in the French Enlightenment* (Geneva, Switzerland: Librairie Droz, 1969), 31.

were Christians and some were atheists.[57] This would have led to interesting discussions in the salon about God, morality, and death.[58] These examples show how different the tone and intent of Lespinasse's salon was from those of other Parisian *salonnières*.

The foremost member of Lespinasse's circle was Jean le Rond d'Alembert, the scientist who put

everyone at ease with his brilliant conversational abilities and his capacity to combine purpose with playful humor.[59] He was particularly adept as a mimic, able to imitate the actors and actresses in character after an evening of theater.[60] He enjoyed being the life of the party. Like Lespinasse, d'Alembert came into the world as an illegitimate child. Upon birth in Paris in November 1717, his mother, Madame de Tencin (the *salonnière* who mentored Madame Geoffrin) placed d'Alembert in a wooden box and left him on the steps of a church, as mothers then did with unwanted children. A priest found the baby and arranged for him to be sent to a wet nurse in Picardy. When d'Alembert's father, an artillery officer named Louis-Camus Destouches-Canon, returned to Paris, he located his son and found a woman from a Parisian artisan family to raise him. Destouches-Canon made provisions to pay for d'Alembert's education and left him an

annuity of 1,200 *livres* a year, which allowed d'Alembert economic independence and a comfortable, but not luxurious, lifestyle.[61] D'Alembert did well in school, received his baccalaureate in 1735, and in his early twenties began to pursue his interest in mathematics and science.

D'Alembert approached these fields as a philosopher. He believed that there was a single, rational system which unified all knowledge, and that this system, like every system, could be studied in constituent parts since the parts and the whole came from the same source.[62] In this way, everything in the universe was interconnected. D'Alembert had little patience for what he called "vague and rash" metaphysics or speculation, insisting instead on the importance "calculation and analysis."[63] He saw little use for intuition or imagination, since everything had to be definite and proven.[64] For d'Alembert this proof did not rely upon an experimental method. He "never held a prism in his hand," one contemporary scientist complained.[65] Rather, d'Alembert was a

---

[57] Lespinasse always attended Catholic mass on Sundays and died reconciled with the Church. See Jebb, *A Star of the Salons*, 331. D'Alembert held a similar position to Hume's, for he was also a skeptic. The two men developed such a close friendship that Hume left d'Alembert £200 upon his death. See Baier, 108.

[58] Smith, Burke, and Hume's prominence in the salons reflected the Anglophilia of many of the *philosophes*. See Ian Buruma, *Anglomania: A European Love Affair* (New York: Random House, 1998), 21-49.

[59] Thomas L. Hankins, *Jean d'Alembert: Science and Enlightenment* (New York: Gordon and Breach, 1970), 16.

[60] Aldis, *Madam Geoffrin*, 162.

[61] Hankins, *Jean d'Alembert*, 18.

[62] Ronald Grimsley, *Jean d'Alembert, 1717-83* (Oxford, U.K., Clarendon Press, 1963), 223, 229.

[63] Grimsley, *Jean d'Alembert, 1717-83*, 223, 255.

[64] Grimsley, *Jean d'Alembert, 1717-83*, 223, 270.

[65] Jérôme Lalande quoted in Hankins, *Jean d'Alembert*, 3.

theoretician who hoped to find mathematical solutions to the questions that troubled him. One specific example of this came in the field of astronomy and the problem of the gravitational forces between the earth, sun, and moon. Sir Isaac Newton determined the gravitational forces between two heavenly bodies in 1687, but Swiss mathematician Leonard Euler posited that Newtonian theory did not account for the effect of a third body.[66] This sent mathematicians racing to find the optimal solution. D'Alembert, Euler, and French mathematician Alexis Clairaut all solved the problem independently of one another in 1747, but whereas Clairaut utilized his background as an experimental and observational scientist to support his solution, d'Alembert relied only upon his analytical ability. This may have been one reason that d'Alembert's cumbersome scientific publications had a reputation for a lack of clarity.[67] In his other mathematical accomplishments, d'Alembert was the first to use partial differential equations in hydrodynamics to solve questions about the resistance of fluids,[68] nearly alone in seeing the differential as the limit of a function,[69] the first to apply techniques used for studying statics to the field of dynamics, and the first to show that imaginary numbers retain the same form when added, subtracted, multiplied, and divided.[70] He also developed a novel solution to the problem of vibrating strings, which continues to play an important role in theoretical physics.[71]

One illustration of how d'Alembert's philosophical approach influenced his mathematical thinking has to do with probability. When tossing a coin, the odds of it landing on "heads" is fifty-fifty. This is true each time the coin is tossed, regardless of the number of previous throws. But d'Alembert rejected this idea, arguing that probability was subjective, not scientific.[72] When gambling, for example, d'Alembert thought that previous outcomes had to be considered since the potential economic effects on a family complicated the calculation. D'Alembert's reasoning can also be seen in the treatment of smallpox. By the 1720s, there was a growing understanding in Western Europe that it was possible to gain immunity to the disease by deliberately placing a small amount of material from a smallpox pustule under the skin of an uninfected person. The patient was likely to develop a mild case of the disease, but it was also possible to die from this inoculation, raising the issue of probability. Was it better to take the risk or not? To d'Alembert's thinking, there had to be more to the equation than a raw calculation of the odds. Human considerations had to enter into the equation as well since the actual mathematical probability provided little comfort to those parents whose children died of smallpox despite having the inoculation. The moral

---

[66] François de Gandt, "Jean Le Rond d'Alembert," *The Princeton Companion to Mathematics*, Timothy Gowers (ed.) (Princeton, New Jersey: Princeton University Press, 2008), 750.

[67] Hankins, *Jean d'Alembert*, 29-37, 63.

[68] Hankins, *Jean d'Alembert*, 49.

[69] J. Morton Briggs, "Jean Le Rond D'Alembert," *Dictionary of Scientific Biography*, Charles Coulston Gillispie (ed.), Volume I, (New York: Charles Scribner's Sons, 1970), 115.

[70] Gandt, "Jean Le Rond d'Alembert," 750. D'Alembert showed this using the formula: $a + bi$, where $i = \sqrt{-1}$.

[71] Grimsley, *Jean d'Alembert, 1717-83*, 5.

[72] Sharon Bertsch McGrayne, *The Theory that Would Not Die: How Bayes' Rule Cracked the Enigma Code, Hunted Down Russian Submarines & Emerged Triumphant from Two Centuries of Controversy* (New Haven, Connecticut: Yale University Press, 2011), 19.   A protégé of d'Alembert's, Pierre Simon Laplace (1749-1827), connected the issue of probability with the problem of gravitational forces: he believed that since it was impossible to obtain exact measurements for celestial bodies, one had to resort to probability to find the most likely data. None of the continental mathematicians, including d'Alembert, were aware of Thomas Bayes (1701-1761), who worked on the issue of conditional probability and developed a method for calculating probability based on previous results. His work, *An Essay towards solving a Problem in the Doctrine of Chances*, was published posthumously in 1763. See McGrayne, 13-20.

question had to be considered as well as the mathematical equation for the solution to be true.[73] Such thinking was undoubtedly influenced by what happened when Lespinasse contracted smallpox in the fall of 1765. She assumed that she possessed immunity to the disease as a result of a severe childhood illness, but this was incorrect: she fell victim to a severe case of the disease at thirty-three. D'Alembert provided most of her care during her slow recuperation, sitting by her bedside day and night. Once the disease had run its course, the *salonnière* found that it left her face horribly scarred and her vision significantly compromised. She continued to suffer from weakness, eye infections, and neuralgia for the rest of her life.[74] Of course, Lespinasse was not alone: one in four French women suffered disfigurement from the disease since, unlike in Great Britain, inoculation was discouraged in France by clerical, legal, and medical authorities.[75]

D'Alembert also won great acclaim in 1751 for his introduction to the famous *Encyclopédie*, the *Encyclopedia or Reasoned Dictionary of the Sciences, Arts, and Crafts*. The project was monumental in its scope, for it sought to document and disseminate human knowledge, incorporating all of the progress made since the Renaissance. As d'Alembert's fellow editor Denis Diderot wrote,

> The purpose of an Encyclopedia is to assemble the knowledge scattered over the surface of the Earth; to explain its general plan to the men with whom we live and to transmit it to the men who come after us; in order that the labors of centuries past may not be in vain during the centuries to come; that our descendants, by becoming better instructed, may as a consequence be more virtuous and happier, and that we may not die without having deserved well of the human race.[76]

D'Alembert's *Discours préliminaire* reflected his view of the universe. He began by establishing a classification for knowledge based on the mental faculty involved: there was memory for history, natural history, and the trades; reason for philosophy, theology, logic, and ethics; and imagination for art, literature, and music. He then succinctly described the contributions of many of the great minds since the Renaissance with Francis Bacon, Descartes, Locke, Leibniz, and Newton receiving the most extensive consideration, and others like La Fontaine, Galileo, Harvey, Huygens, Molière, Montesquieu, Pascal, Poussin, and Racine receiving notable praise.[77] The introduction reflected d'Alembert's religious skepticism and his unqualified endorsement of Locke's ideas about how humans acquire knowledge: "it is to our sensations that we owe all of our ideas," d'Alembert summarized.[78] Thus, the implicit attack on religion, characteristic of the whole *Encyclopédie*, was evident in its opening pages: sensory experience, not divine revelation, was not the measure of

---

[73] Briggs, "Jean Le Rond D'Alembert," 116. The outbreak of the COVID-19 pandemic in 2020 offered a similar opportunity for such considerations and calculations.

[74] de Ségur, *Julie de Lespinasse*, 131-132.

[75] Jebb, *A Star of the Salons*, 210.

[76] Denis Diderot quoted in Charles Coulston Gillispie, "Introduction," *A Diderot Pictorial Encyclopedia of Trades and Industry*, Charles Coulston Gillispie (ed.) Volume 1 (New York: Dover Publications Inc., 1959), ix.

[77] Jean Le Rond D'Alembert, *Preliminary Discourse to the Encyclopedia of Diderot*, Richard N. Schwab (trans.) (Indianapolis, Indiana: Bobbs-Merrill Company, Inc., 1963), 67-100. These leading figures were mathematicians Gottfried Wilhelm von Leibniz (1646-1716) Blaise Pascal (1623-1662); painter Nicolas Poussin (1594-1665); philosophers Francis Bacon (1561-1626), René Descartes (1596-1650), and John Locke (1632-1704), Charles-Louis de Secondat (Montesquieu) (1689-1755); poet Jean de La Fontaine (1621-1695); playwrights Molière (1622-1673) and Jean Racine (1639-1699); and scientists Galileo Galilei (1564-1642), William Harvey (1578-1657), Christiaan Huygens (1629-1695), and Sir Isaac Newton (1642-1727).

[78] Wilson, *Diderot*, 132.

human knowledge. Not surprisingly, the *Discours préliminaire* remains one of the seminal documents of the Enlightenment.

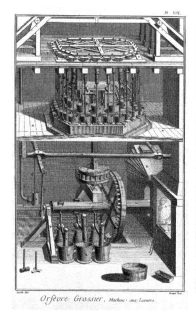 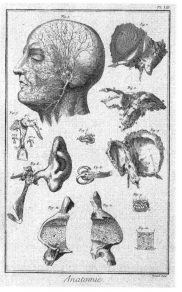 

Orfevre Grossier, Machine aux Lacures.   *Anatomie.*   *Minéralogie, Travail du föle, Mannere de Extremadie.*

The first volume of the *Encyclopédie* was published in June 1751. It included articles on agriculture, anatomy, Arab philosophy, Aristotelianism, bees, Hindu philosophy, silver, steel, and trees. This provided information was not readily available elsewhere, especially to three-quarters of the *Encyclopédie*'s subscribers who were from French provinces or other countries.[79] Subsequent volumes did not hesitate to advance Enlightenment ideals, even if d'Alembert and Diderot had to use innuendo and subtlety to get past the censors; they carefully let the presentation of technological advancements obscure the undertones of political criticism.[80] A few remarkably bold statements did find their way into print, including what Diderot said about political authority:

> No man has received from nature the right of commanding others. Liberty is a present from Heaven, and every individual of the same species has the right to enjoy it as soon as he enjoys reason….True and legitimate power necessarily has limits….It is not the state which belongs to the prince, but rather the prince who belongs to the state.[81]

When the project was completed in 1765, the *Encyclopédie* had grown to twenty-eight volumes, seventeen of text and eleven of detailed illustrations. D'Alembert wrote over 1,500 articles for the massive work, most of which related to topics in mathematics and science. But by the time Lespinasse met d'Alembert in 1754, the burden for shepherding for the *Encyclopédie* to its fruition had passed to Diderot. The two men disagreed over salaries, prestige, editorial responsibility, and how much risk to take in light of the restrictions placed by government censors. D'Alembert was traumatized by the fierce and, to him, quite unanticipated criticism he had received over his entry

---

[79] Wilson, *Diderot*, 7, 135-136. The *Encyclopédie* was arranged alphabetically in French, which means that subjects like "tree," "*arbre*" in French, were in the first volume.
[80] Gillispie, "Introduction," xii-xiii.
[81] Denis Diderot quoted in Wilson, *Diderot*, 142.

about Calvinist Geneva, while Diderot knowingly published works he realized would upset the royal government.[82] D'Alembert's 1754 election to France's most prestigious intellectual society, the *Académie française*, only widened their dissimilarities: while Diderot was doing all of the work, D'Alembert was getting all of the credit. By October 1759, the two men amicably agreed that d'Alembert would continue to submit articles for the *Encyclopédie* but would not seek further editorial control. The two men continued to see each other occasionally, but they were no longer close collaborators.[83] This was one of the reasons why Diderot's visit to Lespinasse's salon fourteen years later was noteworthy.

Diderot's presence in Lespinasse's salon was also unusual because the editor and the *salonnière* had suffered a falling out in 1769. That summer, Diderot wrote a philosophical dialogue in three parts entitled *D'Alembert's Dream*. The first, set when Diderot and d'Alembert first became friends, finds the two men arguing over the nature of the universe; the debate focuses on Diderot's materialism: his belief that humans have no soul and that everything in the universe, including consciousness, is composed solely of matter. In the second part, which takes place the following morning and is based upon Diderot's actual visit to a feverish d'Alembert in 1765, a doctor explains materialism to Lespinasse. In the third and final section, the doctor and Lespinasse discuss the moral implications of a materialist view of humanity and the universe. There are several controversial scenes in the dialogue, including when d'Alembert's character has a wet dream during his feverish delirium. Lespinasse's character does not understand the physical reaction or what to do with the ejaculant, the doctor's advocacy of regular masturbation, or the presentation of homosexuality and bestiality as being a natural consequence of freedom of thought.[84] Diderot held that social constraints robbed individuals of their internal creativity, and only by casting off these constraints could people be free.[85] Therefore, there should be no taboo subjects. This stood quite in contrast with the rules and decorum of the salon—a world Diderot found to be sterile and pointless as a result of its social protocols. *D'Alembert's Dream* was his expression of his frustration with it.[86] Lespinasse first learned of the manuscript in October or November 1769, probably from journalist Jean-Baptiste-Antoine Suard,[87] and she found it grossly offensive on several counts. The mock-Socratic dialogue consistently puts her character in an inferior position and attributes utterly insipid statements to her. She is repeatedly portrayed as prudish, witless, and naïve:

"These questions are too obtuse for me."

---

[82] Diderot was imprisoned in 1749 for publishing "Letter on the Blind for the Use of Those Who See," which argued that morality doesn't come from God, but must be learned through sensory experience. Therefore, each person's morality would differ, based upon the experiences of their life. The work also attacked the validity of God-created design and, therefore, of the existence of God himself. Diderot was far more willing to push the boundaries of acceptable thought than was d'Alembert. See Will and Ariel Durant, *The Age of Voltaire: A History of Civilization in Western Europe from 1715 to 1756 with Special Emphasis on the Conflict Between Religion and Philosophy* (New York: Simon and Schuster, 1965), 628-632.

[83] P. N. Furbank, *Diderot: A Critical Biography* (London: Secker & Warburg, 1992), 200.

[84] For a more detailed summary of the dialogue see L.W. Tancock, "Introduction to D'Alembert's Dream," *Rameau's Nephew and D'Alembert's Dream* (Baltimore, Maryland: Penguin Books, 1966), 134-139; Furbank, *Diderot*, 323-338; and Wilson, *Diderot*, 559-569.

[85] Joseph L. Waldauer, *Society and the Freedom of a Creative Man in Diderot's Thought* (Geneva, Switzerland: Librairie Droz, 1964), 15.

[86] Craveri, *The Age of Conversation*, 362.

[87] Tancock, "Introduction to D'Alembert's Dream," 135.

"No, no say just what you like….And yet, doctor, keep some veils, please, let us have a certain amount of veiling" [since some subjects are too much for me.]

"I only listen for the pleasure of passing things on."[88]

Another issue in the dialogue was that text includes a significant amount of sexual tension between the doctor and Lespinasse's character.[89] This tension had a particular context in 1769 because at the time Paris was awash in rumors about the sexual indulgences of and legal proceedings against the Marquis de Sade, who was accused of severely flogging an unemployed woman he had picked up on Easter Sunday.[90] Diderot's play contains lines that suit that fit the style of Sade's libertine tract *Philosophy in the Bedroom*, and Diderot himself had a libertine streak.[91] At one point in *D'Alembert's Dream*, Lespinasse's character says, "If it was the custom to walk naked in the streets, I would neither be the first or the last to conform. So do whatever you want with me, as long as you instruct me."[92] Even if Diderot had not intended this statement to have sexual undertones, the characterization was inappropriate for who Lespinasse had become by 1769. By then, she had successfully surrounded herself with the greatest minds in Paris and built a reputation for carefully orchestrating a salon with the most unfettered freedom of conversation in the city.[93] As a result of these objections and the damage even the illegal publication of the dialogue would do to Lespinasse's reputation, d'Alembert demanded that Diderot destroy the manuscript. Diderot promised that he would do so.[94] Lespinasse then considered the matter closed but wrote to Suard that Diderot's conduct had been "improper because of his lack of breeding."[95] Diderot's brazen nature also kept him from being invited to Madame Geoffrin's dinners. She saw him as too unpredictable and too difficult to control.[96]

While the *D'Alembert's Dream* controversy remained successfully contained, Lespinasse and d'Alembert were not able to control the one that exploded between Hume and Rousseau. Not only does this episode offer a powerful illustration for how salon society functioned,[97] but it shows how even the brightest minds can succumb to petty and vindictive behavior. The problem began at one of Geoffrin's dinners in late December 1765. British earl Horace Walpole led the guests, including Hume, in joking about Rousseau's "affectations and contradictions." This teasing was cruel since

---

[88] Denis Diderot, *Rameau's Nephew and D'Alembert's Dream*, L. W. Tancock (trans.), (Baltimore, Maryland: Penguin Books, 1966), 226, 230, 233.

[89] Furbank, *Diderot*, 338.

[90] "Chronology," *The Marquis de Sade: Three Complete Novels: Justine, Philosophy in the Bedroom, Eugénie de Franvand and Other Writings* (New York: Grove Press, 1966), 78-79.

[91] Wilson, *Diderot*, 251-252 and Furbank, *Diderot*, 341.

[92] Furbank, *Diderot*, 338.

[93] L.W. Tancock, *Rameau's Nephew and D'Alembert's Dream* (Baltimore, Maryland: Penguin Books, 1966), footnote page 237.

[94] L.W. Tancock, "Introduction to D'Alembert's Dream," 135. The reason the dialogue survives is that Diderot shared the text with Grimm in October 1769. Grimm had a copyist make a second copy of the work, unbeknownst to Diderot. This copy was serialized in 1782, after Lespinasse's death, but received little attention. The first printed edition of the whole play was published in 1830 from a manuscript found in the Russian archives because upon his death, Diderot had his papers shipped to Catherine the Great.

[95] Julie de Lespinasse quoted in Wilson, *Diderot*, 569.

[96] Craveri, *The Age of Conversation*, 302. Madame Geoffrin did, however, continue to see Diderot privately.

[97] Lilti, *The World of the Salons*, 178.

Rousseau was known to be emotionally fragile. He also suffered from paranoia.[98] Walpole purposefully ridiculed a man who was his social inferior simply to enliven the party and to assert his superiority. The next morning, Walpole went further and crafted a letter to Rousseau in the supposed voice of Frederick the Great of Prussia. The letter read:

I admire your talents; I am amused by your dreams….Show your enemies that you can sometimes have common sense….My states offer you a powerful retreat…. [Alternatively], if you persist in racking your brains to find new misfortunes, choose as you may desire; I am King, and I can procure any to suit your wishes….[Furthermore], I shall cease to persecute you when you cease to find your glory in being persecuted.[99]

Walpole shared the letter with several friends, who found it funny and encouraged him to share it more broadly. Walpole had no qualms about doing so, for as he wrote in a letter to the first duke of Montagu in early 1766, "I willingly laugh at mountebanks, political or literary" and so "I was not averse. The copies have spread like wildfire."[100] Rousseau did not see one of these copies before he and Hume left together for London on January 4, 1766, but the news spread to Britain soon enough: the *St. James Chronicle* published the text of Walpole's Frederick the Great letter on April 3. Rousseau responded indignantly, saying that this letter was "fabricated in Paris; and what grieves me and tears my heart especially is that the impostor who wrote it has accomplices in England." By the summer, Rousseau had become convinced that Hume was part of the conspiracy against him.[101] While it is true that Hume had behaved poorly by not defending his friend at Madame Geoffrin's, there is no evidence that he knew of Walpole's letter before he and Rousseau arrived in London. The damage had been done, however, and on July 10 Rousseau wrote an extraordinarily long letter accusing Hume of participating in the conspiracy against him, of intercepting his mail, and of working to alter public perception against him.[102]

To protect his reputation, Hume wanted to rally allies to his side. He wrote to Baron d'Holbach, a well-connected atheist and contributor to the *Encyclopédie*, who on July 5 read Hume's letter at an evening salon to an astonished group, including Lespinasse and d'Alembert. It began, "Jean

---

[98] Leo Darmrosch, *Jean-Jacques Rousseau* (Boston, Massachusetts: Houghton Mifflin Company, 2005), 155, 461-463.

[99] Will and Ariel Durant, *Rousseau and Revolution: A History of Civilization in France, England and Germany from 1756, and the Reminder of Europe from 1715 to 1789* (New York: Simon and Schuster, 1967), 208.

[100] Horace Walpole to George Montague, January 12, 1766 in Durant, *Rousseau and Revolution,* 208.

[101] Durant, *Rousseau and Revolution,* 212.

[102] Rousseau's letter was eighteen folio pages long. See Durant, *Rousseau and Revolution,* 212. Although Rousseau was paranoid and misinterpreted Hume's actions as the events unfolded, there was also some basis for Rousseau's perceptions: Hume did open Rousseau's mail and did snoop into Rousseau's financial affairs. Conversely, however, Rousseau found even Hume's looking at him to be disturbing. See Damrosch, *Jean-Jacques Rousseau,* 419-424.

Jacques is a rascal" and recounted Rousseau's accusations.[103] The next morning, Lespinasse wrote to Hume,

> Alas my God, Monsieur, what has happened between you and Rousseau? What exact deed of darkness has he committed against you? Your friends are again afflicted as they are struck [by the news]. It is inconceivable that a man who is under such obligation to you should strike you in such a way. The sweetness of your habits and the uprightness of your character create great prejudice against him….I would beg you to tell me the details of such bleakness which has led to this. It is not just because of curiosity that I would ask because I believe your every word; rather it would allow me to defend you and your interests against the fanatics of Rousseau, who many hold in high esteem.[104]

D'Alembert enclosed his own note saying, "I would advise you to think twice before putting your grievances before the public, because this kind of personal quarrel often serves to excite the obstinate fanatics still more."[105] Lespinasse initially concurred, but by July 24, Paris' salon gossip had grown so great and so erroneous that she and d'Alembert changed their minds. That evening the leading figures of Lespinasse's salon unanimously agreed with the hostess to tell Hume that he "must at once state your case in print…simply and directly, but without temper or the least acrimony."[106] It was important to claim the high road and protect one's standing if access to *le monde* were to continue.

Hume responded by sending a manuscript outlining his side of the story, which Suard translated into French and Lespinasse and d'Alembert published and distributed in October 1766. Rather than quash the issue, Hume's work helped to carry the details of the dispute across Europe, forcing people to take sides. Voltaire complained, "Is not this something nearly as ridiculous as Jean Jacques himself? I find I am as deep in it as a man eating a supper to which he was not bidden."[107] Madame du Deffand refused to participate, preferring to satirize the whole absurd event.[108] She found nothing wrong in what her dear friend Walpole had done.[109] As for Lespinasse, she believed that Hume's

---

[103] David Hume quoted in de Ségur, *Julie de Lespinasse*, 194. The salon's hostess was Suzanne Curchod, known as Madame Necker (1737-1794). It too was one of Paris' most prestigious salons.

[104] Julie de Lespinasse to David Hume, July 6, 1766 in *Letters of David Hume*, 408. The letter is in French; it was translated for me by Dr. M.A. Claussen of the University of San Francisco.

[105] Jean Le Rond D'Alembert quoted in Grimsley, *Jean d'Alembert, 1717-83*, 146.

[106] de Ségur, *Julie de Lespinasse*, 199. Those present included Lespinasse, d'Alembert, Charles Pinot Duclos, Jean-François Marmontel, André Morellet, Bernard-Joseph Saurin, and Anne-Robert-Jacques Turgot.

[107] Voltaire quoted in Hamel, *Famous French Salons*, 250.

[108] Lilti, *The World of the Salons*, 188-189.

[109] Madame du Deffand's support for Walpole stemmed from her having fallen in love with him at their first encounter in 1765. They carried on a lively correspondence for fourteen years, exchanging at least 955 letters. Although Walpole found Deffand's attention flattering, he also worried that he would become "an international laughing stock" if the extent of her affection became known since she was twenty years older than he. See Joan

reputation had come through the affair intact, and she congratulated him for his "true and humane goodness."[110]

Discussion of the Hume-Rousseau dispute was not limited to the elite salons. Thanks to the continuous rise of literacy and the growth of print culture through the course of the eighteenth century, urban men and women of the middle and even lower classes would have also read, heard about, and discussed the controversy as it unfolded, just as they would have discussed the end of the Seven Years' War in 1763, the marriage of Holy Roman Emperor Joseph II in 1765, Benjamin Franklin's visit to Paris in 1767, or the election of a Clement XIV as pope in 1769. This was made possible by the rise of café culture and rapid increase of coffeehouses, which filled the same role for the middle class that salons did for the aristocracy. Cafés were especially popular because they did not have the violence associated with taverns, and they invited open, unregulated conversation.[111] The arrival of newspapers and periodicals in the 1730s and 1740s promoted and reflected growing literacy rates, as did the number of novels published in France: they jumped four-fold, from 99 novels between 1721 and 1730 to 426 novels between 1771 and 1780.[112] There was also an explosion of *libelles*—tracts that slandered the *ancien régime*'s basis of power and portrayed the aristocracy, the crown, and the Church as degenerate institutions. Descriptions of Louis XV's sex life were particularly popular and made for rich gossip.[113] These lowbrow publications competed with the highbrow treatises of the *philosophes* for attention with government censors, who worked in conjunction with customs officials.

The customs officials examined all books, engravings and printed materials legally entering Paris at one of twenty customs gates surrounding the city. They confiscated all printed matter to remove it temporarily from circulation until each item could be approved by the *Chambre syndicale*.[114] Objectionable materials, such as pornography, political satire, and libelous or slanderous works aimed at prominent persons, were privately shredded or publicly burned, depending on the message the royal authorities wanted to send, but they could also simply be stored in warehouses or sent to the personal libraries of key officials.[115] While the system created so much paperwork that it was unsustainable[116] and while there were plenty of ways to circumvent the established procedures,[117] the efforts of the *Chambre syndicale* show how intensely those with

Hinde Stewart, *The Enlightenment of Age: Women, Letters and Growing Old in Eighteenth Century France* SVEC 2010:09 (Oxford, U.K.: The Voltaire Foundation, 2010), 121-124.

[110] Julie de Lespinasse quoted in Hamel, *Famous French Salons*, 250.

[111] Van Horn, *The Rise of the Public in Enlightenment Europe*, 246-247.

[112] Van Horn, *The Rise of the Public in Enlightenment Europe*, 93, 95. Van Horn notes that rural France lagged considerably behind urban areas in terms of literacy and print culture. In the 1740s, while 60% of urban men and 40% of the urban women were literate, only 35% of the rural men and 13% of the rural women were. See page 85.

[113] One example was the publication of the novel *Tanastès*, written by a Marie-Madeleine Bonafon, who was employed as a chambermaid at Versailles. While she changed the names of Louis XV, Cardinal de Fleury, Madame de Pompadour and others, readers understood all of the references and found it sensational. See Robert Darnton, *Censors at Work: How States Shaped Literature* (New York: W. W. Norton & Company, 2014), 61-69. Darnton, *The Literary Underground of the Old Regime*, 29-30 and 145 also has important commentary on this issue.

[114] Dawson, *Confiscations at Customs*, 3.

[115] Dawson, *Confiscations at Customs*, 15, 30, 120, 137.

[116] Dawson, *Confiscations at Customs*, 145, 149.

[117] Robert Darnton illuminates the complexity of the process as he describes the efforts of one bookseller to import illegal books and other materials to France from publishers in Switzerland. See Darnton, *The Literary Underground of the Old Regime*, 135-144.

political and religious authority resisted the growth of Enlightenment culture. As Attorney General and *Encyclopédie* opponent Jean-Omer Joly de Fleury asserted in 1759, the *philosophes* had "conspired" to "sap the foundations" of the state, and authorities should take a "sword in hand to smash…these sacrilegious and seditious authors."[118]   The demand for prohibited materials, combined with the socialization that occurred among non-elites in cafés and the significant increase in bookstores,[119] made such efforts a rather futile endeavor.

~

Lespinasse's identity as a patron of the rationalist *philosophes* and the reputation of her salon would have remained uncomplicated had it not been for the publication of her anguished love letters in 1809. Released when Napoleon stood at the apex of his power, when Beethoven composed his most heroic music, and when Wordsworth and Coleridge wrote some of their most influential poetry, Lespinasse's letters fed the growing trend of European Romanticism. This changed her reputation considerably. No longer seen as a woman of intellect, she became a woman of passion.

Lespinasse's complicated love triangle began in December 1766, when she met Marquis de Mora, the son of the Spanish ambassador to France. Just twenty-two, Mora was a handsome, charming widower from one of Spain's highest-ranking noble families. Immediately popular everywhere in Paris, the army colonel became the talk of the salons and the court. Mora seems to have enjoyed spending time with the Encyclopedists in particular, but in January 1767, the army recalled the young man to Spain. Despite being twelve years older than Mora, Lespinasse found herself quite infatuated with the Spaniard from their first encounter. She wrote to Baron d'Holbach, "I want to tell you about something which fills my thoughts just now—a new acquaintance who possesses my brain, and I would add, my heart." She described Mora as having a face "full of kindly sympathy," which "imposes confidence and friendship. His character is gentle and attractive without being weak….In a word, I find in this man my idea of perfection."[120] Mora's feelings seem to have been remarkably similar. Through the course of the next seven years, Mora and Lespinasse developed a passionate relationship, interrupted only by the two burdens that kept him in Spain far more than he wished: the demands of the army and his tuberculosis. Interestingly, all of Lespinasse's friends and associates—even d'Alembert, who lived in an apartment in the same building—believed that whether Mora was in Paris or not, their relationship was Platonic. In fact, Mora and Lespinasse were intimate and spoke of marrying one another, over the objections of his family, who thought her unsuitable because of her illegitimate birth.[121]

In June 1772, when Mora was in Spain, Lespinasse met a French army officer, Jacques-Antoine-Hippolyte, Comte de Guibert. Guibert was eleven years younger than Lespinasse, and she quickly found herself equally smitten with the French officer. This time, however, the attraction was not entirely mutual. Guibert seems to have been flattered by the attention Lespinasse showed than

[118] Jean-Omer Joly de Fleury quoted in Darrin M. McMahon, *Enemies of the Enlightenment: The French Counter-Enlightenment and the Making of Modernity* (New York: Oxford University Press, 2001), 21.

[119] Thierry Rigogne, *Between State and Market: Printing and Bookselling in Eighteenth Century France* SVEC 2007: 05 (Oxford, U.K.: The Voltaire Foundation, 2006), 166-167.

[120] Julie de Lespinasse quoted in de Ségur, *Julie de Lespinasse*, 249-250.

[121] de Ségur, *Julie de Lespinasse*, 269-274.

anything else.[122] This made her attraction to him more intense. She wrote him several hundred letters over the next four years, repeatedly declaring her love, while reprimanding him for his inadequacies as a correspondent and berating herself for her unworthiness. Although written in the polite language of *le monde*, these reprimands read more like excoriations, quickly followed by statements of love and self-pity. This was particularly true between May and October 1773, when Guibert was in Germany.[123] On May 24, Lespinasse wrote,

> Did you not promise me news from Strasburg? Are you surprised now that you pledged yourself to write to me so often? Have you regretted the facility with which you yielded to the interest and eagerness shown to you? It is troublesome at a distance of three hundred leagues to have to act for others; there is no pleasure except in following one's own impulse and sentiment. See how generous I am! I offer to return our promise if you now find you have made a mistake. Acknowledge it to me, and I assure you I will not be wounded.[124]

But in her next letter, dated May 30, she wrote,

> I am distracted—worse than that, I am singular; I have but one tone, one colour, one manner; and when they please no longer they chill and weary. You must tell me which of the two effects they have produced. But you must also tell me, if you please, the only news that interests me, namely, how you are.[125]

This pattern of repetitive contradictions, mixed emotions, and successive manipulations continued in her correspondence with Guibert until the day of Lespinasse's death. There is a masochistic quality to many of her letters,[126] including this revealing example from June 6, 1773:

> I have virtuous friends, I have *better still*; and yet I care only for what you are to me….Though your soul is agitated, it is not ill like mine, which passes ceaselessly from convulsion to depression. I can judge of nothing; I mislead myself continually; I take poison to calm me.[127]

The "better still" was Mora. The poison was opium.

---

[122] Craveri, *The Age of Conversation*, 320.

[123] In 1772, Guibert published an influential essay on military strategy (*Essai general de tactique*). This work called for a blending of the traditional infantry deployment in columns (*ordre profound*), which was favored in France, with a linear infantry formation (*ordre mince*), which was favored by Frederick the Great. This work made Guibert a celebrity during his time in Germany. See John A. Lynn, "Nations at Arms, 1763-1815," in *The Cambridge History of Warfare*, Geoffrey Parker (ed.) (New York: Cambridge University Press, 2005), 194.

[124] Mlle. de Lespinasse to Guibert, May 24, 1773 in *Letters of Mlle. De Lespinasse*, 48.

[125] Mlle. de Lespinasse to Guibert, May 30, 1773 in *Letters of Mlle. De Lespinasse*, 51.

[126] Katharine Ann Jensen, *Writing Love: Letters, Women and the Novel in France,1605-1776* (Carbondale, Illinois: Southern Illinois University Press, 1995), 145.

[127] Mlle. de Lespinasse to Guibert, June 6, 1773 in *Letters of Mlle. De Lespinasse*, 52.

~

Most humans have produced and consumed substances to alter their natural consciousness, whether to ease pain, facilitate social interactions, reach spiritual illumination, or escape reality. Albuquerque drank wine, Beklemishev drank vodka, and Go-Mizunoo drank sake, but each of those alcoholic beverages were indigenous to their homelands. What makes Lespinasse's opium use different was that it was a globally-traded narcotic.

Opium poppies originated in the Western Mediterranean and were domesticated 6,000 years ago for their oil.[128] By 1000 BCE, those living in Europe, North Africa, and the Middle East exploited opium poppies as a drug.[129] The ancient Mesopotamians, Egyptians, and Greeks and all used opium for religious or medicinal purposes, and with the expansion of Islam, Arab traders distributed the plant to Turkey, Persia, Afghanistan, and India.[130] Wherever and whenever the opium poppies were cultivated, farmers cut slits in the oval seed pods two or three times a week, just before they ripen, to release a thick, white latex. This substance, which contains various chemical alkaloids, including morphine, is dried and then molded into bricks or rolled into balls for sale and distribution. It is a labor-intensive farming process, but with sufficient toil, one acre of poppies produces about twenty pounds of finished opium.[131]

Renaissance doctors prescribed opium for a wide range of ailments, including abscesses, bellyaches, broken bones, colds, epilepsy, gout, headaches, rheumatism, and ulcers. By the eighteenth century, Europeans either ate the balls of opium or mixed them with alcohol and spices to create laudanum. Both forms were readily available to customers.[132] Scottish surgeon George Young wrote a *Treatise on Opium* (1753), specifically recommending opium and laudanum to women for menstruation, nausea during pregnancy, and hysteria.[133] While doctors at this time did not agree whether opium was a stimulant, a depressant, or a hallucinogenic, many understood that too much of it would kill. When he went into battle against the Austrians in the Seven Years' War in 1758, Frederick the Great had a gold box around his neck with eighteen opium pills inside; he said that if he was to be seriously wounded these pills would be "quite sufficient to take me to that dark bourn when we do not return."[134]

[128] Jennifer Potter, *Seven Flowers and How They Shaped Our World* (New York: Overlook Press, 2013), 100.

[129] Eric Jay Dolin, *When American First Met China: An Exotic History of Tea, Drugs and Money in the Age of Sail* (New York: Liveright Publishing Corporation/W. W. Norton, 2012), 42.

[130] Potter, *Seven Flowers and How They Shaped Our World*, 101-105, 112.

[131] Dolin, *When American First Met China*, 41-42.

[132] Potter, *Seven Flowers and How They Shaped Our World*, 113-116.

[133] Richard Davenport-Hines, *The Pursuit of Oblivion: A Global History of Narcotics* (New York: W. W Norton & Company, 2002), 52.

[134] Davenport-Hines, *The Pursuit of Oblivion*, 56.

The first documented instance of Lespinasse's use of opium occurred in 1764 on the night Madame du Deffand discovered her *petite salon de contrabande*. That dose was large enough that she thought she was doing to die.[135] Despite that scare, her opium use became increasingly frequent with larger and larger doses. After she contracted tuberculosis, probably from Mora, she began coughing up blood. Her doctors prescribed more opium since it was considered to be an effective remedy for that symptom[136] and the lines between prescription and addiction became blurry. It is clear, however, that opium addiction contributed to Lespinasse's death.[137]

~

February 10, 1774 was a powerful turning point in Lespinasse's love triangle. That night, she and Guibert went to the Paris Opéra, having sped through the mostly unlit, narrow, and twisted streets. The driver of their fast-moving carriage didn't concern himself with pedestrians or the mud, excrement, and garbage his wheels threw upon them. Those on the streets were responsible for getting out of the way, despite the absence of sidewalks.[138] Once at the Opéra, the pair exchanged greetings and pleasantries with acquaintances and made their way to their box seat. Rather than listening to the performance, they chatted through the arias. Between acts, they retreated from their seats to the box's antechamber, where there was a comfortable sofa. In the middle of the third act, Guibert took Lespinasse's hand and led her again to the box's antechamber, where they made love for the first time.[139] If she thought this act would solidify her relationship with Guibert or make her happy, she was sorely mistaken. An ambitious, calculating man, Guibert had no intention of devoting his life to the aging Lespinasse. Instead, he soon became involved with a well-born, wealthy sixteen-year old, Mlle. de Courcelles. Guibert did tell Lespinasse of his new relationship but passed it off as merely an *affaire de convenance*. Lespinasse saw it for what it was and wrote, "If we must cease to love, then I must cease to live!"[140] A year and a half later, Guibert and Courcelles were married, but this did not stop Lespinasse from writing or pursuing a relationship with Guibert. Her correspondence continued apace, though in time she came to blame herself as much as him for their status. On October 19,1775, for example, she wrote,

> I loved you: and from that moment I became incapable of what is noble and what is strong. I judge my conduct, *mon ami*; I blame it more than you! When you pronounced my sentence, I ought to have borne it, I ought to have torn myself from you, or from life; there is baseness in seeking to be pitied and comforted by him who strikes us; and that is so true that I undergo, ceaselessly, an awful combat; my soul revolts against your action, my heart is filled with tenderness for you. You are lovable enough to justify that feeling; but you have so mortally affronted me that I must feel humiliated. *Mon ami*, I have told you, often,

---

[135] Aldis, *Madam Geoffrin,* 174. Another source pinpoints the amount consumed at 60 grains and says that the suicide attempt permanently damaged her nervous system. See Claude Manceron, *Age of the French Revolution I, Twilight of the Old Order, 1774-1778*, Patricia Wolf (trans.) (New York, Touchstone Books, 1989), 298.

[136] Jensen, *Writing Love,* 154.

[137] Craveri, *The Age of Conversation*, 323.

[138] Bernier, *Pleasure and Privilege*, 3-4.

[139] de Ségur, *Julie de Lespinasse*, 321.

[140] Jebb, *A Star of the Salons,* 301.

that my situation is now impossible to endure; a catastrophe must come; I know not if it be nature or passion that will bring it about.[141]

Unfortunately for Lespinasse, things were no better on the Mora side of the love triangle: he died of tuberculosis on May 27, 1774 en route to Paris to see her. He had been especially ill since a severe bout with consumption on February 10, which happened to be the same night Lespinasse yielded to her emotions and Guibert's persuasiveness at the Opéra. In his last letter to his beloved, Mora wrote, "I was about to have seen you once more, and now I must die. What a fearful stroke of Fate! But you once loved me, and the thought of you is still sweet to me."[142] Lespinasse came to believe that she caused Mora's death with her betrayal and her heart filled with remorse.[143] This led to a marked increase in her opium use, and her health began to decline precipitously as a result.[144] She died on May 23, 1776.

Even in her final months, none of Lespinasse's contemporaries knew the truth about her love life—not even d'Alembert, who she said was "the only person I ever loved who has not made me unhappy."[145] No one knew of her intimacy with Guibert, and no one understood that she blamed herself for killing Mora. These were secrets she took to the grave and firmly intended for them to remain there with her, but she did not get her wish. The great, final irony of this tragic love story is that in his mourning over Lespinasse's death, d'Alembert turned to Guibert for comfort. Lespinasse made d'Alembert the executor of her will, and in her belongings, d'Alembert found the letters from Mora and an account of their relationship in Lespinasse's handwriting. She specified that d'Alembert should destroy all of these materials, but the mathematician couldn't bring himself to do it. Still not knowing about Lespinasse's relationship with Guibert and not being certain of what to do next, d'Alembert gave Mora's letters to Guibert. In 1809, Guibert's wife published these letters, irrevocably changing history's impression of the *salonnière*.

~

The intellectual persona of Lespinasse's public life, contrasted with the emotional persona of her private life, is curiously well reflected in two letters of condolence d'Alembert received after Lespinasse's death. The first came from Voltaire, who wrote, "This is the moment, my dear friend, when philosophy is very necessary to you….Courage serves for combat, but it does not serve to console us, or make us happy."[146] The second came from Frederick the Great:

> I sympathize with your misfortune in losing a person to whom you were attached. The
> wounds of the heart are keenest of all; and in spite of the fine maxims of philosophy,

---

[141] Julie de Lespinasse to Guibert, October 19, 1775 in *Letters of Mlle. De Lespinasse*, 268.
[142] Marquis de Mora quoted in Jebb, *A Star of the Salons*, 278.
[143] de Ségur, *Julie de Lespinasse*, 321-323.
[144] Jebb, *A Star of the Salons*, 306.
[145] Julie de Lespinasse quoted in Jebb, *A Star of the Salons*, 332.
[146] Voltaire to Jean Le Rond D'Alembert, June 10, 1776 in *Letters of Mlle. De Lespinasse*, 338.

nothing but time will cure them....Our reason is too weak to conquer the pain of a mortal wound."

Frederick then invited d'Alembert to come to Berlin, where "we will philosophize together on the nothingness of life, on the folly of men, on the vanity of stoicism, and all of our being."[147]

Here, then, were two of the most famous Europeans of the eighteenth century expressing opposite ideas about human needs and human nature at the crucial moment of mourning a death. Voltaire urged d'Alembert to turn to reason since no emotions, even courage, could comfort him. Conversely, Frederick the Great urged d'Alembert to recognize the limitations of intellect and accept the power of emotion. In the battle between the mind and the heart, the Enlightenment sought its answer in the former, while its successor, Romanticism, sought its answer in the latter. Julie de Lespinasse straddled these two eras, helping to close out one and anticipate the next.

---

[147] Frederick II to Jean Le Rond D'Alembert, July 9, 1776 in *Letters of Mlle. De Lespinasse,* 332-333.

M

Robert Monckton

1726-1782

At the opening of the Society of Artists exhibition in London on April 9, 1764, the as-yet unrecognized American painter Benjamin West chose to exhibit his first full-length portrait. It depicts an aspiring, but still-tentative, and rather jowly young British officer in full dress uniform. He is positioned in a classical, heroic pose with his left arm outstretched, pointing at the base of a cannon. Light seems to bounce off the gold trimmings of his blue-lapelled red frock coat, black

tricorn hat, and decorated sword handle. Behind him is a background to justify his self-assured pose: the officer has been victorious in the field of battle, dark clouds have begun to clear, smoke rises from a captured fortress, and troops parade enthusiastically behind an oversized flag. Painted just after the conclusion of the Seven Years' War, it is a portrait that lauds eighteenth-century British military prowess and depicts Robert Monckton as an empire-builder.[1] Only a subtle timidity in the major-general's eyes undercuts the patriotic message of war's pride and pomp.

Robert was the second-oldest son of the John Monckton, the First Viscount Galway, and Lady Elizabeth Manners, both of whom came from aristocratic families with well-established Whig* credentials. Like many second sons who were unlikely to inherit property because of primogeniture,* Robert chose to join the army. Thanks to his talent and family connections, he progressed through the infantry ranks

---

[1] Monckton's pose is based on that of Apollo Belvedere, the statue in the Vatican Museums. For more information about Benjamin West and his painting of "Major-General The Honourable Robert Monckton at the Taking of Martinique" (1762), see Stephen Mark Caffey, *An Heroics of Empire: Benjamin West and Anglophone History Painting 1764—1774* (unpublished dissertation) (Ann Arbor, Michigan: UMI Mircoform/ProQuest LLC, 2008), 77-83. Today the painting is in the collection of the National Army Museum, London.

rather quickly. He first experienced the confusion, gore, and heroism of a battlefield in June 1743 at the Battle of Dettingen, during the War of the Austrian Succession.* In its aftermath, he won his captaincy. At the Battle of Fontenoy two years later, Monckton did not play an important role, but his experience in battle helped him to secure the rank of major in 1747.[2] A bit later, he changed infantry regiments and joined the 47th Regiment of Foot, in which he became a lieutenant colonel in 1751.[3]

When his father died just after his appointment as lieutenant colonel, Monckton faced a crossroads. He could either continue to serve in the army or he could take his father's seat in Parliament, representing Pontefract in his home county of Yorkshire. Monckton initially decided to honor his father by moving to London and joining Parliament, but one year of politics changed the young man's mind. By 1752, Monckton was in Canada, having rejoined the 47th regiment and received his first command at age twenty-six. Over the next decade, this determined, prudent, and dutiful man helped lead three military campaigns that significantly changed North American history.

The first occurred in what the British called Nova Scotia and the French called Acadia. In the early 1750s this peninsula was a British territory that was largely occupied by a French population. French settlement began there in 1604, but the colony never enjoyed much attention from its mother country. This prevented the establishment of a stratified socio-economic hierarchy[4] and allowed Catholics and Huguenots to coexist and even work together as they diked marshlands to create new fields. The French also developed lasting, peaceful relationships with the local natives, the Míkmaqs, due to mutual respect, non-competition for resources, and a willingness by most Jesuit missionaries to adapt their message to local needs.[5] There was also considerable intermarriage with the Míkmaqs, for the Acadians came as close as any group to fulfilling explorer

[2] Monckton is not cited in the index of a very detailed account of the battle, which is the basis for my statement that his role was not noteworthy. See Francis Henry Skrine, *Fontenoy and Great Britain's Share in the War of the Austrian Succession, 1741-1748* (Edinburgh, U.K.: William Blackwood and Sons, 1906), 389. The British won at Dettingen, which was the last time a British monarch personally led troops into battle, and the French won Fontenoy, which was the last time a Bourbon monarch personally led troops into battle. For information on the importance of Fontenoy to Louis XV's reign, see Tabetha Leigh Ewing, *Rumor, Diplomacy, and War in Enlightenment Paris*, SVEC 2014:07 (Oxford, U.K.: The Voltaire Foundation, 2014), 157-180.
[3] The 47th Foot is also known as the 47th Lancaster Foot or the Lascelles' Regiment. The information on Monckton's promotions comes from *The Northcliffe Collection* (Ottawa, Canada: F. A. Acland, 1926), 1. This book presents a collection of summaries (called "calendars") of the contents of the Northcliffe Collection, some primary sources in full, and other materials. Monckton's papers form the basis of this collection, which is housed in the Canadian Archives in Ottawa. Because I was not able to visit Ottawa to view the documents in person, I have cited them by the page number in this book.
[4] Carl A. Brasseaux, *The Founding of New Acadia: The Beginnings of Acadians Life in Louisiana, 1765-1803* (Baton Rouge, Louisiana: Louisiana State University Press, 1987), 3.
[5] Gregory Evans Dowd, *War Under Heaven: Pontiac the Indian Nations & the British Empire* (Baltimore, Maryland: The Johns Hopkins University Press, 2002), 20. Another important book about the Jesuits in New France is: Takao Abé, *The Jesuit Mission to New France: A New Interpretation in the Light of the Earlier Jesuit Experience in Japan* (Leiden, Netherlands: Brill, 2011).

Samuel de Champlain dream: "our sons will marry your daughters, and we will be a single people."[6] These factors led Acadia to develop a distinctive, independent character.[7]

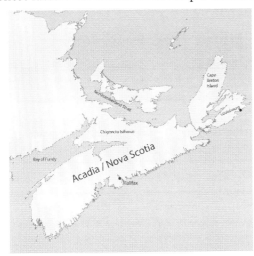

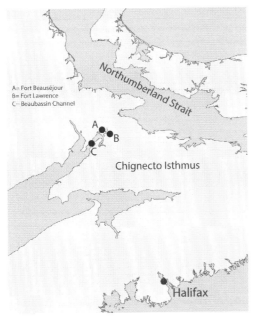

Acadia differed from the tenor of the business-oriented, Puritan colonies of New England in particular. That the Acadians never developed the financial, governmental, and military institutions to support a proto-capitalist economy puzzled the English colonists. As Robert Hale complained in 1731, they "have no taxes to pay, and they trade but little among themselves, everyone raising himself what he wants."[8] Such an atmosphere was almost inconceivable to English mercantilists* and made Acadia a tempting target. This, combined with geopolitical conflicts within Europe, led the British to attack the Acadian settlements in 1613, 1654, 1690, and 1710.[9]

By the Treaty of Utrecht (1713), which ended the War of the Spanish Succession* in Europe and Queen Anne's War in North America, Acadia became a British territory. Article 14 of the treaty gave the Acadians the "Liberty to remove themselves within a Year to any other Place with all of their moveable effects" or to remain and "be subject to the Kingdom of Great Britain." Those choosing to remain in Nova Scotia would "enjoy the free exercise of their religion," Catholicism. Queen Anne added that those Acadians who remained would "retain and enjoy their said lands and tenements without any molestation."[10] Although most Acadians remained in Nova Scotia, two contentious issues persisted. The first was that the Treaty of Utrecht did not delineate the precise borders of Nova Scotia; it just said that France was to surrender "all Nova Scotia or l'Acadie, comprehended within its antient

---

[6] Samuel de Champlain quoted in John Mack Faragher, *A Great and Noble Scheme: The Tragic Story of the Expulsion of the French Acadians from their American Homeland* (New York: W. W. Norton & Company, 2005), 47. The farming Acadians and the hunting-gathering Míkmaqs did not compete for resources because their societies had different economic bases. Despite the political and economic accommodation, there were dire consequences of French settlement: 80-90% of the Míkmaqs died as a result of their first contacts with European diseases. See Faragher, *A Great and Noble Scheme*, 14.

[7] Brasseaux, *The Founding of New Acadia*, 2, 8.

[8] Robert Hale quoted in William Fulkner Rushton, *The Cajuns: From Acadia to Louisiana* (New York: Farrar Straus Giroux, 1979), 34-35.

[9] Jacqueline K. Voorhies, "The Acadians: The Search for the Promised Land," *The Cajuns: Essays on their History and Culture*, Glenn R. Conrad (ed.), 3rd ed. (Lafayette, Louisiana: University of Southwestern Louisiana, 1983), 80.

[10] Treaty of Utrecht and Queen Anne quoted in Voorhies, "The Acadians," 91.

Boundaries."[11] Another round of treaty negotiations after the War of the Austrian Succession also failed to specify the borders but did select a joint commission in 1749 to pinpoint them. When the commission met, it became clear that the two sides were so far apart that no agreement could be reached: the border remained officially undefined.[12]

The second area of disagreement centered upon an oath of loyalty to the British crown. Between 1713 and the early 1750s, British governors repeatedly demanded that the Acadians take such an oath, but the Acadians consistently refused because they saw Queen Anne and kings George I, George II, and George III as staunchly anti-French.[13] The Acadians promised instead to adhere to a policy of strict neutrality in any dispute involving Britain and France. In 1730, they also obtained a verbal agreement with a provincial governor that legitimized this position.[14] Subsequent governors did not, however, recognize this understanding. By the 1750s, British military presence in the region had grown substantially and its new governor, Edward Cornwallis, insisted that the Acadians take an unconditional loyalty oath or "quit the province." If they chose to leave, they would not be allowed to sell their land or other property; they either had to take the oath or lose everything.[15] If this wasn't a hard enough choice, the Míkmaqs complicated the situation by telling the Acadians that they would consider any loyalty oath made to a British monarch to be an act of war against them.[16] The Acadians were stuck between the proverbial hard rocks, and their situation was about to get worse.

In April 1750, British decided to define the Nova Scotia border by building a fort along the banks of a muddy, tidal river called the Missaguash. Their intent was to move the boundary of Nova Scotia west and to capture the fertile land of the Chignecto Isthmus, a land bridge separating the Bay of Fundy from the Northumberland Strait.[17] The French, Acadians, and Míkmaqs initially proved able to fight the intruders off, but the British returned in October with a larger force and easily established Fort Lawrence on the eastern bank of the Missaguash. Once the snows melted, the French responded the following spring by building the much larger Fort Beauséjour on the ridge above the western bank of the Missaguash.[18] The two forts stood just over a mile apart, its men usually watching, and sometimes glaring at, one another.

On August 17, 1752, Lieutenant Colonel Monckton received his orders in Halifax to proceed to Fort Lawrence and assume command. His instructions were typical of those issued to frontier fort commanders. He was to "maintain and defend the Fort" against those who "show any intention to take or annoy it"; to "defend British subjects" from the "Indians, and if he consistently can, to try and chastise such insolence"; to "give full liberty to British subjects trading" in the area; to "prevent any correspondence with the French except what is necessary between him and the French Commandant"; to "allow for the free sale of beer," but "restrain as much as possible the selling to spirituous liquors;" to "prevent the waste or misuse of firewood"; and to send deserters to Halifax

---

[11] Treaty of Utrecht quoted in Faragher, *A Great and Noble Scheme*, 136.
[12] *The Northcliffe Collection*, 1. In 1749, the British definition of Nova Scotia included much of modern New Brunswick. The French, however, maintained that it only included the land east of the Chignecto Isthmus.
[13] Rushton, *The Cajuns*, 37.
[14] Brasseaux, *The Founding of New Acadia*, 14-15.
[15] Edward Cornwallis quoted in Faragher, *A Great and Noble Scheme*, 254. Edward Cornwallis was the uncle of Charles Cornwallis, who surrendered to the Americans at Yorktown in 1781.
[16] Faragher, *A Great and Noble Scheme*, 260.
[17] Today the Missaguash River forms part of the boundary between the Canadian provinces of Nova Scotia and New Brunswick.
[18] Gwyneth Hoyle, "The Siege of Fort Beauséjour," *Beaver*, Vol. 82, Issue 3 (June/July 2002), EBSCOhost.

for punishment.[19] During Monckton's first months as fort commander, he dealt with a wide variety of issues, including the illegal selling of rum; forwarding parcels, letters, and goods from the French to those now living in British territory; missing stores; negotiating new treaties with the Míkmaqs and other tribes; stray French horses; and desertion.[20] He also dealt with larger issues, like a December 1753 uprising of Protestant Germans who had settled on the Chignecto Isthmus with British permission, but who had not received the government provisions they'd been promised. Monckton's orders were to "proceed with all imaginable Dispatch" to the German settlement and "make use of such Measures to Reduce the Inhabitants to Obedience." He proved able to satisfy the immigrants and restore order peacefully, thereby winning the compliments of his superiors.[21]

Word of open conflict in the Ohio Valley between the French and British in the late spring and summer of 1754 convinced Nova Scotia Governor Charles Lawrence that seizing Fort Beauséjour from the French was essential. On November 7, 1754, he ordered Monckton to travel to Boston to meet with Massachusetts Governor William Shirley about the feasibility of raising 2,000 provincial troops "with the greatest privacy and dispatch" for service in spring 1755. If Monckton found Shirley receptive, which Monckton most certainly did, then the lieutenant colonel had tremendously broad powers for a young officer. He was to "hire a sufficient number of Vessels to Transport Your Troops, Artillery, Baggage, and Warlike Stores," including twelve cannon, ammunition, 500 pick axes, 500 shovels, 50 wheelbarrows, 50 horse harnesses, tents, and small arms. To pay for both these supplies and the salaries of the troops, Lawrence gave Monckton "a letter of unlimited credit."[22] No expense should be spared to secure Nova Scotia for the British crown once and for all.

On June 2, 1755, the French guards at Fort Beauséjour spotted the arrival of the first of thirty-four British vessels sailing into Beaubassin, the bay into which the muddy waters of the Missaguash flowed. On board the fleet were 2,000 Massachusetts provincials and 270 British regulars.[23] The two groups had similar entrance qualifications but very different sensibilities. The provincials needed to be between eighteen and forty years old; over five feet, four inches; Protestant; and "able bodied, free from bodily ailments and of perfect limbs."[24] The regular army recruits, or redcoats, were supposed to be between eighteen and forty; at

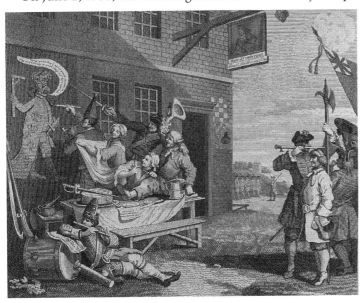

[19] *The Northcliffe Collection*, 7-8.

[20] *The Northcliffe Collection*, 8-14, 17-18.

[21] *The Northcliffe Collection*, 2, 23.

[22] *The Northcliffe Collection*, 25-26.

[23] I. K. Steele, "Monckton, Robert," *Dictionary of Canadian Biography*, vol. 4, University of Toronto/Université Laval, 2003–, accessed January 17, 2020, http://www.biographi.ca/en/bio/monckton_robert_4E.html.

[24] *The Northcliffe Collection*, 28.

least five foot, five inches; able-limbed, and Protestant, but these standards were relaxed when the army's need was great, and there were more Catholics recruits since many concealed their faith.[25] More significantly, the provincials were paid twice as much as the redcoats, lacked meaningful class distinctions within their ranks, had virtually no prior military experience, were employed on a temporary contract, and were frequently sons who would inherit land or other property when their fathers died. Conversely, recruits to the British regulars often were young men in desperate financial situations. They served much longer terms, and by the time they arrived in North America most had had at least some military experience.[26]

The British officers, who frequently were members of the aristocracy and had purchased their commissions, were generally disdainful of soldiers under their command, regardless of origin. They generally believed that the regular army soldiers needed firm, paternalistic guidance, and they made parallels between the hierarchy of the army and the hierarchy of a landed estate.[27] Consequently, most officers held that any type of fraternization between the officers and soldiers risked endangering military operations and represented a violation of the social code that distinguished between aristocratic and common birth.[28] Such attitudes led most officers to believe that while the common soldier might be trained, he could not be trusted. Officers held that soldiers required intense supervision, particularly in battle.[29] As Frederick the Great declared, soldiers "must fear their officers more than any danger" so that they will react instinctively in a moment of crisis.[30] To instill the necessary fear, British officers believed that it was essential to punish soldiers harshly and publicly even for minor infractions. This was usually done by flogging with a cat-o'-nine tails. A member of the drummer corps would whip the cat twice around his head and then bring it down on the offender, often until his back looked like "raw red-chopped sausages" as one young officer remembered.[31] The intent of a flogging was not to kill; it was seen as an important deterrent. If a doctor determined that a man could not endure his entire sentence, the remainder of the punishment would be administered when he was deemed sufficiently fit to tolerate it.[32] There were instances when officers ignored such precautions. In 1762, for example, a provincial witnessed a particularly brutal flogging in Halifax in which three men were punished for

> some trifling offense....One of them was to receive eight hundred lashes, the others five hundred apiece. By the time they had received three hundred lashes, the flesh appeared to be entirely whipped from their shoulders, and they hung as mute and motionless as though they had been long since deprived of life. But this was not enough. The doctor stood by with a vial of sharp snuff, which he would ever and anon apply to their [noses and finding]

[25] Stephen Brumwell, *Redcoats: The British Soldier and War in the Americas, 1755-1763* (New York: Cambridge University Press, 2002), 58-60.
[26] Fred Anderson, *A People's Army: Massachusetts Soldiers and Society in the Seven Years' War* (Chapel Hill, North Carolina: University of North Carolina Press, 1984), 27-28, 33, 38, 55. More precisely, 60% of the British regulars in the American army in 1757 were in their late teens and twenties, under 5'7" and had less than two years of experience. 30% of them were English and Welsh, 50% Scottish and Irish. See Brumwell, *Redcoats*, 73.
[27] Brumwell, *Redcoats,* 71,
[28] Brumwell, *Redcoats,* 70-71, 91.
[29] John A. Lynn, "States in Conflict, 1661-1763," *The Cambridge History of Warfare*, Geoffrey Parker (ed.) (New York, Cambridge University Press, 2005), 180.
[30] Frederick the Great quoted in *The Enterprise of War* (Alexandria, Virginia: Time-Life Books, 1991) 84.
[31] Unidentified officer quoted in Roger Norman Buckley, *The British Army in the West Indies: Society and the Military in the Revolutionary Age* (Gainesville, Florida: University of Florida Press, 1998), 203-204.
[32] Brumwell, *Redcoats,* 106.

that some sign of life remained...the whipping would commence again. It was the most cruel punishment I ever saw inflicted...far worse than death.[33]

British officers were likewise scornful of the provincials since their inexperience meant they could rarely meet the standards of efficiency and responsiveness demanded of the regular soldiers.[34] They were even so disdainful of the provincials' officers that they refused to recognize their ranks.[35] But the provincials were not punished with the same severity as the redcoats; instead, they were simply admonished to show better behavior.[36] This difference did not alleviate the provincials' animosity for the British: they found the British officers absurdly haughty, and criticized the regular soldiers as Godless creatures who broke the Sabbath with impunity.[37] Despite all of these differences and tensions, an acceptance of the chain of command allowed the colonials and the regulars, the officers and the soldiers, to function effectively together as a military unit.

As the ships carrying these men and these tensions approached Beaubassin, the work to improve the defensive fortifications of Beauséjour was still in progress. This work was necessary because, while imposing from afar, the five-bastioned,* earthen-walled fort had significant weaknesses. Its commander, Louis Dupont Duchambon de Vergor, had complained bitterly about the state of the fort when he arrived on August 18, 1754. He reported that, "The curtains are extremely weak. The parade is much too small....All the quarters, of officers and soldiers alike, are poorly built, in bad condition, very damp, and the rain comes in everywhere." He also complained that the "powder magazine is very badly placed, near the gate," and that the well did not function properly, forcing the men to haul water from 700 yards outside the fort.[38] While de Vergor may have been exaggerating the problems to provide an excuse should anything go wrong, there was no denying the fort's major design flaw: the ridge upon which it sat continued to rise behind it, leaving the fort vulnerable to attack from the west. An artillery officer had attempted to compensate for this problem by ordering Acadians from the French side of the border to surround the fort with a trench 6½ feet deep and 16½ feet across, and to use the soil from the ditch to increase the height of the walls. The Acadians had made considerable progress by early June, but the demands of their own farms and a lack of leadership by de Vergor meant that the fort was not fully ready for a battle.[39]

At 6:00 a.m. on June 4, Monckton began his assault. He was methodical about its implementation. Each step had to be completed before the next step could begin, lest the British lose the advantage of their vast superiority of numbers. The first step was to ford the Missaguash, since the French had blown up the only bridge crossing it when the British fleet arrived. French forces tried to stop the British military engineers (sappers) from laying down a temporary bridge, but because their cannons shot over the heads of the British and because Monckton's artillery took out the French guns before they could find the correct range, the British forces crossed the river by

[33] David Perry, *Recollections of an Old Soldier: The Life of Captain David Perry, a Soldier of the French and Revolutionary Wars, Containing Many Extraordinary Occurrences Relating to His Own Private History, and an Account of Some Interesting Events in the History of the Times in Which He Lived No-where Else Recorded* (Windsor, Vermont: Republican & Yeoman Printing Office, 1822), 40-41.

[34] Anderson, *A People's Army*, 61.

[35] Brumwell, *Redcoats*, 18.

[36] Anderson, *A People's Army*, 127-128.

[37] Anderson, *A People's Army*, 111-112; and Brumwell, *Redcoats*, 117.

[38] *The Northcliffe Collection*, 39. A curtain is a defensive wall; a parade is the open ground in the middle of a fort; the powder magazine is the building where gunpowder is stored.

[39] Hoyle, "The Siege of Fort Beauséjour."

noon. Another commander might have pushed forward at that point, taking advantage of his initial success, but Monckton prudently chose to halt and pitch his camp. His men spent the next week hauling heavy artillery and ammunition into place, and one of the leading officers of the provincial troops, John Winslow, captured the high ground above Fort Beauséjour on June 8.[40] As would happen repeatedly over the next seven years when Monckton entered a battle against the French, the remaining steps unfolded with astonishing ease. On June 14, de Vergor received a letter stating that no French reinforcements could arrive in time to help save Fort Beauséjour. This news spread through the fort, creating panic. Eighty Acadians "disappeared into the night," one eyewitness reported.[41] Two days later, the British launched a 13-inch cast-iron shell into the curtain wall near the main gate. The explosion destroyed the fortress' defensive ability, as well as the morale of its occupants.[42] According to provincial ensign Jeremiah Bancroft, de Vergor sent out a "flagg of truse…and Requested a cessation of arme for 48 hours," but "Col. Mungton…demanded ye forte and told them that if they did not give up soon he would hoist his Bloody Flagg and not take it down till he had Destroyed them all."[43] Monckton's refusal to accept anything but an immediate capitulation led de Vergor to suggest terms; Monckton, who had full authority to negotiate, wrote his responses to each of de Vergor's proposals and sent the document back to Fort Beauséjour. De Vergor had little choice and accepted the terms. He also invited the British officers to dine with him that evening, reflecting the values of eighteenth-century gentlemen in war.[44]

The specifics of Monckton's and de Vergor's agreement are significant because of what is said and what is not. Below are de Vergor's proposal and, in italics, Monckton's responses:

> The Commanding Officers…and Garrison of Beauséjour will march out with arms and baggage, drums beating and match lighted. *Granted.*

> The Commandant shall have at the head of the Garrison six pieces of cannon of the largest caliber…with fifty rounds of powder for each cannon. *Not Granted.*

> The necessary conveyances shall be furnished to transport them…where they choose to go. *The Garrison shall be sent directly at the king of Great Britain's charge to Louisbourg by sea.*

> The Garrison shall take with them two hundred quarters of flour and one hundred quarters of bacon. *They shall have a sufficiency of provisions to carry them to Louisbourg.*

> …the Acadians shall not be disturbed for having taken up arms, the more so because they were forced on pain of their lives; no harm shall be done to them. *[No response].*

---

[40] Faragher, *A Great and Noble Scheme,* 305-307.

[41] Jacau de Fiedmont quoted in Hoyle, "The Siege of Fort Beauséjour."

[42] Harrison Bird, *Battle for a Continent* (New York: Oxford University Press, 1965), 43.

[43] Jeremiah Bancroft quoted in Jonathan Fowler and Earle Lockerby, "Operations at Fort Beauséjour and Grand-Pré in 1755: A Soldier's Diary," *Journal of the Royal Nova Scotia Historical Society,* Vol. 12 (2009), 145-184, ProQuest Central.

[44] Francis Parkman, *The Battle for North America,* John Tebbel (ed.) (Garden City, New York: Doubleday & Company, Inc., 1948), 527.

The Acadians shall be permitted to continue to live in their religion, they may have priests, and no violence shall be done to them. *The Acadians having been obligated to take up arms at the forfeiture of their lives shall be forgiven for the part they have now acted.*[45]

The beginning of the document clearly indicates that when the French surrendered, they did so with the honors of war. This was important in the eighteenth-century military environment since it meant that while one side lost, it still retained its dignity. The army's men were still respected as soldiers. The document also states, however, that there are limits to this recognition. The French lost the battle and as a result could not take their most valuable weapons with them, or go wherever they chose. Instead, the British are entitled to keep the cannons and may position their enemies where they would be least threatening. In fact, Monckton furthered this when he specified that, on their honor, the Fort Beauséjour troops could not fight against the British for six months after the surrender. Monckton's responses to the French concerns regarding the Acadians are a triumph of diplomatic language. He does not promise that no harm will come to the Acadians or even that they will have the freedom to worship as Catholics. He only says that they have been forgiven. Monckton worded this so carefully because he knew the wishes of Governor Lawrence: that British Nova Scotia might be rid of its Acadian problem once and for all.

The earliest call for the removal of the Acadians came in 1709, when Scottish trader Samuel Vetch told the Board of Trade, "The greatest part of the inhabitants being removed from thence is absolutely necessary for the security of our own people in case of an attempt from France to recover it, as [well as] to make the natives come over entirely to the interest and obedience of the crown."[46] Vetch called for transporting them to Martinique, but the Board rejected his proposal as impractical. A half century later, Lawrence made the necessary arrangements to overcome the logistical issues, and by the end of July 1755, he was ready to implement his plan. Lawrence and the Halifax Council issued orders for representatives of the Acadians to come to the provincial capital. On July 28, when these one hundred delegates refused to take a loyalty oath to the British monarch, the council's five members voted unanimously for immediate expulsion from Nova Scotia. When they announced their decision later that day, the Acadian representatives were dumbfounded. They had not realized the extent of British resolve.[47] Indeed, they had not understood how significantly the political landscape had changed nor how vulnerable they were as pawns in the increasingly intense mercantilist rivalry between Britain and France.

Lawrence wrote Monckton soon after the vote, and placed him in charge of the removal process. Lawrence said that he should begin with those around Fort Beauséjour, who had taken up arms against the British crown and therefore were "entitled to no favour from the Government." Lawrence also indicated that he had ordered "a sufficient number of Transports" for the removal and urged Monckton to "endeavor to fall upon some stratagem to get the Men, both young & old especially the Heads of Families into your power & detain them till the Transports shall arrive." This was important, Lawrence believed, because with the men in detention, the women and children would be less likely to "attempt to go away and carry off the Cattle." Indeed, it was critical

[45] *The London Magazine, Or, Gentleman's Monthly Intelligencer*, Volume 24 [1755], 349, Google Books.
[46] Samuel Vetch quoted in Faragher, *A Great and Noble Scheme*, 118.
[47] George M. Wrong, *The Rise and Fall of New France*, Volume II (New York: The Macmillan Company, 1928), 771-772. While Monckton was a member of the Halifax Council, he was not present for this vote. The members who did vote were Lawrence; a New England trader, Benjamin Green; a former British officer and current landowner, John Collier; Royal Navy Captain John Rous; a former Massachusetts governor and the current Chief Justice Jonathan Belcher; and the provincial secretary, William Cotterall.

that the Acadians' "whole stock of Cattle and Corn…be secured" so that it might be "applied towards a Reimbursement of the Expence the Government will be at in Transporting them out of the Country." Monckton was also charged with securing "all their Shalops Boats Canoes and every other vessel you can lay your hands upon" to prevent escape.[48] The British did not want the Acadians fleeing westward, where their presence would simply strengthen the French hold on Québec.

Monckton set his plans into motion on August 6. He sent notices to the Acadian men asking to meet the following Sunday at the former French fort so that they might "make arrangements concerning the return of [Acadian] lands." According to ensign Bancroft, about four hundred men showed up at the fort, "but contrary to their expectation the Gate was shut and they confined as Prisoners." Monckton then showed the Acadians "his orders which was that they must be sent off and that the lands and cattle was become forfeited to the King." Eyewitnesses had difficulty describing the Acadian reaction, for as Bancroft said of the Acadians' reaction, "Seing themselves so Decoyed the shame and confusion of face together with Anger so altered their countenense that it can't be expressed."[49] The Acadians tried appealing to Monckton, pointing out that they had responded to the colonel's summons in good faith and that it was utterly unchristian of the British to imprison them in this way. Monckton replied that they would remain in the fort until the transports were ready to take them away and that if their families failed to submit to the transportation plan, the men would be shipped off without them. Monckton did agree to move two hundred of the men a mile away to Fort Lawrence to help relieve the overcrowding.[50] He then sent Colonel John Winslow to use similar tricks to capture other Acadians in communities across the Chignecto Isthmus. Additional orders from Lawrence told Winslow to "destroy all of the Villages…and use every other method to distress as much as can be."[51] This was a scorched earth policy, designed to force the Acadians into submission by leaving them with no viable alternatives. In another letter to Monckton, Lawrence stated his position more emphatically: "you must use the most vigorous measures not only to compel the settlers to board the ships, but also to deprive those who might escape all means of subsistence by burning their homes and destroying in the region all that might enable them to exist" through the winter months.[52]

The first three hundred Acadians affected by the Great Expulsion or *Le Grand Dérangement* were forcibly put aboard the transport ships in Beaubassin on September 10, according to Ensign Bancroft.[53] Monckton thought that the scorched earth policy would persuade more inhabitants to surrender and board the vessels, and he reported his frustration to Lawrence: "the embarkation of the inhabitants here goes on but slow, it being very difficult to collect the women and children."[54] Then, on October 1, 1755, eighty-six Acadian men escaped from Fort Lawrence by digging a tunnel under the walls of the prison. This convinced Monckton that he could not wait any longer: he had to load all the Acadians he had onto transport ships immediately. Lawrence supported this whole-heartedly, writing, "I would have you not wait for the wives and children coming in, but ship off the men without them." To his surprise, Monckton found that as soon as embarkation process

[48] *The Northcliffe Collection*, 81.
[49] Jeremiah Bancroft quoted in Fowler and Lockerby, "Operations at Fort Beauséjour and Grand-Pré in 1755."
[50] Faragher, *A Great and Noble Scheme,* 339.
[51] *The Northcliffe Collection*, 84. Winslow was, however, also ordered to "have all care taken to save the Stock and the Harvest upon the Ground which can be gather'd in any safety" for British use.
[52] Charles Lawrence quoted in Rushton, *The Cajuns,* 49.
[53] Fowler and Lockerby, "Operations at Fort Beauséjour and Grand-Pré in 1755."
[54] Robert Monckton quoted in Faragher, *A Great and Noble Scheme,* 355.

began in earnest, Acadian women and children appeared at the fort so that they might be transported with their husbands.[55]

The British plan for transporting the Acadians to the thirteen British colonies along the Atlantic seaboard called for loading them into the transport ships by the gross tonnage rate per passenger of one half ton per person. This meant that Monckton's men confined 300 people in a space 24 feet wide, 48 feet long, and 15 feet high. To allow the Acadians to lie down, this height was subdivided into three decks, each four feet high. There was no plumbing, no heating, and little ventilation because there was only one storage hatch to the outside.[56] The Acadians were allowed to bring money and a few household items, but most possessions had to be left behind since there was so little room aboard the ships. Moreover, Acadians from communities that had "always been the most Rebellious" were "removed the greatest distance" to discourage their return to Acadia.[57] In the hasty beginning of the embarkation process, family members were separated from one another. As Monckton's aid Brook Watson reported, "I fear some families were divided and sent to different parts of the globe, notwithstanding all possible care was taken to prevent it."[58] The embarkation process continued through mid-December, when the final ship departed with 732 people. In all, through the fall of 1755, almost 7,000 Acadians were uprooted from their homes sent to British colonies that had little enthusiasm for their arrival.[59] As many as 6,000 additional Acadians fled to French territories or joined Míkmaq communities.[60]

The suffering of the Acadians did not end with their departure from their homes. The voyages themselves were horrific: the *Union* was lost at sea; only 207 of the 417 detainees aboard the *Cornwallis* survived the trip to South Carolina as a result of an outbreak of smallpox; and the *Edward* was blown so far off course that it ended up in Antigua, where many of the Acadians contracted malaria. It is estimated that 14% of the transported Acadians did not survive their journey.[61] This percentage parallels the death rate of Africans during the Middle Passage on British ships during the slave trade.[62] Once in the Thirteen Colonies, the Acadians' misery continued. Those arriving in Georgia and South Carolina were accused of trying to destabilize the colonies by altering Indian alliances and promoting Catholicism among slaves.[63] Those under twenty-one who arrived in Pennsylvania, New York, and Massachusetts were separated from their parents and made indentured servants.* And those who arrived in Virginia were refused entry and sent to England, where they were imprisoned for eight years until they were repatriated to France at the conclusion of the Seven Years' War.[64] It wasn't until February 1765 that the first Acadians arrived in New

---

[55] Faragher, *A Great and Noble Scheme,* 356-357.

[56] Rushton, *The Cajuns,* 51.

[57] *The Northcliffe Collection,* 85-86. The 196-ton *Union,* for example, received orders to transport 392 people to Philadelphia, while the 170-ton *Prince Frederick William* took 340 people to Georgia.

[58] Brook Watson quoted in Faragher, *A Great and Noble Scheme,* 357.

[59] Faragher, *A Great and Noble Scheme,* 364-366.

[60] Christopher Hodson, *The Acadian Diaspora: An Eighteenth-Century History* (New York: Oxford University Press, 2012), 45.

[61] Faragher, *A Great and Noble Scheme,* 370-372.

[62] The percentage of deaths for all British slave ships during the slave trade is estimated to be 13%. See Philip D. Morgan, "Slavery in the British Caribbean," *The Cambridge World History of Slavery, Volume 3: AD 1420-AD 1804,* David Eltis and Stanley L. Engerman (eds.) (New York: Cambridge University Press, 2011), 382.

[63] Hodson, *The Acadian Diaspora,* 57.

[64] Rushton, *The Cajuns,* 55. After the war, French ministers wanted the Acadians repatriated from Great Britain or already in France to become colonists in Saint-Domingue (Haiti) or French Guiana, believing that free, white labor would reduce dependence on African slaves and make the colonies more industrious. Those who

Orleans, seeking land for settlement.   They purposefully established their small community far from outside influences in hope that they would be left alone. They refused to assimilate with any of the cultures they encountered during the initial phases of their diaspora. Gradually, more and more Acadians migrated to Louisiana, where they became known as Cajuns.[65]   Meanwhile, the British sought to attract Protestant settlers to Nova Scotia. Governor Lawrence offered 100 acres of woodland to each new family and 50 acres to each child in exchange for small annual rents over a ten-year term. This inducement was successful and by 1764 the population in Acadia had returned to its pre-deportation numbers.[66]

Having captured Fort Beauséjour, expelled the Acadians, and secured greater Nova Scotia for the British crown, Monckton became the province's lieutenant governor in December 1755. Over the next three years, he served as governor twice, handling governmental affairs while Lawrence was away.[67] During his terms of service, Monckton finalized budget reports, ordered food and fuel supplies for British forts, managed the arrival of European Protestant immigrants, and developed a plan to manage French privateers in Nova Scotian waters.[68] It was dull work for a military man, especially during the 1758 campaign, when Monckton remained in Halifax while his men participated in the successful capture of the critical French fortress of Louisbourg on Cape Breton Island. By spring 1759, Monckton was eager to command in the field again.[69] He soon had his chance to help shape the course of North American history for the second time.

---

resettled in French Guiana replicated Acadian land tenure systems in the jungle and were able to preserve Acadian social and cultural systems. See Steven R. Pendery, "Archaeological Dimensions of the Acadia Diaspora," *Archaeological Perspectives on the French in the New World*, Elizabeth M. Scott (ed.) (Gainesville, Florida: University of Florida Press, 2017), 41-44.

[65] Glenn R. Conrad, "The Acadians: Myths and Realities," *The Cajuns: Essays on their History and Culture*, Glenn R. Conrad (ed.), 3rd ed. (Lafayette, Louisiana: University of Southwestern Louisiana, 1983), 10-12. The community numbered about 2,500 people in the mid-1780s. See Hodson, 198.

[66] George F. G. Stanley, *New France: The Last Phase, 1744-1760* (Toronto, Canada: McClelland and Stewart Limited, 1968), 123. The population in 1764 was 12,998, including 2,600 Acadians who had managed to evade deportation.

[67] Steele, "Monckton, Robert."

[68] *The Northcliffe Collection*, 51-55.

[69] Monckton did lead an expedition to burn villages and capture Acadians on the western shore of the Bay of Fundy in September, October, and November 1758, but only 28 Acadians were taken prisoner. See *The Northcliffe Collection*, 64, 99-102, 107. Historians hold varying views on the Acadian removal. A. J. B. Johnston sees a difference between the initial expulsion of the Acadians in 1755 and the St. John River and Petitcodiac River operations, arguing that while the former represented a pre-emptive, strategic act, the later were little more than punitive manhunts with little strategic purpose. See A. J. B. Johnston, "The Acadian Deportation in a Comparative Context: An Introduction," *Journal of the Royal Nova Scotia Historical Society*, 10 (2007), 114-131, ProQuest Central. John Mack Faragher purposefully uses the term "ethnic cleansing" to describe the whole Acadian removal experience (Faragher, *A Great and Noble Scheme*, xix, 470), while from the opening sentence in another historian's work uses the term "genocide" to describe *Le Grand Dérangement*. See Dean W. Jobb, *The Cajuns: A People's Story of Exile and Triumph* (New York: John Wiley & Sons, 2010), 1.

~

Topography often plays a crucial role in military history, and the battle for Québec in the summer of 1759 presents a rich opportunity to examine the interplay of battle strategy and landscape. For Algonquin speakers, this was *kébec*: the place where the river narrows. For the French, Québec was ideally situated for a fortified city: the largest estuarial river in the world flows downstream at a rate of 350,000 cubic feet a second, while tides push brackish water upstream. Navigating the tempestuous currents of the St. Lawrence in the eighteenth century was difficult, which is why the French believed the river to be an impervious barrier.[70] Were this natural moat ever to fail, other natural defenses would protect the city. The narrows at Québec City are created by the large promontory of *Cap Diamant*, which rises 350 feet above the river. This rock formation on the north shore is accompanied by a long, sharp escarpment that follows the river upstream for several miles, creating a natural wall of protection. The only place the city seemed to have any vulnerability to an invading army was downstream, on the north bank's Beauport shore, but extensive mudflats would complicate amphibious assaults and the French had also built extensive fortifications there. The embankment also had two rivers, the St. Charles and the Montmorency, which together limited maneuverability for overland attacks.[71] The city itself, divided between a lower town at river's edge and an upper town high above, was surrounded by stone walls, but these walls were not in sufficiently good repair to withstand a concerted attack from the west. The commander of the French forces in North America, Louis-Joseph de Montcalm-Gozon, was so clear about the limitations of these walls that he reported to Versailles, "If the enemy reaches the foot of [the city's]

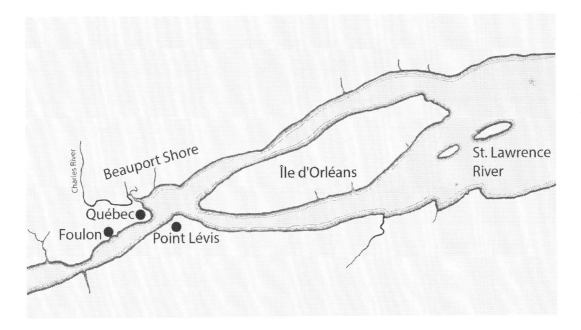

[70] Dan Snow, *Death or Victory: The Battle of Quebec and the Birth of an Empire* (Toronto, Canada: Penguin Canada, 2011) 35, 37, 60. For generations, the French had relied on pilots to navigate each section of the river. See Snow, 9.
[71] Fred Anderson, *Crucible of War: The Seven Years' War and the Fate of Empire in British North America 1754-1766* (New York: Alfred A. Knopf, 2000), 348, 358.

walls, we must capitulate."[72] Hence, Québec's survival largely depended on its considerable natural defenses.

The man who would lead the British forces against these defenses was thirty-two-year-old Major General James Wolfe. Wolfe selected Monckton to be his second in command and appointed him a brigadier general for the campaign, saying, "I couldn't wish to be better supported, your spirit and zeal for the service will help me through all difficulties."[73] The two remaining brigadier generals for the campaign were James Murray, whom Wolfe also selected, and George Townshend, who had been appointed by London. Wolfe was not enthusiastic about Townshend, nor was he on particularly good terms with Vice-Admiral Charles Saunders, upon whom the whole amphibious operation depended. These tensions within the command structure would plague the whole campaign. Worse, the invasion force of 8,500 men was 3,500 men short of the number Wolfe requested, and the invading armada, consisting of 42 men-of-war and 140 transport vessels, departed Louisbourg a month later than Wolfe had wished. This was not a promising start for the confrontation to secure British control of North America, but within just a few weeks, Wolfe found his situation much improved. To the amazement of both the British and the French armies, Saunders had smoothly navigated the treacherous 250-mile St. Lawrence estuary.[74] Wolfe began disembarking his troops on June 26 and 27 and established a base camp on the Île d'Orléans, a large island in the middle of the St. Lawrence, just four miles across from the capital of New France. The siege of Québec had begun.

Wolfe charged Monckton with securing the southern shore of the St. Lawrence and establishing an artillery position at Point Lévis, from where British guns could easily reach the city. At 5:00 p.m. on June 29, Monckton's 3,000 troops began crossing from Île d'Orléans to the south shore. They were divided between regular redcoats, kilt-wearing Highlanders, agile light infantry units, and live-off-the-land rangers, who used the same warfare tactics as the Indians.[75] An unfavorable tide prevented all of the troops from reaching their destination before sunset, but after a June night so cold that there was frost, by early the next morning Monckton and the last of his troops had landed on the south shore. Monckton proceeded up the hill to local church where he posted Wolfe's proclamation to the Canadians.[76] It read:

[72] Louis-Joseph de Montcalm-Gozon quoted in William R. Nester, *The First Global War: Britain, France, and the Fate of North America, 1756-1775* (Westport, Connecticut: Praeger Publishers, 2000), 129-130.

[73] James Wolfe quoted in Snow, *Death or Victory,* 109.

[74] Saunders' passage was aided by a captured Québéquois pilot, who was forced to show Saunders how to navigate a particularly difficult stretch of the river known as the Traverse. A second British squadron, which had been sent to the Gulf of St. Lawrence also navigated the river with the help of a deception by Rear Admiral Philip Durell: he flew the French flag, which brought the French out to pilot the Traverse; these pilots were forced helped the British chart the river. See Nester, *The First Global War*, 133-134. The St. Lawrence was one place where future captain and world explorer James Cook cut his navigational teeth in foreign waters as the master of the *Pembroke*. See Richard Hough, *Captain James Cook: A Biography* (London: Coronet Books, 2003), 23-26.

[75] In this chapter, I carefully use the term "Indian" to identify the native people of North America. In other chapters I use other terms, such as First Nation* people. This choice reflects the belief of many indigenous leaders that the older terminology should be reclaimed. See, for example, Amanda Blackhorse, "Do You Prefer 'Native American' or 'American Indian'?" *Indian Country Today*, May 22, 2015, accessed February 22, 2020, https://tinyurl.com/yd3qljth; and "Native American vs. American Indian: Political Correctness Dishonors Traditional Chiefs of Old," *Native Times*, April 12, 2015, accessed February 22, 2020, https://tinyurl.com/y2navnqe

[76] Abbé H. R. Casgrain, *Wolfe and Montcalm* (Toronto: Oxford University Press, 1926), 105-106.

The King of Great Britain wages no war with the industrious peasant, the sacred orders of religion, or the defenseless women and children: to these, in their distressful circumstances, his royal clemency offers protection. The people may remain unmolested on their lands, inhabit their houses and enjoy their religion in security; for these inestimable blessings, I expect the Canadians will take no part in the great contest between the two crowns. But, if by the vain obstinacy and misguided valour, they presume to appear in arms, they must expect most fatal consequences; their habitations destroyed, their sacred temples exposed to an exasperated soldiery, their harvest utterly ruined, and the only passage for relief stopped up by a formidable fleet.[77]

Having secured one village, Monckton ordered his troops to move west to capture the highest point of the Point Lévis shoreline. They moved in a formal column, protected by the light infantryman and the rangers. At this point, the British forces began to meet significant resistance from hidden, sharpshooting Indians and Canadians. According to Wolfe's personal journal, Monckton was so troubled by this development that he held "a kind of council," seeking the advice of key officers about the wisdom and viability of proceeding.[78] Such indecisiveness was uncharacteristic of Monckton, but perhaps the pressure of commanding his largest force to date weighed on him. In any case, by noon the British had captured the heights of Lévis. They then defended it all afternoon. Late in the day, Monckton ordered the light infantry and the Highlanders to outflank the 400 Canadians and the Indians nearby, and then he personally led the frontal charge against their position.[79] The next day men began hauling dozens of cannons up to the heights to begin the bombardment of Québec.

Despite this success, Monckton's reputation with Wolfe suffered in the subsequent days. When the French launched floating batteries to harass the new British position, Monckton believed that it was a prelude to an amphibious assault. He ordered his men to line up on the beach to greet the French with a volley of musket fire as they landed. Unfortunately for Monckton, the French soldiers never came. Instead, the French floating artillery barges launched twenty-four pound balls into the British battalion, killing fourteen.[80] Although this subjected Monckton to criticism from his men for needlessly risking lives, the tactic of concentrated musketry was a fundamental tenet of eighteenth-century military strategy. The weapon most men held, the flintlock, was not a particularly accurate gun, but it was much faster to load and re-fire than its predecessors. The key to winning a pitched battle in the Seven Years' War was to stand in close formation and deliver as much concentrated firepower as possible.[81] Wolfe ignored this reasoning and continued to criticize his second-in-command. In his private journal, Wolfe described Monckton as having a "dull capacity and may be properly called fat headed, timid, and utterly unqualified."[82] This assessment didn't change on July 1, when Wolfe visited Point Lévis for the first time. The general expected to

---

[77] Nester, *The First Global War,* 136. Wolfe's proclamation also noted that, "the unparalleled barbarity's exerted by the French against our settlements in America might justify the bitterest revenge in the army under my command."

[78] James Wolfe quoted in Snow, *Death or Victory,* 132.

[79] Casgrain, *Wolfe and Montcalm,* 107-108.

[80] Snow, *Death or Victory,* 135.

[81] Daniel Marston, *The Seven Years' War* (Botley, U.K.: Osprey Publishing, 2001), 16. As Fred Anderson notes, "The fate of every infantry battle ultimately rested on the ability of soldiers to withstand the physical and psychological shock of that climactic volley." See Anderson, *Crucible of War,* 360.

[82] James Wolfe quoted in Snow, *Death or Victory,* 136.

find the position well-fortified and secured with the new redoubts he had ordered, but Wolfe was "amazed at the ignorance in the construction" as implemented by Monckton and his men. Wolfe promptly "directed [the construction of] some new works,"[83] and Monckton's reputation had sunk to a new low.

In the month of July, the garrison at Port Lévis shelled the city of Québec continually, the first British ships successfully sailed upstream of the city, and the French easily repulsed two British attempts to dislodge French defenses along the Beauport shore. These events did not change the campaign significantly: the siege was still a stalemate. In mid-August, Wolfe developed an intestinal malady,[84] which combined with his tuberculosis and difficulty urinating, forced him to relinquish his command to Monckton, Murray, and Townshend temporarily.[85] Monckton called for a meeting of the brigadier generals, Admiral Saunders, and other principal naval officers. All agreed that the only solution to the siege was to cut off Québec's supply lines from Montreal by landing the British army west of the city.[86] Realizing that the campaign season was rapidly drawing to a close, the officers wrote to Wolfe on August 29. They stated unanimously that the best course of action was to withdraw from current positions and attempt an assault upriver. Wolfe reluctantly accepted the unified position of his officers, and by the end of the first week of September the British were in position to take their gamble.

Inclement weather delayed the British assault, but on September 12 the foul conditions finally broke and a partially recovered Wolfe issued the order to prepare for battle that night. Monckton, Townshend, and Murray all anticipated receiving detailed instructions from Wolfe as to the specific landing site, but as the day passed into evening, none came. The three brigadier generals wrote a joint letter to Wolfe, frankly saying, "We do not think ourselves sufficiently informed of several parts which may fall to our share in the execution of the descent you intend tomorrow." They urged Wolfe to issue "as distinct orders as the nature of the thing will admit of, particularly to the place or places we are to attack."[87] Wolfe's reply, written at 8:30 p.m. and addressed only to Monckton, began with condescension:

> My reason for desiring the honour of your Company with me [on September 9]…was to shew you, as well as the distance woud permit, the situation of the Enemy, & the place where I mean't they should be attach'd; as you are charged with the duty, I shoud be glad to give you all further light, & assistance in my power–the place is called the *Foulon* distant upon two miles or two miles & a half from Quebec, where you remember an encampment of 12 or 13 Tents & an Abbatis below it–you mention'd to day that you had perceived of breast-work there, which made me imagine you were well acquainted [with] the Place.

The tone of the letter then changed to one of indignation. Wolfe wrote, "It is not a usual thing to point out in the publick orders the direct spot of an attack, nor for any inferior Officer not charg'd [with] a particular duty to ask instructions upon that point." Clearly he was annoyed by the brigadiers generals' questioning of his preparatory planning. Wolfe concluded the letter by taking full responsibility for the attack:

---

[83] James Wolfe quoted in Snow, *Death or Victory,* 138.
[84] Snow, *Death or Victory,* 286.
[85] Anderson, *Crucible of War,* 351.
[86] Christopher Hibbert, *Wolfe at Quebec* (Cleveland, Ohio: The World Publishing Company, 1959), 115-116.
[87] Robert Monckton, James Murray, and George Townshend quoted in Snow, *Death or Victory,* 322.

I had the honour to inform you to day, that it is my duty to attack, the French Army, to the best of my knowledge, & abilities, I have fix'd upon that spot, where we can act [with] most force, & are most likely to succeed, if I am mistaken, I am sorry for it; & must be answerable to his Majesty & the Publick for the consequences.[88]

By midnight, the invasion force had been loaded onto longboats and were waiting for the tide to ebb so that they could drift downriver towards Foulon. Wolfe had told Townshend that Monckton was "charg'd [with] the first Landing & attack at the Foulon,"[89] but during the embarkation process Wolfe changed the plan, choosing to ride with the initial group of boats himself. These first eight boats held the light infantrymen, dressed in unornamented, shortened blue and green jackets for better camouflage, instead of the customary red.[90] They were commanded by Lieutenant Colonel William Howe, whom Wolfe had selected for his physical prowess, family connections, and eagerness to lead the charge up the 175-foot gully to the top of the escarpment and the Plains of Abraham.[91] They were followed by ten boats with troops under Monckton's command.[92] Dozens of other boats followed.

Atop the Plains of Abraham, overlooking the Foulon cove, a hundred Canadian militiamen guarded the break in the escarpment caused by millennia of erosion. They were commanded by Louis de Vergor, the former commandant of Fort Beauséjour, who had been assigned to Foulon

[88] *The Northcliffe Collection*, 412.
[89] *The Northcliffe Collection*, 415.
[90] Brumwell, *Redcoats*, 230.
[91] Anderson, *Crucible of War*, 353.
[92] Snow, *Death or Victory*, 329. The second group of boats included six carrying Bragg's 28th Regiment and four with Kennedy's 43rd Regiment. Both of these regiments were under Monckton's command during the battle.

only two days before.[93] Before retiring for the night, de Vergor had told his sentries to expect a supply convoy coming downriver from Montreal sometime that evening so when the sentries called out to the first British boats and the British responded in passable and reassuring French, the sentries returned to their shelters.[94] This allowed the British troops to land undetected. Howe's light infantry scaled the cliff quickly, subdued a sentry and completely surprised the small French encampment. There was a quick exchange of musket fire as the French emerged from their tents. This awakened de Vergor, who jumped up and tried to flee. A random bullet hit him in the right heel, another one cut into his hand.[95] He fell in a cornfield, still dressed in his nightshirt.[96] Taken prisoner, de Vergor was unable to warn Montcalm. Howe then gave the "all clear" signal, and by 4:00 a.m., Wolfe and the rest of the advance party had begun clamoring out of the boats and struggling up Foulon's gully path.[97] Monckton followed soon after, shadowed by thousands of men ready for a great battle. Once at the French encampment, Monckton paused to acknowledge de Vergor as the first hint of dawn began to glow.[98]

Montcalm learned of the British presence on the Plains of Abraham well after daybreak, and it wasn't until 7:00 a.m. that French troops began moving from Beauport to the Plains of Abraham. By 8:00, the third wave of British troops had landed. Monckton, Townshend, and Murray had organized them so that each regiment was forty yards apart, and within each regiment the men stood in two rows, each man three feet apart. In all, Wolfe had 4,400 men at his command, stretching a half-mile across the farmland, their faces turned toward Québec.[99]

At 10:00, Montcalm ordered his forces to attack the British line. The famous battle only lasted fifteen minutes, for the French troops did not advance in an orderly fashion and fired their initial volley at too far a range to do serious damage to the British line. Wolfe had given strict orders that the redcoats were not to shoot until the French forces were within forty yards. When the French

reached this point, the British let loose a nearly simultaneous volley, so loud it sounded more like a cannon shot than musket fire, according to eyewitness accounts. The French advance wilted under this firepower. Another volley from the men in the second row stopped the advance completely. The French survivors turned and fled for the supposed protection of the city's walls. In the aftermath, 658 men on the British side were counted as killed, injured, or missing, including Wolfe. One musket

[93] Hibbert, *Wolfe at Quebec*, 123.

[94] Bird, *Battle for a Continent*, 294

[95] Bernard Pothier, "Du Pont Duchambon de Vergor, Louis," *Dictionary of Canadian Biography*, vol. 4, University of Toronto/Université Laval, 2003–, accessed January 17, 2020, https://tinyurl.com/yxl3x9gn

[96] Hibbert, *Wolfe at Quebec*, 137-138.

[97] Anderson, *Crucible of War*, 354.

[98] De Vergor was repatriated to France, where he tried to rejoin the army, but his injuries were too severe. In April 1760, he was awarded an invalid's pension. He was never rebuked for failing to prevent the British landing. He died in poverty in 1775. See Pothier, "Du Pont Duchambon de Vergor, Louis."

[99] Snow, *Death or Victory,* 339, 343, 349.

ball shattered his wrist, a second hit his groin, and a third landed in his chest.[100] He bled to death on the battlefield but died knowing of the British victory. A musket ball also found Monckton's chest: it "went through part of my lungs, & was cut out under the blade bone of my shoulder—Just as the French were giving way," the general later wrote.[101] Monckton was taken down the Foulon path and rowed out to the *Lowestoft*, where he received additional medical attention for his wound. On the French side, the causality estimates range from 640 to 1,500 men, including Montcalm. The French general was hit by two musket balls during the retreat and taken back to the city, where he died some eighteen hours later.[102] Québec formally surrendered on September 18. The capital of French North America was finally British.

Monckton recovered from his wounds with astonishing speed, for although he was not present for the French surrender, he took command just a few days later. He must have received the best possible care, but medical science had not progressed significantly in the century since Gijsbert Heeck had sailed for the Dutch East India Company. Internal medicine was still largely defined by imbalances in Galen's four humors, and the specific causes of infection remained elusive. The surgeon treating Monckton aboard the *Lowestoft*, would have removed the musket ball, if it wasn't too deeply imbedded, cleansed the wound, sutured it in a particular style, and applied bandaging.[103] The average surgery survival rate was only 50% since most surgeries involved amputation of a limb.[104] An ordinary soldier would have been transferred to the field hospital on Île d'Orléans, but Monckton was transferred to his private quarters at Point Lévis. This alone improved his chances for survival, for although the connection between a lack of cleanliness and the spread of disease by the mid-eighteenth century was known,[105] most field hospitals were ripe for epidemics and most army encampments were unsanitary.[106] During his recovery, Monckton would have been attended to by female nurses, often conscripted into service from the ranks of the women who traveled with the British army. Some of these women were wives, others were women hoping to find husbands by following the army wherever it went. Still others were prostitutes. These women provided laundry services for the army and many also served as moneylenders, or sold rum illegally to troops.[107] Few wanted to work in the hospitals, which is why so many had to be compelled to do so. In fact, earlier in the campaign, Monckton ordered that

> if any Woman refuse to serve as Nurses in the Hospital, or after having been there Leaves it without being regularly dismissed by the order of the Director, she shall be struck off the Provisn Roll & if found afterwards in any of the camps shall be turned out immediately.[108]

---

[100] Nester, *The First Global War,* 166.

[101] Robert Monckton quoted in D. Peter MacLeod, *Northern Armageddon: The Battle of the Plains of Abraham and the Making of the American Revolution* (New York: Alfred A. Knopf, 2016), 230.

[102] Nester, *The First Global War,* 167.

[103] For more information medical treatment and surgeons during the period of the Seven Years' War, see Catharine L. Thompson, "John Denison Hartshorn: A Colonial Apprentice in 'Physick' and Surgery (Boston)," *Historical Journal of Massachusetts* 38.2 (Fall 2010): 77-103; and Mary C. Gillett, *The Army Medical Department, 1775-1818* (Washington, DC: Center of Military History, United States Army, 1990), 1-19.

[104] Snow, *Death or Victory,* 386.

[105] Gillett, *The Army Medical Department, 1775-1818*, 3, 8-9.

[106] Snow, *Death or Victory,* 283-285.

[107] Brumwell, *Redcoats,* 122-125.

[108] Sarah Fatherly, "Tending the Army: Women and the British General Hospital in North America, 1754-1763," *Early American Studies*, Fall 2012, 566-599, EBSCOhost.

Having recovered some of his strength, Monckton spent the next month serving as *de-facto* governor of Québec. The city was in ruins, the countryside ravaged, the people desperate. Monckton responded by issuing a proclamation to the French Canadians on September 22, 1759, declaring that

> notwithstanding their obstinate refusal to the equitable terms offered to them by Wolfe, and their participating in a war carried on in a barbarous and cruel manner, he, in his desire to show compassion for them, gives them leave to return to their parishes, take possession of their lands and other effects, reap their harvests and practice their religion without molestation, on condition that they surrender their arms, take the oath of fidelity, and remain peaceably in their homes."[109]

In subsequent days, Monckton filled officer vacancies, offering promotions to many men. He managed the numerous requests from Québec residents seeking permission to travel or asking for help. One request came from the nuns operating the Québec hospital, who stated that they were in desperate need of supplies and firewood for the coming winter because they had not able to cut the 600 cords of wood they normally used or to harvest their crops since their fields had been destroyed.[110] Monckton responded positively to most of these requests. He did not treat the residents of Québec with the same harshness he had the Acadians. Conversely, Monckton severely punished British soldiers who were found guilty of robbing or looting: individual soldiers faced sentences of a thousand lashes or hanging as a result of their illegal activities.[111] Indeed, with the hard, Canadian winter fast approaching, Monckton wanted above all else to secure law and order before Admiral Saunders began evacuating the navy on October 18. By October 25, Monckton felt sufficiently secure that Québec would have a peaceful winter,[112] so he turned command over to Murray and left in the second-to-last group of ships, following the currents of the St. Lawrence into the Atlantic Ocean. The *Fowey* arrived in New York on November 17, where Monckton received a cannon salute from Fort George.[113] He was a war hero.

The British capture of Québec City did not end the Seven Years' War or even the battle for North America. The French still held control of the critical towns of Montreal, Detroit, and New Orleans, as well as numerous outposts in what is today Ohio, Indiana, Illinois, and Michigan. The opening months of 1760 were a particularly delicate time, for no one knew if a fleet would arrive to resupply the French in Canada, or if the Ohio Valley Indians would support a peace, or if events in the Asian, African, or European theaters of the war would trump the importance of the Québec victory. Consequently, the commander-in-chief of the British forces in North America, Sir Jeffrey Amherst, sought a prudent and experienced officer to manage the situation on the western frontier and appointed Monckton to the role. On April 29, 1760, Amherst directed Monckton to proceed to

---

[109] *The Northcliffe Collection*, 271.

[110] *The Northcliffe Collection*, 271-277.

[111] MacLeod, *Northern Armageddon,* 274-275.

[112] One reason for this confidence was that Monckton had denied the discharge requests of many soldiers who were eager to return to Britain with Saunders or to accompany Monckton to New York. Instead, Monckton urged the troops to "cheerfully enlist for another year." See Robert Monckton quoted in MacLeod, *Northern Armageddon,* 283-284.

[113] Andrew Cormack, "Observations on the Later Life of Lieutenant-General the Honourable Robert Monckton and the Lives of his Children," *Journal of the Society for Army Historical Research*, 85 (2007), 275-285.

Fort Pitt, secure the Ohio Valley by capturing and building fortresses, and obtain a peace with the Indians.[114]

It was this last order that constituted the most subtle element of Monckton's six months at Fort Pitt. On August 12, he hosted a conference with fifteen chiefs of the Iroquois, Miami, Delaware, Ottawa, Shawnee, Huron, and Potawatomi tribes. One of the leading chiefs was Tamaqua of the Delawares, an even-tempered man who embodied the tribe's tradition as peacemakers. He had opposed war against the British in 1755 and had worked patiently in 1758 and 1759 to convince many tribes that only the restoration of peace would bring back the trade everyone wanted.[115] This desire did not mean that the Indians were pushovers at the negotiating table. In fact, the powerful interior tribes of the American northeast had a history of negotiating favorably with the Europeans through much of the colonial period. This was because neither the French nor the British possessed sufficient soldiers to occupy and control the vast continent. Both nations were dependent upon alliances with key Indian tribes to advance their economic interests and territorial ambitions.[116] Consequently, an essential strategy for many tribes was to try to play the French and the British off against one another, thereby maintaining a balance of power and not allowing either European nation to become too dominant.[117] Monckton knew this, and as a result did not enter into the negotiations lightly.

Monckton opened the conference by reading a letter from Amherst. This letter said that the British did not mean to take possession of Indian lands, but found it necessary to "Build Forts in some parts of your Country, to protect our Trade with you, and prevent the Enemy from taking possession of your Lands, and Hurting both you & Us." Amherst noted that the Indians were "Sensible" and understood that "if we don't Built Forts the French will." He added, "I assure you that no part whatever of your Land Joining the said Forts shall be taken from you, nor any of Our people be permitted to Hunt or Settle upon them, But they shall remain your Absolute property."[118] The discussions, ceremonies, and pledges of good faith from all sides continued until August 17, 1760. The Indians returned prisoners of war, while the British presented their guests with alcohol, desirable merchandise, and gunpowder. Monckton concluded the conference by saying, "it rejoices me to find you all so Hearty in the Renewal of our Antient Friendship, may it continue as long as Sun & Moon endures."[119]

How sincere Monckton was in this statement is certainly debatable, but the French surrender at Montreal a month later changed the political calculus for both the British and the Indians. The British had won control of all of New France. What had once been British requests became

---

[114] *The Northcliffe Collection*, 289. For information about Fort Pitt (which is located in modern Pittsburgh, Pennsylvania) see "Fort Pitt Museum," *John Heinz History Center,* accessed February 2, 2020, https://www.heinzhistorycenter.org/fort-pitt/

[115] Mitchell N. McConnell, "Pisquetomen and Tamaqua: Mediating Peace in the Ohio Country," *Northeastern Indian Lives 1632-1816*, Robert S. Grumet (ed.) (Amherst, Massachusetts: University of Massachusetts Press, 1996) 280, 288-289.

[116] Gary B. Nash, *Red, White, and Black: The Peoples of Early America* (Englewood Cliffs, New Jersey: Prentice-Hall, Inc., 1974), 240.

[117] Neil Salisbury, "Native People and European Settlers in Eastern North America, 1600-1783," *The Cambridge History of the Native Peoples of the Americas*, Volume 1: North America, Part 1, Bruce G. Trigger and Wilcomb E. Washburn (ed.) (Cambridge, U.K.: Cambridge University Press, 1996), 440.

[118] Jeffery Amherst quoted in *Pennsylvania Archives* (1st Series), vol. 3., S. Hazard (ed.) (Philadelphia, Pennsylvania: Joseph Severns, 1852), 746, accessed January 17, 2020 from https://tinyurl.com/y2ovhcb7

[119] Jeffery Amherst quoted in *Pennsylvania Archives* (1st Series), vol. 3., S. Hazard (ed.) (Philadelphia, Pennsylvania: Joseph Severns, 1852), 746, accessed January 17, 2020 from https://tinyurl.com/y2ovhcb7

demands.[120] The Indians lost their position as intermediaries and their bargaining power as a result. Soon the British installed large garrisons throughout the Great Lakes region, which produced a profound resentment among the Indians.[121] Tamaqua, for example, sent a message to Fort Pitt in 1763 condemning the British for "destroying the peace and bringing war"[122] and then took up arms as part of Pontiac's War.[123] Such actions were of little concern in London by that point. Instead, the king issued the Proclamation of 1763, which limited colonial settlement to the eastern side of the Appalachian Mountains and placed the Indians west of the line under the king's protection, thereby denying them both their own sovereignty and any rights as British subjects.[124] It was a tragic precedent.

~

Before the Seven Years' War began, there had been two centers of French colonial commerce and government in North America. The first was Québec with its fur trade and seats of gubernatorial and ecclesiastical administration.[125] That citadel now belonged to British. The second was the sugar-producing Caribbean island of Martinique, and the British soon sought to capture it as well. The man chosen to lead the attack on Martinique was the officer with the most experience in the British army managing amphibious invasions: Major General Monckton.

As in Québec, Martinique's topography dictated the military strategy. The kidney bean-shaped

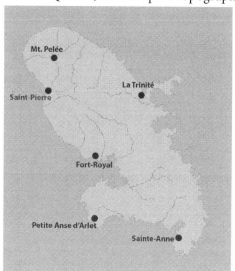

island is forty-three miles long and nineteen miles wide, dominated by a 4,583-foot-high volcano, Mt. Pelée, and blessed with rich soil, ample water and luxuriant vegetation. On his fourth voyage to the Americas, Christopher Columbus declared the island to be "the most wonderful, the most fertile, the sweetest, the most equable, the most charming land in the world."[126] British arrivals echoed this assessment two and a half centuries later, for they were amazed by the lushness and variety of Martinique. Everything from the colorful flowers to the exotic tropical fruits to the smell of the air seemed new and delightful.   Even the landscape astonished them. As one Scot related in 1759, even the wildness of the Highlands could not compare with "Woods, Mountains, canes and continued ravin[e]s" of

[120] McConnell, "Pisquetomen and Tamaqua," 292.

[121] Salisbury, "Native People and European Settlers in Eastern North America, 1600-1783," 445.

[122] Tamaqua quoted in McConnell, "Pisquetomen and Tamaqua," 292.

[123] Dowd, *War Under Heaven*, 129.

[124] Dowd, *War Under Heaven*, 177.

[125] Québec was the only city from which imports could legally arrive and exports could legally depart New France; the colony's Catholic institutions were deeply embedded in the society; and the governor and intendant wielded the power of the Crown. See Allan Greer, *The People of France* (Toronto, Canada: University of Toronto Press, 1997), 44-48.

[126] Christopher Columbus quoted in Joyce Gregory Wyels, "Martinique: Gardens of Bounty and Tears," *Americas* (English ed.) 53.6 (Nov./Dec. 2001), 16-23, ProQuest Central.

this still-untamed isle.[127]   Although that majestic terrain and verdant growth impressed, it also proved enormously challenging in terms of military tactics. The British had, in fact, attempted to take Martinique in 1759, but failed largely because the mission commander neglected to take sufficient account of the topography.[128]   A different approach was in order, and it became Monckton's job to determine what this should be.

Monckton's plan required almost twice as many troops as were involved in the 1759 attempt. This meant pooling troops from North America, Britain, Europe, and the other islands in the Caribbean. The admiralty selected the Barbados as the rendezvous point, and on November 14, 1761, Monckton left New York Harbor with a one hundred ship fleet protected by the 64-gun *Alcide*, the 74-gun *Devonshire*, two other ships with fifty guns, and one with forty guns.[129]   Aboard were thousands of men that Governor-General Jeffery Amherst had assembled on Staten Island for the invasion. They were experienced, "extremely well disciplined" troops who left New York "full of life and courage," according to one civilian observer.[130]   Monckton arrived in Barbados on December 24 to find Admiral George Brydges Rodney's fleet from Britain waiting, and the Caribbean fleet's commander, Admiral James Douglas, already dispatched to blockade Martinique's commercial center of Saint-Pierre.[131]   In preparation for warfare in the tropics, the troops were ordered to rip the lining out of their clothes, to remove the lapels, and, in the case of the Highlanders, to have their "Skirts cut Short." Amherst had urged Monckton to go further and have the men campaign in only their waistcoats,[132] but apparently this was too much of a uniform violation for London to authorize. Properly mustered and supplied, the combined fleet under Rodney's command left Barbados January 7, 1762: eighteen ships of the line, a score of cruisers, four bomb vessels with mortars, just over 13,000 troops, and one thousand White volunteers and conscripted Black slaves from the Barbados.[133]   The fleet arrived off Martinique and joined Douglas two days later, on January 9.

The administrative capital of the island was Fort-Royal. The town's defenses centered upon Fort Saint-Louis, which jutted into Fort-Royal's bay from the north shore. Saint-Louis' triangular bastions, thick ramparts, and arching casements may have given it the look of a medieval castle, and this architecture may have been strategically outdated for the Seven Years' War, but its guns could still do plenty of damage,[134] especially when combined with the guns from Pigeon Island, an

---

[127] Unidentified soldier quoted in Brumwell, *Redcoats*, 140-141.

[128] Unidentified civilian quoted in Brumwell, *Redcoats*, 31.

[129] William Smith, Jr., *The History of the Province of New-York, Volume 2, A Continuation, 1732-1762*, Michael Kammen (ed.) (Cambridge, Massachusetts: The Belknap Press of Harvard University Press, 1972), 262.

[130] Brumwell, *Redcoats*, 2.

[131] Julian S. Corbett, *England in the Seven Years' War: A Study in Combined Strategy, Volume II* (London: Longmans, Green and Co., 1907), 217. Rodney's ship arrived November 22 and the last of his fleet arrived December 9. The Caribbean fleet was led by James Douglas.

[132] Brumwell, *Redcoats*, 147.

[133] Corbett, *England in the Seven Years' War*, 217-218. *The Northcliffe Collection* lists slightly different numbers: 16 ships of the line, 13 frigates, three bombs ships, hospital ships, and 10,311 officers and men (page 310). In *Redcoats* Brumwell states (page 44) that there were 13,288 troops. Nester in the *The First Global War* says there were 14,000 troops on 173 ships (page 217). Another historian gives the figure 16,000 troops. See Mathew Parker, *The Sugar Barons: Family, Corruption, Empire and War in the West Indies* (New York: Walker and Company, 2011), 304. Regardless of which of these figures is correct, the armada was considerable and well equipped to capture Martinique. "White" and "Black" are both intentionally capitalized. See Chapter F, footnote 60.

[134] Roger Norman Buckley, *The British Army in the West Indies: Society and the Military in the Revolutionary Age* (Gainesville, Florida: University of Florida Press, 1998), 373.

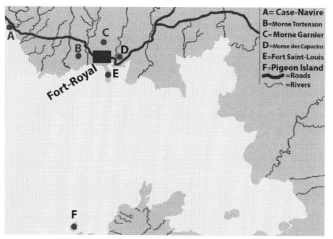

islet off the bay's south shore. In fact, these two guardians of the bay prevented the British from using their naval superiority as well as they had hoped. There just was too much risk of getting caught in a deadly crossfire. The British needed an alternative approach.

Employing the same strategy that kept Montcalm uncertain along the St. Lawrence, Monckton decided to attack the island in several places at once to keep the French off-guard. He requested that Rodney dispatch two ships with two brigades to the southwest corner of the island to take Petite Anse d'Arlet, five frigates to La Trinité to fake a landing on the island's northeast side, and the rest of the fleet to bombard Sainte-Anne in the far south.[135] The troops that landed at Petite Anse d'Arlet marched inland and took the hill high above Pigeon Island, but getting the heavy artillery into position there seemed unrealistic. The island's interior was too rugged to transport the necessary equipment very far. Monckton decided that the only option was to try an amphibious assault on the beach at Case-Navire, some four miles northwest of Fort Saint-Louis. This was the same place where the British had landed to no avail in 1759, but this time the landing went smoothly. The huge fleet bombarded the beach defenses into oblivion, and Monckton established a beachhead at sunset on January 16. The rest of the army disembarked at sunrise the following day.[136]

As with Fort Beauséjour, Fort Saint-Louis' placement suffered from one serious topographical flaw: the hills that overlooked it and surrounded the town. In this case, there were three promontories of concern, each one rising higher to the east. From the road connecting Case-Navire to Fort-Royal, they would have looked like a natural staircase ascending above the town. In the foreground stood Morne Tortenson, followed by Morne Garnier, followed by Morne des Capucins.[137] As British officer Henry Fletcher related in his journal on February 4, 1762, the "Fort becomes Weak by reason of the Many hills which overlook it within Cannon Shot. Whoever is master of these Hills…Commands the Fort."[138] The French had attempted to compensate for this problem by building redoubts and batteries atop all three of the hills. In order to capture the French naval center of the Caribbean, all three would have to be taken.

Monckton's troops went to work on Morne Tortenson on January 24, having spent a week constructing batteries and bringing artillery into place. Following a bombardment near dawn, the light infantry and grenadiers stormed the hillside. According to one eyewitness, at one point the men found themselves in "very smart fire" from French troops and several of them "tumbled to the bottom, [while] others let themselves down by the help of the trees." Then "flinging their muskets on their backs" the advance force "clambered up again as fast as they could."[139] By 9:00 a.m., the

---

[135] Corbett, *England in the Seven Years' War,* 219.

[136] Corbett, *England in the Seven Years' War,* 221-222.

[137] There was little standardization of spelling in the eighteenth century. Alternate spellings for these peaks include Tarnenson, Tortensson, Tortenson, Grenier, and Capuchin.

[138] Henry Fletcher quoted in Buckley, *The British Army in the West Indies,* 364.

[139] Anonymous soldier quoted in Brumwell, *Redcoats,* 235.

British had secured the hilltop and forced the French to retreat to Morne Garnier.[140] Surprised by the speed and ease with which the stronghold had been taken, Monckton positively gushed in his report of the battle: [I am] highly sensible of the Valour of the Troops [I have] the honour to command; the gallant behavior which they have shewn this day will do honour to their Country, and ever distinguish them as Britons."[141] This said, the next hill looked more intimidating. Not only was Morne Garnier taller, but thanks to a steep ravine which separated it from Morne Tortenson, the approach was steeper. During the battle for the second peak on January 27, the British gained a foothold on the Garnier side of the ravine. The French troops then made a crucial mistake: they unexpectedly gave up their secure defensive position, leading a downhill sortie against the British. Monckton's men managed to repulse this attack, and then "pursued by the troops with utmost eagerness up Morne Grenier, by every path, road practicable to run, walk or creep up by." The Martinique defenders then "abandoned their works, Canon, Heights & passes as fast as they saw a red coat in sight," according to a British captain.[142] The British took the third hill, Morne des Capucins, one or two days later, without difficulty.

Because the French governor left Fort-Royal for Saint-Pierre after the capture of Morne Garnier, the residents of the town asked for an independent capitulation on January 29. Monckton refused, wanting to put pressure on the Governor General. The following day, the Islanders appealed again. This time Monckton replied, saying on January 31 that he was "surprised at the inability of the inhabitants to persuade Governor General," but because he was "unwilling to distress the inhabitants" he was now prepared to receive their terms. He expected "hostages from every department of the island" and recommended haste "in order to stop the depredations of the troops."[143] The French Governor General surrendered February 15, and Martinique became a British possession. According to the terms of the final capitulation, the French officers and men surrendered with the honors of war and were transported to France on British ships with their weapons and baggage. All prisoners of war were to be exchanged in accordance with the established agreement. The residents of Martinique had to take a loyalty oath to the British crown, but preserved their right to practice Catholicism freely and openly. They also retained all of their property, including slaves.[144] The British suffered 500 casualties during the month-long campaign.[145] Those who survived were thrilled about the victory, especially since they knew the British army had been defeated in the same spot in 1759. They were also confident about what it meant for the future. As one teenage officer wrote February 27, 1762, "We are now in full Possession of the whole Island: see what we Britons can do! We hope to drive the World before us ere this War be over and I myself being an old Captain."[146] Indeed, with the French surrender, the second citadel of French commerce and civic administration in North America was now in the

---

[140] Corbett, *England in the Seven Years' War,* 223.
[141] Robert Monckton quoted in Brumwell, *Redcoats,* 72.
[142] Harry Gordon quoted in Brumwell, *Redcoats,* 45.
[143] *The Northcliffe Collection,* 319.
[144] *The Northcliffe Collection,* 353-357. Those slaves who had been made free during the siege maintained their free status. Those who were promised their freedom were awarded it. Conversely, however, those free blacks and mulattoes who had taken up arms against the British lost their rights and became slaves.
[145] Anderson, *Crucible of War,* 490.
[146] Anonymous subaltern quoted in Brumwell, *Redcoats,* 116.

hands of Britain's new king, George III. Columbus' Eden could now supply his Majesty's subjects with the sugar they craved.[147]

The capture of Martinique did not end the Seven Years' War. On January 2, 1762, Great Britain declared war on Spain because the British saw an opportunity to acquire additional territories and resources. Admiral Rodney and Monckton learned of this expansion in the conflict during the Martinique campaign, but by mid-February Rodney had not received orders from London about how to protect British interests in the Caribbean. He proposed to Monckton that they take as many ships and men as they could to protect Jamaica from any Spanish threat, but Monckton rejected the proposal, believing that they could not engage in such a bold move without authorization. Monckton could not endorse Rodney's plan, even when he too understood the seriousness of the situation and the need to respond to changing circumstances. This forced Rodney to depart for Jamaica with most of his fleet, but without the supporting troops he also needed. During a stopover at St. Christopher Island (St. Kitts), Rodney learned of London's wishes: he was to prepare the troops on Martinique for transport on a secret mission somewhere in the Caribbean. Although he obeyed orders by returning to Martinique, Rodney also disobeyed orders by sending ten ships to protect Jamaica.[148]

Both Rodney and Monckton easily concluded that the "secret" destination for the mission had to be Havana, the capital of the Spanish Caribbean. They began the necessary preparations, but both men lost their operational command to more senior officers. When the new officers arrived, Monckton had the choice of either joining the campaign or remaining as governor-general of Martinique.[149] When William Anne Keppel, the Earl of Albemarle, arrived on Martinique in mid-April, he sharply criticized Monckton's preparations, and spent the next two weeks reorganizing the transports and troop assignments for the invasion.[150] Naturally, Monckton found this presumptuous. Insulted and in increasingly fragile health, Monckton had little difficulty deciding not to join the Havana campaign.[151] He petitioned for a return to New York, which was granted. Monckton resumed his position as governor of the colony on June 12, 1762, but just over a year later took a leave of absence and returned to England for health reasons.[152]

As is true for many military men, a return home did not bring Monckton an easy life. The transition was harder than he probably ever imagined it would be. Certainly, there were successes: he was exonerated in a court martial in 1764, named governor of Berwick-upon-Tweed in 1765, won another military promotion in 1770, and became the governor of and the Member of

---

[147] For a detailed discussion of the sugar industry, sugar consumption, and the trans-Atlantic slave trade, see Chapter O.

[148] Corbett, *England in the Seven Years' War,* 238-241.

[149] David Greentree, *A Far-Flung Gamble: Havana 1762* (Oxford, U.K.: Osprey Publishing, 2010), 23.

[150] Corbett, *England in the Seven Years' War,* 258-259.

[151] It was fortunate that Monckton did not join the Havana campaign. Yellow fever decimated the troops during the siege: of the 15,000 troops that landed June 7, 1762, only 3,000 were still available for active duty when Havana surrendered August 13. See Parker, *The Sugar Barons,* 304.

[152] John Austin Stevens, *The Memorial History of the City of New York: From its First Settlements to the Year 1892,* Volume 2, James Grant (ed.) (New York: New-York History Company, 1892), 328. Monckton's most important act as governor between June 1762 and June 1763 was to soothe a dispute between the Crown and the colonial legislature over judicial appointments and judicial salaries. He also did not claim any of the emoluments of the governor's office, making him popular with the general public. See Stevens, 408-409 and Alden Chester and Edwin Melvin Williams, *Courts and Lawyers of New York: A History, 1609-1925, Volume 1* (New York: American Historical Society, 1925, 2004), 598-620.

Parliament for Portsmouth in 1778.[153] He also had the company of his American-born wife Susannah and their four children. But all this was tarnished by the crushing burden of debt, caused by unlucky investments in the British East India Company and living beyond his means.[154] By February 1769, Monckton was so pressed by his obligations that the forty-three-year-old borrowed £4,550 and promised to pay his money leaders an annuity of £840 a year for the rest of his life. Even through Monckton proved able to honor this commitment, he was never able to get out of debt altogether. He died in 1782 in Portsmouth, leaving his wife in the care of his niece with an army pension of £50 a year.[155]

Military history both fascinates and frustrates because of its unique ability to change political circumstances, economic patterns, and social conditions with astonishing and capricious speed. One amended order, one wind shift, one bullet's trajectory can make the difference between catastrophe and triumph, permanence and ephemerality. Monckton seems to have appreciated this character of war, for it explains why he moved so methodically with the capture of Fort Beauséjour, why he used the element of surprise against the Acadians, and why he refused to endorse Rodney's plan to protect Jamaica. Monckton understood how much hung in the balance of each and every decision in a military campaign. Throughout his career, he moved purposefully and tenaciously to maximize his odds of success, while undercutting the sway of those uncertain elements he could not control.

---

[153] The court martial stemmed from a formal complaint by Major Colin Campbell, who charged Monckton with verbal and physical mistreatment of him during the Martinique campaign. For more information, see "Proceedings of a General Court Martial Held at the Judge Advocate's Office in the Horse Guards, on Saturday, the 14th, and Continued by Adjournment to Wednesday, the 18th April, 1764, for the Trial of a Charge Preferred by Colin Campbell, Esq., against the Honourable Major General Monckton," accessed January 17, 2020 https://archive.org/details/cihm_52430

[154] Steele, "Monckton, Robert."

[155] Cormack, "Observations on the Later Life of Lieutenant-General the Honourable Robert Monckton." Cormack states that Susannah was a member of the Dutch Reformed Church and that Monckton's three sons entered the British military. The oldest, William, left the army and returned home just before Monckton died; the second, John, died of disease in the Caribbean in 1781; and the third, Robert Philip, continued to serve in the military until his death around 1800. Cormack does not say what became of the daughter Elizabeth.

$\mathcal{N}$

Nguyễn Phúc Ánh

1762-1820

In the opening years of Nguyen Anh's life, no one in the royal family would have bet that the prince would become the founder of the first Vietnamese dynasty to rule both the Red River's fertile valley in the north and the Mekong River's vital delta in the south. No one held such ambitions for him because the odds—both historically and hereditarily—were so heavily stacked against him.

The first obstacle was that the political entity of "Vietnam" did not exist. Rather, what the Vietnamese called Dai Viet in the eighteenth century was dominated by two royal families: the Trinh in the north and the Nguyen in the center and south. Technically, an emperor of the Le Dynasty ruled over all of Dai Viet, but as with Go-Mizunoo and the shoguns, political, economic, and military power no longer rested in the emperor's hands.[1] This meant that Dai Viet was a divided land. The intermittent war the Trinh and Nguyen fought between 1627 and 1672 did not alter this situation, but the subsequent century of peace between the two families allowed the Nguyen to extend Vietnamese migration south toward the Gulf of Siam. This expansion at the expense of the Cham people and Cambodia helped the Nguyen-controlled part of Dai Viet to develop differently than its northern counterpart.[2] Specifically, the south became more commercially focused, was more politically connected to Siam and Cambodia, accepted Mahayana Buddhism, and was governed as a military state. This contrasted with the north, where the Trinh enhanced the role of Confucianism, expanded the role of the civil service examinations and the bureaucracy, and remained more agricultural.[3] Over time, these differences helped the south to

---

[1] Others have made the parallel to Japan in the same period. See, for example, Bruce Lockhart, "Re-assessing the Nguyễn Dynasty," *Crossroads: An Interdisciplinary Journal of Southeast Asian Studies*, Vol.15, No. 1 (2001), 9-53, EBSCOhost.

[2] Li Tana, *Nguyễn Cochinchina: Southern Vietnam in the Seventeenth and Eighteenth Centuries* (Ithaca, New York: Southeast Asia Program Publications, 1998), 11-13.

[3] George Dutton, *The Tây Sơn Uprising: Society and Rebellion in Eighteenth Century Vietnam* (Honolulu, Hawai'i: University of Hawai'i Press, 2006), 22-23 and Li, *Nguyễn Cochinchina*, 59, 71, 103-104. For the background on Mahayana Buddhism, see Chapter G. For the background on Confucianism, see Chapter K.

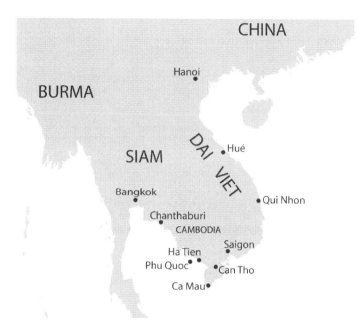

become more affluent than the north.[4] Therefore, when Nguyen Anh was born on February 8, 1762, even the notion of a single Vietnamese state was problematic.

The second obstacle to Nguyen Anh's becoming emperor over the entire crescent of Vietnamese land was that the Nguyen court did not follow the Chinese precept of favoring eldest sons strictly. Instead, the Vietnamese preferred that an adult male ascend the throne, even if the heir was a younger son, or if his mother was a concubine instead of the queen.[5] But this preference was not absolute, so royal succession could still be divisive. This was especially true in 1765, when Nguyen Anh's grandfather, Vo-vuong, died. Vo-vuong had been grooming his second-oldest son, Nguyen Anh's father, as his successor. But near the end of his life, Vo-vuong's will was changed, either by his decision or by his advisors' manipulations. The revised will broke with tradition and designated Vo-vuong's sixteenth son as heir.[6] With this change, Nguyen Anh went from being the young son of the heir apparent to the nephew of an eleven-year-old monarch. It looked like Nguyen Anh would grow up to be merely a minor member of the extended royal family.

The force which overcame this historical and hereditary equation was The Tay Son Uprising. It began in 1771, when a minor tax official and betel nut trader named Nhac could not provide the government with all of the tax proceeds he had been responsible for collecting. Rather than face punishment, Nhac fled to the western highlands where his two brothers, Huệ and Lu, joined him. Over the next two years, the three brothers gathered supporters, and by September 1773 the rebels were ready to make their first move against the Nguyen government. Nhac ordered his men to build a cage, place him inside, lock the cage, and surrender him to government officials in the walled city of Qui Nhon. His Trojan horse moment came when Nhac opened the cage in the middle of the night, killed several guards, and opened the city's gates to his awaiting army. The Tay Son rebels seized control of the provincial capital as the governor fled.[7] In subsequent years, they managed to control much of central Dai Viet.

---

[4] David Chandler, Norman G. Owen, William R. Roff, et al, *The Emergence of Modern Southeast Asia,* Norman G. Owen (ed.) (Honolulu, Hawai'i: University of Hawai'i Press, 2005), 108.

[5] C. Michele Thompson, "Jean Marie Despiau: Unjustly Maligned Physician in the Medical Service of the Nguyễn," *Vietnam and the West: New Approaches,* Wynn Wilcox (ed.) (Ithaca, New York: Cornell Southeast Asia Publications, 2010), 64-65.

[6] Alastair Lamb, *The Mandarin Road to Old Hué: Narratives of Anglo-Vietnamese Diplomacy from the 17th Century to the Eve of the French Conquest* (Hamden, Connecticut: Archon Books, 1970), 88-89.

[7] Dutton, *The Tây Sơn Uprising,* 39-41. Nhac, Huệ and Lu's family name was also Nguyen, but they were not related to Nguyen Anh. In the interest of clarity, I only refer to the brothers by their given name.

The Tay Son brothers attracted an eclectic group of followers, using charisma and propaganda to tap into a variety of social, economic, and political discontents. They flew red banners, evoking a color associated with local deities and the supernatural, and they exploited local legends, claiming to possess, for example, an invincible sword.[8] They also adopted a Robin Hood-type reputation. As a Catholic priest noted in 1774, the Tay Son brothers "appeared to desire equality for all" and the people came to see them as "virtuous and charitable thieves," who would seize "the most luxurious articles" in a wealthy home and distribute them "among the poor, keeping for themselves only rice and victuals."[9] Peasant support for the rebellion grew when new government policies increased their tax burden substantially. Merchants also supported the uprising because of their frustration over the significant decline in trade in southern Vietnamese ports in the late 1760s and early 1770s. These two economic issues were exacerbated by a lack of confidence in the currency in the wake of copper shortages, zinc coin substitutes, and a proliferation of counterfeiting.[10] Ethnic minority groups, including the Cham, the Chinese, and various highland tribes also joined the Tay Son Uprising in large numbers—many bitter over losing their independence as a result of the southward Nguyen expansion.

The critical Tay Son moment for Nguyen Anh came in 1777, when the rebel forces caught up with the retreating royal family in the Mekong River city of Can Tho. The Tay Son captured the king (Nguyen Anh's nephew) and escorted him and the royal family back to Saigon. In a ceremony to celebrate Tay Son's conquests and demonstrate the end of Nguyen rule, the Tay Son publicly beheaded the king and the rest of the royal family, including the women and children. For reasons that remain unclear, Nguyen Anh eluded being taken into custody in Can Tho, thus escaping the October 18 bloodbath.[11]

With his family dead and the Tay Son determined to hunt him down, Nguyen Anh desperately needed protection. He fled into the swamps of Ca Mau in far southeastern Dai Viet[12] and made his way to the port city of Ha Tien on the Vietnamese side of the Cambodian border. There, a man named Mac Thien Tu ruled a semi-autonomous, ethnically heterogeneous, and religiously tolerant fiefdom.[13] Because this fiefdom paid tributes to the Nguyen dynasty, Mac did not hesitate to assist its last surviving heir. Mac traveled to the Siamese[14] port of Chanthaburi and requested the assistance of a well-connected French bishop, Pierre Pigneau de Béhaine. The Bishop of Adran, who had established a seminary near Ha Tien in 1775, provided a ship and sailed to pick up Nguyen Anh. Pigneau arrived at the seminary just in time to save Nguyen Anh from the advancing Tay Son army. He took Nguyen Anh to Tho Chu, a small, far-offshore island in the Gulf of Siam.[15] It was on Tho Chu the bishop and the prince began to develop their fascinating relationship.

---

[8] Li, *Nguyễn Cochinchina*, 149, 152.

[9] Father Diego De Jumilla, quoted in Dutton, *The Tây Sơn Uprising*, 41.

[10] A new land registration system forced peasants to pay taxes on cultivated land they had previously been able to keep hidden, and the government imposed a flat head tax, which affected the peasants the most. As for trade, only sixteen foreign vessels visited the port of Hoi An in 1771, compared to 60-80 vessels in the 1740s. See Dutton, *The Tây Sơn Uprising*, 30-36.

[11] Nghia M. Vo, *Saigon: A History* (Jefferson, North Carolina, McFarland, 2011), 31.

[12] Dutton, *The Tây Sơn Uprising*, 44.

[13] Li Tana, "Mac Thien Tu (1700-1780)," *Southeast Asia, a Historical Encyclopedia from Angkor Wat to East Timor*, Volume 2 (Keat Gin Ooi, ed.) (Santa Barbara, California: ABC-CLIO, 2004), 806-807.

[14] Field Marshal Plaek Phibunsongkhram changed the name of the country from Siam to Thailand in 1939.

[15] Nguyen Phut Tan, *A Modern History of Viet-nam (1802-1954)* (Saigon, Vietnam: Khai-Trí, 1964), 27. In some accounts the island is called Pulau Panjang because this was its eighteenth-century European place name. This

   In late 1777, both Pigneau and Nguyen Anh were in a weak position and needed one another. The Bishop of Adran initially offered to help the prince because he saw the fifteen-year-old's plight as an opportunity to further the expansion of Catholicism among the Vietnamese, while helping to fight Protestant encroachment in the region.[16] If Nguyen Anh were restored to power, Pigneau believed that he could build a Catholic center in the south to compete with the strong Jesuit-based community in northern Dai Viet.[17] For his part, Nguyen Anh saw how much he could benefit from foreign aid as he sought his revenge against the Tay Son, but he also understood that the risks and consequences of foreign assistance. As the two exiles got to know each other, they danced: occasionally beguiling, occasionally guarded, they both wanted to demonstrate trustworthiness and reliability, but they both needed to protect their own interests as well. During their conversations, the bishop introduced Catholicism to the prince, but the issue of ancestor worship quickly interfered. Pigneau saw the Confucian ritual as idolatrous,[18] but given the massacre of the royal family, Nguyen Anh refused to abandon a practice he had been taught to cherish. Indeed, the prince argued that there was something inherently wrong with Christianity if it did not value honoring one's deceased relatives. Pigneau said Christianity most certainly did, just not in the same way. This helped the two to find a workable compromise.[19] With the passage of time, the prince and the bishop eventually developed a fierce loyalty to and respect for one another.

   In late 1777, Nguyen Anh learned that the Tay Son had moved the bulk of their troops to central Dai Viet to protect against a Trinh invasion from the north. The prince returned to the mainland in early 1778 to try to take advantage of the situation and raised an army of Cambodian mercenaries and a navy of Chinese pirates. These forces attacked undermanned Tay Son garrisons, and after a series of quick victories Nguyen Anh captured Saigon and established control over several surrounding provinces. He rallied those loyal to his family, established an administrative structure to govern, and held control over Saigon and the Mekong delta region for the next four years. Then, in 1780, the eighteen-year-old proclaimed himself king of Cochinchina.[20] The Tay Son could not permit this, and in May 1782 they returned

---

identification is not to be confused with the island off the coast of Java called Pulau Panjang today. As the Bishop of Adran, Pigneau was *in partibus infidelibus:* he was the head of a diocese that was not actually in Catholic control. The diocese of Adran was controlled by the Ottoman Empire in the eighteenth century.

[16] James P. Daughton, "Recasting Pigneau de Béhaine: Missionaries and the Policies of French Colonial History, 1894-1914," *Việt Nam: Borderless Histories*, Nhung Tuyet Tran and Anthony Reid (ed.) (Madison, Wisconsin: University of Wisconsin Press, 2006), 291.

[17] Pigneau was a member of the Séminaire des Missions Étrangères (M.E.P.), which bitterly competed with the Jesuits for influence in Vietnam. In the 1780s, there were as many as 400,000 Catholics in the north, but no more than 15,000 in the south, and Pigneau desperately wanted to change that imbalance when he met Nguyen Anh. See Charles Keith, *Catholic Vietnam: A Church from Empire to Nation* (Berkeley, California: University of California Press, 2012), 19.

[18] Joseph Buttinger, *The Smaller Dragon: A Political History of Vietnam* (New York: Frederick A. Praeger, 1958), 262.

[19] Vo, *Saigon,* 34.

[20] Buttinger, *The Smaller Dragon,* 235.

with a vengeance. As brothers Nhac and Huệ arrived in Saigon with the troops from a hundred ships, Nguyen Anh fled to Phu Quoc Island just off the coast from Ha Tien. Meanwhile, the Tay Son forces besieged Saigon's citadel, burned a sizable portion of the city, and massacred more than 10,000 Chinese residents as punishment for the Chinese community's shift of allegiance and increased support for Nguyen Anh.[21] Nhac and Huệ also hoped to destroy the commercial monopoly of these Chinese settlers.[22] Despite this victory, Nhac and Huệ did not stay in southern Dai Viet very long. They were worried about straying too far from their home base in central Dai Viet, and they always faced the challenge of having to fight a two-front war. Therefore, the Tay Son brothers once again left a garrison in Saigon and returned north. This allowed Nguyen Anh to retake Saigon in October 1782. The Tay Son responded with another invasion early in 1783, which again destroyed the Nguyen army and forced the king to flee. This time the Tay Son pursued him toward Phu Quoc island, but a storm obliterated the Tay Son navy and allowed Nguyen Anh to escape. The king's second exile to Phu Quoc, his third to the Gulf of Siam, forced him to recognize that he needed foreign aid to defeat the Tay Son. Rather than look to a Western power, he traveled to Bangkok and met with Siam's new king, Rama I, in spring 1784. Rama I provided Nguyen Anh with 20,000 men and 300 galleys, but as the fleet approached Saigon, the Tay Son were prepared for the attack. They destroyed the Siamese fleet in the Saigon River estuary and killed all but one thousand of the Siamese soldiers.[23] This devastating defeat forced Nguyen Anh to return to Bangkok for a second time as a refugee and guest of Rama I.

Nguyen Anh spent the next three years in Siam. During this formative period, Nguyen Anh learned what it meant to be a monarch of a unified state and what it meant to defeat an army instead of a garrison. Both of these lessons came courtesy of Rama I, who was thirty-five years older than Nguyen Anh. The Siamese monarch had come to power in a *coup d'état* in 1782 and after just two years of rule could point to a number of accomplishments. Fifteen days into his reign, Rama I ordered the capital to be moved to the eastern bank of the Chao Phraya River to protect from Burmese invasions, to alleviate erosion, and to ease overcrowding for the court. By the time Nguyen Anh arrived in Bangkok for the first time in 1784, Rama's new city looked like a capital, with an impressive canal system, an expansive palace compound, a formal audience hall, and elaborate monasteries and temples.[24] Rama I also acted decisively when he issued religious laws designed to restore discipline and dignity to Buddhist monks. He wanted to reestablish the sanctity of the Buddhist monkhood and renew spiritual purity in the wake of what he saw as his predecessor's corrupt practices. He did so by asserting the value of ancient texts[25] and by convening a Buddhist council to revise the Buddhist canon—a enterprise not attempted since 1475.[26] By watching these moves, as well as through Rama I's restructuring of the Siamese bureaucracy, Nguyen Anh beheld an influential model for kingly leadership.

[21] Dutton, *The Tây Sơn Uprising*, 45.

[22] Buttinger, *The Smaller Dragon*, 264.

[23] Dutton, *The Tây Sơn Uprising*, 45-46.

[24] B. J. Terwiel, *A History of Modern Thailand, 1767-1942* (St. Lucia, Queensland: University of Queensland Press, 1983), 72-73, 78.

[25] David K. Wyatt, *Thailand: A Short History* (New Haven, Connecticut: Yale University Press, 1984), 146-147.

[26] Barbara Watson Andaya and Yoneo Ishii, "Religious Developments in Southeast Asia, c. 1500-1800," *The Cambridge History of Southeast Asia, Volume 1, from Early Times to c. 1800*, Nicholas Tarling (ed.) (Cambridge, U.K.: Cambridge University Press, 1992), 566.

Nguyen Anh also gained important military experience during the Burma-Siam War of 1785-1786. The Burmese king, Bodawpaya, drafted a bold plan to attack five areas with over 100,000 troops simultaneously, thereby trying to prevent Rama I from being able to launch an effective defense. According to the plan, the first army was to cross the border in northern Siam, capture Lampang and sweep south to Phitsanulok; the second was to capture Tak and proceed south to Bangkok; the third, led by Bodawpaya himself, was to cross the Three Pagoda Pass and descend on Kanchanaburi and Bangkok from the west; the fourth, departing from Tavoy, and fifth, departing from Mergui, were to capture peninsular Siam, preventing Rama I's tributary states* in the south from providing reinforcements.[27] When Rama I learned of the Burmese preparations in late 1784, he began planning his defense, and Nguyen Anh offered the support of his troops. Once the invasion began, Nguyen Anh's force engaged the Burmese army that departed Tavoy,[28] and performed well,[29] demonstrating to Nguyen Anh and his troops that they possessed the wherewithal to win. As a commander, he also learned that the key to a campaign rested more in controlling personnel than in gaining territory.[30] An outbreak of smallpox and a host of supply issues compromised the Burmese effort in 1785,[31] but a second attempt in 1786 fared no better. In the two-year war, the Burmese army lost some 80,000 men,[32] and Burma was forced to recognize Siam's status as an independent state.[33]

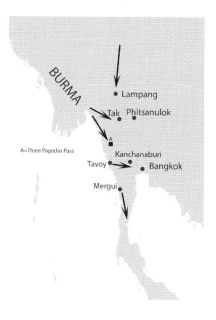

During this period, Nguyen Anh also asked Pigneau, the Bishop of Adran, for his help in obtaining French aid. In early December 1784, Nguyen Anh drafted a letter to "the Great King of Occident" asking for "the necessary relief required for the restoration of my kingdom." Nguyen Anh also asked his royal council to approve a resolution which 1) recognized the need for foreign assistance to defeat the Tay Son; 2) sanctioned Pigneau to negotiate on the Dai Viet's behalf; 3) requested troops, supporting artillery, and ships; 4) authorized the transfer of two sites over which "the King of France will have full sovereignty"; and 5) permitted free trade on all goods between the two nations. Because these were such significant concessions in the minds of the Vietnamese, the council warned Pigneau to negotiate in such a way that any treaty "stipulations will not damage the

---

[27] David K. Wyatt, *Thailand: A Short History* (New Haven, Connecticut: Yale University Press, 1984), 149. Tavoy is now known as Dawei, and Mergui is now known as Myeik.
[28] Thanyathip Sripana, "Tracing Ho Chi Minh's Sojourn in Siam," *Southeast Asian Studies*, 2, no. 3 (December 2013), 527-558, ProQuest Central.
[29] Peter A. Poole, *The Vietnamese in Thailand: A Historical Perspective* (Ithaca, New York: Cornell University Press, 1970), 33.
[30] K. W. Taylor, "Surface Orientations in Vietnam: Beyond Histories of Nation and Region," *The Journal of Asian Studies*, 57, 4 (November, 1998), 949-978, ProQuest Central.
[31] Barbara Watson and Leonard Y. Andaya, *A History of Early Modern Southeast Asia, 1400-1830* (New York: Cambridge University Press, 2015), 314.
[32] Judith L. Richell, *Disease and Demography in Colonial Burma* (Singapore: NUS Press, 2006), 11.
[33] Terwiel, *A History of Modern Thailand, 1767-1942*, 85.

interests" of Dai Viet.[34] To ensure that the bishop would have the proper credentials and credibility, Nguyen Anh gave Pigneau the Royal Seal and entrusted him with the care of his four-year old son, Prince Canh.

Pigneau's embassy landed in Pondicherry, India in February 1785 to discuss the Vietnamese plan with the leading officials in France's Asian headquarters. The Vietnamese proposal was not well received by the newly-arrived governor general, François de Souillac, who wrote that it was "contrary to the interests of France" and "was difficult to be undertaken with any success" anyway.[35] General Coutenceau des Algrains added that there was no reason for France to "indulge herself in such a dream."[36] The general believed that French help would not make a substantial difference since Nguyen Anh had been fighting for eight years without any sustained success. He concluded that the king must either be "without great ability" or "not loved by his subjects."[37] In either case, French military involvement for unclear commercial gains seemed ill-conceived. Discouraged but not resigned, Pigneau pursued alternatives and bided his time. He wrote to the Portuguese to see if they might be interested, and he welcomed the news that both de Souillac and Countenceau would not remain in Pondicherry long. When their replacements arrived, Pigneau pressed his case anew. He found the new officials far more well-disposed to the Vietnamese proposal, but so new to their jobs that they were unwilling to make such an important commitment without consulting with Versailles. Having already spent fifteen months in India, Pigneau felt that it was senseless to wait there any longer. He decided to take Nguyen Anh's case directly to Versailles himself. In June 1786, the bishop, Prince Canh, and their entourage set sail for France aboard *Le Malabar*. The ship arrived in France the following January.[38]

~

In late December 1786, France stood at the edge of bankruptcy. The situation was so bleak that Louis XVI met with one of his administrative councils on December 29 and announced that as a result of the fiscal crisis facing the nation, he "intended to convene an assembly of the most qualified persons," where he would "communicate to them his intentions in regard to the relief of his people, the ordering of his finances, and the reform of several abuses."[39] Louis XVI's decision to call the Assembly of Notables marked a critical turning point in the history of the Bourbon monarchy.

The causes of France's fiscal crisis were complex. The nation still had lingering obligations from the Seven Years' War (1756-1763) and it had borrowed almost 1.3 billion *livres* to finance French participation in the American Revolution, but these debts alone did not constitute a fiscal cataclysm. Great Britain held debt of the same size, and it spent far more of its tax revenue servicing

---

[34] Nguyen Anh quoted in Nguyen Phut Tan, *A Modern History of Viet-nam (1802-1954)* (Saigon, Vietnam: Khai-Trí, 1964), 43-45. The two sites were Côn Sơn Island (Poulo Condore) in the South China Sea and the port of Hội An (Tourane) on the central Vietnam coast.

[35] François de Souillac quoted in Nguyen, *A Modern History of Viet-nam (1802-1954)*, 47.

[36] Coutenceau des Algrains quoted in Nguyen, *A Modern History of Viet-nam (1802-1954)*, 47.

[37] Coutenceau des Algrains quoted in Lamb, *The Mandarin Road to Old Hué*, 142.

[38] Nguyen, *A Modern History of Viet-nam (1802-1954)*, 48-49. The Portuguese did respond favorably, offering to send 56 warships from Goa, but by the time this news had been presented to Nguyen Anh for approval, Pigneau had already left Pondicherry for France.

[39] Louis XVI quoted in Claude Manceron, *Age of the French Revolution, Volume 4: Toward the Brink*, Nancy Amphoux (trans.) (New York: Simon & Schuster, Inc., 1989), 387.

that debt than France did.[40] The difficulty for France rested in three major factors. The first was that France paid a much higher interest rate on its debt than the British did because France, unlike other nations, did not guarantee its bonds. It also had a history of partial defaults, creating greater risk for investors. The penalty for that risk was an interest rate of 4.8% to 6.5%, instead of the 3% to 3.5% the British paid.[41] The second complication was that France signed a free trade agreement with Great Britain in 1786 without providing sufficient transitional support for French industry. British goods flooded the French market, causing as much as a fifty percent drop in production in the manufacturing city of Lille in the late 1780s.[42] The corresponding rise in unemployment stirred considerable resentment. As Englishman Arthur Young stated when he visited Lille in 1787, "the manufacturers will not speak of [the Treaty] with any patience; they wish for nothing but a war," for they believed that a renewed conflict with Great Britain was the only means of escaping ruin. Similarly, Young noted that manufacturers in the city of Beauvais described the treaty as "most pernicious," while the "very respectable commercial gentlemen" in Nantes "were loud against it."[43] The third financial complication France faced was speculation. The end of the American Revolution in 1783 produced a surge in speculative capital, much of it from foreign investors. The French government used this capital to obtain additional credit, exacerbating its problems.   In addition, the 1785 reconstitution of the French East India Company led to wild speculation on the company's shares as investors shared exaggerated expectations about the profit the postwar world would create.[44] When it became known that the company was actually purchasing goods from the British East India Company, instead of from India directly, the French company's stock collapsed. Louis XVI's finance minister Charles Alexandre de Calonne attempted to stop the spiral and prop up the company by secretly buying its shares, but this too became known.[45] The government ended up losing 25 million *livres* in the fiasco.[46] All told, the high interest rates, the unforeseen consequences of the free trade treaty, and the frenzy of speculative investment combined to produce conditions that traditional *ancien regime** solutions could not ameliorate. As Calonne wrote, "It is impossible to tax further, ruinous to be always borrowing, and not enough to confine ourselves to economical reforms."[47] Something had to give.

     After considerable hesitation, Louis XVI called for a meeting of the Assembly of Notables, a noble advisory body that had not met in 161 years. News of the royal decision produced considerable buzz in the salons and cafés of Paris.[48] These rumors and conversations were so electric, they raised national expectations about the possibility of sharing political power.[49] Louis

---

[40] Simon Schama, *Citizens: A Chronicle of the French Revolution* (New York: Alfred A. Knopf, 1989), 62, 65.

[41] Lynn Hunt, "The Global Financial Origins of 1789," *The French Revolution in Global Perspective*, Susanne Desan, Linda Hunt and William Max Wilson (ed.) (Ithaca, New York: Cornell University Press, 2013), 33-34.

[42] Charles Walton, "The Fall from Eden: The Free-Trade Origins of the French Revolution," *The French Revolution in Global Perspective*, Susanne Desan, Linda Hunt and William Max Wilson (ed.) (Ithaca, New York: Cornell University Press, 2013), 49.

[43] Arthur Young, *Travels in France During the Years 1787, 1788, and 1789*, Jeffery Kaplow (ed.) (Garden City, New York: Anchor Books, 1969), 409-410.

[44] Hunt, "The Global Financial Origins of 1789," 39-40, 43.

[45] Walton, "The Fall from Eden," 47-48. Calonne served as finance minister from November 1783 to May 1787.

[46] Hunt, "The Global Financial Origins of 1789," 40.

[47] Charles Alexandre de Calonne quoted in William Doyle, *The Oxford History of the French Revolution*, 2nd ed., (New York: Oxford University Press, 2002), 69.

[48] Manceron, *Age of the French Revolution, Volume 4*, 389.

[49] Manceron, *Age of the French Revolution, Volume 4*, 388.

had no such intentions when he convened the 144 Notables on February 22, 1787 at Versailles. He simply wanted a rubber stamp that would not threaten the perception of French Absolutism.* The Assembly was composed of seven royal princes, 14 high-ranking clerics, 36 nobles of the sword, 38 nobles of the robe, 25 town leaders, 12 representatives of the Third Estate, and 12 counselors of state.[50] No more than five of these men lacked an aristocratic background of some sort.[51] At the opening session, Calonne revealed for the first time the true state of France's budget: the royal treasury collected 475 million *livres* a year in taxes but spent 600 million.[52] This news came as a shock to the Notables, who had little awareness of the government's fiscal problems. Indeed, as far as they knew, all was well: former finance minister Jacques Necker had published a report in February 1781 showing that ordinary government revenues exceeded ordinary government expenditures by 10 million *livres*. France appeared to have a surplus. But Necker had not provided any information on the extraordinary accounts where all the war expenditures were recorded.[53] For six years everyone had been operating under false assumptions. Calonne's proposed remedy to the fiscal crisis was threefold: 1) to replace the nation's convoluted system of taxes, internal tariffs, and exemptions with a new, uniform land tax paid by all subjects; 2) to provide for locally elected assemblies that would assess and administer the tax in order to eliminate fraudulent practices; and 3) to institute a tax paid in cash to replace the *corvée*, which required peasants to provide labor service for roads and other public works. These were radical ideas.[54] Calonne believed that if the old taxes were replaced by more egalitarian ones, the government could weather its financial difficulties and the monarchy would be strengthened as a result. Significantly, the majority of Notables were inclined to support Calonne's ideas, at least initially. They affirmed the idea of tax equity and were willing to forsake their historical privileges because they had come to believe that their economic interests could be better served by a more rational tax structure.[55] Such was the powerful influence of the Enlightenment.*

But what could have been a harmonious, productive gathering turned sour quickly. As the Notables met in sub-committees, their discussions lost focus, and their group identity became stronger. They began to emerge as something other than Louis' subservient sheep. Calonne resented this and made the mistake of printing a pamphlet for popular consumption that criticized the Notables as "rich egotists" not paying their fair share.[56] This hurt Calonne's standing at court, which helped Louis XVI's queen, Marie Antoinette, maneuver for one of her favorites to replace him as finance minister. Louis XVI fired Calonne on April 8 and installed the queen's choice,

[50] Manceron, *Age of the French Revolution, Volume 4,* 397-398. The nobles of the sword were from families that had held noble title for generations. The nobles of the robe were from families that had purchased their noble title. The Third Estate was the term used to designate those who were not noblemen of either type or members of the clergy.
[51] Vivian R. Gruder, *Notables and the Nation: The Political Schooling of the French, 1787-1788* (Cambridge, Massachusetts: Harvard University Press, 2007), 12.
[52] Claude Manceron, *Age of the French Revolution, Volume 5: Blood of the Bastille,* Nancy Amphoux (trans.) (New York: Simon & Schuster, Inc., 1989), 42.
[53] Doyle, *The Oxford History of the French Revolution,* 67. Necker served as finance minister between late June 1777 and mid-May 1781. He also served a second term between late August 1788 and July 11, 1789.
[54] Schama, *Citizens,* 242.
[55] Gruder, *Notables and the Nation,* 38. Not all historians share this assessment of the disposition of the Notables. Some see the body as offering their support only to deceive public opinion. See, for example, Michael P. Fitzsimmons, *The Remaking of France: The National Assembly and the Constitution of 1791* (New York: Cambridge University Press, 1994), 7.
[56] Charles Alexandre de Calonne quoted in Schama, *Citizens,* 245.

Étienne Charles de Loménie de Brienne, the Archbishop of Toulouse.[57] By the third week in May 1787, the more radical Notables, including the Marquis de Lafayette, were calling for a meeting of a truly representational national assembly. Such talk caused Louis to adjourn the Assembly of Notables on May 25 without Calonne's tax plan, or any other alternative, having been approved. This adjournment, and the inability to the Crown to manage France's finances that the adjournment represented, marked the first stage of the political crisis that culminated in the French Revolution.[58]

~

Pigneau and the now seven-year-old Prince Canh arrived in France in February 1787—just in time to experience all of this economic and political turmoil. They made their way from the port of Lorient to Paris, where the bishop gathered news and launched his campaign in the influential salons of the city to woo support for French intervention on behalf of Nguyen Anh. Once well-informed and well-rehearsed, he headed to Versailles to request an audience with Louis XVI.

Versailles was both remarkably open and rigidly exclusive. On the one hand, commoners could come and go through much of the palace as they wanted, but on the other hand, permission to enter certain rooms at particular times was a coveted privilege. As Arthur Young noted that same spring, "the whole palace, except the chapel, seems to be open to all the world; we pushed through an amazing crowd of all sorts of people…many of them not very well-dressed, whence it appears, that no questions are asked." Conversely, it was also clear that the guards at "the door of the apartment in which the King dined, made a distinction, and would not permit all to enter promiscuously." Gradations of distinction were made in personal interactions. Young noticed how Marie Antoinette received people with "a variety of expression[s]. On some she smiled; to others she talked; a few seemed to have the honour of being more in her intimacy. Her return to some was formal and to others distant."[59] Indeed, Versailles retained the character its creator, Louis XIV, intended—a time when

> Frequent fetes, private walks…and excursions were means which the King seized upon in order to single out or to mortify [individuals] by naming the persons who should be there each time, and in order to keep each person assiduous and attentive to pleasing him. He sensed that he lacked by far enough favors to distribute in order to create a continuous effect. Therefore he substituted imaginary favors for real ones.[60]

For Pigneau this meant he had to establish a standing within Versailles' social hierarchy. His two decades of travel and missionary work in Asia gave him a distinguishing novelty and an element of intrigue; the bishop also had with him a more impressive contrivance: the young Vietnamese prince. Dressed in a red silk jacket with gold pompoms and a decidedly un-Vietnamese red Hindu

---

[57] Étienne Charles de Loménie de Brienne served as finance minister from early May 1787 to late August 1788.
[58] Doyle, *The Oxford History of the French Revolution*, 74-75.
[59] Young, *Travels in France*, 11-12.
[60] Louis de Rouvroy, Duke of Saint-Simon, quoted in *The Century of Louis XIV*, Orest and Patricia Ranum (eds.) (New York: Walker and Company, 1972), 81.

turban, Prince Canh became an "Orientalized" sensation.[61] Since he was able to speak charming French, the ladies of the court soon adopted him, and Marie Antoinette bestowed her approval by allowing him to play with her son, the *dauphin*.* This resulted in more tributes, including the composition of a hymn in the Vietnamese prince's honor. It also called for the creation of a new hairstyle, *le chignon à la cochinchinoise*, by the queen's hairdresser, Léonard, who frequently commemorated special events with a new coiffure.[62] Versailles' residents enjoyed such frivolous distractions since they allowed the court, however briefly, to forget the crisis made clear at the Assembly of Notables.

Pigneau and Canh's positive reception by the court, including the endorsement of finance minister Brienne, allowed the bishop to obtain an audience with Louis XVI.[63] On May 6, 1787, Pigneau made his case for helping Nguyen Anh. He argued that intervening in Dai Viet would allow France to secure fortified positions in Indochina from which France would be able to "dominate the seas of China" and "all commerce in this part of the world."[64] In other words, the excellent natural harbors of Dai Viet offered France the best opportunity to challenge British dominance in Asia.[65] Pigneau specifically asked for 1,500 men, seven ships, supporting artillery, Western medicine, food, supplies, and engineering tools.[66] The king and his advisors seemed amicable to the proposal, but announced that they would need to deliberate before making a final decision. Pigneau expected this, but he didn't expect that he would have to wait for seven months before receiving the royal answer.

The reason for the long delay was that France's economic and political upheavals repeatedly caused the concluding negotiations with Pigneau to be postponed. Other issues in mid-1787 were simply more pressing. A troubling civil war in the Dutch Republic pitted republicans against

---

[61] This was a precursor to the nineteenth-century attitude described by Edward W. Said. See Said, *Orientalism* (New York: Vintage Books, 1994), 42.

[62] Stanley Karnow, *Vietnam, A History: The First Complete Account of the War in Vietnam* (New York: Penguin Books, 1984), 55; Louis Henrique, *Les colonies françaises : notices illustrées III. Colonies et protectorats d'Indo-Chine: Cochinchine. Cambodge. Annam. Tonkin* (Paris: Maison Quantin, 1890), 7; Charles-Albert de Moré Pontgibaud, *Mémoires du Comte de Moré: 1758-1837* (Paris, Alphonse Picard, 1898), 119. Other examples of Léonard's work for special occasions included Marie Antoinette's attending the opera with the prince of Sweden in 1771, the arrival of a comet in 1773, and the encouraging progress of the War of American Independence in 1780. See Léonard, *Recollections of Léonard, Hairdresser to Queen Marie-Antoinette*, E. Jules Méras (trans.) (New York: Sturgis & Walton Company, 1909), 94-97, 139, 190.

[63] Nguyen, *A Modern History of Viet-nam (1802-1954)*, 52.

[64] Pierre Pigneau de Béhaine quoted in Buttinger, *The Smaller Dragon*, 238.

[65] Lamb, *The Mandarin Road to Old Hué*, 142.

[66] Buttinger, *The Smaller Dragon*, 263.

royalists, the Americans were convening a constitutional convention in Philadelphia, and most important for the Bourbon monarchy, the appellate court in Paris, the *Parlement*, had become obstinate. According to legal tradition, all royal decrees had to be formally registered with the *Parlement* before they became law. The court could not refuse to register royal decrees, but it could delay their enforcement by asking for clarifications and by making suggestions for revisions. Since twenty-one members of the Paris *Parlement* had served in the hastily dissolved Assembly of Notables, this court was well positioned to thwart royal desires. When Louis XVI presented his tax proposals in July, the *Parlement* boldly refused to register the tax increases until the government made its financial accounts public. The king refused to do this, stating the court had no vetting prerogatives over royal finances.[67] The *Parlement* responded by calling for a meeting of the Estates-General, the legislative body that had not met since 1614; it argued that only the Estates-General could authorize new taxes, and that the "constitutional principle of the French monarchy was that taxes should be consented to by those who had to bear them."[68] This was revolutionary language. The crown responded by quickly taking steps to suppress the spread of such thinking. In August, it exiled the Paris *Parlement* to the city of Troyes, closed print shops and clubs, and assigned police patrols to monitor the city's streets around the clock in an effort to maintain order. These steps did little to change the actual mood in Paris.[69] Englishman Arthur Young sensed this when he wrote in October, "one opinion pervaded the whole company, that they are on the eve of some great revolution in the government" and that everything points to it, from the great confusion surrounding the finances and the deficit, to a king "with excellent dispositions, but without the resources of a mind that could govern in such a moment," from "a court buried in pleasure and dissipation," to "a great ferment amongst all ranks of men, who are eager for some change."[70]

The tug-of-war between the Crown and the Paris *Parlement* culminated on November 19, when finance minister Brienne asked the court to authorize borrowing 420 million *livres* between 1788 and 1792 to pay off short term debts in exchange for cuts to the expenditures of the royal household, the bureaucracy, and the armed forces. Calonne's vision for a new tax structure was dead. The *Parlement* seemed ready to register Louis XVI's budget edicts, but after eight hours of discussion with repeated references to the Estates-General, Louis became frustrated and ordered the *Parlement* to register the loans. All of the day's good will evaporated in stunned silence until the king's cousin, the Duke d'Orleans, stood up, and said, "I beg Your Majesty to allow me to place at your feet and in the heart of his court [the view] that I consider this registration illegal."[71] Dumbfounded, Louis stuttered, "I don't care...it's up to you...yes...it's legal because I wish it."[72] The stage for the final struggle between the monarchy and republicanism had been set.

---

[67] Doyle, *The Oxford History of the French Revolution*, 76-77.
[68] Statement by *Parlement* quoted in Schama, *Citizens*, 264.
[69] Doyle, *The Oxford History of the French Revolution*, 77; and Schama, *Citizens*, 265.
[70] Young, *Travels in France*, 74-75.
[71] Duke d'Orleans quoted in Schama, *Citizens*, 267. William Doyle notes that the Duke d'Orleans was the "head of the junior branch of the royal family and heir to a long tradition of obstructionism." See Doyle, *The Oxford History of the French Revolution*, 80.
[72] Louis XVI quoted in Doyle, *The Oxford History of the French Revolution*, 80. Louis mean to say "it's not up to you."

~

On November 28, 1787, Pigneau signed a treaty with the French minister of foreign affairs, Armand Marc, Comte de Montmorin de Saint-Herem. The treaty acknowledged Nguyen Anh's plight, "having been dispossessed of his states and needing to employ an armed force to cover them." It recognized that Louis XVI was "convinced of the justice of this prince's cause and wishing to give him a sign to indicate his friendship as well as his love of justice, is determined to respond favorably to this request" for aid. The treaty stipulated that

> His Very Christian Majesty…will immediately send to the coasts of Cochinchina and, at his own expense, four frigates, along with the body of troops of 1,200 infantrymen, 200 artillerymen and 250 [non-European soldiers]. These troops will be supplied with all their articles of war, particularly artillery appropriate to these campaigns.

In exchange, "the king of Cochinchina will eventually cede to…the crown of France the absolute control of and sovereignty over the island that forms the principal port of Cochinchina called Hoi Nan [Hoi An]" and to "ensure the suitability of the above-named port…the French will be permitted to make on the mainland all the establishments that they judge necessary." The French also took "control of and sovereignty over the island of Poulo Condore" and were guaranteed "complete liberty to engage in commerce in all lands of the king of Cochinchina, to the exclusion of all other European nations." Louis' subjects were permitted to "travel freely" with a passport, "import all kinds of merchandise from your and other parts of the world," and "export all the resources and merchandise of the country and the neighboring countries, without exception." Moreover, the French did not have to pay any import or export duties "except for those normally assessed on local persons." Finally, Dai Viet also agreed that if the

> very Christian King is attacked or threatened by any power, regardless of what this power might be…the king of Cochinchina commits to send him aid in the form of soldiers, sailors, supplies, vessels, and galleys. This assistance shall be furnished three months after being requested, but it shall not be employed beyond the islands of the Molucccas or the Straits of Sunda.[73]

Interestingly, there was no mention in the treaty about Catholicism or the free practice of religion. It was strictly a military-commercial agreement.

In an addendum to the treaty, Pigneau promised that the Vietnamese would "undertake the expenses resulting from the establishment of fortresses, garrisons, hospitals, warehouses, and lodging units for the commanding officers."[74] This was a significant and expensive concession, but Pigneau had to agree to it order to obtain French assistance. Given France's fiscal state, there would not have been any treaty otherwise.

Pigneau left France with Prince Canh in December 1787, believing that he had accomplished his mission: he had obtained the aid Nguyen Anh thought necessary to defeat the Tay Son. But Pigneau

---

[73] "Treaty of Versailles Between Nguyen Anh and King Louis XVI (1787)," George Dutton (trans.), *Sources of Vietnamese Tradition*, George E. Dutton, Jayne S. Werner and John K. Whitmore (eds.) (New York: Columbia University Press, 2012), 219-222.

[74] Treaty Addendum quoted in Nguyen, *A Modern History of Viet-nam (1802-1954)*, 57.

didn't realize that he also carried a letter which would be his mission's undoing. This letter from the minister of foreign affairs, Montmorin, was addressed to the new governor of Pondicherry, an Irishman in Louis XVI's service named Thomas Conway. In it, Montmorin gave Conway the authority to veto the treaty if he believed it not to be in France's best interest.[75] Because Conway was opposed to any further French expansion in Asia, the disposition of the treaty was a forgone conclusion before Pigneau arrived in Pondicherry in May 1788. Pigneau sent a futile appeal back to Versailles, but he had been duped by Montmorin and no aid would be forthcoming. Pigneau's loyalty to Nguyen Anh would not allow him to return empty-handed, and so the bishop began to raise the necessary men, ships, and equipment in India on his own. It took a year, but on June 19, 1789, Pigneau's chartered ships sailed for Dai Viet.[76]

Pigneau and Prince Canh arrived to find a changed political situation, with the Tay Son having assumed a different character than their altruistic origins of the mid-1770s. By the late-1780s, its leaders had fallen victim to an arrogance that so often accompanies a rise to power. They did not provide peasants with a reduction of either taxes or forced labor, dashing their hopes and undermining their trust.[77] They undertook no fundamental restructuring of the society, perpetuating the problems that existed before their uprising.[78] They took retribution against Buddhist monasteries, destroying temples, forcing monks become soldiers, and melting down sacred bells for arms.[79] They destroyed Christian churches and drafted male Christians into the Tay Son army.[80] They forced children and the elderly to serve on work crews and issued identity cards to monitor population movements.[81] Additionally, the three Tay Son brothers fought among themselves. Between February and June 1787, Nhac, Huệ, and Lu developed an intense, mutual jealousy that turned violent. Although the three eventually came to terms, the egotism of the regime symbolically culminated with Huệ declaring himself emperor of Dai Viet in 1788.[82] By the early 1790s some in the new Tay Son Dynasty-ruled areas that were praying for a victory by Nguyen Anh's forces to provide relief.[83]

The difference in the political situation wasn't only a result of Tay Son problems. Nguyen Anh was also working from a position of greater strength. By summer 1789, he had recruited a multicultural entourage of experts to assist him in conquering Dai Viet. He named a Chinese pirate as his first admiral, chose a Cambodian to be an army commander, and hired Portuguese mercenaries to fight alongside Vietnamese troops. Lest the agreement with the French fall through,

---

[75] Lamb, *The Mandarin Road to Old Hué*, 143-144.
[76] Buttinger, *The Smaller Dragon*, 239.
[77] Buttinger, *The Smaller Dragon*, 240, 265.
[78] J. Kathirithamby-Wells, "The Age of Transition: The Mid-Eighteenth to the Early Nineteenth Centuries," *The Cambridge History of Southeast Asia, Volume 1, from Early Times to c. 1800*, Nicholas Tarling (ed.) (Cambridge, U.K.: Cambridge University Press, 1992), 589.
[79] Dinh Minh Chi, Ly Kim Hoa, Ha Thuc Minh, et al, *The History of Buddhism in Vietnam* (Washington, DC: The Council for Research in Values and Philosophy, 2008), 212.
[80] Dutton, *The Tây Sơn Uprising*, 188. Wynn Wilcox argues, however, that the Tay Son were not as anti-Catholic as typically portrayed. He says that only Nhac persecuted Christians. See Wynn Wilcox, "Transnationalism and Multiethnicity in the Early Nguyễn Phúc Ánh Gia Long Period," *Việt Nam: Borderless Histories*, Nhung Tuyet Tran and Anthony J. S. Reid (ed.) (Madison, Wisconsin: University of Wisconsin Press, 2006), 202.
[81] Dutton, *The Tây Sơn Uprising*, 128, 140.
[82] Dutton, *The Tây Sơn Uprising*, 47-48. Huệ, who was a brilliant general, felt entitled to declare himself emperor after capturing Hanoi from the Trinh in 1786 and after having defeated a Chinese army of 200,000 men in 1788.
[83] Dutton, *The Tây Sơn Uprising*, 168.

Nguyen Anh negotiated an agreement with Portugal to obtain military assistance in exchange for trading rights, territorial concessions, and tolerance of Christianity. He also purchase supplies and ammunition from Chinese, Dutch, English, and Spanish ports, and used a Portuguese captain to transport diplomatic messages on his behalf.[84] In addition, he recruited Burmese, Cambodian, Laotian, Malay, and Siamese soldiers and specialists.[85] By July 1789, when Pigneau arrived back in Dai Viet, Nguyen Anh had captured Saigon for the fourth and final time, and held control of the far south, so he was not disappointed by Pigneau's news.[86] In fact, on February 5, 1790, Nguyen Anh was able to write to Louis XVI, "the wheel of fate turned in our favour; our subjects joined our forces, and thus We were restored to the main part of the kingdom. In the present situation…We consider that our lot is insured." He also stated, "we should not by any means request His Majesty's aid with troops."[87] Nguyen Anh wanted to set his sovereign boundaries and make sure the French did not have a change of heart and decide to intervene.

Nguyen Anh did, however, benefit from the French expertise Pigneau had recruited privately. He instructed the French officers to draft a plan for and supervise the construction of an early modern, European-style fortress in Saigon. This citadel was built with 30,000 laborers and constructed on the site of a previous fortress. It was bordered on three sides by water and was so strong that the Tay Son never threatened Saigon again. In time, Vietnamese engineers learned in time how to erect these Western fortresses without foreign supervision.[88] Similarly, when Nguyen Anh wanted to construct a new fleet, he ordered that an old European vessel be disassembled and rebuilt in the presence of Vietnamese carpenters so that they might learn how to construct such ships. To facilitate the development of this expertise, he established a new shipyard in Saigon, which he visited several hours a day to supervise the work. During his time in the shipyards, Nguyen Anh also became an able carpenter himself.[89] These examples show how important foreign expertise was to Nguyen Anh, but also how effectively he engendered technical autonomy. It was, in fact, this very ability that allowed Nguyen Anh to defeat the Tay Son and win control of all of Dai Viet. He prevailed because he was able to use his naval supremacy to transport whole armies quickly and efficiently.[90] The best example of this came in 1802, when Nguyen Anh surprised the surviving Tay Son leadership[91] by forgoing an opportunity to break a siege at Qui Nhon and instead sailing up the coast to attack northern Dai Viet. Nguyen Anh captured Hanoi, ended the war, and established a new imperial dynasty.[92]

Nguyen Anh was not a magnanimous victor. In August 1802, he gathered the surviving members of the Tay Son Dynasty's royal family, the uprising's commanders, and the commanders' families in his new capital, Hué. In the brutal ceremony that ensued, all of the detainees were

---

[84] Wilcox, "Transnationalism and Multiethnicity in the Early Nguyễn Phúc Ánh Gia Long Period," 195, 197-199.

[85] Taylor, "Surface Orientations in Vietnam."

[86] Lamb, *The Mandarin Road to Old Hué*, 144.

[87] Nguyen Anh quoted in Nguyen, *A Modern History of Viet-nam (1802-1954)*, 71.

[88] Frédéric Mantienne, "The Transfer of Western Military Technology to Vietnam in the Late Eighteenth and Early Nineteenth Centuries: The Case of the Nguyễn," *Journal of Southeast Asian Studies*, 34 (3) (October, 2003), 519-534, EBSCOhost. These were Vauban-style fortresses with star-shaped bastions.

[89] Mantienne, "The Transfer of Western Military Technology." Nguyen Anh's naval interest and personal expertise was quite similar to that of Russia's Peter the Great (1672-1725).

[90] Taylor, "Surface Orientations in Vietnam."

[91] Huệ unexpectedly died in 1792 at the age of forty, which was a devastating blow to Tay Son rule because of his military skill; Nhac died just a year later at fifty.

[92] Dutton, *The Tây Sơn Uprising*, 56.

executed, but not before they had witnessed Nguyen Anh's troops urinate on the exhumed and pulverized bones of Nhac and Huệ. The final death in the ceremony was that of Huệ's nineteen-year-old son, the reigning king, who was pulled apart by four military elephants.[93]   To commemorate his victory and his installation as the first Nguyen emperor, Nguyen Anh published a poem, which concluded in part:

> The entire journey resembled thunder and lightning;
> Their ranks of citadels were all falling tile and flying ash.
> All the false and rebellious [ranks] were captured;
> The guilty ones had now been taken.
> The forces of darkness had been swept away, and all the lands under
> heaven had been cleaned up.[94]

Nguyen Anh then took the new name of Gia Long, which combined the older terms for the southern capital, Saigon (Gia Dinh), and the northern capital, Hanoi (Thang Long).[95]   He also sought to change the name of his land by writing to the Chinese emperor for permission to call it Viet Nam.[96]

   That Nguyen Gia Long had to write to the Chinese emperor for permission to change the name of his country gets to the heart of Vietnam's complex relationship with its northern neighbor. It was an asymmetrical relationship to be sure,[97] but this did not mean that Vietnam never had any power in it.[98] By providing the emperor of China with tributes, Vietnam preserved its political autonomy and eliminated the biggest threat to its security. Vietnamese leaders confirmed their legitimacy by obtaining China's blessing and recognition.[99] This was particularly important for new rulers like Gia Long, who found that offering the Chinese a tribute was a small price to pay. Indeed, in this intricate relationship, it was possible for Vietnam to both celebrate its cultural debt to China and retain its political independence.

   This balance is evident in how the Vietnamese adapted Chinese institutions to their own needs. While Confucian patriarchal values predominated in Vietnam, there were important deviations. Vietnamese women, for example, could inherit land from their parents, and wives retained their rights after their husbands died. This was unique to Vietnam.[100] Similarly, the traditional Confucian social hierarchy (scholars, peasants, artisans, merchants) did not fit well with

---

[93] Buttinger, *The Smaller Dragon*, 266-267.

[94] Gia Long, "Commemoration of the Defeat of the Tay Son" (1802), *Sources of Vietnamese Tradition*, 311-313.

[95] Kathirithamby-Wells, "The Age of Transition," 589.

[96] The Chinese ultimately insisted that that characters be reversed to Nam Viet so that there would be no confusion with a third century BCE kingdom that had resisted Chinese authority. In 1813, the Vietnamese reverted to Dai Viet. In 1838, the Emperor Minh Mang adopted the term Dai Nam. See *Sources of Vietnamese Tradition*, 258. Since Gia Long wanted to call his nation "Vietnam," and since this is the term used today, I henceforth refer to the nation as "Vietnam," regardless of the specific year in question.

[97] Brantly Womack, *China and Vietnam: The Politics of Asymmetry* (New York: Cambridge University Press, 2006), 243.

[98] James A. Anderson, "Distinguishing Between China and Vietnam: Three Relational Equilibriums in Sino-Vietnamese Relations," *Journal of East Asian Studies*, 13, no. 2 (May, 2013), 259-280, ProQuest Central.

[99] Womack, *China and Vietnam*, 135.

[100] Alexander Barton Woodside, *Vietnam and the Chinese Model: A Comparative Study of Nguyễn and Ch'ing Civil Government in the First Half of the Nineteenth Century* (Cambridge, Massachusetts: Harvard University Press, 1971), 45.

Vietnamese society because the nation had not developed a strong craft industry and since the merchants were mostly Chinese immigrants. Because of this, the Vietnamese saw the merchant class more negatively than Chinese society did.[101] Other examples of the differences can be seen in the royal succession tradition, the development of a hybridized writing system, the use of greater ornamentation in Hué's Forbidden City than in Beijing's, and the greater importance of mythic heroes in guiding the actions of the Vietnamese rulers.[102] All of this meant that a qualified, rather than absolute, Confucian state emerged in Vietnam.[103] As such, it also meant that Nguyen dynasty Vietnam differed considerably from that of Kim Hong-do's Joseon Korea. Vietnam did not have the elite Confucian academies or an entrenched scholar-official class like the *yangban*; these institutions fueled a more formal bureaucracy in Korea than in Vietnam.[104]

~

Emperor Gia Long ruled over both northern and southern Vietnam for eighteen years, but it was not as unified a nation as a political map of early nineteenth-century Southeast Asia might suggest. Rather, it remained divided politically, socio-economically, and culturally, despite Gia Long's efforts to create a centralized state focused upon the new imperial capital of Hué.

Gia Long faced enormous political challenges in 1802. While he could have ruled as a military warlord, the forty-year old aspired to something with greater legitimacy, just as Tokugawa Ieyasu had in Japan two hundred years earlier. In fact, Gia Long wanted to refer to himself as the Son of Heaven and use the Chinese standard of possessing a divine mandate. Therefore, when he accepted his imperial title, Gia Long claimed to have defended his people's heritage and asserted himself to be a worthy successor of his Nguyen ancestors. In doing so, he also sought to present his rule as the restoration of a long-established dynasty, rather than as the founding of a new royal line.[105] Because this propaganda was not readily accepted in the north, where the Nguyen family had never ruled, Gia Long had to rely on the coercive power of a local overlord to maintain control of the region.[106] Gia Long supplemented this local authority by creating a nascent centralized government.[107] Following the Chinese model, it consisted six governing boards (appointments, finances, justice, rites, public works, and war) working in coordination with one another with overlapping responsibilities.[108] Officials of 283 districts reported to thirty-one provincial governors, who reported to the six governing boards and Gia Long.[109] Since there was a dearth of experienced talent to populate this bureaucracy as a result of the collapse of the Confucian examination system

---

[101] Woodside, *Vietnam and the Chinese Model*, 30-34.
[102] Woodside, *Vietnam and the Chinese Model*, 11-12, 51-52, 129.
[103] Chandler, Owen, Roff, et al, *The Emergence of Modern Southeast Asia*, 111; and Liam C. Kelley, "'Confucianism' in Vietnam: A State of the Field Essay," *Journal of Vietnamese Studies*, 1, 1-2 (February, 2006), 314-370, ProQuest Central.
[104] Alexander Woodside, *Lost Modernities: China, Vietnam, Korea, and the Hazards of World History* (Cambridge, Massachusetts: Harvard University Press, 2006), 23-29, 72.
[105] Jacob Ramsay, *Mandarins and Martyrs: The Church and the Nguyen Dynasty in Early Nineteenth-Century Vietnam* (Stanford, California: Stanford University Press, 2008), 39-40.
[106] Woodside, *Vietnam and the Chinese Model*, 102. There was also a local overlord in the far south.
[107] Ramsay, *Mandarins and Martyrs,* 34-35.
[108] Woodside, *Vietnam and the Chinese Model,* 67, 69.
[109] Kathirithamby-Wells, "The Age of Transition," 589.

during the Tay Son years, Gia Long filled these positions with military men who had been loyal to him since the 1780s.[110]

The restoration of the examination system was, in fact, a good way to install Confucian values and identify promising candidates for government offices. The first regional exams were held in 1807 at six provincial sites.[111] In the seventh lunar month, candidates gathered at each site to take three rounds of exams, which were held in tents in open fields patrolled by elephants. To promote the quality of responses, candidates were limited to answers of one thousand-words. Two types of proctors supervised the testing and three levels of examiners graded the results. Based on quotas set in advance, the winners were announced publicly eleven days after the last round of testing and were presented with special hats and robes to celebrate their accomplishment.[112] The government held subsequent regional examinations in 1813 and 1819 during Gia Long's reign, and in three-year intervals thereafter.[113] Interestingly, however, because of the lack of qualified individuals and the limited exam tradition in the south, the high-level palace examinations were not held during Gia Long's reign.[114] Hence, it was only with the passage of time that the examination system produced the bureaucrats the government needed.

Another political challenge Gia Long faced was foreign affairs. He needed to inform other nations of his rise to power and wanted to assert his position diplomatically. To facilitate this, in 1800 Gia Long sent one of his most trusted advisors, physician Jean Marie Despiau, to ports in the East Indies to carry the Nguyen standard and to serve notice that Gia Long controlled all trade in Vietnam.[115] He also wanted to change his relationships with his Southeast Asian neighbors. Between 1788 and 1801, Nguyen Anh had sent Rama I a customary gold-and-silver tree as a symbol of his vassalage as a tributary state, but after 1802 Gia Long did not,[116] indicating that Vietnam would no longer be subservient. In time, Vietnam challenged Siam by contesting its control over Cambodia. Gia Long was successful in this effort, and by 1813 Vietnam held dominant sway.[117] Laos, which had allied with Nguyen Anh against the Tay Son, remained in the Vietnam's orbit, offering triennial tributes of elephants and rhinoceros horn to Gia Long.[118] Gia Long remained suspicious of the Western powers and steered his nation towards an isolationist policy. Near his death, Gia Long told his successor, Minh Mang, to treat Europeans cordially but never to ever allow them to win an advantageous position.[119] Gia Long's approach to managing the West was well illustrated in August 1804, when John W. Roberts arrived in Hué to negotiate a commercial

---

[110] Ramsay, *Mandarins and Martyrs,* 35.
[111] Woodside, *Vietnam and the Chinese Model,* 170. None of these sites were in the south, however, because there were so few qualified candidates.
[112] Woodside, *Lost Modernities,* 2-3.
[113] Woodside, *Vietnam and the Chinese Model,* 170-171.
[114] Nola Cooke, "Nineteenth-Century Vietnamese Confucianization in Historical Perspective: Evidence from the Palace Examinations, 1463-1883), *Journal of Southeast Asian Studies,* 25, 2 (September, 1994), 270-312, EBSCOhost. Cooke argues that this limited use of the examination system means that Nguyen Vietnam was less Confucian than usually assumed.
[115] Thompson, "Jean Marie Despiau," 42.
[116] Kathirithamby-Wells, "The Age of Transition,"584.
[117] Wyatt, *Thailand,* 163.
[118] Kathirithamby-Wells, "The Age of Transition," 583.
[119] Buttinger, *The Smaller Dragon,* 242-243, 268. Prince Canh had been the heir apparent, but he died of smallpox on March 20, 1801. Gia Long then named Minh Mang, the son of his second wife, as heir. Others in the court believed that Prince Canh's son had the more legitimate claim. See Thompson, "Jean Marie Despiau," 63.

agreement between the British East India Company and Vietnam. Gia Long granted Roberts an audience but refused to accept his gifts and made no commitments. He made it clear that he was happy to receive British ships in Vietnamese ports but would not grant them preferential treatment. Furthermore, he was quite unwilling to grant any European nation a territorial concession.[120] As his tenure as emperor lengthened, Gia Long's demand for respectful protocol also grew. In 1818, when a French captain arrived on a mission for Louis XVIII, Gia Long refused to receive him because he did not have what the emperor perceived to be sufficiently respectful credentials.[121] The reason for this was simple: Gia Long no longer needed the Western aid he was once so desperate to have.

In addition to the challenges of establishing a government and winning recognition for it, Gia Long faced socio-economic challenges. The rising frustration within the new country is apparent in the 73 popular uprisings Gia Long faced during his eighteen-year reign.[122] This was a continuation of the dissatisfaction Nguyen Anh faced during the final years of the Tay Son war, when he too was brutal in his demands for peasant labor and taxes, even during times of famine.[123] As emperor, Gia Long refused to alleviate the tax and service pressures necessitated by the war. Both were simply redirected towards post-war needs, such as the construction of Hué. Poverty remained widespread as a result.[124] Gia Long did introduce a land reform system in 1804 that he hoped would provide his chief supporters with estates, punish landlords who had supported the Tay Son, allow for government officials to become salaried employees, and distribute land more equitably, but his system achieved very mixed results. Those at the bottom of the social ladder benefited the least.[125] In addition, inflation caused by a vast increase in the amount of silver in circulation ensured that much of the nation continued to face trying economic times through the opening decades of the nineteenth century.[126]

Exerting control of religious practices became both an expression of royal authority and a divisive issue as Gia Long promoted Confucianism and centralization.[127] He was particularly hostile to Buddhism, which he thought to be nonsensical, writing that since "it is predestined whom Buddha saves" the auspicious have no need of Buddha's salvation, "whereas the inauspicious can by no means be saved by Buddha." If human life is predestined, then "misfortune cannot be relieved, nor can blessings be prayed for. Worshipping and praying all get nowhere."[128] This interpretation of the faith, as well its status as a spiritual competitor to Confucianism, led Gia Long to place severe restrictions on the practice of Buddhism.[129] His 1804 edict banned the restoration of Buddhist temples in disrepair, the construction of new Buddhist temples, the casting of bells and

---

[120] Lamb, *The Mandarin Road to Old Hué*, 199.

[121] Jacques Dumarçay, *The Palaces of South-east Asia: Architecture and Customs*, Michael Smithies (ed. and trans.) (New York: Oxford University Press, 1991), 68. Gia Long wanted the captain to carry a personal letter to him from Louis XVIII. Gia Long did provide the French captain with ample gifts, however, to demonstrate Vietnam's goodwill.

[122] Kathirithamby-Wells, "The Age of Transition," 591.

[123] Dutton, *The Tây Sơn Uprising*, 167-168.

[124] Ramsay, *Mandarins and Martyrs*, 98.

[125] Woodside, *Vietnam and the Chinese Model*, 77-80.

[126] Woodside, *Vietnam and the Chinese Model*, 277-279.

[127] Watson and Andaya, *A History of Early Modern Southeast Asia, 1400-1830*, 287.

[128] Nguyen Gia Long quoted in Dinh Minh Chi, Ly Kim Hoa, Ha Thuc Minh, et al, *The History of Buddhism in Vietnam* (Washington, DC: The Council for Research in Values and Philosophy, 2008), 212.

[129] Nguyễn Thế Anh, "From Indra to Maitreya: Buddhist Influence in Vietnamese Political Thought," *Journal of Southeast Asian Studies*, 33, 2 (June 2002), 225-241, ProQuest Central.

statues, and the setting up of altars for religious assemblies. He decreed that all monks had to register with local authorities and reminded the people that "the fates of peoples' lives are fixed: disasters cannot be avoided, and good fortune cannot be actively sought. Praying and confessing faults to solve and eliminate problems are utterly without benefit."[130] The edict also criticized his subjects more generally for their excessive festivals, which could last for ten days and nights and feature "dramatic performances, bawdy songs, and countless rewards and prizes. Eating and drinking were extravagant, and expenditures were incalculable."[131] Gia Long decreed that a district magistrate had to approve spiritual celebrations and that "banquets and singing may last for only one day and night, and prizes and awards may not be excessive."[132] He also placed significant restrictions on the construction and decoration of local temples, promoting instead a ranked hierarchy of temples based on ancestral longevity and proximity to Hué.[133] This was part of Gia Long's effort to glorify his new capital as the center of the nation.

Gia Long's religious edict of 1804 also dealt with Christianity. During the Tay Son struggle, Nguyen Anh tolerated Christianity both out of respect for Pigneau, who died in 1799, and for political considerations. Once in power as emperor, however, Gia Long refused to incorporate in his new legal code an article protecting Christianity.[134] He declared that the faith was

> a religion from distant lands that has been brought into our country by foreigners. It speaks of a hell full of devils and a heavenly paradise full of spirits, and it seeks to persuade the masses to run about as though they were mad and to convince them of this superstition without their realizing it. Henceforth, all the people in villages and hamlets with Christian churches that are in disrepair must report this information to the provincial officials to request permission to repair them, and the construction of new churches is completely prohibited.[135]

These various efforts to regulate spiritual practices were not entirely successful. The Vietnamese remained animists first and foremost, who borrowed elements from Confucianism, Buddhism, Daoism,* and Christianity as their spiritual needs warranted.[136]

~

The Giza Pyramids and the Taj Mahal are famous royal burial sites constructed to make statements for posterity. Gia Long also wanted to make such a declaration, and his tomb complex outside of Hué stands as his final testament. The details of his tomb's architecture and his funeral ceremony are worth exploring because they illustrate the emperor's intentions and values. Indeed, as he

---

[130] "Edict Outlining Propriety and Ritual," *Sources of Vietnamese Tradition*, 320-324.
[131] "Edict Outlining Propriety and Ritual," *Sources of Vietnamese Tradition*, 320-324.
[132] "Edict Outlining Propriety and Ritual," *Sources of Vietnamese Tradition*, 320-324.
[133] Ramsay, *Mandarins and Martyrs,* 38.
[134] Ramsay, *Mandarins and Martyrs,* 47-48.
[135] "Edict Outlining Propriety and Ritual," *Sources of Vietnamese Tradition*, 320-324.
[136] Nola Cooke, "Early Nineteenth-Century Vietnamese Catholics and Others in the Pages of the Annales de la Propagation de la Foi," *Journal of Southeast Asian Studies*, 35, 2 (June, 2004), 261-285, ProQuest Central.

became older, it became most important to him to establish the proper filial and death rituals for the Nguyen Dynasty.[137]

Modeled after the tombs of the Ming Dynasty emperors north of Beijing, construction on Gia Long's funerary compound began five years before he died. Set back from the Perfume River, its design follows the rules of feng shui. It makes use of the forty-two large and small hills that surround the site,[138] thereby allowing nature to provide protection from evil spirits instead of a man-made wall. The complex consists of five major components: a lotus pond, a stele pavilion proclaiming Gia Long's accomplishments, a temple for worshipping Gia Long and his family, an honor courtyard, and the sepulcher.[139] Access to the ancestral temple comes via a broad staircase, which is divided into three sections by four dragon balustrades. At the top of these stairs, a level platform leads to a two-story, free-standing gatehouse pavilion, painted red and decorated with rounded yellow tiles and ornately stylized dragons. Beyond is the temple itself, which repeats the decorative motif of the gatehouse on a grander scale. Its double-eaved, sweeping roof features ceramic friezes of animals, spirits, and plants. The temple's red and yellow interior has three altars, including one of two empty thrones, cloaked with gold silk robes.[140] It is a space symbolizing joyous

---

[137] Kelley, "'Confucianism' in Vietnam."

[138] James Sullivan, *National Geographic Traveler: Vietnam*, 2nd ed., (Washington, DC: National Geographic Society, 2014), 141.

[139] Nguyen Quyhn, "Vietnam: Architecture," *Dictionary of Art*, (Jane Turner, ed.), Volume 32, (New York: Oxford University Press, 1996), 475.

[140] This was the interior's decorative motif in January 2013, but admittedly, it may have been different in the nineteenth century.

reverence. Just to the east of this temple is the honor courtyard. It contains stone elephants, horses, and mandarins facing one another and guarding the entrance to a broad, five-terraced platform with a central staircase. At the top of these stairs, a small doorway leads into a yellow courtyard, where two tall, plain, eight-and-a-half-foot mausoleums with undecorated, triangular roofs stand in the open air. One is for Gia Long, the other for his first wife. The space exudes calm austerity.

By the time Gia Long began to show signs of edema in the fall 1819, the complex was nearly complete. His physician for the previous twenty-five years, Despiau, helped keep the emperor's condition secret until December, when Gia Long became too debilitated to leave his palace chambers. The emperor breathed his last in Despiau's presence on January 20, 1820.[141] Upon the declaration of death, a silk thread, representing his soul, was tied on his ancestor's altar; he was now one of them. Attendants prepared the body with scented oils and special vestments. They made offerings to the corpse, filled the mouth with pearls and precious stones, wrapped it in a shroud, and placed it in a wood coffin. Once the body was properly prepared, the court came to pay its final respects and the coffin was closed. The three-year period of mourning officially began. There was a coronation ceremony for Minh Mang, and astrologers determined that the most auspicious day for Gia Long's burial would be May 27. On May 24, the coffin was carried from the imperial palace to the Perfume River, with Minh Mang following on foot as a nine-gun salute sounded. The body was placed on an imperial barge for its upriver journey, and it arrived near the burial site on May 26. The next day, at six o'clock, as the sun began to set, the master of rites said, "Today we select the auspicious hour and we respectfully seek to place the coffin in the sepulcher." The coffin was then lowered into an outer wooden shell, sealed with resin and then encased in the stone mausoleum.[142] Gia Long was in his final resting place.

These ceremonies and the places built for them illustrate Gia Long's vision for the future of the Nguyen Dynasty and for Vietnam. He hoped that his descendants would follow the model he established and pull Vietnam closer to becoming an unqualified Confucian state. But Vietnam remained a religiously eclectic nation until the end of the Nguyen Dynasty in 1945, demonstrating how difficult it is to bring about such fundamental societal change. Nguyen Anh may have overcome enormous odds to rule over a politically unified Vietnam, but as Emperor Gia Long he could not force his cultural vision upon the Vietnamese people.

---

[141] Thompson, "Jean Marie Despiau," 43, 50, 61.
[142] Dumarçay, *The Palaces of South-east Asia*, 72-73.

O

Richard Oswald

1705-1784

On November 21, 1741, a soap boiler named Samuel Lucas entered Thomas Dickenson's grocery store in Worcester, England and purchased two pounds of a high-quality hyson tea. As the grocer weighed and packaged the bulk green tea leaves from China for Lucas, it is doubtful either man thought about what was involved in bringing that tea to Worcester.[1] In all likelihood, they were simply focused upon the immediate transaction. Similarly, when the British earl Horace Walpole joined two thousand other ticket holders in London's Ranelagh Gardens in early May 1749 to commemorate the end of the War of the Austrian Succession,* his attention was not on how the booths serving tea with milk and sugar obtained their merchandise.[2] Instead, Walpole's focus was on the bands playing French horns, the troops of harlequin actors, the people dancing around a maypole, the gondolas adorned with flags and streamers that plied the canal, and the illuminated orange trees around the amphitheater.[3] He concentrated on the aesthetics, not the logistics. In fact, while most people in eighteenth century Britain didn't realize the enormous complexities involved in bringing sugar and tea to a grocery store or a garden party, there were those like global merchant Richard Oswald who most certainly did.

---

[1] Jon Stobart, *Sugar and Spice: Grocers and Groceries in Provincial England 1650-1830* (Oxford, U.K.: Oxford University Press, 2013), 142, 195.

[2] By the 1720s, the manner in which the British drank tea had changed. It was no longer drunk plain, as in China, or as it had been when tea was first introduced to Europe. Instead, sugar and tea went hand-in-hand for the British of all social classes. See Woodruff D. Smith, "Complications of the Commonplace: Tea, Sugar, and Imperialism," *Journal of Interdisciplinary History*, 23, 2 (Autumn, 1992), 259-279, EBSCOhost.

[3] Horace Walpole, "To Mann, Wednesday 3 May, 1749 OS," *The Yale Edition of Horace Walpole's Correspondence, Volume 20: Horace Walpole's Correspondence with Sir Horace Mann IV*, W.S. Lewis, Warren Hunting Smith and George L. Lam (eds.) (New Haven, Connecticut: Yale University Press, 1960), 46.

Oswald was born in 1705, two years before the Act of Union brought England and Scotland formally together as the United Kingdom of Great Britain.[4] He spent his boyhood in Caithness, mainland Britain's most northerly and quite impoverished shire, where his father was the Presbyterian minister in the coastal village of Dunnet. Like other children in the village, Oswald learned to read and write in a makeshift classroom underneath the steeple of his father's church since the nearest statutory school was impracticably far away.[5] At the age of twenty, Oswald heeded the call of urban life that so many rural youths hear. He moved to Glasgow to work as a clerk in the successful import-export business of his two older cousins. Their firm specialized in Virginia tobacco and the Oswalds were successful and prominent: by 1731 their company had become the fifth largest tobacco firm in the city, importing more than 300,000 pounds of the Chesapeake leaf a year.[6] By helping to keep the firm's records in an office overlooking Glasgow's Old Green, the younger Oswald began to develop his commercial acumen. In fact, he must have been a quick study because in the 1730s Oswald's cousins entrusted him to manage their operations on the American side of the Atlantic.

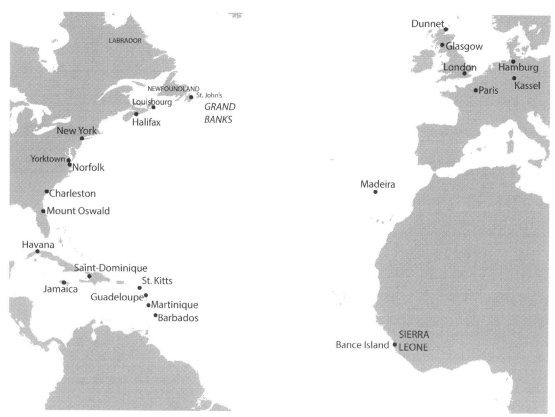

---

[4] Most surviving records list Oswald's birth year as 1705, but his tombstone says he was born in 1700. See David Hancock, *Citizens of the World: London Merchants and the Integration of the British Atlantic Community, 1735-1785* (New York: Cambridge University Press, 1995), 61.

[5] The nearest statutory school in 1706 was in Thurso, about nine miles away. James Traill Calder and Thomas Sinclair, *Sketch of the Civil and Traditional History of Caithness from the Tenth Century*, 2nd ed., (Wick, U.K.: William Roe, 1887), 221.

[6] Hancock, *Citizens of the World*, 61. For information about transatlantic tobacco trade prior to the eighteenth century, see Marcy Norton, *Sacred Gifts, Profane Pleasures: A History of Tobacco and Chocolate in the Atlantic World* (Ithaca, New York: Cornell University Press, 2008).

Oswald spent most of his six years in the Americas in Norfolk, Virginia. He arrived about the time the town received its 1736 charter of incorporation, which came as recognition of the port's growing commercial importance. Highlighted by a few two-story buildings, a courthouse, an Anglican church, and many taverns, Norfolk stood as an *entrepôt* for Tidewater planters, especially as the increased size of ocean-going vessels limited the number that could sail throughout Chesapeake Bay's estuaries. While the port also shipped grain, salted meat, timber, and animal skins, Norfolk's primary export was tobacco, and Glasgow became that commodity's primary destination.[7] As his cousins' agent in America, Oswald was responsible for both selling supplies to planters and for negotiating the purchase price for their crop.[8] His task was facilitated by the fact that tobacco growing had evolved into a carefully regulated industry in the colony. In 1730, the Virginia Assembly began requiring government inspection of all tobacco shipments prior to export.[9] According to these inspection laws, only first growth leaves from each plant were sellable.[10] This policy restricted the quantity of tobacco available for export, which helped maintain higher prices for planters.[11] At an inspection, each hogshead* of tobacco leaves was opened to check for mold and evidence of poorer-quality second growth leaves. Officials burned any tobacco that did not meet the inspection standard.[12] Only once it was certified could Oswald begin haggling over the purchase price. Such practices did not fit well with Adam Smith's Enlightenment* ideas about free trade, but much of the global commerce in the eighteenth century remained rigorously controlled in accordance with mercantilist* values. Such trade was also quite profitable.[13]

In 1741, Oswald returned to Glasgow. In recognition of his work in Virginia, the Carolinas, and Jamaica, Oswald was made a partner in his cousins' firm. As a partner, Oswald aggressively advocated for an expansion of the firm's scope and mission.[14] It soon entered the sugar business.

~

Sugarcane is a grass with species indigenous to both New Guinea and India. Arab traders brought the plant to the Middle East, and the Portuguese introduced it to the Madeira archipelago in the early fifteenth century. By 1452, Madeira's highly profitable sugar mill had become the primary

---

[7] Thomas C. Parramore, Peter C. Stewart, and Tommy L. Bogger, *Norfolk: The First Four Centuries* (Charlottesville, Virginia: University of Virginia Press, 1994), 68-69, 72, 77.

[8] Hancock, *Citizens of the World,* 62.

[9] In addition, non-inspected tobacco could not be used to repay public or private debts. See Gary M. Pecquet, "British Mercantilism and Crop Controls in the Tobacco Colonies: A Study in Rent-Seeking Costs," *Cato Journal*, 22, 3 (Winter, 2003), 467-484, ProQuest Central.

[10] Barbara Hahn, *Making Tobacco Bright: Creating an American Commodity, 1617-1937* (Baltimore, Maryland: The Johns Hopkins Press, 2011), 24.

[11] Pecquet, "British Mercantilism and Crop Controls in the Tobacco Colonies."

[12] Hahn, *Making Tobacco Bright,* 32.

[13] Michael Kwass, "The Global Underground: Smuggling, Rebellion, and the Origins of the French Revolution," *The French Revolution in Global Perspective*, Susanne Desan, Linda Hunt and William Max Wilson (ed.) (Ithaca, New York: Cornell University Press, 2013), 15-16.

[14] Hancock, *Citizens of the World,* 62.

source of Europe's sugar supply.[15] Columbus carried sugarcane shoots to Hispaniola on his second voyage in 1493, where the plant found the humid environment hospitable, but it wasn't until the seventeenth century that sugarcane production exploded in the Caribbean. Barbados became the early production leader as a result of its flat topography, which was ideal for cultivation, its abundance of water and sunshine, and its being a frequent first port of call for Caribbean-bound ships.[16] Initially the work force on the island consisted primarily of White indentured servants* and prisoners, but the ever-increasing demand for sugar led to the dramatic importation of African slaves, beginning in the 1650s. By 1680, there were seventeen African slaves for each White servant living in Barbados.[17]

To create the sugar sold in Thomas Dickenson's grocery store or added to the tea in the Ranelagh Gardens, African slaves began preparing the fields each July or August by burning away old cane and weeds. Then came the arduous job of sowing the tops of three sugarcane plants into a two-foot wide, three-foot long and six-to-nine-inch deep trench. This was the hardest job in the growing and production cycle and the expected work rate in the French Antilles was 28 trenches per hour. Sowing the sugarcane was done almost exclusively by the female slaves, working on what was called the Great Gang. After planting, twelve months of pruning, weeding, and irrigating followed before the cane was ready for harvest. After harvest, the cycle then began immediately again, and many plantation owners rotated their fields to allow for a nearly continuous cycle of sowing and reaping.[18]

The harvesting and processing of the sugarcane required a unique agricultural urgency.[19] It had to be prepared quickly in order to retain the maximum sugar content and to prevent natural fermentation.[20] This meant that within 48 hours the cane had to be cut at ground level, chopped into four-foot segments, transported to the mill, and crushed under the mill roll: a gear-driven machine with three great rollers that worked like a hand-cranked washing machine mangle. In the eighteenth century, a sugar mill's power came from wind, water, animals, or slaves.[21] The exigency of processing cane meant that slave women worked for eighteen to twenty hours a day pushing the cane into the rollers. If a hand got caught in the rollers, it was cut off with a machete so that nothing stopped the flow of production.[22]

---

[15] Sidney M. Greenfield, "Madeira and the Beginnings of New World Sugar Cane Cultivation and Plantation Slavery: A Study in Institution Building," *Caribbean Slavery in the Atlantic World: A Student Reader*, Verene Shepherd and Hilary McD. Beckles (ed.) (Princeton, New Jersey: Markus Wiener Publishers, 2000), 48, 50.

[16] Ian Williams, *Rum: A Social and Sociable History* (New York: Nation Books, 2005), 19, 27-29, 48.

[17] Hilary Mc D. Beckles and Andrew Downes, "The Economics of Transition to the Black Labour System in Barbados, 1630-1680," *Caribbean Slavery in the Atlantic World: A Student Reader*, Verene Shepherd and Hilary McD. Beckles (ed.) (Princeton, New Jersey: Markus Wiener Publishers, 2000), 240-241. "White" and "Black" are both intentionally capitalized. See Chapter F, footnote 60.

[18] Elizabeth Abbott, *Sugar: A Bittersweet History* (New York: Duckworth Overlook, 2009), 81-84, 87. The work of the Great Gang was supplemented by the work of the Second Gang, and on large plantations, the Third Gang. Slaves were assigned to the Great or Second gang based on exhaustion levels; the Third Gang consisted of children, the elderly and the disabled.

[19] Philip D. Morgan, "Slavery in the British Caribbean," *The Cambridge World History of Slavery, Volume 3: AD 1420-AD 1804*, David Eltis and Stanley L. Engerman (eds.) (New York: Cambridge University Press, 2011), 386.

[20] Williams, *Rum,* 11.

[21] Stuart M. Nisbet, "Early Glasgow Sugar Plantations in the Caribbean," *Scottish Archaeological Journal*, vol. 31, no. 1/2 (2009), 115-136, EBSCOhost.

[22] Abbott, *Sugar,* 88.

The roller-crushed cane released juice, which then ran down a channel to the first boiler, where the sap was heated, quicklime was added to clarify it, and any impurities were skimmed off. The amount of quicklime needed varied tremendously, depending on the soil, fertilizer, moisture, and ripeness. The head boiler had to determine the correct amount of quicklime to add, and this determination controlled the quality of the refined sugar the crop would produce.[23] After clarification, the juice flowed to a row of additional boiling pans of decreasing size, which were progressively used to boil off more and more water to encourage crystallization. When the head boiler judged the juice in the final pan to be ready, it was ladled into earthenware vessels and allowed

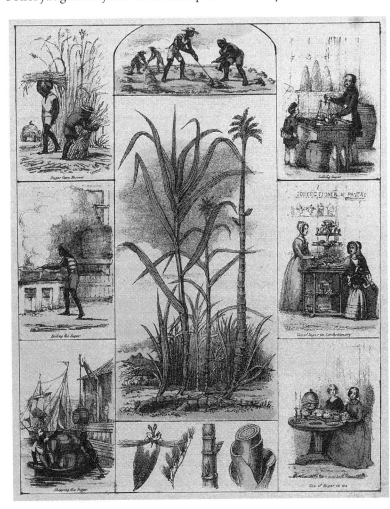

to set. The liquid that did not crystalize dripped out the bottom of the funnel-shaped vessel as molasses.[24] Five months after the sugarcane harvest, the earthenware held a course, brown, muscovado sugar, which was put in hogsheads and transported to Britain for further refining before wholesale and retail purchase.[25]

This production system, and the horrific human toll it exacted, brought large quantities of sugar to Britain and British consumption grew enormously in the eighteenth century as a result. In 1700, annual intake was four pounds per person, but by 1729, it had doubled to eight pounds per person. By mid-century, it was being consumed by members of all social classes and by 1789 British sugar consumption had grown to twelve pounds

---

[23] One hundred pounds of cane might need as little as two ounces or as much as three pounds of quicklime to create the desired quality. Quicklime is calcium oxide (CaO). See Abbott, *Sugar,* 91.

[24] Early Caribbean sugar producers discarded the molasses as a waste product, but when planters learned how to concentrate molasses so it would not ferment, they could sell it to New Englanders, who made it into rum. Rum became the American colonies' major export with its 143 distilleries producing 4.8 million gallons of rum per year by 1770. Rum was also used to buy slaves in Africa, debilitate Native Americans, and placate British sailors. See Williams, *Rum,* 12, 89-90, 99-102, 230-235.

[25] Nisbet, "Early Glasgow Sugar Plantations in the Caribbean."

per person per year.[26] The demand became so great that Britain's Caribbean possessions could not produce sufficient quantities to supply the British appetite. Since the French only consumed 50% of what islands like Saint-Domingue (Haiti), Martinique, and Guadeloupe produced, much of the French Caribbean's sugar ended up being sold in Britain when the two nations were not at war.[27] The French influence also influenced the price of sugar in Britain: taking advantage of their greater production and lower national consumption, French merchants undercut British prices by as much as forty percent.[28] These circumstances caused a marked drop in the retail cost of sugar throughout Britain, and made it possible for a 1774 report to state, "Sugar is so generally in use, by the existence of tea, that even the poor wretches living in almshouses will not be without it."[29] This ubiquity of sugar in the British diet changed the lives of untold millions.

~

Highly successful businessmen often benefit from a lucky break at some point in their careers. Richard Oswald's came in July 1744, when the British navy captured a French ship based in Martinique and confiscated the contents of its hold. Oswald supervised the unloading of the muscovado sugar, coffee, and cocoa in Glasgow, and placed the impounded goods in his firm's warehouse. By selling this free, unexpected merchandise and goods from other prize ships to Hamburg merchants, Oswald reportedly made £15,000.[30] The profits from his other ventures and his own frugality made this a sufficient sum to allow Oswald to leave his cousins in Glasgow and

---

[26] Abbott, *Sugar,* 60. This rate of consumption is small compared to the average American intake today, which is about 180 pounds a year. See Ann Louise Gittleman, "Sugar Savvy 101: The Facts about Sugar and its Kissing Cousins." *Total Health* 30, no. 1 (02, 2008): 44-45,13 ProQuest Central.

[27] Laurent Dubois, "Slavery in the French Caribbean, 1634-1804," *The Cambridge World History of Slavery, Volume 3: AD 1420-AD 1804*, David Eltis and Stanley L. Engerman (eds.) (New York: Cambridge University Press, 2011), 447.

[28] Andrew J. O'Shaughnessy, "The Formation of a Commercial Lobby: The West India Interest, British Colonial Policy and the American Revolution," *The Historical Journal*, Vol. 40, No. 1 (March, 1997), 71-95, EBSCOhost.

[29] Matthew Parker, *The Sugar Barons: Family, Corruption, Empire and War in the West Indies* (New York: Walker and Company, 2011), 297.

[30] The French ship was *L'Heureuse Marie.* The reason Oswald won the right to unload the French cargo rested on his partial ownership of the *Hound*, a ship commandeered by the British navy during the War of the Austrian Succession. See Hancock, *Citizens of the World,* 62. It is unclear whether or not this is the same ship and same circumstances that Hancock mentions on pages 244-245. Hancock also gives two different dates for Oswald's move to London, 1745 and mid-1746.

move to London in mid-1746, where he leased a property and established his own import-export firm.

Oswald's base of operations was 17 Philpot Lane, near the heart of London's commercial and financial center in the eighteenth century.[31] The property featured a narrow, four-story brick Georgian house, which served as both an office and residence. There was also a small yard and a warehouse. The counting house's business was managed from the first floor, with the front room serving as a reception space for clients. There was also a large room for Oswald's clerks, who worked long hours and under constant scrutiny from their boss, and a small study, where

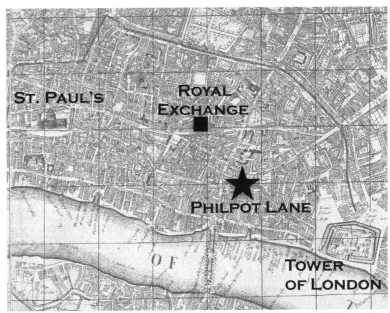

Oswald held private meetings with his key financial partners. Upstairs, on the second floor, there was a dining room and a kitchen, while the third floor housed two bedrooms. These floors were connected by an interior staircase that ran along one side of the house. An attic provided living quarters for some of Oswald's clerks, while a basement provided storage.[32]

British billionaire Richard Branson maintains that "succeeding in business is all about making connections."[33] Oswald believed the same thing, and, upon his arrival in London, he set about trying to establish a network of contacts. He probably began at the Royal Exchange, an arcaded courtyard not far from Philpot Lane, where merchants specializing in goods from different parts of the world met with clients, beginning at noon six days a week.[34] From the Exchange, Oswald likely visited the center of all shipping news, Lloyd's Coffee House on Lombard Street. This establishment published *Lloyd's News*, which kept track of all shipping intelligence and sales. After Lloyd's, Oswald could have headed to Jonathan's Coffee House on Exchange Alley in hope of speaking with stockbrokers.[35] Despite his best efforts, Oswald did not receive a warm reception in establishments like these. This was because London's business community generally resented the Scots, both for their very presence and for their commercial success. It was extraordinarily difficult for someone from Caithness and Glasgow to penetrate London's eighteenth-century commercial networks.

---

[31] Philpot Lane runs north to south; the two cross streets are Fenchurch and Eastcheap. If walking west, it is about a third of the way from the Tower of London to St. Paul's Cathedral. The nearest Tube stop is "Monument" on the Circle and District Lines.

[32] Hancock, *Citizens of the World,* 91-94, 103.

[33] Richard Branson, "Richard Branson: Why You Should Network," Virgin.com, accessed January 19, 2020 http://www.virgin.com/entrepreneur/richard-branson-why-you-should-network

[34] Jerry White, *London in the 18th Century: A Great and Monstrous Thing* (London: Vintage Books, 2013), 174.

[35] Bryant Lillywhite, *London Coffee Houses: A Reference Book of Coffee Houses of the Seventeenth, Eighteenth, and Nineteenth Centuries* (London: George Allen and Unwin Ltd., 1963), 305-308, 330-335.

Oswald turned instead to formal and informal networks created by Scots who had left their homeland in search of better economic opportunities.[36] These men shared Oswald's ambition, competence, and middling socio-economic background.[37] All were in London to make their fortunes in global trade, and all understood that they needed to find inventive ways of minimizing costs. This meant eliminating as many middlemen as possible and controlling the means of production as much as possible. To achieve these goals, Oswald and his five closest associates bought their own ships, hired their own personnel, and contracted their own agents. They also decided in 1748 to purchase an island in West Africa and enter the slave trade.[38]

Bance Island, a fifteen-acre islet in the middle of the Sierra Leone River, became a slave-trading center long before Grant, Oswald & Co. bought it. One owner was the English joint-stock trading monopoly, the Royal African Company (RAC). According to the terms of its September 1672 charter, the RAC possessed an exclusive right to trade in gold, silver, and slaves on the West African coast. It also had the power to build forts, raise troops, fight wars, and confiscate the property of anyone who violated its prerogatives.[39] The company experienced some financial success, but lost control of Bance Island in 1728, when the followers of a Portuguese-Senegambian slave trader attacked and destroyed the island's fortifications.[40] For the next fifteen years, the island reverted to African control and was not used for slaving. Beginning in 1744, a private citizen named George Freyer attempted to establish his own slave-trading center on Bance, but after four years of unprofitable futility he offered his rights to the island for sale. Grant, Oswald & Company purchased Bance Island on July 8, 1748[41] and set their minds to succeeding where Freyer had not.

Oswald and his partners were optimistic about their venture because they had more capital resources than Freyer did. They also knew that Bance Island's location offered several advantages over other slaving stations on the West African coast. It was situated in a broad, deep, estuarial river with protected bays, surrounded by rich timber supplies, fertile soils, abundant supplies of fish and fruit, fresh sea breezes, and ample streams with drinkable water. The island clearly benefited from its adjacent environment.[42] European visitors regularly praised Bance's setting compared to that of other destinations in the African tropics.[43] Its small size made it easier to fortify against attacks by European rivals, and its proximity to experienced slave-trading African tribes facilitated a large volume of transactions. The new proprietors did not take these advantages for granted. Instead,

[36] White, *London in the 18th Century*, 94, 119-120.
[37] Hancock, *Citizens of the World*, 43-44.
[38] Oswald's closest business associates were John Augustus Boyd (1679-1765), John Boyd (1718-1800), Alexander Grant (1705-1772), John Mill (1710-1771) and John Sargent II (1714-1791).
[39] The Royal African Company (RAC) replaced previous English joint stock companies, including Royal Adventures and Gambia Adventures, operating on Bance Island and other stations on the West Coast of Africa, Bance Island is also referred to as "Bence Island" or even just as "Sierra Leone" in many sources. See K. G. Davies, *The Royal African Company* (New York: Atheneum, 1970), 30, 97-98, 388.
[40] The slave trader was José Lopes de Moura. See Hugh Thomas, *The Slave Trade: The Story of the Atlantic Slave Trade, 1440-1870* (New York: Simon & Schuster, 1997), 342, 344.
[41] David Hancock, "Scots in the Slave Trade," *Nation and Province in the First British Empire: Scotland and the Americas, 1600-1800*, Ned C. Landsman (ed.) (Lewisburg, Pennsylvania: Bucknell University Press, 2001), 67. Oswald owned a one sixth share of Grant, Oswald and Company.
[42] Hancock, *Citizens of the World*, 174.
[43] For one example of this attitude see "Report of the Commissioners Sent Out by the British Government to Investigate the State of the Settlements and Forts on the Coast of Africa." *The Monthly Magazine*, April 1, 1817, [No. 296] in *The Monthly Magazine or British Register*, Vol. XLIII, Part I for 1817 (London: Printed for Sir Richard Phillips, 1817), 203.

they took a long-term view. They invested in improvements to the island's facilities and made sure that Bance had the supplies and personnel it needed to prosper. By 1756, the walls of the island's fort had undergone significant repairs and upgrades, its defensive cannons had grown in both size and quantity, and the number of White employees had increased from ten to thirty-five. This made Bance Island one of the most secure and well-staffed White settlements in West Africa.[44]

Oswald and his colleagues also sought to reconstitute some of the fundamental assumptions of the African slave trade. The motivation for this change did not stem from moral considerations but from a desire to increase profits. For Oswald and other slave traders, Africans were simply another commodity to be traded, little different than tobacco or sugar. The questions that kept them up at night were not concerned with the ethics of brutally uprooting millions of humans and transporting them to a foreign land to suffer a life of bondage. Rather, what concerned Oswald and his kin were simply the pertinent economic considerations. Consequently, the partners insisted upon upholding two protocols they believed would produce greater profits.

First and foremost, Grant, Oswald & Company sought to maintain peaceful and positive relationships with local African kings. Bance Island managers, known as agents, were expressly forbidden from kidnapping slaves or waging war on local tribes.[45] This was because the company relied upon these local tribes to provide them with the slaves needed in the Americas. The company fostered positive relationships with these tribes by honoring the prices set by African chiefs. On Bance, transactions were made one slave at a time through a system of bartering. In exchange for each slave, agents offered guns, gunpowder, alcohol, beads, toys, knives, crystal, and seventeen different fabrics, ranging from Indian cottons and Persian silks to German linens and Scottish tartans. In return, the company purchased no fewer than 12,929 individuals between 1748 and 1784, most of whom came from non-coastal areas. The specifics as to how these people were acquired by the coastal tribes in Sierra Leone remains unclear, but war and demographic and economic changes contributed substantially.[46] What is certain is that the region did not have institutionalized slavery prior to development of the Atlantic slave trade and that coastal African chiefs came to control access to slaves in Sierra Leone once that trade began in earnest. This differs from other parts of West Africa, where slavery existed prior to the arrival of the Europeans and where both Christian and Muslim slave traders ventured into the interior themselves.[47] By the eighteenth century, most West Africans who became slaves were prisoners of war, convicted criminals, debtors, sold by relatives, or kidnapped by other Africans.[48]

Second, Grant, Oswald & Company changed the method by which most slave ships acquired their cargos. Along much of the West African coast, ship captains typically conducted their business on board, waiting offshore as their holds slowly filled. This could take as long as five months. The longer the loading took, the more likely the loss of lives.[49] On Bance Island, however, the trade was conducted at the fort, and the company's agents always tried to have slaves to sell so

---

[44] Hancock, *Citizens of the World*, 188.

[45] Hancock, *Citizens of the World*, 199.

[46] Hancock, "Scots in the Slave Trade," 74-75; and Hancock, *Citizens of the World*, 213, 218.

[47] G. Ugo Nwokeji, "Slavery in Non-Islamic West Africa, 1420-1820," *The Cambridge World History of Slavery, Volume 3: AD 1420-AD 1804*, David Eltis and Stanley L. Engerman (eds.) (New York: Cambridge University Press, 2011), 86, 91.

[48] Thomas, *The Slave Trade*, 372-273.

[49] Thomas, *The Slave Trade*, 406.

the ship captains could fill their holds quickly. Not waiting offshore saved lives, improved profit margins, and meant that Bance Island slaves were sold to ship captains at premium prices.[50]

Once Oswald and his associates had Bance Island upgraded and fully operational, the horrid commerce began in earnest. Some of Oswald's ships participated in the traditional triangular trade route, running from Britain to Africa to the Americas and back to Britain. One such early voyage was of the seventy-ton sloop *Carlisle*, captained by Thomas Osborne. It left London on February 1, 1756, loaded with goods from Europe and Asia for African kings, and it arrived off the Senegambia coast six weeks later. Osborne purchased 35 slaves in the region and then proceeded to Bance Island, where he unloaded most of his cargo and replaced it with 158 slaves who had been held in the island's slave yard. Osborne set sail for what was then known as Charles Town, South Carolina with a total of 193 slaves, chained into place in the hull's claustrophobic half decks, lying down shoulder to shoulder. The Atlantic crossing, or Middle Passage, of the ship's triangular trade journey must have been particularly gruesome: the *Carlisle* arrived in Charleston on June 28 with only 150 slaves,[51] a mortality rate of 22%. The conditions on the ship must have been at least as grim as those described by former slave Olaudah Equiano, who endured the Atlantic crossing in 1756:

> The stench of the hold while we were on the coast was so intolerably loathsome, that it was dangerous to remain there for anytime… but now that the whole ship's cargo were confined together, it became absolutely pestilential. The closeness of the place, and the heat of the climate, added to the number in the ship, which was so crowded that each had scarcely room to turn himself, almost suffocated us. This is produced copious perspirations, so that the air soon became unfit for respiration, from a variety of loathsome smells, and brought on a sickness among the slaves, of which many died.[52]

Those who did survive the Middle Passage were traumatized in other ways, for in addition to humiliation, rape, and torture, there was the disorientation and psychological shock of being uprooted from everything they had ever known. As one ship surgeon noted in 1790,

> The slaves in the night were often heard making a howling melancholy kind of noise, something expressive of extreme anguish. I repeatedly ordered the woman, who had been my interpreter in the later part of the voyage, to inquire into the particular causes of this very melancholy noise. She answered that it was because the slaves had dreamed they were back in their own country, only to wake to the reality of the slave ship.[53]

---

[50] Hancock, *Citizens of the World*, 199.

[51] "Voyage 75237, *Carlisle* (1756)," *Voyages: The Trans-Atlantic Slave Trade Database*, accessed January 17, 2020, http://www.slavevoyages.org/voyage/75237/variables. The death rate for slaves on all British ships fell from 10% to 5.65% over the course of the eighteenth century. See Thomas, *The Slave Trade*, 423. The calculated mortality rate on British ships for the whole of the slave trade was about 13%. See Morgan, "Slavery in the British Caribbean," 382.

[52] Olaudah Equiano, *The Life of Olaudah Equiano: or Gustavus Vassa, the African* (Boston, Massachusetts: Isaac Knapp, 1837), 47. Equiano was born in 1745 in a place he called Essaka in the Kingdom of Benin. He purchased his freedom in 1766, became a leading abolitionist in London, and published his vivid memoir in 1789.

[53] Thomas Trotter quoted in Dorothy Schneider and Carl J. Schneider, *An Eyewitness History of Slavery in America: From Colonial Times to the Civil War* (New York: Checkmark Books/Facts on File, 2000), 46.

Once the *Carlisle* arrived in Charleston, the Africans were sold on Oswald's behalf. There were also nine "privileged" slaves, which meant that Captain Osborne sold them on his own for his personal profit.[54] All of the *Carlisle* slaves who disembarked in South Carolina then risked joining the vast numbers who died within three years of their arrival in the Americas.[55]

The *Carlisle* landed in Charleston instead of in Barbados or Jamaica because by January 1756 Oswald had established a special commercial relationship with a local businessman, Henry Laurens. Oswald trusted Laurens and offered him exclusive rights to sell Bance Island slaves in Charleston. Evidence for this trust can be seen in the earliest surviving letter between the two men. Dated April 13, 1756, it was Laurens' response to Oswald's letter of January 17. Laurens tells Oswald that as a result of the falling prices for slaves in Charleston, "we sincerely wish you may order the Sloop [*Carlisle*] to a much better market than ours at present seems to promise."[56] It was also Laurens' practice to share all the financial risks with his slaving partners.[57] Oswald deeply valued such honesty and financial integrity, which was why he was willing to pay Laurens a 9% commission on the sale of each slave sent from Bance Island to Charleston.[58] Laurens also saw to the outfitting of the *Carlisle* for the last leg of the archetypal triangle route, loading

[54] A letter from Henry Laurens to Richard Oswald says that the *Carlisle* only shipped 141 slaves, including 120 from Bance Island. Laurens also states that only five were lost crossing the Atlantic and that all but three were in good health upon arrival. If Laurens' numbers are correct, instead of those used in the Slavevoyages.org database, then the mortality rate abroad the *Carlisle* was only 3.34%. Both sources agree that nine slaves were designated as "privileged." See Henry Laurens to Richard Oswald, June 29, 1756 in *The Papers of Henry Laurens*, Volume 2, November 1, 1755-December 31, 1758, Philip M Hamer and George C. Rogers, Jr. (eds.) (Columbia, South Carolina: University of South Carolina Press, 1970), 233.

[55] The percentage of slaves who died within three years of arrival in the British Caribbean fell over the course of the eighteenth century from approximately one third of the slaves at mid-century to a quarter in 1790. Clearly, the physical and psychological adjustment to the New World remained extraordinarily difficult for a large percentage of those taken from Africa. In the Thirteen Colonies, the slave population sustained itself through natural procreation, but it is unlikely that those who emerged from the Middle Passage greatly enfeebled would live beyond three years. See Philip D. Morgan, "Slavery in the British Caribbean," *The Cambridge World History of Slavery, Volume 3: AD 1420-AD 1804*, David Eltis and Stanley L. Engerman (eds.) (New York: Cambridge University Press, 2011), 382 and Richard Hofstadter, *America at 1750: A Social Portrait* (New York: Vintage Books, 1973), 90-92, 112-113.

[56] Henry Laurens to Richard Oswald, April 13, 1756 in *The Papers of Henry Laurens*, Volume 2, 169. Given the time it took for letters to cross the Atlantic, Oswald could not redirect the *Carlisle* to another port of call, but in this case the symbolism was more important than the practicality.

[57] James Rawley, *London, Metropolis of the Slave Trade* (Columbia, Missouri: University Press, 2003), 89, EBSCOebooks.

[58] Henry Laurens to Richard Oswald, May 24, 1768 in *The Papers of Henry Laurens*, Volume 5, September 1, 1765-July 31, 1768, George C. Rogers, Jr. and David R. Chesnutt (eds.) (Columbia, South Carolina: University of South Carolina Press, 1976), 694. In an effort to reassure Oswald that he is getting a good deal, Laurens notes in this same letter that other Charleston merchants charge a 13% commission and "sometimes more."

the ship's hold with South Carolinian rice. Captain Osborne and his small crew returned to London on December 29, 1756 after a 195-day journey.[59]

Oswald-owned and Company-owned ships did not always participate in traditional triangular trade. Like many other ships plying the Atlantic, Oswald's vessels also took other routes. On August 5, 1760, for example, the one hundred and fifty-ton *Bance Island* set sail from Charleston, bound for Sierra Leone. The ship loaded 352 slaves in Africa and returned to South Carolina on May 30, 1761. Records indicate that 300 slaves survived the trip, giving the voyage a 14.77% mortality rate.[60] Similarly, a decade later, the one hundred-and-eighty-two ton *Charlotte* made the same out-and-back journey. When this ship returned to Charleston on September 5, 1771, the captain reported that only 118 of the 139 slaves leaving Bance Island had survived, giving the trip a mortality rate of 15.11%.[61] Not all of Oswald's ships suffered such high losses or went to and from Charleston. In 1786, the one hundred-and-ten-ton *Mary* loaded 154 slaves at Bance Island and gained two more during the Middle Passage with the birth of two babies. The ship arrived in St. Kitts with 156 men, women, and children and eventually disembarked 151, a mortality rate of 1.95%.[62] Overall, the thirty-three voyages completed by Oswald-owned or partially-owned ships between 1752 and 1787 had a 13.41% fatality rate.[63] This was higher than the overall British average, but even with these loses, as well as the expenses of shipping, insurance, piracy, wages, and overhead, Oswald still made money as a slaver. These profits, between 6% and 10%, were not dramatically different, however, from those of other slavers or from merchants not trading in people.[64] It was not necessary for a mid-eighteenth-century merchant to engage in human trafficking to make a profit. This makes the moral status of those who did more troubling and their financial rationale more dubious.

~

While Robert Monckton sat in Halifax in the summer of 1758, frustrated that he was not participating in the British siege of Louisbourg, Oswald won a bid to supply bread to the British army fighting in the Seven Years' War in Germany. On the European continent, this war stemmed as much from a diplomatic upheaval as it did from the British-French colonial rivalry that Monckton witnessed. Oswald was less concerned with the details of Austria's *rapprochement* with France in the wake of Prussia's rise than he was with the arrival of a lucrative new business

---

[59] Rawley, *London, Metropolis of the Slave Trade*, 92.

[60] "Voyage 26022, *Bance Island* (1760)," *Voyages: The Trans-Atlantic Slave Trade Database*, accessed January 19, 2020, http://www.slavevoyages.org/voyage/26022/variables

[61] "Voyage 78278, *Charlotte* (1771)," *Voyages: The Trans-Atlantic Slave Trade Database*, accessed January 19, 2020, http://www.slavevoyages.org/voyage/78278/variables

[62] "Voyage 82604, *Mary* (1786)," *Voyages: The Trans-Atlantic Slave Trade Database*, accessed January 19, 2020, http://www.slavevoyages.org/voyage/82604/variables

[63] I have computed this percentage based on the records available in the slavevoyages.org database. This percentage is too high if Henry Lauren's numbers for the *Carlisle*'s 1756 trip, as discussed in footnote 54, are correct.

[64] Thomas, *The Slave Trade*, 444. Countries began to abolish their participation in the slave trade as it became unprofitable. The Danes, for example, abolished their slave trade in 1792 specifically for this reason. See James A. Rawley, *The Transatlantic Slave Trade: A History* (New York: W. W. Norton & Company, 1981), 265, 267.

opportunity.[65] He won the bread contract both by luck and by strategy. On the lucky side, none of the conventional provisioners submitted bids, forcing the army to ask for bids from the public. On the strategic side, Oswald's bid was quite low: he agreed to provide bread for the first year of the contract for 75% of the pre-war market rate, undercutting the only other offer. Once he had the contract, Oswald looked to control the means of production as much as possible. He moved to Germany with his wife, Mary Ramsay, who was the only heir of a wealthy Jamaican plantation owner. Upon his arrival in Germany, Oswald set up his own supply depots and bakeries, hired his own employees, and built a few mills to grind the wheat into flour. His reliable deliveries of millions of loaves encouraged the army to renew his contract, but when it did so Oswald charged the army 8% more than the market rate. His third contract had a mark-up of 143%, which is why he made a £112,000 fortune on bread by the end of the war.[66] Little wonder Scottish poet Robert Burns referred to Oswald in a bitter ode as the "Plunderer of Armies!"[67]

In September 1761, a newly-appointed First Commissary-General, Thomas Pownall, conducted a tour of British supply depots and magazines in Germany to ferret out embezzlement, negligence, falsification of records, and shoddy goods.[68] One night, after inspecting Oswald's bread depot in Kassel and finding everything in in good shape, Pownall and Oswald shared an evening meal together. As the former colonial governor of Massachusetts and the former Virginia merchant traded stories about their years in the American colonies, the combination of tales and wine ignited Oswald's desire to own land in the Thirteen Colonies or Canada.[69] An uncharacteristic nostalgia also seems to have influenced Oswald, now in his mid-fifties and thirty years removed from his life in Virginia. The enticing possibilities from Nova Scotia to Florida cried out to Oswald like a siren.

Oswald chose to invest in land in newly-acquired Florida.[70] In July 1764, he won the right to survey 20,000 acres on the east Florida coast. True to form, he was one of the first men to win this right. Oswald had to then find someone to select the particular area, survey it, and register that survey with the provisional governor. Once the survey was registered, the governor awarded the land grant with the provision that the land be settled with White Protestants within a decade.[71] Oswald naturally turned to Henry Laurens to find someone to complete these tasks for him. The surveyor Laurens selected a plot of land forty-five miles south of St. Augustine and ten miles north of modern Daytona Beach at the confluence of the Halifax River and Tomoka River and with access

[65] Isser Woloch, *Eighteenth-Century Europe: Tradition and Progress, 1715-1789* (New York: W. W. Norton & Company, 1982), 41. Prussia's rise under Frederick William I and Frederick the Great threatened Austria's domination of central Europe. After the Prussians captured Silesia during the War of the Austrian Succession (1740-1748), the Habsburgs looked to their traditional enemy, France, to balance Prussia's gains. This produced a diplomatic realignment with Britain, Prussia and Russia pitted against France and Austria.

[66] Hancock, *Citizens of the World*, 221, 227, 231, 233-234, 236-237. Specifically, Oswald delivered 5,395,426 loaves of bread during the war, for which the army paid £191,088. Oswald's costs were just £79,000, leaving him with a handsome profit.

[67] Robert Burns, "Ode, Sacred To The Memory Of Mrs. Oswald Of Auchencruive," *Burns Country*, accessed December 3, 2015, http://www.robertburns.org/works/245.shtml

[68] Charles Assheton Whately Pownall, *Thomas Pownall, M. P., F. R. S., Governor of Massachusetts Bay, Author of the Letters of Junius* (London: Henry Stevens, Son & Stiles, 1908), 167-168.

[69] Hancock, *Citizens of the World*, 153.

[70] Britain acquired East Florida (the non-panhandle part of the modern state) from Spain in the Treaty of Paris (1763), which ended the Seven Years' War.

[71] George C. Rogers Jr., "The East Florida Society of London, 1766-1767," *The Florida Historical Quarterly*, vol. 54, no. 4 (April, 1976), 479-496, EBSCOhost.

to the sea via the Ponce de Leon Inlet. From the outset, however, Laurens was not enthusiastic about the undertaking. He wrote to Oswald:

> Your views of establishing a Farm, plantation & Vineyard in our back settlements, are commendable, Generous & the principles upon which they are extended truly noble; nevertheless, I must not flatter but plainly tell you that the carrying of them into effect, tho not impracticable, will be attended with more difficulty & more expense of Money than you seem to apprehend….The first difficulty that you will encounter is that of obtaining a Sufficient quantity of good land in one body.[72]

Laurens issued a similar warning a few months later, but by February 1765 he had taken out advertisements seeking slaves to work on Oswald's East Florida plantation:

> WANTED, Two Negro Carpenters, two Coopers, three pair of Sawyers, forty Field Negroes, young men and women, some acquainted with indico [sic] making, and all with the ordinary course of Planation work in this country; for which good prices will be given, in cash, or bills upon London: And in cases of no bargain, secrecy if required, may be depended on. — Any person having such Negroes to sell please apply to
> HENRY LAURENS[73]

Despite his misgivings, Laurens purchased the slaves and hired an overseer. The slaves cleared 400 acres, planted indigo and sugar cane, erected barns and stables, and built modest housing to forge the Mount Oswald settlement out of the swamp. By 1770, a sugar mill, distillery, and warehouse had been constructed, and Oswald supplemented the work force with additional slaves from Africa.[74] In 1767, 106 Africans arrived from Bance Island.[75] They were followed by the arrival of the *Charlotte* in 1771 with 115 slaves, and the *Betsy* in 1774 with 82 slaves.[76] By 1780, there were 230 slaves working on Oswald's Florida plantation.[77] These men and women faced unspeakable violence and brutality. In fact, the conditions were such that Oswald's slaves murdered their overseer during a slave rebellion in 1767.[78] Others sought escape, and, like slaves from other nearby plantations, may have joined maroon communities, allied themselves with the Seminoles, joined

---

[72] Henry Laurens to Richard Oswald, July 7, 1764 in *The Papers of Henry Laurens*, Volume 4, September 1, 1763-August 31, 1765, George C. Rogers, Jr. and David R. Chesnutt (eds.) (Columbia, South Carolina: University of South Carolina Press, 1974), 332-333.

[73] "Advertisement, *The Gazette*, February 23, 1765," in *The Papers of Henry Laurens*, Volume 4, 584.

[74] Hancock, *Citizens of the World,* 159.

[75] Jane Landers, *Black Society in Spanish Florida* (Urbana, Illinois: University of Illinois Press,1999), 158.

[76] The *Charlotte* had a mortality rate of 10.16%. See "Voyage 75267, *Charlotte* (1770)," *Voyages: The Trans-Atlantic Slave Trade Database*, accessed January 19, 2020, http://slavevoyages.org/voyage/75267/variables. The jointly-owned *Betsy* departed from another slave island, Iles de Los, off the coast from Conakry, Guinea and landed in St. Augustine with a mortality rate of 9.9%. See, "Voyage 78157, *Betsey* (1774)," *Voyages: The Trans-Atlantic Slave Trade Database*, accessed January 19, 2020, http://www.slavevoyages.org/voyage/78157/variables.

[77] Hancock, *Citizens of the World,* 162.

[78] Lucy B. Wayne, *Sweet Cane: The Architecture of the Sugar Works of East Florida* (Tuscaloosa: University Alabama Press, 2010), 54, EBSCOebooks. The name of this overseer was Samuel Huey or Samuel Hewie. It is unclear how control over the plantation was reestablished, but his replacement was a Native American or mixed-race man named Johnson, who stayed for less than a year. Subsequently, Lt. John Fairlamb, Donald McLean, and Frederick Robinson were in charge of the plantation.

Black militias organized by the British to protect Florida during the American Revolution, or sought refuge in Spanish Florida after 1784.[79] Still others were recaptured or died attempting to free themselves from bondage.

Oswald would not be the last person in Florida's history to lose money pursuing an ill-conceived dream.[80] In Oswald's case, the causes of his problems were numerous. His plantation had poor drainage so the land could not produce sugar cane or indigo of sufficient quality to compete in the marketplace. In fact, the land was poorly suited for growing anything but rice, but rice was a crop in which Oswald had little interest; he could never reconcile his agricultural biases with the location's realities. Unlike Bance Island, Mount Oswald lacked easy access to a viable harbor, which made getting supplies to the plantation difficult, and he never found an overseer he could trust.[81] All of this meant that Oswald never saw any favorable return from his Florida investments. As Laurens succinctly said, Oswald's land would "never make any great progress…for want of Neighbours, Navigation & Markets."[82] Truthfully, this shouldn't have surprised the normally sensible Scot. He had been forewarned well before specious, rosy accounts of Florida's climate and topography reached London, but Oswald ignored Laurens' advice and instead helped fuel the speculation in Florida.[83] The misadventure in Florida was the only poor business decision of Oswald's life, but by this point his financial position was such that he could afford such a mistake.

~

On August 13, 1780, during the American War of Independence, Henry Laurens departed Philadelphia with orders from the Continental Congress to sail to Holland aboard the brigantine *Mercury*. His mission was to "endeavor to borrow Money any where in Europe on Account of the United States of America."[84] Twenty-two days into the voyage, Lauren's ship was overtaken and

[79] See Larry E. Rivers, *Slavery in Florida: Territorial Days to Emancipation* (Gainesville: University Press of Florida, 2000), 6, EBSCOebooks; Sylviane A. Diouf, *Slavery's Exiles: The Story of the American Maroons* (New York: New York University Press, 2014), 40, 44-47, 49-50, 54-56; and Edward Mair, "Slaves and Indians," *History Today* 10, 2 (February 2020), 58–69, EBSCOhost.

[80] See, for example, Edward E. Baptist, *Creating an Old South: Middle Florida's Plantation Frontier Before the Civil War* (Chapel Hill, University of North Carolina Press, 2002), 37-47; Gregg M. Turner, *The Florida Land Boom of the 1920s* (Jefferson, North Carolina: McFarland & Company, 2015), 3-5; and Trevor Burnard, *Planters, Merchants, and Slaves: Plantation Societies in British America, 1650-1820* (Chicago, Illinois: University of Chicago Press, 2015), 128-129.

[81] Hancock, *Citizens of the World*, 160, 162, 165-167. The overseer was the person who was "ultimately responsible for a profitable return on his employer's investment." See Tristan Stubbs, *Masters of Violence: The Plantation Overseers of Eighteenth-Century Virginia, South Carolina, and Georgia* (Columbia, South Carolina: University of South Carolina Press, 2018), 1, EBSCOebooks. Stubbs argues that because of this economic relationship, the "implacably violent, sadistically capricious overseer was largely atypical." (3) He also notes the difficulties Oswald and Laurens had in securing an overseer (40, 42).

[82] Henry Laurens to Richard Oswald, August 12, 1766 in *The Papers of Henry Laurens*, Volume 5, 156.

[83] Early accounts of Florida visitors dramatically shaped impressions in London; these included accounts by William Stork (1766), botanist John Bartram (1766), and Andrew Turnbull (1767). None of these accounts were accurate. See Rogers Jr., "The East Florida Society of London, 1766-1767."

[84] Henry Laurens, "Journal and Narrative of Capture and Confinement in the Tower of London, August 13, 1780-April 4, 1782," in *The Papers of Henry Laurens*, Volume 15, December 11, 1778-August 31, 1782, David R. Chesnutt and C. James Taylor (eds.) (Columbia, South Carolina: University of South Carolina Press, 2000), 332.

captured by the twenty-eight gun British frigate *Vestal*, captained by George Keppel. As the *Vestal* approached, Laurens ordered his most important papers to be burned or thrown overboard. A few minutes later, he ordered his remaining papers destroyed as well, but these did not immediately sink and Keppel's crew fished them out of the ocean and dried them out. Keppel determined that none of the recovered documents contained Laurens' mail and said, "you must certainly have destroyed your Mail, [for] I find nothing of any [subs]tance among these Papers."[85] Laurens admitted that this was correct, and Keppel took Laurens into custody. The *Vestal* then sailed for St. John's, Newfoundland, where Rear Admiral Richard Edwards received Laurens as a gentleman, even after Laurens offered a toast to George Washington instead of King George III. By then end of September, Laurens landed as a prisoner in England and though quite ill was "Committed to the Tower of London on 'suspicion of high Treason'" on October 6.[86] According to the judgment, Laurens was to be guarded around the clock, could not receive letters or visitors, could not have any writing materials, and was not permitted to converse. Locked in two small rooms, together "about 20 feet square," Laurens had to provide for his own food, bedding, and candles for the duration of his internment, as was true of other prisoners of the era.[87] Fortunately, Laurens did not face the absolute confinement prescribed by the court. His slave George was admitted to the Tower October 6, he received his first note from London businessman William Manning on October 8, and Laurens' son, Harry, joined Manning as the prisoner's first visitors on October 14.[88]

Laurens' most important advocate throughout his fifteen-month imprisonment in Tower of London was Oswald. The two men were no longer merely business associates as in the 1750s. Rather, they were close friends. Their friendship began in the early 1770s when Laurens came to England with his three sons to visit the Low Countries, France, and Switzerland and to place his sons in schools in Geneva and England. A typical letter to Oswald from this period finds Laurens casually and conversationally sharing news about his sons, the weather, affairs in France, and his inability to meet Voltaire because of the *philosophe*'s fading health.[89] Similarly, when Laurens prepared to return to South Carolina in September 1774, he wrote to Oswald a letter that expressed a debt of friendship, rather than merely a debt of hospitality.[90] While the American Revolution certainly created tensions between the men, as well as a three-year break in their correspondence, their enduring friendship drove Oswald to look for a solution to Laurens' predicament.[91] The two men met in the Tower for the first time on January 3, 1781, after Oswald returned from a long visit to Scotland. Immediately after that visit, Oswald wrote government officials advocating for Laurens' release on parole.[92] Oswald "pledged the whole of his fortune" as collateral for Laurens'

[85] Laurens, "Journal and Narrative of Capture and Confinement in the Tower of London" 334.

[86] Laurens, "Journal and Narrative of Capture and Confinement in the Tower of London," 336, 338, 341.

[87] Laurens, "Journal and Narrative of Capture and Confinement in the Tower of London," 341, 343-344.

[88] Laurens, "Journal and Narrative of Capture and Confinement in the Tower of London," 344-345.

[89] Henry Laurens to Richard Oswald, May 31, 1773 in *The Papers of Henry Laurens*, Volume 9, April 19, 1773-December 12, 1774, George C. Rogers, Jr. and David R. Chesnutt (eds.) (Columbia, South Carolina: University of South Carolina Press, 1981), 55-57.

[90] Henry Laurens to Richard Oswald, September 22, 1774 in *The Papers of Henry Laurens*, Volume 9, 571-574.

[91] Laurens wrote to Oswald January 4, 1775, but Oswald did not acknowledge that letter until April 12, 1778. Oswald describes the lapse as a "long & unpleasant interval." See Richard Oswald to Henry Laurens, April 12, 1778 in *The Papers of Henry Laurens*, Volume 8, March 16, 1778-July 6, 1778, David R. Chesnutt and C. James Taylor (eds.) (Columbia, South Carolina: University of South Carolina Press, 1992), 107.

[92] Richard Oswald, "Note by Richard Oswald," January 3, 1781 in *The Papers of Henry Laurens*, Volume 15, December 11, 1778-August 31, 1782, David R. Chesnutt and C. James Taylor (eds.) (Columbia, South Carolina: University of South Carolina Press, 2000), 351.

good conduct upon release. He served as a liaison between Laurens and the British government, kept Laurens informed about public opinion, submitted lengthy accounts of Laurens' assessment of the political situation in the Colonies, and provided Laurens with food and money.[93] Though these awkward months, Oswald consistently had to walk the line between remaining a loyal British subject and being a friend to the proud American.

Laurens' release came partially from the work of Edmund Burke. In the aftermath of the American victory at Yorktown, Burke criticized the prisoner exchange system in Parliament and used Laurens as a prime example of the problems he believed existed. This led to a decision to release Laurens on bail while awaiting trial.[94] On December 31, 1781, Laurens left the Tower in a sedan chair, too weak to walk, and appeared before the court, which set bail at £8,000. Oswald posted £2,000, Oswald's nephew, Alexander Anderson, posted another £2,000, and Laurens posted the balance.[95] Three days later, Laurens left for Bath in hope that its famed waters would prove restorative.

~

On April 7, 1782, Oswald and Laurens left London to cross the English Channel, seemingly as friends on a vacation. Once the two men landed at Ostend, however, they headed in opposite directions. Oswald traveled south on a secret diplomatic mission to meet with Benjamin Franklin in Paris, while Laurens proceeded north to meet with John Adams, who was trying to secure diplomatic recognition and loans in the Dutch Republic.[96] Oswald's mission was to begin sounding out Franklin about possible peace terms as a result of the growing opposition in Britain to the war with its American colonies.[97] Oswald's selection for this errand was odd in many ways. He was seventy-seven years old, had no diplomatic experience, had never been to France, and by his own assessment could not speak French properly.[98] He was also blind in one eye and used an ear horn to help him hear.[99] Despite these limitations, the Secretary of State for Home, Colonial, and Irish Affairs, Lord Shelburne, specifically chose Oswald for the mission in hope of appealing to Franklin. Oswald and Franklin were born within a year of one another, were both Physiocrats* and admirers of Adam Smith, and had met at least once, at a London meeting of the East Florida Society in 1765.[100] Oswald was also respected for his expertise with regard to the American colonies, and British officials consulted with him regularly during the war. As early as February 1775, for

---

[93] Laurens, "Journal and Narrative of Capture and Confinement in the Tower of London," 355, 358-359, 364, 374, 379, 381.

[94] David Duncan Wallace, *The Life of Henry Laurens*, (New York: G. P. Putnam's Sons, 1915), 388-389.

[95] Laurens, "Journal and Narrative of Capture and Confinement in the Tower of London," 396-397.

[96] Laurens, "Journal and Narrative of Capture and Confinement in the Tower of London," 401-402.

[97] A House of Commons resolution in February 1782 condemned the war, while one in March essentially called for the recognition of American independence. See David Schoenbrun, *Triumph in Paris: The Exploits of Benjamin Franklin* (New York: Harper & Row Publishers, 1976), 351, 353.

[98] Richard Oswald, "Richard Oswald's Journal, April 18, 1782," *The Emerging Nation: A Documentary History of the Foreign Relations of the United States Under the Articles of Confederation, 1780-1789*, Mary A. Giunta (ed.) (Washington, DC: National Historical Publications and Records Commission, 1996), 348-349.

[99] David McCullough, *John Adams* (New York: Simon & Schuster, 2001), 278 and Hancock, *Citizens of the World*, 65.

[100] Hancock, *Citizens of the World*, 391 and Schoenbrun, *Triumph in Paris*, 355.

example, Oswald had submitted his plan for separating one of the southern colonies from the rest of the rebellious states to take advantage of regional differences; his advice was to try to force a divide between the southern aristocracy and what he called the "Mob of Northern Yeomen," who represented little more than a "Confederacy of Smugglers."[101] More significantly, in August 1781, Oswald had written a memorandum criticizing General Charles Cornwallis' decision to move his troops from the Carolinas to Virginia. He had specifically noted that the Chesapeake Bay would have to be secured by the British navy to prevent an entrapment of Cornwallis' troops.[102] Proved correct by the results of the Battle of Yorktown, Oswald's views held cachet. It also helped that Oswald was, in the words of a contemporary, "devoid of the pride of aristocracy without being suspected of democracy," and that King George III thought Oswald to be the "fittest Instrument for the renewal of…friendly intercourse" between the British and the Americans.[103]

A week after departing London, Oswald arrived in Paris, having experienced several frustrating, if rather typical, eighteenth century travel delays. On the morning of April 15, he went to Franklin's residence in Passy and presented his letters of introduction.[104] As the two men conversed, Oswald made it clear that he was there as a private individual, not as an official representative of the British government. He suggested that it might be desirable for both the British and the Americans to negotiate a separate peace from that with the French.[105] Franklin said that the Americans could only act in concert with France, and suggested that the British should offer the Americans all of Canada as a sign of good faith. Oswald hid his surprise about Franklin's opening offer well, and asked to take Franklin's written comments back to London to consult with Shelburne.[106] Franklin agreed, but first wanted Oswald to go with him to Versailles to meet the French foreign minister, Charles Gravier, Comte de Vergennes. Franklin and Oswald did so on April 18. Vergennes kept the two guests waiting a half hour, paid Oswald a series of condescending compliments upon their introduction, and then asked him if he could speak any French. Vergennes' secretary replied that Oswald understood French, but only if His Excellency spoke slowly.[107] Vergennes was far from impressed, which meant that when Oswald asked Vergennes for specific peace terms, the French foreign minister flatly refused to reveal anything. Not naturally inclined towards deviousness and not innately full of guile, Oswald may have been out of his league in the sophisticated, cunning drawing rooms of Versailles. He did understand the situation well enough to remind Franklin on the trip back to Paris that American and French interests might not always align, especially if the French demands proved unreasonable. Franklin did not respond to this observation, but wrote to Shelburne asking that Oswald be officially credentialed as a representative of the British government.[108] Franklin liked working with Oswald and described him as a man who "seems to

[101] Richard Oswald quoted in W. Stitt Robinson, Jr., "Richard Oswald: Advisor to the British Ministry on the Conduct of the American Revolution," *Richard Oswald's Memorandum: On the Folly of Invading Virginia, the Strategic Importance of Portsmouth, and the Need for Civilian Control of the Military*, W. Stitt Robinson, Jr. (ed.) (Charlottesville, Virginia: University of Virginia Press, 1953), 44-45.

[102] Richard Oswald, "Memorandum 15 Augt" in *Richard Oswald's Memorandum: On the Folly of Invading Virginia, the Strategic Importance of Portsmouth, and the Need for Civilian Control of the Military*, W. Stitt Robinson, Jr. (ed.) (Charlottesville, Virginia: University of Virginia Press, 1953), 12-14, 20.

[103] Benjamin Vaughan and George III quoted in Hancock, *Citizens of the World*, 390-391.

[104] In 1782, Passy was just outside of Paris. Today, Passy is in the 16th Arrondissement.

[105] Oswald, "Richard Oswald's Journal, April 18, 1782," 345-346.

[106] H. W. Brands, *The First American: The Life and Times of Benjamin Franklin* (New York: Doubleday, 2000), 601-602.

[107] Oswald, "Richard Oswald's Journal, April 18, 1782," 348-349.

[108] Schoenbrun, *Triumph in Paris*, 356.

have nothing at heart but the good of mankind."[109] Not only was this the type of man with whom Franklin liked to deal, but it also indicated that Oswald's orientation would not be a major threat to American interests.

Undercut by both British parliamentary politics and the military realities created by the defeat at Yorktown, Oswald never had the opportunity to negotiate from a position of strength. By 1782, the British government was as deeply divided about parliamentary reform and economic reform as it was about negotiating a peace with the Americans.[110] On March 27, Charles Watson-Wentworth, the second Marquess of Rockingham, formed a weak ministry to replace that of Frederick North, who was a strong advocate for continuing the war. About the only thing Rockingham's ministers had in common was an opposition to the preceding government.[111] This internal discord can be seen in the rivalry between Shelburne as the Secretary of State for Home, Colonial, and Irish Affairs and Charles James Fox as the Secretary of State for Foreign Affairs. Shelburne was a monarchist, who believed the king should appoint his cabinet ministers; Fox was a Parliamentarian, who believed in the collective power and responsibility of the cabinet.[112] Both men had an intense personal dislike for one another. Both men also had such a strong desire to direct the peace negotiations with the Americans that each sent his own representative to Paris. Shelburne named Oswald to negotiate with the Americans; to negotiate with the French, Fox appointed Thomas Grenville, a twenty-seven-year old aristocrat with no previous diplomatic experience. Despite clear instructions that Oswald and Grenville collaborate and communicate with one another regularly,[113] the two men failed to keep each other effectively informed.[114] This divided representation weakened Britain's negotiating strength significantly.

The American delegation had its own internal divisions, even if the disunity was less publicly obvious and made less political difference. In June 1781, the American Congress appointed five commissioners to negotiate a peace treaty with the British. Reflecting the non-federalist values of the Articles of Confederation,* the five commissioners represented the regional differences of the as-yet unrecognized nation: John Adams was to speak for New England, John Jay for New York, Benjamin Franklin for Pennsylvania, Thomas Jefferson for Virginia, and Henry Laurens for the Carolinas and Georgia. These five men were not all on good terms. Adams had lost his idolized respect for Franklin, while Franklin had grown tired of Adams' uncompromising righteousness and personal vanity.[115] Adams approached Jay with caution since the two men had disagreed significantly in sessions of the Continental Congress; Jay and Laurens had also quarreled in that setting.[116] Laurens was annoyed with Franklin over how little the Pennsylvanian had done to help while he was imprisoned in the Tower.[117] Fortunately for the Americans, however, only Franklin

[109] Benjamin Franklin quoted in John Cannon, *The Fox-North Coalition: The Crisis of the Constitution, 1782-4* (New York: Cambridge University Press, 1969), 16.

[110] Cannon, *The Fox-North Coalition*, 5-6.

[111] Frank W. Brecher, *Securing American Independence: John Jay and the French Alliance* (Westport, Connecticut: Praeger, 2003), 172.

[112] John W. Derry, *Charles James Fox* (New York: St. Martin's Press, 1972), 151, 154, 157, 159.

[113] Lord Shelburne to Richard Oswald, May 21, 1782, *Memorials and Correspondence of Charles James Fox*, Volume IV, Lord John Russell (ed.) (New York, AMS Press, Inc., 1970), 201.

[114] Derry, *Charles James Fox*, 132.

[115] McCullough, *John Adams*, 197-198, 241-242.

[116] Walter Stahr, *John Jay: Founding Father* (New York: Hambledon and London, 2005), 102-103, 162.

[117] Laurens, "Journal and Narrative of Capture and Confinement in the Tower of London," 385.

and Jay were in Paris through most of peace negotiations; this helped minimize the importance of personal tensions within the delegation.[118]

The negotiations began in May 1782, after Oswald returned to Paris with official authorization to represent the British government[119] and after Grenville arrived in France.[120] They proceeded through the summer and fall and centered upon seven issues: formal recognition of the United States as an independent nation; the new country's northern border; its western border; navigation rights on the Mississippi River; pre-war debts; compensation for the lost property of Loyalists; and fishing rights off Newfoundland. Progress was slow. Gradually, Franklin became increasingly willing to deal with the British independent of French oversight. This was a clear violation of Congress' instructions to defer to French leadership in the peace talks, but Franklin's shift in attitude allowed the conversations to progress.[121] This advance was partly offset by Jay's demand that, as a pre-condition for discussing any other terms, the British crown recognize American independence. He also took exception to the original language of Oswald's commission since it referred to the Thirteen States as Britain's "colonies and plantations" instead of as the "United States of America."[122] It wasn't until October 5 that Oswald presented his revised credentials to the American commissioners and finally satisfied Jay's objections.[123] Only then did the talks begin in earnest. When Adams arrived in Paris from the Dutch Republic at the end of October, he insisted that Britain uphold the American right to fish the Grand Banks and other customary fishing areas and recognize the American need to dry the fish on Canadian shores. The language surrounding this condition was so fraught with disagreement that this issue almost caused the talks to collapse.[124] In the end, Oswald agreed to give the Americans much of what they wanted because he and now-Prime Minister Shelburne realized that the best way to break the American-French alliance was to quickly secure the peace. In fact, Oswald had concluded as early as mid-July that Britain "ought to deal with [the Americans] tenderly, as supposed conciliated friends" because treating them harshly will only push them "into more close connection with [the French] court and our other enemies."[125] Oswald also believed that Atlantic trade would again thrive once it was unencumbered by war. He realized that, having lost the battles of Saratoga and Yorktown, the British should move promptly to make the most of the Atlantic's post-war economic opportunities.

---

[118] Jefferson refused to accept his appointment to the peace commission. This proved fortunate, for Jefferson's decision postponed his fierce disagreements with Adams due to their fundamental differences in attitude and approach. See, for example, Joyce Appleby, *Thomas Jefferson* (New York: Times Books/Henry Holt, 2003), 15-16; and Jon Meacham, *Thomas Jefferson: The Art of Power* (New York: Random House, 2012), 88-89, 103.

[119] The Rockingham cabinet voted on April 23, 1782 to authorize Oswald. See Robinson, Jr., "Richard Oswald," 40.

[120] Grenville met Franklin for the first time on May 9, 1792. See "Benjamin Franklin's Peace Journal, May 9, 1782," *The Emerging Nation: A Documentary History of the Foreign Relations of the United States Under the Articles of Confederation, 1780-1789*, Mary A. Giunta (ed.) (Washington, DC: National Historical Publications and Records Commission, 1996), 376.

[121] Walter Isaacson, *Benjamin Franklin: An American Life* (New York: Simon & Schuster, 2003), 406.

[122] Brecher, *Securing American Independence*, 172.

[123] Isaacson, *Benjamin Franklin*, 409.

[124] "Richard Oswald to Thomas Townshend, November 30, 1782," *The Emerging Nation: A Documentary History of the Foreign Relations of the United States Under the Articles of Confederation, 1780-1789*, Mary A. Giunta (ed.) (Washington, DC: National Historical Publications and Records Commission, 1996), 695.

[125] "Richard Oswald to Lord Shelburne, July 12, 1782," *Memorials and Correspondence of Charles James Fox*, Volume IV, Lord John Russell (ed.) (New York: AMS Press, 1970), 247, 249.

On November 30, 1782, Franklin, Jay, Adams, and Laurens met Oswald in his suite at the Grand Hôtel Muscovite, not far from Saint-Germain-des-Prés, to sign the Preliminary Articles of Peace. The agreement set the longest borders of the United States at the Mississippi River and through the middle of the Great Lakes; ensured that the Mississippi River would remain open to navigation by both British and American citizens; granted Americans the right to fish the Grand Banks and the Gulf of St. Lawrence and to dry and cure fish in any unsettled areas in Nova Scotia and Labrador but not on the island of Newfoundland; assured both British and American creditors that they would not be impeded from collecting debts; made token promises about compensation of Loyalist property confiscated or destroyed during the war; provided for the release of prisoners by both sides; and called for the withdrawal of British troops "with all convenient speed & without causing any destruction or carrying away any Negros, or other property."[126]

The addition of the clause concerning the removal of Black slaves came in the final days of negotiation at the behest of Laurens. It came as a direct result of his pre-war business dealings with Oswald. In 1768, Oswald sold his rights to 5,340 acres in South Carolina to Laurens and John Lewis

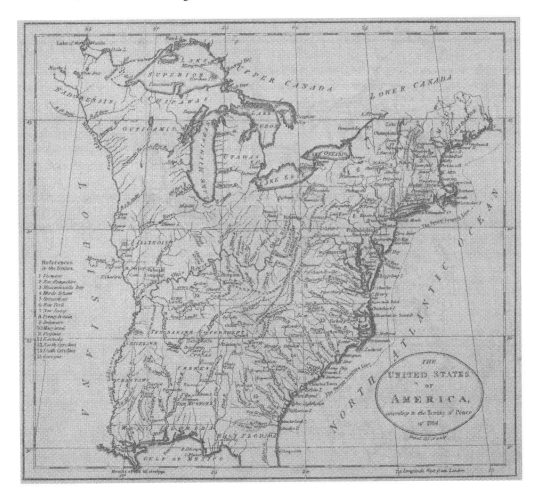

---

[126] "Preliminary Articles of Peace between the United States and Great Britain, November 30, 1782," *The Emerging Nation: A Documentary History of the Foreign Relations of the United States Under the Articles of Confederation, 1780-1789*, Mary A. Giunta (ed.) (Washington, DC: National Historical Publications and Records Commission, 1996), 697-701.

Gervais, a man Oswald had hired during the Seven Years' War to manage one of his German granaries. As part of the deal, Oswald loaned Gervais slaves, including some from his Florida property. At war's end, Gervais still owed Oswald for these slaves, but had no hope of repaying him since all of the slaves had run away during the war. Like many other slaves during the American Revolution, Gervais' slaves fled because the British promised Blacks their post-war freedom in exchange for their wartime assistance. By adding the "Negro clause" to the peace treaty, Laurens offered Oswald a way of recouping his loses.[127] This was the sordid underbelly of the negotiations. Its inclusion in the final treaty meant that another one of the United States' foundational documents would be explicitly tainted with racial considerations.

The British reaction to the preliminary terms Oswald signed was overwhelmingly negative. A typical response was that of Lord Stormont in the House of Lords, who argued that Oswald had been outwitted by the Americans and that the resulting treaty was utterly one-sided as a result. For evidence, Stormont pointed to a particular clause in the preamble and wrote:

> For in return for the manifold concessions on our part, not one has been made on theirs. In truth, the American commissioners had enriched the English dictionary with several new terms and phrases; reciprocal advantages, for instance, meant the advantage of one of the parties.[128]

Such barbs continued unabated through January and February 1783 and eventually resulted in both the collapse of Shelburne's government and Oswald's resignation as peace commissioner.[129] Oswald's replacement, David Hartley, tried to win additional concessions in subsequent months but was unable to make meaningful changes to the agreement. Franklin, Adams, Jay, and Hartley signed the final Treaty of Paris on September 3, 1783. Later that day, the British, French, and Spanish signed a separate agreement at Versailles, officially ending all hostilities.[130] That the Americans signed a different treaty meant that they violated the terms of their alliance with the French.[131] It also meant that Oswald's geopolitical assessment during his first week in France was correct: in the long run, American and British interests were better aligned than Franco-American ones.

Oswald demonstrated his faith in the Anglo-American future eighteen months after he had signed the preliminary agreement with the American commissioners. In late May 1784, he boarded a coach in London with his good friend Laurens and headed to Dover. He made the journey so that

[127] Robert Scott Davis, "Richard Oswald as 'An American': How a Frontier South Carolina Plantation Identifies the Anonymous Author of American Husbandry and a Forgotten Father of the United States," *Journal of Backcountry Studies*, Volume 8, Number 1 (Spring 2014), 19-34, accessed January 19, 2020, http://libjournal.uncg.edu/jbc/article/view/935. When East Florida returned to Spanish control in 1784 as part of the Treaty of Paris, Oswald made arrangements for his slaves to be shipped to South Carolina, Georgia, or British Caribbean islands, where they could be resold. This too helped minimize his financial losses from the American Revolution. See Landers, *Black Society in Spanish Florida*, 159.
[128] Lord Stormont quoted in Cannon, *The Fox-North Coalition*, 52.
[129] Cannon, *The Fox-North Coalition*, 58 and Schoenbrun, *Triumph in Paris*, 388. Shelburne offered his resignation February 24, 1783 and it became official on March 26. For information on how a parliamentary government operates, see Chapter S.
[130] Stahr, *John Jay*, 179-183.
[131] Brecher, *Securing American Independence*, 225.

might see Jay one last time before Jay boarded his ship for New York.[132] As the men spent hours reminiscing over the negotiations and discussing the future of commerce and diplomacy in the Atlantic world, they affirmed their common roots and hope for a peaceful future that was not to be.[133]

~

On November 6, 1784, eight years after Oswald died on his luxurious but not ostentatious Ayrshire estate in southwest Scotland, an anonymous abolitionist published a pamphlet in which a former Jamaican slave named Cushoo meets a friend of his former owner. During their conversation, Cushoo convinces the gentleman to stop consuming sugar and rum until the slave trade is abolished.[134] The clear lesson for the reader is that there are horrifying human consequences for enjoying sweetened tea and other foods made from cane sugar. It is the same lesson that Voltaire's Candide learns in Surinam, where he encounters a slave who has lost his right hand in a sugar factory and his left leg trying to escape the brutality of slavery.[135]

Works like these fueled support for the abolition movement in the late eighteenth and early nineteenth centuries, but Oswald's heirs were not among those who joined the crusade. His wife Mary inherited all of his property on a life-rent basis, which meant that she received the benefits of Oswald's estate until her death but could not distribute or dispose of the assets herself.[136] This meant little changed. Upon Mary's death in 1788, Oswald's nephews, John and Alexander Anderson, followed in their uncle's footsteps and embraced slaving as a profitable venture. When the Andersons inherited a five-ninths share in Bance Island, they purchased the remaining shares from the other owners. They then refurbished the island's facilities, which had fallen into ruin as a result of a French bombardment during the American Revolution. Once the retrofit was complete, the Andersons resumed the slave trade from Bance with the same energy their uncle had. They continued to ship large numbers of Africans across the Atlantic until 1800.[137] Like Oswald, the Andersons did not care to know about the details of the island's slave yard, where in 1791 Anna Falconbridge saw "between two and three hundred wretched victims, chained and parceled out in circles, just satisfying the cravings of nature from a trough of rice placed in the center of each

---

[132] Stahr, *John Jay,* 194. Benjamin Vaughan, who had also been involved in the peace negotiations at Shelburne's urging, was present for these conversations.

[133] War between the United States and Great Britain resumed in 1812.

[134] Anonymous, *No Rum! – No sugar! Or, The Voice of Blood, Being Half an Hour's Conversation between a Negro and an English Gentleman Showing the Horrible Nature of the Slave Trade and Pointing Out an Easy and Effectual Method of Terminating It by an Act of the People* (London: Printed for L. Wayland, 1792), 1-23.

[135] Voltaire, *Candide or Optimism,* Henry Morley and Lauren Walsh (trans.) (New York: Barnes & Noble Classics, 2003), 76-77.

[136] "Correspondence of the Oswald family of Auchincruive, including Richard Oswald (1705-1784)," *Archives Hub,* accessed January 19, 2020, https://tinyurl.com/y5ky7t28. Mary Alexander Ramsay Oswald died December 6, 1788, four years and a month after her husband. Before she died, Mary sought to claim damages as a result of the Treaty of Paris' return of Florida to Spain. She claimed a loss of £9,298 10s. for the value of Mount Oswald but received only £3,921 5s. in the final settlement. See Wayne, *Sweet Cane:* 55-56.

[137] Hancock, *Citizens of the World,* 214-216.

circle."[138] Instead, like Oswald, the Andersons focused their attention on slave prices, overhead costs, mortality rates, and competition. Morality was not a significant concern. Like Oswald, the Andersons knew the right people and the right ways to influence public policy in times of crisis. As a member of Parliament, for example, John Anderson led the victorious charge in 1791 against a bill to prohibit British slave trading along a thousand-mile stretch of the West African coast, including Bance Island.[139] The Andersons also enjoyed their uncle's knack for impeccable timing, for they returned to the slave trade at a particularly lucrative time: between 1791 and 1800, British ships brought almost 400,000 slaves to the Americas and made an average profit of 13%.[140] As a result of their successes, the Anderson brothers did not terminate the Bance Island operation until 1811—four years after Parliament passed legislation outlawing the slave trade.[141] Clearly, Oswald had trained his nephews well in the art of business.

---

[138] A. M. Falconbridge, *Narrative of Two Voyages to the River Sierra Leone during the Years 1791-1793* (London: Frank Cass & Co. Ltd, 1967), 32.
[139] Rawley, *London, Metropolis of the Slave Trade*, 140.
[140] Thomas, *The Slave Trade*, 541.
[141] Hancock, *Citizens of the World*, 216.

P

Lucy E. Parsons

1851-1942

Lucy Parsons was a woman powerful nineteenth-century Americans loved to hate. She demanded social equality instead of social prejudice, economic justice instead of economic discrimination, and revolutionary political change instead of political stability. Despised by those with money and power because she would not compromise her ideals and did not fear arrest, Parsons devoted her life to championing the powerless. For seven decades, she tried to spread her anarchist-socialist message in a country that wasn't able to accept it.

The details of Parsons' early life and family background were vague until recent scholarship unveiled new information.[1] This was because Parsons repeatedly and deliberately tried to hide the details of her childhood from the public over the course of her long life. The reason for this subterfuge was that instead of being of "Spanish-Indian" origins as her husband Albert claimed[2] or of "Spanish and Aztec blood" as friendly contemporaries maintained,[3] Parsons was a descendant of African slaves. Lucia, as she was called then, was born in Virginia in 1851 on a plantation owned by a physician named Thomas J. Taliaferro; contemporaries believed him to be her father because of Lucia's lighter complexion. In late 1862 or early 1863, Lucia joined the thousands whose masters

---

[1] In 2017, Jacqueline Jones published a new biography of Lucy Parsons that convincingly established the details of her childhood. I have relied upon this source to describe the early years of Parsons' life. See Jacqueline Jones, *Goddess of Anarchy: The Life and Times of Lucy Parsons, American Radical* (New York: Basic Books, 2017), ix, 11-12. Jones discovered these details by using modern technological resources and by going back to the original sources from the U.S. Census. See Jacqueline Jones, "The Former Slave Who Became a Radical Agitator (But Never Admitted She'd Been a Slave)," *History News Network*, Columbian College of Arts & Sciences, The George Washington University, accessed March 1, 2020, https://historynewsnetwork.org/article/167965. Prior to the publication of *Goddess of Anarchy*, most scholars relied on the information provided by Carolyn Ashbaugh in her 1976 biography, in which she posited that Parsons was born in Hill County, Texas on a plantation that was owned by James G. and Philip Gathings. See Carolyn Ashbaugh, *Lucy Parsons: An American Revolutionary* (Chicago, Illinois: Haymarket Books, 2012 [reprint]), 267-268.

[2] Albert R. Parsons, *Life of Albert R. Parsons with a Brief History of the Labor Movement in America*, 2nd ed. (Chicago, Illinois: Mrs. Lucy E. Parsons Publisher, 1903), 15.

[3] John Nicolas Beffel, "Four Radicals," *American Mercury*, April, 1932. 441-447.

transported or marched their slaves to Texas to escape war and the threat of emancipation by Union armies.[4] Lucia was joined in this forced migration by her mother Charlotte and her younger brother Tanner. They were settled in McLennan County, north of Waco, where Taliaferro had purchased 200 acres in early 1863.[5] As a house slave, Lucia learned how to cook, clean, and sew.

When the Civil War ended in 1865, Lucia was fourteen or fifteen years old. Now emancipated, Charlotte moved her family, which now included another son, Webster, to Waco.[6] She hoped to take advantage of new employment opportunities and to ensure that her children could benefit from the educational programs created by the Bureau of Refugees, Freedmen, and Abandoned Lands.[7] The Freedmen's Bureau's mission was to offer assistance and relief to former slaves until they became self-sufficient. This included providing transportation for relocation, supplying food and clothing rations, supervising labor contracts to ensure fairness, and issuing marriage licenses to legalize existing relationships between former slaves. The creation of schools for Blacks was a vital part of the Freedmen's Bureau long-term strategy for bringing social change to the former Confederate states during Reconstruction.* This included financing the construction of new schools, hiring teachers, and paying teacher salaries. By the summer of 1866, there were 4,300 Black students attending the 72 Texas schools created by the Freedmen's Bureau and private philanthropic organizations.[8] Lucia was one of these students: in April 1866 she became a pupil in a dirt-floored school in Waco that had been founded by a New Hampshirite, who believed that Black children should only be taught by White men.[9]

When Lucia was sixteen or seventeen, she met her future husband, Albert Parsons, who was White. Albert had joined the Confederate army at the age of thirteen, but after the war became a Radical Republican—someone who favored a genuine transformative Reconstruction of the South, instead of a reconciliatory policy favored by President Andrew Johnson. Albert registered Blacks to vote, collected taxes for the federal government, and edited a pro-Republican newspaper in Waco. As Albert noted, these actions quickly incurred the "hate and contumely" of Texas' White community,[10] and made him a hero among McLennan County's Blacks—a group that faced more

---

[4] For more information on refugeed slaves, see Dale Baum, "Slaves Taken to Texas for Safekeeping during the Civil War," *The Fate of Texas: The Civil War and the Lone Star State*, Charles D. Grear (ed.) (Fayetteville, Arkansas: University of Arkansas Press, 2008), 83-103, EBSCOebooks; and W. Caleb McDaniel, "Involuntary Removals: 'Refugeed Slaves' in Confederate Texas," *Lone Star Unionism, Dissent, and Resistance: Other Sides of Civil War Texas*, Jesús F. de la Teja (ed.) (Norman, Oklahoma: University of Oklahoma Press, 2016), 60-83.

[5] In 1860, there were 663 White families in McLennan County, 40% of which owned at least one slave. By the time Taliaferro arrived two and a half years later with Lucia, Charlotte, and Tanner, these statistics had changed significantly as a result of the war-generated migration. See Jason A. Gillmer, *Slavery and Freedom in Texas: Stories from the Courtroom, 1821-1871* (Athens, Georgia: University of Georgia Press, 2017), 224.

[6] Jacqueline Jones, *Goddess of Anarchy*, 14.

[7] For recent scholarship on the Freedmen's Bureau in Texas see Christopher Bean, *Too Great a Burden to Bear: The Struggle and Failure of the Freedmen's Bureau in Texas* (New York: Fordham University Press, 2016).

[8] *Records of the Field Office for the State of Texas, Bureau of Refugees, Freedmen and Abandoned Lands, 1865-1870* (Washington, DC: United States Congress and National Archives and Records Administration, 2005), 3-5, accessed January 24, 2020, http://www.archives.gov/research/microfilm/m1912.pdf.

[9] Jacqueline Jones, *Goddess of Anarchy*, 17. The man was David F. Davis, a graduate of Phillips Exeter Academy and Dartmouth College, who became a rival of Albert Parsons for influence in the Republican Party in Waco. Lucia's tuition and books were paid for by a Freedman named Oliver Benton, who claimed to have married her. For more information, see Jacqueline Jones, *Goddess of Anarchy*, 16-21, 26. "White" and "Black" are both intentionally capitalized. See Chapter F, footnote 60.

[10] Albert Parsons, *Life of Albert R. Parsons*, 15.

violence between 1869 and 1872 than former slaves did anywhere else in Texas.[11] The reasons for the elevated violence are unclear, but as more and more Whites immigrated to Waco from other parts of the Confederacy to take advantage of new areas of cotton cultivation, the Radical Republicans and Freedmen felt increasingly besieged. Soon it was impossible for them to maintain their electoral majority, either in Waco or at the state level—especially as incidences of violence and voter fraud grew.[12] Lucia and Albert, who were married on September 28, 1872, came to believe that their lives were threatened in the shifting political climate and decided to leave Texas in late 1873.[13] They headed north.

The couple arrived in Chicago as the new year approached. What they found both surprised and captivated them. On the one hand, they did not find a dilapidated city still-reeling from the famous, devastating fire of 1871, which tore through three and a half square miles of urban settlement, destroyed almost 18,000 buildings (including all of the most expensive and important non-residential structures in the city), and left 100,000 people homeless.[14] The Parsonses missed the panic as the blaze approached in the dead of night, forcing many women onto the streets only "dressed in a nightgown and slippers" and a petticoat, many of the men only wearing "nightshirts and pantaloons."[15] They missed the streets jammed full with "carts, carriages, wheel-barrows, and every sort of vehicle," as people of all economic backgrounds desperately tried to save their possessions.[16] They missed both the dread that "the day of judgment had come" with Chicago becoming "Sodom or Pompeii"[17] and the kindness of strangers who provided "coffee and a place to rest" until "a new line of fire" emerged, forcing all to start "on a new race for life."[18] On the other hand, the Parsonses didn't find a city convulsing with the energy of re-construction either. By the time of their arrival, almost all of the rebuilding had been completed and few traces of the fire

---

[11] Randolph B. Campbell, *Grass-Roots Reconstruction in Texas, 1865-1880* (Baton Rouge, Louisiana: Louisiana State University Press, 1997), 178. This level of violence did not occur in Waco in the years immediately following the Civil War because the Freedmen's Bureau was successful in curtailing the maltreatment of Blacks. One reason may have been the continuing presence of Federal troops. As the number of Union soldiers in Texas dropped from 45,000 in 1865 to 500 in 1867, violence against Black people rose. See James Marten, *Texas Divided: Loyalty and Dissent in the Lone Star State, 1856-1874* (Lexington, Kentucky: University of Kentucky Press, 2009), 166, 169, EBSCOebooks.

[12] John David Smith, *We Only Ask for Even-Handed Justice: Black Voices from Reconstruction, 1865-1877* (Amherst, Massachusetts: University of Massachusetts Press, 2014), 104, EBSCOebooks. Smith notes that "black Americans struggled terribly during Reconstruction" as Republicans and the federal courts abandoned freed people. He argues that the Reconstruction devolved into "neo-slavery" (105).

[13] The couple married shortly after the Texas Supreme Court ruled in *Honey v. Clark* that interracial marriage was legal. The Democrat-controlled legislature changed the law shortly thereafter, making interracial marriage illegal. This put the Parsonses at considerable risk. See Jacqueline Jones, *Goddess of Anarchy*, 37-38.

[14] Karen Sawislak, *Smoldering City: Chicagoans and the Great Fire, 1871-1874* (Chicago, Illinois: University of Chicago Press, 1995), 26, 29. The central post office, the courthouse, the customs house, 1600 stores, 60 factories, and numerous banks and hotels were consumed in the flames, which were so hot that iron melted and mortar crumbled.

[15] Aurelia R. King, letter October 21, 1871, quoted in *The Great Chicago Fire: October 8-10, 1871 Described by Eight Men and Women Who Experienced its Horrors and Testified to the Courage of its Inhabitants*, Paul M. Angle (ed.), (Chicago, Illinois: Chicago Historical Society, 1971), 23.

[16] Mary Fales, letter of October 10, 1871, quoted in *The Great Chicago Fire*, 16-17.

[17] King, letter of October 21, 1871, quoted in *The Great Chicago Fire*, 22.

[18] Adeline Rossiter Judd, letter of November 23, 1871, quoted in *The Great Chicago Fire*, 32

remained.[19] Instead, the Parsonses found a city glistening with new buildings and bursting with the civic pride of the well-to-do:

> if the stranger, having missed the sight of the most remarkable conflagration of modern times, would see a still greater wonder, let him visit Chicago...to see the work which has been done....Let him revel for a few days in the spectacle of what a young Western community can do in a single season.[20]

The speed with which Chicago rebuilt was truly remarkable, but underneath the civic pride was a city rupturing with the frustrations and the sorrows of the unemployed and the downtrodden. In the aftermath of the Great Fire, 30,000 people migrated to Chicago to participate in the construction boom, but with the task complete and the national economy in the throes of a depression, the demand for labor quickly shrank. Unemployment soared. On the evening of December 22, 1873, frustrations were so high that ten thousand members of the Chicago working class gathered in the cold and walked to city hall in two silent columns. Illuminated by gas lamps, they marched to present their elected officials with four demands. As Leftists, the protesters fundamentally believed that the government had a responsibility to care for its citizens. They demanded: 1) guaranteed employment for all able to work; 2) assistance for those unable to work; 3) workers' control of the assistance program, and 4) city credit if cash aid was unavailable.[21] The mayor, despite sympathy for the workers' plight, responded that his hands were tied: the city was two million dollars in debt.

Upon the Parsons' arrival in Chicago, Albert was lucky enough to find a job as a printer with the *Chicago Times* as a result of his journalism experience in Waco. He joined the local typographical union. Both he and Lucy were captivated by the class tensions that permeated the city and began working to support the protesters. They were particularly outraged to find that since the Great Fire, the Relief and Aid Society (a private charity operated by the city's wealthiest and most prominent citizens) controlled all welfare efforts in Chicago. They also accepted the rumor that the Relief and Aid Society still had "vast sums of money (several millions of dollars)" in its possession.[22] In fact, the Society had $600,000 of public money still in its coffers, but it refused to distribute these funds because the directors believed that able-bodied men had a responsibility to fend for themselves, and that the Society's on-going programs provided adequately for widows, orphans, and the sick. In other words, the $600,000 was the Society's to keep because it had been more efficient in caring for the needy than anticipated.[23] Such haughty attitudes boiled the Parsons' blood and led both to embrace ideologies that were quite radical for the American political tradition. They became socialists and anarchists.

---

[19] Sawislak, *Smoldering City,* 163, 203. According to the *Chicago Tribune*, the pace of rebuilding was so fast that one brick, stone or iron building of four to six stories was completed each hour of each working day between April 15 and December 1, 1872. The introduction of the derrick allowed for the frantic pace of construction.
[20] Everett Chamberlain, "Five Months After," *The Lakeside Monthly*, April 1872, in *The Great Chicago Fire,* 103.
[21] Sawislak, *Smoldering City,* 266.
[22] Albert Parsons, *Life of Albert R. Parsons,* 16.
[23] Sawislak, *Smoldering City,* 88, 119.

~

In the long wake of the French Revolution and the conservative reaction to it, many different visions competed for radical social change. Karl Marx's publication of the *Communist Manifesto* in 1848 put him in the vanguard and established him as the world's most important radical. In this fifty-

page pamphlet, Marx argued that the specter of social unrest haunted Europe as a result of capitalism's inherent propensity for suppressing the working class. He held that a working-class revolution was inevitable because of the fundamental nature of capitalist competition. Because the capitalist system invariably produces winners and losers, over time those losers would join the ranks of the oppressed as part of the proletariat. Eventually, the proletariat would include so many that its members (who no longer had anything to lose) would rise up, overthrow the established order by force, and then create a different type of society. Oppression would end. Nationalism would wither. Religion would expire. Selfishness would die. No longer would laborers be slaves in an industrial army, prostituting themselves for the benefit of the bourgeoisie.* No longer would the acquisition of private property be the purpose of human existence. Most importantly, the means of production and the wealth created by human labor would be shared by all. "In place of the old bourgeois society, with its classes and class antagonisms, we shall have an association in which the free development of each is the condition for the free development of all."[24]

One of the reasons the *Communist Manifesto* was so influential rested in its methodology and its ability to suggest an end to a historical pattern discussed by the German philosopher Georg Wilhelm Friedrich Hegel (1770-1831). In *Philosophy of History*, Hegel argued that human experience followed a progressive dialectical pattern: for every thesis (or event), there was an antithesis (or reaction), which invariably produced a new, original synthesis (or resolution). This new synthesis, however, cannot last forever, Hegel argued. Its conditions were bound to create a new antithesis, which in turn would produce a new, higher, and original synthesis. For Hegel, there was no end to this algorithm; the historical process was an infinite one.[25] Even more profoundly, Hegel saw this essential pattern occurring in every system, which made Hegelian reasoning

---

[24] Karl Marx and Frederick Engels, *The Communist Manifesto* (New York: Pathfinder Press, 2008), 58.

[25] Henry D. Aiken, *The Age of Ideology: The 19th Century Philosophers* (New York: Mentor Books, 1956), 74. More recent scholarship has questioned whether Hegel deserves full credit for establishing the dialectic model. For the two sides of the dispute, see Leonard F. Wheat, *Hegel's Undiscovered Thesis-Antithesis-Synthesis Dialectics: What Only Marx and Tillich Understood* (Amherst, NY: Prometheus, 2012); and Donald P. Verene, *Hegel's Absolute: An Introduction to Reading the Phenomenology of Spirit* (Albany, New York: State University of New York Press, 2007).

applicable to many different fields. As a young man, Marx found Hegel's ideas to be positively intoxicating.[26] He went on to apply them, arguing that all human conflict was economic, with one class fighting another for control of resources and capital. This process is known as dialectical materialism. In the *Communist Manifesto*, Marx argued that since the proletariat could not oppress itself once it came to power, history's fundamental pattern of one social group exploiting another would end. Dialectical materialism would cease to exist, history would end, and a new world would emerge. This was an extraordinarily powerful message for those desiring social change in the Western world.

Marx's logic did not win over everyone hungering for a different type of society in the nineteenth century, whether in Europe or North America. Members of the radical Left on each continent disagreed over doctrine, strategy, and leadership. In the United States, doctrinal issues focused upon the role of the state and whether politics or economics was the most important force to consider. The strategic questions centered upon: 1) the wisdom of working within existing organizations to promote gradual change; or 2) the necessity of forming new and separate organizations to promote immediate change; and 3) whether violence was a legitimate tool for bringing about social change.[27] The leadership issues focused upon individual egos more than anything else. Many socialists called for the use of the ballot box to advance social change, rejected violence, and saw the state as an entity that should control the means of production and provide for the welfare of its citizens. Others, known as syndicalists, believed in the spontaneous, creative power of autonomous workers' unions to act on their own accord; they embraced violence as a legitimate means of furthering change. A third group, the anarchists, rejected government and hierarchical authority of any kind and advocated a society based upon locally-based, voluntary associations. They saw Marxist ideology as needlessly authoritarian.[28] Despite their differences, these and other Leftist groups benefited from a massive influx of European immigrants over the course of the nineteenth century—many of whom came from Germany and Russia with considerable political acumen. In fact, of the seventeen socialist newspapers published in the United States in 1876, ten were German, three were Bohemian, and one was Swedish, while in the late nineteenth and early twentieth centuries the membership of most of the nation's socialist and communist parties was Eastern European.[29]

~

There were three pivotal events in the history of American labor in the late nineteenth century, one in each of the last three decades of the century. All three had a profound impact on Lucy Parsons' life. The first came in 1877, when, after repeated wage cuts, reduced schedules, and lay-offs in the preceding four years, thousands of railroad workers went on strike. The strikes began in West Virginia on the Baltimore & Ohio Railroad and then expanded to Maryland, Pennsylvania, New York, New Jersey, Indiana, Illinois, and Missouri on various lines. In Chicago, the hub of the Midwest's railroad traffic, the strikes began on July 23. By July 25, Chicago's commercial activity

---

[26] Jonathan Sperber, *Karl Marx: A Nineteenth-Century Life* (New York: Liveright Publishing, 2013), 49.
[27] John Patrick Diggins, *The Rise and Fall of the American Left* (New York: W.W. Norton & Company, 1992), 77-78.
[28] Sperber, *Karl Marx*, 372.
[29] Maldwyn Allen Jones, *American Immigration* (Chicago, Illinois: University of Chicago Press, 1960), 229-230.

had ground to a standstill; without the supplies carried by the railroads, little work was possible. The city was so paralyzed that businesses were losing millions of dollars each day. Combined with some property damage by mobs, this financial loss proved intolerable for Chicago's propertied class. They complained to the mayor, who called for 5,000 "good and experienced citizens" to become deputy police officers. Augmented by 400 members of the Illinois National Guard, the regular police force, a variety of private militia groups, the newly deputized citizens, six companies of United States infantry, and four companies of United States artillery, the forces of law and order had well over 20,000 men in arms. They easily suppressed the disorganized railroad workers. By nightfall on July 26, eighteen were dead, scores were injured, and 400 had been arrested.[30] The four-day strike cost the city's wholesalers $3 million in lost sales and its manufactures $1.75 million in lost production,[31] but the long-term consequence was even more severe: its outcome bred mistrust and resentment on both sides—an ill will that would not easily be forgotten. In short, the gulf between the city's haves and its have-nots grew greater as a result of those July days.

In the early stages of the strike, Albert spoke to a crowd of 15,000, and though counseling moderation and peaceful protest, he urged the crowd to

> fight for our wives and children, for with us it is a question of bread and meat. Let the grand army of labor say who shall fill the legislative halls of the country. Go to the ballot-box and say that the government of the United States shall be the possessors of all of railway lines in this country....[Let us] take out of their hands the means by which they now enslave us...and if the capitalist engages in warfare against our rights, then we shall resist him with all the means that God had given us.[32]

When Albert showed up for work the next day, he found that he had been blacklisted: he would never work for the *Times* or for any other newspaper in Chicago again. With Albert unable to obtain employment, Lucy realized that she would have to support her family. Therefore, she expanded the seamstress business she had begun in 1875. Calling it "Parsons & Co., Manufacturers of Ladies' and Children's Clothing," Lucy hired more workers and began manufacturing uniforms and suits for hotels, restaurants, and other service industries.[33] This unusual enterprise showed Lucy's independent streak. Before the development of the inexpensive sewing machine, most women employed in the garment industry worked in sweatshops in "unspeakable conditions" for "endless hours" and "starvation wages," according to an article in *Ladies Garment Worker*.[34] In Chicago, for instance, seamstresses earned as little as $1.50 a week producing coats which would retail for as much as $15 a piece.[35] Lucy refused to let capitalists so ruthlessly benefit from her labor. Indeed, seeing the conditions others faced and deeply embittered over the response of the capitalists

---

[30] Philip S. Foner, *The Great Labor Uprising of 1877* (New York: Monad Press, 1977), 149-156.

[31] Bessie Louise Pierce, *A History of Chicago, Volume III: The Rise of the Modern City, 1871-1893* (New York, Alfred A. Knopf, 1957), 251. Nationally, over 100,000 workers participated in the 1877 strikes; at least a thousand ended up in jail and over a hundred workers were killed. As a result of this labor unrest, National Guard armories were built in cities around the country to help quell future disturbances. See Howard Zinn, *A People's History of the United States, 1492-Present* (New York: HarperCollins Publishers, 1999), 251.

[32] Albert Parsons quoted in Foner, *The Great Labor Uprising of 1877*, 143-144.

[33] Jacqueline Jones, *Goddess of Anarchy*, 48, 55, 69-70.

[34] John H. M. Laslett, *Labor and the Left: A Study of Socialist and Radical Influences in the American Labor Movement, 1881-1924* (New York: Basic Books, 1970) 101.

[35] Ashbaugh, *Lucy Parsons*, 51.

to the railroad strike, Lucy soon concluded that the interests of labor and capital were utterly irreconcilable.[36] She put her frustrations on paper and published her first work in *National Socialist* in December 1878. Her parody of a Byron poem painted a vivid picture of capitalist oppression. By 1885, she proclaimed, let

> every dirty, lousy tramp arm himself with a revolver or knife and lay in wait on the steps of the palaces of the rich and stab or shoot their owners as they come out. Let us kill them without mercy, and let it be a war of extermination and without pity. Let us devastate the avenues where the wealthy live as Sheridan devastated the beautiful valley of the Shenandoah.[37]

Lucy had found her uncompromising political voice.

The second major event in American labor history of the late nineteenth century was Chicago's Haymarket Riot of May 4, 1886. In the decade since the railway strikes of 1877, labor agitation had centered upon the establishment of an eight-hour work day. In Chicago, the anarchists had gained a prominent role in this fight, led by Albert and his friend August Spies. They had broken with East Coast anarchists, who held that intermediate goals such as the establishment of trade unions or negotiating for shorter hours, higher wages, and better working conditions were mere sops and wouldn't change the fundamental nature of capitalism. Albert and Spies held a more pragmatic view, arguing that it was necessary for anarchists to support the eight-hour movement in order to win the hearts of workers and dominate Chicago's unions.[38] At an eight-hour rally on May 3, outside the McCormick Harvester Machine Company plant, the trouble began. When McCormick strikebreakers tried to leave the plant, they were prevented from doing so by 500 strikers and 6,000 other unionists; the police intervened to protect the scabs and attacked the strikers, killing one and injuring many more. Outraged, Spies called for a protest rally the next evening, May 4. To advertise the gathering, Spies had 20,000 handbills printed, a few hundred of which

---

[36]Lucy Parsons, "On the 'Harmony' Between Capital and Labor, or the Robber and the Robbed," *Lucy Parsons Freedom, Equality & Solidarity: Writings and Speeches, 1878-1937*, Gale Ahrens (ed.), (Chicago, Illinois: Charles H. Herr Publishing Company, 2004), 39-40. Based on these beliefs, Parsons came to reject imperialist-capitalist wars later in her life. She was so opposed to the Spanish-American War that she had her mixed-race, eighteen-year-old son, Albert Jr., committed to a psychiatric institution to prevent him from enlisting as he desired. Parsons also opposed World War I because for her the wage class could not benefit as capitalists did from promoting nationalism. See Lucy Parsons, "Workers and War," *Lucy Parsons Freedom, Equality & Solidarity*, 151.
[37] Lucy Parsons quoted in Ashbaugh, *Lucy Parsons*, 59.
[38] James Weinstein, *The Long Detour: The History and Future of the American Left* (Boulder, Colorado: Westview Press, 2003), 25. The fact that Chicago was the center of the 8-hour movement made this stance especially necessary. See Ray Ginger, *Eugene V. Debs: The Making of an American Radical* (New York, Collier Books, 1962), 64.

called for workingmen to "Arm Yourselves and Appear in Full Force!"[39] These handbills and other written materials, quickly caught the attention of the police.

At 8:30 p.m. on May 4, about 1,300 people gathered at Haymarket Square, which could accommodate the hoped-for crowd of 20,000. Standing in a wagon's box to be seen by the assemblage, Spies spoke first, followed by Albert, who had just returned from a trip to Cincinnati. Another anarchist labor leader, Samuel Fielden, began to speak about 10:00 p.m., as a storm approached.[40] When first raindrops fell, the crowd began to disperse, and Albert and Lucy decided to take their children to a near-by meeting hall while Fielden finished his remarks. Even the mayor left, believing that any potential for trouble had abated.[41] As Fielden was about to finish his speech and release the 200 remaining listeners, a police column of 176 men approached and told Fielden and the crowd to leave. Fielden protested that this was a peaceful gathering and they had the right to free assembly, but he and Spies acquiesced and began climbing down from the wagon. Just then, someone detonated a bomb, killing seven policemen and seriously wounding twenty-three.[42] The police responded by opening fire on the remaining crowd. According to the initial account in the *Chicago Tribune*, "an incessant fire" from police revolvers could be heard for "nearly two minutes and at least 250 shots were fired. The air was full of bullets" as the police "as dangerous as any mob of Communists" were "blinded by passion and unable to distinguish between the peaceable citizen and the Nihilist assassin."[43] When the dust settled, the police had shot three civilians and wounded several dozen.[44]

From the meeting hall a block away, Albert and Lucy saw the flash of light from the exploding bomb, joined others in scrambling for cover, and contemplated the "ominous" sound that Lucy later

---

[39] Philip S. Foner, "Editor's Introduction," *The Autobiographies of the Haymarket Martyrs* (New York, Monad Press, 1977), 5. That this text was printed bilingually in German and English shows the influence of Eastern European immigration in Chicago's working class community.

[40] Foner, "Editor's Introduction," 6.

[41] Beffel, "Four Radicals," 441-447.

[42] Timothy Messer-Kruse, *The Trial of the Haymarket Anarchists: Terrorism and Justice in the Gilded Age* (New York: Palgrave MacMillan, 2011), 3.

[43] "A Hellish Deed," *Chicago Tribune*, May 5, 1886, 1, https://chicagotribune.newspapers.com/image/349711596/

[44] Messer-Kruse, *The Trial of the Haymarket Anarchists*, 188.

recalled "turned me cold."[45] Once it seemed safe, the family made their way home. A friend, Lizzie Holmes, convinced Albert that he had to get out of town,[46] which was sound advice since city officials saw the bombing as an opportunity to destroy the anarchist movement in Chicago and were making scores of arrests.[47]

Lucy was one of the first targets of the crackdown, partly because of the police's determination to find Albert and partly because of her own rhetoric. She was, in fact, arrested three times the day after the bombing alone,[48] her house was repeatedly ransacked in the subsequent days, and her son, age six, was subjected to verbal threats and physical abuse.[49] By May 10, hundreds of anarchists, socialists, and labor leaders were in jail, and by May 27, thirty-one persons had been indicted by a grand jury as accessories to murder and for conspiracy. Albert, who was hiding in Wisconsin, was indicted in absentia. In the next few weeks, some of the accused turned state's evidence or plea bargained; others simply had the charges against them dropped. By June 21, when the trial began, there were eight defendants, including Albert, who unexpectedly walked into the courtroom to stand trial with his comrades. The all-male, middle-class jury, consisting of clerks, salesmen, a bookkeeper, and a school principal,[50] was not impressed by his voluntary surrender and on August 20 returned a guilty verdict for all eight men. Seven, including Albert, were given a death sentence, and one was sentenced to fifteen-years in prison.[51]

It was at this moment, with the reading of the verdicts, that Lucy's public life truly began. With enormous poise, she walked up to her condemned husband, shook his hand and said, "My husband, I give you to the cause of liberty. I now go forth to take your place....I, too, expect to mount the scaffold. I am ready."[52] Two hours later, she was on a train to Cincinnati to begin a seven-week speaking tour to raise the money for the appeals process and to educate Americans about anarchism. To Lucy this meant the elimination of "every law, every title deed, every court, and every police officer or soldier," for she considered statutes to be "human tricks" and voting to be a "modern delusion."[53] She wanted to abolish the state and the wage system that supported it. Such

---

[45] Lucy Parsons quoted in Beffel, "Four Radicals," 441-447.
[46] Ashbaugh, *Lucy Parsons,* 76.
[47] Weinstein, *The Long Detour,* 25.
[48] "A Historical Trial: The Great Crime of May 4 and the Men Who Perpetrated It," *Chicago Tribune,* August 21, 1886, 2, https://chicagotribune.newspapers.com/image/349276924/
[49] Ashbaugh, *Lucy Parsons,* 85.
[50] "A Historical Trial: The Great Crime of May 4 and the Men Who Perpetrated It." The jurors were relatively young: seven were in their 20s and five in their 40s. The youngest, S. C. Randall, was 22 and a salesman with a seed company. Many of the jurors did not have a strong religious affiliation, although they all had been raised in the Protestant tradition. None were Jewish, Orthodox Christian, or Roman Catholic.
[51] Timothy Messer-Kruse has challenged the traditional historical interpretation that the trial was unfair and that the accused were unjustly sentenced to death. He argues that the accused anarchists did know to varying degrees about the bombing and wanted to use the trial to promote their ideology instead of providing a strong defense. See Messer-Kruse, *The Trial of the Haymarket Anarchists,* 184-185.
[52] Lucy Parsons quoted in Ashbaugh, *Lucy Parsons,* 104.
[53] Lucy Parsons quoted in Steve J. Shone, *American Anarchism* (Leiden, Netherlands: Brill, 2013), 78, 83, EBSCOebooks.

views meant that she was a threatening presence in many communities. In Cleveland, for example, she was refused access to the rented meeting hall when the owner learned the topic of her speech, so she so stood on a chair in the street and declared,

This building has been closed against me by a damnable capitalist, but I will show them all they cannot down me....I will take the red flag of the [Paris] Commune and plant it all over New England in mills and factories.[54]

Similarly in Orange, New Jersey, the proprietor tried to renege on the contract, but Lucy helped forced open the entrance and spoke to a hundred people as scheduled; the police refused to intervene since the anarchists had a contract and were meeting peacefully.[55] In Philadelphia, Lucy attracted one thousand people and spoke of how the Constitution "is not worth the paper it's written on," predicting that everyone present would eventually be called an anarchist and arrested.[56] At the Cooper Institute in New York, the mood was festive with a brass band playing the "Marseillaise" and a choir singing revolutionary hymns as the large crowd yelled its support. At the end of her remarks, Lucy pulled out a scarlet silk handkerchief and said that upon her death, either at the scaffold or by natural causes, she wanted to be wrapped in anarchist red.[57] It brought down the house. Before a group of Yale University students in New Haven, she repeated what she had told other varied crowds: "You may have expected me to belch forth great flames of dynamite and stand before you with bombs in my hands. If you are disappointed, you have only the capitalist press to thank for it."[58] This ability to reach crowds both large and small, to impress those both friendly and hostile, confirmed Lucy's reputation as a great orator.

Lucy's tour achieved its goal of raising money and increasing public awareness: Albert and his fellow inmates received a stay of execution from the Illinois Supreme Court in November 1886. It was, however, a false victory. Ultimately, the same court upheld the jury's original verdict and the United States Supreme Court refused to hear the cases. At noon on November 11, 1887, Albert and the three other defendants who had refused to ask the governor for a commuted sentence, were

---

[54] Lucy Parson quoted in "Lucy Parsons Talks: Preaching Anarchy in the Streets of Cleveland," *The New York Times*, October 16, 1886, 5, ProQuest Historical Newspapers. The Commune was the name of the socialist government which briefly governed Paris in 1871.

[55] "Hall Was Hired and Mrs. Parsons Insisted on Lecturing in it," *The New York Times*, October 25, 1886, 2, ProQuest Historical Newspapers. Arriving in New Jersey, Lucy was received at the train station by "two little girls offer[ing] her a huge bouquet of red roses and then a number of women stepped from the welcoming crowd and kissed the dusky representative of Anarchy." See "Mrs. Parsons Warmly Received," *Chicago Tribune*, August 21, 1886, 10, https://chicagotribune.newspapers.com/image/349262675/

[56] Lucy Parsons quoted in "Philadelphia Anarchists: Mrs. Parsons Appealing for the Chicago Anarchists," *The New York Times*, November 1, 1886, 1, ProQuest Historical Newspapers.

[57] "Socialists and Anarchists: They Listen to one of Mrs. Lucy Parsons's Familiar Speeches," *The New York Times*, November 5, 1886, 2, ProQuest Historical Newspapers. Today, the Cooper Institute is the Cooper Union for the Advancement of Science and Art.

[58] Lucy Parsons quoted in Ashbaugh, *Lucy Parsons,* 108.

hanged from the gallows. Lucy did not get to say goodbye to her husband. As the trap door of the gallows opened that gray day, she was huddling naked in a jail cell a few blocks away with her two naked children clinging to her for warmth. All three had been arrested that morning when they tried to gain permission to see Albert, and all had been stripped under the assumption that one carried a bomb. Lucy and her children did not have their clothes returned to them until 3:00 p.m., when they were allowed to leave and claim Albert's body. "Most of the police were drunk. It was a day of celebration for them," Lucy said bitterly.[59] Two days after the executions, 250,000 people lined the route to the Waldheim Cemetery to pay their respects. Albert and his compatriots had to be buried outside the city limits since no Chicago cemetery was willing to inter their bodies.

The third major event in American labor history in the late nineteenth century, the Pullman Strike of 1894, was also centered in Chicago. In the words of Theodore Dreiser, Chicago then "possessed a high and mighty air calculated to overawe and abash the common applicant and to make the gulf between poverty and success seem both wide and deep."[60] For the poor, Chicago was a place of filth and squalor with "no basement too dark, no stable loft too foul, no rear shanty too provisional, no tenement room too small" to become a work space for the colonies of German, Irish, Italian, Polish, Russian, French-Canadian, and Jewish immigrants, according to the social reformer Jane Addams.[61] In these neighborhoods, mountains of garbage buried sidewalks, carcasses of dead animals slowly rotted, and vermin multiplied. Chicago's infant mortality rate was high and the drinking water supply was so routinely compromised by the city's unreliable sewage system that poor mothers often preferred giving their children pasteurized beer instead of water.[62] Its air was fouled with coal dust and the deafening noise of trains, streetcars, and iron-wheeled carriages passing day and night.[63] It was also dangerous. In neighborhoods like Hell's Half-Acre and Satan's Mile, rough saloons and crass bordellos dominated storefronts and petty thieves and organized gangs looted casual passers-by. These areas were so full of vice and mayhem that even Chicago's hardened police officers never entered them alone.[64]

Conversely, Chicago was also a city of enormous pride and wealth. It had recently hosted World's Columbian Exposition to celebrate the 400th anniversary of Columbus' landing in the Western Hemisphere. Its skyline featured impressive buildings that set the standard for

---

[59] Lucy Parsons quoted in Beffel, "Four Radicals," 441-447.

[60] Theodore Dreiser, *Sister Carrie* (New York: New American Library, 1980), 20.

[61] Jane Addams quoted in Jean Bethke Elshtain, *Jane Addams and the Dream of American Democracy* (New York: Basic Books, 2002), 98.

[62] Andrew Kersten, *Clarence Darrow: American Iconoclast* (New York: Hill and Wang, 2011), 33.

[63] Erik Larson, *The Devil in the White City: Murder, Magic and Madness at the Fair that Changed America* (New York: Vintage Books, 2003), 28.

[64] Herbert Asbury, *Gem of the Prairie: An Informal History of the Chicago Underworld* (DeKalb, Illinois: Northern Illinois University Press, 1986), 113, 122.

commercial office space;[65] its streetcar lines extended into the countryside in anticipation of future growth; and it had become the nation's second largest city. Chicago's leading citizens were men of confidence and ambition, whose fortunes came from a combination of innovation, ruthlessness, and corruption. They lived in Victorian mansions with mansard roofs and wrought-iron fences. They decorated with flamboyant wallpaper, crystal chandeliers, stately molding, marble busts, delicate porcelains, gold clocks, life-size oil paintings, and richly upholstered, dark-wood furniture. They would have wholeheartedly agreed with Baptist minister Russell Conwell, who told more than six thousand audiences that, "The opportunity to get rich, to attain unto great wealth is...within the reach of almost every man and woman....I say that you ought to get rich and it is your duty to get rich" because "money is power" and "you can do more good with it than without it."[66]

George Pullman was perhaps the boldest of Chicago's robber barons. In addition to building a near-monopoly in passenger railroad cars, he built his own company town south of the city to combine his production needs and social values. He hoped to create a community that would be "ennobling and refining" by enforcing regulations that promoted responsibility, morality, cleanliness, and sobriety.[67] These included a banning taverns and factory cafeterias (to encourage men to spend their lunches and evenings at home), discouraging women from working outside the home, prohibiting what he believed to be immoral entertainment, and even forbidding workers from sitting on their stoops in shirtsleeves.[68] The Pullman Palace Car Company owned the stores, the church, and the library—everything except the public school. The town's housing was hierarchical: executives resided in well-appointed, detached houses; foremen and other company officials lived in row houses; and single, male laborers either rented rooms in private homes or occupied boarding houses. Rents for all of these living spaces were substantially higher than in surrounding areas, but Pullman's salaries prior to 1893 largely compensated for this discrepancy. Employees complained that the company didn't acknowledge merit or longevity, didn't provide a pension, didn't tolerate criticism, and didn't hesitate to intimidate employees before they entered a voting booth.[69] Employees were not required to live in Pullman, but with daily garbage daily and indoor plumbing, the sanitary conditions were much better than in Chicago itself, and residents felt safer than in other neighborhoods. For those who embraced its social regulations, it was a good place to live. As one journalist said, "The corporation does practically everything but sweep your room and make your bed, and the corporation expects you to enjoy it and hold your tongue."[70] This understanding changed in 1893, when the nation experienced a sharp recession after two decades of erratic economic growth. Pullman began cutting wages. A federal study concluded that Pullman cut wages 25%, but workers argued that it was much more and some statistics bear this out: bi-monthly salaries for a seamstress were cut in half, from $16.87 to $8.28, and the overall company bimonthly average salary fell 35% from $25.53 to $16.85.[71] Most problematically, Pullman did not

---

[65] H.W. Brands, *American Colossus: The Triumph of Capitalism, 1865-1900* (New York: Anchor Books, 2010), 303.

[66] Russell Conwell quote in "Acres of Diamonds," *The Study of American History, Volume II, Reconstruction to the Present* (Guilford, Connecticut: The Dushkin Publishing Group, 1974), 42-43.

[67] George Pullman quoted in David Ray Papke, *The Pullman Case: The Clash of Labor and Capital in Industrial America* (Lawrence, Kansas: University Press of Kansas, 1999), 12.

[68] Janice L. Reiff, "A Modern Lear and His Daughters: Gender in the Model Town of Pullman," *The Pullman Strike and the Crisis of the 1890s: Essays on Labor and Politics*, Richard Schneirov, Shelton Stromquist, and Nick Salvatore (ed.), (Urbana, Illinois, University of Illinois Press, 1999), 66, 69.

[69] Ginger, *Eugene V. Debs,* 124, 128.

[70] Unidentified Pittsburgh journalist quoted in Brands, *American Colossus,* 519.

[71] Reiff, "A Modern Lear and His Daughters: Gender in the Model Town of Pullman," 77. Pullman also laid

make any adjustments to the town's rents or to store prices. Employees were quickly squeezed to the breaking point.

The Pullman Strike began May 11, 1894, when the employee grievance committee voted to walk out, after meeting with company officials who refused to make concessions in salaries or prices. The company also refused to agree to arbitration. The employees knew that their odds of success were small, but a month later, when the American Railway Union (ARU) voted to join the strike by refusing to handle any trains carrying Pullman passenger cars, a local protest became a national issue. The ARU's president was Eugene V. Debs, who worried that his year-old union wasn't ready to handle the strike of this magnitude, but the rank and file membership was outraged by Pullman's actions and buoyed with confidence from the ARU's unexpected strike victory against the Great Northern Railroad earlier that year. At its convention on June 26, the ARU voted to strike and 125,000 workers closed ranks, refusing to move Pullman cars. This brought twenty railroads around the nation to a standstill.[72] Debs specifically ordered members to move any trains that carried government mail cars so that the ARU wouldn't violate the Interstate Commerce Act, but the railroad owners found a counter strategy: they attached mail cars to trains that normally did not normally carry them (such as suburban lines), thereby threatening to inconvenience the general public and prompting the federal government to intervene. President Grover Cleveland ordered federal troops into Chicago on July 4 and a few days later declared martial law in response to the violence triggered by their presence. The strike collapsed, Pullman felt vindicated, and Debs, arrested for interfering with interstate commerce, spent six months in jail. He emerged from prison as a socialist, writing, "As long as workingmen vote the same ticket [Democrat or Republican] their masters vote they must expect to be doomed to slavery."[73]

Lucy Parsons took note of this shift and wondered if Debs might help foster a new vision for America, for he too was known as a great orator. It is odd, however, that she was not more visibly active in the Pullman strike itself. There are no surviving records of her speaking to strikers or joining the picket lines or being arrested during this time. In fact, in the *Chicago Tribune*, there is only one mention of Parsons during the entire strike: that she spoke to "a small audience" in her home on May 28 on the subject of liberty.[74] This doesn't fit well with Parsons' history of agitation, her fearlessness in confronting the law, or her partiality for the limelight. It also doesn't match the *Tribune*'s fixation with finding new opportunities to criticize radicals for being un-American, as it had in the aftermath of the Haymarket Riot.[75] One possible reason for Parsons' lack of visibility

---

off employees, cutting his staff from 5,500 in July 1893 to 3,300 in May 1894.

[72] Ginger, *Eugene V. Debs,* 138. When the strike began, the ARU did not have a strike fund to support workers.

[73] Eugene Debs quoted in Harold W. Currie, *Eugene V. Debs* (Boston, Massachusetts: Twayne Publishers /G.K. Hall and Company, 1976), 32.

[74] "Lucy Parsons Talks of Liberty," *Chicago Daily Tribune*, May 28, 1894, 2, https://chicagotribune.newspapers.com/image/349451897/

[75] Lauren L. Basson, *White Enough to be American?: Race Mixing, Indigenous People and the Boundaries of State and Nation* (Chapel Hill, North Carolina: University of North Carolina Press, 2008), 150-151. This assessment of the *Tribune* needs to be balanced against the fact that the paper also prominently published verbatim statements from anarchists and socialists, allowing radicals to speak for themselves. See, for example, "Social Democracy at Parting of the Ways," *Chicago Tribune*, September 21, 1897, 1, https://chicagotribune.newspapers.com/image/349874129/.

was that she knew she was becoming overshadowed as the nation's premier anarchist by another woman, Emma Goldman. Goldman was the insider who knew all the right people, the intellectual who spoke four languages, and the fresh face people wanted to see, while Parsons was the darker, working-class outsider, who, in Goldman's words, was merely another anarchist's wife, "millions of miles removed" from substantive ideas.[76] This was unfair, since Parsons had done far more than ride her late husband's coattails to fame. It was also ironic, since the two proud women held many beliefs in common. Goldman once defined anarchism as

> the liberation of the human mind from the dominion of religion; the liberation of the human body from the dominion of property; liberation from the shackles and restraint of government. Anarchism stands for a social order based on the free grouping of individuals for the purpose of producing real social wealth; an order that will guarantee to every human being free access to the earth and full enjoyment of the necessities of life, according to individual desires, tastes, and inclinations.[77]

Parsons would have agreed with all of this, as well as with Goldman's view that women's suffrage was a useless cause since obtaining the vote wouldn't really change the status of American women as long as the capitalist structures remained in place. The two women did disagree with one another about marriage and sex, and this difference helped fuel Goldman's prominence. Goldman saw marriage as furthering oppression against women and advocated for free love,[78] but Parsons publicly emphasized the importance of the traditional family and the value of monogamy.[79] As Parsons once succinctly said, "Variety in sex relations and economic freedom have nothing in common. Nor has it anything in common with Anarchism, as I understand Anarchism; if it has, then I am not an Anarchist."[80] This position put her at odds with even close Leftist friends, such as fellow *Alarm* editor Lizzie Holmes, who believed that sexual freedom would help bring about emancipation for women.[81] Goldman won radical support by casting aside Victorian sensibilities, proclaiming that "marriage and love have nothing in common"[82] and that love was the "harbinger of hope, of joy, of ecstasy…the defier of all laws."[83] As Goldman's celebrity grew, she became the

[76] Emma Goldman quoted in Roxanne Dunbar-Ortiz, "Afterward," in *Lucy Parson Freedom, Equality & Solidarity*, 170. Another scholar summarizes Goldman's view by saying Goldman saw Parsons as "an opportunist who took advantage of her husband's notoriety." See Donna M. Kowal, *Tongue of Fire: Emma Goldman, Public Womanhood, and the Sex Question* (Albany, New York: State University of New York Press, 2016), 11.
[77] Emma Goldman, *Anarchism and Other Essays* (New York: Dover Publications, 1969), 62.
[78] Kowal, *Tongue of Fire*, 17-18. This advocacy for free love did not mean, however, that men and women could be as promiscuous as they wanted to be in Goldman's eyes (37). Another valuable source on Goldman's attitudes towards free love and marriage, as well as to her relationships is Paul Avrich and Karen Avrich, *Sasha and Emma: The Anarchist Odyssey of Alexander Berkman and Emma Goldman* (Cambridge, Massachusetts: The Belknap Press of Harvard University Press, 2012).
[79] Parsons may have advocated for the traditional family publicly, but she did not hold herself the same standard in her own life. See Ashbaugh, *Lucy Parsons*, 201.
[80] Lucy Parsons quoted in Ashbaugh, *Lucy Parsons*, 204.
[81] Wendy Hayden, *Evolutionary Rhetoric: Sex, Science, and Free Love in Nineteenth Century Feminism* (Carbondale, Illinois: Southern Illinois University Press, 2013), 47-49, EBSCOebooks. Lizzie May Hunt Swank Holmes (1850-1926) grew up on a free love commune in Berlin Heights, Ohio, but by the end of the nineteenth century she questioned if free love would provide women with freedom. Instead, she "urged a more complex view of women's oppression," according to Hayden (page 48).
[82] Goldman, *Anarchism and Other Essays*, 227.
[83] Goldman, *Anarchism and Other Essays*, 236.

voice that defined what anarchism stood for in the United States, and Parsons found herself increasingly eclipsed by a woman fifteen years her junior. As the 1890s progressed, Parsons' growing frustration with her decreased national prominence may have created a sense of dejection, which could explain her notable absence in the Pullman Strike.

~

Idealists never surrender, and with the passage of three more years, Parsons optimistically returned to the radical stage, albeit in a diminished role. She was present in June 1897 when Debs decided to terminate the ARU and replace it with a broader movement called Social Democracy of America.[84] From the beginning, Social Democracy suffered from factionalism, but Parsons was initially captivated by its willingness to accept all workers, regardless of gender or race, and by its goal to establish a colony with public ownership of the means of production and distribution in a new western state.[85] People could join the colony for $500, which could be paid for in $5 weekly installments over a two-year period. The first edition of the organization's newspaper, *The Social Democrat*, proclaimed that concentrating socialism in a colony will "advance the cause of Socialism to a tremendous extent" because its members were engaged in "a great and holy work."[86] Social Democracy's official seal honored the American utopian tradition and the optimism of the organization's first convention: it featured a sun rising over a pastoral scene and body of water, surrounded by the words, "Labor is the Source of All Wealth and All Civilization."[87] This fit well with Parsons' belief that society could be organized on the basis of working "two or three or four hours a day of easy, of healthful labor."[88] She joined the Board of Directors and chaired a chapter of the organization, known as Branch 2.[89] The group estimated that it needed to raise $2.5 million to buy the land and finance starting costs, but a year later it had raised less than a tenth of one percent of that amount, and the outbreak of the Spanish-American War made alternative financing, such as bonds, infeasible.[90] By the time Social Democracy held its second convention in June 1898, Debs and Parsons had become estranged over the use of violence as a permissible strategy; the two could not reconcile the ideological differences between anarchism and socialism. Parsons saw Debs as a dictatorial leader,

---

[84] Ira Kipnis, *The American Socialist Movement, 1897-1912* (Chicago, Illinois: Haymarket Books, 2004), 51-52.

[85] These new states were Montana, North Dakota, South Dakota, and Washington, which were admitted to the Union in 1889; Idaho and Wyoming, which were admitted in 1890; and Utah, which was admitted in 1896.

[86] Cyrus Field Willard, "Colonization Department" *Social Democrat*, January 6, 1898, Volume 5, Issue 1, 3, microfilm.

[87] I saw the seal in the Eugene V. Debs House in Terre Haute, Indiana. I am grateful to the librarians of Indiana State University and to the museum's Karen Brown for arranging a special tour for me.

[88] Lucy Parsons quoted in Shone, *American Anarchism*, 85.

[89] Jacqueline Jones, *Goddess of Anarchy*, 249.

[90] Willard, "Colonization Department."

who was deluded in believing that the ballot box could make a meaningful adjustment to class structure in the United States.[91] Debs maintained,

> There is no connecting link between the platform of Social Democracy and anarchy….Ours is a peaceable organization, which seeks to educate the people to the use of peaceful means of reform. We believe in the ballot, not in bullets.[92]

Parsons' and Debs' personal rift was symbolic of the factionalism within Social Democracy of America. At its second convention, the organization was so divided over its goals that the party split in two with 52 delegates voting to continue with the colonization plan and 37 delegates voting to form a new "a class-conscious, revolutionary, social organization," the Social Democratic Party.[93] The colonists went to the state of Washington and established a community, the Burley Colony, which lasted until 1913.[94] Meanwhile, the Social Democrats with Debs as their leader, eventually merged with other socialist parties to become the Socialist Party of America in 1901.[95] By the presidential election of 1912, the united socialists had gained sufficient momentum and support that Debs earned 6% of the national popular vote—the highest tally for any Leftist party in American history. This success was a direct result of Debs' personal appeal. Without him on the ticket in 1916, the Socialists garnered 300,000 fewer votes than four years before, and the party never regained the level of success it achieved in 1912.[96]

---

[91] Lucy Parsons, "Forcible Revolution to Come," *Chicago Tribune*, September 21, 1897, 1, https://chicagotribune.newspapers.com/image/349874129/.

[92] Eugene V. Debs quoted in "Toss Out the Rabid: Branch 2, Social Democracy Given a Cold Deal," *Chicago Tribune*, September 19, 1897, 1, https://chicagotribune.newspapers.com/image/349872339/.

[93] Ginger, *Eugene V. Debs*, 214.

[94] During its fourteen years of existence, the colony's 150 residents built a lumber mill, a fruit cannery and a cigar factory but ultimately supply and demand issues doomed its economic model. Members of the community also disagreed with one another over whether to require manual labor of all members. See Chris Henry, "Utopian Colony Failed, but Burley Thrives a Century Later," *McClatchy-Tribune Business News*, January 14, 2012, n.p., ProQuest Central. Interestingly, the Burley Colony held all property communally and did not allow for private property. A study shows that the American utopian communities that allowed for some element of private property were more successful than those that did not. See Clifford F. Thies, "The Success of American Communes," *Southern Economic Journal*, vol. 67, no. 1 (July, 2000), 186-199, ProQuest Central.

[95] The merging groups were Debs' Social Democrats; a large faction of the Socialist Labor Party, which broke away from Daniel De Leon's authoritarian leadership; and independent socialist entities from Iowa and Texas. See Ginger, *Eugene V. Debs*, 224. For a detailed biography of De Leon, see Stephen Coleman, *Daniel De Leon* (New York: St. Martin's Press/Manchester University Press, 1990). Coleman argues (page 5) that De Leon was a man who made "plenty of enemies. Those who have not detested him, however, have tended to worship him."

[96] James Chace, *1912: Wilson, Roosevelt, Taft & Debs—The Election that Changed the Country* (New York: Simon & Schuster Paperbacks, 2004), 239.

Parsons had a more prominent role in the inaugural convention of the International Workers of the World (IWW) in June 1905 in Chicago. She shared the dais with Debs, Mother Jones, and the organization's president Bill Haywood, who declared the event the "Continental Congress of the Working Class."[97] The IWW was in many ways the type of organization Parsons had sought all along, and she threw her heart into it, editing and raising money for one of the organization's newspapers, *The Liberator*.[98] The IWW was a syndicalist organization, open to both skilled and unskilled workers, regardless of race or gender.[99] Its goal was to bring all workers together into one union to take control of the means of production without a particular political affiliation. It was willing to use direct action, general strikes, and sabotage to achieve its goals.[100] As a result of this inclusivity and purposefulness, the inaugural convention attracted over 200 delegates, who represented trade unionists, socialists, anarchists, and many other hues of radical opinion.[101] At the opening convention, Parsons took the floor and told the delegates that she wasn't there to represent any one group or branch or association as some were, but instead wanted to represent the great mass who are "downcast and miserable" so that she might raise her "voice and mingle it with yours in the interest of humanity."[102] A day later, she gave a major speech—often considered the finest of the convention[103]—about the status of working-class women and the future of the industrial unionism. She began by noting that "men have made such a mess of it in representing" women. She argued that women are "the slaves of the slaves" because they are "exploited more ruthlessly than men." She cautioned that meaningful change required hard work and sacrifice, not just enthusiastic speeches and celebratory conventions. Then she outlined what it would take to become a "revolutionary Socialist" and to realize the goal that "the land shall belong to the landless, the tools to the toiler, and the products to the producers." Parsons argued that since workers already had a numerical superiority, all they lacked was class consciousness. They simply needed to become better informed and educated in order to bring about social change. She urged her audience to

---

[97] William D. Hayward quoted in Peter Cole, David Struthers, and Kenyon Zimmer, "Introduction," *Wobblies of the World: A Global History of the IWW*, Peter Cole, David Struthers, and Kenyon Zimmer (eds.) (London: Pluto Press, 2017), 3.

[98] The fact that Parsons purposely placed the IWW's logo on the newspaper's masthead symbolizes her strength of her support for the organization, at least until 1912, when she left the organization and joined the Syndicalist League of North America. By 1912 Parsons thought that the IWW had become too centralized an organization, and she believed in a strategy of disrupting mainstream labor unions like the AFL from within. See Kenyon Zimmer, "A Cosmopolitan Crowd: Transnational Anarchists, the IWW, and the American Radical Press," *Wobblies of the World*, 34, 38. One illustration of the changes in the IWW that Parsons objected to can be found in Bill Haywood's statement from 1912: "I, for one, have turned my back on violence. It wins nothing. When we strike now, we strike with our hands in our pockets." Bill Haywood quoted in Diggins, *The Rise and Fall of the American Left*, 81-82.

[99] This was a fundamentally different approach to unionism than the American Federation of Labor, which was the most important labor organization at the time. The AFL was primarily an association of craft unions for white, skilled male workers, while the IWW welcomed women, African Americans, Chinese Americans, and unskilled laborers.

[100] Diggins, *The Rise and Fall of the American Left*, 81.

[101] Ginger, *Eugene V. Debs,* 254-255.

[102] Lucy Parsons, "Speeches at the Founding Convention of the Industrial Workers of the World," *Lucy Parsons Freedom, Equality & Solidarity,* 77.

[103] Franklin Rosemont, *Joe Hill: The IWW & the Making of a Revolutionary Workingclass Counterculture* (Oakland, California: PM Press, 2015), no page, Kindle edition.

turn our eyes eternally and forever towards the rising star of the industrial republic of labor, remembering that we have left the old behind and have set your faces towards the future. There is no power on Earth that can stop men and women who are determined to be free at all hazards. There is no power on Earth so great as the power of intellect. It moves the world and it moves the Earth.[104]

The revolution Parsons dreamed of never occurred in the United States, perhaps because of what has been described as a "search for order," especially by White middle-class Americans, who were caught in between the titanic opposites of crushing poverty and copious wealth.[105] These Americans wanted to realize societal improvements to lessen economic chasm, but they did not want to change the fundamental nature of the American political or economic system. The achievements of the Progressive Movement, such as the graduated income tax, the direct election of senators, women's suffrage, and the establishment of state and national parks and monuments, were hailed by the middle class as meaningful reforms. For someone like Parsons, however, these changes were merely methods of ameliorating and distracting and delaying. The differences between the policies of the mainstream political parties were like the differences between Tweedledum and Tweedledee.[106] American capitalists went along with Progressive changes because they came to realize that they could benefit from the rationalization of the economy and predictability in politics championed by Theodore Roosevelt.[107] Industrialists also knew that making concessions would undercut Debs' and Parsons' radical message, thereby minimizing any risk to their advantageous position. Indeed, Progressivism insured that the industrial elite held onto what they had. In the end, most Americans were more suspicious of big labor than of big business[108] and there was very little change in the class divide as a result of the Progressive Era.[109] In addition, the inherent political conservatism of the majority of European immigrants undercut the ability of Leftist parties to attract more voters.[110]

A series of events in the aftermath of World War I also contributed to overcoming Parsons' dream creating an anarchist-socialist society. Between 1918 and 1920, the nation was seized with a paralyzing, almost hysterical fear of that which was different or unknown. Mistrusting innovation and change, many Americans supported what they thought they heard in Warren G. Harding's presidential campaign message of "a return to normalcy."[111] The first assault came with the appearance of the Great Influenza in 1918, which terrorized the nation with the speed and

---

[104] Lucy Parsons, "Speeches at the Founding Convention of the Industrial Workers of the World," *Lucy Parsons Freedom, Equality & Solidarity,* 78-83.

[105] Robert H. Wiebe, *The Search for Order, 1877-1920* (New York: Hill and Wang, 1967), 165.

[106] Louis Auchincloss, *Theodore Roosevelt* (New York: Times Books-Henry Holt and Company, 2001), 125.

[107] Gabriel Kolko, *The Triumph of Conservatism: A Reinterpretation of American History, 1900-1916* (New York: The Free Press, 1977), 284-285.

[108] Joan Hoff Wilson, *Herbert Hoover: Forgotten Progressive* (Boston, Massachusetts: Little, Brown and Company, 1975), 34.

[109] Neil A. Wynn, *From Progressivism to Prosperity: World War I and American Society* (New York: Holmes & Meier Publishers, Inc., 1986), 21.

[110] Maldwyn Allen Jones, *American Immigration*, 231.

[111] John W. Dean, *Warren G. Harding* (New York: Times Books-Henry Holt and Company, 2004), 100. Dean shows that Harding was not calling for a resurrection of the past, but rather for sensible, ordinary progression. A Library of Congress article supports this idea, arguing that Harding was "rejecting the activism of Theodore Roosevelt and the idealism of Woodrow Wilson." See "Presidential Election of 1920," *American Leaders Speak: Recordings from World War I*, Library of Congress, accessed March 3, 2020, https://tinyurl.com/yytuplhd.

randomness with which it attacked. The influenza was so noxious that healthy people died within as little as six hours of the first sign of infection, and many of the infected suffered from acute delirium and other mental disorders after other symptoms passed. Out of a total population of 105 million, 675,000 Americans died. Worldwide, at least five percent of the population succumbed to the most-deadly virus the planet has ever witnessed.[112]

The influenza attack was followed by a horrific series of race riots in 1919, which also spread considerable mistrust and fear. While the riots were frequently triggered by small, localized events, they were fundamentally about differing expectations and economic opportunity: Black veterans arrived home from Europe believing that their wartime service earned them a better place in American society, while most Whites saw the wartime service as an aberration and sought to return Blacks to their subservient, pre-war status. In Chicago, for example, the crisis began when five Black teenagers swimming off a raft in Lake Michigan on a hot July afternoon crossed into a "Whites Only" beach area. One young man drowned after being hit by a rock thrown by a White man objecting to racial mixing on the segregated beach. When the teens sought help and identified the perpetrator, a White police officer on duty refused to act. Word of the incident quickly spread and hundreds of angry Blacks and offended Whites faced off against one another. After rocks were thrown and shots were fired, Chicago found itself embroiled in days of uncontrolled violence. The *Defender*, a Black newspaper, described the situation vividly, noting that "every hour, every minute, every second, finds patrols backed up and unloading their human freight branded with the red symbol of this orgy of hate. Many victims have reached the hospitals, only to die before kind hands could attend to them" because of the onslaught of victims. Things were so tense that "undertakers on the South Side refused to accept bodies of White victims. White undertakers refused to accept Black victims. Both for the same reason. They feared the vengeance of the mobs."[113] By the time the riot ended, twenty-three Blacks and fifteen Whites were dead, 342 Blacks and 195 Whites had been injured, and twice as many Blacks as Whites had been arrested.[114] This was only one of more than twenty-five riots which occurred across the nation during the "Red Summer" of 1919. In addition, vigilantes lynched over eighty African Americans and burned another eleven at the stake before the year ended.[115] In such a venomous atmosphere, it is not surprising that Parsons continued to falsify her racial origins and deny her African American heritage.

A third source of post-war fear was the failure of the Allied intervention to overthrow Lenin's communist government in Soviet Union. During the Red Scare of 1919-1920, the word "Bolshevik" became synonymous with treason, and treason became associated with anyone possessing Left-of-center political views. When Seattle workers, for example, called for a general strike in February 1919 to respond to the 99% rise in the cost of living since 1914, they were seen as betraying the nation instead of supporting their families. Later in the spring, a May Day bomb plot was

---

[112] John M. Barry, *The Great Influenza: The Epic Story of the Deadliest Plague in History* (New York: Viking, 2004), 242, 379-380, 397, 460. The outbreak of COVID-19 in the winter of 2019-2020 generated considerable discussion about the 1918 pandemic. There was greater agreement about the number of deaths in the United States than globally, but 50 million deaths worldwide is a commonly accepted figure. See Douglas Jordan, "Discovery and Reconstruction of the 1918 Pandemic Virus," *Centers for Disease Control and Protection*, [2019], accessed May 17, 2020, https://www.cdc.gov/flu/pandemic-resources/reconstruction-1918-virus.html

[113] The *Defender* quoted in *American Violence: A Documentary History*, Richard Hofstadter and Michael Wallace (ed.) (New York: Alfred A. Knopf, 1971), 246-247.

[114] William M. Tuttle, Jr., *Race Riot: Chicago in the Red Summer of 1919* (New York: Atheneum, 1970), 4-10, 64.

[115] At least ten of these victims were black veterans, some of whom were still in uniform when they were killed. Wynn, *From Progressivism to Prosperity,* 181, 189.

discovered which had targeted thirty-six national leaders such as Supreme Court justice Oliver Wendell Holmes, billionaires John D. Rockefeller and J.P. Morgan, and Attorney General A. Mitchell Palmer. A coordinated bomb attack aimed at federal judges, major city mayors, and Palmer followed on June 2. Palmer responded with a crackdown against the radical Left. In a coordinated series of raids, thousands of people were arrested without warrants, denied legal representation, and deported.[116] One person who suffered this persecution was George Markstall, Parsons' companion for the last three decades of her life.[117] He was arrested by the Secret Service and charged with threatening the life of President Woodrow Wilson by calling him a "grafter." After Markstall's arrest, federal and Chicago city officials announced that they would deport every anarchist leader in the Midwest at the first act of sabotage or bomb explosion.[118] For Parsons, the episode's suppression of free speech and resulting police oppression was eerily reminiscent of the

Haymarket events. America was clearly not going to be a nation with much tolerance for radicals.

Not that this stopped Parsons from continuing her quixotic path. In the 1920s, she could be found hawking pamphlets and copies of *Life of Albert R. Parsons* from tattered shopping bags around town, or speaking occasionally at alternative coffee shops.[119] She was active in the Communist Party's International Labor Defense, which was dedicated to generating public awareness about and providing legal assistance for imprisoned radicals. But with the passage of time she found herself to be increasingly politically isolated. Not only had so many of her generation's Leftist compatriots died, but the founding of the Soviet Union and the Comintern had changed the political landscape.[120] In the 1930s, she found much to criticize. Parsons believed Franklin D. Roosevelt's New Deal* program was the "wind that has blown the radical movement to Hell," and that the broad expansion of government represented "despotism…on horseback riding at high speed."[121] By 1934, she had concluded that "anarchism is a dead issue in American life today."[122] Such discouragement did not prevent her from appearing two years later at a May Day rally to mark the fiftieth anniversary of the Haymarket bombing. At the fiftieth anniversary of the executions, Parsons, blind and hobbled at eighty-six, spoke with youthful vehemence, condemning capitalism

---

[116] Robert K. Murray, *Red Scare: A Study in National Hysteria, 1919-1920* (McGraw Hill Book Company, 1964), 7, 34, 71, 78, 193, 213, 222.

[117] Markstall worked in many trades during his life and was active in the Socialist Party in Omaha and Kansas City before meeting Parsons. They were arrested together in Los Angeles in April 1913. The couple was reportedly married in 1927, but no marriage certificate has been found. See Jacqueline Jones, *Goddess of Anarchy*, 289-290, 332.

[118] "Hold Radical in Chicago: Alleged to Have Said President Had Better Be Out of the Way," *The New York Times*, June 6, 1919, 1, ProQuest Historical Newspapers. Upon his arrest, Markstall was taken to a "psychopathic hospital for evaluation." See "Reds' 'Mailman,' Crones' Friend, Seized in Raid," *Chicago Tribune*, June 6, 1919, 3, https://chicagotribune.newspapers.com/image/355038959/

[119] Jones, *Goddess of Anarchy*, 316, 321-322.

[120] Jones, *Goddess of Anarchy*, 316, 320, 326. For more information on the International Labor Defense, see Rebecca Hill, *Men, Mobs, and Law: Anti-Lynching and Labor Defense in U.S. Radical History* (Durham, North Carolina: Duke University Press, 2008), 209, 214-216.

[121] Lucy Parsons quoted in Jacqueline Jones, *Goddess of Anarchy*, 334.

[122] Lucy Parsons quoted in Jacqueline Jones, *Goddess of Anarchy*, 336.

and injustice in no uncertain terms.[123] In May 1938, there was a brief mention of Parsons in the *Chicago Tribune* noting that she "now lives quietly in a cottage on the northwest side of Cicero," and has "a mild-mannered, alert little body whose chief interest seems to be the chickens she fondly tends." The column suggested that because the woman who was once "one of the most dangerous characters in America," and who liked to quip that she'd "been in more jails than any woman in America" now listened to Father Coughlin, she could no longer be considered a threat.[124] Naturally, Parsons realized her limitations, but that did not stop her from speaking to more than a thousand strikers of the Farm Equipment Workers' Union on February 22, 1941, or from riding on the Union's float in the May Day parade that spring, or from agitating crowds in the summer heat in front of a department store while pleading for 'beautiful anarchy.'"[125]

~

Lucy Parsons died a horrible death. On March 7, 1942, a fire broke out in her Chicago home. Blind and increasingly frail, she was unable to get herself out of the house in time to escape the flames. She was almost 90.

The *New York Times* article announcing Parsons death is telling because of what was said and what was not. It quite unintentionally confirms the struggle she faced to gain recognition and legitimacy. Appearing on page 36, the article was sandwiched between a story about an automobile accident on a New Jersey turnpike and a story about a murder warrant in Manhattan. It is a mere 443 words long. The article makes no mention of her fiery oratory or voluminous writing. Eighty percent of the text is actually devoted to Albert Parsons, the Haymarket Riot, and the circumstances of the house fire that killed her.[126] Her significance reduced to twenty percent of her own obituary, Lucy was slighted by the nation's newspaper of record. Her accomplishments were marginalized because the world she envisioned never materialized. Even more symbolically, her Waldheim Cemetery gravestone in the shadow of the Haymarket Martyrs' Monument lists the year of her birth incorrectly by eight years. The proud, obstinate radical might not have expected anything more for

---

[123] Jacqueline Jones, *Goddess of Anarchy,* 339-340.

[124] "A Line O' Type of Two," Chicago *Tribune*, May 4, 1938, 12. https://chicagotribune.newspapers.com/image/370986838/. Father Charles Coughlin was a conservative Catholic priest with a popular, national radio program in the 1930s. He frequently attacked socialism and the New Deal and advocated for American isolationism. See Donald Warren, R*adio Priest: Charles Coughlin, the Father of Hate Radio* (New York: The Free Press, 1996).

[125] "Strikers Rally at Entrance of Tractor Plant," *Chicago Tribune*, February 23, 1941, 13, https://chicagotribune.newspapers.com/image/372233210/; Herma Clark, "When Chicago Was Young," Chicago *Tribune*, August 17, 1941, 104, https://chicagotribune.newspapers.com/image/372248103/; and Jacqueline Jones, *Goddess of Anarchy,* 341. Significantly and symbolically, the strike on February 22, 1941 involved picketers at the International Harvester's McCormick Works, which was the same factory where police had attacked strikers in 1886, thereby triggering the Haymarket events.

[126] "Lucy Parsons Is Burned to Death in Chicago; Husband was Hanged After Haymarket Riot," *The New York Times*, March 8, 1942, 36, ProQuest Historical Newspapers. The newspaper article in the *Chicago Tribune* was more substantial, providing a picture of her from 1915, and a picture of the burned house. It also documents the fact that the FBI confiscated her library of 1500 books, as well as all of her personal papers. These have never been seen since. See "Lucy Parsons, Blind Anarchist, Burned to Death," *Chicago Sunday Tribune*, March 8, 1942, 10, https://chicagotribune.newspapers.com/image/371264529/

her epitaph or her obituary, however, having humbly but feistily written in 1937, "Oh Misery, I have drunk thy cup of sorrow to its dregs, but I am still a rebel."[127]

---

[127] Lucy Parsons, "November 11: Fifty Years Ago," *Lucy Parson Freedom, Equality & Solidarity,* 165.

Q

Naser al-Din Shah Qajar

1831-1896

Six months before Naser al-Din Shah Qajar died, the British envoy in Tehran wrote to the foreign office in London describing Iran and its monarch in the bleakest terms:

> The Administration is, and has been for generations, corrupt right through. The first idea of every Persian official is illicit gain. No doubt the proceedings of the Shah and others who ought to set an example tend to increase the prevailing corruption, but they have not created it. Its roots lie deep in the national character. Of all the Asiatics with whom I have had to deal, the Persians appear to me to be the most shameless liars and thieves. And there is no patriotism upon which one can work. Patriotism here is replaced by national conceit, which makes the Persians look down upon all other countries, but will not make them sacrifice the smallest personal interest for the good of their own.[1]

The envoy's late nineteenth-century sense of racial superiority may be distasteful, but his grim assessment of Iran's state in 1895 was not altogether incorrect. Indeed, the promise with which Naser al-Din Shah Qajar began his reign almost five decades before had long vanished; where there was once potential, only frustration stood. This situation, however, was not entirely of the shah's making.

Nasir al-Din ascended the throne at seventeen as the fourth monarch of Iran's Qajar dynasty. The most important man in the new shah's youth was not his father or another male relative. Instead, it was Amir Kabir, a reformer of humble origins who eventually became Nasir al-Din's leading minister.[2] The reason for this unusual circumstance was that Nasir al-Din's father,

---

[1] Sir Mortimer Durand quoted in Firuz Kazemzadeh, *Russia and Britain in Persia, 1864-1914* (New Haven: Yale University Press, 1968), 290. Many of the sources used in the chapter refer to the nation as Persia, but this is largely a Western term. Iran is the preferred indigenous placename.

[2] Many figures in Iranian history are known more by their titles than by their personal names. In the interest of simplicity, I have chosen to identify such individuals by their most well-known title throughout the text, despite

Muhammad Shah, and his mother, Mahd 'Ulya, did not enjoy a happy marriage.[3] Several of their children had died in infancy, and Mahd 'Ulya's outspoken independence led Muhammad Shah to

avoid her whenever possible. Muhammad Shah also demoted Mahd 'Ulya, making her a temporary wife instead of a permanent one.[4] Because their relationship was so strained, Muhammad Shah wanted little to do with Nasir al-Din. In fact, the king did not see the prince between ages four and eight and had nothing to do with the prince's educational development and training. Muhammad Shah even waited until seven months before he died to send the prince to Tabriz to govern the northwest Iranian province of Azerbaijan—the custom for the heir apparent.[5] As a result, Nasir al-Din was not as well prepared as he might have been to govern the nation when his father died in September 1848 of complications from gout. The new shah had to rely on the help of experienced advisors like Amir Kabir.

Because the sixty-three-year-old Qajar dynasty had never experienced a peaceful succession between monarchs, it was essential for Nasir al-Din to secure the capital, Tehran. This was not an altogether straightforward task because the new king was in Tabriz, 400 miles away, and did not have an army at his disposal. Rather, he had to raise one, as was the custom for provincial governors.[6] This required money, which Muhammad Shah had not provided. Therefore, Nasir al-Din needed to borrow funds from Tabriz merchants to secure his throne. At first, the merchants balked at the royal request, not being sure that the new king would repay them once he was in Tehran. This obstinacy forced Nasir al-Din to turn to the British and Russian consuls in Tabriz, both of whom happily guaranteed the loans in order to increase their influence with the new Qajar king.[7] Thus from the very beginning of his reign, Nasir al-Din's had his fortunes tied to the machinations of foreign diplomats.

After consulting with royal astrologers to determine the most auspicious timing, Nasir al-Din entered Tehran with his paid troops on October 20, 1848. He found the capital peaceful, thanks to

---

the anachronisms this choice produces. In this case, Amir Kabir was a prestigious Qajar military title given to the army's commander-in-chief; it was awarded to Mirza Taqi Khan Farahani (1807-1852) by Nasir al-Din Shah in 1848, despite the man's non-aristocratic family background.

[3] Mahd 'Ulya means "queen mother." She was born Princess Malek Jahan and lived from 1805 to 1873.

[4] Abbas Amanat, *Pivot of the Universe: Nasir al-Din Shah Qajar and the Iranian Monarchy, 1831-1896* (Berkeley, California: University of California Press, 1997), 26, 31, 41. Temporary wives were kept as sexual companions for a specified time period and a specified sum, but this was not the equivalent of prostitution. See Janet Afary, *Sexual Politics in Modern Iran* (New York: Cambridge University Press, 2009), 60, 65.

[5] Ann K. S. Lambton, *Qajar Persia: Eleven Studies* (Austin, Texas: University of Texas Press, 1988), 16; and Amanat, *Pivot of the Universe*, 38, 63-65.

[6] Gavin R. G. Hambly, "Iran During the Reigns of Fath 'Ali Shāh and Muḥammad Shāh," *The Cambridge History of Iran, Volume 7, From Nadir Shah to the Islamic Revolution*, Peter Avery, Gavin Hambly, and Charles Melville (eds.) (New York: Cambridge University Press, 1991), 159.

[7] Amanat, *Pivot of the Universe*, 91. Over the course of Nasir al-Din's long reign, Great Britain and Russia competed to gain the more influential hand in Iran. While Britain has traditionally been seen as the more influential, University of Delaware historian Rudi Matthee argues that Russia's involvement was "more direct, invasive, and consequential than that of the British." See Rudi Matthee, *Russians in Iran: Diplomacy and Power in the Qajar Era and Beyond* (London/New York: I. B. Tauris, 2018), 1-2.

his mother, who had taken charge upon Muhammad Shah's death and ordered palace troops to quell local riots in her son's name.[8] At his first public audience, Nasir al-Din sat on a marble throne adorned in the symbols that linked the Qajar monarch to Iran's past. These included a twenty-four-pound jeweled crown designed by the dynasty's founder; armlets brandishing two famous diamonds an Iranian army took from the Mughals in 1739; and a diamond sword associated with the Shi'a faith.[9] One of the king's first acts was to appoint Amir Kabir as his chief minister. With this appointment, Nasir al-Din wrote,

> I have delivered all affairs of Persia into your hands and hold you responsible for the good, or bad, that may ensue. We have this day made you First Person in Persia. We have every trust and confidence in your justice, and treatment of our people; and in no one else do we put any faith except in you.[10]

This endorsement gave Amir Kabir an unprecedented political and military influence that he immediately set out to use.

The new chief minister's vision for Iran differed substantially from those of his predecessors. Amir Kabir hoped to replace the decentralized administrative systems that characterized much of Iran's history with a strong national government with streamlined procedures to overcome its tribal disunity, economic inertia, and technical backwardness. He wanted to modernize Iran's educational, judicial, and military structures. By doing so Amir Kabir looked to create a strong, well-financed monarchical state that could stand proudly amongst the nations of the world.[11] He began his efforts by cutting the salaries and pensions the government paid out in order to restore the empty treasury.[12] Then he encouraged the shah to limit the practice of appointing men to offices in exchange for a payment so that merit might replace what he saw as graft.[13] In 1851, Amir Kabir conducted the first new land tax assessment of the Qajar dynasty in another effort generate revenue for the state.[14] The reforming minister also sought change the relationship between the state and the 'ulama—the clerical body of religious scholars and jurists. He wanted to limit the 'ulama's authority by requiring state approval of all its rulings, thereby bringing secular oversight to religious courts. He also sought to limit the right of religious authorities to provide asylum in places other than holy shrines,[15] and challenged tradition by wanting to abolish torture as a form of punishment with the country.[16] In other areas, Amir Kabir undertook a smallpox vaccination campaign to

---

[8] Lambton, *Qājār Persia*, 16.

[9] Amanat, *Pivot of the Universe*, 100. The shah who led the invasion of Mughal India was Nadir Shah (1688-1747). He expanded Iranian territory and founded the short-lived Afsharid dynasty. The large diamonds are the Koh-i-Noor (105 carats), which is now a part of the British crown jewels, and the Daria-i-Noor (182 carats), which may still be a part of the crown jewels of Iran.

[10] Nasir al-Din Shah Qajar quoted in Amanat, *Pivot of the Universe*, 101.

[11] Amanat, *Pivot of the Universe*, 104, 127, 131.

[12] Lambton, *Qājār Persia*, 287.

[13] Amanat, *Pivot of the Universe*, 126.

[14] Lambton, *Qājār Persia*, 81.

[15] Hamid Algar, *Religion and State in Iran 1785-1906: The Role of the Ulama in the Qajar Period* (Berkeley, California: University of California Press, 1969), 129-133.

[16] Willem Floor, "Change and Development in the Judicial System of Qajar Iran," *Qajar Iran: Political, Social and Cultural Change, 1800-1925*, Edmund Bosworth and Carole Hillenbrand (eds.) (Edinburgh, U.K: Edinburgh University Press, 1983), 120.

improve public health[17] and created a department of translation so that Nasir al-Din might be kept well informed about the contents of foreign journals. He also founded the nation's first weekly newspaper in February 1851 to disseminate information and explain government actions.[18]

The chief minister's most lasting reform was the founding of a polytechnic school in Tehran, Dar al Fonun. Amir Kabir believed that instead of sending students abroad to learn Western military science and medicine, Iran would benefit more by bringing European instructors to Iran to teach students, who in time could become teachers themselves. Inaugurated December 29, 1851, Dar al Fonun initially enrolled 105 teenage boys, 58% of whom studied military sciences and 19% of whom studied medicine. The language of instruction was French and students progressed at their own pace. Although the inaugural class didn't graduate until 1858, as it struggled to meet the expectations of its Austrian instructors, eventually most students graduated in four or five years.[19] As he waited for the college to produce new officers, Amir Kabir proposed other military reforms. He imposed a new quota system on each village and tribe, which allowed for six months of service, six months of leave, and a paid salary;[20] he appointed a doctor to each military regiment and founded the first state military hospital to help wounded soldiers;[21] and he proposed creating all-Christian regiments within the Iranian army in order to draw upon as many talented men as possible.[22] His overall military goal was to develop a Western-trained and Western-equipped army that could defend Iran against foreign powers.

Amir Kabir's vision and actions generated intense opposition in Qajar Iran. This began within the court, as members of both the harem and the government who benefited from existing socio-political systems feared a loss of revenue and status. Leading the objections was Nasir al-Din's mother, Mahd ʿUlya. Like Ibrahim's mother as valide sultan of the Ottoman Empire, Mahd ʿUlya held the highest rank and commanded the largest salary within the harem.[23] Her motivation went beyond financial considerations, and, because the harem of the Qajar court was far less sequestered than the one in Istanbul, she was a nimble political force.[24] Not only did she see the prime minister's inspirational sway as a threat to her own ability to influence the shah and his policies, but she sensed

[17] Willem Floor, *Public Health in Qajar Iran* (Washington, DC: Mage Publishers, 2004), 41. For a detailed discussion of smallpox vaccination, see Chapter R. In Iran, there was never a national smallpox outbreak, but it was endemic in the Persian Gulf port of Bushire. See Floor, *Public Health*, 33.

[18] Peter Avery, "Printing, the Press, and Literature in Modern Iran," *The Cambridge History of Iran, Volume 7*, 820-821.

[19] Monica M. Ringer, *Education, Religion and the Discourse of Reform in Qajar Iran* (Costa Mesa, California: Mazda Publishers, Inc., 2001), 70-78.

[20] Lambton, *Qājār Persia*, 23, 72, 98. Under the quota system, the number of men each village or tribe had to supply was proportionally based on their tax assessment.

[21] Floor, *Public Health in Qajar Iran*, 189-190.

[22] Daniel Tsadik, *Between Foreigners and Shiʿis: Nineteenth Century Iran and its Jewish Community* (Stanford, California: Stanford University Press, 2007), 43.

[23] Guity Nashat, "Marriage in the Qajar Period," *Women in Iran from 1800 to the Islamic Republic*, Lois Beck and Guity Nashat (eds.) (Urbana, Illinois, University of Illinois Press, 2004), 57.

[24] Afary, *Sexual Politics in Modern Iran*, 67-68, 74.

that Amir Kabir was not above treachery against her.[25]   In fact, in an effort to eliminate competing influences, the prime minister at one point suggested to Nasir al-Din that he shoot his mother and claim it was an accident.[26]   Hence, from the opening months of the shah's reign, Amir Kabir and Mahd 'Ulya were locked in an intense struggle over the direction of the court and the country. The battle also played out beyond the capital, as provincial officials across Iran resisted the prime minister's efforts because they benefited from the decentralized status quo. Even Iran's topography stood in opposition to Amir Kabir's vision: with limited arable land, few navigable rivers, rugged mountain ranges, and insufficient natural ports, Iran's environment resisted the goals of modernization.[27] The greatest opposition, however, came from the *ulama*, which saw Amir Kabir's aspirations as a dire threat to Iran's uniqueness as a Shi'a state.

~

Most Muslims today believe that the before he died in 632 the Prophet Muhammad did not designate a caliph—the temporal successor and protector of the faith. Therefore, it was incumbent upon the community to select someone to govern in the moment of transitional crisis. These Sunni Muslims recognize the legitimacy of Abu Bakr, a wealthy merchant and Muhammad's father in law, as the appropriate choice. Sunni Muslims also recognize the legitimacy of the successors of Abu Bakr who held the caliphal title. This includes the family that moved the capital of the caliphate to Damascus in 661, the Umayyads.* Some Muslims today, however, believe that Muhammad did, in fact, designate a successor, his cousin and son-in-law, 'Ali ibn Abi Talib. These Shi'a Muslims believe in the importance of a divine and blood connection between Muhammad and his successors, holding that it was inappropriate for the Muslim community to select a successor since 'Ali had a blood connection to the Prophet. For the Shi'a, the recognition of Abu Bakr and the Umayyads is an unfathomable heresy.[28]   Only imams* with a genetic connection to Muhammad and who possess Muhammad's charisma can lead Islam faithfully.[29]   Shi'a Muslims also look to an event in 680, when Muhammad's only surviving grandson, Imam Husayn ibn Ali, was killed in the Iraqi desert at the Battle of Karbala. The brutal killing of the imam and 72 of his adult male followers by an Umayyad army, followed by the presentation of their decapitated heads on pikes in Damascus and the degradation of their wives and children, defines the distinctive essence of the Shi'a faith.[30] The events at Karbala are as essential to their beliefs as the passion and crucifixion of Jesus are to Christians.[31]

---

[25] Amanat, *Pivot of the Universe*, 106.

[26] Guity Nashat, "Introduction," *Women in Iran from 1800 to the Islamic Republic*, Lois Beck and Guity Nashat (eds.) (Urbana, Illinois, University of Illinois Press, 2004), 13.

[27] Charles Issawi, "European Economic Penetration, 1872-1921," *The Cambridge History of Iran, Volume 7*, 590.

[28] Hamid Dabashi, *Shi'ism: A Religion of Protest* (Cambridge, Massachusetts: The Belknap Press of Harvard University Press, 2011), 60, 81.

[29] Ofra Bengio and Meir Litvak, "Introduction," *The Sunna and Shi'a in History: Division and Ecumenism in the Muslim Middle East*, Ofra Bengio and Meir Litvak (eds.) (New York: PalgraveMacMillan, 2011), 2.

[30] Kamran Scot Aghaie, *The Martyrs of Karbala: Shi'i Symbols and Rituals in Modern Iran* (Seattle, Washington: University of Washington Press, 2004), 8-10.

[31] Elaine Sciolino, *Persian Mirrors: The Elusive Face of Iran* (New York: The Free Press, 2000), 174.

The followers of the largest sect within the Shi'a branch of Islam are known as Twelvers.[32] They believe that there have been twelve imams, each of whom was a divinely inspired, blood descendent of Muhammad. Each of these men possessed a special purity and understanding, and each appointed his successor, just as Muhammad did 'Ali. Twelvers also believe that before the eleventh imam died in 874, he designated his young son as the next imam. This twelfth successor is known as the Hidden Imam because he disappeared from public view as an infant. For the next seventy years, a period known as the Lesser Occultation, the Hidden Imam only communicated with four designated agents; when the last of these men died in 940, the period of Greater Occultation began, and it continues to this day.[33] Twelvers anticipate the return of the Hidden Imam, holding that it will bring a violent day of reckoning, the defeat of the Sunni, and the conquest of the world.[34]

Until this happens, who is to have spiritual and political authority over the faithful? The shahs of Iran's Safavid Dynasty (1501-1736) answered this question by wielding a mighty and charismatic power over the *'ulama*. They were able to do so because they had claim as direct descendants of Muhammad and because they had established Shi'a Islam the state religion of Iran.[35] The Qajars, who succeeded the Safavids in the late eighteenth century, could not make such claims. They were simply Turcoman pastoralists and warriors from northeastern Iran who defeated other tribal contenders in battle and then established their capital at Tehran.[36] Although the Qajars had no spiritual mandate, the dynasty's first shahs still hoped to win the support of the *'ulama* in order to legitimize their rule.[37] Had Iran been Sunni, this might have been possible, but as a Shi'a nation this goal was almost impossible since at its core Shi'ism holds that only the Hidden Imam possesses sufficient merit to rule.[38] For the Shi'a, all secular government is ultimately illegitimate and unjust.[39] This fundamental assertion, combined with the absence of a strong secular government in the second half of the eighteenth century, allowed the *'ulama* to assert increasing influence as the century progressed. By the time Nasir al-Din ascended the throne in 1848, the *'ulama* saw the monarchy as a subservient institution. The clergy firmly believed that because the Qajar shah was not a religious scholar, he was duty-bound to follow the *'ulama*'s rulings.[40]

This assertion of religious authority produced tensions within the *'ulama* as two interpretative schools developed, one strictly constructional, one not. The Akhbari school attracted doctrinal purists, who believed that the Quran and other early writings about Muhammad provided sufficient instructions for governance and should be taken literally. They also maintained that it was necessary for all Shi'a, regardless of their training, to submit to these teachings. Its counterpart, the Usuli school, found this interpretation and practice too limited and instead asserted that those who were well trained in jurisprudence could independently interpret Islam's sacred documents. To the Akhbari, such a position was blasphemous because it diminished the importance of the imams and

---

[32] There are many other Shi'a branches in addition to the Twelvers. These sects largely emerged as a result of disagreements over which imams had the legitimate and lineage tracing back to Muhammad.

[33] Algar, *Religion and State in Iran*, 3.

[34] Moojan Momen, "Millennialism and Violence: The Attempted Assassination of Nasir al-Din Shah of Iran by the Babis in 1852," *Nova Religio*, 12.1 (2008), 57-82, ProQuest Central.

[35] Bengio and Litvak, "Introduction," 4.

[36] Mansoureh Ettehadieh Nezam-Mafi, "Qajar Iran, 1795-1921," *The Oxford Handbook of Iranian History*, Touraj Daryaee (ed.) (New York: Oxford University Press, 2012), 319-321.

[37] Dabashi, *Shi'ism*, 167-168.

[38] Algar, *Religion and State in Iran*, 5, 21.

[39] Lambton, *Qajar Persia*, 195, 279.

[40] Hamid Algar, "Religious Forces in the Eighteenth- and Nineteenth-Century," *The Cambridge History of Iran, Volume 7*, 714.

because such behavior was akin to Sunni practices. In this conflict for over leadership and doctrine, the more practical approach of the Usuli school prevailed.[41] Those with sufficient training could authoritatively interpret Muhammad's teachings. This gave the 'ulama a plasticity and energy during Nasir al-Din's reign that it had not possessed in earlier centuries.

~

During the thousandth anniversary of the Twelfth Imam's Occultation in 1844,[42] a man named Sayyid 'Ali Muhammad Shirazi announced that he had received a revelation from God. He claimed to be the Bāb—the doorway or gateway—to the Hidden Imam. This assertion was a direct challenge to the authority of the 'ulama, who considered the Bāb's pronouncement to be sacrilegious because a new revelation from God annulled Muhammad's status as the final prophet.[43] Over the next several years, the Bāb advanced his claims, attracted followers, and articulated his criticisms of the 'ulama. He was arrested, questioned, and jailed numerous times. By 1848, the Bāb was in solitary confinement in Tabriz and made to stand trial. Significantly, Nasir al-Din presided.

The Bāb was popular in Tabriz, despite the 'ulama's influence and opposition to him. This meant that at the trial Nasir al-Din found himself caught between the clerics and the public. He handled this awkwardness reasonably well, successfully presenting himself as an impartial judge. Nasir al-Din demonstrated sympathy to the Bāb at the beginning of the proceedings by offering the accused an honored seat. This won the Qajar prince public support. Nasir al-Din even said that if the Bāb's claims were shown to be true, then the Bāb would rule Iran instead of the shah.[44] Once the trial got underway, Nasir al-Din and members of the local 'ulama asked the Bāb to locate places on a globe, to speak Arabic in the style of the Quran, and to perform a miracle. These tests did not go well: the prince had to correct a syntax error and there was no miracle. The Bāb then proclaimed that he was more than an intermediary: that he was the Hidden Imam himself. Not accepting this, Nasir al-Din had the Bāb declared insane. The defendant was then re-imprisoned and tortured to make him recant his extraordinary claim, but he never did.[45] In response to an armed rebellion by his most radical followers in July 1850, the Bāb was executed on Amir Kabir's order.[46] Nasir al-

---

[41] Algar, *Religion and State in Iran*, 34-36. Schools of Islamic law also differed in their interpretation of the law for people who are mute. The Shafi'is school held that a Muslim needed to be able to move lips and tongue in prayer if physically able to do so, whereas the Hanafi school held that merely the intention to pray outloud was sufficient. See Sara Scalenghe, *Disability in the Ottoman World, 1500-1800* (New York: Cambridge University Press, 2014), 36.

[42] The Islamic calendar begins with Muhammad's flight from Mecca to Medina (622 by the Christian calendar). The Twelfth Imam went into hiding in 260 (or 873), making 1260 (or 1844) the thousandth anniversary of his Occultation.

[43] Algar, *Religion and State in Iran,* 137-138.

[44] Amanat, *Pivot of the Universe,* 84-86.

[45] Amanat, *Pivot of the Universe,* 86-88.

[46] One of the best-known radicals was a woman named Tahereh Qorrat al-Ayn. She possessed a sound theological understanding, was an eloquent speaker, and unlike the Bāb advocated violence as a legitimate means of producing change. Shortly before the Bāb's trial, she took charge of a Bābi conference, calling for armed rebellion as she threw off her veil in the middle of a speech, much to the astonishment of the assembled men. After two years in hiding she was arrested in January 1850 and executed in September 1852. For more details, see Dabashi, *Shi'ism,* 183-199.

Din's government then hunted down, arrested, and punished the Bāb's followers, who may have once numbered 100,000.[47] By the end of the year, the movement had been driven underground.

In Tehran, a cadre of surviving Bābis, no more than 70 men, began to organize their revenge.[48] They planned to assassinate Nasir al-Din and stage an armed rebellion in the resulting disarray. About two hours after dawn on August 15, 1852, the shah set out for a hunting trip from a summer palace in the foothills north of the city. As he did so, three men approached and appeared to offer him a petition to right an injustice. Because this was such a common occurrence, the would-be assassins surprised Nasir al-Din when they took guns from their pockets instead of papers. The ill-prepared Bābi conspirators, however, were poor marksmen and had only loaded their weapons with partridge shot; each fired, one at a time, but only a few pellets hit the shah and these left only minor wounds. Royal guards killed two of the assailants, spared a third for questioning, and captured a fourth conspirator waiting nearby.[49] In the aftermath of the attack, there was renewed persecution of those suspected of being Bābi adherents. Thirteen more suspects were forced to reveal the names of others associated with the Tehran cell. In the end, twenty-three Bābis were executed, many after experiencing brutal public torture, including being shod like horses or having burning candles placed in holes cut in their flesh. Those who didn't know of the plot but seemed sympathetic to it were exiled. Nasir al-Din certainly wanted to eradicate the Bābi problem, and he had no compunction about his government's brutality towards the Bābis. But the shah could never be sure of complete success, and this fact haunted him.[50]

In these opening years of Nasir al-Din's rule, there was a second prominent execution—one that also tarnished the shah's reputation significantly. This was the execution of Amir Kabir in January 1852. The prime minister's downfall came not only from the opposition generated by the 'ulama and Mahd 'Ulya. It also came from Nasir al-Din's transition from an underprepared seventeen-year old prince to a brash twenty-year old king. The shah came to resent Amir Kabir's nagging admonitions for him to work faster, to prioritize more effectively, and to spend less money. Nasir al-Din believed that he had learned enough from Amir Kabir and wanted to govern without his mentor's meddling interference.[51] It was a sophomoric faith in himself. In November 1851, Nasir al-Din dismissed Amir Kabir as his prime minister and reorganized the government to separate the ministries of domestic affairs, and foreign affairs, and the army. Nasir al-Din then exiled the former prime minister to the city of Kashan, but three months later changed his mind and ordered the

[47] Momen, "Millennialism and Violence," 58.
[48] Momen, "Millennialism and Violence," 67.
[49] Various accounts of this assassination attempt do not entirely align, including the date of the attempt. I have constructed this account based on Amanat, *Pivot of the Universe*, 204-205; Momen, "Millennialism and Violence," 69-70; and Ḥasan-e Fasā'i, *History of Persia Under Qājār Rule*, Heribert Busse (trans.) (New York: Columbia University Press, 1972), 302-304.
[50] See Amanat, *Pivot of the Universe*, 209-215; Fasā'i, *History of Persia Under Qājār Rule*, 304; and Momen, "Millennialism and Violence," 70.
[51] Amanat, *Pivot of the Universe*, 119-126.

execution. He may have been manipulated into making this decision by Mahd 'Ulya and her conservative allies in the court, who reinforced the shah's fear that his former mentor was trying to depose him.[52] Regardless of the precise reason for the decision, the international outcry to it was vociferous. The British government, for example, decried Amir Kabir's death as a "shameless and barbarous transaction" which produced feelings of "utmost horror and indignation."[53] With this decision, any hope for meaningful reform in Iran died too, as the conservatives held sway through the 1850s and 1860s. Iran stagnated.[54]

~

Nasir al-Din is best known for being the first shah to journey peacefully beyond Iran's borders. He made four trips in all—each of which illustrates complex diplomatic, socio-economic, and religious issues Iran faced in the last half of the nineteenth century. These trips also provide unparalleled insight into who Nasir al-Din was in his middle age.

The shah's first trip, in 1870, was to the Shi'a holy shrines in Ottoman-controlled Iraq. Nasir al-Din's timing may not have been altogether coincidental: Iran and the Ottoman Empire were about renew negotiations to settle their long dispute over the partially undefined border between them.[55] The novelty of the trip drew considerable attention in diplomatic circles, with the Russians and the British offering opposing opinions to the Sublime Porte* as to the wisdom of the shah's tour. Istanbul agreed with the British position that the visit would facilitate border negotiations and improve Ottoman-Iranian relations. It ordered the governor of Iraq to afford Nasir al-Din every consideration and respect.[56] The royal entourage left Tehran September 17 and travelled southwest

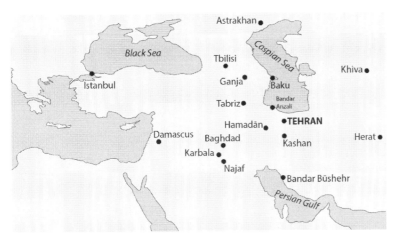

through the provinces of Markazi, Hamadan, and Kirmanshah, reaching the border with Ottoman Iraq two months later. That it took two months for the shah's retinue to travel 450 miles, an average of seven and a half miles per day, illustrates the astonishing fact that there were no paved roads in Iran in 1870. Everyone and everything, including the shah, typically travelled by

---

[52] Nezam-Mafi, "Qajar Iran, 1795-1921," 330.

[53] Lord Malmesbury quoted in Amanat, *Pivot of the Universe*, 163.

[54] Nikki Keddie and Mehrdad Amanat, "Iran Under the Later Qājārs, 1848-1922," *The Cambridge History of Iran, Volume 7*, 182, 184.

[55] Sabri Ateş *The Ottoman-Iranian Borderlands: Making a Boundary, 1843-1914* (New York: Cambridge University Press, 2013), 203.

[56] Meir Litvak, *Shi'i Scholars of Nineteenth-Century Iraq: the 'Ulama' of Najaf and Karbala'* (New York: Cambridge University Press, 1998), 171.

horse, camel, or mule; wheeled vehicles were nearly useless on the caravan tracks that had been used for millennia.[57]

The Sunni governor of Iraq met Nasir al-Din at an uncontested point on the border and escorted the shah to Baghdad. Over the next several days, Nasir al-Din made pilgrimages to the site were the Seventh Imam and the Ninth Imam were buried, to the sepulcher of the first Muslim convert from Iran, and to the ruins of the Sassanid capital. In a strategic ecumenical gesture, Nasir al-Din also visited the tomb of the founder of an influential Sunni school of jurisprudence.[58] On November 28, the shah made a second trip to the tombs of the Twelver Imams and presented gifts to the guardians of the sanctuary. He and his party then set up camp on the banks of the Euphrates before proceeding to the holy city of Karbala. There, at the entrance to the courtyard surrounding the mosque, Nasir al-Din dismounted and walked on foot to the shrine of Imam Husayn. This gesture, as well as his genuine tears of mourning over the events at Karbala, were well-received by the local clergy as a sign of the shah's humility.[59] On December 6, Nasir al-Din departed Karbala for Najaf, the site of 'Ali's shrine. When he arrived at the city gate the next day, the shah recorded, "we dismounted from the carriage and entered the town on foot in the company of all the servants and pashas…And I felt a spiritual tranquility whose description is not in my power."[60] His heartfelt reaction led him to sponsor an extensive refurbishment and enhancement of the 'Ali's shrine and give a large-carat diamond hat pin to the mosque; this symbol of Qajar power was to be hung above 'Ali's tomb, thereby associating Nasir al-Din closely with the saint.[61] After this emotional visit, Nasir al-Din paid his respects at the grave of the founder of the Qajar dynasty.[62] On December 13, he made another visit to 'Ali's tomb and then departed for Karbala and Baghdad, where he made a third visit to the site where the Seventh Imam and the Ninth Imam were buried. Nasir al-Din's pilgrimage concluded with a visit to the shrines of the Tenth and Eleventh Imams in Samarra before beginning his return journey to Tehran. The repeated visits to shrines in Baghdad, Karbala, and Najaf are telling, for they illustrate the extent of Nasir al-Din's personal faith. Far more than going through the motions, the shah affirmed his deep piety and his solid understanding of Shi'a theology. He also enjoyed demonstrating the extent of his faith by distributing gifts generously.[63] This has been the royal prerogative in many societies, including Eleni's Ethiopia, Kim's Korea, and Lespinasse's France.

The trip to Iraq was important beyond the shah's own spiritual edification. One consequence was that Nasir al-Din received *de facto* recognition outside Iran as the leader of the Shi'a. This came both through the deference that Ottoman officials accorded the shah and through an interaction at Husayn's shrine. When the muezzin chanted the call to prayer, he did not include a reference to 'Ali. Nasir al-Din implored the muezzin to include this reference, as was the tradition in Iran, and

---

[57] Lambton, *Qajar Persia*, 114, 208.

[58] Fasā'i, *History of Persia Under Qajar Rule*, 370. The Seventh Imam was Mūsá ibn Ja'far al-Kāzim and the Ninth Imam was his grandson, Muhammad ibn 'Alī ibn Mūsā. They are buried in the Al Kādhimiya mosque in a suburb of Baghdad. The Sassanid capital was Ctesiphon. The influential Sunni scholar was Imam Abū Hanīfah. The first Iranian convert was a companion of Muhammad's named Salmān al-Fārisī.

[59] Fasā'i, *History of Persia Under Qajar Rule*, 371.

[60] Nasir al-Din quoted in Fasā'i, *History of Persia Under Qajar Rule*, 371.

[61] Amanat, *Pivot of the Universe*, 434.

[62] The Qajar dynasty's founder was Āghā Mohammad Khān Qājār (1742–1797), who was assassinated and sent to Najaf for an honored burial by his successor, Fath-Ali Shah Qajar (1772-1834).

[63] Algar, *Religion and State in Iran*, 124, 155.

the muezzin did so, thereby restoring the old tradition.[64] The second consequence was that the Ottomans and the Iranians came to border agreements involving the transport of pilgrims and corpses to holy sites, a closer monitoring of the frontier to limit the movement of tribes and fugitives, and non-intervention in disputed lands.[65] This helped soothe tensions between the monarchical states. Third, the trip rekindled Nasir al-Din's interest in reform, for increasingly he came to respect the advice of his ambassador to Istanbul, Mirza Husain Khan. The shah realized that Mirza Husain Khan had a vision and proficiency that might reinvigorate the government after two decades of failed ministerial experiments and stagnation. Therefore, the shah ordered the ambassador to return with him to Tehran.[66]

Once in the capital, Nasir al-Din promoted Mirza Husain Khan quickly, making him the prime minister in November 1871. This was a critical decision because Mirza Husain Khan's vision for a stronger centralized government with cabinet ministers and a European model of administration renewed tensions with the 'ulama. This tension undercut the gains Nasir al-Din had made with the clergy as a result of his Iraqi pilgrimage.[67] Mirza Husain Khan was, however, popular with the general public because he opened his own grain stores during a drought-caused famine in the early 1870s and his authoritarian style helped minimize hoarding and speculation during the crisis.[68] Most importantly, Mirza Husain Khan was convinced that Nasir al-Din should continue to travel abroad to witness the advantages of industrial progress personally.[69] This encouragement led the shah to make the first of three trips to Europe. Each of these trips received extensive media coverage in Europe and the United States because the press and the public were fascinated by the Shah's extravagance.[70]

On April 19, 1873, less than three weeks after his mother died, Nasir al-Din departed Tehran with an entourage that included ministers, relatives, governors, generals, foreign diplomats, servants, the court photographer, the shah's personal physician, and members of the harem.[71] The trip's complex preparations prevented an extended mourning period for the queen mother, and the shah may not have wanted one anyway. The forty-two-year old had long wanted to visit Europe, and he may have found Mahd 'Ulya's death liberating, given the complexities of their relationship.[72] The shah did write

---

[64] Litvak, *Shi'i Scholars of Nineteenth-Century Iraq,* 172.

[65] Ateş *The Ottoman-Iranian Borderlands,* 203-204.

[66] Keddie and Amanat, "Iran Under the Later Qājārs, 1848-1922," 184. The man's full name was Mirza Husain Khan Moshir od-Dowleh Sipahsālār (1828–1881). His family had risen through the ranks, with each generation becoming increasingly prominent within the court. Mirza Husain Khan's grandfather was a court barber, his father was a high-level bureaucrat.

[67] Algar, *Religion and State in Iran,* 170-171.

[68] Keddie and Amanat, "Iran Under the Later Qājārs, 1848-1922," 186.

[69] Keddie and Amanat, "Iran Under the Later Qājārs, 1848-1922," 185.

[70] See, for example, an article about Nasir al-Din's visit to Russia in May 1873, which noted that the cost of the Russian reception in Astrakhan was 200,000 francs; that the shah travelled with so many rubies that their value could not be estimated; and that he wore a uniform "covered in diamonds…valued at 8,000,000 francs." "The Shah on His Travels," *Chicago Tribune,* June 10, 1873, 2, https://chicagotribune.newspapers.com/image/466248911

[71] Nasir al-Din Shah Qajar, *The Diary of H.M. the Shah of Persia During His Tour Through Europe in A.D. 1873: A Verbatim Translation,* Sir James W. Redhouse (trans.) (London: John Murray, 1874), 1, 18-20.

[72] Amanat, *Pivot of the Universe,* 172.

> It has now been a year of planning for the journey to farangistan [Europe]. So it's obvious what we've seen and endured in terms of the chatter of the public and...inside the harem....[W]e must put on our boots and set off.[73]

Before his departure, Nasir al-Din left the government in the hands of his son, Crown Prince Mozaffar ad-Din Shah Qajar, and an uncle. He also gathered the army together and had a proclamation read. It stated:

> All the officers and soldiers of the army of the capital shall know: the day of departure of the shah to Europe in order to visit the powerful and mighty rulers and kings who are related to us in friendship has arrived...It is our royal intention to promote the affairs of the army and your welfare [while in Europe]...[W]e expect every soldier during our absence to climb upon the steps of our service and to protect the order of the empire under the command of our officers.[74]

The first stop on the tour was Russia, which the shah reached by sailing across the Caspian Sea, accompanied by Russian naval vessels. Docking at Astrakhan, the delegation transferred to Russian boats for the voyage up the Volga River, and at Tsaritsin (Volgograd), the party boarded the tsar's personal train for the trip to Moscow. It was Nasir al-Din's first time riding a train, and he was impressed by the train's speed of five leagues an hour and by its luxurious interior appointments.[75] After a four-day visit to Moscow, where the shah visited the Kremlin and attended his first ballet,[76] he arrived in St. Petersburg on May 22. He was met at the station by Alexander II, the crown princes, and high-ranking army officers. The two monarchs boarded an open carriage and proceeded down Nevsky Prospect towards the Winter Palace as men and women shouted their greetings and approval on a pleasant and sunny day.[77]

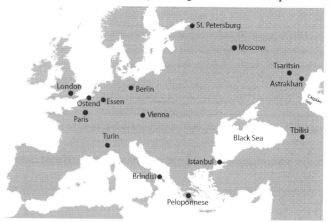

One wonders if the two sovereigns realized how much they had in common as they rode together in the carriage. Both had survived assassination attempts. Both had begun their reigns embracing a spirit of reform but had become more reactionary as they aged. In the tsar's case, Alexander had emancipated the serfs in 1861, believing it was better to free the serfs from above

---

[73] Nasir al-Din Shah Qajar quoted in Neghmeh Sohrabi, *Taken for Wonder: Nineteenth-Century Travel Accounts for Iran to Europe* (New York: Oxford University Press, 2012), 73.

[74] Nasir al-Din Shah Qajar quoted in Fasā'i, *History of Persia Under Qājār Rule*, 378.

[75] Nasir al-Din Shah Qajar, *The Diary of H.M. the Shah*, 23, 28, 32-33.

[76] Nasir al-Din Shah Qajar, *The Diary of H.M. the Shah*, 34, 38.

[77] Nasir al-Din Shah Qajar, *The Diary of H.M. the Shah*, 42-43.

than risk revolution from below.[78] In other early reforms, he offered the Poles self-governance, asked the Finnish Parliament to write a constitution,[79] and overhauled Russian governmental systems to allow for more local authority and control. Alexander also created an independent judiciary with trial by jury in criminal cases and a recognition that all Russians held equal standing under the law.[80] By 1873, this energy for modernization had dissipated. As Russia's discouraged, reform-minded minister of war noted at the end of that year:

> What an amazing and lamentable comparison with the situation as it was when I entered the top echelons of the government thirteen years ago! Then everything surged forward; now everything drags back. Then the sovereign was sympathetic to progress, he moved things forward himself; now he has lost confidence in everything he himself created, in everything that surrounds him, even himself. With such a state of affairs is it possible for me alone to keep my footing amidst the debris of the shipwreck, and would it not be excusable for me to decide to lay down my arms? One soldier doesn't make an army.[81]

An advocate for modernization in Iran might have offered a similar assessment of Iran and its shah in 1873.

Nasir al-Din's first state visit was not without mishap. In Moscow, the shah became aware that his visit was encumbered by the presence of his favorite wife, Anis od-Dowleh, and her servants. Prime Minister Mirza Husain Khan worried about the press coverage the veiled harem women produced and asked the shah to send his wife back to Tehran. Anis od-Dowleh objected vigorously, but Nasir al-Din agreed with his minister that harem traditions, even those of the looser Qajar court, were incompatible with projecting the image of the shah being on equal footing with European sovereigns. Anis od-Dowleh returned to Tehran, ostensibly for health reasons, but she would not forget the slight.[82] In St. Petersburg, Nasir al-Din attempted to accommodate local customs by bowing to the people on Nevsky Prospect,[83] and eating breakfast at the same table as his courtiers at Prince Oldenburg's palace,[84] but the Russian nobility took little notice of these efforts and instead ridiculed the shah for his behavior—especially his table manners.[85] While Nasir al-Din received the prestigious Order of St. Andrew, Alexander II undercut its symbolism by voicing his concern that anti-Russian factions in Iran were purposefully misrepresenting the tsar's sentiments

---

[78] Alexander II said this to the Russian Assembly of Nobles in March 1856. The details of the emancipation of the serfs did not satisfy nobles or peasants, conservatives or radicals, due to disagreements over land allotments. Edward Radzinsky, *Alexander II: The Last Great Tsar* (New York: Free Press, 2005), 117, 134.

[79] Radzinsky, *Alexander II,* 145-147.

[80] Nicholas V. Riasanovsky, *A History of Russia* (New York: Oxford University Press, 1993), 374-377. Military reforms came in 1874.

[81] Dmitrii Alekseevich Milutin, "Count Dmitrii Milutin on the year 1873," *Source Book for Russian History from Early Times to 1917, Volume 3: Alexander II to the February Revolution,* George Vernadsky (ed.) (New Haven, Connecticut: Yale University Press, 1972), 625.

[82] Mehrdad Kia, "Inside the Court of Naser od-Din Shah Qajar, 1881-96: The Life and Diary of Mohammad Hasan Khan E'temad os-Saltaneh," *Middle Eastern Studies,* 37, 1 (January 2001), 101-141, EBSCOhost.

[83] Nasir al-Din Shah Qajar, *The Diary of H.M. the Shah,* 42-43.

[84] Moritz Deutschmann, *Iran and Russian Imperialism: The Ideal Anarchists, 1800-1914* (New York: Routledge Taylor and Francis Group, 2016), 86. Normally, the shah ate alone as a symbol of the fact that he had no equal.

[85] Kazemzadeh, *Russia and Britain in Persia,* 113.

to the shah. This remark caused great embarrassment for Nasir al-Din, who had hoped to impress the tsar.[86]

The cool reception Nasir al-Din received in the Romanov court was in part a by-product of an agreement between the government of Iran and a London businessman named Paul Julius Freiherr von Reuter. Known as the Reuter Concession, this 1872 agreement granted the entrepreneur a seventy-year monopoly to build all roads, railways, and tramways; exploit most mines and forests; construct irrigation systems and sell the water obtained from them; establish a central bank; and have first right to establish monopolies for factories, mills, postal systems, and telegraphs. Mirza Husain Khan had been a strong advocate for the agreement.[87] One of few conditions in the contract was that Reuter had to begin construction of a railroad from the Caspian Sea to Tehran within fifteen months.[88] Because of its extraordinarily sweeping scope, the Reuter Concession generated bitter opposition both in Iran and Russia. Many Iranians saw the concession as a threat to the nation's cultural identity and its sovereignty; most Russians worried that it would result in a complete British domination of Iran. Looking for some way to soothe Russian feelings, Nasir al-Din's promised his hosts that if the Reuter did not fulfill the contract terms, Iran would look for Russian development aid instead.[89]

After seven days of tense meetings, awkward meals, and an array of performances, troop reviews, Hermitage visits, and midnight balls, the harem-less royal party took its leave of Alexander II and St. Petersburg, traveling west on the tsar's train. At the border of the new German Empire, the delegation transferred from the tsar's personal train to a faster German one and arrived in Berlin on May 31. Like many travelers, Nasir al-Din's sophistication grew daily as he gained a means of comparison. In his diary, he noted in detail how different Russia and East Prussia were in terms of their population density, infrastructure, cultivated land, and personal liberty.[90] In Berlin, he noticed how the city had more gas lamps than St. Petersburg.[91] He also compared ballet performances, pointing out differences in costumes and commenting on the relative quality of the dancers.[92] This growing sophistication meant that his time with Kaiser Wilhelm I and Otto von Bismarck did not produce major embarrassments, but there were sufficient annoyances that many Berliners were happy to send the shah on his way.[93] This mattered less for Nasir al-Din and Iran because even a newly unified Germany did not possess the geopolitical importance for Iran that Russia or Great Britain did.

After a week in Berlin, Nasir al-Din continued west, where he visited two sites that left great impressions. The first was Alfred Krupp's cannon and gun manufacturing plant, which was the first great factory the shah had seen. Krupp had made a name for himself at the Crystal Palace exposition

---

[86] Kazemzadeh, *Russia and Britain in Persia,* 113. Alexander's remark may have implied that the main culprit was Mirza Husain Khan, a known Anglophile.

[87] Keddie and Amanat, "Iran Under the Later Qājārs, 1848-1922," 187.

[88] Hamid Algar, *Mīrzā Malkum Khān: A Study in the History of Iranian Modernism* (Berkeley, California: University of California Press, 1973), 116-117.

[89] Kazemzadeh, *Russia and Britain in Persia,* 114.

[90] Nasir al-Din Shah Qajar, *The Diary of H.M. the Shah,* 69.

[91] Nasir al-Din Shah Qajar, *The Diary of H.M. the Shah,* 75.

[92] Nasir al-Din Shah Qajar, *The Diary of H.M. the Shah,* 80.

[93] William Howard Russell, "The Shah of Persia," *Chicago Tribune,* June 29, 1873, 7, https://chicagotribune.newspapers.com/image/466250265. Russell describes the Shah as "proud, willful, sensual, and arbitrary." He notes with disdain that Nasir al-Din displayed an "utter indifference to engagements," for he kept a parade in Potsdam waiting for several hours, delayed the start of a "gala theater in his honor," and skipped a scheduled breakfast altogether.

in 1851 by producing a 4,300-pound single steel ingot and winning a gold medal.[94] By 1873, nations around the world considered Krupp-made armaments to be the standard against which all others were judged, and the Essen plant was flooded with orders.[95] Nasir al-Din wrote with amazement at what he saw:

> Guns of every description, such as large cannon for forts, cannon for ships, and cannon for field use in campaigns, are all manufactured here. His plant and workshops resemble a mighty city. He employs 15,000 workmen, for the whole of whom he has erected houses and lodgings, paying them salaries and wages….[The steam hammers are] like mountains. When the hammer strikes the gun, the earth floor of the workshop emits a sound and trembles. It was a marvelous thing.[96]

The second memorable site combined natural beauty with modernity. It was the Rhine River Valley, which struck the luxury-loving shah as an Eden:

> The river Rhine is like a paradise. On both sides of it, everywhere, there were castles, pavilions, populousness, cultivation, railroads; and trains incessantly ply backwards and forwards. Numerous steam-ships, like the one in which we were sitting, navigated it upwards and downwards, carrying passengers and travellers, goods and merchandize….The whole of the hills are covered with woods and vineyards, and one is never satiated with gazing on them. At each moment some new feature, some new castle or palace of a different style of architecture, comes in sight, which have been built by men of wealth as summer-residences, where they take their pleasure and enjoy life. Truly, for the purposes of a promenade, no place could be better than these regions…[for] in front of them are orchards, flower-gardens, and the like, which surpass all powers of description.[97]

From Germany, the royal embassy continued to Belgium, where Nasir al-Din spent five days. He met with King Leopold II, observed Parliament in session, witnessed a Catholic procession, and took note of the freedom of the press.[98] On June 18, he sailed from Ostend to Dover, where he was met by Queen Victoria's younger sons, Prince Alfred and Prince Arthur. The royal party then boarded a train to London that "travelled at so furious a rate that it was impossible for one to distinguish any place."[99] Once in the capital, the shah was overwhelmed by what he saw:

> It is impossible to describe the prosperity, the populousness, the extent of the city, the number of lines of railway over which incessantly the trains come and go in every direction, the smoke of the manufactories, and the like…The Lord of the Universe has bestowed upon them power and might, sense and wisdom, and enlightenment.[100]

---

[94] William Manchester, *The Arms of Krupp, 1587-1968* (New York: Bantam Books, 1968), 76-78. The official name of the event was the The Great Exhibition of the Works of Industry of All Nations.

[95] Manchester, *The Arms of Krupp,* 150.

[96] Nasir al-Din Shah Qajar, *The Diary of H.M. the Shah,* 96.

[97] Nasir al-Din Shah Qajar, *The Diary of H.M. the Shah,* 119-120.

[98] Nasir al-Din Shah Qajar, *The Diary of H.M. the Shah,* 126, 130-131.

[99] Nasir al-Din Shah Qajar, *The Diary of H.M. the Shah,* 141.

[100] Nasir al-Din Shah Qajar, *The Diary of H.M. the Shah,* 141-142.

This was the impression the British government hoped to give any head of state or important visitor, even if this impression ignored the fact that according to one expert, "never was the contrast between rich and poor so great and to the poor so stinging, as it is at the present time."[101] Indeed, as noted in an influential pamphlet a few years later, many in the capital failed to realize the extensiveness of London's "pestilential human rookeries." Tens of thousands lived in eight-foot-square rooms accessed by "passages swarming with vermin" and courts "reeking with poisonous and malodorous gases" that never saw the sun or were "visited by a breath of fresh air."[102] That was the London Nasir al-Din didn't see. Instead, he stayed in Buckingham Palace.

On June 20, Nasir al-Din took the train to Windsor Palace to meet Queen Victoria. The visit was not a given because Victoria had resisted receiving royal visitors since her husband's death in 1861; in fact, the queen once wrote that she would only see "those that are very nearly related to her, and for whom she need not alter her mode of life."[103] Only after Victoria was persuaded of the geopolitical necessity of the visit did she yield. Even then, she objected to paying for the expenses of the Shah's trip. Prime Minister William Gladstone had to ask Parliament to provide the necessary funds, except for the shah's "entertainment under your Majesty's roof."[104] Victoria was, therefore, not well-disposed to the shah's visit. When the day came, the queen "felt nervous and agitated" as she dressed,[105] but she needn't have worried: Nasir al-Din's visit was satisfactory for both monarchs. As the shah hoped, Victoria took note of his coat "covered with very fine jewels [and with] enormous rubies as buttons" as well as his "sword belt and epaulettes made entirely of diamonds, with an enormous emerald in the

centre of each."[106] Nasir al-Din was honored that Victoria "advanced to meet us at the foot of the staircase," thereby affirming his equivalent royal stature.[107] Victoria found Nasir al-Din to be "very

[101] Thomas Wright, *Our New Masters* (London: Strahan & Co., 1873), 40.
[102] Andrew Mearns, *The Bitter Cry of Outcast London: An Inquiry into the Condition of the Abject Poor* (London: James Clarke & Co., 1883), 4.
[103] Queen Victoria quoted in Christopher Hibbert, *Queen Victoria: A Personal History* ([Cambridge, Massachusetts]: Da Capo Press, 2001), 346.
[104] William Gladstone, "Mr. Gladstone to Queen Victoria, March 29, 1873," *The Letters of Queen Victoria, Second Series: A Selection of Her Majesty's Correspondence and Journal Between the Years 1862 and 1878*, Volume II, 1870-1878, George Earle Buckle (ed.) (London: John Murray, 1926), 251.
[105] Queen Victoria, "Extract from the Queen's Journal, June 20, 1873," *The Letters of Queen Victoria, Second Series,* 258.
[106] Queen Victoria, "Extract from the Queen's Journal, June 20, 1873," *The Letters of Queen Victoria, Second Series, Volume II,* 259. The sword belt was also described by one reporter as "a treasure-house in itself. The sheath is studded with rubies, emeralds, and diamonds, which shame their setting of purist gold." See Russell, "The Shah of Persia," 7.
[107] Nasir al-Din Shah Qajar, *The Diary of H.M. the Shah,* 148.

agreeable and pleasing" and took honor in the fact the she was the first woman to whom the Iranian Order of the Lion and the Sun had ever been presented.[108] Similarly, the shah relished that Victoria "with her own hand" presented him with the British Order of the Garter, "one of the most esteemed English Orders."[109] Even the luncheon went smoothly, with no breaches of etiquette, perhaps because Nasir al-Din had read Victoria's book about Scotland and took "delight" in the presence of a Scottish pipe band marching around the tables during dessert.[110] About the only thing that struck Victoria as odd about Nasir al-Din was that he "ate fruit all through luncheon, helping himself from the dish in front of him and [only] drank quantities of iced water."[111] This was notable to her only because Iranians ate fruit in vast quantities by nineteenth century European standards.[112]

Victoria was not alone in her nervousness over the Qajar royal visit. Many in London understood the vital role Iran could play in the unfolding Anglo-Russo rivalry, now often referred to as the Great Game.[113] In 1864, Alexander II formally decided to continue Russia's expansion into Central Asia, for as his vice chancellor announced, "the interests of border security and trade relations require…civilized states" to gain control over "its neighbors, whose wild and unruly customs render them very troublesome." This initial action must be repeated "farther and farther into the heart of savage lands" for "prosperity, safety, and cultural progress" to be maintained. Like other nations, Russia does so "not so much from ambition as from dire necessity."[114] This imperialist ideology was used to justify the Russian conquest of Tashkent in 1865, which became the base of operations for further regional expansion. The conquest of the Emirate of Bukhara followed in 1868. On the eve of Nasir al-Din's arrival in London, the Russians occupied the Khanate of Khiva bordering the Caspian Sea.[115] Many in London believed that this rapid advance represented direct threat to British control of India.[116] British Prime Minister Benjamin Disraeli described it a few years later as "a struggle for Empire," and in this struggle there could be no compromises.[117] If Iran could provide a buffer to Russian expansion, or if Iran could be prevented from entering Russia's orbit, then it was important to treat its shah with all due respect and courtesy. So Nasir al-Din spent the next two weeks enjoying sight-seeing tours, military parades, social gatherings, concerts, and plays. His hosts went so far as to name a new ship in the Royal Navy after

---

[108] Queen Victoria, "Extract from the Queen's Journal, June 20, 1873," *The Letters of Queen Victoria, Second Series, Volume II*, 260.

[109] Nasir al-Din Shah Qajar, *The Diary of H.M. the Shah*, 149.

[110] Queen Victoria, "Extract from the Queen's Journal, June 20, 1873," *The Letters of Queen Victoria, Second Series, Volume II*, 260. The book was *Leaves from the Journal of Our Life in the Highlands* (1868).

[111] Queen Victoria, "Extract from the Queen's Journal, June 20, 1873," *The Letters of Queen Victoria, Second Series, Volume II*, 260.

[112] Willem Floor, *Agriculture in Qajar Iran* (Washington, DC: Mage Publishers, 2003), 286.

[113] Rudyard Kipling coined this term in his novel *Kim*.

[114] Aleksandr Mikhailovich Gorchakov, "Gorchakov's Justification of the Russian Advance into Central Asia, 1864," *Source Book for Russian History from Early Times to 1917, Volume 3*, 610.

[115] Dilip Hiro, *Inside Central Asia: A Political and Cultural History of Uzbekistan, Turkmenistan, Kazakhstan, Kyrgyzstan, Tajikistan, Turkey, and Iran* (New York: Overlook Duckworth, 2009), 25-26 and Hugh Seton-Watson, *The Russian Empire, 1801-1917* (London: Oxford University Press-Clarendon Press, 1967), 442-443. Khiva was captured on June 10, 1873.

[116] Peter Hopkirk, *The Great Game: The Struggle for Empire in Central Asia* (New York: Kodansha America, 1992), 5.

[117] Benjamin Disraeli, "The Earl of Beaconsfield to Queen Victoria, August 8, 1880," *The Letters of Queen Victoria, Second Series: A Selection of Her Majesty's Correspondence and Journal Between the Years 1862 and 1885*, Volume III, 1879 1885, George Earle Buckle (ed.) (London: John Murray, 1928), 129.

him.[118] Little wonder he wrote that everything about the British was "extremely well regulated and governed, and admirable." From personal wealth to the arts, from commerce to the pleasures of leisure time, Great Britain was in Nasir al-Din's mind "the chief of all nations."[119]

The shah's visit to Britain was not only one of decadent enjoyments. While staying in Buckingham Palace, he met with business and civic leaders, including representatives of the Jewish community, who pressed the Qajar monarch to do a better job of protecting his Jewish subjects.[120] Although Iranian Jews had some official protection, they were regularly discriminated against. During the first two decades of Nasir al-Din's reign, there had also been several instances of outright persecution: in 1856 Jews were forcibly deported; in 1860 Jews were assaulted, imprisoned, fined, and tortured for supposedly mocking Shi'a holy days; and in 1865, they were intensely harassed in the city of Hamadan. Jewish leaders throughout Europe knew about these incidents, as well as about daily prejudices. Upon the announcement of the shah's trip, they organized a well-coordinated campaign to meet with Nasir al-Din. In Berlin, Amsterdam, London, Paris, Rome, and Istanbul, Jewish leaders called upon the shah to change inheritance laws, stop illegal taxes, end zoning restrictions in commercial areas, permit Jews to testify in courts of law, and more. The shah responded positively to all of these pleas: on June 24, for example, he promised to promote religious freedom and civil rights. In Paris on July 12, he issued an edict stating that "no acts of violence or oppression should be perpetrated against the Jews." Nasir al-Din believed Jews, who played a critical economic role in Iran, should be treated with fairness and toleration; they should be protected from harm as were his other subjects. But discrimination and persecution continued despite the shah's wishes.

On July 5, Nasir al-Din bid farewell to the nation that impressed him so much, believing that the British were sad to see him go.[121] This was an understandable, if exaggerated perception, for even one as seasoned as Mark Twain was taken aback by the size of the crowds that greeted the shah: "The streets for miles are crammed with people waiting whole long hours for a chance glimpse of the shah. I have never seen any man 'draw' like this one."[122] In reality, Nasir al-Din was more of a curiosity than a beloved figure. Some found him outrageous, calling the Shah as "His Oriental Toploftical Elevatedness."[123] Soon a West End burlesque show opened that featured a caricature of the shah initially flashing his jewels but ending up with nothing but pawn tickets.[124]

After a rough voyage across the English Channel, a crossing that left Nasir al-Din and everyone else in the royal party seasick, the entourage made its way by train to Paris.[125] Over the next thirteen days, Nasir al-Din toured many of the area's famous sites, including Versailles, Notre Dame, the Arc de Triomphe, Les Invalides, the Luxembourg Palace, and the Louvre. He also enjoyed the

[118] Nasir al-Din Shah Qajar, *The Diary of H.M. the Shah*, 164.

[119] Nasir al-Din Shah Qajar in *The Diary of H.M. the Shah*, 214.

[120] The information for this paragraph is based upon the indispensable work of Daniel Tsadik, *Between Foreigners and Shi'is: Nineteenth-Century Iran and its Jewish Minority* (Stanford, California: Stanford University Press, 2007), especially pages 32, 47, 50 57, 90-92. Another valuable source about Jews being forcibly deported is Haideh Sahim, "Two Wars, Two Cities, Two Religions: The Jews of Mashhad and the Herat Wars," *The Jews of Iran: The History, Religion, and Culture of a Community in the Islamic World*, Houman M. Sarshar (ed.) (New York: I.B. Tauris, 2014), 75-108.

[121] Nasir al-Din Shah Qajar, *The Diary of H.M. the Shah*, 215.

[122] Mark Twain quoted in Afshin Marashi, *Nationalizing Iran: Culture, Power, and the State, 1870-1940* (Seattle, Washington: University of Washington Press, 2008), 24.

[123] "Personal," *Chicago Tribune*, July 9, 1873, 3, https://chicagotribune.newspapers.com/image/349284968

[124] "England and the Orient," *New York Times*, June 15, 1878, 1, ProQuest Historical Newspapers.

[125] Nasir al-Din Shah Qajar, *The Diary of H.M. the Shah*, 216.

Sèvres factory, the zoo in the Bois de Boulogne, and shopping in the hundreds of stores in the Palais Royal, where the shah spent a substantial amount of money.[126] Significantly, Nasir al-Din's description of his time in France possesses a different tone from his other journal entries. Instead of a daily account as he had done, and as he would later, the shah's report for republican France is essentially one long entry for his thirteen days there. Its tone is matter-of-fact and flat; the enthusiasm in describing his visits elsewhere is missing, replaced by ennui. The reason for this change may rest in the political diversity of France's post-Franco-Prussian War* landscape, which he saw as a weakness. The Qajar monarch did not view France's head of state as his equal the way he held Alexander II, Wilhelm I, Leopold II, and Victoria to be; for Nasir al-Din, true, legitimate political authority could only come from royalty. This meant that the shah concluded that France was no longer one of Europe's great nations.[127] Some of the press noticed the change in disposition and concluded that the Shah is "thoroughly disgusted with Paris."[128] Switzerland proved no more reassuring, for he found the Swiss to have "very strange customs of administration" and no army.[129]

Nasir al-Din's normal narrative tone returned after crossing into Italy on July 24. King Victor Emmanuel II met him in Turin and presented him with "some most beautiful and costly" gifts; clearly, the shah was on far more familiar turf and far more comfortable as a result.[130] From there, he continued to Vienna to attend the 1873 World Exposition and to meet with Emperor Franz-Joseph I. The shah found Vienna's low-lying terrain troubling and unhealthy; he commented upon the city's issues with potable water and an outbreak of cholera at length.[131] Doing so gave him the opportunity to point out to his Iranian readers that Europe was not always as far advanced as they might assume.[132] This commentary served to mitigate criticisms about public health conditions in Iran, where cholera outbreaks were devastating, human sewage polluted groundwater, bodies were not buried at sufficient depth, soap was not readily available, and vermin thrived in many homes.[133]

From Vienna, Nasir al-Din had to retrace his steps back through the Alps to Italy since the Balkans did not yet have a connecting rail network that could take him to Istanbul.[134] After a six-day trip from Vienna to Brindisi, the shah boarded the Ottoman sultan's yacht, which Nasir al-Din found to be more beautiful and richly decorated than any thus far encountered on his trip.[135] This and another ship took the Qajar embassy across the Ionian Sea, around the Peloponnese of Greece,

---

[126] Nasir al-Din Shah Qajar, *The Diary of H.M. the Shah*, 225-258.

[127] Sohrabi, *Taken for Wonder*, 97.

[128] "Untitled," *Chicago Tribune*, July 31, 1873, 4, https://chicagotribune.newspapers.com/image/349286172.

[129] Nasir al-Din Shah Qajar, *The Diary of H.M. the Shah*, 220, 287.

[130] Nasir al-Din Shah Qajar, *The Diary of H.M. the Shah*, 288, 296.

[131] Nasir al-Din Shah Qajar, *The Diary of H.M. the Shah*, 325-327.

[132] Sohrabi, *Taken for Wonder*, 97-98.

[133] Floor, *Public Health in Qajar Iran*, 18, 59, 61, 63. In the nineteenth century, there were cholera outbreaks in 1821, 1829, 1845-1847 (which killed 10% of Tehran's population), 1851-1853 (which killed another 15,000 to 16,000 people in Tehran), 1868-1869, and 1889-90.

[134] *The Orient Express* did not complete its first run from Paris to Istanbul until June 1883. See Christian Wolmar, *Blood, Iron, and Gold: How the Railroads Transformed the World* (New York: Public Affairs, 2010), 258.

[135] Nasir al-Din Shah Qajar, *The Diary of H.M. the Shah*, 357.

through the Aegean and up the Dardanelles. They arrived in Istanbul August 18, greeted by 3,000 Iranians waving from five steamers.[136] Although Nasir al-Din visited the Topkapı Palace that Ibrahim I and Kösem knew so well, he did not stay there, for by the mid-nineteenth century the Ottoman court had moved to the more-European styled Dolmabahçe Palace overlooking the Bosporus. During his week in Istanbul, Nasir al-Din attended diplomatic soirées, spent time sightseeing, and made a pilgrimage to Hagia Sophia, where he prayed in the "very imposing and ancient mosque" that had "though the lapse of time…fallen from its original splendor." While the shah clearly appreciated the building's historical and spiritual significance, it did not fit with his natural proclivity for the contemporary and the embellished. This led him to poetically compare Hagia Sophia to "a venerable tree from which the freshness of youth has departed."[137] Nasir al-Din had become a keen observer and a more sophisticated man as a result of his 1873 European journey.

By late August, Nasir al-Din needed to return to Tehran for there were worrisome reports coming from home. The Qajar embassy made its way across the Black Sea by ship, through modern Georgia to Tbilisi by train, over dusty roads to Baku by carriage and horseback, and down the Caspian Sea on the same Russian ship that had taken them to Astrakhan almost four months before. It was a depressing journey, marked by "poor and miserable" towns, "parched and disagreeable" soil, "excessively sultry" weather, and accommodations quite unlike the grand chambers of St. Petersburg, London, and Vienna. Nasir al-Din described the governor's house in Ganja, Azerbaijan, for example, as "a very wretched tenement." On another night he chose sleep in a tent rather than endure what was available otherwise.[138] Even the Caspian did not cooperate, becoming so violent that people "threw off their finery in the midst of heavings and vomitings," and the shah wondered if he might end both the trip and his life capsized.[139]

Circumstances did not improve once Nasir al-Din finally returned to his homeland. In the port of Bandar Anzali, he was met by the members of the 'ulama, who presented him with petitions demanding that Mirza Husain Khan be removed as prime minister. While the shah had been away, a leading cleric had issued a fatwa* asserting that it was a religious duty to remove the Anglophile and advocate for Westernizing reform.[140] In addition, Nasir al-Din's favorite wife, Anis od-Dowleh, had been rallying opposition in secular circles to the Reuter Concession and Mirza Husain Khan. She was determined to avenge the affront of not being allowed to complete the royal trip. With the religious community and the court united in their anger about what the trip represented and the role Mirza Husain Khan played in it, the shah had little choice but to dismiss his prime minister.[141] To soothe the tumult, Nasir al-Din also had to cancel the Reuter Concession, which he did on the grounds that Reuter had not begun construction of a railroad within the agreed fifteen months. In reality, some minimal work had been done, but as a diplomatic letter to the governments of Europe explained, Reuter had broken his promise to cover all of the costs of the shah's first European trip. Combined with the lack of sufficient progress on the railroad, the Qajar government concluded that Reuter was incapable of performing a "thousandth part of what he had engaged to do." The businessman was instead guilty of "mere speculation."[142] The repudiation of the concession and Mirza Husain Khan's dismissal as prime minister represented important victories for Iran's

---

[136] Nasir al-Din Shah Qajar, *The Diary of H.M. the Shah*, 367-368.
[137] Nasir al-Din Shah Qajar, *The Diary of H.M. the Shah*, 383.
[138] Nasir al-Din Shah Qajar, *The Diary of H.M. the Shah*, 416-417, 419.
[139] Nasir al-Din Shah Qajar, *The Diary of H.M. the Shah*, 425-426.
[140] Hajji Mulla 'Ali Kani was the cleric who issued the *fatwa*. See Algar, *Religion and State in Iran*, 177.
[141] Kazemzadeh, *Russia and Britain in Persia*, 117-118.
[142] Mirza Husain Khan quoted in Kazemzadeh, *Russia and Britain in Persia*, 126-127.

conservative forces. As after the fall of Amir Kabir, the promise of meaningful reform in Iran again evaporated. For the second time in two decades, Nasir al-Din's enthusiasm for change had been overcome by clerics and the court.

~

The shah's second trip to Europe came just five years after his first. Tied to the another world exposition, the 1878 journey proved to be less controversial in Iran; with the forces of conservatism still ascendant, the shah's travels were not threatening.[143] Nasir al-Din argued that this journey was necessary because the "continuous invitations from the exalted kings for get-togethers, etc., which were accepted with happiness and pleasure" in 1873 had prevented him from gaining a "complete knowledge" of European "industries, customs, good traditions, laws, and military methods" for Iran's benefit.[144] He wanted to gain more practical knowledge. The lack of a diplomatic focus also made the trip less burdensome for European governments, which was welcomed news in most capitals since diplomatic attention that summer focused the Congress of Berlin.*

Nasir al-Din did meet with Alexander II and Franz Joseph I during brief visits to St. Petersburg and Vienna. He asked the both monarchs for military instructors to improve Iran's army and both agreed.[145] This was important, for despite the early promise of the polytechnic school Dar al Fonun, the shah's army in the 1870s and 1880s remained hopelessly outdated. Its capacity in the field was undercut by insufficient training and equipment, the lack of a clear command structure, and the competing authority of tribal leaders.[146] Though dapper on parade, it was not an effective fighting force. Another problem involved the falsification of muster roles that allowed officers to collect pay for non-existent soldiers. Some of these officers were civilians who had simply purchased their rank in order to make profit off the state.[147] The request for Austrian and Russian military advisors was Nasir al-Din's attempt to correct these problems. The Russians proved to be more influential, because they created the Persian Cossack Brigade. This unit became closely connected to the shah and helped further Russian influence in Iran.[148] The British objected to the arrival of these military advisors and the creation of the brigade, but Nasir al-Din responded forcefully: "Persia is not Afghanistan….She is an independent Power, and always considers it her interest to be on friendly and cordial footing with all Powers, especially with those of England and Russia."[149] In other words, the shah would do what he believed to be in Iran's best interest, regardless of British sensibilities. This was a remarkable position for Nasir al-Din to take, given that the British had occupied the Iranian port of Bandar Būshehr and stopped Iran's domination of the Afghan border during the Anglo-Persian War in 1856-1857.[150]

[143] Algar, *Religion and State in Iran,* 179.
[144] Nasir al-Din Shah Qajar quoted in Sohrabi, *Taken for Wonder,* 88.
[145] Stephanie Cronin, "Building a New Army: Military Reform in Qajar Iran," *War and Peace in Qajar Iran: Implications Past and Present,* Roxane Framanfarmaian (ed.) (New York: Routledge, 2008), 63.
[146] Deutschmann, *Iran and Russian Imperialism,* 90.
[147] Cronin, "Building a New Army," 64-65.
[148] Deutschmann, *Iran and Russian Imperialism,* 92.
[149] Nasir al-Din Shah Qajar quoted in Kazemzadeh, *Russia and Britain in Persia,* 167.
[150] The strategic city of Herat was in Iranian territory during the Safavid Dynasty (1501–1736) but was subsequently lost. The Qajars tried to retake the city in 1838 and 1856. The British hoped to create a unified

Nasir al-Din also visited France during this second European trip, mainly to experience the Exposition Universelle in Paris. There was no grand welcome in Paris since the trip was not an official one. The shah was simply met at the train station by a lieutenant colonel and escorted to his twenty-nine-room suite at the Grand Hotel near the Opera House. According to a newspaper report, the shah's luggage included thirty-six large boxes of gold coins to pay for his travel expenses, perhaps necessary since there were rumors of unpaid bills from his first visit to the city.[151] At the Exposition Universelle, Nasir al-Din was proud of the Iranian pavilion, believing that it compared favorably to those of other non-European countries. He took special satisfaction that the Ottoman Empire was not represented "due to war and troubles" because its absence affirmed Iran's position as the most stable nation in the Near East.[152]

While the shah was in France, he received a proposal for a concession on Iran's only navigable river, the Karun, which flows into the Persian Gulf.[153] The British had argued as early as 1871 that opening this river to steamboats would facilitate trade and stimulate the Iranian economy, but Nasir al-Din had resisted.[154] By 1878, still smarting from the fallout of the Reuter Concession, Nasir al-Din's position was even more entrenched. The issue for the Qajar monarch was not economic: many countries had granted incentivizing dispensations for the development of their railroads, including the United States, Canada, and Russia.[155] Rather, the issue was sovereignty. He worried that by allowing another nation's steamboats to ply the Karun, Iran's territorial integrity would be compromised; he fretted that Iran would follow India's fate and become a British colony.[156] As he forcefully wrote in January 1879,

> For fifty years you [the British] have carried on trade with Persia, and there has never been a word; what has happened now that you want the Karoon River? Moreover, such rivers as these, are like the door of one's house; and why should you desire to enter by

---

Afghanistan as a buffer state between India and Russian expansion in Central Asia and saw Herat as an essential component of that goal. When Iranian forces finally captured Herat in October 1856, the British declared war against Nasir al-Din. The British navy attacked the Persian Gulf port of Bandar Būshehr in December 1856 and subsequently won a battle in the interior. Overwhelmed by British military superiority, Nasir al-Din sued for peace. The peace treaty was lenient, but required the Iranians to withdraw from Herat. For more information, see Amanat, *Pivot of the Universe*, 255-356, 231-232, 277-306.

[151] "Marvelous Works of Art: Treasures at the Trocadero. Fortunes in Jewels and Antiques—the Shah among the Curiosities…" *New York Times*, June 30, 1878, 4, ProQuest Historical Newspapers.

[152] Nasir al-Din Shah Qajar quoted in Sohrabi, *Taken for Wonder*, 99.

[153] Heidi A. Walcher, *In the Shadow of the King: Zill al-Sultān and Isfahān under the Qājārs* (New York: I. B. Tauris & Co. Ltd., 2008), 59.

[154] Sir Mortimer Durand quoted in Kazemzadeh, *Russia and Britain in Persia*, 149.

[155] In the United States, the Pacific Railway Act of 1864 gave companies like the Union Pacific and the Central Pacific bonds at very advantageous rates and vast tracts of land that they could sell for profit. The Canadian Pacific and Northern Pacific also won extraordinary land grants. See Richard White, *Railroaded: The Transcontinentals and the Making of Modern America* (New York: W.W. Norton, 2011), 22-24. In Russia, the tsar allowed the Society of Russian and Foreign Capitalists to build a 2700-mile railroad network in 1857. The Russian network connected Warsaw to St. Petersburg, Moscow to Kursk and Nizhny-Novgorod; it also connected the Baltic and Caspian Seas. Under the terms of the agreement, the Society was to maintain the network for 85 years, at which point it would become state property. The government paid 5% interest on the amount calculated for the construction costs. See "Decree on Railways, January 26, 1857," *Source Book for Russian History from Early Times to 1917, Volume 3,* 607. The Society had both Russian and foreign investors, distinguishing it somewhat from most of the concession arrangements in Iran.

[156] Walcher, *In the Shadow of the King,* 60.

force and without consent?... Without any kind of preamble all at once you insist and precipitate matters. If my consent is asked for, I decline to give it.[157]

The river remained underutilized for the next decade.

In late spring 1888, a new British envoy, Sir Henry Drummond Wolff, arrived in Tehran and pressed the shah for concessions. Wolff firmly believed that the problems of underdeveloped nations could only be solved through the rapid infusion of foreign capital.[158] He argued that the "opening of the Karun would be to give Persia what she urgently needed—an easy highway from some of her richest and most inaccessible provinces....Khuzistan, with little care, could be made a second Egypt."[159] This was exactly what opponents of increased Western influence feared the most, but Wolff was nothing if not persistent. He pushed and the shah resisted. By the fall, they found a compromise: Iran would allow "commercial steamers of all nations without exception" to transport merchandise on part of the Karun;[160] in return, Iran obtained for the first time an assurance that Great Britain would respect its borders and help ensure that Russia would as well.[161] With this agreement Nasir al-Din had soothed relations with the British, taken a step to protect his country against Russian aggression, and had not granted a true concession to any one beneficiary. In fact, the most successful shipping company on the internationalized Karun ended up being Iranian.[162] The agreement with Wolff did, however, create something of a slippery slope: it gave many the impression that Iran was now open for monopolistic foreign investment.

This impression proved to be a correct one. While Nasir al-Din wanted to preserve Iranian political independence, the shah was, by his late fifties, prone to yielding to indulgence and temptation, as Wolff realized. As the British envoy wrote in confidential letter to his Russian counterpart, the shah's

> existence is an anxious one....He knows how precarious is his position—that it is at the mercy of influences which he cannot resist. Once his position is solidly guaranteed, there is reason to believe that he would willingly lend himself to the counsels given by enlightened and well-disposed allies.[163]

Wolff believed that if presented with the right opportunity and sufficient financial incentives, Nasir al-Din would make deals that would enrich both British businessmen and himself. The first opportunity to test this premise came in January 1889, when both Nasir al-Din's prime minister and foreign minister were both in London and agreed to meet to talk about the Reuter Concession cancelled fifteen years earlier.[164] By the end of the month, the two Qajar ministers had signed an agreement with George Reuter to create the Imperial Bank of Persia. This sixty-year concession

---

[157] Nasir al-Din Shah to Mirza Husain Khan, [January 1879], quoted in Kazemzadeh, *Russia and Britain in Persia,* 161-162.

[158] Keddie and Amanat, "Iran Under the Later Qājārs, 1848-1922," 191.

[159] Sir Henry Drummond Wolff, *Rambling Recollections*, Volume II, (London: MacMillan and Co. Limited, 1908), 343.

[160] Wolff, *Rambling Recollections*, 344.

[161] Walcher, *In the Shadow of the King,* 73.

[162] Walcher, *In the Shadow of the King,* 75-76.

[163] Sir Henry Drummond Wolff to Prince Dolgorouki, June 13, 1888 in Wolff, *Rambling Recollections*, 348.

[164] The prime minister was Mirza Ali Asghar Khan Amin al-Soltan, and the foreign minister was Mirza Abbas Khan Qavam od-Dowleh. George Reuter was Paul Julius Freiherr von Reuter's second son.

gave Reuter "the exclusive right of issuing notes," which were to become "legal tender for all transactions in Persia."[165] The government granted the bank a tax-exempt status in exchange for a 6% share of the bank's net profit and the right to borrow money. It was the first of many important concessions, and it provided the context under which Nasir al-Din's third trip to Europe unfolded.

The trip began, as had the first two, with a visit to St. Petersburg. Nasir al-Din was forever trying to balance an overture to Britain with a corresponding one to Russia. He saw maintaining an equilibrium between the two nations as the only way for Iran to remain one of the few uncolonized lands in Asia and Africa. But by summer 1889, the Russians had lost faith in the shah's neutrality and fairness. They suspected he had become a devout Anglophile, and they pointed to the creation of the Imperial Bank as a confirmation. Consequently, a royal invitation from the tsar was not readily forthcoming, and once it finally arrived, Iranian and Russian officials bickered over the length of the visit and the size of the Qajar delegation. By the time Nasir al-Din arrived in St. Petersburg, the Russian court's attitude was hostile; they mocked the shah's French and ridiculed his mannerisms.[166] Even when shah wept at the site of Alexander II's 1881 assassination,[167] Russian hearts remained unmoved: Nasir al-Din received only perfunctory gifts during his state visit.[168]

The Qajar delegation arrived in Britain on July 1. Wolff had been making arrangements in the capital for much of the spring. He wanted Nasir al-Din to gain "a more extensive knowledge of the country" than he had acquired in 1873, when his appointments "had principally been confined to festivities near the metropolis" of London.[169] Wolff specifically wanted the shah to meet with men who could impress him with wealth and opportunity. Over the course of the next four weeks, the shah was wooed by more industrialists and financiers, mayors and aristocrats, than he had been in 1873. There were social engagements with the Rothschilds and the dukes of Norfolk and Westminster; speeches and meals with the civic leaders in Birmingham, Liverpool, Manchester, Glasgow, and Edinburgh; and manufacturing tours of shipyards, steel works, and armament factories. The schedule was so packed with events that the shah repeatedly gave into fatigue. Even the royals contributed more willingly than on the previous visit, with Victoria cheerfully seeing Nasir al-Din on three occasions.[170] On July 4, Abdullah

1=Dover
2=Liverpool
3=Manchester
4=Edinburgh
5=Glasgow

Sassoon, a leading Jewish merchant in the India trade, rented the Empire Theater in London and threw an ostentatious ball in the shah's honor.[171] Every detail about the evening was designed to impress Nasir al-Din, including an extravagant display of roses.[172] In gratitude, the shah presented

[165] Kazemzadeh, *Russia and Britain in Persia*, 210-211.

[166] Kazemzadeh, *Russia and Britain in Persia*, 212, 219-220.

[167] Deutschmann, *Iran and Russian Imperialism*, 86.

[168] Kazemzadeh, *Russia and Britain in Persia*, 221.

[169] Wolff, *Rambling Recollections*, 351.

[170] Wolff, *Rambling Recollections*, 356-364.

[171] Walcher, *In the Shadow of the King:* 165. Abdullah Sassoon (1818-1896) was known as Sir Albert David Sassoon in London. For more information on the Sassoon family and its business operations, see Peter Stansky, *Sassoon: The Worlds of Philip and Sybil* (New Haven: Yale University Press, 2003).

[172] "Stories about the Shah: How Europe has Impressed Him This Time," *New York Times*, July 28, 1889, 6. ProQuest Historical Newspapers.

Sassoon with the Order of the Lion and the Sun—the same honor he had given Victoria in 1873. This might seem like a disproportionate response to a businessman's hospitality, but Sassoon's son was one of the directors of the Imperial Bank of Persia, and everyone present understood the importance of bringing complementary needs together to maximize profits.

The most important concession that came out of this milieu involved tobacco. Known as the Tobacco Régie and signed by Nasir al-Din in March 1890, this agreement granted a close friend of Wolff's a monopoly to buy, manufacture, sell and export tobacco in Iran for fifty years. In exchange, the royal treasury was to receive £15,000 a year plus 25% of the company's net profits. This was not as attractive an arrangement for the shah as it might seem.[173] Unlike railroads or banks, Iran's tobacco industry was already well-established. The Tobacco Régie suddenly made Iran's independent wholesale and retail merchants *de facto* employees of a British-owned company. They now had to work on commission instead of for themselves.[174] Opposition to this arrangement grew slowly. Newspaper articles printed abroad began appearing in November 1890, and protest leaflets were surreptitiously posted in mosques in January 1891.[175] The first formal petition reached Nasir al-Din in February 1891.[176] Outright protests began in the spring. There was a notable public disturbance in Tehran on May 22,[177] and clerics in Shiraz refused to enter their mosques until the Tobacco Régie's local agent had been expelled from the city.[178] The *ulama*'s leadership in the protest grew as the months passed; in July a prominent cleric sent a telegram to the shah protesting the tobacco concession,[179] and in October leading Islamic jurists wrote to Nasir al-Din arguing that the presence of the Tobacco Régie violated the Quran since it required Muslims to be managed by infidels.[180] Opposition became more intense in the fall, when the six month transitional grace period in November. In response, one prominent tobacco merchant in Isfahan burned his tobacco rather than surrender it to the Régie. This action inspired Isfahan residents to begin the nation's first smoking boycott.[181] In other cities, merchants closed bazaars rather than allow the monopoly to continue.[182] In early December, a *fatwa* declared that smoking tobacco was akin to making war on the Hidden Imam,[183] and the nation responded with overwhelming obedience. Even the harem supported the smoking ban and were said to have broken their water pipes as a symbol of their opposition.[184] Surrounded by near-universal defiance, Nasir al-Din cancelled the Tobacco Régie in January 1892, but the consequences were profound. Not only did he have to take out a forty-year loan from the Imperial Bank to pay the immense fine for breaking the contract, but it undercut the shah's position significantly. The sense of the shah as an absolute monarch had been proven

---

[173] By comparison, the Tobacco Régie for the Ottoman Empire gave the sultan £630,000 a year. Wolff's friend was Major Gerald Talbot, who subsequently sold the monopoly to the Imperial Tobacco Corporation of Persia for a substantial profit. See Nikki R. Keddie, *Religion and Rebellion in Iran: The Tobacco Protest of 1891-1892* (Frank Cass & Co. Ltd., 1966), 35, 39.

[174] Kazemzadeh, *Russia and Britain in Persia,* 249.

[175] Keddie, *Religion and Rebellion in Iran,* 44, 46.

[176] Kazemzadeh, *Russia and Britain in Persia,* 254.

[177] Algar, *Religion and State in Iran,* 206-207.

[178] Kazemzadeh, *Russia and Britain in Persia,* 257.

[179] Algar, *Religion and State in Iran,* 210-211. This man was Sayyid Mohammed Hassan Husayni Nouri Shirazi (1814-1896).

[180] Kazemzadeh, *Russia and Britain in Persia,* 261.

[181] Keddie, *Religion and Rebellion in Iran,* 94-95.

[182] Nezam-Mafi, "Qajar Iran, 1795-1921," 333.

[183] Keddie, *Religion and Rebellion in Iran,* 95-96.

[184] Nezam-Mafi, "Qajar Iran, 1795-1921," 333.

illusory.[185] This vulnerability empowered every other constituency to act against the Qajar sovereign, including Nasir al-Din's assassin.

~

Jamal al-Din al-Afghani was one of the most influential Muslim theologians of the nineteenth century. Through his eclectic writings and extensive travels, Afghani's words reached a diverse cross-section of the Middle East. To some he was a Pan-Islamic, anti-imperialist reformer who inspired independence movements; to others, he stood as a bulwark against modernization and change. He might best be described as a neo-traditionalist who sought to reconcile Islam and the West by using the teachings of the Quran and other foundational Islamic works.[186] Muslims of many stripes found hope and justification in Afghani's messages. One was a disaffected cloak maker named Mirza Riza Kirmani, who met Afghani in Tehran in 1886 or 1887 and become a devotee.[187] Afghani had long held that despotic governments should be replaced by republican ones,[188] and by early 1890 he was holding secret meetings in Tehran aimed at securing political change in Iran. Shortly before Nasir al-Din intended to move against the cleric's subversive activities, Afghani took sanctuary in the Shrine of Shah Abdol Azim south of Tehran.[189] This protected him from civil authority for seven months, but in January 1891 Nasir al-Din violated the sanctity of the holy site and ordered his cavalry to arrest Afghani so that he might be expelled from the country. This action alienated the shah from his subjects just as the protests against the Tobacco Régie were about to erupt.[190]

Mirza Riza Kirmani remained in Tehran and began distributing leaflets as a member of a secret anti-Qajar, pro-Afghani group. He was arrested, released, and rearrested.[191] He spent four years in prison. In 1895, he traveled to Istanbul to meet with Afghani, who was so set upon revenge that he once said, "I only want the Shah to die, his belly to be split, and him to be put in his grave."[192] Afghani sent Mirza Riza Kirmani back to Tehran to complete this task.

On May 1, 1896, Nasir al-Din visited the Shrine of Shah Abdol to express his gratitude to God for allowing him to rule Iran for almost fifty years. Although the shah customarily had popular Shi'a sites vacated prior to his arrival, on this occasion he did not. After Nasir al-Din had completed his prayers, Mirza Riza Kirmani approached as if to offer him a petition. As in 1852, what came out of the man's coat was not a piece of paper but a gun. Firing at point blank range, Mirza Riza Kirmani hit Nasir al-Din's heart.[193] As the Qajar sovereign bled to death, a group of women attacked Mirza Riza Kirmani, severing one ear, but before they could tear the assassin limb from

---

[185] Walcher, *In the Shadow of the King*, 162. The fine was for £500,000 at 6% interest.
[186] Nikki R. Keddie, *Sayyid Jamāl ad-Dīn al-Afghānī: A Political Biography* (Berkeley, California: University of California Press, 1972), 1-2, 422.
[187] Keddie, *Sayyid Jamāl ad-Dīn al-Afghānī*, 279.
[188] Keddie, *Sayyid Jamāl ad-Dīn al-Afghānī*, 107.
[189] Keddie, *Sayyid Jamāl ad-Dīn al-Afghānī*, 320-322. The Shrine of Shah Abdol Azim is in Rey, Iran; it commemorates a descendent of the Second Imam and a companion of the Ninth Imam. Like other Muslim holy sites, it offered *bast*, protection from civil authority. Violating *bast* was a controversial act.
[190] Algar, *Religion and State in Iran*, 200.
[191] Sir Thomas Edward Gordon, *Persia Revisited* (London: Edward Arnold, 1896), 185-187.
[192] Jamāl al-Din al-Afghani quoted in Keddie, *Sayyid Jamāl ad-Dīn al-Afghānī*, 405.
[193] Amanat, *Pivot of the Universe*, 440.

limb, he was taken into custody. Then, in a macabre effort to stifle panic, the prime minister loaded the shah's body into the royal carriage and pretended to converse with him as the royal carriage and set off for Golestan Palace.[194]

Nasir al-Din's long reign and its relative stability produced wistfulness among Iranians once he was gone. What was supposed to be a fiftieth jubilee celebration became a funeral. The official mourning began with the dead shah lying in state in the Takiah Dawlat, the royal theater he had built for productions of Shi'a passion plays or *ta'ziya*. The *ta'ziya* commemorated the martyrdom of Husayn at the Battle of Karbala. The symbolic association between Husayn and Nasir al-Din was poignant and intentional, including a life-size portrait of the shah and an image Imam 'Ali above the funeral bier.[195] Nasir al-Din was presented to the mourners as a martyr assassinated by the Bābis, for there was suddenly a greater appreciation for the things he had done, rather than those he hadn't. A photograph of the scene at the Takiah Dawlat shows men in uniform gathered in a large semi-circle around a coffin covered in flowers and decorated with garlands; dozens are wiping away their tears.[196] Expressions of grief continued during the funeral procession, which included Jews, who genuinely appreciated the efforts Nasir al-Din had made to protect them.[197]

---

[194] Keddie and Amanat, "Iran Under the Later Qājārs, 1848-1922," 197.

[195] Ingvild Flaskerud, *Visualizing Belief and Piety in Iranian Shiism* (New York: Continuum, 2010), 25, 29.

[196] Unknown photographer, "The Late Nasir al-Din Shah Lying in State in the Takiah Dawlat," 1896. Albumen silver photograph, 8 1/2 x 11 in., Brooklyn Museum, 1997.3.80, accessed January 25, 2020, https://www.brooklynmuseum.org/opencollection/objects/161186

[197] Tsadik, *Between Foreigners and Shi'is,* 175-176.

After the funeral, a new *ta'ziya* play was written and produced that memorialized and depicted the shah's assassination; this emotional dramatization fortified the comparison between Nasir al-Din and Husayn.[198] This was a fitting homage in many ways, since the flamboyant shah treasured and encouraged the *ta'ziya*. The *'ulama*, however, found the production's theatrical and emotional nature shameful.[199] The conflict between Nasir al-Din and Iran's clergy remained as palpable as it had throughout his reign. The conflict was also evident in the Shah Abdol Azim shrine four years later, when the elaborately carved marble tombstone for Nasir al-Din finally arrived. It featured a full-length sculpture of the shah lying on his back, dressed in a European-style military uniform with a long sword, wearing his distinctive aigrette of diamonds on his head. The carving spoke of Western influence, modernity, and decadence. It offended the *'ulama*'s sensibilities, which is why Nasir al-Din's tomb was removed from the shrine after the Islamic Revolution in 1979.[200]

~

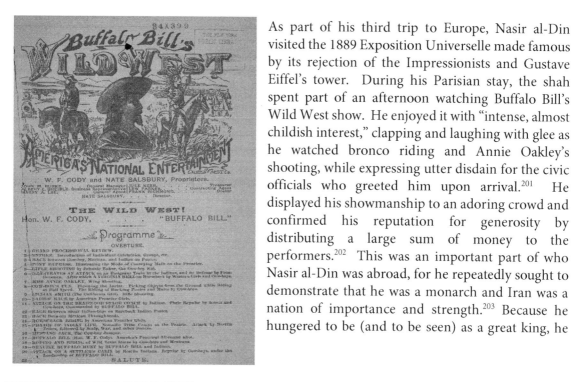

As part of his third trip to Europe, Nasir al-Din visited the 1889 Exposition Universelle made famous by its rejection of the Impressionists and Gustave Eiffel's tower. During his Parisian stay, the shah spent part of an afternoon watching Buffalo Bill's Wild West show. He enjoyed it with "intense, almost childish interest," clapping and laughing with glee as he watched bronco riding and Annie Oakley's shooting, while expressing utter disdain for the civic officials who greeted him upon arrival.[201] He displayed his showmanship to an adoring crowd and confirmed his reputation for generosity by distributing a large sum of money to the performers.[202] This was an important part of who Nasir al-Din was abroad, for he repeatedly sought to demonstrate that he was a monarch and Iran was a nation of importance and strength.[203] Because he hungered to be (and to be seen) as a great king, he

[198] Peter Chelkowski, "Majlis-i Shâhinshâh-i Îrân Nâsir al-Dîn Shah," *Qajar Iran: Political, Social and Cultural Change, 1800-1925*, 231.

[199] Algar, *Religion and State in Iran,* 20, 158-159.

[200] When the tomb was removed in 1979 it disappeared for many years. In the mid-1990s it resurfaced and was placed in a museum in the Golestan Palace in Tehran. I am grateful to Omid Ahmadian for determining this for me and for translating the content of this website: https://tinyurl.com/y5qkhdov

[201] "Fêting the Shah," *New York Herald* (European edition), August 2, 1889, 1, quoted in Jill Jones, *Eiffel's Tower: The Thrilling Story Behind Paris's Beloved Monument and the Extraordinary World's Fair that it Introduced* (New York: Penguin Books, 2009), 189. "Buffalo Bill" was the nickname of William Frederick Cody (1846-1917).

[202] Jones, *Eiffel's Tower,* 190.

[203] Amanat, *Pivot of the Universe,* 427; and Sohrabi, *Taken for Wonder,* 100.

always had a public relations campaign to win.[204] This was a major reason for his extensive travel within Iran, his visits to Shi'a holy sites in Iraq, and the three trips to Europe.

Several personality traits limited Nasir al-Din's ability to achieve greatness. The shah possessed a puerile impishness and impulsiveness, as well as a strong proclivity for indulging himself, as many primary sources document. He loved practical jokes that victimized his ministers and courtiers, such as the time he secretly had the air valve on a rubber boat opened "mid-lake, leaving the richly-dressed courtiers floundering in the water."[205] He had a habit of changing his plans at the last second, ruining the preparations of his hosts, as when he spontaneous decided to climb the stairs of Eiffel's Tower instead of attending a welcome ceremony in his honor at the Trocadéro.[206] He ate incessantly, got drunk regularly, and assembled the second largest harem of the Qajar dynasty as his desire to be surrounded by women increased as he aged.[207] Other examples of Nasir al-Din's lack of moderation include hunting, from which it was always important to return with an impressive trophy;[208] his insistence on being the beneficiary of gifts, even from his officials and courtiers;[209] and the vast accumulation of objects and wealth housed in the Royal Museum.[210] These

characteristics became increasingly noticeable in the final decade of his reign, as the shah became increasingly disillusioned by the responsibilities of government and the constraints he faced. In fact, they became embodied by the shah's relationship with favorite young nephew, Malijak.[211] Nasir al-Din's fawning over Malijak meant that the boy became a major-general, was allowed to precede the prime minister in official ceremonies,[212] and often wore "a huge portrait of the Shah, set in diamonds, around his neck."[213] Malijak accompanied the shah to Europe in 1889, and Nasir al-Din permitted the eleven-year-old to break all rules of decorum, much to the horror of his hosts. At an operatic gala in Paris, for example, Malijak was "the nuisance of the party" as he mocked the dancing of performers and "utterly spoiled

---

[204] This desire to win the public relations campaign is reflected in one grudging account of the Shah's time in Paris. It held that the Shah had "acquired the democratic habit of shaking hands with crowds of strangers. He is not as skillful in this as an American president, but he does well for an indolent Oriental." See "Personals," *Chicago Tribune*, July 29, 1889, 4 https://chicagotribune.newspapers.com/image/349270364.

[205] George Nathaniel Curzon, *Persia and the Persia Question*, Volume I (London: Longmans, Green, and Co., 1892) 399.

[206] "At the Big Exposition: The Shah Likes President Carnot's Name. Features of the Great Show that Sits at the Feet of the Aspiring and Airy Eiffel Tower," *New York Times*, August 18, 1889, 9, ProQuest Historical Newspapers.

[207] E. Yarshater, "Observations on Nâsir al-Dîn Shah," *Qajar Iran: Political, Social and Cultural Change, 1800-1925*, 8, 11; and Nashat, "Marriage in the Qajar Period," 56-57. Nasir al-Din had 85 wives when he died, perhaps compensating for the fact that he may have been impotent by the 1880s.

[208] Kia, "Inside the Court of Naser od-Din Shah Qajar, 1881-96."

[209] Kia, "Inside the Court of Naser od-Din Shah Qajar, 1881-96."

[210] George Nathaniel Curzon, *Curzon's Persia*, Peter King (ed.) (London: Sidgwick & Jackson, 1986), 94.

[211] "Malijak" was Nasir al-Din's nickname for his nephew. The boy's real name was Ḡolām-ʿalī Khan. He was born in 1879. In 1886, Nasir al-Din gave the boy the title ʿAzīz-Al-Solṭān or "the beloved of the sovereign." After Nasir al-Din's death, Malijak lost all that had been left to him and died in poverty in Tehran in 1940. For more information see "ʿAzīz-Al-Solṭān," Encyclopaedia Iranica, August 18, 2011, accessed February 12, 2020, http://www.iranicaonline.org/articles/aziz-al-soltan-golam-ali-khan

[212] Yarshater, "Observations on Nâsir al-Dîn Shah," 9.

[213] Curzon, *Persia and the Persia Question*, Volume I, 400.

the solemnity" of the occasion, but Nasir al-Din ignored the social clues and took delight by Malijak's scandalous behavior.[214]   Another witness was fascinated by the shah's presence but complained that "the nasty little boy he has with him is always doing something unpleasant."[215] This evidence shows that by his late middle age, Nasir al-Din had become far more focused upon personal gratification than on leading Iran into the twentieth century.

In fact, while the shah obtained the latest photographic equipment,[216] enjoyed inventions like the phonograph,[217] and admired Western technology generally, he came to believe that it was best if Iran did not experience the benefits of Europe's material culture.[218] He believed the reforms accompanying the infusion of Europe's goods and technology threatened the Qajar regime. Nasir al-Din was not alone in this assessment, for in the end few Iranians in the 1880s and 1890s wanted meaningful reform. The 'ulama didn't because they thought that change would diminish their power and threaten the uniqueness of the Shi'a state. Government officials and members of the court didn't because they saw change as a threat to their traditional sources of income. The British and the Russians didn't because each feared its counterpart and rival would benefit disproportionately. Surrounded by factions each looking out for its own interest, it is hardly surprising that Naser al-Din Shah Qajar ended up choosing to do the same thing.

---

[214] "Boulanger is a Sphinx: Even His Silence Seems Mysterious. The Shah and His Infant Nuisance. South American Interests and other Parisian Gossip," *New York Times*, August 19, 1889, 2, ProQuest Historical Newspapers.

[215] Henry C. Leffler quoted in "Caught at the Hotels," *Chicago Tribune*, October 6, 1889, 6, https://chicagotribune.newspapers.com/image/371138924.

[216] Carmen Pérez González and Reza Sheikh, "From the Inner Sanctum: Men Who Were Trusted by Kings," *The Eyes of the Shah: Qajar Court Photography and the Persian Past*, Jennifer Y. Chi (ed.) (Princeton, New Jersey: Princeton University Press, 2015), 143.

[217] "Stories about the Shah,"6.

[218] Amanat, *Pivot of the Universe*, 424.

R

William Redfern,

1774-1833

On the Australian winter day of July 26, 1814, the convict ship *Broxbornebury*, under the command of Captain Pitcher, came upon another vessel, the *Surry,* some ninety miles south of the entrance to Sydney's famous harbor. As the *Broxbornebury* drew near, Pitcher determined that the *Surry*'s "safe conduct into…Port was despaired of" unless he provided the *Surry* with "some person capable of navigating her in."[1] He ordered one of his officers to take charge of the distressed vessel. When Mr. Nash boarded the *Surry*, the problem become clear: its "Captain, two Mates, the Surgeon, twelve of the Ship's Company, Sixteen Convicts, and Six Soldiers were lying dangerously ill with fever."[2] Within the next few days, most of these men were dead of typhus, bringing the death total for the voyage to fifty, including thirty-six prisoners.[3]

This news deeply disturbed the governor of New South Wales, Lachlan Macquaire, because it wasn't an isolated incident. In fact, it was the third time that year that a convict ship had arrived in Australia amid a medical crisis. The first ship had been the *General Hewitt*, whose captain had confined the prisoners below deck, regardless of the weather conditions, on each of the forty-six days the ship called at various ports. By the time the *General Hewitt* had arrived in Sydney on February 7 after a 165-day voyage, thirty-four of the three hundred convicts had died.[4] Three months later, the *Three Bees* arrived in Sydney from Ireland on May 7, having lost nine of its 219 Irish convicts en route. An additional seven men died of scurvy during the 192-day journey, and

---

[1] "Ship News," *The Sydney Gazette and New South Wales Advertiser*, July 30, 1814, 2, accessed January 25, 2020, http://trove.nla.gov.au/

[2] William Redfern, "Surgeon Redfern to Governor Macquarie," *Historical Records of Australia*, Series I, Volume VIII (Sydney, Australia: Library Committee of the Commonwealth Parliament, 1916), 281.

[3] Lachlan Macquarie, "Governor Macquarie to the Commissioners of the Transport Board," *Historical Records of Australia*, Series I, Volume VIII, 274.

[4] D'Arcy Wentworth, William Redfern and Edward Luttrell, "Proceedings of a Medical Court of Enquiry Holden at Sydney in New South Wales, 16th of March, 1814," *Historical Records of Australia*, Series I, Volume VIII, 245, 247. The *General Hewitt* spent twenty-seven days loading prisoners along the Thames, nine days in the Madeira Islands, and ten days in Rio de Janeiro.

fifty-five others had to be hospitalized because of their "dreadful State."[5] Macquarie recognized the arduous nature of the convict voyages to Australia, but he believed that the illness and death aboard these three ships were more a consequence of negligence than bad luck. This is why he ordered the convening of a "medical Court of Enquiry to examine the very great and unusual mortality,"[6] and

why he entrusted the writing the summary report to his close friend and the colony's most capable doctor, William Redfern.

Redfern's report of September 30, 1814 detailed the sailings of the three ships and the medical conditions each faced. Based on extensive interviews with surviving officers and non-convict passengers, he chronicled the care and treatment of the prisoners, noting everything from their pre-embarkation environment to the quality of the rations on the voyage. Redfern took particular interest in ventilation and sanitation issues, chronicling the amount of time convicts were permitted on deck, the frequency and type of fumigation procedures used, and how often convicts washed their clothes. He also recorded those instances when a ship's captain abused his power by withholding wine, food, supplies, and medicine from the prisoners so that he might profit from the sale of unused items once in New South Wales. As the doctor assembled this information, four broad patterns emerged. These became the basis of Redfern's recommendations for the future transportation of convicts to Australia.

The first suggestion involved the clothing the prisoners were issued. Redfern found that prisoners departing the British Isles in the summer months, had suitable clothing because their journeys benefited from "nearly or entirely Avoiding the Winter" in either hemisphere. But he also found that the standard issue of cloth "Jackets and Waistcoats, duck trowsers…coarse linen Shirts, Yarn Stockings and Woolen Caps" was insufficient if the ships departed Britain late in the year because then the prisoners endured "the rigor of two Winters" during their long voyage. He worried the standard issue and a winter departure caused illness since "the body does not possess the power of instantaneously adopting itself to very great and sudden transitions, nor of supporting their effects with impunity." Redfern recommended what he described as an inexpensive, "trifling change" for winter voyages: that the "Duck or Harn Trowsers be exchanged for Cloth Ones, that Flannel Waistcoats and Drawers be Supplied; And that an Additional Blanket be issued to each person." This simple modification would improve the health of the prisoners since they would be warmer during the day and not have to sleep in their clothes at night, which he believed was a "baneful custom" that spread "the effluvia arising from the human body…thus rendering it [a] more virulent…Contagion." Redfern found it inexcusable that prisoners were not supplied with sufficient fresh water to wash their clothes while at a port of call, believed that soap was not typically

[5] Redfern, "Surgeon Redfern to Governor Macquarie," 279.
[6] D'Arcy Wentworth, William Redfern and Edward Luttrell, "Medical Officers to Secretary Campbell," *Historical Records of Australia*, Series I, Volume VIII, 244.

issued to prisoners in sufficient amounts, and held that all prisoners should be required to wash themselves in cold water at least every other day.[7]

Redfern's second suggestion for improving prisoner health and diminishing mortality centered on diet. He found that the official food allowance was "quite sufficient provided it be duly served out," but he lamented that frequently this was not done. He recommended that the government adjust the provisions for travel through the tropics. Not only should butter be eliminated as a provision, but flour, suet, and plumbs should be substituted for the ration of salt beef. He also recommended tripling the provision of wine for the voyage. Providing each prisoner with a quarter of a pint a day "would be attended with the most beneficial consequences…by assisting to maintain the Vigor of the System, Counteract debility arising from bad weather, confinement below, and despondency." Redfern also wanted "a small portion of lime juice and sugar" added to the wine and directed that it be "served out" on deck "and drunk at the tub by each individual." This would furnish each convict with an antiscorbutic and each of them "would then know the quantity he was daily entitled to."[8]

The third recommendation focused upon air, "the great Pabulum of Life." Redfern asserted that it was to "ignorance or inattention in regulating its influence…[that] the ill state of health and great Mortality Are Chiefly to be attributed." He noted how the close confinement of bodies for a long period of time generated "a most subtle poison" and, given the conditions aboard the three ships, "It is only to be wondered at that so few died." Redfern believed that the best solution was to allow the prisoners as much access to the deck as possible. He pointed out that, "not one of the Transports, employed exclusively in bringing out female Convicts, has had a Contagious disease Among them" because the female prisoners had "unrestrained Access to the deck." Redfern then boldly recommended that no convict ship sail with more prisoners "than the deck is capable of holding." He also specified how regular fumigations of the convict prison should occur and held that "the Prison and Hospital ought to be white washed every two or three Weeks with Quicklime" to help prevent the spread of disease.[9]

The last recommendation centered upon personnel. Redfern argued that the quality of the convict ships' doctors was decidedly poor, either due to inexperience or irresponsibility. He found that few possessed the wherewithal to withstand abusive captains and masters, who have "little claim to education, refined feeling, or even common decency," and who "generally treat their Surgeons as they do their Apprentices and men with rudeness and brutality." Redfern contended that the appointment of naval surgeons with command authority would solve this problem, for only these men were "Accustomed to Sea practice, who know what is due to themselves as Men, and as officers with full power to exercise their Judgment without being liable to the Controul of the Masters of the Transports." He believed that by extending this power to medical personnel the regulations could be enforced so that "the poor Convicts" could avoid becoming "the unhappy Victims of the Captain's brutality and the Surgeon's Weakness, want of Skill, or drunkenness." He wanted these surgeons to have the authority to enforce regulations, monitor supplies, prevent illegal trade, and protect the welfare of the prisoners.[10]

The thoroughness, empathy, and insight that Redfern exhibited in his report quickly caught the attention of London officials. They ordered a wholesale adoption of his recommendations. The

[7] Redfern, "Surgeon Redfern to Governor Macquarie," 281-285.
[8] William Redfern, "Surgeon Redfern to Governor Macquarie," 285-287. An antiscorbutic is a food that fights scurvy by providing Vitamin C.
[9] Redfern, "Surgeon Redfern to Governor Macquarie," 287-290.
[10] Redfern, "Surgeon Redfern to Governor Macquarie," 290-291.

results were both immediate and profound: the death rate fell from the 11.3% abroad the *General Hewitt* to less than 1% on all voyages between 1816 and 1820, despite a tripling in the number of convict ships sailing to Australia.[11]   The acceptance of Redfern's four major recommendations saved thousands of lives. His report stands as one of the most important documents in Australia's colonial history.

It was also a deeply personal document for Redfern, for when he used the phrase, "the poor Convicts," the surgeon wasn't speaking in the abstract. Only thirteen years earlier, Redfern himself had been transported to the New South Wales penal colony as a criminal.

~

The details of Redfern's life prior to his transportation remain frustratingly uncertain. There is circumstantial evidence that he was born in Ireland and grew up in or near the town of Trowbridge in Wiltshire, England, although one official record says he was born in Canada.[12]   His childhood education was solid: as an adult he demonstrated familiarity with the classics and his writing was vivid and clear.[13]   The details of Redfern's medical education are also a mystery, but at some point in his early twenties Redfern went to London and passed the examination of the Company of Surgeons. To do this, he would have needed some previous training, perhaps an apprenticeship with an older brother or a local doctor in Trowbridge. He might also have been drawn, like many other medical students, to Edinburgh—the recognized center of medical education in Britain in the late eighteenth century. Both the medical school at the University of Edinburgh and the Edinburgh Royal College of Surgeons offered experiential instead of theoretical approaches to teaching medicine. The university also had the benefit of being inexpensive, tolerant, and flexible: it enrolled students of all Christian faiths and allowed them to select their own coursework, pay only for the courses they took, and leave whenever they saw fit.[14]   This atmosphere would have served Redfern well prior to his moving to London. In January 1797, he received his commission as first surgeon's mate with the Royal Navy.[15]

It was not the ideal time for a twenty-three-year-old novice surgeon to join the navy. Of the 120,000 men in naval service during the Napoleonic Wars,[16] only one fifth were genuine volunteers

---

[11] Alan Brooks and David Brandon, *Bound for Botany Bay: British Convict Voyages to Australia* (Kew, Richmond, Surrey, U.K.: The National Archives, 2005), 170.

[12] This record is his enlistment form for the Royal Navy. It may be a clerical error, or Redfern may have said he was born in Canada in order to hide his Irish birth.

[13] Edward Ford, *The Life and Work of William Redfern* (Sydney: Australasian Medical Publishing Company Limited, 1953), 12; and Edward Ford, "William Redfern (1774-1833)," *Australian Dictionary of Biography,* Volume 2, (Carleton, Australia: Melbourne University Press, 1967), accessed January 25, 2020, http://adb.anu.edu.au/biography/redfern-william-2580

[14] Roy Porter, *The Greatest Benefit to Mankind: A Medical History of Humanity*, (New York, W. W. Norton & Company, 1998), 289-292. Porter also notes that most doctors in New South Wales in 1810 received their training in Edinburgh. It seems likely that Redfern would be in this group, although Porter does not specifically mention him.

[15] Ford, *The Life and Work of William Redfern*, 12. Redfern passed the examination of the College of Surgeons, but he did not obtain a formal diploma from them before his naval commission arrived.

[16] N. A. M. Rodger, *The Command of the Ocean: A Naval History of Britain, 1649-1815* (New York: W. W. Norton & Company, 2004), 639.

like Redfern; the rest had been pressed into service or lured with bounties.[17] Conditions were ghastly, even in home waters, with men enduring rancid food, fouled water, and living conditions comparable to the worst tenements on land. Sailors had scurvy even while in port.[18] Shore leave was almost never permitted for fear of desertion.[19] The men were, in fact, so underappreciated that a seaman's pay had not increased in 145 years,[20] while those of a merchant sailor had increased fourfold over the same period.[21] Even soldiers in His Majesty's army fared better: they had received a salary increase in 1795, while some sailors had not received any pay at all in four years.[22] As one of Redfern's fellow surgeons wrote in a report to his commander,

> Untoward fortune has often placed me in situations where I could not practice my profession agreeable to its principles, or the feelings of my conscience, but I never was in a situation more replete with anxiety than the present as Surgeon of the *Sandwich*.[23]

In spring 1797, these conditions prompted two mutinies, one successful and one not. The first began at Spithead, the protected body of water between the Isle of Wight and the entrance to Portsmouth's harbor. The Admiralty had ignored the petitions that sailors sent requesting a pay increase and better food so the seamen of the Channel Fleet refused an April 16 order to weigh anchor. They took control of the ships and offloaded unpopular officers. The sailors swore their loyalty to the Crown, elected representatives to negotiate, promised to return to duty if the French fleet suddenly arrived, and maintained discipline and order throughout the uprising. After considerable hand-wringing, Parliament approved the salary increase on May 9 and the sailors won the concession that unpopular officers would be replaced. George III gave his consent to the deal and provided a royal pardon for the mutineers.[24] The second mutiny in the spring 1797 occurred at Nore, near where the River Thames joins the North Sea. Encouraged by the success at Spithead, the sailors at Nore sought more, including shore leave for all men, pardons for deserters, payment of all back wages prior to the next sailing, a fairer distribution of prize money, changes in court martial procedures, and an agreement that no officer could return to a ship without the consent of the crew.[25] But the Admiralty was in no mood to give any further concessions and responded to the Nore demands by cutting off shore supplies to the rebel ships on May 28. The mutineers, reinforced with ships from the North Sea, attempted to blockade the Thames and cut off London. A fortnight passed without significant change and enthusiasm for the mutiny waned among many

---

[17] Leonard F. Guttridge, *Mutiny: A History of Naval Insurrection* (Annapolis, Maryland, Bluejacket Books, 2006), 45.
[18] Ford, *The Life and Work of William Redfern*, 5.
[19] Peter Burke, *Celebrated Naval and Military Trials* (London: Wm. H. Allen & Co., 1866), 230.
[20] Rodger, *The Command of the Ocean*, 446. Rodger also supplies detailed salary tables by rank between 1647 and 1807 on pages 618-627.
[21] Daniel A. Baugh, "The Eighteenth Century Navy as a National Institution," *The Oxford Illustrated History of the Royal Navy* (Oxford, U.K.: Oxford University Press, 1995), 145.
[22] Guttridge, *Mutiny*, 47; and Ford, *The Life and Work of William Redfern*, 5.
[23] Ford, *The Life and Work of William Redfern*, 33.
[24] Rodger, *The Command of the Ocean*, 445-447. The sailors were also angered by the Quota Acts, which paid large bounties to landlubbers that could have gone to experienced seamen. See Ellen Gill, *Naval Families, War, and Duty in Britain, 1740-1820* (Woodbridge, U.K: The Boydell Press, 2016), 217.
[25] Keith Grint, *The Arts of Leadership* (Oxford, U.K.: Oxford University Press, 2000), 88; and Gill, *Naval Families, War, and Duty in Britain*, 220.

of the men; several ships stopped participating in the blockade and surrendered. By June 13, all of the recalcitrant ships were back in the Admiralty's control.

One of these ships was the much-discontented, 64-gun *Standard*, with its new surgeon's mate William Redfern. The *Standard* was a leader in the North Sea reinforcements that joined the mutiny: she was one of the first to disobey orders off Great Yarmouth, one of the first nine ships to raise the red flag of mutiny at Nore, and one of the last to surrender on June 13. Its crew was also one of the last to be court-martialed. The late August verdicts were harsh: thirteen crew members of the *Standard* and sister ship *Inflexible* were sentenced to death, including Redfern.[26] He was not listed on the rosters of the men who directed the Nore Mutiny,[27] but in the eyes of the naval judges, Redfern exhibited motivational leadership at a critical juncture, when he urged the mutiny's leaders "to be more united amongst themselves" so that they might succeed.[28] This was enough to warrant the death sentence, but on account of his youth the judges commuted Redfern's sentence to life imprisonment. Redfern was not alone in this clemency. Of the 412 men court-martialed, 59 were originally sentenced to death, but only 29 of them were hanged. Other mutineers were imprisoned for various terms or flogged.[29]

There are four primary motivations for punishing criminals: deterrence, retribution, incapacitation, and reformation.[30] The problem in late-eighteenth and early-nineteenth-century Britain was that these motivations were often in conflict, and a new consensus had yet to emerge on how best to manage the nation's rising crime rate. Many argued for banishment to a faraway land via transportation. Until the American Revolution broke out in 1775, the American colonies had served this purpose well, absorbing 50,000 criminals as indentured servants* for seven and fourteen-year terms.[31] Advocates for transportation argued that surely another suitable location could be found. Critics of transportation responded with powerful arguments. For some, it was a question of morality since they saw parallels between the Atlantic slave trade and the shipping of criminals across an ocean to provide convict labor.[32] For others, it was a question of restitution: some far-flung destination should not benefit more from convict labor than Britain itself; a criminal's debt to society would be better paid with hard labor closer to home.[33] Still others envisioned a comprehensive reform of penal system—one which would realize the full potential of the Penitentiary Act of 1779. This meant establishing hygienic prisons with daily regimentation and demeaning labor, uniforms and solitary confinement, and salaried officials and standardized meals. It also meant providing prisoners with the ability to reduce the length of their sentences

---

[26] William Johnson Neale, *The Mutiny at Spithead and the Nore: with an Enquiry into its Origins and Treatment; and Suggestions for the Prevention of Further Discontent in the Royal Navy* (London: Thomas Tegg, 1842), 183-184, 244, 399.

[27] Ford, *The Life and Work of William Redfern*, 8.

[28] John Thomas Bigge, *Report of the Commissioner into the State of the Colony of New South Wales* (London: The House of Commons, June 19, 1822), 84.

[29] Grint, *The Arts of Leadership*, 94-95.

[30] Norval Morris and David J. Rothman, "Introduction," *The Oxford History of the Prison: The Practice of Punishment in Western Society*, Norval Morris and David J. Rothman (eds.) (New York: Oxford University Press, 1998), ix-x.

[31] Brooks and Brandon, *Bound for Botany Bay*, 22. Sending criminals to the American colonies was authorized in 1718 with the Transportation Act. This helped alleviate the labor shortage, particularly in Virginia and Maryland, where 80% of the indentured servants shipped from Britain worked on tobacco plantations.

[32] J. B. Hirst, *Convict Society and Its Enemies: A History of Early New South Wales* (Sydney, George Allen & Unwin, 1983), 21-22, 32.

[33] Brooks and Brandon, *Bound for Botany Bay*, 24.

with good behavior.[34] By constructing institutions that produced penitent individuals able to return to society, the cycle of crime could be broken, advocates held. The problem was that this approach was far more expensive than transportation. In 1786, key officials in Parliament, including Home Secretary Thomas Townshend, Lord Sydney, chose the bottom line over reform. On August 18, Sydney ordered the Treasury to

> take such measures as may be necessary for providing a proper number of vessels for the conveyance of 750 convicts to Botany Bay, together with such provisions, necessaries, and implements for agriculture as may be necessary for their use after their arrival.[35]

The eighty-one-year history of transporting convicts to Australia had begun.

By the time Redfern was sentenced to life imprisonment in 1797, the colony of New South Wales was well-established. It had even begun to thrive, leaving the terrible uncertainty of the starvation years behind. Word trickled back to Britain that the colony was, in fact, much more than a jail.[36] Letters from early convicts who had completed their sentences or were pardoned told of beginning a new life. As time passed, the number of people with this status increased: 74% of the colony's White residents were convicts in 1790, but only 32% were in 1800. Moreover, the atmosphere had changed in the mid-1790s so that supervision over the convicts was more relaxed.[37] Such news led one chief justice to argue in 1810 that transportation to Australia was little more than "a summer's excursion, an easy migration to a happier and better climate."[38] Such critiques were unfair, but Redfern must have heard enough encouraging news to decide at some point within his first four years of confinement to submit a request to be transported to Australia. When authorities honored Redfern's request, he joined over a hundred prisoners aboard the *Minorca*, which set sail on June 21, 1801 from Spithead. Fourteen other men convicted of mutinous activities between 1797 and 1799 were also on board the *Minorca* for the 176-day voyage to Sydney.[39]

These mutineers were not typical passengers on convict ships. In fact, prisoners charged with political offenses comprised only 2% of the 162,000 men and women transported to Australia between the first arrival in Sydney harbor in 1787 and the end of penal transportation to Western Australia in 1868.[40] More typical were people like Thomas Pevett, who stole and killed a ewe in 1801, or Mary Preston, who stole a watch and money from a drunk man as he vomited in the street in 1809. In 1842, fourteen-year-old William Burton was transported to Van Diemen's Land (Tasmania) for a seven-year sentence because he stole a pair of shoes from a cart in Ipswich, while nineteen-year-old Elizabeth Mandeville received a seven-year sentence for stealing money in 1808

---

[34] Randall McGowan, "The Well-Ordered Prison: England 1780-1865," *The Oxford History of the Prison*, 80. None of these characteristics were a part of the early modern prison experience.

[35] Lord Sydney, "Lord Sydney to the Lords Commissioners of the Treasury," *Historical Records of New South Wales*, Vol. 1, Part 2: Phillip, 1783-1792 (Sydney: Charles Potter Government Printer, 1892), 14.

[36] Hirst, *Convict Society and Its Enemies*, 78-79.

[37] F. K. Crowley, "The Foundation Years, 1788-1821," *Australia: A Social and Political History*, Gordon Greenwood (ed.) (New York: Frederick A. Praeger, 1955), 7, 13. "White" and "Black" are both intentionally capitalized. See Chapter F, footnote 60.

[38] Brooks and Brandon, *Bound for Botany Bay*, 33.

[39] "Convict Indents: First Fleet, Second Fleet and Ships to 1801, NRS 1150," Record # 1150_4_3999_000063, accessed October 4, 2019, http://srwww.records.nsw.gov.au/indexesold/searchform.aspx?id=77

[40] Brooke and Brandon, *Bound for Botany Bay*, 13, 63.

on Dyott Street in London's Bloomsbury neighborhood.[41] Indeed, most of the crimes prompting transportation involved property rather than treason. They were also most frequently committed by the uneducated urban poor. Most were not first-time offenders.[42]

Many convicts struggled as much emotionally from their banishment as they did physically from the rigors of the passage to Australia. As pickpocket George Barrrington noted in his journal in 1791, as if the goodbyes to family weren't hard enough, the last sight of England "brought a fresh pang to the bosom of one who in all probability was bidding it adieu forever."[43] Even for the best educated, the experience was incomprehensible. As one convict wrote,

> But, take [me] J[ohn] Grant brought up in a free country with the noblest Ideas of Independence & Liberty & place him in a distant colony where slavery predominates—To expect him to settle in such a place is as if you bid fish live upon dry land, or fowls of the air in the ocean.[44]

Convicts in Sydney in the opening years of the nineteenth century were treated differently than those transported to the American colonies in the eighteenth century. In North America, the British government took no responsibility for the convicts; merchants simply transported them across the Atlantic and sold them for the duration of their sentence to the highest bidder. In Australia, the government closely monitored the convicts, whether they were assigned to government service or to private individuals.[45] In the assignment system in the early 1800s, those working for the government worked ten-hour days, beginning at dawn, Monday through Friday, and a six-hour day on Saturday. They were required to attend church services on Sundays. They also needed to work some of the remaining hours of the week to provide for their own housing since the government only supplied them with food and clothes. These convicts were employed in government construction projects, stone quarries, slaughterhouses, lumberyards, dockyards, and road gangs.[46] The convicts in private assignment were known as servants and referred to their employers as masters.[47] After 1804, these masters had to keep a convict for at least a year and were required to provide the necessary food, clothing, and housing because this reduced government costs significantly. It also meant that only government convicts wore distinctive, identifiable clothing.[48] Privately assigned convicts also had their late afternoons free and had the right to work for additional employers if they could earn more by doing so. Because there was no established currency in the colony at the turn of the century, all convicts were paid for the work done outside the prescribed working hours with alcohol, tea, sugar, and tobacco.[49] Those who possessed special

---

[41] L. L. Robson, *The Convict Settlers of Australia: An Enquiry into the Origins and Character of the Convicts Transported to New South Wales and Van Diemen's Land 1787-1852* (Carlton, Victoria, Australia: Melbourne University Press, 1965), 48, 54, 78-79.

[42] John Hirst, "The Australian Experience: The Convict Colony," *The Oxford History of the Prison: The Practice of Punishment in Western Society*, Norval Morris and David J. Rothman (eds.) (New York: Oxford University Press, 1998), 237.

[43] George Barrington quoted in Brooks and Brandon, *Bound for Botany Bay,* 81.

[44] John Grant*, John Grant Journal, 1805-1810*, W. S. Hill Reid, Joan O'Hagan and others (ed. and trans.) National Library of Australia, Manuscript # MS 737, item #42, page 54.

[45] John Hirst, "The Australian Experience: The Convict Colony," *The Oxford History of the Prison*, 241.

[46] Crowley, "The Foundation Years," 17-19.

[47] Hirst, *Convict Society and Its Enemies,* 32.

[48] Crowley, "The Foundation Years," 22.

[49] Hirst, *Convict Society and Its Enemies,* 37-40.

skills, such as carpenters and bricklayers, or those with an education, such as clerks and surgeons, were assigned to the most attractive jobs and had the opportunity to earn the most outside pay.[50] In the early 1800s female convicts were usually employed as domestic servants. Because they were not allowed to live alone as male convicts were, they usually slept in the kitchen, which was detached from the house. This meant that women had far less freedom than men in the penal colony, which bred resentment and prompted disruptive behavior in many women.[51]

Convicts in private service were not supposed to be physically punished by their masters. Instead, when a disciplinary issue arose, masters were required to bring the convicts before a magistrate, who would hear the case and decide the punishment. This was a burdensome requirement, and many masters came to adopt the common wisdom that the carrot worked better than the stick for controlling convict behavior and getting work done. Incentives replaced maltreatment. Even convicts in government service had the right to appear before a magistrate before a flogging could be administered.[52] Convicts who committed crimes in the colony and who were deemed incorrigible and beyond redemption were frequently sent to more isolated outposts like Van Diemen's Land and Norfolk Island, where conditions were harsher. In April 1803, for example, Robert Jillet was found guilty of stealing 77 pounds of salt pork in a wheelbarrow from the government store. He was found guilty and initially sentenced to death but was subsequently sent to Norfolk Island with his wife Hailey and "several of the Store Attendants whose conduct had been such as to render them suspected."[53] If the Jillets needed medical care during their sentence on the island, they would have received it from Redfern. He had been assigned to Norfolk in May 1802 because the island desperately needed a doctor, even one who, according to one official document, was "a dangerous character to Society."[54]

Located a thousand miles northeast of Sydney and 700 miles northwest of Auckland, Norfolk Island was first charted by James Cook in 1774. It originally drew the attention of British authorities because two of its natural resources, tall pines and flax, might provide important naval stores. All

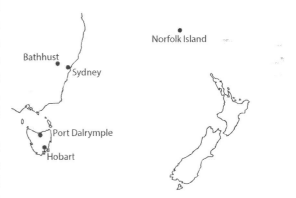

that was needed was labor for the uninhabited island, so a detachment of the First Fleet settled on Norfolk two months after the first prisoners arrived in New South Wales. When the pine trees proved insufficiently strong for masts and the flax production proved insufficiently ample for sails, the island simply became a prison, accompanied by a few free settlers and a military garrison.

A dearth of primary documents makes it difficult to assess the harshness of the conditions during the early years of the Norfolk penal colony.[55] There are glimpses, however, that it was

---

[50] Crowley, "The Foundation Years," 18.

[51] Hirst, "The Australian Experience," 244.

[52] Hirst, *Convict Society and Its Enemies,* 57-58, 66, 71.

[53] "Court of Criminal Jurisdiction," *The Sydney Gazette and New South Wales Advertiser,* April 10, 1803, 1, and "Sydney," *The Sydney Gazette and New South Wales Advertiser,* April 24, 1803, 4, accessed January 28, 2020, http://trove.nla.gov.au/

[54] Ford, *The Life and Work of William Redfern,* 11.

[55] Robson, *The Convict Settlers of Australia,* 118. Robert Hughes presents the island as a place of horrific sadism, but Anne-Maree Whitaker reports that this characterization of the Foveaux administration of the island is

brutal. A marine named John Easty, bound for England in 1792, recorded in his diary that Norfolk was "a poor, miserable place" where "all manners of cruelties and oppression [are] used." The "flogging and beating the people to death" is so sad "that it's better for the poor, unhappy creatures to be hanged almost than to come under the command of such tyrants."[56] Convict John Grant, whose time on Norfolk overlapped with Redfern's, wrote that the island was a study in contrast between its natural beauty and its human barbarity. In his private journal Grant said that the "superb trees" and "a mountain rising on one side" form "a spectacle of the greatest Beauty when approached from the sea." He noted that the island was "completely protected" by "a violent surf continually pounding on the rocks surrounding it" and that "the exquisite Beauty of the interior of the land, amply repays the curiosity of all those who visit it. I was never so struck by a place…. Abundance reigns around us!" This contrasted with Grant's assessment of those in charge of the island, including Lieutenant-Governor Joseph Foveaux.

> I am anxious that these truths be promulgated… for the System prevailing here makes me sick to the depths of my soul….[The] System rouses aversion in [the convicts] for all effort—the Military weighs on them—Slavery prevails—Dissolute individuals do as they wish—overwhelming the natural bent of man in that charming setting so well adapted for its display….The blood of many innocent Men cries out for Vengeance against this Foveaux: May it please Providence that…he atones for his abuse of Power on the Scaffold.[57]

Grant was an agitator, critical of almost everything in colonial Australia except the convicts.[58] He described the colony's free settlers as "lazy buggers and almost Spiritless, incapable of supporting themselves at home, and consequently throwing themselves on the Charity of the nation for an Establishment here."[59] Having little toleration for authority, he was constantly at odds with island officials. Hence, Grant's description may be exaggerated.

Redfern had only been on Norfolk for a few months when Foveaux gave him a conditional pardon and recommended him for a full pardon to Governor Philip Gidley King in Sydney. King granted the full pardon on June 19, 1803, and Redfern became a free man, even in Britain. It had been less than six years since his conviction for mutiny and less than two years since his departure from England aboard the *Minorca*. Clearly the decision to come to Australia had been a good one. He was able to go anywhere or do anything he wished. Interestingly, Redfern chose to remain on Norfolk, serving as the island's surgeon and earning a government salary.[60] If the conditions on the island were as bad as Easty and Grant say, with convicts being grossly, regularly, and purposefully mistreated, then Redfern becomes a willing accomplice to the viciousness. His only source of

---

based upon documents that were forged in the 1850s. (See Robert Hughes, *The Fatal Shore: The Epic of Australia's Founding* (New York: Vintage Books, 1988), 113-119; and Anne-Maree Whitaker, "From Norfolk Island to Foveaux Strait: Joseph Foveaux's Role in the Expansion of Whaling and Sealing in Early Nineteenth Century Australasia," *The Great Circle*, Vol. 26, No. 1 (2004), 51-59, EBSCOhost. There is more historical consensus about the second iteration of the island's penal settlement (1825-1855), when conditions were so brutal that convicts attempted to seize the island three times. See Hirst, "The Australian Experience," 254.

[56] Hughes, *The Fatal Shore*, 111. I have corrected this quotation for spelling and punctuation errors.

[57] Grant, *John Grant Journal*, 44.

[58] N. S. Lynravn, "Grant, John (1776–?)" *Australian Dictionary of Biography*, Volume 1, (Carleton, Australia: Melbourne University Press, 1966), accessed January 28, 2020, http://adb.anu.edu.au/biography/grant-john-2118

[59] Grant, *John Grant Journal*, 62.

[60] Bigge, *Report of the Commissioner into the State of the Colony of New South Wales*, 84.

redemption would be a deep desire to alleviate convict suffering, using his medical training for that purpose. The less appealing possibility is that Redfern was simply a cruel co-conspirator. Significantly, there is evidence to support both possibilities as he became older. On one side, Redfern was known to possess a violent temper. In late 1810s he beat hospital employees and convict servants with "unjustifiable severity," and in the late 1820s he physically attacked a newspaper editor in the street for publishing an article that criticized Redfern's reputation.[61] Redfern's proclivity for violence may have been a learned behavior he developed on Norfolk. On the other side, there is evidence of Redfern's deep commitment to helping those in need. He traveled significant distances outside of Sydney to help patients, and his extensive philanthropic work benefited many groups.[62] Redfern took a special interest in education and supported the creation of free public schools in Sydney, including the establishment of a special school for Aboriginal children in Parramatta.[63] He gave generously whenever asked. In 1826, the *Sydney Gazette and the New South Wales Advertiser* hinted at the inherent tension in Redfern's persona:

> His methods or his manner…may not be so winning or seductive as might be wished, but then his experience, his skill and his practice…make ample amends for any apparent absence of overflowing politeness.[64]

In short, Norfolk made Redfern a complicated man.

On September 17, 1807, a notice went up on Norfolk announcing the plan for the island's evacuation. The island had become too expensive to operate since it was not producing the anticipated exports. The convicts and free settlers were to be shipped to Van Diemen's Land. The order divided the free settlers into three groups and said that proportional "Grants of Land are to be made (free of Expense) on their arrival in the Settlement of Port Dalrymple or of Hobart Town (according to their option)" and that a new house would be erected "at the Public Expense of equal value to the house which they shall have left behind." Those with the highest priority would receive food and clothing for "Two Years at the public expense," as well as "the Labour of four Convicts for the first nine months and Two for fifteen months longer." These convicts were also to be clothed and fed at the public expense. Residents in the remaining two categories received similar benefits but for shorter terms. All three groups were to be "supplied from the Stores with Implements of Husbandry as well as other implements and Tools equivalent to such as they… may not have it in their power to remove."[65] Clearly, the government wanted to make the evacuation and transition as economically palatable as possible. Records indicate that even though he owned 48 acres on

---

[61] Bigge, *Report of the Commissioner into the State of the Colony of New South Wales*, 86 and "Case of Assault," *The Australian*, January 23, 1828, 3, accessed October 4, 2019, http://trove.nla.gov.au/

[62] Norman Dunlop, "William Redfern, the First Australian Medical Graduate, and His Times," *Journal and Proceedings*, Royal Australian Historical Society, Vol. XIV, 1928, Part II, 40.

[63] "Government and General Orders," *The Sydney Gazette and the New South Wales Advertiser*, December 10, 1814, 1, accessed October 4, 2019, http://trove.nla.gov.au/ and "General Meeting," *The Sydney Gazette and the New South Wales Advertiser*, March 15, 1817, 2, accessed October 4, 2019, http://trove.nla.gov.au/

[64] Dunlop, "William Redfern," 43.

[65] "Notice for Withdrawing the Settlers and the Inhabitants of Norfolk Island, 1807, Sept. 17," [Manuscript] #MS 523, National Library of Australia, Canberra. For information the early history settlement of Port Dalrymple (today's George Town, Tasmania), see James Backhouse Walker, *The Discovery and Occupation of Port Dalrymple*, Open Access Repository, University of Tasmania, accessed March 25, 2020, https://eprints.utas.edu.au/16731/2/1890-Walker-discovery_of_port_dalrymple.pdf

Norfolk, Redfern chose to go to Sydney instead of accepting this offer. He left the island on May 15, 1808 aboard the schooner *Estamina*, hoping to win an appointment in the Sydney hospital. He was accompanied by a servant and his first wife, who must have once been a convict herself.[66]

Redfern arrived in Sydney at an interesting turning point in the colony's history. He found that Governor William Bligh, famous for the *Bounty* mutiny, was in prison after a military *coup d'état*

against him five months before. While the *coup* is known today as the Rum Rebellion, the divisive issue involved property, not alcohol: did the Crown continue to own the land in Sydney or did those who had built their own houses and cultivated their own gardens on city land have any legal title to it? Bligh was the first governor who attempted to reassert and clarify the exclusivity of Crown ownership, but because 85% of Sydney's population believed that they held title by "naked possession," Bligh's cancellation of leases and evictions of occupants created significant resentment. The crisis was not resolved until Governor Lachlan Macquarie arrived from England in December 1809 and upheld the right of private property.[67] Redfern was the only physician to side with Bligh throughout the conflict, believing that he had been unfairly removed from office and that the best interests of the colony were served by remaining loyal to gubernatorial authority.[68] This meant that when Foveaux returned from England and assumed command as lieutenant governor, he happily appointed Redfern assistant surgeon of the hospital in Sydney with a salary of almost £137, plus housing quarters and food supplies.[69] Foveaux felt little trepidation in making the appointment since he knew Redfern's work from their years together on Norfolk and since the rest of the medical community was in disgrace for siding with the rebels. He had no qualms about issuing Redfern the vouchers necessary to operate the hospital, which by December 1808 totaled just over £577.[70] Foveaux did not have any official certification to prove that Redfern was a qualified surgeon, however,[71] which led the thirty-four year old doctor to insist that he be examined by three of Sydney's surgeons who had supported the *coup*. Foveaux reported to London on September 1, 1808 that doctors Thomas Jamison, John Harris, and William Bohan "have examined Mr. William Redfern touching his Skill in Medicine

[66] Ford, *The Life and Work of William Redfern*, 11.

[67] Grace Karskens, "The Early Colonial Presence, 1788-1822," *The Cambridge History of Australia, Volume I: Indigenous and Colonial Australia*, Alison Bashford and Stuart Macintyre (ed.) (New York: Cambridge University Press, 2013), 114-115.

[68] Dunlop, "William Redfern," 47.

[69] Lachlan Macquarie, "List of Persons Holding Civil and Military Employments in His Majesty's Colony of New South Wales and its Dependencies, April 30, 1810," *Historical Records of Australia*, Series I, Volume VII, 327.

[70] Joseph Foveaux, "Lieutenant-Colonel Foveaux to Viscount Castlereagh, December 31, 1808," *Historical Records of Australia*, Series I, Volume VI, 703-704.

[71] Ford, "William Redfern."

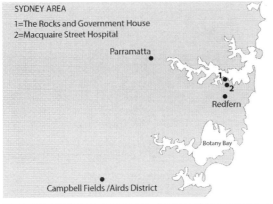

SYDNEY AREA
1=The Rocks and Government House
2=Macquaire Street Hospital

and Surgery" and "find him qualified to exercise the Profession of a Surgeon."[72] London confirmed Redfern's appointment on July 26, 1811.[73]

Redfern began his medical work in Sydney in the Dawes Point Hospital, in the area known as The Rocks. It was located in the area of George Street, Nurse's Walk, and Surgeon's Court, just west of where the Contemporary Museum of Art stands today. Constructed in 1796 with convict labor, the hospital consisted of a collection of single-story, whitewashed brick buildings with steeply pitched roofs, stone foundations, and small windows. This compound provided not only rooms for convict patients, a house for the principal surgeon, and a house for the assistant surgeons. By 1810, they were all in what Macquarie described as "a most ruinous state and very unfit for the reception of the sick."[74] He issued orders early in his tenure for the construction of a new hospital. The ambitious governor wanted a substantial structure to confirm his vision for the colony as a redemptive community instead of merely a place to house unwanted British prisoners.[75] His plan called for a two-story main building, 131.5 feet long, 26 feet wide, and 36 feet high, with both stories surrounded by wide verandas. White Doric columns, spaced symmetrically around the whole exterior, were to give the facility a sense of classical stateliness and prestige. Inside, each floor was to contain four wards, sixty feet long, designed to accommodate 20 patients each. At either end of this building would stand another structure in the same style. The northern one would serve as the home of the principal surgeon and two staff surgeons, while the southern one would house four assistant surgeons. The plan for the compound also included two detached kitchens, servant quarters, stables, and a coach house.[76] Macquarie wanted Sydney to become "as fine and

[72] Joseph Foveaux, "Certificate of Examination of William Redfern, Sept. 1, 1808," *Historical Records of Australia*, Series I, Volume VI, 647.

[73] Robert Jenkinson, Second Earl of Liverpool, "Earl of Liverpool to Governor Macquarie July 26, 1811," *Historical Records of Australia*, Series I, Volume VII, 362.

[74] Ford, *The Life and Work of William Redfern*, 14.

[75] Karskens, "The Early Colonial Presence," 117.

[76] J. Frederick Watson, *The History of the Sydney Hospital from 1811 to 1911* (Sydney, W.A. Gullick, 1911), 16-17.

Opulent a Town as any one in His Majesty's other foreign Dominions." [77] The hospital was to be an early showcase of this aspiration.

The problem was that the governor had no way to pay for such a grand project, nor did any colonist. This forced both the governor and those wanting to secure the contract to be creative. Three men stepped forward in July 1810 and offered to construct the hospital compound in exchange for the exclusive right to import 45,000 gallons of rum to the colony over the next three years. They also wanted this rum excused from government taxes. Macquarie had no right to exempt the contractors, but he did agree to give them a six-month delay in payment of the duty, the labor of 20 convicts for the duration of the project, draft animals and 80 oxen for slaughter. With the details settled, the governor laid the cornerstone October 30, 1810. He did not wait for London's approval to build what became known as the Rum Hospital, but he did not expect significant objections because the colony would obtain a new hospital at no cost to the Crown. Unfortunately for the governor, London officials were critical of his actions. They especially objected to the fact that one of the contractors, D'Arcy Wentworth, also served as the hospital's principal surgeon. [78] But everyone knew that by the time Macquarie learned of these concerns, it would be too late to stop the project. Patients moved into the new hospital from Dawes Point in March 1816, almost two years later than the contract originally specified. [79]

Redfern had no objections to the original plans of the hospital, but upon occupancy found it to be "defective, in not having the several conveniences of wash-house, storerooms, and water-closets." Only five of the eight wards in the central building could be used for patients since three had been requisitioned for civil and criminal courts and storage. [80] Still, as the man responsible for day-to-day operation of the facility, Redfern decided to get on with it, despite collecting a salary that was only 40% of that of the hospital's principal surgeon, D'Arcy Wentworth. [81]

~

Medical knowledge had improved, albeit unevenly, in the 160 years since Gijsbert Heeck sailed with the Dutch East India Company. In some areas, knowledge had even improved in the six decades since Robert Monckton's wounds on the Plains of Abraham. But significant limitations and frustrations remained. Perhaps the situation in the early nineteenth century is best captured by the words of pathologist and anatomist Matthew Baillie, who wrote, "I know better perhaps than another man, from my knowledge of anatomy, how to discover disease, but when I have done so, I

---

[77] *The Governor: Lachlan Macquarie* [exhibition brochure], Helen Cumming, Kathryn Lamberton, Cathy Perkins (eds.) (Sydney: State Library of New South Wales, 2010), 8.

[78] Watson, *The History of the Sydney Hospital*, 18-24.

[79] John Thomas Bigge, *Report of the Commissioner of Inquiry on the State of Agriculture and Trade in the State of the Colony of New South Wales* (London: The House of Commons, March 13, 1823), 105.

[80] Bigge, *Report of the Commissioner of Inquiry on the State of Agriculture and Trade*, 106-107.

[81] In 1817, Redfern was paid £136, 17s, 6d, while D'Arcy Wentworth received £365, 0s, 0d, and first assistant surgeon James Mileham received £182, 10s, 0d. See "List of Names, etc., of Persons Holding Civil and Military Appointments in the Territory of New South Wales and Its Dependencies on the 31st of March, 1817," *Historical Records of Australia*, Series I, Volume IX, 244. It is clear from these salaries and the reputations of the men that having a higher position and salary was more a function of seniority than responsibility or talent. Redfern also received rations, fuel, light, and lodging as part of his salary. See Dunlop, "William Redfern," 27.

don't know better how to cure it."[82]   This was because in the early nineteenth century, there was still no knowledge of microscopic pathogens.[83] Combined with a lack of equipment, it was difficult to distinguish between various diseases. A fever could be the result of everything from the flu to malaria, typhoid to typhus.[84] The solution remained to try to purge the body of what ailed it: bloodletting, cupping, and clystering remained standard treatments. For most surgeons in this period, a moderate bleeding was eight to twelve ounces, while a heavy one was sixteen to twenty ounces.[85] Doctors used an array of medicines, herbs, and toxins to combat various maladies. These included using opium to stop diarrhea, wine to stimulate the appetite, and mercury to calm inflammations and treat venereal diseases. New drugs like oxide of zinc, aconite, castor oil, magnesia, and sarsaparilla became part of physicians' arsenal. In surgery, there had been advances: some surgeons were able to complete the removal of kidney stones in less than three minutes, utilize internal sutures, and treat patients with cataracts. They used alcohol and turpentine on wounds to fight what they called putrefaction; this helped kill bacteria and fight infection.[86]

Perhaps the most significant change came in fighting smallpox.   Vaccination replaced inoculation, thanks to the work of Edward Jenner, who injected cowpox into an eight-year-old boy in hopes of making him immune to much more virulent smallpox. It did, and by 1800 much of Europe had benefited from his discovery and technique. Getting the cowpox vaccine to Australia proved quite challenging, however, since the lymph had difficulty surviving in hot and humid environments.   There were three possible methods of do so: in a dried state, such as on a cloth thread; in a fluid state, using a lancet; or through direct arm-to-arm transfers from an infected person to an uninfected person.[87] Of these three, the arm-to-arm method had the greatest success. Sydney's assistant surgeon John Savage hoped to use this method aboard the *Glatton* in September 1802. His plan was to keep the vaccine alive through the successive vaccination of convicts, but the captain and ship's surgeon refused to cooperate, and the lymph was dead by the time the ship arrived in Sydney in March 1803. Fourteen months later, the *Coromandel* arrived with samples that had

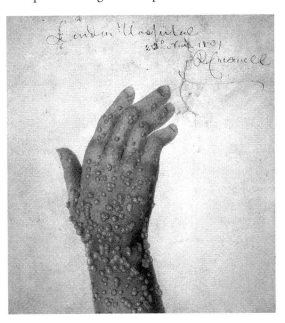

---

[82] Matthew Braillie quoted in Roy Porter, *The Greatest Benefit to Mankind: A Medical History of Humanity*, (New York, W. W. Norton & Company, 1998), 266.

[83] Brooks and Brandon, *Bound for Botany Bay,* 177.

[84] Mary C. Gillett, *The Army Medical Department, 1775-1818* (Washington, DC : Center of Military History, United States Army, 1990), 3-4.

[85] Gillett, *The Army Medical Department,* 6. Gillett notes that in the 1790s American physician Benjamin Rush went much further, advocating the removal of a quart of blood at a time, repeatable two to three times a day. See page 2.

[86] Gillett, *The Army Medical Department,* 7-8, 15-16; and Porter, *The Greatest Benefit to Mankind,* 269, 278.

[87] Andrea Rusnock, "Catching Cowpox: The Early Spread of Smallpox Vaccination, 1798-1810," *Bulletin of the History of Medicine,* 83, 1 (Spring 2009), 17-36, ProQuest Central.

been prepared by the Royal Jennerian Society, and packed in a variety of ways to improve the odds of success. None of these official samples survived, but a lymph "put up in a different manner" and sent privately to John Savage did. In June 1804, Sydney's surgeons began vaccinating the town's children. By the end of the antipodean winter, over four hundred children had become immune to smallpox, but many parents in New South Wales refused to allow their children to be vaccinated. Without any new carriers, the cowpox could not survive and within a year the lymph was no longer available in the colony. [88] Meanwhile, the cowpox vaccine spread through other parts of the world. In 1803, Spain's Charles IV ordered royal surgeon Francisco Xavier Balmis to spread the vaccine through Spanish territories. Using arm-to-arm vaccination with orphans from Santiago de Compostela and supplied with 2,500 copies of a pamphlet with color engravings and detailed instructions, Balmis and his assistants succeeded in bringing cowpox to Cuba, Mexico, Guatemala, Panama, Argentina, Chile, Peru, Philippines, China, and other territories.[89] Similar efforts took the lymph across Siberia, through the Mediterranean, and to the Middle East and India.

~

Redfern's career running the Sydney hospital between 1808 and 1819 captures the transitional state of the medical profession in the early nineteenth century quite well. There is evidence suggesting Redfern was near the forefront of the profession, and there is also evidence showing that his thinking was outdated. On the progressive side, Redfern was considered the foremost obstetrician in the colony.[90] He helped delivery many babies at a time when other surgeons, such as John Savage and James Mileham, refused to assist women in labor because they did not consider midwifery to be a part of their job.[91] Similarly, Redfern understood the advantage of smallpox vaccination and recognized the public health importance of maintaining a supply of vaccine. He had been the surgeon who had administered the vaccinations on Norfolk Island in 1805. When a new sample arrived in New South Wales from India in 1809, Redfern argued that those "in the superior ranks of life" must "impress on the minds of the poorer orders of people, whose ignorance renders them too susceptible to the grossest and most unfound prejudices, the usefulness, safety, and superior advantages of this new plan of inoculation."[92] Redfern specifically recommended that in order to preserve this new supply of the vaccine that only a few children should be vaccinated at one time. Unfortunately, parental resistance to vaccination continued and this sample died, making it necessary to obtain more lymph from Britain and elsewhere in succeeding decades. Despite

[88] Michael Bennett, "Smallpox and Cowpox Under the Southern Cross: The Smallpox Epidemic of 1789 and the Advent of Vaccination in Colonial Australia," *Bulletin of the History of Medicine*, 83, 1 (Spring 2009), 37-62, ProQuest Central.

[89] Rusnock, "Catching Cowpox."

[90] Edward Ford, *Medical Practice in Early Sydney: With Special Reference to the Work and Influence of John White, William Redfern, and William Bland* (Sydney: Australasian Medical Publishing Company Limited, 1955), 27.

[91] Vivienne Parsons, "Savage, John, 1770-?)" *Australian Dictionary of Biography*, Vol. 2, (Carleton, Australia: Melbourne University Press, 1967), accessed February 21, 2020, http://adb.anu.edu.au/biography/savage-john-2631 and Vivenne Parsons, "Mileham, James (1763-1824) Vol. 2, 1967, accessed February 21, 2020, http://adb.anu.edu.au/biography/mileham-james-2451. Both men were court-martialed for refusing aid to the women in labor.

[92] Bennett, "Smallpox and Cowpox Under the Southern Cross."

Redfern's progressive smallpox orientation, he also frequently used very traditional treatments. On October 6, 1814, for example, when Mrs. Macquarie's curricle hit a blind boy in the street, the governor's wife sent for Redfern, hoping that he might save the boy's life. Redfern's treatment consisted of bleeding him. [93] Redfern was also prone to believing in tall tales and suspect folk remedies. One of his surviving, unpublished medical notebooks contains a recipe for pill made from rhubarb and crab eyes. It also prescribes rubbing a toad's leg on a victim's sores, applying egg whites to a burn, treating kidney stones with blackberry syrup, and forcing salt down the throat of an epileptic during a seizure.[94]

Redfern's primary responsibility in the new Macquarie Street Hospital was to provide for the medical needs of convicts. Those in government service received unconditional care, while those assigned as servants to free men received treatment if their masters provided for the patient's first fourteen days of rations. If an assigned servant's illness lasted longer than a fortnight, the master could return the convict to government care or take the convict back once he or she was discharged from the hospital. Other individuals also received treatment at the Macquarie Street Hospital, including all civil officers of the Crown, merchant seaman whose captains paid for the services, and poor, free settlers who had the governor's permission to enter the hospital.[95] Redfern usually began his rounds at 8:00 a.m., checking individually on each patient in the wards. At each bed, he would order a prescription, which a convict clerk recorded. Later in the morning, Redfern saw the outpatients, including the poor who could not pay for care and had not yet obtained the governor's dispensation. He then went to the supply storage rooms, prepared the medicines, and gave them to his apprentice, Henry Cowper, for distribution to the patients. By noon, Redfern considered his official duties for the day completed. As he left for his extensive and expensive private practice, the Macquarie Street Hospital took on a more casual atmosphere, with patients looking after themselves and their own needs. They cooked their own food in the wards, sold their unwanted rations from the verandas to townspeople to obtain tea and sugar, and managed without the assistance of nurses or attendants through the night. Between 1816 and 1818, men and women

were assigned to the same wards, which were locked at night, so there was little sense of privacy or safety. Overcrowding meant the bodies of the dead were left in the hallways until coffins could be made for them. These conditions were not dissimilar to those found in London hospitals of the period.[96]

Redfern's management of the hospital received considerable criticism in an important report assessing the status of Australian penal colony. In 1819, the Crown appointed John Bigge as a special commissioner and sent him to Australia to determine how the transportation system could be made a greater deterrent for crime in Britain. Bigge was also charged with evaluating the effectiveness of colonial officials. In his final report, Bigge blamed Redfern for the

[93] Lachlan Macquarie, "Governor Macquarie to Under Secretary Goulburn, December 15, 1817," *Historical Records of Australia*, Series I, Volume IX, 733. Not surprisingly, the boy died.

[94] William Redfern (?), *William Redfern Notebook, 1795-1825*, Microfilm, Mitchell Library, Sydney, Call no. MAV/FM3/709, pages 2, 18, 40, 45, 47, accessed April 15, 2015. The original is badly damaged but presumed to be authentic. It is owned by a descendent of Redfern.

[95] Watson, *The History of the Sydney Hospital,* 38.

[96] Watson, *The History of the Sydney Hospital,* 39-44; Dunlop, "William Redfern," 13; Ford, *Medical Practice in Early Sydney,* 23; and Bigge, *Report of the Commissioner of Inquiry on the State of Agriculture and Trade,* 105.

atmosphere at the new hospital. The commissioner was outraged by the "impropriety, not to say criminality" of Redfern's habit of using government-supplied medications for patients in his private practice. He called this outright "fraud," and noted that Redfern "never imported medicine on his own account" and "partook more largely from the medical stores of government than any other person." Because Redfern refused to allow Bigge to see the ledgers of his private practice, the commissioner was not absolutely able to determine if Redfern gave medicine to non-convict patients for free or if "they constituted a distinct source of profit to him." Bigge believed that because medical supplies were always in short supply in the colony, Redfern's actions were "very prejudicial to the lower order of patients in the colonial hospital" since they reduced "to them the supplies of the most useful medicines."[97] If Redfern was guilty of malpractice, his patients did not seem to object too strenuously. Quite the contrary, they praised his skill, devotion, and expertise. In fact, patients of all classes and backgrounds appreciated him so much they even tolerated his idiosyncratic style, which was far more gruff than gracious.[98] At a time when most physicians earned their reputations primarily on the basis of their bedside manner, this was unusual.[99] In fact, Redfern's reputation as an effective doctor within the community was stellar. Even Bigge had to admit that Redfern's practice was "more extensive and successful than that of any other medical practitioner in the colony."[100] Other Sydney doctors did not enjoy such laudable reputations. Many patients of other local doctors found the heavy bleedings so objectionable that they called the hospital the "Sydney Slaughterhouse," and sought their medical care from alternative practitioners in The Rocks.[101]

As a result of his public reputation, his long service to the hospital, the customary use of a seniority system, the unquestioned support of Macquarie, and a promise from London, Redfern fully expected to become the hospital's principal surgeon when D'Arcy Wentworth retired in May 1818. Instead, a naval surgeon named James Bowman received the post and arrived in the colony in the fall. Redfern was humiliated. He resigned his job as assistant surgeon on October 18, 1819. In his resignation letter, he expressed his "severe and mortifying disappointment" at having failed to receive the appointment, despite his "reasonable expectations" that he would as a result of his "long, laborious and I trust useful service of Eighteen Years." Redfern ended the letter by saying that since "my most sanguine hopes and best prospects in life are thus utterly blasted, I have, therefore the honor of thus tendering my resignation."[102] Five days later, Macquarie announced the news to the public in the *Sydney Gazette and the New South Wales Advertiser*. The governor praised Redfern's "superior Professional Skill, Steady Attention, and active zealous performance of the numerous important Duties entrusted to him." He concluded:

> With these Impressions and the strongest Sense of his superior Talents and Merits His Excellency desires Mr. Redfern to accept the Assurance that he will carry into his Retirement His Excellency's best Wishes for his future Happiness and Prosperity.[103]

---

[97] Bigge, *Report of the Commissioner into the State of the Colony of New South Wales*, 84-86.

[98] Dunlop, "William Redfern," 43; and Ford, *The Life and Work of William Redfern*, 19.

[99] Porter, *The Greatest Benefit to Mankind*, 256.

[100] Bigge, *Report of the Commissioner into the State of the Colony of New South Wales*, 84.

[101] Ford, *Medical Practice in Early Sydney*, 22, 27.

[102] William Redfern, "Assistant Surgeon Redfern to Governor Macquarie, October 18, 1819," *Historical Records of Australia*, Series I, Volume X, 273.

[103] "Government and General Orders," *The Sydney Gazette and the New South Wales Advertiser*, October 23, 1819, 1, accessed January 28, 2020, http://trove.nla.gov.au/

What made Redfern's failure to secure the promotion especially painful was the fact that it was far from the first rejection he had received. In fact, Redfern's social standing handsomely illustrates the limitations that any former convict, or Emancipist, faced in Sydney society. Redfern might be respected as a physician, but, like other Emancipists, he found himself repeatedly excluded from social functions in the homes of the free settlers. This meant that landowner and prominent citizen John Macarthur could write to his wife,

> if I had as much a power as I have inclination, Mr. Redfern's reward for the service he has rendered [their daughter] Elizabeth should be as great as the skill he has manifested in discovering and applying an efficacious remedy to her extraordinary disease.[104]

But it also meant that this reward could not include an invitation to dinner. In the minds of many free settlers in Australia, once a man was a convict, he was always a convict. As Bigge reported, "It is this difficulty…that constitutes the formidable impediment…to bring back into society…[all] persons who have been once rendered infamous."[105]

From the outset of his governorship in 1810, Macquarie fought against this bias, which had to be overcome if his vision of a redemptive colony might be realized. As he wrote to London, "I was very much surprised and Concerned on my Arrival here, at the extraordinary and illiberal Policy I found had been adopted" by my predecessors "respecting those Men who had been originally sent to this Country as Convicts, but who, by long Habits of Industry and total Reformation of Manners, had not only become respectable, but by many Degrees the most useful members of the community." Macquarie complained that these elite former convicts had "never been Countenanced or received into society." He decided "to adopt a new line of conduct" and invite these men to Government House. Redfern was one of the first four men to receive such an invitation, along with D'Arcy Wentworth, "an opulent Farmer" Andrew Thompson, and "an opulent Merchant" Simeon Lord, who owned the largest private house in New South Wales.[106] But even the governor's seal of approval was not enough to change the prevailing attitudes in key circles, including the military. When, for example, Redfern came to dine at the regimental mess at the invitation of a senior officer, all of the junior officers walked out in protest, refusing to associate with the doctor because he had once been a convict.[107]

This attitude was not just about social snobbery. It was also about the existing elite's political and economic position. By 1820, the colony's demographics had changed significantly: more adults had been born in New South Wales than had freely migrated there. In addition, 18% of the colony's adults held pardons or had completed their sentences.[108] The colony was no longer composed only of the convicts and the free. Many of the people in these changed demographics were becoming successful. Convicts Jane Meredith and Thomas Parment provide one such example. Both

---

[104] Ford, *The Life and Work of William Redfern*, 20.

[105] Bigge, *Report of the Commissioner into the State of the Colony of New South Wales*, 90.

[106] Lachlan Macquarie, "Governor Macquarie to Viscount Castlereagh March 8, 1810," *Historical Records of Australia*, Series I, Volume VII, 275-276.

[107] Hirst, *Convict Society and Its Enemies*, 155.

[108] Crowley, "The Foundation Years," 13. These tensions were exacerbated in the 1820s by the influx of decommissioned soldiers from the Napoleonic Wars, many of whom were still on half pay and wanting land. See Angela Woollacott, *Settler Society in the Australian Colonies: Self-Government and Imperial Culture* (Oxford, U.K.: Oxford University Press, 2015), 15.

transported in 1815, she was a needle worker in Devon, and he was a surgeon. She was sent to the women's factory at Parramatta in 1819 for misbehavior; he completed his sentence and went to Parramatta looking for a wife. Their marriage freed Jane, and the couple went on to have four children and own 720 acres of land a hundred miles north of Sydney.[109] Indeed, by 1821 over fifty percent of the male Emancipists owned land or were tradesmen.[110] The free immigrants, however, believed that such economic clout threatened to disrupt their influence. The idea of extending full civil rights to the Emancipists would constitute a social revolution in New South Wales.[111]

The tensions over the rights and status of Emancipists came to a head from an unexpected quarter in January 1820, when a Parramatta judge accused a litigant, Edward Eagar, of being "a revolutionist."[112] Eagar then sued Judge Barron Field for damages. At trial in April, Fields' attorney argued that because Eager was an Emancipist, he had no right to sue because no pardon could restore his legal standing vis-à-vis those who never lost theirs. This brought the issue of Emancipist rights to the forefront. If the Emancipists could not sue, they could not own property or hold office.[113] They were certainly not free men. In this line of reasoning, landowners with property that had once belonged to an Emancipist would also lose clear title to their land.[114] The Emancipists didn't obtain permission to meet to discuss the problem until January 1821, but at that meeting Redfern was unanimously elected chair. The assembly resolved to submit a petition to the King and Parliament for recognition of their civil rights and agreed that representatives should take the petition to London. Over the next 10 months the petition gathered 1,367 signatures. Redfern and Eager set sail for London on October 25, 1821 aboard the *Duchess of York*.[115]

Redfern was an impolitic choice for the Emancipists' cause because his name carried so much notoriety. Not only was there his past as a mutineer, but there was his impatience and violent temper. Redfern had also been at the center of a controversy involving the appointment of Emancipists to government posts. In the fall of 1819, on the heels of Bowman's appointment as principal surgeon, Macquarie had appointed Redfern as magistrate of a district west of Sydney called Airds. Bigge objected to this decision, saying that Redfern's appointment was "replete with Danger to the Community."[116] This insulted Macquarie, who went a step further and appointed his close friend as a magistrate for all of New South Wales. Bigge was beside himself with disbelief, and both he and Macquarie appealed to London for support of their position. This issue was whether or not it was appropriate for Emancipists to serve the colonial government. The Secretary of State

---

[109] Robson, *The Convict Settlers of Australia*, 141.

[110] Robson, *The Convict Settlers of Australia*, 125.

[111] R. M. Hartwell, "The Pastoral Ascendancy, 1820-1850," *Australia: A Social and Political History*, Gordon Greenwood (ed.) (New York: Frederick A. Praeger, 1955), 56.

[112] Edward Eagar was involved in many legal cases. In 1815, he was disbarred by Judge Jeffrey Hart Bent for not having the right credentials under a new Charter of Justice. In 1819, when he brought suit in England to recover a debt, he was denied standing because his pardon had not yet "passed the Great Seal," meaning that it had not received final confirmation. To streamline the story, I have chosen to begin with the Field case instead. For more details, see Hirst, *Convict Society and Its Enemies*, 158; and N. D. McLachlan, "Eagar, Edward (1787-1866)," *Australian Dictionary of Biography*, Volume 1 (Carleton, Australia: Melbourne University Press, 1966), accessed January 28, 2020, http://adb.anu.edu.au/biography/eagar-edward-2013

[113] C.M.H. Clark, *A History of Australia, Volume I: From the Earliest Times to the Age of Macquarie* (Carlton, Australia: Melbourne University Press, 1963), 355-357.

[114] Hirst, *Convict Society and Its Enemies*, 159.

[115] Clark, *A History of Australia, Volume I*, 359.

[116] John Thomas Bigge, "Mr. Commissioner Bigge to Governor Macquarie November 2, 1819," *Historical Records of Australia*, Series I, Volume X, 219.

for War and the Colonies, Earl Bathurst, sided with Bigge, saying that although he appreciated Macquarie's "Intentions and Motives," His Majesty "is nevertheless compelled to disapprove of the course you have thought it advisable to pursue." Bathurst indicated that while it was possible for former convicts to serve in "situations of trust," there was no pressing necessity to do so in Redfern's case: "it is impossible for His Majesty to sanction Mr. Redfern's nomination…[his] Name should not appear in the New Commission for the Peace."[117] This announcement signaled how much the mood in London had changed in regard to Macquarie's policies after a decade of his governorship. Men with a different vision for the colony were in ascendancy.

Despite these impediments, the petition Redfern and Eager filed was successful, and the Emancipists secured the essential rights they sought. The New South Wales Act of 1823 validated all prior pardons and ensured that all future pardons would be valid from the date of the governor's signature. This secured Emancipist property and allowed them legal standing in court. The act also created the colony's first legislative assembly and a supreme court, even if real power remained in the hands of the governor and the Parliament in London.[118]

~

Returning to Australia in 1824, Redfern brought with him two commodities that illustrate his shift in vocation from medicine to agriculture: verdelho grape vines from the Madeira Islands and Merino sheep from Portugal and Spain. This shift, and the accompanying move to the countryside, was good for Redfern's soul. Not only did it help him overcome the disappointment of having lost the principal surgeon position, but his fortunate timing allowed him to take advantage of a significant change in Australia's land use policy.

Prior to the end of Macquarie's administration, freed convicts could receive thirty-acre land grants, as well as the tools, seed, and livestock they needed to create a new livelihood. The goal was to create a viable, post-penal population for the colony, using the model of the yeoman farmer. In 1825, however, as a result of the recommendations Bigge made to the Crown, a new land policy arose. It awarded land in 1,920 acre parcels and allowed one person to purchase as many as five parcels, payable in quarterly installments. Even better for those with capital, the purchase price was refundable if the landowner maintained a reasonable number of convict laborers on his property. This policy concentrated land ownership employed an increased number of convicts and created something akin to a plantation-style society.[119] According to the plan, Australia would serve as a center of wool production, helping feed British industrialization. The reason for the dramatic increase in parcel size was that sheep require more grazing land than thirty-acre plots allow. As White Australians continued to explore and settle the interior of New South Wales, they encountered grasslands that seemed ideal for large herds. In 1813, explorer George Evans, for example, lauded what became the Bathurst area, writing, "the grass here might be mowed it is so thick and long." It is "the best grass I have seen in any part of New South Wales; the hills are also covered the fine pasture, the Trees being so far apart must be an acquisition to its Growth; it is in

---

Henry Bathurst, Third Earl Bathurst, "Earl Bathurst to Governor Macquarie July 10, 1820," *Historical Records of Australia*, Series I, Volume X, 310.
[118] Hirst, *Convict Society and Its Enemies,* 159, 170, 172.
[119] Jack Kociumbas, *The Oxford History of Australia*, Volume 2, 1770-1860, (Melbourne, Australia: Oxford University Press, 1992), 32, 134-136; and Hirst, "The Australian Experience," 251.

general the sweetest in open Country."[120]
When Evans took Macquarie and Redfern to
see the Bathurst area two years later, the
official account of the trip described the land
by saying, "It is impossible to behold this
grand scene without a feeling of admiration
and surprise." It is "designed by nature for
the occupancy and comfort of man."[121] This
land was, of course, already occupied, but, as
in the American West, Australian pastoralists saw the land as uninhabited and unutilized,   rich
enough to sustain vast flocks of sheep. What they failed to appreciate was that the Aboriginals had
created these grasslands over thousands of years. Through the careful, repeated, purposeful, and
reverent use of fire, Aboriginal Australians manipulated and controlled their environment. They
burned the richest land yearly to manage the underbrush and limit the damage of wildfires, but left
the least fertile land alone for generations. Their sophisticated land management system allowed
them to honor their spiritual beliefs and usually to live with significant free time and freedom from
want.[122] When the pastoralists set their flocks loose upon the land, the sheep disrupted the
ecological balance and rapidly destroyed the pastureland.[123] Large landowners then sought more
land, as well as government support for these acquisitions. Men like Governor Richard Bourke
were more than happy to oblige; in the 1830s he wrote, "sheep must wander or they will not thrive,"
and "sheep are erratic animals and the doctrine of concentration is ill-applied to them. Our wool
is our wealth, and I am disposed to give ample runs."[124]

   Redfern was far from being the largest landowner in New South Wales, but he certainly did
benefit from government land policies, either through the grants Macquarie awarded him on
account of their friendship or from the ability to purchase the larger tracts after 1825. At his death,
Redfern owned over 23,000 acres scattered between Bathurst and Sydney.[125] His favorite of these
was his 2,620 Campbell Fields estate in the Airds District, which he had first seen with Macquarie
in 1810 and named after Macquarie's wife.[126] This was where he retired with his second wife, Sarah
Wills, and his two sons when he returned from the Emancipist mission to London. Redfern was as
successful an agriculturalist as he was a doctor. As early as 1817, he was able to provide the
government stores with as much fresh meat as any other rancher in the colony. Significantly, of

[120] George William Evans quoted in Bill Gammage, *The Biggest Estate on Earth: How Aborigines Made Australia*
(Sydney: Allen & Unwin, 2011), 188.
[121] J. T. Campbell, "Government and General Orders, June 10, 1815," *Historical Records of Australia*, Series I,
Volume VIII, 574.
[122] Gammage, *The Biggest Estate on Earth,* 123-128, 138, 160-162.
[123] Kociumbas, *The Oxford History of Australia*, Volume 2, 126. White-Aboriginal relations were complex
because the white settlers and squatters took land and triggered violent Aboriginal responses and yet needed
Aboriginal cooperation because of labor and knowledge. See Woollacott, *Settler Society in the Australian Colonies,*
8-9. Henry Reynolds pioneered scholarship about violent Aboriginal responses white encroachment. See his
books *Forgotten War* (Sydney: University of New South Wales, 2013) and *The Other Side of the Frontier: Aboriginal
Resistance to the European Invasion of Australia* (Sydney: University of New South Wales, 2006), which was first
published in 1982.
[124] Richard Bourke quoted in Hartwell, "The Pastoral Ascendancy, 1820-1850," 81.
[125] Philip Norrie, *Wine Doctors of Sydney* (Lane Cove, Australia: Organon, 1994), 3. Redfern's 23,190 acres was
the equivalent of 36.23 square miles.
[126] Dunlop, "William Redfern," 37.

the top six providers in 1817, Redfern was the only one with a convict heritage.[127] Even Bigge grudgingly recognized him as one of the eight property owners who exhibited "the best state of cultivation" and made "the greatest improvement" to the land in the colony.[128]

Redfern used both free and convict labor to help him work his estates. Like other pastoralists, he took advantage of how the convict system changed in the 1820s to better meet the needs of agriculture and British industrialization.[129] As a result of Bigge's recommendations, convicts were no longer able to earn money on their own time, they had to surrender any assets to the government until the completion of their sentence, and they were assigned to secondary penal stations, such as re-opened  Norfolk Island, for misbehavior. The revised goal was to punish the convicts with hard labor, rather than rehabilitate the banished and incorporate them into society. Even those with skills were assigned to unskilled manual labor as part of their punishment. According to Bigge, transportation had to be expanded to meet the growing needs of the pastoralists.[130] Bigge had originally been sent to Australia to determine if a system of "general discipline, constant work, and vigilant superintendence" could make the colony an "object of real terror."[131] Thanks to Bigge's recommendations, many new convicts answered in the affirmative until the last consignment arrived in Australia in 1868.[132]

~

The bookend to the frustrating uncertainty of Redfern's youth is the obscurity of his final years. In 1828, Redfern took his nine-year-old son, William Lachlan Macquarie Redfern, to Edinburgh to complete his education. He financed this decision and the change of residence by selling £25,000 worth of sheep and cattle the previous year.[133] He must have chosen Edinburgh intentionally, but

---

[127] "Deputy commissary General's Office," *The Sydney Gazette and New South Wales Advertiser*, December 27, 1817, 1, accessed October 4, 2019, http://trove.nla.gov.au/ The other five were H. M. Arthur, James Birnie, William Howe, George Thomas Palmer, and William Charles Wentworth.

[128] Bigge, *Report of the Commissioner of Inquiry on the State of Agriculture and Trade,* 13.

[129] Convict labor could not always meet the needs of the pastoralists. In 1832, for example, the Redferns took out an advertisement seeking twelve shepherds who were "Free or Ticket of Leave Men, producing testimonials of good conduct, and of a proper knowledge in the tending and care of Sheep" for a wage of "Twenty Pounds per Annum, with weekly Rations." See "Classified Advertising," *The Sydney Gazette and New South Wales Advertiser*, May 31, 1832, 4, accessed October 4, 2019, http://trove.nla.gov.au/

[130] Kociumbas, *The Oxford History of Australia,* Volume 2, 153-158.

[131] Hirst, *Convict Society and Its Enemies,* 87.

[132] Transportation ended at different times in different parts of Australia. New South Wales received its last convicts in 1840, Tasmania in 1853, and Western Australia in 1868. In each of these locations, the convicts still had to complete their terms, so the convict penal system endured for years after these dates.

[133] "Shipping Intelligence," *The Sydney Gazette and New South Wales Advertiser*, May 14, 1827, 2, accessed October 4, 2019, http://trove.nla.gov.au/. Sheep cost between £15 and £25 a head in the mid 1820s, depending on the breed, so Redfern would have sold between 1000 and 1600 sheep to finance his move. (See Ian M. Parsonson,

he left no specific explanation. Perhaps Redfern wanted to return to a city he knew, the city where he may have once studied medicine. What is clear is that he and William lived at 18 Lothian Street, just a few yards from the University of Edinburgh's Old College.[134] Five years passed, with Redfern in living in Scotland and his wife, Sarah, remaining in New South Wales. During this interval, she managed family affairs from their Campbell Fields estate.[135] In 1830, their younger son, Joseph Foveaux Redfern, died. Redfern must have then encouraged Sarah to join him in Edinburgh, for on March 10, 1833, she left Sydney on the barque *Norfolk*, accompanied by a servant.[136] Unfortunately, she did not arrive in time: the *Norfolk* docked in London two days after Redfern's July 17 death.

~

In June 1992, the Australian High Court issued a landmark decision upholding Aboriginal land rights for the first time. In *Mabo v Queensland [No. 2],* it dismissed the long-held concept that prior to the arrival of the First Fleet the continent was *terra nullius* or unowned land because the Aboriginals had no recognizable system of law. The court ruled instead that the Meriam people had their own laws governing property and that these had to be recognized in common law.*[137] In other words, native title had existed across the continent in 1788, even if the High Court was only now recognizing this fact.[138] The High Court ruled that Aboriginal land rights existed where the government had not specifically awarded the land previously and where Aboriginals had maintained a connection to it.[139] It was a ruling that seemed to mark a key turning point in Australian history, and the nation's prime minister at the time, Paul Keating, wanted to take full advantage of the opportunity. Just one week after the decision, he told Parliament that the court's decision did "not interfere with private property rights," but it did make Australia "far better prepared psychologically to proceed with the process of reconciliation." Keating argued that for Australia to become "a truly civilised, advanced nation," it must abolish its "arrogance, ignorance, and complacency," and "eradicate this injustice and prejudice" once and for all.[140] The prime minister set out to devote his administration to the realization of these ideals.

The *Australian Ark: A History of Domesticated Animals in Australia* (Collingwood, Victoria, Australia: Csiro Publishing, 2000), 40-42, EBSCOebooks.

[134] *The Post-Office Annual Directory for 1833-34* (Edinburgh: Ballantyne and Co., 1833), 73, 139, accessed January 28, 2020, https://tinyurl.com/y4u9gqxj. At this point, the Georgian building lacked its dome.

[135] Sarah's management included dealing with a crop-damaging wildfire and the reassignment of convicts. See "Domestic Intelligence," *The Sydney Gazette and New South Wales Advertiser*, December 12, 1831, 4 and "Return of All Assigned Convicts Between the 1st Day of January and the 31st Day of March, 1832," *The Sydney Gazette and New South Wales Advertiser*, June 14, 1832, 2, accessed January 28, 2020, http://trove.nla.gov.au/

[136] "Shipping Intelligence," *The Sydney Gazette and New South Wales Advertiser*, March 12, 1833, 2, accessed January 28, 2020, http://trove.nla.gov.au/

[137] Lisa Strelein, *Compromised Jurisprudence: Native Title Since Mabo*, (2nd ed.) (Canberra: Aboriginal Studies Press, 2009), 1, EBSCOebooks.

[138] David Day, *Paul Keating: The Biography* (Sydney: Fourth Estate/HarperCollins Publishers Australia Pty Limited, 2015), 370.

[139] Paul Kelly, *The March of Patriots: The Struggle for Modern Australia* (Carlton, Victoria, Australia: Melbourne University Press, 2009), 201.

[140] Paul Keating quoted in Day, *Paul Keating,* 371.

The most famous moment in Keating's effort came on December 10, 1992, when he appeared before a hostile and distrustful crowd to launch Australia's participation in the International Year of the World's Indigenous People. The venue was a park in Redfern, a poor, inner-city neighborhood just south of Sydney's central business district, which is named after the Emancipist doctor who owned one hundred acres in the area nearly two centuries before.[141] Keating's audience was predominately Aboriginal, but the message was not for them as much as it was for White Australians.[142] Keating began tentatively, facing both catcalls and disinterest, but as he spoke, the audience slowly began to acknowledge his words:[143]

> The starting point might be to recognise that the problem starts with us non-aboriginal Australians. It begins, I think, with that act of recognition. Recognition that it was we who did the dispossessing. We took the traditional lands and smashed the traditional way of life. We've brought the diseases. The alcohol. We committed the murders. We took the children from their mothers. We practiced discrimination and exclusion. It was our ignorance and our prejudice. And our failure to imagine these things being done to us. With some notable exceptions, we failed to make the most basic human response and enter into hearts and minds. We failed to ask – how would I feel if this were done to me? As a consequence, we failed to see that what we were doing degraded all of us.[144]

With these words, the forty-eight-year-old Keating became the first Australian prime minister to acknowledge his nation's racial history in such a direct way.[145] His words resonated because they were decades ahead of the current discourse about multicultural sensitivity. Keating didn't use his governmental authority to tell Aboriginal Australians what they knew they had experienced. Rather, Keating spoke as a White man about the White experience. This gave him an authenticity his audience appreciated, and it allowed him to facilitate multicultural conversation during the remainder of his term.[146] As part of his eighteen-minute address, Keating also indicated that the mistreatment wasn't only in the past but was unequivocally linked to the problems facing the

[141] Increasing numbers of Aboriginals from other parts of Australia settled in Redfern through the course of the twentieth century, attracted by inexpensive rents and nearby factory and railroad jobs. By the 1950s, Redfern had a decidedly Leftist political bent and the reputation for accommodating many of society's outcasts, including Aboriginals. By the 1960s, many buildings were in poor shape and calls for demolition and urban renewal began. High rises for public housing replaced individual houses and unemployment soared. For more information on Redfern's history, see Terry Irving and Rowan Cahill, *Radical Sydney: Places, Portraits, and Unruly Episodes* (Sydney: University of New South Wales Press Ltd., 2010), 266-272, 328-333.
[142] Don Watson, *Recollections of a Bleeding Heart* (Sydney: Vintage/Random House, 2003), 288.
[143] Watson, *Recollections of a Bleeding Heart*, 289.
[144] Paul Keating, "Keating Speech: The Redfern Address 1992," *Australian Screen of the National Film and Sound Archive*, accessed January 28, 2020, http://aso.gov.au/titles/spoken-word/keating-speech-redfern-address/extras/
[145] "FED: Elders mark 20 years since Keating speech," AAP General News Wire [Sydney], Dec 9, 2012, ProQuest Central.
[146] The literature regarding effective ways to have multicultural conversations is vast. A few books that stand out include: Helen Fox, *"When Race Breaks Out": Conversations about Race and Racism in College Classrooms* (3rd ed.) (New York, Peter Lang Publishing, Inc., 2017); Glenn E. Singleton, *Courageous Conversations About Race: A Field Guide for Achieving Equity in Schools* (Thousand Oaks, California: Corwin/Sage, 2015); Irhad Manji, *Don't Label Me: An Incredible Conversation for Divided Times* (New York: St. Martin's Press, 2019); and Ibram X. Kendi, *How to be Antiracist* (New York: One World, 2019).

Aboriginal community in the 1990s.[147] It makes sense, therefore, that on the twentieth anniversary of the Redfern speech, Aboriginal leaders hailed Keating's courage for not only saying what he said but for saying it in Redfern.[148] In fact, Keating's words stand as one of the most important speeches in Australian history.[149]

The racial reconciliation Keating called for has remained elusive for Australia through the opening decades of the twenty-first century, with the community of Redfern remaining a potent symbol of the divide. Two episodes stand out. In the first, in February 2004, unemployment in Redfern stood at 33%, Aboriginal men rarely lived long enough to collect a pension, customary Aboriginal rites of passage were not passed along to the young, and both taxi cabs and public buses refused to enter the neighborhood at night.[150] A seventeen-year old Aboriginal, Thomas Hickey, died after falling off his bicycle and impaling himself on a guardrail. Believing that the police caused the death by chasing the youth in a patrol car, about a hundred and fifty Redfern residents participated in a protest riot. They set fire to the Redfern railway station, threw Molotov cocktails and bricks, and injured thirty police officers. The police ended the protest by using high-pressure water hoses against the participants.[151] Community leaders blamed the police for both Hickey's death and the resulting violence. As Aboriginal activist Lyall Munro said, "These young people are very, very upset about what happened [to Hickey]" and "they are very upset about what's happening to their young friends on a continual basis." He noted that, "this is an everyday occurrence—the harassment and intimidation of our young people. You could interview every Aboriginal kid [in Redfern]…and the majority will tell you that they've all been bashed by the police."[152] Describing the level of desperation and frustration in the community, Munro added that, "If Palestinian kids can fight…tanks with sling shots, our kids can do the same."[153] While emotions cooled as the months passed, the issues that prompted them did not.

---

[147] Keating's connection to the present differed from the four-minute speech Prime Minister Kevin Rudd gave in February 2008, when the Australian government issued an official apology to Aboriginal Australians. Rudd only addressed the past and took no responsibility for contemporary conditions. See Denise Cuthbert and Marian Quartly, "Forced Child Removal and the Politics of National Apologies in Australia," *American Indian Quarterly*, 37, no. 1 (Winter, 2013), 178-202, 285, ProQuest Central. For a transcript of the speech, see "Apology to Australia's Indigenous Peoples," accessed July 17, 2020, https://tinyurl.com/y6ksfgh2

[148] Gail Mabo, audio recording in, "Redfern Marks Keating Speech, 20 Years On," ABC [Australian Broadcasting Corporation] News Online, accessed October 4, 2019, https://tinyurl.com/y3e6xg7q

[149] Keating's speechwriter, Don Watson, claims to have been the actual author of the speech. Keating vehemently denies this, and the two men had a falling out with the publication of Watson's book *Confessions of a Bleeding Heart* cited above.

[150] Claire Scobie, "'They're Treating Our Kids Like Dogs. It's Got to Stop'": It's Known as the Block, but for Many Aborigines It's Also Home. In the Wake of the Redfern Riots, Claire Scobie Reports from Australia on the Anger in Sydney's Forgotten Ghetto," *The* [Glasgow] *Herald*, February 18, 2004, ProQuest Central.

[151] David Fickling, "Inquiries Begin into Boy's Death and Sydney Riot: Fatal Accident Involving an Aboriginal Teenage Cyclist Sparks Violence in the Poor Suburb of Redfern Leaving Dozens Injured," *The* [Manchester] *Guardian*, February 17, 2004, ProQuest Central.

[152] Lyall Munro quoted in Molly Bishop, "Nine-hour Sydney Street Battle Leaves 40 Injured," *Birmingham Post*, February 17 2004, 10, ProQuest Central.

[153] Lyall Murno quoted in Roger Maynard, "Police Deny Chase Led to Aborigine Death Riot," *The* [London] *Times*, February 17, 2004, 14, ProQuest Central.

The second episode began in May 2014 after several years of increased gentrification and real estate speculation in Redfern.[154] Aboriginal leader Jenny Munro established a tent city or embassy on a vacate lot in the heart of Redfern to prevent the construction of a $70 million commercial development known as the Pemulwuy Project. Munro and her supporters demanded that it include sixty-two low-income housing units for Aboriginals. Two issues made the situation particularly complex. The first was that the lot was part of The Block, the symbolic heart of Redfern's Aboriginal community. The second was that the land was owned by the Aboriginal Housing Company (AHC), which was created in the 1970s to provide housing for Aboriginals. The AHC purchased the lot with a government grant. Munro maintained that "this is about black housing on black land," while the leader of the AHC, Mick Mundine, argued that Pemulwuy's commercial components had to be built first to help finance the desired housing.[155] The Aboriginal community was pitted against itself, with the city government and the police refusing to intervene in the intra-Aboriginal dispute. By 2019, the tensions had not abated. The AHC received approval for a plan to construct a twenty-four-story student accommodation tower on The Block in March and construction began in June. Munro characterized the decision by the New South Wales Independent Planning Commission as an attempt to practice social engineering and destroy Aboriginal identity.[156]

The name of Redfern stands, then, for two very different concepts in Australian history. It represents both a story of second chances and a story of unfulfilled promises. It exemplifies two justifications for punishment and penance, and it embodies the thorny difficulties involved in realizing racial reconciliation. Hence, Redfern is a place name that suitably captures the intricate complexities of Australian history.

---

[154] Redfern's median weekly rent jumped from $255 to $500 between 2006 and 2016, which was well above the national average of $355 in 2016. The Aboriginal population in Redfern dropped from 35,000 people in 1968 to just 300 in 2011. See Megan Gorrey, "Redfern's Soaring Rents Push Aboriginal Community to the Fringe," *The Sydney Morning Herald*, June 6, 2019, accessed January 28, 2020, https://tinyurl.com/yy2j3zhd

[155] Jenny Munro quoted in "Stalemate on The Block in Redfern as Protesters Defy Trespass Notice," *ABC [Australian Broadcasting Corporation] Regional News*, March 2, 2015, n.p., EBSCOhost; and Rick Feneley, "The Block, the Violence and the Bitter Feud Blocking Mick Mundine's Vision," *Sydney Morning Herald*, May 17, 2015, accessed January 28, 2020, https://tinyurl.com/y5gagjas

[156] Jamie McKinnell and Liv Casben, "The Block Plans Approved for 24-Storey Student Tower in Redfern," *Australian Broadcasting Corporation*, March 3, 2019, accessed January 28, 2020, https://tinyurl.com/y65bokt9

S

Catherine Wilson Malcolm Sheppard,[1]

1847(?)-1934

Women around the world fought for the right to vote through the course of the late nineteenth and early twentieth centuries. In Argentina, the campaign's leader was Alicia Moreau de Justo, while in Finland it was Alexandra Gripenberg. Iceland's Bríet Bjarnhéðinsdóttir and the Philippines' Pura Villanueva Kalaw led the suffrage campaign in their countries, just as Millicent Fawcett and Emmeline Pankhurst did in Great Britain, and Susan B. Anthony and Elizabeth Cady Stanton did in the United States. The honor of achieving the world's first successful suffrage campaign at the national level, however, belongs to another fascinating woman: New Zealand's suffragist and prohibitionist Kate Sheppard.

The details of Sheppard's childhood remain obscure, but it is clear that she developed an early appreciation for music from her father, and received both a strong education and a well-defined sense of morality from her uncle, with whom she presumably lived for an extended period after her father died.[2] This uncle was a minister in Free Church of Scotland in the Highland coastal community of Nairn.

The Free Church was a Calvinist, evangelical, and presbytery church that separated from the government-supported Church of Scotland in 1843, primarily because its members did not want the state to appoint its ministers.[3] It also separated because its members believed that it was both essential and practical for a church to impose standards of moral behavior on the society. This belief, combined with its insistence on the doctrine of predestination and the legalistic tone of its

---

[1] Catherine preferred to be called "Katherine" or "Kate." Malcolm was her maiden name, but in the interests of simplicity, she is identified as "Sheppard" throughout the chapter.

[2] This assessment derives from two sources, which disagree over the date of Sheppard's birth and the date of her father's death. See Judith Devaliant, *Kate Sheppard, A Biography: The Fight for Women's Votes in New Zealand – the Life of the Woman Who Led the Struggle* (Auckland, New Zealand: Penguin Books, 1992), 5; and Tessa K. Malcolm, "Sheppard, Katherine Wilson," *Dictionary of New Zealand Biography, Te Ara - The Encyclopedia of New Zealand*, updated May 2013, accessed January 29, 2020, http://www.TeAra.govt.nz/en/biographies/2s20/sheppard-katherine-wilson

[3] Peter Hilis, *The Barony of Glasgow: A Window onto Church and People in Nineteenth Century Scotland* (Edinburgh, U.K.: Dunedin Academic Press, 2007), 9, EBSCOebooks.

manifesto, made the Free Church the central voice of Puritanism in Scotland.[4] Soon, however, the Free Church developed internal disagreements over other doctrinal issues and divided again between its Lowland and Highland affiliates.[5] In the more conservative Highlands, the Free Church emphasized the importance of observing the Sabbath strictly and favored imposing temperance on a society that consumed three times the volume of spirits per capita that England did.[6] These Highlanders worshiped in churches without stained glass windows, printed hymnals, or instrumental music. Their ministers often spoke in Gaelic instead of English[7] and delivered their lengthy sermons without the benefit of prepared texts.[8] They also organized revival events and offered critical financial support for congregations in isolated areas.[9] All of this gave the conservative Free Church of the Highlands a character distinct from other churches in late nineteenth century Britain.

This was the formative atmosphere in which Sheppard was raised in Nairn. She also spent time in Dublin, where her mother and some of her siblings lived. In November 1868, twenty-one-year-old Sheppard, her mother, her two brothers, and one of her sisters left the port of Gravesend on the River Thames aboard the three-masted *Matoaka* for its penultimate voyage. They were bound for Christchurch, New Zealand, where Sheppard's older sister, Marie, had emigrated to marry a Scottish businessman. Emigrants typically had to provide their own mattresses, blankets, towels, toiletries, silverware, and plates for the long voyage. They also had to prove that they had sufficient clothing. For men, this meant six shirts, two pairs of new shoes, and two complete suits. For women, it meant two flannel petticoats, two pairs of strong shoes, and two durable dresses. A typical contract promised to provide ten cubic feet of luggage space and specified the food ration per week, which included salt beef, salt pork, biscuit, flour, rice or oatmeal, raw sugar, tea, butter, raisins, suet, pickles, mustard, salt, pepper, six ounces of lime juice, and 21 quarts of water.[10] The *Matoaka*'s 89-day voyage to New Zealand via Cape Town was half as long as William Redfern's had been to New South Wales in 1801, but it was still an extended time at sea.

The trip would have been full of new experiences for Sheppard, some of which would have shocked the puritanical sensibilities of her uncle, if not those of Sheppard herself. Crossing the equator, for example, she would have had to participate in the traditional Baptism at the Line ceremony, when a member of the crew, dressed as Neptune, assumed control of the ship and initiated newcomers to the southern hemisphere. A Scottish seaman aboard the *County of Peebles* named George Moore Sinclair kept an illustrated diary that documented the event in 1877 quite well. Sinclair recorded with glee that Neptune held a trident "comprised of a spoon, knife & fork,"

---

[4] Andrew L. Drummond and James Bulloch, *The Church in Victorian Scotland, 1843-1874* (Edinburgh, U.K.: The Saint Andrew Press, 1975), 1, 10, 21, 28.

[5] See James Lachlan MacLeod, *The Second Disruption: The Free Church in Victorian Scotland and the Origins of the Free Presbyterian Church* (East Linton, U.K.: The Tuckwell Press, 2000) for a thorough discussion of the Highland-Lowland division.

[6] Drummond and Bulloch, *The Church in Victorian Scotland*, 21-27. Free Church objected to operating trains between Edinburgh and Glasgow on Sundays. In 1839, there were 7.5 pints of spirits consumed per capita in England versus 23 pints per capita in Scotland.

[7] MacLeod, *The Second Disruption*, 131.

[8] J. M. Reid, *Kirk and Nation: The Story of the Reformed Church of Scotland* (London: Skeffington & Son Ltd., 1960), 127, 149-150.

[9] Patricia Meldrum, *Conscience and Compromise: Forgotten Evangelicals of Nineteenth-Century Scotland* (Carlisle, U.K.: Paternoster, 2006), 45, 124.

[10] J. Laughton Johnston, *A Kist of Emigrants* (Lerwick, U.K.: The Shetland Times, Ltd., 2010), 67. This contract was from 1874.

wore a crown, and "a flowing white robe." His beard was "composed of rope yarn red and white." As he walked to his throne, "two large sharks walked by his side, one carrying the razor and strap" and the other the "brush and pot." Neptune asked the captain if he "had any objection to making a few sailors," to which the captain replied, "'go ahead, sir, go ahead!'" Neptune handed out punishments to the neophyte crew as his assistants in the shark costumes applied a black lather to each man's face and shaved each roughly. The passengers watched, laughing hysterically, until Neptune turned on them as well, pouring buckets of salt water over men's heads.[11] Women were typically not exempt from the initiation ceremony. On some ships, they were sprinkled with salt water instead of being drenched, but they also had to kiss Neptune's "wife," or take an unpleasant sniff from her smelling bottle.[12] Sinclair noted that there were plenty of shrieks aboard the *County of Peebles*, and that the next day, "the whole lower rigging is flapping with drying garments of all descriptions."[13] Another unusual experience for Sheppard would have been the celebration of Christmas because none of the Scottish kirks celebrated the holiday or other feast days as Catholics and Anglicans did.[14] On Sinclair's ship, the crew and passengers joined together to have "jolly good dinner below," a seaman and a passenger were married, and "the captain came down in the midst of our festivities to taste the pudding" made by Mrs. Bailey and gave us "6 bottles of figg" to enjoy. One crew member marked the occasion by putting on "a clean pair of socks," and Sinclair described day as "a very nice time," which filled him with a warm "feeling all through."[15] Sheppard probably encountered something like this as she saw the Southern Cross for the first time.

The *Matoaka*, which was lost at sea on its return journey to England, landed in Lyttelton, New Zealand, near Christchurch, on February 8, 1869, and Sheppard began immediately settling into a new life. Because Christchurch had more churches than any other city in New Zealand, she had a wealth of options to meet her spiritual needs.[16] She began attending the local Presbyterian church, but left it to join the Trinity Congregational Church in April—perhaps because of the greater role music played among the Congregationalists. Sheppard's involvement with Trinity was a seminal experience for her: she began to develop her capacity for leadership. Not only did she help with the fundraising for the construction of a new church, which opened in January 1874 with the singing of the Gloria from Wenzel Müller's Twelfth Mass, but Sheppard also taught Sunday school and chaired a women's group.[17] It was also during her early years in Christchurch that she married an Anglican businessman, Walter Sheppard, eleven years her senior. Their only child was born in 1880.[18]

---

[11] George Moore Sinclair, *Diary Kept on Board the County of Peebles, 1877-1879*, 32-33. [photocopy], MSY-6857, Alexander Turnbull Library, Wellington, New Zealand.
[12] Henning Henningsen, *Crossing the Equator: Sailor's Baptism and Other Initiation Rites*, (Copenhagen, Denmark: Munksgaard, 1961), 75.
[13] Sinclair, *Diary Kept on Board the County of Peebles*, 32-33.
[14] Reid, *Kirk and Nation*, 43.
[15] Sinclair, *Diary Kept on Board the County of Peebles*, 41-42. The six bottles of "figg" could refer to a liquor made from figs or to figs preserved in bottles for the voyage.
[16] Geoffrey W. Rice, *Christchurch Crimes and Scandals, 1876-99* (Christchurch, New Zealand: Canterbury University Press, 2013), 15.
[17] Devaliant, *Kate Sheppard*, 11. In the nineteenth century, many people attributed this work to Wolfgang Mozart. For more information on the debate, see Mark Everist, *Mozart's Ghosts : Haunting the Halls of Musical Culture* (New York : Oxford University Press, 2012), 129-156.
[18] Douglas Sheppard died in Glasgow, Scotland from pernicious anaemia in 1910. Sheppard did not have any grandchildren.

~

In 1879, American suffragist and prohibitionist Frances Willard won the presidency of the Woman's Christian Temperance Union (WCTU), ousting the standing president after a two-year fight.[19] This was a milestone for the organization because Willard had a transformative vision for the group. She wanted to empower the WCTU politically by teaching its members, and American women generally, that femininity and domesticity were not incompatible with a woman's rightful participation in the democratic process. Since the WCTU had traditionally been opposed to women's suffrage, this transformation could not happen overnight. Rather, Willard sought to lead the organization through a series of steps that would migrate organizational opinion. One step was to convince WCTU members

that they should have the right to vote solely on liquor issues so that they could protect their children and homes from the nefarious effects of alcohol. Willard was convincing, and the WCTU officially endorsed this position in 1881.[20] Willard's victory rested in her adept understanding of political strategy, which was based on an unapologetic appeal to "the average woman" on her own terms.[21] Through the course of the 1880s and early 1890s, Willard took the WCTU much further. Influenced by gradualist approach of Fabian Socialism,* she became convinced that the prohibition issue was too narrow a focus of concern if women hoped to change to society. Willard, therefore, adopted her "Do Everything" policy, which called for using an array of tactics to fight for broad social change.[22] She also began to reach out abroad, seeking ties with women's temperance and suffrage leaders in other countries. With these steps, Willard transformed a small, limited group into the largest women's organization in the United States.[23]

When Willard learned in late October 1884 that the American West Coast's WCTU superintendent, Mary Clement Leavitt, had been invited to speak in Honolulu, Hawai'i, Willard saw a unique opportunity. Just six days before her departure, Willard convinced Leavitt to expand her trip into a worldwide campaign that would promote the ideals of the WCTU and investigate

---

[19] The name of the organization is frequently misspelled in both primary and secondary sources, using "Women's" instead of "Woman's." See, for example, the illustration on page 440.

[20] Ruth Bordin, *Frances Willard: A Biography* (Chapel Hill, North Carolina: University of North Carolina Press, 1986), 100, 103-104, 108, 111.

[21] Carol Mattingly, *Well-Tempered Women: Nineteenth-Century Temperance Rhetoric* (Carbondale, Illinois: Southern Illinois Press, 1998), 163. There was a strong implication that this "average" woman was a white, native-born, educated, middle class, evangelical Protestant. See Lisa McGirr, *The War on Alcohol: Prohibition and the Rise of the American State* (New York: W.W. Norton & Company, 2016), 7, 9, 17, 43-44-45, 128-129.

[22] Bordin, *Frances Willard,* 130, 145-146, 210.

[23] Patricia Grimshaw, "Women's Suffrage in New Zealand Revisited: Writing from the Margins," *Suffrage & Beyond: International Feminist Perspectives*, Melanie Nolan (ed.) (New York: New York University Press, 1994), 35.

the viability of establishing a new international temperance organization.[24] The second stage of Leavitt's eight-year journey was the trip from Hawai'i to New Zealand. Her speeches generated considerable enthusiasm in Auckland, Dunedin, Oamaru, and Invercargill before Leavitt arrived in Christchurch.[25] There, she spoke to a standing-room-only crowd at the Royal Theater on May 10, 1885. One local paper described her as "an elderly woman, very plainly attired, with a mild voice, a pleasant smile when speaking, and a noticeable American accent." The paper reported that she spoke about how the human body was "a wonderful piece of mechanism belonging to God" that should not be abused.[26] Sheppard may have been present to hear this first address in Christchurch, but she must have attended Leavitt's fifth speaking engagement in the city, held at Trinity Congregational Church on the evening of May 14. At this speech, Leavitt appealed to mothers to abstain from drinking alcohol to set an example for

their children. She argued that the craving of alcohol was cultivated or inherited, rather than natural.[27] By the time Leavitt left for Australia, she had established seven new chapters of the WCTU, one in each of the principal cities of New Zealand.[28] Three more chapters would follow by the end of 1885.[29] Christchurch became one of the strongholds for temperance in the colony.[30]

In June 1885, Sheppard began her political activism with the Christchurch chapter of the Woman's Christian Temperance Union by working on a campaign to ban women from being employed as barmaids and to ban the sale of alcohol to minors.[31] She collected 4,800 Christchurch signatures supporting the ban on barmaids and made arrangements for the petition to be properly received in Parliament, but subsequently learned that the petition, as well as others from other parts of New Zealand, had been quickly dismissed.[32] Sheppard concluded from this experience that women had no political power because they could not vote. If there was to be any progress in prohibition in the colony, women would first have to win their suffrage.[33] This realization led

[24] "Untitled," *Oamaru Mail*, Volume IX, Issue 2880, April 18, 1885, 2, "Papers Past," National Library of New Zealand, accessed January 29, 2020, http://paperspast.natlib.govt.nz/cgi-bin/paperspast. All subsequent references to nineteenth century newspapers published in New Zealand come from this website.

[25] "Local & General," *Star* [Canterbury], Issue 5303, 6 May 6, 1885, 3.

[26] "Mrs. Leavitt," *The Press* [Christchurch], Volume XLI, Issue 6129, May 11, 1885, 3.

[27] "Gospel Temperance Union," *Star* [Canterbury], Issue 5310, May 15, 1885, 3.

[28] "Untitled," *Oamaru Mail*, Volume X, Issue 3034, September 3, 1885, 2. By late 1889 Leavitt had travelled 70,000 miles in five years and "addressed audiences of all colors in all lands, without fee and without hope of any reward," according to an admiring column in the *Chicago Tribune*. See "Personals," *Chicago Tribune*, October 29, 1889, 4, https://chicagotribune.newspapers.com/image/371159366.

[29] Megan Cook, "Women's movement - Women's [sic] Christian Temperance Union," *Te Ara - the Encyclopedia of New Zealand*, accessed January 30, 2020, http://www.teara.govt.nz/en/womens-movement/page-2

[30] Rice, *Christchurch Crimes and Scandals*, 16.

[31] Devaliant, *Kate Sheppard*, 19, 21.

[32] Devaliant, *Kate Sheppard*, 22.

[33] Patricia Grimshaw, *Women's Suffrage in New Zealand* (Auckland, New Zealand: Auckland University Press, 1972), 37.

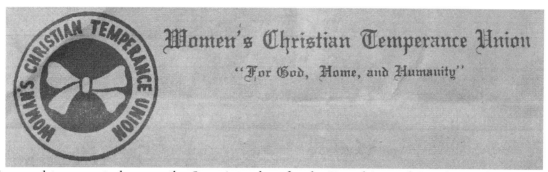

Sheppard to agree to become the Superintendent for the Franchise and Legislation for the New Zealand Woman's Christian Temperance Union when the organization held its national convention in Christchurch in February 1887.[34] One of her first steps was to ensure that each New Zealand chapter appointed a woman who would be responsible for suffrage advocacy and activism and would submit weekly reports to Sheppard.[35] In this way, Sheppard set high expectations for participation and progress, and she monitored changes in the political atmosphere throughout the colony. A year later, as president of the WCTU, Sheppard wrote a one-page leaflet, "Ten Reasons Why the Women of New Zealand Should Vote." The publication argued that because women were not children, lunatics, or convicts, and because they were "affected by the prosperity of the Colony," they possessed "an inherent right to a voice in the construction of laws which all must obey." It also asserted that government would be improved by women voters because their participation would foster less corruption; promote diverse perspectives; support "a deeper interest in the constant preservation of peace, law, and order; and elect candidates with higher moral standards.[36]

Sheppard's early work had precedents. In 1869, Mary Ann Müller anonymously wrote and published a ten-page pamphlet entitled *An Appeal to the Men of New Zealand*. In it she bemoaned the fact that a woman "may be a householder, have large possessions, and pay her share of taxes towards the public revenue" and yet remain part of "a wholly unrepresented body of the people." She objected to the fact that educated women are "degraded below the level of the ploughman, who perhaps can neither read nor write," and that "most girls of eighteen are better informed on many subjects of general information" than boys of the same age. Echoing Mary Wollstonecraft, Müller noted that New Zealand women are "brave and strong, with an amount of self-reliance, courage, and freedom from conventionalities," but that their minds are "weakened and famished by disuse."[37] This pamphlet, which was widely read and discussed, challenged New Zealand men to become world leaders and grant women the vote. In 1878, James Wallis, a Member of Parliament (MP) from Auckland, took up this challenge and introduced the first franchise bill to include women. Although the bill was defeated, it did have supporters. Later that parliamentary session, Wallis moved to strike the word "male" from another bill governing elections. His amendment

---

[34] Devaliant, *Kate Sheppard*, 24.

[35] Grimshaw, *Women's Suffrage in New Zealand*, 37.

[36] Kate Sheppard, "Ten Reasons Why the Women of New Zealand Should Vote," *New Zealand History*, Ministry for Culture and Heritage, accessed January 30, 2020, https://tinyurl.com/y4fc46cj

[37] Mary Ann Müller (a.k.a. Fémmina), *An Appeal to the Men of New Zealand* (Nelson, New Zealand: J. Hounsell, Bookseller and Stationer, 1869), Hilda Kate Lovell-Smith Papers, MSI–Papers–1376-10, Alexander Turnbull Library, Wellington, New Zealand.

failed 26-36. In 1879, similar vote failed 19-27.[38] Other attempts were made by other legislators in 1880, 1881, 1887, and 1890, but none of these efforts resulted in a change of law.[39]

There were a number of reasons why men opposed women's suffrage. Those who made their livelihood producing, distributing, and selling of alcohol were convinced that the Prohibitionists were correct about the effects of the women's vote: the passage of a suffrage bill "would be the death blow of the liquor traffic."[40] Hence, brewers' and vintners' associations lobbied MPs vigorously against the passage of any legislation. Politicians were not certain how women would vote; many worried that the infusion of women's votes would change the balance of power in Parliament.[41] It was, therefore, politically safer to maintain an exclusive male franchise. Other opponents of women's suffrage argued that they lacked the proper constitution for voting; that they would be fiscally irresponsible; that polling places were too ruckus and ill-mannered for women to attend; and that women would be too influenced by their ministers and priests. Still others claimed that giving women the vote would create undue discord between the sexes as wives neglected their homes; that no one would be able to care for children on election day; and that women had not actually demonstrated that they wanted the right to vote.[42]

Sheppard seized upon the tangibility of this last argument and in 1891 set out to show the Parliament in Wellington the extent of women's desire for democratic participation. She began organizing petitions for both the House of Representatives and the Legislative Council. Utilizing her WCTU chapter superintendents to assemble canvassers and collect the signatures in towns around the colony, Sheppard collected 10,085 signatures, which were pasted onto rolls of wallpaper and forwarded to Sir John Hall, one of her strongest allies in Parliament.[43] Hopes for the passage of suffrage legislation had never been higher.

~

In the British parliamentary system, bills are usually presented to the House of Commons by members of the government's cabinet, but they can also be sponsored by other MPs. All bills must be presented three times. The first reading is generally a formality, during which it is given its official title. Debate occurs at the second reading. The sponsor of a bill opens the discussion and

---

[38] *How We Won the Franchise in New Zealand* [pamphlet] (Wellington, New Zealand: The W.C.T.U. of N.Z., [1925?]), 6-7.

[39] Melanie Nolan and Caroline Daley, "International Feminist Perspectives on Suffrage: An Introduction," *Suffrage & Beyond: International Feminist Perspectives*, Melanie Nolan (ed.) (New York: New York University Press, 1994), 3.

[40] Reverend E. Walker quoted in "Prospects of the Liquor Traffic," *Hawera & Normandy Star*, Volume XVIII, Issue 3101, April 19, 1892, 2.

[41] Devaliant, *Kate Sheppard,* 56.

[42] Kate Sheppard, *Woman Suffrage in New Zealand* (London: Woman Suffrage Alliance, [1907]), 4-8. Additional information may be found in Raewyn Dalziel, "Presenting the Enfranchisement of New Zealand Women Abroad," *Suffrage & Beyond: International Feminist Perspectives*, Melanie Nolan (ed.) (New York: New York University Press, 1994), 51-55, and Grimshaw, *Women's Suffrage in New Zealand,* 77.

[43] *How We Won the Franchise in New Zealand,* 11. Sheppard's relationship with Hall was so close that she wrote many of his modern-sounding speeches. See Tom Brooking, *Richard Seddon, King of God's Own: The Life and Times of New Zealand's Longest-Serving Prime Minister* (Auckland, New Zealand: Penguin Books, 2014), no page, Kindle edition.

other members of the House weigh in. An initial vote is taken at the end of this debate, and then the bill is referred to committee, where amendments are often introduced. When the amended bill is reported out of committee, the full House debates it for a second time. After the third and final reading, a vote is taken, and if a majority is in favor, the bill passes to the House of Lords. The House of Lords lost its power to veto Commons' legislation in 1911, but it is able to delay the implementation of most bills for one year. Technically, the king or queen may veto parliamentary legislation, but this has not happened since 1707.[44]

Late nineteenth-century New Zealand followed the same parliamentary traditions, with the House of Representatives standing in place of the House of Commons and the Legislative Council, appointed by the prime minister, serving in place of the House of Lords. Royal approval for colonial legislation came from the governor. Today, New Zealand has a unicameral legislature that meets in Wellington.

The New Zealand Parliament has two other important traditions. First, in the nineteenth century, the House of Representatives included four seats for representatives of the indigenous people of the islands, the Maori; the unicameral Parliament today has retained these specially designated seats. Second, legislators are allowed to pair with one another: in order to facilitate an absence by one member, a known opponent will agree not to vote as well. This professional courtesy cancels out the effect an absence would have on the outcome of a controversial vote.

~

The second reading of Sir John Hall's Female Franchise Bill came on August 24, 1891. The debate began at 2:30 p.m., broke for a two-hour dinner recess, and lasted until 1:30 a.m.. Hall reasoned that every human being who was bound by laws had some right in their formulation and rejected the view that voting would have a negative effect on women's character. He noted that women taxpayers already had the right to vote in local elections without degrading them in the least. Henry Fish, the leading opponent to women's suffrage, described the cause's leaders as fanatics and promised to offer amendments in committee that would lessen support for the bill by making it more radical; these amendments included the right for women to become members of Parliament. In the end, the second reading passed 33 to 8.[45] In committee, an effort to delay implementation of the bill was rejected, but the amendment allowing women to run for Parliament passed 30-24. The third reading passed by a voice vote, and the bill was sent to the Legislative Council, where it was defeated on the second reading 17 to 15.[46] Because the two Maori representatives voted against the bill, some suffragists blamed the defeat on them.[47]

This defeat did not leave Sheppard discouraged, for rarely in democratic politics is an issue decided once and for all. Rather, as she wrote in her new temperance publication, the *Prohibitionist*:

[44] Samuel E. Finer, "Great Britain," *Modern Political Systems*, 3rd ed., Roy C. Macridis and Robert E. Ward (eds.), (Englewood Cliffs, New Jersey: Prentice Hall, Inc., 1972), 108-111, 118-120.
[45] "House of Representatives," *Timaru Herald*, Volume LIII, Issue 5224, August 25, 1891, 3.
[46] Devaliant, *Kate Sheppard*, 67, 69.
[47] Patricia Grimshaw, Politicians and Suffragettes: Women's Suffrage in New Zealand, 1891-1893," *NZ Journal of History*, Volume 4, No. 2 (October, 1970), 160-177, accessed January 30, 2020, http://www.nzjh.auckland.ac.nz/document?wid=1603&page

> The battle for the franchise has been fought and lost. Our defeat however was almost a victory. To have carried the Women's Suffrage Bill through the Lower House, and to be beaten in the Upper House by so small majority as two, is little short of a triumph for the large hearted men who are fighting so stoutly for our cause.[48]

Others were also impressed by the progress. One newspaper editorial noted that what had three or four years earlier been "universally regarded" as an "idle dream of a few faddists," women "of the masculine sort," and "weakminded men better fitted by Nature for petticoats" had become "one of those things which are certain to come about in the near—probably very near—future."[49] Sheppard knew that, having come so close, it was time to redouble the WCTU's suffragist efforts, rather than to surrender in frustration.

The 1892 campaign also ended in defeat, despite the fact that Sheppard sent twice as many petition signatures to Parliament as the year before.[50] This time the petition outlined four reasons for awarding suffrage: 1) that "Governments derive their just powers from the consent of the governed;" 2) that "the physical weakness of women naturally disposes them to exercise habitual caution, and to feel a deep interest in the constant preservation of peace, law, and order;" 3) that mothers "are particularly invested in legislation bearing upon the education and moral welfare of the young;" and 4) that women who own land and pay taxes face "taxation without representation," which "is tyranny."[51] One reason for the increased visible support was that Sheppard benefited from the creation of the Women's Franchise League (WFL). This organization expanded the pool of available volunteers because it was open to all women who supported the suffrage cause, regardless of their temperance beliefs. The WFL went out of its way not to undercut Sheppard's leadership or to fracture the suffrage movement as it expanded the breadth of the suffrage appeal.[52] What doomed the effort in 1892 was not the Legislative Council *per se*, but rather their amendment requiring women to vote by mail through a designee, just as some migrant workers did. The lower house opposed this intrusion to the secret ballot and this disagreement between the two branches stopped the bill. Although the colony did not have formal political parties in the late nineteenth century, one historian has argued that this was more a power struggle between two political factions than a commentary on suffrage itself.[53] This was an especially frustrating outcome for Sheppard, who wrote, "*both houses are agreed as to womanhood suffrage*, the only bone of contention being as to the manner of voting."[54] That technicality left New Zealand women "still grouped with criminals, lunatics, and aliens," according to the WCTU report summarizing the previous twelve months.[55]

1893 was a scheduled election year, so suffragists felt a particular urgency to secure a parliamentary victory as the year began. Sheppard launched another petition drive in February. She didn't mind that the work was a repetition of what she had done before. Rather, Sheppard held the firm conviction that the petition process was "invaluable" because there was "a vast amount of ignorance and indifference to overcome" and the drive showed the "women of the colony the

---

[48] Kate Sheppard quoted in Devaliant, *Kate Sheppard*, 69.
[49] "Woman Suffrage," *Ashburton Guardian*, Volume XIII, Issue 2647, April 19, 1892, 2.
[50] *How We Won the Franchise in New Zealand*, 11. There were 20,274 signatures in 1892.
[51] Petition quoted in "Miscellaneous. Female Suffrage," *Hawke's Bay Herald*, Volume XXVIII, Issue 9321, March 18, 1893, 5.
[52] Devaliant, *Kate Sheppard*, 80.
[53] Grimshaw, *Women's Suffrage in New Zealand*, 70-73.
[54] Kate Sheppard quoted in Devaliant, *Kate Sheppard*, 90. The italics are Sheppard's.
[55] WCTU Report quoted in "Miscellaneous. Female Suffrage," *Hawke's Bay Herald*, March 18, 1893, 5.

reasons why the franchise should be granted."[56] In Christchurch, Sheppard assigned door-to-door canvassing routes to members of the WCTU and the Canterbury Women's Institute, which had been founded in 1892 as a broad-based group dedicated to social change.[57] WCTU superintendents and leaders from other organizations developed similar plans in other communities. In fact, at least a third of the women who helped on the 1893 petition drive were not affiliated with a temperance group.[58] There was also an increased effort to reach women in rural areas, as volunteers carried petitions on horseback, collecting signatures on isolated farms throughout the colony.[59] Sheppard also worked to keep spirits high by speaking at public meetings and writing encouraging words to help motivate her supporters:

> Although we are still political outcasts, the promised land is in sight! Year-by-year we have been winning our way….Our forces have been gaining in numbers, not by any transient wave of enthusiasm, but by sheer, logical reasoning, and the hard work performed by members….Let us work and hope on, and this privilege must soon be ours![60]

But the suffragists lost a key ally in April, when the sympathetic premier, John Ballance, died. He had been a proponent of the franchise for women since 1879.[61] A firm opponent of women's suffrage, Richard Seddon, replaced him, which meant that Hall and Sheppard faced new obstacles in Parliament.

After its second reading, the House of Representatives debated the government's Electoral Bill in committee on July 28. During the debate, Hall presented Sheppard's 1893 petitions with dramatic flair. He began by placing a few pieces of paper on the desk, which produced a round of jeers. Then he brought into the chamber an enormous coil of sheets glued onto wallpaper and slowly began to unroll all 300 yards of it.[62] This was an impressive display, but Hall did not trust Seddon, and so decided to introduce his own women's suffrage bill, just as he had in 1891. At the second reading of his own bill on August 9, Hall presented additional petitions, bringing the total of signatures to 31,872, or three times as many as had been sent to Parliament two years before. This

---

[56] Kate Sheppard quoted in "Miscellaneous. Female Suffrage," *Hawke's Bay Herald*, March 18, 1893, 5.

[57] Devaliant, *Kate Sheppard, a Biography*, 101, 105.

[58] Ian Tyrrell, *Woman's World, Woman's Empire: The Woman's Christian Temperance Union in International Perspective, 1880-1930* (Chapel Hill, North Carolina: University of North Carolina Press, 1991), 225.

[59] Marilyn J. Waring, "How the Vote Was Won," *Ms*, 3, no. 4 (January 1993), 16, ProQuest Central.

[60] Kate Sheppard quoted in "Miscellaneous. Female Suffrage," *Hawke's Bay Herald*, March 18, 1893, 5.

[61] "Woman Suffrage," *Ashburton Guardian*, April 19, 1892, 2.

[62] Devaliant, *Kate Sheppard*, 109-110, and Grimshaw, *Women's Suffrage in New Zealand*, 89.

represented about a quarter of the adult women living in New Zealand and included women from every class, region, and denomination.[63] When the bill moved to committee, there was sharp disagreement as to whether or the bill would include the enfranchisement for Maori women. When one MP argued that Maori women were not sufficiently well-educated to vote, two representatives objected strenuously. Such a roar erupted on the floor that the chair ruled that the exclusion of Maori women be struck from the bill's language.[64] This allowed the government's bill to sail through the lower house with a voice vote at the third reading, and all attention shifted to the Legislative Council.

Seddon did not lead a major fight in the House of Representatives because he had packed the upper house with new appointments and was confident that the bill would once again be defeated there.[65] On August 17, the government's Electoral Bill received its second reading and debate began. Over the next few days, amendment after amendment was offered to try to undermine the bill, but none of these passed and the bill moved on to its third reading. The final vote in the Legislative Council came on September 8, 1893. Seddon had assured his brewer and vintner allies that he had the votes to defeat the legislation, but he had miscounted. Seddon then pressured a new councilor to break his promised pairing. When two councilors who had long been opposed to women's suffrage learned of Seddon's attempt to violate the assembly's cherished traditions, they switched their votes in disgust. The Electoral Bill granting women the right to vote in national elections passed 20-18.[66]

Neither Sheppard or Hall could be certain of victory until the royal governor signed the bill. Upset members of the Legislative Council appealed to the governor to reject the bill on the grounds that such a momentous change could not be enacted so close to a scheduled election. Others hoped to delay the bill's implementation by asking that it be sent to Queen Victoria for approval. Both proponents and opponents of the bill bombarded the governor's office with telegrams, and the alcohol lobby submitted petitions with over 10,000 names of those opposing women's suffrage.[67] After ten days of political wrangling, on September 19, Seddon announced the governor's assent. This was met with loud applause in the House of Representatives,[68] but there were no women present to enjoy the moment of victory. For the first time during the legislative session, the ladies' gallery was empty because many of the frequent observers were attending a fashionable wedding across the street.[69] Seddon telegraphed Sheppard, "Electoral Bill assented to by his Excellency the governor at a quarter to twelve this day, and now trust that all doubts as to the sincerity of the Government in this very important matter have been effectively removed."[70]

---

[63] Charlotte Macdonald, "Suffrage, Gender and Sovereignty in New Zealand," *Suffrage, Gender, and Citizenship: International Perspectives on Parliamentary Reforms*, Irma Sulkunen, Seija-Leena Nevala-Nurmi, and Pirjo Markkola (eds.) (Newcastle-upon-Tyne: Cambridge Scholars Publishing, 2009), 21.

[64] "Parliamentary Gossip," *Auckland Star*, Volume XXIV, Issue 187, August 9, 1893, 2.

[65] Waring, "How the Vote Was Won," 16.

[66] Grimshaw, *Women's Suffrage in New Zealand*, 92-93 and Waring, "How the Vote Was Won," 16. Tom Brooking argues that the evidence for this being the reason for the outcome is thin because it rests on a single letter from MP Alfred Saunders to Sheppard. See Brooking, *Richard Seddon, King of God's Own,* no page, Kindle edition.

[67] Grimshaw, *Women's Suffrage in New Zealand,* 93-94.

[68] "Women Franchise," *Press* [Christchurch], Volume L, Issue 8592, September 20, 1893, 5.

[69] "Women Enfranchised," *Otago Daily Times*, Issue 9848, September 20, 1893, 2.

[70] Richard Seddon quoted in "The Struggle for the Suffrage," *Star* [Canterbury], Issue 4752, September 20, 1893, 3.

Sheppard proclaimed the day to be the "beginning of a new and happy era," for the colony, but characteristically deflected praise away from herself, saying that victory came through the hard work of many individuals. She wrote, "We have discovered no new methods, no royal road. We believe that the secret of our success lies in the fact that those men and women who were interested in Womanhood Suffrage worked hard and continuously."[71]   Sheppard's opponents also acknowledged this assessment, even as they bemoaned their defeat. As the Brewers', Wine & Spirit Merchants & Licensed Victuallers' Association annual report in 1894 said, "the late election presents a somewhat startling object lesson to the trade and public generally.   The results achieved…show what organization can accomplish as opposed to apathetic indifference."[72] With the election just ten weeks away, Sheppard focused more of her attention on the immediate future: women only had six weeks in which to register. The excitement of being the first women in the world to cast a ballot in a national election naturally led many women to register immediately. In Christchurch, for example, on the morning of September 20, women lined up in droves at the registrar's office.[73] In Auckland, women made a large number of applications on both the afternoon of September 19 and the morning of September 20.[74] Women who lived far from a registrar picked up the forms at local post offices or had the forms mailed to them.[75] Although most suffrage opponents quietly accepted the change, there were other reactions to the suffrage news. According to one Christchurch newspaper, "some wags hoisted a garment suggestive of a petticoat government" on a flagpole near the Canterbury Women's Institute, but it was quickly removed by "early dawn." The paper ventured that the "perpetrators of joke…are now trembling under a threat of the ladies' vengeance at the ballot box."[76]

---

[71] Kate Sheppard, *Franchise Report for 1893 of the New Zealand Women's* [sic] *Christian Temperance Union* (Invercargill, New Zealand: Ward, Wilson and Co., Printers, 1893), 4, accessed August 8, 2015,
http://collections.tepapa.govt.nz/Object/397630/download

[72] Martin Kennedy, "Brewers', Wine & Spirit Merchants & Licensed Victuallers' Association of New Zealand Fourth Annual Report of the Executive Council, 1894," 2, in *Letter Book of the Brewers', Wine & Spirit Merchants & Licensed Victuallers' Association of New Zealand*, MS-Papers-1629-06, Alexander Turnbull Library, Wellington, New Zealand.

[73] "The Struggle for the Suffrage," *Star,* September 20, 1893, 3.

[74] "The Auckland Women," *Auckland Star,* Volume XXIV, Issue 223, September 20, 1893, 5.

[75] "Women! Register!," *Hawke's Bay Herald*, Volume XXVIII, Issue 9482, September 20, 1893, 2.

[76] "The Struggle for the Suffrage," *Star,* September 20, 1893, 3.

Eighty percent of New Zealand's women registered in time to participate in the November 28 election.[77] This was a remarkable accomplishment for Sheppard and the other suffragists, who were stuck by the way "the men and women who denounced the idea of women voting…now displayed a most amusing alacrity in enrolling women."[78] Indeed, both liberal and conservative politicians suddenly found themselves courting women assiduously. Conservatives did so because the general consensus, as reported by one newspaper, was that "the conservatism of women in social and religious matters would be actively exerted in the political sphere."[79] Liberals did so in hope of counterbalancing this perceived bias and of preserving their control of Parliament.[80] Rather than choosing sides, Sheppard and the WCTU urged women to vote for the candidate that best embodied their shared values. Sheppard believed that "on no account should a woman vote for a man of immoral life."[81] When the day of the election came, Sheppard was delighted to see that the "rowdyism that so often disgraces" pre-election meetings "was noticeably absent," and she applauded the festive atmosphere the day produced with people enjoying holiday picnics and with men and women behaving respectfully since the pubs were closed.[82] She believed that this was what an election day should be: men and women civilly and dutifully participating together in the democratic process without a drop of alcohol in sight.

The voters returned a resounding victory for the liberals in 1893. Interestingly, for all the debate over suffrage, women's votes did not significantly influence the outcome: even though 83% of registered women voted, women only composed 41% of the participating electorate.[83] Moreover, most women voted the same way their fathers, brothers, and husbands did. This pattern did not discourage Sheppard because she believed that women helped elect higher quality men to office. She described the new colonial Parliament as "cleansed and purified" as a result of the election.[84]

~

Accompanied by her husband and her son, Sheppard left on a life-changing trip to Great Britain in late March 1894. The family traveled aboard a new French steamer, the three-masted, two stacked *Armand Béhic*, which stopped in Auckland, Sydney, Melbourne, and Adelaide before crossing the Indian Ocean. In these ports, Sheppard gave encouragement and advice to local suffragists, and gave interviews to the local press.[85] Sheppard had become a celebrity and her fame brought plenty,

---

[77] Macdonald, "Suffrage, Gender and Sovereignty in New Zealand," 22.

[78] Sheppard, *Franchise Report for 1893*, 3.

[79] "The Elections," *Star* [Canterbury], Issue 4813, 29 November 1893, 2.

[80] Prior to the passage of the Electoral Bill of 1893, the suffrage issue cut through New Zealand's political factions in unexpected ways. Seddon, for example, was a liberal who opposed suffrage, and Hall was a conservative who supported it, but not all liberals were opposed to women's suffrage nor all conservatives for it.

[81] Sheppard, *Franchise Report for 1893*, 3.

[82] Sheppard, *Franchise Report for 1893*, 3.

[83] In 1893, there were 193,536 registered male voters, of whom 129,782 voted. For women, 109,461 registered and 90,290 voted. See Sheppard, *Woman Suffrage in New Zealand*, 4-5.

[84] Sheppard, *Franchise Report for 1893*, 3.

[85] See, for example, "Page 1 Advertisements Column 1," *New Zealand Herald* [Auckland], Volume XXXI, Issue 9472, March 30, 1894, 1. For examples of interviews, see "Women's [sic] Christian Temperance Union. Female Suffrage in New Zealand. Interview with Mrs. Kate Sheppard," The Advertiser [Adelaide], April 3,

if not too much, attention. The voyage across the Indian Ocean offered a respite, but because the *Armand Béhic* passed through the Suez Canal instead of rounding Africa, Sheppard was back in the public eye quickly enough.[86]

The trip to Britain was important for several reasons. First, she had the opportunity to attend the World Woman's Christian Temperance Union (WWCTU) conference, where she met Frances Willard for the first time. Sheppard was most impressed by the organization's president. In fact, she aspired to the qualities Willard offered seemingly without effort:

> Mrs. Willard is an ideal President….She is able to give her whole mind to the question under discussion. No desultory conversation is allowed to fritter away precious time….If her brain is quick, so are her sympathies….[She has] a keen sense of humour, which adds to her charm, and helps to brighten many a discussion."[87]

Other women impressed Sheppard too. One was Margaret Sibthorp, who Sheppard described as "one of the pioneers in advanced thought, advocating the principle of perfect freedom for women."[88] Sibthorp published a monthly periodical, *Shafts*, which advocated for economic independence for women and equal protection for women under the law, including equal pay for

equal work.[89] The social justice publication also offered a forum for addressing other social concerns in need of reform, including prostitution, vivisection, and prisons. As Sibthorp wrote, "The aim of *Shafts* is to awaken thought; to induce people to ask why, to question—is the condition of things which I see around me right or just? Is this that I have believed, spiritually morally, socially, the truth?"[90] These were inspiring questions for Sheppard—ones that she would begin to do something about once she returned to New Zealand.

Not everything about Sheppard's British interlude was uplifting. In one of the most important moments of the trip, her confidence for public speaking was shaken severely. She spoke to a large gathering of suffrage and temperance groups on June 9, 1894 without incident, and again before a crowd of 500 in July.[91] She also spoke at the WWCTU conference in June 1895. Either here or shortly after, she embarrassed herself, becoming tongue-tied with

---

1894, 7, and "Women's Franchise in New Zealand. An Interview with Mrs. Sheppard," South Australian Register [Adelaide], April 3, 1894, 7, accessed January 30, 2020, http://trove.nla.gov.au/
[86] The Suez Canal opened November 17, 1869, eight months after Sheppard arrived in Christchurch. This is why her first time seeing the canal was in 1894, by which time it was an essential feature of the British imperial communication and transport system.
[87] Kate Sheppard, *The White Ribbon: For God and Home and Humanity*, Volume 1, Number 2 (August, 1895), 1.
[88] Kate Sheppard, *The White Ribbon*, Volume 1, Number 10 (April, 1896), 3.
[89] Sheppard, *The White Ribbon,* Volume 1, Number 10 (April, 1896), 3.
[90] Margaret Sibthrop quoted in Michelle Elizabeth Tusan, *Women Making News: Gender and Journalism in Modern Britain* (Urbana, Illinois: University of Illinois Press, 2005), 129.
[91] Dalziel, "Presenting the Enfranchisement of New Zealand Women Abroad," 43.

nervousness. Although friends reassured her that she was a strong public speaker, Sheppard never recovered from the incident. She never again spoke to an international audience of any size or attended another international conference. In 1904, there was an opportunity for her to speak at the International Congress of Women meeting in Berlin, but she had an emotional breakdown, spent several weeks in bed, and instead sent a written report.[92] This was also when Sheppard began to experience other serious health problems. In November 1895, she had an operation, which may have been a hysterectomy, but the medical details remain unclear. What is certain is that she intentionally sought out female doctors in London to perform the necessary operation.[93]

~

New Zealand's 1893 debate over the suffrage question occurred while MPs were also considering major revisions to the colony's alcohol policy. According to the Alcoholic Liquors Sale Control Act passed that September, local licensing districts were expanded to correspond to the borders of parliamentary districts, and every three years the voters in these districts would elect members of a Licensing Committee. This committee would determine the number of liquor licenses available, based on the voter's directive. Voters had three choices for this directive: they could elect to retain the existing number of establishments, reduce the number, or ban the sale of alcohol altogether. In order for a district to enact prohibition, 50% of the registered voters had to vote in the election, and of these, 60% had to choose the no-licensing option. If that threshold was not met, then these votes were reallocated to the ballots asking for a reduction in the number of licenses within the district.[94] The act also barred children under sixteen from consuming alcohol in a pub, forbade the off-site alcohol sales to children under thirteen, and further restricted the hours pubs could be open.[95] Most controversially for those in the alcohol industry, the act provided no compensation to those businesses adversely affected by a district ban.[96] Hence, the act was a compromise between the wet and dry camps. For the Prohibitionists, although it was difficult to win an outright ban, the law made it readily possible for

---

[92] Devaliant, *Kate Sheppard,* 141, 179.

[93] Devaliant, *Kate Sheppard,* 142. Devaliant also suggests that Sheppard had a miscarriage at some point (139).

[94] "The Act of 1893," *An Encyclopedia of New Zealand,* A. H. McLintock (ed.), accessed January 30, 2020, http://www.teara.govt.nz/en/1966/prohibition/page-4 ; and Brooking, *Richard Seddon, King of God's Own,* no page, Kindle edition.

[95] "Friday, September 29, 1893," *The Otago Daily Times,* Issue 9856, September 29, 1893, 2.

[96] Tom Brooking, *Richard Seddon, King of God's Own: The Life and Times of New Zealand's Longest-Serving Prime Minister* (Auckland, New Zealand: Penguin Books, 2014), no page, Kindle edition.

them to win a reduction in the number of pubs serving alcohol. Prime Minister Seddon wanted a compromise because he believed that a more restrictive prohibition bill, such as one that only required a bare majority of votes to ban alcohol, would result in an outburst of public divisiveness that would jeopardize his government.[97]

In accordance with the complicated terms of this new act, New Zealanders cast their ballots for the Licensing Committees for the first time in March 1894. The results shocked the alcohol producers, distributors, and sellers. Of the 107,518 men and women who voted, 46% elected to ban alcohol licensing altogether, and another 15% voted to reduce the number of licenses available.[98] With 61% of the electorate wanting to impose limits upon the alcohol trade, the alcohol interests knew that they would have to organize themselves effectively in order to protect their interests and livelihoods. If they did not succeed in doing so, the Brewers', Wine & Spirit Merchants & Licensed Victuallers' Association predicted that the colony would be completely dry within nine years.[99] Hence, the association worked to secure amendments to the existing law by pressing their influence with MPs. Its members especially wanted to see changes to the eligibility requirements for serving on Licensing Committees and to operating hours.[100] Lobbyists were sure to use the findings of Gilbert Stringer, who had been hired by the Association to investigate the effects of prohibition in Maine, Kansas, and Iowa. Stringer reported that prohibition led normally law-abiding citizens to break the law, resulted in a population decline as people left dry states, and utterly failed to decrease drinking.[101] There was, then, to be an all-out war between the Prohibitionists and the alcohol lobby in New Zealand, even though both alcohol consumption and public drunkenness in New Zealand were actually lower in the late nineteenth century than they had been at midcentury.[102] While prohibition was never enacted nationwide, at its highest point, 12 of the nation's 76 parliamentary districts were dry.[103]

When Sheppard returned to New Zealand in January 1896, she did not concentrate her energies solely on this war. In fact, while she certainly continued to believe in prohibition and again became president of the NZWCTU, Sheppard had come to possess a more encompassing understanding of the nature of social reform. By talking to women from around the world, she had gained a much better grasp of how the key social issues facing women and children were interconnected. Banning liquor was not necessarily the ultimate cure-all. Sheppard had, in short, internalized Willard's Do Everything philosophy as a result of her time in Britain.

[97] Brooking, *Richard Seddon, King of God's Own,* no page, Kindle edition.
[98] "The Act of 1893," *An Encyclopedia of New Zealand,* A. H. McLintock (ed.), accessed January 30, 2020, http://www.teara.govt.nz/en/1966/prohibition/page-4
[99] Kennedy, "Brewers', Wine & Spirit Merchants & Licensed Victuallers' Association of New Zealand Fourth Annual Report of the Executive Council, 1894," 2.
[100] "Alcoholic Liquors Sale Control Act 1893 Suggested Amendments," and "Conference Meeting," in *Minute Book* [of the Brewers', Wine & Spirit Merchants & Licensed Victuallers' Association of New Zealand], 12-13. MS-Papers-1629-02, Alexander Turnbull Library, Wellington, New Zealand.
[101] "How Prohibition Works," *Wanganui Herald,* Volume XXVII, Issue 8255, August 22, 1893, 2.
[102] Rice, *Christchurch Crimes and Scandals,* 16, 227-228.
[103] Most of these districts were in rural areas, provincial towns, or the suburbs of major cities. See "The No-License Era," *New Zealand History,* Ministry for Culture and Heritage, accessed January 30, 2020, http://www.nzhistory.net.nz/politics/temperance-movement/no-license-era

~

In 1888, Frances Willard, Susan B. Anthony, and other American women leaders met in Washington, DC with representatives from Canada, Denmark, Finland, France, Great Britain, India, Ireland, and Norway to form the International Council of Women (ICW). This umbrella organization was dedicated to coordinating the reforming efforts of women around the world, and it urged individual nations to form their own national councils to find common ground and synchronize the work within each nation. While Sheppard was in London, she received a letter from ICW member Eva McLaren, who urged her to help found New Zealand's National Council of Women (NCW) with the aid of Lady Anna Stout, a suffragist with connections to elite society. Sheppard was receptive to the proposal, and when she returned to New Zealand, she began working to sponsor the inaugural meeting.[104] As Stout wrote, the NCW's goal was to "increase the sum total of womanly courage, efficiency, and *esprit de corps*; that it would tend to widen the horizon by bringing together women of the most diverse views on all subjects" so that they might find "common ground," despite their radically different perspectives and views.[105] Stout stressed that

> If our women could be made to realize that by co-operation, organisation, sympathy, and charity we could mould ourselves into such a powerful army that we could overcome the most indomitable foe, we should have no difficulty in storming the ramparts of prejudice and winning our battle for justice, home, and humanity. We must first overcome the foes that are in ourselves.[106]

These were strong words and ambitious goals, to be sure, but twenty-five women representing twelve organizations took up the call and met in Christchurch in April 1896.

The delegates, who elected Sheppard president over Stout, met in the former hall of the provincial council. This gave their meetings a formal ambience and allowed many to observe the proceedings from the public galleries. The scope and nature of the women's debate, as well as the convention's setting, helped the NCW to become known as the Women's Parliament. During their week-long convention, the delegates passed formal resolutions on a wide range of topics, only some of which dealt with the home and family. These upheld the necessity of a direct referendum, called for an elected executive and the reform of the Legislative Council, appealed for reforms in the criminal justice system, and advocated for the abolition of capital punishment.[107] Other resolutions demanded that "the conditions of divorce for men and woman should be made equal"; that laws be changed so that women maintained their legal rights upon marriage; and that women should be able to attach "a certain just share of her husband's earnings or income for her separate use, payable,

---

[104] Eva McLaren originally implied that Sheppard would be the president of the NCW, but later asked Stout to become the president and Sheppard to become secretary. See Roberta Nicholls, "The Collapse of the Early National Council of the Women of New Zealand, 1896-1906," *New Zealand Journal of History*, Volume 27, No. 2 (October, 1993), 157-172, accessed January 30, 2020, http://www.nzjh.auckland.ac.nz/document.php?wid=774

[105] Anna Stout, *The National Council of Women of New Zealand* [pamphlet]([Christchurch, New Zealand]: Christchurch Press Company, Ltd., [1896]), 1, MS-Papers-1376-10, Alexander Turnbull Library, Wellington, New Zealand.

[106] Stout, *The National Council of Women of New Zealand*, 1.

[107] "National Council of Women," *Southland Times* [Invercargill], Issue 13431, April 17, 1896, 2.

if she so desire it, into a separate account."[108] Still more resolutions called for reforming inheritance laws so that at least a third of a man's property went to his wife and at least a third to his children; pushed for police reform to improve efficiency; and insisted on the repeal of the Contagious Diseases Act, which compelled women suspected of prostitution, but not their clients, to submit to a compulsory medical examination for venereal disease.[109] Sheppard reported that the delegates also discussed "Pauperism, Single Tax, Land Nationalism, Constructive Socialism…Technical Education, the Problem of Purity, Old Age Pensions, Undesirable Immigrants" and more.[110] Together, these resolutions and discussions championed the equality of women and the special role women had to play in making New Zealand a better society.

Reactions to the NCW's resolutions varied widely. Some in the press gave credit to the delegates for their professionalism and seriousness, noting how they worked from prepared speeches,[111] while others hailed Sheppard's leadership as "a capital choice."[112] One paper lauded the "unselfish utterances of women genuinely concerned in the redressing of grievances for the sake of common humanity" and cautioned that "this is no hysterical sisterhood, to be treated with contempt." Rather, they are a "band of women… who have manifestly call out socialistic problems, and are prepared to speak the truth" without "political bias."[113] Other newspapers maintained that some of the NCW's ideas were "impracticable" and if carried out "would probably be found to have erred greatly."[114] Still others criticized the Sheppard and the other delegates for the speed with which they worked:

> We are very much disappointed with the manner in which the business before the Council has been dispatched….The policy of hurry-scurry indulged in by the Council strikes us as being calculated to bring their deliberations into grave distrust, if not contempt.[115]

Sheppard admitted that the breadth was "sufficient to satisfy even a glutton for work," but she also believed that this array of issues needed attention since Parliament was not addressing them.[116] The general public's greatest concern centered upon the concept of the economic independence of married women, with many wondering if such a change would threaten the fabric of society.[117]

Unfortunately for long-term success of the NCW, Sheppard was not able to prevent factionalism from undermining the organization. This was quite different from the suffrage campaign, where there had been far less egotism and disagreement as a result of the united focus upon a singular goal. Stout was among the first to leave, complaining that the council did not represent a sufficient breath of organizations and that the Christchurch members held too much control over the agenda.[118] The NCW leadership then divided, quite publicly, between pacifists and nationalists over the Second Boer War.*   Later, when Sheppard's more politically radical, less strategically

[108] "National Council of Women," *Otago Daily Times*, Issue 10645, April 14, 1896, 6.
[109] "Women's Council," *Star* [Christchurch], Issue 5543, April 18, 1896, 5.
[110] Sheppard, *The White Ribbon*, Volume 1, Number 10 (April 1896), 4.
[111] "The Women's Convention," *The Hawera & Normanby Star*, Volume XXXII, Issue 3232, April 23, 1896, 2.
[112] "What the Women in the Convention Were Like," *Evening Post* [Wellington], Volume LI, Issue 95, April 22, 1896, 4.
[113] "What the Women in the Convention Were Like," *Evening Post*, April 22, 1896, 4.
[114] "The Women's Convention," *The Hawera & Normanby Star*, April 23, 1896, 2.
[115] "Women in a Hurry," *The Marlborough Express* [Blenheim], Volume XXXI, Issue 89, April 20, 1896, 2.
[116] Sheppard, *The White Ribbon*, Volume 1, Number 10 (April 1896), 4.
[117] Nicholls, "The Collapse of the Early National Council of the Women of New Zealand."
[118] Devaliant, *Kate Sheppard*, 151.

compromising successor assumed the presidency, the NCW lost much of its public relations savvy.[119] The organization folded in 1906.[120]

Sheppard's participation in the NCW did not preclude her continued work with the WCTU. She continued to edit the WCTU's chief publication, *The White Ribbon*, and in those years when she wasn't the president, she served as the group's chief liaison to the supportive members of Parliament. She tended to be more vocal in the WCTU meetings than those of the NCW,[121] illustrating how much she still cared about the issue of temperance, and how much she still embodied the WCTU's mission. Like her fellow Prohibitionists and the Free Church worshippers of her youth, Sheppard wanted to improve public virtue. This meant working to fight any erosion of the sanctity of the Sabbath, such as operating trams on Sundays, and protesting the content of a new school reader, which failed to promote pupils' "advancement intellectually & morally" because much of its language was "slangy and vulgar."[122] The WCTU promoted outreach efforts with kindergartens, schools, young women, prisons, and the press. It also appointed and funded separate superintendents to monitor literature, relief work, and narcotics use. Other superintendents promoted hygiene, food reform, and the use of unfermented wine. There was also a specific superintendent devoted to working with the Maori.[123]

On January 29, 1840, Governor William Hobson arrived in New Zealand with orders from the Crown to obtain British sovereignty over the islands by negotiating a treaty with the Maori chiefs. He invited the tribal leaders to meet with him, drafted a treaty without the aid of legal counsel, and had it translated into Maori. Less than a week later, forty chiefs and Hobson signed the three articles of the Treaty of Waitangi. In Hobson's eyes, the first article of the treaty held that the Maori had ceded "all rights and powers of Sovereignty" to the British Crown, but because the Maori copy of the treaty used the term "governorship" instead of "sovereignty," the Maori's understanding of the first article was undoubtedly quite different.[124] This may not have been as much as a deliberate deception as a desire to make the treaty more palatable to the Maori.[125] The second article of the treaty was also open to different interpretations. The English version guaranteed the Maori "the full exclusive and undisturbed possession of their Lands and Estates Forests Fisheries and other properties," while the Maori version confirmed "the unqualified exercise of their chieftainship over

[119] Nicholls, "The Collapse of the Early National Council of the Women of New Zealand, 1896-1906."

[120] The NCW was revived in 1918 by Sheppard and other women. Sheppard served as president for its first year, but resigned for medical reasons in 1919. See Devaliant, *Kate Sheppard*, 208-209.

[121] Devaliant, *Kate Sheppard*, 147, 151.

[122] *Convention Minutes, New Zealand Christian Temperance Union, 1895-1905*, March 20, 1895, and April 8, 1896, Alexander Turnbull Library, Wellington, New Zealand, 79-057-09/09, accessed April 22, 2015.

[123] *Convention Minutes, New Zealand Christian Temperance Union, 1895-1905*, March 22, 1895, 79-057-09/09, Alexander Turnbull Library, Wellington, New Zealand.

[124] Donald Denoon, "Land, Labor and Independent Development," *The Cambridge History of the Pacific Islanders*, Doland Denoon (ed.) (New York: Cambridge University Press, 1997), 166. For a thorough exploration of the legal issues surrounding the Treaty of Waitangi, see Mark Hickford, *Lords of the Land: Indigenous Property Rights and the Jurisprudence of Empire*. New York: Oxford University Press, 2012.

[125] J.M.R. Owens, "New Zealand Before Annexation," *The Oxford History of New Zealand*, W.H. Oliver (ed.) (Wellington, New Zealand: Oxford University Press, 1981), 52.

their villages and over their treasures all." The third article confirmed "royal protection" to the Maori and imparted to them "all the Rights and Privileges of British subject[s]." It remains the least disputed part of the text.[126]   Once the Treaty of Waitangi had been signed, additional copies were made and sent throughout what the Maori called Aotearoa to be signed by the chiefs who had not attended the initial ceremony. In the end, 530 Maori chiefs did so, and Hobson formally declared British sovereignty over the islands in May 1840.

That the British were willing to sign a treaty with the Maori illustrates how differently Victorian Britons saw the native people of Aotearoa than the Aboriginal Australians. The British respected the Maori as warriors, but considered most Aborigines to be little more than bothersome nuisances.[127] Some Victorians even argued that the Maori were descendants of the Aryans in India, and, therefore, shared a common ancestry with northern Europeans. The Maori and the British could both be seen as pioneers, who traveled vast distances to settle together in the South Pacific. This supposed racial connection helped explain why Maori military resistance had been so effective in the 1850s and 1860s. It also showed how distinct New Zealand and Australia were and why New

Zealand should not become a part of a federation of Australian territories.[128] One influential author proclaimed that as a distant branch of the Caucasians, "no finer colored race exists in the world" than the Maori.[129] That most Maoris were practicing Christians by 1840 only validated Victorian sensibilities.[130] Such attitudes also help explain why after 1867 the Maori held their own seats in Parliament—something unique in British colonies.[131] It also explains why there was no attempt to ban

[126] Denoon, "Land, Labor and Independent Development," 166.

[127] M. P. K. Sorrenson, "Maori and Pakeha," *The Oxford History of New Zealand*, W.H. Oliver (ed.) (Wellington, New Zealand: Oxford University Press, 1981), 169; and Nolan and Daley, "International Feminist Perspectives on Suffrage," 11-12.

[128] Donald Denoon, "New Economic Orders: Land, Labour, and Dependency," *The Cambridge History of the Pacific Islanders*, Doland Denoon (ed.) (New York: Cambridge University Press, 1997), 224.

[129] Edward Tregear quoted in James Belich, *Paradise Reforged: A History of the New Zealanders from the 1880s to the Year 2000* (Auckland, New Zealand: Allen Lane/Penguin Press, 2001), 209.

[130] John Garrett, *To Live Among the Stars: Christian Origins in Oceania* (Suva, Fiji: World Council of Churches/Institute of Pacific Studies, University of the South Pacific, 1982), 69.

[131] Augie Fleras, "From Social Control Towards Political Self-Determination? Maori Seats and the Politics of Separate Maori Representation in New Zealand," *Canadian Journal of Political Science*, Volume 18, No. 3 (September 1985), 551-576, EBSCOhost.

interracial marriages in New Zealand as in other British territories.[132] All told, the British desired Maori assimilation in the colony, and they believed that the Maori were far closer to attaining this than other native peoples in their empire.

Despite this general orientation on the part of the White[133] settlers, there was still extensive conflict with the Maori over control of land in the second half of the nineteenth century. According to the Treaty of Waitangi, the Maori should have retained control over all land they did not sell, but by the 1860s the colonial government began confiscating land as a punishment for Maori rebellions and making that land available for White settlement. Much of what was confiscated included the most arable tracts.[134] The Maori lost more land after the Supreme Court ruled in 1877 that "no body politic existed capable of making a cession of sovereignty," and, therefore, the Treaty of Waitangi did not preserve Maori land rights.[135] By 1891, the Maori held just 18% of the land they held in 1840, and most of this land was difficult to make profitable because of its remoteness, lot size, or scattered dispersal.[136] The percentage of Maori land holdings continued to drop significantly in the opening decades of the twentieth century,[137] leaving most Maori to live in makeshift camps in ghastly conditions.[138] This grim economic situation, combined with a large late nineteenth-century population decrease meant that many White New Zealanders believed extinction of the Maori was a very real, if unintentional, possibility.[139]

The women of the WCTU demonstrated their desire to fight this decline and worked to improve life for the Maori. They firmly believed that alcohol had at least as negative an impact on the Maori as it did on Whites. WCTU members visited Maori towns, took pledges of abstinence, and worked with tribal leaders to spread the word about the evils of alcohol consumption. In the last three months of 1894, for example, two North Island WCTU members visited thirteen settlements, primarily along the remote Whanganui River.[140] According to the 1896 report of the superintendent for Maori relations, such efforts met with success; the WCTU was certainly well-received in Maori communities. As one chief said, "I shall not fail to warn [my people] against 'waipiro' [alcohol] as you are doing now." Another chief said,

[132] Sorrenson, "Maori and Pakeha," 173-175; and Denoon, "Land, Labor and Independent Development," 192.
[133] "White" and "Black" are both intentionally capitalized. See Chapter F, footnote 60.
[134] Sorrenson, "Maori and Pakeha," 173-175; Denoon, "Land, Labor and Independent Development," 170.
[135] James Prendergast quoted in Donald Denoon, "Land, Labor and Independent Development," 171.
[136] R. M. Burdon, *The New Dominion: A Social and Political History* (Wellington, New Zealand: A. H. & W. H. Reed, 1965), 276-277.
[137] Although the Maori held almost 11 million acres in 1891, they held only 4.8 million in 1920. After 1920, all Maori lands were overseen by the Native Trust Office. See Belich, *Paradise Reforged*, 192; and Burdon, *The New Dominion,* 277.
[138] Sorrenson, "Maori and Pakeha," 173-175; and Denoon, "Land, Labor and Independent Development," 192. The economic plight of the Maori was such that the International Workers of the World (IWW) made efforts to reach out to the Maori community and to champion its cause. The first IWW newspaper published in the Southern Hemisphere, the *Industrial Unionist,* included articles in Maori by its sixth issue and specifically called upon the Maori to rise up and join in class struggle. See Mark Derby, "Ki Nga Kaimahi Maori Katoa ("To All Maori Workers"): The New Zealand IWW and the Maori," *Wobblies of the World: A Global History of the IWW*, Peter Cole, David Struthers, and Kenyon Zimmer (eds.) (London: Pluto Press, 2017), 186-202.
[139] Belich, *Paradise Reforged,* 191.
[140] "The Maori Temperance Mission," *Evening Post* [Wellington], Volume XLIX, Issue 3, January 4, 1895, 4.

I wish the good lady had come many years ago. She might have saved many lives, men, women, and even children, who have all died from the 'waipiro.' See how few of us there are left, and once we were a powerful, numerous tribe. This is the work of the 'waipiro'.[141]

The WCTU also sponsored multiracial, alcohol-free social events in an effort to forge closer connections between the Maori and White communities. The social held in Wellington in 1895 was so successful that the superintendent called for similar events to be held annually. To the superintendent's mind, it was only proper etiquette for the WCTU to offer such cordiality: "Besides being a return and recognition of the hospitality shown by the Maoris to us when visiting the districts, it also gives an opportunity for the display of Maori talent in singing and speechmaking," she reported.[142] She took particular note of the comments of a young Maori chief in Manakau in November 1895, for they echoed her understanding of why these interactions were so important. The chief said it was the "first time he had ever been invited to meet the Maori and Pakeha [Whites] together or see them so friendly together."[143] While it is true that the publication of such comments was part of the inspiring, self-promotional nature of the WCTU newspaper, the comments also illustrate the organization's commitment to improving the dire conditions many Maori faced.

~

In June 1894, Sheppard wrote that "the time has come when a man must allow his wife the freedom of her individuality; she is a human being with thoughts and aspirations."[144] It wasn't until the opening years of the twentieth century, however, that Sheppard acted upon this ideal in her personal life. When her husband, Walter, went to live in England in March 1905, Sheppard chose to remain in New Zealand and moved into the home of her close friends, William and Jennie Lovell-Smith. Since she did not need to do this for financial reasons, there has always been speculation that there must have been something else that motivated Sheppard's decision, such as a romance with William.[145] Regardless of the exact nature of the relationship the three initially shared, they eventually made an agreeable accommodation. They happily traveled to India, Italy, Austria, Switzerland, France, and England together in 1912, where they enjoyed the sightseeing, reconnections with relatives, and each other's company.[146] After Jennie died in 1924, William married Sheppard, perhaps to legitimize their relationship. They enjoyed a little more than three years together before he died. Sheppard lived for another six years before dying in 1934 at eight-six.

During the last three decades of Sheppard's life, her interest in and commitment to women's and temperance issues never waned. She continued to write, to make occasional appearances at conferences and meetings, and to participate in church and civic events, though her health

---

[141] "Work Among the Maoris: The [New Zealand] Superintendent's Second Annual Report," *The White Ribbon: For God and Home and Humanity*, Volume 1, Number 10 (April, 1896), 9.
[142] "Work Among the Maoris," 9.
[143] "Work Among the Maoris," 9.
[144] Kate Sheppard quoted in Dalziel, "Presenting the Enfranchisement of New Zealand Women Abroad," 55.
[145] Devaliant, *Kate Sheppard*, 186-187.
[146] Devaliant, *Kate Sheppard*, 201-202.

prevented her from retaining formal leadership positions for any length of time.[147] During this period, she consistently reiterated the views she expressed in her inspirational and resolute speech at the 1903 WCTU convention, entitled, "Women's Disabilities." In this speech, she proclaimed, "I do not know whether there exists a state of absolute, individual freedom, [but I do know that] the struggle for freedom goes ceaselessly on, and those who abandon the struggle are degenerates." She described New Zealand as being "seriously affected by our mono-sexual system of representation," and observed that women could still not serve on juries, could not enter into financial partnerships without their husbands' consent, were not allowed to work overtime without a permit, and were discriminated against in the laws involving illegitimate children. Sheppard noted, in particular, the way that women were held to the same standards and yet, in many cases, received just half the pay. This added up to condemning women to "a distinctly inferior economic position."[148] To Sheppard, this was as objectionable as not having the right to vote.

On October 3, 1896, the importers of Sri Lanka's Suratura Tea took out a full-page advertisement in a supplement to the *Auckland Star*, depicting the meeting of the National Council of Women in Christchurch the previous April. In the ad, the twenty-five attendees gather around an oblong table, each holding a cup of tea or having one on the table in front of them. Sheppard sits to the immediate left of the head of the table. The ad's subtitle reads, "What might have been the opinions and report of the Fair Sex had a committee reported upon the various descriptions of food in New Zealand." The fictitious report is spread down the length of the table and is presented in the form of a resolution. It proclaims that "after several prolonged sittings" during which the committee taste-tested "numerous different brands," the organization declared that "Chinese Teas are objectionable from the fact that the leaves are often rolled by *hand*, thus impregnating the leaf with perspiration." It also asserts that Suratura provided the "most satisfaction for flavor, aroma, purity, and economy" because it is "not blended with China, Indian, or other Teas," is "packed where grown," and "arrives fresh weekly." Therefore, Suratura is "entitled to the first place and should be used by all classes," the resolution's text concludes. This message is reinforced by various quotations rising from the mouths of the delegates. One describes the beverage as "delicious," while another proclaims it as "a gift divine." The longest quote states that, "when we obtain seats in the Upper House we should use the influence we would then possess" to pass a law "making it compulsory for everyone to drink Suratura Tea on account of its purity and economical properties."[149] All of the women depicted in the ad are identified by name and all of the likenesses are true.

---

[147] Judith Devaliant notes that Sheppard worked on the WCTU display at the New Zealand International Exposition in Christchurch in 1906-1907 (Devaliant, *Kate Sheppard*, 188), participated in the Grand Suffrage Procession in London in 1908 (195), attended her last WCTU convention in 1918 (205), and helped revive the NCW in 1918-1919 (208).

[148] K. W. Sheppard, "Women's Disabilities," Hilda Kate Lovell-Smith Papers, MS-Papers–1376-10, Alexander Turnbull Library, Wellington, New Zealand. Accessed April 22, 2015.

[149] "The National Council of Women held at Christchurch, April 1896 / Suratura Tea," [Advertisement], supplement to *The Otago Daily Times* October 17, 1896, lithograph by Wm Gregg & Co., Agents for Otago, 1896, courtesy of Hocken Collections, Uare Taoka o Hākena, University of Otago, accession number 15,892. The ad also appeared in other newspapers in New Zealand, such as the *Auckland Star* on October 3, 1896. There are other examples of companies associating themselves with women's movements. See, for example, a soap ad with quotes from American WCTU national treasurer Helen M. Barker as saying, "Wool Soap is an

This ad is a particularly adroit piece of marketing because it appeals to divergent audiences, depending upon interpretation. Because of its large size, many could have seen it as an homage to the NCW and as a celebration of the progress women had made by 1896. Alternatively, others could have seen the ad as ridiculing the organization and the values it upheld. Either way, both

excellent article, and every woman will be benefited by using it." "Wool Soap," [advertisement], *Chicago Tribune*, June 29, 1898, 4, https://chicagotribune.newspapers.com/image/349860371

feminism's supporters and opponents would associate Suratura Tea with their own viewpoint, and more tea would be sold.

There's little doubt which interpretation Sheppard would have had. It would have disturbed her considerably. Because she was she opposed to habitual consumption of tea, she would have been offended by the association between her likeness and a drink she thought akin to poison.[150] Sheppard would have also seen the ad as a pointed mockery of the important proceedings of the NCW and an attack on the integrity of its leadership. The ad's resolution lampooned the importance of the NCW's work on behalf of women and children by equating tea drinking with divorce rights, equal pay, and other social reforms. It also advocated for the substitution of one vice for another. Even the notion that the primary issue for post-1893 New Zealand feminism concerned the proper consumption of tea would have been patently offensive to someone of Sheppard's sensibilities.

Sheppard was never one to recoil from a challenge. As objectionable as the Suratura Tea advertisement was, she would have been inspired her to redouble her efforts to make New Zealand a healthier, more equitable place.

---

[150] Devaliant, *Kate Sheppard,* 174.

T

Ta'unga

1818?-1898

Upon his birth on the South Pacific island of Rarotonga, Ta'unga lay swathed in a giant taro leaf filled with warm water as men positioned ceremonial weapons between the umbilical cord and the boy's stomach. In the ensuing ceremony, the cord was tied off with a piece of tapa cloth and then cut with a bamboo knife. Ta'unga's father announced the boy's name, which meant "priest" or "skilled person." In accordance with tradition, he also proclaimed the name of his son's god. Later, the father placed the bamboo knife before the idol representing Ta'unga's personal god, where it remained untouched until the bamboo decayed and rejoined the earth.[1]

The polytheistic world of Ta'unga's birth did not remain that way for long: by the time he was ten, Christianity had a strong presence on Rarotonga, thanks to the work of men in service of the London Missionary Society (LMS). This organization's origins date to September 1794, when Scottish Evangelist David Bogue published the first issue of *Evangelical Magazine*, which called upon Nonconformists* who believed in infant baptism to coordinate their missionary efforts in unchristian lands.[2] Bogue noted that Catholics, Anglicans, Methodists, and Baptists had already entered the missionary field, but not Evangelicals, who generally believed in the self-governance of each congregation. He wrote:

> We alone (and it must be spoken to our shame) have not sent messengers to the heathen, to proclaim the riches of redeeming love. It is surely full time that we had begun. We are

---

[1] Jon Joassen, *A Book of Cook Islands Maori Names* (Suva, Fiji: Institute of Pacific Studies, University of the South Pacific, 2003), 8-9, 62.

[2] Bogue's decision to publish this periodical was prompted by a letter from two Baptist missionaries working in India; this letter had been sent to Bristol's Baptist minister John Ryland and called for the creation of a non-denominational missionary society. Ultimately, Bogue decided to make his pitch only to those who believed in infant baptism, thereby excluding the Baptists. See Richard Lovett, *The History of the London Missionary Society 1795-1895*, Volume 1 (London, Henry Frowde/Oxford University Press, 1899), 4-5.

able. Our number is great. The wealth of many thousands is great….Nothing is wanting but for some persons to stand forward and begin.[3]

Bogue's appeal received considerable support in London, as had a similar appeal in the Midlands a year earlier.[4] A growing Evangelical consensus had emerged in England that it was time to fulfill the words that Jesus had given to his disciples: "Go into all the world and preach the gospel to the whole creation," (Mark 16:15). On November 4, 1795, Bogue met with seventeen London ministers in a small room above Baker's Coffee House,[5] just down an alley from the Royal Exchange and in the neighborhood where Richard Oswald had spent so much time.[6] These men began planning how to realize Evangelical hopes. By the following September, a board of directors for the new Missionary Society[7] was in place and there were clear standards for the recruitment of volunteers. The board maintained "it is not necessary that every missionary should be a learned man; but he must possess a competent measure of that kind of knowledge which the object of the mission requires."[8]   The board sought "Godly men who understand the mechanic arts," who could document their "experience in the Christian life," and who could win the unanimous support of the admissions committee.[9] In November 1795, the directors of the Missionary Society expanded its applicant pool significantly by allowing married men and their wives to apply instead of only single men.

The directors wanted men and women with practical skills and middle-class aspirations because they expected the missionaries to show Pacific Islanders how to build walled houses and make Western clothes to cover their naked bodies.[10] In other words, part of the missionary goal was to bring a British definition of Christian civilization to the Pacific. This attitude stemmed from an Enlightenment* confidence that all races possessed the potential to evolve and was akin to the ideals of many late eighteenth and early nineteenth century abolitionists. It also, however, prescribed a particular code of behavior.[11] As Edward Said has pointed out, "cultures have always been inclined to impose complete transformations on other cultures, receiving these other cultures not as they

---

[3] David Bogue quoted in *John Morison, The Fathers and Founders of the London Missionary Society: A Jubilee Memorial Including a Sketch of the Origin and Progress of the Institution* (London: Fisher, Son & Co./The Caxton Press, [1844]), x.

[4] This appeal came in 1793 from Birmingham's Edward Williams, who convened a meeting of supportive ministers. See *Morison, The Fathers and Founders of the London Missionary Society,* ix.

[5] Tom Hiney, *On the Missionary Trail: A Journey Through Polynesia, Asia, and Africa with the London Missionary Society* (New York: Atlantic Monthly Press, 2000), 6.

[6] More precisely, Baker's Coffee House was on Exchange Alley (now called Change Alley), which opened onto Cornhill, the street on the south side of the Royal Exchange. Baker's Coffee House was one storefront away from Jonathan's Coffee House, where stockbrokers liked to gather, and where Oswald undoubtedly tried to make contacts upon his arrival in London in 1746. See Bryant Lillywhite, *London Coffee Houses: A Reference Book of Coffee Houses of the Seventeenth, Eighteenth, and Nineteenth Centuries* (London: George Allen and Unwin Ltd., 1963), 97-99, 305-309, and unpaginated map.

[7] The original name of this organization was the Missionary Society. In 1818, it changed its name to London Missionary Society. Whether called the Missionary Society or LMS in the text, it was one organization.

[8] Lovett, *The History of the London Missionary Society,* 43.

[9] Lovett, *The History of the London Missionary Society,* 44. Those who were able to win at least 2/3 of the votes had their cases investigated further; those who did not win 2/3 were rejected.

[10] Malama Meleisea and Penelope Schoeffel, "Discovering Outsiders," *The Cambridge History of the Pacific Islanders,* Donald Denoon (ed.), (Cambridge, U.K.: Cambridge University Press, 1997), 143.

[11] Lawrence James, *The Illustrated Rise & Fall of the British Empire,* abridged by Helen Lownie (New York: St. Martin's Press, 1999), 91, 94.

are but as, for the benefit of the receiver, they ought to be."[12] By seeking to impose Georgian cultural sensibilities such as privacy, modesty, and tidiness, the London Missionary Society's representatives brought more to the Pacific than their faith. While such cultural imperialism is objectionable to

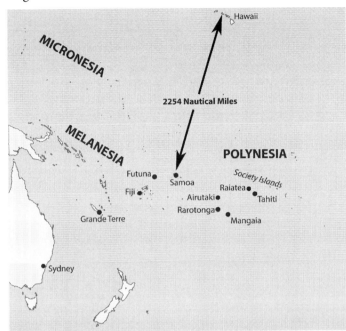

most modern minds, in the nineteenth century such an intervention was seen as a laudable endeavor. In 1899, the history of the LMS proudly proclaimed that "Wherever the Gospel has come, *civilization has followed* in its train....[Today] the whole of Polynesian life has been lifted up to a much higher level" as a result of Christianity's presence.[13]

The Society's first mission departed in August 1796 and sailed via Cape Horn for Tahiti. The choice of Tahiti stemmed from the positive accounts of the island left by James Cook and William Bligh.[14] After seven-months aboard the Society's small ship the *Duff*, the eighteen missionaries were eager to disembark, but they did not find the welcoming arms they expected. The king of Tahiti, Pōmare I, refused to allow the proselytizers to land, let alone engage in their work, because the Tahitians had discovered that there were unintended consequences of contact with Europeans. What the Tahitians once saw as a straightforward and reasonable exchange of resources—hospitality and sexual pleasure for tools and weapons—became a complicated deal that included new diseases.[15] By the mid-1790s, the Tahitians were a guarded and altogether different population from the one Cook and Bligh had met earlier in the century. Only the efforts of a marooned, English-speaking sailor from Sweden allowed the *Duff*'s hopefuls to land: Peter Haggerstein, who had lived in Tahiti for four years and was trusted, convinced Pōmare I to permit access. This hurdle crossed, others quickly emerged. The work proved far harder than the missionary artisans imagined, partly because they were so isolated and partly because without

[12] Edward Said, *Orientalism* (New York: Vintage Books, 1994), 67.

[13] Lovett, *The History of the London Missionary Society,* 470-471. UC-Berkeley's David Shaw King has argued that Evangelicals "were progressive. They were vehemently opposed to slavery, infanticide, human sacrifice, warfare. They brought writing, taught literacy, and print books; in doing so they fixed Polynesian languages. They urged the elevation of women in Polynesian society. Unlike the American missionaries in Hawai'i, for example, their aim was to establish spiritual rather than territorial or economic dominion." See David Shaw King, *Missionaries and Idols in Polynesia* (San Francisco, California: Beak Press, 2015), 5.

[14] John Garrett, *To Live Among the Stars: Christian Origins in Oceania* (Geneva: World Council of Churches ; Suva, Fiji : Institute of Pacific Studies, University of the South Pacific, 1982), 9. Cook visited in 1769, 1773, and 1776; Bligh did so in 1788-1789 and 1792.

[15] Matt K. Matsuda, *Pacific Worlds: A History of Seas, Peoples, and Cultures* (New York: Cambridge University Press, 2012), 134-135.

seminary training they didn't understand the complexities of conversion.[16] Most problematically, the Evangelists spoke very little Tahitian.[17] These obstacles resulted in some missionaries declaring their desire to leave Tahiti; others expressed their anxiety through emotional collapses or erratic behavior. Two members of the contingent quit the mission in hope of integrating into the local culture and marrying.[18] When a British ship bound for Sydney moored off the Tahitian coast in March 1798, eleven of the original eighteen jumped at the chance to move to Australia as free settlers, many fearful of the rising potential for Tahitian aggression against them. Only seven missionaries remained faithful to their assignments.[19] These stalwarts developed a Tahitian dictionary, which led to the delivery of the first Tahitian language sermon in February 1802.[20] The transformative moment for the missionaries came in 1808, when Pōmare II evacuated Tahiti for nearby Mo'orea as a result of a military defeat: the two surviving missionaries joined the king and over the next five years proved able to convert Pōmare II's army. When Pōmare II recovered his throne in 1815 by recapturing Tahiti, the London Missionary Society gained its first permanent foothold in the Pacific. Prominent Evangelist John Williams pictured Tahiti becoming the "fountain from whence the streams of salvation" could flow.[21]

PAPEIHA.

Williams' vision was predicated upon being able to identify and train Polynesians to serve as indigenous pastors who could spread the Word and provide spiritual care.[22] Williams saw this as an essential phase for Evangelical Christianity because the LMS lacked a sufficient number of White[23] missionaries to cover the vastness of the Pacific. One of Williams' most effective recruits was Papeiha, who grew up on the second largest of the Society Islands, Raiatea, and who introduced Christianity to Rarotonga in July 1823, when Ta'unga was about five years old. Papeiha did more to further LMS's interests on Rarotonga in two years than all of its missionaries had in twenty years on Tahiti.[24] This effectiveness stemmed from a

---

[16] In fact, there were only four trained ministers in the original group. See Garrett, *To Live Among the Stars,* 12-13. It should be noted that what is meant by the terms "convert" and "conversion" for Christianity has changed over time and remains an issue of scholarly debate between historians, anthropologists, and sociologists. See David W. Kling, "Conversion to Christianity," *The Oxford Handbook of Religious Conversion,* Lewis R. Rambo and Charles E. Farhadian (ed.) (New York: Oxford University Press, 2014), 621-622.

[17] Matsuda, *Pacific Worlds,* 146.

[18] Hiney, *On the Missionary Trail,* 14-15.

[19] Robert William Kirk, *Paradise Past: The Transformation of the South Pacific, 1520-1920* (Jefferson, North Carolina: McFarland & Company, Inc., Publishers, [2012]), 49.

[20] Matsuda, *Pacific Worlds,* 147.

[21] John Williams quoted in Raeburn Lange, *Island Ministers: Indigenous Leadership in Nineteenth Century Pacific Islands Christianity* (Christchurch, New Zealand: Macmillan Brown Centre for Pacific Studies, University of Canterbury and Canberra, Australia: Pandanus Books, Research School of Pacific and Asian Studies, Australian National University, 2005), 42.

[22] Many scholars remain frustrated with having to use the terms Polynesia, Melanesia, and Micronesia to describe cultural and geographical regions in the Pacific, but, in the words of one anthropologist, they remain a "useful shorthand." See Jocelyn Linnekin, "Contending Approaches," *The Cambridge History of the Pacific Islanders,* Donald Denoon (ed.), (Cambridge, U.K.: Cambridge University Press, 1997), 8-9.

[23] "White" and "Black" are both intentionally capitalized. See Chapter F, footnote 60.

[24] Richard Gilson, *The Cook Islands, 1820-1950,* Ron Crocombe (ed.) (Wellington, New Zealand: Victoria University Press in association with the Institute of Pacific Studies of the University of the South Pacific, 1980), 21.

variety of sources. First, Papeiha had had missionary experience prior to his arrival on Rarotonga. He had helped introduce Christianity to another one of the Cook Islands, Aitutaki, in October 1821, where he had seen first-hand how important it was to secure the support of the chiefs before approaching the people with the new religion.[25] By the time he arrived on Rarotonga, Papeiha knew his top priority was to establish a meaningful relationship with the island's political leaders. Papeiha succeeded so well that he married the daughter of the first high chief to convert.[26] Second, Papeiha was not averse to taking risks. When John Williams first sought to bring the Gospel to the island of Mangaia in June 1823, for example, Papeiha overcame the inhabitants' initial resistance and tentativeness by confronting the people by himself. As Williams recorded,

> Papeiha offered to leap into the sea and swim through the surf. Being accoutered for his daring exploit, he went into the boat; and on reaching the reef, which extended but a few yards from the shore…this devoted man dived into the sea and was borne on top of a billow to the shore,

where he attempted to negotiate for the settlement of missionaries on the island.[27] Third, Papeiha had luck on his side. On Aitutaki, the death of a key chief's daughter encouraged the Aitutakians to question their native religion and to accept the power of Christianity.[28] Papeiha was also fortunate to arrive on Rarotonga accompanied a high chief's relative, who had been kidnapped more than nine years earlier and given up for lost. Papeiha's recovery of the woman built goodwill and facilitated his entrance into Rarotongan society.[29] Fourth, Papeiha possessed an uncompromising resolution and zeal, allowing him to realize gains where less confident and more subtle men would not. He was purposefully confrontational: he demanded that he be allowed to accompany Rarotongan priests to their rituals; and he insisted that Jehovah replace the Rarotongan gods outright, rather than be integrated with them.[30] His influence grew so quickly that within one a year Papeiha obtained a renunciation of both idolatry and cannibalism by the Rarotongans, who lived in such fear that Papeiha and another Polynesian pastor became virtual despots on the island.[31]

---

[25] Lovett, *The History of the London Missionary Society*, 253.

[26] Lange, *Island Ministers*, 63.

[27] John Williams, *A Narrative of Missionary Enterprises in the South Sea Islands* (London: J. Snow, 1837), 78-79. On this particular occasion, Papeiha's risk-taking did not end well: although he thought he had secured a peaceful agreement with the Mangaians, he had not. Later that day, when Papeiha, two other native pastors and their wives returned to the island with supplies, ready to establish a mission, they nearly lost their lives and had to be evacuated.

[28] Lovett, *The History of the London Missionary Society*, 257.

[29] The woman's name was Taperu. She was kidnapped from Rarotonga by a captain of a sandalwood trader, Philip Goodenough, who left her on Aitutaki in 1814. Williams and Papeiha found her on Aitutaki in 1821, and brought her, as a convert, back to Rarotonga in 1823. Taperu's social rank made her words and her faith powerful. She died in 1881. See William Robson, *James Chalmers: Missionary and Explorer of Rarotonga and New Guinea* (New York and Chicago: Fleming H. Revell, n.d.), 35; and Gilson, *The Cook Islands*, 5.

[30] Gilson, *The Cook Islands*, 21.s

[31] Marjorie Tuainekore Crocombe, "Introduction," *Cannibals and Converts: Radical Change in the Cook Islands*, Marjorie Tuainekore Crocombe (ed. and trans.) ([Suva, Fiji]: Institute of Pacific Studies, University of the South Pacific, 1983), 19-20.

~

Ta'unga never recorded his earliest memory growing up near Rarotonga's eastern village of Ngatangiia, but it may have been the day in February 1824 when Papeiha arrived at the request of local chiefs and burned all of the village's idols and sacred gathering space, the *marae*.[32] Because Ta'unga's father was a Rarotongan priest, who probably opposed the advent of the new religion, Papeiha's actions would have been especially memorable to the five or six year-old.[33] But no event

in Ta'unga's childhood had more impact than the appearance of British missionaries Charles and Elizabeth Pitman in May 1827, and the subsequent establishment of a permanent Christian mission in Ngatangiia. Charles Pitman reversed Papeiha's excesses and deepened the Rarotongans' understanding of the faith. Specifically, he returned to its rightful owners land that Papeiha had confiscated,[34] and he ordered the construction of a school so that people might come to understand written language instead of seeing it as a mysterious form of prayer.[35] Ta'unga enrolled in the new school. He was such a good student that after only four years of instruction, Pitman sent him to the Titikaveka district in the southern part of the island to teach children there. Each morning at sunrise, the fourteen-year old walked the two miles from Ngatangiia to Titikaveka to teach his classes, accompanied by a man who taught the adults.[36] By 1833, Ta'unga understood Christian theology well enough to be able to write a sophisticated and personalized statement of faith. His penmanship in Rarotongan was also so pleasing that

Pitman sent a copy of it to London as evidence of the mission's progress.[37]

Such growth did not preclude resistance to Christianity on Rarotonga in the late 1820s and early 1830s. Opponents refused to move into the Christian villages, occasionally raided them, and even

---

[32] Maretu, *Cannibals and Converts: Radical Change in the Cook Islands*, 60.

[33] R. G. and Marjorie Crocombe, *The Works of Ta'unga: Records of a Polynesian Traveler in the South Seas, 1833-1896* (Canberra: Australian National University Press [1968]), 1, 5.

[34] Marjorie Tuainekore Crocombe, "Introduction," 19.

[35] A. Buzacott, *Mission Life in the Islands of the Pacific, Being a Narrative of the Life and Labours of the Rev. A. Buzacott*, J. P. Sunderland and A. Buzacott (ed.) (London, John Snow and Co., 1866, reprinted Suva, Fiji: Institute of Pacific Studies, University of the South Pacific, 1985), 63.

[36] R. G. and Marjorie Crocombe, *The Works of Ta'unga*, 5. The man's name was Iro.

[37] R. G. and Marjorie Crocombe, *The Works of Ta'unga*, 6-7. Ta'unga never learned to read or write English.

committed arson.[38] Ngattangiia's wattled, plastered, and thatched church, for example, was destroyed by fire in July 1829, and the arsonist was never caught.[39] There was even a plot to murder another British missionary on the island, Aaron Buzacott, as well as the chiefs who supported him and his mission.[40] Ta'unga himself was not immune to the cultural conflicts produced by the arrival of Christianity. In 1836, the eighteen-year-old followed Rarotongan custom and impregnated a woman as a sign of his virility. For refusing to obey the Christian doctrine of abstinence prior to marriage, Pitman dismissed Ta'unga from the church. Eventually, Ta'unga won back Pitman's approval and was restored to his former position, but the episode illustrates the complexities of the Christian transition on the island.[41]

By 1840, the work of Reverends Buzacott, Pitman, and William Wyatt Gill, as well as the native pastors like Ta'unga, had begun to make Rarotonga something more than a nominally Christian society. While it is true that some had done little more than reorient their beliefs to accommodate Jehovah,[42] others had made what the British considered to be greater progress.[43] When the captain of *HMS Sulphur*, Sir Edward Belcher, visited that year, he was impressed by what he saw and how much Rarotonga had been transformed:

> [Mr. Buzacott] soon made his appearance, and conducted us to his house, which for neatness and comfort surpasses anything we have met among missionaries. The roads, enclosures, church, school, and private residences, are an age in advance of Tahiti. Neatness and regularity prevail, and the appearance of the resident chief, as well as of those about him, reflects the highest credit on the present missionary…it reminds me but what I expected of Tahiti if their laws had been enforced.[44]

Another symbol of this transformation was the establishment of a college in the main town of Avarua to train native pastors for missionary work. Founded in 1839 by Buzacott, the Takamoa

---

[38] Gilson, *The Cook Islands*, 33.

[39] Maretu, *Cannibals and Converts*, 81, 83.

[40] Buzacott, *Mission Life in the Islands of the Pacific*, 44-45.

[41] R. G. and Marjorie Crocombe, *The Works of Ta'unga*, 7. The mother was a Titikaveka woman, Teanini. Ta'unga chose a Christian name for his son, Daniel, which also indicates the complexities of the transition. Daniel was adopted and raised by Iro, who once walked with Ta'unga to teach in Titikaveka. Daniel was also known as Daniela because all Rarotongan words end in a vowel, as noted by the Crocombes on page xviii.

[42] Gilson, *The Cook Islands*, 31-32.

[43] Historian Marc David Baer outlines four stages in the full conversion to any faith, even if these stages do not follow a linear path. The first is acculturation, when the converts make changes to their diet, dress, habits, customs, holidays, architecture, and language. The second step is hybridity, when the converts practice the old and new beliefs simultaneously as they attempt to reconcile conflicting ideas. The third stage is syncretism, when the indigenous faithful merge the two belief systems to create a new synthesis. An example of this would be what happened in Peru when Diego Fernández de Córdoba was viceroy. The final stage in the conversation process is transformation, when the faithful seek to intensify the depth or purity of their convictions in order to demonstrate their devotion. This often means purging of the hybrid and syncretic elements that had allowed a religion to grow originally. See Marc David Baer, "History and Religious Conversion," *The Oxford Handbook of Religious Conversion*, 25-34. In another work, Lewis R. Rambo outlines a seven-stage process for conversion and argues that it is a "malleable" and "complex process that transpires over time." See Lewis R. Rambo, *Understanding Religious Conversion* (New Haven, Connecticut: Yale University Press, 1993), 168, 170, EBSCOebooks.

[44] Sir Edward Belcher, *Narrative of a Voyage Round the World Performed in Her Majesty's Ship Sulphur During the Years 1836-1842, Volume 2* (London: Henry Colburn Publisher, 1843), 15.

Institute initially enrolled five male students, two bachelors and three married men. The married men lived with their wives in the "comfortable detached stone cottages," which were situated on both sides of a "wide, noble road." These student houses had both front and rear gardens, as well as a neat footpath, Buzacott boasted.[45] The wives received training from Mrs. Buzacott while the men took their theology courses. Ta'unga

desperately wanted to be a part of Takamoa's inaugural class, but he was told that he was still too young to qualify for admission. On March 16, 1841, however, Buzacott and Gill interviewed Ta'unga and accepted him into the college two weeks later.[46]

Ta'unga spent the next year studying at Takamoa. On Mondays and Fridays, he attended divinity lectures. On Tuesdays, he read from the New Testament in Rarotongan, while on Thursdays, he read from the Old Testament in Tahitian. On Wednesdays he wrote out the lectures of LMS founder David Bogue, so that he would have his own copies once in the field.[47] As he read and learned, Ta'unga undoubtedly asked Buzacott a wide range of theological, practical, and cultural questions like these:

> "If Christ knew that Judas was bad at heart, why did he not put him down?"
> "If people go out to fish at night, should they have a prayer in the canoe at daylight?"
> "What is the meaning of a cymbal? Is it an animal or what?"
> "Why does Paul say to the Corinthians that things offered to idols are not to be eaten; and to Timothy he says, every creature of God is good?"
> "Should people shave their beards on the Sabbath-day?"
> "Is it right to beat a child on the Sabbath-day?"
> "What is the meaning of the bottomless pit?"[48]

Because LMS members wanted to replicate a desirable standard of living in new missions across the Pacific, Takamoa students also received training in skills such as house construction and furniture building. They also had to grow their own food in an on-site garden.[49] Clearly, Buzacott did not want his charges to have idle hands.

---

[45] Buzacott, *Mission Life in the Islands of the Pacific*, 133, 211.

[46] R. G. and Marjorie Crocombe, *The Works of Ta'unga*, 8.

[47] Buzacott, *Mission Life in the Islands of the Pacific*, 133-134.

[48] While I have not been able to find examples of student questions from Takamoa in the 1840s, these questions were asked by native students at Malua Theological College in Samoa. The college was founded by Reverend George Turner in 1844. Presumably the students at Takamoa asked similar questions. See George Turner, *Nineteen Years in Polynesia: Missionary Life, Travels, and Researches in the Islands of the Pacific* (London, John Snow, 1861), 137-138.

[49] Buzacott, *Mission Life in the Islands of the Pacific*, 135.

The Takamoa program was designed to be a four-year course of study, but the demand for native pastors was such that many students in the college's early years departed before completing their coursework.[50] This was true of Ta'unga. When he learned that the missionary ship *Camden* was heading west to establish new missions in Melanesia in March 1842, Ta'unga eagerly volunteered to join this Christian vanguard.[51] The send-off was poignant and grand, as Buzacott recorded:

> Several hundreds were collected at sea-side, every one of whom was anxious to give us a parting token of their kindness by a hearty shake of the hand. It was a most affecting scene. It was overpowering to witness the streaming eyes of men and women…[many of whom] we regarded as our spiritual children, begotten again by the Spirit of God.[52]

It took the *Camden* four months to reach Ta'unga's destination, which was the village of Tuauru on the southeastern shore of Grande Terre, the largest island of New Caledonia. During the voyage, the Camden stopped on Samoa and on the New Hebrides island of Tanna. Both times local missionaries approached Ta'unga, urging him to join an existing mission, rather than establish a new one.[53] According to a letter he wrote to Pitman, Ta'unga struggled with these offers but refused to accept them without a clear indication from God:

> I was constantly praying to God to tell me what He really wished me to do and I asked Him many times what island He wanted me to go to. But still it was not revealed to me. So I told them that it was not intended that I should stay there.[54]

As a consequence of these unanswered prayers, Ta'unga was the last of the eleven Takamoa-trained Rarotongans to be dropped off as the *Camden* made its way to Sydney. While many native pastors

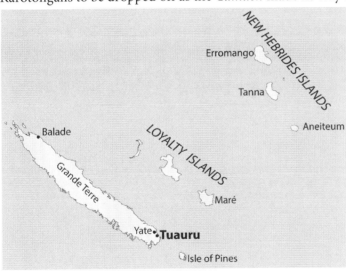

were simply assigned destinations, Ta'unga was given unusual independence as a result of his exceptional abilities.

Upon the *Camden*'s arrival at Tuauru on July 20, 1842, Buzacott went ashore to offer the local Kanak chief, Uadota, presents and to negotiate for the safety of three native pastors: Ta'unga and Samoans Taniela and Noa.[55] This was relatively easy to do since a similar arrangement had been made a year before for another Rarotongan pastor and since the

---

[50] Lange, *Island Ministers,* 67.

[51] R. G. and Marjorie Crocombe, *The Works of Ta'unga,* 10.

[52] Buzacott, *Mission Life in the Islands of the Pacific,* 154.

[53] Today, the New Hebrides islands are the nation of Vanuatu.

[54] Ta'unga quoted in R. G. and Marjorie Crocombe, *The Works of Ta'unga,* 26.

[55] Buzacott, *Mission Life in the Islands of the Pacific,* 170. Buzacott was accompanied by *Camden*'s captain and another white LMS minister, Thomas Slatyer.

Samoans were already known in Tuauru.[56] The next day, Buzacott and the *Camden* departed, leaving the three Pacific pastors living with Uadota, in what was for Ta'unga a very foreign land.

Ta'unga initially struggled with the cultural and environmental differences he encountered in the land of the Kanak, as well as with Melanesia generally. He describes the Kanak as being "a very strange kind of people" who speak "a strange language [that] sounds like the noise made by turkeys." He complains that the Kanak are "degraded" because they "walk about without clothing, both men and women." And he laments the fact that the shadow of the mountains created a

persistent mist that made the island "a very cold land."[57] Similarly, Ta'unga sees the Melanesians living on the island of Tanna as having "a wild appearance and evil-looking faces. It is a land of people who are black and naked. Their houses are bad. The only clothes worn by the women are the leaves of trees."[58] Certainly some of these attitudes can be attributed to Ta'unga's acculturation as a representative of the LMS, but Polynesians and Melanesians often struggled to understand each other's worldview.[59] This problem became more acute when Christianized Polynesians and unchristianized Melanesians encountered one another. The Kanak religion, for example, placed supreme value in the collective experience, whereas Evangelical preaching introduced the concept of individualism.[60] Similarly, differing sexual norms and behaviors existed between Polynesians and Melanesians.[61] Such varying perspectives and customs created the cultural dissonance Ta'unga

felt upon his arrival at Tuauru.

Despite these challenges, both sides looked to find common ground and adapt to the new circumstances. For their part, the Kanak welcomed Ta'unga and his fellow Polynesians as distant relatives and honored guests, which was not a particularly uncommon Melanesian approach.[62] The villagers provided the LMS missionaries with ample food, without an expectation of remuneration, and they harvested the timber to build the guests a new house. The chief also responded to Ta'unga, Taniela, and Noa's requests to assemble the village to hear the Christian message, and he urged them to accept the faith. Conversely, Ta'unga began to learn the language with Noa's assistance, while Taniela accepted the invitation to attend two great feasts on different parts of the island.[63]

[56] In April 1841, the *Camden* dropped a Rarotongan named Mataio off at Tuauru, but he died a few months later; the two Samoans, Taniela and Noa, remained. See Archibald Wright Murray, *Missions in Western Polynesia: Being Historical Sketches of these Missions from the Commencement in 1839 to the Present Time* (London, John Snow, 1863), 281-283.

[57] Ta'unga quoted in R. G. and Marjorie Crocombe, *The Works of Ta'unga,* 31, 34.

[58] Ta'unga quoted in R. G. and Marjorie Crocombe, *The Works of Ta'unga,* 22.

[59] Matsuda, *Pacific Worlds,* 235.

[60] Pothin Wete, "The Development of the Political Awareness of the Kanak Evangelical Church in New Caledonia and the Loyalty Islands from 1960 to 1987 and its Theological Implications: Possibility for a Kanak Liberation Theology," (thesis for bachelor of divinity, Pacific Theological College, Suva, Fiji, September 1988), 16-17. This work is available at Hamilton Library, University of Hawai'i-Mānoa.

[61] Alice Bullard, *Exile to Paradise: Savagery and Civilization in Paris and the South Pacific, 1790-1900* (Stanford, California: Stanford University Press, 2000), 36.

[62] A warm welcome and the exchange of gifts was also a Polynesian expectation; see Garrett, *To Live Among the Stars,* 4, 190.

[63] Ta'unga quoted in R. G. and Marjorie Crocombe, *The Works of Ta'unga,* 32-36.

These multi-day ceremonial gatherings, sometimes involved five or six thousand people. They included speeches that traced the lineage of patrilineal and matrilineal groups, events that allowed coastal and mountain peoples to exchange goods, and dances that mimicked warfare and provided practical training for battle.[64] Because they were a vital component of Kanak culture, it made sense for the missionaries to experience these gatherings. This mutual good will meant that Ta'unga soon won the villagers' agreement to stop working on the Sabbath and to attend religious instruction instead. He also began teaching the Kanak to read and write individual letters as the first step towards literacy. Most importantly, he won Uadota's allegiance. Ta'unga was sufficiently proud of the progress he had seen in Tuauru that within a month of his arrival, he declared, "The land is now in a pleasing state."[65] To be sure, the Tuauruans could not legitimately be called Christians, but they were open to the new faith.

The motivations for welcoming Catholic and Protestant missionaries were not entirely spiritual. Across the Pacific, political, economic, and social motivations were influential as well. In the nineteenth century, Pacific island cultures generally had a desire to acquire Western technology and goods. Trade, therefore, became an essential component of any missionary equation.[66] Chiefs particularly sought access to trade because the wealth it generated helped to increase perceptions of their *mana*—a supernatural essence that allowed the possessor to shape the world around him.[67] By associating themselves with the missionaries, the authority of the single Christian God, and the material resources the Europeans could provide, the chiefs enhanced their *mana* significantly.[68] This infusion of *mana* was critical because the adoption of Christianity also benefited those at the other end of the social spectrum. In Samoa, for example, the adoption the new faith tended to flatten the social hierarchy by taking away the chiefs' sacred authority and by altering marriage customs.[69] Similarly, Christianity absolved lower-ranking Kanak of various cultural obligations to the local elite.[70] On Rarotonga, communities that had been defeated in war and forced to surrender their prime land were happy to return from the mountains to coastal lands in Christian villages since doing so improved their living conditions and food supplies.[71] Throughout the Pacific, a desire for literacy also played a motivational role. Some hoped that learning to read and write would allow them to participate more equitably in the world economy. Others hoped to either affirm or

[64] Raymond Ammann, *Kanak Dance and Music: Ceremonial and Intimate Performances of the Melanesians of New Caledonia, Historical and Actual* (Nouméa, New Caledonia: Agence de Développement De La Culture Kanak, 1997), 56-63, 83-87.
[65] Ta'unga quoted in R. G. and Marjorie Crocombe, *The Works of Ta'unga,* 36-37.
[66] Meleisea and Schoeffel, "Discovering Outsiders," 143.
[67] The nature and influence of *mana* features prominently in academic discussions of the Pacific cultures. For a recent summary of much of this scholarship, see Paul van der Grijp, *Manifestations of Mana: Political Power and Divine Inspiration in Polynesia* (Zürich, Switzerland: Lit Verlag, 2014), 51-64. For a short criticism of van der Grijp's work, see G. E. Marcus, "Manifestations of Mana: Political Power and Divine Inspiration in Polynesia," *Choice,* 52.5 (January 2015), 854, ProQuest Central.
[68] Vanessa Smith, *Literary Cultures and the Pacific: Nineteenth-Century Textual Encounters* (Cambridge, U.K.: Cambridge University Press, 1998), 57; and Gilson, *The Cook Islands,* 24.
[69] Malama Meleisea, *The Making of Modern Samoa: Traditional Authority and Colonial Administration in the Modern History of Western Samoa* (Suva, Fiji: Institute of Pacific Studies, University of the South Pacific, 1987), 13. With Christianity, chiefs were to have many children by one wife, instead of many children by different wives. This altered the landscape of ruling familial alliances.
[70] Ammann, *Kanak Dance and Music,* 5.
[71] Michael P. Reilly, "Transforming Mangaia's Spiritual World: Letters from the Early Christian Community of Oneroa," *Journal of the Polynesian Society,* 116, no. 1 (March 2007), 35-57, EBSCOhost.

alter their position in an island's social hierarchy by becoming literate.[72] These socio-economic issues led many islanders into missionary classrooms, even when they were not particularly interested in the religious teachings that accompanied the instruction.[73]

Counterbalancing these enticements were several deterrents to receiving LMS missionaries. Foremost among them was disease, which caused a population decline in the Society Islands from an estimated 200,000 in 1769 to just 16,000 in 1797.[74] A similar decline on Grande Terre reduced the population from 80,000-100,000 in 1774 to 20,000 in 1900.[75] Islanders across the Pacific quickly realized the connection between the arrival of trading vessels and missionary ships and an outbreak of deadly illnesses within their populations. On the island of Tanna in modern Vanuatu, for example, an undiagnosed epidemic killed two Samoan pastors within a year of their arrival in November 1839; dysentery hit the island after missionary George Turner's visit in 1842; a trading ship brought smallpox in April 1853; and a measles outbreak ensued in 1860. After each of these encounters with the outside world, the Tannese responded punitively.[76] Similarly, the Kanak in northern Grande Terre called tuberculosis "christiano" because the association between the new disease and the French Catholic missionaries was so strong,[77] and they attacked the French mission at Balade in 1847 as a result of their fear of European diseases.[78] Another example comes from the island of Futuna, where an epidemic broke out in March 1843 after the arrival of two LMS pastors, Apela and Samuela. The Futunese responded by killing Apela and one of Samuela's daughters and throwing their bodies into the sea; then the exasperated residents attacked Samuela and demanded that his wife marry a chief. When Samuela's wife refused, the Futunese "beat her brains out. They cooked the bodies of Samuela and his wife," distributed them widely, and divided up the Samoans' property.[79] Such violence continued in this part of Melanesia for decades. In 1872, LMS member Maggie Whitecross Paton reported in a letter home that missionary J. D. Gordon was "tomahawked by a suspicious Native, who regarded him as bringing disease" to the island of Erromango.[80] Given this pattern, Ta'unga was fortunate not to suffer more than he did. After a series of epidemics in Tuauru, the Rarotongan wrote, "The people would not come near us, for they thought that we were the cause of the sickness. This belief was an obstacle to the work of God."[81] At one point, the situation was so tense that Tuauru's chief feared for Ta'unga's life, but the Rarotongan was never harmed the way other LMS pastors were.

---

[72] Smith, *Literary Cultures and the Pacific,* 57; and Gilson, *The Cook Islands,* 70-72.

[73] Jocelyn Linnekin, "New Political Orders," *The Cambridge History of the Pacific Islanders,* Donald Denoon (ed.), (Cambridge, U.K.: Cambridge University Press, 1997), 201.

[74] Hiney, *On the Missionary Trail,* 57.

[75] "Kanak Identity in New Caledonia," *Living Heritage, Kanak Culture Today,* Peter Brown (ed.) (Noumea, New Caledonia: Agency for the Development of Kanak Culture, 2000), 6; and Ammann, *Kanak Dance and Music,* 3. Ammann states that the declines were higher in other parts of the Pacific, including Vanuatu and the Marquesas Islands.

[76] Featuna'i Liua'ana, "Errand of Mercy: Samoan Missionaries to Southern Vanuatu, 1839-1860," *The Covenant Makers: Island Missionaries in the Pacific,* Doug Munro and Andrew Thornley (ed.) (Suva, Fiji: Pacific Theological College and the Institute of Pacific Studies, University of the South Pacific, 1996), 52-55; and Linnekin, "New Political Orders," 199.

[77] Bullard, *Exile to Paradise,* 41.

[78] Ammann, *Kanak Dance and Music,* 3.

[79] Turner, *Nineteen Years in Polynesia,* 364; and Liua'ana, "Errand of Mercy," 57.

[80] Maggie Whitecross Paton, *Letters and Sketches from the New Hebrides* (New York: A. C. Armstrong and Son, 1895), 126.

[81] Ta'unga quoted in R. G. and Marjorie Crocombe, *The Works of Ta'unga.* 60.

Another significant deterrent to accepting missionaries was the enormous personal risk that conversion required. Many missionaries recognized that they were not making a simple request. As Maggie Whitecross Paton noted,

> it is like taking a great leap into the dark to risk the anger of their gods by coming to Worship. For what proof have they, at first, that we are leading them into the right way? True, they see that we wish to be kind; but the idea of any one coming among them simply for their good is a doctrine they cannot understand.[82]

When Pacific islanders calculated that the risk had become too great, such as in times of significant stress, new converts reverted to their former religious practices. Ta'unga witnessed this: after one epidemic, most people in the district, not just in the village of Tuauru, fled because they feared contagion. Once resettled, they resumed their polytheistic practices, quite assured that any allegiance to Jehovah was a mistake.[83] There were also social deterrents to conversion. Missionary George Turner noted, for example, that once "the children were getting wiser" than the adults on the Vanuatuan island of Aneiteum, the adults forced the pastors to close the school.[84] It was simply too disruptive to Aneiteum society to allow children to possess more knowledge than their elders. Finally, the character and the quality of the missionaries themselves could be a deterrent. Samoan pastors, for example, saw themselves as superior to the Melanesians they were proselytizing and expected to be revered. They also had a reputation for being quick to anger. Such qualities undercut their effectiveness in some communities.[85] For many communities, Whiteness gave authority, regardless of personal righteousness or behavior.[86] In these places, European missionaries were strongly preferred to indigenous pastors. As Maggie Whitecross Paton noted in 1865, missionaries

> tried to induce the Natives [on Aneiteum] to receive the Native Teachers we had brought from Maré but without success. They would readily have taken a white Missionary; but the Chief would not promise protection to the Teachers.[87]

Clearly, men like Ta'unga faced considerable obstacles when they attempted to introduce Christianity into a new society.

~

Ta'unga spent almost three years living in Tuauru, during which he had several brushes with death. The first came when he attempted to walk north to the village of Yate, where he hoped to share the

---

[82] Paton, *Letters and Sketches from the New Hebrides*, 72.

[83] R. G. and Marjorie Crocombe, *The Works of Ta'unga*, 60.

[84] Turner, *Nineteen Years in Polynesia*, 366.

[85] Sione Latukefu, "Pacific Islander Missionaries," *The Covenant Makers: Island Missionaries in the Pacific*, Doug Munro and Andrew Thornley (ed.) (Suva, Fiji: Pacific Theological College and the Institute of Pacific Studies, University of the South Pacific, 1996), 28, 32.

[86] Patricia Grimshaw and Andrew May, "Reappraisals of Mission History: An Introduction," *Missionaries, Indigenous Peoples and Cultural Exchange*, Patricia Grimshaw and Andrew May (ed.) (Portland, Oregon: Sussex Academic Press, 2010), 2.

[87] Paton, *Letters and Sketches from the New Hebrides*, 17.

Gospel with a new community. About a mile and a half beyond the boundary of the Tuauru district, Ta'unga found himself being followed by two men who were "besmeared with charcoal from head to foot. Their faces were completely covered. Only their teeth and the whites of their eyes stood out clearly. It was impossible to see who they were."[88] Ta'unga asked for directions to the chief, and the two men said they would show him the way. The three men then proceeded along the path single file, with Ta'unga in the vulnerable middle position. The party proceeded over one steep ridge and then another, until, after about five miles, they came to a stream. Ta'unga took a long drink of water as the two warriors talked in Gradji about whether this was the right moment to kill their captive. Ta'unga recalled:

> They thought I did not understand the Gradji language. When I heard what they said I stood up in the water and called out, 'I want to go into the bush to relieve myself.' So I went downstream and when I reached a bend near the path whence we came, they could not see me. So I clambered up the path and started running [for Tuauru].[89]

A second vulnerable moment came on Ta'unga's way home from another village in the region. He was again accosted for being in a place where he had no permission to travel.   Ta'unga recounted that he ran from his potential abductors,

> reached the inlet and jumped into it and began crossing to the other bank. They threw spears at me in the water. One went over my head and landed in front of me, while the other just missed my ear.

> A wave carried me to the other side of the inlet and I rested on a rock there. They jumped into the water too, but they didn't quite make this bank for the current swept them back into the inlet. They persisted, however, and finally reached this side, exhausted. I ran on again with them in pursuit.

> When I reached the top of another ridge I slowed down. Again they threw spears but I managed to dodge them. One passed my side and the other went under my feet, landing ahead of me. I picked them up and when they saw I had them in my hands they turned back.

> I returned to the village and, on reaching our house, I collapsed on the mat.[90]

The Kanak chief, Uadota, scolded Ta'unga for his foolishness and unbeknown to the pastor, made arrangements for his warriors to capture the men who had endangered the Rarotongan. One of the two men was killed, but the other was captured alive. When Ta'unga learned of this news, he says he rushed out to find "the live man all trussed up to the post of the cook house" and the ovens burning, for

---

[88] Ta'unga quoted in R. G. and Marjorie Crocombe, *The Works of Ta'unga*, 55.

[89] Ta'unga quoted in R. G. and Marjorie Crocombe, *The Works of Ta'unga*, 56.

[90] Ta'unga quoted in R. G. and Marjorie Crocombe, *The Works of Ta'unga*, 56-57. The Crocombes note that one of Ta'unga's manuscripts presents these two stories as separate events, but a later one from 1879 presents them both as part of a single episode. They conclude on page 55, "It is likely that in the intervening thirty-two years the two incidents became compounded in his mind."

it was nearly time to kill the second man. Then I called out saying, 'share out our man. Give me my share for I must go.' And they answered, 'Wait till the other has been killed. When that is done, then they will be divided out.' But I insisted, 'Divide them. Give me my share.' So they brought me one of the arms [of the man who had died and already been cut up] and I called out, 'I won't accept that. Give me the live man. That is my share—let that be your gift to me.' There was an instant silence, not one of them spoke for a long time. At last one called out, 'Let him take the live man,' and another said, 'No. He might set him free.' I replied, I want him as a servant to cook my food and to weed my food patch,' and all the chiefs agreed.[91]

Out of gratitude for saving his life, the servant remained in Ta'unga's service even after the pastor left Grande Terre.[92]

The third time Ta'unga's life was in jeopardy, he faced an army, not individual warriors acting on their own. The army was from the Isle of Pines, which lies thirty miles off the southern tip of Grande Terre. The residents of Tuauru and neighboring districts were subjects of the chief of the Isle of Pines, Matuku, and paid him tributes.[93] Since 1840, Matuku's warriors had been decimated by the diseases left by the twenty-one[94] missionary and sandalwood ships that had visited his island, and he became determined to rid his people of Western influence as a result. That meant stopping the trading ships and removing the pastors. Matuku's warriors' first attack came against the trading vessel *Caroline*, when it visited in July 1842, but the crew of the *Caroline* repelled the islanders. When another sandalwood ship, the *Star*, arrived in early November 1842, Matuku took another approach and ordered thirty of his men to request permission to board the ship so that they might sharpen their axes on the ship's grindstone. This was not an unusual request, and the captain of the *Star* readily agreed in an effort to facilitate trade. Once on board, Matuku's warriors positioned themselves strategically around the deck, and then suddenly and simultaneously attacked the crew, killing all seventeen. Later, the two LMS pastors from Samoa, who had been expelled from the Isle of Pines, and two other passengers were put to death, cooked, and eaten. Valuables from the *Star* were confiscated and the ship was burned.[95] In the aftermath of these events, Matuku met with Uadota, the chief of Tuauru. Matuku said "You must kill the two teachers at Tuauru also. Do not leave them or we shall all die. They are the cause of all the deaths on these islands."[96] Uadota resisted Matuku's orders, but placated him by taking a sacred axe to be used to kill Ta'unga. Matuku soon learned that Uadota had not completed the assigned task and took matters into his own hands, ordering a fleet of twenty canoes to sail for Tuauru. When the Tuauruans saw the canoes

[91] Ta'unga quoted in R. G. and Marjorie Crocombe, *The Works of Ta'unga*, 58.
[92] The would-be assassin and servant's name was Navie. He died in 1846 on Rarotonga. See R. G. and Marjorie Crocombe, *The Works of Ta'unga*, 58.
[93] "Matuku" is what Ta'unga called the chief. This was actually the man's title; his name was Touru. In the interest of consistency and simplicity, I have used the names that Ta'unga did. See Garrett, *To Live Among the Stars*, 191.
[94] Ta'unga quoted in R. G. and Marjorie Crocombe, *The Works of Ta'unga*, 63.
[95] Dorothy Shineberg, *They Came for Sandalwood: A Study of the Sandalwood Trade in the South-West Pacific, 1830-1865* (St. Lucia, Australia: University of Queensland Press, 2014), n.p. Google Books.
[96] Ta'unga quoted in R. G. and Marjorie Crocombe, *The Works of Ta'unga*, 46.

approaching, Uadota urged Ta'unga to flee into the mountains, but Ta'unga steadfastly refused. According to his account, he, Noa, and another pastor,[97] instead

> got all dressed up [and] waited for our doom, having placed our souls in the hands of God….We were sitting in our house all dressed up when we heard the children of the Village shrieking as they fled through the bush. So we said to ourselves, 'Here they come.' We had just finished our third prayer and were commencing the fourth one when they arrived within sight of our house…
>
> [The warriors] formed into [two] lines which reached right to the door. I was sitting in the doorway…my heart wept when the chief arrived calling out, 'Ta'unga and Noa. Ta'unga and Noa. Who are you to create all this trouble? Where did you find these things that caused all of our customs and our gods to disappear?'[98]

At this point, Matuku stood at the end of the two lines of his soldiers, whose greased bodies and guns, swords and axes glistened in the sun. The Isle of Pines chief shouted that he was going to cut off and burn the three pastors' penises. Instead of being intimidated or becoming angry, Ta'unga rose out of his chair and walked alone down the rows of men until he stood face to face with Matuku, who had a spear in his left hand and an axe in his right. Ta'unga joyfully exclaimed "Greetings!," causing Matuku to step back, even as he berated and insulted the pastor. Ta'unga then greeted Matuku in the name of Jehovah, which caused the chief to put his axe in his left hand and extend his right to shake hands with Ta'unga.[99] Ta'unga began to tell the chief about God and Christian sin. When Ta'unga finished his oration, Matuku presented him with a large quantity of food and invited him to become the pastor of the Isle of Pines. Matuku promised that his people would renounce idolatry. Ta'unga reported later that he did not trust Matuku's sincerity and so refused the offer because there had been no real change of heart. There had simply been a change in strategy.[100] This change, however, did diffuse the confrontation and allowed Ta'unga to escape death once again.

When the next missionary ship called at Tuauru in May 1845, Ta'unga and Noa met it off-shore. Ta'unga could claim that he had made meaningful progress towards the Christianization of the community over the previous three years: some people now wore clothes and as many as seventy people were attending services and not working on the Sabbath.[101] Ta'unga had not become discouraged that the majority of people had not accepted God. He attributed their reluctance to presence of the Devil, for he "was the instigator of all the evils which befell man, namely, the worship of idols, the killing of men, thieving, lying, adultery, vengeance, jealousy, and all [other] evils imaginable."[102] Reverends Archibald Wright Murray and George Turner may have been pleased with the progress Ta'unga documented, but they were also quite concerned for the safety of the native pastors, given the wars on Grande Terre and the new orders from chief of the Isle of Pines to kill Ta'unga and Noa. As Turner noted, "The people [of Tuauru] had a meeting and wept over

---

[97] The other pastor was Teura, who was also from Rarotonga. He replaced Taniela, who by this point had returned to Samoa. Teura died of tuberculosis in July 1844.

[98] Ta'unga quoted in R. G. and Marjorie Crocombe, *The Works of Ta'unga,* 64-65.

[99] Ta'unga quoted in R. G. and Marjorie Crocombe, *The Works of Ta'unga,* 66.

[100] Ta'unga quoted in R. G. and Marjorie Crocombe, *The Works of Ta'unga,* 67.

[101] Ta'unga quoted in R. G. and Marjorie Crocombe, *The Works of Ta'unga,* 75.

[102] Ta'unga quoted in R. G. and Marjorie Crocombe, *The Works of Ta'unga,* 71.

it. They could not kill their teachers; but as they are a conquered tribe, and under the feet of the old tyrant, they felt sadly afraid of the consequences of refusal."[103] Murray added that while Noa wanted to depart, Ta'unga wanted to stay, "notwithstanding the perilous circumstances in which they were placed…We could not, however, think of leaving him alone."[104] Therefore, Murray and Turner ordered Ta'unga to abandon his mission and sail with them for Samoa. Ta'unga vigorously objected, saying, "No, I won't go. I am going back to ashore….If I die, I die. If I live, I live….Life and death are not matters which are left in my hands." The reverends did not accept this reasoning, insisting, "you do not have the right to say what is to happen to you. We decide what is right for you. Do not exalt yourself above us."[105]

In this astonishing moment, Murray and Turner revealed the true complexities of the relationship LMS missionaries had with native pastors. On the one hand, the Polynesians were hailed as pioneers who could provide the necessary mediation between the civilized world and the untamed lands of Melanesia. They were necessary and important. On the other hand, the use of indigenous pastors was seen as a stopgap measure until authoritative, White missionaries could intercede. They were fallible and superfluous.[106] While Murray and Turner possessed a genuine concern for Ta'unga's welfare and safety, their feelings for the pastor were muddied by their own sense of racial and spiritual superiority. Murray and Turner saw Ta'unga as being *their* servant, as well as God's. They would not abide the Rarotongan's passionate expression of autonomy and allow him to remain in the village of Tuauru. With little choice but to follow orders, Ta'unga sailed with the missionaries to Samoa. Murray and Turner intended the retreat from Grande Terre to be a temporary one, but the London Missionary Society never reestablished itself on the island.

The LMS did not give up on the New Caledonian region entirely. After sailing east for a day, the *John Williams* came in sight of two of the Loyalty Islands. As the ship approached, Murray and Turner asked Ta'unga where he would prefer to be posted; Ta'unga chose Maré, perhaps not realizing that the island had had two Samoan pastors stationed there since 1841.[107] It proved to be an unhappy choice, for Ta'unga quickly found himself at odds with his fellow pastors. Samoans and Rarotongans frequently experienced frustration with one another because each group regarded itself as bearing greater prestige. The Samoans believed they possessed a superior culture, while the Rarotongans believed they possessed superior spiritual expertise since they had helped to bring Christianity to Samoa.[108] In other words, the paternalism White missionaries could exhibit towards native pastors was replicated between different Pacific peoples themselves. Maré exemplified this pattern: even after Ta'unga built the Samoans a new house and learned Maré's language, the Samoans refused to allow the newcomer to assist with preaching. Hence, there was very little for Ta'unga to do on the island. He did manage to befriend and convert the son of a chief, and he developed a relationship with the chief himself as he learned about Maré's customs and history.[109]

---

[103] Turner, *Nineteen Years in Polynesia*, 417.

[104] Murray, *Missions in Western Polynesia*, 289.

[105] Ta'unga quoted in R. G. and Marjorie Crocombe, *The Works of Ta'unga*, 75.

[106] Smith, *Literary Cultures and the Pacific*, 57; and Gilson, *The Cook Islands*, 81-83.

[107] R. G. and Marjorie Crocombe, *The Works of Ta'unga*, 24-25.

[108] R. G. and Marjorie Crocombe, *The Works of Ta'unga*, 40.

[109] Ta'unga quoted in R. G. and Marjorie Crocombe, *The Works of Ta'unga*, 77-78. The Samoans were Tataio and Iakopo.

Ta'unga noted chief's stories about capturing and eating Europeans,[110] for there may have been as many as forty White sailors killed on Maré between 1843 and 1845.[111] According to Ta'unga, cannibalism was "rife" on Maré. He found "their customs were frightening to experience and horrid to behold,"[112] perhaps because he perceived Melanesian anthropophagy as differing from the flesh-eating practices Ta'unga witnessed as a boy on Rarotonga. Whereas Rarotongan tradition prescribed cannibalism as an act of revenge, the Melanesians, both on Grande Terre and in the Loyalty Islands, waged war to satisfy their craving for human flesh.[113] From Ta'unga's perspective, what was once a means to an end on Rarotonga became the end unto itself in Melanesia, and he found this particularly objectionable:

> When the battle was over, they all returned home together, the women in front and the men behind. The womenfolk carried the flesh on their backs; the coconut-leaf baskets were full up and the blood oozed over their backs and trickled down their legs. When they reached their homes the earth ovens were lit at each house and they ate the slain. Great was their delight, for they were eating well that day… the flesh was dark like sea-cucumber, the fat was yellow like beef fat, and it smelt like cooked birds, like pigeon or a chicken. The share of the chief was the right hand and the right foot. Part of the chief's portion was brought for me, as for the priest, but I returned it. The people were unable to eat it all; the legs and the arms only were consumed.[114]

Ta'unga also recounted witnessing a live man being amputated:

> He got hold of the victim and chopped off one of his hands. The man screamed as it was cut off. Then he cut off the other hand, while the victim twisted and squirmed. When that was done he cut off one leg and then the other. But the man did not die. His trunk was the only thing left. Still he did not die. Then the head was cut off and he at last expired. I was overcome with grief and tried to stop them but they would not listen because I did not know the language, so I was unable to tell them the right way of life.[115]

Ta'unga's wrote these passages for his mentor Charles Pitman, shortly after his departure from the Loyalty Islands in October 1846. He may have used sensationalized language in order to generate

---

[110] The role of cannibalism in various cultures is a subject of debate. See, for example, Gananath Obeyesekere, *Cannibal Talk: The Man-eating Myth and Human Sacrifice in the South Seas* (Berkeley, California: University of California Press, 2005) and Tracey Banivanua-Mar, "Cannibalism and Colonialism: Charting Colonies and Frontiers in Nineteenth-Century Fiji," *Comparative Studies in Society and History,* 52.2 (Apr 2010): 255-281, ProQuest Central.

[111] Turner, *Nineteen Years in Polynesia,* 401. Ta'unga's account puts the number at 28.

[112] Ta'unga quoted in R. G. and Marjorie Crocombe, 79.

[113] Peggy Brock, Norman Etherington, Gareth Griffiths, and Jacqueline Van Gent, *Indigenous Evangelists and Questions of Authority in the British Empire, 1750-1940* (Leiden, Netherlands: Koninklijke Brill, 2015), 167-168. These scholars note that Ta'unga was "judgmental" of the New Caledonians and saw himself as superior to them.

[114] Ta'unga quoted in R. G. and Marjorie Crocombe, *The Works of Ta'unga,* 91-92.

[115] Ta'unga quoted in R. G. and Marjorie Crocombe, *The Works of Ta'unga,* 93.

a reaction within the LMS community or to reinforce his cultural superiority over the Melanesians.[116] Alternatively, he may have genuinely been outraged by the behaviors he witnessed.

By the mid-1840s Ta'unga saw himself as being a deeply committed Christian, who differed substantially from those he sought to convert. He had sufficient experience to have confidence in his ability to answer complex theological questions in ways that non-believers could understand. When asked about the nature of the soul and if all men had one, for example, Ta'unga responded:

> Not one man is without a soul!...The soul comes from God. He created Adam from the soil and when He made him he looked like a man, from his head to his two feet, but they were useless. And God then breathed life into him, that was his soul, and he became a live man, and that soul was the part that God intended should live. It is only through ignorance that souls die.[117]

~

Ta'unga's next missionary assignment was quite different than anything he had yet experienced. Rather than continue his work on the Christian frontier, trying to sway non-believers, his LMS supervisors selected Ta'unga to direct a continuing mission in Samoa. His specific assignment was on the Manu'a Islands, where anthropologist Margaret Mead did her early and revolutionary field work in 1925 and 1926.[118] Ta'unga's primary concern no longer centered upon the initial steps of the conversion process. Now he undertook the continuing pastoral responsibility for helping Christians sustain their faith and maintain their adherence to Western behavioral norms. It was an altogether new challenge: the difficulties of generating elation and joining a new population differed from sustaining those feelings over time.[119]

---

[116] Brock, Etherington, Griffiths, and Van Gent, *Indigenous Evangelists and Questions of Authority in the British Empire,* 167-168.

[117] Ta'unga quoted in R. G. and Marjorie Crocombe, *The Works of Ta'unga,* 83.

[118] In 1928, Mead published *Coming of Age in Samoa,* in which she argued that adolescence was primarily a culturally-determined experience, rather than a biological one. In 1983, anthropologist Derek Freeman bitterly contested the conceptual and methodological validity of Mead's work. Recent scholarship largely holds that Freeman's attack was excessive: that while Mead made some errors as a young anthropologist, her work was essentially correct. See Derek Freeman, *Margaret Mead and Samoa: The Making and Unmaking of an Anthropological Myth* (Cambridge, Massachusetts: Harvard University Press, 1983); Paul Shankman, The *Trashing of Margaret Mead: Anatomy of an Anthropological Controversy* (Madison, Wisconsin: University of Wisconsin Press, 2009).

[119] Lewis R. Rambo notes that "When people cannot maintain a sense of euphoria and empowerment, an inevitable loss of energy may initiate a new crisis…This issue is a serious problem for any tradition that advocates total, complete, and sudden conversion" as Evangelicals do. See Rambo, *Understanding Religious Conversion,* 136.

Ta'unga arrived on Manu'a's main island of Ta'u in mid-1849, having enjoyed a ten-month visit home to Rarotonga and having spent a year and a half studying at Samoa's Malua Institute, a theological college that had opened in 1844. He was well-received by the 820 people who lived on Ta'u, partly because everyone, including Ta'unga, assumed that his appointment would be temporary.[120] Ta'unga believed that he would soon return to Melanesia, and the Manu'ans had confidence that another Englishman would be appointed to replace the LMS preacher who had "reached their hearts" and in 1844 led the Manu'ans to experience "their first powerful" Pentecostal* awakening.[121] These expectations were never realized; instead, Ta'unga led the Manu'ans for almost thirty years.

During his first six years in the Manu'a Islands, Ta'unga concentrated his efforts on preaching, teaching, and managing schools. He supervised ten teachers and eleven assistant teachers, raised the level of instruction to a commendable standard, collected greater tithes* to support LMS efforts elsewhere, and built a coral-walled church.[122] He could again point to a significant progress in a short amount of time. When he wasn't working, Ta'unga devoted his energies towards his new family. In 1853, he overcame his European supervisors' preference that he wed a Samoan, and instead married a Rarotongan woman named Ngapoko. The two had met when Ta'unga returned

home in 1847, and Ta'unga insisted that no other woman would do. The couple had two children[123] and worked together, each teaching single-sex classes. Ngapoko proved to be particularly effective in the classroom; in 1862, the Evangelist couple "arranged a competition between her class and mine," Ta'unga wrote. "Her class is of women, mine is of men. But I have been beaten, my wife won the competition! All of the women have completed their training and have been received into the church. My group is still struggling along....She has carried out her share of the work faithfully and well."[124]

It was also during this time that Ta'unga promoted the adoption of laws banning smoking and tattooing. The prohibition against tattoos especially put Ta'unga at odds with his flock, since tattoos were an essential part of Samoan culture, even after the arrival of Christian missionaries. It was so important, in fact, that no Samoan male could be considered a man or could find a wife until he had been

---

[120] R. G. and Marjorie Crocombe, *The Works of Ta'unga,* 116, 118-119, 121.

[121] Thomas Bullen quoted in "Samoas. Work of God at Manua," *The Evangelical Magazine and Missionary Chronicle*, Volume XXIII (July 1845) (London, Thomas Ward and Co., 1845), 378. The preacher was Matthew Hunkin, who married a high-ranking Samoan wife. After six years of work (1843-1849) on Manua'a, Hunkin resigned his post to become a trader and landowner in his wife's village on Tutuila. See R. P. Gilson, *Samoa 1830 to 1900: The Politics of a Multi-cultural Community* (Melbourne, Australia: Oxford University Press, 1970), 90, 143.

[122] R. G. and Marjorie Crocombe, *The Works of Ta'unga,* 119-120.

[123] R. G. and Marjorie Crocombe, *The Works of Ta'unga,* 122-123. The children were a boy named Samuel and a daughter named Maria. The word for Samuel in Rarotongan is Tamuera. I have used the English term to confirm that Ta'unga's son had a Christian name.

[124] Ta'unga quoted in R. G. and Marjorie Crocombe, *The Works of Ta'unga,* 130.

tattooed from his mid-torso to his knees.[125] An expert applied this body art over the course of two or three months, using a piece of human bone cut like fine-toothed comb; the bone was dipped into a "mixture of candle-nut ashes and water, and tapping it with a little mallet, it sinks into the skin….As it extends over such a large surface, the operation is a tedious and painful affair," Reverend George Turner noted in 1861.[126] Most LMS missionaries were adamantly opposed to the practice, both because they saw it as a mutilation that tarnished the body given by God and because it maintained a connection to pagan beliefs.[127] As Reverend Archibald Wright Murray wrote:

> As practiced among the heathen, besides being barbarous and useless itself, [tattooing] was always accompanied by a variety of abominable customs.   A whole train of evils generally accompany such practices. Hence, on *relative* grounds, it is often of great importance to get practices discontinued, which, in themselves are comparatively harmless.[128]

Ta'unga's strict adherence to LMS wishes had important consequences by the 1860s. Given the choice between Christianity and manhood, many young men choose the latter and left home to obtain their tattoos elsewhere. They did so despite being forbidden by law from returning to Manu'a, and the population on Ta'unga's islands declined as a result.[129] Ultimately, however, the effort to stop tattooing largely failed in Samoan archipelago, quite unlike what happened in the Cook Islands or the Society Islands. Recognition of Samoan resolve finally came in 1875, when the Mission Committee for Samoa agreed to allow church members to have tattoos.[130]

Samoans were not able to resist other aesthetic and social changes. The custom had been for men to grow their hair long and for women to keep it short except when pregnant, but the reverse became fashionable with the spread of Christianity, in accordance with European sensibilities. This changed the Samoan definition of beauty[131] and corresponded with a broad alteration of the role of women in Samoan society. In the pre-Christian era, Samoan women held a revered status, for they were seen both as peacemakers with decision-making prerogatives and as divine vessels that could attract the supernatural.[132] They were vital to a village's contentment. With the arrival of Christianity, male missionaries and pastors assumed these roles and encouraged women to focus

---

125 William B. Churchward, *My Consulate in Samoa: A Record of Four Years' Sojourn in the Navigators Islands with Personal Experiences of King Malietoa Laupepa, His Country, and His Men* (London: Richard Bentley and Son, 1887), 392.

126 Turner, *Nineteen Years in Polynesia,* 181-182.

127 Therese Mangos and John Utanga, "The Lost Connections: Tattoo Revival in the Cook Island," *Fashion Theory: The Journal of Dress, Body & Culture*, 10, no.3 (September, 2006), 315-331. Academic Search Premier, EBSCOhost.

128 Archibald Wright Murray, *Forty Years' Mission Work in Polynesia and New Guinea from 1835-1875* (New York: Robert Carter & Brothers, 1876), 224.

129 N. A. Rowe, *Samoa Under the Sailing Gods* (London and New York: Putnam, 1930), 73.

130 Gilson, *Samoa 1830 to 1900,* 136. The Committee also agreed to allow smoking and card playing. The survival of the tattooing tradition allowed Margaret Mead to observe it when she did fieldwork in Manu'a in the mid-1920s; she noted how the tattooing patterns allowed for a differentiation based on social rank. See Margaret Mead, *Social Organization of Manu'a* (Honolulu, Hawai'i: Bernice P. Bishop Museum, 1969), 80.

131 Jeannette Marie Mageo, "Hairdos and Don'ts: Hair Symbolism and Sexual History in Samoa," *Frontiers*, 17, 2 (1996), 138-167, ProQuest Central.

132 Latu Latai, "Changing Covenants in Samoa? From Brothers and Sisters to Husbands and Wives?" *Oceania*, Vol. 85, Issue 1 (2015), 92-104, ProQuest Central.

their attention on domestic duties as defined by Victorian standards.[133] Women like Ngapoko hoped to provide the necessary example.

Ta'unga's standing in the Manu'a Islands took a sharp negative turn in 1855, when he began to administer the ordinances of baptism and the Lord's Supper directly to his parishioners, instead of having an English missionary from Tutuila periodically do so. Granting Ta'unga these responsibilities was a notable recognition of the pastor's skills and experience; it came twenty years before the 1875 decision to ordain all native pastors in Samoa.[134] The London Missionary Society was also tacitly acknowledging that the need for White missionaries was greater elsewhere.[135] Ta'unga's proficiency and the needs of the global organization did not matter to the Manu'ans, however. They knew the LMS only provided a salary to its White missionaries, not to its native pastors, so they protested the liturgical change by refusing to contribute to the collection for the Rarotongan pastor's livelihood. The Manu'ans hoped to squeeze Ta'unga out and have a White missionary assigned to them permanently.[136] An intervention by Reverend Thomas Powell only produced a promise for minimal assistance for Ta'unga. Five years later, the situation was so problematic that Powell reported to London although Ta'unga felt the community's rejection of him keenly, he was willing to remain at his post. In reality, Ta'unga did not have a choice; once again, he had to do as he was told. By 1862, after seven years of impasse, both the Manu'ans and Ta'unga recognized that no change in missionary assignments would be forthcoming. Ta'unga and the Manu'ans were bound together. This realization meant that the people once again took up an annual collection for their pastor,[137] but continued to hope that they would obtain the appointment of a White missionary in Manu'a. Even Ta'unga was deferential to the spiritual expertise of his White superiors. In 1862, he wrote to Reverend William Wyatt Gill, "The islands are still pressing for a European missionary to serve them….We pray to God that He may bring it about."[138] This orientation is striking because it illustrates how even though political colonialism did not exist in the Pacific in the mid-nineteenth century, cultural colonialism did. As in other parts of the world, Western civilization was defined by its racial domination.[139] Manu'an perceptions of racial superiority and inferiority were, therefore, deeply embedded in their desires for a White missionary.

By the 1860s, Ta'unga faced many of the same problems as other Christian leaders working in the Pacific with converted populations, but Manu'a's relative isolation, reduced the intensity of his experience.[140] The challenge was really no longer one of proselytizing pagans. Rather, the task now

---

[133] Fei Taule'ale'ausumai, "Wounded Healers," *International Congregational Journal*, 13, no. 2 (Winter, 2014), 67-75, EBSCOhost.

[134] Lange, *Island Ministers,* 93-94.

[135] Gilson, *Samoa 1830 to 1900,* 130-131.

[136] R. G. and Marjorie Crocombe, *The Works of Ta'unga,* 121.

[137] R. G. and Marjorie Crocombe, *The Works of Ta'unga,* 121.

[138] Ta'unga quoted in R. G. and Marjorie Crocombe, *The Works of Ta'unga,* 131.

[139] For an interesting discussion of the intersection of race, culture, and identity in the nineteenth century, see Robert J. C. Young, *Colonial Desire: Hybridity in Theory, Culture and Race* (New York: Routledge, 1995), 90-95. Other scholars characterize the atmosphere as "pre- or proto-colonial" and argue that Ta'unga did not experience "the racism and disempowering impact of a colonized society." See Brock, Etherington, Griffiths, and Van Gent, *Indigenous Evangelists and Questions of Authority in the British Empire,* 165.

[140] Manu'a was the center of Samoan political authority until the sixteenth century, but when Tongan rule of Samoa ended, it shifted west to the larger islands. This shift left Manu'a politically isolated from the rest of the archipelago and resulted in greater social stability and fewer wars. See Malama Meleisea, *Lagaga: A Short History of Western Samoa* (Suva, Fiji: University of the South Pacific, 1987), 31-32; and Gilson, *Samoa 1830 to 1900,* 58. As the British consul confirmed in 1887, the Manu'ans "have a king of their own, and their own laws, and

was to nourish Christian faith, sustain denominational loyalty, and prevent the return of unwanted behavior. When the Catholics purchased land on Upolu for a cathedral in 1852 and when Wesleyan Methodists reopened their Samoan mission on Upolu in 1857, the door opened for doctrinal competition. In some areas, people also retained a devotion to local spirits or to the cults established in the 1820s with the arrival of Christianity.[141] There was also competition from other powerful forces. By the 1860s, the European settler economy was booming as traders and capitalists, led by the Hamburg company J.C. Godeffroy & Sohn, purchased large tracts of land from Samoans to develop copra and cotton plantations.[142] This increased commercialization and contact with the outside world and transformed a port like Apia on Upolu into what the LMS representatives saw as a den of iniquity and sin with grog shops, gambling, and prostitution. As the American Commodore William Mervine confirmed in 1856, Apia was

> composed of a heterogeneous mass of the most immoral and dissolute Foreigners that ever disgraced humanity….Responsible to no law for their conduct—certainly none that the natives have the power or disposition to enforce against them—there exist anarchy, riot, debauchery which render life and property insecure.[143]

This meant that LMS villages were soon near settlements with a very different lifestyle. The presence of such a counterculture quashed all hope of building a solely Christian community in the South Pacific.[144] Moreover, the presence of expansive and frequent European and American commercial activity, as opposed to the occasional visits by single ships earlier in the century, promoted conflict between Samoans. As British consul William Churchward noted, most of the disputes on Samoa were a product of "mischievous White interference with native affairs."[145] All this meant that LMS representatives in the Pacific had to adapt to a changing landscape to maintain the support of the Evangelical faithful.

LMS pastors and missionaries employed all of the tools in their arsenal to combat these developments. One of these centered upon status: LMS churches made a definite and purposeful distinction between congregants identified as converts and those who were in full fellowship with the church and could take communion. The adults who could demonstrate their knowledge of Protestant Christian tenets, and who consistently upheld behavioral standards, were interviewed for full membership.[146] Those who were admitted, but later engaged in improper behavior, could have their privileges withdrawn temporarily or could be excommunicated altogether; excluded members could also be readmitted once they had redeemed themselves, as Ta'unga had in his

keeping pretty much to themselves, neither interfere with politics on the other islands, nor are interfered with from them." See Churchward, *My Consulate in Samoa,* 42.

[141] Meleisea, *Lagaga,* 52, 55, 62, 64. These cults included one to Sio Vili, a Samoan who had travelled on a whaling ship to Sydney, who, upon his return in the early 1820s, became a self-proclaimed prophet. For more detailed information on the Wesleyans in Samoa, see Margaret Reeson, *Pacific Missionary George Brown 1835-1917: Wesleyan Methodist Church* (Canberra: Australian National University, 2013).

[142] Meleisea, *The Making of Modern Samoa,* 33-36. Copra is the dried meat of a coconut.

[143] William Mervine quoted in Gilson, *Samoa 1830 to 1900,* 179-180.

[144] Gilson, *Samoa 1830 to 1900,* 179.

[145] Churchward, *My Consulate in Samoa,* 390.

[146] Gilson, *The Cook Islands,* 31.

youth.[147] This ability to include and exclude within an island community was a potent tool for maintaining influence among many Samoans. It helped the church to sustain spiritual enthusiasm with full members and manage those who suffered spiritual lapses. Ta'unga utilized these techniques in early 1862, when he and Powell slowly admitted converts to full membership: ten on February 15, ten on February 22, fifteen on March 1, twenty-seven on April 5, five on April 19, and eleven on May 3. Ta'unga and Powell also chose ten people from the small island of Olosenga to join the church on the main island of Ta'u in full fellowship, thereby exploiting the existing island hierarchy within the Manu'a group.[148]

The LMS representatives also used the people's desire for books and education to their advantage. The literary culture on the islands grew out of the elementary schools, which held annual competitions in reading, writing, arithmetic, geography, and Scriptural history, and awarded prizes to winners.[149] This orientation meant that when the LMS published ten thousand copies of a revised edition of the Old and New Testaments in Samoan in 1860, all were quickly purchased.[150] Copies of geography, astronomy, and math texts were widely available, as well as works like *The Pilgrim's Progress*.[151] Ta'unga recognized the value of this literary culture and participated in it: during his final years in Samoa, he wrote a history of the Manu'a group.[152]

In 1870, Ta'unga began to express his wish to retire and return home to Rarotonga, but Powell and the other missionaries in Samoa refused his requests for eight years. It wasn't, therefore, until October 1, 1879, that Ta'unga saw his homeland again. The sixty-one-year old was accompanied by his wife Ngapoko and their children.[153]

~

Rarotonga was a wholly different place from the one Ta'unga remembered from his youth. Upon his arrival in Avarua, the main buildings at the Takamoa Institute could provide a comforting familiarity, but so much else would have startled the pastor. First and foremost in Ta'unga's eyes may have been the new church with gothic windows that opened in December 1853. Sixty-four

---

[147] Annual LMS reports detail membership statistics, including baptisms, church attendance, full membership, excommunications, etc.. See, for example, *The Report of the Directors to the Fortieth General Meeting of the Missionary Society, Usually Called the London Missionary Society on Thursday, May 15, 1834* (London, [unknown], 1834), 3-18.

[148] Ta'unga quoted in R. G. and Marjorie Crocombe, *The Works of Ta'unga*, 128. Defining behavioral standards for missionaries was also important, as in the case of Reverend Alexander Simpson in Tahiti in the 1840s. Simpson was accused of having taken "improper liberties," which included telling obscene jokes, drunkenness, sexual assault, and extramarital affairs. In December 1850, the LMS directors in London forced Simpson to retire because his behavior had generated such gossip that his moral reputation was ruined. The directors realized that ministers with poor reputations threatened to destabilize the authority and effectiveness of the entire Mission. See Emily J. Manktelow, "Thinking with Gossip: Deviance, Rumour, and Reputation in the South Seas Mission of the London Missionary Society," *Subverting Empire: Deviance and Disorder in the British Colonial World*, Will Jackson and Emily J. Manktelo (eds.) (New York: Palgrave MacMillan, 2015), 104, 111, 117-118.

[149] Lovett, *The History of the London Missionary Society*, 394.

[150] Lovett, *The History of the London Missionary Society*, 387.

[151] Murray, *Missions in Western Polynesia*, 460.

[152] R. G. and Marjorie Crocombe, *The Works of Ta'unga*, 140.

[153] R. G. and Marjorie Crocombe, *The Works of Ta'unga*, 143-144. Also traveling with the family were Samuel's Samoan wife, Paiau, and the daughter of the high chief of Manu'a.

feet long, forty feet wide and constructed of coral block walls three feet thick, the whitewashed church featured a large bell tower, and interior galleries on three sides.[154] Aaron Buzacott adored it, but the Earl of Pembroke found it quite incongruous with the island setting, describing it in 1870 as a "vile black and white abomination paralyzing one of the most beautiful bits of scenery in the world."[155]

Activity in the port certainly would have caught Ta'unga's attention, for Avarua's docks were far busier, with as many as 50 ships calling there each year in the early 1880s. Not only was the volume greater, but the nature of business had changed as well. Bartering no longer dominated transactions; instead, a cash economy had emerged, with the inexpensive Chilean dollar serving as the primary currency.[156] Other changes were readily apparent. Fashions had changed for the island's elite; by the late 1870s and early 1880s, they rode in carriages, wore Western uniforms and colorful dresses, carried parasols, and ate food from tin cans. The recognized sovereign of the island, Makea Takau Ariki, behaved quite differently than the old chiefs had. She compared herself to Queen Victoria and imitated the court's ceremonies and traditions as best she could.[157] Makea also impaired the long-standing alliance between the ruling class and the Protestant missionaries when she sought to regulate the island's economy to her own advantage.[158]

In 1879, Makea revised the legal code, adding specific punishments and fines for various crimes in an attempt to acknowledge the island's changing state of affairs. Foreigners deserting their ships were fined $10; captains could not leave sick crewmen on Rarotonga without permission and the payment of $30; and there could be no debt accumulation between foreigners and Rarotongans. Murder was punishable by death except in cases of self-defense; intentional arson resulted in spending three years in irons if the culprit had no land; fornication resulted in a fine of $4 per person; and stealing

a pig necessitated the payment of four pigs to the owner. Widows were entitled to remain on their

[154] Buzacott, *Mission Life in the Islands of the Pacific*, 219.

[155] Earl of Pembroke quoted in Louis B. Wright and Mary Isabel Fry, *Puritans in the South Seas* (New York: Henry Holt and Company, 1936), 204.

[156] Alexander H. Spoehr, "Rarotonga in 1887: A Historical Geography of an Island in Transition," (unpublished master's thesis, University of Hawai'i-Mānoa, 1973), 70, 74. This thesis is available at Hamilton Library, University of Hawai'i-Mānoa. The Chilean dollar had been introduced to the South Pacific by J.C. Godeffroy & Sohn in the early 1860s. The company bought the large coins with little silver content at a discount and passed them off at face value in the Pacific. British sterling was too expensive for most Rarotongans and other Pacific islanders to acquire and use.

[157] Gilson, *The Cook Islands*, 51

[158] Jeffrey Sissons, Nation and Destination: Creating Cook Islands Identity ([Suva, Fiji]: Institute of Pacific Studies; [Rarotonga, Cook Islands]: University of the South Pacific Centre in the Cook Islands, 1999), 13.

husband's land unless they remarried or committed three crimes; children were punished by working on public works projects; and there was a 9:00 p.m. curfew.[159] The problem with these clear societal expectations was that the police proved unable to enforce the laws. There were too many violations and the fines were too difficult to collect. Europeans, in particular, flouted the laws regularly. They had also gained permission to marry Rarotongan women.[160]

There were other changes on Rarotonga. As he passed around the northeast end of the island on his way to the village of Ngatangiia, Ta'unga would have seen the copra, cotton, and coffee plantations operated by foreign overseers; a new species of taro introduced from Hawai'i; and the groves of lime and orange trees planted to cater to the needs of whaling ships.[161] When he sat down to eat a meal prepared in his honor, Ta'unga's plate held foods that had not been a part of the island's diet in the 1840s, including beef, turkey, duck, sweet potatoes, tomatoes, turnips, carrots, cabbage, rice, tapioca, and pineapple.[162] Such changes came with great costs: whereas the population was estimated to be 7,000 people in 1828, by 1843 it had fallen to 3,300, and by the 1880s, was down to 1,800.[163] As was true in Tahiti and New Caledonia, this rapid population decline was the direct result of increased European contact.

Rarotonga had also changed religiously while Ta'unga was on his missions. As had happened in Samoa with increased commercialization, Rarotonga lost its potential to become a Christian sanctuary. The missionaries were no longer held in awe by the majority. By the 1880s those who had full church membership constituted only a quarter of the island's population.[164] Moreover, people were no longer willing to work for the church for free. The advent of a cash economy meant that people expected to be paid for their work, even for baking the bread for communion.[165] Alcohol, "that curse of all curses" had come to the island and the "churches have suffered fearfully from it. Our young men have given themselves up to intoxication and one after another falls victim," Reverend James Chalmers wrote in 1867. The problem became so pronounced that Chalmers began mixing wine and coconut milk for communion and eventually "confined ourselves entirely to [using] the cocoanut milk."[166]

Tellingly, Ta'unga did not become disheartened by the changes he saw. Rather, it fortified his commitment to continue his life's work: instead of retiring, he continued serving as a pastor. He began in eastern Rarotonga, but in 1882 Rarotonga's leading missionary, William Wyatt Gill, asked Ta'unga to take over the mission on Ma'uke, a volcanic island 150 miles northeast of Rarotonga. Ta'unga spent about a year on Ma'uke compensating for the limitations of his predecessor, and then returned home, where he worked for several years with Gill on a new translation of the Bible

[159] Makea, *The Blue Laws of Rarotonga* (Rarotonga(?): unknown publisher, 199?), 1-9. This was originally printed at the Mission-House Rarotonga in 1879. The publication is available at Hamilton Library, University of Hawai'i-Mānoa.

[160] Richard Gilson, *The Cook Islands, 1820-1950*, Ron Crocombe (ed.) (Wellington, New Zealand: Victoria University Press in association with the Institute of Pacific Studies of the University of the South Pacific, 1980), 48, 53.

[161] Spoehr, "Rarotonga in 1887," 63-67.

[162] Buzacott, *Mission Life in the Islands of the Pacific,* 240-241.

[163] Spoehr, "Rarotonga in 1887," 25.

[164] Gilson, *The Cook Islands,* 53.

[165] Gilson, *The Cook Islands,* 48.

[166] James Chalmers quoted in Richard Lovett, *James Chalmers His Autobiography and Letters*, 6th ed. (London, The Religious Tract Society, 1903), 83, 92.

in Rarotongan. The last large project of his life was translating a Biblical history from Samoan into Rarotongan.[167]

Ta'unga died in August 1898, either on the same day his wife Ngapoko did or shortly thereafter. They share a single gravesite overlooking the sea.[168]

~

The Christianization of the Pacific was unusual for a number of reasons. Because its impetus came from individuals rather than governments, there was no accompanying colonial bureaucracy, as happened so prominently in Latin America. Because different denominations fought for control of particular islands, there was greater sectarianism than in Africa. Most importantly, because indigenous pastors like Ta'unga were so essential to the messianic enterprise, their cultural interactions differed from those Europeans and Pacific Islanders experienced directly. As cultural intermediaries, indigenous pastors allowed conversion to happen.[169]

Some White missionaries recognized this crucial role better than others. Moderates publicly acknowledged the value native pastors brought, but still criticized them for their limitations. As Cook Islands missionary William Nicol Lawrence wrote in his annual report in 1888,

> Our teachers [pastors] have done their work conscientiously and well; they have wrought according to their ability, but we want a better class of teachers if they are to make progress. Their education is too limited; they are too near the level of their congregations. The people are growing more in intelligence than holiness; their material prosperity is more marked than their spiritual prosperity.[170]

Conservatives went further, loading criticism upon indigenous pastors and the people they served. Reverend George Harris argued that there was an "inherent weakness in the race" and that pastors were too "yielding to the whims and fancies of their people."[171] Like so many others, Harris saw the indigenous pastors as an inferior, if necessary, stopgap until Europeans could arrive. Murray, Turner, and Powell partially shared these attitudes, which is why native pastors appear so infrequently in their accounts. It is also why Murray and Turner denied Ta'unga the opportunity to return to Tuauru to gather his belongings in 1845. This meant that his journal documenting three years of his day-to-day life in the village was lost.[172] When a missionary ship unexpectedly arrived in Manu'a to take Ta'unga home in 1879, he did not have sufficient time to pack and his history of Manu'a was never recovered.[173] Hence, two of Ta'unga's manuscripts were forsaken simply because a European itinerary was seen as more important than a native pastor's texts. Similarly, when the LMS directors decided to send a deputation to Samoa in 1888 to assess the spiritual status of the archipelago, the committee proclaimed the need for a uniform code of

[167] R. G. and Marjorie Crocombe, *The Works of Ta'unga,* 144-146.
[168] R. G. and Marjorie Crocombe, *The Works of Ta'unga,* 147.
[169] Garrett, *To Live Among the Stars,* 118.
[170] William Nicol Lawrence quoted in Lovett, *The History of the London Missionary,* 370.
[171] George Alfred Harris quoted in Lange, *Island Ministers,* 74-75.
[172] Ta'unga quoted in R. G. and Marjorie Crocombe, *The Works of Ta'unga,* 76.
[173] R. G. and Marjorie Crocombe, *The Works of Ta'unga,* 140.

discipline as a result of "the conditions of Samoan life, and the infantile weaknesses of the Samoan character....Samoan Christians have not yet conquered their characteristic national and social weaknesses" after 50 years of nominal Christianity.[174]   Even by the end of Ta'unga's life, conservative missionaries were not ready to treat Christians in the Pacific as peers. As William Nicol Lawrence wrote in 1895, "The time has not yet come when we can safely leave these native Christian communities to meet alone, unaided, the difficulties of their position."[175]   The LMS directors agreed with him. With continuing confidence in their preeminence, the directors worried that a premature recognition of Pacific autonomy would cause the demise of its young churches.[176]

Progressive missionaries, who were in the minority, viewed the situation in the Pacific differently. An early missionary in Samoa, George Barden, documented the work of a Rarotongan pastor named Teava at length and proclaimed, "the assistance he rendered me in many ways was of inestimable value" for "among all the native brethren...I do not know that there is one more deserving of esteem than Teava....Teava and his kind wife were our steadfast friends and helpers, rejoicing with us in our joys and sympathizing with us in our sorrows."[177] For Barden, there was sense of partnership. Over time, progressive missionaries became more adamant in their support for the pastors. James Chalmers, for example, wrote as early as 1874, "I think it is time [that] these

ENGLISH.	Marquesan Islands. 139° to 141° W. Lon. 7° to 10° S. Lat. MARQUESAS.	Society Islands. 148° to 153° W. Lon. 16° to 18° S. Lat. TAHITI.	Sandwich Islands. 154° to 160° W. Lon. 18° to 20° N. Lat. HAWAII.	Hervey Islands. 157° to 160° W. Lon. 18° to 22° S. Lat. RAROTONGA.	Humphrey's Island. 161° 4' W. Lon. 10° 28' S. Lat. MANAHIKI.	Navigator's Islands. 168° to 173° W. Lon. 13° 30' to 14° 30' S. Lat. SAMOA.	Savage Island. 169° W. Lon. 19° S. Lat. NIUE.	Bowditch Island. Union Group. 171° W. Lon. 9° to 11° S. Lat. FAKAAFO.	Friendly Islands. 173° to 175° W. Lon. 18° to 21° S. Lat. TONGA.	Fiji Islands. 178° W. Lon. 17° S. Lat. BAU.
Sun	Oumati	Ra & Mahana	La	La	La	La	La	La	La'a	Singa
Moon	Mahina	Ava'e	Mahina	Ma'ama	Marama	Masina	Fetu	Mahina	Mahina	Vula
Star	Fetii	Feti'a	Hoku	Etu	Fetu	Fetu	Fetu	Fetu	Feti	Kalokalo
Cloud	Ao	Ata	Ao	Ao	Ao	Ao	Aho	Ao	Ao	Demitangi
Heavens	Ani	Ra'i	Lani	Langi	Langi	Langi	Langi	Langi	Langi	Langi
Rain	Ua	Ua	Ua	Ua	Ua	Ua	Uha	Ua	Uha	Uha
Lightning	Uia	Uira	Uwila	Uila	Uira	Uila	Chila	Uila	Uhila	Liva liva
Thunder	Fatutii	Patiri	Hekili	Mangunga	Patitiri	Faititili	Paka le langi	Faititili	Faijili	Kurukuru
Wind	Matani	Mata'i	Makani	Matangi	Matangi	Matangi	Matangi	Matangi	Matangi	Thangi
Light	Mannu	Maramarama	Malamalama	Ao	Malamalama	Malamalama	Malamalama	Ao	Maua	Rarama
Darkness	Potana	Poiri	Poeleelo	Pouri	Pouri	Pouriuri	Pouriuri	Po	Fakapouri	Bu tapu
North		Apato'a	Akau			Matu	Malangi		Tokelau	Vua likai
South		Apato'erau	Kukulu hema			Tonga	Malangi		Potubonga	Theva
East		Tehitia o te ra	Hikina			Sasae	Tokilau		Hahake	Thake
West		Te to'a to'a o te ra	Komohana			Sisifo	Maluifohifo		Hihifo	Ra
Cold	Anu	Maariri	Anu	Anu	Makariri	Ma'alili	Makalili	Ma'a lili	Mokoiia	Lilina
Heat	Vea	Mahanahana	Uela	Ma'ana	Vevela	Vevela	Mafana	Vevela	Mafana	Katakata
Mountain	Mauna	Mau'a	Knahini	Maunga	Maunga	Maunga	Mounga	Maunga	Mounga	Ulunivanua
Land	Fenua	Fenua	Honua	Enua	Henua	Fanua	Fonua	Fenua	Fonua	Vanua
Sand	Onetai	One	One	'One	One	Oneone	Oneone	Oneone	Oneone	Nokotuu
Stone	Kea	O fa'i	Pohaku	Toka	Fatu	Ma'a	Maka	Fatu	Maka	Vatu
Water	Vai	Vai & pape	Uai	Vai	Vai	Vai	Vai	Vai	Vai	Wai
Sea	Tai	Miti	Kai	Tai	Tai	Sami	Tahi	Moana	Tahi	Wasawasa
Tree	Akau	Raau	Laau	Rakau	Lakau	La'au	Lakau	Lakau	Akau	Uto
Bread Fruit	Mei	Uru	Aenei	Kulu		Ulu	Me	Talo	Mei	Uto
Taro	Tao	Taro	Kalo	Taro		Talo	Talo	Talo	Taro	Ndalo
Cocoa Nut	Echi	Haari	Niu	Niu	Ni	Niu	Niu	Niu	Niu	Niu
Yam	Buauhi	Uhi	Uhi	Ui		Ufi	Ufi		Ufi	Uvi
Sugar Cane	To	To	Ko	To		Tolo	To	To	To	Ndovu
Banana	Meika	Mei'a	Maia	Meka		Fa'i	Futi		Hopa	Vundi
Canoe	Vaka	Vaa	Kaa	Vaka	Vaka	Va'a	Vaka	Vaka	Vaka	Wanka leya
Ship	Tepe (ship)	Pahi	Ua'a	Pai	Pahi	Vaa papa langi	Vaka tonga	Folau tana	Vaka papa langi	Waka
Fish	Ika	Ia	Lawaia	Ika	Ika	I'a	Ika	Ika	Ika	Ika
Pig	Puaka	Pua'a	Puaka	Puaka		Pua'a	Puaka		Puaka	Kori
Dog	Nuhe	Uri	Ilio	Mango		Uri			Kuri	Ton
Fowl	Moa	Moa	Manu	Moa	Moa	Moa	Moa	Moa	Moa	Ngakobakoa
Ant	Ko	Ro	Nonanona	Lo	Loa	Loi	Lo	Lo	Loa	Kalavo
Rat	Kiore	Iore	Iole	Kiore	Kiore	Imoa	Kumaa	Kiuoa	Kuma	Bokawanga
Fire	Ahi	Auahi	Ahi	A'i	Ahi	Afi	Afi	Afi	Afi	Yalo
House	Fae	Fare	Hale	Are	Fare	Fale	Fale	Fale	Fale	Ngasau
Arrow	Kouin	Ohe	Puapana			Aufana	Kaufana		Kahe	Dakai
Bow	Para	Fana	Kakaka			Aufana	Kaufana	Fana	Akau	Nairran
Club	Akau toa	Raau	Neua	Lupo	Tuki	Uatongi	Lakau		Tao	Moto
Spear	Pakeo	Mabae	Iho	Tao	Tao	Tao	Tao	Tao	Abo	Singa
Day	Ao	Ao	Laoloa	La	Po	Ao	Aho	Po	Aho	Levu
Night	Po	Po & Ru'i	Po	Po	Po	Po	Po	Po	Po	Lailai
Great	Nui	Rahi	Nui	Mata	Rahi	Tele	Lahi	Tele	Lahi	Voleka
Small	Iti	Iti	Uuku	Ngiti	Iti	Itiiti	Tote	Iisiu	Iki	Yawa
Near	Atuata	Fatata	Kokoke	Vaitata	Epiri	Latalata	Tata mai	Late mai	Ofi	Vinaka
Distant	Mamao	Tentea e	Loihiaku	Mamao	Mamao	Mamao	Mamao	Mamao	Lelei	Tha
Good	Meitai	Maita'i	Maikai	Meitaki	Kino	Leanga	Kelea	Lesunga	Kovi	Von
Bad	Pe	Ino	Ino	Kino	Poa	Leanga	Koa	Fott	Kasi	Mandra
Few	Hou	Opi & hou	Hou	Ou	Tahito	Tuai	Pepe		Mamao	Duaudana

churches were left to their own resources....So long as native churches have foreign pastors so long

---

[174] Report quoted in Lovett, *The History of the London Missionary Society*, 399, 402.

[175] William Nicol Lawrence quoted in Lange, *Island Ministers*, 75.

[176] Lange, *Island Ministers*, 74.

[177] George Barden quoted in Murray, *Forty Years' Mission Work in Polynesia and New Guinea*, 110-111.

Improbable Voices
489

will they remain weak and dependent."[178]   Perhaps the best example of a missionary who appreciated indigenous people and culture was William Wyatt Gill, who worked on Mangaia and Rarotonga between 1845 and 1883. He noted how much the Cook Islanders wished to preserve their history and knowledge of pre-Christian songs and stories. He wrote,

> Two courses lay open to me—either to ignore their ancient religion and their undoubted history or to study both for their own sake, and especially with a view to understand native thought and feeling. I chose the latter course.[179]

This gave the missionary considerable insight and made him more sympathetic to the native pastors, whose assistance he lauded. Gill was especially grateful for Ta'unga's work as a linguist, asserting with confidence that Ta'unga was "acknowledged to be the best living authority on the Rarotongan language." On the publication of a new translation of the Bible, Gill noted, "If my work is a success, it is due mainly to the untiring aid of Ta'unga."[180] As the end of the nineteenth century approached, the most progressive missionaries went so far as to question the integrity of the whole LMS endeavor in the Pacific. They had seen the havoc the missionary and commercial impact had brought. As Chalmers wrote in 1890,

> Isn't it sad that a people so free, kind, and truly attractive should be dying out? Strong drink is a fearful agent, but it cannot alone be blamed for the sad decrease [in population]. I blame clothing, change in housing, and the introduction of foreign food as much as strong drink. I feel persuaded were these natives to return to the manner of living their forefathers they would again increase. The introduced changes are too great.[181]

Ta'unga would not have agreed with this assessment. As he admonished the students at the Takamoa Institute in 1862,

> Be strong, every one of you, do not be indolent, that you may be men of courage—fearless warriors, but not with the weapons of war. Arouse the remaining islands, that the kingdom of grace may spread rapidly throughout this world. Let us do the work of Jesus while we still have a little life. We who have pioneered this work are now aging. Our time in short and our end is uncertain. It is up to God. Pray to God, all of you, on our behalf, so that our remaining life may be lengthened and we may continue the work together.[182]

For Ta'unga, eternal salvation was worth any earthly cost.

[178] James Chalmers quoted in Lovett, *James Chalmers,* 109.
[179] William Wyatt Gill, *From Darkness to Light in Polynesia* (London: The Religious Tract Society, 1894), 8-9.
[180] William Wyatt Gill quoted in Lovett, *The History of the London Missionary Society,* 358.
[181] James Chalmers quoted in Lovett, *James Chalmers,* 369.
[182] Ta'unga quoted in R. G. and Marjorie Crocombe, *The Works of Ta'unga,* 134.

U

Walter Ulbricht

1893-1973

John Gunther was a well-known and respected mid-twentieth century journalist, who dedicated his career to helping Americans understand the world around them. In 1965, he published an anthology that featured his assessments of leading political figures from the previous thirty years with Hitler and Stalin, Mao and Chiang Kai-Shek, Gandhi and Tito, de Gaulle and Khrushchev all receiving the expected attention. Even lesser-known men like Léon Blum, Lázaro Cárdenas, and Kwame Nkrumah had long chapters about them, but East Germany's Walter Ulbricht did not.[1] He wasn't even mentioned in passing in the chapter about West Germany's Konrad Adenauer and Willy Brandt. This is telling, for only with the passage of time has the architect of the Berlin Wall emerged as one of the most intriguing figures of the decades surrounding World War II. In fact, Ulbricht was a master political strategist and organizer who sought to build a model socialist state for other nations to emulate.

Ulbricht grew up as the oldest child in an atheist, pacifist family of five in a rather seedy neighborhood of Leipzig—a city with greater Leftist support than other parts of Germany.[2] His father was an artisan tailor who struggled to thrive in an increasingly industrialized Germany. The family's economic circumstances meant that in their tenement flat they proudly hung a portrait of Socialist Democratic Party (SPD) leader August Bebel, rather than one of Kaiser Wilhelm II.[3] As a

---

[1] See John Gunther, *Procession* (New York: Harper & Row, 1965). In addition to the figures mentioned above, Gunther included profiles of well-known figures of Kemal Ataturk, Winston Churchill, Dwight D. Eisenhower, Emperor Hirohito, Douglas MacArthur, Benito Mussolini, Gamal Abdel Nasser, Jawaharlal Nehru, Franklin Delano Roosevelt, Haile Selassie, Albert Schweitzer, Leon Trotsky, Harry S. Truman, and Earl Warren. He even included profiles of figures many Americans would have trouble identifying today, such as Great Britain's Alec Frederick Douglas-Home, Liberia's William Vacanarat Shadrach Tubman, Morocco's Thami El Glaoui, Tunisia's Sidi Mohammed Lamine Pasha, and Romania's Magda Lupescu. For information on Gunther and his career, see Ken Cuthbertson, *Inside: The Biography of John Gunther* (New York: Bonus Books, 1992).
[2] Sean Dobson, *Authority and Upheaval in Leipzig, 1910-1920: The Story of a Relationship* (New York: Columbia University Press, 2001), 87-89.
[3] Carola Stern, *Ulbricht: A Political Biography* (New York: Frederick A. Praeger Publishers, 1965), 4-8. As the first biography of Ulbricht in English, this book remains an important source of information on Ulbricht's early life,

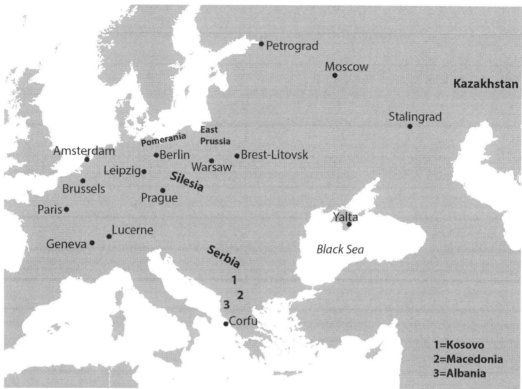

schoolboy, Ulbricht was bookish and shy. The family could not afford to continue his education after eight years of schooling, so he became an apprentice to a cabinetmaker, for whom he worked ten-hour days. Upon completing his apprenticeship in May 1911, Ulbricht and two friends set out to explore the world and satisfy their wanderlust. Their travels blended the traditions of early modern journeymen roaming in search of work and those of idealistic, turn-of-the-century hiking clubs embracing the outdoors.[4] During his travels that summer and fall, Ulbricht visited Bohemia, Austria, Bavaria, Switzerland, and Italy. He spent the subsequent winter working as a cabinetmaker near Lucerne.[5] At some point in his travels, Ulbricht contracted diphtheria, which damaged his larynx and left him with an unpleasant falsetto voice for the rest of his life,[6] but he was strong enough in the spring to continue on to Geneva and Amsterdam. He returned to Leipzig in early fall 1912.

Ulbricht's political life began at this point, although near the end of his life he claimed to have had class consciousness and been a "member of the Socialist working class youth movement from

---

but Stern's anti-communist Cold War bias tints her account almost as much as the official East German biographies do. Stern was an agent for the United States' Counter Intelligence Corps after World War II. She left East Germany for West Berlin in 1951.

[4] Ulbricht was a member of the Young Workers' Education Association. Other examples of hiking organizations include Die Naturfreunde or Nature Friends, which had 200,000 largely socialist members in Austria, Germany, and Switzerland in the early twentieth century; and the Wandervogel Committee for Schoolboys' Rambles, which was a Romantic middle-class hiking society with nationalistic overtones. See Rebecca Solnit, *Wanderlust: A History of Walking* (New York: Viking Penguin, 2000), 155-158.

[5] Stern, *Ulbricht*, 9, 11.

[6] Frederick Kempe, *Berlin 1961: Kennedy, Khrushchev, and the Most Dangerous Place on Earth* (New York: Berkley Books, 2011), 94.

1908 onwards."[7] His decision to join the SPD wasn't unexpected, given his family's tradition, sociopolitical circumstances, and orientation, but he quickly left it as a result of World War I. In August 1914, when the SPD's leader proclaimed the party's support for the war, Ulbricht saw the party as betraying everything for which socialism stood.[8] Holding true to the Marxist idea that the common interests of the proletariat transcended national boundaries, Ulbricht believed that the SPD had surrendered its principles to the interests of capital. It was an unforgivable betrayal for the pacifist Marxist. Tellingly, Ulbricht then chose to chart his own course. This was Ulbricht's first important political decision; it was also his first experience negotiating the landmines of party factionalism that would dominate his political career. Armed with his pacifist upbringing and Marxist conviction, Ulbricht began distributing anti-war pamphlets that fall. He was soon reported to the authorities.[9]

Ulbricht was drafted into the Imperial German Army on May 23, 1915 and received training as a wheelwright on account of his woodworking skills.[10] Supplying an army with wooden wagon wheels was particularly important on the Eastern Front, where the combatants never developed the complex trench system prevalent in France and Belgium. Instead, field position and maneuverability defined tactical strategy.[11] This made the wheelwright's job crucial for military operations. Ulbricht was assigned to the Serbian front in time for the Central Powers' campaign to knock Serbia out of the war in October and November 1915, but he seems to have devoted much

[7] Walter Ulbricht, *The Lessons of History and the Struggle of Peace* (Dresden: Verlag Zeit im Bild, [1970]), 5.

[8] The SPD leader was Hugo Haase. In a speech before the Reichstag, he said, "in the hour of danger, we will not leave our own Fatherland in the lurch….Guided by these principles, we herewith approve the desired war credits." Hugo Haase quoted in Heinrich August Winkler, *Germany: The Long Road West, Volume 1: 1789-1933* (New York: Oxford University Press, 2006), 301. Haase was personally opposed to the party's decision to support the war but felt an obligation to represent the majority view of the SPD leadership.

[9] Catherine Epstein, *The Last Revolutionaries: German Communists and Their Century* (Cambridge, Massachusetts: Harvard University Press, 2003), 20. In fact, the SPD leaders may have been the ones to report Ulbricht.

[10] Mario Frank, *Walter Ulbricht: eine deutsche Biografie* (Berlin: Siedler Verlag, 2001), 52. I am grateful to Dr. M.A. Claussen of the University of San Francisco and former Marin Academy colleague Karsten Windt for their assistance in translating portions of Frank's book for me.

[11] Norman Stone, *The Eastern Front, 1914-1917* (London: Hodder and Stoughton, 1975), 92.

of his attention toward political agitation. He secretly distributed revolutionary leaflets among the troops, and spent his time on leave lecturing Leipzig youth about worker solidarity and war resistance.[12] Such actions did not win Ulbricht the affection of his fellow soldiers, who repeatedly subjected him to humiliating military punishments as a result of his political convictions.[13] Ulbricht's words fell on deaf ears in part because the Austro-Hungarian, German, and Bulgarian offensive was so successful. By the end of 1915, the Central Powers had occupied all of Serbia, including Kosovo, and had forced the Serbian army to retreat over the Albanian mountains to be evacuated to the Greek island of Corfu.[14] Ulbricht spent much of the rest of the war in Macedonia, where he contracted malaria in October 1917. He then spent the next three months recovering in a field hospital.[15] He was eventually transferred to Galicia on the Eastern front, but when the Russians signed the Treaty of Brest-Litovsk* on March 3, 1918, Ulbricht joined the hundreds of thousands of German troops transferred to the trenches on the Western Front.[16] As his troop train neared Leipzig, Ulbricht leapt from the train and went AWOL, only to be caught a few days later. After completing his prison sentence, he was sent to Belgium and reassigned to the same unit with which he had served on the Eastern Front. Once again, he was arrested for possessing what officials deemed to be revolutionary propaganda. In early November 1918, Ulbricht escaped a temporary prison south of Brussels with the help of prison guards, and deserted the army for a second time. He spent the last days of the war trying to organize a workers' and soldiers' council before returning to Leipzig in November 1918.[17]

As a twenty-five-year old with a growing political conviction but little political party experience, Ulbricht found himself engulfed by the tumultuous political waters of the new Weimar Republic. It was a time when, as one American diplomat noted, "political opinion has been in a constant state of flux" with the parties of the radical left gaining strength, although ordinarily "Germany is not fertile soil for Bolshevism."[18] This atmosphere generated great optimism in Ulbricht. He joined the Independent Social Democratic Party of Germany (USPD) since he could not forgive the SPD for its stance during World War I. After the brutal murders of Rosa Luxemburg and Karl Liebknecht in January 1919, however, Ulbricht became increasingly involved with the party they founded, the Communist Party of Germany (KPD).[19] Ulbricht formally joined the KPD in

---

[12] Frank, *Walter Ulbricht,* 53.

[13] Epstein, *The Last Revolutionaries,* 20.

[14] H. P. Willmott, *World War I* (New York: Dorling Kindersley Publishing, 2003), 120-121. The Serbs fought off the first three campaigns against them, all in 1914.

[15] Frank, *Walter Ulbricht,* 53.

[16] On November 1, 1917, the number of German troops on the Western Front was 3.25 million, but by April 1, 1919, it was over 4 million men. The number of divisions grew from 147 to 191. See David Stevenson, *With Our Back to the Wall: Victory and Defeat in 1918* (Cambridge, Massachusetts: The Belknap Press of Harvard University Press, 2011), 36.

[17] This account of Ulbricht's last year of activities in the First World War blends details from several sources. See Epstein, *The Last Revolutionaries,* 20; Frank, *Walter Ulbricht*, 53; and Stern, *Ulbricht,* 14. The prison was near Charleroi, Belgium.

[18] Ellis Loring Dresel, "Report of a Journey to Germany by Ellis Loring Dresel and Lithgow Osborne to the American Commission to Negotiate Peace," May 10, 1919, Box 1, Ellis Loring Dresel Papers, Hoover Institution Archives, Stanford University.

[19] Luxemburg and Liebknecht originally founded the Groupe Internationale, but it subsequently changed its name to the Spartacus League in 1916. After the war, Luxemburg and Liebknecht founded the Kommunistische Partei Deutschlands (KPD) on December 31, 1918. See Elżbieta Ettinger, *Rosa Luxemburg: A Life* (Boston: Beacon Press, 1986), 195, 241-242.

December 1920,[20] having witnessed the inability of the Left to coordinate a national general strike. He had also seen how the bourgeoisie* successfully secured its political and economic position, and how essential it was to have military support to secure general order.[21] These were lessons Ulbricht would never forget.

Ulbricht's greatest strengths lay in his organizational skills and in his uncanny ability to remember names, faces, and the details of people's lives, even decades after he met them.[22] He used these strengths, as well as his willingness to follow instructions from his superiors carefully, to win appointment as the KPD district secretary for Thuringia in late March 1921. He moved to Jena without his wife and daughter[23] and began to attend key party events and meetings, including the Fourth Congress of the Communist International or Comintern. Convened in Petrograd on November 5, 1922 and moved to Moscow four days later, the Fourth Congress was where Ulbricht

---

[20] Epstein, *The Last Revolutionaries,* 20-21, 23. Carola Stern says that Ulbricht was at the founding meeting of the Leipzig chapter of the KPD in January 1919 and implies that he was a member at that point. See Stern, *Ulbricht,* 21.

[21] While there were regional strikes throughout Germany in February 1919, these strikes did not have sufficient coordination to present a united front to the Weimar government. The bourgeois counterstrikes included doctors, pharmacists, shopkeepers, civil servants, and university faculties. On May 10-11, 1919, Major General Georg Maercker occupied Leipzig, imposed martial law, and arrested all USPD and union leaders. See Dobson, *Authority and Upheaval in Leipzig,* 238, 244-245, 252, 262, 264, and 292.

[22] Kempe, *Berlin 1961*, 95.

[23] Stern, *Ulbricht*, 128-129. Martha Ulbricht was a seamstress, who remained in Leipzig with the daughter, Dorle, through the war. Ulbricht sent her money regularly until the Nazi seizure of power in 1933. He divorced Martha in 1951.

met Lenin.[24] The personal connection to the founder of the Soviet Union gave the young German Communist a heightened sense of legitimacy that he utilized throughout his life. Ulbricht also witnessed how Lenin justified his New Economic Policy* and with it, the return to a market economy. He watched Lenin account for past mistakes and make tactical compromises. He heard Lenin say that "our economic offensive…had run too far ahead" because the USSR had not provided adequate resources to the masses. This made the "direct transition to purely socialist forms, to purely socialist distribution… beyond our available strength." Ulbricht took note as Lenin said, "We have only just begun to learn, but are learning so methodically that we are certain to achieve good results."[25] From the Fourth Congress, Ulbricht learned that once the Communists were in control, it was permissible to adjust tactics in the process of building a socialist state. The overarching goal did not change, but the means for attaining that goal could change, if political and economic circumstances demanded it. Compromises might be made as long one never lost sight of the final destination. This was the essential lesson Ulbricht internalized from his first trip to Moscow and his one and only encounter with Lenin.

It would be decades, however, before Ulbricht was in power and could express such strategic flexibility. The delay was due in part to Stalin's rise to power, the Comintern's increasing insistence that its directives be obeyed, and the fractiousness of the KPD during the 1920s. As a result of an inner-party power struggle in 1923 and 1924, in which he bet on the wrong horse and lost his seat on the Central Committee, Ulbricht learned that he was better off adhering to Moscow's wishes than articulating an independent voice.[26] His mentor became Ernst Thälmann, a charismatic KPD delegate from Hamburg, who was elected into the Comintern's leadership at its Fifth Congress in June and July 1924. Thälmann became chairman of the KPD in September 1925 because of Stalin's support.[27] Thälmann's unquestioned loyalty to Moscow led him to purge the KPD of independent intellectuals, who might challenge policies on ideological grounds; to refuse any cooperation with the SPD, even if that delayed the revolution, because all bourgeois parties possessed "more or less a fascist character"; and to support Stalin's policy of Socialism in One Country,* which put the needs of the USSR first.[28] Thälmann's election allowed Ulbricht to return to office as well, for he supported the official party line carefully. In 1928, he was elected as one of Westphalia's representatives to the Reichstag, and, in 1929, he became the KPD district secretary for Berlin and Brandenburg. This put him in the national spotlight, as was true for his Nazi counterpart, Joseph Goebbels. While these two district party officials on opposite ends of the political spectrum made common cause during a Berlin transit strike in November 1932, they more typically railed against each other. On January 22, 1931, for example, a debate between Ulbricht and Goebbels ended in a

[24] Hope M. Harrison, *Driving the Soviets up the Wall: Soviet-East German Relations, 1953-1961* (Princeton, New Jersey: Princeton University Press, 2005), 14.
[25] Vladimir Ilyich Lenin, "Five Years of the Russian Revolution and the Prospects of the World Revolution Report to the Fourth Congress of the Communist International, November 13, 1922," *Marxist Internet Archive*, accessed February 4, 2020, https://www.marxists.org/archive/lenin/works/1922/nov/04b.htm
[26] The KPD dispute was between those on the right (led by Heidrich Brandler, who believed in cooperating with the SPD and using parliamentary means to achieve revolutionary change), and those on the left (led by Ruth Fischer and Arkadi Maslow, who saw any cooperation with the "bourgeois" SPD as a betrayal of the working class and who advocated direct action to achieve social change). Ulbricht initially sided with Brandler, who was replaced by Fischer and Maslow in 1924. See Stern, *Ulbricht*, 26-27; and Epstein, *The Last Revolutionaries*, 22-24.
[27] Russel Lemmons, *Hitler's Rival: Ernst Thälmann in Myth and Memory* (Lexington, Kentucky: University Press of Kentucky, 2013), 37.
[28] Lemmons, *Hitler's Rival*, 44-46.

riot after the Communists tried to prevent Goebbels from speaking by singing the "The Internationale" at the end of Ulbricht's opening remarks. Several days later, after the murder of two KPD members by National Socialist thugs, Ulbricht stood in the Reichstag and accused Goebbels and the Berlin police chief of conspiring to destroy the unemployed, and urged Communists to defend themselves.[29]   The two parties would fight at the polls and in the streets for the next two years.

~

On February 7, 1933, forty members of the KPD leadership secretly met at a riverside restaurant outside of Berlin. In the aftermath of Hitler's appointment as the Chancellor eight days before, Thälmann admitted that the Communists had underestimated the danger the Nazis posed and called for the creation of a united front with the Social Democrats and various trade unionists to lead a General Strike against the new government. After a decade of refusing to work with the SPD or any other group, Thälmann asked the KPD to reverse course completely and join a broad anti-Hitler coalition. His call was months, if not years, too late. This became abundantly clear when Ulbricht got word in the middle of Thälmann's remarks that the meeting's secrecy had been compromised and that the Nazis were en route to arrest the KPD leadership. The meeting broke up and everyone, including Ulbricht, went into hiding.[30] Thälmann was located and arrested in early March. He joined over 100,000 other Communists in Nazi prisons and concentration camps by year's end.[31] Other KPD leaders, including Wilhelm Pieck, established the headquarters for the now-exiled German Communist Party in Paris in May 1933, but Ulbricht remained in Germany as the party's local Operational Director, leading resistance efforts within Germany and maintaining contact with Pieck through letters passed by secret curriers.[32] In October 1933, Ulbricht's Berlin landlord confronted him with a newspaper that identified the him as a man wanted by the state. Ulbricht fled to Paris. He was lucky to have escaped.

By September 1934, Ulbricht and Pieck were stationed in Moscow. They were the first KPD leaders to learn of Stalin's decision to adopt a United Front strategy against fascism along the lines of the one Thälmann had articulated before his arrest. At the Comintern's Seventh World Congress a year later, the policy was formally adopted.[33]   Henceforth, as the general secretary of the Comintern told the delegates, "establishing unity of action of all sections of the working class in the

[29] Ralf Georg Reuth, *Goebbels*, Krishna Winston (trans.) (New York: Harcourt Brace & Company, 1993), 125-126, 155.

[30] Epstein, *The Last Revolutionaries*, 45-46; and Lemmons, *Hitler's Rival*, 59-60.

[31] Epstein, *The Last Revolutionaries*, 47.

[32] Jean-Michel Palmier, *Weimar in Exile: The Antifascist Emigration in Europe and America*, David Fernbach (trans.) (New York: Verso, 2006), 111-112, 301-302. Palmier says Ulbricht did this from Danzig, but Carola Stern says he was living in Berlin by July 1933. See Stern, *Ulbricht*, 54. One example of Ulbricht's agitation effort is an essay he wrote on February 15, 1933. In it he called for workers to join together regardless of political affiliation to take direct action rather than waiting for detailed instructions. This was necessary, Ulbricht argued, because Hitler's government was far stronger than the Brüning government had been. See Walter Ulbricht, "Everything for the Anti-Fascist United Front," *Whither Germany? Speeches and Essays on the National Question* (Dresden, Germany: Zeit im Bild Publishing House, 1966), 75-79.

[33] Epstein, *The Last Revolutionaries*, 60-61.

struggle against fascism" was of paramount importance.[34] As Pieck reiterated in October 1935, the KPD may have overestimated the readiness of the masses for revolution, but workers could still join with other political factions in a unified struggle against fascism.[35] But there was a difference between what was said and what was actually done: the KPD did not cooperate effectively with other leftist groups. Ulbricht, for example, purposefully thwarted the overtures of potential allies in Paris, and he was quite inflexible when he met with the SPD leadership in Prague in November 1935 to negotiate a common platform.[36] His obstinance derived in part from his faithfulness to Lenin's doctrine. In *The State and Revolution* (1917), Lenin had held that "petty-bourgeois democracy is never able to understand that the state is the organ of the rule of a definite class which *cannot* be reconciled with its antipode (the class opposite to it)."[37] In other words, in the struggle for power it was not possible for Leninist Communists to compromise; as the vanguard for revolution, they had to assume the sole leadership position. This unwillingness to form an effective Popular Front with socialists, centrists, and other non-fascists directly led to the fascist victory in the Spanish Civil War and the expansion of Stalin's Great Purge in the Soviet Union.

Stalin's intolerance for any deviation in interpretation or independence in action meant that between 1930 and 1938 over 3.8 million people in the Soviet Union were arrested for supposedly betraying revolutionary ideals or threatening the world's only Communist state. Victims of Stalin's vindictiveness included 1.8 million party members who lost their party memberships; over 33,000 military officers who were demoted; the wives of these men who were sent to labor camps for up to eight years; more than 767,000 kulaks* and other agrarians, who were put in gulags or were killed; and 350,000 foreign nationals, such as Koreans, Iranians, and Poles, who were sentenced to forced labor or death. At the height of the terror in 1937 and 1938, 87% of those arrested received sentences and 52% of those sentences resulted in executions.[38] Stalin justified these acts by arguing that as socialism evolved, the class struggle had intensified and the nation had not kept pace with these changes. Instead, officials had become complacent. Stalin argued that "leading comrades" had failed to discern the presence of "diversionists, spies and murderers" in their midst and had been so "naïve that at times they themselves assisted in promoting the agents" of hostile foreign governments to key posts.[39] Such language was sufficiently vague to include anyone Stalin wanted to eliminate.

Another group that drew Stalin's attention were the German Communists living in the Soviet Union. As with Stalin's other purges, it began with a particular target—those working in war-related industries—but soon it spread to include those even suspected of having close contacts with Germans. Eventually, 76% of the 55,000 who were arrested were shot.[40] Even Ulbricht did not

[34] Georgi Dimitrov, "Unity of the Working Class against Fascism: Concluding Speech before the Seventh World Congress of the Communist International," August 14, 1935, *Marxist Internet Archive*, accessed February 4, 2020, https://www.marxists.org/reference/archive/dimitrov/works/1935/unity.htm#s1

[35] Gregory W. Sandford, *From Hitler to Ulbricht: The Communist Reconstruction of East Germany, 1945-1946* (Princeton, New Jersey: Princeton University Press, 1983), 5.

[36] Eric D. Weitz, *Creating German Communism, 1890-1990: From Popular Protests to Socialist State* (Princeton, New Jersey: Princeton University Press, 1997), 296; and Palmier, *Weimar in Exile*, 349-350.

[37] V. I. Lenin, "The State and Revolution," *Essential Works of Lenin*, Henry M. Christman (ed.) (New York: Dover Publications, 1987), 274.

[38] Robert Gellately, *Stalin's Curse: Battling for Communism in War and Cold War* (New York, Alfred A. Knopf, 2013), 35-42.

[39] Josef Stalin quoted in Robert Conquest, *The Great Terror: A Reassessment* (New York: Oxford University Press, 1990), 177.

[40] Gellately, *Stalin's Curse*, 44.

escape scrutiny. In late 1937, the Comintern recalled him from Paris to face charges of Trotskyism.*[41] Ulbricht saved himself by offering savvy answers to the questions posed and by demonstrating his loyalty to Stalin's purification quest: he gave evidence against fellow KPD members, ending many of his rivals' careers, if not lives.[42] Ulbricht betrayed his German comrades because he understood that as long as Stalin dominated European communism, any deviation from Stalin's policy was politically, if not personally, fatal. Because resistance was futile, the only choice was between his life and somebody else's; Ulbricht chose his own and hoped to be remembered as something more than a martyr.

Ulbricht's loyalty to Stalin was so firm in this period that when the Third Reich and the USSR signed a non-aggression pact in August 1939, shocking the world, Ulbricht did not waver in his support. He did not object, for example, when Stalin surrendered several hundred German Communists to Nazi officials at Hitler's request.[43] Instead, he quickly adjusted to the new line of thought, arguing that the emerging war in Western Europe was an imperialist war that would destroy capitalism; the USSR was wise to avoid it.[44] In February 1940, Ulbricht stated that British imperialism was "the most reactionary force in the world." It was a greater threat to "democratic liberties" than Nazism.[45] He also convinced despairing KPD émigrés a year that the war's destruction would usher in revolutions across Europe and that it was their job to help prepare for this inevitability.[46] Even when Hitler launched Operation Barbarossa in June 1941, exposing Stalin's gross miscalculations, Ulbricht maintained his absolute support for the Soviet dictator. During this part of his life, Ulbricht was the consummate foot soldier.

Although never a dynamic speaker, Ulbricht spent much of the war trying to hearten, educate, persuade, and indoctrinate various audiences. The Comintern issued orders to Ulbricht and Wilhelm Pieck to begin assisting the Red Army's Political Administration in developing a propaganda campaign to target and discourage Nazi soldiers. This campaign included radio broadcasts, which were overseen by Ulbricht, and the publication of a multitude of written materials.[47] Typically printed on either half or quarter-sheets of paper, the flyers presented images of warm, well-fed, and freshly-shaven German POWs playing music and cards, writing letters home, or relaxing the day away. Others showed cartoons of orphaned German children, incapacitated German veterans, and cheating wives spending elegant nights with Nazi officials.

---

[41] The person who made the charge against Ulbricht was Willi Münzenberg, a German Communist propagandist. Ulbricht and Münzenberg had a long-standing personal dislike for one another. See Sean McMeekin, *The Red Millionaire: A Political Biography of Willy Münzenberg, Moscow's Secret Propaganda Tsar in the West* (New Haven, Connecticut: Yale University Press, 2003), 278, and 289, EBSCOhost.

[42] Stern, *Ulbricht*, 77; and Epstein, *The Last Revolutionaries*, 62.

[43] Anne Applebaum, *Iron Curtain: The Crushing of Eastern Europe, 1944-1956* (New York: Doubleday, 2012), 43.

[44] Weitz, *Creating German Communism*, 302.

[45] Walter Ulbricht quoted in Roger Moorhouse, *The Devils' Alliance: Hitler's Pact with Stalin, 1939-1941* (New York: Basic Books, 2014), 114-115.

[46] Applebaum, *Iron Curtain*, 56.

[47] Epstein, *The Last Revolutionaries*, 83.

There were even cartoons comparing Napoleon's and Hitler's invasions of Russia, surrounded by the skulls of the dead. Many of the flyers were signed by Ulbricht, Pieck and other surviving German Communist leaders in an effort to support the idea that the campaign was an authentically German one.[48] One leaflet from 1942 noted that "Hundreds of thousands of corpses of German soldiers cover the battlefields from the North Cape to the Black Sea" and then said,

> You have been told that you must fight and sacrifice for Germany because Germany is 'a state of the people'....But do you govern the country? Do you make the laws? Do you decide on the fateful questions of Germany, on war and peace? Do you own all the riches of a country which were created by the work of your hands and the work of your fathers and grandfathers?....You can see from all of this that the greatest disaster for Germany is that it is not the people who are master in their house, that is not the people who have to decide in Germany, but a handful of highly placed rich men...[who] make war with your hands to subjugate and plunder foreign peoples....It does not matter to them that in doing so millions of German people perish, for they calculate that for every dead German they receive half a dozen other cheap workers. Your sacrifices at the front are senseless. You are fighting for a lost cause. Hitler can never subdue the mighty 200 million people of the Soviet Union defending a homeland which really belongs to them....You are fighting against yourselves, for you are fighting for the cause of your worst enemies...for servitude....Take aim at the greedy and bloodthirsty German plutocrats! Overthrow Hitler and his clique!...Make yourself masters in the German house![49]

At other points in the war, Ulbricht took his message directly to a targeted audience. In December 1941, for example, Ulbricht traveled from Moscow to German POW camps in Kazakhstan in order to identify potential defectors,.[50] In late 1942, he was on the front lines at Stalingrad, leading trucks mounted with loudspeakers blaring propaganda messages. This was dangerous work since such trucks were obvious targets for Nazi hand grenades. It was also frustrating work since there were few results, at least initially.[51] This led Nikita Khrushchev to poke fun at Ulbricht on Christmas Eve for having not earned his dinner since there had not been any defections that day.[52] Insulted but not discouraged, Ulbricht redoubled his efforts. As the tide of the war began to shift after Stalingrad, Ulbricht recruited a small group of lower-ranking Wehrmacht officers to join what became the National Committee for Free Germany (NKFD).[53]

---

[48] See Klaus Kirchner Collection, February-May, 1942, Box 2, Items 846-926 and 1212; Box 3, Item 1515, Hoover Institution Archives, Stanford University.

[49] Walter Ulbricht, "Who is Master in the German House?," *Whither Germany? Speeches and Essays on the National Question*, 109-112.

[50] Wolfgang Leonard, *Child of the Revolution*, C.M. Woodhouse (trans.) (London: Ink Links Ltd., 1979), 148.

[51] Epstein, *The Last Revolutionaries*, 84.

[52] Harrison, *Driving the Soviets up the Wall*, 58-59.

[53] Epstein, *The Last Revolutionaries*, 84. Although some 2000-3000 POWs completed anti-fascist training each year, the NKFD proved unable to attract many high-ranking Nazi officers. See Weitz, *Creating German Communism*, 307. One exception came later in the war, when Field Marshal Paulus spoke on *Freies Deutschland* radio in August 1944, saying "Germany must rid itself of Adolph Hitler and get a new head of government to end the war and bring about circumstances that will enable our people to go on living and enter into peaceful, yes friendly, relations with our present enemies." Friedrich Paulus quoted in Wilhelm Adam and Otto Rühle,

Formed in mid-July 1943, the NKFD brought German POWs and German Communist émigrés together to spearhead propaganda efforts to promote popular uprisings at home, encourage troop desertions on the front, and anticipate the postwar period.[54] Ulbricht's crucial task during this period was to develop a plan for the political leadership of postwar Germany.[55]

The Committee's leading members understood that Germany's population had been bombarded with anti-Communist messages since 1933, and that these messages had to be taken into account when shaping a postwar strategy. The Battle of Stalingrad made this even more vital since the Nazi defeat resulted in an increased intensity in Nazi propaganda. Joseph Goebbels, for example, declared in February 1943 that "the hordes from the steppe" represented a "terrifying historical threat" that drove "all previous threats to the Occident into the shadows." He told Germans that Jews would then hurl "the world into deepest disorder, thereby bringing about the destruction of cultures thousands of years old, in which it never shared."[56] Such messages, as well as the postwar relationship between the Allies, convinced Stalin that the NKFD's first goal should not be the establishment of a socialist state, but rather a program of denazification in cooperation with Western allies.[57] In fact, the NKFD's goal became to provide Germany a "strong democratic constitution…the complete abolition of all laws based on national and social hatred; a re-establishment and broadening of political rights and social services; economic and commercial freedom" and the prosecution of Nazi war criminals.[58] This postwar strategy led Stalin to dissolve the Comintern in May 1943. As a member of the Comintern's Executive Committee, Ulbricht helped draft the resolutions and construct the language to justify the action.[59]

When he was not traveling during the war, Ulbricht lived in Moscow's Hotel Lux with the other members of the Working Commission of the National Committee for Free Germany and hundreds of other leading Communist émigrés. Despite its name, the residence was far from luxurious. The conditions were poor, with infestations of rats and cockroaches, communal showers and kitchens, and the smell of diapers and disinfectant permeating the hallways. Stalin's secret police monitored all movements and conversations with diligence. They routinely removed residents from their rooms at night in order to torture them for information.[60] In fact, by fall 1939, 170 Hotel Lux residents had disappeared, leaving 600 others who were intensely, if forcibly, loyal to Stalin.[61] Room assignments at the Hotel Lux were made on the basis of an émigré's importance, and by January

---

With Paulus at Stalingrad, Tony Le Tissier (trans.) (Barnsley, South Yorkshire: Pen and Sword Military, 2015), 262, EBSCOhost.

[54] Leonard, *Child of the Revolution,* 259-260. Leonard says that prior to the Tehran Conference between Stalin, Churchill, and Roosevelt (November 28-December 1, 1943), the focus of the NFKD was to get Wehrmacht officers to withdraw from Soviet territory and to win an honorable peace for Germany. As the military situation changed, the NFKD increasingly focused on postwar considerations.

[55] Epstein, *The Last Revolutionaries,* 84

[56] Joseph Goebbels quoted in Reuth, *Goebbels,* 315-316.

[57] Sandford, *From Hitler to Ulbricht,* 9, 13.

[58] Leonard, *Child of the Revolution,* 238-239.

[59] For information on the decision to dissolve the Comintern and the debate on the wording of the resolutions, see *Dimitrov and Stalin 1934-1943: Letters from the Soviet Archives,* Alexander Dallin and F. I. Firsov (eds.) (New Haven, Connecticut: Yale University Press, 2000), 226-251.

[60] Frank, *Walter Ulbricht,* 154-155. During the 1930s and 1940s, many of the world's leading communists lived at the Hotel Lux, including China's Zhou Enlai, Hungary's Mátyás Rákosi, Italy's Palmiro Togliatti, Vietnam's Ho Chi Minh, and Yugoslavia's Josip Broz Tito. See Salvi Luca, "Togliatti and the Hotel Lux." *World Affairs* 154, no. 3 (1992): 115-18, EBSCOhost.

[61] Moorhouse, *The Devils' Alliance,* 116.

1944 Ulbricht's living quarters reflected his status. He and his personal secretary (and girlfriend), Lotte Kuhn, lived in a prestigious ground floor room with a private shower, kitchen and telephone.[62]

The rapid advance of Soviet troops through the Ukraine and much of Poland in the first half of 1944, as well as Allied successes in Normandy and Italy, convinced the Working Commission of the National Committee for Free Germany that an adjustment to their postwar goals was both feasible and necessary. In August 1944, the Commission issued a revised "Action Program" that called for the expropriation of all Nazi property, the punishment of Nazi war criminals and war profiteers, and the nationalization of public utilities, banks, transportation, key industries, and major corporations.[63] This represented a significant shift from the organization's earlier policy, for it identified the first steps in transforming postwar Germany—regardless of what other political parties in Germany believed should happen. Stalin spoke publicly about a unified Germany, open elections and temporary zones of occupation, but for Ulbricht and Pieck only the creation of an imposed Communist state could break the Nazi contagion, and they were determined not to waste the opportunity the advancing Red Army provided.[64]

Having captured Warsaw on January 17, 1945 and crossed the Oder River into Germany later that month, the Soviets prepared for the final assault on Berlin. Capturing the capital and the area to the Elbe River was a central Soviet goal, for Stalin hoped to obtain uranium, scientific equipment, and atomic expertise prior to the American arrival.[65] Intelligence reports in Moscow had indicated that British forces were about to launch a campaign to take Berlin and that the Nazis were negotiating an independent peace with the Western Allies.[66] Although this intelligence was in error, Stalin believed the race for Berlin had to be won as quickly as was logistically possible. By mid-April, 2.5 million Soviet troops, 6,250 tanks, and 7,500 aircraft were positioned on the city's outskirts. On April 16, the Soviets launched more than a million rounds of artillery pieces at the defensive Nazi line in twenty-four hours, leaving many survivors so shell-shocked that they were incapable of fighting.[67] In houses 40 miles away, pictures fell off the walls.[68] But this largest Soviet bombardment of the war did not open the roads to Berlin. Instead, SS troops and members of the Hitler Youth continued intense street fighting in the center of the city until May 2, when the Nazis finally capitulated. The Soviets suffered 352,000 casualties in the sixteen-day battle.[69]

The city the Red Army captured was, in the words of German playwright Bertolt Brecht, "a pile of rubble outside Potsdam."[70] In fact, 90% of Berlin's buildings lay in ruins,[71] and, depending on the neighborhood, between a third and a half of the city's pre-war housing was uninhabitable.[72]

---

[62] Frank, *Walter Ulbricht*, 154-155. Lotte Kuhn (1903-2002) married Ulbricht in 1953.

[63] Sandford, *From Hitler to Ulbricht,* 15.

[64] Epstein, *The Last Revolutionaries,* 85.

[65] Antony Beevor, *The Fall of Berlin 1945* (New York: Viking, 2002), xxxiv, 138, 307.

[66] Gellately, *Stalin's Curse,* 109.

[67] Beevor, *The Fall of Berlin 1945,* 217. On April 16, 1945, Soviet troops fired 1,236,000 rounds.

[68] Antony Beevor, "Introduction," *A Woman in Berlin: Eight Weeks in the Conquered City, A Diary by Anonymous,* Philip Boehm (trans.) (New York: Henry Holt and Company, 2005), xiii.

[69] Beevor, *The Fall of Berlin 1945*, 365-366, 372; and Gellately, *Stalin's Curse,* 117. In the battle, 78,291 Soviet soldiers died and 274,184 Soviet soldiers were wounded.

[70] Bertolt Brecht quoted in Eli Ruben, *Amnesiopolis: Modernity, Space and Memory in East Germany* (New York: Oxford University Press, 2016), 20.

[71] Beevor, "Introduction," xv.

[72] Emily Pugh, *Architecture, Politics and Identity in Divided Berlin* (Pittsburgh, Pennsylvania: University of Pittsburgh Press, 2014), 31. Only 380,000 of the 1,562,000 apartments survived without damage. In East Berlin, one third of the domiciles built by 1939 had been destroyed. See Ruben, *Amnesiopolis,* 20.

There was little running water, electricity, or food. Competition for everything was exacerbated by the fact that Berlin had absorbed millions of German refugees from East Prussia, Silesia, and Pomerania fleeing the Soviet advance.[73] Common people plundered what they could, while economic and government officials fled west, taking with them knowledge, supplies, and records.[74] Many of the U-Bahn tunnels were under water, and 95 of the city's tram system had been destroyed.[75] Disease became an increasing problem as typhus, diphtheria, and tuberculosis plagued the city.[76] As one Allied news correspondent summarized:

> [Berlin] is a city of the dead. As a metropolis it has simply ceased to exist. Every house within miles of the center seems to have had its own bomb….The scene beggars description. "The *Blitz* of London was a bank holiday compared to this," one of my colleagues remarked….I have seen Stalingrad; I have lived through the London *Blitz*…but the scene of utter destruction, desolation, and death which meets the eye in Berlin…is something that almost baffles description….The town is literally unrecognizable….If Stalingrad, London, Guernica, Rotterdam, Coventry wanted avenging, they have had it…no mistake about it.[77]

But for Berlin's women, this wasn't nearly the worst of it. Berlin also became a horrifically dangerous place as Soviet troops raped indiscriminately and with impunity in the opening days of the occupation. Victims, often subjected to multiple assaults, were as young as ten and as old as eighty, and not a night went by without hearing the cries of brutalized women.[78] All told, as many as 130,000 Berlin women were raped by Soviet troops in the weeks, months, and years that followed.[79] The violence became so commonplace that women talked about their experiences openly and without shame. Many women decided that it was better to become the companion of a member of the officer corps in order to obtain a level of protection and minimize the risk of acts of sadism.[80]

---

[73] Richard J. Evans, *The Third Reich at War* (New York: Penguin Press, 2009), 711. In January 1945, 50,000 German refugees arrived by train a day. Nazi figures from February 1945 estimated that 8 million people fled west in advance of the Red Army.

[74] Sandford, *From Hitler to Ulbricht,* 23.

[75] Beevor, *The Fall of Berlin 1945,* 46, 419. The U-Bahn is the underground subway.

[76] For the whole Soviet Occupied Zone for 1945-1946, there were 149,580 cases of diphtheria; 129,000 cases of typhus; and 56,780 cases of tuberculosis. See Mary Fulbrook, *The People's State: East German Society from Hitler to Honecker* (New Haven, Connecticut: Yale University Press, 2008), 89.

[77] Harold King, "Devastated Berlin: Newsman Describes the Capital of the Third Reich as a Modern Carthage, May 9, 1945," *Hitler's Third Reich: A Documentary History,* Louis L. Snyder (ed.) (Chicago, Illinois: Nelson-Hall,1981), 537-538.

[78] Norman M. Naimark, *The Russians in Germany: A History of the Soviet Zone of Occupation, 1945-1949* (Cambridge, Massachusetts: The Belknap Press of Harvard University, 1995), 80, 82; and Alexandra Richie, *Faust's Metropolis: A History of Berlin* (New York: Carroll & Graf Publishers, Inc., 1998), 589-592.

[79] Beevor, "Introduction," xx.

[80] *A Woman in Berlin: Eight Weeks in the Conquered City, A Diary by Anonymous,* 64, 70-71, 115, 131, 147. Historians now know that the author was a journalist named Marta Hillers who lived in Berlin's Tempelhof District. See Kempe, *Berlin 1961,* 14-15.

~

Walter Ulbricht rarely drank,[81] but on April 29,1945, the day before Hitler committed suicide as Soviet troops approached his Berlin bunker, he raised a vodka toast with the nine members of his advance team in Wilhelm Pieck's apartment at the Hotel Lux.[82] His team's broad mission was to take "all necessary measures for normalizing the life of the German populace as quickly as possible" in cooperation with Soviet military officials.[83] This meant everything from reestablishing local political authority and restoring public services to rekindling a peacetime economy and resurrecting public faith. And this all needed to be done before the Americans, British, and French took possession of their zones in Berlin in accordance with the Yalta Agreements.[84] Ulbricht, now fifty-one, believed he was ready for the monumental task worthy of a toast. While Pieck ostensibly remained the KPD's chairman, his poor health and age meant that Ulbricht had become the man in charge.[85] Full of optimism and faith in his ability, Ulbricht deemed his time had come. In fact, he even expected Berliners to welcome his return as a proven anti-fascist leader.[86]

Early the next morning, Ulbricht and his team boarded a Douglas DC-3 with Soviet insignia for the flight west. The plane touched down on a military landing strip near the Oder River. The party clambered into an army truck for the two-hour drive to the Soviet military headquarters at Bruchmühle, 19 miles east of Berlin. There they were welcomed by one officer as the "new German government," as if all were a *fait accompli*.[87] On May 1, Ulbricht went into Berlin to assess the situation for himself. That night he told his team that "our task will be to build up German agencies for self-government in Berlin. We shall tour the various districts of Berlin and try to pick out those democratic Anti-Fascists who are best suited to build up a new German regime."[88] Working in pairs, each group would assume responsibility for a particular district and report on their findings and progress each night. When Ulbricht visited the Neukölln District, for example, he found a surviving group of KPD members already at work trying to provide basic services. Ulbricht greeted these go-getters coolly, making it clear that as the party's leader in Berlin, he would approve all decisions and personnel assignments.[89] Ulbricht can be criticized for his authoritarian bent in this situation, but few others in Germany appreciated the full complexity of situation. Not only did Ulbricht have to account for the presence of independently-minded Soviet military commanders who began running neighborhoods like personal fiefdoms,[90] but he also had to suppress the voices calling for an immediate Bolshevik revolution in Germany. Ulbricht knew that such talk would

---

[81] Stern, *Ulbricht*, 131.

[82] Leonard, *Child of the Revolution*, 287.

[83] Orders to Walter Ulbricht quoted in John Dornberg, *The Other Germany* (New York: Doubleday & Company, Inc., 1968), 29.

[84] Dornberg, *The Other Germany*, 32.

[85] John Rodden, *Textbook Reds: Schoolbooks, Ideology, and East Germany Identity* (University Park, Pennsylvania: Pennsylvania State University Press, 2006), 44. Pieck was born in 1876, making him 17 years older than Ulbricht. Pieck died in 1960. There has not been a significant biography written about him in English.

[86] Lemmons, *Hitler's Rival*, 119.

[87] Leonard, *Child of the Revolution*, 292-293.

[88] Walter Ulbricht quoted in Leonard, *Child of the Revolution*, 297.

[89] Leonard, *Child of the Revolution*, 299-300.

[90] Naimark, *The Russians in Germany*, 12-15.

panic the bourgeoisie and undermine the professed goal of establishing a multi-party democracy.[91] He realized that locally organized, anti-fascist relief committees were too politically diverse to be useful to him; they undercut Communist influence by including a broader spectrum of anti-fascists.[92] Ulbricht also had a profound mistrust of the Germans themselves since they had failed to support the KPD and prevent the rise of the Nazi party.[93] All this meant that Ulbricht thought he had to be unyielding if he had any hope of implementing his carefully calculated plan.

This plan centered on developing local government. Each of Berlin's twenty districts would have a mayor who represented the predominant class of the neighborhood: middle class districts would have bourgeois mayors, working class districts would have Social Democratic (SPD) ones. Furthermore, in Ulbricht's words, "at least half" of all the civil service posts in each district "must in any case be held by members of the bourgeoisie or Social Democrats."[94] The catch was that in every district the senior deputy mayor had to be a Communist and party members would administer the crucial areas of education, labor, personnel, police, and public safety for each district. Members of other political parties would handle the offices of church affairs, health, social welfare, and traffic.[95] As Ulbricht said, "It's got to look democratic, but we must have everything in our control."[96] When the city-wide government was inaugurated on May 17, 1945, a full month before the Western Allies entered Berlin to occupy their zones, Ulbricht had already ensured that the government's composition met his requirements. Of the sixteen leading members of the municipal administration, seven were Communists; these seven controlled the communications, financial, labor, personnel, police, and social welfare departments.[97]

The restoration of civic government, combined with the efforts of the Soviet military, facilitated measurable progress throughout Berlin. On May 11, new ration cards were issued that provided for surprisingly generous portions, passenger rail service was restored to some cities by May 14, and a special medical clinic for raped women was opened on May 23.[98] On May 13, radio broadcasts

resumed, and on May 18, an opera company gave a live, on-air performance that symbolically featured works by Beethoven and Tchaikovsky.[99] By the end of the month, many parts of the city had water and electricity restored to individual residences, and part of the S-Bahn returned to service on June 8.[100] This progress was replicated elsewhere: one month after liberation, the larger cities of eastern Germany had their electricity, water, sewage systems restored; access to food and medical care; and had cinemas and theaters

---

[91] Naimark, *The Russians in Germany,* 254-256.

[92] Sandford, *From Hitler to Ulbricht,* 27.

[93] Weitz, *Creating German Communism,* 319.

[94] Walter Ulbricht quoted in Leonard, *Child of the Revolution,* 303.

[95] Dornberg, *The Other Germany,* 32-33.

[96] Walter Ulbricht quoted in Leonard, *Child of the Revolution,* 303.

[97] Dornberg, *The Other Germany,* 33.

[98] *A Woman in Berlin,* 168, 178, 193-194, 212. The minimum amounts per person were 300g of bread, 400g of potatoes, 20g of meat, 9g of fat, 30g of a grain, and 15g of sugar a day. There were also monthly allowances for coffee, salt, and tea.

[99] Applebaum, *Iron Curtain,* 174-175. The opera company was Deutsche Oper Berlin.

[100] *A Woman in Berlin,* 198, 223, 247.

reopened.[101] In some respects, normal life returned—a Herculean accomplishment for Ulbricht, the Communist leaders in other cities, and their bureaucratic and technical supporters. As Ulbricht said at the fifteenth anniversary of the Democratic Republic of Germany (GDR) in 1964, "today this sounds so simple," but it was "not merely a matter of climbing out of the morass of hunger, want, and material and spiritual ruin. It was more a matter of establishing at the same time the basis for a social and national renewal."[102]

This success did not mean that all problems had ended. In some ways, they had grown. Boys prostituted themselves for food during the summer of 1945,[103] and Soviet troops continued to abuse women and take advantage of their position as conquerors. Ulbricht would not tolerate criticism of the Soviet army in public,[104] but on July 12 he and Pieck complained to Georgi Zhukov, the head of the Soviet Military Administration in Germany (SMA), about the on-going attacks on German citizens.[105] On August 3, Zhukov responded by issuing an order that reprimanded Soviet troops for "robbery," "physical violence," and "scandalous events," and noted that the soldiers' behavior adversely affected German public opinion of the Red Army.[106] The order did little good, however, and the problems persisted until the founding of the GDR in October 1949.[107]

The economic challenges were vast, in part because they were wholly intertwined with the political goal of denazification. Ulbricht held that those who had benefited economically from Nazi rule should be punished, and the only way to punish was to restructure the economy. He began with land reform because a consensus existed across the political spectrum that the great Junker* estates and the property of Nazi war criminals should be confiscated.[108] On June 25, 1945, Ulbricht told a convention of the now-reconstituted KPD that eastern Germany's large estates should be expropriated and this land redistributed to small farmers. He then rallied support for his plan in the countryside and advised local officials about the process he envisioned.[109] The seizure of all farms over 100 hectares began September 3. In the Thuringian town of Saalfeld, for example, 5,800 hectares were taken from 26 people identified as Nazi war criminals and were redistributed to over 2,300 people.[110] By October 1947, 32% of the farmland in the Soviet occupation zone had been expropriated, creating 210,276 new peasant farms averaging a little over eight hectares each.[111] This transfer of land broke the power of the rural gentry[112] and met important Communist social goals,

[101] Naimark, *The Russians in Germany,* 257.
[102] Walter Ulbricht, *The Way to the Completion of the Socialist Construction of the German Democratic Republic* (Berlin, The Council of State of the German Democratic Republic, 1964), 11.
[103] Patrick Major, *Behind the Berlin Wall: East Germany and the Frontiers of Power* (New York: Oxford University Press, 2011), 27.
[104] Leonard, *Child of the Revolution,* 311-312.
[105] Naimark, *The Russians in Germany,* 118.
[106] Georgi Zhukov quoted in Beevor, *The Fall of Berlin 1945,* 413.
[107] Naimark, *The Russians in Germany,* 89.
[108] Naimark, *The Russians in Germany,* 142. Many made a direct association between the Junkers' militarism and the rise of the Nazis.
[109] Sandford, *From Hitler to Ulbricht,* 85.
[110] Andrew Port, *Conflict and Stability in the German Democratic Republic* (New York: Cambridge University Press, 2007), 29.
[111] André Steiner, *The Plans that Failed: An Economic History of the GDR,* Ewald Osers (trans.) (New York: Berghahn Books, 2010), 27. 6,330 farms over 100 hectares and 8,332 smaller farms were confiscated; this land was redistributed to 500,000 people. See Ralph Jessen, "Mobility and Blockage During the 1970s," *Dictatorship as Experience: Towards a Socio-Cultural History of the GDR* (Konrad H. Jarausch, ed., and Eve Duffy, trans.) (New York: Berghahn Books, 1999), 343.
[112] Sandford, *From Hitler to Ulbricht,* 116.

but it was an economic disaster because many of the new farmers did not have the necessary fertilizer, draft animals, and farm equipment to be successful. Many also found that the farm sizes were too small so the agricultural yield per hectare in 1946 was only 57% of what it had been in ten years earlier.[113] Agricultural production remained a thorn in Ulbricht's side for decades.[114]

For the industrial sector, Ulbricht wanted to nationalize factories and other means of production in order to punish manufacturers and managers for their Nazi allegiance. As he said in September 1945,

> with company managers or stockholders we do not differentiate between active Nazis and others. Members of the Hitler party and its affiliated organizations who were company directors or held management positions must be removed in all cases. For the position of the manager is so important that one can lend no credence to any claim of 'I was only a nominal Nazi.'[115]

The Soviet Military Administration supported Ulbricht in this approach in late October 1945 when it issued orders to begin repossessing industrial property formally. Public backing for this action was confirmed eight months later, when voters approved a carefully worded referendum that asked, should the "factories of war criminals and Nazi criminals" be placed in "the hands of the people?" In industrialized Saxony, 78% of the voters agreed.[116] This support, which came in the aftermath of an intense propaganda campaign, helped justify the continuation of the nationalization process for the next two and a half years. As the process progressed, it included medium-sized industrial assets but did not eliminate all private property or all privately-held corporations. In fact, one third of the economy in the Soviet zone remained in private hands by the end of 1948, which represented about 40% of industrial production.[117] As Ulbricht said about seizing raw materials, "Take what you

need from the really big ones, from the war profiteers, but leave the little ones in peace."[118] In the immediate postwar period, his goal was to punish former Nazis and to take control of major industries, not to destroy all vestiges of the market economy.

The development economic policy in eastern Germany was complicated by war reparations. At the Potsdam Conference in July and early August 1945, Stalin reiterated his expectation from Yalta that the USSR receive half of the twenty billion dollars the Germans were to pay to the Allies. Because the

---

[113] Steiner, *The Plans that Failed,* 33. Steiner points out (page 27) that only 25% of these small farmers had ploughs while only 20% had a harrow.

[114] Burghard Ciesla, "Winner Takes All: The Soviet Union and the Beginning of Central Planning in Eastern Germany, 1945-1949," *The East German Economy, 1945-2010: Falling Behind or Catching Up?* (Hartmut Berghoff and Uta Andrea Balbier, eds.) (New York: Cambridge University Press—German Historical Institute, 2013), 70.

[115] Walter Ulbricht quoted in Sandford, *From Hitler to Ulbricht,* 190.

[116] Applebaum, *Iron Curtain,* 237; and Steiner, *The Plans that Failed,* 29. Votes in the other Länder followed Saxony's lead.

[117] Ciesla, "Winner Takes All," 70.

[118] Walter Ulbricht quoted in Sandford, *From Hitler to Ulbricht,* 196.

Americans and British did not want a repeat of the World War I reparations fiasco, they agreed that the United States, Great Britain, France, and the USSR should each take its share of the reparations from its zone of occupation. This meant that, although there was more industrial wealth in the western zones to pay for reparations, the real burden fell primarily from the eastern zone.[119] In fact, although 45% of the industrial capacity and 60% of the transportation facilities in the eastern sector had been destroyed during the war,[120] by late summer 1945, lines of boxcars stretching over 60 miles had been loaded with industrial material and were headed to Moscow.[121] More shipments followed in 1946 until 80% of the automobile industry that had not been destroyed in the war had been taken away. Similarly, 75% of the iron, 75% of the machine tool, 66% of the textile machinery,

50% of the chemical industry, and 33% of the pharmaceutical industry were removed.[122] Whole factories were simply dismantled and shipped. All told, the Soviets took about 30% of the surviving postwar industry from eastern Germany. They only stopped there because they feared that they were leaving an economic wasteland where there was no work.[123] The Soviets also took as reparations over 300,000 works of art, millions of documents from archives, and the entire collections of twenty-five libraries.[124] After 1946, reparations continued but were paid for through levies on production until 1954.[125] All of this stood in contrast to what happened in Western Europe, where the Marshall Plan infused $13 billion in economic assistance between 1948 and 1950.[126] Simply put, Ulbricht faced significantly different economic challenges than his counterparts in West Germany.

---

[119] Michael Neiberg, *Potsdam: The End of World War II and the Remaking of Europe* (New York: Basic Books, 2015), 198. The Soviets also received a percentage of the western zone's surviving industrial structure until the American stopped delivering materials in May 1946. The urban areas of the Soviet zone suffered more bomb damage during the war than did the cities in the western zone. See Fulbrook, *The People's State,* 50.

[120] Sandford, *From Hitler to Ulbricht,* 37.

[121] Steiner, *The Plans that Failed,* 17

[122] Steiner, *The Plans that Failed,* 19.

[123] Major, *Behind the Berlin Wall,* 25; and Jochen Laufer, "From Dismantling to Currency Reform: External Origins of the Dictatorship, 1943-1948," *Dictatorship as Experience: Towards a Socio-Cultural History of the GDR* (Konrad H. Jarausch, ed., and Eve Duffy, trans.) (New York: Berghahn Books, 1999), 77-78. Ironically, much of the industrial material the Soviets hauled away was not effectively utilized.

[124] Richie, *Faust's Metropolis,* 610-612, 1044.

[125] Randall W. Stone, *Satellites and Commissars: Strategy and Conflict in the Politics of Soviet-Bloc Trade* (Princeton, New Jersey: Princeton University Press, 1996), 30.

[126] John Agnew, J. Nicholas Entrikin, "Introduction," *The Marshall Plan Today: Model and Metaphor* (John Agnew, J. Nicholas Entrikin, eds.) (New York: Routledge, 2004), 14.

Political challenges also surfaced in the opening years of Ulbricht's administration. While the support of the Soviet Military Administration gave the KPD certain advantages when Stalin permitted the reestablishment of political parties in the Soviet zone on June 9, 1945, Ulbricht's problem was that the KPD was not the most popular party in the Soviet sector; as before the war, the SPD was. Eager to take advantage of this situation, the leader of the Social Democrats, Otto Grotewohl, proposed an immediate unification between the SPD and the KPD, but Ulbricht thwarted the proposal, saying that "a process of ideological clarification" had to come before "organizational unity" could occur.[127] Ulbricht needed time to consolidate his leadership position and to plan how to overcome the popularity of the SPD. By fall 1945, the two men found their positions reversed: Grotewohl was now resisting the merger idea because of his increasing suspicions of Soviet intentions, and Ulbricht was now advocating for it. The two sides together were finally forced together through a combination of Soviet pressure; the decision of the Social Democrats in the American, British and French zones to forsake their comrades in the Soviet zone; and the embarrassing showing by Communist parties in elections in Hungary and Austria in November.[128] At a meeting in December 1945 between the thirty highest-ranking KPD members and the thirty highest-ranking SPD members, the two sides hashed out the details for the merger. A theoretical justification was supplied by Ulbricht's KPD rival, Anton Ackerman, who provided the same organizational leadership in Dresden that Ulbricht had provided in Berlin during Soviet occupation. In his essay, "Is there a Separate German Road to Socialism?," Ackerman argued that the USSR did not present the sole model for the development of socialism, and that because Germany faced different realities and circumstances, it could develop along different lines.[129] This appealed to the socialists, who wanted independence from Moscow, and it helped facilitate the union, but support for the merger was not universal. In mid-February, the Central Committee of the SPD voted only 8-3 for unification with the Communists.[130]

On April 21, 1946, over a thousand delegates from the two parties sat together in mixed seating in the Admiralspalast, a large Berlin theater that had escaped significant damage during the war. As the ceremony to create the Socialist Unity Party of Germany (SED) began, Wilhelm Pieck and Otto Grotewohl entered from opposite sides of the stage. They met in the middle, surrounded by leaders of both parties and shook hands to the wild applause of the approving audience. Then a large ceremonial wooden club, which had once belonged to SPD leader August Bebel and which had not been seen in years, was presented, evoking further emotion and enthusiasm. After speeches by Pieck and Grotewohl, Ulbricht read the formal resolution to create the SED. It was unanimously approved by the delegates, and Grotewohl and Pieck were elected as joint chairmen.[131]

By the time the SED met for its First Party Conference in January 1949, the world was a different place and the SED was a different party. The Cold War was hot as a result of the Berlin Airlift, the

[127] Walter Ulbricht quoted in Mike Dennis, *The Rise and Fall of the German Democratic Republic, 1945-1990* (Harlow, United Kingdom: Longman/Pearson Education Limited, 2000), 23.
[128] Naimark, *The Russians in Germany*, 275-279; Sandford, *From Hitler to Ulbricht*, 147. The communists in Austria only won 5.41% of the vote and four seats in parliament while the Socialists won 76. See Rolf Steininger, *Austria, Germany, and the Cold War: From the Anschluss to the State Treaty 1938-1945* (New York: Berghahn Books, 2012), 49. In Hungary, the communists won 16.95% of the vote, finishing third behind the Socialists. See Dae Soon Kim, *The Transition to Democracy in Hungary: Árpád Göncz and the Post-Communist Hungarian Presidency* (New York: Routledge, 2013), 31.
[129] Leonard, *Child of the Revolution*, 348-349. Many sources call the title of the essay, "Is there a Special German Road to Socialism?"
[130] Naimark, *The Russians in Germany*, 282.
[131] Leonard, *Child of the Revolution*, 354-356.

announcement of the Truman Doctrine, the Communist *coup d'état* in Czechoslovakia, and the outbreak of war in Vietnam. Israel had become a nation, Yugoslavia's Josip Broz Tito had broken away from Stalin, and India and Pakistan had separated from both Great Britain and one another. While these events were unfolding, Ulbricht was, under Stalin's orders, hard at work reshaping the SED into a party in which Lenin's concept of democratic centralism prevailed. This meant that while there could be disagreements during policy discussions, all party members were bound by the decisions of its governing body—a body that Ulbricht dominated. There could be no loyal opposition or continuing discussion.[132] Uniformity was necessary, Ulbricht argued, in order to intensify the class struggle so that various socialist goals could be met. As he said in 1948, "our task is…to cross the road to the complete elimination and liquidation of capitalist elements in the countryside as well as in the cities. This task is, to put it bluntly, that of socialist construction."[133] The Communist state would need to be carefully assembled, and only a disciplined, Leninist party— one purged of individualists and malcontents—could achieve this. Rather than power for power's sake, this was a genuine effort to create a different and better type of society.[134] Of course those who were purged, like Anton Ackerman, former members of the SPD, and former KPD members who had not been in Moscow with Ulbricht during the war, saw the situation differently, but to his credit, Ulbricht never engaged in Stalinist show trials or arranged for his opponents to mysteriously disappear. Rather, Ulbricht's purges of leading SED figures resulted in forced retirements or reassignments to obscure, low-level jobs in the emerging bureaucracy.[135] This is one of the reasons scholars have struggled to fit Ulbricht's state within the conventional definitions of a dictatorship.[136]

Ulbricht's formal push for what he termed the Construction of Socialism came in conjunction with the SED's Second Party Conference in July 1952. By this time, Stalin had given up hope of a resolution with the West for a unified Germany, so he endorsed Ulbricht's plan. This far-reaching policy called for the collectivization of agriculture, the elimination of almost all private business, the growth of heavy industry, the establishment of work norms to increase productivity, an expansion of the armed forces and police, greater state control over education, a suppression of religious expression, and a reorganization of regional administration.[137] In other words, the Construction of Socialism was Ulbricht's attempt to transform the three-and-a-half-year-old German Democratic Republic (GDR) into a Soviet-style state with a planned economy. It was a decision that nearly ended Ulbricht's political career.

---

[132] Epstein, *The Last Revolutionaries,* 179.
[133] Walter Ulbricht quoted in Weitz, *Creating German Communism,* 346.
[134] Fulbrook, *The People's State,* 5-6, 9.
[135] Dornberg, *The Other Germany,* 59. In September 1948, Ackerman was blamed for promoting "false and dangerous" ideas with the publication of the 1946 essay "Is there a Separate German Road to Socialism?" He was forced to recant it and was removed from all leadership positions by 1953. See Epstein, *The Last Revolutionaries,* 177. Leaders of other political parties, such as Georg Dertinger of the Christian Democratic Union and Karl Hamann of the Liberal Democratic Party, faced long jail terms. See Jens Gieseke, *The History of the Stasi: East Germany's Secret Police, 1945-1990,* David Burnett (trans.) (New York: Berghahn Books, 2014), 33.
[136] Mary Fulbrook uses the term "participatory dictatorship" to describe the GDR. See Fulbrook, *The People's State,* 12. For other discussions of the relationship between the SED and definitions of dictatorship, see Jürgen Kocha, "The GDR: A Special Kind of Modern Dictatorship," and Konrad H. Jarausch, "Care and Coercion: The GDR as Welfare Dictatorship," and Michael Lemke, "Foreign Influences on the Dictatorial Development of the GDR, 1949-1955," in *Dictatorship as Experience: Towards a Socio-Cultural History of the GDR* (Konrad H. Jarausch, ed., and Eve Duffy, trans.) (New York: Berghahn Books, 1999), 19-24, 59-60, 98-102.
[137] Dennis, *The Rise and Fall of the German Democratic Republic,* 57-60.

~

In early 1952, the GDR began construction of a premier housing project along a broad two-kilometer East Berlin street renamed Stalinallee.[138] In an effort to keep costs down and to quicken the pace of construction, the government asked citizens to either donate 300 hours of labor or loan the project 3% of their annual income in return for the right to participate in the lottery for one of the 2,600 apartments. Propaganda posters reinforced the message, emphasizing the speed of construction that a cooperative spirit produced.[139] Some 45,000 East Berliners participated, salvaging 35 million bricks from the city's rubble while singing chanteys and winning awards for their productivity.[140] Rejecting Le Corbusier's Modernism* that dominated postwar architecture in the West, Ulbricht called for something more than "American boxes" and "Hitleresque barracks" that could be built as easily in "America as Africa."[141] He called for a monumental architectural style that would create palaces for workers to live in, raise national consciousness for the values of the socialist state, and celebrate and educate the workers who had created it.[142] The result, some of which was ready in time for Stalin's last birthday in December 1952, featured forty-six eight-story apartment buildings with shops, restaurants and entertainment venues on the ground floor and comfortable residential units with high-ceilings, central heat, private bathrooms, balconies, marble staircases, elevators, and telephones.[143] Stalinallee impressed at a time when many East Germans lived in housing without central heat, toilet facilities or even running water.[144]

The success of the Stalinallee project was part of what made the workers uprising on June 16-17, 1953 so symbolic and troubling. In mid-May, as part of his Construction of Socialism program, Ulbricht announced an increase in productivity norms that required workers to produce an additional 10% before being able to earn bonuses. On the surface, this was not unreasonable since the old norms were regularly exceeded by 175 to 200%.[145] But wages in the GDR were so low that workers had to obtain high bonuses to support themselves. In addition, supplies of butter, margarine, oil, sugar, and meat were rare that spring as East Germany faced its first food crisis since 1947.[146] By mid-June, the government had admitted that "a series of mistakes have been made," but this announcement did not include an adjustment in prices, a reduction in productivity norms or a change in Politburo leadership.[147] On June 15, fed-up construction workers at three different job sites refused to work and instead held meetings to draft petitions to the government. The next day, about eighty workers in Stalinallee's Block 40 decided, rather spontaneously, to present their

---

[138] For a history of the planning for Stalinallee and East Berlin as a capital city, see Paul Stangl, *Risen from Ruins: The Cultural Politics of Rebuilding East Berlin* (Stanford, California: Stanford University Press, 2018).

[139] David Heather, *DDR Posters: The Art of East German Propaganda* (Munich, Germany: Prestel, 2014), 68-73.

[140] "Uncle Joe's Miracle Mile in Red Berlin," *Life Magazine*, Vol. 33, No. 25 (December 22, 1952), 27-30.

[141] Walter Ulbricht quoted in Pugh, *Architecture, Politics and Identity in Divided Berlin*, 42.

[142] Ed Taverne, "The Last Avenue of the 'Other' Europe: The Stalinist Universe of the Karl-Marx-Allee in Berlin," *European Review*, Vol. 13, No. 2, (May, 2005), 207-218, ProQuest Central.

[143] Kempe, *Berlin 1961*, 181; and Pugh, *Architecture, Politics and Identity in Divided Berlin*, 42.

[144] Ruben, *Amnesiopolis*, 21-22. Most East Germans lived in residences built before 1918. Ruben's statistics, such as 35% of the dwellings in the GDR not having any indoor plumbing, are for 1961. The percentages would have been higher in 1953.

[145] Steiner, *The Plans that Failed*, 60.

[146] Steiner, *The Plans that Failed*, 59.

[147] Richard Millington, *State, Society and the Memories of the Uprising of 17 June 1953 in the GDR* (New York: Palgrave Macmillan, 2014), 3.

petition *en masse* instead of sending a small delegation to the Council of Ministers building as originally planned. As these men marched west, they were joined by so many other Berlin workers that some 5,000 protesters arrived at 97 Wilhelmstraße, only to find the ministry doors locked. While a government spokesman eventually appeared, the crowd was not mollified by his announcement that the increased work norms would not be enforced. The protesters wanted more significant reforms, and some began calling for a general strike for June 17. On the way back to Stalinallee, the workers commandeered a government van with a loudspeaker attached to its roof. This turned the petition march into a protest, as the loudspeakers broadcast an appeal for a general strike. The news spread like wildfire throughout Berlin and the whole GDR, due in part to Western radio coverage.[148]

The pattern of events on June 17 was repeated in cities throughout the country. As shifts began, workers in industrial plants, construction sites, and shops began their day talking about whether to participate in the general strike. There was little coordinated or organized leadership; in most places, someone simply proved sufficiently convincing to provoke action.[149] Once people walked off the job, marches, demonstrations, and protests followed until Soviet tanks and troops restored order, in many cases by suppertime. In the city of Magdeburg, for example, workers in two major plants decided to join the strike by 8:45 a.m., which resulted in 10,000 protestors marching towards the center of the city. By noon, 100,000 Magdeburgers were in the streets, and there were attacks on SED buildings and officials. Protesters took over the communications office, vandalized the police headquarters, and attempted to seize the prison, but the local Soviet military commander responded to the official request for help, and by that evening 3,500 had been arrested.[150] In the town of Saalfeld, one thousand striking construction workers marched to the Maxhütte Steel Mill, calling upon the steel workers to join them. When the steel workers refused to join, only 600 of the construction workers continued their protest, marching to the center of town. At this point, the SED district secretary declared a state of emergency and Soviet troops arrived, dispersing the crowd by 7:00 p.m.[151] In East Berlin, about 115,000 people went on strike or participated in demonstrations.[152] As one large group marched down the main street of Unter den Linden, they provocatively sang the third verse of *Deutschland, Deutschland über Alles*, West Germany's new national anthem. Later, at the Brandenburg Gate, a group tore down the Soviet flag and throughout the government sector, windows were broken and fires set. The nervous SED leaders, including Ulbricht, decided to leave the city with their families. At midday, Soviet tanks fired their first shots. These were followed by bullets from the guns of the East German *Volkspolizei*, the People's Police. Working together, the Soviet military and the *Volkspolizei* brutally restored order to city by that evening.[153] All told, there were about 90 deaths and 10,000 arrests over the two days as hundreds of

---

[148] This account is based on a blending of several sources because various details, including the number of people involved, are not in agreement. See Baring, *Uprising in East Germany*, 41-49, 67; Dennis, *The Rise and Fall of the German Democratic Republic*, 65; and Richie, *Faust's Metropolis*, 683.

[149] Baring, *Uprising in East Germany*, 68.

[150] Millington, *State, Society and the Memories of the Uprising of 17 June 1953 in the GDR*, 13-14.

[151] Port, *Conflict and Stability in the German Democratic Republic*, 73-74.

[152] Dennis, *The Rise and Fall of the German Democratic Republic*, 66-67.

[153] Richie, *Faust's Metropolis*, 684-685. Another account holds that a crowd of 25,000 gathered in front of the Council of Ministries by 9:00 a.m.; 80-100 of these demonstrators overpowered the 500 members of the Volkspolizei and State Security and nearly succeeded in occupying the government seat. Soviet troops arrived and cleared the area around 97 Wilhelmstraße by noon, but fighting continued through the afternoon and evening in other parts of the city. See Christian F. Ostermann, *Uprising in East Germany 1953: The Cold War, the*

communities and about a half million East Germans registered their dissatisfaction with GDR President Pieck, GDR Prime Minister Grotewohl, and SED General Secretary Ulbricht. The events associated with June 17 were the largest protest in the GDR's forty-year history until autumn 1989.[154]

Ulbricht was unable to respond effectively to the crisis because so much of his attention was consumed by power struggles in both Moscow and the SED Politburo. Stalin's unexpected death in March 1953 created an unstable situation. One of the leading contenders to replace Stalin was Lavrenti Beria—a man who opposed Ulbricht's Construction of Socialism and who had so little respect for GDR that he questioned the purpose of its existence.[155] In fact, Beria insisted that Ulbricht abandon his signature policy and replace it with the "New Course." This program called for non-collectivized farms, the restoration of private enterprise, lower prices, and an emphasis on manufacturing consumer goods. East Germany's official newspaper, *Neues Deutschland*, published these goals four days before the Stalinallee protests began.[156] This represented a notable embarrassment and reprimand for Ulbricht, and led two of his rivals on the Politburo, Rudolf Herrnstadt and Wilhelm Zaisser, to attack him. On July 7, Herrnstadt and Zaisser forced a vote to remove Ulbricht from office, and the Politburo voted 9-2 to do so.[157] This decision could not stand without Soviet blessing, so the next day, Ulbricht and Grotewohl flew to Moscow to seek Soviet assistance. Upon their arrival, they learned that Beria had been arrested for "criminal anti-party and anti-governmental activities" in late June. He had been charged with being "an agent of international imperialism" who sought to force the GDR to adopt the New Course so that it might be transformed "into a bourgeois government."[158] This news meant Ulbricht could return to East Berlin with Moscow's support and the ability to oust his rivals. By the end of the month both Herrnstadt and Zaisser had been expelled from the SED, and Ulbricht was in as strong a position as ever.[159] To help prevent future protests and to gather increased intelligence on malcontents,

---

German Question, and the First Major Upheaval Behind the Iron Curtain (New York: Central European University Press, 2001), 164.

[154] Historians do not agree on the statistics for June 16-17. The number of towns with disturbances range from 272 (Baring, *Uprising in East Germany,* 52) to 373 (Dennis, *The Rise and Fall of the German Democratic Republic,* 67) to 560 (Harrison, *Driving the Soviets up the Wall,* 35). Estimated arrests range from 5,000 to 10,000 (Steiner, *The Plans that Failed,* 62) to 13,000 (Dennis, *The Rise and Fall of the German Democratic Republic,* 68). There were 11,646,100 working age adults in the GDR in August 1950, so as large as the 1953 protests were, most workers did not participate, either because of loyalty to the regime or fear of retribution. See Wolfgang F. Stolper, *The Structure of the East Germany Economy* (Cambridge, Massachusetts: Harvard University Press, 1960, 27.

[155] Andrei Gromyko, *Memoirs* (New York: Doubleday, 1989), 317. Beria is quoted as saying, "all we need is a peaceful Germany, whether it is socialist or not isn't important." See Kempe, *Berlin 1961,* 23.

[156] Victor Baras, "Beria's Fall and Ulbricht's Survival," *Soviet Studies,* Vol. 27, No. 3 (July 1975), 381-395, EBSCOhost.

[157] A. James McAdams, *Germany Divided: From Wall to Reunification* (Princeton, New Jersey: Princeton University Press, 1993), 40. Only Erich Honecker and Hermann Matern voted no.

[158] Charges against Lavrenti Beria quoted in Harrison, *Driving the Soviets up the Wall,* 40-41. Richard Millington says that Ulbricht and Grotewohl flew to Moscow on July 10, 1953. See Millington, *State, Society and the Memories of the Uprising of 17 June 1953 in the GDR,* 172.

[159] After his expulsion from the SED, Rudolf Herrnstadt was given a job at an archive. He died of lung cancer in 1966. Wilhelm Zaisser was pensioned and died in 1958. In conjunction with these two expulsions, Ulbricht purged large numbers of SED officials at district and local levels. For a detailed discussion of the conflict with Herrnstadt and Zaisser and the subsequent party purges, see Peter Grieder, *The East German Leadership, 1946-73: Conflict and Crisis* (Manchester, U.K.: Manchester University Press, 1999), 52-91.

Ulbricht began expanding the importance of the Ministry of State Security (MfS or Stasi) in the GDR. Although the secret police ministry employed 4,000 agents in 1952, it had 10,000 by 1955.[160]

   This change of events allowed Ulbricht to hold true to his vision of the GDR as a centrally planned, socialist state. He wanted East Germans to embrace the slogan "as you work today, so you will live tomorrow."[161] Life was about securing the future and the creation of the ideal socialist state. While the SED did take meaningful steps to increase the standard of living in the aftermath of the June 16-17 uprising,[162] after almost thirty years of hardship caused by the Depression, the War, and Soviet occupation, East Germans did not want to hear about continued sacrifices. They wanted tangible, immediate, and sizeable benefits. For many citizens this increasingly meant moving to West Germany—the nation Ulbricht described in 1954 as a fascist land of "big landlords, bankers, and armaments tycoons."[163] Between 1945 and 1961, 3.5 million people disagreed with Ulbricht's assessment and left the GDR. This exodus amounted to one sixth of the nation's population.[164] The vast majority of these refugees did so for economic, not political or ideological reasons. Nearly half fled alone. This was especially true of young men looking to  take advantage of West Germany's growing job market for skilled labor.[165] By the late 1950s, the problem was more than total number of losses: the composition of the departees emigrating also took its toll. Engineers and scientists left for the West because they disliked the travel restrictions, the state's centralized planning, the emphasis on quantity over quality, and the difficulties of keeping pace with technological advances in the West. They also resented having to participate in the harvest each fall. In a state with grand technological goals, the loss of 7,554 mechanical engineers and the loss of 2,035 electrical engineers was acutely felt, especially since younger professionals were the most likely to leave.[166] Other groups that departed in significant numbers were farmers, Christians, academics, doctors and other health professionals, and those coerced by the state to spy or join the military.[167]

---

[160] David Childs and Richard Popplewell, *The Stasi: The East German Intelligence and Security Service* (New York: Palgrave, 1996), 59.

[161] SED slogan quoted in Ruben, *Amnesiopolis*, 28.

[162] Millington, *State, Society and the Memories of the Uprising of 17 June 1953 in the GDR*, 175. The SED increased wages, lowered prices, eliminated major food shortages, reduced power outages, increased the number of consumer goods available, released some political prisoners, and returned land to farmers.

[163] Walter Ulbricht, "The Present Situation and the Struggle for the New Germany," *Whither Germany? Speeches and Essays on the National Question*, 161.

[164] Major, *Behind the Berlin Wall*, 56.

[165] Major, *Behind the Berlin Wall*, 74-75, 79. Only 14.2% of the refugees were considered political by West Germany authorities; 47% emigrated alone.

[166] Dolores L. Augustine, *Red Prometheus: Engineering and Dictatorship in East Germany, 1945-1990* (Cambridge, Massachusetts: MIT Press, 2007), 87-88, 91-93. The losses in mechanical engineering fields occurred between January 1959 and May 1960; the losses in electrical engineering fields occurred between January 1958 and April 1959.

[167] Major, *Behind the Berlin Wall*, 66-71.

Getting to West Germany between 1945 and 1961 was not nearly as difficult as one might assume. While access across the border that ran from the Baltic Sea to Czechoslovakia was significantly curtailed in 1952, the borders within Berlin remained largely open in accordance with the agreements made at Potsdam in 1945. This meant that fleeing to West Germany was really just a matter of traveling to West Berlin, and this was something that millions of East Germans legally did each year. In fact, between spring 1950 and spring 1961, 13.1 million East Germans received official permission to travel to West Germany and West Berlin on visas and inter-zonal passes. In addition, 63,000 East Berliners travelled to West Berlin each day for work in early 1961.[168] Hence, there was plenty of opportunity for what became known as the flight from the Republic or *Republikflucht*. Significantly, Ulbricht took responsibility for this emigration: in 1961 he said, "In my assessment, 60 per cent of *Republikfluchten* can be ascribed to deficiencies in our own work."[169] This did not mean surrendering to capitalism or giving up. Rather, it meant taking the necessary steps to stop the emigration hemorrhage so that lasting adjustments could be made in the GDR's socialist experiment.

~

In the late afternoon of Saturday, August 12, 1961, Ulbricht hosted a garden party for a carefully selected group of government officials at a country estate on the Großer Döllnsee, an oblong lake almost 40 miles northeast of central Berlin. Having a summer party at the House Among the Birches was not unusual, but on that particular afternoon there were several anomalies. Not only was Erich Honecker, Ulbricht's trusted protégé, absent, but the surrounding woods were full of a large number of military personnel and the chefs were required to spend the night. Some guests were nervous, but after hours of mingling, drinking, and dining, most had relaxed. At 10:00 p.m., as most of his guests were ready to depart, Ulbricht announced that they would have to remain until the open border between socialist and capitalist Europe had been secured; only once Operation Rose had closed passage between East and West Berlin would they be permitted to leave. Ulbricht then asked his captive government officials to register their approval of the operation, which they naturally did.[170]

A garden party in the woods may seem like historical minutia, but given the complexities of the operation to erect the Berlin Wall, it also squarely illustrates Ulbricht's ability to organize and account for a myriad of details. He planned for every contingency and anticipated every variable. In this case, he invited, and then held captive, anyone who might threaten the success of the operation, and he purposefully distracted Western intelligence operatives by giving the appearance that all was normal on a summer Saturday afternoon and evening.[171] Such tenacity complemented

---

[168] Major, *Behind the Berlin Wall*, 89-90, 94.

[169] Walter Ulbricht quoted in Major, *Behind the Berlin Wall*, 82.

[170] Kempe, *Berlin 1961*, 339-340, 345-346; and Frederick Taylor, *The Berlin Wall: 13 August 1961 - 9 November 1989* ([New York?], HarperCollins eBooks, 2014), no page, Kindle edition. The House Among the Birches had once been the home of Hermann Göring's personal hunter; it was not Göring's retreat residence as many sources indicate. Göring's actual retreat, Carinhall, was on a split of land in between Großer Döllnsee and Wuckersee. Carinhall was blown up as the Red Army advanced on April 28, 1945, but the House Among the Birches survived the war, became a retreat center for high ranking SED members, and today stands as a hotel.

[171] Kempe, *Berlin 1961*, 340.

the multitude of Ulbricht's preparations in the months beforehand. He had purchased from British and West German firms a sufficient amount of barbed wire to encircle West Berlin and had the manufacturing labels removed to avoid any diplomatic fallout; he had badgered Khrushchev relentlessly and took advantage of his vulnerabilities until the Soviet leader consented to the proposal; he had calculated the troop density needed to hold key points along the border, such as Potsdamer Platz, until the barbed wire could be unrolled; he had designated the precise amounts of ammunition that would be available on the front line; and he had coordinated statements of support from the Warsaw Pact to arrive an hour after Operation Rose had begun. Most importantly, Ulbricht had carefully selected the men to implement his orders and had utilized the nation's overlapping security forces—the border troops, the riot police, the *Volkspolizei*, the factory militias, the National People's Army, and the agents of the Ministry of State Security (MfS or Stasi)—to monitor one another if one any unit didn't follow its orders.[172] The Soviet army was also available in case something went wrong. From a logistical standpoint, it was Ulbricht's finest hour.

The erection of the Anti-Fascist Defense Rampart, as it was officially called by the GDR, was a repressive act for many East Germans, but it was positively liberating for Ulbricht: he began articulating policies that were far more liberal than those he had previously pursued in an effort to remake East German society. The former Stalinist released nearly 16,000 political prisoners,[173] reformed the penal code, and forced the Stasi to adhere to published laws and to refrain from extraordinary or extralegal measures that might have been permissible during the crises of the state's early years.[174] As early as 1962, Ulbricht began to speak in favor of economic reforms to modernize the East German economy and increase its productivity. He wanted the GDR to reach his 1958 goal of exceeding West Germany's per capita consumption in consumer goods and foodstuffs.[175] It was

time for socialism to prove its superiority as an economic system, and Ulbricht was eager for the challenge. As he told the SED's Sixth Congress in January 1963, the time for "appeals to morale and ideological consciousness" was over because they were not enough to overcome consumers' material concerns; therefore, the GDR had to "move away from old dogmas" and embrace economic change.[176] At another point, Ulbricht explicitly emphasized, "what is at stake is a complete transformation, and not a mere correction."[177] Given Ulbricht's proclivity for planning,

---

[172] See Harrison, *Driving the Soviets up the Wall*, 142-143, 180, 186, 205; Kempe, *Berlin 1961*, 324-326; Major, *Behind the Berlin Wall*, 113-114.

[173] Gerhard Besier and Katarzyna Stokłosa, *European Dictatorships: A Comparative History of the Twentieth Century* (Newcastle-upon-Tyne, U.K.: Cambridge Scholars Publishing, 2013), 499.

[174] Gieseke, *The History of the Stasi*, 54-55.

[175] Steiner, *The Plans that Failed*, 90, 109.

[176] Walter Ulbricht quoted in Monika Kaiser, "Reforming Socialism? The Changing of the Guard from Ulbricht to Honecker During the 1960s," *Dictatorship as Experience: Towards a Socio-Cultural History of the GDR* (Konrad H. Jarausch, ed., and Eve Duffy, trans.) (New York: Berghahn Books, 1999), 327.

[177] Walter Ulbricht quoted in Kaiser, "Reforming Socialism?," 329.

he explored the issues thoroughly before setting forth on his bold mission: he and two key Politburo members, Erich Apel and Günter Mittag, organized discussions with thousands of economic, technical, and scientific experts. Then they tested various approaches in small-scale experiments and evaluated the outcomes. By July 1963, they were satisfied with their plan, and the GDR adopted the New Economic System.[178]

The NES made profits, rather than production, the basis of evaluating the success of state-owned enterprises. It gave these enterprises greater freedom to manage resources, set production schedules, and reinvest their own profits. It gave more autonomy and responsibility to factory managers, and allowed for incentive bonuses for workers, based on both their individual performance and the performance of the enterprise. It also set more realistic prices for raw materials. Finally, it gave priority to industries like chemicals, electronics, cybernetics, and die tools so that they might be more competitive for export in the world market.[179] The primary goal of the NES was to change the production structure to improve domestic supplies while continuing scientific and technological advancement.[180] Ulbricht, Apel, and Mittag did not abandon the values of economic central planning, but the NES did explicitly reject the idea that the Soviet Union would serve as the fundamental economic model for the GDR. Instead, Ulbricht offered a new paradigm for socialist governments,[181] saying that Stalin had "relied heavily on the instrument of bureaucracy because he had lost confidence in the masses and his cadre. Stalin's distrust evolved from a lack of faith in the persuasive power of Communist ideas. The result was over-centralization."[182] This was the exact problem Ulbricht wanted to offset with the NES.

The New Economic System was one of five initiatives Ulbricht outlined in a speech honoring the nation's fifteenth anniversary in October 1964. He opened the speech by challenging the GDR to turn over "a new leaf," which he believed would allow the nation to complete its construction of the socialist state. A second element of his New Leaf program called for reframing the relationship between the two German states through mutual diplomatic recognition and working towards the long-term goal of reunification.[183] As early as December 1956, Ulbricht had been trying to develop a political confederation between the two Germanys, but few in the West took him seriously.[184] Working from a place a greater strength after the construction of the Berlin Wall, Ulbricht tried again appealed to the West German leadership. He believed that "the shaping of relations between

---

[178] Kaiser, "Reforming Socialism?," 327. The NES was based on the work of two economists, Fritz Behrens and Arne Benary, who believed in decentralized economic decision-making. In 1957, Ulbricht denounced the pair, but once the Wall was in place he began exploiting their ideas. See Jonathan R. Zatlin, *The Currency of Socialism: Money and Political Culture in East Germany* (New York: Cambridge University Press, 2007), 48.
[179] Epstein, *The Last Revolutionaries*, 181; Port, *Conflict and Stability in the German Democratic Republic*, 175-176; and Kaiser, "Reforming Socialism?," 327-328. Most enterprises, such as automobile manufacturing, were overseen by a Vereinigungen Volkseigener Betriebe (VVB), which, according to one description, "can be considered a form of trust that has control over the operations of enterprises in a given economic field....Each VVB is responsible for fulfilling that part of the economic plan over which it has jurisdiction and for facilitating implementation of directives from the State Planning Commission and synthesizing the recommendations from the individual enterprises below." See Martin Schnitzer, *East and West Germany: A Comparative Economic Analysis* (New York: Praeger Publications, 1972), 230.
[180] Ulbricht, *The Way to the Completion of the Socialist Construction of the German Democratic Republic* (Berlin, The Council of State of the German Democratic Republic, 1964), 35-36.
[181] Epstein, *The Last Revolutionaries*, 181.
[182] Walter Ulbricht quoted in Dornberg, *The Other Germany*, 87-88.
[183] Ulbricht, *The Way to the Completion of the Socialist Construction of the German Democratic Republic*, 5.
[184] McAdams, *Germany Divided*, 28.

the German Democratic Republic and the West German Federal Republic is solely the affair of the German states and their governments and parliaments."[185] Foreign powers had no role to play; it was a German matter that had to be mutually decided if Europe was to have long-term peace. This concept challenged the prevailing views of the bifurcated Cold War world.

The third element of Ulbricht's New Leaf proposal asserted the goal of forming friendly relations with all nations. Documents reveal that Ulbricht wanted to base the GDR's foreign policy "on the anti-imperialist and anti-colonial traditions of the German working class" and to give special attention to the emerging nations in Africa and Asia.[186] As Ulbricht told his diplomatic corps in 1960, it was the GDR's duty to "promote to the best of its ability…[the] struggle for political and economic liberation" in these parts of world. This meant that by 1963, East Germany forbade trade with the Republic of South Africa so that it could "stand firmly at the side of the people of South Africa in their struggle against the terrorist and apartheid regime."[187] Similarly, Ulbricht's government condemned the Netherlands for its actions in West Irian in 1957; Belgium and the United States for their actions in the Congo in 1960 and 1961; Portugal for its policies in Angola and Goa in 1961; the United States for its intervention in Vietnam in 1962; and South Africa for its actions in Namibia in 1966. Each of these condemnations contained criticism of West Germany's support for the opposite side.[188] Ulbricht reserved special criticism for Israel, for he saw Zionism as an extension of Western imperialism.[189] This criticism increased substantially after the Six-Day War* broke out in June 1967, for Ulbricht distinguished between Israel's existence and expansion and the "suffering and injustice inflicted by the criminal Hitler regime on the Jewish citizens of Germany and other European states."[190] East Germany's anti-Zionism was so strong that it remained the only Warsaw Pact member that did not establish diplomatic relations with Israel.[191]

The fourth element of the New Leaf, authored by a man raised as a pacifist, urged West Germany to eliminate nuclear weapons from its territory to help safeguard world peace. As Ulbricht wrote to the West German chancellor in 1964,

> the risk of a nuclear war breaking out because of power-political interests, or even by accident, increases by leaps and bounds as the number of states possessing nuclear weapons grows. For this reason and in view of the dangers threatening our nation I consider it an urgent necessity to appeal to you to relegate to the background what separates you and me in our political views, and to take joint steps to avert the danger of nuclear war. For the

---

[185] Walter Ulbricht to Professor Ludwig Erhard, Chancellor of the Federal Republic of Germany, May 26, 1964 in *Whither Germany? Speeches and Essays on the National Question*, 319.

[186] Walter Ulbricht quoted in *The GDR: A Staunch Ally of the Emergent Countries* (Dresden: Verlag Zeit in Bild, 1971), 6.

[187] Walter Ulbricht quoted in *The GDR: A Staunch Ally of the Emergent Countries*, 7.

[188] *The GDR: A Staunch Ally of the Emergent Countries*, 33, 47-50, 67-68, 77-79.

[189] Jeffery Herf, *Undeclared Wars with Israel: East Germany and the Western Far Left*, 1967-1989 (New York: Cambridge University Press, 2016), 1, 33, 37-38, 46-51, 57-58, 455. In addition to showing the extent of Ulbricht's and the GDR's aggressive anti-Zionist stance, Herf dismisses Ulbricht's broader appeals to peace and justice on page 7 as "rhetorical fog."

[190] Walter Ulbricht quoted in Jeffery Herf, *Undeclared Wars with Israel: East Germany and the Western Far Left*, 1967-1989 (New York: Cambridge University Press, 2016), 38.

[191] Herf, *Undeclared Wars with Israel*, 4.

sake…of the existence and health of future German generations…I hope you will realize that is necessary to agree without any delay on the total renunciation of nuclear weapons.[192]

The fifth and final element of Ulbricht's New Leaf for 1964 called for changes in the GDR's relationship with the Soviet Union, based upon "friendship, mutual assistance and cooperation."[193] Ulbricht's use of the word "mutual" was particularly important for it implied a reciprocity on the basis of equal standing. In fact, Ulbricht wanted the Soviet Union to recognize the GDR as a sovereign state and true partner, rather than as a satellite. As he bluntly said during a trip to Moscow a few years later, "We want to develop ourselves as a genuine German state. We are not Byelorussia, we are not a Soviet republic. So genuine cooperation" is necessary.[194] Such status would allow East Germany to pursue independent policies, interpret Marxism differently, and provide alternative models to those of the USSR.[195]

The five elements of Ulbricht's New Leaf program were a startling departure from established policy. The proposal was especially threatening to two men in particular: the new leader of the Soviet Union, Leonid Brezhnev, who ousted Khrushchev on October 13, 1964, and Ulbricht's former ally and protégé Erich Honecker. Neither of these men agreed with the new orientation Ulbricht articulated, and both began working to undermine Ulbricht's position and authority. Brezhnev circumvented Ulbricht's effort to wrest control over the Warsaw Pact's foreign policy priorities,[196] and rejected Ulbricht's request for increased oil shipments.[197] In the aftermath of the Prague Spring* in 1968, the Soviet leader issued the Brezhnev Doctrine, asserting that Warsaw Pact countries could not adopt policies that jeopardized "socialism in their own country nor the fundamental interests of the other socialist countries" and that intervention was permitted when such threats occurred.[198] This doctrine could be applied to Ulbricht's independence and reforms, if necessary. Brezhnev also had a personal dislike for Ulbricht, finding him to be haughty, overbearing, and insufferable. This didn't help the SED leader's long-term job security.[199] Meanwhile, Honecker attacked the NES in December 1965, when it became clear that Ulbricht's reforms would not produce the expected growth. Honecker thought that the adoption of costs and prices as measures of success betrayed the planned economy. He noted the difficulties both suppliers and producers had in adjusting to the new economic model.[200] Hoecker did not believe the NES could ever work, so he acted to have the NES scaled back and replaced with a program that

---

[192] Walter Ulbricht to Professor Ludwig Erhard, Chancellor of the Federal Republic of Germany, January 6, 1964 in *Whither Germany? Speeches and Essays on the National Question*, 313.

[193] Ulbricht, *The Way to the Completion of the Socialist Construction of the German Democratic Republic*, 5.

[194] Walter Ulbricht quoted in Epstein, *The Last Revolutionaries*, 185. Byelorussia is the nation of Belarus today.

[195] M. E. Sarotte, *Dealing with the Devil: East Germany, Détente, and Ostpolitik, 1969-1973* (Chapel Hill, North Carolina: University of North Carolina Press, 2001), 17.

[196] Laurien Crump, *The Warsaw Pact Reconsidered: International Relations in Eastern Europe, 1955-1969* (New York: Routledge, 2015), 118, 124.

[197] Sarotte, *Dealing with the Devil*, 19.

[198] Brezhnev Doctrine quoted in Sarotte, *Dealing with the Devil*, 17. Sarotte points out that Ulbricht was deeply opposed to the reform movement in Czechoslovakia in 1968 and only trusted himself to offer alternative interpretations and programs. This attitude came from his standing as one of the senior communist leaders in the world and one of the few still alive who had met Lenin.

[199] Harrison, *Driving the Soviets up the Wall*, 232-233.

[200] Zatlin, *The Currency of Socialism*, 49.

restored emphasis to central planners.[201]   Operating more covertly, Honecker also purposefully mismanaged, ignored, or contravened many of Ulbricht's directives.[202]

All of the tensions produced by the New Leaf program came to a head in 1970, just after SPD candidate Willy Brandt was elected chancellor of West Germany. Brandt's determined policy to improve relations with West Germany's Communist neighbors, known as *Ostpolitik*, put many political and economic issues on the table. Ulbricht was eager to engage in negotiations,[203] but Brezhnev was unwilling to let Ulbricht have a decisive or independent role. He insisted that Soviet negotiations with the Federal Republic had to take priority over inter-German talks.[204] As a result, the Soviets and the West Germans signed the Treaty of Moscow in August 1970. Ulbricht was so fully excluded from the negotiations that he learned about the treaty's details only after the fact.[205] Such diplomatic marginalization, combined with his failing health, made Ulbricht vulnerable. Honecker pounced in December 1970 with the publication of "On the Correction to the Economic Policies of Walter Ulbricht at the 14th Meeting of the Central Committee of the SED." This detailed essay charged Ulbricht with failing to provide sufficient consumer goods to the population, incurring unacceptable foreign debts, behaving with "arrogance in relation to the Soviet Union," and inappropriately "referring to the GDR and its experiences as a model at every opportunity."[206] Ulbricht responded in January 1971 by attempting to goad the Central Committee into organizing a new party congress to affirm his position, but he was not able to gain sufficient support.[207] A few weeks later, thirteen of the twenty SED Politburo members wrote an extraordinary joint letter to Brezhnev, which charged Ulbricht with pursuing "a personal line," and putting himself above the Party. They asked for Brezhnev's help to get Ulbricht to resign.[208] Brezhnev did not act upon this request immediately, though he had plenty of opportunity to do so since Ulbricht spent most of February and March staying at a spa outside of Moscow. Ulbricht still held sufficient status to speak on the opening day of the Twenty-Fourth Congress of the Communist Party of the Soviet Union on March 30, 1971—much against Honecker's wishes. Two weeks later, however, Brezhnev held a five-hour meeting with Ulbricht where the Soviet leader made his wishes clear. Ulbricht formally resigned as First Secretary of the Central Committee of the Socialist Unity Party of Germany on May 3.[209]

Retirement did not suit Ulbricht well. He had a heart attack on June 14, but lived to face the indignity of being blamed by Honecker for every problem the GDR faced, while simultaneously being air-brushed out of the historical record. Honecker sought to eradicate the cult of personality that Ulbricht had built over the years.[210] Not only was Ulbricht's Berlin house demolished, but

---

[201] Steiner, *The Plans that Failed*, 116-117, 120. As a result of this attack on the NES, its key author, Erich Apel, committed suicide. The revised plan was known as the Economic System of Socialism.

[202] Kaiser, "Reforming Socialism?," 332, 334.

[203] Epstein, *The Last Revolutionaries*, 184; and Dennis, *The Rise and Fall of the German Democratic Republic*, 134.

[204] Dennis, *The Rise and Fall of the German Democratic Republic*, 134-135.

[205] Sarotte, *Dealing with the Devil*, 67-69.

[206] Erich Honecker quoted in Sarotte, *Dealing with the Devil*, 101.

[207] David Binder, "The Quick Decline and Fall of Walter Ulbricht," *New York Times*, June 22, 1971, 2, ProQuest Historical Newspapers.

[208] Sarotte, *Dealing with the Devil*, 106.

[209] Sarotte, *Dealing with the Devil*, 107-109, 233-234. Sarotte notes (page 110) that in late April or very early May, Honecker took an armed guard with him to visit Ulbricht at Großer Döllnsee and gave orders to seal the compound. This suggests that Honecker had to force Ulbricht to sign the resignation letter.

[210] Rodden, *Textbook Reds*, 43-44, 47. According to Rodden, Honecker's cult of personality "remained comparatively subdued."

memorials and plaques bearing his name were removed, stamps bearing his image were withdrawn from circulation, publications he had written were cleared from public libraries, and schools, stadiums, and factories named after him were renamed.[211]   Honecker's condemnation was so thorough that he secretly destroyed some of Ulbricht's files, distributed files which left unfavorable impressions, spitefully denied Ulbricht tickets to attend the fifty-fifth celebration of the Bolshevik Revolution, and subjected his one-time mentor to Stasi surveillance.[212]   This meant that Ulbricht lived his final days foreshadowing what millions of East Germans would experience in the 1970s and 1980s as the state security apparatus grew to become an omnipresent institution that permeated daily life.[213]

Ulbricht died August 1, 1973 at the age of eighty.   The initial news reports in the GDR were muted and brief, minimizing the role that the founder of the nation had played in his twenty-six years at the helm.   Brezhnev, however, took exception to this coverage and insisted that Ulbricht be given a full state funeral. Although the Soviet leader chose not to attend the August 8 ceremony, tens of thousands of East Germans made the opposite decision, despite the rain, and lined the processional route through East Berlin to the crematorium.   The outpouring of recognition caught SED officials by surprise since Ulbricht was never a beloved figure and since so much effort had been put into discrediting him.   But ordinary East Germans understood the importance of the moment:[214]   the father of the German Democratic Republic was dead.[215]

~

Walter Ulbricht sought to build an egalitarian society that was both a humane alternative to capitalism and a socialist state independent of the Soviet Union.[216]   In many ways, he succeeded in this quest. His long fight for recognition of East German sovereignty was finally realized with the GDR's admission to the United Nations in 1973.   Ulbricht also restored eastern Germany as an industrial center in Europe, and did so while providing heavily-subsidized or free education, food, health care, and housing to its citizens.[217]   In addition, East Germany experienced a profound social

---

[211] Paul Betts, "When Cold Warriors Die: The State Funerals of Konrad Adenauer and Walter Ulbricht," *Between Mass Death and Individual Loss: The Place of the Dead in Twentieth-Century Germany*, Alon Confino, Paul Betts, and Dirk Schumann (eds.) (New York: Berghahn Books, 2008) 163; Fulbrook, *The People's State*, 40; and Epstein, *The Last Revolutionaries*, 186.

[212] Sarotte, *Dealing with the Devil*, 184; and Epstein, *The Last Revolutionaries*, 186.

[213] There is considerable scholarship on the role the Ministry for State Security (MfS) played in the GDR. East Germany had perhaps the largest and most pervasive security apparatus in world history with 91,000 fulltime employees and 176,000 informants in 1989 for a population of 16 million. These are ratios that far outstripped those for the USSR, or Nazi Germany. The Stasi's methods were notably less brutal in the 1980s and they were in the 1950s. See Gieseke, *The History of the Stasi*; Gary Bruce, *The Firm: The Inside Story of the Stasi*, (New York: Oxford University Press, 2010); and Mike Dennis, *The Stasi: Myth and Reality* (New York: Routledge, 2014).

[214] Betts, "When Cold Warriors Die," 167-169.

[215] Mike Dennis uses the term "father" to describe Ulbricht, saying that he "defended with great stubbornness what he perceived to be the GDR's fundamental interests against both the Soviet Union and West Germany. If anyone deserves the title of father of the GDR, it was Ulbricht." See Dennis, *The Rise and Fall of the German Democratic Republic, 1945-1990,* 138.

[216] McAdams, *Germany Divided*, 72.

[217] The GDR claimed in 1970 that it was one of the world's top ten industrial countries, ranking ninth and West Germany ranking fourth. See Martin Schnitzer, *East and West Germany: A Comparative Economic Analysis* (New

transformation during the Ulbricht years that can be seen in two ways. The first involves the experience of East German women. The government genuinely wanted to see meaningful social change for women,[218] and the results, though incomplete, were impressive. The number of women employed outside the home, for example, rose from 44% in 1950 to 70% in 1970.[219] More specifically, the number of women employed in industry jumped from 25.5% in 1949 to 42.4% in 1970,[220] and the number of women working in agriculture who received technical training rose from 8.5% in 1960 to 62% in 1970.[221] In 1965, a new family code was passed that increased women's financial independence, made divorce easier, and gave both parents equal responsibility for parenting; it specifically guaranteed women the "right to develop their abilities for their own and society's interests," which, combined with a significant expansion in access to abortion after 1968, gave women control of their lives.[222] There is also evidence that women enjoyed more satisfying sex lives than their West German counterparts as a result of this independence.[223] A second way of illustrating this social change is education. Between 1947 and 1966, the number of kindergartens in the GDR quadrupled while the number of class seats tripled, giving East German children far greater access to early education than their West German counterparts.[224] At the university level, the percentage of students from working class backgrounds jumped from just 4% to 53% between 1945 and 1958, and the total university enrollment increased by 61% between 1960 and 1971 as the SED sought to build a population with scientific and technical expertise.[225] The state's emphasis on education produced considerable upward social mobility in East German society during Ulbricht's tenure, allowing the GDR to claim it had the highest standard of living among the world's Communist nations.[226]

York: Praeger Publications, 1972), 386. Since 1989, historians have shown that East German statistics are often unreliable, while economists have found ways of compensating for the compromised data. See Hans-Peter Brunner and Peter Allen, "A Regional Development Approach: Transport, International Trade, and Investment Modeled in Space," *International Trade Issues*, Robert V Weeks (ed.) (New York: Nova Science Publishers, 2006), 27.

[218] Fulbrook, *The People's State,* 170.

[219] Sandrine Kott, *Communism Day-to-Day: State Enterprises in East German Society*, Lisa Godin-Roger (trans.) (Ann Arbor, Michigan, University of Michigan Press, 2014), 184. The percentage was 81% in 1989.

[220] Peter Hübner, "Stagnation or Change? Transformation of the Workplace in the GDR," *Dictatorship as Experience: Towards a Socio-Cultural History of the GDR* (Konrad H. Jarausch, ed., and Eve Duffy, trans.) (New York: Berghahn Books, 1999), 291.

[221] Dagmar Langenhan and Sabine Ross, "The Socialist Glass Ceiling: Limits to Female Careers," *Dictatorship as Experience: Towards a Socio-Cultural History of the GDR* (Konrad H. Jarausch, ed., and Eve Duffy, trans.) (New York: Berghahn Books, 1999), 185. The effects of Ulbricht's vocational policy for women can be seen even in the 2020s: the percentage of women in the former GDR who work outside the home remains larger than in other parts of Germany, and the wage differential between men and women in the former GDR is far less than in Bavaria, Baden-Württemberg, Lower Saxony, and the key cities of Bremen and Hamburg. See "Why is Germany's Pay Gap So Large?" *The Economist*, Vol. 434, No. 9285 (March 14, 2020) 41.

[222] Family Code of the German Democratic Republic of December 20, 1965 quoted in Fulbrook, *The People's State,*152; and Langenhan and Ross, "The Socialist Glass Ceiling,"179.

[223] Kristen R. Ghodsee, *Why Women Have Better Sex Under Socialism* (New York: Nation Books, 2018), 133-137.

[224] Jean Edward Smith, *Germany Beyond the Wall: People, Politics…and Prosperity* (Boston, Massachusetts: Little, Brown and Company, 1969), 161. In the mid-1960s, only 20% of West German children attended nursery schools or kindergartens.

[225] Jessen, "Mobility and Blockage During the 1970s," 345, 348.

[226] Richard F. Staar, *Communist Regimes in Eastern Europe*, 4th ed., (Stanford, California: Hoover Institution Press, 1982), 123. In fact, Czechoslovakia had a higher standard of living into the 1970s. The GDR's standard of living became the highest in the 1980s as a result of on-going subsidies from West Germany. See Bulent

Naturally, these successes came with costs. Conformity became a pervasive social expectation and those who did not conform were subjected to harassment, if not imprisonment.[227] The Stasi instilled fear. The government awarded privileges to those who demonstrated their loyalty. The GDR did not have open elections, and political power became concentrated in the hands of a very few. Censorship was ubiquitous and all publications were subjected to a multilayered approval process. Journalists, authors, and artists internalized expectations so thoroughly that they became self-censors.[228]   Christians and intellectuals faced persecution, while schools and youth organizations became indoctrination centers.[229] Substantial environmental damage occurred as the dire consequences of pollution and toxic dumping became secondary to the needs of industry.[230] Travel and freedom of movement were carefully regulated within the country, and there were 72,000 people imprisoned for attempting to cross the Berlin Wall after its construction.[231] Most visibly, the availability and quality of consumer goods lagged far behind the standards in the West.

For Ulbricht, giving up personal freedoms and appliances in order to secure a proud socialist future was a deal well worth making. As he said in 1968, coercion in the GDR "differs from the compulsion in capitalist class society in the fact that it is applied in the interests of safeguarding the socialist order. One must always proceed from the question in whose interest and for what purpose compulsion is being employed."[232] In other words, better to compel for social equity than for the interests of idle capital.

Gokay, *Eastern Europe Since 1970: Decline of Socialism to Post-Communist Transition* (New York: Routledge, 2013), 52, 60.

[227] Fulbrook, *The People's State,* 8-10.

[228] Simone Barck, Christoph Classen, and Thomas Heimann, "The Fettered Media: Controlling Public Debate," *Dictatorship as Experience: Towards a Socio-Cultural History of the GDR* (Konrad H. Jarausch, ed., and Eve Duffy, trans.) (New York: Berghahn Books, 1999), 214, 216, 218. For additional information on censorship in the GDR see other essays in *Dictatorship as Experience*; and Robert Darton, *Censors at Work: How States Shaped Literature* (New York: W. W. Norton & Company, 2014), 148-197.

[229] John Rodden, *Repainting the Little Red Schoolhouse: A History of Eastern German Education, 1945-1995* (Oxford: Oxford University Press, 2002), 17, 62, 155.

[230] Joyce Marie Mushaben, *Becoming Madam Chancellor: Angela Merkel and the Berlin Republic* (New York: Cambridge University Press, 2017), 223; Daniel Charles, "East German Environment Comes into the Light," *Science,* vol. 247, no. 4940, 1990, 274+, EBSCOhost.

[231] Major, *Behind the Berlin Wall,* 147.

[232] Walter Ulbricht, *The Role of the Socialist State in the Shaping of the Developed Social System of Socialism* (Dresden: Verlag Zeit im Bild, 1968), 24. [Documents of the National Policy of the GDR, No. 6, 1968, Grafischer Grosbetrieb Völkerfreundschaft, Dresden, Translated by Intertext, Berlin, GDR], Norman Allderdice Collection, Box 123, Folder 24, #2000C53, Hoover Institution Archives, Stanford California.

$\mathcal{V}$

Heitor Villa-Lobos

1887-1959

When Brazilian composer Heitor Villa-Lobos was nine, his father Raul told him an Amazonian Indian legend. In the story, a beautiful maiden enjoyed bathing near the mouth of the Amazon River at dawn. Because of her exceptional beauty, the river gods calmed the waters, allowing her to enjoy the sun's warm rays of welcome. One day, the god of the tropical winds noticed her morning ritual and, in an attempt to seduce her, lavished her body with a gentle, perfumed breeze. Much like Narcissus, the maiden rebuffed the wind god, having become entranced by the exquisiteness of her own reflection. The angered wind god then punished the vain maiden by blowing her sweetened scent into the nostrils of a monster, who became crazed with desire. The monster destroyed everything in his path until he found the self-absorbed maiden staring at her reflection in the morning light. Suddenly, the maiden's shadow and the monster's shadow became one. Horrified by what she seemed to have become, the maiden ran from the river, pursued by the monster "into the abyss of her own desire."[1]

This legend must have made a significant impression on the young Villa-Lobos because it became the basis of his groundbreaking 1917 symphonic poem* *Amazonas*. The score for this one-movement work begins softly and grows steadily, almost as if the listener is entering the jungle for the first time to become increasingly surrounded by the unexpected sounds of a new and intimidating environment. The score ends eleven minutes later in frenzy and discord as the monster chases the maiden from the river. To achieve these effects, Villa-Lobos broke with European music tradition in a number of ways. Not only did he include instruments not typically associated with orchestral music, such as the violinophone and the viola d'amore,[2] but he also created unpredictable sounds from the traditional instruments by having half of the violins, violas,

---

[1] Heitor Villa-Lobos quoted in David Appleby, *Heitor Villa-Lobos: A Life, 1887-1950* (Lanham, Maryland: The Scarecrow Press, 2002), 42-43.

[2] Appleby, *Heitor Villa-Lobos,* 43. The violinophone is a violin with an attached horn attached that magnifies the violin's sound and gives it a distinctive tone. A viola d'amore has a set of sympathetic strings underneath the strings which are played; these additional strings vibrate in sympathy to create a different sound than a regular viola.

cellos, and double basses play broken chords while the other half did not.[3]   He also purposefully evoked the cries of Amazonian songbirds.[4] The result was so bold that the first orchestra to practice *Amazonas* did so under protest: the members of the string section tied handkerchiefs to their bows in order to register their dissatisfaction with the music and what was being asked of them. Consequently, the first public performance of *Amazonas* was cancelled and no one heard the work until it was performed for a Parisian audience in 1929.[5] By that point Villa-Lobos had become known as a revolutionary composer whom critics and audiences either seemed to love or hate.

Villa-Lobos' musical rise was unusual in that he did not have substantial formal training. As a boy, Heitor enjoyed staying up late and listening to his father Raul play chamber music with his friends on Saturday nights. This interest helped convince Raul to begin teaching Heitor to play the cello at age six by using a modified viola the boy could hold between his legs.[6] Two years later, Heitor began playing the clarinet thanks to an accident. One day, Heitor snuck into his father's room, was caught touching his father's clarinet, and dropped the instrument on the floor. Heitor's punishment was that he had to teach himself to play a scale on the clarinet; when he managed to do this very quickly, Raul extended the father-son lessons to both instruments.[7]   Prior to his unexpected death in 1899, Raul was an exacting, if encouraging, teacher, who liked to quiz his son on key characteristics of an array of European compositions. He also made a point of taking Heitor to musical performances to expand the boy's musical appreciation and sophistication.[8] Unfortunately, Villa-Lobos' mother, Noêmia, did not share in her husband's faith in music. In fact, Noêmia knew how hard it was to make a decent living as a musician because her own father had been unable to so, and she insisted that Raul pursue a career that could support a growing family.[9] In 1890, Raul landed a job as an assistant librarian at the National Library in Rio de Janeiro in part to satisfy Noêmia's expectations, but his untimely death meant that Noêmia, now a single parent with four children, transferred her musical anxieties from her husband to Heitor.[10] Noêmia pressed her eldest son to pursue medicine, but Villa-Lobos was stubborn. As a teenager, he regularly snuck out of the house at night to listen to Rio de Janeiro's street musicians, and at age sixteen he moved in with an aunt, who was a pianist and more supportive of his musical dreams.[11] During this time Villa-Lobos also taught himself to play the guitar.

---

[3] Gerard Béhague, *Heitor Villa-Lobos: The Search for Brazil's Musical Soul* (Austin, Texas: University of Texas, 1994) 55. The technical term for this technique is arpeggiated figures.

[4] Candance Slater, *Entangled Edens: Visions of the Amazon* (Berkeley, California: University of California Press, 2002), 280.

[5] Simon Wright, *Villa-Lobos* (New York: Oxford University Press, 1992), 19.

[6] David Appleby, *The Music of Brazil* (Austin, Texas: University of Texas Press, 1983), 118-119.

[7] Appleby, *Heitor Villa-Lobos,* 9.

[8] Heitor Villa-Lobos quoted in Gerard Béhague, "Villa-Lobos, Heitor," *The New Grove Dictionary of Music and Musicians*, 2nd ed., Stanley Sadie (ed.), Volume 26 (New York: Oxford University Press, 2001), 613. David Appleby indicates that Raul died of smallpox (*Heitor Villa-Lobos,* 10), but another biographer says that Raul died of malaria. See Lisa M. Peppercorn, *The World of Villa-Lobos in Pictures and Documents* (Aldershot, U.K.: Scolar Press, 1996), 22.

[9] Appleby, *Heitor Villa-Lobos,* 3.

[10] These children were Heitor's older sister Bertha (1886-1976), younger sister Carmen (1888-1970), and younger brother Othon (1897-1918). Noêmia also gave birth to three or four other children who died at birth or in infancy. Both Heitor and Othon were born prematurely. See Peppercorn, *The World of Villa-Lobos in Pictures and Documents*, 26.

[11] David Appleby, *The Music of Brazil* (Austin, Texas: University of Texas Press, 1983), 119; and Appleby, *Heitor Villa-Lobos,* 14.

In the opening years of the twentieth century, Villa-Lobos sought to support himself by playing diverse musical genres in a variety of venues. He served as a supporting cellist for orchestral concerts and a teetering opera company; he entertained Rio de Janeiro's aristocracy with waltzes, polkas, and other European dance music; he accompanied shows in silent movie houses and vaudeville theaters; he played in city cafes with varying degrees of prestige; and he even performed in bordellos.[12] Through this assortment of settings, Villa-Lobos met Brazilians from around the country who joined together to form *choros*—ethnically diverse instrumental ensembles that featured a soloist improvising on a familiar melody. Each *choros* could have different instruments, but they often included flute, viola, clarinet, trombone, ophicleide, guitar, and an assortment of Brazilian instruments such as a *cavaquinho* (a type of ukulele), an *atabaque* (a hand drum), and maracas.[13] By playing with these *ad hoc* bands, Villa-Lobos learned the art of improvisation and met Brazilians from very different backgrounds than his own. Villa-Lobos was quite young to be accepted by these musicians, but because he played a variety of instruments, took initiative, and read music, his skill and personality overcame his age and experience.[14]

Villa-Lobos gained further exposure to Brazil's musical complexity when he traveled to various parts of the vast country between 1908 and 1912. Exactly where he went and how long he spent in each place remains a matter of speculation because Villa-Lobos did not document his whereabouts by keeping a journal or by writing to his family during this period.[15] The specifics are also difficult to document accurately because as the years passed, Villa-Lobos relished the opportunity to entertain music critics and friends with exaggerated accounts of his survival in the Brazilian jungle. On one occasion, for example, Villa-Lobos said that he had been captured by Amazonian cannibals and had spent three days watching funeral

---

[12] Appleby, *Heitor Villa-Lobos*, 16-17; Wright, *Villa-Lobos*, 4; Peppercorn, *The World of Villa-Lobos in Pictures and Documents*, 39; and Thomas G. Garcia, "The 'Choro,' the Guitar and Villa-Lobos," *Luso-Brazilian Review*, 34, 1 (Summer 1997), 57-66, EBSCOhost.

[13] Gerard Béhague, "Choro," *The New Grove Dictionary of Music and Musicians*, 2nd ed., Stanley Sadie (ed.), Volume 5: Canon to Classic rock (New York: Oxford University Press, 2001), 766; and Garcia, "The 'Choro,' the Guitar and Villa-Lobos."

[14] Appleby, *Heitor Villa-Lobos*, 16.

[15] In 1930, Villa-Lobos admitted that he hated to write letters, and it is known that he threw most of the ones he received away. If he wrote any letters to his family during his travels, none of them have survived. In fact, the oldest known letter by Villa-Lobos is from 1927. See Lisa Peppercorn, "Introduction," *The Villa-Lobos Letters*, Lisa M. Peppercorn (ed. and trans.) (London: Toccata Press, 1994), 9-10. Appleby confirms that Villa-Lobos was out of touch with his family for over a year at a time. See Appleby, *Heitor Villa-Lobos,* 25.

ceremonies before he was rescued. On another occasion, Villa-Lobos asserted that he used a gramophone to conduct musical experiments on an Indian population that had had no prior contact with civilization.[16] On a third occasion, he recounted that he had seen a man-eating flower in action: we came upon "a large circular flower called the sensitive plant. My friend approached it, and it closed around him. I drew my knife! I slashed it without effect! I [then] thought of my saxophone," and decided to play a drawn-out melody. "The plant opened, expanded, freeing my friend!"[17] Coming from a man never mistaken for modest, these stories cast doubt upon his claim to have visited remote places in the modern states of Acre, Goiás, Roraima, Mato Grosso, Minas Gerais, and Tocantins over the course of three complicated trips.[18] It is known that Villa-Lobos travelled to the southern state of Panará because he gave a concert in Paranaguá in April 1908 that

included his own works and those by several European composers.[19] It is also true that Villa-Lobos financed a trip to the Amazon by selling off rare books he inherited from his father. At the Teatro Amazonas in Manaus, he gave two concerts that featured well-known works by Mendelssohn, Chopin, and Verdi, as well as his own piece for voice and piano, *Japoneza op. 2*.[20] Even if Manaus was the only place in the Brazilian hinterland that Villa-Lobos visited, he would have travelled there by ship via Salvador, Recife, Natal, São Luís, and Belém, and then up the Amazon River via Santarém. This journey would have allowed him to experience unfamiliar sights and sounds. It would have a been a revelatory journey, as it was even for a seasoned *National Geographic* reporter, who wrote twenty years later about this part of the world with a sense of awe:

> From the air, you see how close primeval forests crowd Pará. Its streets end in the jungle…In equatorial dawn and dusk it smells of jungle….Giant mango trees, when in fruit pelted with rocks by small boys, shade the wide cobblestoned street of its better quarters. Along its water front you smell smoked crude rubber, the half-tanned skins of jaguars and snakes, pineapples, piles of Brazil nuts ready for shops bound for New York or Liverpool….You smell, too, the shop of the wild-animal dealer, its front gaudily painted with a Noah's Ark of jungle creatures. He shows you bright, shrill macaws, lewd monkeys, and snarling jaguars; and anteaters, living now not on ants, but on fresh eggs broken into a dish; and cunning little capybaras, or "river pigs", and the scarlet ibis, a stork, a white owl

[16] Lisa Peppercorn, "Villa-Lobos's Brazilian Excursions," *Villa-Lobos: Collected Studies* (Aldershot, U.K: Scolar Press, 1992), 25.

[17] Heitor Villa-Lobos quoted in Ralph Gustafson, "Villa-Lobos and the Man-Eating flower: A Memoir," *The Musical Quarterly*, 75, 1 (Spring 1991), 1-11, EBSCOhost.

[18] Peppercorn, "Villa-Lobos's Brazilian Excursions," 26.

[19] Appleby, *Heitor Villa-Lobos*, 20, 22. An article in *Time* magazine also asserts that Villa-Lobos financed his Amazon trip by selling his father's books. See "Tropical Thunderstorm," *Time*, Latin American ed., Vol. LXV, no. 5, (January 31, 1955), 44.

[20] Peppercorn, *The World of Villa-Lobos in Pictures and Documents*, 47; and Appleby, *Heitor Villa-Lobos*, 20, 23, 119. A program for Villa-Lobos' appearance in Manaus does not list the year, but the concerts were either in September 1911 or September 1912.

in a black mask; rare parrots, multicolored wild ducks; and an electric eel which give you a distinct shock when you stick a wire into his water barrel and touch him.[21]

Little wonder Villa-Lobos found his travel experiences, whatever they were, worthy of exaggeration in later life.

Soon after his return to Rio de Janeiro in late 1912, Villa-Lobos met Lucília Guimarães, a graduate of the Instituto Nacional de Música who taught piano at the Colégio Sacré-Coeur. The relationship proved to be a transformative one since Lucília's family heartily supported Villa-Lobos' pursuit of a musical career and welcomed him into the family,[22] and since Lucília became a key interpreter of the 35-year-old's music.[23] The two were married on November 12, 1913, and Villa-Lobos moved into the Guimarães' home. Over the next year and a half, Villa-Lobos wrote constantly, composing almost 100 pieces, but he remained largely underappreciated by those with influence. His first break came on July 31, 1915, when a well-known and respected Rio conductor included Villa-Lobos' *Suite característica* in the orchestral program. This was followed in November by an exclusive concert of Villa-Lobos' music at which Lucília was the principal pianist.[24]

The next important step in Villa-Lobos' rise to recognition came in 1918, when the well-known

Polish-American pianist Arthur Rubinstein was in Rio de Janeiro as part of a South American tour. Two students from the national conservatory told Rubinstein about a musical "genius," who "was twice expelled from the conservatory for rejecting any intervention or criticism from the teachers."[25] Intrigued, Rubinstein decided that he had to meet this unusual man and had the two students escort him to the Cinema Odeon, where Villa-Lobos was still part of the *choros* that accompanied silent films. At the intermission, Villa-Lobos and his compatriots broke away from the film's clichéd tunes and played what Rubinstein described as "music, real music! It was made up of Brazilian rhythms" that were "treated in a completely original way. It sounded confused, formless, but very attractive."[26] The piece was *Amazonas*. Rubinstein was so impressed that he asked to meet Villa-Lobos. The introduction went well as long as Rubinstein praised Villa-Lobos' work, but when Rubinstein asked if Villa-Lobos had written anything for the piano, Villa-Lobos rudely responded, "Pianists have no use for composers. All they want is success and money."[27] Rubinstein took offense and walked away. Fortunately, Villa-Lobos reconsidered his words and behavior and sought to make amends. Several days later, he appeared with his band at Rubinstein's hotel room at 8:00 a.m. and played several pieces. As he listened, Rubinstein became "convinced that I was facing a great composer who had something to say."[28] The two men struck up a lasting friendship, and Rubinstein played

[21] Frederick Simpich, "Skypaths Through Latin America," *The National Geographic Magazine*, Vol. LIX, No. 1 (January, 1931), 1-79.

[22] Appleby, *Heitor Villa-Lobos*, 29.

[23] Peppercorn, *The World of Villa-Lobos in Pictures and Documents*, 59.

[24] Appleby, *Heitor Villa-Lobos*, 34-35.

[25] Arthur Rubinstein, *My Many Years* (New York: Alfred A. Knopf, 1980), 90.

[26] Rubinstein, *My Many Years*, 91.

[27] Villa-Lobos quoted in Rubinstein, *My Many Years*, 91.

[28] Rubinstein, *My Many Years*, 92.

the first suite of Villa-Lobos' piano series called *A Prole do Bebê* (The Baby's Family) as part of his last concert in Rio. Although the audience booed the composition, Rubinstein's international influence meant that Villa-Lobos' works began to appear on concert programs within Brazil.

~

Just as the sinking of the *Lusitania* helped to bring the United States into World War I after a firm policy of neutrality, Germany's U-boat campaign did the same for Brazil. On April 5, 1917, a German submarine sank a Brazilian freighter, shocking the nation. Germany attacked the Brazilian ship for the same reason it attacked other neutral ships in the Atlantic: to prevent supplies arriving to Great Britain and France. In Brazil's case, the country had benefited greatly from exporting foodstuffs during the war as a neutral country. In fact, the value of bean exports jumped from $24,000 to $10,000,000 between 1915 and 1917, while the value of sugar exports rose from $3,000,000 to $15,000,000. On October 23, after the Germans sank a fourth ship flying a Brazilian flag, Brazil declared war on the German Empire. It was the only South American country to do so. Joining the Allies gave Brazil a seat at Versailles.[29]

As a victor, Brazil sought to remember the horrors of the war and celebrate the peace. In 1919, the president of Brazil asked the director of the Instituto Nacional de Música to organize a commemorative concert to that end. The director asked three composers to each write symphonies about war, victory, and peace; Villa-Lobos was not initially one of the director's choices, but when one composer declined the invitation, Villa-Lobos was selected in his place that May.[30] As summer 1919 passed without Villa-Lobos showing evidence of progress, however, Lucília began to fret about the looming deadline. All she saw that summer was her husband going to movies and playing French billiards. When she confronted Villa-Lobos in July, he told her that he had already composed the symphony in his head. Only a few days before the first rehearsal, Villa-Lobos wrote down the score for *Sinfonia no. 3, A Guerra*. This symphony rivaled Strauss and Wagner in the scale of its production: 164 musicians, including 26 first violins, 24 second violins, 12 violas, 12 cellos, 12 basses, and a 37-member vocal ensemble.[31] When Villa-Lobos drew five curtain calls on opening night, it was clear the composer had deserved the commission. One critic hailed it as "full of life, rich in ideas, energy, and movement, graphically describing the horrors of the struggles of humanity during the past five years."[32] Villa-Lobos wrote two more symphonies to complete the commission, *Sinfonia no. 4, A Vitória* (1919) and *Sinfonia no. 5, A Paz* (1920). The income this commission produced allowed Villa-Lobos and Lucília to move out of the Guimarães' home to their own apartment. Brazil had begun to recognize its genius.

In the aftermath of World War I, Modernism* represented Brazil's cultural avant-garde. The movement's greatest advocates, led by writer Mário de Andrade, created works of literature, art,

---

[29] E. Bradford Burns, *A History of Brazil*, 2nd ed. (New York: Columbia University Press, 1980), 352-353. Brazil won both of its demands at Versailles, thanks to American support: 1) Germany had to pay for the Brazilian coffee it seized in German ports at 1914 prices; and 2) Brazil got to keep German vessels it seized in Brazilian ports in 1917.
[30] Peppercorn, *The World of Villa-Lobos in Pictures and Documents*, 71. The Brazilian president was Epitácio da Silva Pessoa, and the director was Abdon Filinto Milanês.
[31] Lisa Peppercorn, "Foreign Influences in Villa-Lobos's Music," *Villa-Lobos: Collected Studies*, 55.
[32] Júlio Reis quoted in Appleby, *Heitor Villa-Lobos*, 34-35.

and music that attempted to forsake the nineteenth century's long cultural influence. Brazilian Modernists were keen to do so because so much of that influence was seen as a manifestation of Europe's cultural hegemony as opposed to Brazilian or even South American inspirations. As Andrade noted, "modernism in Brazil was a rupture, it was an abandonment of principles and consequential techniques, it was a revolt against what the nation's thinking was then."[33] The spark that lit the movement's fire in Brazil came in December 1917, when a Brazilian Expressionist* painter, Anita Malfatti, presented her solo exhibition in São Paulo. The public found Malfatti's bold colors and distorted figures jolting; one influential art critic went so far as to declare her insane,[34] but a small group of intellectuals were inspired by Malfatti's freshness and its break with Brazilian tradition. They began to write and to seek out other artistic innovators, and as the months passed the group's postwar energy came to coincide with the hundredth anniversary of Brazil's independence from Portugal. To the budding group of Brazilian Modernists, it seemed fitting to gather to celebrate the next step in Brazil's cultural development and independence. The result was the February 1922 *Semana de Arte Moderna* (Week of Modern Art), which was organized by Andrade and which was held in São Paulo to signify a symbolic break with Rio de Janeiro's colonial origins and conservative traditions. As Andrade said, Rio may have been more international, but São Paulo "was much more modern in spirit," and it was only through São Paulo that modernism might spread across the country.[35]

The program for the *Semana de Arte Moderna* featured lectures, poetry readings, and concerts—all designed to educate the audience about Modernist principles, both theoretically and experientially. Unfortunately for the performers, including Villa-Lobos, the audience did not receive the lesson well. People threw fruit and vegetables at the stage and shouted insults so loudly that at times it was impossible to hear the speakers or the music. There was even a fist fight between a young baritone vocalist and a heckler.[36] Villa-Lobos' holding a large share of the Week's musical program made him a repeated target. Hampered by a kidney ailment that swelled his ankles and covered his feet in sores, Villa-Lobos couldn't wear formal shoes and had to shuffle across the stage. The audience mocked the conductor's attire and movements, sarcastically clapping in rhythm.[37] Despite this embarrassment, Villa-Lobos' faith in himself did not waiver. He emerged from the *Semana de Arte Moderna* convinced that he had something unique to share with the world that went beyond both Modernism and conventional chamber and orchestral music. In 1923 he wrote, "[I] will never, ever change to please public taste….What I can say for certain is that my art is my own and cannot conform to this intoxication that is called modernism. [In this trend] I see only horrible imitation. [Instead], I follow my own way, my own path."[38]

The *Semana de Arte Moderna* convinced Villa-Lobos that the only way that he could gain the international attention he craved was to go to Europe. Funding such a trip posed a significant challenge, but a member of the Brazilian Congress introduced a bill to help pay for it, as Congress

[33] Mário de Andrade, "The Modernist Movement," Richard Correll (trans.), *Portuguese Studies* 24, no. 1 (November 2008): 95-115, EBSCOhost.

[34] Kristin G. Congdon and Kara Kelley Hallmark, *Artists from Latin American Cultures: A Biographical Dictionary* (Westport, Connecticut: Greenwood, 2002), 159.

[35] de Andrade, "The Modernist Movement."

[36] Appleby, *The Music of Brazil*, 91.

[37] Appleby, *Heitor Villa-Lobos,* 57.

[38] Villa-Lobos quoted in Appleby, *Heitor Villa-Lobos*, 66.

had done for other composers in an effort to promote international appreciation for Brazil.[39] The allotted funds could not cover all of the costs, but friends came to his rescue, and Villa-Lobos sailed for France on June 30, 1923.[40] He did so wanting to give Parisian audiences something they had never heard. This meant leaving nineteenth-century chamber and orchestral music behind while offering something that Brazilian popular music didn't. This was no small challenge since the pioneering samba band Oito Batutas, led by famous musicians Pixinguinha and Donga, had been wildly received by Parisian audiences in early 1922. The band's reception was so enthusiastic, in fact, that many Parisians saw it as being emblematic of Brazilian culture.[41] Villa-Lobos realized that the exotic turned heads, for in the 1910s he had seen how a Paraguayan guitarist provocatively marketed himself as the elaborately-dressed, guitar-playing Indian from the jungle.[42] Villa-Lobos knew he had to be as tantalizing, if less garish, to win the attention of Parisians. He had to produce something special, thereby tackling the issue that Brazilian author Coelho Neto thought bedeviled the nation in 1910: urban Brazil produced nothing original. "Even our views are imported," Neto bemoaned.[43] Villa-Lobos' solution was to switch his style away from both Romanticism and Modernism and embrace indigenous Brazilian music in a new way.[44] In 1923, either just before his departure from Rio de Janeiro or just after his arrival in Paris, he wrote *Nonetto: Impressão Rápida de Todo o Brasil* (*A Brief Impression of the Whole of Brazil*).[45] The fourteen-minute, one movement piece is scored for flute, piccolo, oboe, clarinet, saxophone, bassoon, celesta, harp, piano, a mixed chorus with as many as twelve parts, and, most distinctively, a percussion section that requires eighteen instruments and at least two players. The work sought to capture the vastness and diversity of world's fifth largest country, and by using instruments which were either unknown by or rarely used for European audiences, Villa-Lobos created a sound that melded and synthesized both popular and orchestral Brazilian music.[46] When *Nonetto* premiered in Paris on May 24, 1924, it shocked the audience with its new sounds, but supportive critics heard understood that the Brazilian composer offered something genuine and unprecedented. As one said,

> Villa-Lobos is intellectually and emotionally alive to all that goes on around him. His is a nature that seeks to transcribe everything it finds in life. In him the elements of savage races and exquisitely civilised peoples meet and this union of temperamental extremes is

[39] These composers included Antônio Francisco Braga, Antônio Carlos Gomes, Alexandro Levy, and Alberto Nepomuceno. See Peppercorn, *The World of Villa-Lobos in Pictures and Documents*, 88.
[40] Appleby, *Heitor Villa-Lobos,* 61.
[41] Marc A. Hertzman, *Making Samba: A New History of Race and Music in Brazil* (Duke University Press: Durham, North Carolina, 2013), 107, 109.
[42] Wright, *Villa-Lobos*, 5-6. The Paraguayan guitarist was Agustín Barrios Mangoré. In his advertisements, he was "Nitsuga Mangoré, the Paganini of the Guitar, from the Jungles of Paraguay." "Nitsuga" is Agustin spelled backwards.
[43] Coelho Neto quoted in Thomas E. Skidmore, *Black into White: Race and Nationality in Brazilian Thought* (Durham, North Carolina: Duke University Press, 1993), 97.
[44] Peppercorn, "Foreign Influences in Villa-Lobos's Music," 53.
[45] The disagreement over the date is discussed in Elisa Macedo DeKaney, "Eight Choral Works by Heitor Villa-Lobos (1887-1959)," *The Choral Journal*, no. 4 (2007): 8-17, EBSCOhost.
[46] This description comes from several sources: Wright, *Villa-Lobos*, 40-41; Appleby, *Heitor Villa-Lobos*, 67-68; and DeKaney, "Eight Choral Works by Heitor Villa-Lobos (1887-1959)." The unknown instruments include a puíta (a drum), the reco-reco (scrapers), and the xucalho (a rattle). The rarely used items included coconut shells, a whistle, and a china plate scraped with a knife.

the determining cause of his rare sensibility…He is a creator of ambiances, of spiritual worlds and vistas, not an imitator of them.[47]

This reception convinced Villa-Lobos that he had to return to Brazil to raise funds to support an extended European stay. He arrived back in Rio in October 1924.[48]

Villa-Lobos' return to his homeland was not only about finding a patron. Before he could return to Europe, he had to compose new material that would promote his reputation as a unique artist. Over the next twenty-six months, he devoted much of his time and energy to writing new music. The composer also looked for new sources of inspiration, which led him to the National Library to research Brazilian musical traditions. He examined Indian instruments in the library's collection, and he read early European accounts of Brazil, which included descriptions of Indian and African melodies and customs, as well as helpful illustrations.[49] He listened to the recorded cylinders that a Brazilian anthropologist had collected from the Parecís Indians in 1912.[50] Villa-Lobos also frequented samba venues, for by the mid-1920s many White urban intellectuals saw samba as defining Brazil's authentic national music.[51] From all of these sources and influences, as well as from his own sense of what moved him and what impressed others, Villa-Lobos began to produce what many music historians and musicologists see as the finest works of his career. As for the financial obstacles, Arthur Rubinstein once again proved pivotal in the development of Villa-Lobos' career. The two men renewed their friendship when Rubinstein was in Rio for another concert tour. Known as a late-night carouser,[52] Villa-Lobos took the pianist club-hopping on those nights when he wasn't performing, so that he might experience the richness of the city's musical scene, including samba. Rubinstein heard a variety of instruments that were new to him and became convinced that Villa-Lobos had to return to Paris so that he might bring his version of amalgamated Brazilian music to more European audiences. Therefore, Rubinstein approached a member of the

[47] Irving Schwerké, *Le Jazz est mort! Vive le Jazz!*, 201, 203. This book was privately published by the author and presents a collection of his writings. It does not give a place of publication, a publisher, or a date of publication. I obtained copy number 1,040 from the rare book collection at Dominican University of California, thanks to librarian Anne Reid. Based on internal textual references, I believe it was published in 1926. The title of the essay quoted here is Irving Schwerké, "Villa-Lobos: Rabelais of Modern Music," *The League of Composers Review*, January 1925.
[48] Latin American Music Center, Jacobs School of Music, Indiana University, "1924," *Heitor Villa-Lobos Website*, accessed December 4, 2017, http://villalobos.iu.edu/1924
[49] The works included Hans Staden's *Zwei Reisen nach Brasilien, 1548-1555*; Jean de Léry, *Histoire d'un Voyage Fait en la Terre du Brésil, Autrement Dite Amérique*; Johann Baptist von Spix and Karl Friedrich Philipp von Martius' *Reise in Brasilien in den Jahren 1817-1820*; drawings by Jean-Baptiste Debret, who was in Brazil from 1816 and 1831; and engravings by Johann Moritz Rugendas. See Peppercorn, *The World of Villa-Lobos in Pictures and Documents*, 100-101, 104, 109, 113-114.
[50] Appleby, *Heitor Villa-Lobos*, 81-82. The anthropologist was Edgar Roquette Pinto (1884-1954).
[51] Hermano Vianna, *The Mystery of Samba: Popular Music and National Identity in Brazil*, John Charles Chasteen (ed. and trans.) (Chapel Hill, North Carolina: University of North Carolina Press, 1999), 2; and Brian Owensby, "Toward a History of Brazil's 'Cordial Racism': Race beyond Liberalism," *Comparative Study of Society and History*, 47.2 (April, 2005), 318-347, ProQuest Central. Vianna notes on the first page of his book that one night in 1926, Villa-Lobos, anthropologist Gilberto Freyre, historian Sérgio Buarque de Holanda, district attorney Pedro Prudente de Morass Neto, and classical composer and pianist Kuciano Gallet went out together to hear samba greats Donga, Pixinguinha, and Patrício. "White" and "Black" are both intentionally capitalized. See Chapter F, footnote 60.
[52] Vianna, *The Mystery of Samba*. 7.

wealthy family that owned the newly-opened, art deco Copacabana Palace, Carlos Guinle, and asked him to sponsor Villa-Lobos. Rubinstein's appealed to Guinle's vanity:

> How would you like to be celebrated after your death Carlos?...Right here in Brazil lives an authentic genius, in my opinion the only one on the whole American continent. His country does not understand his music yet, but future generations will be proud of him. Like all great creators, he has no means of making his works known in the world unless he is helped by some great Maecenas. I thought of you first of all, knowing your understanding, your patriotism, and your great generosity. The composer is Heitor Villa-Lobos, a future famous name in the history of Brazil, and if you are ready to help him, your name will always be linked with his.[53]

The heavy-handed pitch worked, and Villa-Lobos soon found himself with substantial funds and use of use of a Left Bank apartment at 11 Place St. Michel, which was owned by the Guinle family.[54] Villa-Lobos and Lucília departed for Paris in December 1926.

   In 1927, Villa-Lobos gave two concerts of his own works at the thousand-seat Salle Gaveau, each of which received enormously positive responses from Parisian audiences and the local press. These concerts introduced European audiences to a series of works he called *Chôros*, which might have taken their name from the Brazilian instrumental street ensembles but were really something more. The program for the October 24 concert included *Chôros no. 2*, a three-minute dialog between a

---

[53] Rubinstein, *My Many Years,* 154-155.
[54] Appleby, *Heitor Villa-Lobos,* 72.

flute and a clarinet. It begins with sharply dissonant tones and timbres, but very slowly allows the two instruments to increasingly complement one another. An independent voice is retained until the final note, when the flute and the clarinet join in harmony.[55] Contrastingly, *Chôros no. 8*, which was also on the program that night, is a full orchestral piece that requires eight percussionists playing an array of Afro-Brazilian instruments and offers little resolution. It purposefully evokes what the Parisian audience would have perceived and enjoyed as exotic and primitive,[56] just as Josephine Baker's *Danse Sauvage* did on opening night at the Revue Négre two years earlier.[57] A December 5 concert continued this theme with *Chôros no. 3* and *Chôros no. 10*. The former, known also as *Pica-Pau* (Woodpecker), is a four-minute choral work for male voices that is based on a Parecís Indian melody collected by a Brazilian anthropologist in 1908. The voices are accompanied by clarinet, saxophone, bassoon, three horns, and a trombone, thereby merging the Amerindian base with Rio's popular street music and Western musical traditions.[58] There may also be an purposeful attempt to refer to the Afro-Brazilian musical tradition.[59] The latter, subtitled *Rasga o Coração* (Break the Heart), fuses traditions in an even more powerfully with a popular *choros* musical phrase, the words of a well-known Brazilian poet, and two Indian melodies with different scales and bird sounds.[60] In fact, *Chôros no. 10* is considered to be a work that unites the urban individual with the vastness of the Brazilian jungle, thereby revealing a vision for the nation's future.[61] In doing this, *Chôros no. 10* echoes the goals of Brazil's 1891 constitution, which called for designating "a zone of 14,400 square kilometers in the central plateau of the Republic…which will at an opportune moment demarcate the establishment…of the future federal Capital."[62]

Villa-Lobos followed these concerts with a campaign to enhance his reputation for epitomizing the Other, just as Baker had done. In mid-December 1927, he gave an interview to music critic Lucie Delarue Mardrus in which he told fanciful, even outrageous stories about his travels in Amazonia as a young man, knowing that these stories would generate more enthusiasm for his work. This calculated publicity stunt was effective: conducting invitations rolled in from the capitals of Europe, and although most of these offers were never realized, they proved to Villa-Lobos that his name was on the lips of many culturally important Europeans.[63] The composer's name was also spoken in Brazil as word spread of his success, but not all of the talk was positive. In

---

[55] Appleby, *Heitor Villa-Lobos*, 81. The *Chôros* were not written in numerical order and the numbers do not hold any special significance.

[56] Carol A. Hess, *Representing the Good Neighbor: Music, Difference, and the Pan American Dream* (New York: Oxford University Press, 2013), 90-91.

[57] Phyllis Rose, *Jazz Cleopatra: Josephine Baker and Her Time* (New York: Vintage Books, 1991), 18-19. The opening night was October 2, 1925.

[58] DeKaney, "Eight Choral Works by Heitor Villa-Lobos (1887-1959)." This anthropologist was also Edgar Roquette Pinto (1884-1854).

[59] Béhague, *Heitor Villa-Lobos*, 78-80.

[60] Appleby, *The Music of Brazil*, 131-132. The poet was Catulo da Paixão Cearense, who deeply appreciated Villa-Lobos' use of his words; thirty years later, however, Cearense's relative sued Villa-Lobos for plagiarism. The case was settled in Villa-Lobos' favor. See Wright, *Villa-Lobos*, 72.

[61] Wright, *Villa-Lobos*, 70-71.

[62] "Making the Federal District, Constituent Assembly," Amy Chazkel (trans.), *The Rio de Janeiro Reader: History, Culture, Politics*, Daryle Williams, Amy Chazkel and Paulo Knauss (eds.) (Durham, North Carolina: Duke University Press, 2016), 148.

[63] Appleby, *Heitor Villa-Lobos*, 73, 76. The invitations came from Amiens, Amsterdam, Barcelona, Berlin, Brussels, Liege, Lisbon, Madrid, Poitiers, and Vienna. The Brussels invitation did materialize, but as with Igor Stravinsky's debut of *Rite of Spring* in Paris in 1913, the Belgian audience rioted as supporters and detractors physically fought with one another over the value and meaning of the works that challenged the musical canon.

fact, as Villa-Lobos' popularity grew in Europe, it waned in Brazil. The reason was that just as elite Brazilians fretted in 1922 that Pixinguinha and Donga's samba band tour would leave the impression that all Brazilians were Black, many of the nation's affluent Whites believed that Villa-Lobos' music said Brazil was nothing but a wild land full of cavorting, darker-skinned men and women constantly surrounded by disturbing jungle sounds.[64]

The reality was that Brazil in the 1920s was a multicultural society still dealing with the long shadow of slavery. It had the ignoble distinction as being the last nation in the Americas with legalized slavery; it wasn't abolished until 1888. Perhaps more problematically, the abolition of slavery failed to change society significantly. The 750,000 former slaves were left to fend for themselves and lingered at the bottom of the social ladder. Political power remained concentrated in the hands of a White agrarian oligarchy that continued to focus Brazil's economy on agricultural exports.[65] This White-Black socio-economic division was complicated by the presence of the descendants of free Blacks, pervasive interracial relationships, and immigration.[66] Many politicians and intellectuals in the late nineteenth and early twentieth centuries supported European immigration and interracial liaisons, believing that miscegenation would eventually end perceived Black inferiority, while sparing Brazil the racial tensions that characterized United States' history.[67] Whiteness would triumph in time, peacefully and gradually. Villa-Lobos shared this view. He saw European culture as superior to all others and wanted darker-skinned Brazilians to embrace White culture to escape their lower social standing.[68] One of Villa-Lobos' good friends, anthropologist Gilberto Freyre, helped change the national discourse about race by arguing that Brazil's unique amalgamation of Whites, Blacks, and Indians gave the country an unparalleled strength. Freyre frankly said that "the majority of our countrymen are the near descendants of either masters or of slaves, and many of them have sprung from the union of slave-owners with slave women" to form "so perfect…[a] fusion" that the "curious observer of today has the impression that they have grown up together fraternally" and "complement one another with their differences." He argued that Brazil was moving in the direction of "a broad democratization…of interhuman relationships" and possessed "a national sentiment tempered by a sympathy for the foreigner that is so broad as to become, practically, universalism." To Freyre, Brazil was "marching onward toward a social democracy" because of its diversity, not in spite of it.[69] This argument was widely accepted in the

---

[64] Hertzman, *Making Samba*, 107; and Appleby, *Heitor Villa-Lobos,* 76. Theodore Roosevelt's account of his exploration of Amazonia in 1913-14 created a similar image for Americans of Brazil as only a dangerous wilderness; as Roosevelt said, "In this dense jungle, when the sun is behind clouds, a man without a compass who strays a hundred yards from the river may readily become hopelessly lost." See Theodore Roosevelt, *Through the Brazilian Wilderness* (New York: Charles Scribner's Sons, 1914), 158.

[65] Emilia Viotti da Costa, *The Brazilian Empire: Myths and Histories* (Chapel Hill, North Carolina: University of North Carolina Press, 2000), xxvi-xxvii, 166, 171, 199, 233.

[66] In 1872, Brazil had a population of 9.9 million, 15.2% of whom were slaves and 42% of whom were "free colored." See Skidmore, *Black into White*, 41. In terms of immigration, over 2.2 million people arrived between 1872 and 1910. The highest numbers came from Italy, Portugal, Spain, and Germany. See Thomas Skidmore, *Brazil: Five Centuries of Change* (New York: Oxford University Press, 1999), 72-73.

[67] Skidmore, *Black into White,* 76.

[68] Jerry Dávila, *Diploma of Whiteness: Race and Social Policy in Brazil, 1917-1945* (Durham, North Carolina: Duke University Press, 2003), 6.

[69] Gilberto Freyre, "Preface to the English-Language Edition," *The Masters and the Slaves: A Study in the Development of Brazilian Civilization,* Samuel Putnam (trans.) (New York: Alfred A. Knopf, 1946), xi-xiv. The extent of Freyre's friendship with Villa-Lobos is seen in Freyre's dedication of his book *New World in the Tropics* (1959) to "Heitor Villa-Lobos, my friend." The composer died a few months later.

1930s and 1940s because it was the only way to alter the perception of Brazil as a second-class nation.[70]   National pride demanded that Brazil embrace its demographic realities, but racial prejudice or discrimination persisted nonetheless.[71]   Villa-Lobos himself displayed such bias, despite his intellectual and musical debt to Afro-Brazilians and Brazilian Indians. In 1941, he composed an ethnomusicological map of the world to explain the influences that shaped Brazil's musical culture. Europe's contributions dominated Villa-Lobos' schema, and Africa's influence appeared to be far less important than Brazilian reality would suggest.[72]

~

In the 1830s, coffee replaced sugar as Brazil's primary export. By the last decade of the nineteenth century, coffee had become so dominate that it comprised 64.5% of the nation's exports, whereas rubber stood at 15% and sugar at just 6%.[73] By 1928, Brazil's consul general in New York went so far as to say that "coffee represents three-quarters of Brazilian exports, which means that coffee is…our real money….Coffee is practically Brazil itself."[74] Given this economic domination, coffee plantation owners in the major producing state of São Paulo sought to brandish a corresponding political influence at the national level. This assertion was resented by those in the other eighteen states and this interstate conflict came to a head in the aftermath of the national election of 1930. This election pitted a Paulista,* Júlio Prestes, against Rio Grande do Sul's Getúlio Vargas. Prestes won the election on March 1, but four months later, when Vargas' running mate was assassinated in Recife, those angered by the outcome of the election marched on Rio de Janeiro, supported by their state's military forces. In order to prevent a possible civil war, the national army decided to support the approaching rebels and to prevent Prestes from taking office. Vargas arrived in the capital on November 3, swaggering with gaucho style.[75] It would be fifteen years before this quasi-fascist left the presidential palace.

---

[70] Brian Owensby, "Toward a History of Brazil's 'Cordial Racism': Race beyond Liberalism," *Comparative Study of Society and History*, 47.2 (April, 2005), 318-347, ProQuest Central.

[71] By the 1970s Freyre's ideas were challenged by academics who noted that racial prejudice and discrimination continued. Studies have shown that this prejudice has continued since then. A survey of adults in Rio de Janerio in 2000 found that Cariocas of all racial groups agree that racial prejudice exists and that this prejudice results in discrimination against Blacks. See Stanley R. Bailey, *Legacies of Race: Identities, Attitudes and Politics in Brazil* (Stanford, California: Stanford University Press, 2009), 97-98. As the twenty-first century has progressed, little has changed: Blacks remain marginalized in education, employment opportunities, and health care, as many studies have shown. See, for example, John Burdick, *The Color of Sound: Race, Religion, and Music in Brazil* (New York: New York University Press, 2013), 6-7. A 2013 study of racial prejudice in Brazilian children confirmed that aversive racism (subconscious discrimination) continues to persist, so attitudes are apt to continue. See Dalila Xavier de França and Maria Benedicta Monteiro, "Social Norms and the Expression of Prejudice: the Development of Aversive Racism in Childhood," *European Journal of Social Psychology*, 43, 4 (June, 2013), 263-271, EBSCOhost.

[72] Hertzman, *Making Samba,* 146-149.

[73] Burns, *A History of Brazil*, 196.

[74] Sebastião Sampaio, "Brazilian-American Coffee Relations: the Sao Paulo Coffee Institute at the Annual Coffee Convention in Chicago," *Brazil*, No. 6, 1st year (November 1928): 9-12, Box 144, Campaign and Transition: Subject, Trips—Latin America "A"—Trips—Latin America Brazil—K, Herbert Hoover Papers, Herbert Hoover Presidential Library, West Branch, Iowa.

[75] Skidmore, *Brazil: Five Centuries of Change*, 107-108.

These political events had a profound effect on Villa-Lobos' life. The composer had met Prestes during the presidential campaign and had proposed to him that Brazil adopt a program of national music education. Prestes responded favorably, so when Prestes won the election Villa-Lobos began to assemble a curriculum for São Paulo state. Vargas' *coup d'état* dashed Villa-Lobos' hopes initially, but because the composer's ideas fit so well with Vargas' nationalistic plans, Villa-Lobos was permitted to continue. Villa-Lobos spoke before the São Paulo legislature, which, after some debate, accepted his proposal. He then launched a 54-town tour within the state to promote popular understanding of serious music. This tour was not particularly successful: attendance was poor and the works by Beethoven, Chopin, Villa-Lobos, and others were often too long for the uninitiated. Villa-Lobos once again demonstrated little tact, for he repeatedly criticized the public's greater interest in *fútbol* than music. His sullying of the national pastime resulted in audiences throwing rotten eggs at the stage and the musicians needing to leave more than one town abruptly.[76] Despite these setbacks, the tour still impressed those in influential positions. On April 18, 1931, Vargas issued a decree that created a new government entity, the Superintendência de Educação Musical e Artística (SEMA), and made music instruction compulsory in the public schools in the state of Rio de Janeiro. Villa-Lobos was to lead this program, so he and Lucília moved back to Rio in late 1931; his formal appointment came the following April, giving Villa-Lobos a stable income for the first time in his life.[77]

Villa-Lobos embraced his new job with vigor, believing in the transformative power of music. He began by training music teachers and organizing school choirs. In 1932, he published his *Guia Prático*, a practical guide for choral instruction that included 137 folk songs from around the country that he had arranged.[78] These songs were designed to instill a patriotic fervor, the spirit of *brasilidade* (Brazilian-ness) in children. Learning the songs and being a part of a chorus would foster what he saw as essential collective discipline.[79] By practicing songs like "Hymn to the Sun of Brazil," and "Hymn to President Vargas" in small groups for weeks in advance, and by using a standardized system of hand gestures, Villa-Lobos could then direct as many as 40,000 children at a nationalist rally, such as Flag Day or Day of the Fatherland. To create both a visual and aural effect, he had the children, all dressed in the same attire, wave their arms in unison as they sang. The results produced memorable experiences for both the performers and the audience.[80] These concerts were not altogether different from the rallies German boys and girls experienced as members of Hitler Youth in the 1930s, which is why Villa-Lobos received criticism from Mário de

---

[76] The tour was from January to September 1931. Villa-Lobos made most of the logistical arrangements himself, and this process left him exhausted. Not all of the concerts were poorly received: in Botucatú on February 14, 1931, flowers replaced rotten eggs and he was awarded a gold medal. The quote attributed to Villa-Lobos about football is: "Soccer causes human intelligence to detour from the head to the feet!" For more information, see David E. Vassberg, "Villa-Lobos as Pedagogue: Music in the Service of the State," *Journal of Research in Music Education*, 23, 3 (Autumn 1975), 163-170, EBSCOhost; and Appleby, *Heitor Villa-Lobos*, 95-100.

[77] Appleby, *Heitor Villa-Lobos*, 100-101. The full name of the new government office was Superintendência de Educação Musical e Artística do Departamento de Educação da Prefeitura do Distrito Federal.

[78] Wright, *Villa-Lobos*, 108-109.

[79] Vassberg, "Villa-Lobos as Pedagogue." Some groups were largely excluded from *brasilidade*, including those of Chinese descent, who faced racist representations in samba song lyrics, discrimination because of anxiety over economic competition, and restricted immigration. See Ana Paulina Lee, *Mandarin Brazil: Race, Representation, and Memory* (Stanford, California: Stanford University Press, 2018), 140-143.

[80] Appleby, *Heitor Villa-Lobos*, 106, 111; and Dávila, *Diploma of Whiteness*, 160, 164.

Andrade and others for his participation.[81] Villa-Lobos pushed the criticisms aside, believing in the importance of instilling an ideology through a common experience that emphasized discipline-instilled camaraderie.[82] As he said, the "socializing power of collective singing teaches the individual to forfeit…the egoistic idea of excessive individuality, integrating him into the community." Participation in choral music was for Villa-Lobos an "eminently nationalistic" educational tool.[83] It helped to construct what is called a common cultural citizenship.[84]

These beliefs and practices fit well with Vargas' goals and policies for the nation. Because the Brazilian Empire (1822-1889) had a centralization of political power, the Republic's constitution gave more power to the states. States in the Republic, for example, could levy their own tariffs, assume their own loans, and raise their own armed forces. This shift meant that the federal government's percentage of tax revenues fell from 81.5% in 1856 to 54.2% in 1929, while state and local tax revenue correspondingly increased through this same period.[85] Vargas believed this situation needed correction; he was determined to restore centralized authority in the nation. He may have admired the totalitarian regimes that emerged in Europe in the 1920s and 1930s, but Vargas he was not a leader of a far right-wing political party, and he did not succumb to fascist dogma.[86] Instead, just as university professor Antonio de Oliveira Salazar came to dominate the military dictatorship and suppress the nation's leading fascists in Portugal, Vargas proved able to do so in Brazil.[87] He also quashed Brazilian Communists after an attempted uprising by Leftist military officers in 1935; the specter of Comintern agitation allowed him to declare a national emergency, suspend habeas corpus, and utilize military tribunals instead the courts. Two years later, Vargas bypassed the Constitution's term limits, staging a *coup d'état* against his own government and establishing Brazil's first dictatorship.[88] In a radio address on November 10, 1937, Vargas justified his actions by saying, "In periods of crisis…the democracy of parties, instead of offering a certain opportunity for growth and progress…subverts the hierarchy, menaces the fatherland, and put in danger the existence of the nation by exaggerating competition and igniting the fires of civil discord."[89] He presented himself as the only person who could save Brazil from its economic difficulties and its emerging political extremism.

---

[81] Flávio Oliveira, "Orpheonic Chant and the Construction of Childhood in Brazilian Elementary Education," *Brazilian Popular Music and Citizenship*, Idelber Avelar and Christopher Dunn (eds.) (Durham, North Carolina: Duke University Press 2011), 59.

[82] Dávila, *Diploma of Whiteness*, 160. Dávila expressly makes the parallel to Leni Riefenstahl's rallies and notes that the rallies in Brazil were "nationalistic even by the high standard of the 1930s." For information on the role of music in Hitler Youth see Michael H. Kater, *The Twisted Muse: Musicians and Their Music in the Third Reich* (New York: Oxford University Press, 1999), 130-135.

[83] Heitor Villa-Lobos quoted in Appleby, *Heitor Villa-Lobos,* 102.

[84] Idelber Avelar and Christopher Dunn, "Introduction: Music as Practice of Citizenship in Brazil," *Brazilian Popular Music and Citizenship*, 3.

[85] Skidmore, *Brazil: Five Centuries of Change*, 105.

[86] Robert O. Paxton, *The Anatomy of Fascism* (New York: Alfred A. Knopf, 2004), 197; and Hertzman, *Making Samba,* 173.

[87] Martin Blinkhorn, *Fascism and the Right in Europe 1919*-1945 (New York: Routledge, 2013), 56, 80; and Paxton, *The Anatomy of Fascism*, 193. The fascist movement in Portugal was National-Syndicalism, the "Blue Shirts," and was led by Francisco Rolão Preto; Salazar suppressed the movement in 1934 and exiled Preto. For a detailed discussion of the fascist movement in Brazil, the Ação Integralista Brasileira (AIB), which was led by Plínio Salgado, see Sandra McGee Deutsch, *Las Derechas: The Extreme Right in Argentina, Brazil, and Chile, 1890-1939* (Stanford, California: Stanford University Press, 1999), 248-307.

[88] Robert M. Levine, *Father of the Poor?: Vargas and his Era* (New York: Cambridge University Press, 1998), 47.

[89] Getúlio Vargas quoted in Burns, *A History of Brazil*, 407.

With the establishment of the *Estado Novo* (New State), Vargas disbanded all political parties; gave the police broad powers to interrogate, torture, and imprison dissidents; created an Office of Press and Propaganda to impose censorship on the media and the performing arts; purged the education ministry of progressives; imposed religious education in schools; banned speaking foreign languages publicly and imposed Portuguese as the official language; increased the military budget by 49%; and reorganized labor into corporatist syndicates* that

denuded unions, made strikes illegal, and gave the state the right to arbitrate wages, benefits, and working conditions.[90] This was a significant shift from the Republic's values of democratic liberalism, but there were limits too: Vargas' *Estado Novo* was conservative, authoritarian, and nationalistic, but it was not a fascist state that was dedicated to war or to racial purity.[91] Quite conversely, Vargas sought a peaceful national unity and a loyalty that superseded political parties, class differences, and ethnic groups.[92] Examples of this orientation include the government's attempts to bring Brazilians together through Carnival, samba, and *fútbol*. Not only did the government subsidize samba schools and influence samba lyrics in the 1930s, but it also determined performance themes, regulated costumes and instruments, and broadcast samba music to every corner of the nation to provide for a common and identifiable cultural experience.[93] Similarly, amateur soccer became professionalized during the Vargas years with greater control of fans, construction of new stadiums, explicit support for multi-racial national teams, and prescribed media coverage for the sport.[94] The creation of a National Sports Council helped suppress regional sports federations and banned women from playing *fútbol* to protect the nation's morality and fertility rate.[95] Vargas also supported Villa-Lobos' mass choral program as a way of promoting national identity; he may not have personally liked music, but he understood the value of 30,000 children singing the national anthem, as happened in the Independence Day ceremonies in 1939.[96]

Vargas' chance to celebrate the *Estado Novo* on the international stage came with the 1939 World's Fair in New York. Many of the pavilions and exhibit areas of the participating sixty nations emphasized their cultural heritage, but Brazil's entry was notably and forwardly Modernist. The two-story, fluid, L-shaped building was designed by Brazilian architects Lúcio Costa and Oscar Niemeyer. They took Le Corbusier's principles of Modernist architecture and gave them a tropical

---

[90] Daryle Williams, *Culture Wars in Brazil: The First Vargas Regime, 1930-*1945 (Durham, North Carolina: Duke University Press, 2001), 83-85; Burns, *A History of Brazil*, 409; Dávila, *Diploma of Whiteness*, 158; Levine, *Father of the Poor?*, 55; and Skidmore, *Five Centuries of Change*, 114-117.

[91] Paxton, *The Anatomy of Fascism*, 197.

[92] Jens R. Hentschke, *Reconstructing the Brazilian Nation: Public Schooling in the Vargas Era* (Baden-Baden, Germany: Nomos Verlagsgesellschaft, 2007), 48, 455.

[93] Owensby, "Toward a History of Brazil's 'Cordial Racism'."; and Hertzman, *Making Samba*, 195-196.

[94] There are a number of pertinent essays in *Soccer in Brazil*, Martin Curi (ed.) (New York: Routledge, 2015); see in particular, Bernardo Borges Buarque de Holanda, "The Fan as Actor: the Popularization of Soccer and Brazil's Sports Audience," 13, 16; Martin Curi, "Arthur Friedenreich (1892-1969): A Brazilian Biography," 22, 24; and Ronaldo Helal and Antonio Jorge Soares, "The Decline of the 'Soccer-Nation': Journalism, Soccer and the National Identity in the 2002 World Cup," 133.

[95] David Goldblatt, *Futebol Nation: The Story of Brazil Through Soccer* (New York: Nation Books, 2014), 61.

[96] Wright, *Villa-Lobos*, 115.

sensibility: curved exterior walls, an undulating interior balcony, an inviting rampway, and a rear garden with a lily pond and forty-one rare Amazonian birds.[97] Critics praised the pavilion's openness, natural light, and informative exhibits.[98] One appreciated the "cool restraint" of the restaurant's "semi-circular wall of dark polished walnut with a peach-colored leather bench running around its base," the view from the wall of clear glass opposite, and the enticing aroma from the coffee bar.[99] This stood in contrast to the other parts of the Fair's international zone, including Japan's Shinto* temple, Thailand's gold-trimmed royal barges, Peru's exhibit on Incan life, and Italy's artistic treasures from antiquity.[100] As Brazil's ambassador said at the inauguration ceremony, Brazil was "conscious of its right to be optimistic" and hoped that visitors to the pavilion would see "what we are today" and "gain a glimpse of that which we shall be tomorrow."[101] Brazil had shown itself to be exceptional in Latin America, and this fit well with the Fair's goal of generating optimism for the future during the Depression.[102]

Brazil also made a significant musical impression during the Fair's eighteen-month run in Flushing Meadows. In the opening weeks of the Fair, another respected Brazilian composer and conductor, Walter Burle Marx, led the New York Philharmonic Symphony in two concerts. The first featured "an extraordinary variety of material" and "gave the impression of a significant creative ferment" occurring within Brazil, according to *New York Times* music critic Olin Downes.[103] The program included four works by Villa-Lobos: *Chôros no. 8* and three selections

[97] Williams, *Culture Wars in Brazil,* 83-85; and Antonio Pedro Tota, *The Seduction of Brazil: the Americanization of Brazil During World War II,* Lorena B. Ellis (trans.) (Austin, Texas: University of Texas Press, 2009), 61. Le Corbusier's five key architectural principles were: 1) use of pilotis to lift a building off the ground; 2) an unobstructed and unadorned façade; 3) an open floor plan; 4) horizontal windows to let in more light; and 5) a roof garden. To see how Niemeyer applied these principles in Brazil, see illustration for the 1939 World's Fair.
[98] For critiques of the pavilion, see Zilah Quezado Deckker, *Brazil Built: The Architecture of the Modern Movement in Brazil* (London: Spon, 2001), 54-61.
[99] Charlotte Hughes, "For Gourmets and Others: From Cosmopolitan Brazil," *New York Times,* July 2, 1939, D7, ProQuest Historical Newspapers.
[100] John Markland, "'Abroad' at the Fair," *New York Times,* June 4, 1939, XX1, ProQuest Historical Newspapers. There were other Modernist pavilions, including Australia's and Great Britain's.
[101] Carlos Martins Sousa quoted in "Tropical Background Sets Off the Brazilian Display: Brazil's Pavilion Opened by Envoy," *New York Times,* July 2, 1939, 9 ProQuest Historical Newspapers.
[102] Hess, *Representing the Good Neighbor,* 100; and Tota, *The Seduction of Brazil,* 60.
[103] Olin Downes, "Brazilian Music is Played at Fair," *New York Times,* May 5, 1939, 33, ProQuest Historical Newspapers. In addition to Villa-Lobos, the concert included works by Brazilians Antônio Carlos Gomes (1836-1896), Francisco Paulo Mignone (1897-1986), Oscar Lorenzo Fernández (1897-1948) and Walter Burle Marx (1902-1990).

from Villa-Lobos' suites honoring Johann Sebastian Bach, the *Bachianas brasileiras*.[104] The second concert, five nights later, included *Chôros no. 10*, which Downes hailed as "the greatest score of the evening" because it

> is a truly primitive and unconscious score. The composer hears, not as some conservatory told him to listen, but with a pair of ears as keen and unspoiled as those of a wild animal. Those ears have not been trained to fool him. He hears sounds in nature; he puts down those sounds, and not substitute harmonies, as they occur in his consciousness.[105]

Once again, Villa-Lobos had made a name for himself by giving a new audience something that they had never before heard. Significantly, the first commercial recordings of Villa-Lobos' works were produced in conjunction with the Fair.[106]

Not all of Villa-Lobos' music was well-received during this period. In October 1940, near the end of the Fair's run, the Museum of Modern Art hosted a Festival of Brazilian Music that showcased much of Villa-Lobos' work to date. At the final concert in the series, Arthur Rubinstein played *Rudepoêma* (Savage Poem), which Villa-Lobos had dedicated to Rubinstein and presented to him in 1926. The festival program billed *Rudepoêma* as "perhaps the most difficult piano composition ever written." Rubinstein considered it "to be a monumental attempt to express the origins of the native Brazilian *caboclos*, their sorrows and joys, their wars and peace, finishing with a savage dance."[107] Critics were not convinced. Canadian musicologist Colin McPhee excoriated *Rudepoêma*, arguing that while it may be the most difficult composition ever written, "it was also surely one of the worst."[108] Another critic wrote that while Villa-Lobos' "harmonizations are…far from banal…they are never profound and rarely distinguished."[109] Even the normally supportive Olin Downes found it "weak in development" and noted that "the piano becomes excessively pulsatile; it has to be beaten as a madman would beat his drum."[110] The work was too experimental for many ears.[111] But these reviews did not undermine Villa-Lobos' overall reputation. In fact, as a result of his general reception at the Fair, there was a growing interest in having the Brazilian composer conduct his own works in the United States.

In May 1944, Villa-Lobos wrote to his old Parisian friend Serge Koussevitzky, then music director of the Boston Symphony Orchestra, saying that he could now accept the invitations to appear in the United States and asking for Koussevitzky's help in organizing a concert tour. Villa-Lobos proposed the program, detailed a rehearsal schedule, and wrote that "as for the expenses, I shall ask only for the tickets, accommodation for two persons, and the royalties for hire and

[104] Written between 1930 and 1945, the nine works of the *Bachianas brasileiras* were Villa-Lobos' best effort to synthesize and integrate Modernist Brazilian music with Bach's oeuvre. Villa-Lobos admired Bach more than any other composer and saw him as providing what Villa-Lobos called "the most sacred gift to the world of art" and "the plainsong of the earth." Appleby, *Heitor Villa-Lobos,* 119-121; and Wright, *Villa-Lobos,* 86.
[105] Downes, "Brazilian Music on Fair Program," 33. This evening's program also included a suite by Mignone.
[106] Wright, *Villa-Lobos,* 93. The recorded works were *Bachianas brasileiras no. 1* and *Bachianas brasileiras no. 2*.
[107] Rubinstein, *My Many Years,* 252. *Caboclos* are Portuguese-speaking people who have descended from Amazonian tribes; they often also have White ancestors. See Daniel Leonard Everett, *Don't Sleep, There are Snakes: Life and Language in the Amazonian Jungle* (New York: Pantheon Books, 2008), 159.
[108] Colin McPhee quoted in Hess, *Representing the Good Neighbor,* 126.
[109] Virgil Thomson quoted in Hess, *Representing the Good Neighbor,* 125.
[110] Olin Downes, "Brazilian Series of Concerts Ends," *New York Times,* October 21, 1940, 21, ProQuest Historical Newspapers.
[111] Béhague, *Heitor Villa-Lobos,* 100.

performance."[112] Those tickets were international airline tickets on Pan American Airways, and they were not easy things to obtain in 1944.

The primary reason centered upon the role Pan Am served during World War II. Seven weeks before Franklin D. Roosevelt proclaimed in late December 1940 that the United States "must be the great arsenal of democracy" by supplying Great Britain with the resources it needed to fight Nazi aggression and four months before the Lend-Lease Act* became law, the War Department signed the Airport Development Program agreement with Pan Am's chairman Juan Trippe to pay for the construction of military-grade airfields and support facilities in fifteen countries in Latin America. Soliciting a private company for the construction was the only way for the United States to maintain its international neutrality and not irritate local governments, while still building the infrastructure the War Department believed was necessary "for the defense of the Western Hemisphere."[113] In this way, Pan Am became an essential agent of American geo-political and military concerns,[114] even if Roosevelt worried that Trippe would happily put his airline's interests ahead his country's when the opportunity arose.[115] In fact, Trippe may have been doing just this when he met with Winston Churchill in London in June 1941 and proposed that Pan Am take over air supply operations for the Royal Air Force in Africa.[116] Having an American company provide American war matériel through Brazil to Egypt and the Middle East through the Lend-Lease program certainly violated the spirit of American neutrality laws, but Roosevelt believed that it was crucial for these supplies arrive as quickly as possible. Government lawyers found the necessary loopholes, to come up with a plan: if Pan Am sold needed planes to the American government and then leased those same planes back from the government, and if Pan Am stayed out of active combat zones, the supply route could operate legally. Pan Am could also legally own and operate all of the accompanying ground facilities for such a complex operation.[117] Soon, Pan Am linked Miami with Brazil, West Africa, the Sudan, India, and China, providing vital war supplies for Allied forces in multiple theaters much faster than shipping by sea. On the return trips, Pan Am brought the U.S. important raw materials from Africa and Latin America, such as rubber, quinine-producing

---

[112] Heitor Villa-Lobos to Serge Koussevitzky, May 22, 1944, in *The Villa-Lobos Letters*, 75-77.

[113] Jennifer Van Vleck, *Empire of the Air: Aviation and the American Ascendancy* (Cambridge, Massachusetts: Harvard University Press, 2013), 83-84 and 87-88. The contract with Pan Am was signed November 2, 1940. The Lend-Lease Act was signed into law by Roosevelt on March 11, 1941. The fireside chat in which Roosevelt sought to win support for the bill was broadcast December 29, 1940. For a text of the fireside chat see John Woolley and Gerhard Peters, "Franklin D. Roosevelt, XXXII President of the United States: 1933-1945, 154 – Fireside Chat, December 29, 1940," *The American Presidency Project*, accessed February 7, 2020, http://www.presidency.ucsb.edu/ws/index.php?pid=15917. Vargas had offered Roosevelt access to existing coastal air bases in Brazil in 1937, but Roosevelt declined the offer because he couldn't give the appearance of preparing for war. See Skidmore, *Brazil: Five Centuries of Change*, 119-120.

[114] Dan Hagedorn, *Conquistadors of the Sky: A History of Aviation in Latin America* (Gainesville, Florida: University of Florida Press, 2008), 407; and Van Vleck, *Empire of the Air*, 87-88, 100.

[115] Marylin Bender and Selig Altschul, *The Chosen Instrument, Pan Am, Juan Trippe: The Rise and Fall of an American Entrepreneur* (New York: Simon and Schuster, 1982), 340.

[116] Van Vleck, *Empire of the Air*, 135-136.

[117] Deborah Wing Ray, "The Takoradi Route: Roosevelt's Prewar Venture Beyond the Western Hemisphere," *Journal of American History*, 62, 2 (September 1975), 340-358, EBSCOhost. As part of the legal maneuvering, several subsidiaries were created, including Atlantic Airlines, Pan American Airways-Ferries, Pan American Airways-Africa Ltd., and the Pan American Airways Company. As Ray notes, "All of these operations overlapped in practice; on paper none of them overlapped. The arrangement was a legal *tour de force*."

cinchona bark for malaria, and essential minerals.[118] After the military took over these ferrying operations in late 1942,[119] Pan Am continued to fly, providing air service to military personnel and high priority civilian passengers.[120] Roosevelt, for example, flew the *Dixie Clipper* to Casablanca in January 1943 to meet Churchill for one of their wartime conferences. Villa-Lobos' American concert tour was hardly in the same category of importance, which was one of the reasons why the conductor's arrival in the United States was delayed by almost a week.

Other factors contributed to the delay, including some diplomatic reluctance over the propriety of Villa-Lobos' bringing a female companion on the tour. The press believed that the woman was his wife, but this was not the case.[121] In 1932, Villa-Lobos had fallen in love with Arminda Neves d'Almeida, a student-teacher at an institute for music teachers that he directed. The affair between the twenty-year-old and the forty-five-year-old continued for several years until May 1936, when Villa-Lobos wrote to his wife Lucília after attending an international music conference in Prague. He declared,

> I cannot live in the company of someone from whom I feel completely estranged, isolated, [by whom I feel] constricted, in short without any affection save certain gratitude at your faithfulness during many years in my company.

> *I proclaim our absolute freedom.*   I do so, however, with a quiet conscience, in the knowledge that I have done everything to ensure that you lack nothing. It was entirely through my own efforts that I secured for you the excellent positions you now hold, as a result of which you earn more than I do and have better prospects.

> My wish is that you will never feel any rancor towards me or anyone else, but to accept with calm and resignation that our situation could not end any other way than this.[122]

In response, Lucília defended herself, citing her indefatigable efforts supporting Villa-Lobos financially and musically for almost a quarter-century, and her legal rights as a wife since divorce was impossible in Brazil at the time. She did not, however, stand in Villa-Lobos' way, nor did she express bitterness in her memoirs over the outcome of their relationship.[123] By 1944, when Villa-Lobos wanted to bring Arminda with him to the United States, the couple had been together for over a decade, but by Brazilian law they could not apply for a standard visa as husband and wife.[124] This situation added to the travel complications and delays.

---

[118] William A. Krusen, *Flying the Andes: The Story of Pan American-Grace Airways and Commercial Aviation in South America, 1926-1967* (Tampa, Florida: University of Tampa Press, 1997), 129.
[119] John D. Carter, "The Early Development of Air Transport and Ferrying," Wesley Frank Craven and James Lea Cate, *The Army Air Forces in World War II, Volume One: Plans and Early Operations* (Washington, DC: Office of Air Force History, 1983), 338.
[120] Oliver E. Allen, *The Airline Builders* (Alexandria, Virginia: Time-Life Books, 1981), 166.
[121] "Villa-Lobos Takes a Trip," *Time*, 44, 23 (December 4, 1944), 90.
[122] Heitor Villa-Lobos to Lucília Villa-Lobos, May 28, 1936 in *The Villa-Lobos Letters*, 56-57.
[123] Appleby, *Heitor Villa-Lobos*, 117; and Lucília Villa-Lobos to Heitor Villa-Lobos, June 14, 1936 in *The Villa-Lobos Letters*, 57-59.
[124] Villa-Lobos circumvented the difficulty by obtaining permission to travel under a diplomatic passport. See Appleby, *Heitor Villa-Lobos*, 159.

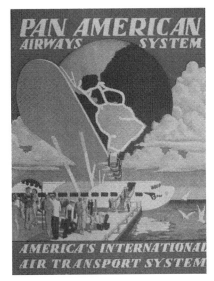

Eventually, Villa-Lobos and Arminda procured the necessary documents, Pan Am issued the couple the hard-to-obtain tickets, and they began their long journey to Los Angeles for his first public event in the U.S. Because they were not able to get a reservation to fly the preferred route via Belém, Brazil; San Juan, Puerto Rico; and Miami as planned, the couple had to fly via Buenos Aires, Santiago, Lima, and Mexico City on two Pan Am subsidiaries, Pan American-Grace Airways (Panagra) and Compañía Mexicana de Aviación (CMA). In each of these cities, Villa-Lobos and Arminda had overnight stops. After the taxing five-day trip, Villa-Lobos and Arminda arrived in Los Angeles at 5:35 p.m. on November 21—just about the time the conductor was supposed to appear at an Occidental College commencement ceremony to receive an honorary degree. The Los Angeles police provided them with a siren-blaring escort through the city's streets, getting the Brazilians to the ceremony on time and giving Villa-Lobos the sensational entrance and impression he so very much wanted to make in America.[125] Unfortunately, actual events in Los Angeles did not similarly inspire. At Occidental, Villa-Lobos' acceptance speech had to be translated since the conductor spoke no English, and the translator took advantage of the situation to poke fun of Vargas, the *Estado Novo*, and Villa-Lobos' role as a government official in the undemocratic state.[126] Worse, Villa-Lobos' concert, conducting the Werner Janssen Symphony of Los Angeles on November 26, attracted only a small, unenthusiastic crowd.[127] This inauspicious debut did not discourage Villa-Lobos particularly. Instead, he drew upon the abundant confidence that allowed him as a young man to scorn professors at the *Instituto Nacional de Música* or arrive in Europe believing that he had something to teach Parisians, rather the other way around. If Angelenos had missed the point of his music, that was their fault, not his.

---

[125] The details of Villa-Lobos' itinerary and the story of the police escort come from Appleby, *Heitor Villa-Lobos*, 141-142 (which states that the couple flew via Argentina and had the escort); Hess, *Representing the Good Neighbor*, 131 (which states that the couple arrived in Los Angeles on November 21); and the *Pan American World Airways Latin American Time Tables*, October 1944, page 5 (personal collection). To arrive in Los Angeles on November 21, the couple would have had to fly from Rio to Buenos Aires on another Pan Am subsidiary, Panair do Brasil, on November 17. The rest of their routing would have proceeded as follows: depart Buenos Aires 8:00 a.m. and arrive Santiago 2:20 p.m. on November 18; depart Santiago 6:45 a.m. and arrive Lima at 5:25 on November 19; depart Lima 5:00 a.m. and arrive Mexico City at 3:10 p.m. on November 20; and depart Mexico City at 7:00 a.m. and arrive in Los Angeles at 5:35 p.m. on November 21. Intermediate and refueling stops on the route included Córdoba and Mendoza, Argentina; Antofagasta and Arica, Chile; Arequipa and Chiclayo, Peru; Guayaquil, Ecuador; Santiago de Cali, Colombia; Balboa, Canal Zone (Panamá); the capital cities of Costa Rica, Nicaragua, Honduras, El Salvador, and Guatemala; and Tapachula, Guadalajara, Hermosillo, and Mexicali, México. Most of the planes used for this route were probably DC-3s.

[126] Hess, *Representing the Good Neighbor,* 132. The translator was Brazilian author Érico Veríssimo, who was a visiting professor at the University of California-Berkeley that fall. The two men, both possessing considerable egos, did not get along well. See also Appleby, *Heitor Villa-Lobos,* 142-143.

[127] Peppercorn, *The World of Villa-Lobos in Pictures and Documents*, 176. The concert included *Rudepoêma, Symphony no. 2*, and *Chôros no. 6.*

Villa-Lobos was not so arrogant that he misunderstood the importance of positive reviews. Shortly after he and Arminda arrived in New York and took up residence at the Waldorf-Astoria on December 12, the conductor met *New York Times* columnist Olin Downes. By disentangling nationalism and patriotism, Villa-Lobos tried to make his music and his résumé more palatable to a nation fighting Nazi Germany:

> The distinction is most important. Patriotism in music and capitalizing upon it, is very dangerous. You cannot produce great music in that way. You will have instead propaganda. But nationalism—power of the earth, the geographic and ethnographic influences the composer cannot escape: the musical idioms and sentiments of people and environment—these origins, in my opinion, are indispensable to a vital and genuine art.[128]

The opening months of 1945 witnessed the highlights of Villa-Lobos' concert tour and honors. He was celebrated by the New York League of Composers with a concert of eleven of his works at the Museum of Modern Art on January 28; he conducted the New York Philharmonic on February

8 and 9; he appeared as a guest conductor at the Boston Symphony Orchestra on February 23 and 24, and he participated in a special series of performances held at the University of Chicago on February 27.[129] The events culminated on March 14 with Serge Koussevitzky conducting the Boston Symphony Orchestra at Carnegie Hall. The program featured an orchestral version of *Rudepoêma* and *Chôros no. 12*, Haydn's *Symphony No.102 in B-flat major*, and Schumann's *Symphony no. 1*. Later that evening, a reception held in Villa-Lobos' honor at the Waldorf Astoria attracted the famous and well-connected. It was an event at which people wanted to be seen. Attendees included American musicians Marion Anderson, Aaron Copland, Duke Ellington, Benny Goodman, Cole Porter; international conductors, vocalists, and pianists; New York politicos Nelson Rockefeller and Fiorello Henry La Guardia; Brazilian diplomats and businessmen; and members of the press, including Olin Downes. Not all of these celebrities really cared for Villa-Lobos' music. Copland, for example, described it as being outstanding only in its abundance and criticized it for its lack of coherence and unity.[130] But such views did not interfere with the festivities or with Villa-

---

[128] Heitor Villa-Lobos quoted in Olin Downes, "Hector Villa-Lobos: Visiting Brazilian Composer Discusses Sources of Nationalism," *New York Times* Dec 17, 1944; X7, ProQuest Historical Newspapers.

[129] Appleby, *Heitor Villa-Lobos*, 144-147. One critic of the Chicago event was not fully impressed with *Bachianas brasileiras*, writing that "much of the tone is beautiful, and the slow movement is richly instrumental, but the fugue gets off to a boogie woogie start and lands in monotony." See Claudia Cassidy, "Virtuosity Flares in Milstein's Tschaikowsky; Villa-Lobos at Mandel Hall," *Chicago Tribune*, February 28, 1945, 17, https://chicagotribune.newspapers.com/image/371129722/

[130] Howard Pollack, *Aaron Copland: The Life & Work of an Uncommon Man* (New York: Henry Holt and Company, 1999), 229.

Lobos' satisfaction with the evening. Having long aspired to fame, on that night Villa-Lobos knew he had arrived.

Villa-Lobos returned to a Brazil that was bursting with mixed emotions as a result of its participation in World War II. The nation's road to war began with Vargas' agreeing to let Pan Am expand airport facilities. By mid-1941, the Brazilians were honoring American requests to prohibit the sale of strategic materials to the Axis powers, to concentrate Brazilian troops in the Northeast, and to construct a naval base in Natal. Vargas' officials were also considering requests to meet with representatives of the American General Staff, to participate in joint military maneuvers with the Americans and to allow for detailed aerial surveys of the country as part of a coordinated defense policy.[131] The bombing of Pearl Harbor finalized the Brazilian position, for as Vargas said, "There is no doubt about our attitude. Let us proclaim it at once: we stand solidly with the United States."[132] In late January 1942, therefore, Vargas overrode military concerns over Brazil's preparedness a twentieth-century war, and he ended Brazilian neutrality by breaking off diplomatic and commercial relations with Germany, Italy, and Japan. Many Brazilians greeted this news favorably, but it wasn't until eight months later, when a single U-Boat sank five Brazilian passenger ships and killed 607 people, that Brazil declared war on Germany and Italy. In August 1943, Brazil created an expeditionary force, the racially-diverse Força Expedicionária Brasileira (FEB), to send combat troops to Europe.[133] It was the only Latin American country to do so. Support for Brazil's participation in the war was counterbalanced by frustrations with the nation's economic and political situation. The war caused a loss of important export markets, led to skyrocketing costs of living, and created shortages of everything from meat and milk to gasoline and newsprint. It also made the *Estado Novo* increasingly untenable, as Vargas himself realized, since it seemed nonsensical for Brazilians to fight against dictatorships when Brazil did not have a democratic government.[134] Vargas set an election date for December 2, 1945 and allowed for the return of open political activity, but the military did not believe the sincerity of his intentions and ousted him from office on October 29, 1945.[135] Brazil then re-embraced democracy, but only until 1964, when the military ended the Second Republic with another *coup d'état*.

~

In the last decade of his life, Villa-Lobos continued to be enormously productive, despite battling bladder cancer and jet setting between New York, Paris, and Rio de Janeiro. He received numerous

[131] "The Ambassador in Brazil ([Jefferson] Caffery) to the Secretary of State [Cordell Hull]," June 4, 1941, *Foreign Relations of the United States Diplomatic Papers, 1941, The American Republics*, Volume VI, (Washington, D.C.: U.S. Government Printing Office, 1941), 497, accessed December 2, 2017, http://digital.library.wisc.edu/1711.dl/FRUS.FRUS1941v06

[132] Getúlio Vargas quoted in Burns, *A History of Brazil*, 411.

[133] Neill Lochery, *Brazil: The Fortunes of War: World War II and the Making of Modern Brazil* (New York: Basic Books, 2014), 165, 169-170, 211.

[134] Lochery, *Brazil: The Fortunes of War*, 43, 51, 130-131, 147, 233-225; and Skidmore, *Brazil: Five Centuries of Change*, 123-124. The cost of living in Rio de Janeiro almost doubled between 1939 and 1945.

[135] The election was held as scheduled and pitted two military officers. Eúrioco Gaspar Dutra won the open election; the communist party won 10% of the vote. Vargas returned to the presidency after winning the 1950 election. He committed suicide in 1954 in the face of another impending military *coup d'état*. See Skidmore, *Brazil: Five Centuries of Change*, 128-129, 135-138.

commissions as a result of his international fame; in fact, he earned $100,000 a year through commissions, royalties, conducting fees, and his government salary at a time when the average American family's income was $4,237.[136] There were commissions for movie soundtracks and ballets, choral works and string quartets, symphonies and guitar concertos. It was an extraordinary diversity of work. One of the more unusual commissions in this period was to write the score for a Broadway musical, *Magdalena*, which opened September 20, 1948 at the Ziegfeld Theater. Villa-Lobos called it "a musical adventure," but "misadventure" might be more apt: the production's libretto was plagued by what a *Time* magazine reviewer called "all of the stock melodrama of opera and the seediest monkeyshines of operetta; they have lavished on South America all the tritest features of the tropics."[137] Set in Colombia in the watershed of the Magdalena River, the musical centered on the travails of pagan Indians being exploited by a petty dictator-general until a newly Christianized Indian princess offers the impoverished emerald miners hope and salvation. This plot played upon Latin American stereotypes as offensively as the casting did with its "blond, blue-eyed Indians who wear gaucho costumes from the Argentine, Ecuadorian hats and Peruvian ponchos, and sing Brazilian music in perfect English."[138] Villa-Lobos may have been attracted to the commission because of the potential to adapt folk music; his score drew heavily from the *Guia Prático*, the *Bachianas brasileiras*, and the *choros* of his youth.[139] Critics generally praised the score, despite its closer connection to the music of urban Brazil than that of rural Colombia. One critic noted that "disentangled from the appalling libretto and lyrics of *Magdalena*, the score might be stimulating, especially since the orchestrations are unhackneyed."[140] Another argued that while the libretto was "dull here and there," what made *Magdalena* "exciting is its music" since Villa-Lobos "has created one of the busiest and more imaginative musical show scores on record."[141] Such assessments meant that the shortcomings of the $300,000 production, which was characterized as a "mulligan stew" in the *New Republic*, did not fall upon Villa-Lobos' shoulders.[142] Villa-Lobos could not have done much to rescue the show, for the time the production was in previews in Los Angeles and San Francisco, he was in New York having his cancerous bladder removed.

[136] Appleby, *Heitor Villa-Lobos,* 149; and "100 Years of U.S. Consumer Spending: Data for the Nation, New York City, and Boston: 1950," *Bureau of Labor Statistics,* August 3, 2006, 25, accessed February 7, 2020, https://www.bls.gov/opub/uscs/report991.pdf
[137] "Four of a Kind," *Time*, Vol. LII, No. 4 (October 4, 1948), 59.
[138] Alfred Frankenstein quoted in Hess, *Representing the Good Neighbor*, 138. Frankenstein was a critic with the *San Francisco Examiner*. The production was in previews in Los Angeles and San Francisco in the summer of 1948.
[139] Thomas George Caracas Garcia, "American Views of Brazilian Musical Culture: Villa-Lobos' *Magdalena* and Brazilian Popular Music," *The Journal of Popular Culture*, Vol. 37, No. 4 (May, 2004) 634-647, ProQuest Central. Villa-Lobos never received the completed libretto, so he wrote the music without knowing the whole storyline. For more information on the production, see Gustafson, "Villa-Lobos and the Man-Eating flower;" and Appleby, *Heitor Villa-Lobos*, 159-160.
[140] Brooks Atkinson, "At the Theatre: Heitor Villa-Lobos, Brazilian Composer, Has Written the Musical Score for 'Magdalena'," *New York Times*, September 21, 1948, 31. ProQuest Historical Newspapers.
[141] John Chapman, "Two Musicals in New York Win Plaudits," *Chicago Tribune*, September 26, 1948, 117, https://chicagotribune.newspapers.com/image/370940619/
[142] Cecil Smith, "Music: Novelties on the West Coast." *New Republic* 119, no. 7 (August 16, 1948): 26. *Complementary Index*, EBSCOhost. The stated costs of the production vary considerably according to the source. The $300,000 is an estimate.

Villa-Lobos completed another unusual commission in the last decade of his life, a ballet based on the controversial 1920 Eugene O'Neill play *The Emperor Jones.* The play centers upon an African

American who tyrannically rules a Caribbean island, faces rebellion, and eventually dies in the jungle, consumed by terror and memories after encountering a witchdoctor.[143] Given the setting and Villa-Lobos' reputation for evoking the authentic sounds of the tropical wilderness, Empire State Music Festival officials believed that he was ideal choice for choreographer José Limón's adaptation in July 1956. The play fit with the outdoor Festival's commitment to "brand-new works or very, very old ones" that were rarely presented in more traditional venues.[144] Reviews of the ballet's world premiere, at which Villa-Lobos conducted, were generally positive. As one critic noted, Villa-Lobos' music enhanced the choreography "admirably, building up to a stunning climax in the scene of primitive incantation."[145] Because of this success, Villa-Lobos was asked back to the Festival a year later for a performance of the "Emperor Jones" music without the accompanying ballet. That concert also featured *Caixinha de Boas Festas* (The Surprise Box), a ballet suite for orchestra written in 1932, and Bach's *Prelude and Fugue no.6 in D minor,* which Villa-Lobos had transcribed. The concert illustrates how well the Brazilian continued to believe that Bach defined a universal music experience since it offered "the most spiritual expression of human solidarity."[146]

Magdalena and *Emperor Jones* were not, however, particularly characteristic of Villa-Lobos' overall output in the 1950s. Instead, much of his attention centered upon composing symphonies and concertos that largely abandoned the inspirations from folk music and nationalism.[147] He particularly wanted to appeal to American audiences, resulting in an arguably less individualized sound.[148] His Ninth Symphony, for example, offers a decidedly somber second movement (*Adagio*) that is quite unlike the rest of his *oeuvre*.[149] Such concessions did not reduce Villa-Lobos' showmanship, and he refused to allow his deteriorating health to interfere with his schedule. At the January 1955 debut of his Eighth Symphony, commissioned by the Philadelphia Symphony Orchestra, he "strode to the podium, grey hair tucked behind his ears, coattails dangling rakishly

[143] For an analysis of the play and O'Neill's depiction of race in it, see Garrett Eisler, "Backstory as Black Story: The Cinematic Reinvention of O'Neill's The Emperor Jones," *Eugene O'Neill Review* (2010), 148-162, EBSCOhost. There was also a film adaptation of the play by director Dudley Murphey in 1933.

[144] Frank Forest quoted in "Opera Under Canvas," *Time*, LXXIV, No. 6 (August 10, 1959), 51.

[145] "Ballet: 'Emperor Jones': Premiere of Work by Limon at Ellenville," *New York Times*, July 13, 1956, 24, ProQuest Historical Newspapers.

[146] "Villa-Lobos Conducts: His 'Emperor Jones' Heard at Empire State Festival," *New York Times*, July 13, 1957, 10, ProQuest Historical Newspapers; and Heitor Villa-Lobos quoted in Appleby, *Heitor Villa-Lobos,* 119.

[147] Stephen Estep, "Villa-Lobos: Symphonies 8,9,11." *American Record Guide*, 2017, 205, EBSCOhost; and Philip Scott, "Villa-Lobos Symphonies Nos. 8, 9, 11," *Fanfare: The Magazine for Serious Record Collectors*, 41, no. 2 (November 2017): 524-525, EBSCOhost; and Appleby, *Heitor Villa-Lobos,* 156.

[148] Lisa Peppercorn, "Villa-Lobos's Last Years," *Villa-Lobos: Collected Studies*, 92-93; and Simon Wright, *Villa-Lobos* (New York: Oxford University Press, 1992), 120.

[149] Philip Scott, "Villa-Lobos Symphonies Nos. 8, 9, 11," *Fanfare: The Magazine for Serious Record Collectors*, 41, no. 2 (November 2017): 524-525, EBSCOhost.

below his calves," and he conducted the orchestra through the work with confidence.[150] What was lost was some of Villa-Lobos' exceptionality. Reviewers accused him of unimaginatively prolonging his compositions. They took note of how he was "composing furiously between concerts" to keep up with the commissions while traveling between three continents.[151] This resulted in an Eleventh Symphony whose "essential material is superficial, even banal, suitable for some popular medium, not for symphony," according to one review of its premiere at Carnegie Hall.[152] But not all of Villa-Lobos' work in the 1950s was weak: his last four string quartets are considered exceptional,[153] as is the rewritten *Concerto for Guitar and Orchestra*, which Andrés Segovia commissioned and the two men premiered together with the Houston Symphony Orchestra on February 6, 1956. The work is considered to be one of Villa-Lobos' finest and illustrates his desire to move beyond the features typical of Brazilian folk music.[154]

Villa-Lobos turned seventy in March 1957. This prompted a series of awards, recognizing his contributions and confirming status as Latin America's most important composer of the twentieth century. Brazil proclaimed 1957 to be the "Villa-Lobos Year," and São Paulo made him an honorary citizen.[155]   In New York, where he spent his birthday and finished composing his Twelfth Symphony, Villa-Lobos gathered with friends at City Hall for an award ceremony and asked a friend for a cigar.[156] The president of the city council presented him with a scroll that hailed his "distinguished and exceptional service" for promoting cultural relationships between the peoples of the North and South America. Mayor Richard Wagner hailed him as a

> talented interpreter of music; inspired teacher who led the movement to make the folk music of Brazil an important social force in the lives of her youth; creative genius whose fresh and vigorous imagination has recreated the native music of the Brazilian people in new forms.[157]

Villa-Lobos skillfully used the ceremony as both a promotional and educational opportunity: after receiving the award, he demonstrated the Brazilian instruments that would be used later that month by the Philadelphia Symphony Orchestra under his direction. Combined with his insistence to the press that it was impossible for him to use musical notations to communicate his intent for these

---

[150] "Tropical Thunderstorm," *Time*, Latin American ed., Vol. LXV, no. 5, (January 31, 1955), 44. The unnamed critic described it as being "as prodigal with melodies as a bargain basement with its wares, innocently loaded with hints of other compositions, but still characteristic and convincing."
[151] "Tropical Thunderstorm," 44; and Stephen Estep, "Villa-Lobos: Symphonies 8,9,11," *American Record Guide*, 2017, 205, EBSCOhost.
[152] Howard Taubman, "Music: New Symphony: Villa-Lobos' Eleventh Has Premiere Here," *New York Times*, March 22, 1956, 40, ProQuest Historical Newspapers.
[153] Appleby, *Heitor Villa-Lobos*, 163.
[154] The original piece was commissioned by Segovia in 1951, but it did not include a cadenza (a solo). Segovia refused to play it as a result. Arminda eventually badgered Villa-Lobos into writing the cadenza, which he inserted between the second and third movements. For more information about the work and the premiere, see Wright, *Villa-Lobos*, 123; Graham Wade and Gerard Garno, *A New Look at Segovia, His Life, His Music*, Volume 1 (Pacific, Missouri: Mel Bay Publications, 2000), 166; and John Patykula, "A Look at the 1956 Premiere of Villa-Lobos' Immortal 'Concerto for Guitar,' Performed by Andrés Segovia," August 2, 2017, *Classical Guitar*, accessed February 7, 2020, https://tinyurl.com/yxlfavl6
[155] Peppercorn, "Villa-Lobos's Last Years," 101.
[156] Peppercorn, *The World of Villa-Lobos in Pictures and Documents*, 280; and Gustafson, "Villa-Lobos and the Man-Eating flower."
[157] Richard Wager quoted in Béhague, *Heitor Villa-Lobos*, 28-29.

instruments and his ubiquitous cigar, the event captured the essence of both Villa-Lobos' musical significance and personality.[158]

By 1959, Villa-Lobos' medical condition had seriously deteriorated; his kidneys could no longer function properly, and he developed uremia. On July 12, he conducted for the last time at an Empire State Music Festival concert consisting entirely of his works. The next day, he flew to Rio de Janeiro, now an eighteen-hour trip with a single stop in Caracas, so that he might receive an award recognizing his life's work.[159] This extraordinary schedule for a terminally ill man landed him in the hospital for the subsequent 35 days, but he returned home in late August. On September 7, he and Arminda attended a concert at Rio's Teatro Municipal that featured his 1958 work of sacred music, *Magnificat alleluia*. This one-movement tribute to the Annunciation alternates between an alto soloist and a chorus, both of which are supported by an orchestra with piccolo, flute, oboe, clarinet, bassoon, contrabassoon, horn, trumpet, trombone, tuba, timpani, and strings. An organ doubles the impact of the orchestra. As with much of the sacred music that Villa-Lobos wrote between 1905 and 1958, *Magnificat alleluia* upholds Catholic tradition while simultaneously adding a Brazilian flavor.[160] When the work commissioned by Pope Pius XII concluded, the audience turned to Villa-Lobos' box and gave him an uninhibited ovation that left the maestro visibly moved; he waved back to them in acknowledgement of their affection.[161] It was his last appearance in public.

In his final interview with a member of the press three months earlier, Villa-Lobos complained about his fellow countrymen, saying the vast majority could not appreciate his music or accomplishment:

> I did everything I could to bring about a true musical culture in Brazil. It's useless. The country is dominated by mediocrity. Every time a mediocre person dies, five more are born....Art is not of the people....The distinction must always be made; there is spontaneous music, people-to-people music. Then there is art music, music for the aristocracy.[162]

[158] John Briggs, "Villa-Lobos, 70, Hailed by City; Composer Thumps in Brazilian: Proper Way to Play the Reco-Reco," *New York Times*, March 5, 1957, 33, ProQuest Historical Newspapers. The Philadelphia Symphony Orchestra concert included Villa-Lobos' 1939 choral work *Cantata Profana: Mandu-Carara* on March 28 and 29, 1957. The instruments Villa-Lobos demonstrated were the camisão (a drum made of goatskin stretched over a square frame); the cabaça (a gourd filled with pumpkin seeds that has more seeds strung on the outside); the reco-reco (a rattle with notches which is played by running a stick along the notches); and the caracaxa and xucalho, which are similar to maracas.
[159] Appleby, *Heitor Villa-Lobos,* 170; and *Pan American World Airways System Timetable,* January 1-31, 1958, 16, accessed February 7, 2020, http://www.timetableimages.com/ttimages/pa/pa58/pa58-09.jpg. The eighteen hour trip replaced the four or five day odyssey travelers faced in the 1940s. This same timetable notes that it was possible to fly "around the world in less than 80 hours." The award was the Carlos Gomes Medal.
[160] Jill Burleson, "Villa-Lobos's Música Sacra," *Choral Journal,* 49, no. 12 (June 2009), 10-19, EBSCOhost; and Hoffmann Urquiza Pereira, "A conductor's study of Villa-Lobos's Magnificat-Alleluia and Bendita Sabedoria," Ph.D. dissertation, Louisiana State University, 2005, 116-117, 124, accessed February 7, 2020, http://digitalcommons.lsu.edu/gradschool_dissertations/1535
[161] Peppercorn, "Villa-Lobos's Last Years," 103.
[162] Heitor Villa-Lobos quoted in Appleby, *Heitor Villa-Lobos,* 169-170.

One leading authority believes that this quote is quite uncharacteristic of who Villa-Lobos was throughout his gregarious life.[163] There is, however, an element of truth in what Villa-Lobos said: in the ceremonies after the composer's death on November 17, his body lay in state in a former government building so that people could pay their respects. Hundreds did so,[164] but not thousands or tens of thousands, as would have happened for a more populist national hero. Villa-Lobos believed that all children have within them the art of music,[165] and yet he could not translate this belief into something most people could fully appreciate. The public preferred the emerging sounds of Brazilian bossa nova and international rock 'n roll. Classical music belonged to the elite, as it always had, despite Villa-Lobos' intense efforts, both as a composer and as a government official, to change the paradigm.

Villa-Lobos' funeral was the last major civic event Rio de Janeiro hosted as the nation's capital.[166] Four months later, Brasília was inaugurated as the new capital as the country sought to realize the potential of its hinterland and leave the legacies of colonialism behind. As president Juscelino Kubitschek proclaimed, "We have turned our back on the sea and penetrated to the heartland of the nation. Now the people will realize their strength."[167] He predicted that within twenty years Brazil would stand as "the world's fourth greatest power, ahead of all others except the U.S., Russia, and China."[168] Kubitschek also hoped that Brazil's international influence would be cultural, which

---

[163] Wright, *Villa-Lobos*, 139.

[164] Appleby, *Heitor Villa-Lobos*, 172. The building was the former site of the Ministério de Educação e Cultura (Ministry of Education and Culture).

[165] Appleby, *Heitor Villa-Lobos*, 181.

[166] Wright, *Villa-Lobos*, 138. A chorus of children sang one of his thirty-five sacred a cappella pieces, *Silêncio*, at the gravesite at the Cemitério São João Batista in the Botafogo neighborhood. See Appleby, *Heitor Villa-Lobos*, 172; and Gerard Béhague, "Santoro, Cláudio," *The New Grove Dictionary of Music and Musicians*, Vol. 22, 2nd ed., Stanley Sadie (ed.) (New York: Oxford University Press, 2001), 260-262.

[167] Juscelino Kubitschek quoted in "Kubitschek's Brasilia: Where Lately the Jaguar Screamed, a Metropolis Now Unfolds," *Time,* Vol. LXXV, no. 17 (April 25, 1960), 34.

[168] Juscelino Kubitschek quoted in "J.K. in a Hurry," *Time*, Vol. LXXIV, no. 18 (November 2, 1959), 24.

is why he announced in August 1960 that Brasília would host a new symphony orchestra. In order to attract world-class musicians, he offered salaries comparable to those of Brazilian senators.[169] As with so many of the lofty ambitions for Brasília, this goal was not realized. The temporary housing that emerged in the haste of Brasília's five-year construction evolved into permanent underclass *favelas* and compromised Lúcio Costa's urban plan for the city; with the existence of these slums, Costa's goal of promoting democracy by bridging class differences through the shared amenities that surrounded his Superquadra apartment buildings, such as libraries, movie theaters, and shopping areas became implausible.[170] The nation also suffered from runaway inflation because the construction of Brasília was facilitated by the printing of more money; the annual inflation rate in 1959, for example, was 35.9%. When it rose to 89.9% in 1964, the military staged a *coup d'état*.[171] The subsequent military dictatorship eroded Costa's visionary goals further and intellectuals fled the capital. One who left for Europe was Brazilian composer and conductor Cláudio Santoro. With the relaxation of authoritarianism in Brazil and the passage of an amnesty law that applied to both the military and the opposition in 1979, however, Santoro returned to Brasília to establish the *Orquestra Sinfônica do Teatro Nacional* (the National Theater Symphony Orchestra).[172] This meant that after a nineteen-year absence, Brazil's Modernist capital once again had its own proud orchestra to present the music of Villa-Lobos and the other great composers of the twentieth century.

---

[169] Allen Hughes, "The World of Music: Brasilia: It Will Have Orchestra with Many of Its Men Engaged in U.S.A.," *New York Times*, August 29, 1960, X9, ProQuest Historical Newspapers.

[170] Farés El-Dahdah, "Introduction: the Superquadra and the Importance of Leisure," *CASE: Lucio Costa, Brasilia's Superquadra* (Munich, Germany: Prestel Verlag, 2005), 12-13.

[171] Thomas Skidmore, *Brazil: Five Centuries of Change*, 147-148, 156.

[172] Gerard Behague, "Santoro, Cláudio," *The New Grove Dictionary of Music and Musicians*, Vol. 22, 2nd ed., Stanley Sadie (ed.) (New York: Oxford University Press, 2001), 260-262. For more information on the orchestra, see http://www.cultura.df.gov.br/nossa-cultura/orquestra-sinfonica.html

W

Miriam Guilisieyi Khamadi Were,[1]

1940-

In September 1961, Kenyan exchange student Miriam Were stood in front of the imposing red brick facade of William Penn College's administration building in Oskaloosa, Iowa. How she got there defies quick explanation, for it is a story that begins three hundred years earlier and unites the history of three continents. It is a story of faith and conflict, ambition and hope.

In the 1640s, a young Englishman named George Fox felt unfulfilled by any of the religious options before him. The Conforming Anglicans and the Catholics were too hierarchical in their governance, while the Puritans were too hypocritical in their lives: what they preached and how they behaved did not align.[2] He wanted congruity between what people did on Saturday nights and what they said on Sunday mornings. Fox questioned if spiritual authority resided in a pope or an archbishop, or even in a group of elders, as was true of the Presbyterians in Scotland. After many days of fasting and prayer in 1647, Fox heard a voice tell him that the Divine Spirit resided in him and in *every* individual, if only they would open up their hearts and follow their own Inner Light. Christians didn't need an ecclesiastical bureaucracy to tell them what to believe. They didn't even need a local priest or minister. Rather, Christians simply needed to accept God on their own by cultivating the seed within themselves.[3] When Fox began to share his beliefs, he attracted followers by the hundreds, especially from northeastern England. The Society of Friends, commonly

---

[1] Were, pronounced "where-way," is Miriam's married name; Khamadi is her maiden name, but, in the interests of simplicity, she is referred to as Were throughout the chapter.

[2] Margaret Hope Bacon, *The Quiet Rebels: The Story of the Quakers in America* (Wallingford, Pennsylvania: Pendel Hill Publishers, 1999), 11.

[3] Ane Marie Bak Rasmussen, *A History of the Quaker Movement in Africa* (New York: I. B. Tauris & Company Ltd., 1995), 3.

known as the Quakers, was born. Part of the attraction of Fox's message rested in its optimism: humanity was not depraved and condemned to Hell as many Christian denominations held. Rather, all were equal before God and all could find spiritual fulfillment and happiness.[4] This message threatened the existing order, for both the established churches and the government found these Quaker beliefs blasphemous. That Fox's Quakers refused to take oaths to anyone but God, refused to pay the obligatory tithes* to the Church of England, refused to honor social distinctions and customary titles, and by 1660, refused to participate in war only made the group more objectionable to authorities, both spiritual and secular. Persecutions resulted, including public whippings and brandings. In one notorious case in 1656, a man was committed to the pillory for two hours for public humiliation, then flogged with 310 lashes. He was then mutilated by having a "B" for blasphemer branded onto his forehead and a hole bored through his tongue with a hot iron.[5] By the time the Act of Toleration was passed in 1689 (which allowed for the freedom of religion for English Protestants), Fox had been arrested and sent to prison eight times, along with 15,000 of his followers.[6]

By the eighteenth century, Quakerism had spread to the English colonies in America, most notably to Pennsylvania, which was founded in 1682 by William Penn. By this time, most Quakers practiced Quietism: their religious services, called "meetings," were held in silence until a member of the congregation was moved to speak by the Holy Spirit. Quietists believed that only by becoming absolutely still and silent could a person become ready to receive God's guidance. Because Quakers did not want to speak falsely and because they wanted to be sure that their words were truly inspired, months might pass before anyone spoke at a meeting. Over time, this repeated absence of God's presence left many Quakers feeling disheartened and unworthy. This void emerged just as an evangelical movement known as the Second Great Awakening swept the young nation. During this revivalist period, Americans increasingly sought to demonstrate their faithfulness through emotional expressions: they gathered by the thousands to hear testimonials, be inspired by sermons, and experience transformative conversions. Membership in the Methodist and Baptist churches grew dramatically between 1800-1830 as a result of their revivalist style, which encouraged participatory singing, clapping, and shouting. New sects like the Church of Latter-Day Saints (Mormons) entered the religious landscape of the United States. One man living on the Kentucky frontier wrote about his experience, saying,

> The circuit preacher exhorted...[and the] congregation nearly all rose from their seats and began to fall upon the floor like trees thrown down by a whirlwind...some shouting for joy, others crying aloud for mercy....I attempted to reply, but had lost the power of speech— my tears flowed freely, my knees became feeble, and I trembled like Belshazzar.[7]

As Quakers interacted with Methodists and Baptists in Indiana and other frontier states, many desired to connect the Society of Friends tradition with the energy of the Second Great Awakening.[8]

---

[4] Bacon, *The Quiet Rebels*, 23.

[5] Will and Ariel Durant, *The Age of Louis XIV* (New York: Simon and Schuster, 1963), 199. The man's name was James Nayler (1618-1660).

[6] Durant, *The Age of Louis XIV*, 18.

[7] Jacob Young, *Autobiography of a Pioneer or the Nativity, Experience, Travels and Ministerial Labors of Rev. Jacob Young with Incidents, Observations and Reflections*, (Cincinnati, Ohio: L. Swormstedt & A. Poe, 1857), 41.

[8] Peter W. Williams, *America's Religions: From their Origins to the Twenty-first Century* (Urbana, Illinois: University of Illinois Press, 2002), 132.

Ultimately, this response to the rise of evangelicalism split the Quakers in two, dividing those who believed in the traditional, Quietist ways from those who believed in modernization: to be led by ministers, have more structured meetings, and actively expand the Society of Friends by sending missionaries abroad. Descendants of this evangelical faction sent the first Quaker missionaries to Kenya in 1902.[9]

From the missionary standpoint, the timing of the Friends Africa Industrial Mission was fortuitous because by then the effects of Britain's imperialist policies in Africa were quite evident. In 1884, representatives from Great Britain, Germany, France, Portugal, Belgium, the United States, and nine other European countries met in Berlin to discuss the future of Africa. The conference's host, Otto von Bismarck, wanted to avoid a European war caused by issues emerging in Africa. Much of the discussion concerned the ownership of and trade within the Congo River basin, but the diplomats also established the rules for colonizing the rest of the continent. These rules required Europeans to negotiate treaties with African chiefs, to create colonial borders cooperatively with other European nations, and then to occupy the land, forcibly when necessary.[10] Attendees at the Berlin Conference also agreed that a European nation had to demonstrate "effective occupation" of an area to retain their claim to it.[11] This escalated the "Scramble for Africa," a race to occupy the continent's interior and extract its resources for the benefit of the mother country. The Europeans set territorial boundaries with little regard to indigenous cultures so certain ethnic groups like the Maasai were divided between two different colonies (modern Kenya and Tanzania) with rival colonial masters (the British and the Germans); groups with enormous cultural differences, like the Hausa and Igbo in Nigeria, were forced together in one colony. These actions disrupted African life significantly and led to many problems once the colonies achieved independence in the 1960s. That there were no African representatives at the conference revealed the fundamental orientation nineteenth century imperialists had towards the continent. It was a place to be civilized and Christianized, enlightened and educated. In return, Africa and Africans could, quite justifiably, be exploited. As Rudyard Kipling wrote, Europeans had to take up the White Man's Burden, with its "savage wars of peace," its "new-caught, sullen peoples," and its "mouth of famine" in order to reap the rewards of glory, profit, and the "judgment of your peers."

In today's Kenya and Uganda, the British subjugated native peoples by employing the same techniques Europeans had utilized in West Africa during the Atlantic slave trade. Through a combination of commercial inducements, exploitation of intertribal animosities, and superior technology, the British were able to control much of the East African interior by the end of the nineteenth century.[12] This subjugation facilitated the construction of a railroad from Mombasa on the coast to Kisuma on Lake Victoria in 1901. This made the Kenyan highlands far more accessible and desirable for White settlement. The British then distributed vast tracts of land to White settlers

---

[9] Quakers in Kenya today are experiencing a divide between those who prefer slow songs and traditional sermon styles with limited charismatic appeal and those want amplified music, dancing, and technological innovations. As was true in nineteenth-century America, the style of Quaker worship can differ considerably among meetings in the same district or region. See George Busolo, Oscar Malande, Ann K. Riggs, and Theoneste Sentabire, "Quakers in Africa," *The Cambridge Companion to Quakerism*, Stephen W. Angell and Pink Dandelion (eds.) (Cambridge, U.K./ New York: Cambridge University Press, 2018), 206, 211-212.

[10] Edward Reynolds, *Focus on Africa* (Lexington, Massachusetts: D.C. Heath and Company, 1994), 39-40.

[11] Brian Athow and Robert G. Blanton, "Colonial Style and Colonial Legacies: Trade Patterns in British and French Africa," *Journal of Third World Studies*, 19.2 (Fall, 2002), 219-241, ProQuest Central.

[12] A. E. Afigbo, E.A. Ayandele, R.J. Gavin, J.D. Omer-Cooper, and R. Palmer, *The Making of Modern Africa*, Volume 1, The Nineteenth Century (Harlow, England, Longman Group, 1986), 337-338.

in order to grow export crops like coffee. They restricted Africans to designated reserves, which were akin to reservations for Native Americans in the United States, and taxed them to support the expenses of the colonial government.[13] British officials had little concern about the massive social changes brought about through these Imperialist policies, as long as they did not incite rebellion or interrupt the flow of natural resources coming from the colony. The reason for this indifference rested in a deep-seated prejudice against the native peoples. In the words of the British High Commissioner Sir Charles Eliot, the African

> is too indolent in his ways, and too disconnected in his ideas, to make any attempt to better himself or undertake any labour which does not produce a speedy result. His mind is far nearer the animal world than is that of the European or Asiatic and exhibits something of the animal's placidity and want of desire to rise beyond the stage he has reached.[14]

Such attitudes were enshrined in law. Colonial officials in the East Africa colony established strict segregation laws similar to those in South Africa during Apartheid or in the American South during the Jim Crow era. All public services and conveniences, from hospitals to cinemas, from post offices to lavatories, were racially divided. In the minds of the British, Kenya was a colony for

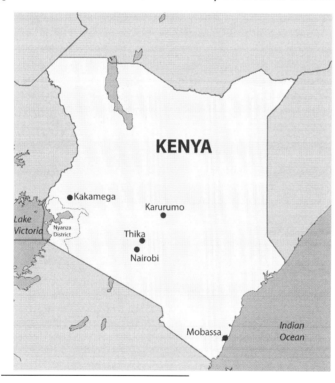

gentlemen and Blacks were not considered gentlemen.[15] Thus, British colonial officials, like their German, French, Belgian, and Portuguese counterparts in other parts of Africa, established a comfortable life for themselves while suppressing native autonomy.

The Quakers, who were the first Christian missionaries in western Kenya, had a decidedly different attitude. Blessed with a thousand acre land grant in a fertile area with a good water supply, they tried to establish a "a self-supporting, self-propagating native church."[16] Their goal was to teach Africans the Word of God and a set of practical skills that would help them find meaningful work in the colonial Kenyan economy. This

---

[13] Rasmussen, *A History of the Quaker Movement in Africa*, 33. All colonies were expected to be profitable, though few were. Taxing Africans was one way to increase revenue and manage expenses. "White" and "Black" are both intentionally capitalized. See Chapter F, footnote 60.

[14] Wunyabari O. Maloba, *Mau Mau and Kenya: An Analysis of a Peasant Revolt* (Bloomington, Indiana: Indiana University Press, 1998), 25.

[15] David Anderson, *Histories of the Hanged: The Dirty War in Kenya and the End of the Empire* (New York: W. W. Norton & Company, 2005), 80.

[16] Rasmussen, *A History of the Quaker Movement in Africa*, 20. The Quakers' goals paralleled those of the London Missionary Society in many ways. See Chapter T for more information.

coincided nicely with African desires in the early twentieth century, since by then many Kenyan chiefs saw the importance of literacy for their communities. In fact, the key to the mission's success was the establishment of a network of Quaker primary and secondary schools. After World War I, western Kenyans flocked to them. By 1950, there were 33,000 students in Quaker schools, as well as 17,000 adults with full membership in western Kenya.[17]

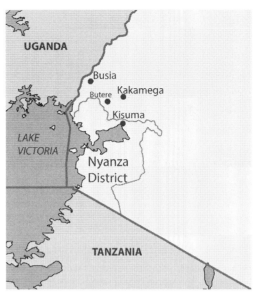

Miriam Khamadi Were was one of these students and her parents were two of these Friends. Were was the couple's seventh child. Like her brothers and sisters, she began her primary education in a Quaker school near the western Kenyan town of Kakamega. In the equivalent of the fifth grade, Were gained acceptance to a Friends boarding school for girls, having scored well on the Certificate Entrance Examination. In 1957, she was a member of the inaugural class at Butere Girls' High School. She graduated from Butere in 1960 with an interest in medicine but wasn't sure how to pursue that goal at a time when women were discouraged from pursuing careers in the natural sciences. Fortunately, a nurse at a Quaker youth camp saw Were's potential and recommended her to the head of the local Quaker mission, who arranged for her attendance at Iowa's William Penn College.[18] The assistance included admission and tuition but, as was true for Barack Obama, Sr., who was admitted to the University of Hawai'i in 1959, other obstacles remained. In order to obtain a student visa, Were and Obama had to have guaranteed transportation back to Kenya and $300 in cash. Fortunately for both, Kenya's national independence leader Tom Mboya had teamed up with an American businessman to create the Air Lift program "to meet the grave shortage of facilities for higher education in our own country and the urgent need for such education in aid of our over-all development and political emancipation," Mboya explained.[19] Between 1959 and 1963 planes chartered by the African American Students Foundation (AASF) brought 800 East Africans to the United States for their collegiate education. Obama was one of the program's 81 inaugural students in 1959; Were followed a year later as one of AASF's 289 second-year students, 53 of whom were women.[20]

---

[17] Conversion was not a requirement to attend school. There were 18,000 pupils in 1931 and 33,000 pupils in 1949. In terms of church membership, there were 51 African Friends members in 1914; 1,013 in 1920; 7,500 in 1929; and 17,000 in 1950. Today there are more Quakers living in Kenya than in any other country in the world. See Rasmussen, *A History of the Quaker Movement in Africa*, 44, 46, 50, 63, 94, 96.

[18] Esther Lwakabamba, "Penn Graduate Creates Legacy by Changing World," *The Statesmen Status*, May 6, 2015, accessed December 15, 2017, https://statesmenstatus.wordpress.com/2015/05/06/penn-graduate-creates-legacy-by-changing-world/ William Penn College changed its name to William Penn University in 2000.

[19] Tom Mboya, "To Aid African Students," *New York Times*, November 24, 1959, 36, ProQuest Historical Newspapers.

[20] Tom Shachtman, *Airlift to America: How Barack Obama Sr., John F. Kennedy, Tom Mboya, and 800 East African Students Changed Their World and Ours* (New York, St. Martin's Press, 2009), 7-9, 21-22, 92-93, 175, 201. The businessman was William X. Scheinman, who founded his own airplane parts company, Arnav Aircraft Associates. Not all of the Air Lift students were well received. When forty African students picketed the

When Were arrived in Oskaloosa, Iowa and stood in front of the William Penn College's Prairie-style administration building in September, 1960, she did so as the first African to ever set foot on the campus. Like other Air Lift students, she faced a host of cultural adjustments, both large and small: Were didn't own panty hose or a suitable coat, faced homesickness and racial tensions, and suffered from limitations in her academic preparation. Because she had never had any exposure to chemistry, on the first day of class she didn't know what the number two stood for in the formula H_2O. When she asked about it, her classmates laughed at her, but the professor defended Were and then worked with her outside of class to compensate. This help, combined with her faith and an uncommon determination, allowed Were to conclude her freshman year successfully.[21] By the time she was a sophomore, Were had made many of the necessary adjustments. In a feature she wrote for the student newspaper in February 1962, Were sounds like a typical American college student, complaining about term papers and due dates, worrying about her preparedness for final exams, and enjoying the novelty of still-new experiences—which in her case included gift exchanges at Christmas and trips to the bowling alley. The one thing Were clearly struggled with was the winter; she was unprepared for the beauty of the snow and the fierceness of the cold. She concluded the article begging to have her remains sent home to Africa should she not survive the season. "It's too cold to have a grave in the snow," Were poetically wrote.[22] As an upperclassman, Were was active in the Student Christian Association and the Model United Nations, and she was published in the prestigious *Beloit Poetry Journal*.[23]

One of the reasons Were thrived at William Penn was its Quaker heritage. As the college's 1963-64 handbook proclaimed, William Penn strives "to build lives which will reflect both culture and character, to inspire a spirit of service which will honor God and benefit man, and to guide in the selection of and preparation for life's great callings." It seeks to uphold the ideals of "democracy, sincerity, integrity, and simplicity."[24] These goals applied to both women and men, which meant that all students were encouraged to engage in a serious collegiate education and discuss important issues. This was not a given in the late 1950s and early 1960s, when many women were encouraged to think more about marriage than intellectual accomplishment, when academic discourse still smarted from the loyalty oaths and persecutions of the McCarthy era, and when college students

Belgian, French, and British consulates in Chicago in February 1961 to protest the assassination of the Democratic Republic of Congo's Patrice Lumumba, the *Chicago Tribune* decried their actions, saying, such "demonstrations…do not speak well very well for the type of students we are bringing to this country. Maybe these students don't think they are Communists, but they couldn't do more to promote the communist cause if they tried. One would think they would have enough appreciation for the educational opportunities this country is affording them to avoid associating themselves with communist causes and demonstrating against American interests." See "No Appreciation," *Chicago Tribune*, February 22, 1961, 16, https://chicagotribune.newspapers.com/image/376538237
[21] Lwakabamba, "Penn Graduate Creates Legacy by Changing World." Tellingly, many other Air Lift students had this same type of determination: only 2% of the students who participated in the program dropped out and returned to East Africa. See Shachtman, *Airlift to America*, 198.
[22] Miriam Khamadi, "Initiation to Winter," *The Penn Chronicle*, February 2, 1962, [Vol. LXXIV, No. 7], 1-3, courtesy of the Wilcox Library Archives, William Penn University, Oskaloosa, Iowa.
[23] Were's poem was published in *The Beloit Poetry Journal*, Vol. 16, No. 2 (Winter 1965-66), accessed December 15, 2017, http://www.bpj.org/PDF/V16N2.pdf#zoom=100&page=26. The information about her other activities comes from the William Penn College yearbook, *Quaker 64*, courtesy of the Wilcox Library Archives, William Penn University.
[24] *William Penn College 1963-64* [Bulletin and Student Handbook], 8, courtesy of the Wilcox Library Archives, William Penn University.

on many campuses could be characterized by their insularity and disinterest.[25] Were also thrived in Oskaloosa because its social atmosphere had a certain familiarity. At William Penn, students were prohibited from dancing, drinking, and smoking, and students and faculty were required to attend chapel programs and attend church regularly, either at a Friends Meeting "or at some other church of their choice."[26] These expectations fit with those Were had known as a child. Moreover, such behavioral regulations were not altogether unusual for students in the early 1960s. At Oregon's George Fox College, another Quaker institution, "attendance at programs inconsistent with Christian principles" was "seriously discouraged," students were required to attend chapel four times a week, and students were specifically prohibited from "social dancing, the use of 'playing cards,' alcoholic beverages, or tobacco."[27] Ohio's Findlay College, which was affiliated the Church of God, still required weekly room inspections and specified acceptable dress for public areas, but recent liberalizations allowed students to smoke and for men to be present in the lounge of the women's dorm until 1:00 a.m. on weekend nights.[28] Public institutions also had notable restrictions. Idaho's Boise Junior College maintained a dress code and expected its students to "present satisfactory evidence of good moral character" by showing "proper respect for good order, morality, and integrity…in keeping with the standards that identify a lady or a gentlemen."[29] At Western Kentucky State College, freshmen were required to attend chapel every Wednesday morning, and women had curfews and were required to have escorts after 7:00 p.m.[30] Similarly, University of Maryland—College Park enforced curfews and quiet hours during this era.[31] The early 1960s then were a time when the atmosphere at many American colleges remained quite traditional. The protests that engulfed so many campuses in the later 1960s had yet to emerge.[32]

As Were was working her way toward a bachelor's degree in natural science, her homeland was working toward independence. When Were was still in primary school, the poorest members of Kenya's largest ethnic group, the Kikuyu, began a guerrilla war against British rule. This insurgency

---

[25] Wini Breines, *Young, White, and Miserable: Growing Up Female in the Fifties* (Boston, Massachusetts: Beacon Press, 1992), 73-77; and Christopher J. Lucas, *American Higher Education: A History* (New York: Palgrave Macmillan, 2006), 245, 275.

[26] *William Penn College 1963-64*, 12.

[27] *Student Handbook, 1963-1964*, 6, 14, George Fox University Archives, accessed February 9, 2020, https://tinyurl.com/yymqmero. The institution changed its name to George Fox University in 1996.

[28] *Findlay College Bulletin, Student Handbook, 1963-64*, Vol.1, Number 3 (July 1963), Margaret Magoon (ed.), Findlay College Student Senate and the Public Relations Office, 28-31, *University of Findlay Memory*, accessed December 15, 2017, http://cdm17127.contentdm.oclc.org/cdm/singleitem/collection/myfirst/id/14/rec/16. The institution changed its name to the University of Findlay in 1989.

[29] *Boise Junior College Student Handbook 1963-64*, [8], retrieved accessed February 9, 2020, http://scholarworks.boisestate.edu/student_handbooks/6/. The institution became a four-year college in 1965 and became Boise State University in 1974.

[30] *Student Handbook* [1963], Western Kentucky State College, Bowling Green, Kentucky, WKU Student Activities, Organizations & Leadership, "UA12/2/34 Student Handbook," WKU Archives Records, Paper 2941, accessed February 9, 2020, http://digitalcommons.wku.edu/dlsc_ua_records/2941. The institution became Western Kentucky University in 1966.

[31] *M Book, Class of '67*, Liz Hall (ed.), July 1963, 37, The Student Government Association of the University of Maryland—College Park, accessed February 9, 2020, https://tinyurl.com/yxw68tch

[32] The trigger for these campus protests, the Free Speech Movement at the University of California-Berkeley, began October 1, 1964. By that time, Were was back in Kenya. Two recommended sources on the Free Speech Movement and the development of campus activism at Berkeley and elsewhere, see *The Free Speech Movement: Reflections on Berkeley in the 1960s*, Robert Cohen and Reginald E. Zelnik (eds.) (Berkeley, California: University of California Press, 2002); and W. J. Rorabaugh, *Berkeley at War: the 1960s* (New York, Oxford University Press, 1989).

is now known as the Mau Mau. Initially, its participants were not bound together by a single political ideology; they did not possess a unified leadership or enjoy a coherent strategy.[33] Instead, Mau Mau rebels shared a variety of grievances. Some were transplanted, landless squatters, who had been removed from their ancestral lands by the White coffee plantation landlords; these men could not fulfill their cultural traditions because without property, they could not marry.[34] Others came from the ranks of the urban unemployed, who suffered from high inflation and a marked discrimination in wages when they could find work.[35] These groups responded to their intolerable socio-economic situation by attacking White farms and livestock, assassinating British collaborators, and creating havoc in urban areas. In response to the expanding violence, the British colonial government declared a state of emergency in October 1952. This unified the groups, transforming the scattered rebels into a Kikuyu-dominated guerrilla army held together by loyalty oaths.[36] After the British created a passbook system to monitor Kikuyu movement, they arrested Jomo Kenyatta and other national leaders, despite their repeated public denunciations of Mau Mau violence. The British also forcibly detained at least 150,000 Kikuyu. Consequently, Black support for the Mau Mau guerrillas only grew. With each camp holding as many as ten thousand more people than they were designed to accommodate, the detention centers became crucibles for a plethora of diseases, including typhoid, malaria, tuberculosis, and dysentery. [37] Even scurvy was a problem. In fact, historians compare the conditions in the camps with those in Nazi Germany or Stalinist Russia.[38] Hundreds of thousands of additional Kenyans were held in 800 villages surrounded by barbed wire. In all, nearly the entire Kikuyu population of 1.5 million people was eventually detained by colonial officials during the Mau Mau.[39] The Kikuyu could not withstand the superiority of British force, and by 1956, the rebellion collapsed. Significantly, however, the state of emergency lasted until 1961 because the British imposition of greater force only succeeded in promoting nationalist feelings in the colony, uniting Mau Mau rebels and more conventional political organizations under the same umbrella.[40] With India and Pakistan gaining their independence in 1947, and with Ghana gaining its independence in 1957, Kenyan nationalists knew time was on their side. As British Prime Minister Harold MacMillan said on a trip to South Africa in 1960, "The wind of change is blowing through this continent. Whether we like it or not, this

---

[33] Maloba, *Mau Mau and Kenya,* 11. The local population recognized different Mau Mau geographical groups as being distinct from one another. See Greet Kershaw, *Mau Mau from Below* (Athens, Ohio: Ohio University Press, 1997), 220.

[34] Frederick Cooper, *Africa Since 1940: The Past of the Present* (New York: Cambridge University Press, 2002), 72.

[35] Cooper, *Africa Since 1940,* 33, 37, 39. The average inflation rate between 1939 and 1951 was almost 7% per year. In terms of wages, the highest paid African earned less than half the wage of the lowest paid Asian in Kenya, and the highest paid African male earned one tenth the wage of the lowest paid European. This meant that the wage for the lowest paid African worker was very poor indeed.

[36] Piers Brendon, *The Decline and Fall of the British Empire, 1781-1997* (New York: Alfred A. Knopf, 2008), 560-561.

[37] Anderson, *Histories of the Hanged,* 5, 318-320.

[38] Caroline Elkins, *Imperial Reckoning: The Untold Story of Britain's Gulag in Kenya* (New York: Henry Holt and Company, 2005), 151, 153.

[39] Elkins, *Imperial Reckoning,* xiv. In terms of total Mau Mau casualties, official records indicate that 1,819 Africans died and 916 Africans were wounded. This contrasts with the 32 Europeans killed and 26 wounded during the conflict. In fact, more Europeans died of traffic accidents in Kenya between 1952 and 1960 than were killed in the Mau Mau. See Anderson, *Histories of the Hanged,* 84.

[40] Bethwell A. Ogot, "Mau Mau & Nationhood," *Mau Mau & Nationhood: Arms, Authority & Narration,* ed. E.S. Atieno Odhiambo and John Lonsdale (Athens, Ohio: Ohio University Press, 2003), 20.

growth of national consciousness is a political fact. We must all accept it as a fact."[41] The Mau Mau was not successful, but independence was imminent anyway.[42]

Were witnessed Kenyan independence from afar. In her article in the student newspaper, written the day before the Union Jack was lowered and Kenya's new flag rose on December 12, 1963, she noted that "history tells of uprisings and these are often condemned though little attention is often paid to the oppression that led to it." She also noted that Kenyatta was not the first leader to be

> connected with an uprising that later led to people taking a fair share of decision-making in the matters of their country...[including] the Commander-in-Chief of the 13 colonies during the American War of Independence and the first president of the United States, George Washington.[43]

Were was clearly proud of her country, and like many Kenyans, loyal to its established national leader, Kenyatta. How much she must have wanted to be in her homeland that day, joining the quarter of a million people who gathered to watch the formal ceremonies in Nairobi or celebrating in her hometown of Kakamega.

Were's final semester in Oskaloosa came in spring 1964 as the Beatles appeared on the Ed Sullivan show, the Ford Mustang made its debut, Barry Goldwater battled for the Republican presidential nomination, Malcolm X left the Nation of Islam, and as two all-White juries in Jackson, Mississippi failed to convict a White supremacist for the murder of Medgar Evers. Such events certainly drew Were's attention, just as President Kennedy's assassination had in the fall, but as a senior in the pre-medical program, Were's course load demanded priority. The recommended course of study for the year was 26 units in physical chemistry, anatomy and physiology, bacteriology, and either math or German. She also had to take six units in philosophy and religion and complete an internship to provide her with practical field experience for a future career.[44] She was able to do this while being an active member of the student body, illustrating Were's determination. University records show that as an upperclassman Were served as the secretary-treasurer of the

[41] Harold Macmillan quoted in "'The Wind of Change' - Harold Macmillan's Africa Tour of 1960," *The National Archives*, accessed February 9, 2020, https://tinyurl.com/y4slnus2

[42] On June 6, 2013, the British government agreed to an out-of-court settlement £13.9 million to the 5,228 Kenyans who were found to have been tortured and sexually abused during Mau Mau, but the government stopped short of issuing a formal apology because doing so would increase its legal liability. Several thousand Kenyans have refused to recognize this settlement, and litigation continues. See Daniel Howden and Kim Sengupta, "59 Years Late, but Mau Mau Accept an Almost-Apology," *The Independent*, London, June 7, 2013: 8, ProQuest Central.

[43]Miriam Khamadi, "Kenya Looks to Independence," *The Penn Chronicle*, Vol. LXXV, No. 12, (December 11, 1963), 2. Courtesy of the Wilcox Library Archives, William Penn University.

[44] *William Penn College 1963-64* [Bulletin and Student Handbook], 22-24. Courtesy of the Wilcox Library Archives, William Penn University.

International Club, attended a Model United Nations conference at Iowa State University, and was a member of the Student Christian Association that offered programing on Wednesday nights. She also participated in a debate over government funding for higher education for qualified high school graduates.[45] Were certainly deserved the applause she received when she received her diploma on May 25.

After graduation, Were enrolled in Uganda's Makerere University, earning a postgraduate diploma in education.[46] This credential enabled her to return to Kakamega to begin a career teaching high school biology, chemistry, and physical education. The town, like so many provincial capitals in Africa's new nations, was full of both problems and promise. Kakamega was home to just under five thousand people. Unlike many Kenyan towns, it was connected by a paved road to Nairobi. It ranked tenth in the country for letters mailed per week, supported 12,500 newspaper subscriptions, and had 85+% voter turnout for the 1963 Assembly election. Kakamega was surrounded by a wealthy province with a high average salary of over £100 per year as a result of the region's primary industry, sugar cane production. But Kakamega lacked rail access, had a relatively modest rate of one telephone conversation every five and a half minutes, and had only one radio for every 50 people. There was just one television set in town.[47] Overall, Kakamega was a literate, relatively prosperous community, which enjoyed a better position than the average Kenyan town in 1964.[48]

Like most beginning teachers, Were sought to replicate her best educational experiences in her new classroom. She wanted to give her public school students the privileged academic preparation she had received in Quaker schools.[49] Were quickly found this impossible because so many of her students were too sick to learn. They could not make the necessary progress they needed to in order to become leaders of the new nation. In fact, in a typical year only forty to fifty percent of her district's primary school students passed the national exam to qualify to enter Were's secondary

---

[45] "International Club Seeks New Members," *The Penn Chronicle*, September 30, 1963 [Vol. LXXV, No. 4, page 1; *1964 Quaker* [yearbook]; and email correspondence with Julie Hansen, Librarian and Archivist, June 17, 2017. Courtesy of the Wilcox Library Archives, William Penn University.

[46] Miriam Khamadi Were, "Community Health, Community Workers, and Community Governance," *Africa's Health Challenges: Sovereignty, Mobility of People, and Healthcare Governance*, Andrew F. Cooper, John J. Kirton, Franklyn Lisk, and Hany Besada (eds.) (Farnham, U.K., Ashgate, 2013), 111.

[47] Edward W. Soja, *The Geography of Modernization in Kenya: A Spatial Analysis of Social, Economic and Political Change* (Syracuse, New York: Syracuse University Press, 1968), 32, 33, 36, 39, 41, 43, 44, 46.

[48] Soja, *The Geography of Modernization in Kenya,* 108, 111.

[49] I use the term "public school" in the American sense, not the British one. The Kenyan government nationalized all schools in 1963, requiring all instruction to conform to national regulations, thereby absorbing Quaker schools into the national school system. Therefore, Were could not have taught in the type of school in which she had received her primary and secondary education. See "Friends Schools in Kenya from Independence in 1963 to the Present Day," *Quakers in the World*, accessed February 9, 2020, http://www.quakersintheworld.org/quakers-in-action/149

school.[50]   Realizing that the future of her country was quite literally at stake as a result of her teaching experiences, Were took two steps to try to change the Kenya's prognosis. The first was to publish a series of young adult fiction novellas so that secondary school students could read stories with both literary merit and cultural meaning. *The Eighth Wife*, for example, discusses polygamy and the challenges a young Kenyan woman has fitting into an established family; *The Boy In Between* addresses the tribulations of being a teenager and a middle child in mid-century Kenya.[51] Were's second important decision, and the more personally transformative one, came in 1968, when she decided to earn a medical degree. She believed that as a doctor who specialized in public health, she could help improve the well-being of Kenyan children and the future of her country. This was exactly the type of visionary commitment Tom Mboya hoped to produce when he began the Air Lift Program.[52]

In 1973, Were earned bachelor of medicine and bachelor of surgery degrees at the University of Nairobi in 1973, where she was named the best all-around medical student in her graduating class. She briefly worked in Kenya's Ministry of Health, but in October 1974 she was recruited to join the Faculty of Medicine's Department of Community Health. Soon after her arrival, Were proposed that the Faculty spearhead a latrine-building program to improve sanitary conditions in Kenya, but her male colleagues dismissed her ideas as beneath a doctor's dignity. They also took to calling Were the Professor of Latrines.[53] Tellingly, such ridicule did not dissuade Were from her commitment to find practical solutions to the nation's public health issues. She instead advocated for "People's participation in their own health care."[54] In 1975, she won a scholarship to pursue her master's and doctoral degrees in public health at The Johns Hopkins University. Her Ph.D. fieldwork took her back to Kakamega, where she established a community-based health care system, despite incredulity from both her medical peers and government officials about the odds for the project's success.[55] Were's program was designed to empower carefully selected local citizens to provide basic health care services directly to the district's 134,000 people. These services included vaccinating children, improving sanitation, supplying contraceptives and family planning services, and providing basic first aid. The health care workers were paid by a tax which the people of the Kakamega region agreed to levy against themselves, thanks to Were's facilitation. This gave the residents ownership of the venture, rather than relying upon outside aid to fund the project.   Were also insisted the health care workers approach all patients respectfully, even when patient beliefs were unsound in the eyes of Western medicine. This created exceptional community support. Customarily, for example, mothers in Western Kenya placed cow dung on the umbilical cord at

---

[50] Soja, *The Geography of Modernization in Kenya,* 65.

[51] The books were: *Boy in Between* (Nairobi: Oxford University Press 1969); *The Eighth Wife* (Nairobi: East Africa Publishing Company, 1972); *High School Gent* (Nairobi: Oxford University Press, 1972); and *Your Heart is My Heart* (East African Publishing House, 1980). All of these titles were republished in 2005 by Nairobi's MvuleAfrica Publishers. See World Cat, www.worldcat.org.

[52] Tom Mboya was a member of the Luo tribe, who was educated in Catholic schools and began his professional career as a sanitation inspector. As a pan-Africanist, he developed close ties to Ghana's Kwame Nkrumah and founded his own political party, People's Congress Party. In 1960, as negotiations for independence approached, Mboya joined the Kenya African National Union (KANU) and became its Secretary General. Upon independence, Mboya was elected to parliament. He was assassinated in 1969 at the age of 38.

[53] Were, "Community Health, Community Workers, and Community Governance," 111.

[54] Were, "Community Health, Community Workers, and Community Governance," 112.

[55] Miriam K. Were, "Kakamega, Kenya: A Promising Start Derailed," *Just and Lasting Change: When Communities Own Their Futures,* Daniel Taylor-Ide and Carl E. Taylor (eds.) (Baltimore, Maryland: Johns Hopkins Press, 2002), 169.

birth; now expectant mothers were told that this practice was dangerous, but the choice was left to the mother, lest the health care workers be seen as a police force monitoring good and bad parenting.[56] In time, the region's acceptance of the program was so extensive that households were eagerly participating in demographic surveys, developing community gardens, protecting water sources, building latrines, and establishing daycare centers. Perhaps most significantly, because 99% of the health care workers were women, the project helped redefine gender relationships in the region.[57] Years later, Were's revealed her overall strategy when she wrote, "In Africa, if it doesn't happen in the communities, it doesn't happen. And when it happens in the communities, it happens in the nation."[58]

In 1978, the World Health Organization (WHO) and the United Nations Children's Fund (UNICEF) held the world's first international conference on primary health care in Alma-Ata, USSR—today's Almaty, Kazakhstan. The conference's declared that health care was a fundamental human right, that the world's "gross inequality" in health care was "unacceptable," and that by the year 2000 everyone on the planet should enjoy "a level of health that will permit them to lead a socially and economically productive life."[59] During the Alma-Ata conference, Kenyan officials presented the results of the Kakamega Project to the delegates, and Were's work received international recognition for the first time.[60] This gave her cachet with international agencies and diplomats. But this exposure also came with a cost at the local level: as the Kakamega Project attracted international observers and outside funding, private donors and governmental agencies began setting priorities. They also began controlling the distribution of medicine and making demands on the health care workers. The Kenyan Ministry of Health formally assumed control of the program in 1982. "The consequence [of their directives] was to institutionalize a people's process," Were observed twenty years later.[61]   Indeed, the loss of autonomy, caused by the international attention obtained in Alma-Ata, eroded the fundamental nature of the community-based health care project. This was ironic because the conference delegates had specifically proclaimed their faith in "the spirit of self-reliance and self-determination" in essential health care.[62] Unfortunately, the agencies and governments the delegates represented proved unable to adhere to these values.

Were rode the wave of international recognition well, even as it took her further and further away from direct care. She became a bureaucrat, an advisor, and a spokesperson, campaigning through various international agencies for the health care needs of women and children. She spent fifteen years living in Ethiopia, overseeing the $10 million budget of UNICEF's Health and Nutrition Office there in the 1980s, and serving as the head of the World Health Organization's

---

[56] Miriam K. Were, "Communicating on Immunization to Mothers and Community Groups," *Assignment Children*, 69-72, (1985), 429-442.

[57] Were, "Kakamega, Kenya," 173. The Kakamega Project increased the use of household latrines from 1% in October 1977 to 91% in January 1980. It also reduced disease in the district by increasing the use of dishracks, keeping homes free of stagnant water, keeping grass cut within 16 meters of a dwelling, cleaning up water sources, and immunizing children. See Were, "Community Health, Community Workers, and Community Governance," 113-114.

[58] Were, "Community Health, Community Workers, and Community Governance," 115.

[59] "Declaration of Alma-Ata," International Conference on Primary Health Care, *World Health Organization*, 1, accessed February 9, 2020, http://www.who.int/publications/almaata_declaration_en.pdf

[60] Sarah Boseley, "Miriam Were: Bringing Health Care to African Villages," *The Lancet*, 371, 9629 (June 14, 2008), 1991, ProQuest Central.

[61] Were, "Kakamega, Kenya" 176.

[62] "Declaration of Alma-Ata," 2.

mission in Addis Ababa for three difficult years of transitional governments in the 1990s. Between 1993 and 2000, Were was the director of the United Nations Population Fund (UNFPA) in Ethiopia; this agency focuses on reproductive health rights around the world. In climbing this professional ladder, Were can be criticized for becoming a part of the administrative oversight she found to be so obtrusive and inefficient when she was in Kakamega. She can also be criticized for becoming part of an international assembly of governmental agencies that some argue have done more harm than good in Africa as a result of the cycle of indebtedness they perpetuate.[63] It should be noted, however, that Were continued to promote local authority and to advocate for respecting patient rights whenever possible. In 1985, for example, she called for using metaphorical language that uneducated patients could understand in order to prevent disease and improve preventive measures like immunizations.[64] She also developed a reputation for representing the disenfranchised and for speaking her mind. At a major interagency conference in 1993, Were thought the meeting's pompous chair was ignoring critical women's issues and, despite the newness of her UNFPA appointment, launched "the most blistering assault I have ever witnessed," according to Stephen Lewis, Canada's former ambassador to the United Nations. "She was eloquent and forceful and unremitting and demanded that equality be present in all the decisions...and recommendations. It was very impressive and very moving."[65] In this moment, Were showed that she could move effectively between her job as the insider bureaucrat and her calling as the outsider activist.

During her time in Addis Ababa, Were dealt with corruption and famine, ethnic divisions and civil war, and radical ideologies and political demagogues. These were things to be expected in many other African countries in the late twentieth century. What wasn't expected, and what changed the landscape of public health in Africa more dramatically than anything else, was the arrival of a new disease: HIV/AIDS. This pandemic, which had claimed the lives of 30 million people by 2011, ensured that WHO and UNICEF's 1978 goal of providing adequate health care for all would not and could not be reached.

~

It is amazing what genetic mutations can reveal about the political, social, economic, and personal history of humanity. In the case of HIV, scientists now know, with remarkable precision, both when and where the HIV virus entered the human population. They know both how and why it

---

[63] Zambian economist Dambisa Moyo argues that except for emergency humanitarian relief, foreign aid to African countries is "an unmitigated, political, economic, and humanitarian disaster" because the vast amounts of aid (whether as grants or loans) foster corruption, foment conflict, undercut exports, promote inflation, reduce savings, prevent the establishment of real capital markets, and erode trust in society. See: Dambisa Moyo, *Dead Aid: Why Aid is Not Working and How There is a Better Way for Africa* (New York: Farrar, Straus and Giroux, 2009), xix, 49, 58-62.

[64] Were, "Communicating on Immunization to Mothers and Community Groups."

[65] Boseley, "Miriam Were: Bringing Health Care to African Villages." In 2003, Stephen Lewis won Canada's highest honor for lifetime achievement for his work as a diplomat and humanitarian activist. He is the founder of AIDS-Free World, and the board chair of the Stephen Lewis Foundation, which is dedicated to fighting AIDS in Africa. Lewis has also been Deputy Executive Director of UNICEF, a member of an international panel to investigate the Rwandan genocide, and the U.N.'s special envoy for HIV/AIDS in Africa.

spread. And they know what helps stop its spread and what doesn't. The story of the evolution of this one virus reveals the history of intimate human behavior in the twentieth century.

HIV stems from a similar virus in chimpanzees, called simian immunodeficiency virus (SIV). This virus has infected the central chimpanzee (*pan troglodytes troglodytes*) for several hundred years and is transmitted by sexual intercourse. It spread to humans who came into contact with chimpanzee blood.[66] This had probably happened many times prior to the twentieth century, when native peoples in southern Cameroon and northern Republic of Congo (Brazzaville) hunted for bush meat, but because this part of Africa was so remote, the hosts died before the disease could spread.[67] By the early twentieth century, central Africa was less isolated. The agreements at the Berlin Conference and the resulting Scramble for Africa brought Europeans in contact with remote peoples, especially in areas with valuable natural resources. In central Africa, ivory was initially the desired commodity, used for everything from piano keys and billiard balls to corsets and combs. Later, with the popularization of the bicycle and the invention of the automobile, rubber became essential. The Germans, French, Portuguese, and Belgians all used brutal forced-labor systems to extract rubber from their colonies, killing tens of millions of people in the process.[68] Untold more had their way of life drastically altered as new transportation networks facilitated the growth of early urbanization along the central African coast.

The first human to contract HIV and carry it to the outside world lived shortly before or after World War I in southeastern Cameroon, near what is today Lobéké National Park.[69] This person

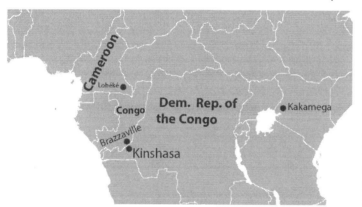

was one of the thousands of porters, traders, and hunters who passed through the region as a result of the rubber and ivory trade. He or she came in contact with chimpanzee blood during the butchering process and then either traveled downstream to Léopoldville (modern Kinshasa) or had sex with those who did. Statistics show that the capital of the Belgian colony had a gender imbalance of ten males to each female in 1910, and that prostitution was rife thanks to its tacit toleration by the colonial administration.[70] This gave HIV the incubator it needed to spread, but the growth of HIV is also unquestionably tied to efforts to eradicate other infectious diseases. Efforts to combat African sleeping sickness, malaria, hepatitis, leprosy, syphilis, yaws, and other

[66] Jacques Pepin, *The Origins of AIDS* (New York: Cambridge University Press, 2011), 41. A second edition of this book is scheduled for publication in late 2020. See Helen Branswell, "HIV's Genetic Code, Extracted from a Nub of Tissue, Adds to Evidence of Virus' Emergence in Humans a Century Ago," *Stat*, July 16, 2019, accessed February 7, 2020, https://tinyurl.com/y592wjca
[67] Craig Timberg and Daniel Halperin, *Tinderbox: How the West Spread the AIDS Epidemic and How the World Can Overcome It* (New York: Penguin Press, 2012), 50-51.
[68] Adam Hochschild, *King Leopold's Ghost* (Boston, Massachusetts: Houghton Mifflin Company, 1998), 233, 280.
[69] Jacques Pepin uses the year 1921 as the best estimate but says that the range for human infection is 1908-1933. See Pepin, *The Origins of AIDS*, 41. Craig Timberg and Daniel Halperin use the year 1908 as the best estimate, but say the range for human infection is 1884-1924. See Timberg and Halperin, *Tinderbox*, 35, 50.
[70] Pepin, *The Origins of AIDS*, 73, 94.

diseases intravenously often used improperly sterilized medical equipment. Since HIV transmission is ten times more likely through the sharing infected needles than through sexual intercourse, contaminated injections must have also contributed to HIV's spread.[71] By 1960, the extensive diversity in the HIV virus in Kinshasa meant that multiple strains existed simultaneously in the city as the virus evolved.[72]

The four major subtypes of HIV spread around the world from the Kinshasa incubator, often through the actions of a few individuals. Geneticists, for example, can trace how HIV moved from Kinshasa heterosexuals in the 1960s to San Francisco homosexuals in the 1970s.[73] In 1961, the United Nations Secretary General, Dag Hammarskjöld, called upon French-speaking professionals to come to the Democratic Republic of the Congo to help stabilize the former Belgian colony. As many as 10,000 Haitians responded to Hammarskjöld's request and moved to Africa. Some of these professionals had sex with Kinshasa prostitutes and became infected with HIV. When they returned to Haiti, they brought the virus to the Western Hemisphere.[74] The virus spread quickly in the hemisphere's poorest country due to prostitution centered in the Porte-au-Prince suburb of Carrefour. Here, bisexual Haitian men infected vacationing American homosexuals.[75] These gay men, took the virus to Miami, New York, and San Francisco, where a rampant, rebellious promiscuity allowed the HIV virus to spread quickly, eventually devastating the gay community.[76] Similarly, the histories of the other HIV sub-types can be traced. One spread up the West African coast; a third spread from Southern Africa to India and Southeast Asia; and the fourth spread across the continent to East Africa.[77]

---

[71] Pepin, *The Origins of AIDS*, 103, 224-225. Geneticists have proven that the oral polio vaccine was not a source of HIV transmission, as Edward Hooper theorized in *The River: A Journey to the Source of HIV and AIDS* (Boston, Massachusetts: Little, Brown, and Company, 1999). Similarly, the idea of there being Patient Zero who was responsible for the spread of the disease among homosexual men, as theorized by Randy Shultz in *And the Band Played On* (New York: St. Martin's Press, 1987), has also been set aside because of the discovery of a simple clerical error. See Zhen Gong, Xiaoyu Xu, and Guan-Zhu Han, "'Patient 0' and the Origin of HIV/AIDS in America," *Trends in Microbiology*, 25, 1 (2017), 3–4, EBSCOhost.

[72] Michael Worobey, et al., "Direct Evidence of Extensive Diversity of HIV-1 in Kinshasa in 1960," *Nature*, 455, 7213 (October 2, 2008), ProQuest Central. This viral diversity was also evident in the spread of SARS-CoV-2 during the COVID-19 pandemic. See Charlie Campbell, Yunnan Yuxi, Yunnan and Alice Park, "Inside the Global Quest to Trace the Origins of COVID-19—and Predict Where It Will Go Next," *Time*, July 23, 2020, accessed August 21, 2020, https://time.com/5870481/coronavirus-origins/

[73] Recently and similarly, scientists have traced the history of different strains of SARS-CoV-2 (COVID-19) by documenting mutations in the virus. See Peter Fimrite, "Scientists Unlock Genome To Track Outbreak's Spread," *San Francisco Chronicle*, May 19, 2020, A1.

[74] Timberg and Halperin, *Tinderbox*, 72.

[75] "Researchers Reporting U.S.-Haitian AIDS Tie," *New York Times*, October 20, 1983, A22, ProQuest Historical Newspapers.

[76] In the 1970s and early 1980s, many American gay men were having hundreds of anonymous sexual encounters a year. Sexually transmitted diseases were widespread within the gay community, but the attitude was that they could easily be cured with penicillin, as was true until the early 1970s, when drug resistances began to develop. Many gays thought of STDs as "an occupational hazard," rather than something to avoid. See Cokie and Steven V. Roberts, "The Venereal Disease Pandemic," *New York Times*, November 7, 1971, SM62, ProQuest Historical Newspapers. Such attitudes fueled the anonymous sex club culture—a $100 million industry by the late 1970s.

[77] There are two great ironies regarding this global spread. The first is that HIV is actually a very fragile virus. Exposure to air kills it, and it requires the right circumstances to transmit sexually. The vaginal lining frequently and saliva usually inhibits HIV transmission, which is why unprotected anal sex is the most risky sexual

One place the East African strain settled was in the slums of Nairobi. Here, as in Kinshasa and Carrefour, sex was the means by which poor women obtained basic necessities to live. Sex was "the last resort for ensuring that rent is paid and that children do not go to bed hungry," a 1999 study concluded.[78] Because these women were paid as little as seven cents for each sexual encounter, they had to service multiple men each day in order to earn a enough to support themselves, even at the frightfully minimal standard of a Nairobi slum. This increased their risk of infection and led to more HIV-infected people. Unfortunately, the public health care services available to these Nairobi residents were abysmal. In 1993, a major clinic serving the slums did not have gloves for the staff to examine patients, rarely had a sufficient supply of syringes and needles, and did not have sealed containers for used needles or blood samples. The clinic's one sterilization machine only worked sporadically so gynecological equipment wasn't sanitized between patients. During the rainy season, the clinic's patients had to wait in knee-deep water because the building no longer had a proper roof. In these conditions, the clinic itself probably spread HIV and other diseases.[79] Moreover, boxes of condoms sat untouched despite advertising campaigns because women believed that male sexual behavior would not change and that they would be subjected to violence if they asked men to use them.[80] As a result of this multitude of problems, HIV infection rates for pregnant women jumped from 2% in 1986[81] to 16.2% in 1993.[82] In other parts of Kenya, the situation was even worse, for unlike Nairobi, where the HIV infection rate eventually stabilized, provincial cities and small towns experienced accelerating HIV infection rates in pregnant women as the 1990s progressed:

Town[83]	1990	1993/4	1995	1996/7
Kisumu	19.2%	19.6%	25.3%	34.9%
Busia	17.1%	22.2%	22.0%	28.1%
Mombasa	10.2%	16.5%	15.8%	17.4%
Kakamega	5.3%	8.6%	11.7%	10.0%
Thika	2.5%	9.6%	19.6%	23.1%
Karurumo	---	2.0%	10.3%	26.6%

---

behavior. The second irony is that HIV works slowly. Once it resides in a new host, it can survive for decades, unlike Ebola, which kills its hosts quickly. See Timberg and Halperin, *Tinderbox,* 39.

[78] Eliya Msiyaphazi Zulu, F. Nii-Amoo Dodoo and Alex Chika Ezeh, "Urbanization, Poverty and Sex: Roots of Risky Sexual Behaviors in Slum Settlements in Nairobi, Kenya," *HIV and AIDS in Africa: Beyond Epidemiology,* Ezekiel Kalipeni, Susan Craddock, Joseph R. Oppong, Jayati Ghosh (eds.) (Malden, Massachusetts: Blackwell Publishing, 2004), 170. For the historical context of prostitution in Nairobi and its contrast with prostitution in the AIDS era, see Luise White, *The Comforts of Home: Prostitution in Colonial Kenya* (Chicago: University of Chicago Press, 1990), especially pages 217-219.

[79] Karen M. Booth, *Local Women, Global Science: Fighting AIDS in Kenya* (Bloomington, Indiana: Indiana University Press, 2004), 31-32.

[80] Booth, *Local Women, Global Science,* 3.

[81] Booth, *Local Women, Global Science,* 64.

[82] Maryinez Lyons, "Mobile Populations and HIV/AIDS in East Africa," *HIV and AIDS in Africa: Beyond Epidemiology,* 179.

[83] Pepin, *The Origins of AIDS,* 179. Cultural practices like polygamy and wife inheritance (widows being required to marry a male relative of their deceased husband) have played a significant role in increased infection rates in rural areas. See Wairagala Wakabi, "Kenya's Mixed HIV/AIDS Response," *The Lancet,* 369.9555 (January 6-12, 2007), 17-18, ProQuest Central.

Much of the blame for this escalation rests with the Kenyan government, which was slow to respond to the crisis in the 1980s. It created a national program to try to control the spread of AIDS in 1987, but it was more concerned with obtaining international funding and protecting the blood supply for tourists going on safari than talking with Kenyans about sexual risk and behavior.[84] African homophobia meant years were lost before health professionals, let alone the general public, accepted that fact that the "gay plague" of San Francisco and New York was the same disease infecting so many Africans.

~

In the December 2002, Mwai Kibaki won the Kenyan presidential election, ending forty years of rule by Jomo Kenyatta's political party.[85] Kibaki promised at his inauguration that Kenya would enjoy a new era: "I am inheriting a country which has been badly ravaged by years of misrule and ineptitude....[The] government will no longer be run on the whims of individuals," he proclaimed.[86] Miriam Were was one of the people Kibaki selected to improve government accountability. He appointed her chair of the National AIDS Control Council (NACC) in March 2003, proclaiming that the agency, "must be re-energized...[with its resources] channeled directly to those in need without recourse to intermediaries."[87] This was music to Were's ears. The reorientation was necessary because the NACC had become riddled with corruption, nepotism, and incompetence.[88] The agency's chairperson was embezzling $25,000 a month and "left the council in complete disarray," according to Canada's Stephen Lewis. Were set to work immediately, and with her "commanding presence," "calm determination," and "great dexterity" to manage the issues, she imposed order.[89] Were also had essential support from top as Kibaki launched his "total war on AIDS," ordering 50 million condoms from a German manufacturer and distributing them in hair salons, banks, and restaurants.[90] In 2003, Kibaki saw to it that Kenya participated in its first World

---

[84] Booth, *Local Women, Global Science,* 65-66. The National AIDS Control Program (NACP) was originally designed to be 8% Kenyan financed and 92% donor financed. When the Kenyan government failed to provide any funds whatsoever, the program lost credibility and violated Were's philosophy of the necessity of community engagement.

[85] As in the United States, two visions for Kenya's political and economic character have competed since the nation's founding. The first, a strong centralized government dominated by the Kikuyu and promoting capitalism, was that of President Kenyatta. The second was a devolved political system with strong local authority and, for some, a redistribution of wealth and African Socialism; this was the vision of an increasingly oppressed minority. See Daniel Branch, *Kenya: Between Hope and Despair, 1963-2011* (New Haven, Yale University Press, 2011), especially pages 16, 53, 58.

[86] Mwai Kibaki quoted in Marc Lacey, "Kenya Joyful as Moi Yields Power to New Leader," *New York Times,* December 31, 2002, A8, ProQuest Historical Newspapers.

[87] Mwai Kibaki, "President Mwai Kibaki's Speech During the Official Launch of War Against HIV/AIDS at State House, Nairobi on 23rd March 2003," accessed November 22, 2012 from http://www.statehousekenya.go.ke/speeches/kibaki/2003230301.htm

[88] Joseph Ngome, "Reporting on HIV/AIDS in Kenya," *Nieman Reports,* 57, 1 (Spring, 2003), 44-45, ProQuest Central.

[89] Stephen Lewis, telephone interview with Derek Dwight Anderson, January 17, 2013.

[90] Emily Wax, "In Another Break with Past, Kenyans See Hope on AIDS; Moi's Successor Promotes a 'Total War,'" *The Washington Post,* May 21, 2003, A1, ProQuest Central.

AIDS Day to raise awareness at a time when few African leaders were willing to talk publicly about sexual practices and sexually transmitted disease prevention.

When Were took over the NACC, the estimated HIV rate in Kenya was 9.4% of the overall population. [91] Though down from an all-time high of 13.4% in 2000, Were knew that the nation could not rely on that trend continuing. In 2005, she launched an innovative program with the major Kenyan cellular phone company and a Danish wireless company; it allowed Kenyans to access information about HIV/AIDS simply by sending a short text message.[92] Then Were insisted that the government develop a strategic plan, including a systematic survey of the population. In Were's opinion, this was the only way to ensure the effectiveness of national and international programs because it was the only way to identify needs precisely and work with local populations directly. Because of her reputation for efficacy and candor, Were's approach gained traction. By 2005, the strategic plan was in place, and by December 2007, the national survey was underway. The results showed that HIV infection rates had dropped 50% over the previous ten years and that deaths from AIDS had dropped 29%. It also found that most new infections were occurring in heterosexuals with multiple partners, but that men who had sex with other men, especially in prison, were the most at-risk population.[93] Recognizing this sexual diversity and recommending changes to Kenyan laws "that criminalise and discriminate against the most-at-risk populations" certainly broke new ground, and Were deserves credit for this breakthrough. The report repeatedly calls for more decentralized approaches to HIV prevention and care, reflecting Were's health care philosophy.[94]

The report also called for a national circumcision policy for all Kenyan men, even those from ethnic groups that do not traditionally practice it. The reason was that several studies showed that uncircumcised men had a much higher likelihood of contracting and spreading HIV than circumcised men because the tissues of the foreskin are particularly susceptible to transmission.[95]

---

[91] National AIDS and STD Control Programme (NACCOP), *Sentinel Surveillance of HIV & STD's in Kenya, 2006* (Nairobi, Kenya: Ministry of Health, 2006), accessed November 22, 2012, http://www.nascop.or.ke/library/3d/Sentinel%20Surveillance_2006_FINAL_REPORT.pdf.

[92] "Project Launched to Provide AIDS Information Via Mobile Phones," *BBC Monitoring Africa*, December 22, 2005, ProQuest Central.

[93] Kenya National AIDS Control Council, "Kenya: HIV Prevention Response and Modes of Transmission Analysis," (Nairobi, Kenya: 2009), iii-iv, accessed November 23, 2012, http://www.nacc.or.ke/images/stories/Documents/KenyaMOT22March09Final.pdf

[94] Kenya National AIDS Control Council, "Kenya: HIV Prevention Response and Modes of Transmission Analysis."

[95] Timberg and Halperin, *Tinderbox,* 105.

A correlation between circumcision and HIV was suggested as early as 1989, but the international health community did not act until the third millennium began. In 2005, a South African study was stopped because the interim analysis showed a 60% reduction in HIV transmission risk for circumcised men. Scientists believed that to continue the trial without notifying participants of those findings would have been immoral. Similarly, a 2006 Kenyan study and a 2006 Ugandan study were both stopped because of a 51-53% reduction in risk.[96] Because the part of Kenya with the lowest percentage of circumcised males is in the Nyanza district (49% versus 86% nationally), and because the Nyanza district is near Kakamega, Were knew the community and how to approach the work. In November 2008, the Kenyan government launched a voluntary medical circumcision program with the goal of circumcising 860,000 men by 2013. These men were mostly from the Luo ethnic group, the largest ethnic group in Kenya which does not traditionally practice circumcision.[97] The procedures were performed free-of-charge by trained clinicians instead of by medical doctors, thereby employing the community health techniques Were used in Kakamega thirty years before. The effort has been a success: HIV rates in Kenya have continued to fall, reaching 5.6% in 2012 and 4.7% in 2018 for those between the ages of 15 and 49.[98] Worldwide,

---

[96] Marie-Louise Newell and Till Bärnighausen, "Male Circumcision to Cut HIV Risk in the General Population," *The Lancet*, 369. 9562 (February 24-March 2, 2007), 617-619, ProQuest Central. These results have been replicated more recently as well. See Quentin Awori, et al. "Use of Topical Versus Injectable Anaesthesia for ShangRing Circumcisions in Men and Boys in Kenya: Results from a Randomized Controlled Trial." *PLoS One,* 14.8 (2019) ProQuest Central; and Kudzaishe Mangombe and Ishmael Kalule-Sabiti, "Knowledge about Male Circumcision and Perception of Risk for HIV among Youth in Harare, Zimbabwe," *Southern African Journal of HIV Medicine*, 20, 1 (2019), 855, accessed February 22, 2020, https://tinyurl.com/yxqckh6n. The World Health Organization continues to stand by the efficacy of the procedure (see "WHO to Develop New Guidelines on Male Circumcision," *World Health Organization*, May 2018, accessed February 9, 2020, https://tinyurl.com/yxa7qxr2. Some scientists have criticized the methodology of the original studies and expressed concerns that circumcision advocacy is a culturally insensitive and strategically unwise practice on a diverse continent with limited financial and human resources. See Michael Garenne, Alain Giomi, and Christophe Perrey, "Male Circumcision and HIV Control in Africa: Questioning Scientific Evidence and the Decision-Making Process," *Global Health in Africa: Historical Perspectives in Disease Control*, Tamara Giles-Vernick and James L. A. Webb, Jr. (eds.) (Athens, Ohio: Ohio University Press, 2013), 191-198, 205.

[97] Amy Herman-Roloff, Robert Bailey and Kawango Agot, "Factors Associated with the Safety of Voluntary Medical Male Circumcision in Nyanza Province, Kenya," *Bulletin of the World Health Organization*, 90. 10 (October, 2012), 773-781, ProQuest Central. Circumcision provides longer-term protection as well. A study of men from this same area showed that 66 months after circumcision, Kisumu men were less than half as likely to become infected as uncircumcised men. See: Nathan Seppa, "Male Circumcision Lowers HIV Rate," *Science News*, 182.4 (August 25, 2012), 11, ProQuest Central.

[98] Davies O. Kimanga, et al, "Prevalence and Incidence of HIV Infection, Trends, and Risk Factors Among Persons Aged 15–64 Years in Kenya: Results from a Nationally Representative Study," *Journal of Acquired Immune Deficient Syndrome*, 66, Supplement 1, (May 1, 2014), s13-s26, accessed February 9, 2020, US National Library of Medicine, National Institutes of Health, National Center for Biotechnology Information, doi:10.1097/QAI.0000000000000124, https://tinyurl.com/y6oqlhgq; and "Kenya," *UNAIDS*, 2019, accessed February 9, 2020, https://tinyurl.com/y3ovx2cw. Kenya remains a leader in voluntary male circumcision, despite concerns that the push to meet annual government goals is compromising the quality of care and adherence to established protocols. See Adam Gilbertson, Barrack Ongili, Frederick S. Odongo, et al, "Voluntary Medical Male Circumcision for HIV Prevention among Adolescents in Kenya: Unintended Consequences of Pursuing Service-Delivery Targets." *PLoS ONE* 14, no. 11 (November 4, 2019): 1, EBSCOhost.

circumcision has probably averted the spread of HIV infections more than all other factors combined.[99]

In recognition of this work and her life's work of community advocacy, the Kenyan, Italian, British, and Japanese governments all presented Were with significant awards and honors between 2005 and 2008. At the Fourth Tokyo International Conference on African Development in 2008, for example, the presentation ceremony for the First Hideyo Noguchi Africa Prize was hosted by the Prime Minister Yasuo Fukuda and attended by the Emperor and Empress of Japan and forty other heads of state. Lauded for overcoming cultural taboos through frank discussion and for being a beacon of hope for millions, Were responded in her acceptance speech by noting that significant work remained: reducing the disease burden and improving public health is crucial "for the creation of wealth and improvement of the overall socioeconomic situation in Africa….Healthy people, creation of wealth, and social stability are some of the requirements for us, the people of Africa, to get out of the indignity in which most of us live."[100]

Were retired as chair of the National AIDS Control Council in 2009. As Canada's Stephen Lewis said, "Miriam established a focus" for the fight against AIDS's spread in Kenya which "sustained and enhanced existing programs. She had a lasting impact on government policy," and helped Kenya turn a corner during her tenure at NACC. This helped give Kenya "one of the best [HIV/AIDS] programs in Africa."[101] Since her official retirement, Were has continued her AIDS work and taken on new responsibilities. She serves as one of fourteen commissioners for the Global Commission on HIV and the Law, and she is one of the Champions for an AIDS-Free Generation in Africa, which advises heads of state on AIDS policy. Were has also become active in the movement for Universal Health Coverage. She is proud of the connection between this effort and the publication of the Maternal and Child Health Handbook "as a global tool for improving mother and child health" because "if we improve the health of all African mothers and children, we shall improve the health of all Africans."[102] In December 2018, Were gave the closing address at the MCH Handbook conference in Bangkok, where she noted that there was considerable work yet to do: the adolescent fertility rate for girls between the ages of 15 and 19 remains very high in eastern and central Africa and only 16 of Africa's 54 countries use the Handbook's policy recommendations.[103] In addition to these activities, Were served as the chancellor of Kenya's Moi University from 2013-2018. She also works with a youth advocacy and empowerment organization she founded in 1995 called the UZIMA Foundation, and she continues to advocate for building a comprehensive system of community-based health care. As Were recently said,

---

[99] Timberg and Halperin, *Tinderbox,* 177.

[100] Miriam K. Were quoted in Kiyoshi Kurokawa, "Hideyo Noguchi Africa Prize," *The Global Forum Update on Research for Health,* Volume 5 (Woodbridge, U.K: Pro-Brook Publishing, 2008), 34, accessed February 21, 2020, https://tinyurl.com/yxhdqjp4

[101] Stephen Lewis, telephone interview with Derek Dwight Anderson, January 17, 2013.

[102] Miriam K. Were quoted in "Updates on Activities of Prof Miriam Khamadi Were (The Laureate of the First Hideyo Noguchi Africa Prize for Medical Services)," *The Cabinet Office,* Government of Japan, 2019, accessed February 7, 2020, https://tinyurl.com/y2gvvwvp

[103] Miriam K. Were, "MCH Handbook in Africa," Eleventh International Conference on Maternal and Child Health: Leaving No One Behind from Asia to the World, Bangkok, Thailand, December 12-14, 2018, *MCH Handbook* accessed February 7, 2020, https://tinyurl.com/y5rhdz2m. The adolescent fertility rate is defined as the number of births per 1000 women, ages 15-19.

"my experience has shown me that where there is community health that is effectively managed, it becomes the foundation of the health system….We need to listen to the people to know what they are already doing right so that we don't interfere with it."[104]

Now in her eighties, Were remains a woman of remarkable energy and personal conviction. She regularly spreads her message of hope and activism at college graduations and international conferences. What is especially striking is how consistent Were's message has remained over fifty years of public service, and how closely connected that message is to the ideas of George Fox and William Penn. It is a message of respecting all individuals, regardless of wealth or education, ethnicity or belief. It is a message of optimism that the world will get better and that individuals can make a difference. And it is a message—and a lifetime—built on the basis of Were's favorite prayer:

> Lord,
> Make me an instrument of peace;
> Where there is hatred,
>   Let me sow love;
> Where there is injury,
>   Let me sow pardon;
> Where there is doubt,
>   Let me sow faith;
> Where there is despair,
>   Let me sow hope;
> Where there is darkness,
>   Let me bring Light;
> Where there is sadness,
>   Let me sow Joy![105]

As Were recently said, "focusing only on the health problem often ignores the fact that one is dealing with a human being and that the person has rights. Therefore, in your dealings with people, especially when they are sick, endeavor to be compassionate."[106]

---

[104] "Miriam Were's ICHC Plenary Highlights." *MCSP Global*, April 19, 2017, accessed February 22, 2019, https://www.youtube.com/watch?v=EqUnkPZr6Vk. This interview occurred at the Institutionalizing Community Health Conference in Johannesburg, South Africa, March 27-30, 2017.

[105] This prayer is an adaptation of the Prayer of St. Francis. Were shared it with an audience in Fukushima, Japan in 2008, when she won the Hideyo Noguchi Africa Prize in 2008.

[106] Miriam K. Were quoted in "Updates on activities of Prof Miriam Khamadi Were (The Laureate of the First Hideyo Noguchi Africa Prize for Medical Services)," The Cabinet Office, Government of Japan, 2019, accessed February 7, 2020, https://www.cao.go.jp/noguchisho/english/award/01/message_miriamwere2019.html

X

Xu Xiangqian

1901-1990

In a July 1936 interview, Mao Zedong identified eighteen men, other than himself, who had been instrumental in the development of the Chinese Communist Party (CCP) through the first fifteen years of its existence.[1] Most of these men did not live long enough to witness the end of Mao's dominance of China, let alone hold high office in the post-Mao era, but Xu Xiangqian did. In fact, although Xu only ranked fifteenth on Mao's list, he was the only one in the group to earn China's highest military rank and to serve on the Politburo after Mao's death. Given the competitive factionalism of Chinese communism in the twentieth century, this represents a noteworthy accomplishment. Above all else, Xu was a survivor.

Xu was born into a small land-owning family in northern Shanxi province as the fourth child and second oldest son. Because his father, who held a Qing Dynasty bachelor's degree, was a teacher, Xu received a solid primary and secondary education. He then matriculated to a teachers' college in the provincial capital of Taiyuan. After graduation, Xu married, had a daughter, and taught middle school in his hometown of Wutai. Everything looked as if he would follow in his father's footsteps, even if such a future failed to capture Xu's imagination. His real interest was political change: in 1915, Xu led his classmates in student demonstrations against Japanese imperialism after Japan issued the Twenty-One Demands.* Similarly, Sun Yat-sen's articulation of the Three Principles of the People (nationalism, democracy, and social welfare) motivated twenty-

---

[1] The interview was conducted by American journalist Edgar Snow on July 25, 1936 in Yanan, the CCP base in Shaanxi province at the end of the Long March. Mao's order was 1) Zhu De, 1886-1976; 2) Wang Ming, 1904-1974; 3) Zhang Wentian, 1900- 1976; 4) Zhou Enlai, 1898-1976; 5) Bo Gu, 1907-1946; 6) Wang Jianxiang, 1906-1974; 7) Peng Dehuai, 1898-1974; 8) Li Weihan, 1896-1984; 9) Deng Fa 1906-1946; 10) Xiang Ying, 1898-1941; 11) Xu Haidong, 1900-1970; 12) Chen Yun, 1905-1995; 13) Lin Biao, 1907-1971; 14) Zhang Guotao, 1897-1979; 15) Xu Xiangqian, 1901-1990; 16) Chen Changhao, 1906-1967; 17) He Long, 1896-1969; and 18) Xiao Ke, 1907-2008. See Edgar Snow, *Red Star Over China* (New York: Grove Press, 1968), 448-449. For this chapter I have generally used the Pinyin system for Romanization of Chinese characters, even if the original source, such as Snow's book, used the Wade-Giles system. The only exceptions are for those proper nouns that are still better known today by their Wade-Giles spellings, such as Chiang Kai-shek, instead of Jiǎng Jièshí. Xu's name in the Wade-Giles system is Hsü Hsiang-chien.

two-year old Xu to disappoint his father, abandon his wife and daughter, and move to Guangzhou—the center of nationalist political activity in 1924.[2]

Upon his arrival in the southern port city, Xu joined Sun Yat-sen's Kuomintang or National Party (KMT) and applied for admission to the Whampoa Military Academy.[3] Sun Yat-sen had founded the institution earlier that year in order to generate a loyal, dependable, and professional army that would serve the KMT and its nationalist cause. Funding for the venture came from the Soviet Union because it fit with orthodox Marxist doctrine: China needed to overthrow the vestiges of its feudal past, eradicate Western imperialism, and become a bourgeois* national state before revolutionary socialism could take root. It also needed a strong army to defeat the regional warlords that dominated the country. Because the Comintern saw the Kuomintang as the most likely organization positioned to facilitate such political change,[4] they gave Sun the funds to establish the

---

[2] The account of Xu's early life comes from his interview with Helen Foster Snow in the summer of 1937. See Helen Foster Snow, *The Chinese Communists: Sketches and Autobiographies of the Old Guard* (Westport, Connecticut: Greenwood Publishing, 1972), 149.

[3] The Whampoa Military Academy is known today as the Huangpu Military Academy in Pinyin.

[4] Jonathan D. Spence, *The Search for Modern China* (New York: W.W. Norton & Company, 1990), 335-336. Spence notes that the Soviets supported a unified China as a bulwark against possible Japanese expansion in eastern Russia.

academy. The Comintern also sent officers to serve as faculty members.[5] Whampoa superintendent Chiang Kai-Shek hired additional instructors and made admission decisions, approving candidates from both the Kuomintang and the Chinese Communist Party.[6] In June 1924, the first class of 500 hopeful cadets, including Xu, assembled on an island ten miles downriver of Guangzhou and stood before Sun and Chiang.[7] Over the next six months, the cadets learned military tactics and weaponry, but three-quarters of their time was devoted to a political indoctrination in the Three Principles of the People and its importance for the Kuomintang.[8] Considerable attention was also given to Chiang's military philosophy that encouraged risk taking, self-sacrifice, unity, discipline, and loyalty. Soldiers were taught to fight even in the face of defeat and death, to obey their commanders unquestioningly, and to be aggressive in their tactics and actions.[9] The resulting military-political orientation became known as the "Whampoa Spirit." It was a neo-Confucian expectation of conduct that Sun Yat-sen and Chiang Kai-shek hoped would become a characteristic of the KMT as a whole. In his opening address at the First National Congress of the Kuomintang on January 20, 1924, Sun declared,

> All members of the party must possess spiritual unity. In order that all members of the party may be united spiritually, the first thing is to sacrifice freedom, the second is to offer ability. If the individual can sacrifice his freedom, then the whole party will have freedom. If the individual can offer his ability, then the whole party will possess the ability.[10]

This spirit was put to an early test because the precarious Kuomintang government in Guangzhou was surrounded by the troops of hostile warlords.[11] This pressure led Chiang to

---

[5] The Soviet's gift was for 2.7 million yuan in initial start-up funding, plus 100,000 yuan a month for on-going expenses. See Jay Taylor, *The Generalissimo: Chiang Kai-shek and the Struggle for Modern China* (Cambridge, Massachusetts: The Belknap Press of Harvard University, 2009), 45.

[6] Xiaobing Li, *A History of the Modern Chinese Army* (Lexington, Kentucky: University Press of Kentucky, 2007), 37-38; and Taylor, *The Generalissimo*, 47.

[7] Sources do not agree on the number of cadets in the first class; figures range from 350 to 700. Jay Taylor uses the figure of 500, which seems the most reasonable. See Taylor, *The Generalissimo*, 47.

[8] Spence, *The Search for Modern China*, 339; and Taylor, *The Generalissimo*, 46. Another historian states that the majority of the curriculum was devoted to combat skills and physical fitness; See Peter Worthing, "The Eastern Expeditions of 1925: A Defining Moment in the History of the Nationalist Military," *Modern China Studies*, vol. 17, no. 2 (June 2010), 18-44, EBSCOhost. Regardless of the exact proportions, the curriculum certainly had both practical and ideological components.

[9] Peter Worthing, *General He Yingqin: The Rise and Fall of Nationalist China* (Cambridge, U.K.: Cambridge University Press, 2016), 39.

[10] Sun Yat-sen quoted in Lyon Sharman, *Sun Yat-sen: His Life and Meaning, a Critical Biography* (Stanford, California: Stanford University Press, 1968), 258.

[11] Of particular concern was Chen Jiongming (1878-1933), who dominated either the civil or military governorship of Guangdong between 1911 and 1923. Chen broke with Sun Yat-sen in 1922. For information on Chen, see Leslie H. Dingyan Chen, *Chen Jiongming and the Federalist Movement: Regional Leadership and Nation Building in Early Republican China* (Ann Arbor, Michigan: University of Michigan Press, 1999); and Humphrey Ko, *The Making of the Modern Chinese State: Cement, Legal Personality and Industry* (Singapore: Palgrave Macmillan, 2016).

condense two years of training into six months.[12]   The first Whampoa graduation was held that winter and upon graduation, Xu was made a squad commander at age twenty-three.[13]   His first combat mission came three months later, in February 1925, when Whampoa's First and Second Training Regiments attacked the fortified town of Danshui in eastern Guangdong province as part of the First Eastern Expedition. The town's sixteen-foot walls formed an intimidating barrier, but a

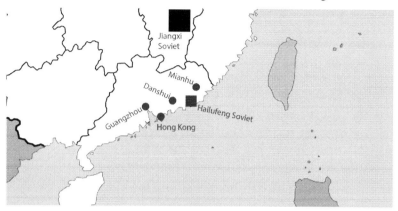

morning artillery barrage on February 15 opened up a small breach at the wall's southeast corner and soldiers from Chiang's two regiments formed human ladders by standing on each other's shoulders to scale the walls. The town soon fell, providing the Whampoa troops with additional guns and ammunition, as well as much needed confidence. A month later in the village of Mianhu, the two Training Regiments scored another victory over a warlord garrison, despite poor intelligence, numerical inferiority, and heavy casualties. These two battles confirmed for many the legitimacy of the Whampoa system and set the tone for the KMT army's future approach to battle.[14]

At the end of the First Eastern Expedition, Chiang Kai-shek sent Xu north to work as a political officer. Xu spent the next two and a half years in central and northern China, battling warlords, instructing troops, helping to establish a branch of the Whampoa Military Academy in Wuhan, teaching future officers, and recovering from illness.[15] Most significantly, in late 1926 or early 1927, Xu joined the Chinese Communist Party.[16] He must have done so without drawing the attention of key Kuomintang officials because although Chiang conducted a ruthless purge of Communists in mid-April 1927,[17] Xu retained his position as a member of the Wuhan Whampoa Special Cadet's

[12] Worthing, "The Eastern Expeditions of 1925."

[13] James Zheng Gao, *Historical Dictionary of Modern China, 1800-1949* (Lanham, Maryland: Scarecrow Press, 2009), 91; and Helen Foster Snow, *The Chinese Communists,* 149. Sources do not agree on the graduation date of the first class, but either late December or early January is most likely.

[14] The two Training Regiments had somewhat different experiences in these battles, but I have been unable to determine whether Xu was in the First, which took the lead in both battles and suffered the largest casualties, or in the Second, which helped turn the tide to win both battles. At Mianhu, the First Regiment may have been outnumbered ten to one and may have suffered a casualty rate of 70%. See Worthing, "The Eastern Expeditions of 1925."

[15] Xu was one of the few Whampoa graduates who became an instructor at Whampoa. See Donald W. Klein and Anne B. Clark, *Biographical Dictionary of Chinese Communism, 1921-1965* (Cambridge, Massachusetts: Harvard University Press, 1971), 1055. Nie Rongzhen was another.

[16] Klein and Clark, *Biographical Dictionary of Chinese Communism, 1921-1965,* 349.

[17] Chiang's suppression included what is known as the Shanghai Massacre or the April 12 Incident, when the KMT and its opium mafia allies crushed Shanghai's communist-controlled General Labor Union. They then arrested and executed known Communists. A British official estimated that 400 were killed and many more arrested. In subsequent weeks, Chiang's communist suppression occurred in many cities, killing thousands. This was the start of the Chinese Civil War. See among other sources Philip Short, *Mao: A Life* (New York: John Macrae-Henry Holt, 1999), 179-180; Elizabeth J. Perry, *Shanghai on Strike: The Politics of Chinese Labor* (Stanford, California: Stanford University Press, 1992), 90-92; and Taylor, *The Generalissimo*, 66-68.

Training Regiment. This position allowed him to infiltrate the staff of an important Nationalist general, Zhang Fakui, and to work as a Communist spy for several months. By early August, however, Zhang had become suspicious of those with connections to the Special Regiment. He disarmed the unit and moved it to Jiangxi province. Probably thinking himself in grave danger, Xu escaped from Zhang's army and traveled to Wuhan and Shanghai to make contact with CCP officials. The Party ordered Xu to return to Guangzhou to begin fomenting unrest.[18] Ironically, by the end of the year, General Zhang also ended up in Guangzhou with the Special Regiment still intact.

Xu's specific mission was to help organize the urban component of a provincial uprising that would unite Guangzhou's working class with rebelling peasants from the countryside. This would give the CCP a revolutionary base.[19] Xu was to work closely with the now-Communist commander of the Special Regiment, Ye Jianying.[20] On December 7, 1927, a congress of peasants, workers, and soldiers met secretly to coordinate operations and set the date for what became known as the Guangzhou Uprising or Guangzhou Commune. The steering committee, which was led by two Comintern representatives, then decided to make the uprising be a military operation instead of a part of a general strike. Both Xu and Ye disagreed with this fatal decision, believing that success depended upon generating a broad basis of worker support. The operation began anyway in the early morning hours of December 11.[21] Xu and Ye may not have understood that by late 1927 the Guangzhou labor movement was deeply divided after repeated failures to bring about change. The Comintern leaders saw a military intervention as necessary, even if risky, because without CCP action, the Party jeopardized losing the working class support it had worked so hard to generate.[22]

During the Uprising, Xu served as captain of the Sixth Detachment. This put him in charge of 600 largely unarmed and untrained men with whom he couldn't communicate because he didn't speak Cantonese.[23] Always relying on a translator or on written instructions was an obvious disadvantage in battle, but initially the Uprising proceeded as planned. The rebels seized the police headquarters and key government buildings, but they failed to capture the arms depot, to isolate the city's communications and transportation networks, or to receive support from rural areas. These failings, combined with the death of a Comintern representative on the second day of fighting, ensured that the Guangzhou Uprising collapsed within 72 hours. In the aftermath, those suspected of Communist ties were rounded up and shot in groups of fifty; 6,000 died in these

---

[18] Helen Foster Snow, *The Chinese Communists*, 150; and Klein and Clark, *Biographical Dictionary of Chinese Communism*, 349 and 1004-1005.

[19] S. Bernard Thomas, *'Proletarian Hegemony' in the Chinese Revolution and the Canton Commune of 1927* (Ann Arbor, Michigan: Center for Chinese Studies, University of Michigan, 1975), 22. The CCP did not understand the situation in the countryside surrounding Guangzhou. This meant the idea of a coordinated urban-rural undertaking was unrealistic. See Arif Dirlik, "Narrativizing Revolution: The Guangzhou Uprising (11-13 December 1927) in Workers' Perspective," *Modern China*, 23, 4 (October 1997), 363+, EBSCOhost.

[20] Ye Jianying had secretly become a communist on July 18, 1927, two weeks before Xu's departure from the Special Regiment. See Klein and Clark, *Biographical Dictionary of Chinese Communism,* 1004.

[21] Gao, *Historical Dictionary of Modern China*, 75; and Thomas, *'Proletarian Hegemony' in the Chinese Revolution and the Canton Commune of 1927*, 23-24. The Comintern representatives were Heinz Heumann and Zhang Tailei. The date for the uprising was moved forward two days, from December 13 to December 11, once it was learned that Zhang Fakui was sending reinforcements to help suppress the Communists.

[22] Dirlik, "Narrativizing Revolution."

[23] Helen Foster Snow, *The Chinese Communists*, 150.

executions.[24] Some escaped the bloodbath, including the largely intact Special Regiment. These 1,200 men retreated into eastern Guangdong province, while Ye went to British-controlled Hong Kong.[25] Xu evaded capture and caught up with his former students in the Special Regiment as they retreated. Together they traveled 180 miles east to the closest friendly base, the Hailufeng Soviet on the Guangdong coast, passing through land that Xu had first seen during the First Eastern Expedition. He arrived in the Hailufeng Soviet in January 1928.[26]

The leader of Hailufeng was Peng Pai, a Guangdong native who had been born into a prominent landowning family but who had become a revolutionary in his early twenties. In 1921, he wrote a newspaper article calling for the abolition of private property. At the Fifth CCP Congress in 1927, Peng joined with Mao in calling for the confiscation of all land for the benefit of the masses. For Peng, revolutionary change in China had to come from the rural peasantry, not urban workers. He put this belief into practice in eastern Guangdong in late 1927 when he created China's first soviet.*[27] Xu admired Peng and enjoyed working with him, but the 1,200 men of the Special Regiment and the 800 men of the Red Army were no match for the Kuomintang troops bent on destroying the Hailufeng Soviet, especially because the Communists had difficulty recruiting new soldiers. As Xu said,

> The local peasants didn't want to join the regular Red Army because they didn't understand our dialect nor we theirs. I had great difficulty with my work in Hailufeng because I still could not speak Cantonese!...We couldn't get any new recruits, and the army decreased daily."[28]

In fact, by March 1928, when the Hailufeng Soviet collapsed, only 60 of the 1,200 men in the Special Regiment were still alive. Xu was one of those who escaped, thanks to the help of Communist agents. Xu made his way to Shanghai, where his former Whampoa teacher and leading Politburo member Zhou Enlai gave him an important new assignment.[29]

~

Between June 1929 and August 1932, Xu served as the military commander of the Oyuwan Soviet.[30] The Communist base, located in the Dabie Mountains where the provinces of Hubei, Henan, and Anhui all meet, had advantages that the Hailufeng Soviet did not. Oyuwan's rugged terrain provided relative safety, a defensible position, and access to urban areas in three political

---

[24] Thomas, *'Proletarian Hegemony' in the Chinese Revolution and the Canton Commune of 1927*, 25-27; and Dirlik, "Narrativizing Revolution." The Comintern representative who died was Zhang Tailei.

[25] Klein and Clark, *Biographical Dictionary of Chinese Communism,* 1005.

[26] Helen Foster Snow, *The Chinese Communists,* 150.

[27] Klein and Clark, *Biographical Dictionary of Chinese Communism,* 720-723.

[28] Xu Xiangqian quoted in Helen Foster Snow, *The Chinese Communists,* 151.

[29] William W. Whitson, *The Chinese High Command: A History of Communist Military Politics, 1927-71* (New York: Praeger Publishers, 1973), 127. At this point, Zhou's title was head of the Organizational Bureau of the Standing Committee of the Politburo. Zhou was in charge of day-to-day Party affairs. See Barbara Barnouin and Yu Changgen, *Zhou Enlai: A Political Life,* (Hong Kong: The Chinese University Press, 2006), 41.

[30] The name came from the three ancient names for the provinces of Hubei (E), Henan (Yu) and Anhui (Wan); consequently, some sources refer to the Soviet as "E-Yu-Wan."

jurisdictions. The residents of these agriculturally poor highlands were more inclined to embrace revolutionary change than peasants in wealthier regions. In addition, the CCP had recently recognized the legitimacy of rural-based guerrilla warfare, despite the departure from Marxist theory that this represented.[31] With these advantages, the Oyuwan Soviet quickly grew in size and importance, though surrounded by Nationalist-controlled territories.[32]

By destroying part of the Peking-Hankow railway, disrupting shipping on the Yangtze and Han Rivers, routing a Nationalist regiment in open combat, and capturing much-needed armaments in summer 1930, the Oyuwan Soviet attracted the attention of Chiang Kai-shek and the Nationalist leadership.[33] Their response, the first of five Encirclement Campaigns, was the KMT's attempt to eradicate the Communists from their Dabie Mountains base, as well as from their soviets in other parts of China.[34] The First Encirclement Campaign, which was launched in December 1930, quickly showed the effectiveness of Xu's tactics. He overcame the Nationalists' superiority in numbers and equipment by using mobility to his advantage. Rather than engage the enemy in large-scale battles, Xu used lightning strikes to unexpectedly and quickly attack the enemy before retreating. The Nationalist commanders could never be certain where Xu's main forces were concentrated; they were continually subjected to ambushes, resulting in high KMT casualties.[35] In the early spring 1931, the Nationalist troops withdrew in frustration. During the Second Encirclement Campaign in late spring and early summer 1931, the Nationalists fared no better.

Xu never made his military decisions in isolation. Like all commanders, he worked in conjunction with a political commissar, who represented the Party and ensured that the military followed the intentions of the Central Committee. In the Chinese Communist system, the primary purpose of the military was to serve the interests of the Party. To instill this, each military unit, down to the company level, had a political commissar.[36] In this way, the CCP guaranteed that the army was *its* army, rather than an independent entity. In other words, it was the commissar's job to outline policy on behalf of the Party, and it was Xu's job to implement that vision through military means. Both the commanding officer and the political commissar had to sign an order for it to be valid,[37] which meant that commissars needed to be in frequent contact with Party leaders. The problem during this early period of Xu's work in the Oyuwan Soviet was that communication with Party leadership was difficult and erratic, giving Xu considerable autonomy. In April 1931, however, this situation changed when representatives of the Central Committee arrived to assert their control over the Soviet.[38] The group included Zhang Guotao, a man who would shape Xu's career in critical ways.

---

[31] Robert W. McColl, "The Oyüwan Soviet Area, 1927-1932," *The Journal of Asian Studies*, 27, 1 (November, 1967), 41-60, EBSCOhost. The official endorsement of rural-based guerrilla warfare came at the Sixth National Congress of the CCP, which was held in Moscow from July to September 1928.

[32] Edgar O'Ballance, *The Red Army of China: A Short History* (New York: Frederick A. Praeger, 1963), 45, 63. By the summer of 1931, the Oyuwan Soviet governed about two million people.

[33] Whitson, *The Chinese High Command*, 128.

[34] McColl, "The Oyüwan Soviet Area, 1927-1932." The most famous of the other soviets was the Jiangxi–Fujian Soviet, led by Mao Zedong. Not all sources agree on the dates for each of the Five Encirclement Campaigns. Although there were brief breaks in the conflict, there was almost continuous warfare between the Nationalists and the Communist bases between mid-1930 and late 1934.

[35] Whitson, *The Chinese High Command*, 131.

[36] Li, *A History of the Modern Chinese Army*, 53.

[37] Whitson, *The Chinese High Command*, 44.

[38] Whitson, *The Chinese High Command*, 132.

Zhang was born into a wealthy landowning family in Jiangxi province, and in 1916 he was sent to study at Peking University. He became fascinated with Marxism and was an active protester in the May Fourth Movement.* In July 1921, Zhang represented Beijing Marxists at the First CCP Congress in Shanghai. This made him, like Mao, one of the thirteen founding members of the Party. The Congress put Zhang in charge of Party recruitment, discipline, and organization, giving him a greater influence than Mao had at that time.[39] As the decade progressed and the CCP formulated its early policies, Mao and Zhang repeatedly disagreed. They also had divergent career experiences that helped shape their later decisions. Zhang, for example, consistently opposed any Communist cooperation with the Nationalists and voted against resolutions to do so in both July 1922 and May 1927; Mao believed that cooperation was strategically important for the fledgling party. In addition, Mao never left China, but Zhang gained extensive international experience: he became China's representative to the Comintern in 1921 and lived in Moscow from June 1928 to January 1931.[40] The two narcissists[41] particularly clashed over the merits of guerrilla warfare, with Mao calling for a peasant-led "People's War" to usher in revolutionary change, and Zhang lauding the value of a professionally-trained soldiers, tactical maneuvers, and superior firepower.[42] Most fundamentally, their rivalry for control of the Party stemmed most from their own raw quest for power.[43] Therefore, by the time Zhang reached the Oyuwan Soviet, he was a man with an ambitious mission who would not tolerate dissent.

Fortunately, Xu had the same orientation to military operations that Zhang did: Xu too believed in the value of a specialized military that utilized established tactics and was led by a well-trained officer corps. He was not a proponent of Mao's reliance on peasant guerrilla soldiers. Indeed, Xu was first and foremost a military manager—a man whose greatest interests lay in tactics and military professionalism.[44] Upon his arrival in April 1931, Zhang was impressed with the proficiency of Oyuwan's troops, and he came to appreciate Xu's leadership as a result.[45] The two men bonded quickly. This connection became vital later in 1931, when Zhang became convinced that the Soviet was full of Nationalist sympathizers. In the subsequent shakeup, Zhang replaced most of the army's top commanders, took charge of most operations, and brought in a new political commissar, Chen Changhao, to root out potential traitors. Chen was zealous in this work: by late November 1931 he boasted that he had "mobilized the masses to run a check on every red soldier and officer" in the Oyuwan Soviet, which had "eliminated 1,000 traitors…and nearly 2,000 rich peasants." Chen believed that it was essential to continue "to use disciplinary means to deepen and intensify the effort to purge counterrevolutionaries…so that every soldier can fully understand that only the political programs of the [Communist Party] offer salvation."[46] At one point, Xu too was

---

[39] Klein and Clark, *Biographical Dictionary of Chinese Communism,* 38-39.

[40] Klein and Clark, *Biographical Dictionary of Chinese Communism,* 39-40; and Short, *Mao,* 139.

[41] Much has been written about Mao's personality but for his identity as a narcissist, see Michael M. Sheng, "Mao Zedong's Narcissistic Personality Disorder and China's Road to Disaster," *Profiling Political Leaders: Cross-cultural Studies of Personality and Behavior,* Ofer Feldman and Linda O. Valenty (eds.) (Westport, Connecticut: Praeger Publishers, 2001), 111-120.

[42] Whitson, *The Chinese High Command,* 136.

[43] Short, *Mao,* 329.

[44] Whitson, *The Chinese High Command,* 35.

[45] Whitson, *The Chinese High Command,* 133.

[46] Chen Changhao, "The Great Victory of Purging Counterrevolution Allies in the E-Yu-Wan Soviet (22 November 1931)," *The Rise to Power of the Chinese Communist Party: Documents and Analysis,* Tony Siach (ed.) (London: East Gate, 1996), 548-549.

questioned, but he exonerated himself to Zhang and Chen's satisfaction. He retained his rank,[47] although what became known as the Fourth Front Army actually belonged to Zhang by this point. Xu was smart enough to realize the danger in crossing a man as ruthless as Zhang and so accepted the *de facto* demotion without objection. Unfortunately, Xu suffered more than the loss of prestige: one victim of Zhang's purges was Xu's second wife, who was tortured for information and killed when she refused to denounce her husband.[48]

Chiang Kai-shek's efforts to eradicate the Communist stronghold at Oyuwan persisted through the next two and a half years. Despite scoring several key victories against KMT troops early in 1932, the tactical situation for the Soviet did not decidedly change: it was isolated from other Communist-controlled areas, from major cities, and from sources of supply. By June, Chiang had 400,000 troops encircling the Oyuwan Soviet and by August the Nationalists had begun to construct a series of concentric trenches, ever tightening the noose as Nationalist planes dropped bombs on Communist positions. Zhang decided that holding the Dabie Mountains base was an untenable long-term position.[49] In addition, the Fourth Front Army had lost 35,000 soldiers in the previous ten months.[50] Therefore, without consulting the Central Committee, Zhang decided in late August 1932 to try to break free from the Nationalist encirclement and move the Fourth Front Army west to fertile Sichuan to establish a new soviet there. Oyuwan was to be abandoned, except for a small guerrilla force that would continue to harass Nationalist troops and serve Communist interests as best it could.[51] It was probably Xu's job to figure out how best to withdraw. He chose to move the majority of his forces across the Dabie Mountains from the western slopes to unite with a smaller group of Communist troops defending the highland's eastern edge. From there, a total force of 16,000 swung around the northern edge of the Dabie Mountains and broke through the concentric Nationalist lines in the west.[52] Despite intense bombing by the KMT's air force, Xu was able, at the cost of many lives, to hold the breach open long enough for the rest of his army to pass through.[53] The Fourth Front Army's Long March had begun.

---

[47] Salisbury, *The Long March: The Untold Story* (New York: Harper & Row, 1985), 247.

[48] Sun Shuyun, *The Long March: The True Story of Communist China's Founding Myth* (New York: Doubleday, 2006), 127.

[49] Whitson, *The Chinese High Command*, 137. In the early 1932 victories, Xu's troops captured 15,000 rifles and 20,000 prisoners, as well as machine guns, howitzers, and mortars.

[50] Sun, *The Long March*, 126.

[51] The commander Xu assigned to the guerrilla forces was Xu Haidong (no relation), who eventually had to flee the Dabie Mountains base. In September 1934, Xu Haidong led his troops north into Shaanxi, where he met with Mao's army in October 1935. Xu Haidong later became a senior general in the People's Liberation Army. See McColl, "The Oyüwan Soviet Area."

[52] Whitson, *The Chinese High Command*, 138-139. The town where Xu's western and eastern units met was the capital of the Oyuwan Soviet, Chinchiachai; according to the website Geographic.org, which uses data from the National Geospatial-Intelligence Agency website, the town no longer exists as a result of the construction of a reservoir. Whitson doesn't detail how Xu's combined force returned to the Nationalist western line, so the swing around the northern end of the Dabie Mountains is a presumption on my part. It fits, however, with Xu's use of maneuverability and surprise whenever possible. Whitson says that the break through the Nationalist lines occurred at Hok'ou. I believe that the current place name for this place is Hekouzhen. Another source says that the breakthrough came at a point on the Peking-Hankow Railway where the Nationalist forces were weakest, and as best as I can determine, Hekouzhen was on the railroad line. See Edward L. Dreyer, *China at War, 1901-1949* (London: Longman Group, 1995), 186.

[53] O'Ballance, *The Red Army of China*, 85.

Xu and Zhang's Long March is not as well-known as Mao's, but it came two years before and was as much a retreat as a strategic relocation. The 1,500-mile journey to northeastern Sichuan took the Fourth Front Army through Henan and southern Shaanxi. At one point, they were within 25 miles

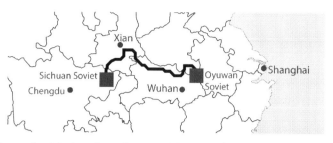

of Xian, threatening to capture the city from the Nationalists, but KMT troops beat them back and forced them south across the Daba Mountains and into Sichuan.[54] By the time they arrived in late 1932, the Fourth Front Army had lost almost half its personnel and much of its weaponry.[55]

In Sichuan, the Communists found a situation ripe for socio-economic change. There were districts where farmers readily made their supplies of grain, animals, foodstuffs, and supplies available to the Red Army because their frustration with the provincial government was so great.[56] Not only did Sichuan farmers face land tax rates that were four times higher than anywhere else in China, but they had been forced to pay future taxes as much as 50 years in advance by petty warlords who fought battles for entertainment.[57] Sichuan also faced an opium problem, for it was one of the three top cultivation regions in China in the 1920s and 1930s. Warlord encouragement for cultivation was so strong that famines resulted when farmers planted too many poppies and not enough grain. Local consumption of opium was also deleterious: about fifty percent of the Sichuan population smoked opium regularly and perhaps ten percent of the population qualified as addicts.[58] Xu noted the extent of the opium problem and was proud of the fact that the Communists campaigned against opium use. In doing so, the Communists won considerable support from eastern Sichuan women, who enthusiastically supported a ban.[59] The Fourth Front Army attracted large numbers of new recruits with their promises of socio-economic change. In fact, within two years of its arrival in Sichuan, the Fourth Front Army grew

---

[54] Klein and Clark, *Biographical Dictionary of Chinese Communism*, 908.

[55] Whitson, *The Chinese High Command*, 138-139. This left the army with about 9,000 soldiers, 8,000 rifles, 50 machine guns and no artillery.

[56] Douglas Robertson, "Reds Still Active in Yangtse Region: Definite Results of Nanking's Campaign Achieved in Only One Area," *New York Times*, July 1, 1934, E8, ProQuest Historical Newspapers.

[57] Norman D. Hanwell, "Red China on the March." *Nation* 143, no. 13 (September 26, 1936): 359, EBSCOhost.

[58] Edward R. Slack, *Opium, State, and Society: China's Narco-Economy and the Guomindang, 1924-1937* (Honolulu: University of Hawaii Press, 2001), 7, 11, 14, 43, EBSCOebooks. Other recommended sources on opium in China include Timothy Brook and Bob Tadashi Wakabayashi, *Opium Regimes: China, Britain, and Japan, 1839-1952* (Berkeley: University of California Press, 2000) and Barbara Hodgson, *Opium: A Portrait of the Heavenly Dream* (San Francisco, California: Chronicle Books, 1999).

[59] Helen Praeger Young, *Choosing Revolution: Chinese Women Soldiers on the Long March* (Urbana, Illinois: University of Illinois Press, 2001), 154-155; Helen Foster Snow, *The Chinese Communists,* 158; and Whitson, *The Chinese High Command,* 140-141. One scholar disagrees, saying that Zhang and Xu did not interfere with the production of opium because it was Sichuan's largest cash crop. See Salisbury, *The Long March*, 247.

ten-fold to 80,000 soldiers.[60] Armed with the infusion of manpower, the new Soviet expanded rapidly until it controlled fourteen counties in eastern Sichuan with a population of nearly one million. This confluence of factors allowed Zhang Guotao to establish a new government, the Sichuan-Shaanxi Soviet, which held its first congress for 3,000 delegates in May 1933.[61] But these successes did not put the Soviet out of danger. Sichuan warlords united in the face of a common enemy, and Xu and Zhang Guotao once again found themselves encircled by hostile and well-armed forces. They waged an almost continuous war for the next two years, until April 1935, but repeatedly found themselves at a disadvantage. As Xu recalled,

> The foundation of the new soviet had not had time to become well consolidated. Since the masses did not yet understand the meaning of revolution thoroughly, they could not struggle for the salvation of their soviets or, in the end, even for their own immediate interests. The masses were easily suppressed by the reactionary forces and subsided into passivity…[and] the new recruits had had no experience in warfare and no training.[62]

None of these challenges led Xu and Zhang to quit the Sichuan Soviet. Rather, it was the news that Mao and his First Front Army had abandoned the Jiangxi Soviet and were headed west.

~

In the pouring late afternoon rain of June 25, 1935 Mao stood underneath an oilcloth canopy in front of a makeshift parade ground in central Sichuan mountain hamlet of Fubian, waiting for the arrival of his guest, Zhang Guotao. The head of the Fourth Front Army appeared on a white horse accompanied by a dozen mounted men, including Xu. In a well-orchestrated moment, Zhang jumped down off his horse and embraced Mao as thousands of civilians and soldiers cheered with enthusiasm and soggy red banners with white inscriptions flapped heavily. After ascending the temporary platform and delivering speeches to mark the occasion, Mao and Zhang walked up the valley with arms around each other's shoulders to the village of Lianghekou, where Mao was staying in a lamasery. That night, the officers of the First and Fourth Armies, including Xu, enjoyed a hearty banquet in the lamasery, toasting one another, their reunion, and their survival.[63]

Beneath the professed unity and happiness lay deep differences and suspicions. This began with Zhang and

---

[60] Klein and Clark, *Biographical Dictionary of Chinese Communism,* 351.

[61] Helen Foster Snow, *The Chinese Communists*, 158. The Sichuan-Shaanxi Soviet is also known as the Tung-Na-Pa Soviet—a name derived from the principal towns in the soviet, according to the Wade-Giles System. These towns were Tungchiang, Nanchiang, and Pachou, which are Tongjiang, Nachong, and Bazhong in Pinyin.

[62] Xu Xiangqian quoted in Helen Foster Snow, *The Chinese Communists*, 159.

[63] Dean King, *Unbound: A True Story of War, Love, and Survival* (New York: Little, Brown and Company, 2010), 197; and Salisbury, *The Long March*, 242-243.

Mao's rivalry, which was now fifteen years old and had not diminished with their physical separation. They still disagreed about cooperating with the Kuomintang and using peasants for guerrilla warfare. By summer 1935, they had also come to different conclusions about the Japanese presence in China. Mao believed the CCP should form a united front with the KMT to confront the Japanese aggression, while Zhang preferred an independent course.[64] Zhang and Xu commanded a force that was at least seven (and perhaps eleven) times larger than Mao's, and its personnel were far better clothed and fed than Mao's. These facts exacerbated the mistrust between them.[65] Further down the chain of command, officers on both sides believed that their experience over the previous four years was not being sufficiently respected by their counterparts. The Fourth Front Army had built two successful soviets from scratch and had repeatedly produced and trained a powerful army; the First Front Army had faced the brunt of Chiang Kai Shek's attention during the Encirclement Campaigns, had marched thousands and thousands of miles through difficult terrain, and had executed tactics brilliantly.[66] Both sides had plenty to be proud of, but each side promoted itself and the importance of its own experience. More fundamentally, the two long-separated armies had developed different characters, especially with regards to women. Whereas Mao's army only had 30 women during its Long March, most of whom were married to senior officers and all of whom were forced to abandon their babies at birth, the Fourth Front Army had 2,000-3,000 women in its ranks and women were allowed to keep their newborns.[67] There was even a female-led unit, the Independent Women's Regiment, which Xu made quite clear was to be a combat unit, not a support unit. He once told the regiment's commander,

> Yours is a fighting unit, not a reserve unit for wives. From now on, men should not visit your regiment without a reason. Your women should not fall in love and should not marry. Anyone who wants to marry must leave [the unit].[68]

Xu's treatment of women as professional soldiers was distinctive, as was true of his treatment of non-Han populations in the territories the Fourth Front Army controlled. In fact, Xu and Zhang's army generally enjoyed better relations with minorities than Mao's army did.[69] Taken together, all of these factors meant that the odds of forming a single, unified Red Army were slim.

---

[64] Spence, *The Search for Modern China*, 408.

[65] Estimates of the Fourth Front Army's troop strength range from 45,000 to 80,000; estimates of the First Front Army's size range from 7,000 to 10,000. See among other sources, Li, *A History of the Modern Chinese Army*, 58; Salisbury, *The Long March*, 243-244, 381; and Short, *Mao*, 329.

[66] Two examples of this brilliance can be seen at Kunming and the crossing of the River of Golden Sands and at the crossing of the Dadu River at Luding Bridge. For details see Salisbury, *The Long March*, 178-187 and 220-230.

[67] Sun, *The Long March*, 121-122; and Salisbury, *The Long March*, 79. Sun uses the figure of 3,000 women; most other sources say 2,000.

[68] Xu Xiangqian quoted in Sun, *The Long March*, 130-131. The Women's Independent Regiment's commander was Zhang Qiuqin, 1904-1968, who was not related to Zhang Guotao. Zhang Qiuqin joined the CCP in 1924, studied in Moscow, was a member of the Oyuwan Soviet and briefly was even a political commissar. She died in the Cultural Revolution.

[69] Whitson, *The Chinese High Command*, 145; King, *Unbound*, 198. The two armies also differed in the use of titles and corporal punishment: the Fourth being seen as the more traditional and less Revolutionary than the First, which banned beatings and tended to refer to people as "comrade" instead of by their job title. The Fourth was also considered to have more disciplined troops.

Mao and Zhang's power struggle for control of the army and the Party quickly centered upon the issue of where the combined armies should go to establish a new, secure base of operations: Mao wanted to continue north, aiming for northern Shaanxi or eastern Gansu; Zhang argued for heading southwest to the Sichuan-Tibet border region. The two men tussled and danced for the rest of June, but on the last day of the month, the combined army headed north over a 13,500-foot mountain, the first of three high peaks the Communists would cross before reaching the Maoergai River Valley 100 miles to the northeast. From this valley, the Long Marchers would try to capture the Nationalist garrison at Songpan and seize control of the only road into Gansu. Mao seemed to have won the tug-of-war. When troops under Zhang's command subsequently failed to secure Songpan and Nationalist reinforcements blocked the Gansu road,[70] Mao sensed it was time to put Zhang in his place and assert the preeminence of the Party over the Fourth Front Army's military superiority. At a Politburo meeting on July 20, Mao saw to it that Zhang was asked to give an evaluation of the Oyuwan Soviet and an account of his decision to abandon it. At the conclusion of Zhang's remarks, Mao pounced on his rival, accusing him of committing serious errors of judgment.[71] Politically outmaneuvered and deeply offended, Zhang looked for an escape. On August 6, as the joint army approached the vast, 11,000-foot high basin known as the Grasslands, Zhang proposed that the First and Fourth Armies once again divide, but with the twist that its leading officers and some units swap sides. The Left Column, composed primarily of Fourth Army troops, would be led by the First Army's Zhu De. Zhang would serve as the Left Column's political

[70] Salisbury, *The Long March*, 257.
[71] Alexander V. Pantsov, *Mao: The Real Story* (New York, Simon & Schuster, 2012), 285.

commissar. Conversely, the Right Column, composed primarily of First Army troops, would be led by the Fourth Army's Xu and Chen Changhao. Mao would serve as its Party leader. The women on the Long March were also divided between the two columns, with most joining Mao and Xu.[72] Zhang's plan called for the two reconstituted armies to cross the Grasslands separately and reunite once they arrived in Gansu province. Mao agreed to adopt Zhang's plan.

The Grasslands, which flower in summer, looked beautiful at a distance but beneath the waist-high grass lurked trouble. For the six days the forty mile crossing required, simply finding a safe pathway was trick: as one eyewitness said, "a deceptive green cover hid a Black viscous swamp, which sucked in anyone who broke through the thin crust."[73] Added to this challenge came the fact that there was no firewood, no shelter, no potable water, and very little food. Daytime rain alternated with nighttime snow flurries. The Right Column's Marchers, dressed in rags, were overcome with both dysentery and malaria as they trudged through the water and muck. Casualty rates were so high that Mao's First Front Army suffered more losses crossing the Grasslands than it did climbing through the Snowy Mountains.[74] It was a brutal experience that none of the survivors would forget. Once across the giant bog, the Right Column's survivors set up camps in and around the Tibetan village of Baxi.[75] On September 3, Mao received a message from Zhang saying that the Left Column had attempted its crossing, but that a tributary of the Yellow River was so flooded that it was impossible to continue north; he was ordering his troops west to the town of Aba to obtain food and supplies.[76] Mao responded by urging Zhang to reconsider, but Zhang refused. More critically, Zhang seems to have also sent a secret message, ordering Xu and Chen Changhao to bring the Right Column back across the Grasslands to join him in Aba.[77] This shocking message of September 9 was intercepted by Mao-loyalist Ye Jianying, with whom Xu had worked during the Guangzhou Uprising. Ye took the message to Mao, who approached Xu and Chen that afternoon; Mao asked them to ignore Zhang's orders and continue moving north.

Xu faced the biggest choice of his military career. On the one hand, he possessed an institutional loyalty to the Communist Party and its leadership; on the other hand, Xu had developed a fierce personal loyalty to Zhang. Such conflicting loyalties were not unique to Xu, for they are a common difficulty in the military.[78] In this decisive moment, Xu's personal loyalty to Zhang won the day:

---

[72] King, *Unbound*, 223.

[73] Otto Braum quoted in Pantsov, *Mao*, 286.

[74] Short, *Mao,* 332. Exact figures do not exist, but as many as 1,000 men and women in the First Front Army may have died. See King, *Unbound,* 239.

[75] Tibetan cultural influence in the 1930s extended well beyond the modern political borders of Tibet. While many of the places mentioned in this section of the chapter lie within the borders of Sichuan today, they were culturally Tibetan areas at the time of the Long March.

[76] There are two easily confused communities called Aba in northern Sichuan. The first is on the Aqu Qu and is at GPS Coordinates 32° 54'25.6896"N, 101°42' 49.3776"E; the second is on the Suomo River and is at GPS Coordinates 31° 55'18.2424"N, 102° 14'17.9268 E, according to the website LatLong.net. (See https://www.latlong.net , accessed February 21, 2020.) Zhang retreated to the first one.

[77] This story is repeated in a variety of sources, including the detailed account in Salisbury, *The Long March*, 275-277. It also corresponds with official Chinese accounts, although the actual telegram from Zhang to Xu and Chen has never been made public. This fact has led some historians to question whether it ever existed. One author says that "recently available evidence" indicates that the fault for the Zhang-Mao split rests with Mao, who was paranoid about a plot against him. See Li, *A History of the Modern Chinese Army*, 58.

[78] Andrew Scobell, *China's Use of Military Force Beyond the Great Wall and the Long March* (New York: Cambridge University Press, 2003), 56-58.

Xu and Chen both told Mao the Right Column would re-cross the Grasslands. They had picked Zhang, instead of Mao, to be their Chairman.

This decision left Mao with few options but to flee. At 2:00 a.m. on September 10, those loyal to Mao moved north into the night. Chen learned of Mao's clandestine departure just before dawn. Chen reported to Xu, "A strange thing has happened. The First Army has pulled out. Shall we send troops after them?" Xu had a reputation for being dour, but Mao's sudden departure produced a strong emotional reaction in the thirty-three-year old. The sense of betrayal was overwhelming, for as Xu recorded in his memoirs,

> I did not know what to think. I sat on the bed speechless for half an hour. Why? Why did they not tell us? I had not expected it at all. My heart was heavy, and my head numb….I was in such a bad mood. I threw myself on the bed, covered by head with a quilt and did not speak a word.[79]

With order needing to be restored in the chaotic camp, Xu finally answered Chen's question about pursuit. Xu responded rhetorically but poignantly: "Have you ever seen the Red Army attacking the Red Army?"[80] Xu had made his second career-changing decision in less than twelve hours; he was not going to start an intra-Communist civil war. Rather, each side was free to go its own way. Mao loyalists proceeded north into Gansu and then crossed southern Ningxia before settling in the arid northern Shaanxi town of Yanan.[81] Zhang loyalists, including Xu and Chen Changhao, went south, crossing the Grasslands for a second time to join Zhang in Aba. Zhang did not, however, give Mao's men the same choice. Zhu De, for example, became a virtual prisoner: his horse was slaughtered, his personal bodyguard was removed, and he was prevented from seeing his wife.[82] Other Maoist supporters were shot.[83]

Because the story of the Long March typically centers upon Mao, what happened to Zhang and Xu after their reunion in Aba is less well-known. Zhang quickly began to try to assert his authority over Chinese communism. He held anti-Mao rallies in Aba and Zhuokeji, declaring the Politburo and the Central Committee illegitimate. On October 5, 1935, Zhang created a new Provisional Central Committee, naming himself as its Party Secretary. He appointed those loyal to him, including Xu and Chen, to the most important positions, but he also chose military figures with Maoist loyalties for his new Central Committee as well. This included Zhu De, for Zhang knew that he would need broad military support if he ever hoped to win his power struggle with Mao.[84] To impress these men, Zhang launched a rather audacious military campaign to capture a major city for the Communists for the first time. His choice was Sichuan's provincial capital, Chengdu. By November 11, the Fourth Front Army was within sixty miles of the city, having scored victories over a local warlord's troops before the ferocious battle for the town of Baizhang began. At Baizhang, the tide turned against Zhang's plans: the Communists were forced to retreat to the Snowy Mountains, and by February 1936 disease, desertion, and death had claimed 50% of the

---

[79] Xu Xiangqian quoted in Sun, *The Long March*, 159. He is characterized as a "dour man" in Short, *Mao*, 334.

[80] Xu Xiangqian and Chen Changhao quoted in Salisbury, *The Long March,* 277.

[81] Mao loyalists who went north included Zhou Enlai, Lin Biao, Nie Rongzhen, Peng Dehuai, and Ye Jianying.

[82] Salisbury, *The Long March*, 314.

[83] Pantsov, *Mao*, 289.

[84] Salisbury, *The Long March*, 311.

once-formidable army.[85] Quick pursuit by warlord and Nationalist forces compelled Zhang and Xu to move further west. To put themselves out of enemy range, in late February they led their army over a 17,950-foot mountain—the highest route undertaken by any troops during the Long March. Reaching the Tibetan borderlands in the dead of winter was another test of endurance; it required not only a staged assault with base camps like those used to climb Mt. Everest, but also required speed since the army had to complete the passage before storms descended.[86] Fortunately for the Fourth Army, the casualty rate for this part of the journey was not as high as one might suspect.

Once in Tibetan lands, the Communists faced a local population that was suspicious of, if not hostile to, their arrival. The early years of the twentieth century had fundamentally altered the relationship between Tibet and China. Rather than being Tibet's protector, China had become Tibet's foe. As the Thirteenth Dalai Lama said in 1913,

> During the time of Genghis Khan and Altan Khan of the Mongols, the Ming Dynasty of the Chinese, and the Qing Dynasty of the Manchus, Tibet and China co-operated on the basis of a patron and priest relationship. A few years ago Chinese authorities in Sichuan and Yunnan endeavoured to colonise our territory….[Consequently] the patron-priest relationship has faded like a rainbow in the sky.[87]

By the 1930s, these concerns had grown, although the Nationalists had largely convinced Tibet's religious leaders that they were lesser of two evils. The Communists stood for atheism, but the KMT had sent deferential envoys, contributed four thousand Chinese silver dollars to monasteries, and adopted policies to protect Buddhist property. This led Tibetan leaders to publish writings and to speak to local leaders supporting the Nationalists and criticizing the Communists.[88] In response, the Communists adopted a propaganda campaign of their own. They promised to treat the Tibetans "kindly and peacefully," appealed directly to peasants for help, and held rallies urging Tibetan women to reject cultural traditions and modernize. Zhang and Xu, now based in the city of Garzê, also responded by trying to do more socially and politically than create another soviet. They announced the establishment of an independent Tibetan People's Republic. They promised the new state political autonomy and its own army if it signed an "eternal treaty of friendship with the Red Army," and would "unconditionally help the Red Army get grain, fodder, and wool; arrange for guides, translators, and other laborers for the front; find homes for and look after the wounded."[89] Unconditional help hardly represented autonomy, but the Fourth Army desperately needed Tibetan food, clothing, shelter, and labor. In fact, the army's needs completely outstripped the land's ability to support it. The Tibetans suffered unduly as a result, although the army tried to

---

[85] King, *Unbound,* 266-268, 270. In the battle of Baizhang, Zhang lost 10,000 soldiers while the Sichuan forces lost 15,000. King's estimate of the size of the Fourth Army in February 1936 is 40,000. The local warlord in the battle at Baizhang was Liu Xiang (1888-1938).

[86] King, *Unbound,* 279-280. The mountain was Danglingshan.

[87] Thirteenth Dalai Lama, Ngawang Lobsang Thupten Gyatso Jigdral Chokley Namgyal (1876-1933), quoted in Sam van Schaik, *Tibet: A History* (New Haven, Connecticut: Yale University Press, 2011), 190-191.

[88] Gray Tuttle, *Tibetan Buddhists in the Making of Modern China* (New York: Columbia University Press, 2005), 190-192, EBSCOebooks. The leaders were the Ninth Panchen Lama, Thubten Choekyi Nyima (1883–1937), and the Norlha Qutughtu, Sönam Rapten (1865-1936).

[89] Tibetan People's Republic Constitution quoted in Sun, *The Long March,* 163. One leader of the rallies urging social change for women was Zhu De's wife, Kang Keqing, 1911-1992.

pay for what it took. As one eyewitness said, "They left money in our storage place too. But what was the use of money when there was no food to buy? We couldn't eat the silver dollars."[90]

Whatever his long-term intentions may have been for Tibet, events in other parts of the world altered Zhang's plans. In January 1936, Zhang received word from Mao that one of Zhang's long-term friends had come from Moscow with important news: the Comintern had called upon "all compatriots…no matter how different past and present attitudes of various parties and organizations are on political issues" to "stop the Civil War in order to concentrate all our strength" towards "the sacred cause to resist Japan and save the nation."[91] Mao and Zhang were to put aside their own differences, as well as their differences with Chiang Kai-shek, and work together as a united front to impede Japanese expansion. Stalin feared a two-front war against the Soviet Union and the believed that the best way to prevent it was to get the various Chinese factions to work together.[92] Just after this news broke, another group of Long Marchers, He Long's Second Front Army, arrived in Garzê from Hunan.[93] The arrival of another army had a number of consequences: it increased the number of those who wanted to move north to join Mao, it produced armed conflict with the Tibetans as a result of the increased competition for resources,[94] and it triggered a reorganization of the military leadership. First Front Army officers returned to the top posts, including Zhu De as commander-in-chief of military operations.[95] This reshuffling resulted in a demotion for Xu as the combined armies headed north for what would be his third crossing of the dreaded Grasslands. The man who once led the Oyuwan Soviet had been surpassed by more ambitious, cunning men.

According to several accounts, the July 1936 crossing of the Grasslands was the most arduous of the three. Severe weather complicated the normal perils of the swamp, and the armies had to cross a much broader area as they moved from the southwest to the northeast corners of the expanse. What had taken six days on Xu's first crossing now took fourteen. Food was in such short supply that people ate animal hides and leather from belts, shoes, and rifle straps. Comrades stole from one another. Those without tents froze to death in nighttime snowstorms, and some were killed by huge hailstones by day. Women abandoned babies after giving birth because no infant could survive in such difficult conditions. When the Marchers, especially those not in the vanguard, deviated from the established pathway in search of food, they frequently drowned. Many others drowned at the end of the crossing, wading chest-deep through a freezing, swollen river even though they did not know how to swim. There are no definite records of the casualty rates for the third crossing, but the Second Front Army alone lost over 7,000.[96]

For Xu and the Fourth Front Army, leaving the Grasslands was not the end of their difficulties. In fact, worse was yet to come. In September 1936, Stalin promised to send war matériel, including

---

[90] Nima quoted in Sun, *The Long March*, 177.

[91] "Message to Compatriots on Resistance to Japan to Save the Nation (1 August 1935)," *The Rise to Power of the Chinese Communist Party: Documents and Analysis*, 695. Zhang's friend was Lin Yuying.

[92] Salisbury, *The Long March*, 317-318.

[93] He Long's force included Xiao Ke's Sixth Army group, which was one of the first groups to evacuate Jiangxi in advance of Mao's First Front Army. Xiao joined He Long in Hunan in October 1935. Zhang reported that He Long arrived in Garzê with 5000 men, but other sources use a figure of 15,000 and 20,000. There is greater agreement that He left Hunan with about 40,000 men. This puts the Second Front Army's losses prior to its arrival in Garzê at between 50 and 80%. See Whitson, *The Chinese High Command*, 150; and Klein and Clark, *Biographical Dictionary of Chinese Communism*, 300.

[94] Sun, *The Long March*, 167.

[95] Salisbury, *The Long March*, 318. The First Front Army's Liu Bocheng was named chief-of-staff.

[96] Young, *Choosing Revolution*, 110-113; Sun, *The Long March*, 171-175; and King, *Unbound*, 288-290.

planes to rifles, to the Chinese Communists.[97] In order to reach Soviet territory and take possession
of the thousands of tons of equipment, the Communists would have to cross the Yellow River and
secure the Silk Road's Hexi Corridor in Gansu Province. Mao assigned the Fourth Front Army to
this task because he still feared the size of Zhang's army and the political influence this size would
carry once Zhang reached Yanan.[98] The fact that Zhang strongly advocated for opening the
Corridor only made the scheme more appealing to Mao. Zhang chose Xu to be the commander-
in-chief of the operation and selected Chen Changhao as his political commissar. On October 24
what became known as the Western Legion began crossing on sheepskin rafts to the western bank
of the Yellow River at Jingyuan, about ninety miles northeast of Gansu's capital Lanzhou. After
about 20,000 of the army's 35,000 soldiers had crossed, including Xu and the Independent
Women's Regiment, Nationalist forces attacked the eastern bank to prevent more troops from
crossing to the western side. Xu didn't understand why more troops had not crossed before the
Nationalists arrived; he was even more puzzled as to why the 31st Corps had been ordered to return
to the eastern side without his permission. The answer lay in Mao's political struggle with Zhang:
Mao realized that the Nationalists' attack at Jingyuan, combined with the mission to western China,
could eliminate his rival's influence completely.[99]

Therefore, Xu and Chen found themselves on the western bank of the Yellow River with a
diminished army, no logistical support, and a near-impossible mission that required them to pass
through 1,500 miles of hostile territory to reach the Soviet border. The hostility came from Chinese

[97] Sun, *The Long March,* 211.
[98] Li, *A History of the Modern Chinese Army,* 63.
[99] Sun, *The Long March,* 212, 233, 239. Xu and Chen's army was also known as the Western Route Army.

Muslims, who were led by the Ma warlord family. As the Western Legion passed into the Hexi Corridor—a narrow band wedged between the Gobi Desert and the Qilian Mountains and punctuated by occasional oases—Ma forces began what proved to be quite an effective and ruthless campaign to eradicate the Communists from their lands. In early December, the Ma killed or captured half of the Ninth Army Group in the town of Gulang. In early January 1937, all three thousand men in the Fifth Corps were killed at Goatai, and another four thousand were lost at Nijaying within a week.[100] The Women's Regiment fought bravely when the Ma broke through the walls of Linze, but lost 400 in the initial battle and many more trying to break free of the subsequent Ma siege. By mid-January Xu and Chen had lost half their army in ten weeks; there were now only 10,000 men and women under their command.[101] They cabled Mao, asking for additional troops and supplies or for permission to withdraw, but Mao refused to help and refused to let them retreat. Instead, Mao castigated Xu and Chen for their "lack of confidence." Mao wrote,

> The commanders of the Western Legion have lost any belief in themselves to defeat the enemy and finish their task….Judging from your strength and the enemy's you should certainly win. The Central Committee sincerely hopes that you will reflect thoroughly on your losses, learn your lessons, confess your mistakes past and present, and carry out all our instructions in the Bolshevik spirit of self-criticism.[102]

This response convinced Xu and Chen that they would have to take matters into their own hands. In early March, they ordered the army to flee to the Qilian Mountains. Wang Quanyuan, the commander of the Women's Regiment, begged Xu to be allowed to form the rear guard that would enable the other troops to escape. Xu hesitated but eventually yielded to Wang's appeals. More than 500 of the 800 women under Wang's command died in the subsequent Ma attack, but the remaining core of the army and the rest of its leadership escaped. Most of the women who survived the Ma attack were caught, raped, imprisoned, and eventually sent to Ma labor camps.[103]

On March 16, 1937, Xu and Chen received orders to come to Yanan to account for themselves and the disaster.[104] Accompanied only by an elite guard, they used the army's remaining gold and silver to gain safe passage and make their way to Northern Shaanxi.[105] Xu left Li Xiannian, a man he had known since the Oyuwan Soviet, in command of the remnants of the Western Legion, which numbered less than 2,000 by this point. Li led his men over the Qilian Mountains, into the Qaidam salt basin, and then westward towards the city of Ürümqi. Only 393 men survived the trek, arriving on May 8. Li appealed for asylum in the Soviet Union, but this request was denied.[106] Not only would the Soviets not bring

---

[100] Sun, *The Long March*, 237.

[101] King, *Unbound*, 309-314.

[102] Mao Zedong quoted in Sun, *The Long March*, 238.

[103] Young, *Choosing Revolution*, 233-239; and Sun, *The Long March*, 239-241. The surviving women, most of whom remained loyal to the CCP, were refused re-admission to the Party until 1989 because of fears that they had been ideologically compromised.

[104] Salisbury, *The Long March*, 320.

[105] King, *Unbound*, 317.

[106] Georgi Dimitrov, the Bulgarian head of the Comintern, supported Li Xiannian's request for asylum, but Soviet official Vyacheslav Molotov, and presumably Stalin, opposed it. See *Dimitrov and Stalin 1934-1943: Letters from the Soviet Archives*, Alexander Dallin and F. I. Firsov (eds.) (New Haven, Connecticut: Yale University Press, 2000), 109.

the promised war matériel to the Chinese border, but they would not help those who had been sent on the fool's errand to obtain it.[107] Probably at Xu's urging, the CCP sent an official to find Li and his men. This effort was successful: Li was flown to Langzhou and the other survivors were brought back to Communist territory by truck.[108] This episode brought the endurance test of the Long March to an end, but it left deep scars on its survivors. In fact, Xu was described as having so much anxiety in summer 1937 that observers thought him "neurotic."[109] They didn't appreciate the cause of his anxiety.

~

Between 1937 and 1949, as China fought the Sino-Japanese War, World War II, and its Civil War between the Nationalists and Communists, Xu focused on slowly and carefully rebuilding his reputation. He did not play a nationally prominent role for many years, serving only as a battalion commander, a deputy divisional commander, and a guerrilla warfare organizer in various provinces.[110] During this time he was carefully monitored,[111] because of his role in the Western Legion's tragedy and his long association with Zhang Guotao, who defected to the KMT in 1938 and later fled to Hong Kong.[112] That Xu was able to largely restore his reputation by the time Mao proclaimed the existence of the People's Republic of China on October 1, 1949 was a result of his essential role in the Battle of Taiyuan.

Ever since Xu was a boy growing up in Shanxi, his home province had been dominated by a warlord named Yan Xishan, who came to power in 1911 at the age of twenty-eight. By the late

---

[107] Stalin did transfer one million dollars in cash to the CCP between November 1936 and January 1937, so there was tangible support from the Soviet Union during this period. See Li, *A History of the Modern Chinese Army*, 63.

[108] Klein and Clark, *Biographical Dictionary of Chinese Communism,* 500-501. Another source puts the total number of survivors at 436. See Gao, *Historical Dictionary of Modern China,* 126. Like Xu, Li was a survivor, despite his association with this episode and with Zhang. Li survived Mao's purges and became the president of the People's Republic of China between 1983-1988. See Harrison E. Salisbury, "Li Xiannian, Tough Survivor, " *New York Times,* July 18, 1985, 1, ProQuest Historical Newspapers.

[109] See Helen Foster Snow, *The Chinese Communists,* 148.

[110] Much of the guerrilla work was done in Shandong Province. Xu also worked with He Long in Shanxi, Shaanxi, and other provinces. See Klein and Clark, *Biographical Dictionary of Chinese Communism,* 351-352. Klein and Clark note that Xu was ill in 1941-1942 and without assignment. In the military's organization, each army had three corps, each corps had three divisions, each division had three battalions, each battalion had three companies, each company had three platoons, and each platoon had three squads. Therefore, being a battalion commander was not a high rank for someone of Xu's experience and expertise. See Kenneth Allen, "Introduction to the PLA's Administrative and Operational Structure," *The People's Liberation Army as Organization,* James C. Mulvenon and Andrew N. D. Yang (eds.), Volume 1.0, (Santa Monica, California: RAND Corporation, 2002), 11.

[111] In 1939, when Xu was in Shandong, the Party leadership determined that a "strong commissar must be assigned" if Xu was to be promoted to the commander of all CCP forces in Shandong. This political commissar was "an impulsive and out-going thirty-three-year-old" named Zhu Rui. Because extroverted Zhu and reserved Xu did not get along well, they were recalled to Yanan in summer 1940. See Sherman Xiaogang Lai, *A Springboard to Victory: Shandong Province and Chinese Communist Military and Financial Strength, 1937-1945* (Leiden, Netherlands: Brill, 2011), 39-40, 112-113. This source also has more details on Xu's military campaigns during this time.

[112] Zhang emigrated to Canada in 1968 and died in Toronto in 1979.

1920s, Yan had developed a reputation for emphasizing the development of provincial infrastructure and industry, while maintaining as much political independence from Chiang Kai-shek as possible.[113] Twenty years later, Taiyuan had become an intensely fortified, reasonably industrialized city, but Yan was paying the price for his independence: by February 1947, Communist forces, attacking from both the north and the south, had captured much of Shanxi and the Nationalists were not enthusiastic about coming to Yan's rescue.[114] The troops pressuring Yan had largely been recruited locally and trained by Xu, who appealed to a broad range of Shanxi residents as a result of his own middle class origins in the province.[115] By July 1948, the direct siege of Taiyuan had begun, and Xu, accompanied by men he had worked with for years, had been named to orchestrate the final assault on the city.[116] This was not an easy task, for Yan had built a complex system of defenses, including concentric pillboxes, blockhouses, and trenches surrounding the city to supplement its 40-foot thick walls. At the end of World War II, he had also hired Japanese mercenaries to help defend him. Xu did have the advantage of controlling the surrounding mountains and was able to pound the city with artillery.[117] The siege of Taiyuan was the longest in the Chinese Civil War and one of the bloodiest in all military history. As on the Western Front during World War I, it became a war of attrition with Xu's troops needing to capture each pillbox, blockhouse, and trench before victory could be secured.[118] Xu realized that with his 30,000 men he lacked sufficient manpower to tackle such an impenetrable fortress, and asked for reinforcements on November 8. Mao denied this request, convinced that Taiyuan needed to wait until both Beijing and the port of Tianjin had been captured.[119] This decision delayed Xu's final assault on the city until April 1949, and gave Yan Xishan time to escape by airplane to Nanjing. As new troops slowly arrived, Xu managed supplies of food and equipment for the growing army and partnered the new forces with those already in position. He also oversaw self-criticism meetings when misunderstandings arose between various Communist units. Because of illness, however, he had to hand much of the battlefield's operational control over to another general, Peng Dehuai.[120] Peng found that the casualty rates became exceedingly high as the Communist encirclement drew closer and they tried to dislodge the 100,000 surprisingly loyal defenders and Taiyuan's one million supporting laborers. During the siege, starvation within the city was so extensive that people went

[113] Hallett Abend, "Yen the Straddler, on Fence 16 Years," *The New York Times*, October 24, 1927, 7, ProQuest Historical Newspapers.

[114] Benjamin Welless, "Shansi's Warlord in Unique Battle," *The New York Times*, February 9, 1947, 33, ProQuest Historical Newspapers.

[115] Whitson, *The Chinese High Command*, 177.

[116] Harry H. Collier and Paul Chin-Chih Lai, *Organizational Changes in the Chinese Army, 1895-1950* (Taipei, Taiwan: Office of the Military Historian, 1969), 302; and Whitson, *The Chinese High Command*, 177.

[117] Robert Doyle, "Everybody Fight Together," *Time*, November 15, 1948, 33-34. Chiang Kai-Shek urged Yan to expand his defensive systems around Taiyuan in 1939 because of concerns over Communist growth in Shanxi. See Taylor, *The Generalissimo*, 163.

[118] Dominic Meng-Hsuan Yang, "Noble Ghosts, Empty Graves, and Suppressed Traumas: The Heroic Tale of 'Tiayuan's Five Hundred Martyrs' in the Chinese Civil War," *Historical Reflections*, 41, 3 (Winter 2015), 109-124, EBSCOhost; and Whitson, *The Chinese High Command*, 353.

[119] Christopher R. Lew, *The Third Chinese Revolutionary War, 1945-49: An Analysis of Communist Strategy and Leadership* (London: Routledge, 2009), 125.

[120] Xu Xiangqian, *Xu Xiangqian Hui Yi Lu* (Beijing, China: Zhong Guo Ren Min Jie Fang Jun Chu Ban She, 2007), 570-597. I am grateful to Uldis Kruze, Professor of History at the University of San Francisco, for reading this chapter and summarizing it for me.

blind because of malnourishment, while some resorted to cannibalism.[121] On April 19, after a week of intense fighting, the First Artillery Division's 3,000 guns finally turned the city's defenses to rubble. Fires broke out everywhere in the city. Six days later, after particularly vicious street fighting, the siege was over.[122] Despite heavy losses, the siege of Taiyuan helped restore Xu's military reputation as a commander: he had coordinated the conquering of that which was thought to be impenetrable, despite being severely outnumbered. The restoration of Xu's standing meant that with the establishment of the People's Republic, he was elected to the CCP's Central Committee, selected as chief of the People's Liberation Army's General Staff, and appointed to the powerful Party's Central Military Commission.[123]

~

Xu was never a robust man, and through the course of the 1950s he was frequently ill as the physical and mental ordeals of the Oyuwan Soviet, the Long March, the Western Legion, and the Battle of Taiyuan caught up with him. It is also true, however, that feigning illness was a socially acceptable way for Chinese officials to behave when they found themselves in opposition to major policy decisions; some of Xu's absences and sick leaves during this decade may have had more to do with politics than health.[124] Regardless of the precise balance, it is clear that in the 1950s Xu made important contributions, won high honors, and steered clear of chaos.

In May 1951, as the Korean War waged along the 38th Parallel, Mao tapped Xu to head a delegation of military commanders and technology experts to travel to Moscow to negotiate an arms deal with the Soviet Union. Xu, then forty-nine, was an unusual choice for the secret mission, but unlike Ye Jianying, Xu had not opposed the intervention in Korea. Rather, Xu had watched from the safety of a coastal sanitarium until the final decision had been made. Once back in Beijing, Xu simply described the decision as "wise."[125] This meant that Xu was a neutral figure who Mao thought could get the job done, even though Xu had never been abroad. Xu's unpublicized mission was to buy weapons and equipment for sixty infantry divisions and to obtain advanced technology so China might develop its own weapon production in accordance with the Sino-Soviet Mutual

---

[121] Yang, "Noble Ghosts, Empty Graves, and Suppressed Traumas." Another source says that Xu only had 15,000 troops against the 135,000 defenders. See Robert Weatherley, *Mao's Forgotten Successor: The Political Career of Hua Guofeng* (New York: Palgrave Macmillan, 2010), 37.

[122] Whitson, *The Chinese High Command*, 353. The story of 500 officials committing suicide with the potassium cyanide Yan showed to *Time* reporter Robert Doyle in November 1948 is a myth. Rather, only forty-six people committed suicide, while most officials simply surrendered to the Communists when the city fell. See Yang, "Noble Ghosts, Empty Graves, and Suppressed Traumas."

[123] This body is sometimes identified as the Central Military Affairs Commission (CMC) or the Military Affairs Commission (MAC), but its full name is the Military Commission of the Central Committee of the Chinese Communist Party. It has always been the primary body for determining the nation's military policy. See Allen, "Introduction to the PLA's Administrative and Operative Structure," 1-2.

[124] Scobell, *China's Use of Military Force Beyond the Great Wall and the Long March*, 88.

[125] Scobell, *China's Use of Military Force Beyond the Great Wall and the Long March*, 86-87, 89. Zhu De and Peng Dehnai, who ended up commanding the Chinese "volunteers" in Korea, were the two most important leaders to support the intervention. Lin Biao, He Long, and Liu Bocheng joined Ye Jianying in arguing against the Korean action.

Assistance and Alliance Treaty of 1950.[126] In his account of the mission, Xu admitted that the delegation "had little experience in [the] modernization of our army or in international diplomacy," which meant that "the meeting schedule, negotiating agenda, and almost everything concerning the arms purchase talks were basically determined by the Soviets."[127] Despite this disadvantage, Xu appreciated the depth of the hospitality the mission received. He did become frustrated in June and July by the Soviets' insistence that the delegation tour steel mills, tractor factories, and army bases, as well as Leningrad, Stalingrad, and Caspian Sea resorts. This extensive tour showed Xu, however, that the USSR was incapable of providing what the Chinese wanted in 1951. As Xu wrote,

> Our political propaganda at home at the time emphasized only how strong and powerful the Soviet Union was, but did not mention its difficulties and problems. As Chinese, we could not even imagine these problems had we not gone there to observe them ourselves....We saw a shortage of daily goods and empty shelves in every grocery store....In some remote regions like the Far East and New Siberia, the Soviet people live in even worse poverty than the Chinese people.[128]

His eyes opened to Soviet realities, Xu returned from Moscow with weapons, even if they were generally antiquated and of poor quality. During the nine-day journey on the Trans-Siberian Railway, Xu contracted a high fever, which degenerated into pleurisy. His condition was serious enough that Zhou Enlai sent medical experts to attend to his illness. Even with this care, it took Xu a long time to recover.[129]

Important institutional changes came to the People's Liberation Army (PLA) in the next few years, and Xu generally supported all of them. Most tellingly, the army's culture was changed to embrace greater centralization and modernization. Between the founding of the Red Army in 1927 and the Korean War, field commanders had considerable latitude because of the nature of guerrilla warfare; relationships between soldiers and commanders were generally informal, reflecting an egalitarian, revolutionary spirit.[130] In fact, this culture was a source of pride within the army, for as general Zhu De once noted, "We regard officers and men alike as individual human beings on equal footing. The only difference between them is in matters of duty."[131] In the post-war world, however, it became clear that the army needed to adopt greater formality and to refine its organizational systems. Specifically, the Korean War had shown the PLA how much more advanced the American army was in terms of both weapons and logistics. Xu's friend Nie Rongzhen noted, "we entered the war in haste and were not well prepared." The PLA's "weapons were in disarray...our transportation means were backward and primitive...the soldiers did not

---

[126] Xu Xiangqian, "The Purchase of Arms from Moscow," *Mao's Generals Remember Korea*, Xiaobing Li, Allen R. Millett, and Bin Yu (trans.) (Lawrence, Kansas: University Press of Kansas, 2001), 141. The future General Secretary of the CCP and President of the PRC, Jiang Zemin, was also a member of this delegation.

[127] Xu, "The Purchase of Arms from Moscow," 142.

[128] Xu, "The Purchase of Arms from Moscow," 145.

[129] Xu, "The Purchase of Arms from Moscow," 146. The Soviet Union also exchanged obsolete weapons with North Korea for rice and other goods before the war began. See Alexander Kim and Kyonghyuon Min, "On the Arms Trade Between the Democratic People's Republic of Korea and the Soviet Union in 1949 and 1950," *The Historian*, no. 3 (2015), 518-536, EBSCOhost.

[130] Ellis Joffe, *Party and Army: Professionalism and Political Control in the Chinese Officer Corps, 1949-1964* (Cambridge, Massachusetts: East Asian Research Center, Harvard University, 1967), 24-26; and Li, *A History of the Modern Chinese Army*, 122.

[131] Zhu De quoted in Joffe, *Party and Army*, 31.

have enough to eat; their clothes were too thin against the cold, so they suffered large, non-battle losses."[132] The fact that the Chinese were only able to supply their troops with 10% of the ammunition deemed necessary convinced the Central Military Commission to institute reforms.[133] In 1954 and 1955, therefore, the PLA adopted new policies, which established a clear sequence of ranks, introduced hierarchical insignia, delineated specific criteria for promotions, provided for fixed salaries, and introduced male conscription.[134] Between 1950 and 1958, the PLA also adjusted its composition; the percentage of infantry troops dropped significantly as the percentages of artillery, tank, engineering, air force, and navy units correspondingly grew.[135] Perhaps most symbolically, the PLA began presenting awards and honors for exceptional service. These included bestowing the rank of marshal upon ten men in September 1955 to recognize the importance of their military contributions and their service to the Party. Xu was one of these ten marshals.[136] It was all a far cry from the years when everyone in the PLA wore the same insignia and Zhe De's dog was trained to bark "at anybody who does not wear a red-starred cap."[137] The PLA was coming of age.

This maturation and the professionalism embedded in it eventually gave Mao pause, especially after the criticism generated during the Hundred Flowers Movement.* By June 1957, Mao had launched an anti-rightist campaign that resulted in over 500,000 people being purged from positions or sent to labor camps. Both civilian and military officials had been put on notice that opposition to Mao was ruinous.[138] Then in January 1958, Mao called for a "permanent

---

[132] Nie Rongzhen, "Beijing's Decision to Intervene," *Mao's Generals Remember Korea*, 50-53. Nie's friendship with Xu went back to Whampoa Military Academy in the mid-1920s.

[133] Nie, "Beijing's Decision to Intervene," 58.

[134] Joffe, *Party and Army*, 34-37.

[135] Li, *A History of the Modern Chinese Army*, 126. Infantry representation in the armed forces dropped from 61.1% in 1950 to 42.3% in 1958.

[136] The ten marshals were Chen Yi, Peng Dehuai, He Long, Lin Biao, Liu Bocheng, Luo Ronghuan, Nie Rongzhen, Xu Xiangqian, Ye Jianying, and Zhu De. These ten are the only men to be awarded this rank in the PRC. As part of the PLA's reforms, many rank gradations developed. These included, for example, four types of generals: senior generals, regular generals, lieutenant generals, and major generals. The other high honors awarded in the mid-1950s were: 1) the Order of August 1 for exceptional service between 1927 and 1945, given to 131 people; 2) the Order of Independence and Freedom for service between 1937-1945, given to 117 people; and 3) the Order of Liberation for service between 1946-1950, given to 570 people. Xu was given all three of these service awards.

[137] Kang Keqing quoted in Helen Foster Snow, *The Chinese Communists*, 151.

[138] Frank Dikötter, *The Tragedy of Liberation: A History of the Chinese Revolution, 1945-1957* (New York: Bloomsbury Press, 2013), 292-295. Walter Ulbricht was deeply relieved by Mao's abandonment of the Hundred Flowers Movement. In February 1957, Ulbricht said, "Our main problem is not 'to tell all flowers to bloom,' but rather to find the right selection of flowers, and to grow what is truly new and useful, without tolerating the noxious growth of noxious weeds under the pretext that they are flowers." See Hope M.

revolution," in which China would engage in a series of constant revolutionary reforms that would allow the nation to achieve Communist ideals. Without perpetual reform, Mao said "people would…be covered in mold."[139]   This applied to the PLA as much as it did to other sectors of society, because PLA officers had taken advantage of the army's new culture and were adopting the selfish habits that had characterized the Nationalist and warlord armies.[140]   Therefore, at a summer military conference held in 1958 and attended by one thousand high-ranking officers, it was decided that the PLA should engage in a careful study of Mao's military works to inculcate the "proletarian ideology" into its ranks, thereby "smashing the purely military point of view, dogmatism, and individualism."[141]   Such ideals fit well with Mao's launching of the Great Leap Forward* in May 1958 since PLA's resources were used to help implement a collectivization program that placed villagers in giant communes. The resulting famine killed 45 million people.[142]   Fourteen months later, one of Xu's fellow marshals, Peng Dehuai, gently criticized the Great Leap Forward, saying that "an excessive number of capital construction projects were hastily started" because of "a lack of experience" and a "deep understanding of the law of planned and proportionate development of the socialist economy,"[143] Mao responded by purging Peng and more than 1,800 of his allies.[144] Having experienced the consequences of not following Mao's dictums, Xu seems to have made a point of staying quiet through these upheavals.[145]

~

By the mid-1960s, the principal political and military leaders of China had known each other and worked both for and against one another for decades. Many of the relationships went back forty years to the beginnings of Chinese communism.[146] Xu maintained solid working relationships with a broad range of these men, but of one Xu's chief rivals was China's defense minister, Lin Biao. This made Xu's arrival at Lin's residence on the evening of January 24, 1967 startling. Anything that

Harrison, *Driving the Soviets up the Wall: Soviet-East German Relations, 1953-1961* (Princeton, New Jersey: Princeton University Press, 2005), 80.

[139] Mao Zedong quoted in Pantsov, *Mao*, 285.

[140] Harlan W. Jencks, *From Muskets to Missiles: Politics and Professionalism in the Chinese Army, 1945-1981* (Boulder, Colorado: Westview Press, 1982), 52.

[141] PLA newspaper quoted in Joffe, *Party and Army*, 124.

[142] Frank Dikötter, *The Cultural Revolution: A People's History, 1962-1976* (New York: Bloomsbury Press, 2016), 9-10; and Joffe, *Party and Army*, 85. The PLA more than doubled its manpower for non-military purposes in 1958 as compared to 1957. It also provided transportation for the backyard furnaces, produced non-military equipment for industrial use, and used 70,000 officers to supervise 4,000 communes.

[143] Peng Dehuai, *Memoirs of a Chinese Marshal: The Autobiographical Notes of Peng Dehuai*, Zheng Longpu (trans.) (Beijing, Foreign Language Press, 1984), 511, 514.

[144] Li, *A History of the Modern Chinese Army*, 178.

[145] Klein and Clark, *Biographical Dictionary of Chinese Communism*, 353.

[146] Xu had known Zhou Enlai since 1924 and Ye Jianying since 1927. Other examples of long-term relationships include Mao and Zhou Enlai, who first met in 1926; Zhou, Deng Xiaoping, and Marshal Nie Rongzhen, who first met in France in 1921; and Marshals He Long, Zhu De, Lin Biao, and Chen Yi, who had fought together in the Nanchang Uprising in 1927.

could bring Xu and Lin together outside of an officially scheduled meeting indicated that something critical was afoot.

By January 1967, the Cultural Revolution had been raging for seven months. Its chaos had become so pervasive that students at military academies were attacking senior officers, replicating what students at civilian institutions had done as the Red Guards.[147] Even worse, basic functionality in the navy, air force, and the PLA's General Staff Headquarters had ceased because too many personnel had become involved in identifying and arresting "reactionaries."[148] For Xu, now vice-chairman of the Central Military Commission and member of the Politburo, this was unfathomable. If the military lost all order, nothing would protect China from dissolving into complete anarchy. This, Xu feared, would allow a foreign power to take advantage of the situation.[149] China risked becoming as weak as it was in the late Qing Dynasty. For Xu and his allies, the Revolution had to be saved from its worst excesses. This position put Xu at odds with the Central Cultural Revolution Group, which was led by Radicals Chen Boda and Jiang Qing (Madame Mao). They fervently believed that:

Although the bourgeoisie has been overthrown, it is still trying to use the old ideas, culture, customs, and habits of the exploiting classes to corrupt the masses, capture their minds, and endeavor to stage a comeback. The proletariat must do the exact opposite: it must meet every ideological challenge posed by the bourgeoisie head-on. Our present aim is to topple those in power who are taking the capitalist road, to criticize reactionary scholarly "authorities," criticize the ideology of the bourgeoisie and all exploiting classes. We must reform art and literature, reform all parts of the superstructure that do not accord with the socialist base of our country. Our purpose in doing this is to stabilize and develop our socialist system.[150]

---

[147] Roderick MacFarquhar and Michael Schoenhals, *Mao's Last Revolution* (Cambridge, Massachusetts: The Belknap Press of Harvard University Press, 2006), 176; Scobell, *China's Use of Military Force Beyond the Great Wall and the Long March*, 95-96; and Dikötter, *The Cultural Revolution,* 130-131.

[148] Hu Angang, *Mao and the Cultural Revolution, Volume 2: The Red Guards March for Mao* (Honolulu, Hawai'i: Silkroad Press, 2017), 28.

[149] Gao Wenqian, *Zhou Enlai: The Last Perfect Revolutionary: A Biography*, Peter Rand and Lawrence R. Sullivan (trans.) (New York: Public Affairs, 2007), 151. Marshals Ye Jianying and Nie Rongzhen agreed with Xu in this assessment.

[150] "The 'Sixteen Point Decision,' *The Search for Modern China: A Documentary Collection*, Third ed., Janet Chen et al (ed.) (New York: W. W. Norton & Company, 2014), 450. The Sixteen Points were adopted by the Eleventh Plenum of the Central Committee in August 1966. The quote comes from the first point, "A New Stage in the Socialist Revolution."

Such attitudes held sway on January 23, when an official government publication posited that "when genuine proletarian Leftists ask the army for help, the army should send troops to actively support them."[151] Xu immediately realized the quagmire this represented: how was the PLA supposed to determine who was "genuine" and who was not among competing Leftist groups? He decided to suggest an alternative policy and push Lin Biao into action by calling upon him at home the next evening.[152] Lin responded positively to Xu's concerns, which encouraged Xu to follow up with a  letter the next morning, He wrote, "Although the army must resolutely support real leftists and carry on internal class struggle at the local level, I worry that we may fail to control the army and thus suffer serious side effects."[153] Over the next several days, Marshals Xu, Ye Jianying, Nie Rongzhen, and others developed what became known as the Eight Orders. Opposed by the Radicals on the Central Cultural Revolution Group, these Orders were approved by Mao and issued publicly on January 28. They called for the PLA to prevent illegal arrests and house searches, prohibit attacks on PLA members by other groups, require traveling soldiers to return to their units, provide additional education to soldiers, and more.[154] It was a critical step in trying to establish limits as to what the Cultural Revolution meant. Then Mao went a step further. At Central Cultural Revolution Group meeting on February 10, Mao sharply criticized Chen Boda and Jiang Qing, calling them selfish and incompetent.[155] He also issued an order for the PLA to take control of banks, post offices, newspapers, broadcast communications, prisons, warehouses, and police forces in certain essential areas.[156] Xu and his allies believed the time was right to assert their power over the Radicals.

At a meeting of the Standing Committee of the Politburo on February 11, 1967, the marshals pounced. Ye Jianying spoke first, accusing Chen Boda of making "a mess of the party, a mess of the government, and a mess of the factories and the countryside" and "still you are not satisfied. You insist on making a mess of the army as well! What are you up to, going on like this?" More passionately, Xu pounded his fist on the table as he exclaimed, "What is it that you want? The army is a pillar of the proletarian dictatorship, but you are making a mess of it; it's as if you didn't want this pillar. Are you suggesting none of us are worth saving?" Xu then invoked a Red Guard leader named Kuai Dafu and condescendingly asked, "Do you want people like Kuai Dafu to command

---

[151] *Zhongfa* quoted in MacFarquhar and Schoenhals, *Mao's Last Revolution*, 175.

[152] Scobell, *China's Use of Military Force Beyond the Great Wall and the Long March*, 97-98, 237, and Hu, *Mao and the Cultural Revolution, Volume 2*, 30.

[153] Xu Xiangqian quoted in Hu, *Mao and the Cultural Revolution, Volume 2*, 30.

[154] Hu, *Mao and the Cultural Revolution, Volume 2*, 31-32; and Yan Jiaqi and Gao Gao, *Turbulent Decade: A History of the Cultural Revolution*, D.W.Y. Kwok (trans.) (Honolulu, Hawai'i: University of Hawai'i Press, 1996), 125. Xu and Lin Biao had to go directly to Mao and bypass the Central Cultural Revolution Group in order to get this done. Xu and the other marshals originally proposed six points, discussion added a seventh, and Mao added an eight, which is why they are known as the Eight Orders.

[155] Pantsov, *Mao*, 523. Ye Jianying was present at the February 10 meeting, which is how Xu and others found out about Mao's criticism.

[156] Hu, *Mao and the Cultural Revolution, Volume 2*, 34. By mid-February 1967, the PLA was also in complete control of ten of China's twenty-nine political divisions.

the army?" The meeting's chair, Zhou Enlai, became nervous about the exchange, but did not stop the proceedings, allowing another radical leader, Kang Sheng, to respond to Xu by pointedly saying, "The army does not belong to you, Xu Xiangqian. What makes you think you are so special?" Xu defended himself, saying "We've devoted our whole lives to this army. Do you think soldiers of the People's Army will simply let a few of you destroy it?" Ye then rhetorically asked the Radicals, "Can the revolution do without the party leadership? Does one not need an army?" Nie Rongzhen supported Ye, saying, "only persons with despicable intentions could persecute veterans and strike them from behind." At this point, there was an awkward pause as the two sides glared at one another across the room. Zhou quickly adjourned the meeting because it was not following the published agenda.[157]

Five days later, the Standing Committee met again and the attack against the Radicals resumed. But over the course of the three-hour meeting, the marshals and their allies went too far and seemed to attack the legitimacy of the Cultural Revolution itself, rather than just the leadership of the Central Cultural Revolution Group. When Mao learned of the details of this second meeting, he became furious. He even threatened to step down and lead a guerrilla war against those who opposed the Cultural Revolution.[158] This reaction caused many to backpedal quickly, including Ye Jianying, who was perfectly willing to let Xu take the fall.[159] In the end, only those perceived to be the harshest critics of the Radicals were forced to take leaves of absence from their posts. This included Xu. As a leading member of what became known as the February Countercurrent he was then subjected to seven intense, self-incriminating interrogations known as Struggle Meetings between February 25 and March 18.[160] With his intentions misrepresented and his statements used against him, Xu had again hit bottom. In late April, however, Mao held a unity meeting with the participants of the February Countercurrent, and invited Xu to appear on the rostrum at the May Day celebrations. This was Mao's signal that Xu was not going to be ostracized.[161] He would still be allowed to work for the Party. It remains unclear why Mao resuscitated Xu when he did, but whatever Mao's reason, Xu was fortunate to survive the Cultural Revolution. Millions of others, including fellow marshals He Long and Peng Dehuai, did not.[162]

---

[157] The dialogue of the February 11 meeting is presented in a variety of sources, but to obtain what seems to be the full transcript, I blended these sources: Dikötter, *The Cultural Revolution*, 136; Gao, *Zhou Enlai:* 154-155; MacFarquhar and Schoenhals, *Mao's Last Revolution*, 192; Pantsov, *Mao*, 524; and Scobell, *China's Use of Military Force Beyond the Great Wall and the Long March*, 100-101.

[158] Dikötter, *The Cultural Revolution,* 136-138.

[159] Pantsov, *Mao,* 526. Xu and Ye had a more fluid relationship than Xu did with many of the senior leaders in the PLA. Unlike Nie Rongzhen, who was a reliable friend and ally for Xu after the Long March, Xu and Ye were sometimes allies and other times foes.

[160] MacFarquhar and Schoenhals, *Mao's Last Revolution*, 196. Marshal Chen Yi and CCP official Tan Zhenlin were the other two prominent individuals who were punished for the February Countercurrent. Ye Jianying, Li Xiannian, and others were largely absolved.

[161] MacFarquhar and Schoenhals, *Mao's Last Revolution*, 198.

[162] Both He Long and Peng Dehuai were first arrested in December 1966 at the urging of Jiang Qing and were subsequently subjected to struggle meetings and repeated torture. He died in 1969, Peng in 1974, both as a result of the mental and physical abuse they suffered. Xu did not escape all of the Radicals' public attacks after Mao's intervention. In June 1967, there was a "Down with Xu Xiangqian" poster campaign, which accused Xu of being a "big time bomb" and a "typical careerist and conspirator." See Yong Zhou, *A Great Trial in Chinese History: The Trial of the Lin Biao and Jiang Qing Counter-Revolutionary Cliques, Nov. 1980-Jan. 1981* (Oxford, U.K.: Pergamon Press, 1981), 165. It is estimated that as many as two million died during the Cultural Revolution, although Jiang Qing and the Gang of Four were only found guilty of killing 34,800 people. See "Introduction," *Memoirs of a Chinese Marshal: The Autobiographical Notes of Peng Dehuai*, 10; R. Keith Schoppa, *Twentieth Century*

In the last two decades of Xu's life, there are three years that stand out, for in each Xu took a policy position that broke with convention. His decisions in 1969, 1979, and 1989 illustrate his matured thinking and mark him with an unpredictability unusual in a senior military officer and bureaucrat.

In late February 1969, Mao gave Xu, Chen Yi, Nie Rongzhen, and Ye Jianying the directive to evaluate China's international standing and to analyze its future foreign policy, especially in light of the Soviet invasion of Czechoslovakia and the issuance of the Brezhnev Doctrine in 1968.[163] To keep the marshals' work secret and to protect them from the still-powerful Radicals, Mao assigned each to work in a different factory outside of Beijing.[164] While the men prepared their reports, the international situation changed on March 2, when Chinese border troops in Manchuria crossed the frozen Ussuri River and attacked Soviet positions around a disputed island. The Soviets responded to the Chinese ambush on March 15 with a tank assault that resulted in hundreds of casualties, but they were not able to dislodge the Chinese troops. With the military situation in flux, the marshals' initial reports, which had concluded the Soviets would not launch a full-scale war against China in the immediate future, were drawn into question.[165] In May, Mao asked the four marshals to prepare a new report, and Zhou Enlai told them to not "be restricted by any established framework" so that they might help to develop Mao's strategic thinking.[166] On July 11, Xu, Chen, Nie, and Ye submitted their revised conclusions. They argued that while both "U.S. imperialists" and "Soviet revisionists" were "representatives of the international bourgeoisie class" and while both "take China as the enemy," the new American president, Richard Nixon, sees "China as a 'potential threat' rather than a real threat." The Americans would not launch a large-scale war against China, but the Soviets "have made China their main enemy, imposing a more serious threat to our security."[167] Indeed, the marshals saw the Americans as "sitting on top of the mountain to watch a fight between two tigers," hoping that their battle would weaken both communist nations, but the marshals also

<hr/>

China: A History in Documents (New York: Oxford University Press, 2004), 140; Yan and Gao, *Turbulent Decade*, 202-205, 208-314; Pantsov, *Mao,* 518; and Dikötter, *The Cultural Revolution*, xvi.

[163] The Brezhnev Doctrine held that the USSR could intervene in Warsaw Pact countries which adopted policies that jeopardized socialism. See Chapter U for more context and details.

[164] Lorenze M. Lüthi, "Restoring Chaos to History: Sino-Soviet-American Relations, 1969," The *China Quarterly*, 210 (2012), 378-397, ProQuest Central. Lüthi notes that Xu, Chen, Nie, and Ye all were attacked by Lin and Jiang at the Twelfth Plenum of the Eighth Central Committee in October 1968. As long as the Radicals retained power, Xu and other military moderates were vulnerable.

[165] The first report was submitted March 18, the second by April 1, the third on July 11, and the fourth on September 17. See Chen Jian, *Mao's China and the Cold War* (Chapel Hill, North Carolina: University of North Carolina Press, 2001), 246; and Lüthi, "Restoring Chaos to History." The island is known as Zhenbao Island by the Chinese and Damansky Island by the Russians. The March 2 attack caused 31 Soviet fatalities and an unknown number of Chinese casualties. The March 15 response resulted in 91 Chinese casualties and over 200 Soviet casualties.

[166] Zhou Enlai quoted in Chen, *Mao's China and the Cold War*, 247. The marshals were initially reluctant to present anything that went against the policies established at the CCP's Ninth National Congress that April.

[167] "Report by Four Chinese Marshals—Chen Yi, Ye Jianying, Xu Xiangqian, and Nie Rongzhen—to the Central Committee: 'A Preliminary Evaluation of the War Situation,'" July 11, 1969 quoted in Chris Tudda, *A Cold War Turning Point: Nixon and China, 1969-1972* (Baton Rouge, Louisiana: Louisiana State University Press, 2012), 23.

concluded that the Americans were more concerned with the Soviets and wanted China to resist the USSR.[168] This represented a significant shift in understanding at a time when China officially held that the United States was "the most ferocious enemy of the people of the whole world."[169] In September, with the PLA completely mobilized for outright war with the Soviet Union as a result

of a major clash along the Xinjiang border and a subsequent Soviet threat to launch a nuclear attack on China, the marshals took this new paradigm even further. In their final report, Xu, Chen, Nie, and Ye called for playing "the American card."[170] They hoped to change China's geopolitical mindset, as well as its overall position, by taking advantage of the rivalry between the Cold War superpowers. This change in approach paved the way for Nixon's famous mission to China in February 1972. It would be an exaggeration to say that Xu and his fellow marshals were responsible for Nixon's trip, but they did open the door to make that visit possible.

Xu's late-life unconventionality may best be seen in relation to China's weak execution of its 1979 invasion of Vietnam. Now seventy-seven and defense minister, Xu was less enthusiastic about the initiative than China's new *de facto* leader, Deng Xiaoping, but as a respected tactician he formulated the PLA's battle plan for the attack anyway.[171] When Chinese troops performed poorly in the attack, which occurred at 26 sites along the 797-mile border with a goal of capturing five provincial capitals, Xu saw it as a confirmation of how much the PLA needed reform. The facts that officers panicked, supplies didn't arrive, communications didn't work, intelligence reports failed, and casualty rates were too high all pointed to the desperate need for change.[172] China hadn't fought an international war since the 1962 Sino-Indian War and its inexperience showed. As Xu dispassionately said in the war's aftermath, in "this military operation against Vietnam we have gained experience in all aspects, [and this] will lead to a very good postmortem. We can analyze which things went well and which things went wrong—all beneficial to our future work."[173] Xu specifically wanted to update Mao's People's War doctrine, which emphasized defensive positions and numerical superiority over technology and efficiency. Although Xu didn't originate the idea of a "people's war under modern conditions," he forcefully supported it. This distinguished him

---

[168] "Report by Four Chinese Marshals," quoted in Tudda, *A Cold War Turning Point*, 24.

[169] Lin Biao, "Report to The Ninth National Congress of The Communist Party of China," (Delivered on April 1 and adopted on April 14, 1969), *Marxist Internet Archive*, accessed February 15, 2020, https://www.marxists.org/subject/china/documents/cpc/9th_congress_report.htm

[170] Lüthi, "Restoring Chaos to History," and Dikötter, *The Cultural Revolution*, 245. The Soviet attack in Xinjiang came on August 13, 1969. In the aftermath, the Soviets threatened a nuclear strike against the Chinese nuclear base at Lop Nor. Mao and Zhou then mobilized the PLA. In October, Chinese fears over a Soviet attack were so strong that the CCP leadership, including Xu, was evacuated to different parts of China with orders to begin preparations for guerrilla warfare.

[171] Scobell, *China's Use of Military Force Beyond the Great Wall and the Long March,* 133. Scobell describes Xu as a "progressive" (139).

[172] Ezra F. Vogel, *Deng Xiaoping and the Transformation of China* (Cambridge, Massachusetts: Belknap Press of Harvard University Press, 2011), 530-531. According to Xu's plan, the campaign to capture the five cities should have taken one week; instead, it took three. For the Chinese, 25,000 were killed and 37,000 wounded.

[173] Xu Xiangqian quoted in Scobell, *China's Use of Military Force Beyond the Great Wall and the Long March*, 133. As part of this postmortem, all soldiers were required to write summaries of their experiences. See Zhang Xiaoming, "China's 1979 War with Vietnam: A Reassessment," *The China Quarterly*, 184 (2005), 851-74, ProQuest Central. Zhang's article also provides a description and assessment of the battles and the preparations for the war.

from men like Ye Jianying, who continued to believe in the importance of the Maoist doctrine.[174] As Xu wrote in October 1979,

> We must equip ourselves with advanced military thinking to meet the needs of modernizing our national defense and [our] needs in a future war….War is now conducted in a way different from that in the past….[Therefore] our military thinking must tally with changing conditions.[175]

In other words, as Xu also wrote, in order to advance China's military thinking, "we must combine Marxist-Leninism-Mao Zedong thought with the practice of modern warfare." Only by "realistically solv[ing] problems regarding the theory and practice of building a people's army" will it be possible for China to "launch…a people's war under modern conditions."[176] In many ways, this was the Mao-Zhang debate from the 1920s and 1930s about guerrilla fighters versus professional soldiers, updated for the nuclear era.

As part of this modernization program, Deng began downsizing the PLA. As early as 1975, Deng had said that the army could be summarized in five words: "bloating, laxity, conceit, extravagance, and inertia," and through the late 1970s and 1980s, he made drastic cuts.[177] Whereas the PLA had 6.1 million troops in 1975, by 1982 it was almost two million soldiers smaller. By 1988 the PLA was almost half the size it had been when Mao died in 1976.[178] Most significantly for Xu, Deng imposed a retirement system on the military as part of the modernization program. Like Nie Rongzhen and Ye Jianying, Xu was forced to resign his positions in 1985, but he retained many of the privileges that went with being a senior military official, including a substantial income.[179] Since Xu resented Deng's broken promise to support Mao's designated successor Hua Guofeng, Xu may not have wanted to continue to work with Deng anyway. As Xu wrote, "Deng Xiaoping is manipulative; you can't work with him."[180]

The final example of Xu's unconventionality is his reaction to the student protesters in Tiananmen Square in spring 1989. On the evening of May 21, the day after the declaration of martial law, seven students from the Chinese Science and Technology University went to Xu's residence, asking him to comment because bloodshed seemed likely if PLA troops tried to suppress the democracy movement. Unlike Nie Rongzhen, who also received a student

---

[174] Thomas W. Robinson, "Chinese Military Modernization in the 1980s." *The China Quarterly*, no. 90 (1982): 231-52, EBSCOhost. Ye wasn't opposed to modernization *per se*, just deviation from Mao's doctrine.

[175] Xu Xiangqian quoted in Joffe, "'People's War Under Modern Conditions.'" The first person to articulate the idea of a "people's war under modern conditions" was Su Yu (1907-1984), who attained the rank of Grand General.

[176] Xu Xiangqian quoted in V. K. Kapoor, "The Ultimate Victory," *SP's Land Forces*, October 1, 2010), ProQuest Central.

[177] Deng Xiaoping quoted in MacFarquhar and Schoenhals, *Mao's Last Revolution,* 389.

[178] Vogel, *Deng Xiaoping and the Transformation of China,* 526. The PLA was 5.2 million in 1979; 4.2 million in 1982; and 3.2 million in 1988. The military budget also decreased in this period, from 4.6% of GNP in 1979 to 1.4% of GNP in 1991 (page 541).

[179] Vogel, *Deng Xiaoping and the Transformation of China,* 547.

[180] Xu Xiangqian quoted in "The Views of Two Marshals and Eight Generals," Zhang Liang, *The Tiananmen Papers*, Andrew J. Nathan and Perry Link (eds.) (New York: Public Affairs, 2002), 264-265, n 47.

delegation that night, Xu did not speak directly to his visitors. Instead, a member of his staff, speaking on Xu's behalf and with his explicit consent, told the students,

> the troops are carrying out the martial law tasks to restore the capital's normal order and safeguard the situation of stability and unity. These tasks are by no means targeted at the students. Army comrades are, under no circumstances, willing to see a bloody incident and will do everything to avert such an incident. Please do not listen to rumors. It is hoped that the students will return to school as quickly as possible and help the government to calm down the situation with a rational attitude.[181]

The students in Tiananmen Square perceived this statement and Nie's similar statement to mean that the venerable marshals were on their side and that they had told Deng not to use force against them.[182] In fact, Xu and Nie may have telephoned Deng to object to the use of force against the students,[183] for Xu had also said at one point, "Let us hope it [martial law] is never directed at the students."[184] It wasn't that Xu sympathized with the democracy movement *per se*, but he was decidedly opposed to the use of military force against it. This view put Xu and Nie on the same side as the eight generals who wrote to Deng on May 20, saying, "We request that troops not enter the city and that martial law not be carried out in Beijing."[185] These statements departed markedly from the attitudes of the hardliners, who were unapologetic about imposing martial law and using violence to clear the Square.[186] What Xu really wanted was for the protest to end without bloodshed. He wanted order restored, and he did not want to see the reputation of the army to which he had devoted his life sullied by an attack on defenseless people. In this attitude, he was only a step away from the rhetorical question that had shaped his career fifty-four years before: "Have you ever seen the Red Army attacking the Red Army?"[187] Such thinking about the human consequences of military actions made Xu an unconventional figure in the context of twentieth-century China's brutal history.

~

Countries, especially new ones forged in war, need military heroes, which is why Xu and nine other important commanders were awarded the rank of marshal in 1955. In the sixth year of the People's

[181] "Students Visit Marshals Nie Rongzhen and Xu Xiangqian," *Beijing Spring 1989: Confrontation and Conflict— The Basic Documents*, Michel C. Oksenberg, Marc Lambert, Melanie Manion (eds.) (London: Routledge, 2015), 316.

[182] Philip J. Cunningham, *Tiananmen Moon: Inside the Chinese Student Uprising of 1989* (Lanham, Maryland: Rowman & Littlefield Publishers, 2014), 279, EBSCOebooks.

[183] Scobell, *China's Use of Military Force Beyond the Great Wall and the Long March*, 251.

[184] Xu Xiangqian quoted in "The Views of Two Marshals and Eight Generals," Zhang, *The Tiananmen Papers*, 265. Nie went further, saying, "Under no circumstances should there be shedding of blood."

[185] "The Views of Two Marshals and Eight Generals," Zhang, *The Tiananmen Papers*, 264-265.

[186] "The Leaders Take Stock," Zhang Liang, *The Tiananmen Papers*, Andrew J. Nathan and Perry Link (eds.) (New York: Public Affairs, 2002), 420-424. As Deng said, "Our use of martial law to deal with the turmoil was absolutely necessary. In the future…we will use severe measures to stamp out the first signs of turmoil as soon as they appear."

[187] Xu Xiangqian and Chen Changhao quoted in Salisbury, *The Long March*, 277.

Republic, they had both the proper political credentials and sufficient meritorious service to warrant high recognition. With the changing values of the Cultural Revolution, most of these men lost their high standing, and only some lived long enough to recover it during Deng's era. This rise and fall, determined by political considerations instead of military ones, suggests that more universal criteria should be applied when evaluating the career of a leading officer.

In *The Art of War*, the fifth-century Chinese military strategist Sun Tzu (d. 470 BCE) wrote that it was essential for an army to have a commander who stood for "the virtues of wisdom, sincerity, benevolence, courage, and strictness."[188] Against this standard, Xu Xiangqian compares favorably. He possessed the wisdom to cope with the machinations of an intensely political arena and the courage to stand up for what he believed. As China's president Jiang Zemin noted at a 2001 ceremony to mark Xu's one hundredth birthday, Xu opposed separatism within the party during the Long March and maintained his belief in the value of unity during the Cultural Revolution.[189] At both moments, Xu championed a viewpoint that went against the mainstream and accepted the adverse personal consequences. He did so as a result of his sincerity and strictness, both of which stemmed from his intense sense of loyalty, first to Zhang, then to Mao, but always to the army in service to the CCP. Xu believed that an army should be governed by rules, led by principled individuals, and judged by its professionalism. This is why, despite having sympathy the Tiananmen protesters, Xu wrote the PLA a letter on June 13, 1989 expressing his "lofty tribute to all the officers and men of the martial law command," and offering his condolences for their losses in the line of duty.[190]

The PLA did what the Party told it to do.

---

[188] For Sun Tzu, these traits in a commander were one of the five constants in war; the others were moral law, Heaven, earth, and method and discipline. Sun Tzu saw moral law as that which "causes the people to be in complete accord with their ruler." Heaven is that which "signifies night and day, cold and heat, times and seasons." Earth comprises "distances, great and small; danger and security; open ground and narrow passes; the chances of life and death." And method and discipline is defined as "the marshaling of the army in its proper subdivisions, the gradations of rank among the officers, the maintenance of roads by which supplies may reach the army, and the control of military expenditure." Sun Tzu, *The Art of War*, Lionel Giles (trans.) (New York: Barnes & Noble Classics, 2003), 74-75.

[189] "Jiang Addresses Meeting to Mark Late Marshal's 100th Birthday," *Xinhua News Agency*, November 7, 2001, EBSCOhost.

[190] Xu Xiangqian quoted in Scobell, *China's Use of Military Force Beyond the Great Wall and the Long March*, 155.

y

Ahmed Zaki Yamani

1930-

The June 6, 1977 issue of *Time* magazine featured an extraordinary advertisement purchased by the Kingdom of Saudi Arabia. The eight-page spread, entitled "A Special Relationship," saluted the thirty-two year "strategic, economic, and human partnership" between the nation with the world's largest proven oil reserves and the United States. It featured historical photographs of Franklin D. Roosevelt and Dwight Eisenhower meeting with Saudi kings, showcased Arabs working alongside Americans in Saudi refineries and universities, underscored the kingdom's modern architecture and infrastructure, highlighted the positive impact the kingdom's development had had on the American economy, and celebrated the country's "unique religious responsibility" to maintain the "religious and moral values of Islam" as the guardian of Mecca and Medina. The advertisement even included a photograph of four teenage girls sitting in a courtyard at their school, laughing as they casually enjoyed bottles of Coca-Cola and shared a package of European-made TUC crackers. Dressed in open-collar white blouses and long blue skirts, the young women seem far removed from the expected *abaya* or a *niqab*.[1] The overall intent of the advertisement was to make Saudi Arabia appear modern and approachable. By offering the American reader the image of a friendly, reliable ally in an unpredictable world, the unprecedented promotion was doing in print what the kingdom's minister of petroleum and mineral resources, Ahmed Zaki Yamani, regularly did in person with both delicacy and panache.

---

[1] Kingdom of Saudi Arabia, "A Special Relationship: A Report by the Kingdom of Saudi Arabia," [Advertisement], *Time*, vol. 109, no.23 (June 6, 1977), 45-52. An *abaya* is a loose-fitting cloak that covers all but a woman's head, hands and feet; the *niqab* is a face veil that has an opening for the eyes. TUC crackers were first made in Belgium in 1958; the acronym stands for the Trade Union Corporation. See "Mondelēz International Brand Family," *Mondelēz International*, 2018, accessed February 17, 2020, https://eu.mondelezinternational.com/brand-family

For a quarter century, Yamani managed[2] what Saudis regularly refer to as their "gift from God."[3] His virtuosity during this time stemmed from his ease in both the Western and Arab worlds. He gained this fluency during his college years at the University of Cairo and during his postgraduate study in the United States. This began at New York University, where he studied American statutory law and British common law.* He lived off-campus, on the Upper East Side, so that he could both observe *halal** and visit fashionable Midtown music clubs.[4] Before finishing his master's degree in Comparative Jurisprudence in 1955, Yamani met an Iraqi woman named Laila who was also studying at NYU. They eventually married and had three children. Before returning to Saudi Arabia, Yamani moved to Boston and enrolled at Harvard Law School, where he completed a one-year Master of Laws program designed for international students with previous legal experience.[5] By the time he received the two graduate degrees, Yamani had gained a significant cross-cultural fluency. What this allowed him to do later in life was choose attire that honored those with whom he was meeting, insist that his non-Muslim guests eat midday during Ramadan, and send Christmas cards to Western friends with a genuine appreciation of the holiday.[6] Indeed, he was as comfortable in a tailored suit in London as he was wearing a white thobe* in Riyadh.[7] Similarly, Yamani was as content speaking in English or French as he was in Arabic as a result of his education.

Returning to Saudi Arabia at age twenty-six, Yamani began working in the kingdom's Finance Ministry. He also established a private law practice and wrote newspaper columns that explained *Shari'a*, Islamic law. This fit well with his family background, for both Yamani's father and grandfather had held the rank of grand mufti—the foremost interpreter of religious law in a Muslim nation.[8] Within just a few years, Yamani gained a distinguished reputation as legal expert in both *Shari'a* and Western law, in part because of the way he viewed legal precedent. On the one hand, Yamani argued that the religious elements of *Shari'a* provided Saudi Arabia with a "model code of ethics—so lacking in Western law—the purpose of which is to strengthen secular principles by giving them a sense of dependence on divine guidance." This was necessary because "the spirit and general principles of *Shari'a* are as valid today as they were…many centuries ago and as the they will be tomorrow."[9] On the other hand, Yamani also saw *Shari'a* as being an "organic creature" that had to adapt to changing circumstances. It should not be beholden to a single interpretative school of jurisprudence.[10] For Yamani, it was important to examine the "purpose and wisdom

---

[2] I use the term "managed" because, as Daniel Yergin notes, Yamani "could not dictate or solely determine Saudi policy, but he could shape it. His style of diplomacy, his mastery of analysis and negotiation, and his skill with the press all gave him decisive influence. His power was augmented by simple longevity, the fact that he ended up being 'there' longer than anyone else." See Daniel Yergin, *The Prize: The Epic Quest for Oil, Money & Power* (New York: The Free Press, 2008), 621.

[3] See, for example, Abdullah Jumah quoted in Ellen R. Wald, *Saudi, Inc.: The Arabian Kingdom's Pursuit of Profit and Power* (New York: Pegasus Books, 2018), xvii. Abdullah Jumah was the CEO of Saudi Aramco from 1995 to 2008.

[4] Jeffery Robinson, *Yamani: The Inside Story* (New York: The Atlantic Monthly Press, 1989), 41-42.

[5] "Degree Programs," *Harvard Law School*, 2018, accessed February 21, 2020, https://tinyurl.com/y4dujdz7

[6] Robinson, *Yamani*, 7, 9, 43.

[7] "The Emissary from Arabia," *Time*, Vol. 102, no. 25 (December 17, 1973), 34.

[8] Yamani's father was the grand mufti in Indonesia and Malaysia when Yamani was a boy, and Yamani's grandfather was once the grand mufti for the Ottoman Empire in Arabia. See Robinson, *Yamani*, 39.

[9] Ahmad Zaki Yamani, *Islamic Law and Contemporary Issues* (Jeddah, Saudi Arabia: The Saudi Publishing House, [1967]), 13.

[10] Yamani, *Islamic Law and Contemporary Issues*, 13. The four main schools of jurisprudence for Sunni Muslims are Hanafi, Shafi, Maliki and Hanbali. They differ in the interpretation of primary sources, the weight given to

underlying" the texts "rather than only their literal meaning." He distinguished between the "Quranic rules and commands," which are very few in number and which are "a sacred and immutable source of law," and the "vast body of legal opinions produced by Muslim jurists and scholars," which are "not religiously binding on Muslims."[11] What this meant is that even as a young professional Yamani developed a keen sense of legal subtlety. He used this skill early in his career when he successfully represented the Arabian-American Oil Company (Aramco) in a Saudi court against a suit filed by a merchant from the eastern city of Hofuf.[12] Clearly, Yamani was able to walk with confidence between two different worlds.

In late 1957, Saudi Crown Prince Faisal bin Abdulaziz Al Saud requested that Yamani pay him a visit. Faisal had a knack for identifying young talent, and he liked to surround himself with erudite and urbane individuals.[13] The king had noticed Yamani's newspaper writings and legal successes and needed someone who understood Western systems of budgeting, banking, and the law. At the conclusion of their discussion, the Crown Prince asked Yamani to be his chief legal advisor. Yamani accepted the assignment without hesitation or conditions.[14] This was important, for Faisal and his older brother, King Saud, had long been rivals, and Faisal sensed that an outright struggle for power was eminent.[15] Faisal wanted to be surrounded by talented men he could trust in such circumstances, and he wanted some of these men to have Western experience. Yamani met the criteria nicely. So began a professional relationship that developed into deep friendship over the next seventeen years.[16]

In 1959, Faisal named Yamani to be a minister of state without portfolio. When he joined the cabinet at twenty-nine, Yamani became the youngest Saudi to ever hold a cabinet post. This did more than raise eyebrows; it generated resentment in royal circles towards the talented commoner from Mecca.[17] What Yamani soon learned as a result of joining Faisal's inner circle was that the nation was not in strong fiscal shape, despite the discovery of Saudi Arabia's vast oil reserves just before World War II. In fact, the kingdom was on the verge of bankruptcy: it lacked a certifiable budget, faced a currency shortage, held insufficient gold reserves, and owed $120 million to foreign banks in 1958.[18] Part of the problem lay in the House of Saud itself, which through the 1950s made no distinction between the king's private funds and those of the state. Royals saw all of the nation's wealth as their own private property and ran the kingdom as a family business.[19] They spent

---

secondary sources, and other factors. For a discussion of the differences in legal schools of interpretation for Shi'a Muslims, see Chapter Q.

[11] Ahmad Zaki Yamani, "Forward," Hasson Hathout, *Reading the Muslim Mind* (Burr Ridge, Illinois: American Trust Publications, 1995), xxiv, xxv and xxviii.

[12] Scott McMurray, *Energy to the World: The Story of Saudi Aramco*, Vol. 2 (Houston, Texas: Aramco Services Company, 2011), 10.

[13] Alexei Vassiliev, *King Faisal of Saudi Arabia: Personality, Faith, and Times* (London: Saqi Books, 2012), 265-266.

[14] Robinson, *Yamani*, 48.

[15] At their father's deathbed in November 1953, Saud bin Abdulaziz Al Saud and Faisal had promised to cooperate with one another, but the brothers never abandoned their animosity. By the late 1950s they were unwilling to work together to solve problems. See Robert Lacey, *The Kingdom* (New York: Harcourt Brace Jovanovich, 1981), 318; and Vassiliev, *The History of Saudi Arabia*, 335.

[16] Robinson, *Yamani*, 52.

[17] Robert Sherrill, *The Oil Follies of 1970-1980: How the Petroleum Industry Stole the Show (and Much More Besides)* (Garden City, New York: Anchor Press/Doubleday, 1983), 131.

[18] Vassiliev, *The History of Saudi Arabia*, 341; and Lacey, *The Kingdom*, 321, 324.

[19] Saïd K. Aburish, *The Rise, Corruption and Coming Fall of the House of Saud* (New York: St. Martin's Press, 1995), 275; Robert Lacey, *Inside the Kingdom: Kings, Clerics, Modernists, Terrorists, and the Struggle for Saudi Arabia* (New York: Viking, 2009), 38; Robinson, *Yamani*, 13; and Vassiliev, *The History of Saudi Arabia*, 402.

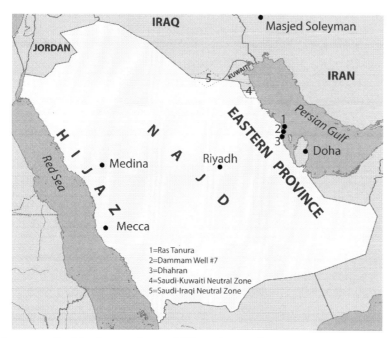

1=Ras Tanura
2=Dammam Well #7
3=Dhahran
4=Saudi-Kuwaiti Neutral Zone
5=Saudi-Iraqi Neutral Zone

accordingly, embracing the Arabian custom that saw gift giving as a measure of prosperity.[20] When Faisal's predecessor and brother King Saud ordered a palace outside of Riyadh demolished and replaced with a more lavish one, he was operating within the boundaries of established royal behavior.[21] His nation was named *Saudi* Arabia; it belonged to the princes of the House of Saud. But by 1958 the kingdom could not afford royal extravagance. King Saud had abolished the tax on *hajj* pilgrims, long an important source of revenue, because God had given him oil,[22] but these oil revenues fell in 1956 and 1957 with the closure of the Suez Canal during the Suez Crisis.*[23] Saud also had political difficulties. In February 1958, he was accused of involvement in a conspiracy to assassinate Egyptian president Gamal Abdel Nasser after Nasser's creation of the United Arab Republic.*[24] Soon the financial and political situation became such that Faisal, with the support of nine of his brothers, announced that he would take over the day-to-day operations of the kingdom. Saud officially remained king, but the power of the monarchy belonged to Faisal, who quickly began to institute changes to establish a budget and control royal spending.[25] Then, in March 1962, Faisal appointed Yamani to the post that made him

---

[20] Wald, *Saudi, Inc.*, 53. A similar Arabian custom is offering hospitality and sanctuary to strangers. This custom developed in response to the challenges of the Arabian environment. See David F. Long, *Culture and Customs of Saudi Arabia* (Westport, Connecticut: Greenwood Press, 2005), 64.

[21] Lacey, *The Kingdom*, 299.

[22] In one of his legal writings, Yamani outlines the Islamic view of personal property. He notes, "all property is owned by God," and he quotes the medieval Persian legal scholar, Al-Zamakshari (1075-1144), who wrote, "He supplied you with it and permitted you to reap its benefits, and made you heirs and successors in disposing with it, but it is not really yours and you are only God's agents and representatives." See Yamani, *Islamic Law and Contemporary Issues*, 19-20. This applied as much to oil as anything else. Robert Lacey confirms that King Saud and the other royals held this belief too. See Lacey, *The Kingdom*, 301.

[23] Robert Vitalis, *America's Kingdom: Mythmaking on the Saudi Oil Frontier* (Stanford, California: Stanford University Press, 2007), 185.

[24] Vassiliev, *The History of Saudi Arabia*, 354.

[25] Faisal remained in power until December 1960, but resigned his posts when Saud refused to approve the budget Faisal had prepared. Saud then held power for the next 15 months, as the factional struggle in the royal family brewed. In March 1962, when Saud had to go to the United States for medical treatment, he appointed Faisal regent, but upon Saud's return he found that thanks to the influence of an anti-royalist revolution in Yemen, the Saudi royal family had rallied around Faisal. Saud formally abdicated on November 3, 1964 and left Saudi Arabia in March 1965. He died in 1969. See Lacey, *The Kingdom*, 335-338, 345-356; and Vassiliev, *The History of Saudi Arabia*, 358-368.

famous. As the new minister of petroleum and mineral affairs, Yamani quickly became the face of the kingdom's most important industry.

~

In 1744, an ambitious emir named Muhammad bin Saud met an itinerate Muslim preacher named Muhammad ibn Abd al-Wahhab, who emphasized the importance of Allah's absolute singularity: nothing can describe God and nothing is like God.[26] Al-Wahhab held that the greatest sin was worshipping anything but Allah Himself; even the worship of something closely associated with Allah was so wrong that it was beyond redemption or forgiveness.[27] The focus of all prayer had to be upon Allah, not upon saints, relics, tombs, or other objects. According to al-Wahhab's austere reading of the Quran, any distraction from the absolute, singular authority of Allah compromised the integrity of Islam altogether. Even the Prophet Muhammad was not to be worshipped or venerated.[28] It was a powerful message, but also a controversial one because the sage men of the 'ulama in Arabia saw it as a threat to their prestige and their capacity to interpret the Quran.[29] Consequently, al-Wahhab looked for a secular leader to help him spread of his beliefs. When he met Muhammad bin Saud in 1744, two men easily came to a mutually beneficial understanding: the emir would help al-Wahhab spread his teachings through military conquest, while the preacher provided Muhammad bin Saud with a religious justification for expansion. Each man agreed to support the other and not to infringe upon the other's realm of authority.[30] This recipe worked well as more and more of Arabia slowly came under the control of bin Saud and what non-followers called Wahhabism.[31]

Muhammad bin Saud died in 1765 and al-Wahhab died in 1792, but the relationship between the emirate and the ultra-monotheistic faith did not end. Instead, Saudi-Wahhabi forces pursued their *jihad* north into Iraq with righteous fury. In 1802, they attacked the holy Shi'a city of Karbala, where they massacred thousands, including women, children, and the elderly; destroyed the mosques and tombs of 'Ali, Husayn, and other imams; and confiscated large quantities of jewels,

---

[26] Reza Aslan, *No god but God: The Origins, Evolution, and Future of Islam* (New York: Random House, 2005), 150-151.

[27] James Noyes, *The Politics of Iconoclasm: Religion, Violence, and the Culture of Image-Breaking in Christianity and Islam* (New York: I. B. Tauris & Co. Ltd., 2013), 69-70. The oneness of Allah is known as *tawhid* and takes three forms: the oneness of lordship of Allah, the oneness of the worship of Allah, and the oneness of the names and qualities of Allah. To believe in something other than *tawhid* is to commit *shirk*.

[28] Vassiliev, *The History of Saudi Arabia*, 74.

[29] Ayman S. Al-Yassini, "Saudi Arabia: The Kingdom of Islam," *Religion and Societies: Asia and the Middle East*, Carlo Caldarola (ed.) (Berlin, Germany: Walter de Gruyter & Company, 1982), 62-63; Noyes, *The Politics of Iconoclasm*, 68; and Aslan, *No god but God,* 199, 242.

[30] John S. Habib, "Wahhabi Origins of the Contemporary Saudi State," *Religion and Politics in Saudi Arabia: Wahhabism and the State*, Mohammed Ayoob and Hasan Kosebalaban (eds.) (Boulder, Colorado: Lynne Rienner Publications, 2009), 57-58.

[31] As Robert Lacey notes the term "Wahhabism" is not well-received by many Saudis today because it implies that the followers of al-Wahhabi's teachings are members of a sect, instead of being the purest, truest Muslims. Many Saudis prefer the term *Muwahhidun* instead, but because this word usually translates into English as "Unitarians" and applies to a group of Christians as well, the Wahhabi terminology remains common. See Lacey, *The Kingdom*, 56, and Lacey, *Inside the Kingdom*, xix.

gold, weapons, fabrics, and precious books.[32] Then, in 1803, the Wahhabis turned their attack to the Hijaz region in western Arabia and the cities of Mecca and Medina, which quickly surrendered. For the next fifteen years, the Wahhabis raided Iraq and battled with Ottoman-Egyptian forces for control of the Hijaz and Islam's holiest cities, but by 1818 the first Saudi-Wahhabi state faced its demise as a result of overextension, rebellious local populations, and a string of military defeats.[33] A second, more fractious and less fervent[34] Saudi state existed between 1824 and 1891, but it too succumbed: the al-Rahman tribe from northern Najd forced the father of modern Saudi Arabia, Abdul Aziz, and his father to flee Riyadh.[35]

In January 1902, when Abdul Aziz was twenty-six, he led a band of forty men to the outskirts of Riyadh in what easily could have been a quixotic attempt to recapture the city and reestablish al-Saud rule over the region of Najd in central Arabia. On one legendary night, however, Abdul Aziz's men cut down a large date palm, used it as a ladder to scale the city's walls, and occupied the governor's palace. They killed the governor, subdued his troops, released prisoners, and reestablished al-Saud rule in Riyadh.[36] With the city's capture, Abdul Aziz strategically sought to overcome the mistakes of his ancestors. He began his rule by working to soothe tribal jealousies and win over rivals with charm and diplomacy. One of the ways he did this was to encourage the settlement of nomadic tribesmen in strategically situated, urban colonies; this bound them together through a common commitment to use war to spread Wahhabi doctrine.[37] These tribesmen became known as the Ikhwan, and they helped Abdul Aziz's expand his territory in the Najd region. Later, after Abdul Aziz gained access to the Persian Gulf by occupying much of the Eastern Province unilaterally, he offered the Ottoman Empire his cooperation and signed a treaty with the Sublime Porte* in May 1914.[38] Abdul Aziz did this because his repeated attempts to court British support had failed to gain traction. The outbreak of the First World War, however, changed Saudi and British geopolitical considerations: by mid-1915, the British archeologist and Arab expert Gertrude Bell and others had convinced the British government to send Abdul Aziz almost £10,000 a month to change the emir's alliance.[39] These bribes worked, partially because Abdul Aziz had financial difficulties as a result of the ways in which the war disrupted *hajj* traffic and the corresponding tax revenues. In December 1915, Abdul Aziz signed the Treaty of Darin, which recognized him and

---

[32] Vassiliev, *The History of Saudi Arabia*, 96-98; and Aslan, *No god but God*, 244.

[33] James Wynbrandt, *A Brief History of Saudi Arabia*, 2nd ed. (New York: Facts on File, 2010), 137-140.

[34] Habib, "Wahhabi Origins of the Contemporary Saudi State," 59.

[35] Abdul Aziz's full name was Abdulaziz ibn Abdul Rahman ibn Faisal ibn Turki ibn Abdullah ibn Muhammad Al Saud (1875-1953). He is also referred to as Ibn Saud in many Western sources.

[36] Wald, *Saudi, Inc.*, xi-xiii.

[37] M. E. Yapp, *The Making of the Modern Near East, 1792-1923* (New York: Longman Inc., 1987), 261. By 1912, there were 10,000 people living in the Ikhwan settlement of Arṭawiyya (Al Artawiyah). John S. Habib notes that the Ikhwan were "taught that abandoning the desert for a life in the town was a virtual reenactment of the Prophet Muhammad's own migration, or hijra, from Medina to Mecca, from the realm of polytheism (*dar al-kufr*) to the realm of faith (*dar al-Islam*)." See Habib, "Wahhabi Origins of the Contemporary Saudi State," 65.

[38] Jacob Goldberg, "The 1914 Saudi-Ottoman Treaty: Myth or Reality?," *Journal of Contemporary History*, 19, 2 (April 1984), 289-314, EBSCOhost. According to the terms of the treaty, Abdul Aziz recognized Ottoman sovereignty over Najd and the Eastern Province, surrendered his right to engage in an independent foreign policy, and declared himself to be a subject of the Porte. In return, he was appointed the Sultan's governor for Najd and the Eastern Province, had his descendants recognized as the legitimate local leaders in much of Arabia, and had the right to determine the strength of Ottoman garrisons in the region.

[39] Janet Wallach, *Desert Queen* (New York: Anchor Books, 1999), 152. Georgina Howell's *Gertrude Bell: Queen of the Desert, Shaper of Nations* (Farrar, Straus and Giroux, 2006) is also a valuable source about a fascinating woman.

his descendants as the legitimate rulers of the Najd and the Eastern Province along the Persian Gulf. It also transformed his lands into a British protectorate.[40]

In the aftermath of World War I, the Treaty of Sèvres partitioned the Ottoman Empire; created British mandates in Mesopotamia and Palestine; established French mandates in Syria and Lebanon; and allowed for the independence of the Hijaz region. Western diplomats hoped this

independence would mean that the holy cities of Mecca and Medina would be governed by a reliable partner, Sharif Hussein bin Ali.[41] Reflecting its relative lack of importance at the time, most of Arabia was left to determine its own postwar situation.[42] This suited Abdul Aziz well for several years, for it allowed his army of nomadic tribesmen, the Ikhwan, to expand Wahhabi influence northward and to conquer long-standing rivals, such as the al-Rahman tribe in northern Najd.[43] By 1922, however, the Ikhwan were conducting raids into the Transjordan and Iraq, and this risked British reprisals. Abdul Aziz insisted that the Ikhwan cease their raids, arrested leading perpetrators,[44] and negotiated with the British to define the border between his territory and that of the British mandates. In December, the Uqair Protocol set the boundaries and established two neutral zones

---

[40] The Treaty of Darin is also referred to as the Anglo-Saudi Treaty of 1915 in many sources. The specific parts of the Eastern Province which were recognized as belonging to Abdul Aziz were Al-Hasa, Qatif, Jubai, and their surrounding areas. The treaty specifically excluded Iraq, Jordan, Kuwait, Bahrain, Qatar, and Oman as having any Saudi claim. See Askar H. al-Enazy, *The Creation of Saudi Arabia: Ibn Saud and British Imperial Policy, 1914-1927* (New York: Routledge, 2010), 52-54; and Habib, "Wahhabi Origins of the Contemporary Saudi State," 61.

[41] The Treaty of Sèvres (1920) also ceded land in Thrace and around Izmir to Greece; established the independent state of Armenia; promised the establishment of a Jewish homeland in Palestine in accordance with the Balfour Declaration of 1917; created substantial zones of influence in Anatolia for Britain, France, Italy, and Greece; and left the Sultan with a crippled state. The harsh terms of this treaty helped spark the Ataturk-led Turkish War of Independence, resulting in the signing of the Treaty of Lausanne in 1923. The Lausanne treaty recognized the Republic of Turkey and established its modern borders.

[42] Clive Leatherdale, *Britain and Saudi Arabia, 1925-1939: The Imperial Oasis* (New York: Frank Cass and Company, 1983), 26.

[43] Askar H. al-Enazy argues that this and subsequent expansion was not Abdul Aziz's design or ambition: his "early foreign policy motivation was primarily defensive and preservationist, and was completely consistent with the non-aggressive principles of Wahhabism." Al-Enazy also states that the "often aggressive attitude towards non-Wahhabi Muslims contrasts sharply with Wahhabism's pragmatic, even benevolent attitude towards non-Muslim peoples," and holds that Saudi expansion was a result of British policy in the region. See al-Enazy, *The Creation of Saudi Arabia*, 2, 118. In a review of this work, Robert Lacey is skeptical of these assertions, while acclaiming other aspects of the book. See Robert Lacey, "The Creation of Saudi Arabia: Ibn Saud and British Imperial Policy, 1914–1927 Al-Enazy Askar H." *Journal of Islamic Studies*, no. 2 (2012): 242-244, EBSCOhost.

[44] Michael Darlow and Barbara Bray, *Ibn Saud: The Desert Warrior Who Created the Kingdom of Saudi Arabia* (New York: Skyhorse Publishing, 2012), 283.

near Kuwait.[45] This curtailed any further expansion to the north, which is why Abdul Aziz redirected the Ikhwan's attention westward against Sharif Hussein. The Hijaz region soon fell, which allowed Abdul Aziz to enter Mecca as a pilgrim dressed in a simple white robe in October 1924.[46] But the capture of Islam's holiest city did not satisfy the some of the leaders of the Ikhwan, who pressed for additional conquests and fiercer adherence to Wahhabism in the lands Abdul Aziz now controlled. In 1929, they revolted against their emir, but their movement was quashed by troops loyal to Abdul Aziz.[47] This victory prompted him to declare himself the king of a new country, the Kingdom of Saudi Arabia, in 1932.

As Abdul Aziz struggled to dominate Arabia in the opening decades of the twentieth century, petroleum extraction became a commercially viable industry in the Middle East. The first major discovery of oil came as a result of a concession Naser al-Din Shah Qajar's son granted to an Australian mining magnate in 1901. According to the terms of this concession, William Knox D'Arcy and his consortium had 60 years to "probe, pierce, and drill at their will the depths of Persian Soil" for oil, except in five provinces bordering Russia and the Caspian Sea. In return, the D'Arcy consortium paid the Qajar monarch £20,000 in cash, £20,000 worth of company stock, and 16% of the venture's future profits.[48] It took seven years and a £400,000 investment for D'Arcy's speculative mission to strike oil, but on May 26, 1908, a drilling team hit pay dirt at 1,180 feet near the Iranian city of Masjed Soleyman, in the southwestern province of Khuzestan.[49] This find led other entrepreneurs to hunt for oil elsewhere in the region. On October 15, 1927, drillers working just north of Kirkuk, Iraq tapped a large oil field at 1,500 feet that produced a gusher that soaked villages in the area.[50] These finds suggested that the potential for oil in the Middle East was vast and would require cooperative management on a global scale. In 1928, oil company executives reached two important agreements. The first, known as the Red Line Agreement, was signed in Ostend, Belgium on July 31 by representatives of from British, Dutch, French, and American oil

---

[45] Darlow and Bray, *Ibn Saud,* 289-290. This delineation of the border between what became Saudi Arabia and Iraq disrupted 10,000 years of grazing patterns for nomadic tribesmen. The creation of two diamond-shaped neutral zones helped alleviate this because the resources of the Iraq Neutral Zone and the Kuwait Neutral Zone were to be split 50-50 between Iraq and Saudi Arabia, or between Kuwait and Saudi Arabia. These resources included the oil that lay underneath. The Kuwait Neutral Zone lasted until 1966, when the new border divided the zone in half. The Iraq Neutral Zone lasted until July 1975, when it too was divided in half. See *The Middle East and North Africa* (London: Europa Publications, 2004), 986.
[46] Habib, "Wahhabi Origins of the Contemporary Saudi State," 63.
[47] Darlow and Bray, *Ibn Saud,* 343-358.
[48] Mozaffar ad-Din Shah Qajar quoted in Mostafa Elm, *Oil, Power, and Principle: Iran's Oil Nationalization and its Aftermath* (Syracuse, New York: Syracuse University Press, 1992) 8. Mozaffar ad-Din Shah Qajar, Naser al-Din Shah Qajar's son, ruled from 1896-1907 and was forced to create a national assembly and establish a constitutional monarchy in 1906.
[49] Elm, *Oil, Power, and Principle,* 12. Elm discusses the process of negotiating for and financing of D'Arcy's concession, as well as the finding oil in Iran on pages 6-13. A more detailed account can be found in Roger Howard, *The Oil Hunters: Exploration and Espionage in the Middle East* (London: Hambledon Continuum Books, 2008), 13-81. Speculators were hoping to find oil in Iran because of its proximity to the oil fields surrounding Baku, Azerbaijan, which were producing 200,000 barrels a day by 1900. Oil had first been discovered near Baku in 1870. See *The Petroleum Handbook,* 6th ed. (Amsterdam, The Netherlands: Elsevier Science Publishers B.V., 1983), 26, Google Books.
[50] Howard, *The Oil Hunters,* 148. The first oil was found in Bahrain on June 1, 1932 at just over 2,000 feet, and in Kuwait on February 23, 1938 at a depth of 3,672 feet.

companies.[51] In this pact, the companies agreed to share the wealth produced from all crude extracted between the Suez Canal and Iran, except Kuwait, with each receiving a 23.75% share. The companies also agreed they would not develop oil fields in the region without the support of the other members.[52] The second agreement, which remained secret until 1952, was negotiated by four leading executives, who gathered at Achnacarry Castle in the Scottish Highlands in late August. By day, the representatives of Standard Oil of New Jersey (Esso/Exxon), Royal Dutch/Shell, the Anglo-Persian Oil Company (BP), and Gulf Oil shot grouse, bagged red deer, and caught brown trout.[53] By night, they enjoyed drams of exquisite single malt scotch, glasses of elegant Châteauneuf-du-Pape, hand-rolled Cuban cigars, and the fine local cuisine[54] as they discussed the best way to limit the supply of crude oil worldwide in order to increase profits.[55] Before the four executives left the Highlands, they agreed to adhere to production quotas, to share facilities, and to limit construction of new refineries. They also agreed to supply a market from the nearest geographical source, while continuing to charge for long-distance shipping fees.[56] This allowed the companies to pool their resources but pretend to be in stiff competition. These two agreements positioned member companies well, but they could not anticipate all possible contingencies. Those oil companies which were not signatories, for example, were free to pursue their own best interests. This meant that the Red Line Agreement and the Achnacarry Agreement were not a firewall against all competition. Eyeing the vast desert of Arabia, Standard Oil of California took advantage of this limitation and in 1933 signed an independent concession with Saudi Arabia's Abdul Aziz.

~

In mid-April 1939, a caravan of 500 cars and 2,000 people departed Riyadh—an undeveloped city of 40,000 residents whose water was still drawn from earthen wells by camels pulling wooden water wheels; whose airport consisted of a strip of sand, a simple windsock, and no permanent buildings;

---

[51] The Red Line Agreement was signed by 1) the Anglo-Persian Oil Company (which became British Petroleum); 2) the Royal Dutch/Shell Oil Company; 3) France's Compagnie Française des Pétroles (which became Total); and 4) the Near East Development Corporation, which represented Standard Oil of New Jersey (Esso/Exxon), Socony (Mobil), Gulf Oil, the Pan-American Petroleum and Transport Company, and Atlantic Refining (Arco).

[52] "The 1928 Red Line Agreement," *Bureau of Public Affairs, Office of the Historian, Department of State*, accessed February 16, 2020, https://history.state.gov/milestones/1921-1936/red-line. The remaining 5% share went to an influential Armenian-British businessman named Calouste Gulbenkian. Kuwait was reserved for British companies alone and was excluded from the agreement.

[53] The four men were Sir John Cadman of Anglo-Persian Oil Company (BP), Henri Deterding of Royal Dutch/Shell, William Mellon of Gulf Oil, and Walter Teagle of the Near East Development Corporation, which represented Standard Oil of New Jersey (Esso/Exxon).

[54] For an account of the Achnacarry menus, see Struan Stevenson, *The Course of History: Ten Meals that Changed the World* (New York: Arcade Publishing, 2019), 148-151. On pages 154-166, Chef Tony Singh provides modern recipe equivalents for all of the dishes Stevenson describes.

[55] Within a year, Socony (Mobil), Texas Oil Company (Texaco), and Atlantic (Arco) had joined the Achnacarry Agreement cartel. See Shukri Ghanem, *OPEC: The Rise and Fall of an Exclusive Club* (London: KPI, 1986), 13-14; and Robert Sherrill, *The Oil Follies of 1970-1980: How the Petroleum Industry Stole the Show (and Much More Besides)* (Garden City, New York: Anchor Press/Doubleday, 1983), 531.

[56] Yergin, *The Prize,* 247.

and whose major thoroughfare was an unpaved road.[57] The entourage included Abdul Aziz, seventeen other members of the royal family with their attendants and servants, officials from the California oil company, and one American woman dressed in male clothes so as not to offend Wahhabi sensibilities.[58] Their destination was the Persian Gulf town of Dhahran, which was just south of Dammam Well Number 7, where the first Saudi oil had been struck on March 4, 1938 at a depth of 4,724 feet.[59] Their purpose was to celebrate not just the discovery of oil, but also its readiness for market. On the commemorative day, May 1, 1939, Abdul Aziz boarded an oil tanker in the new port of Ras Tanura for a reception with the rest of the royal party and California oil officials. The day culminated with the presentation of new automobiles for the king and his chief financial advisor, Abdullah Suleiman, just before the king turned the valve which piped crude from the storage tanks into the ship.[60] Saudi Arabia's "gift from God" was ready for export to the world.

When officials from Standard Oil of California (Socal) first met with Abdul Aziz in 1933, the king had little faith that oil would be discovered underneath the sands of his kingdom. His biggest hope was that the agreement would alleviate his dire need for cash and that drilling would produce new sources of water.[61] This is why the king and Suleiman agreed to such unfavorable terms with the Americans. The original concession agreement gave Socal "the exclusive right, for a period of 60 years, to explore, prospect, drill for, extract, treat, manufacture, transport, deal with, carry away, and export" oil and oil products from most of the Eastern Province. It also gave Socal permission to build the facilities it needed in order to accomplish these tasks, promised Socal preferential consideration for future concessions in other parts of the kingdom, and exempted Socal from all taxes and duties. This surrendered substantial sovereignty.[62] In exchange, Abdul Aziz received loans of £50,000 in gold paid over eighteen months; an annual rent of £5,000 in gold until oil was discovered; a royalty of £100,000 in gold, paid over two years, once discovery had been made in commercial quantities; and a fee of four shillings in gold per ton of all oil sold from storage.[63] Abdul Aziz had such meager expectations from the Socal venture that he believed he was getting £55,000 for nothing.[64]

[57] Lacey, *The Kingdom*, 280-281; and Wald, *Saudi, Inc.*, xiv. Lacey's description of the wells and the airport is from 1946. The estimated population is from 1932.

[58] Wallace Stegner, *Discovery!: The Search for Arabian Oil* (Vista, California: Selwa Press, 2007), 135. The woman was Anita Burleigh, wife of a California Arabian Oil Company official. Casoc was a subsidiary of Standard Oil of California (Socal). Casoc became a joint partnership between the Standard Oil of California and the Texas Oil Company (Texaco) in 1936.

[59] This famous well produced 32 million barrels of oil during its 44 years of production. In 1999, Crown Prince Abdullah declared Dammam No. 7 to be "Prosperity Well" because of its importance to the history of Saudi Arabia. See Loring M. Danforth, *Crossing the Kingdom: Portraits of Saudi Arabia* (Oakland, California: University of California Press, 2016), 32.

[60] Stegner, *Discovery!*, 139.

[61] Wald, *Saudi, Inc.*, 9.

[62] Aburish, *The Rise, Corruption and Coming Fall of the House of Saud*, 277.

[63] Vassiliev, *The History of Saudi Arabia*, 316-317. The loans and the royalties were paid out of profits due to the government, instead of being in addition to the profits.

[64] Wald, *Saudi, Inc.*, 9.

World War II hampered the development of the oil industry in the kingdom, but by 1946 Standard Oil of California and Texaco saw that, even working together, they lacked sufficient capital to develop Saudi Arabia's oil potential. They approached Standard Oil of New Jersey (the company that became Exxon) and Socony Vacuum (later Mobil) to join them as partners in the Arabian American Oil Company or Aramco.[65] This venture expanded production significantly: Aramco extracted nine times more oil from Saudi Arabia in 1950 than

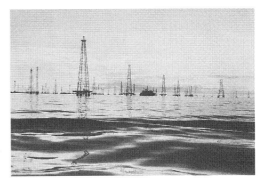

Socal's subsidiary had just five years earlier.[66] Such production helped make Aramco the largest American company operating overseas and produced such unprecedented profits that a year with a 200% return disappointed.[67] Naturally, this volume caught Saudi attention. The Americans were exploiting Saudi resources to produce vast wealth, yet the monarchy was not benefiting proportionately. In 1950, Abdullah Suleiman made it clear to an Aramco vice-president that Saudi Arabia was determined to get its fair share. The kingdom wanted to renegotiate the terms of the concession. This news scared Aramco executives, who decided at their November board meeting to offer the Saudis a 50-50 profit sharing arrangement. One reason Aramco was willing to do this was that, according to American tax rules at the time, foreign income taxes were tax deductible. Since Aramco's American tax rate was 38%, the company could soothe Saudi frustrations by offering the profit-sharing arrangement and still pay less overall tax as a result of the tax deduction.[68] Another factor was that Aramco had tens of millions of dollars invested in the development of the industry, which it could ill afford to lose.[69]

American trepidation in the face of Saudi discontent also stemmed from events in Latin America. In 1937, Bolivia nationalized its oil industry, and a year later Mexico followed suit.[70] In 1943, the world's largest petroleum exporter, Venezuela, passed its Hydrocarbons Act, which boosted royalties to 16.66% and imposed the world's first income tax on international oil companies. The net effect of these two fees was that the oil companies suddenly had to share 50% of their profits with the national government. Venezuela's unprecedented and unexpected action, one of the most important in Venezuela's history, established a new standard in relations between

---

[65] Socal, the forerunner of Chevron, owned 30% of Aramco; Texaco held 30%; Standard Oil of New Jersey, held 30%; and Socony Vacuum held 10%. Socony Vacuum was the product of a merger of Standard Oil of New York and Vacuum Oil in 1931.

[66] Vassiliev, *The History of Saudi Arabia*, 319. Production in 1945 was 21.3 million barrels and in 1950 was 199.5 million barrels.

[67] Lacey, *The Kingdom*, 291.

[68] Wald, *Saudi, Inc.,* 55, 57, 68-70, 75.

[69] Socal had invested $10 million in Saudi Arabia even before the drilling on Dammam Well No. 7 began in 1936. See Wald, *Saudi, Inc.,* 16. Removing much of the infrastructure was impractical.

[70] The nationalization of the oil industry in Mexico is celebrated as a national holiday. Although international economist Noel Maurer argues that the conditions in Mexico in 1938 did not fit the typical criteria for nationalization (rising corporate profits, a diminished likelihood of punishment, and declining costs associated with expropriation), the action itself showed that there was sufficient potential for civil unrest to force a government to intervene, with dire costs to the foreign companies. See Noel Maurer, "The Empire Strikes Back: Sanctions and Compensation in the Mexican Oil Expropriation of 1938," *The Journal of Economic History*, vol. 71, no. 3 (September 2011), 590-615, EBSCOhost.

governments and foreign oil companies.[71] After World War II, Venezuela's development minister, Juan Pablo Pérez Alfonzo, armed with copies the 50-50 profit sharing arrangement translated into Arabic, travelled to the Middle East to share its details with the other oil producing states.[72] This forced Aramco's board in November 1950 to offer Saudi Arabia the same deal it had offered Venezuela.[73]

Pérez Alfonzo's motivation for reaching out to Arab leaders had several components. Although a fierce nationalist, Pérez Alfonzo was also a realist. He knew that Venezuela's petroleum industry still required foreign assistance, despite its quarter century lead on Saudi Arabia.[74] His objective was changing, not severing, the relationship with foreign oil companies. As Pérez Alfonzo said in November 1945,

> the defense of our national economy and the necessity of using foreign capital for development of our natural resources can be harmonized without trouble....It is in Venezuela's best interest to permit development of its oil petroleum resources under the present arrangement of foreign capital and technicians. There is no intention to nationalize the industry or expropriate properties.[75]

Since nationalization was not a viable option, Pérez Alfonzo had to strengthen his hand by building alliances with other oil producers. This had to be done quickly: Pérez Alfonzo realized that because the United States was moving from being a net exporter of oil to a net importer in the postwar boom, it would buy cheaper oil from the Middle East if it could. In order to preserve Venezuela's market share, it was important for other oil producing nations strike similar 50-50 profit-sharing agreements.[76] Pérez Alfonzo's trip to Iraq, Iran, and Saudi Arabia in 1948 was a bold attempt to persuade other them to work together to overcome the disadvantageous concession agreements they had made in the opening decades of the twentieth century. This effort was cut short, however,

---

[71] Stephen G. Rabe, *The Road of OPEC: United States Relations with Venezuela, 1919-1976* (Austin, Texas: University of Texas Press, 1982), 87; and Terry Lynn Karl, *The Paradox of Plenty: Oil Booms and Petro-States* (Berkeley, California: University of California Press, 1997), 85, 87. Although the 1943 law established the 50-50 precedent, there were technicalities. See Francisco Parra, *Oil Politics: A Modern History of Petroleum* (London and New York: I. B. Tauris, 2004), 15. Parra says that "rising oil prices in 1946 and 1947 again resulted in a shortfall in payments." This situation led to an amended law in November 1948 "to provide for an additional tax (*Impuesto Adicional*) to be set at whatever amount was needed to bring total tax payments by each company to a minimum of 50% of its pre-tax profits....Although the 1943 Hydrocarbons Law was designed to produce a 50/50 split of profits, it was therefore not until 1948 that 50/50 became a legal reality."

[72] Raul Gallegos, *Crude Nation: How Oil Riches Ruined Venezuela* (Lincoln, Nebraska: University of Nebraska Press, 2016), 64; and Miguel Tinker Sales, *The Enduring Legacy: Oil, Culture, and Society in Venezuela* (Durham, North Carolina: Duke University Press, 2009), 218-219.

[73] Thanks to the vastness of Saudi reserves and the efficiency of its production per well, however, the 50-50 deal did not adversely affect Aramco's bottom line. Between 1949 and 1951, the company's profits still rose by 300%. See Aburish, *The Rise, Corruption and Coming Fall of the House of Saud*, 275; and Lacey, *Inside the Kingdom*, 279.

[74] The Venezuelan government issued the first oil concession in 1910, twenty-three years before Abdul Aziz granted his concession. The Caribbean Oil Company struck oil in commercial quantities in 1914 at a depth of 443 feet, which was a thousand feet closer to the surface than many fields in the Middle East. See Gallegos, *Crude Nation,* 57.

[75] Juan Pablo Pérez Alfonzo quoted in Sales, *The Enduring Legacy*, 210.

[76] Karl, *The Paradox of Plenty*, 88; and Federico Vélez, *Latin American Revolutionaries and the Arab World: From the Suez Canal to the Arab Spring* (New York: Routledge, 2016), 137.

when the Venezuelan military staged a *coup d'état* against president Rómulo Gallegos in November 1948, forcing Pérez Alfonzo into exile.[77]

All had not been lost. Pérez Alfonzo had planted a seed that Saudi Arabia's oil director, Abdullah Tariki, began to cultivate. By the time he visited Mexico and Venezuela on a fact-finding mission in September 1951, Tariki's had become quite hostile to the international oil companies, especially Aramco.[78] Part of the antagonism was philosophical, for Tariki was an ardent Arab nationalist, but part of his animosity was personal: Tariki had faced racial discrimination while obtaining his master's degree in petroleum engineering at the University of Texas in the late 1940s, and he was repeatedly insulted by Aramco officials in Dhahran. In fact, despite having a White American wife, Aramco initially refused to allow Tariki to live in the senior staff compound because his presence would violate the camp's decidedly Jim Crow culture.[79] In 1956, Tariki quietly surveyed Middle Eastern nations to learn the specifics of each nation's still-secret concession terms. He learned that although there were subtle differences, the basic stipulations disadvantaged Arab nations and Iran because all involved extended timelines, vast areas, and no possibility of renegotiation. The concessions also allowed oil companies near-total control of both production levels and prices.[80] In the mid-1950s, Tariki determined that Aramco was not actually sharing 50% of the profits with the Saud monarchy; the ratio was closer to 68% to 32% because, in addition to the IRS tax break, any determination of profit came after the company's expenses—even extravagant ones—had been deducted. In addition, Aramco sold Saudi oil to Socal, Mobil, and Texaco at discounted rates, but these companies neglected to pass the savings onto their customers.

---

[77] The *coup d'état* of November 24, 1948 replaced a democratically-elected government with a military dictatorship. The junta was soon dominated by Colonel Marcos Pérez Jiménez, who had an emphatic pro-American business orientation. Under Pérez Jiménez, strikes became illegal, no new taxes were imposed, oil production increased, and oil company profits soared. Pérez Alfonzo's party, Acción Democrática, was outlawed and those leaders who didn't flee Venezuela were imprisoned. Pérez Jiménez enjoyed the full support of the Eisenhower administration because of his pro-business, anti-leftist orientation. After nearly a decade in power, however, Pérez Jiménez faced opposition from within the military by frustrated younger officers and a general public that sought the restoration of democracy. See Miguel Tinker Salas, *Venezuela: What Everyone Needs to Know* (New York: Oxford University Press, 2015), 85-86, 90-92; John Lombardi, *Venezuela: The Search for Order, the Dream of Progress* (New York: Oxford University Press, 1982), 225-226; and Rabe, *The Road of OPEC*, 126-129, among other sources.

[78] Wald, *Saudi, Inc.*, 126.

[79] While in Texas, Tariki was repeatedly mistaken for a Mexican or Mexican-American and therefore discriminated against. The Aramco camp, like its counterparts in Mexico and Venezuela in the 1930s, segregated employees by race and provided the best accommodations and amenities only to whites. The atmosphere was intentionally similar to that of the Jim Crow American South. Tariki was proud to have broken through this barrier. He once noted, "I was the first Arab to penetrate into the tight Aramco compound, and I never saw such narrower people." Tariki's wife was reproved by a group of Aramco wives for marrying an Arab. See "Saudi Arabia: Sticking Point," *Time*, Vol. LXXII, No. 17 (October 27, 1958), 25-26, and "Middle East: Oil Politics," *Time*, Vol. LXXIII, No. 17 (April 27, 1959), 22. For detailed information on the Dhahran camp, see Vitalis, *America's Kingdom*, 22-26, 252-255. For information on similar situations in Venezuela, see Sales, *The Enduring Legacy*, 143-145. "White" and "Black" are both intentionally capitalized. See Chapter F, footnote 60.

[80] Tariki was joined on this fact-finding mission by Mohammed Salman, the Arab League's director of petroleum affairs, and Anes Qasem, a Palestinian lawyer who worked for Libya. See Christopher R. W. Dietrich, *Oil Revolution: Anticolonial Elites, Sovereign Rights, and the Economic Culture of Decolonization* (New York: Cambridge University Press, 2017), 68.

This meant that Saudi Arabia was effectively being excluded from its full share of the sales of its own oil.[81]

In April 1959, the Arab Petroleum Congress met in Cairo to examine what could be done legally to change the nations' relationships with the world's largest oil companies,[82] known as the Seven Sisters.[83] Venezuela's Pérez Alfonzo, now back in office, attended the conference as an observer. He told the attendees that Middle Eastern oil was being sold at too low a price in Western Europe, and that the region's countries needed to work together to not increase production.[84] During one of the quieter days of the conference, Pérez Alfonzo, Tariki, and representatives from Kuwait, Iran, and the United Arab Republic slipped away to the suburb of Maadi for a private meeting. These men agreed that it was important for their nations to put aside their differences and begin working together. They needed to collaborate to resist unilateral price changes by oil companies, gain a greater share of profits, and create their own national oil companies and regulatory agencies. Their agreement, known as the Maadi Pact, was the first step in the establishment of the Organization of the Petroleum Exporting Countries (OPEC).[85]

~

Zaki Yamani became Saudi Arabia's minister of petroleum and mineral resources in March 1962, after King Faisal fired Tariki for a combination of impertinence, radicalism, and insubordination. Tariki had become a celebrity among ardent Arab nationalists for his vocal criticisms of Aramco and other Western oil companies and for his praise for Iran's Mohammad Mosaddeq, the Iranian prime minister who had nationalized the nation's oil industry before being overthrown in a CIA-led *coup d'état* in 1953.[86] Tariki's orientation and methods were discomfiting to Faisal's conservative nature. Faisal believed that Tariki was overstepping his authority, forgetting that he

---

[81] Lacey, *The Kingdom*, 330-331. The discounted rate Aramco provided its parent companies was as much as 18%. Another expert puts the Saudi percentage of profits at only 22%. See Vitalis, *America's Kingdom,* 134.
[82] Dietrich, *Oil Revolution,* 70.
[83] The Seven Sisters were the companies that by 1980 became British Petroleum, Chevron, Exxon, Gulf, Mobil, Royal Dutch Shell, and Texaco. These companies were more partners than competitors because they shared mutual interests in the Middle East. It wasn't until Idaho's Senator Frank Church held hearings in 1974 and 1975 that the interlocking relationships these corporations had with one another and with Compagnie française des pétroles (CFP) or Total became fully understood. Church's subcommittee determined, for example, that the Abu Dhabi Petroleum Corporation was owned by BP (23.75%), Shell (23.75%), Total (23.75%), Exxon (11.876%), and Mobil (11.876%); and the Iranian Consortium consisted of BP (40%), Chevron (7%), Exxon (7%) Gulf (7%), Mobil (7%), Shell (7%), Texaco (7%), Total (6%). See Anthony Sampson, *The Seven Sisters: The Great Oil Companies and the World They Made* (New York: Viking Press, 1975), 169.
[84] "Venezuela Spurs Arabs in Oil Talks," *The New York Times*, April 18, 1959, 6, ProQuest Historical Newspapers. Pérez Alfonzo was Venezuela's minister of mines and hydrocarbons from February 1959 to January 1963, during the second government of Rómulo Betancourt.
[85] The other men present in the meeting were Ahmed Sayyid Omar of Kuwait, Manucher Farmanfarmaian of Iran, Iraq's Mohammed Salman of the Arab League's Petroleum Committee, and Seleh Nesim of the United Arab Republic. See M. S. Vassiliou, *Historical Dictionary of the Petroleum Industry* (Lanham, Maryland: Scarecrow Press, 2009), 316-317, EBSCOhost. OPEC was officially established in Baghdad in September 1960; for a detailed account of its creation see Ghanem, *OPEC*, 27-35.
[86] Wald, *Saudi, Inc.,* 132.

worked for the king, rather than for himself or for the nation as a whole.[87] The final straw came when Tariki publicly accused Faisal of siphoning 2% of the profits from a Japanese joint-venture project in order to benefit of one of Faisal's brothers-in-law.[88] Faisal pushed Tariki into exile and appointed Yamani, who had proven loyalty and a decidedly different personal temperament.[89] This meant that Yamani served as Saudi Arabia's representative to OPEC. He also chaired Petromin, the national Saudi oil company formed in 1962 that Saudis hoped would one day replace the Arabian American Oil Company (Aramco).[90] In addition, he administered a substantial governmental bureaucracy with financial, geological, technical, and legal departments.[91]

One of Yamani's first actions as Minister of Petroleum and Mineral Resources was to fly to San Francisco to attend an Aramco board meeting. No one at Aramco knew what to expect of the thirty-one-year old, but Yamani proved to be so level-headed, gracious, and disarming that he was invited to informal social events with company executives.[92] This helped Yamani to establish a new, less adversarial, relationship with the Americans and overcome Tariki's reputation for being hotheaded, arrogant, and anti-American.[93] Yamani's goals were not substantially different than Tariki's, for Yamani candidly said, "The problem of prices is a historical problem. In this subject, we want nothing more than justice." He added, "if we desire to ensure our revenues from petroleum or even their increase, we cannot be blamed since we are the owners of this natural wealth."[94] Tariki and Yamani differed in their styles of the delivery and in their expectations for the speed of change. Yamani's demeanor made his even aggressive statements more palatable to American ears, just as his understanding that Saudi Arabia was not yet ready for complete control of its oil fields fit well with King Faisal's desire to preserve American relations.[95] By the time Yamani attended his first OPEC conference in April 1962, he possessed the wherewithal to support an Iranian resolution that Western oil companies should fairly compensate OPEC nations for the inherent value of a precious, nonrenewable resource; at the same time, he could preserve positive relations with Aramco.[96] Later that year, Yamani began putting his personal stamp on the organization: because the oil companies refused to recognize OPEC but regularly met with him, Yamani decided to put himself into the middle of the equation. He convinced several key OPEC members to allow him to serve as their chief representative and then invited oil company executives to a meeting. Once gathered, Yamani announced that other OPEC members were present at his invitation as well. "Frankly, there was

[87] Aburish, *The Rise, Corruption and Coming Fall of the House of Saud*, 253.
[88] Vitalis, *America's Kingdom*, 233-234.
[89] Aburish, *The Rise, Corruption and Coming Fall of the House of Saud*, 257; and Robinson, *Yamani*, 48.
[90] Steffen Hertog, "Petromin: The Slow Death of Statist Oil Development in Saudi Arabia," *Business History*, 50 (5) (2008), 645-667.
[91] Fouad Al-Farsy, *Saudi Arabia: A Case Study in Development* (London: Stacey International, 1978), 109.
[92] Robinson, *Yamani*, 52-53. One of these events was a family birthday party hosted by Socal's vice president George T. Ballou.
[93] These qualities made Tariki a hero for many Arabs and simultaneously upset many Americans. One Aramco official who met him as a young geologist said, Tariki was "very supercilious, almost insulting…[and] so anti-American…it showed." See Richard Wallace ("Brock") Powers, "American Perspectives of Aramco, the Saudi-Arabian Oil-Producing Company, 1930s to 1980s : Oral History Transcript, 1995," 415, Regional Oral History Office, Bancroft Library, University of California-Berkeley, accessed February 16, 2020, https://archive.org/details/aramcooilproduc00hickrich.
[94] Ahmed Zaki Yamani quoted in Dietrich, *Oil Revolution*, 104.
[95] Vassiliev, *King Faisal of Saudi Arabia*, 344.
[96] Dietrich, *Oil Revolution*, 111. The resolution called for compensation for the "intrinsic value of petroleum." Pérez Alfonso and Tariki also viewed oil as having special value because of its limited supplies and essential role in industrialized economies.

nothing much they could do about it….They were finally seeing OPEC."[97] Three years later, in 1965, Yamani moved the organization's headquarters from Geneva to Vienna after Switzerland refused to give OPEC full diplomatic recognition. The Austrian capital was Yamani's choice because it had one of the Europe's great opera houses.[98]

Despite Yamani's efforts, OPEC remained internally divided and weak throughout the 1960s. At the November 1964 meeting in Jakarta, for example, a rift opened between those countries which advocated for a gradual change in the contracts with oil companies and valued international arbitration and those nations which wanted immediate change and saw arbitration as an affront to national sovereignty.[99] More problems emerged the following year. At the July 1965 meeting in Tripoli, members agreed to a 20% increase in total production, but, because the increases were not evenly distributed, no country honored the agreement. Nine months later in Vienna, OPEC made another attempt to control production—a defining element of a true cartel—but its members again failed to follow through on the deal they had negotiated.[100] No event showcased OPEC's limitations more than the Six-Day War* in 1967, when Arab members pushed for an oil embargo against the United States and Great Britain for their support of Israel. When Iran and Venezuela refused to participate, seeking to take advantage of the anticipated oil shortage, the embargo lost all hope of influencing American or British policy. Yamani bemoaned OPEC's inability to use its resources effectively, saying that if OPEC failed to use its oil as a weapon, "we are behaving like someone who fires a bullet into the air, miss[es] the enemy, and allow[s] it to rebound on himself."[101]

Just when it looked like OPEC was destined to remain an organization that oil importers could largely ignore, the international oil market shifted from a buyers' market to a sellers' market. Demand began to outstrip supply. This shift came as the result of many factors, including, the Six-Day War's closure of the Suez Canal and the Trans-Arabian Pipeline to Lebanon, the drop in Nigerian oil production as a result of the Biafran War,* and a peak in American oil production.[102] OPEC responded to the changing circumstances by trying to improve its members' position. It resolved at its December 1970 meeting in Vienna "to establish 55 per cent as the minimum rate of taxation on the net income of the oil companies operating in Member Countries," and to enter into negotiations to secure more attractive deals.[103] Several OPEC members took far more radical measures. In late February 1971, Algeria seized 51% control of all French oil interests within its

[97] Ahmed Zaki Yamani quoted in Robinson, *Yamani*, 55.
[98] Robinson, *Yamani,* 55.
[99] The gradualists were Saudi Arabia, Iran, Kuwait, Libya, and Qatar. Iraq, Venezuela, and Indonesia formed the block Christopher R. W. Dietrich calls the "insurrectionists." See Dietrich, *Oil Revolution,* 113.
[100] Ghanem, *OPEC,* 78, 80-81. Ghanem defines a cartel as a group that limits production to control price.
[101] Ahmed Zaki Yamani quoted in Sampson, *The Seven Sisters,* 175.
[102] Dietrich, *Oil Revolution,* 196. Dietrich describes the complex interplay between the Nixon administration and the governments of Iran, Libya, and Saudi Arabia between 1969 and 1972. See pages 159-223.
[103] "Resolution XXI. 120," [December 28, 1970], *OPEC Official Resolutions and Press Releases, 1960-1980* (New York: Pergamon Press, 1980), 99.

borders and nationalized all oil and gas pipelines.[104] Libya nationalized the operations of British Petroleum that December in the wake of a diplomatic dispute.[105] Iraq followed suit in June 1972.[106]

Yamani was not tempted by this nationalization movement. As he once said, rapid nationalization risked "kill[ing] the goose that lays the golden eggs." Instead, Yamani preferred a strategy of "squeezing the goose without killing it."[107] In fact, Yamani outlined his philosophical approach to the issue as early as 1968. In a speech at the American University of Beirut entitled "Participation vs. Nationalism, a Better Means to Survive," Yamani argued that a gradual Saudi integration into Aramco's operations would serve his nation's long-term interests better than nationalization. What he wanted was joint ownership, for he believed that such a participatory partnership was "the only way to ensure stability in the market...to safeguard the security of our future income from oil, and to ensure that we do not find ourselves at the mercy of adverse market forces which we would be powerless to influence or control."[108] Yamani worried about Saudi Arabia's limiting itself only to the profits from the extraction of its petroleum resources. He thought increased wealth would come from greater proximity to the retail market, and the best way to do this was to gain control of Aramco. As he said in Beirut, "our main target is the downstream operations because these are the key to the stability of prices in the world markets."[109] Yamani understood that in the late 1960s and early 1970s many oil producing nations still needed Western expertise and marketing to make full use of their most precious resource.[110] This is why, in June 1968, OPEC stipulated that "when a Member Government is not capable of developing its hydrocarbon resources directly, it may enter into contracts" with outside operators. Under Yamani's influence, the resolution also held that such governments "shall seek to retain the greatest measure possible of participation in and control over all aspects of operations," and that the "the terms and conditions of such contracts shall be open to revision at predetermined intervals."[111] While Aramco officials initially dragged their heels over participation, ultimately they accepted the strategy because the alternatives for them were so much worse. As Aramco's president and CEO said, "Participation was Yamani's idea that the government would buy into Aramco and become a

---

[104] "French Oil Assets Seized by Algeria," *New York Times*, Feb 25, 1971, 1, ProQuest Historical Newspapers.

[105] Raymond H. Anderson, "Libya Seizes British Oil Concern, Charging a London Conspiracy in Iran's Occupation of 3 Islands." *New York Times*, Dec 08, 1971, 11, ProQuest Historical Newspapers. On November 30, 1971, Great Britain formally ended its protectorate of the Trucial States in the Persian Gulf, which were comprised of the sheikhdoms of Abu Dhabi, Ajman, Dubai, Fujairah, Ras al-Khaimah, Sharjah, and Umm Al Quwain. Iran seized the small but strategically valuable islands of Abu Musa, Greater Tunbs, and Lesser Tunbs that same day. This prompted the Libyans to nationalize British Petroleum assets in protest for what they perceived to be an anti-Arab conspiracy by the British and Iranians. For more information on this dispute and the events that led to the creation of the United Arab Emirates, see Vassiliev, *The History of Saudi Arabia*, 380-383; and Dietrich, *Oil Revolution*, 241-242.

[106] "Iraq Takes Over Big Oil Company After Talks Fail," *New York Times*, June 2, 1972, 1, ProQuest Historical Newspapers.

[107] Ahmed Zaki Yamani quoted in Sherrill, *The Oil Follies of 1970-1980*, 132.

[108] Ahmed Zaki Yamani quoted in Ghanem, *OPEC*, 108-109.

[109] Ahmed Zaki Yamani quoted in Ghanem, *OPEC,* 109. "Downstream" is an economic term that means those operations that are closer to retail; "upstream" involves those operations closest to the raw materials.

[110] Peter Ellis Jones, *Oil: A Practical Guide to the Economies of World Production* (New York: Nicolas Publishing Company, 1988), 34-35.

[111] "Resolution XVI. 90," [June 24-25, 1968], *OPEC Official Resolutions and Press Releases, 1960-1980* (New York: Pergamon Press, 1980), 81.

true participant." He added, "through this method, the Saudis would become a shareholder and fight off the rest of the producing governments, who were hell-bent to nationalize."[112]

In December 1972, Yamani announced on the radio that after rigorous negotiations through the course of the summer and fall, he had secured a landmark deal for Saudi participation in Aramco. The final agreement provided for an immediate 25% Saudi ownership of the American company and timetable for gradually increasing that control: by January 1, 1982, Saudi Arabia would own 51% of Aramco. In compensation, Saudi Arabia agreed to pay Aramco approximately $500 million.[113] Significantly, this compensation was only for the above-ground investments Aramco had already made in Saudi Arabia, rather than for any rights to Saudi oil reserves underground, which were the essential part of Abdul Aziz's original concession. The leading Aramco negotiator bemoaned, "We never got any payment for the reserves, which were a terrific value."[114] In flipping the power dynamic between the American oil company and the Saudi royal family, Yamani made Aramco's owners "instruments of nations whose interests did not necessarily parallel our own," as former Secretary of State Henry Kissinger once complained. Yamani's formula was, in fact, "a revolution permitting OPEC governments to establish prices unilaterally."[115] Yamani was so proud of his success that he boasted that his agreement was four times better than the one the Shah of Iran had reached earlier that year.[116] Yamani's negotiating skill, which stemmed from his unique combination of perspicaciousness, cultural sensitivity, and geniality, had served King Faisal exceptionally well.[117]

~

On October 6, 1973, Egyptian and Syrian forces attacked Israeli positions along the Suez Canal and in the Golan Heights in an effort to recapture the occupied territories Israel had gained during the Six-Day War. Yamani was en route to Vienna to negotiate new oil prices with representatives of the major oil companies when he learned the news.[118] The outbreak of the Yom Kippur War did not in itself change Yamani's bargaining strategy. He knew that, allowing for inflation, oil prices

---

[112] Frank Jungers quoted in McMurray, *Energy to the World,* 41.

[113] Wald, *Saudi, Inc.,* 183. In late 2019, Aramco had the largest initial public offering (IPO) in history: within the first six days of trading, its valuation reached $2.03 trillion. This outstripped the combined value of ExxonMobil, Chevron, Total, BP, and Royal Dutch Shell. It also far outdistanced the value of companies such as Apple and Microsoft, which were both worth $1.2 trillion in late 2019. See Stanley Reed, "Now Saudi Arabia's Aramco Is Worth $2 Trillion," *San Francisco Chronicle,* December 17, 2019, D2.

[114] George Piercy quoted in Robinson, *Yamani,* 69.

[115] Henry Kissinger, *Years of Upheaval* (Boston, Massachusetts: Little, Brown and Company, 1982) 868-869.

[116] James Bamberg, *British Petroleum and Global Oil, 1950-1975* (Cambridge, U.K.: Cambridge University Press, 2000), 472. According to the Shah Mohammad Reza Pahlavi's agreement, Iran received a 20% share, compared to Saudi Arabia's 25% share, and there was no provision for an eventual majority ownership.

[117] In a confidential memorandum to President Gerald Ford dated August 23, 1975, Senate Majority Leader Mike Mansfield, a Democrat from Montana, described Yamani as "perspicacious." See "Memorandum from Mike Mansfield to the President, August 23, 1975," in Box 9, folder "Congressional Leadership Meetings with the President - 9/4/75: Bipartisan" of the John Marsh Files at the Gerald R. Ford Presidential Library, accessed February 16, 2020, https://www.fordlibrarymuseum.gov/library/document/0067/1562903.pdf

[118] Faisal had been hesitant to let Yamani attend the meeting in Vienna, or an earlier one in San Francisco, but the reasons for the king's behavior only became clear once Yamani was en route. See Lacey, *The Kingdom,* 397-398; and Robinson, *Yamani,* 84-85.

were less in 1970 than they had been in 1958,[119] and he was determined to obtain a substantial increase in the official, posted price.[120] On October 8, 1973, Yamani met with Exxon's George Piercy and Shell's André Bénard in Yamani's suite on the top floor of the Intercontinental Hotel in Vienna. They were joined by Iran's oil minister Jamshid Amouzegar. Yamani began the negotiations by asking for a $3 or 100% increase in the posted price. The oil executives countered with 45¢ or 15% increase. Six days later, the two sides were little closer to finding a compromise: Yamani held firm with a price over $5 a barrel, while the oil executives remained under $4 a barrel. With this impasse, Piercy and Bénard announced that they needed time to consult with government officials in Washington, The Hague, and London.[121] This stalling tactic annoyed Yamani, who responded with silence, and the meeting broke up without a settlement. The next day, when Piercy telephoned Yamani and asked about next steps, Yamani said, "You can hear it on the radio."[122] On October 16, representatives from the Organization of Arab Petroleum Exporting Countries (OAPEC) met in Kuwait and set the posted price unilaterally at $5.11 per barrel. Yamani said, "This was the moment for which I have been waiting a long time. The moment has come. We are masters of our own commodity."[123] This victory meant that oil producers would never again negotiate prices with Western oil companies. Instead, OPEC and OAPEC would set them. The victory also propelled Yamani into the limelight. Media from around the world hung on his every word for the next thirteen years.[124]

Just before 9:00 p.m. on October 17, the Riyadh airport security chief received a call ordering him to close the airport to all traffic except for one private jet arriving from Kuwait. Two black Cadillacs and a police escort then rushed Yamani from the tarmac to King Faisal's palace. In Yamani's pocket was an unlined piece of paper filled with his handwriting that included corrections, deletions and amendments.[125] It was the announcement that, during the Kuwait summit, the members of OAPEC had agreed that they would reduce oil production by at least 5% each month until Israel withdrew from the Occupied Territories and restored Jerusalem to Arab control.[126] It also contained the announcement that OAPEC wanted an oil embargo against Israel's supporters, but had ultimately left the decision up to each Arab government. According to Yamani, Faisal did not what to impose the embargo on the United States,[127] but when

---

[119] Wald, *Saudi, Inc.,* 184-186; and Lacey, *The Kingdom,* 186.

[120] "Posted price" is a term that originated in the early days of oil well drilling. It was the price at which the owner of a particular oil well was willing to sell his oil. Today, it is the published price for oil purchased in lots at tanker terminals. It is not the real price. An analogy is the window price tag at a car dealership: it is a starting point for the sale, not the final price.

[121] Wald, *Saudi, Inc.,* 185; and Lacey, *The Kingdom,* 404.

[122] Ahmed Zaki Yamani quoted in Lacey, *The Kingdom,* 405.

[123] Ahmed Zaki Yamani quoted in Thomas W. Lippman, *Inside the Mirage: America's Fragile Partnership with Saudi Arabia* (Boulder, Colorado: Westview Press, 2004), 156.

[124] John Greenwald, "Wild Goodbye to Mr. Oil," *Time,* Vol. 128, no. 19 (November 10, 1986), 42.

[125] William Powell, *Saudi Arabia and Its Royal Family* (Secaucus, New Jersey: Lyle Stuart Inc., 1982), 78-80.

[126] Vassiliev, *The History of Saudi Arabia,* 335; and Lacey, *The Kingdom,* 393. Saudi Arabia and Kuwait immediately cut their production 10%.

[127] Robinson, *Yamani,* 94.

the Nixon administration, then quite consumed by the Watergate Scandal,[128] foolishly asked Congress for a $2.2 billion aid package for Israel in the last weekend of the war,[129] Faisal took the request as a personal insult. He declared *jihad* and ordered that all oil shipments to the United States immediately cease.[130] Yamani then called Aramco's CEO Frank Jungers and told him that Aramco would have to enforce the embargo. Jungers complied.[131] The company's relationship with the kingdom would never be the same: the balance of power had decisively and permanently shifted.

In December 1973, the oil ministers of Saudi Arabia, six Gulf States, and Iran met in Tehran to set a new round of prices. Although oil had sold for as much as $17 per barrel on the open, spot market since the start of the embargo, the ministers agreed to a posted price of $11.65. They considered the action "moderate" in "hope that the consuming countries will refrain from further increase of their export prices."[132] In other words, OAPEC decided not to raise oil prices as much as it could in hope that the West would not retaliate by raising the prices of industrially produced goods. OAPEC's decision was not well-received by King Faisal, who chided Yamani for agreeing to such a large increase.[133] It was also not well-received by American consumers—most of whom didn't know that the United States was an oil-importing nation.[134] Not only had the posted price jumped four-fold in just three months, but cutbacks for consumers loomed. In early December, President Nixon announced on television that because of rising cost of imported petroleum products, the U.S. needed to cut heating oil sales through the winter by 20%; limit the sale of gasoline in order to reduce private driving use by 30%; lower highway speeds to 50 mph for cars and 55 mph for trucks and buses to diminish consumption; and enforce a ban on unnecessary outdoor lighting, including Christmas lights.[135] With the arrival of the new year, the situation only worsened as the American bill for imported oil skyrocketed from $3.9 billion to $24 billion between 1972 and 1974. Countries that relied more heavily on imported oil than the United States suffered considerably more. By the end of 1974, for example, Japan's inflation rate hit 24% as a result of its $18 billion bill for oil imports, and the nation saw its first decline in economic growth since 1945 as a result. Similarly, Great Britain faced its worst economic crisis since the Depression; Italy had

---

[128] October 20, 1973 was the date of the "Saturday Night Massacre," when Nixon ordered Attorney General Elliot Richardson to fire Special Prosecutor Archibald Cox because of Cox's insistence that Nixon surrender his White House tapes. See "Richard Nixon Stumbles to the Brink," *Time*, Vol. 102, no. 18, (October 29, 1973), 12-19.

[129] The assessment that the timing of the announcement was foolish was Henry Kissinger's. See Kissinger, *Years of Upheaval*, 873.

[130] Lacey, *The Kingdom*, 412. Faisal may not have been willing to go along with an embargo until the announcement of the aid package. See Robinson, *Yamani*, 94. King Faisal, Yamani, other Saudis, and even American oil executives repeatedly warned the American government about the connection between the potential use of oil as a political weapon and support for Israel's control of the Occupied Territories, especially Jerusalem. See Lacey, *The Kingdom*, 398-402; and Vassiliev, *The History of Saudi Arabia*, 391. Nixon surprisingly did not listen to at least the oil executives, despite his political indebtedness to American oil companies, especially those in California. See Joan Hoff, *Nixon Reconsidered* (New York: Basic Books, 1994), 262-263.

[131] Wald, *Saudi, Inc.*, 191-192.

[132] "Press Release, No. 18-73," [December 24, 1973], *OPEC Official Resolutions and Press Releases, 1960-1980* (New York: Pergamon Press, 1980), 143.

[133] William D. Smith, "Faisal: He Changed the Balance of Power," *New York Times*, March 30, 1975, 125, ProQuest Historical Newspapers.

[134] Meg Jacobs, *Panic at the Pump: The Energy Crisis and the Transformation of American Politics in the 1970s* (New York: Hill and Wang, 2016), 4.

[135] "A Time of Learning to Live with Less," *Time*, Vol. 102, no. 23, (December 3, 1973), 29-30.

to borrow more than $13 billion to cover its trade deficit; and Greece witnessed Europe's highest gas prices at $2.50 a gallon—a cost so challenging that the government turned off the floodlights to the Acropolis to save money.[136] Those hardest hit by the spike in petroleum prices were the underdeveloped nations. These countries saw staggering increases in their foreign debt as they attempted to pay the new energy prices. The ratio of Zambia's debt to its exports, for example, grew from 5.7% in 1970 to 28.5% in 1973. In Peru, the ratio escalated from 13.9% to 32.2%. Brazil's debt, the highest in the world in 1979, reached $49 billion.[137] Debt servitude on this scale destined such nations to poverty for generations[138] and made day-to-day living difficult. In Sri Lanka, for example, where the price of fertilizer rose 375%, the rice harvest fell 40%.[139] Millions were left hungry as a result.

In contrast, the oil producers witnessed a vast infusion of cash into their economies as a result of the oil boom. In fact, between 1970 and 1974, the world witnessed history's largest transfer of wealth without war up to that point.[140] Nigeria's revenues from oil exports, for example, grew from $1.2 billion in 1972 to $9.2 billion in 1974, while Iran's jumped from $2.4 billion to $20.9 billion in the same two-year period.[141] In Venezuela, income from a single barrel of crude soared 587% between 1972 and 1975, which allowed the nation's new president, Carlos Andrés ("Cap") Pérez, to dream about transforming not just Venezuelan society, but all of Latin America. After his election in December 1973, Pérez secured emergency powers from the legislature that allowed him to issue more than a hundred decrees to establish price controls, create jobs, increase wages, expand social services, support agriculture, promote non-petroleum industries, and grant scholarships to send 10,000 students a year abroad for education. He also offered loans to the World Bank and provided aid to other Latin American nations suffering from the rise in oil prices.[142] His vision, known as La Gran Venezuela, was to "generate an order of social justice" in order to foster democracy in his country and throughout the region.[143] Thanks to the oil revenues, Venezuelans soon attained a per capita income that put them on par with West Germany,[144] and possessed sufficient cachet as a tourist destination to warrant Concorde Supersonic Service by Air France in 1976.[145] Similarly, as the world's largest oil producer, Saudi Arabia benefited the most from the price increases of the first energy crisis. As Yamani noted, "It was an extraordinary and unprecedented period in our history."[146] The nation's annual income from oil revenues rose from $2.8 billion in 1972 to $28.9 billion in 1974.[147] This infusion of capital fueled urban migration, promoted the establishment of a Saudi middle class, increased the numbers of immigrant workers, expanded basic literacy in Saudi

---

[136] "Faisal and Oil: Driving Toward a New World Order," *Time*, Vol. 105, no. 1 (January 6, 1975), 12.

[137] Paul Hallwood and Stuart W. Sinclair, *Oil, Debt & Development: OPEC in the Third World* (London: George Allen & Urwin, 1981), 91.

[138] John P. Powelson, "Oil Prices and the World Balance of Payments," *OPEC: Twenty Years and Beyond*, Ragaei El Mallakh (ed.) (Boulder, Colorado: Westview Press, 1982), 188, 192.

[139] "Faisal and Oil," 12.

[140] Karl, *The Paradox of Plenty*, xv, 3.

[141] "Faisal and Oil," 26.

[142] "The Petrolear Society," *Time*, Vol. 104, no. 25 (December 16, 1974), 46; and Karl, *The Paradox of Plenty*, 124.

[143] Carlos Andrés Pérez quoted in "Cap Pérez: No Longer Martyrs," *Time*, Vol. 104, no. 25 (December 16, 1974), 48.

[144] Karl, *The Paradox of Plenty*, 120. The per capita income rose from about $1250 to $2300 in 1975, thereby making Venezuela Latin America's wealthiest nation. See Rabe, *The Road of OPEC*, 188.

[145] Gallegos, *Crude Nation*, 74.

[146] Ahmed Zaki Yamani quoted in Robinson, *Yamani*, 129.

[147] "Faisal and Oil," 26.

children, and caused new roads, hospitals, universities, hotels, and airports to spring up almost overnight.[148] Not everyone in Saudi Arabia, however, was pleased by the enormity of these changes and their social consequences. As early as the mid-1960s there was significant skepticism in the nation about the impact of Western influences. As one Saudi said, "Modernization we want, we need, and we will have, but on our own terms."[149] King Faisal himself shared this ambivalence. He was as troubled by the changes oil wealth generated as he was by the rapidity with which these changes occurred. Faisal believed that the speedy influx of Western consumer goods and modern life threatened the Bedouin social fabric of the nation. He worried that he could be leading his people to damnation.[150] Perhaps to alleviate some of his guilt, Saudi Arabia provided extensive grants to Muslim nations without oil reserves, such as Afghanistan, Bangladesh, Morocco, Pakistan, and Sudan.[151]

~

In 1975, Yamani's faced two traumatic events. The first came mid-morning on March 25, when Kuwait's new oil minister, Abdul Mutaleb Kazimi, came to the royal palace to pay a short visit to King Faisal. Instead of a business meeting, it was just a chance for the king and the Kuwaiti minister to share a coffee and exchange courtesies in the Arab custom. A television crew was on hand to capture the moment. When the Kuwaitis arrived in the antechamber to the king's office, Kazimi found one of the king's many nephews, Prince Faisal bin Musaid, waiting in the modest room, apparently also for a scheduled appointment. Because the Kazimi and the prince knew each other, they greeted one another, and the nephew easily melded into the Kuwaiti delegation. Yamani arrived in the reception room a few minutes later to facilitate the diplomatic exchange between the king and the new oil minister. At 10:25, when King Faisal entered his office, Yamani went in to brief him. The king then walked into the anteroom to greet his guests. After welcoming Kazimi, the king turned to kiss his nephew. The prince pulled out a pistol from under his thobe and fired three times. The first shot hit the king in his neck, cutting the jugular vein; the second went through his ear; and the third grazed his forehead. Several more shots were also fired. At one point, Yamani, who was standing next to the king when the prince first fired, found the gun pointing at him. Bodyguards wrestled the prince to the ground and tied him up. The king, still barely alive, was rushed to the hospital, but his loss of blood was too great. He died within an hour, and was buried in an unmarked grave in accordance with Wahhabi teachings.[152] Saudi Arabia lost its king, and Yamani lost a man who had been like a father to him. He went into a period of deep mourning that lasted for months.[153]

---

[148] Vassiliev, *The History of Saudi Arabia*, 411, 428-429, 433-434; and Lacey, *The Kingdom*, 421.

[149] Anonymous source quoted in Thomas J. Abercrombie, "Saudi Arabia: Beyond the Sands of Mecca," *National Geographic*, Vol. 129, no. 1 (January 1966), 5.

[150] Lacey, *The Kingdom*, 423.

[151] Hallwood and Sinclair, *Oil, Debt & Development*, 113-114, 121, 123. Some non-Muslim countries also received aid, such as South Korea, which received $20.8 million in 1977. But this was a fraction of the increase South Korea saw in its total oil bill of $614.9 million.

[152] This account of King Faisal's death comes from a variety of sources, including Robinson, *Yamani*, 141-143; "The Death of a Desert Monarch," *Time*, Vol. 105, no. 14 (April 7, 1975), 15, 18; Vassiliev, *King Faisal of Saudi Arabia*, 443-444; and Lacey, *The Kingdom*, 426-427.

[153] Robinson, *Yamani*, 150-151.

The second traumatic event came when Yamani was in Vienna for an OPEC meeting. On December 21 at 11:40 a.m., five men and one woman approached a Ringstrasse office building across the street from Vienna University and asked a group of reporters standing on the snowy sidewalk if the oil ministers were still meeting inside.[154] Receiving a positive answer, the casually dressed group carrying sports bags purposefully strode into the lobby, walked past a security guard, and charged up the stairs to the second floor, where they pulled out machine guns and began firing. After shooting the three security officers, throwing a grenade down the staircase, and destroying the telephone switchboard, the terrorists burst into the conference room where the delegates were meeting and opened fire. Yamani dove under the conference table as the gunmen shot bullets everywhere. The room was quickly secured by the terrorists. In the silence that followed, Yamani heard someone speaking English ask the ominous question, "Have you found Yamani?" His heart sank. The notorious terrorist Carlos the Jackal, who Yamani knew had a death list with his name on it, now held the lives of 60 hostages in his hands. A long afternoon followed as the Austrian government considered Carlos' demands: 1) his pro-Palestinian, anti-Israeli manifesto be read on the radio; 2) his compatriot who had been wounded in the initial attack be released from the hospital and allowed to rejoin the terrorists; and 3) a bus with curtains drawn take him, his compatriots, and the hostages to the airport, where a fully fueled DC-9 would fly them wherever he wanted. The Austrian government agreed to these terms on the condition that all Austrians be released. At 6:22 p.m., 38 minutes before Yamani's scheduled execution, Austrian radio began reading Carlos' statement. The next morning, the Jackal loaded the remaining 41 hostages onto the specially outfitted bus, rode to the airport, boarded the plane, and flew to Algeria, where he planned to begin releasing hostages in stages. The first group of officials to be released were from Ecuador, Gabon, Indonesia, Nigeria, and Venezuela, because they were seen as neutral parties. From Algiers, the Jackal planned to fly to other Arab capitals, slowly releasing his prisoners, except for Yamani and Iranian oil minister Jamshid Amouzegar, whom Carlos repeatedly threatened with execution. In fact, as Yamani said later, "Their decision to assassinate us was final even if their demands were met."[155] The Jackal's plans were foiled in Tripoli, when the longer-range Boeing 707 was not delivered as arranged. Carlos decided to fly back to Algiers, where, after intense negotiations with Algerian officials, the drama ended and all of the hostages were released. Yamani expressed his gratitude to the Algerians, saying, "Without the intervention of our Algerian brethren, their firmness and wisdom, we would not have escaped death."[156] Austrian officials assumed that Carlos and his compatriots would be arrested and extradited, but as part of the deal the Algerians allowed the Carlos to go free. It is estimated that he did so with $20 million in payment for not killing any of the hostages.[157] Upon Yamani's release, his family flew from Switzerland to Algiers to find a

---

[154] In 1975, OPEC's headquarters was on the part of the Ringstrasse named after Vienna's anti-Semitic mayor Dr. Karl Lueger. In 2012, the city renamed this portion of the boulevard Universitätsring. See Bethany Bell, "Vienna Street Severs anti-Semite Link," *BBC News*, April 21, 2012, accessed February 16, 2020, https://www.bbc.com/news/world-europe-17797696

[155] Ahmed Zaki Yamani quoted in "Had Execution Set Says Saudi Oil Chief," *Chicago Tribune*, December 25, 1974, 14. https://chicagotribune.newspapers.com/image/382221046.

[156] Ahmed Zaki Yamani quoted in "Had Execution Set Says Saudi Oil Chief," 14.

[157] This kidnapping account is based upon a variety of sources, but especially John Follain, *Jackal: The Complete Story of the Legendary Terrorist Carlos the Jackal* (New York: Arcade Publishing, 1998), 81-98; and Robinson, *Yamani*, 152-172. There are minor discrepancies in the accounts, including the time that Carlos' manifesto was first read on the radio (Folain says 6:22 p.m. while Robinson says 5:20 p.m.), but since both authors interviewed Yamani, the fundamental details align. Other sources for the account include: 1) Clyde H. Farnsworth "Terrorists Raid OPEC Oil Parley in Vienna, Kill 3," *The New York Times*, Dec 22, 1975, 1,

grateful man who was convinced that he had barely escaped death for the second time in nine months.[158] Yamani arrived back in Saudi Arabia four days later to a hero's welcome.

The shared trauma of the kidnapping did not bring Yamani and Iranian oil minister Jamshid Amouzegar closer together. Instead, they feuded just as bitterly as they had at the April 1975 OPEC meeting in Vienna, when Amouzegar wanted at least a 20% hike in prices and Yamani argued for no more than 10%.[159] Their feud became increasingly evident at the OPEC meeting in Bali in May 1976, when the two men again locked horns over price increases. This time Yamani vigorously opposed even a nominal rise, while Amouzegar, supported by Algeria, Libya, and Venezuela, demanded a substantial price increase to compensate for inflation. Because a unanimous vote was required for any price adjustment, Yamani won the day, but OPEC's rupture loomed.[160] In fact, relations between the members were so fractured that the organization's press releases could only comment on procedural matters and by-laws, not policies.[161] At the next meeting, held in Doha, Qatar in December 1976, eleven nations agreed impose a 15.4% price increase over the course of the next twelve months, bringing the price to $12.70 a barrel, but Saudi Arabia and the United Arab Emirates refused to agree. Yamani walked out of the meeting and flew to Riyadh to consult with King Khalid, who was King Faisal's half-brother and heir. When Yamani returned to Doha, he announced that Saudi Arabia would go its own way, only raising prices 5%. Saudi oil would cost $12.08 a barrel and Saudi Arabia would increase its production.[162] The adoption of the two-tiered pricing system undercut OPEC's power, but Yamani was firm about the correctness of the decision. He said, "We live in a small world. If the rest of it suffers economically, we also suffer, no matter how high we raise the price of oil."[163]

The pressures on OPEC and the politics of world pricing for oil grew in the years that followed. On December 3, 1978, Iran's exiled spiritual leader Ayatollah Khomeini declared in France that "to strike in the oil sector is to do the will of God."[164] He wanted his followers to undercut Shah Mohammad Reza Pahlavi's major source of income. By December 25, Khomeini's followers had ensured that Iran had stopped exporting oil altogether. Because Iran was the world's second largest oil producer, this action sparked the decade's second international energy crisis. Yamani attempted to compensate for the changing circumstances in Iran by increasing Saudi production by two million barrels a day, but panic overtook the markets anyway.[165] This was despite the fact that there

---

ProQuest Historical Newspapers; 2) "Curtain Descends in Algiers on OPEC Terrorists' Fate," *New York Times*, Dec 24, 1975, 4, ProQuest Historical Newspapers; 3) "Murder Plan Laid to OPEC Raiders," *New York* Dec 25, 1975, 8, ProQuest Historical Newspapers; 4) Robert D. McFadden, "Terrorists Free All Of Hostages, Give Up In Algiers," *New York Times*, Dec 23, 1975, 1, ProQuest Historical Newspapers; and 5) "The Terrorists' Bold Gamble in Vienna," *Time*, Vol. 106, no. 26 (December 20, 1975), 20.

[158] Yamani separated from his first wife, Laila, in 1964; they had three children. Upon their separation, Yamani lived alone for nine years before signing his marriage contact (the *milka*) with his second wife, Tammam, in Mecca on March 23, 1975, two days before King Faisal's assassination. There are five children from the second marriage.

[159] "OPEC's Price Doves Win a Big One," *Time*, Vol. 106, no. 14 (October 6, 1975), 54.

[160] "Temporary Standoff at Bali," *Time*, Vol. 107, no. 24 (June 7, 1976), 66-69.

[161] "Press Release No. 5-76, Vienna, June 28, 1976," *OPEC Official Resolutions and Press Releases, 1960-1980* (New York: Pergamon Press, 1980), 163-164.

[162] The OPEC Supercartel in Splitsville," *Time*, Vol. 108, no. 26 (December 27, 1976), 52-53.

[163] Ahmed Zaki Yamani quoted in "The OPEC Supercartel in Splitsville," *Time*, Vol. 108, no. 26 (December 27, 1976), 52-53.

[164] Sayyid Ruhollah Mūsavi Khomeini quoted in Pierre Terzian, *OPEC: the Inside Story* (London: ZED books, 1985) 258.

[165] Yergin, *The Prize,* 665-667.

was actually an oil glut in December 1978.[166] The large Western oil companies drove prices higher because they hoarded supplies—a practice they began when Jimmy Carter banned all trade with Iran on November 13, 1978.[167] The outbreak of the Iraq-Iran War in September 1980 also fueled consumer anxieties. OPEC nations with limited reserves, like Algeria and Libya saw a new price spike as an opportunity that couldn't be missed[168] and greed took over. Soon, oil prices were like a runaway train: crude jumped from $13 a barrel in early 1978 to $40 a barrel in late 1980.[169] As with the 1973-1974 energy crisis, the impact on the world economy was profound as both industrial nations and developing nations struggled to manage inflation. Yamani, however, distinguished between the two events:

> There is no doubt that the initial dramatic increases in the oil prices that occurred in 1973-74 were economically justifiable, corrective measures that went a great distance in redressing the injustices of the oil companies' price regime. What happened in 1979-80, however, deprived OPEC of its touch with the economic realities which had given it the very justification for its actions in breaking loose from the oil companies' control and pricing regime. Very sadly, the dramatic increase in revenues of the producer countries proved to be too heady in the circumstances and gave OPEC many illusions as to how you could use its oil. The result was that political rather than economic considerations became dominant in the process of forming OPEC policies.[170]

In other words, political and emotional responses had unnaturally manipulated the laws of supply and demand in 1979-80. For Yamani, this was anathema, for he had an unshakeable faith in free trade and private enterprise. As he once said, "human initiative [is] a fundamental will of God" and the "free system has always functioned with admirable success and efficiency to the benefit of people everywhere."[171]

Those in the petroleum industry know that oil is a commodity particularly prone to boom and bust cycles. The next bust came in the 1980s, when a three-year, worldwide recession began the decade.[172] Demand for oil quickly fell. Ironically, this came just as the expansion of oil fields in the North Sea, Alaska, and Mexico allowed supplies and production to grow. By 1982, non-OPEC nations surpassed the production of OPEC members for the first time in twenty years.[173] While average prices fell to about $26 a barrel in August 1985, Yamani tried to keep prices from falling further by having Saudi Arabia become a flexible producer: the kingdom adjusted its production levels, usually with cutbacks, in an effort to stabilize prices. Although Saudi Arabia produced 10.3 million barrels a day in 1981, by June 1985 it produced only 2.0 million barrels a day. This strategy

[166] Sherrill, *The Oil Follies of 1970-1980*, 413.
[167] Sherrill, *The Oil Follies of 1970-1980*, 460.
[168] "The OPEC Supercartel in Splitsville," 52.
[169] "The Seven Lean Years," *Time*, Vol. 116 no. 25 (December 22, 1980), 54.
[170] Ahmed Zaki Yamani, "Forward," Fadhil J. Al-Chalabi, *OPEC at the Crossroads* (New York: Pergamon Press, 1989), ix.
[171] Ahmed Zaki Yamani, "Control and Decontrol in the Oil Market," *Vital Speeches of The Day*, 49, no. 16 (June 1983), 482, EBSCOhost. In the same speech, given at the University of Kansas, Yamani also admitted, however, that "oil price volatility" was "one of those things which do not conform to the model of a free market mechanism. The only means of combating it lies in control by a public authority."
[172] "Global Economic Slump Challenges Policies," *International Monetary Fund*, January 2009, accessed February 16, 2020, https://tinyurl.com/y5ge4g5c
[173] Charles P. Alexander, "The Humbling of OPEC," *Time*, Vol. 121, no. 6, (February 7, 1983), 43.

had two problems: 1) it was predicated upon other OPEC members honoring official prices and not exceeding their assigned production quotas; and 2) it caused a decline in the kingdom's revenue from $100 billion to $37 billion over the same four-year period. OPEC members did not respect the quota system, and Saudi Arabia faced an untenable budget deficit.[174] In response, Yamani announced that Saudi Arabia would stop propping up prices. He urged all oil-producing nations, OPEC members or not, to cut back their production. When his concerns went unheeded, Yamani decided to teach OPEC a lesson: he would let prices fall, for knew that Saudi Arabia could make more money selling 4.2 million barrels a day (mbd) at $20 a barrel than it could selling 2.3 mbd at $27.[175] As he told an Oxford University audience in September 1985, "Most of the OPEC member countries depend on Saudi Arabia to carry the burden and protect the price of oil. Now the situation has changed. Saudi Arabia is no longer willing or able to take that heavy burden and duty."[176] His nation would no longer be taken for granted. Saudi Arabian oil began flooding the market after another failed OPEC meeting in Geneva in December 1985, and prices began to fall. By April 1986, oil prices had fallen from $26 a barrel to $11, and by the end of the summer the bust was so complete that a barrel of oil sold for $7 in some markets.[177]

Yamani might have weathered this collapse if he had had a positive relationship with King Fahd, who had become the Saudi monarch in 1982. Fahd, however, resented Yamani's international prominence and increased proclivity for speaking as an authority on Saudi foreign policy issues not involving oil. Between 1982 and mid-1986, the king and his minister's relationship deteriorated to overt hostility. In truth, Yamani had become increasingly arrogant as the years passed. In a shocking *faux pas* in December 1980, for example, he used the first person singular when describing how Saudi oil policy was set. An interviewer asked Yamani if Saudi Arabia had plans to cut production and he replied, "If I returned to a ceiling of 8.5 million barrels per day, that would immediately affect you."[178] The answer made it seem as if he alone determined production levels and prices instead of the House of Saud. Such behavior from a commoner was unacceptable to King Fahd and other members of the royal family. The time was ripe for managerial change. The final break came in October 1986, when Fahd sent Yamani a cable during an OPEC meeting that ordered Yamani to set the price of oil at $18 a barrel and allow for an increase in Saudi Arabia's production quota. Yamani initially refused to present Fahd's idea because it was an impossibly unrealistic policy given market conditions, but did eventually agree to announce it. The problem was that he did so with such condescension that everyone saw Yamani's manner as an insult to his king.[179]

On October 29, 1986, Yamani was in his Riyadh home playing the French card game Belote when the evening news began its broadcast. The lead story was that King Fahd had fired Yamani as oil minister. This was how Yamani learned that his twenty-four-year service to the House of Saud had come to an end. His reaction reflected his characteristic composure: he simply sighed

---

[174] John S. De Mott, "Twinkle, Twinkle, Fading Star," *Time*, Vol. 126, no. 5 (August 5, 1985), 44; and "Breaking Rank," *Time*, Vol. 126, no. 13 (September 30, 1985), 66.
[175] Stephen Koepp, "Spoiling for an Oil-Price War," *Time*, Vol. 126, no. 25 (December 23, 1985), 44; and Robinson, *Yamani,* 271.
[176] Ahmed Zaki Yamani, "Debate at the Oxford Energy Seminar, 13 September 1985," *OPEC and the World Oil Market: The Genesis of the 1986 Price Crisis* (Oxford, U.K.: Oxford University Press, 1986), 166.
[177] Tom Bower, *Oil: Money, Politics, and Power in the 21st Century* (New York: Grand Central Publishing, 2009), 53.
[178] Ahmed Zaki Yamani quoted in "Some Blunt Talk from OPEC," *Time*, Vol. XXX, no. XXX (December 22 1980), 57.
[179] Robinson, *Yamani,* 32 and 278; Wald, *Saudi, Inc.,* 217; and Lacey, *Inside the Kingdom,* 91.

and went back to his game. He felt complete acceptance, accompanied by a sense of relief,[180] for as Yamani believed, "The Muslim who must be at peace with others must be at peace with himself. This is a necessary effect of the Muslim's total submission to the will of God."[181] Even the announcement that a long-standing rival was to replace him as minister did not produce a reaction. "It's the king's decision, and that's life," Yamani told a friend in Geneva.[182] The rest of the world, however, did not share Yamani's calm. The news sent shock waves globally, catching Reagan administration officials by surprise and sending oil prices seesawing wildly for over a week.[183] King Fahd was also worried about what Yamani's dismissal might mean. He initially forbade Yamani to leave the country and essentially put the oil celebrity under house arrest.[184]

~

Yamani's fiercest critics dismiss him as a media-hungry, powerless showman—a mere spokesman for Saudi royal policy—instead of an influential member of government.[185] While it is certainly true that Yamani enjoyed the spotlight, his ability to move seamlessly between the Arab and Western worlds meant that his influence did not end with his dismissal. Those who studied, covered, and worked in the petroleum industry still turned to Yamani for his expertise. In 1994, for example, he was a leading speaker at the Fifth Repsol-Harvard Seminar on Petroleum Policy, addressing experts in government, industry, and academia from Africa, Europe, Latin America, and North America on the problem of low oil prices. Yamani argued that consumers should be worried about another price spike.[186] Two years later, he was the keynote speaker at the Seventh Repsol-Harvard Seminar. In that speech, he analyzed the state of the world oil market and expressed his deep concern about the ways in which political pressures—particularly those of Americans—negatively affected the laws of supply and demand.[187] In 1990, Yamani founded a think tank, the Centre for Global Energy Studies in London, which until its closure in March 2014 offered independent evaluations of the economics and geopolitics of the petroleum industry.[188] The Centre came to be respected for its in-depth analyses of specific problems, such as Iraq's oil potential if

[180] Robinson, *Yamani*, 279.
[181] Ahmad Zaki Yamani, "Forward," in Hathout, *Reading the Muslim Mind*, xiii.
[182] Ahmad Zaki Yamani quoted in John Greenwald, "Wild Goodbye to Mr. Oil," *Time*, Vol. 128, no. 19 (November 10, 1986), 42. The rival was Hisham Nazer (1932-2015). He was oil minister from 1986 to 1995.
[183] Greenwald, "Wild Goodbye to Mr. Oil," 42. Prices initially "dropped more than a $1.10 a barrel in New York City and then climbed nearly $2 to about $15.25 by week's end."
[184] Robinson, *Yamani*, 280.
[185] See, for example, Aburish, *The Rise, Corruption and Coming Fall of the House of Saud*, 261, where Yamani is characterized as "a dispensable technocrat," who did not affect Saudi oil policy, who was not respected by King Faisal, whose most meaningful legacy was simply to illustrate "the banality of glamour."
[186] Ahmed Zaki Yamani, "Introductory Remarks and Comments," *Barcelona 1994*, accessed February 16, 2020, https://imagenes.repsol.com/es_eu/03BARCEL~1__53601_tcm9-67091.pdf
[187] Ahmed Zaki Yamani, "The State of The World Oil Market," *Granada 1996*, accessed February 16, 2020, https://sites.hks.harvard.edu/fs/whogan/Repsol_Seminars/Repsol_Seminars_2000/Repsolco.pdf
[188] "About CGES," *Centre for Global Energy Studies*, accessed February 16, 2020, https://web.archive.org/web/20140303144837/http://www.cges.co.uk:80/about-us.htm

United Nations sanctions were lifted in 2000,[189] and for sponsoring conferences on controversial topics for the industry, such as climate change.[190] This evidence suggests that Yamani was more than a flash in the pan and more than a mouthpiece for the Saudi monarchy. One journalist assessed Yamani as being "Mr. Oil" at the time of his dismissal,[191] but his influence on the industry outlasted his tenure as Saudi oil minister by decades. One economist went so far as to declare Yamani to be one of the three most important people in history of petroleum, along with early oil tycoons John D. Rockefeller and Henri Deterding.[192] Not bad for a commoner, who consistently worked to find common ground between producers and customers of black gold.

[189] Fadhil J. Chalabi, "Iraq and the Future of World Oil." *Middle East Policy*, 7, 4 (2000), 163-173, ProQuest Central.

[190] Paul Rogers, "Climate Change: Canary to Ghost," *OpenDemocracy*, November 21, 2013, ProQuest Central.

[191] Greenwald, "Wild Goodbye to Mr. Oil," 42.

[192] Jones, *Oil,* 313. For a detailed account of Standard Oil's Rockefeller and Royal Dutch Shell's Henri Deterding, see Peter B. Doran, *Breaking Rockefeller: The Incredible Story of The Ambitious Rivals Who Toppled an Oil Empire* (New York: Penguin Books, 2016).

Z

Kirsten Zickfeld

1971-

A few months before pioneering climatologist Kirsten Zickfeld was born in Saarbrücken, West Germany, the United Nations celebrated its twenty-fifth anniversary. In his closing remarks on October 24, 1970, Secretary-General U Thant told the General Assembly:

> As we watch the sun go down evening after evening through the smog across the poisoned waters of our native earth, we must ask ourselves seriously whether we really wish some future universal historian on another planet to say, "With all their genius and with all their skill, they ran out of foresight and air and food and water and ideas;" or, "they went on playing politics until their world collapsed around them;" or, "when they looked up, it was already too late." If the United Nations does nothing else, it can at least serve a vital purpose in sounding the alarm."[1]

U Thant's query has yet to be answered fully, but his words serve as the *raison d'être* for Zickfeld's professional life. She has devoted herself to developing climatic models to warn humanity about the unparalleled risks it faces.

Fluent in four languages and able in two others, it is not much of a stretch to call Zickfeld a citizen of the world. She completed her secondary school education at Il Liceo Classico "F. A. Gualterio" in Orvieto, Italy with a perfect score on her exam for university entrance.[2] She entered the Free University Berlin to study physics in October 1991—just a year after East Germany and

---

[1] U Thant quoted in Henry Tanner, "U.N. Condemns Racism as Special Session Ends: U.N. Ends Special Jubilee Session," *New York Times*, October 25, 1970, 1, ProQuest Historical Newspapers. For an analysis of U Thant's tenure as Secretary-General, see A. Walter Dorn, "U Thant: Buddhism in Action," *The UN Secretary-General and Moral Authority: Ethics and Religious in International Leadership*, Kent J. Kille (ed.) (Washington, DC: Georgetown University Press, 2007), 143-186.

[2] Most of this personal biography comes from a 2011 version of Zickfeld's curriculum vitae, downloaded February 19, 2020, https://apps.neb-one.gc.ca/REGDOCS/File/Download/867571.

West Germany had formally unified. Berlin may have been a city in fascinating transition,[3] but Zickfeld stayed on task: she finished her first two years of required coursework on schedule and completed a year of additional study at the University of Edinburgh in Scotland. She also participated in a community service project in Peru. Returning to Berlin in April 1994, Zickfeld began working towards the German equivalent of a master's degree, the *Diplom*. Her thesis, "Femtosecond Relaxation Dynamics of Small Silicon Clusters: Structural Change, Fragmentation, and Metallization," involved manipulating the electrons of silicon atoms with different pulses of lasers and helped her to finish the *Diplom* with distinction in March 1998.[4] At the time, only 43% of the university graduates in Germany were women, only 10% of university professors were women, and most of the women who pursued academic careers did so in the humanities and social sciences.[5] As something of a pioneer, Zickfeld decided to pursue a Ph.D. in climate physics through a joint program sponsored by Potsdam University and the Potsdam Institute for Climate Impact Research. Over the next five years, she completed her coursework and worked as a research associate on a planetary ocean currents project called the Integrated Assessment of Changes in the Thermohaline Circulation. This group developed conceptual climate models, studied the stability of the Indian monsoon, and analyzed circulation patterns in the Atlantic Ocean. It also contributed to international climate assessments sponsored by the United Nations. During this period, Zickfeld also delivered numerous professional papers at international conferences, investigated the impact of the paper industry on peat forests in Indonesia, and made repeated trips to Nicaragua (and one to Laos) to participate in local development programs. In March 2004, Zickfeld graduated *summa cum laude* and earned awards for the originality of her thesis, "Modeling Large-scale Singular Climate Events for Integrated Assessment." Her first postdoctoral appointment was also at the Potsdam Institute for Climate Impact Research, but her second postdoc took her to Canada, where she joined the School of Earth and Ocean Sciences at the University of Victoria. After two years, Zickfeld secured a job with the Canadian Centre for Climate Modelling and Analysis in Victoria, and in August 2010 she won a tenure-track job at Simon Fraser University in Vancouver. Today, Zickfeld is an extensively-published associate professor in the Department of Geography at Simon Fraser, where she leads her own climate research lab and works with graduate students from around the world. Zickfeld's background is of interest, however, for more than the contents of her résumé. Part of what makes her the right person to conclude *Improbable Voices* is the compelling dialogue that can be found between her life and the world around her. What follows is a chronological attempt to integrate German, Canadian, and international environmental policy with Zickfeld's own highly specialized work.

In the years shortly after Zickfeld's birth, West Germany emerged as an environmental leader. With Willy Brandt's election in October 1969, a new interior minister, Hans-Dietrich Genscher,

[3] Works on the effects of reunification on Berlin politically, economically, socially, and architecturally include: 1) Katharine Burgess, "Putting Berlin Back Together: Planning Policy after the Fall of the Wall." *Planning*, Vol. 81 Issue 3 (2015), 26-31, EBSCOhost; 2) Dora Damjanović, "The Reunification of Germany & Global Social Evolution," *Cadmus*, Vol. 3 Issue 5 (2018), 44-56, *ProQuest*; and 3) the essays in *Cultural Topographies of the New Berlin*, Karin Bauer and Jennifer Ruth Hosek (eds.) (New York: Berghahn, 2018).
[4] Zickfeld graduated "*sehr gut*" or "very good," one step below "*hervorragend*" or "excellent." One website that clearly explains German degrees and grades, see "The Tertiary Education Landscape," and "Understanding & Converting German Grades," *Singapore Students' Association of Germany*, accessed February 19, 2020, http://ssag.eu/.
[5] Stefan Fuchs, Janina Von Stebut and Jutta Allmendinger, "Gender, Science, and Scientific Organizations in Germany," *Minerva: A Review of Science, Learning & Policy*, 39, 2 (Summer 2001), 175-201, EBSCOhost.

presented the nation with its first comprehensive environmental policy. In defining and promoting environmental protection, Genscher's legislation set air quality standards, restricted airplane noise, established a leaded gasoline law, regulated trash removal, instituted forest and nature protection, banned the use of the pesticide DDT, created new government agencies, and more.[6] The federal push to protect the environment soon joined with a grassroots anti-nuclear movement.[7] This powerful combination prompted West Germany to consider policies in the 1970s that other industrial nations had not. While the United States, France, and Great Britain responded to the challenge of Ahmed Zaki Yamani's 1973 and 1979 oil crises by attempting to expand their energy supplies, West Germany began to consider ways of decoupling energy consumption from economic growth.[8] In other words, leftist West German politicians presented conservation as a way of promoting quality of life without compromising national prosperity. This was a very different strategy from that of increasing nuclear energy production, as the French did, or exploiting new oil discoveries, as the British and Americans did. This unique political situation, combined with the influence of other social movements in the 1970s, such as feminism, led to the formation of the Green Party in West Germany in 1980.[9] It became the inspiration for green parties around the world.[10]

As Zickfeld was concluding her primary school education, West Germans were confronted with visual evidence of the nation's environmental failings: 76% of the country's fir trees were dying off as a result of acid rain.* The forests celebrated in the works of Johann Wolfgang von Goethe and the Brothers Grimm faced ruin as numerous deciduous species fell victim to this pollution.[11] Caused primarily by sulfur dioxide emissions from coal burning industrial plants and automobiles, the threat of *Waldsterben* or forest death was such a visceral blow to the German psyche that politicians of all stripes joined together to protect the woodlands.[12] Indeed, as late as 1979, West Germany had opposed an international agreement on air pollution designed to fight acid rain, but by 1982 *Waldsterben* had convinced German leaders to join the accord.[13] By July 1983, West German cars were required to have catalytic converters to help filter emissions, and West German power plants were ordered to adopt desulfurization mechanisms within five years.[14] By the mid-1980s, an ecological consciousness emerged as West Germans altered their spending habits,

[6] Frank Uekötter, *The Greenest Nation?: A New History of German Environmentalism* (Cambridge, Massachusetts: The MIT Press, 2014), 86-87, EBSCOhost. Genscher was a member of the Free Democratic Party of Germany (FDP), which was the junior partner in the government with Brandt's Social Democratic Party of Germany (SPD).

[7] Andrew S. Tompkins, *Better Active Than Radioactive!: Anti-nuclear Protest in 1970s France and West Germany* (Oxford, U.K.: Oxford University Books, 2016), 2-4.

[8] Stephen G. Gross, "Reimagining Energy and Growth: Decoupling and the Rise of a New Energy Paradigm in West Germany, 1973-1986," *Central European History*, 50, no. 4 (December 2017): 514-546, EBSCOhost.

[9] Saskia Richter, "Petra Kelly, International Green Leader: On Biography and the Peace Movement as Resources of Power in West German Politics, 1979-1983," *German Politics and Society*, vol. 33, no. 4 (2015): 80-96, EBSCOhost.

[10] Per Gahrton and Caroline Lucas, *Green Parties, Green Future: From Local Groups to the International Stage* (London: Pluto Press, 2015), 34, EBSCOebooks.

[11] Anastasia Toufexis, "Turning Green into Yellow," *Time*, Vol. 123, no. 2 (January 9, 1984), 54.

[12] Uekötter, *The Greenest Nation?,* 114.

[13] Armin Rosencranz, "The Acid Rain Controversy in Europe and North America: A Political Analysis," *Ambio*, Vol. 15, No. 1 (1986), 47-51, EBSCOhost. The formal name of the agreement was the Convention on Long Range Transboundary Air Pollution.

[14] Uekötter, *The Greenest Nation?,* 114.

supported organic farming, and created Federal Ministry for the Environment, Nature Conservation, and Nuclear Safety with cabinet-level status.[15] The governmental integration of nuclear safety and ecology was a regulatory response to the Chernobyl Nuclear Power Plant accident on April 26, 1986—an event which led the Green Party to initiate their "Chernobyl Is Everywhere" campaign to rally opposition to nuclear energy and nuclear weapons.[16] Soon, the Greens were calling for West Germany's withdrawal from NATO*[17] and the party's message resonated: in the federal election of January 1987, the Greens won 8.3% of the vote and more seats in Parliament that ever before.[18]

While Zickfeld was in Italy completing her secondary schooling, the world became a different place. The era witnessed the fall of Berlin Wall, the reunification of Germany, Nelson Mandela's release from prison in South Africa, the suppression of China's nascent democracy movement in Tiananmen Square, the separation of the Baltic States from the Soviet Union, and a legacy from the Gulf War that is still visible.[19]   Additionally, the world's most successful international environmental treaty to date, the Montreal Protocol, was signed by 24 nations in September 1987. This agreement froze the use of ozone-damaging chlorofluorocarbons (CFCs) at 1986 levels and mandated a 20% reduction of CFCs by 1994 and a 30% reduction by 1999. Upon the Protocol's signing, a diplomat explained its significance: "Never before in the history of science and law has the international community agreed to take such radical steps to avert a problem" before it "has begun to take its toll."[20] In fact, signatories adhered so well to its terms that it was possible to accelerate timetables and repair the threat more quickly.[21] This was possible because ozone depletion had such clear and tangible consequences and because there were readily available substitutes for refrigerants and propellants.[22] It also meant that the Montreal Protocol was signed just 28 months after the discovery of the ozone hole above Antarctica was announced.[23] Subsequent climate change negotiations proved to be far more problematic.

[15] Uekötter, *The Greenest Nation?,* 120-122.

[16] Erik Eckholm, "Nuclear Disaster: The Ever-Widening Impact; After Accident at the Soviet Station, Nuclear Power is Questioned Again," *New York Times*, May 02, 1986, A10, *ProQuest Historical Newspapers.*

[17] James M. Markham, "Green Party Asks Break with NATO: Conference Draws Up Election Program That Also Seeks Abolition Of A-Power," *New York Times*, May 21, 1986, A8, *ProQuest Historical Newspapers.*

[18] James M. Markham, "Kohl Keeps Power by Narrower Edge in West Germany," *New York Times,* January 26, 1987, A1, *ProQuest Historical Newspapers.* In the previous federal election, the Greens won 5.6% of the vote.

[19] Thomas E. Ricks, *Fiasco: The American Military Adventure in Iraq* (New York: Penguin Press, 2006), 3-11.

[20] Mostafa K. Tolba quoted in Dianne Dumanoski, "24 Countries Sign Treaty to Protect Ozone Layer," *Boston Globe*, Sep 17, 1987, 12, *ProQuest Historical Newspapers.* Tolba was the executive director of the United Nations Environment Programme (UNEP).

[21] Supporters of this view include former United Nations Secretary-General Kofi Annan. See "International Day for the Preservation of the Ozone Layer, 16 September," *United Nations*, 2018, accessed February 19, 2020, https://www.un.org/en/events/ozoneday/background.shtml

[22] Joshua P. Howe, *Behind the Curve: Science and the Politics of Global Warming* (Seattle, Washington: University of Washington Press, 2014), 152.

[23] For an account of the discovery of the ozone hole by one of the original British scientists, see Jonathan Shanklin, "Reflections on the Ozone Hole," *Nature*, No. 7294 (2010): 34-35, EBSCOhost.

~

Given the extent of the world's current climatic issues today, it is astonishing how long scientists and politicians have known about the consequences of increasing levels of atmospheric carbon dioxide (CO_2). In the nineteenth and early twentieth centuries, scientists and engineers saw a clear connection between climate, and CO_2, and other compounds.[24] After World War II, greater clarity and precision in atmospheric measurements and predictions emerged, primarily because the American government increased funding to determine how changes in the atmosphere might affect nuclear weapons testing and defense preparation during the Cold War.[25] In 1953, Gilbert Plass, a Canadian-born physicist working at Johns Hopkins University, used the analogy of a giant greenhouse to explain the effects of continued CO_2 emissions. He predicted that at the then-current rate of increase, the planet would see a 1.5° Fahrenheit rise in temperature every hundred years. Plass noted that the warming trend would be compounded by decreased cloud cover and lower levels of precipitation. He believed that only after thousands of years would the planet be able to absorb a sufficient amount of the industrial CO_2 to begin to lower earth's temperature.[26] Many scientists in the 1950s disagreed with Plass, for they assumed that excess CO_2 would simply be absorbed by the oceans. The director of the Scripps Institution for Oceanography in La Jolla, California, Roger Revelle, realized in 1957 that while industrial CO_2 might initially be absorbed by the oceans, it could just as easily be re-released into the atmosphere, thereby compounding the problem Plass had identified.[27] What Revelle and his Scripps colleagues needed, however, was good data to prove their supposition. To get this, Revelle recruited a chemist named Charles David Keeling, who had developed instruments for measuring minute concentrations of CO_2.[28] Keeling placed an infrared gas analyzer atop Mauna Loa, Hawai'i in March 1958. His first measurement showed a CO_2 level of 313 parts per million (ppm). Subsequent measurements, which Keeling first published in 1960, showed two patterns: 1) CO_2 levels rose and fell over the course of a single year; and 2) each subsequent year registered an increase in CO_2 levels. Taken together, Keeling's records showed how the planet breathes as Northern and Southern Hemispheres alternate seasons and how each passing year amplified the potential for CO_2 to change the earth's delicate atmospheric balance.[29] This led Revelle and his colleague Hans Seuss to write, "Thus, human beings are now

---

[24] Examples include French physicist Joseph Fourier, who in 1824 determined that the earth's atmosphere retained heat; Irish physicist John Tyndall, who showed that water vapor and CO_2 absorbed heat readily and hypothesized that changes to either could have climatic effects; and Swedish chemist Svante Arrenius, who is discussed at the end of this chapter. See Benjamin Lieberman and Elizabeth Gordon, *Climate Change in Human History: Prehistory to the Present* (London/New York: Bloomsbury Academic, 2018), 142.

[25] Howe, *Behind the Curve*, 17, 40.

[26] "Invisible Blanket," *Time*, Latin American ed., vol. LXI, no. 21 (May 25, 1953), 46. Plass' prediction has proven quite correct.

[27] Howe, *Behind the Curve*, 19.

[28] For an account of Keeling's work before being recruited by Revelle, see Rob Monroe, "The History of the Keeling Curve," *Scripps Institution of Oceanography*, April 3, 2013, accessed February 19, 2020, https://scripps.ucsd.edu/programs/keelingcurve/2013/04/03/the-history-of-the-keeling-curve/

[29] William Cronon, "Forward," Howe, *Behind the Curve*, ix.

carrying out a large scale geophysical experiment…[by] returning to the atmosphere and oceans the concentrated organic carbon stored in sedimentary rocks for hundreds of millions of years."[30]

Detailed knowledge of the effects of this experiment soon began to emerge. In 1965, Revelle submitted a report to President Lyndon B. Johnson that predicted the anticipated environmental changes were "not controllable through local or even national efforts."[31] Instead, the problem required a coordinated global undertaking. The first comprehensive attempt to initiate such a bold endeavor occurred the year after Zickfeld was born, when 1,200 delegates from 113 nations met in Stockholm, Sweden in June 1972 for the United Nations Conference on the Human Environment (UNCHE). At the time, the Keeling Curve measurements from Mauna Loa read 330 ppm.[32] The secretary-general of the conference was Canadian billionaire-turned-diplomat Maurice Strong, who made his fortune in the oil and gas industries.[33] U Thant asked Strong to chair the groundbreaking meeting because of his work in international development in the 1960s.[34] Before the conference opened, Strong outlined its potential and aspirations:

> Today, more than ever, one can say with validity…that no nation—no matter what its boundaries—is an island to itself. Insularity is an anachronism, now dispelled by the environmental reality that water and air, even more than land, are links with, rather than barriers to, the rest of the world….For, in the final analysis, any viable solution will be contingent upon bold new steps to bring about vastly improved conditions of life for all people. Only thus can we realize at this juncture in human history, the concept of a planet held in trust for future generations; only thus can we affirm the inescapable physical unity and interdependence of the biosphere, and the need for all the world's people to co-operate in preserving it, sharing it, and managing it for the whole human family.[35]

Unfortunately, these lofty, communal ideals were not fully realized, as Cold War tensions constrained the deliberations. East Germany, for example, was not allowed to participate in the conference because it was not a member of the United Nations or one of its specialized agencies. This exclusion led the Soviet Union and some of the other Warsaw Pact countries to boycott the Stockholm meeting.[36] In addition, Sweden accused the United States of practicing "ecocide" in

---

[30] Roger Revelle and Hans E. Suess, "Carbon Dioxide Exchange between Atmospheric and Ocean and the Question of an Increase in Atmospheric CO2 during the Past Decades," *The Global Warming Reader: A Century of Writing about Climate Change*, Bill McKibben (ed.) (New York: Penguin Books, 2011), 41-42.

[31] Roger Revelle quoted in Nathaniel Rich, *Losing Earth: A Recent History* (New York: Farrar, Straus and Giroux, 2019), 23.

[32] "Atmospheric Concentrations of CO2 from Mauna Loa, Hawaii," *Carbon Dioxide Informational Analysis Center, U.S. Department of Energy*, last modified June 8, 2015, accessed August 2, 2019, https://cdiac.essdive.lbl.gov/trends/co2/recent_mauna_loa_co2.html. All Keeling Curve statistics between 1958 and 2015 are taken from this source. Although 330 ppm is just 0.033% of the total atmosphere, small changes in the percentage of CO2 lead to significant changes.

[33] For an account of Strong's complicated relationship with the environment and his industrial ties, see David Segal, "Strong's Wrongs," *New Republic*, vol. 206, no. 25 (June 22, 1992), 13, EBSCOhost.

[34] Sam Roberts, "Maurice Strong, Environmental Champion, Dies at 86," *New York Times*, December 2, 2015, 1, *ProQuest Historical Newspapers*.

[35] Maurice Strong, "The Stockholm Conference," *The Geographical Journal*, vol. 138, no. 4 (December 1972), 411-417, EBSCOhost.

[36] In 1972, the German Democratic Republic applied for membership in the World Health Organization for the fourth time. A month before the Stockholm conference, the GDR's application was rejected 70-28 with 25

Vietnam with its use of defoliants and large-scale bombing,[37] and other members of the Non-Aligned Movement* viewed the West's push towards environmentalism as an extension of imperialism that would force developing nations into perpetual servitude.[38] The UNCHE did produce a treatise that endorsed 26 principles and made 109 recommendations. The Declaration on the Human Environment condemned racial discrimination, colonial oppression, and the use of nuclear weapons. It called on nations to protect wildlife, prevent the pollution of the seas, and safeguard "natural ecosystems" for "the benefit of present and future generations." It welcomed the "transfer of financial and technological assistance" to minimize the effects of natural disasters and underdevelopment, and it proclaimed that humans had a "solemn responsibility to protect and improve the environment for present and future generations." The declaration also maintained that "the environmental policies of all States should enhance and not adversely affect the present or future development potential of developing countries." Indeed, "economic and social development is essential for ensuring a favourable living and working environment" and an "improvement of the quality of life."[39] There was only one reference to carbon dioxide in the lengthy report, and it was buried deep inside the recommendation section: the UN is to "take steps to ensure proper collection, measurement, and analysis of data relating to the environmental effects of energy use" including the "monitoring of environmental levels resulting from emission of carbon dioxide, sulphur dioxide, oxidants, nitrogen oxides" and other particulates resulting "from releases of oil and radioactivity."[40] The focus, then, was on fact-finding and record-keeping, not on limiting CO_2 concentrations as pollutants. This decision was a product of what many developing countries saw as inherent tension between development and protection, between economic growth and ecological conservation. As Indian Prime Minister Indira Gandhi asked the delegates, "how can we speak to those who live in villages and in slums about keeping the oceans, the rivers, and the air clear, when their own lives are contaminated at the source?" We must have a higher standard of living for the earth's impoverished people "without despoiling nature of its beauty, freshness, and purity so essential to our lives."[41] This is a tension that has continued to dominate climate policy discussions ever since, despite the hopes for sustainable development. This shortcoming, combined with the voluntary, non-binding nature of the Stockholm agreement, is why the UNCHE was so important: it set the imperfect precedent for all subsequent diplomatic summits on the environment.[42]

---

abstentions. This made the GDR ineligible to attend the UNCHE. The Soviets did participate extensively in the preparation for the conference, but did not send a delegation to Stockholm. This boycott was joined by Bulgaria, Czechoslovakia, and Poland. Warsaw Pact member Romania did participate. The GDR did not gain membership in the United Nations until September 18, 1973. See "U.N. Agency Rejects East German Bid," *New York Times*, May 20 1972, 3; and Gladwin Hill, "1,200 Gather in Stockholm for Parley on Environment: Delegates from 90% of the World Arrive in Stockholm for Conference," *New York Times*, June 5, 1972, 1, *ProQuest Historical Newspapers*; and *Report of the United Nations Conference on the Human Environment, Stockholm, 5-16 June 1972*, (New York: United Nations, 1973), 43, accessed February 19, 2020, https://tinyurl.com/y3ltadfd

[37] Gladwin Hill, "U.S., at U.N. Parley on Environment, Rebukes Sweden for 'Politicizing' Talks," *New York Times,* June 8, 1972, 13, *ProQuest Historical Newspapers*.

[38] Elke Seefried, "Rethinking Progress: On the Origin of the Modern Sustainability Discourse, 1970–2000," *Journal of Modern European History,* Vol. 13, No. 3 (2015), 377-400, EBSCOhost.

[39] *Report of the United Nations Conference on the Human Environment, Stockholm, 5-16 June 1972*, 4-5.

[40] *Report of the United Nations Conference on the Human Environment, Stockholm, 5-16 June 1972*, 19.

[41] Indira Gandhi quoted in Robert Bendiner, "Third-World Ecology: At Stockholm: On Balance, an Awareness that Early Concern for Environment is Cheaper and Saner," *New York Times*, June 26 1972, 33. *ProQuest Historical Newspapers*.

[42] Howe, *Behind the Curve*, 83.

Even with the agreement's fundamental contradictions and limitations, both the West German and the Canadian delegations left Stockholm sufficiently pleased with the outcome. The Canadians were particularly satisfied by the language concerning the rights of coastal states to prevent maritime pollution by enforcing environmental standards on all international vessels. This was important because the language set a precedent in the emerging field of international environmental law that worked in Canada's interests.[43] The West Germans were pleased to have minimized the diplomatic impact of the Warsaw Pact boycott and looked forward to taking the next steps in protecting the environment.[44] As Chancellor Willy Brandt later said, "Neither the individual nor the community can live at the expense of nature….Noise, air, and water pollution and disturbances of the ecological balance do in fact jeopardize the benefits of economic growth and productivity." Therefore, polluters must be punished for their criminal acts, for "mankind as a whole has an elementary right to a decent environment."[45] Similarly, delegates from other nations left Stockholm buoyant that they had agreed to a set of principles and made substantial recommendations. In fact, a number of delegates thought they had accomplished a small miracle.[46] As conference Secretary-General Maurice Strong said in 1973, "it was nothing short of remarkable that—given the tensions and realities of international life—113 nations were able to convene in less than two weeks to achieve wide agreement on virtually all the specific proposals placed before the Conference."[47] The Stockholm meeting resulted in the establishment of government environmental agencies in over 115 countries, the creation of thousands of conservation groups around the world, and the growth of public awareness about environmental issues.[48]

Exactly twenty years later, as Zickfeld was finishing her first year of university and as the Keeling Curve had risen to 359 ppm, Maurice Strong chaired another pivotal climate meeting as diplomats gathered in Rio de Janeiro for the United Nations Conference on Environment and Development in June 1992. The Rio Earth Summit, as it was informally known, dwarfed the scale of the Stockholm meeting, attracting representatives of 172 governments, including 108 heads of state;

---

[43] The Canadians objected to oil tanker traffic through the Northwest Passage and the potential for environmental disaster in the delicate Arctic ecosystem. When the *S. S. Manhattan*, a supertanker owned by Humble Oil, evoked the principle of freedom of the seas and completed a voyage to Alaska in September 1969, the Canadian public and Pierre Trudeau's government objected vigorously. The language of the Stockholm agreement gave the Canadian government international permission to limit such traffic in the future. See Michael W. Manulak, "Multilateral Solutions to Bilateral Problems: The 1972 Stockholm Conference and Canadian Foreign Environmental Policy," *International Journal*, vol. 70, no. 1 (2015), 4-22, EBSCOhost.

[44] Kai Hünemörder, "Environmental Crisis and Soft Politics: Détente and the Global Environment, 1968-1975," *Environmental Histories of the Cold War*, Corinna R. Unger, and John Robert McNeill (eds.) (Washington, D.C./ New York: German Historical Institute/Cambridge University Press, 2010), 265-266, EBSCOhost. The Stockholm conference was one of the last times the West Germans worked under the constraints of the Hallstein Doctrine, which maintained that West Germany was the only legitimate government of the German people and that it would not have diplomatic relations with nations, other than the Soviet Union, which recognized East Germany diplomatically. For more on the Hallstein Doctrine, see Randall E. Newnham, "Embassies for Sale: The Purchase of Diplomatic Recognition by West Germany, Taiwan and South Korea," *International Politics*, vol. 37, no. 3 (2000), 259-283, *ProQuest Central*.

[45] Willy Brandt, "Federal Republic of Germany Policy Statement," *Vital Speeches of the Day*, vol. XXXIX, no. 9 (February 15, 1973): 258-266, EBSCOhost.

[46] Gladwin Hill, "Sense of Accomplishment Buoys Delegates Leaving Ecology Talks," *New York Times,* June 18, 1972, 14, ProQuest Historical Newspapers.

[47] Maurice F. Strong, "One Year After Stockholm: An Ecological Approach to Management," *Foreign Affairs*, vol. 51, no. 4 (July 1973), 690-707, EBSCOhost.

[48] Philip Elmer-Dewitt, "Summit to Save the Earth: Rich vs Poor," *Time*, vol. 139, no. 22 (June 1, 1992), 42.

2,400 representatives of non-governmental organizations; and 10,000 journalists. Another 17,000 people attended a parallel conference called the Global Forum.[49] In conjunction with these meetings, the city also hosted several other events: an Indigenous Peoples' Conference on Territory, Environment, and Development, featuring 600 leaders from indigenous communities in Australia, Brazil, Canada, Scandinavia, and Russia; a trade show called EcoBrazil '92, promoting green technology from Brazil and around the world; and scores of museum exhibits and cultural events, including a ballet set to the music of Heitor Villa-Lobos entitled *Forest of the Amazon*.[50] All told, over 30,000 people travelled to Rio de Janeiro to attend an official event.

The enormous scale of the Rio Earth Summit and the optimism it generated reflected four painstaking years of preparation, which were largely triggered by the formation of the Intergovernmental Panel on Climate Change (IPCC) in March 1988. This organization was created by the World Meteorological Organization and the United Nations Environment Programme to develop a consensus on climate change between governments, rather than only between scientists or environmentalists.[51] Staffed by government scientists and policymakers, the IPCC is divided into three main working groups, each with a different focus. Working Group I assesses the scientific basis of climate change, seeking to determine what might happen; Working Group II assesses the potential impacts of climate change, seeking to determine the socio-economic consequences; and Working Group III assesses how to mitigate the effects of climate change, seeking to determine what might be done now and in the future.[52] Every five years, the three working groups recruit volunteer scientists from around the globe, who are nominated by their governments and international organizations on the basis of their expertise and professional standing. Once selected, these IPCC scientists work to evaluate and summarize the available scientific literature. Their drafts undergo extensive review and commentary.[53] Their synthesized, peer-reviewed final report is not prescriptive: they may present projections and discuss the implications of those projections, "but they do not tell policymakers what actions to take."[54] The process has been pejoratively described as "byzantine,"[55] which is why Ronald Reagan's White House officials endorsed it as a strategy to limit the influence of scientists in the political process.[56] But it is also a rigorous system that produces the consensus-driven, intergovernmental language that is so necessary for international agreements.

---

[49] "UN Conference on Environment and Development (1992)," *United Nations Department of Public Information*, May 23, 1997, accessed July 25, 2019, https://www.un.org/geninfo/bp/enviro.html

[50] Andrea Dorfman, "Summit to Save the Earth: Sideshows Galore," *Time*, vol. 139, no. 22 (June 1, 1992), 59.

[51] Howe, *Behind the Curve*, 155, 159.

[52] Christopher Shaw, *The Two Degrees Dangerous Limit for Climate Change: Public Understanding and Decision Making* (London/New York: Routledge, 2016), 58.

[53] The IPCC's Fifth Assessment Report (2014), for example, received a total of 142,631 comments by experts and policymakers during its review process. See "IPCC Factsheet: How Does the IPCC Review Process Work?," Revised January 15, 2015, accessed February 19, 2020, https://tinyurl.com/y65mjh6t

[54] "IPCC Factsheet: What is the IPCC?," *Intergovernmental Panel on Climate Change*, August 30, 2013, accessed February 19, 2020, https://www.ipcc.ch/site/assets/uploads/2018/02/FS_what_ipcc.pdf

[55] Bill McKibben, "The Coming Meltdown," *The New York Review of Books*, January 12, 2006, accessed February 19, 2020, https://www.nybooks.com/articles/2006/01/12/the-coming-meltdown/

[56] Gerald Kutney, *Carbon Politics and the Failure of the Kyoto Protocol* (London/New York: Routledge, 2014), 137-138; and Richard Elliot Benedick, *Ozone Diplomacy: New Directions in Safeguarding the Planet*, (Cambridge, Massachusetts: Harvard University Press, 1998), 321.

In June 1988, three months after the IPCC was founded, a conference on the earth's changing atmosphere opened in Toronto.[57] It was called by Prime Minister Brian Mulroney, a conservative from Québec, who unexpectedly became Canada's greenest head of state.[58] He fought against acid rain, securing binding commitments from all seven of Canada's eastern provinces to cut sulfur dioxide emissions by 50%. With his own house in order, Mulroney began pushing the United States to act.[59] In April 1988, Mulroney criticized the Reagan Administration's call for more research on acid rain, saying that it was "unacceptable" in the face of the available scientific information. He added, "If I'm a good neighbor, the United States would be pretty upset with me if I were dumping my garbage in your backyard. That's exactly what's happening, except that this garbage is coming from above."[60] By standing up to the United States and by negotiating the Montreal Protocol limiting the use of ozone-damaging chlorofluorocarbons, Mulroney solidified Canada's international environmental leadership. Indeed, by gathering three hundred scientists and policymakers from forty-six nations together in Toronto, Mulroney epitomized Canada's consistent advocacy for an international climate treaty in the 1980s.[61] Most impressively, the Toronto meeting was designed to be the first scientific meeting that would raise public awareness about climate change.[62] It was also the first time that an international conference discussed specific CO_2 emission reductions.[63] At the meeting's conclusion, attendees recommended that by 2005 governments reduce emissions to 22% of 1988 levels, and the public took notice. These limitations would allow all nations to adjust gradually to the restrictions, while reaching the goal of limiting future global temperature changes to no more than 2° Celsius.[64]

The end of the Cold War presented the world with a unique opportunity to set aside national interests and redefine the character of its international relations.[65] But four years after Toronto, when the Rio Earth Summit began, clear divisions remained. As in Stockholm, these centered upon differences between industrialized nations and developing nations. Those with ample resources largely looked to maintain their high standard of living and preserve diverse ecosystems, while those with limited resources did not want to be penalized to solve a problem they did not create. Representatives from Latin America, Africa, and Asia—the Global South—argued that decadent consumption by the industrialized North caused the problem of global warming, so the North should sacrifice and solve the problem. Bolivia, Laos, and Zambia should not suffer economically because Great Britain, Japan, and the United States had emitted too much CO_2 in the twentieth century. As the president of Brazil said, "You can't have an environmentally healthy planet in a

---

[57] The official name of the conference was "Our Changing Atmosphere: Implications for Global Security."
[58] May, "Brian Mulroney and the Environment," 381.
[59] May, "Brian Mulroney and the Environment," 385.
[60] Brian Mulroney quoted in John F. Burns, "Canada to Press on Acid Rain: Canada Losing Patience with U.S. on Acid Rain," *New York Times*, April 25, 1988, A1, *ProQuest Historical Newspapers*. In Canada, maple sugar trees in Québec and salmon fishing in Nova Scotia were especially affected by acid rain.
[61] Silvia Maciunas and Géraud de Lassus Saint-Geniès, "The Evolution of Canada's International and Domestic Climate Policy: From Divergence to Consistency?," *Centre for International Governance Innovation*, Paper 21, April 2018, accessed February 20, 2020, https://tinyurl.com/y4x4qqcw
[62] May, "Brian Mulroney and the Environment," 387.
[63] Naomi Klein, *This Changes Everything: Capitalism vs. the Climate* (Toronto: Alfred A. Knopf-Canada, 2014), 73.
[64] Klein, *This Changes Everything*, 55. Christopher Shaw contends that the idea of specific limits emerged in the 1970s and that the first reference to the two-degree celsius limit came in a 1995 study by the German Advisory Council on Global Change (WBGU). See Shaw, *The Two Degrees Dangerous Limit for Climate Change*, 25.
[65] Elmer-Dewitt, "Summit to Save the Earth," 42.

world that is socially unjust."[66] To solve the problem of global warming, the legacies of empire and imperialism had to be addressed as well.[67] Such fundamental issues were beyond the scope of what the North was willing to consider, and at the mid-point of the conference, it appeared that the negotiations would collapse.[68] For many, noble aspirations simply withered in the face of economic realities: there were limits to the economic burden that wealthy nations were willing to assume. As a member of the German delegation said, "the noble words that were spoken reduced themselves in the final phase to paying."[69] Leaders of environmental organizations were even more frustrated. According to one British eyewitness, they confronted Maurice Strong on June 6, "laying down the gauntlet" with a ten-point plan "to save the summit from failure." Their demands included

> legally binding targets and timetables for reducing greenhouse gas emissions, a reduction of consumption by the North, global economic reform to improve the terms of trade for the South, more financial commitment from the North…a ban on the export of hazardous waste, recognition of the rights of indigenous peoples, and an end to nuclear weapons and nuclear power.[70]

These demands were politically unrealistic, but the global visibility of the Earth Summit made it critical for the delegates and world leaders to leave Rio de Janeiro with an agreement. Complete failure was not a viable option. This awareness led to counties to seek the ratification of three treaties. The first, the Framework Convention on Climate Change, charged nations, in the words of George H.W. Bush, to "establish national climate change programs" and "detail the programs and measures they will undertake to limit greenhouse emissions and adapt to climate change."[71] The second, the Convention on Biological Diversity, had three main goals: "conservation of biodiversity; sustainable use of biodiversity; [and] fair and equitable sharing of the benefits arising from the use of genetic resources."[72] The third treaty, the Convention to Combat Desertification, sought, as Bill Clinton said, to "mitigate the effects of drought on arid, semi-arid, and dry sub-humid lands…by stimulating more effective partnerships between governments, local

---

[66] Fernando Collor de Mello quoted in Philip Elmer-Dewitt, "Summit to Save the Earth: Rich vs Poor," *Time*, vol. 139, no. 22 (June 1, 1992), 43.

[67] Amitav Ghosh, *The Great Derangement* (Chicago, Illinois: University of Chicago Press, 2016), 87, 146. Ghosh also argues that imperialism helped to delay climate change because imperial policies often prevented the development of industry in Asia (109-110); that industrialization in Asia in the 1980s accelerated the climate change crisis; and that no solution to the problem will work unless it works in Asia (90-91).

[68] Eugene Linden, "Rio's Legacy," *Time*, vol. 139, no. 25 (June 22, 1992), 44.

[69] Hubert Weinzierl quoted in Uekötter, *The Greenest Nation?*, 129. Weinzierl has been an environmental leader in Germany for many decades. See "Den organisierten Naturschutz aus der Nische in das Zentrum unserer Gesellschaft gerückt," *Deutsche Bundesstiftung Umwelt DBU* (German Federal Environmental Foundation), September 23, 2014, accessed February 20, 2020, https://tinyurl.com/y4pyvxwb

[70] Fiona Godlee, "Rio Diary: A Fortnight at the Earth Summit," *British Medical Journal*, July 11, 1992, 102-105, EBSCOhost. Godlee was the longtime editor of the *British Medical Journal*.

[71] George H.W. Bush, "Statement on Signing the Instrument of Ratification for the United Nations Framework Convention on Climate Change," *George H.W. Bush Presidential Library & Museum*, October 13, 1992, accessed February 20, 2020, https://bush41library.tamu.edu/archives/public-papers/4953

[72] "Convention on Biodiversity," *The United Nations*, no date, accessed February 20, 2020, https://www.un.org/en/events/biodiversityday/convention.shtml

communities, non-governmental organizations, and aid donors."[73] Canada's Brian Mulroney was the first international leader to sign the three Rio conventions,[74] but because none of the treaties included specific, mandatory obligations, his signature did not mean as much as it should have. The desertification treaty was so innocuous, that, in his message to the Senate for ratification, Clinton noted the United States could actually meet its obligations "under existing law and ongoing assistance programs."[75] Where there were specifics, such as in the biological diversity treaty, the United States refused to become a signatory.[76] There were also endless qualifications. The Framework treaty, for example, stated in Article 3 that "measures taken to combat climate change, including unilateral ones, should not constitute…a disguised restriction on international trade."[77] In other words, nations did not have to fight climate change if doing so would adversely affect profits. While many delegates tried to put a positive spin on the outcomes from the 1992 Rio Earth Summit,[78] Maurice Strong was honest. He pointed out that while the delegates had been meeting, 5,000 tons of CO_2 had entered the atmosphere each minute and more than a quarter of a million children had been born, "most of them poor, all facing an uncertain future."[79]

Five years later, while Zickfeld was working on her *Diplom* in physics and as CO_2 emissions reached 365 ppm, 2,200 delegates from 161 countries[80] met in Kyoto, Japan to try to apply specific emission targets to the broad principles proclaimed in Rio de Janeiro. The summit's premise was that 38 nations with developed economies would meet an explicit CO_2 reduction target by 2012. In the end, members of the European Union, many of the central and eastern European aspirants to the EU, and Liechtenstein, Monaco, and Switzerland agreed to an 8% reduction from their 1990 emission levels. The United States agreed to 7%, while Canada, Hungary, Japan, and Poland agreed to 6%. Croatia agreed to 5%. A few nations, such as New Zealand, Russia, and the Ukraine only had to maintain their current level of CO_2 emissions until 2012, while three nations, Australia, Iceland, and Norway, were actually allowed to increase their rates of pollution because they were already producing less CO_2 than in 1990.[81] During the negotiations, the Clinton administration pushed for the development of a cap-and-trade system, which would allow nations to buy carbon credits to offset their emissions. The Americans wanted to be able to purchase a part of another industrialized nation's quota, and to be given credits for implementing environmentally-friendly

[73] Bill Clinton, "Message to the Senate Transmitting the United Nations Convention to Combat Desertification," *Government Publishing Office*, August 2, 1996, accessed February 20, 2020, https://www.govinfo.gov/content/pkg/PPP-1996-book2/pdf/PPP-1996-book2-doc-pg1248.pdf
[74] May, "Brian Mulroney and the Environment," 381.
[75] Clinton, "Message to the Senate Transmitting the United Nations Convention to Combat Desertification."
[76] The United States did not initially sign the treaty out of concern that it threatened the biotechnology industry and risked American patent protection. The U.S. has also never ratified it. See Keith Schneider, "White House Snubs U.S. Envoy's Plea to Sign Rio Treaty," *New York Times*, June 5 1992, 2. *ProQuest Historical Newspapers*.
[77] "United Nations Framework Convention on Climate Change, Article 3 Principles," quoted in Klein, *This Changes Everything*, 77.
[78] James Brooke, "U.N. Chief Closes Summit with an Appeal for Action," *New York Times*, June 15 1992, 1, *ProQuest Historical Newspapers*.
[79] Maurice Strong quoted in Godlee, "Rio Diary."
[80] Michael D. Lemonick, "Turning Down the Heat," *Time*, vol. 150, no. 26 (December 22, 1997), 24.
[81] David G. Victor, *The Collapse of the Kyoto Protocol and the Struggle to Slow Global Warming* (Princeton, New Jersey: Princeton University Press, 2001), 27-28. The 15 members of the EU in 1997 were: Austria, Belgium, Denmark, Ireland, Finland, France, Germany, Greece, Italy, Luxembourg, Netherlands, Portugal, Spain, Sweden, and the United Kingdom. The aspiring EU members who agreed to the 8% reduction were Bulgaria, Czech Republic, Estonia, Latvia, Lithuania, Romania, Slovakia, and Slovenia.

projects in developing nations.[82] They saw these cap-and-trade accommodations as an expedient way to avoid the thorny issue of an outright carbon tax and reasoned the system would help mitigate the economic impacts of Kyoto's ambitious goals. The Europeans saw cap-and-trade as an excuse to pollute and criticized it for violating the whole spirit of environmental protection and cooperation.[83] As Germany's then-environmental minister Angela Merkel said, "The aim cannot be for industrial countries to satisfy their obligations solely through emission trading and profit."[84] Facilitating a compromise, the Canadians brought the two sides together.[85] The Americans got their cap-and-trade, while the Europeans got their specific and binding targets. The Canadians also secured recognition of forests as being key absorbers of carbon. By calculating these carbon sinks into the emission equation for each nation, Canada eased its own burden while maintaining its image as an international environmental leader.[86] Of the developed nations, Germany may have benefited the most from the Kyoto Protocol, for it found it could meet much of its target simply by continuing to close inefficient power plants in the former East Germany.[87] Great Britain also looked to have an easier road to its target because of its switch from coal to natural gas in the 1990s.[88]

Almost 200 nations eventually ratified the Kyoto Protocol, but the United States was not among them, despite the fervent hopes of Vice-President Al Gore. The reason largely stemmed from a decision Angela Merkel made in 1995: to bridge the North-South divide that had undermined the Rio Earth Summit, Merkel convinced delegates meeting in Berlin in preparation for Kyoto to absolve developing countries from both binding and voluntary CO_2 emission targets.[89] This was a revolutionary shift. It won enormous support from the nations of the Global South, who thought the move would allow them time to industrialize and become competitive in global markets. But it frightened American businessmen for exactly the same reason: how could emerging economies like China's, Brazil's, and India's not have *any* CO_2 restrictions—especially since China produced 12% of the world's CO_2 emissions between 1960 and 2010?[90] How could American businesses compete in such a market? In light of these concerns, the U.S. Senate passed a resolution 95-0 declaring that United States "should not be a signatory to any protocol" which would "result in serious harm to the U.S. economy" or which would "mandate new commitments to limit or reduce greenhouse gas emissions" unless that agreement also applied to developing countries "within the same compliance period."[91] In other words, what became known as the Berlin Mandate doomed

---

[82] Victor, *The Collapse of the Kyoto Protocol*, 4.
[83] Howe, *Behind the Curve*, 192-193.
[84] Angela Merkel quoted in Klein, *This Changes Everything*, 218.
[85] Maciunas and de Lassus Saint-Geniès, "The Evolution of Canada's International and Domestic Climate Policy."
[86] Maciunas and de Lassus Saint-Geniès, "The Evolution of Canada's International and Domestic Climate Policy." The authors note that Canada's domestic environmental policy did not reflect its international environmental reputation during the Kyoto period.
[87] Kutney, *Carbon Politics and the Failure of the Kyoto Protocol*, 197-198.
[88] Lemonick, "Turning Down the Heat," 24. Coal burning produces far more greenhouse gases than burning natural gas. In fact, a new natural gas power plant will emit 50 to 60 percent less carbon dioxide than a new coal plant does. See "Environmental Impacts of Natural Gas," *Union of Concerned Scientists*, June 19, 2014, accessed February 20, 2020, https://tinyurl.com/w44pss5
[89] Kutney, *Carbon Politics and the Failure of the Kyoto Protocol*, 197.
[90] Kutney, *Carbon Politics and the Failure of the Kyoto Protocol*, 156. At 12% China was in second place as an emitter, behind the United States, which produced 24% between 1960-2010.
[91] "S.Res.98 - A Resolution Expressing The Sense Of The Senate Regarding The Conditions For The United States Becoming A Signatory To Any International Agreement On Greenhouse Gas Emissions Under The

any chance that the agreements reached in Kyoto would be ratified by the United States. Canada did ratify and its government issued three plans between 2000 and 2005 to try to meet its Kyoto obligations, but none of these proved to be successful in reducing emissions.[92] In fact, by 2007, Canada's emissions were 27% above 1990 levels, instead of moving towards its goal of 6% below. This led new Conservative Party Prime Minister and fierce Kyoto critic Stephen Harper to conclude that it was impossible for Canada to meet its Kyoto target without doing significant damage to the nation's economy.[93] Therefore, in 2011, Canada became the only ratifying country to withdraw from the Protocol. The Kyoto debacle was so acute that Yamani's 1973 and 1979 oil spikes, and the conservation they induced, did more to reduce CO_2 emissions than the Protocol did.[94]

~

Despite the failures in Rio and Kyoto, climate scientists kept working to document what they knew to be true and to convince policymakers and the general public of the grave danger the planet faced.[95] Zickfeld had her first opportunity to contribute to that effort as a research associate at the Potsdam Institute for Climate Impact Research, when she became a contributing author to the IPCC's Third Assessment Report.[96] From January 1999 to December 2000, Zickfeld collaborated on a project entitled, "Integrated Assessment of Climate Protection Strategies." This group's work was eventually incorporated into conclusions of the Third Assessment, which was published in 2001. Zickfeld's contribution to the 893-page report was small to be sure, but it showed her how the IPCC's mission of summarizing the work of individual scientists could lead to recommendations for policymakers on a global scale. In fact, the first conclusion in the report was that "an increasing body of observations gives a collective picture of a warming world and other changes in the climate system." Zickfeld had been part of that collective picture. The report also pointedly stated that "greenhouse gases and aerosols due to human activities continue to alter the atmosphere in ways that are expected to affect the climate," and that "global average temperature and sea level are projected to rise" under all possible scenarios. The assessment held that scientists' "confidence in the ability of models to project future climate has increased" because there is "new and stronger evidence that most of the warming observed over the last 50 years is attributable to human activities" and that "human influences will continue to change atmospheric composition

United Nations Framework Convention On Climate Change," *United States Congress*, July 25, 1997, accessed February 20, 2020, https://www.congress.gov/bill/105th-congress/senate-resolution/98
[92] Maciunas and de Lassus Saint-Geniès, "The Evolution of Canada's International and Domestic Climate Policy."
[93] "Canada's House Backs Steep Emission Cuts," *New York Times*, February 15 2007, 1. *ProQuest Historical Newspapers*.
[94] Steven Stoft, *Carbonomics: How to Fix the Climate and Charge it to OPEC* (Nantucket, Massachusetts: Diamond Press, 2008), 4.
[95] The climate models developed by scientists in the 1970s, 1980s, and 1990s have proven to be astonishingly accurate in predicting the planet's climate situation in 2020. See Zeke Hausfather, Henri F. Drake, Tristan Abbott, and Gavin A. Schmidt, "Evaluating the Performance of Past Climate Model Projections," *Geophysical Research Letters*, Vol. 47, Issue 1, (January 16, 2020), https://doi.org/10.1029/2019GL085378
[96] "Kirsten Zickfeld, Curriculum Vitae," *Government of Canada*, accessed February 20, 2020, https://apps.neb-one.gc.ca/REGDOCS/File/Download/867571.

throughout the 21st century," bringing about "anthropogenic climate change" for many centuries.[97] Indeed, though couched in the compromise language of international diplomacy, the Third Assessment sent a clear warning for the new century that the situation was dire.[98]

In March 2004, with the Keeling Curve at 378 ppm, Zickfeld became a professional climatologist with her doctorate in hand. In doing so, she overcame many of the discriminatory practices and behaviors most female German scientists still faced at the beginning of the twenty-first century, including institutional bias, less support and mentorship, fewer networking opportunities, and outright sexism.[99] The focus of her dissertation was on thermohaline circulation: how ocean temperatures and salinity in the oceans create planetary, deep-water movements of seawater that are distinct from surface currents driven by wind or tides—and how this circulation may relate to climate change. This field was not much in the public's eye until, two months after Zickfeld's graduation, Twentieth Century Fox released the popular climate disaster movie *The Day After Tomorrow*. Directed by Germany's Roland Emmerich and starring Jake Gyllenhaal, Dennis Quaid, and Emmy Rossum, the film depicted a sudden cessation of the North Atlantic thermohaline circulation (or THC) system, which transfers saltier, warmer water from the tropics north to the Arctic and subsequently brings cold water south to the tropics. In the movie, this collapse in ocean circulation left New York City swamped by a wave and then plunged into a sudden deep freeze. This made for great visual effects, which helped *Tomorrow* to become 2004's seventh highest grossing film in the United States. It made over $544 million worldwide.[100] It also influenced public perceptions about climate change in Germany, Great Britain, Japan, and the United States,[101] although its scientific premise was flawed.[102] Like historians, scientists can become easily frustrated by factual misrepresentations in popular culture, but what Zickfeld and her Potsdam Institute mentor Stefan Rahmstorf objected to more was the publication of a study commissioned by Bjørn Lomborg, a scientist who had published the controversial book *The Skeptical Environmentalist* in 2001.[103] Lomborg hired two scientists from the Danish Meteorological Institute to complete the

---

[97] *Climate Change 2001: The Scientific Basis*, J.T. Houghton et al, (eds.) (Cambridge, U.K.: Intergovernmental Panel on Climate Change/Cambridge University Press, 2001), 2-17, accessed February 20, 2020, https://www.ipcc.ch/report/ar3/wg1/

[98] Bill McKibben, "Some Like It Hot," *New York Review of Books*, July 5, 2001, accessed July 19, 2019 https://www.nybooks.com/articles/2001/07/05/some-like-it-hot/

[99] Fuchs, Von Stebut, and Allmendinger, "Gender, Science, and Scientific Organizations in Germany."

[100] "The Day After Tomorrow," *IMDb (Internet Movie Database)*, accessed February 20, 2020, https://www.imdb.com/title/tt0319262/?ref_=ttfc_fc_tt

[101] Anthony A. Leiserowitz, "Before and After *The Day After Tomorrow*," *Environment* 46, no. 9 (November 2004), 22-37, EBSCOhost; and Fritz Reusswig, "The International Impact of *The Day After Tomorrow*." *Environment* 47, no. 3 (April 2005): 41-43, EBSCOhost. These articles discuss studies and professional conversations about the impact of the film in shaping perceptions of climate change. Leiserowitz concludes that the film "had a significant impact on the climate change risk perceptions" of Americans who saw the film. Reusswig notes that while there were shifts in Germany and Japan, they were less notable because "public discourse is much more influenced by the assumption that climate change is predictable or that it already happens."

[102] Michael E. Mann, "Do Global Warming And Climate Change Represent A Serious Threat To Our Welfare And Environment?," *Social Philosophy & Policy*, vol. 26, no. 2 (2009), 193-230, *ProQuest Central*; and Robin L. Murray and Joseph K. Heumann, *Monstrous Nature: Environment and Horror on the Big Screen* (Lincoln, Nebraska: University of Nebraska Press, 2016), 194, EBSCOhost.

[103] Bjørn Lomborg, *The Skeptical Environmentalist: Measuring the Real State of the World* (Cambridge, U.K.: Cambridge University Press, 2001). This book argues that the world is not the verge of environmental catastrophe or breakdown, but is instead making tremendous progress. Children, for example, in both the industrialized and developing world will have a higher standard of living today than ever before (351-352). The

study and its release its results to coincide with the movie's May 2004 premiere. The Danes argued that although "abrupt changes" in Atlantic thermohaline circulation were "highly unlikely," the models they used supported "the prediction of a gradual decline in the strength of the Atlantic" deep-water currents. Therefore, the risk of a high impact like the one portrayed in *The Day After Tomorrow* "cannot be ruled out."[104] For Zickfeld and Rahmstorf, this was irresponsibly provocative. It was also sloppy science. They wrote a cutting critique of the study and its conclusions, showing that it had ignored important scholarship, failed to consider uncertainties like future meltwater from the Greenland ice cap, and mistook the fundamental nature of risk assessment.[105] Zickfeld was especially annoyed because she had recently published the results of her own study that showed how "the stability of the THC is dependent upon the rate of climate change." This meant that the likelihood of the collapse of North Atlantic thermohaline circulation was entirely conditional on how quickly temperatures increased and how much effort people made to mitigate that increase.[106] There wouldn't be a sudden collapse of the THC, even if it gradually slowed over time as temperatures increased. *The Day After Tomorrow* was fiction, and the work of the Danish scientists was rash.

Another response to the movie came between July and September 2004, when Zickfeld and another Potsdam Institute graduate student conducted interviews with twelve leading climate change experts, using a 60-page interview protocol they had developed over the preceding two years.[107] The interviewees represented a cross-section of scientific backgrounds, schools of thought,

---

scientific community widely criticized the book for its undue optimism. The scientists Lomborg hired were Steffen Malskær Olsen and Erik Buch. See for example, David Pimentel, "Skeptical of the Skeptical Environmentalist," *Skeptic* 9, no. 2 (June 2002), 90-94, EBSCOhost. For an example of a supportive review of the book, see Andrew McAfee, "Pessimism and Its Discontents," *Chronicle of Higher Education* 61, no. 11 (November 14, 2014), B9, EBSCOhost.

[104] S. M. Olsen and E. Buch, 2004, "A Review of the North Atlantic Circulation, Marine Climate Change and its Impact on North European Climate," Copenhagen, Denmark: Institut for Miljøvurdering (Environmental Assessment Institute), 2004, accessed July 20, 2019, De Økonomiske Råd (Danish Economic Councils), https://tinyurl.com/y6dhylwe

[105] Stefan Rahmstorf and Kirsten Zickfeld, "Thermohaline Circulation Changes: A Question of Risk Assessment," *Climatic Change* 68, no. 1-2 (January, 2005), 241-247, *ProQuest Central*.

[106] Kirsten Zickfeld, Thomas Slawig, Stefan Rahmstorf, and Richard Greatbatch, "A Low-Order Model for the Response of the Atlantic Thermohaline Circulation to Climate Change," *Ocean Dynamics* 54, no. 1 (February 2004): 8-26, EBSCOhost. In this study, Zickfeld and her colleagues built a model with four interconnected boxes with different volumes and salinities to simulate the North Atlantic Ocean, the South Atlantic Ocean, the tropics, and the deep Atlantic, which is how cold, less saline water returns to the tropics to begin the process again. They concluded that "use of a dynamic four-box model of the Atlantic to mimic the response of the THC as simulated by comprehensive climate models was successful," and that the simple model "represents a useful tool for exploring the basic physical mechanisms underlying the response of the THC to climate change." Zickfeld and a colleague did another study on the THC in 2003 and expanded that study in 2008. The conclusion of the 2008 study was that "short-term mitigation efforts are not required to preserve the THC," but "in light of the huge uncertainty associated with the allowable range of CO_2 emissions" it would be wise to "abandon business-as-usual paths…if the risk of a THC shutdown is to be kept low." See Kirsten Zickfeld and Thomas Bruckner, "Reducing the Risk of Atlantic Thermohaline Circulation Collapse: Sensitivity Analysis of Emissions Corridors." *Climatic Change*, vol. 91, no. 3-4 (December 2008), 291-315, *ProQuest Central*.

[107] Kirsten Zickfeld, Anders Levermann, M. Granger Morgan, Till Kuhlbrodt, Stefan Rahmstorf, and David W. Keith, "Expert Judgements on the Response of the Atlantic Meridional Overturning Circulation to Climate Change." *Climatic Change* 82, no. 3-4 (June 2007): 235-265, *ProQuest Central*. The scientists were well-published meteorologists, oceanographers, and climatologists associated with universities, research institutes, and

and nationalities. Each was asked over the course of a lengthy interview to evaluate the possible effects of global climate change on the Atlantic Meridional Overturning Circulation (AMOC), which is a more precise term for studying ocean dynamics than THC.[108] In the survey, the scientists concurred with one another that heat and freshwater fluctuations from melting ice and vertical mixing are the most important factors in evaluating the current state and future trends for AMOC, but they admitted that the factors influencing the vertical mixing remained the least well understood part of ocean circulation. The experts also agreed that even a partial collapse of AMOC would lead to cooling in the North Atlantic, but they disagreed as to the probability of a complete collapse in the face of rising CO_2 levels. If, for example, the amount of CO_2 in the atmosphere doubled, most of the experts foresaw a weakening of AMOC with an eventual recovery, but there was little agreement over how long that recovery would take or how intense the weakening would be. If the amount of CO_2 in the atmosphere quadrupled, then the predictions became even more varied, with only two of the twelve forecasting a complete, permanent AMOC collapse. There was agreement, however, that the greater the temperature increase, the greater the probability of AMOC's collapse.[109] This shows that while scientists may disagree on the specifics of climate change, particularly around scale and timeline, there is scientific consensus that rising temperatures will have a profound impact on the planet and its residents.

In January 2006, with the Keeling Curve at 382 ppm, Zickfeld departed Germany and moved to British Columbia to take a position as a postdoctoral research associate at the University of Victoria's School of Earth and Ocean Sciences. She left a nation where eco-friendly legislation enjoyed broad support and where the Green Party was well-established[110] to enter one where federalism promoted significant differences in environmental policy and where the Green Party lacked parliamentary representation.[111] Indeed, Canada in 2006 was a nation that was so divided

---

government agencies in Canada, the Faroe Islands, Germany, Japan, Switzerland, the United Kingdom, and the United States. The interviews were five to seven hours long.

[108] According to scientists associated with the National Oceanic and Atmospheric Administration's Geophysical Fluid Dynamics Laboratory in Princeton, New Jersey, the terms AMOC and THC are "often used interchangeably, but have distinctly different meanings. The AMOC is defined as the total (basin-wide) circulation in the latitude depth plane," but does not explain what drives the circulation. "In contrast, the term 'THC' implies a specific driving mechanism related to creation and destruction of buoyancy." The problem, however, is that the THC isn't actually observable or quantifiable in the field because it is so "difficult to cleanly separate overturning circulations into a 'wind-driven' and 'buoyancy-driven' contribution" as the global conveyor belt completes its process of circulating the oceans over hundreds of years. Therefore, to allow for both factors, the term "AMOC" is often used in the literature. See Thomas L. Delworth et al, "Chapter 4: The Potential for Abrupt Change in the Atlantic Meridional Overturning Circulation," *Abrupt Climate Change: Synthesis and Assessment Product 3.4* (Washington, DC: U.S. Geological Survey / National Oceanic and Atmospheric Administration / National Science Foundation, December, 2008), 262-263, accessed February 20, 2020, https://tinyurl.com/y5kgnvgp. For the purposes of the study, and because of the ambiguity in the use of the term among scientists, Zickfeld defined the AMOC as "the basin-scale deep overturning circulation in the Atlantic which transports warm surface water northwards and cold water southwards at depth."

[109] Zickfeld, Levermann, Morgan, Kuhlbrodt, Rahmstorf, and Keith, "Expert Judgements on the Response of the Atlantic Meridional Overturning Circulation to Climate Change."

[110] Uekötter, *The Greenest Nation?*, 153. In the 2005 federal election, the Green Party of Germany won 8.1% of the vote and secured 55 seats in the Bundestag.

[111] Kutney, *Carbon Politics and the Failure of the Kyoto Protocol*, 137-138. For a discussion of Canadian federalism and the Constitution, see *Framing Canadian Federalism: Historical Essays in Honour of John T. Saywell*, Dimitry Anastakis and Penny Bryden (eds.) (Toronto, Canada: University of Toronto Press, 2009); and Alain-G. Gagnon, *Contemporary Canadian Federalism: Foundations, Traditions, Institutions* (Toronto, Canada: University of Toronto Press, 2009). In the January 2006 federal election, the Green Party of Canada finished a distant fifth,

and soul-searching that the newly-resurgent, but still-unproven, Conservative Party did not win a parliamentary majority. As a result of his party's fragile minority mandate, Conservative leader Stephen Harper had to seek different alliances for each piece of legislation, rather than form a true coalition government.[112] What Harper proved able to do, however, over the course of his ten-year prime ministership was launch a concerted attack on environmental protections. His government's policies resulted in enormous budget cuts to the departments and agencies responsible for environmental protection. Harper also increased threats to endangered species, reduced ecosystem protection for fisheries, removed thousands of lakes and streams from federal protection, increased ocean dumping, and restricted or laid off government scientists. There was also significant harassment of non-governmental agencies opposed to his policies.[113] For Harper, such changes were necessary and justified by the 2008 recession. As the official government speech stated in March 2010,

> Our strategy is clear: we must combine the best of our intellectual and natural resources to create jobs, growth and opportunity....We are the world's seventh largest crude oil producer with the second largest proven reserves. We are the third largest natural gas producer, the third largest hydroelectric generator, the largest producer of uranium, and by far the largest supplier of energy resources to the world's largest marketplace. To support responsible development of Canada's energy and mineral resources, our Government will untangle the daunting maze of regulations that needlessly complicates project approvals, replacing it with simpler, clearer processes that offer improved environmental protection and greater certainty to industry.[114]

Canada's oil and natural gas-producing provinces used this policy orientation to centralize regulatory responsibility for environmental issues in pro-industry agencies, limit opportunities for the public to object to development projects, and disregard the implications of the cumulative effects of environmental degradation. In British Columbia, for example, the Oil and Gas Activities Act was updated in 2010 to give the Oil and Gas Commission, instead of the Ministry of Environment, control over permits for road construction and water use. In Alberta, the provincial government attempted to prevent environmental organizations from submitting commentary on tar sands development, and in Newfoundland, government agencies made no comprehensive

winning 4.48% of the popular vote nationally. Because it did not win in any districts (known as a "riding"), the Green Party did not gain a seat in Parliament.

[112] Peter C. Newman, "Stephen Harper, Born-Again Canadian," *Maclean's* vol. 119, no. 6 (February 6, 2006), 40, EBSCOhost. The modern Conservative Party in Canada was born in 2003 with the merger of the Progressive Conservative Party and the Canadian Alliance (Reform Party). The election in 2006 was the current Conservative Party's first election.

[113] Jocelyn Stacey, "The Environmental, Democratic, and Rule-of-Law Implications of Harper's Environmental Assessment Legacy," *Review of Constitutional Studies*, vol. 21, no. 2 (2016): 165-185, EBSCOhost; David Schindler, "Harper's Assault on Environmental Protection and Science," *Canadian Dimension*, Vol. 49, Issue 4 (2015), EBSCOhost; and Klein, *This Changes Everything*, 381-382.

[114] Governor General of Canada Michaëlle Jean, quoted in "Text of Stephen Harper Government's Speech from the Throne," March 3, 2010, *Georgia Straight*, accessed February 21, 2020, https://tinyurl.com/y5bfouyz. The governor general is the British crown's representative in Canada, carrying out the monarch's constitutional and ceremonial duties there. This duty includes reading the text of the government's speech before Parliament once a year. The words, though stated by Jean, may be considered to be Harper's.

assessment on the impact of offshore oil drilling on marine environments.[115] But federalism, did allow for the passage of some pro-environment legislation during the Harper years. In British Columbia, the government passed a carbon tax in 2008 that was made more palatable to voters by cuts to other taxes, and Ontario closed the last of its coal plants in 2014.[116] In addition, a protest movement called Idle No More, which was organized by four First Nation* women, raised awareness for environmental rights and indigenous rights in Canada, as well as the intersectionality of these rights.[117] On the international stage, however, Canada became an obstructionist participant in climate talks during the Harper years, as nations worked towards the Copenhagen climate summit in 2009.[118] Canada consistently blocked resolutions calling for binding commitments on CO_2 emissions or on aggregate targets for the largest CO_2 emitters. Canadian representatives also blocked references to the UN Declaration on the Rights of Indigenous Peoples, thus separating environmental issues and indigenous rights internationally. On his way to Copenhagen, Canada's environment minister argued that it was his job to "put Canada's best interests forward, and we are doing that."[119] As the negotiator for the thirty-seven members of the Alliance of Small Island States (AOSIS) said of the Canadians, "it's like they're thumbing their nose at the process. And as we've gotten closer to putting numbers on the table, I think Canada has become more problematic," repeatedly using diverting strategies to stifle progress.[120] When the Copenhagen negotiations again only produced a series of non-binding agreements, the Harper government was quietly pleased.[121]

As a postdoctoral student adjusting to living in a new country, Zickfeld proved to be quite productive. She published two papers in 2007 about the ways in which changes in the wind patterns in the Southern Hemisphere affect the Southern Ocean around Antarctica. Zickfeld did not travel

[115] Angela V. Carter, Gail S. Fraser, and Anna Zalik, "Environmental Policy Convergence in Canada's Fossil Fuel Provinces?: Regulatory Streamlining, Impediments, and Drift," *Canadian Public Policy / Analyse de Politiques*, vol. 43, no. 1 (2017), 61-72, EBSCOhost.

[116] Joshua S. Goldstein and Steffan A. Qvist, *A Bright Future: How Some Countries Have Solved Climate Change and the Rest Can Follow* (New York: Public Affairs, 2019), 199, 207. Ontario was able to close the coal plants through upgrades to its nuclear power plants. Some environmentalists do not see this as a step in the right direction, but Goldstein and Qvist argue that developing nuclear power is an essential component for combating climate change.

[117] See among other sources Niigaan Sinclair, "Idle No More: Where Is the Movement 2 Years Later?," *The Canadian Broadcasting Corporation (CBC)*, December 7, 2014. 2014, EBSCOhost; Marc Woons, "The Winter we Danced: Voices from the Past, the Future, and the Idle no More Movement," *The Canadian Journal of Native Studies* vol. 35, no. 1 (2015), 177-182. ProQuest Central; and Ionut Nicolescu, "Cases of Equality: Idle No More and the Protests at Standing Rock," *Canadian Journal of Urban Research*, vol. 27, no. 2 (Winter 2018): 1-13, EBSCOhost. Another important First Nation protest gained international awareness in February 2020 over the construction of the $5 billion, 420-mile Coastal GasLink pipeline in British Columbia, which is to pass through land belonging to the Wet'suwet'en tribe. The protests shut down freight and passenger service Canada, causing a significant economic disruption and a crisis for Justin Trudeau's government. The controversy not only pitted environmentalists against industry, but it has also divided the Wet'suwet'en community. See, for example, "Shut down Canada," *The Economist*, February 22, 2020, 36; and Randy Baker, "A Who's Who of the Wet'suwet'en Pipeline Conflict," *CBC News*, February 26, 2020, https://tinyurl.com/y5c5ohub

[118] Maciunas and de Lassus Saint-Geniès, "The Evolution of Canada's International and Domestic Climate Policy."

[119] Jim Prentice quoted in Jonathon Gatehouse, "Suddenly the World Hates Canada," *Maclean's* vol. 122, no. 50 (December 28, 2009), 18, EBSCOhost.

[120] M. J. Mace quoted in Gatehouse, "Suddenly the World Hates Canada," 18.

[121] "Harper Leaves Copenhagen As Climate Talks End In Confusion," *CityNews* [Toronto, Canada], December 18, 2009, accessed February 21, 2020, https://tinyurl.com/yy2dvdrh

to do this. Instead, she used a climatic model developed at the University of Victoria that allows users to enter variables into mathematical equations to measure probable outcomes. The model allows climatologists to consider a large number of factors simultaneously, including ocean circulation, thermodynamics, moisture levels in the atmosphere, CO_2 emissions, vegetation patterns, the amount of sea ice, the proportion of the sun's light and radiation reflected by the surface, and more.[122] In the first paper, Zickfeld and her colleagues reported the results of eight simulations related to carbon dioxide absorption and the phenomena of intensifying poleward winds. This was important because the Southern Ocean has been a major carbon sink, helping to absorb CO_2 emissions caused by industrialization. They predicted that the intensifying poleward winds would bring "increased precipitation over South Africa, southeastern South America, and Australia," thereby increasing the "global terrestrial carbon pool." This meant that the winds would help decrease the amount of carbon in the atmosphere because the increase in precipitation would increase the amount of land vegetation. This was encouraging news for those concerned with climate change, but the report "emphasized the necessity to take into account changes in the terrestrial biosphere when making inferences about the effects of changing winds on atmospheric CO_2 concentrations."[123] In the second paper, Zickfeld and her colleagues showed that "neither CO_2 emissions alone...or poleward-intensified winds alone...can account for the overall pattern of Southern Ocean temperature change." Instead, it was the combination of changing wind patterns, which themselves were a product of human actions, and the increased CO_2 emissions that contributed to warming sea temperatures around Antarctica. The second study also contained a major finding: some of the models used in the IPCC's Fourth Assessment in 2007 did not adequately account for the effects these winds were having on the Antarctic Circumpolar Current.[124] This meant that the Fourth Report had underestimated the climate change impacts on the Antarctic.

In November 2008, with the Keeling Curve at 384 ppm, Zickfeld began working as a research scientist at the Canadian government's Centre for Climate Modeling and Analysis in Victoria, BC. A year later, she published a groundbreaking work that proved to be so important that it won her the prestigious President's Prize of the Canadian Meteorological and Oceanographic Society in 2018. The paper's importance stemmed not only from the experimental results she obtained, but also from the originality of her method. Instead of approaching the experiment as other climatologists might, Zickfeld flipped the operating supposition on its head. Whereas climatologists had typically inputted data into climate models and then evaluated the models' results, Zickfeld began with the desired goal and then determined what would need to be done to reach that goal. By inverting the established premise and normal method of analysis to determine what would classify as dangerous levels of anthropogenic interference—the amount of human-caused CO_2 emissions that would be truly harmful to the planet—Zickfeld pushed the field in a new direction. The new paradigm was so novel that other scientists wrote articles describing her

---

[122] The official name of the model is the University of Victoria Earth System Climate Model (UVic ESCM) and for these experiments, she used version 2.8. The model's lead designer was Andrew J. Weaver.
[123] Kirsten Zickfeld, John C. Fyfe, Oleg A. Saenko, Michael Eby, and Andrew J. Weaver, "Response of the Global Carbon Cycle to Human-induced Changes in Southern Hemisphere Winds," *Geophysical Research Letters*, Vol. 34, (June 2007), L12712, accessed February 21, 2020, from *Semantic Scholar, Allen Institute for Artificial Intelligence,* https://pdfs.semanticscholar.org/044c/c6d2c91259641f37fc4930705f9474525b08.pdf
[124] John C. Fyfe, Oleg A. Saenko, Kirsten Zickfeld, Michael Eby, and Andrew J. Weaver," The Role of Poleward-Intensifying Winds on Southern Ocean Warming," *Journal of Climate*, vol. 20, no. 21 (Nov 01, 2007). 5391-5400. *ProQuest Central.*

approach and findings.[125] With her new approach, Zickfeld showed that to hold average global temperature increases to 2° Celsius, then two things must happen: 1) CO_2 concentrations in the atmosphere cannot exceed 450 ppm and 2) the total amount of carbon dioxide emitted between the years 2000 and 2500 cannot exceed 590 petagrams of carbon.[126] If these levels are exceeded, then carbon dioxide will have to be artificially removed from the atmosphere in order to have the earth eventually stabilize its temperature at 2° Celsius. Zickfeld's models also determined that regardless of whether the earth's temperature stabilizes in the year 2150 or 2200 or 2300, CO_2 concentrations in the atmosphere won't stabilize until about 2350.[127] This finding illustrated how the ocean's thermal inertia and ability to absorb CO_2 profoundly affects climate models. The oceans have helped mitigate the effects of greenhouse gas emissions, but because they continue to absorb excess planetary heat, oceans will also ensure that recovery will take considerable time.

In August 2010, with the Keeling Curve at 388 ppm, Zickfeld left her position as a government scientist and joined the faculty of the department of geography at Simon Fraser University, where she founded her own climate lab to train graduate students and to work with postgraduate students. She also continued to conduct her own prolific research, which soon included another landmark study. In 2012, Zickfeld and Damon Matthews, a geographer-climatologist from Concordia University in Montreal,[128] were the first to find that even if all carbon emissions ceased immediately, the Earth's temperature would continue to rise by a few tenths of a degree for a decade before slowly returning to 2012 levels in about 2212. In other words, even if every airplane, car, factory, and power plant had ceased polluting in 2012, it would still take two centuries for the earth's atmospheric temperatures to return to those same levels. The timeline is even longer for ocean temperatures because of the ocean's thermal inertia. Matthews and Zickfeld concluded, "sea-level rise would be expected to continue for many centuries, even following the elimination of all emissions."[129] Zickfeld acknowledged in an interview that "it's totally unrealistic to believe we can

---

[125] Matthew H. England, "Alexander Sen Gupta, and Andrew J. Pitman, "Constraining Future Greenhouse Gas Emissions by a Cumulative Target," *Proceedings of the National Academy of Sciences*, 106 (39) (September 29, 2009), 16539-16540, accessed February 21, 2020, https://www.pnas.org/content/106/39/16539.

[126] One petagram of carbon (PGC) is a billion metric tons. To illustrate this size, the Pacific Marine Environmental Laboratory determined that if one 60-foot long railroad hopper car holds 100 tons of coal, then it would take a train 156,500 miles long to haul the coal equivalent of one PGC. See "The Carbon Cycle," *Pacific Marine Environmental Laboratory, National Oceanic and Atmospheric Administration*, no date, accessed February 21, 2020, https://www.pmel.noaa.gov/co2/story/Carbon+Cycle.

[127] Kirsten Zickfeld, Michael Eby, H. Damon Matthews, and Andrew J. Weaver, "Setting Cumulative Emissions Targets to Reduce the Risk of Dangerous Climate Change," *Proceedings of the National Academy of Sciences (PNAS)*, September 22, 2009, 106 (38) 16129-16134, accessed February 21, 2020, https://www.pnas.org/content/106/38/16129

[128] Matthews earned his bachelor's at Simon Fraser and his Ph.D. from the University of Victoria, so the Zickfeld and Matthews knew many of the same people, although they did not overlap chronologically at either institution. They also collaborated on a 2011 study that explored the relationship between carbon uptakes on land and in the ocean. See Kirsten Zickfeld, Michael Eby, H. Damon Matthews, Andreas Schmittner, and Andrew J. Weaver. "Nonlinearity of Carbon Cycle Feedbacks," *Journal of Climate* 24, no. 16 (August 15, 2011): 4255-4275, EBSCOhost. For a brief biography of Matthews, see "Damon Matthews, Ph.D.," *Concordia University*, 2018, accessed February 21, 2020, https://www.concordia.ca/faculty/damon-matthews.html .

[129] H. D. Matthews and Kirsten Zickfeld, "Climate Response to Zeroed Emissions of Greenhouse Gases and Aerosols," *Nature Climate Change* 2.5 (2012): 338-341. *ProQuest Central.*

stop all emissions now," but added that knowing this helps us to understand how difficult it will be "to keep the projected global rise in temperature under 2° Celsius."[130]

~

As was true with the summits in Stockholm, Rio de Janeiro, and Kyoto, the climate negotiations in Paris in December 2015 were the culmination of years of preparatory negotiations involving many individuals. What made the largest difference between the failed talks in Copenhagen in 2009 and the hopeful ones in Paris lay in the decisions and actions of six heads of state. In November 2014 with the Keeling Curve at 397 ppm, Barack Obama met with Xi Jinping in Beijing to talk specifically about climate change and the upcoming Paris summit. Both leaders agreed to specific CO_2 limits for the first time; the United States committed itself to an emissions reduction of 26%-28% below its 2005 level by 2025, and with China committed itself to capping its CO_2 emissions by 2030. Obama and Xi made these pledges, acknowledging that "human activity is already changing the world's climate system" in such ways that "urgently require enhanced actions," because they hoped doing so would "inject momentum into the global climate negotiations and inspire other countries to join in coming forward with ambitious actions as soon as possible."[131] This announcement broke the twenty-year deadlock between the two nations over climate change policy.[132] Six months later, Pope Francis I provided more momentum with his influential encyclical letter *Laudato Si'*, which lucidly and forcefully called for the urgent need to address ecological issues and social justice issues simultaneously.[133] He described climate as "a common good," criticized "throwaway culture," and noted that the digital world "can stop people from learning how to live wisely, to think deeply, and to love generously." Frances also stated that there are moral and ethical limits to private property, technology, and consumption, and he declared with both realism and frustration,

> It is remarkable how weak international political responses [to the climate crisis] have been. The failure of global summits on the environment make it plain that our politics are subject to technology and finance. There are too many special interests, and economic interests easily end up trumping the common good and manipulating information so that their own plans will not be affected.[134]

Thirteen weeks before the opening of the Paris summit, Fiji's Prime Minister Josaia Voreqe "Frank" Bainimarama gathered government leaders and other prominent individuals from fifteen Pacific

---

[130] Kirsten Zickfeld quoted in Anthony Watts, "Give up Canada, You're Toast," *Watts Up with That?*, March 7, 2012, accessed February 21, 2020, https://wattsupwiththat.com/2012/03/07/give-up-canada-youre-toast/

[131] The White House Office of the Press Secretary, "U.S.-China Joint Announcement on Climate Change," *National Archives*, November 11, 2014, accessed February 21, 2020, https://tinyurl.com/yd6kxfj6

[132] Coral Davenport, "A Climate Deal, 6 Fateful Years in the Making: Stung by Failure in Copenhagen in '09, 195 Nations Felt New Urgency," *New York Times,* December 14 2015, 2. *ProQuest Historical Newspapers.*

[133] Ghosh, *The Great Derangement*, 150-151, 157.

[134] Francis I, "Encyclical Letter Laudato Si' of the Holy Father Francis on Care for our Common Home," *The Holy See*, May 25, 2015, accessed July 25, 2019 https://tinyurl.com/o6sowft. Significantly, Francis repeatedly used the words "environmental crisis" or "ecological crisis" to describe the climate problem.

nations together to hammer out a common strategy for the Paris talks.[135] The result was the Suva Declaration, which demanded that any agreement in Paris "limit global average temperature increase to below 1.5°C above pre-industrial levels," "be legally binding," and provide "increased support for adaptation measures" in threatened Pacific nations with "100% grant financ[ing]."[136] It was a bold resolution given the results of past climate conferences and how much harder it would be to limit the temperature increase to 1.5°C, but as Bainimarama said,

> There are those who say it may already be too late to avert disaster for our coastal communities and to prevent three of our number—Kiribati, Tuvalu and the Marshall Islands—from disappearing beneath the waves altogether. But we in the Pacific are not prepared to simply sit back weakly and allow this to happen. We are gearing up for the biggest struggle Pacific Islanders have ever faced—the fight for our survival. And we intend to take that fight with other islands and low-lying nations all the way to Paris and do everything in our power to get the world to finally sit up and take notice.[137]

In October 2015, Bainimarama applauded the election results in Canada, which brought Liberal Party leader Justin Trudeau to power after almost a decade of Tory rule. During the campaign, Trudeau had vowed to reestablish Canada's role as an international climate leader and had called for putting a price on carbon.[138] Bainimarama had followed the election closely because he knew that a change in government in Canada had the potential to change the character of the Paris negotiations. Canada would no longer be the obstacle it had been during the Stephen Harper years. In his congratulatory message to Trudeau, Bainimarama wrote, "Fiji wholeheartedly welcomes your commitment to increase Canada's involvement in international peacekeeping and strengthening its efforts to tackle the cataclysmic effects of climate change."[139]

Added to this this potent mix of political leadership in 2015 was Germany's Chancellor Angela Merkel. In the wake of Greece's debt crisis, the influx of Syrian refugees, and Russia's seizure of the Crimea, she had become both Europe's moral center and its most powerful leader.[140] Part of this authority came from her ability to stand firm in her beliefs, but also in her willingness to alter course in the face of new evidence. After Japan's Fukushima Daiichi nuclear plant meltdown in 2011, Merkel orchestrated a significant change to Germany's energy and environmental policy. Trained as a physical chemist, she had long been a supporter of nuclear power, but she withdrew that support after Fukushima and decided to close all of Germany's nuclear power plants by 2022. Merkel said,

[135] Justin Worland, "That Sinking Feeling: How Pacific Countries Joined Together to Confront Climate Change Before It's Too Late," *Time*, vol. 193 no. 24 (June 24, 2019), 31-36.
[136] "Suva Declaration on Climate Change," *Pacific Islands Development Forum*, September 2-4, 2015, accessed July 25, 2019, http://pacificidf.org/wp-content/uploads/2016/02/ecopy-Declaration.pdf
[137] Josaia Voreqe Bainimarama quoted in "Fijian PM Calls on Australia to Abandon Coalition of the Selfish, Stop Lobbying Pacific Leaders Not to Attend PIDF," *Pacnews*, September 2, 2015, *ProQuest Central*.
[138] Maciunas and de Lassus Saint-Geniès, "The Evolution of Canada's International and Domestic Climate Policy."
[139] Josaia Voreqe Bainimarama quoted in "Fijian PM Congratulates Canada's Trudeau on Election," *Cihan News Agency*, October 24 2015, *ProQuest Central*.
[140] Nancy Gibbs, "The Choice: 2015 Person of the Year," *Time*, vol. 186, no. 25-26 (December 21, 2015), 49-50; and Matthew Qvortrup, *Angela Merkel: Europe's Most Influential Leader* (New York: Overlook Duckworth, 2016), 327-337; and Joyce Marie Mushaben, *Becoming Madam Chancellor: Angela Merkel and the Berlin Republic* (New York: Cambridge University Press, 2017), 243.

> Without a doubt, the dramatic events in Japan were a deep blow for the world and for me personally….[We have] to recognize…that even in a high-technology land like Japan, the risks inherent in nuclear energy cannot be mastered….The residual risks of atomic energy are only acceptable if you believe that human error will never intervene….I accepted the residual risks nuclear energy prior to Fukushima because I utterly believed that such a catastrophe could never happen in a high-technology land with security standards as high as humanly possible. But now is has happened.[141]

With this switch, Merkel harnessed her motto, *Wir schaffen das* ("We can do this")[142] and led Germany toward a policy of *Energiewende*, a fast "energy turnaround" to renewable sources in order to reduce the nation's greenhouse gas emissions to at least 80% of 1990 levels by 2050.[143] By 2018, Germany could generate 40% of its net electricity production from renewable sources while exporting surplus electricity to neighboring countries.[144] But this progress has been undercut because Germany continues to operate its lignite coal-burning plants, which produce large amounts of CO_2. Some argue that Germany's renewable energy resource growth will struggle to compensate for the pending closure of the nuclear power plants,[145] but it is clear that Merkel exploited the rare political consensus generated by the Fukushima nuclear accident to pass green legislation and end divisiveness about nuclear power.[146]

Despite the forward movement provided by Obama, Xi, Francis, Bainimarama, Trudeau, and Merkel, there was considerable doubt that an agreement could be reached as the December 2015 Paris summit opened. But after two weeks of intense weeks of negotiations, leaders agreed to work to keep the global temperature rise in the twentieth-first century to "well below 2 degrees Celsius above pre-industrial levels and to pursue efforts to limit the temperature increase even further to 1.5 degrees Celsius." To accomplish this, each nation would make "nationally determined contributions" beyond what was already being done to limit greenhouse gases. For each signatory, these contributions were to "reflect its highest possible ambition" with the understanding that the nations of the world had "common but differentiated responsibilities and respective capabilities." In addition, developed nations were to "provide financial resources to assist" developing countries "with respect to both mitigation and adaptation."[147] This meant that while the pleas of the Pacific Island nations were incorporated into the accord and while there were binding commitments under

---

[141] Angela Merkel quoted in Mushaben, *Becoming Madam Chancellor*, 228.

[142] Mushaben, *Becoming Madam Chancellor,* 313.

[143] Christine Sturm, "Inside the *Energiewende*," *Issues in Science & Technology* vol. 33, no. 2 (Winter 2017), 41–47, EBSCOhost. For more about Germany's energy future, see Karoline Steinbacher and Sybille Röhrkasten, "An Outlook on Germany's International Energy Transition Policy in the Years to Come: Solid Foundations and New Challenges," *Energy Research & Social Science* 49 (March 1, 2019), 204–208, EBSCOhost.

[144] Bruno Burger, "Net Public Electricity Generation in Germany in 2018," *Fraunhofer Institute for Solar Energy Systems ISE*, January 5, 2019, 7, 12, accessed February 21, 2020, https://tinyurl.com/y3u5ctru

[145] Goldstein and Qvist, *A Bright Future,* 34, 39. Goldstein and Qvist argue that it will be impossible for renewables to meet the world's energy needs in the future and that nuclear power is the only viable alternative to cut CO2 emissions substantially in the timeframe available.

[146] Mushaben, *Becoming Madam Chancellor*, 232-234; and Uekötter, *The Greenest Nation?*, 153-154.

[147] "Paris Agreement," *United Nations Climate Change*, December 12, 2015, accessed February 21, 2020, https://tinyurl.com/y7rfhdjt. The language "common but differentiated responsibilities and respective capabilities" was originally used in the United Nations Framework Convention on Climate Change (UNFCCC) treaty at the Rio de Janeiro conference in 1992.

international law to fight climate change for the first time, each nation was permitted to determine its own specific course of action. This left plenty of room for noncompliance. Despite these significant limitations, some worry that the Paris Agreement will prove to be the climax of international cooperation on the environment for the foreseeable future.[148] After all, various forms of populist nationalism have come to dominate countries as culturally diverse as Bolivia, Brazil, Hungary, India, Israel, the Philippines, Turkey, and the United States,[149] and Great Britain voted for Brexit, albeit by a slim margin. In addition, Donald Trump began the four-year withdrawal process from the Paris Agreement on June 1, 2017, even though the Keeling Curve had climbed to 410 ppm.[150] Given this decision, there are those who put the odds of meeting even a 2°C goal at less than five percent.[151]

These discouraging predictions are counterbalanced by efforts to increase the chances of attaining the goals of the Paris Agreement. In April 2016, the IPCC agreed to prepare a special report on the impact of global warming of 1.5°C above pre-industrial levels, using the systems of its regular assessments. Governments and influential organizations nominated 541 experts as potential authors and editors for the report.[152] Canada nominated Zickfeld, and the IPCC selected her to be one of the lead authors for the first chapter, which provided framing and context for the rest of the report. This was an honor that recognized her contributions in the advancement of scientific knowledge. Chapter 1 makes it clear that "human influence has become a principal agent of change on the planet" and that, as of 2017, "human-induced warming [had] reached approximately 1°C…above pre-industrial levels." It notes that significant portions of the global population have already experienced a 1.5°C temperature increase, which has "already resulted in profound alterations to human and natural systems."[153] In other words, the *Special Report: Global Warming of 1.5°C* speaks with a certainty that previous IPCC documents lacked. It possesses such a such candor and clarity that it may be seen as a last-chance clarion call to action.[154] Given the nature of diplomatic language, the report is a surprisingly radical document: the first chapter

[148] Bill McKibben, "A Very Grim Forecast," *The New York Review of Books*, November 22, 2018, accessed February 21, 2020, https://www.nybooks.com/articles/2018/11/22/global-warming-very-grim-forecast/
[149] For an interesting analysis of three major types of populism (anti-establishment, cultural, and socio-economic) and the ability of populists to stay in power, see Jordan Kyle and Limor Gultchin, "Populists in Power Around the World," *Tony Blair Institute for Global Change*, November 7, 2018, accessed February 21, 2020, https://institute.global/insight/renewing-centre/populists-power-around-world
[150] "The Keeling Curve," *Scripps Institution of Oceanography*, July 31, 2019, accessed August 2, 2019, https://tinyurl.com/y6sbpnwb.
[151] Nathaniel Rich, *Losing Earth: A Recent History* (New York: Farrar, Straus and Giroux, 2019), 4. Rich notes that retired NASA scientist and environmental activist Jim Hansen calls a two-degree Celsius rise "a prescription for long-term disaster." Hansen became famous in June 1988, when he testified before Congress that he was 99% confident that global warming was being caused by human actions and that it was "time to stop waffling." See James Hansen, *Storms of My Grandchildren: The Truth about the Coming Climate Catastrophe and Our Last Chance to Save Humanity* (New York: Bloomsbury USA, 2009), xv.
[152] "Preface," *Special Report: Global Warming of 1.5°C*, The Intergovernmental Panel on Climate Change (April 2019), vii, accessed February 21, 2020, https://www.ipcc.ch/sr15/download/
[153] "Chapter 1: Framing and Context," *Special Report: Global Warming of 1.5°C*, The Intergovernmental Panel on Climate Change (2019), 51, 53, accessed February 21, 2020, https://www.ipcc.ch/sr15/download/
[154] David Wallace-Wells notes that in not wanting to be alarmist, scientists in the past have not been as honest with the general public as they could have been. He sees the *Special Report* as giving scientists permission to be less cautious in their conclusions: "It is ok, finally, to freak out." See David Wallace-Wells, *The Uninhabitable Earth: Life After Warming* (New York: Tim Duggan Books, 2019), 157.

appeals not just for action, but action that is consistent with the UN Sustainable Development Goals. This means finding ways to limit global warming to 1.5°C while also eradicating poverty and hunger, securing gender equality, protecting ecosystems, and providing access to clean water, sanitation, quality education, and affordable energy for all humanity. Chapter 1 notes that this will "require substantial societal and technological transformations," but unapologetically proclaims that such changes are desirable and necessary. Specifically, there should be a

> decoupling of economic growth from energy demand and CO_2 emissions; leap-frogging development to new and emerging low-carbon, zero-carbon and carbon-negative technologies; and synergistically linking climate mitigation and adaptation to global scale trends (e.g., global trade and urbanization) that will enhance the prospects for effective climate action, as well as enhanced poverty reduction and greater equity.[155]

Zickfeld was also selected to be a contributing author for the report's second chapter, entitled, "Mitigation Pathways Compatible with 1.5°C in the Context of Sustainable Development." She also served as an expert reviewer for other portions of the 630-page document. As Zickfeld said in an interview upon the publication of *Special Report: Global Warming of 1.5°C,* Chapter 2 is important because it provides the specific means to attain the goals outlined in Chapter 1: "What gives me hope is that with this report for the first time we have put out a blueprint or a roadmap [for] how this 1.5 degrees can be achieved." The *Special Report* outlined policies, finance mechanisms, and the scale of the technological transition that's required, "and so now it is on policy makers to take this on and act.[156] Chapter 2 states that, based on Zickfeld's research, "limiting global mean temperature increase at any level requires global CO_2 emissions to become net zero at some point in the future."[157] That is, to limit temperatures, we must at some point stop putting anthropogenic CO_2 into the atmosphere. This will require "large-scale transformations of the global energy–agriculture–land-economy system, affecting the way in which energy is produced, agricultural systems are organized, and food, energy, and materials are consumed."[158] The growth of renewable energy needs to be such that power sources will be "almost decarbonized" by 2050;[159] industry needs to develop "new sustainability-oriented low-carbon industrial processes;"[160] buildings around the world need to be newly-built or renovated to high green standards; and the demand for transportation needs to decrease through urban planning, increased vehicle load capacity, and the use of buses and trains over cars and airplanes. In addition, vehicles should be fueled by electricity whenever possible.[161] Higher agricultural yields, reforestation, eating less meat and reducing food

[155] "Chapter 1: Framing and Context," 56, 73-75.
[156] "Action Needed in All Sectors to Stop Climate Change Disaster: Kirsten Zickfeld," *Prime Time Politics, Cable Public Affairs Channel* (CPAC), October 11, 2018, *YouTube video*, 13:14, posted by CPAC, https://www.youtube.com/watch?v=Hp5K03kWpxI
[157] "Chapter 2: Mitigation Pathways Compatible with 1.5°C in the Context of Sustainable Development," *Special Report: Global Warming of 1.5°C,* The Intergovernmental Panel on Climate Change (2019), 108, February 21, 2020, https://www.ipcc.ch/sr15/download/
[158] "Chapter 2: Mitigation Pathways Compatible with 1.5°C in the Context of Sustainable Development," 108.
[159] "Chapter 2: Mitigation Pathways Compatible with 1.5°C in the Context of Sustainable Development," 136.
[160] "Chapter 2: Mitigation Pathways Compatible with 1.5°C in the Context of Sustainable Development," 140.
[161] "Chapter 2: Mitigation Pathways Compatible with 1.5°C in the Context of Sustainable Development," 142.

waste will also be important.[162] Chapter 2 also calls for the development of a rigorous carbon pricing system and a "major shift in investment patterns," from fossil fuels to renewable energy sources.[163]

The differences between enacting these recommendations and not enacting them are the differences between a 1.5°C and 2°C temperature increase above pre-industrial levels. These differences include:

- 420 million fewer people being frequently exposed to extreme heat waves;
- 65 million fewer people being exposed to exceptional heatwaves;
- 10.4 million fewer people being exposed to the impact of sea level rise;
- *Any* chance to save the planet's existing tropical coral reefs;
- A 50% reduction in the number of vertebrate & plant species threatened by extinction;
- A 50% reduction in the number of people threatened by water scarcity worldwide;
- Limiting the geographical range of vector-borne diseases like malaria & dengue fever;
- Limiting the risk of heavy precipitation in Canada, northern Europe and northern Asia;
- Limiting the intensity of cyclones;
- Limiting ocean acidification, species shifts, and a general decline in ocean productivity;
- Greater cereal yields in Africa, Southeast Asia and Central and South America;
- Greater economic growth in Africa, Brazil, India, Mexico, Southeast Asia;
- A decreased risk of poverty in Africa and Asia;
- A decreased risk of flooding globally;
- A substantially reduced risk of extreme drought in the Mediterranean region (southern Europe, northern Africa, the Near East) and Southern Africa.[164]

On the whole, the *Special Report: Global Warming of 1.5°C* answers challenge posed by an Antoine de Saint Exupéry quote that appears before the report's Table of Contents: "Pour ce qui est de l'avenir, il ne s'agit pas de le prévoir, mais de le rendre possible" or "As for the future, it is not a question of predicting it, but of making it possible."[165] Zickfeld is rightfully proud of this work.

~

In 1903, the Swedish Nobel Prize-winning Chemist Svante Arrhenius noted that the

slight percentage of carbonic acid in the atmosphere may by the advance of industry be changed to a noticeable degree in the course of a few centuries. That would imply that there

[162] "Chapter 2: Mitigation Pathways Compatible with 1.5°C in the Context of Sustainable Development," 148.
[163] "Chapter 2: Mitigation Pathways Compatible with 1.5°C in the Context of Sustainable Development," 153. Some financial analysts argue that, given the increased viability of renewable energy sources, continuing to invest in the fossil fuel industry is a mistake. See Bill McKibben, "A Future without Fossil Fuels?" *New York Review of Books*, April 4, 2019, 4-6.
[164] "Chapter 3: Impacts of 1.5°C of Global Warming on Natural and Human Systems," *Special Report: Global Warming of 1.5°C*, The Intergovernmental Panel on Climate Change (2019), 177-181, accessed February 21, 2020, https://www.ipcc.ch/sr15/download/.
[165] The quote comes from the French author's posthumous 1948 work *Citadelle*. The translation is by Google Translate.

is no real stability in the percentage of carbon dioxide in the air, which is probably subject to considerable fluctuations in the course of time.[166]

Arrhenius was correct that industry—as well as population growth and rampant consumerism—would produce sufficient CO_2 to create a noticeable level of climatic change at the planetary level in the late twentieth and early twenty-first centuries. He was also right that the amount of CO_2 in the earth's atmosphere is not fixed and can be changed. As Zickfeld and one of her graduate students have shown, ocean temperatures and sea levels will inevitably rise because of our past actions,[167] but it is still possible to lessen the most adverse impacts of those changes. The amount of additional global warming "depends on future rates of emission reductions."[168] It is not about what humans have done; it's about the decisions humanity makes in the very near future.

The challenge is too daunting for a single solution. We can no longer fix the problem with regulations or treaties or technological innovations alone.[169] Even multiple strategies and new technologies will require all the collective expertise, political cooperation, and financial expenditure humanity can muster.[170] But if governments follow the prescriptions of IPCC's 2018 *Special Report* and its November 2019 supplement,[171] we can ameliorate future conditions for our grandchildren

---

[166] Svante Arrhenius, *Worlds in the Making: The Evolution of the Universe*, H. Borns (trans.) (New York and London: Harper & Brothers, 1903), 54.

[167] Dana Ehlert and Kirsten Zickfeld, "Irreversible Ocean Thermal Expansion Under Carbon Dioxide Removal," *Earth System Dynamics* 9, no. 1 (January 2018): 197-210. EBSCOhost. Ehlert completed her Ph.D. in April 2017 and is currently working as a postdoctoral researcher at the GEOMAR Helmholtz Centre for Ocean Research Kiel, Germany. See "Thesis Defense—Congratulations to Dana Ehlert," Department of Geology, Simon Fraser University, April 13, 2017, https://www.sfu.ca/geography/news-and-events/kudos-archives/kudos-2017/20170413-ehlert-thesis-defence.html; and "Dana Ehlert," GEOMAR Helmholtz Centre for Ocean Research Kiel, accessed February 21, 2020, https://www.geomar.de/en/mitarbeiter/fb2/bm/dehlert/

[168] "Chapter 1: Framing and Context," 51.

[169] Andrew Revkin, "Climate: The More Things Change…" *National Geographic*, Vol. 234, no. 1 (July 2018), 17-20.

[170] John L. Brooke, *Climate Change and the Course of Global History: A Rough Journey* (New York: Cambridge University Press, 2014), 560. The necessary financial commitments are daunting: one study estimated that it will cost $320 billion a year in private investment until 2050 to achieve the necessary emission reductions and establish a carbon-neutral economy. See Jeremy B. C. Jackson and Steve Chapple, *Breakpoint: Reckoning with America's Environmental Crisis* (New Haven, Connecticut: Yale University Press, 2018), 201-202.

[171] The UN Environment Program (UNEP) issued an updated report in November 2019 which concluded the planet must reduce its greenhouse gas emissions by 7.6% each year between 2020 and 2030 in order to meet the 1.5°C goal. See United Nations Environmental Programme, *Emissions Gap Report 2019* (Nairobi, Kenya: UNEP, 2019), accessed February 21, 2020, https://tinyurl.com/ttfwzrx. With President Donald Trump announcing in June 2017 that the "United States will cease all implementation of the non-binding Paris Accord and the draconian financial and economic burdens the agreement imposes on our country," and with the United States' formal withdraw from the agreement on November 4, 2019, the prospect of the world meeting the 7.6% reduction goal appears slim. See Donald Trump, "Statement by President Trump on the Paris Climate Accord," June 1, 2017, *The White House*, accessed February 21, 2020, https://tinyurl.com/yazkrs3d; and Michael R. Pompeo, "On the U.S. Withdrawal from the Paris Agreement," November 4, 2019, *Department of State*, accessed February 21, 2020, https://tinyurl.com/yyldo364

and great grandchildren.[172] What is required is a global, communal decision to act quickly,[173] to choose what's best for everyone on the planet, instead of what is best for the self.[174] It means finally abandoning what social critic and historian Christopher Lasch identified in 1979 as a culture of narcissism. It means taking a sincere interest in the past and rejecting the appearance of success over substantial accomplishment. It means discouraging rampant consumerism as a way of life and living for the betterment of future generations instead of our own.[175]

Despair and resignation will not combat the twenty-first century's climatic issues, but hope and will power still just might.

---

[172] The COVID-19 outbreak in 2019-2020 made it clear that it is possible to make a meaningful, dramatic impact on the environment quickly. The planet witnessed a 17% drop in CO_2 emissions in April 2020 as compared to April 2019 as a result of the economic downturn caused by the pandemic and the planet was on target to see a 4% to 7% decrease in CO_2 emissions for the year. If such changes could come from a multifaceted global plan instead of a health crisis, the economic impact of the changes would not be nearly so great. For the full report, see Corinne Le Quéré et al, "Temporary Reduction in Daily Global CO_2 Emissions During the COVID-19 Forced Confinement," *National Climate Change*, May 19, 2020, accessed May 20, 2020, https://doi.org/10.1038/s41558-020-0797-x

[173] In November 2019, scientists examined nine areas in the world where climate change may alter the ecosystem so much as to tip the balance toward a catastrophic outcome. The scientists determined that "the evidence from tipping points alone suggests that we are in a state of planetary emergency: both the risk and urgency of the situation are acute." They called for governments to act immediately to limit "abrupt and irreversible climate changes." The nine tipping point areas were the Amazon rainforest, Arctic sea ice, Atlantic Ocean circulation, boreal forests, coral reefs, the Greenland ice sheet, permafrost zones, the West Antarctic Ice Sheet, and the J. Wilkes Basin in East Antarctica. See Timothy M. Lenton et al, "Climate Tipping Points— Too Risky to Bet Against," Nature, November 27, 2019, accessed February 22, 2020, https://www.nature.com/articles/d41586-019-03595-0

[174] Certainly not everyone agrees with this premise. Duke University ethicist Walter Sinnott-Armstrong, for example, presents thirteen philosophical principles that might be used to assert that individuals have a moral obligation not to promote global warming, but he dismisses each of them. Instead, he argues that our real moral obligation is to "let governments do their job to prevent the disaster of excessive global warming" because the scale of the problem is too vast for individual actions. See Walter Sinnott-Armstrong, "It's Not *My* Fault: Global Warming and Individual Moral Obligations, *Climate Ethics: Essential Readings*, Stephen M. Gardiner, Simon Caney, Dale Jamieson, and Henry Shue (eds.) (New York: Oxford University Press, 2010), 332-344, EBSCOhost.

[175] Christopher Lasch, *The Culture of Narcissism: American Life in an Age of Diminishing Expectations* (New York: Warner Books, 1979), 21-25, 33, 116-117, 137-138. These are only a few of Lasch's major points in a book that still makes for provocative reading in the 2020s. This is particularly true in the light of the rise of social media and personalized technology: numerous studies have documented the connections between narcissism and social media. One study has suggested that narcissistic behavior has become so ubiquitous through social media's prevalence that narcissism can now be considered a normalized behavior. See Christina Frederick and Tianxin Zhang, "Narcissism and Social Media Usage: Is There No Longer a Relationship?" *Journal of Articles in Support of the Null Hypothesis*, Vol. 16, No. 1 (2019), 23+, EBSCOhost.

GLOSSARY

ABSOLUTISM: A political theory which holds that all power should be concentrated in the hands of a monarch, rather than being shared between a monarch and a legislative assembly or social classes such as the nobility or the bourgeoisie.* In philosophy, the theory is associated with Thomas Hobbes (1588-1679). In political history, it is associated with Louis XIV of France (1638-1715).

ACID RAIN: Precipitation that contains a high level of acidity as a result of having incorporated sulfur dioxides (SO_2) or nitrogen oxides (NOx) that are produced by burning of fossil fuels or emitted from volcanoes. This precipitation often affects trees, bodies of water, and buildings made of limestone or marble by lowering their pH.

ANCIEN RÉGIME: A French term that is broadly used to describe government and society in France before the French Revolution in 1789.

ARTICLES OF CONFEDERATION: A form of American government from 1781-1789 which was designed to maintain the power of the individual states and keep the central government weak. The system provided for each state having one vote in Congress.

BASTION: A part of a fortress which projects out from its main walls and which offers additional firing angles for the defenders in a siege.

BIAFRAN WAR: In May 1967, areas in southeastern Nigeria declared their independence from the rest of the country and attempted to create the Republic of Biafra. This secession attempt stemmed from ethnic tensions between Muslims and Christians in the aftermath of Nigeria's independence from Great Britain in 1960. Also known as the Nigerian Civil War, the conflict became notorious when the Nigerian government blocked food and other essential supplies from reaching Biafra, causing a massive famine and the deaths of millions. The war ended in January 1970 with the defeat of the secessionists.

BOURGEOISIE: French term for those belonging to the upper middle class in the socio-economic hierarchy of eighteenth-century France. They were wealthy but not of noble blood. Typical members of the bourgeoisie were merchants, lawyers, and bureaucrats.

CARAVANSERAI: An inn in the Muslim world with an interior courtyard that provides secure stables, lodging, and storerooms for caravans and other travelers.

CARAVEL: A small, shallow-keeled, fast vessel with a triangular sail mounted at an angle to the main mast. Maneuvering this sail allowed the ship to sail against an on-coming wind by a process of tacking or zigzagging. Given the dominant wind patterns, this sailing technology was essential for sailing south along the African coast.

COLUMBIAN EXCHANGE: A term for the plants, animals, and diseases that were transferred from the Americas to Europe and Africa and vice versa as a result of European ships traveling across the Atlantic Ocean in the late fifteenth and sixteenth centuries. Examples of the Exchange include cacao, maize, potatoes, tobacco, and probably syphilis traveling *from* the Americas; and coffee, horses, measles, smallpox, sugarcane, and African slaves traveling *to* the Americas.

COMMON LAW: The part of English law that is based on custom and judicial precedent.

CONGRESS OF BERLIN (1878): This diplomatic conference, sponsored by Otto von Bismarck, was held in the wake of the Russo-Turkish War of 1877-1878, during which the Russians entered the outskirts of Istanbul and forced the Ottoman Empire to sign the humiliating Treaty of San Stefano. This treaty gave Russia additional territories in the Caucasus region, provided for Serbian and Romanian independence, created the state of Bulgaria with generously-drawn borders, and forced the Ottomans to pay a large indemnity. These terms were not well received in London and Vienna because the British and the Austrians feared that the Treaty would allow Russia to become too dominant in the Balkans and the eastern Mediterranean. In an effort to avoid a general European war, Bismarck held the Congress of Berlin in June and July 1878. He proved able to convince the Russians to modify the terms of the Treaty of San Stefano so that Russia still retained the new territories in the Caucasus region and the indemnity; Bulgaria lost its much of its legal status and size; Britain won control of Cyprus; France gained Tunisia; and Austria was allowed to occupy Bosnia and Herzegovina. Conflicts over the Balkans would eventually precipitate World War I.

CORPORATIST SYNDICATES: These industrial organizations owe their origins to the political ideology of Corporatism: for society to function effectively and properly, both workers and employers should be grouped into industrial and professional corporations that are controlled by and serve the state.

CHIAROSCURO: In Western painting, the use of heightened contrasts of light and dark, often to increase a sense of depth and volume.

DAOISM (or Taoism): A Chinese philosophical and religious tradition associated with a sixth century BCE man named Laozi (or Lao Tzu). It emphasizes the importance of acting in harmony with nature and the natural order. Because civilization is seen as a corruption of the natural order, the Dao or the Way is a method of restoring original purity and becoming one with the universe.

DAUPHIN: The oldest son and heir-apparent of the King of France.

DUMA: An advisory council to the crown prince or tsar in Russia, usually consisting of noblemen.

DUTCH REVOLT: This was the first phase in the Eighty Years' War (1568-1648) or the Dutch War of Independence. This conflict between Spain and her territories in the Low Countries lasted between 1568 and 1609 and was followed by a truce that lasted for twelve years. In 1621, the conflict resumed as a result of the outbreak of the Thirty Years' War.*

THE ENLIGHTENMENT: An intellectual movement that prized reason. It dominated European thought in the eighteenth century.

EPIPHANY: In the Orthodox Christian tradition, Epiphany commemorates Jesus' baptism in the Jordan River by John the Baptist. In the Catholic tradition, the feast day commemorates the arrival of the three Magi in Bethlehem to celebrate Jesus' birth.

EUCLIDEAN GEOMETRY (or plane geometry): The branch of mathematics developed by Euclid (Alexandria, Egypt, c. 300 BCE) that uses axioms and theorems to explain the areas and volumes of physical objects.

EXPRESSIONISM: An early twentieth-century artistic movement that sought to convey an array of emotions by using bold colors and by intentionally distorting and exaggerating identifiable objects.

FABIAN SOCIALISM: The political philosophy articulated by the members of the Fabian Society, which was founded in London in 1884. Fabian Socialists rejected revolution as the best means to attain socio-economic change and instead advocated for a gradual, evolutionary path to a democratic, socialist state. The group's name comes from the cautious Roman general Fabius Cunctator, who in the Second Punic War with Carthage fought a war of attrition and avoided pitched battles.

FATWA: An interpretative ruling on a point of Islamic law issued by an authoritative cleric.

FIRST NATIONS: A term used to designate the various indigenous peoples of Canada.

FRANCO-PRUSSIAN WAR: In July 1870, France declared war on Prussia, ostensibly because of the possibility of a Prussian prince becoming the King of Spain. The real cause of the war was the growth of Prussian power as a result of German unification under Otto von Bismarck's leadership. The war lasted just over six months and resulted in Germany's acquisition of the French provinces of Alsace and Lorraine, the collapse of Napoleon III's Second French Empire, and the birth of France's Third Republic.

GREAT LEAP FORWARD: Mao Zedong's disastrous socio-economic plan from 1958 to 1962 that tried to industrialize China quickly by forming large-scale communes. These communes prioritized the quantity of industrial production over the quality, used backyard steel furnaces to reach manufacturing goals, and created a massive famine by disregarding agricultural needs.

GUILDS: The medieval and early modern associations of artisans and craftsmen that established standards for a particular trade and trained apprentices in the profession.

HALAL: An Arabic term signifying that which is permissible according to Islamic Law. The word is most commonly used to designate food, especially meat, that has been prepared in the proper manner.

HANSEATIC LEAGUE (or Hansa): A late-medieval trading association that agreed to common laws to protect merchants, adhered to protectionist commercial practices, and sought to fight piracy. The origins of the League date to 1241, when the German towns of Hamburg and Lübeck entered into a formal alliance. By 1300, the League's members had come to dominate northern European trade from London to Russia. The League finally dissolved in 1669.

HAMMAM: A public bathing house with a steam room or sauna and separate facilities for men and women. This is often a central part of the social fabric in a Turkish community, but *hammams* may also be found in other Muslim countries.

HOGSHEAD: A volume measurement defined by a large cask or barrel; while there was some variety due to differences in the diameters of barrels, a hogshead was typically 63 gallons.

HOLY ROMAN EMPIRE: The political entity that loosely held central Europe together from the tenth century to 1806. Seven electors (the Archbishops of Mainz, Trier, and Cologne; the King of Bohemia; the Count Palatine of the Rhine; the Duke of Saxony; and the Margrave of Brandenburg) selected a member of a leading European royal family to rule over the collection of principalities, duchies, kingdoms, and fiefdoms that stretched from Antwerp to Vienna, Hamburg to Florence. By the early modern period, the emperor was usually a member of the Spanish or Austrian branches of the Habsburg family.

HUNDRED FLOWERS MOVEMENT: A Maoist campaign begun in May 1956 to encourage freedom of speech in the wake of Nikita Khrushchev's denunciation of Joseph Stalin. The campaign encouraged criticism of the Communist Party and utilized an ancient Chinese expression, "Let a hundred flowers bloom, and a hundred schools of thought contend," to embolden participation. By June 1957 the movement had become too threatening and was suppressed.

ICONOSTASIS: A wall that separates the public areas of an Orthodox church from those reserved for clerics. The iconostasis prevents the public from seeing the altar in an Orthodox Christian church during religious services. The wall is usually covered with icons, which are religious paintings of Orthodox saints.

IMAM: Most commonly, this term is used for a Muslim cleric who leads the faithful in prayer. It can also be used to describe someone of scholarly renown. In the Shi'a tradition, the imam is the man God has selected to lead the Islamic community.

INDENTURED SERVANTS: In exchange for transportation to the British colonies in North America, these people were subject to a five to seven-year labor contract. Upon the completion of their contract, indentured servants became free.

JAINISM: An ancient religion from India which emphasizes the importance of *ahimsa* (nonviolence), rejects the caste system, and practices yoga as the means of purifying and liberating the soul. Jains worship twenty-four *Tirthankaras* or liberated souls, and concentrate on their adherence to the Three Jewels (right knowledge, right faith, and right practice). The last *Tirthankara* was a man named Vardhamana Mahavira, who lived in the sixth century BCE. Jains also believe that at some point in the future another twenty-four *Tirthankaras* will live.

JUNKERS: Members of the conservative landholding aristocracy in Prussia and Eastern Germany who often also served as military officers.

KULAKS: Prosperous Russian peasants.

LEND-LEASE: Adopted in March 1941, this system allowed the United States, despite being officially neutral, to provide war matériel for World War II to Great Britain, China, the Soviet Union, and other anti-fascist nations of vital strategic importance. Once the United States entered the war, Lend-Lease was expanded to help many Allied nations.

LITTLE ICE AGE: Between 1300 and 1850, many parts of the earth experienced a decrease in mean temperatures. This resulted in an expansion of glaciers and sea ice, decreased crop yields, famine, and migration.

MACHIAVELLIAN: An adjective used to describe the political values and personal attributes Niccoló Machiavelli (1469-1527) outlined as being necessary for effective leadership in his treatise *The Prince*. It argues that it is more important for rulers to be feared than loved and that it is necessary for them to act in their own best interests, ruthlessly if necessary, in order to gain and then maintain political power.

MAUNDY THURSDAY or Holy Thursday: Held the Thursday before Easter, this holy day commemorates the Last Supper. The liturgy includes the rite of foot washing, replicating Jesus' washing the feet of the Apostles (John, 13:1-17).

MAY FOURTH MOVEMENT: An anti-imperialist social reform movement in China begun during student protests in Beijing on May 4, 1919. The protesters objected to the clauses in the Treaty of Versailles that ended World War I, particularly the provisions that allowed for Japan to gain control of the German concessions in Shandong Province. The movement resulted in China refusing to sign the Treaty and promoted debate about China's ideological future.

MERCANTILISM: An economic theory that holds that careful regulation, instead of free trade, is the best way to maximize profits and growth for one nation while simultaneously taking away profits from competing countries.

METROPOLITAN: In the Russian Orthodox Church, all bishops hold equal spiritual authority, but those bishops who hold leading administrative ranks within the church are often called by different titles and have more prestige and temporal influence. A Metropolitan is one of these figures. He is the archbishop of an important area known as a province.

MODERNISM: A global architectural, artistic, literary, musical, and philosophical movement in the late nineteenth and twentieth centuries that sought to break away from established styles and doctrines.

NATO: The North Atlantic Treaty Organization is an alliance of nations formed in April 1949. Member nations promise to provide mutual defense in case of an attack. Its creation helped to increase tension during the early years of the Cold War. Initial members included Belgium, Canada, Denmark, France, Iceland, Italy, Luxembourg, the Netherlands, Norway, Portugal, the United Kingdom, and the United States. Greece, and Turkey joined in 1952, followed by West Germany in 1955.

NEW DEAL: This was the umbrella term for a set of policies American president Franklin D. Roosevelt initiated after taking office in 1933 to help the United States recover from the stock market crash of 1929 and the resulting Great Depression.

NEW ECONOMIC POLICY: In 1918, after the Soviet Union withdrew from World War I with the Treaty of Brest-Litovsk,* Lenin adopted an economic policy known as War Communism. This policy nationalized industries and trade to the point that private enterprise virtually ceased to exist. It hoped to transform an agrarian nation into a socialist state very quickly. This proved to be impossible and created an economic disaster and widespread famine. By spring 1921, Lenin had pivoted to the New Economic Policy, which allowed for the temporary return of private enterprise.

NON-ALIGNED MOVEMENT: In response to post-World War II decolonization and the Cold War, a group of leaders from the developing world formed an organization dedicated to representing the needs of nations not formally in the American or Soviet alliance systems. These leaders included Egypt's Gamal Abdel Nasser, Ghana's Kwame Nkrumah, India's Jawaharlal Nehru, Indonesia's Sukarno, and Yugoslavia's Josip Broz Tito.

NONCONFORMIST: A Protestant who does not recognize the doctrines and practices of an established church. In England, a nonconformist would be a Protestant who was not a member of the Church of England (an Anglican). In Scotland, a nonconformist would be a Protestant who was not a member of the Church of Scotland (a Presbyterian).

PAPAL NUNCIO: The Vatican's ambassador to another nation.

PAULISTA: A resident of São Paulo, Brazil.

PENTECOSTAL: The adjective describing a group of Protestants who seek baptism with the Holy Spirit. Believers see this post-conversion union as being manifested in "speaking in tongues," the power to heal, and other supernatural experiences.

PHYSIOCRATS: The eighteenth-century economic and political theorists who saw agriculture was the basis of the economy, opposed mercantilism*, and advocated for free trade within certain limitations.

POLITIQUE: A person who believes that the overall interests and stability of the state outweigh the importance of religious doctrine in decision making. The term is often associated with the Reformation.

PRAGUE SPRING: In the spring of 1968, Communist Czechoslovakian leader Alexander Dubček initiated a series of liberalizing reforms that promoted civil rights and greater local autonomy. This initiative did not satisfy democracy advocates within Czechoslovakia, and it threatened the leaders of other Warsaw Pact countries. In August 1968, the Soviet Union invaded Czechoslovakia in order to suppress the reform movement and depose Dubček.

PRIMOGENITURE: The legal or customary process by which the eldest-born son inherits the bulk of his father's estate in its entirety, leaving other sons and all daughters with little wealth generated from the father's property or title.

PURGATORY: A state of being after death in which humans pay for their earthly sins before gaining admission to Heaven.

RECONSTRUCTION: In American history, this term refers to the period after the Civil War and involves the conditions under which the rebellious Southern states would be readmitted to the Union. Under President Andrew Johnson, the terms of readmission were fairly lenient, for the Tennessean's goal was not to punish the eleven seceding states excessively. In 1868, however, a new group of Senators and Congressmen was elected, who believed that the Southern states should undergo a transformative process before being readmitted to the Union. From 1869 to 1877, Congress imposed "Radical Reconstruction" on the South in order to protect former slaves and institute reform.

SAMURAI: The members of Japan's traditional warrior caste.

SECOND BOER WAR: This conflict in South Africa was fought between the two Boer states (Transvaal and the Orange Free State) and the British Empire between 1899 and 1902. The Boers were the descendants of Dutch settlers in South Africa, who also fought against the British in the First Boer War between December 1880 and March 1881. The Second Boer War is often described as a preview of twentieth-century conflicts because of the ways in which the Boers used guerrilla war tactics while the British adopted scorched earth policies and built concentration camps to house the civilian population. The Second Boer War is also known as the Anglo-Boer War or the South African War.

SCHOLASTICISM: A medieval method of didactic investigation which critically examined theological questions through specific rules of inquiry and discussion in an attempt to reconcile reason and revelation.

SCIENTIFIC REVOLUTION: Denotes the process in the sixteenth and seventeenth centuries when many educated Western Europeans came to accept the heliocentric model of the universe and the idea that there were rational, mathematical explanations for natural phenomenon. The gradual acceptance of the theories of Copernicus, Kepler, Galileo, and Newton gave science and rational thought greater cultural cachet and set the stage for the Enlightenment* in the eighteenth century.

SHINTO: or "the way of the Kami" is the indigenous, polytheistic, and animist religion of Japan devoted to natural spirits and anthropomorphic and conceptional deities.

SHOGUN: A military ruler in Japan before 1868.

SIX-DAY WAR: In June 1967, Israel launched attacks on Egypt, Syria, and Jordan in response to what the Israelis saw as Arab preparations for war. The six days of fighting resulted in significant victories for the Israelis as they captured the Gaza Strip, the Sinai Peninsula, the West Bank of the Jordan River, and the Golan Heights.

SPANISH ARMADA: Philip II's military operation in 1588 to invade England, depose Elizabeth I, and restore Catholicism. The final plan called for 130 ships to sail from Spain to Flanders, pick up a Spanish army there, and transport it to England for the invasion. The plan came within just a few hours of succeeding, but when the winds changed, the Spanish fleet was blown into the North Sea and had to circumnavigate the entire British Isles to return to Spain. The extent of the Spanish loss remains the subject of historical debate with the estimated number of ships lost ranging from 44 to 65 and the number of Spanish casualties ranging from 10,000-15,000.

SOVIET: A council that serves as the local government in a particular area, especially during periods of revolutionary change. It seeks to represent workers and peasants in accordance with Marxist theory.

SOCIALISM IN ONE COUNTRY: Stalin's political and economic strategy to concentrate all resources to secure the communist revolution in the Soviet Union in the late 1920s and early 1930s. Rather than attempting to export revolution to other nations, the needs of the Soviet Union were to take priority over those of communist parties in other parts of the world. The opposing strategy was Trotskyism.*

SUBLIME PORTE: A phrase used to describe the government of the Ottoman Empire. The term comes from the name of a gateway in the Topkapı Palace in Istanbul. It is used the same way "Number 10 Downing Street" represents the British government or "Foggy Bottom" represents the American State Department.

SUEZ CRISIS: In July 1956, Egyptian president Gamal Abdel Nasser nationalized the Suez Canal as a result of the American and British decision not to help him finance the construction of the Aswan High Dam in Upper Egypt. France, Great Britain, and Israel then intervened militarily in order to reopen the Canal, but the United States forced the three allies to withdraw and Egypt retained control of the Canal.

SYMPHONIC POEM: The term for a one-movement orchestral composition that is inspired by a story or event.

TARTARS or Tatars: A Turkic-speaking, Muslim ethnic group in southern Russia, which led raids upon Muscovy even after the period of Mongol domination. Different branches controlled the Crimea, Kazan, and Astrakhan.

THIRTY YEARS' WAR: A series of military conflicts between Protestants and Catholics, as well as between European monarchs fighting to extend their political influence, that engulfed Europe between 1618-1648. The conflicts ended with the Treaty of Westphalia, which recognized religious toleration for Catholics, Lutherans, and Calvinists in most of the Holy Roman Empire* and formalized the independence of the Dutch Republic and Switzerland.

THOBE or Thawb: The ankle-length garment worn as a robe by Arab men.

THREE-FIELD SYSTEM: A method of farming which rotates crops and leaves one third of the fields fallow in order to restore nutrients to the soil and increase agricultural yields over time. It was developed in Western Europe around 800 CE but was not used in Russia until the late Middle Ages.

TITHE: A mandatory tax paid to the government or a contribution to an ecclesiastical organization, usually amounting to ten percent of a total income.

TREATY OF BREST-LITOVSK: Signed March 3, 1918, this treaty ended World War I between Germany and the Soviet Union. According to the treaty's harsh terms, the Soviet Union surrendered the Ukraine, Poland, Finland, and the Baltic States and land in the Caucasus to the Central Powers. It also had to pay a large indemnity.

TRIBUTARY STATE: A nominally independent nation or region that regularly demonstrates its subordinate position to a dominating kingdom in the pre-modern era. In some instances, this homage is made only in symbolic terms, but in many cases the tribute is paid in material goods.

TROTSKYISM: The ideology of Leon Trotsky (1879-1940), who argued that in order to preserve communism in the Soviet Union, the revolution needed to be exported to other nations. His concept of a permanently unfolding communist revolution stood in opposition to Stalin's policy of Socialism in One Country.*

TWENTY-ONE DEMANDS: In January 1915, Japan issued an ultimatum to China, asserting its prerogative to benefit from 21 economic and political privileges in China, as European nations did. These concessions involved railways, ports, mining rights, appointments, and more. These demands created considerable anti-Japanese sentiments in China.

UMAYYADS: The family that established a caliphate in Damascus, Syria in 661 and that ruled an empire stretching from Spain to India. The Umayyads were overthrown in 750 at the Battle of the Zab and the caliphate passed to the Abbasids.

UNITED ARAB REPUBLIC: Egypt's president Gamal Abdel Nasser dreamed of a pan-Arab state. The creation of the United Arab Republic between Egypt and Syria in February 1958 was meant to be the first step in that direction. Syria withdrew from the union in 1961 after a military *coup d'état*, and Egypt stopped using the designation in 1971.

WAR OF THE AUSTRIAN SUCCESSION (1740-1748): In October 1740, Holy Roman Emperor and Habsburg monarch Charles VI died without a male heir. His will designated his eldest daughter, Maria Theresa (1717-1780), as sovereign of Austria, Bohemia, Croatia, Galicia, Hungary, Transylvania, and other territories. This inheritance was challenged by Bavaria, France, and Prussia because it contradicted a legal tradition established by Clovis, King of the Franks (466-511 CE), that excluded women from inheriting property. The eight-year war resulted in Maria Theresa retaining her throne but losing the key province of Silesia to Prussia.

WAR OF THE SPANISH SUCCESSION (1701-1714): On November 1, 1700, Spain's king Charles II died childless. According to his will, the grandson of France's Louis XIV, Philip of Anjou, was to inherit an undivided Spanish empire. This threatened to unite the crowns and territories of France and Spain. Great Britain, Prussia, the Dutch Republic, and the Holy Roman Empire* were particularly opposed to this and formed an anti-French alliance. The resulting war ended with Philip retaining the Spanish throne, but with Spain surrendering important European territories, including the Spanish Netherlands (Belgium), Gibraltar, Minorca, Milan, Naples, Sardinia, and Sicily to the victors. In this way, the Bourbons controlled Spain, but could not prevent the division of Charles II's inheritance.

WHIGS: In British history, the term was originally used to describe rebellious Presbyterians who sought to bring Calvinism to Scotland in the sixteenth century. By the Glorious Revolution of 1688, the term was applied to those who supported a constitutional monarchy over an absolutist one. In American history, a Whig was initially a colonist who supported the American Revolution against the British crown. In the nineteenth century, Whigs were members of a political party that opposed the authoritarianism of Andrew Jackson.

ZOROASTRIANISM: A religion from Iran with a hereditary priesthood that was founded by Zarathushtra in the sixth century BCE. Zarathushtra emphasized the struggle of good and evil in the world and revered the epitome of goodness and the creator of the world, Ahura Mazda. Ahura Mazda's evil opposite was

Ahriman. Zoroastrianism became the official religion of the Sassanian Dynasty in 224 CE, but with the rise of Islam many Zoroastrians moved east to India.

SUGGESTIONS FOR FURTHER READING:

Presenting a comprehensive bibliography for a world history of this length and diversity is more than a daunting prospect: it threatens to overwhelm to the point of being unhelpful. In an effort to mitigate this problem, I have chosen to highlight no more than a dozen recently-published and noteworthy secondary works for each chapter. It is my hope that this approach will prove more valuable, enlightening, and practical for those wishing to learn more.

Despite this choice, I am quick to acknowledge the importance of primary sources, and the debt I have to many other secondary authors. I hope that the footnotes throughout the text clearly document my appreciation for these works as well. In fact, my greatest enjoyment as a researcher came when reading older works, for oftentimes they proved to be the most helpful and influential. This was a welcomed reminder of the continued value of old books and the scholarship of yesteryear.

Chapter A:

Asher, Catherine B. and Cynthia Talbot. *India Before Europe.* New York: Cambridge University Press, 2006.

Bethencourt, Francisco and Diogo Ramada Curto (eds.). *Portuguese Oceanic Expansion, 1400-1800.* New York: Cambridge University Press, 2007.

Crowley, Roger. *Conquerors: How Portugal Forged the First Global Empire.* New York: Random House, 2015.

Doniger, Windy. *The Hindus: An Alternative History.* New York: Penguin Group, 2010.

Disney, A. R. *A History of Portugal and the Portuguese Empire*, Volumes 1 and 2. New York: Cambridge University Press, 2009.

Ferreira, Susannah Humble. *The Crown, the Court, and the Casa da Índia: Political Centralization in Portugal 1479-1521.* Leiden, Netherlands: Brill, 2015.

Henn, Alexander. *Hindu-Catholic Encounters in Goa: Religion, Colonialism, and Modernity.* Bloomington, Indiana: Indiana University Press, 2014.

Moffett, Samuel Hugh. *A History of Christianity in Asia, Volumes I and II.* Maryknoll, New York: Orbis Books, 2005.

Russell, Peter. *Prince Henry "the Navigator:" A Life.* New Haven, Connecticut: Yale University Press, 2000.

Chapter B:

Bell, David N. *Orthodoxy: Evolving Tradition.* Collegeville, Minnesota: Liturgical Press, 2008.

Bucher, Greta Bucher. *Daily Life in Imperial Russia.* Westport, Connecticut: Greenwood Press, 2008.

Casillo, Robert and John Paul Russo. *The Italian in Modernity.* Toronto: University of Toronto Press, 2011.

Freely, John and Ahmet S. Cakmak, *Byzantine Monuments of Istanbul.* New York: Cambridge University Press, 2010.

Gruber, Isaiah. *Orthodox Russia in Crisis: Church and Nation in the Time of the Troubles.* DeKalb, Illinois: Northern Illinois Press, 2012.

Kasper, Cardinal Walter (ed.). *The Petrine Ministry: Catholics and Orthodox in Dialogue.* New York: The Newman Press, 2006.

Merridale, Catherine. *Red Fortress: The Secret Heart of Russia's History.* London: Allen Lane/ Penguin Books, 2013.

Perrie, Maureen (ed.). *The Cambridge History of Russia, Volume 1: from Early Rus' to 1689.* Cambridge, UK: Cambridge University Press, 2006.

Siecienski, Anthony Edward. *The Papacy and the Orthodox: Sources and History of a Debate.* New York: Oxford University Press, 2017.

Sulikowska, Alexsandra. *The Icon Debate: Religious Images in Russia in the 15th and 16th Centuries.* Frankfurt am Main: Peter Lang, 2016.

Chapter C:

Eire, Carlos M. N. *Reformations: The Early Modern World, 1450-1650*. New Haven, Connecticut: Yale University Press, 2018.

Derksen, John D. *From Radicals to Survivors: Strasbourg's Religious Nonconformists over Two Generations, 1525-1570*. Utrecht, Netherlands: Hes & DeGraaf Publishers, 2002.

Gordon, Bruce. *Calvin*. New Haven, Connecticut: Yale University Press, 2009.

Hendrix, Scott H. *Martin Luther: Visionary Reformer*. New Haven: Yale University Press, 2015.

Kaplan, Debra. *Beyond Expulsion: Jews, Christians, and Reformation Strasbourg*. Stanford, California: Stanford University Press, 2011.

MacCulloch, Diarmaid. *The Reformation*. New York: Viking, 2004.

Maltby, William. *The Reign of Charles V*. New York: Palgrave, 2002.

Marty, Martin. *Martin Luther*. New York: Penguin Group, 2004.

Old, Hughes Oliphant. *The Reading and Preaching of the Scriptures in the Worship of the Christian Church, Volume 4: The Age of Reformation*. Grand Rapids, Michigan: W.B. Eerdmans, 2002.

Rummel, Erika (ed.). *The Correspondence of Wolfgang Capito Volumes 1, 2, 3*. Toronto: University of Toronto Press, 2005, 2009, 2015.

Tracy, James D. *Europe's Reformations, 1450-1650*. Lanham, Maryland: Rowman & Littlefield Publishers, 2002.

Chapter D:

Aughterson, Kate (ed.). *The English Renaissance: An Anthology of Sources and Documents*. New York: Routledge, 2002.

Barone, Robert W. *A Reputation History of John Dee, 1527-1609: The Life of an Elizabethan Intellectual*. Lewiston, New York: The Edwin Mellen Press, 2009.

Burton, Dan and David Grandy. *Magic, Mystery and Science: The Occult in Western Civilization*. Bloomington, Indiana: Indiana University Press, 2004.

Childs, Jessie. *God's Traitors: Terror and Faith in Elizabethan England*. Oxford, U.K.: Oxford University Press, 2014.

Dooley, Brendan (ed.) *A Companion to Astrology in the Renaissance*. Leiden: Brill, 2014.

Doran, Susan. *Queen Elizabeth I*. New York: New York University Press, 2003.

Mancall, Peter (ed.). *Bringing the World to Early Modern Europe: Travel Accounts and Their Audiences*. Leiden, the Netherlands: Koninklijke Brill NV, 2006.

Page, Sophie. *Magic in the Cloister: Pious Motives, Illicit Interests, and Occult Approaches to the Medieval Universe*. University Park, Pennsylvania: Pennsylvania State University Press, 2013.

Parry, Glyn. *The Arch-Conjuror of England: John Dee*. New Haven, Connecticut: Yale University Press, 2011.

Woolley, Benjamin, *The Queen's Conjuror: The Life and Magic of Dr. Dee*. London: Flamingo, 2002.

Wright, Anthony D. *The Counter-Reformation: Catholic Europe and the Non-Christian World*. London: Routledge, 2017.

Young, Francis. *Magic as a Political Crime in Medieval and Early Modern England: A History of Sorcery and Treason*. London/New York: I.B. Tauris, 2018.

Chapter E:

Baldridge, Cates. *Prisoners of Prester John: The Portuguese Mission to Ethiopia in Search of the Mythical King, 1520-1526*. Jefferson, North Carolina: McFarland & Company, 2012.

Crummey, Donald. *Land and Society in the Christian Kingdom of Ethiopia*. Urbana, Illinois: University of Illinois Press, 2000.

Denysenko, Nicholas E. *The Blessing of Waters and Epiphany: The Eastern Liturgical Tradition*. Farnham, U.K.: Ashgate Publishing Limited, 2012.

Gomez, Michael A. *African Domination: A New History of Empire in Early and Medieval West Africa*. Princeton, New Jersey: Princeton University Press, 2018.

Hassen, Mohammed. *The Oromo and the Christian Kingdom of Ethiopia, 1300-1700*. Woodbridge, Suffolk, U.K.: James Currey, 2015.

Henze, Paul B. *Layers of Time*. New York: Palgrave, 2000.

Labrand, John. *Bringers of War: Portuguese in Africa During the Age of Gunpowder and Sail from the Fifteenth to the Eighteenth Century*. London: Frontline Books, 2013.

Marcus, Harold G. *A History of Ethiopia*. Berkeley, California: University of California Press, 2002.

Pankhurst, Richard. *The Ethiopians*. Malden, Massachusetts: Blackwell Publishers, 2001.

Ramos, Manuel João and Isabel Boavida (eds.). *The Indigenous and the Foreign in Christian Ethiopian Art: On Portuguese-Ethiopian Contacts in the 16th and 17th Centuries*. Aldershot, U.K.: Ashgate Publishing Limited, 2004.

Salvadore, Matteo. *The African Prester John and the Birth of Ethiopian-European Relations, 1402-1555*. New York: Rutledge, 2017.

Chapter F:

Buschmann, Rainer F., Edward R. Slack Jr., and James B. Tueller. *Navigating the Spanish Lake: The Pacific in the Iberian World, 1521-1898*. Honolulu, Hawai'i: University of Hawai'i Press, 2013.

Candiani, Vera S. *Dreaming of Dry Land: Environmental Transformation in Colonial Mexico City*. Stanford, California: Stanford University Press, 2014.

Cañeque, Alejandro. *The King's Living Image: The Culture and Politics of Viceregal Power in Colonial Mexico*. New York: Routledge, 2004.

Conover, Cornelius. *Pious Imperialism: Spanish Rule and the Cult of the Saints in Mexico City*. Albuquerque, New Mexico: University of New Mexico Press, 2019.

Curcio-Nagy, Linda A., *The Great Festivals of Colonial Mexico City: Performing Power and Identity*. Albuquerque, New Mexico: University of New Mexico Press, 2004.

Gates, Jr., Henry Louis. *Blacks in Latin America*. New York: New York University Press, 2011.

Lane, Kris. *Potosí: The Silver City that Changed the World*. Oakland, California: University of California Press, 2019.

Lowney, Chris. *A Vanished World: Muslims, Christians, and Jews in Medieval Spain*. New York: Oxford University Press, 2006.

Mannarelli, María Emma. *Private Passions and Public Sins: Men and Women in Seventeenth Century Lima*. Albuquerque, New Mexico: University of New Mexico Press, 2007.

Nesvig, Martin Austin. *Ideology and Inquisition: The World of the Censors in Early Mexico*. New Haven, Connecticut: Yale University Press, 2009.

Silverblatt, Irene. *Modern Inquisitions: Peru and the Colonial Origins of the Civilized World*. Durham, North Carolina: Duke University Press, 2004.

Villa-Flores, Javier and Sonya Lipsett-Rivera (eds.) *Emotions and Daily Life in Colonial Mexico*. Albuquerque, New Mexico: University of New Mexico Press, 2014.

Chapter G:

Adolphson, Mikael, Edward Kamens, and Stacie Matsumoto (eds.). *Heian Japan: Centers and Peripheries*. Honolulu, Hawai'i: University of Hawai'i Press, 2007.

Armstrong, Karen. *Buddha*. New York: Viking Penguin, 2001.

Crompton, Louis. *Homosexuality & Civilization*. Cambridge, Massachusetts: The Belknap Press of Harvard University Press, 2003.

Doak, Kevin Michael. *Xavier's Legacies: Catholicism in Modern Japanese Culture*. Vancouver, British Columbia: University of British Columbia Press, 2011.

Downer, Lesley. *Women of the Pleasure Quarters: The Secret History of the Geisha*. New York: Broadway Books, 2001.

Graham, Patricia Jane. *Faith and Power in Japanese Buddhist Art, 1600–2005*. Honolulu, Hawai'i: University of Hawai'i Press, 2007.

Lillehoj, Elizabeth. *Art and Palace Politics in Early Modern Japan, 1580s-1680s*. Leiden, Netherlands: Koninklijke Brill, 2011.

Neill, James. *The Origins and Role of Same-Sex Relations in Human Societies*. Jefferson, North Carolina: McFarland and Company, 2009.

Orzech, Charles D., Henrik H. Sørensen and Richard K. Payne (eds.). *Esoteric Buddhism and the Tantras in East Asia*. Leiden, Netherlands: Koninklijke Brill, 2011.

Parker, Geoffrey. *Global Crisis: War, Climate Change and Catastrophe in the Seventeenth Century*. New Haven, Connecticut: Yale University Press, 2013.

Pitelka, Morgan and Alice Y. Tseng (eds.). *Kyoto Visual Culture in the Early Edo and Meiji Periods: The Arts of Reinvention*. New York: Routledge, 2016.

Seduction: Japan's Floating World. San Francisco, California: Asian Art Museum, 2015.

Chapter H:

Bosma, Ulbe, and Remco Raben. *Being "Dutch" in the Indies: A History of Creolisation and Empire, 1500-1920*. Athens, Ohio: Ohio University Press, 2008.

Bruijn, Iris. *Ship's Surgeons of the Dutch East India Company: Commerce and the Progress of Medicine in the Eighteenth Century*. Leiden, Netherlands: Leiden University Press, 2009.

Clulow, Adam. *The Company and the Shogun: The Dutch Encounter with Tokugawa Japan*. New York: Columbia University Press, 2014.

Dash, Mike. *Batavia's Graveyard*. New York: Three Rivers Press, 2002.

Derks, Hans. *History of the Opium Problem: The Assault on the East, ca. 1600-1950*. Leiden, The Netherlands: Koninklijke Brill NV, 2012.

Hochstrasser, Julie Berger. *Still Life and Trade in the Dutch Golden Age*. New Haven, Connecticut: Yale University Press, 2007.

Mak, Geert. *Amsterdam*. Cambridge, Massachusetts: Harvard University Press, 2000.

Levine, Allan. *Scattered Among the Peoples: The Jewish Diaspora in Twelve Portraits*. Woodstock, New York: The Overlook Press, 2003.

Maiuro, Marco and Federico De Romanis (eds.). *Across the Ocean: Nine Essays on Indo-Mediterranean Trade*, Leiden, The Netherlands: Brill, 2015.

Ruangsilp, Bhawan. *Dutch East India Company Merchants in the Court of Ayutthaya: Dutch Perceptions of the Thai Kingdom, c. 1604-1765*. Leiden, The Netherlands: Koninklijke Brill NV, 2007.

Chapter I:

Boyar, Ebru and Kate Fleet (eds.). *Ottoman Women in Public Space*. Leiden: Brill, 2016.

Crowley, Roger. *City of Fortune: How Venice Ruled the Seas*. New York: Random House, 2011.

Finkel Caroline. *Osman's Dream: The History of the Ottoman Empire*. New York: Basic Books, 2006.

Imber, Colin. *The Ottoman Empire, 1300-1650: The Structure of Power*. London: Red Globe Press, 2019.

Mossensohn, Miri Shefer. *Ottoman Medicine: Healing and Medical Institutions, 1500-1700*. Albany, New York: State University of New York Press, 2009.

Özgüleş, Muzaffer. *The Women Who Built the Ottoman World: Female Patronage and the Architectural Legacy of Günuş Sultan*. London: I. B. Tauris & Company Ltd., 2017.

Parker, Geoffrey. *Global Crisis: War, Climate Change and Catastrophe in the Seventeen Century*. New Haven, Connecticut: Yale University Press, 2013.

Power, Mick. *Madness Cracked*. New York: Oxford University Press, 2014.

Scalenghe, Sara. *Disability in the Ottoman World, 1500-1800*. New York: Cambridge University Press, 2014.

Streusand, Douglas E. *Islamic Gunpowder Empires: Ottomans, Safavids, Mughals*. Boulder, Colorado: Westview Press, 2011.

Walthall, Anne (ed.). *Servants of the Dynasty: Palace Women in World History*. Berkeley, CA: University of California Press, 2008.

White, Joshua M. *Piracy and Law in the Ottoman Mediterranean*. Stanford, California: Stanford University Press, 2018.

Chapter J:

Chandra, Satish. *Essays on Medieval Indian History.* New Delhi, India: Oxford University Press, 2005.

Curry, John J., and Erik S. Ohlander (eds.). *Sufism and Society: Arrangements of the Mystical in the Muslim World, 1200-1800.* New York: Routledge, 2012.

Eraly, Abraham. *The Mughal World: India's Tainted Paradise.* London, U.K.: Weidenfeld & Nicolson, 2007.

Faruqui, Munis D. *The Princes of the Mughal Empire, 1504-1719.* New York: Cambridge University Press, 2012.

Gandhi, Supriya. *The Emperor Who Never Was: Dara Shukoh in Mughal India.* Cambridge, Massachusetts: Belknap Press of Harvard University Press, 2020.

Jaffrelot, Christophe (ed.). *Hindu Nationalism: A Reader.* Princeton, New Jersey: Princeton University Press, 2007.

Koch, Ebba. *The Complete Taj Mahal and the Riverfront Gardens of Agra.* New York: Thames & Hudson, Inc., 2006.

Lal, Ruby. *Empress: The Astonishing Reign of Nur Jahan.* New York: W. W. Norton & Company, 2018.

Lal, Ruby. *Domesticity and Power in the Early Mughal World.* Cambridge, U.K.: Cambridge University Press, 2005.

Nicoll, Fergus. *Shah Jahan: The Rise and Fall of the Mughal Emperor.* London: Haus Publishing, 2009.

Preston, Diana and Michael. *Taj Mahal: Passion and Genius at the Heart of the Moghul Empire.* New York: Walker & Company, 2007.

Truschke, Audrey. *Aurangzeb: The Life and Legacy of India's Most Controversial King.* Stanford, California: Stanford University Press, 2017.

Chapter K:

Jungmann, Burglind. *Pathways to Korean Culture: Paintings of the Joseon Dynasty, 1392-1910.* London: Reaktion Books, 2014.

Kim, Hyongeong Han. *In Grand Style: Celebrations in Korean Art During the Joseon Dynasty.* San Francisco, California: Asian Art Museum, 2013.

Knell, Simon J., et al (ed.). *National Museums: New Studies from around the World.* New York: Routledge, 2011.

Oh, Ju-seok, *The Art of Kim Hong-do.* New York: Art Media Resources, 2005.

Song-mi, Yi. *Korean Landscape Painting: Continuity and Innovation Through the Ages.* Elizabeth, New Jersey: Hollym International Corporation, 2006.

Walthall, Anne (ed.). *Servants of the Dynasty: Palace Women in World History.* Berkeley, California: University of California Press, 2008.

Woo, Wyunsoo (ed.). *Treasures from Korea: Arts and Culture of the Joseon Dynasty, 1392-1910.* Philadelphia, Pennsylvania: Philadelphia Museum of Art, 2014.

Chapter L:

Baier, Annette C. *The Pursuits of Philosophy: An Introduction to the Life and Thought of David Hume.* Cambridge, Massachusetts: Harvard University Press, 2011.

Bromwich, David. *The Intellectual Life of Edmund Burke: From the Sublime and Beautiful to American Independence.* Cambridge, Massachusetts: Belknap Press of Harvard University, 2014.

Craveri, Benedetta. *The Age of Conversation.* New York: New York Review of Books, 2005.

Damrosch, Leo. *Jean-Jacques Rousseau.* Boston, Massachusetts: Houghton Mifflin Company, 2005.

Darnton, Robert. *Censors at Work: How States Shaped Literature.* New York: W. W. Norton & Company, 2014.

Kale, Steven. *French Salons: High Society and Political Sociability from the Old Regime to the Revolution of 1848.* Baltimore, Maryland: The Johns Hopkins University Press, 2004.

Lilti, Antoine. *The World of the Salons: Sociability and Worldliness in Eighteenth Century Paris.* New York: Oxford University Press, 2015.

McGrayne, Sharon Bertsch. *The Theory that Would Not Die: How Bayes' Rule Cracked the Enigma Code, Hunted Down Russian Submarines & Emerged Triumphant from Two Centuries of Controversy*. New Haven, Connecticut: Yale University Press, 2011.

McMahon, Darrin M. *Enemies of the Enlightenment: The French Counter-Enlightenment and the Making of Modernity*. New York: Oxford University Press, 2001.

Pelletier, Louise. *Architecture in Words: Theatre, Language and the Sensuous Space of Architecture*. New York: Routledge, 2006.

Potter, Jennifer. *Seven Flowers and How They Shaped Our World*. New York: Overlook Press, 2013.

Van Horn, James. *The Rise of the Public in Enlightenment Europe*. Cambridge, U.K.: Cambridge University Press, 2001.

Chapter M:

Abé, Takao. *The Jesuit Mission to New France: A New Interpretation in the Light of the Earlier Jesuit Experience in Japan*. Leiden, Netherlands: Brill, 2011.

Anderson, Fred. *Crucible of War: The Seven Years' War and the Fate of Empire in British North America 1754-1766*. New York: Alfred A. Knopf, 2000.

Brumwell, Stephen. *Redcoats: The British Soldier and War in the Americas, 1755-1763*. New York: Cambridge University Press, 2002.

Dowd, Gregory Evans. *War Under Heaven: Pontiac the Indian Nations & the British Empire*. Baltimore, Maryland: The Johns Hopkins University Press, 2002.

Faragher, John Mack. *A Great and Noble Scheme: The Tragic Story of the Expulsion of the French Acadians from their American Homeland*. New York: W. W. Norton & Company, 2005.

Hodson, Christopher. *The Acadian Diaspora: An Eighteenth-Century History*. New York: Oxford University Press, 2012.

Jobb, Dean W. *The Cajuns: A People's Story of Exile and Triumph*. New York: John Wiley & Sons, 2010.

Nester, William R. *The First Global War: Britain, France, and the Fate of North America, 1756-1775*. Westport, Connecticut: Praeger Publishers, 2000.

Parker, Mathew. *The Sugar Barons: Family, Corruption, Empire and War in the West Indies*. New York: Walker and Company, 2011.

Scott, Elizabeth M. (ed.). *Archaeological Perspectives on the French in the New World*. Gainesville, Florida: University of Florida Press, 2017.

Snow, Dan. *Death or Victory: The Battle of Quebec and the Birth of an Empire*. Toronto: Penguin Canada, 2011.

Chapter N:

Chandler, David, Norman G. Owen, William R. Roff, et al. *The Emergence of Modern Southeast Asia*. Honolulu, Hawai'i: University of Hawai'i Press, 2005.

Desan, Susanne, Linda Hunt and William Max Wilson (eds.). *The French Revolution in Global Perspective*. Ithaca, New York: Cornell University Press, 2013.

Dutton, George. *The Tây Sơn Uprising: Society and Rebellion in Eighteenth Century Vietnam*. Honolulu, Hawai'i: University of Hawai'i Press, 2006.

Gruder, Vivian R. *Notables and the Nation: The Political Schooling of the French, 1787-1788*. Cambridge, Massachusetts: Harvard University Press, 2007.

Keith, Charles. *Catholic Vietnam: A Church from Empire to Nation*. Berkeley, California: University of California Press, 2012.

Tran, Nhung Tuyet and Anthony Reid (eds.). *Viêt Nam: Borderless Histories*. Madison, Wisconsin: University of Wisconsin Press, 2006.

Vo, Nghia M. *Saigon: A History*. Jefferson, North Carolina: McFarland & Company, 2011.

Wilcox, Wynn (ed.). *Vietnam and the West: New Approaches*. Ithaca, New York: Cornell Southeast Asia Publications, 2010.

Watson, Barbara, and Leonard Y. Andaya. *A History of Early Modern Southeast Asia, 1400-1830.* New York: Cambridge University Press, 2015.

Chapter O:
Abbott, Elizabeth. *Sugar: A Bittersweet History.* New York: Duckworth Overlook, 2009.
Baptist, Edward E. *Creating an Old South: Middle Florida's Plantation Frontier Before the Civil War.* Chapel Hill: University of North Carolina Press, 2002.
Burnard, Trevor. *Planters, Merchants, and Slaves: Plantation Societies in British America, 1650-1820.* Chicago, Illinois: University of Chicago Press, 2015.
Diouf, Sylviane A. *Slavery's Exiles: The Story of the American Maroons.* New York: New York University Press, 2014.
Hahn, Barbara. *Making Tobacco Bright: Creating an American Commodity, 1617-1937.* Baltimore, Maryland: The Johns Hopkins Press, 2011.
Isaacson, Walter. *Benjamin Franklin: An American Life.* New York: Simon & Schuster, 2003.
Parker, Matthew. *The Sugar Barons: Family, Corruption, Empire and War in the West Indies.* New York: Walker and Company, 2011.
Stahr, Walter. *John Jay: Founding Father.* New York: Hambledon and London, 2005.
Stobart, Jon. *Sugar and Spice: Grocers and Groceries in Provincial England 1650-1830.* Oxford, U.K.: Oxford University Press, 2013.
Stubbs, Tristan. *Masters of Violence: The Plantation Overseers of Eighteenth-Century Virginia, South Carolina, and Georgia.* Columbia, South Carolina: University of South Carolina Press, 2018.
White, Jerry. *London in the 18th Century: A Great and Monstrous Thing.* London: Vintage Books, 2013.
Williams, Ian. *Rum: A Social and Sociable History.* New York: Nation Books, 2005.

Chapter P:
Brands, H.W. *American Colossus: The Triumph of Capitalism, 1865-1900.* New York: Anchor Books, 2010.
Cole, Peter, David Struthers, and Kenyon Zimmer (eds.). *Wobblies of the World: A Global History of the IWW,* London: Pluto Press, 2017.
Bean, Christopher. *Too Great a Burden to Bear: The Struggle and Failure of the Freedmen's Bureau in Texas.* New York: Fordham University Press, 2016.
De la Teja, Jesús F. (ed.). *Lone Star Unionism, Dissent, and Resistance: Other Sides of Civil War Texas.* Norman, Oklahoma: University of Oklahoma Press, 2016.
Kowal, Donna M. *Tongue of Fire: Emma Goldman, Public Womanhood, and the Sex Question.* Albany, New York: State University of New York Press, 2016.
Hayden, Wendy. *Evolutionary Rhetoric: Sex, Science, and Free Love in Nineteenth Century Feminism.* Carbondale, Illinois: Southern Illinois University Press, 2013.
Gillmer, Jason A. *Slavery and Freedom in Texas: Stories from the Courtroom, 1821-1871.* Athens, Georgia: University of Georgia Press, 2017.
Jones, Jacqueline. *Goddess of Anarchy: The Life and Times of Lucy Parsons, American Radical.* New York: Basic Books, 2017.
Messer-Kruse Timothy. *The Trial of the Haymarket Anarchists: Terrorism and Justice in the Gilded Age.* New York: Palgrave MacMillan, 2011.
Shone, Steve J. *American Anarchism.* Leiden, Netherlands: Brill, 2013.
Sperber, Jonathan. *Karl Marx: A Nineteenth-Century Life.* New York: Liveright Publishing, 2013.
Smith, John David. *We Only Ask for Even-Handed Justice: Black Voices from Reconstruction, 1865-1877.* Amherst, Massachusetts: University of Massachusetts Press, 2014.

Chapter Q:
Ateş, Sabri. *The Ottoman-Iranian Borderlands: Making a Boundary, 1843-1914.* New York: Cambridge University Press, 2013.

Beck, Lois, and Guity Nashat (eds.). *Women in Iran from 1800 to the Islamic Republic*. Urbana, Illinois, University of Illinois Press, 2004.

Bengio, Ofra and Meir Litvak (eds.). *The Sunna and Shi'a in History: Division and Ecumenism in the Muslim Middle East*. New York: PalgraveMacMillan, 2011.

Dabashi, Hamid. *Shi'ism: A Religion of Protest*. Cambridge, Massachusetts: The Belknap Press of Harvard University Press, 2011.

Framanfarmaian, Roxane (ed.). *War and Peace in Qajar Iran: Implications Past and Present*. New York: Routledge, 2008.

Deutschmann, Moritz. *Iran and Russian Imperialism: The Ideal Anarchists, 1800-1914*. New York: Routledge Taylor and Francis Group, 2016.

Hiro, Dilip. *Inside Central Asia: A Political and Cultural History of Uzbekistan, Turkmenistan, Kazakhstan, Kyrgyzstan, Tajikistan, Turkey, and Iran*. New York: Overlook Duckworth, 2009.

Jones, Jill. *Eiffel's Tower: The Thrilling Story Behind Paris's Beloved Monument and the Extraordinary World's Fair that it Introduced*. New York: Penguin Books, 2009.

Matthee, Rudi. *Russians in Iran: Diplomacy and Power in the Qajar Era and Beyond*. London/New York: I. B. Tauris, 2018.

Sarshar, Houman M. (ed.), *The Jews of Iran: The History, Religion, and Culture of a Community in the Islamic World*. New York: I.B. Tauris, 2014.

Sohrabi, Neghmeh. *Taken for Wonder: Nineteenth-Century Travel Accounts for Iran to Europe*. New York: Oxford University Press, 2012.

Tsadik, Daniel. *Between Foreigners and Shi'is: Nineteenth Century Iran and its Jewish Community*. Stanford, California: Stanford University Press, 2007.

Chapter R:

Brooks, Alan, and David Brandon, *Bound for Botany Bay: British Convict Voyages to Australia*. Kew, U.K.: The National Archives, 2005.

Cahill, Rowan. *Radical Sydney: Places, Portraits, and Unruly Episodes*. Sydney: University of New South Wales Press Ltd., 2010.

Day, David. *Paul Keating: The Biography*. Sydney: Fourth Estate/HarperCollins Publishers Australia Pty Limited, 2015.

Gammage, Bill. *The Biggest Estate on Earth: How Aborigines Made Australia*. Sydney: Allen & Unwin, 2011.

Gill, Ellen. *Naval Families, War, and Duty in Britain, 1740-1820*. Woodbridge, U.K: The Boydell Press, 2016.

Kelly, Paul. *The March of Patriots: The Struggle for Modern Australia*. Carlton, Australia: Melbourne University Press, 2009.

Reynolds, Henry. *Forgotten War*. Sydney: University of New South Wales, 2013.

Rodger, N. A. M. *The Command of the Ocean: A Naval History of Britain, 1649-1815*. New York: W. W. Norton & Company, 2004.

Strelein, Lisa. *Compromised Jurisprudence: Native Title Since Mabo*. Canberra: Aboriginal Studies Press, 2009.

Woollacott, Angela. *Settler Society in the Australian Colonies: Self-Government and Imperial Culture*. Oxford, U.K.: Oxford University Press, 2015.

Chapter S:

Belich, James. *Paradise Reforged: A History of the New Zealanders from the 1880s to the Year 2000*. Auckland, New Zealand: Allen Lane/Penguin Press, 2001.

Brooking, Tom. *Richard Seddon, King of God's Own: The Life and Times of New Zealand's Longest-Serving Prime Minister*. Auckland, New Zealand: Penguin Books, 2014.

Hickford, Mark. *Lords of the Land: Indigenous Property Rights and the Jurisprudence of Empire*. New York: Oxford University Press, 2012.

Hilis, Peter. *The Barony of Glasgow: A Window onto Church and People in Nineteenth Century Scotland*. Edinburgh, U.K.: Dunedin Academic Press, 2007.

McGirr, Lisa. *The War on Alcohol: Prohibition and the Rise of the American State*. New York: W.W. Norton & Company, 2016.

MacLeod, James Lachlan. *The Second Disruption: The Free Church in Victorian Scotland and the Origins of the Free Presbyterian Church*. East Linton, U.K.: The Tuckwell Press, 2000.

Meldrum, Patricia. *Conscience and Compromise: Forgotten Evangelicals of Nineteenth-Century Scotland*. Carlisle, U.K.: Paternoster, 2006.

Rice, Geoffrey W. *Christchurch Crimes and Scandals, 1876-99*. Christchurch, New Zealand: Canterbury University Press, 2013.

Sulkunen, Irma, Seija-Leena Nevala-Nurmi, and Pirjo Markkola (eds.) *Suffrage, Gender, and Citizenship: International Perspectives on Parliamentary Reforms*. Newcastle-upon-Tyne: Cambridge Scholars Publishing, 2009.

Chapter T:

Bullard, Alice. *Exile to Paradise: Savagery and Civilization in Paris and the South Pacific, 1790-1900*. Stanford, California: Stanford University Press, 2000.

Grijp, Paul van der. *Manifestations of Mana: Political Power and Divine Inspiration in Polynesia*. Zürich, Switzerland: Lit Verlag, 2014.

Grimshaw, Patricia and Andrew May (eds.). *Missionaries, Indigenous Peoples and Cultural Exchange*. Portland, Oregon: Sussex Academic Press, 2010.

Hiney, Tom. *On the Missionary Trail: A Journey Through Polynesia, Asia, and Africa with the London Missionary Society*. New York: Atlantic Monthly Press, 2000.

Jackson, Will and Emily J. Manktelo (eds.). *Subverting Empire: Deviance and Disorder in the British Colonial World*, New York: Palgrave MacMillan, 2015.

King, David Shaw. *Missionaries and Idols in Polynesia*. San Francisco, California: Beak Press, 2015.

Kirk, Robert William. *Paradise Past: The Transformation of the South Pacific, 1520-1920*. Jefferson, North Carolina: McFarland & Company, 2012.

Lange, Raeburn. *Island Ministers: Indigenous Leadership in Nineteenth Century Pacific Islands Christianity*. Christchurch, New Zealand: Macmillan Brown Centre for Pacific Studies, University of Canterbury / Canberra, Australia: Pandanus Books, Research School of Pacific and Asian Studies, Australian National University, 2005.

Matsuda, Matt K. *Pacific Worlds: A History of Seas, Peoples, and Cultures*. New York: Cambridge University Press, 2012.

Rambo, Lewis R. and Charles E. Farhadian (eds.) *The Oxford Handbook of Religious Conversion*, New York: Oxford University Press, 2014.

Reeson, Margaret. *Pacific Missionary George Brown 1835-1917: Wesleyan Methodist Church*. Canberra: Australian National University, 2013.

Shineberg, Dorothy. *They Came for Sandalwood: A Study of the Sandalwood Trade in the South-West Pacific, 1830-1865*. St. Lucia, Australia: University of Queensland Press, 2014.

Chapter U:

Applebaum, Anne. *Iron Curtain: The Crushing of Eastern Europe, 1944-1956*. New York: Doubleday, 2012.

Augustine, Dolores L. *Red Prometheus: Engineering and Dictatorship in East Germany, 1945-1990*. Cambridge, Massachusetts: MIT Press, 2007.

Dennis, Mike. *The Stasi: Myth and Reality*. New York: Routledge, 2014.

Epstein, Catherine. *The Last Revolutionaries: German Communists and Their Century*. Cambridge, Massachusetts: Harvard University Press, 2003.

Fulbrook, Mary. *The People's State: East German Society from Hitler to Honecker*. New Haven, Connecticut: Yale University Press, 2008.

Harrison, Hope M. *Driving the Soviets up the Wall: Soviet-East German Relations, 1953-1961*. Princeton, New Jersey: Princeton University Press, 2005.

Herf, Jeffery. *Undeclared Wars with Israel: East Germany and the Western Far Left*, 1967-1989. New York: Cambridge University Press, 2016.

Kempe, Frederick. *Berlin 1961: Kennedy, Khrushchev, and the Most Dangerous Place on Earth*. New York: Berkley Books, 2011.

Major, Patrick. *Behind the Berlin Wall: East Germany and the Frontiers of Power*. New York: Oxford University Press, 2011.

Millington, Richard. *State, Society and the Memories of the Uprising of 17 June 1953 in the GDR*. New York: Palgrave Macmillan, 2014.

Ruben, Eli. *Amnesiopolis: Modernity, Space and Memory in East Germany*. New York: Oxford University Press, 2016.

Stangl, Paul. *Risen from Ruins: The Cultural Politics of Rebuilding East Berlin*. Stanford, California: Stanford University Press, 2018.

Chapter V:

Appleby, David. *Heitor Villa-Lobos: A Life, 1887-1950*. Lanham, Maryland: The Scarecrow Press, 2002.

Burdick, John. *The Color of Sound: Race, Religion, and Music in Brazil*. New York: New York University Press, 2013.

Curi, Martin (ed.). *Soccer in Brazil*. New York: Routledge, 2015.

Dávila, Jerry. *Diploma of Whiteness: Race and Social Policy in Brazil, 1917-1945*. Durham, North Carolina: Duke University Press, 2003.

Hagedorn, Dan. *Conquistadors of the Sky: A History of Aviation in Latin America*. Gainesville, Florida: University of Florida Press, 2008.

Hertzman, Marc A. *Making Samba: A New History of Race and Music in Brazil*. Durham, North Carolina: Duke University Press, 2013.

Hess, Carol A. *Representing the Good Neighbor: Music, Difference, and the Pan American Dream*. New York: Oxford University Press, 2013.

Lochery, Neill. *Brazil: The Fortunes of War: World War II and the Making of Modern Brazil*. New York: Basic Books, 2014.

Paxton, Robert O. *The Anatomy of Fascism*. New York: Alfred A. Knopf, 2004.

Tota, Antonio Pedro. *The Seduction of Brazil: the Americanization of Brazil During World War II*. Austin, Texas: University of Texas Press, 2009.

Van Vleck, Jennifer. *Empire of the Air: Aviation and the American Ascendancy*. Cambridge, Massachusetts: Harvard University Press, 2013.

Williams, Daryle, Amy Chazkel and Paulo Knauss (eds.). *The Rio de Janeiro Reader: History, Culture, Politics*. Durham, North Carolina: Duke University Press, 2016.

Chapter W:

Anderson, David. *Histories of the Hanged: The Dirty War in Kenya and the End of the Empire*. New York: W. W. Norton & Company, 2005.

Branch, David. *Kenya: Between Hope and Despair, 1963-2011*. New Haven, Connecticut: Yale University Press, 2011.

Brendon, Piers. *The Decline and Fall of the British Empire, 1781-1997*. New York: Alfred A. Knopf, 2008.

Cooper, Andrew F., John J. Kirton, Franklyn Lisk, and Hany Besada (eds.) *Africa's Health Challenges: Sovereignty, Mobility of People, and Healthcare Governance*. Farnham, U.K.: Ashgate, 2013.

Cooper, Frederick. *Africa Since 1940: The Past of the Present*. New York: Cambridge University Press, 2002.

Elkins, Caroline. *Imperial Reckoning: The Untold Story of Britain's Gulag in Kenya*. New York: Henry Holt and Company, 2005.

Giles-Vernick, Tamara and James L. A. Webb, Jr. (eds.). *Global Health in Africa: Historical Perspectives in Disease Control*. Athens, Ohio: Ohio University Press, 2013.

Moyo, Dambisa. *Dead Aid: Why Aid is Not Working and How There is a Better Way for Africa*. New York: Farrar, Straus and Giroux, 2009.

Pepin, Jacques. *The Origins of AIDS*. New York: Cambridge University Press, 2011.

Shachtman, Tom. *Airlift to America: How Barack Obama Sr., John F. Kennedy, Tom Mboya, and 800 East African Students Changed Their World and Ours*. New York: St. Martin's Press, 2009.

Timberg, Craig and Daniel Halperin. *Tinderbox: How the West Spread the AIDS Epidemic and How the World Can Overcome It*. New York: Penguin Press, 2012.

Williams, Peter W. *America's Religions: From their Origins to the Twenty-first Century*. Urbana, Illinois: University of Illinois Press, 2002.

Chapter X:

Barnouin, Barbara and Yu Changgen, *Zhou Enlai: A Political Life*. Hong Kong: The Chinese University Press, 2006.

Cunningham, Philip J. *Tiananmen Moon: Inside the Chinese Student Uprising of 1989*. Lanham, Maryland: Rowman & Littlefield Publishers, 2014.

Dikötter, Frank. *The Tragedy of Liberation: A History of the Chinese Revolution, 1945-1957*. New York: Bloomsbury Press, 2013.

King, Dean. *Unbound: A True Story of War, Love, and Survival*. New York: Little, Brown and Company, 2010,

Li, Xiaobing. *A History of the Modern Chinese Army*. Lexington, Kentucky: University Press of Kentucky, 2007.

MacFarquhar Roderick and Michael Schoenhals, *Mao's Last Revolution*. Cambridge, Massachusetts: The Belknap Press of Harvard University Press, 2006.

Pantsov, Alexander V. *Mao: The Real Story*. New York: Simon & Schuster, 2012.

Scobell, Andrew. *China's Use of Military Force Beyond the Great Wall and the Long March*. New York: Cambridge University Press, 2003.

Sun, Shuyun. *The Long March: The True Story of Communist China's Founding Myth*. New York: Doubleday, 2006.

Taylor, Jay. *The Generalissimo: Chiang Kai-shek and the Struggle for Modern China*. Cambridge, Massachusetts: The Belknap Press of Harvard University, 2009.

Tudda, Chris. *A Cold War Turning Point: Nixon and China, 1969-1972*. Baton Rouge, Louisiana: Louisiana State University Press, 2012.

Vogel, Ezra F. *Deng Xiaoping and the Transformation of China*. Cambridge, Massachusetts: Belknap Press of Harvard University Press, 2011.

Chapter Y:

Danforth, Loring M. *Crossing the Kingdom: Portraits of Saudi Arabia*. Oakland, California: University of California Press, 2016.

Doran, Peter B. *Breaking Rockefeller: The Incredible Story of The Ambitious Rivals Who Toppled an Oil Empire*. New York: Penguin Books, 2016.

Darlow, Michael and Barbara Bray. *Ibn Saud: The Desert Warrior Who Created the Kingdom of Saudi Arabia*. New York: Skyhorse Publishing, 2012.

Dietrich, Christopher R. W. *Oil Revolution: Anticolonial Elites, Sovereign Rights, and the Economic Culture of Decolonization*. New York: Cambridge University Press, 2017.

Gallegos, Raul. *Crude Nation: How Oil Riches Ruined Venezuela*. Lincoln, Nebraska: University of Nebraska Press, 2016.

Jacobs, Meg. *Panic at the Pump: The Energy Crisis and the Transformation of American Politics in the 1970s*. New York: Hill and Wang, 2016.

Lacey, Robert. *Inside the Kingdom: Kings, Clerics, Modernists, Terrorists, and the Struggle for Saudi Arabia*. New York: Viking, 2009.

Noyes, James. *The Politics of Iconoclasm: Religion, Violence, and the Culture of Image-Breaking in Christianity and Islam*. New York: I. B. Tauris & Co. Ltd., 2013.

Vassiliev, Alexei. *King Faisal of Saudi Arabia: Personality, Faith, and Times*. London: Saqi Books, 2012.

Vélez, Federico. *Latin American Revolutionaries and the Arab World: From the Suez Canal to the Arab Spring*. New York: Routledge, 2016.

Vitalis, Robert. *America's Kingdom: Mythmaking on the Saudi Oil Frontier*. Stanford, California: Stanford University Press, 2007.

Wald, Ellen R. *Saudi, Inc.: The Arabian Kingdom's Pursuit of Profit and Power*. New York: Pegasus Books, 2018.

Chapter Z:

Ghosh, Amitav. *The Great Derangement*. Chicago, Illinois: University of Chicago Press, 2016.

Goldstein, Joshua S. and Steffan A. Qvist. *A Bright Future: How Some Countries Have Solved Climate Change and the Rest Can Follow*. New York: Public Affairs, 2019.

Howe, Joshua P. *Behind the Curve: Science and the Politics of Global Warming*. Seattle, Washington: University of Washington Press, 2014.

Klein, Naomi. *This Changes Everything: Capitalism vs. the Climate*. Toronto: Alfred A. Knopf-Canada, 2014.

Kutney, Gerald. *Carbon Politics and the Failure of the Kyoto Protocol*. London/New York: Routledge, 2014.

Lieberman, Benjamin and Elizabeth Gordon. *Climate Change in Human History: Prehistory to the Present*. London/New York: Bloomsbury Academic, 2018.

McKibben, Bill (ed.). *The Global Warming Reader: A Century of Writing about Climate Change*. New York: Penguin Books, 2011.

Rich, Nathaniel. *Losing Earth: A Recent History*. New York: Farrar, Straus and Giroux, 2019.

Shaw, Christopher. *The Two Degrees Dangerous Limit for Climate Change: Public Understanding and Decision Making*. London/New York: Routledge, 2016.

Tompkins, Andrew S. *Better Active Than Radioactive!: Anti-nuclear Protest in 1970s France and West Germany*. Oxford, U.K.: Oxford University Books, 2016.

Uekötter, Frank. *The Greenest Nation?: A New History of German Environmentalism*. Cambridge, Massachusetts: The MIT Press, 2014.

Wallace-Wells, David. *The Uninhabitable Earth: Life After Warming*. New York: Tim Duggan Books, 2019

Pages numbers in **bold** indicate passages with particular depth or significance.

226, 228-229, **237-238**, 280-282, **308-309**, 323, 329, 334, 341, 378.

Suez Canal: 448, 614, 619, 626, 628, 675.

Suez Crisis (1956-1957): 614, 675.

Sufism: 220-223, 231.

Suffrage and suffragists: 367, 371, 435, **438-447**, 448-449, 452, 457.

Sugar and sugarcane: 189, 210, 230, 300, 304, 329, **331-334**, 337, 342-343, 337, 342-343, 351, 409, 414, 423, 436, 505, 511, 530, 537, 564, 648, 669.

Suleiman the Magnificent (1494-1566): 87, 213.

Sunni: 220, 381-383, 386, 612.

Sun Tzu (544 BCE-496 BCE): 609.

Sun Yat-sen (1866-1925): 577-579.

Surat: 217, 227.

Surgeons, see Doctors.

Suva Declaration (2015): 661.

Switzerland and Swiss: 86, 88-90, 264, 334, 395, 456, 492, 623, 633, 650, 675.

Sydney: 407, 413-431, 447, 464, 469, 483.

Symphonic poem: 525, 675.

Symphonies: 530, 546, 548-550.

Symphony orchestras: 541-542, 545-546, 549-553.

Syndicalism: 358, 370.

Tahiti and Tahitians: 463-464, 467-468, 484, 486.

Taiyuan: 577, 596-598.

Takamoa Institute: 467-469, 484, 489.

Tanna Island: 469-470, 472.

Taoism, see Daoism.

Tapadas: 151.

Tariki, Abdullah (1919-1997): 623-625.

Tartars or Tatars: 60, 67, 164, 675.

Tasmania, see Van Diemen's Land.

Tattoos and tattooing: 480-481.

Ta'unga (1818?-1898):

childhood and upbringing: 461, 464-466.

education of: 466, 468-469.

on Manu'a, Samoa: 479-484.

on Maré, New Caledonia: 477-479.

in Tuaura, New Caledonia: 469-477.

relationships with European missionaries: 467-470, 476-477, 480, 484, 487-488.

relationships with indigenous missionaries: 469, 477.

relationships with indigenous converts: 475, 479-484, 486.

return to Rarotonga and last years: 484-487.

Taxes: 41, **42-43**, 48, 60, **61**, 62, 78, 80, 82, 112, **116-117**, 118, 127, 131, 133, 143-144, 159, 165, 203-204, 207, 210, **227**, 228, 241, 243, 247-248,

281, 308-309, **313-318**, 320, 325, 354, 371, 379-380, 394, 400, 420, 440, 442-443, 452, 539, 558, 565, 586, 614, 616, 620, **621**, 622-623, 626, 651, 657, 675.

Tay Son: 308-311, 319-322, 324-326.

Ta'ziya: 403-404.

Tea: 166, 174, 193, 242, **329**, 332, 334, 351, 414, 423, 436, **457-459**, 505.

Temperance, see prohibition.

Tepehuanes people: 146-147.

Tehran: 377-378, 380, 382, 384-387, 389-390, 395-396, 399, 401-402, 404-405, 501, 630.

Tetzel, Johannes (1465-1519): 75-76.

Thälmann, Ernst (1886-1944): 496-497.

Thailand, see Siam.

Theravada Buddhism: 186.

Thermohaline circulation: 640, 653-655.

Tiananmen Square (1989): 607-609, 642.

Third Rome: 56-57, 64.

Thirty Years' War (1618-1648): 179, 190, 206, 670, 675.

Thobe or thawb: 612, 632, 675.

Three-field system: 61, 675.

Tibet and Tibetans: 162, 589-590, 592-593.

Tabriz: 378, 383.

Tithe: 78, 83, 131, 480, 556, 675.

Tobacco: 189, 192, 242, **330-331**, 337, 401, 412, 414, 561, 669.

Tobacco Régie (1891): 401-402.

Tōfukumon'in (1607-1678): 157-158, 160-161, 164, 172, 174, 202, 217.

Tokugawa Hidetada (1579-1632): 157-158, 168.

Tokugawa Iemitsu (1604-1651): 158, 164-165, 168, 171, 173, 175.

Tokugawa Ieyasu (1543-1616): 158-160, 172-173, 323.

Toledo, Francisco de (1515-1582): 152.

Tombs, see Graves.

Topkapı Palace: 195-197, **199-204**, 206-209, 211, 213, 237, 396, 675.

Townshend, George (1724-1807): 292, 294-296.

Toyotomi Hideyoshi (1537-1598): 158, 163-164.

Trade, see Commerce.

Trains, see Railroads.

Transportation, of criminals to Australia: **407-410, 412-414**, 423, 429.

Trans-Siberian Railway: 599.

Transubstantiation: 58, 86.

Trials: 53, **67-68**, 78, 109, 136, 305, 345, **362-363**, 370, 383, 389, 426, 457, 510, 563.